Turbulent Peace

Turbulent Peace

The Challenges of Managing International Conflict

Edited by Chester A. Crocker,
Fen Osler Hampson, and Pamela Aall

UNITED STATES INSTITUTE OF PEACE PRESS
Washington, D.C.

United States Institute of Peace
1200 17th Street NW
Washington, DC 20036

First published 2001

Printed in the United States of America

The paper used in this publication meets the minimum requirements of American National Standards for Information Science—Permanence of Paper for Printed Library Materials, ANSI Z39.48-1984.

Library of Congress Cataloging-in-Publication Data
Turbulent Peace: the challenges of managing international conflict / edited by Chester A. Crocker, Fen Osler Hampson, and Pamela Aall.
    p. cm.
  Includes bibliographical references and index.
  ISBN 1-929223-29-3 (Cloth) — ISBN 1-929223-27-7 (pbk.)
  1. International relations. 2. Pacific settlement of international disputes. 3. Mediation, International. 4. Peace. I. Crocker, Chester A. II. Hampson, Fen Osler. III. Aall, Pamela R.

JZ5595 .T87 2001
327.1'7—dc21   2001040294

Contents

Foreword

Richard H. Solomon
President, United States Institute of Peace

In 1996, the United States Institute of Peace published *Managing Global Chaos: Sources of and Responses to International Conflict.* The book's editors, Chester A. Crocker, (chairman of the Institute's board of directors), Fen Osler Hampson (a former Institute fellow), and Pamela Aall (then deputy director of the Institute's Education and Training program), sought to distill into a single volume some of the most insightful and instructive analysis of international conflict and its prevention, management, and resolution in the first years after the end of the Cold War. They succeeded admirably. Former secretary of state George Shultz commented that "the sweep, insight, and ideas presented in *[Managing Global Chaos]* make for genuinely rewarding reading." *Foreign Affairs* observed that the volume "represents the collective wisdom of a high-powered group of foreign policy practitioners and scholars." Readers agreed. The book sold remarkably well, especially to colleges and universities.

Now, five years later and a decade into the post–Cold War era, Crocker, Hampson, and Aall have taken a fresh look at the state of international conflict and its management. In *Turbulent Peace,* they have brought together nearly fifty top-flight scholars and practitioners and arranged their work to form a comprehensive, multifaceted assessment of the contemporary world and new perspectives on ways of preventing, containing, and resolving its conflicts. I am confident that readers of this new compendium will be impressed by the results of the editors' industry in updating their previous work. That said, some readers may question whether a sequel to the 1996 volume was really necessary. After all, only a handful of years have passed since the publication of *Managing Global Chaos.* How much could have changed?

"A week is a long time in politics," British prime minister Harold Wilson once remarked. In much the same vein, we may say that in the fields of international relations and conflict resolution, five years can bracket the transition to a different era. Back in 1996, when *Managing Global Chaos* first appeared, we were more or less content to describe ourselves as living in "the post–Cold War world." It was evident, of course, that the world was no longer orchestrated according to the logic of the superpower standoff, but still we tended to contrast events in the mid-1990s with the relative stability that had prevailed until the Eastern bloc disintegrated at the end of the preceding decade. Hence our perception of the world of the mid-1990s was one of relatively unstructured conflict, or "chaos."

I would not say now that our perception was wrong. With one Cold War protagonist (the Soviet Union) having disappeared, the other (the United States) uncertain how to behave, several other actors (the European Union and China, for instance) edging their way toward center stage, and with numerous ethnic and religious conflicts or humanitarian crises born of failing states occupying the attention of policymakers in the world's major capitals, the era seemed truly chaotic.

Five years later, however, much has changed. If we have yet to find the right name with which to dub our age, we are profoundly uncomfortable referring to it merely as the postscript to a former era. "Post–Cold War world" no longer suffices. We know that we are in a new time and to some degree in unfamiliar territory.

Many features of today's international landscape would have been recognizable to earlier generations: violence and instability in the Great Lakes region of Africa; fighting in Kashmir between Indian and Pakistani forces; clashes between Israelis and Palestinians; China rattling its saber at Taiwan; the United States talking of putting up its own nuclear umbrella. Yet these enduring conflicts now coexist with other features that only *seem* to have been around for decades: Russia struggling to adapt to democracy and capitalism; NATO looking for a mission; Europe searching for the political will and military wherewithal to deal with

its own conflicts; the United Nations—indeed, the entire international community—wrestling *continually* with the contending principles of respect for national sovereignty and protection of human rights; and everyone trying to keep up with the information revolution and a globalizing economy.

Moreover, these post–Cold War phenomena have now been with us long enough that we have begun to plot their development and to discern patterns within them. We have, as it were, new historical reference points. We can now draw interesting comparisons with events as recent as 1995, as well as with those of 1985 and 1975.

Turbulent Peace presents ample proof of the ability to recognize trends in phenomena of quite recent vintage. Take, for example, the high incidence of intrastate conflict, which has been perhaps the most conspicuous feature and undoubtedly the most disheartening aspect of the recent international landscape. One author argues forcefully, however, that the skyrocketing course of intrastate conflict in the 1990s may now have not only slowed but reversed. Another sea-change, widely acknowledged, is that whereas the early 1990s witnessed an overly optimistic embrace of the possibilities of a "new world order," the years immediately thereafter saw an overly pessimistic retreat from the dangers of military intervention in failed and fractured states, a wariness that has since diminished to the extent that several new and sizable missions have been launched.

The past five years have added significantly to the rich if not always rewarding history of post–Cold War peace enforcement interventions: cases such as Kosovo, East Timor, and the Democratic Republic of the Congo have been added to the roster of earlier ventures in places such as Somalia, Haiti, Cambodia, and Bosnia (the full list now runs to more than forty). Thus the contributors to this volume can draw on a wealth of recent case material—a situation that does not necessarily lead to consensus, for although the contributors may cite the same cases, they have very different assessments of the wisdom of these recent operations and very different conceptions of what circumstances, if any, justify intervention.

Our authors address many issues other than intervention, of course. For instance, proponents of reconciliation and promotion of the rule of law have watched truth commissions in South Africa and Guatemala complete their work. They have witnessed the creation (on paper) of a permanent international criminal court to deal with genocide, war crimes, and crimes against humanity. And they have seen General Pinochet and President Milosevic discover that those accused of human rights abuses are not always beyond the reach of justice, either at home or abroad.

In short, as the chapters in this volume attest, we have entered a new (albeit still evolving and nameless) era, and no one who wishes to understand the character of our times can afford to ignore the kind of analyses offered in *Turbulent Peace*. Chester Crocker, Fen Hampson, and Pamela Aall have assembled a truly impressive cast of writers. Eminent and influential figures from both the scholarly and the policymaking communities here present authoritative, often provocative, assessments of the fluid global scene. The coverage is extensive, the opinions varied. One need only look at, say, the chapters that make up part II, "Intervention Strategies and Their Consequences," to see the diversity of views and the dynamism of the debate.

Students of contemporary international relations and their professors will find *Turbulent Peace* indispensable. This one volume captures the state of the art in international conflict management. Each of the main schools of thought is represented, each of today's most pressing issues is addressed. Taken individually, the chapters offer penetrating, often passionate, analyses of specific sources of or solutions to violent conflict. Taken together, they form a comprehensive, well-balanced survey of the many causes of war and the many options for its prevention, management, or resolution.

By bringing the best in contemporary thinking on international conflict management to the attention not only of professional analysts, diplomats, and policymakers but also of students, scholars, and indeed all citizens interested in securing a more peaceful world, *Turbulent Peace* reflects and advances the fundamental mission of the United States Institute of Peace. Since its establishment in 1984, the Institute has supported research on an extensive range of subjects pertinent to international relations and conflict management, and has disseminated the fruits of that research to a remarkably wide range of audiences. In reaching out to varied groups, we do our best to present information in a form that meets the needs of both students and practitioners. For instance, in the field of education, the Institute disseminates resources that include teaching texts, collections of cases of peacemaking (see, for instance, *Herding Cats: Multiparty Mediation in a Complex World*), and in-depth analyses of critical conflicts and issues, such as Ted Robert Gurr's *Peoples versus States*, John Paul Lederach's *Building Peace*, and Raymond Cohen's *Negotiating across Cultures*. The Institute also works directly with faculty both in the United States and abroad to improve teaching in the field of conflict analysis and management. We have been pleased to see the enthusiastic reception accorded *Managing Global Chaos* in colleges and universities throughout the United States and abroad. We trust that *Turbulent Peace* will likewise prove a valuable resource for educators and students.

Perhaps one of those students will finally coin an appropriate name for this new era, a time that has clearly outgrown the moniker "post–Cold War world." Or perhaps a scholar or policymaker will hit upon a suitable phrase. And maybe my insightful and productive colleagues Crocker, Hampson, and Aall have already found the right answer in "turbulent peace."

Acknowledgments

Turbulent Peace represents a vibrant community of individuals interested in the basic questions on the nature of conflict and peacemaking. Like all thriving communities, it depends on the support and goodwill of many people, some of whom appear in the book but many of whom contributed to the effort in other ways. Dick Solomon played a critical role in the development of both *Managing Global Chaos* and *Turbulent Peace,* and without his continuing enthusiasm and encouragement neither of these projects would have seen the light of day. Similarly, the contributions of Harriet Hentges, Chick Nelson, Patrick Cronin, Bernice Carney, Joe Klaits, David Smock, and Judy Barsalou have enriched this work, and each in their different ways have helped turn idea into reality. Kimberly Spring and Janice Hoggs were superb in keeping track of complex and ever-changing information and material and in organizing the editors. Aleksandar Jovovic and Naren Kumarakulasingam have given much substantive expertise and practical support to many aspects of the project, and Jeff Helsing and Heather Kerr Stewart have been generous with ideas and advice based on their constant interactions with faculty and students.

Once again, we have presented the Publications program at the Institute with a behemoth of a book and once again they have risen beautifully to the challenge. Thanks go especially to Nigel Quinney, whose clear thinking, fine hand, firm management, and—as always—good sense and good humor have shaped this book at every step along the way. Dan Snodderly's contributions have ranged from the weighty to the minute; without his support, this book would not have happened. To his colleagues in publications—Marie Marr, Kay Hechler, Mike Chase, Michael Soneson: our deepest appreciation for your work as well.

Finally, to the many teachers and students who commented critically and constructively on *Managing Global Chaos* and urged us to undertake this sequel, we would like to add a special word of thanks. Your search for answers at the end of the Cold War was the inspiration for the first volume and we hope that this second volume provides some answers but also broadens and deepens your search. We are now beginning to understand the landscape and landmarks of peacemaking. This book can suggest their dimensions and define some obstacles, but the task of charting a reliable and appropriate path to peace is still a challenge for all of us.

Introduction

Chester A. Crocker,
Fen Osler Hampson,
and Pamela Aall

THE UNITED STATES INSTITUTE OF PEACE, established by Congress in 1984, came into being just as the Cold War began to wane. By the early 1990s, the foundations of the former Soviet Union had cracked, shuddered, and finally collapsed with a rapidity that stunned experts and casual observers alike. The battle of the Titans—the organizing principle for international relations in the second half of the twentieth century—was over and the world anticipated an era of peace. Little thought was given to what peace entailed except that it meant the end of the perpetual state of tension and of the underlying threat of nuclear annihilation. With the end of the Cold War eastern European states would make peaceful transitions to democracy, African and Latin American states—freed from the demands of the ideological war between the two superpowers —would move ahead with peaceful economic development, and Asian countries would continue to ride the economic wave of the 1980s to a peaceful prosperity.

Within a few years, conflicts erupted in the Balkans, Nagarno-Karabakh, Tajikistan, Chechnya, Somalia, Ethiopia, Rwanda, Zaire, Liberia, and Haiti. Ethnic tensions intensified in other parts of Central Asia, Africa, and Southeast Asia. Fighting continued in Northern Ireland, the Middle East, El Salvador, and Guatemala. It became clear that peace had not broken out; instead, the very nature of conflict had changed. Conflicts became internal, setting neighbor against neighbor, ethnic group against ethnic group, religion against religion. Breaking all accepted rules of war, these conflicts targeted civilians and slaughtered noncombatants— men, women, and children—just because they belonged to the wrong group. As focused as these conflicts were on their internal quarrels, they also spread like wildfire, threatening to produce regional conflagrations out of local ones. And sometimes it seemed that they were adopting one of the most pernicious characteristics of wildfire: spreading unseen underground only to ignite in another part of the forest.

In this transformed world, the work of the Institute is increasingly wide ranging. Through its multidisciplinary and practical approach, the Institute seeks to understand the complex causes of present-day conflict and has focused on all aspects of the response to conflict—research and analysis; policy development and implementation; mediation, facilitation, and dialogue; peacekeeping and peace enforcement; rule of law and transitional justice; education; practitioner training; and the challenges of reconciliation. Taking seriously its mandate as an educational organization, the Institute has also looked for ways to present this understanding to the next generation of policymakers and practitioners and to the scholars who are teaching them in colleges and universities across the country. In 1996 we gathered the fruits of ten years' experience in analyzing conflict and designing strategies for its prevention and containment into one volume entitled *Managing Global Chaos: Sources of and Responses to International Conflict.* Our objective was to present much of the best thinking on our past experience and current options and to give shape to the field of conflict analysis and management—its new dynamics, security challenges, and actors.

Although many things have changed since we assembled the first edition, we considered retaining the title *Managing Global Chaos* for this new volume. The notion of chaos has not lost its power or relevance, bearing in mind the particular sense in which we use the term. In using "chaos," we are drawing by analogy on chaos theory in the natural and mathematical sciences. In this sense, chaos refers to the potential of even seemingly minor, distant events to have unpredictable and potentially dramatic effects on the security and stability of other places in a world that is both ever more tightly interconnected and, ironically, ever more differentiated and decentralized in its political, social, and economic structures. We do not argue that the world is already chaotic or doomed to descend into anarchy, as some observers claim.[1] Still less do we posit that cultural clashes,

irrational responses to globalization pressures, and the absence of structured underpinnings that make behavior comprehensible are causing new levels of vicious brutality in global conflict.[2] In fact, as Ted Robert Gurr's chapter in this volume argues, there are reasons to be cautiously optimistic because both the frequency and the intensity of ethnic and intercommunal conflict declined during the past decade.[3] Another positive sign is that a significant number of the conflicts that did occur were settled through negotiation. It is too early to proclaim the easing of intergroup conflict and movement toward political settlement as trends. Nor do these happenings provide grounds for complacency, given the fragile nature of many of the negotiated settlements that were reached and the obvious potential for brewing discontent in some neighborhoods to erupt into violent conflict. It is for this reason that we have chosen to give this volume the new title of *Turbulent Peace: The Challenges of Managing International Conflict,* a title we hope captures the changing circumstances of the world in which we live.

Vulnerability and sensitivity to political and security shock effects can be a function of this very diversity and lack of centralized authority structures. In the Middle East, for example, the unsettled nature of the peace process between Palestinians and Israelis, punctuated as it has been by the recurring eruption of violence, has consequences that go well beyond the region and the immediate interests of the parties to the conflict. One need look no further than the impact of the fortunes of the peace process on the price of energy and the pocketbooks of consumers in oil-importing nations to appreciate the considerable vulnerabilities that are involved when a peace process in a critical region of the world goes sour. Likewise, domestic and secessionist violence brought on by the collapse of authoritarian governments in Asia, such as Suharto's regime in Indonesia, contributed significantly to the growing instability of global capital markets and a rapid loss of investor confidence in what came to be known as the "Asian crisis." Civil unrest in countries as near as Guatemala and Mexico and as far away as Sudan, Somalia, and Ethiopia in the Horn of Africa prompted massive flights of refugees not just into neighboring countries but around the globe. And the United States has come to understand what many other countries have known for some time: the enormous risks and dangers that are posed by terrorist attacks on their military personnel, on their diplomats, and even at home as aggrieved groups and the criminal organizations they give rise to take out their frustrations on us.

Certain patterns of events—for instance, "failed" or "failing" states, warlord predation, and secessionism—also produce a pattern of responses, giving rise, in turn, to changed patterns of violence and conflict. Similarly, the success or failure of response mechanisms operating in the name of an amorphous "international community" can have decisive "feedback" effects—positive or negative—in regions beyond the locus of an immediate conflict scenario. As the wars in the Balkans in the 1990s reveal all too vividly, no region—in this case Western Europe—is immune to unrest along its borders, and "foreign wars" may be just hours away by air or road. Some regions and subregions may approach chaotic conditions right under the noses of others that are thriving in the newly liberalized global system, freed from the burdens of bipolar, East-West confrontation. The "chaos" phenomenon in security and conflict studies closely parallels the more widely recognized economic and political repercussions of globalization under the integrative influence of the new technologies combined with uneven local and regional capabilities to adapt to resulting change.

The sovereignty of individual states and the respect for the sanctity of state borders that characterized the fundamental nature of interstate relations over the past 350 years are also being eroded or, at the very least, redefined.[4] States are challenged from within as subnational groups declare their separate identities

and seek separate recognition. It is increasingly evident that this phenomenon is not confined to the "new" states of the developing world, but also affects some very old states in Europe and Asia. States are also challenged from the outside by supranational, intergovernmental, or nongovernmental bodies that have asserted the right to intervene—by force if necessary—in the domestic affairs of sovereign states in order to defend individuals from mass violence or to protect them from gross violations of human rights.[5] The extraneous and seemingly uncontrollable forces brought about by rapid technological innovation and change also challenge the authority of states in other ways. The "traditional" media—radio and television—also affect conflict processes and pressures for intervention through the so-called CNN effect.[6] But so too do new communications technologies. It is a cliché to say that the Internet has suddenly made us all—at least those of us who have access to computers—citizens of a global cyber-village where information and chat rooms are accessed at the mere click of a finger. The velocity of information flows, financial transactions, international investment, and even environmental change is not only changing our perceptions of how we see ourselves as citizens and how we relate to our own governments. It is also affecting the legitimacy of governments and the capacities and prospects of some states to thrive or even to survive. The point here is not to argue whether the change in national sovereignty is a good or bad thing, but to recognize that the diffusion of power throughout the international system has added whole new layers of complexity to efforts to maintain international order.

This diffusion of power in all of its varied meanings makes it all the more important that we take a multifaceted and multidimensional approach to conflict analysis and conflict management. This approach needs to recognize that states no longer have the legitimacy and the monopoly on power and the use of force that they once enjoyed and that as some states break apart or are wracked by internal conflict the unsettling consequences and shock waves can spill across borders, infect the surrounding region, and even reverberate into the international system.

One of the challenges for both students and practitioners of international conflict management is to make intellectual sense out of all of this chaos and complexity and to understand that there are real alternatives and a wide range of potential response strategies to different conflict situations.[7] To point out that the world and its conflicts are complex is not very helpful if we stop there. The task of the policy analyst, wherever he or she sits—in the classroom, in the State Department, in the United Nations, or in the office of a nongovernmental organization in some war-torn society—is to understand what drives and sustains these seemingly intractable conflicts so that interventions aimed at helping the parties resolve these conflicts or assisting the victims do not make the situation worse or further exacerbate tensions.

The levels-of-analysis approach, developed in Jack Levy's opening chapter to this volume, offers a useful framework that gives some insight into the "causes" or "vectors" that influence conflict processes and contribute to the escalation of violence. In practical terms, no serious scholar or professional authority argues for a "single-factor" explanation of conflict and war. Leading scholars on war causation—from Geoffrey Blainey, Raymond Aron, and Bernard Brodie[8] to Michael Howard, whose classic essay is included in this volume—argue against single-factor analyses, which have never been useful in explaining war events except in terms of circular or tautological arguments (e.g., wars occur because there is nothing to prevent them). Still less are they useful today when political leaders in war-torn societies have become ever more entrepreneurial and creative in describing their struggles in terms that will "sell," shading the rhetoric to the market if need be. And just as there is no single cause of conflict,

there is no single solution. Understanding complexity and the dynamics of the various levels is as important to the analysis of conflict resolution as it is to the analysis of conflict.

A CHANGING LANDSCAPE

In this present volume, although we continue to use a multidimensional chaos paradigm, we do so within a geopolitical landscape that has changed markedly since the mid-1990s. Specifically, we are speaking here of five emerging dynamics that characterize the setting for conflict analysis and management in the current period and run through the different sections of this book.

The first of these is the return of geopolitics, those endemic and hegemonic conflict patterns between states that have long characterized the international system, together with rising concerns about how such contests will be conducted in today's technological environment. For much of the first post–Cold War decade, analysts focused, and not without reason, on ethnic and internal wars that have formed the overwhelming majority of contemporary conflicts. Like a pendulum, this focus may occasionally have gone too far, to the extent of obscuring the vital linkage between internal wars and the regional "bad neighborhoods" in which they occur and which often constitute the leading triggers of the conflict's outbreak or provide a lethal milieu for its spread. The concentrated focus on internal conflict may also have distracted us from appreciating the continued salience in certain regions of endemic, interstate rivalry or hostility based on the sorts of factors (concern for regional primacy, changing power relations, security dilemmas, regime legitimacy contests, the absence of universally accepted regional or subregional "rules of the game") that scholars have long recognized as conflict spurs or accelerants.

When combined with the recent attention in the scholarly and policy communities to so-called rogue actors and the reality of continued, if not accelerated, diffusion of sensitive weapons technologies to unstable regions, the return of geopolitics points to a legitimate global concern for dampening regional interstate confrontations. Similarly, it points to the value of enhancing efforts to erect confidence- and security-building measures and antiproliferation regimes ranging from small arms to nuclear weapons. The return to open warfare and overt nuclear testing in South Asia is only the most dramatic illustration of this concern. In 1998–2000, the Horn of Africa witnessed the largest-scale and costliest conventional interstate warfare on the African continent since World Wars I and II, as the Eritreans and Ethiopians engaged in a seemingly pointless test of wills over an impoverished and barren landscape where the border was never demarcated. In the Taiwan Straits, the struggle for legitimacy and to decide who will set the terms for the ultimate reunification of China has produced open threats of the use of force on one side and of unilateral secession on the other. Accordingly, this new edition of the volume includes expanded coverage of the sources of and responses to regional conflicts that pertain to this pattern.[9]

The second emerging issue that we have chosen to highlight in the volume is that one-dimensional debates about interventionism and isolationism miss a much richer reality of challenges and trade-offs in conflict management revolving around questions of sociopolitical context, timing, sequencing, and grasping the stages and cycles in the life of a conflict. All too often, we believe, the intervention debate has been handled as if the only real issue is military intervention, as distinguished from other types of third-party-assisted processes by a range of external actors. Worse, within the ambit of the military intervention field, the debate has been framed as if the issue is simply a "yes or no" matter and, within that, an up or down vote on support for UN peacekeeping. This sort of framing of the question trivializes

the real issues of public policy choice. In this volume, we have insisted on a broader look at the concept of intervention, touching on issues of feasibility and strategic management; the concept of mediatory peacemaking as a strategic enterprise; ethical imperatives; the impartiality dilemma; the specific types of peacekeeping that have worked and those that have not; the phasing of intervention; the range of external, third-party, roles (official and nonofficial) in conflict management; and the problems associated with intervention that freezes or prolongs conflicts rather than actually managing or resolving them.[10]

Of particular importance in looking at this complex equation is the effort to pull together from case studies the lessons learned from post–Cold War experience. The purpose is to make a start in identifying certain principles and concepts that can lead to doctrines of best practice in third-party interventions (1) by different sets of actors, (2) by using different instruments and techniques, (3) in distinct types of societies, and (4) at various points in the conflict life cycle. Once again, the value of tackling the conflict management agenda in this way is that it links theory directly to practical application. In practice, the question most likely to arise is not, "Which kind of intervention works better, NGO-led track-two initiatives to open a channel between the sides or a big-power effort to summon the parties to a Camp David summit?" Rather, the question will likely be, "How do we know when the first option is needed or when only the second has hope of success?"

A third emerging theme this volume treats is the continuing and still unresolved dialogue among scholars and practitioners about the interaction between conflict management, on the one hand, and democratization, the rule of law, civil-society institution building, and other elements of what can broadly be called governance (or nation building), on the other hand.[11] Negotiated political transitions (e.g., from communist dictatorship, from apartheid, from oppressive military or one-man rule) place a sharp focus on the significance of these issues since they impose on peacemakers and warring parties alike a seemingly stark choice between priorities (reconciliation, power sharing, justice, accountability to local or international authorities, adherence to democratic norms and universal legal principles, the quest for peace and stability). Given the predominant role of Western governments and publics and Western-oriented intergovernmental and nongovernmental organizations in the peacemaking field —and the reality that most violent conflicts occur in or between transitional or developing societies—the potential clash of values and priorities is further underscored. Western diplomats and activists naturally bring with them certain expectations about democratic practices and human rights standards. The idea that peace can and should be imposed by outsiders is itself derived from this set of Western-derived assumptions and priorities.

Increasingly, the scholar and the practitioner are beginning to ask awkward but essential questions about the proper sequence and priorities to be adopted in addressing these questions. Must basic governance questions be resolved and fundamental political or social change occur before there can be stability and peace? Or is the greatest source of contemporary chaos and political turbulence the weakening of state institutions and capabilities and their replacement by rival and even less legitimate power sources? If the former thesis is correct, then peacemaking and conflict management should consciously be placed on the back burner until political conditions ripen not for negotiated settlements but for legitimate governance, which will bring in its wake a just order. If the latter hypothesis is true, then the first order of business is for the international community to lend support to the strengthening of the sovereign and legitimate capacity of states in deeply troubled societies. Under this approach, it is democratic norms and Western sensibilities that must be placed on the back

burner in the interests of reestablishing political order and arresting unguided turbulence by keeping an external hand on the levers of power until local authorities can reassert themselves. We have not attempted to resolve this debate —a modern version of age-old debates in political theory—but rather try to reflect it fairly in the context of conflict management theory and practice.[12]

The fourth emerging theme is the need for more explicit recognition—by practitioners and scholars alike—that there is much truth to the nostrum "it depends" when analyzing conflict sources and appropriate remedies. The simple fact is that societies and polities differ dramatically in their capacity to cope with external or internal shocks and pressures. A typology of societies and conflicts could advance thinking in the academic and policy communities about what works, when and where. What triggers the outbreak of an uncontrollable conventional warfare in one context could inspire the launch of a fast and effective special mission by the European Union or the Organization for Security and Cooperation in Europe in another setting. Some regions are replete with security-related institutions and mechanisms adept at forestalling, preempting, and channeling conflicts before they turn violent. These security-surplus or security-exporting regions—sadly too few in number—stand in marked contrast to security-deficit regions where supplies of tinder and matches far outweigh the stock of fire extinguishers.

We believe it is becoming essential in the conflict management field to speak candidly about these distinctions. Erudite discourse on the limits of UN peacekeeping or the promise of nongovernmental initiatives for postconflict peacebuilding needs to be situated within typologies of conflict settings. To illustrate, peace initiatives that have borne fruit in Northern Ireland and South Africa would not likely gain the same traction in societies such as Sierra Leone and Afghanistan, where the vital infrastructure of civil society remains far less developed and institutionalized. Remedies depending on the presence and conduct of stable, coherent actors make sense in places where such actors are the key decision makers.[13] Those remedies can lead, however, to illusions and wishful thinking when, literally, there is no one in charge. To take another example, in assessing the context for the insertion of peacekeepers, the policymaker needs the benefit of a plain-spoken analysis about the intentions and capabilities of local actors and, as Doyle suggests in his chapter, to weigh this judgment against the likely capacity of the outside force to cope over the lifetime of the intervention.

These four themes—the return of geopolitics, the debate on intervention, the push and pull between conflict management and post-conflict governance issues, and the recognition that different societies require different peacemaking strategies—run through this volume.[14] Their presence testifies to the fact that we are only just beginning to understand how to reach peace. Some peacemaking efforts over the past dozen years have been successful: Cambodia, El Salvador, Guatemala, and even the seemingly intractable conflict in Northern Ireland, which yielded at last to the persistent mediation by three distinguished outsiders—former U.S. senator George Mitchell, former Finnish prime minister Harri Holkeri, and General John de Chastelain of Canada. Some efforts, however, have not met with the same success. Conflict reignited yet again in Angola despite the agreements that had been reached at Lusaka, despite UN engagement, and despite strong U.S. support for the UN mediator. The U.S. effort to broker peace between the Israelis and the Palestinians in the last days of the Clinton administration was badly derailed by the outbreak of violence in the region. And some efforts—involving the same region, the same players, and the same mediators using the same techniques—have produced very different results. In the Balkans, for instance, U.S. assistant secretary of state Richard Holbrooke, with the aid of NATO, used coercive peacemaking to strong-arm the Bosnian Serbs, Croats, and Muslims into agreement. The same coercive approach failed, however, during the Serb-Kosovar Albanian negotiations in Rambouillet and as a result brought NATO into direct armed conflict with the Serbs. In general, the record over the past decade points to a highly mixed track record, with most cases falling somewhere in between pure success and downright failure.

With the passage of time, assessments of the record of international interventions become more, not less, problematic. For example, the lessons of Cambodia are more difficult to read than we initially thought. Did the collapse of the power-sharing arrangement between Hun Sen and Prince Norodom Ranarridh mean that democratic elections after conflict produce at best an unstable result, prey to renewed conflict? Or did the decision to include the Khmer Rouge in this early government leave gaping wounds that prohibited reconciliation? Or were these all necessary steps toward a sustainable peace—steps in a long, slow process requiring patience, persistence, and open-ended commitment by all concerned? Did the international community do too much or too little to make peace endure in Cambodia? Can outsiders help to bring peace at all, and if so, how can they help?

This brings us to our fifth overarching theme. Over the past decade, we have learned a great deal about the complications of reaching a negotiated agreement and of creating from that negotiated settlement a sustainable peace.[15] We have learned about the fragility of agreements, the difficulties in coordinating an international response, the challenges of implementation, the influence of spoilers, the unpredictable results that elections can produce, and the strong resistance to reconciliation. It is clear that we live in turbulent times and that a negotiated conflict settlement often leads to a turbulent peace. This peace is not an end state in itself but needs to be nurtured into its next phase: a stable, functioning government, society, and culture in which conflicts are settled through negotiation rather than through violence.

This turbulence refers not only to postconflict situations. At the lower end of the conflict spectrum, we are reminded of an interesting feature of post–Cold War conflict events: the occurrence in places such as Central Asia, Indonesia and the Philippines, Central Africa, and the Balkans of violent, turbulent situations that hover somewhere between war and peace. We do not propose in this volume a new theory for explaining and responding to political violence below the threshold of outright war. A number of our chapters on conflict sources shed an especially bright light on the phenomenon of turbulence.[16] Managing such turbulence cannot simply be swept aside as somehow beneath the proper concern of the international community: this turbulence is the breeding ground for other phenomena that affect the health of the global system—criminality of all sorts, the rise of predators and warlords ("rogues," to some), environmental and health disasters[17]—and that postpone indefinitely vitally needed investment, growth, and improved standards of governance. Low-level violence of this sort is capable of dismantling and destabilizing negotiated settlements, reversing fragile progress. Yet the remedies for sustained turbulence in rough neighborhoods are by no means obvious in our postimperial and postcolonial age.

Christoph Bertram points out that it is impossible to recognize the full character of your own period as you live through it.[18] Living in a period of transition, as we do now, makes this recognition even more difficult. We do not have a term for our age beyond the weak description "the post–Cold War period." We do know, however, that our age is marked by change and by the roiling seas produced by change. We hope that the contributions in this volume serve to underscore the gravity of the challenge and the long road that still lies ahead in security and conflict studies.

STRUCTURE OF THIS BOOK

As discussed above, there have been important developments over the past five years, both in the scholarly fields related to conflict management and on the ground where war and peace occur. This volume seeks to capture these changing dynamics. It includes some contributors to *Managing Global Chaos*, who have rewritten their chapters to reflect these changes. It also includes many new authors, who have been commissioned to treat new issues and to reflect the widened range of viewpoints in areas of lively debate. Unfortunately, the hard limits of space forced us to drop a number of excellent chapters, including the seven case studies, that were included in the earlier volume. For students interested in the evolution of thought and practice in the field of conflict analysis and management, these chapters are well worth seeking out from *Managing Global Chaos*.

This volume focuses on two dimensions of the conflict field: sources and responses. Of these two dimensions, the first has attracted the most attention from scholars within the field of international relations. In recent years, however, attention to responses to conflict has increased, driven by a growing desire among students and faculty on the one hand and policymakers and practitioners on the other hand to come up with workable solutions to seemingly intractable conflagrations. The unceasing explosions of internal conflicts in the 1990s may have presented very difficult challenges to practitioners but they also touched the lives of individuals around the world as the news networks reported on mass civilian killings in Rwanda, Bosnia, Liberia, and Sierra Leone. In the face of these contemporary wars, student and faculty concern expanded beyond understanding the causes of these conflicts to identifying and applying solutions. This volume, as did its predecessor, dedicates a major part of its pages to the practical, political, ethical, and operational considerations of conflict management. Recognizing that all sorts of diverse institutions play a role in responding to conflict, the book explores many different kinds of institutional capacities and devotes several sections to the use of both coercive and diplomatic methods of making or encouraging peace.

Analyzing conflict and peacemaking is not easy. Each conflict is unique and has its own set of causes and dynamics. Consequently, each response has to be unique. There are some tools —general though they may be—that can help to conceptualize the field and thereby increase understanding of these complex factors. It is to some of these tools that we now turn.

Table 1 ("Illustrative Strategies for Managing a Turbulent World") relates various conflict management strategies and techniques, including the use of force, negotiated interventions, and track-two diplomacy, to the discussion of sources of conflict. The first section of the book is based on the typology in Jack Levy's chapter, which is itself modeled on the work by Kenneth Waltz that defined a levels-of-analysis approach to the study of conflict.[19] Using Levy's three different levels of analysis —the systemic, subsystemic, and individual levels—the left-hand column of the table demonstrates that there is potentially a wide range of factors that can influence conflict processes and that for any given conflict a variety of different factors and forces can play out across these different levels. Using the same levels-of-analysis approach, part I of the volume captures the wide array of conflict sources from a rich variety of scholarly and disciplinary backgrounds and in some respects speaks to the left-hand column of the table. Although some of the writers in this section of the book stress the continued importance of systemic sources of conflict—that is, sources of conflict that arise from the anarchic nature of the international system and transnational forces and processes that increasingly operate at the global level— others point to the importance of subsystemic

factors, including the growing importance of culture, ethnicity, identity, and personality in conflict processes, especially within states.

Part II of the volume examines the ongoing debate about intervention, focusing primarily, though not exclusively, on the role of coercive versus noncoercive strategies and instruments of intervention. The essays in this section bring a diverse range of opinions and insights to the ongoing debate among scholars and practitioners about intervention methods, techniques, and timing, particularly when military intervention is an option. At one end of the spectrum is the viewpoint that international intervention to end intrastate conflicts is inconclusive and generally tends to be counterproductive. At the other end some argue that the international community has a moral commitment to intervene when confronted with evidence of genocide and massive human rights abuses. As the essays in this section demonstrate, these debates play out at different levels—the political, the moral, and the practical or expedient. As the introductory essay to part II argues, however, much of the debate tends to focus on the use of force, ignoring the fact that there are other strategies and instruments of intervention, ranging from formal diplomacy to a wide variety of track-two interventions. Furthermore, intervention strategies—whether they involve the use of (or the threat to use) force or diplomacy or some other method of negotiation and mediation (i.e., peaceful intervention techniques)—must be carefully tailored to the appropriate source of conflict or level of analysis, explicitly recognizing that many different factors and forces are at play in any given conflict.

In part III we focus on the role of negotiation, mediation, and preventive statecraft as specific tools and methods of conflict management. Negotiation is rightly viewed as a means to an end (diplomatic negotiations in the area of arms control, for example, are directed at developing new arms control regimes; a

Table 1. Illustrative Strategies for Managing a Turbulent World

Sources of Conflict (see Part I)	Coercive Strategies and Instruments (see Part II)	Negotiation, Mediation, and Other Political Instruments (see Parts II and III)	Institutions and Regimes of Security and Conflict Management (see Part IV)	Peacebuilding (see Part V)
Level 1: Systemic Factors				
Anarchy and changing balance of power, breakup of empires (e.g., Soviet Union)	Power balancing, alliances and alignments	Concert-based strategies of negotiation (e.g., Concert of Europe)	Collective security/cooperative security	Kantian confederation of democratic states
Regional and hegemonic rivalries	Power balancing, alliances and alignments, military-assistance programs, sanctions	Diplomatic engagement/isolation, pressures and incentives for adherence to arms regimes, engagement	Strengthened arms regimes, expanded/new collective security institutions	New/expanded institutions for regional economic cooperation and integration
Weapons proliferation and innovation that change existing power balances or lead to new sources of threat in the international system	New offense-defense strategies and technologies (e.g., missile defense, information warfare, high-tech weaponry)	Negotiated understandings and agreements (e.g., through the G-8 and other forums), preventive diplomacy	Arms control regimes and confidence-building measures	
Global nonmilitary security threats (e.g., transnational criminal networks, economic destabilization, environmental degradation, population pressures)	International criminal courts, Interpol, bilateral cooperation against criminal mafias	Negotiated understandings and agreements (e.g., through the G-8 and other forums), preventive diplomacy	International regimes and other kinds of international governance responses to enhance cooperation at both global and regional/subregional levels	

Level 2: States and Societies

Transitional states	Peace enforcement, conflict suppression, targeted sanctions, coercive diplomacy	Mediation, dialogue, track-one and -two diplomacy, financial inducements, aid and trade conditionality	Collective security initiatives, regional organizations (membership inducements, threats of expulsion or nonmembership)	Good governance, reconciliation, reconstruction, development assistance, civil-society institution building, rule of law, truth commissions, preventive diplomacy
State collapse	Rapid reaction force, military protectorates	Multilateral and bilateral assistance programs, financial bail-outs, aid and trade conditionality, administrative/political protectorates	Temporary multilateral governance structures	
Ethnopolitical/religious extremism	Rapid reaction force, safe havens, coercive diplomacy, deterrence, preventive diplomacy	Negotiated autonomy, cross-cultural negotiation, circumnegotiation, minority rights protection policies, aid and trade conditionality	Constitutional and electoral reforms, power sharing, federalism, consociational democracy	Support for reconciliation measures (political, social, religious, etc.), strengthening civil society, strengthening minority rights protection, monitoring governance structures (e.g., autonomy or power-sharing arrangements)
Warlord economies	Targeted sanctions, boycotts, arms embargoes	External monitoring and transparency	Codes of conduct for multinationals	
Rogue states	Coercive diplomacy, deterrence, preventive diplomacy, support for armed opposition, sanctions	Isolation/engagement, support for nonviolent opposition	Institutional arrangements based on common interest (e.g., KEDO)	

continued on next page

Table 1. Illustrative Strategies for Managing a Turbulent World *(cont.)*

Sources of Conflict (see Part I)	Coercive Strategies and Instruments (see Part II)	Negotiation, Mediation, and Other Political Instruments (see Parts II and III)	Institutions and Regimes of Security and Conflict Management (see Part IV)	Peacebuilding (see Part V)
Level 3: Leadership and Human Agency				
Bad leaders	Coercive intervention and diplomacy, targeted sanctions	Support for nonviolent opposition	Denial/expulsion for multilateral institutions	Criminal courts/tribunals
Spoilers	Military containment, legal threats, asset seizures	Engagement or isolation and delegitimization	Multilateral incentives and pressures	Power sharing or continued isolation
Elite cultural cognitive barriers to cooperation		Secret diplomacy and back channels, confidence-building measures, international support for risk taking by the parties themselves, track-two workshops		Conflict transformation initiatives, civil-society building

mediated intervention by a third party in an intrastate conflict is directed at ending violence and perhaps establishing a detailed road map that charts the way to a lasting peace settlement). However, such factors as the timing and sequence of negotiations, the choice of negotiating partners, the selection of a mediator(s), and the forum within which negotiations are conducted can exercise a decisive influence on outcomes, including whether a settlement or arms control treaty is reached or not. The essays in part III discuss the utility of different negotiation and mediation instruments at both diplomatic and unofficial levels and the impact different kinds of negotiated interventions can have on peace processes.

Table 1 illustrates that more than one set of intervention strategies or response mechanisms may be necessary to address sources of conflict at different levels of analysis. Furthermore, these different strategies and responses may, in fact, complement one another and therefore should not be viewed as mutually exclusive options. Part IV of the volume develops this theme, examining the role of international institutions and regimes in the conflict management equation. The essays in this section suggest that although international organizations such as the United Nations remain highly relevant to the maintenance of international peace and security, there is growing recognition that their activities and efforts must be complemented by an increasingly diverse portfolio of institutions, including regional and subregional organizations and nongovernmental organizations. The essays in this section also attempt to distill much of the knowledge and experience gained over the past decade about the utility of these different institutions and their comparative advantages in different conflict settings.

Once a negotiated agreement is reached, there may be the temptation to conclude that the job is done. Nothing could be further from the truth. As the essays in part V demonstrate, the challenges of consolidating the peace and moving from a settlement to a genuine process of reconciliation are as formidable as they are varied. During the consolidation phase of a peace process, important choices have to be made, such as whether to prosecute those accused of war crimes or whether to use other means (e.g., truth commissions) to achieve national reconciliation. There is no easy answer to, or ready-made formula for addressing, these challenges. However, in the five years since the publication of *Managing Global Chaos*, scholarly and policy understandings of what these precise challenges are and what the priorities should be in moving from settlement to reconciliation have grown enormously. The greatly expanded list of topics covered in this section reflects our enlarged understanding about not only the scope of these challenges but also the obvious limitations to social and political engineering carried out on a local or even a nationwide scale.

Figure 1 ("The Life Cycle of International Conflict Management") takes a different perspective, relating many of the different approaches to conflict management available to peacemakers to different points on the conflict cycle. It does not incorporate sources of conflict, as table 1 does, but instead focuses on the dynamics of conflicts and the timing of appropriate responses. The bell curve on the chart represents in idealized form the pattern of a conflict, showing how a conflict escalates toward the outbreak of violence and then de-escalates toward rapprochement and reconciliation. The curve also indicates the types of conflict management techniques that may be effective at particular points of the conflict cycle. For instance, at the bottom of the curve, before violence has broken out or after settlement has been reached, approaches that stress developing capacity to handle disputes peacefully—institution building, good governance, transparency, rule of law, fact finding, education, practitioner training, development assistance—may be not only appropriate but essential to the prevention of conflict or consolidation of peace. At the higher end of the curve, after

Figure 1. The Life Cycle of International Conflict Management

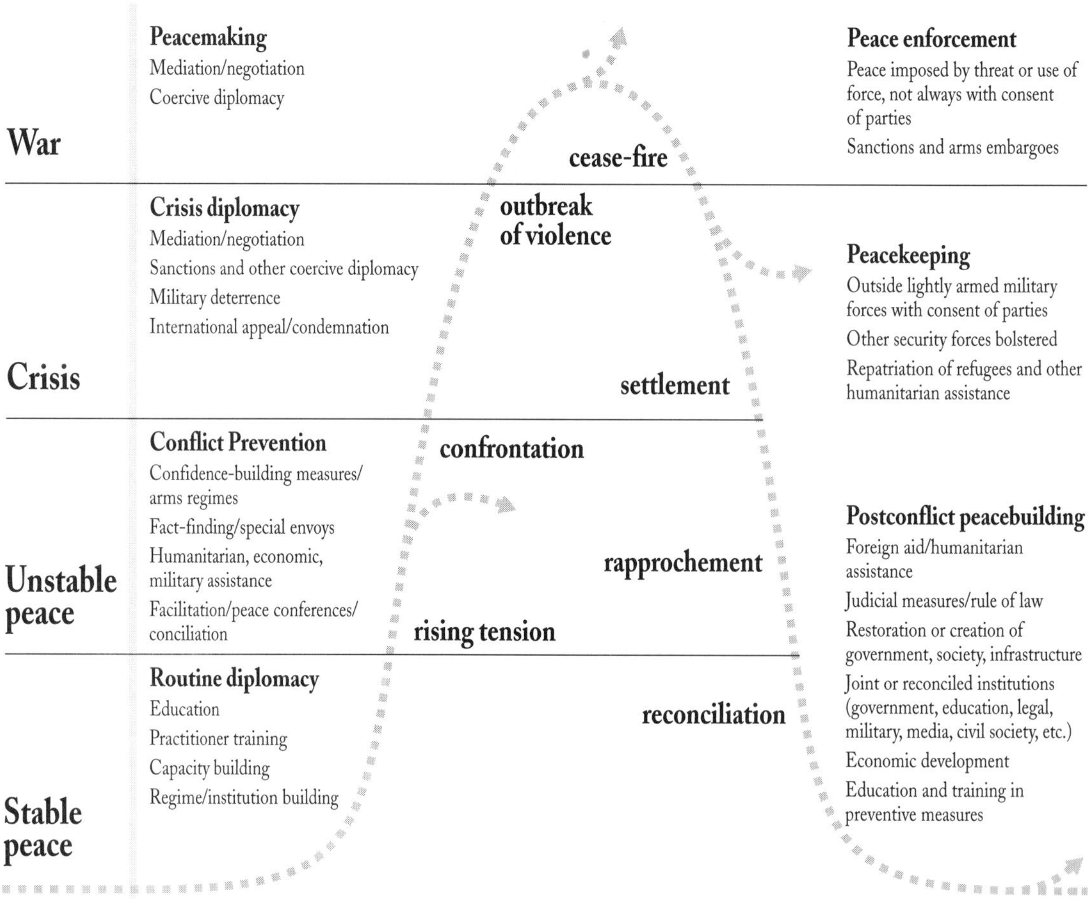

War

Peacemaking
Mediation/negotiation
Coercive diplomacy

Peace enforcement
Peace imposed by threat or use of force, not always with consent of parties
Sanctions and arms embargoes

cease-fire

Crisis diplomacy
Mediation/negotiation
Sanctions and other coercive diplomacy
Military deterrence
International appeal/condemnation

outbreak of violence

Peacekeeping
Outside lightly armed military forces with consent of parties
Other security forces bolstered
Repatriation of refugees and other humanitarian assistance

Crisis

settlement

Conflict Prevention
Confidence-building measures/arms regimes
Fact-finding/special envoys
Humanitarian, economic, military assistance
Facilitation/peace conferences/conciliation

confrontation

rapprochement

Postconflict peacebuilding
Foreign aid/humanitarian assistance
Judicial measures/rule of law
Restoration or creation of government, society, infrastructure
Joint or reconciled institutions (government, education, legal, military, media, civil society, etc.)
Economic development
Education and training in preventive measures

Unstable peace

rising tension

Routine diplomacy
Education
Practitioner training
Capacity building
Regime/institution building

reconciliation

Stable peace

Source: Adapted from figure 2.1 in Michael S. Lund, *Preventing Violent Conflict: A Strategy for Preventive Diplomacy* (Washington, D.C.: United States Institute of Peace Press, 1996), 38.

the outbreak of large-scale violence, the antagonists may be closed to these kind of approaches and respond only to strong incentives and disincentives of both a political and a more coercive nature: mediation, political and economic sanctions, and military engagement in the peace mission.

In looking at this curve, it is important to remember that individual conflicts rarely follow this idealized pattern. Some double back on themselves, swinging from tenuous settlement to renewed conflict, as happened in Angola in the 1990s. Some never quite develop into full-fledged conflicts, but simmer uneasily for years, as happened in Indonesia before the outbreak of fighting over East Timor. Even so, the chart does provide a useful means of understanding general conflict dynamics and identifying appropriate approaches to conflict management.

In these rapidly changing times, none of the essays in this volume can provide the last word on any given subject. But they do represent, in our opinion, some of the best thinking and research on the topics they address. Our basic aim for this book is to provide a closer representation of post–Cold War realities and experience while also capturing some of what we are learning and offering some snapshots of a moving target: the full complexity of contemporary conflict management in a turbulent world. We hope that the essays and insights in this volume will therefore not only illuminate but also stimulate and provoke.

NOTES

1. For example, see Robert D. Kaplan, "The Coming Anarchy," *Atlantic Monthly* 273, no. 2 (February 1994): 44–76.

2. For a critical view of a range of writings on chaos and anarchy, see Yahya Sadowski, *The Myth of Global Chaos* (Washington, D.C.: Brookings Institution, 1998). Sadowski argues that the end of the Cold War may have changed the world, its ills, and their remedies less than imagined by what he terms the optimists and pessimists.

3. See the chapter by Ted Robert Gurr (chapter 11) in this volume.

4. See, for example, J. A. Mathews, "Power Shift," *Foreign Affairs* 76, no. 1 (January-February 1997): 51–66.

5. Kofi Annan, *Annual Report of the Secretary-General*, United Nations, General Assembly, Official Records, Fifty-Fourth Session, September 20, 1999.

6. See the chapter by Warren Strobel (chapter 40).

7. See the chapters by Bruce Jentleson (chapter 15), Chantal de Jonge Oudraat (chapter 21), Joseph Nye (chapter 22), Louis Kriesberg (chapter 25), Saadia Touval and I. William Zartman (chapter 26), P. Terrence Hopmann (chapter 27), Raymond Cohen (chapter 28), Harold Saunders (chapter 29), Rolf Ekeus (chapter 31), and Alain Destexhe (chapter 38).

8. Geoffrey Blainey, *Causes of War* (New York: Free Press, 1973); Raymond Aron, *Peace and War* (Garden City, N.Y.: Doubleday, 1966); and Bernard Brodie, *War and Politics* (New York: Macmillan, 1973), esp. 276–340, "Some Theories on the Causes of War."

9. See chapters by Michael Howard (chapter 2), Charles Kupchan (chapter 3), Geoffrey Kemp (chapter 5), Michael Brown (chapter 13), Lawrence Freedman (chapter 20), Michael Krepon and Lawrence Scheinman (chapter 36), and David Yost (chapter 34).

10. See the chapters by Phil Williams (chapter 7), Paul Collier (chapter 10), Connie Peck (chapter 33), William Schabas (chapter 35), Mary Anderson (chapter 37), and John Paul Lederach (chapter 49).

11. On the challenges of democratization, see the chapter by Edward Mansfield and Jack Snyder (chapter 8).

12. Among the chapters that deal with this tension between governance and conflict management are those by Edward Luttwak (chapter 16), Pamela Aall (chapter 23), Fen Hampson (chapter 24), Michael Doyle (chapter 32), William Schabas (chapter 35), Roy Licklider (chapter 41), Pauline Baker (chapter 44), Roland Paris (chapter 45), Timothy Sisk (chapter 46), and Neil Kritz (chapter 47).

13. On the role of leadership in peacemaking, see the chapter by Janice Gross Stein (chapter 12).

14. This volume makes its own contributions toward this agenda, but we also want to point interested readers to other work that shares the aim of deriving concepts of best practice, such as Melanie C. Greenberg, John H. Barton, and Margaret E. McGuinness, eds., *Words over War: Mediation and Arbitration to Prevent Deadly Conflict* (Lanham, Md.: Rowman and Littlefield, 2000); and Barnett R. Rubin, ed., *Cases and Strategies for Preventive Action* (New York: Century Foundation Press, 1998).

15. For a sampling of the breadth of lessons learned over the past decade, see the chapters by Chester Crocker (chapter 14), Stanley Hoffmann (chapter 17), Richard Betts (chapter 18), Richard Haass (chapter 19), Nicole Ball (chapter 42), Stephen John Stedman (chapter 43), and R. Scott Appleby (chapter 48).

16. See the chapters by Phil Williams (chapter 7), Mohammed Ayoob (chapter 9), Paul Collier (chapter 10), Ted Robert Gurr (chapter 11), and Michael Brown (chapter 13).

17. On criminality and other political economy pathologies of conflict, see the chapters by Jean-Marie Guehenno (chapter 6), Paul Collier (chapter 10), and Virginia Haufler (chapter 39). On the relationship between environmental degradation and conflict, see the chapter by Nils Petter Gleditsch (chapter 4).

18. Christoph Bertram, "Naming a New Era: The Interregnum," *Foreign Policy* (summer 2000).

19. Kenneth N. Waltz, *Man, the State, and War: A Theoretical Analysis* (New York: Columbia University Press, 1959).

Contributors

Chester A. Crocker is the James R. Schlesinger Professor of Strategic Studies at Georgetown University and chairman of the board of directors of the United States Institute of Peace. From 1981 to 1989 he was assistant secretary of state for African affairs; as such, he was the principal diplomatic architect and mediator in the prolonged negotiations among Angola, Cuba, and South Africa that led to Namibia's transition to democratic governance and independence, and to the withdrawal of Cuban forces from Angola. He is the author of *High Noon in Southern Africa: Making Peace in a Rough Neighborhood,* and coeditor of *Managing Global Chaos: Sources of and Responses to International Conflict; African Conflict Resolution: The U.S. Role in Peacemaking;* and *Herding Cats: Multiparty Mediation in a Complex World.* He is also an adviser on strategy and negotiation to U.S. and European firms.

Fen Osler Hampson is professor of international affairs at the Norman Paterson School of International Affairs, Carleton University, Ottawa, Canada. He is the author of five books, including *Nurturing Peace: Why Peace Settlements Succeed or Fail,* and coeditor of twenty others, including *Managing Global Chaos: Sources of and Responses to International Conflict* and *Herding Cats: Multiparty Mediation in a Complex World.* His most recent book is *Madness in the Multitude: Human Security and World Disorder* (Oxford University Press, 2001). Hampson was a peace fellow at the United States Institute of Peace in 1993–94.

Pamela Aall is director of the Education Program at the United States Institute of Peace and has been acting director of the Education and Training Program at the Institute. Before joining the Institute, she was a consultant to the President's Committee on the Arts and the Humanities, and to the Institute of International Education. She held a number of positions at the Rockefeller Foundation and has worked for the European Cultural Foundation and the International Council for Educational Development. She is coeditor of *Managing Global Chaos: Sources of and Responses to International Conflict* and *Herding Cats: Multiparty Mediation in a Complex World,* and coauthor of *Guide to IGOs, NGOs, and the Military in Peace and Relief Operations.*

Mary B. Anderson, a development economist, is president of the Collaborative for Development Action, Cambridge, Massachusetts.

R. Scott Appleby teaches courses in American religious history and comparative religious movements. Formerly, he chaired the religious studies department of St. Xavier College, Chicago, and was codirector of the American Academy of Arts and Sciences' Fundamentalism Project.

Mohammed Ayoob is University Distinguished Professor of International Relations at James Madison College, Michigan State University.

Pauline H. Baker is president of the Fund for Peace and an adjunct professor at the Graduate School of Foreign Service, Georgetown University. She was a grantee of the United States Institute of Peace in 1997 and 2000.

Nicole Ball is visiting senior research fellow at the Center for International Development and Conflict Management, University of Maryland, College Park.

Richard K. Betts is Leo A. Shifrin Professor of War and Peace Studies in the School of International and Public Affairs, Columbia University. He was an Institute grantee in 1992.

Michael Brown is director of the M.A. in security studies program and director of the Center for Peace and Security Studies at the Edmund A. Walsh School of Foreign Service, Georgetown University. He was an Institute grantee in 1998.

Raymond Cohen is professor of international relations at the Hebrew Univeristy of Jerusalem. He was a fellow at the United States Institute of Peace in 1988–89 and in 1996.

Paul Collier is director of the Development Research Group of the World Bank. He is on leave from the University of Oxford, where he is professor of economics and director of the Centre for the Study of African Economics.

Alain Destexhe is a senator in the Belgian Parliament, a former president of the International Crisis Group, and secretary general of Doctors Without Borders (Médicins Sans Frontières).

Michael W. Doyle is director of the Center of International Studies and Edwards S. Sanford Professor of Politics and International Affairs at Princeton University. He was an Institute grantee in 1996.

Rolf Ekeus is the OSCE's High Commissioner on National Minorities and chairman of the governing board of SIPRI (the Stockholm International Peace Research Institute). He is a former Swedish ambassador to the United States and the OSCE, and former executive chairman of the United Nations Special Commission on Iraq.

Lawrence Freedman is professor at the Department of War Studies at King's College, London, in the University of London.

Nils Petter Gleditsch is research professor at the International Peace Research Institute (PRIO), Oslo; editor of the *Journal of Peace Research;* and professor of international relations at the Norwegian University of Science and Technology in Trondheim. He was an Institute grantee in 1996.

Jean-Marie Guehenno is United Nations undersecretary general for peacekeeping operations.

Ted Robert Gurr is Distinguished University Professor at the University of Maryland, College Park, and director of the Minorities at Risk Project. He was a peace fellow at the United States Institute of Peace in 1988–89 and an Institute grantee in 1988, 1989, 1994, and 1999.

Richard N. Haass is director of policy planning in the U.S. State Department. He is a former vice president and director of Foreign Policy Studies and Sydney Stein, Jr., Chair in International Security at the Brookings Institution.

Virginia Haufler is associate professor of government and politics at the University of Maryland.

Stanley Hoffmann is Paul and Catherine Buttenwieser University Professor at Harvard University. He was chairman of the Center for European Studies at Harvard from 1969 to 1995. He was an Institute grantee in 1992.

P. Terrence Hopmann is professor of political science and director of the Program on Global Security of the Thomas J. Watson Jr. Institute for International Studies at Brown University, Rhode Island. He was an Institute grantee in 1999.

Sir Michael Howard is emeritus professor of modern history at the University of Oxford and life president of the International Institute for Strategic Studies.

Bruce W. Jentleson is director of the Terry Sanford Institute of Public Policy and professor of public policy and political science at Duke University. He was a senior fellow at the United States Institute of Peace in 1999.

Chantal de Jonge Oudraat is an associate at the Carnegie Endowment for International Peace in Washington, D.C.

Geoffrey Kemp is director for regional strategic programs at the Nixon Center, Washington, D.C. He was an Institute grantee in 1988, 1993, 1994, and 1999.

Michael Krepon is president emeritus of the Henry L. Stimson Center. He was an Institute grantee in 1993.

Louis Kriesberg is professor emeritus of sociology and Maxwell Professor Emeritus of Social Conflict Studies at Syracuse University, where he was also founding director of the Program on the Analysis and Resolution of Conflicts. He was an Institute grantee in 1987.

Neil J. Kritz is director of the Rule of Law Program at the United States Institute of Peace.

Charles A. Kupchan is associate professor of international affairs at the School of Foreign Service and Government Department of Georgetown University and senior fellow at the Council on Foreign Relations. He was an Institute grantee in 1999.

John Paul Lederach teaches and works in international peacebuilding for the Joan B. Kroc Institute for Peace at Notre Dame University and is a distinguished scholar at Eastern Mennonite University's Conflict Transformation Program. He was an Institute grantee in 1995.

Jack S. Levy is Board of Governors' Professor of Political Science at Rutgers University.

Roy Licklider is professor of political science, Rutgers University. He was an Institute grantee in 1989 and 1995.

Edward N. Luttwak is senior fellow at the Center for Strategic and International Studies, Washington, D.C.

Edward D. Mansfield is professor of political science at Ohio State University. He was an Institute grantee in 1996.

Joseph S. Nye, Jr., Don K. Price Professor of Public Policy, is dean of the Kennedy School. He returned to Harvard in 1995 after serving as assistant secretary of defense for international security affairs and as chair of the National Intelligence Council.

Roland Paris is assistant professor of political science and international affairs at the University of Colorado, Boulder.

Connie Peck is senior coordinator of the Programme in Peacemaking and Preventive Diplomacy at the United Nations Institute for Training and Research. She was an Institute grantee in 1993 and 1994.

Harold H. Saunders is director of international affairs at the Charles F. Kettering Foundation. He was formerly assistant secretary of state for Near Eastern and South Asian affairs. He was an Institute grantee in 1987 and 1996.

William A. Schabas is director of the Irish Centre for Human Rights at the National University of Ireland, Galway, where he also holds the professorship in human rights law.

Lawrence Scheinman is Distinguished Professor of International Policy, Monterey Institute, and was assistant director of the U.S. Arms Control and Disarmament Agency responsible for nonproliferation and regional arms control in the Clinton administration.

Timothy D. Sisk is on the faculty of the Conflict Resolution Program at the University of Denver and a senior research associate at the Graduate School of International Studies. He is a former program officer and research scholar at the United States Institute of Peace.

Jack L. Snyder is Robert and Renée Belfer Professor of International Relations at the Institute of War and Peace Studies, Columbia University. He was an Institute grantee in 1996.

Stephen John Stedman is senior research scholar at the Center for International Security and Cooperation at Stanford University. He was an Institute grantee in 1995.

Janice Gross Stein is director of the Munk Centre for International Studies and Harrowston Professor of Conflict Management and Negotiation in the Department of Political Science at the University of Toronto. She was an Institute grantee in 1988.

Warren P. Strobel is a senior editor at *U.S. News & World Report*, responsible for covering national security and intelligence. He was a fellow at the United States Institute of Peace in 1994–95 and an Institute grantee in 1997.

Saadia Touval teaches in the conflict management program the Nitze School of Advanced International Studies, Johns Hopkins University, Washington, D.C. He was formerly professor of political science and dean of the Faculty of Social Sciences at Tel Aviv University. He was a fellow at the United States Institute of Peace in 1993–94.

Phil Williams is professor of international security in the Graduate School of Public and International Affairs at the University of Pittsburgh. He was an Institute grantee in 1999.

David S. Yost is a professor at the U.S. Naval Postgraduate School in Monterey, California. He was a senior fellow at the United States Institute of Peace in 1996–97.

I. William Zartman is the Jacob Blaustein Professor of Conflict Resolution and International Organization at the Nitze School of Advanced International Studies, Johns Hopkins University, Washington, D.C. He was a visiting fellow at the United States Institute of Peace in 1992–93 and an Institute grantee in 1988, 1996, and 1998.

PART I
THE SOURCES AND CHANGING GLOBAL CONTEXT OF CONFLICT

1

Theories of Interstate and Intrastate War

A Levels-of-Analysis Approach

Jack S. Levy

A GLANCE THROUGH the table of contents of this volume reveals how dramatically our perceptions of international conflict have changed since the end of the Cold War. Conventional concerns about superpower confrontation, the balance of power, alliances, arms races, and deterrence have given way to new concerns about regional conflicts, ethnonational wars, religious militancy, resource scarcity and environmental degradation, preventive diplomacy, peacekeeping, and humanitarian intervention. This shift in focus reflects some unmistakable changes in patterns of warfare: over the past five centuries war between the great powers has significantly increased in severity but diminished in frequency; over the past five decades war has shifted away from the great powers and away from Europe to other actors in other regional systems, and away from interstate wars to intrastate wars; and the distinction between interstate and intrastate wars has itself begun to blur.[1]

Although some argue that the end of the Cold War has changed "all the answers and all

the questions,"[2] the theme of change must be tempered by that of continuity. The world has changed in profound ways over the millennia, but many of the factors that play a central role in contemporary international conflicts would have been familiar to Thucydides, who wrote his history of the Peloponnesian War over twenty-four hundred years ago.[3] Thucydides' argument that "the strong do what they can and the weak suffer what they must" is as relevant for contemporary ethnonational conflicts as it was for the Peloponnesian War, and many of the "nontraditional" causes of war discussed in this volume (refugees from environmental disasters, for example) exert their influence through causal paths (like external scapegoating) that played a central role in many of the great power wars of the past.

My aim in this chapter is to put many of the explanations and arguments discussed in the individual chapters in this volume into a larger theoretical context and to integrate the sources of continuity and the sources of change into a single overarching framework. I select some of the leading theories of international conflict, identify their key variables, specify the causal paths through which they affect decisions for war and peace, highlight some of the key interaction effects between variables at different levels of analysis, and suggest which of these theories are likely to be most useful for understanding changing patterns of warfare in the new global system. I include both traditional theories of international war and new theories of ethnonationalism, population movements, and environmental change. I try to provide in the limited space available an overview of contending theories rather than detailed evidence, examples, or analytical critiques.

I organize this theoretical review around a "levels-of-analysis framework," which was first systematized by Kenneth Waltz and then widely used by scholars in the analysis of the causes of interstate wars. I show that, with some modifications, this framework can also be useful for analyzing the intrastate wars of the contemporary era.[4]

THE LEVELS-OF-ANALYSIS FRAMEWORK

The levels-of-analysis framework suggests that the causes of war can be analyzed at the level of the individual, the nation-state, and the international system. The individual level focuses primarily on human nature and predispositions toward aggression and on individual political leaders and their belief systems, personalities, and psychological processes. The nation-state (or national) level includes both governmental variables, such as the structure of the political system and the nature of the policymaking process, and societal factors, such as the structure of the economic system, the role of public opinion, economic and noneconomic interest groups, ethnicity and nationalism, and political culture and ideology. International system- (or systemic-) level causes include the anarchic structure of the global system, the number of

major powers in the system, the distribution of military and economic power among them, patterns of military alliances and international trade, and other factors that constitute the external environment common to all states. In a later work Waltz collapsed the individual and nation-state levels to create a simplified dichotomy of nation (or unit) level and system level. Others have disaggregated the nation-state level into distinct governmental and domestic- or societal-level factors.[5]

Scholars generally use the levels of analysis as a framework for classifying independent variables that explain state foreign policy behaviors and international outcomes. This leads us to ask such questions as whether the causes of war are to be found primarily at the level of the individual, the nation-state, or international system, and how variables from different levels interact in the foreign policy process.

The levels-of-analysis framework is sometimes used in a different way, to refer not to the independent causal variables but instead to the dependent variable—that is, to the unit of analysis or type of actor (individual, organization, group, state, or system) whose behavior is to be explained. In this second sense the systemic level of analysis refers to explanations of patterns and outcomes in the international system, the dyadic level to explanations of the strategic interactions between two states, the national level to explanations of state foreign policy behaviors, the organizational level to explanations of the behaviors of key governmental organizations (the U.S. Department of Defense, for example), and the individual level to explanations of the preferences, beliefs, or choices of individuals.[6] In this essay I use levels of analysis to refer to independent causal variables.

It is logically possible and in fact usually desirable for explanations to combine causal variables from different levels of analysis, because whether war or peace occurs is usually determined by multiple variables operating at more than one level of analysis. Among the factors contributing to Iraq's invasion of Kuwait in 1990, for example, were the poor condition of Iraq's economy (a domestic or societal-level variable), Iraq's need for higher oil prices and the refusal of Arab oil-producing states to lower production levels and thus allow prices to rise (a systemic variable), and Saddam Hussein's propensities for risk taking (an individual-level variable). Similarly, a unipolar system, global political economy, and democracy work together to reinforce peace, as Charles Kupchan argues in chapter 3 of this volume. Michael Brown's classification (chapter 13) of the sources of internal war in terms of bad leaders, bad domestic problems, bad neighborhoods, and bad neighbors can be framed in terms of levels of analysis: the first is an individual-level factor, the second a domestic-level factor, and the third a regional system factor, and the fourth refers to the external environment of a particular state.

The preceding examples illustrate the use of independent causal variables from various levels to explain state decisions for war. We can also use causal variables from different levels to explain the foreign policy preferences of individual leaders. We have to be careful whenever we use causal variables at one level to explain behavior or outcomes at a "higher" level. Individual- or domestic-level variables, for example, do not provide a logically complete explanation of aggressive state policies unless they are combined with a "theory of foreign policy" that explains how the preferences of individual actors or domestic publics are translated into a foreign policy decision for the state. Saddam Hussein's beliefs and personality may help explain the origins of the 1990–91 Persian Gulf War, but only in conjunction with the highly centralized structure of the Iraqi regime, which allowed Saddam to make policy in the absence of any significant internal constraints. Political leaders cannot always implement their preferred policies. U.S. president William McKinley preferred to avoid war with Spain in 1898, but because of domestic pressures for war McKinley "led his country unhesitatingly toward a war which he did not want for a cause in which he did not believe."[7]

Similarly, explanations of state foreign policy preferences or behaviors do not generally provide a logically complete explanation for war or peace. Because war and peace are both dyadic or systemic outcomes resulting from the interactions of two or more states, an explanation for war and peace requires the inclusion of dyadic- or systemic-level causal variables.[8] While attempts to secure peace through a policy based on the idea of si vis pacem, para bellum (if you want peace, prepare for war) are sometimes effective, they can also backfire, provoke the adversary rather than deter him, and lead to war through a conflict spiral. Alternatively, a strategy of advancing peace by adopting a conciliatory policy toward the adversary often works, but it might also fail by undermining a state's credibility, leading the adversary to increase its demands in the expectation that further concessions will be forthcoming, and result in war by miscalculation.[9] A theory of war is technically incomplete without a theory of bargaining or strategic interaction that explains how states respond to each other's actions and how they act in anticipation of each other's responses.

Although the levels-of-analysis framework has traditionally been applied to states and to interstate relations, with some modifications it can also be applied to a wide range of nonstate actors, from international organizations like the United Nations to nonstate entities like the Kosovar Albanians or transnational criminal enterprises (see Phil Williams's analysis in chapter 7 of this volume). We could ask whether decisions for UN intervention are driven more by the imperatives of the situation, by politics within the United Nations, or by the leadership of the secretary-general; whether the behavior of a particular nonstate communal group is influenced primarily by the external threats and opportunities it faces, by pressures from subgroups within it (including its military arm), or by the particular beliefs and charisma of an individual leader; or whether the behavior of an international drug ring is driven by rational calculations of profit and loss given the political economy of the international drug traffic, by political infighting within the organization, or by the risk-taking propensities of individual leaders. Although the levels-of-analysis framework can be applied to any actor, the framework assumes that the actor in question is sufficiently organized that it has a decision-making body with the authority to act on behalf of the group. If the group is more amorphous, so that we cannot speak of a single group policy with inputs from different levels, it is harder to apply the levels-of-analysis framework.

Although the levels-of-analysis framework is very useful, it is not perfect. It is better for classifying the sources of a particular state's foreign policy (or the policies of any organization) than for explaining wars or other outcomes that are the product of the strategic interaction of two or more actors, though if we are cognizant of the need to explain dyadic-level outcomes the limitations of the framework can be minimized. The levels-of-analysis framework is also more useful in classifying variables than in classifying theories. Although Waltz applied his different "images" of conflict to theories,[10] most of the theories he focused on (human nature and aggressive-instinct theories, Marxist-Leninist theories of imperialism or Kantian theories of republican states, and Rousseau's systems theory based on anarchy) were "monocausal," or single-factor, theories, or at least theories for which the key variables all derived from a single level of analysis.

Although we still have some single-level theories (systemic-level realist theories, including balance-of-power theory and power transition theory, for example), most of our theories of war and peace have become more complex and involve variables from two or more levels of analysis. Liberal theories of economic interdependence and peace, for example, include both political leaders' fears of the economic costs of war and their deterrent effect on conflict (a dyadic-level factor) and the influence of domestic economic groups that have a vested interest in the continuation of peace (a societal-level factor). Contemporary theories of both globalization and conflict incorporate the structure of the global economy, internal economic sources of economic expansion and contraction, domestic pressure groups, and economic ideologies, as Kupchan demonstrates in chapter 3 and Jean-Marie Guehenno in chapter 6. Theories of environmental scarcities include both systemic-level sources of resource scarcities and environmental refugees along with their societal-level impact, including changing demographic balances and incentives for scapegoating, as Nils Petter Gleditsch argues in chapter 4. Rational choice theories emphasize the maximization of interests under constraints, but interests include both state interests and external constraints (systemic level) and the interests of elites in maintaining their own political power in the face of domestic constraints (societal level). We can often use the levels-of-analysis framework to classify the individual components of these theories, which is very useful, but not the theories themselves.

In addition, some important variables are themselves difficult to classify because they cut across the different levels of analysis. The impact of oil on the U.S. decision to intervene against Iraq in the Persian Gulf War had both systemic and societal components; the Bush administration's wish to maintain access to oil at reasonable prices involved concerns about the impact of higher oil prices on the economies of the United States, its key allies, and newly democratizing states of the former Soviet bloc, and perhaps about the economic interests of U.S.-based oil companies.[11] Oil companies are both domestic actors in the U.S. political system and transnational actors in the global political economy, and it is not always clear how best to classify them. Economic variables in general often have an international and domestic component and are difficult to classify in terms of a single level. Nevertheless, by leading us to recognize the various components of a complex concept or factor (such as the implications of oil for national economic interests and for private economic interests, or the importance of credibility for states and for individual leaders), the levels-of-analysis framework serves a useful role.

Despite its limitations, the levels-of-analysis framework is still more useful than most other frameworks for classifying alternative explanations of the causes of war and peace, and I use it here in that capacity. I focus primarily on theories of interstate war, because until recently that is the realm of the most systematic theorizing about international conflict. In the process I consider the possible application of some of these theories to the kinds of intrastate wars that plague the contemporary world, and I also relate some contemporary theories of ethnonational conflict to older theories of great power war.

SYSTEMIC-LEVEL SOURCES OF INTERNATIONAL CONFLICT

The traditional literature on the causes of war has been dominated by the realist paradigm, a systemic-level approach that incorporates several distinct theories. These theories all posit that the key actors are sovereign states that act rationally to advance their security, power, and wealth in an anarchic system, which is characterized by the lack of a legitimate authority to regulate disputes and enforce agreements between states. Anarchy, along with uncertainties regarding the present and future intentions of the adversary, induces political leaders to focus on short-term security needs and on their relative position in the system, adopt worst-case thinking, build up their military strength, and utilize coercive threats to advance their interests, influence the adversary, and maintain their reputations. The core realist hypothesis is that international outcomes are determined by, or

at least are significantly constrained by, the distribution of power between two or more states, though different conceptions of power and of the nature of the system lead to different theories and different predictions about what those specific outcomes are.[12]

In the realist worldview, wars occur not only because some states prefer war to peace (such as Hitler's Germany in 1939), but also because of the unintended consequences of actions by those who prefer peace to war and who are more interested in preserving their security than in extending their influence. Even defensively motivated efforts by states to provide for their own security through armaments, alliances, and deterrent threats are often perceived as threatening by others, which leads to counteractions and conflict spirals that become difficult to reverse. This is the "security dilemma"—actions to increase one's security may only decrease the security of others and lead them to respond in ways that decrease one's own security.[13] It is often said that World War I was a classic case of an "inadvertent war" between states that did not seek war but that became locked in a conflict that spiraled out of control.[14]

The leading realist theory is balance-of-power theory, which posits the avoidance of hegemony as the primary goal of states and the maintenance of an equilibrium of power in the system as the primary instrumental goal. The theory predicts that states, and particularly great powers, will build up their arms and form alliances to balance against the primary threats to their interests and particularly against any state that threatens to secure a hegemonic position over the system. Balance-of-power theorists argue that the balancing mechanism almost always works successfully to avoid hegemony, either because potential hegemons are deterred by their anticipation of a military coalition forming against them or because they are defeated in war after deterrence fails.[15] In this view, the two world wars of this century and the European war against Napoleonic France a century before were each "balance-of-power wars" that resulted from the formation of a military coalition to block a threatening state from achieving a position of dominance.

The general realist proposition that states act to advance their interests, defined primarily in terms of security, and that the distribution of power is the primary determinant of international outcomes has clear relevance for regional and ethnonational conflicts in the contemporary world.[16] The idea that states have "neither permanent friends nor permanent enemies, just permanent interests" (in the words of Lord Palmerston, the mid-nineteenth-century British leader) applies to contemporary conflicts as well as to the great power politics of earlier centuries.[17] So does the idea that states facing rapidly rising adversaries may be tempted to initiate a preventive war in order to defeat the adversary while the opportunity is still available, which is reflected in Michael Howard's argument (chapter 2) that "the causes of war remain rooted, as much as they were in the pre-industrial age, in perceptions by statesmen of the growth of hostile power and the fears for the restriction, if not the extinction, of their own."[18]

An important alternative to balance-of-power theory is "power transition theory," a form of hegemonic theory that shares realist assumptions but that emphasizes the existence of order within a nominally anarchic system. Hegemons commonly arise and use their strength to create a set of political and economic structures and norms of behavior that enhance the stability of the system at the same time that they advance their own security. Differential rates of growth lead to the rise and fall of hegemons, however, and the probability of a major war grows as the hegemon loses its dominant position and reaches a maximum at the point when the declining leader is overtaken by the rising challenger.[19]

Hegemonic theory has direct implications for the contemporary world. As Kupchan (chapter 3) argues, unipolarity under U.S. leadership contributes to stability in the contemporary world, but with the inevitable decline of U.S. hegemony new instabilities will arise, especially in East Asia. In particular, many fear the consequences of the continued rise of Chinese power and the dangers of a Sino-American conflict as the point of a power transition approaches, which is estimated to occur in about three decades.

In power transition theory, it is the combination of equality of power and change in power that is destabilizing. We can separate the static component, which posits that at the dyadic level war is least likely when one state has a preponderance of power over another and most likely when there is an equality of power. This is the "power preponderance hypothesis." It is based on the logic that under conditions of preponderance the strong are satisfied and do not have the incentives for war and the weak, though dissatisfied, lack the capability for war.

The power preponderance hypothesis, which draws strong support from empirical studies,[20] is reflected in many arguments about ethnonational conflict—that ethnonational wars that end in decisive victories are far less likely to be followed by renewed violence than are negotiated settlements based on roughly equal power,[21] or that a situation characterized by the strong dominance of one ethnic group is less prone to violent conflict than one characterized by an equality of power or a moderate imbalance of power between the two groups.[22] The latter argument is challenged, or at least qualified, by those like Paul Collier (chapter 10), who emphasizes the stabilizing effects of ethnic diversity, and Ted Robert Gurr (chapter 11), who argues that the effects of ethnic geography can be mitigated by commitments to protect the rights of minorities.

Arguments about the consequences of a particular distribution of power between ethnonational groups need to be placed within a larger political context. Ethnonational minorities are often secure within stable political systems characterized by strong centralized state or imperial institutions (the communist political systems in the former Soviet bloc, for example), but the collapse of state power leaves ethnonational communities in a condition of "emerging anarchy." With uncertainty about their future and with fear for their security, these groups define their highest priority to be security against physical and economic threats. Nationalism is basically the desire among a group to create a state capable of dealing with such threats and providing protection for the group.

Such ethnonational groups may have no hostile intentions toward other groups but still desire to build up their military strength for protection. In doing so, however, they only threaten the security of others, resulting in misperceptions, conflict spirals, and the preventive use of force by those perceiving temporary but vanishing advantages. Thus ethnonational groups in a condition of weakening centralized authority face an "ethnic security dilemma" that is comparable to the security dilemma facing states in the international system, with many of the same consequences.[23] This is a realist explanation for ethnonational conflict, with the unit of analysis shifted from states to ethnonational communities or other identity groups that seek security in an anarchic system without external guarantees of protection.

This perspective generates a number of propositions about the intensity of the ethnic security dilemma and hence the likelihood of violence. Violence is most likely if there is a low congruence between state territorial borders and ethnonational boundaries and if ethnic groups are intermingled (rather than each being concentrated in its own area). This reduces the legitimacy of states, leaves many ethnic minorities outside the boundaries of their nation-states, and makes protection more difficult. It increases the likelihood of secessionist wars by captive peoples to withdraw from the territory of a larger state and create their own state, and of irredentist wars by ethnic groups in one state to retrieve ethnically kindred people and their territory from another state. If, however, state boundaries correspond with ethnonational

boundaries, state armies can protect their own ethnonational groups. Similarly, if ethnic minorities are concentrated in certain areas within a state, it is easier for them to protect themselves than if they are dispersed.[24]

Realist theories, which have long dominated the analysis of the causes of interstate wars, and which now provide an important explanation for ethnonational wars, have recently been challenged from a number of directions. One such challenge comes from liberal international theory, which is really a set of related theories sharing a broad set of assumptions and which suggests that under certain conditions the violence-prone character of an anarchic system can be ameliorated and levels of warfare significantly reduced. The primary components of this liberal theory of peace are free trade, democratic political systems, and international institutions.[25]

I focus here on the liberal theory that trade promotes peace (commercial liberalism), and then on the democratic peace proposition (republican liberalism). I leave aside theories of the peaceful effects of international institutions (institutional liberalism). Although there are well-developed theories of the effects of international institutions on cooperation between states, particularly in the international political economy, the effects of institutions on decisions for war and peace are less well developed. Such theories may help explain the role of external intervention in stabilizing or destabilizing regional conflicts and civil wars (see the essays in part II of this volume), but they are less likely to explain variations in war and peace among the great powers.[26]

The idea that trade and other forms of economic interdependence promote peace goes back to Adam Smith and David Ricardo. Scholars advance a number of interrelated theoretical arguments in support of this proposition, the most compelling of which is that trade generates economic advantages for both parties (otherwise they would not trade) and that the anticipation that war will disrupt trade and lead to a loss of the benefits of trade deters political leaders from initiating militarized conflict.[27] Liberal theorists also argue that the prosperity generated by trade promotes a culture of acquisitiveness that dampens the martial spirit, and that trade empowers certain domestic groups that have vested interests in the continuation of trade and therefore in the maintenance of the peace that supports that trade.[28]

Mercantilists and economic nationalists, reflecting a realist perspective, criticize the liberal economic theory of war on a number of grounds. They argue, first, that the magnitude of the effects of trade on decisions for war and peace is small relative to that of military and diplomatic considerations, pointing to the fact that high levels of economic interdependence in 1914 did not deter the great powers from becoming involved in an enormously destructive general war. Realists also argue that the causal arrow between trade and peace might be reversed: rather than trade promoting peace, it may be that peace creates conditions for trade and prosperity. It is more plausible to argue that the absence of conflict leads to Arab-Israeli trade than to argue that Arab-Israeli trade plays a significant role in reducing political conflict.

Realists question the implicit liberal assumption that trade is always more efficient than military coercion in expanding markets and investment opportunities and in promoting state wealth. They concede the validity of this assumption for the contemporary system, at least for advanced industrial states (but not necessarily for parts of Africa or elsewhere in the developing world), but argue that it is not universally valid; for much of human history military force has been a useful instrument to promote state wealth as well as power. Thus the anticipated gains from war outweigh the anticipated losses from a disruption of trade. Many liberal theorists concede this point but argue that as the foundations of wealth and power have historically shifted from territory to industrialization and now to knowledge-based forms of production, the economic value of territorial

conquest has diminished, at least for advanced industrial states. As a result, trade is economically efficient and peace promoting in the Western world in the contemporary era.[29]

Realists also question whether trade always has a negative effect on international conflict. They argue that political leaders are less influenced by the possibility of gains from trade in an absolute sense than by concerns about relative gains, by the fear that the adversary will gain more from trade and convert those gains into further economic gains, political influence, and military power.[30] Concerns about the strategic implications of trade, exacerbated by domestic pressures for protectionist policies, especially during economic downturns, can transform economic competitions between trading partners into strategic rivalries that sometimes escalate to war.

In addition, while the economic interdependence created by trade generates mutual dependence between trading partners, this dependence is often asymmetrical, and the less dependent party may be tempted to use economic coercion to exploit the adversary's vulnerabilities and influence its behavior relating to security as well as economic issues. These tendencies are reinforced by demands for protectionist pressures from domestic economic groups that are especially vulnerable to external developments, particularly in bad economic times, and by leaders' temptations to bolster their domestic support through hard-line foreign policies. These can lead to retaliatory actions, conflict spirals, and war. The U.S. oil embargo against Japan in 1940, for example, set off a conflict spiral that contributed to the Pacific War.

Whether the deterrent effects of the gains from trade outweigh the potentially destabilizing effects of economic asymmetries and economic competitions, and whether the latter escalate to trade wars and militarized conflicts, is ultimately an empirical question that analysts have only recently begun to analyze systematically. The evidence so far suggests that on average trade contributes to peace but that the effect is rather modest.[31] Because of debates about the best way to test the trade-promotes-peace hypothesis,[32] because the relationship is only modest in strength, and because of numerous cases in which economic interdependence either fails to prevent war or perhaps even contributes to it, the current evidence in support of the liberal economic theory of peace must be treated as provisional. Scholars need to give more attention to the *conditions* under which trade either promotes peace or exacerbates conflict.

Although the liberal economic theory of peace, like so many other theories of international conflict, was developed with the experience of the European great powers in mind, the theory, along with the realist critique, has enormous relevance for the contemporary world. The pacifying effects of trade have undoubtedly contributed to the condition of stable peace among the advanced industrial democracies of the European Union. Whether the lure of prosperity through trade will have a comparable effect in the Middle East, or whether it will be too weak to overcome long-standing hostilities between Arabs and Israelis, is a critical question for the future. Another critical set of questions concerns economic rivalries. Will the leading military powers, who face diminishing military security threats after the end of the Cold War, at least for a while, respond by shifting their competition to the economic realm, and will this result in economic rivalries that exacerbate political hostilities between them?[33] Will competition among developing states for scarce resources be resolved peacefully, or will the demands of economic development combine with political differences to generate economic rivalries and resource wars?

It is conceivable that economic rivalries, fueled by parochial domestic interests and by hard-line publics sympathetic to the appeals of economic nationalism, could escalate into strategic rivalries and then possibly into crises or military confrontations. Although the militarization of commercial rivalries was an important path to war between great powers in the seventeenth century,[34] this pattern is much less likely to repeat itself in the future, at least for the great powers. New developments in military technology render war too costly for one advanced industrial power against another, and the globalization of markets and finance makes free trade an efficient strategy for the accumulation of economic wealth, at least for advanced capitalist states. This has been reinforced by the growth of liberal economic theory and decline of mercantilist doctrines. Changing technology has also increased the range of domestic substitutes for key natural resources, which lessens the competition for scarce natural resources. Thus it is hard to imagine that the political leaders of advanced industrial states would conclude that their economic interests might be better served by a strategy of military conquest than a strategy of free trade. The Pacific War between Japan and the United States serves as a cautionary tale, however, because Japan's need for oil and other resources in Southeast Asia in the face of a U.S. oil embargo was a key motivation leading to Japan's initiation of the war. That was an extraordinarily high-risk war for a great power, however, and the development of nuclear weapons magnifies those risks many times over.

These arguments are less compelling for much of the Third World, where military force can be used without the fear of mutual destruction, and where norms against the use of force are much weaker than in the West. In addition, territory and territory-based resources remain an important element of military power and economic wealth; the demand for already limited resources is further exacerbated by growing populations and limited infrastructures, so that natural resources make an attractive target for military conquest.

The potentially explosive impact of resource scarcities in the developing world has generated a growing literature on environmental scarcity and its implications for international conflict. One of the central themes in this literature is the neo-Malthusian argument that rapidly growing and increasingly urbanized populations competing for scarce resources—coupled with the degradation of those resources by desertification, deforestation, rising sea levels, pollution, and environmental disasters—will generate famines, economic and social problems, environmental refugees, political instabilities, and serious domestic and international crises.[35] This is most likely to arise for developing countries, which generally lack the wealth and institutional capacity to respond effectively to environmental disruptions.[36]

The combination of population growth, uneven resource distribution, and the environmental degradation of scarce resources leads to scarcities that can contribute to violent conflict in a number of ways. The most direct path is through "simple-scarcity" conflicts or "resource wars" between states, in which one state uses military force against another for the primary purpose of gaining access to key economic and strategic resources. The primary factor leading to Iraq's invasion of Kuwait in 1990, for example, was the goal of gaining control over Kuwait's vast oil supplies as a means of reviving the Iraqi economy, eliminating an oppressive debt, and in doing so further consolidating Saddam's hold on political power. This case is consistent with Thomas Homer-Dixon's argument that conflicts over nonrenewable resources tend to be more destabilizing than disputes over renewable resources. The potential exception here is water: disputes over river water may be a particularly serious point of conflict in the future.[37]

Simple scarcity conflicts or "resource wars" are not the only path from environmental scarcity to war. Perhaps even more likely is an indirect path that goes through societal and governmental responses to systemically induced pressures. These responses include scapegoating against external states and against refugees who might conceivably be blamed for the problem.[38] I return to these in the next section,

on societal-level causes of war. For now, it suffices to hypothesize that economic competition over limited resources is more likely to arise, and more likely to take on a strategic dimension and escalate to war, for contemporary Third World states than for advanced industrial states.

The sources of state behavior and international patterns in realist balance-of-power theory and power transition theory, and also in some versions of liberal economic theories of trade and peace, are found primarily at the systemic level.[39] With the exception of some diehard realists, however, scholars have increasingly recognized that systemic structures cannot by themselves provide a fully satisfactory explanation of variations in war and peace, and this has led to increasing challenges to realism and other systemic-level theories from theoretical perspectives linked to the societal, bureaucratic/organizational, and individual levels. The argument is not only that these other levels of analysis will become increasingly important in the future, but also that their influence on international behavior in the past has been seriously underestimated.[40]

SOCIETAL-LEVEL SOURCES OF INTERNATIONAL CONFLICT

After decades of neglect, domestic variables now occupy center stage in the study of international conflict. Although one long-standing approach to international conflict, Marxism-Leninism, has waned in influence, another, Kantian liberal theory, has suddenly developed into one of the most vibrant research enterprises in the field, as scholars examine the "democratic peace" and related aspects of the security behavior of democratic states.[41] Scholars have also devoted much attention to the diversionary theory of war and, more recently, to the impact of domestic political economy and political culture on war and peace. The increasing importance of intrastate wars, particularly ethnonational wars, has generated considerable interest in ethnonationalism, the political capacity of states, environmental scarcity and degradation, population movements, and other factors that either operate at the societal level or include societal factors as a major step in the hypothesized causal chain leading to war. Societal-level groups can affect intrastate wars either indirectly, through their influence on state policies (which is how they affect interstate wars), or directly, through their own military actions, because in internal wars organized identity groups are themselves independent actors.

Although Immanuel Kant spoke of a "pacific union" among democracies,[42] and although many have argued that democracies behave differently than do nondemocratic states in international relations, it was not until a number of studies in the mid-1980s offered systematic evidence that democracies rarely if ever go to war with each other that the "democratic peace" became a central focus of scholarly research in international relations. What is striking about this finding is that in a realm as complex as international relations, in which the actions and interactions of states are so historically contingent, and in which the regularized laws of physics are only a dream to scholars in search of a science of international relations, the absence of war between democracies "comes as close as anything we have to an empirical law in international relations."[43] Although interest in the democratic peace began with a strong empirical finding, it was intensified by the fact that the observed pattern contradicted realist theory,[44] constituted the core of an emerging liberal theory of peace and war, reinforced the ideological foundations of U.S. foreign policy, and provided some basis for optimism that the persistent pattern of international war might one day be broken.

To say that democracies rarely if ever fight each other is not necessarily to say that democracies are more peaceful than other kinds of states. Most of the evidence suggests that democracies are as likely as authoritarian states to get involved in wars; they often fight imperial wars; in wars between democracies and autocracies they are more likely to be the initiators than the targets; and they occasionally engage in covert action against each other.[45] But the fact remains that they have been nearly immune from war against each other and that there are few if any unambiguous cases of actual wars between democracies.[46] Scholars have also demonstrated that the relative absence of war between democracies cannot be explained by the fact that democratic dyads trade a lot with each other and that potential conflicts between democracies in the period since World War II were suppressed by U.S. hegemonic power or by other economic or geopolitical factors correlated with democracy.

The growing consensus that democracies rarely if ever fight each other is not matched by any agreement on how to best explain this strong empirical regularity, and in the absence of a convincing theoretical explanation there are few grounds for predicting whether the democratic peace will continue into the future. Theorizing about the democratic peace is in its early stages, and new theories will undoubtedly be proposed, but at the present time there are three general types of models.

The "democratic culture and norms model" suggests that democratic societies are inherently averse to war, and particularly to the casualties from war, and that the norms of peaceful conflict resolution that have evolved within democratic political cultures are extended to relations between democratic states. Consequently, when democracies become involved in disputes with each other they resolve their differences through norms of bounded competition rather than through force.

The "institutional constraints model" emphasizes the checks and balances and the dispersion of power that preclude democratic leaders from taking unilateral military action and imposing aggressive wars on a citizenry that must bear most of the costs of those wars. This, combined with the role of a free press that ensures an open debate, means that democracies are more deliberate in their decisions with respect to war.

One can question whether the aversion to casualties is an inherent feature of democracies or a historically contingent aspect of U.S. and European political culture beginning in the later twentieth century (see Geoffrey Kemp's discussion in chapter 5). One can also question the institutional model's assumption that leaders have more warlike preferences than do their domestic publics, a point to which we return in our subsequent discussion of the diversionary theory of war. The institutional and cultural models also have difficulty explaining the fact, confirmed repeatedly in empirical studies, that democracies often fight and often initiate wars.

Proponents of the institutional and cultural models respond by arguing that because there are fewer internal constraints on the use of force by authoritarian leaders, autocrats often attempt to exploit the conciliatory tendencies of democracies. This undermines democratic political leaders' expectations that their peaceful conflict resolution strategies will be reciprocated, reduces their internal constraints on the use of force, and provides additional incentives for democratic regimes to use force against authoritarian regimes to eliminate their violent tendencies. This is plausible, but the institutional and cultural models have more trouble explaining why democracies have frequently initiated imperial wars against weaker opponents despite the absence of any risk of being exploited by the latter, or why democracies have fought wars against autocracies with an intensity disproportionate to any plausible security threat.

A third explanation of the democratic peace is the "signaling model," which is based on the "transparency" of democratic political systems ensured by a free press and open political competition. Transparency makes it obvious whether democratic political leaders involved in international crises have the support of the political opposition and the public. Without domestic support, democratic political leaders cannot implement military threats that might escalate to war. The adversary understands this and will adopt a harder line in crisis bargaining. Democratic leaders anticipate the adversary's resolve and avoid getting into crises in the first place unless they anticipate domestic support. This means that if democracies do get into crises, the adversary will then assume that the leader has domestic support and consequently that the leader will be highly resolved. As a result, the adversary behaves more cautiously. Thus crises bargaining involving democratic states is less likely to be characterized by misperceptions regarding the adversary's resolve and thus is less likely to escalate to war because of misperceptions.[47] In this way the signaling model better incorporates the strategic interaction between democratic states and their external adversaries than does either the cultural or institutional model.

The democratic peace also has important policy implications, for it suggests that by promoting the development of democracies around the world the United States can contribute to the elimination of war as well as to the establishment of liberal institutions and political freedom. Some researchers question this prescription, however, and argue that although well-established democratic dyads are peaceful, the *process* of transition to democracy can be a particularly destabilizing period, and that democratizing states occasionally go to war against other states and even against each other. Edward Mansfield and Jack Snyder argue in chapter 8 that the democratization process brings new social groups with widely divergent interests into the political process at a time when the state lacks the institutional capacity to accommodate conflicting interests and respond to popular demands. This can create enormous social conflict, which is often exacerbated if democratization is coupled with the introduction of market forces into nonmarket economies, which leads to popular pressures for state protection against the pain of economic adjustment.

Democratization can be particularly destabilizing in multiethnic societies where ethnic groups are uncertain about how fully their rights will be protected, especially if the state in transition is too weak to maintain a monopoly of violence to protect those rights, as Mohammed Ayoob (chapter 9) and Gurr (chapter 11) each argue. Elites competing for mass political support are tempted to make nationalist appeals and engage in external scapegoating in order to bolster their internal support. This scapegoating is particularly appealing to those elites whose interests are threatened by the democratization process and who believe that an external enemy might help reverse that process and strengthen centralized political power at home.[48]

While these theoretical linkages are plausible, most of the evidence suggests that states in the process of democratization are *not*, on average, more war prone than are other states. Violence is most likely to occur in the very early stages in the transition away from authoritarianism, not as states move closer to democracy.[49] Still, there are enough historical cases of democratizing states becoming involved in wars, through processes similar to those hypothesized above, to justify more research on the conditions under which this is likely to happen.

One example is the French Revolution, and another is Serbia under Slobodan Milosevic.[50] A key causal mechanism in these cases involves a political leader conducting an aggressive foreign policy, perhaps including the use of force, to increase his or her domestic political support. This pattern is not restricted to democratizing states, of course, but is a strategy that political leaders in a variety of states have adopted through the ages, ranging from the Athenian "Sicilian expedition" during the Peloponnesian War to the Argentinian invasion of the Falkland Islands in 1982.[51]

While scholars have often alluded to external scapegoating, it was not until the 1980s that they began to systematically investigate this phenomenon. The "diversionary theory of war" is theoretically grounded in social identity theory and the in-group/out-group hypothesis (see chapter 12, by Janice Gross Stein), which posits that conflict with an out-group increases the cohesion of a well-defined in-group.[52] Political leaders facing substantial domestic unrest or political opposition at home anticipate this response and sometimes take belligerent action, including the use of force, in order to rally domestic support. They often set the stage for their scapegoating by promoting historical myths that glorify their people's own history and to demonize the adversary.[53]

Internal political insecurity does not always lead to external scapegoating, however, and this raises the question of the conditions under which leaders are most likely to adopt this strategy. Among the conditions that scholars have identified are low to moderate levels of domestic political support and legitimacy, poor economic performance, and the perception that a diplomatic or military victory is feasible with minimal costs. Another possible variable is regime type, and some have suggested that democratic leaders, because of their electoral accountability, may have greater incentives for scapegoating than do authoritarian leaders, but empirical support for this hypothesis is mixed.[54]

Political leaders must balance incentives for scapegoating against its potential costs, however, and recent evidence suggests that democratic leaders who initiate wars, particularly losing wars, are more likely to be removed from office than are nondemocratic leaders.[55] This provides one possible basis for explaining the finding that democratic states tend to win a disproportionate number (75–80 percent) of the wars that they fight: because of the anticipated political costs of military defeat, democratic leaders are more cautious in their decisions for war (whether driven by scapegoating or other motivations) than are authoritarian leaders and tend to start only those wars they are likely to win.[56]

The fact that democratic leaders occasionally engage in diversionary action raises the interesting question of how often they scape-goat against other democracies.[57] Scholars have not yet examined this question, or the broader question of whom states select for diversionary targets. Presumably some states or groups make more useful targets than others for the purposes of rallying domestic support, but diversionary theory lacks a theory of targets. One obvious hypothesis is that because of the emotions generated by ethnic loyalties and the historical grievances associated with them, ethnic rivals make particularly useful targets for scapegoat-ing by political elites.

With the explosion of ethnic conflicts after the end of the Cold War, scholarly attention has shifted from interstate to intrastate warfare, with particular attention paid to the questions of how violent ethnonational conflicts arise, the conditions under which they end, and the pos-sible role of international intervention in the termination of ethnic wars.[58] Because cultural awareness is increasing, and because conflicts over culturally defined identities are more dif-ficult to resolve through compromise than are conflicts over tangible strategic or economic re-sources, some argue that the primary sources of international conflict in the future will be cultural rather than ideological or geopolitical, based on a "clash of civilizations" between eth-nically and religiously defined peoples.[59]

A common view of ethnonational conflicts is the "primordialist," or "ancient hatreds," ap-proach, which takes ethnic identity as a social category that is fixed by birth and sees ethnic conflict as a persistent and "natural" phenom-enon.[60] In this view, strong centralized political institutions can suppress ancient rivalries, but the collapse of those institutions (the collapse of the Soviet Union or Yugoslavia, for example) "removes the lid" on those rivalries and allows peoples to take action to settle long-suppressed grievances. Many scholars are skeptical of the primordialist view, in part because the ancient hatreds hypothesis fails to explain why violent ethnic conflicts have broken out among some ethnic communities but not others, when those

violent conflicts occur, and how intensely they are fought.[61]

An alternative perspective is the "instrumen-talist" approach, which suggests that ethnic dif-ferences are not natural but instead are manipu-lated by political leaders or elites to advance other interests. By invoking historical myths that glorify one's own people and demonize others, leaders can play the "ethnic card" in order rationalize the economic sacrifices neces-sary to support costly defense efforts, mobilize mass armies, strengthen the institutions of cen-tralized state power, and bolster their own do-mestic political support, possibly through the use of military force. Thus instrumentalist theories of ethnic conflict implicitly build on the foundations of diversionary theory.[62] As Collier argues in chapter 10, group leaders can also use the symbols of ethnicity for the rhetor-ical rationalization of predatory economic be-havior, whether directed toward the accumula-tion of wealth as a self-interested end in itself or as a necessary means for sustaining a rebellion.

However easy it may be for political leaders to use ethnic mobilization as a means to sell their policies domestically in order to advance other ends, ethnic mobilization and the poli-cies based on it are not always easy to turn back. As Stein argues in chapter 12, images of the enemy, once established, are highly resistant to change, and political leaders can easily become entrapped politically by overselling their poli-cies to the public and creating new domestic coalitions in support of those policies. Thus ethnic-based policies tend to take on a momen-tum of their own.

Another way in which ethnonational conflict can contribute to international conflict is by increasing migration across borders.[63] Inter-national migration has increased significantly after the end of the Cold War and is now de-fined by numerous scholars as a national secu-rity issue and source of conflict within and be-tween states.[64] Communal conflicts, violent secessionist movements, and the political and economic oppression from which they derive create incentives for ethnic minorities to migrate in search of security or to join their national homelands. Large-scale population movements may be the deliberate aim of governmental policy as well as the unintended consequence of communal conflict, as demonstrated by ethnic cleansing in the Balkans during the Bosnian and Kosovo wars. Governments sometimes adopt forced emigration as a strategy for achieving cultural homogeneity or the dominance of one ethnic community over another, eliminating political dissidents, colonizing areas beyond borders, scapegoating against a prosperous but unpopular ethnic minority, destabilizing another state, or influencing that state's policies.[65]

Population movements can contribute to conflict within and between states through a number of different causal paths.[66] Immigrants can generate social conflict within the host or receiving country by putting added strain on scarce resources, particularly in large urban areas. Migrations can change land distribution, economic relations, and the balance of political power among ethnic, religious, or other social groups; undermine state capacity to create markets and other institutions that facilitate adaptation to environmental change; generate a perceived threat to the host country's cultural identity; trigger a social backlash by indigenous people in response to perceived threats to economic security or social identity from migrants; and generally increase communal conflict, political instabilities, and the likelihood of civil strife.[67]

Migrations may also contribute to international conflict by serving as a focal point for relations between home and host countries. Host countries that cannot easily assimilate the new immigrants or deal with the consequent economic problems and social instabilities may attempt to influence the home government to stop or slow the flow of refugees or eliminate the conditions that gave rise to them. If cooperative efforts fail, governments may resort to coercive threats and possible military action

to block the flow of refugees. Hard-line actions against the migrants' home country can also serve as a useful scapegoating strategy for political leaders who want to bolster their internal political support.

In summary, while resource scarcity can lead directly to international conflict through "resource wars," a more common path to conflict runs through its intervening social consequences. Scarcity generally leads to economic decline and declining standards of living, perceptions of a zero-sum game among different social groups, attempts by these groups to pass the costs of decline onto others, class conflict and social discontent, challenges to the legitimacy of the regime, pressures on democratic political institutions and free-market systems, and an increasing probability of civil strife or external scapegoating.[68]

INDIVIDUAL-LEVEL SOURCES OF INTERNATIONAL CONFLICT

Individual-level theories trace international conflict to individual political leaders (of states or nonstate actors), the content of their belief systems or their "operational codes" about world politics, the psychological processes through which they acquire information and make decisions, and their personalities and emotional states. Because of these variables, key decision makers vary in their preferences for foreign policy goals, their images of the adversary, and/or their beliefs as to the optimum strategies to achieve their goals and meet those threats. This means that different decision makers in the same situation will not behave in the same way. Unlike in systemic- and societal-level theories, individuals make a difference in state foreign policy behavior.[69]

The foreign policy behavior of states (or policies of nonstate groups) can be affected by the psychological processes involved in individual judgment and decision making as well as by the content of their belief systems. There has been more and more evidence from social psychology to demonstrate that people are limited in their cognitive abilities to process information, that their perceptions of their environment are shaped by their prior beliefs as much as by the objective evidence, that they utilize heuristics or cognitive shortcuts in lieu of more normatively rational decision rules, and that these heuristics can produce some rather serious discrepancies between the perceptions of individuals and the "real world."[70] Because of space limitations I focus here on the consequences of misperceptions for international conflict behavior but not the psychological processes that generate these misperceptions.

Misperception-based explanations are often seen as necessary causes of wars, on the assumption that if each side had correctly assessed its adversary's intentions and the likely outcome of the war, the parties could have agreed to a settlement commensurate with that anticipated outcome while avoiding the costs of fighting.[71] The concept of misperception is extremely difficult to define analytically or measure empirically, however, and there are a plethora of types of misperceptions, but the ones most likely to have a major impact on the processes leading to war are misperceptions of the capabilities and intentions of adversaries and third parties.[72] These categories apply to the relations between ethnic groups as well as between states. Ethnic groups in conflict, for example, are concerned not only with the intentions and capabilities of rival groups but also with the likelihood and effect of international intervention.

Exaggeration of the hostility of the adversary's intentions is particularly important. In the short term it can induce one to take counteractions (in the extreme case, a preemptive strike) that trigger a conflict spiral and unnecessary war, and in the long term it can lead to an arms race or system of alliances and counteralliances. Underestimation of the adversary's hostility by a status quo state can contribute to war by erroneously undercutting incentives to build up military capabilities in the long term or to demonstrate resolve in the short term, either of which undermines deterrence. Alternatively, the underestimation of the adversary's resolve by an aggressive state may lead it to make more coercive military threats in the expectation that the adversary will back down, which results in a conflict spiral. Misperceptions of the adversary's intentions may derive from secondary misperceptions of the adversary's value structure, its definition of its vital interests, its definition of the situation, its expectations about the future, and the domestic or bureaucratic constraints on its freedom of action. The failure of U.S. leaders to understand how important it was to the Chinese to prevent a U.S.-backed regime from being established in North Korea in 1950 and how important it was to the North Vietnamese to unify their country played a significant role in U.S. involvement in two major land wars in Asia after World War II.

Misperceptions of adversary capabilities can also be critical. The underestimation of adversary capabilities relative to one's own generates military overconfidence and the common belief that a rapid military victory involving minimal costs is very likely. The overestimation of adversary capabilities may lead one to overreact and initiate an arms buildup that is followed by an arms race and conflict spiral. Alternatively, it can lead to excessive passivity that undermines deterrence. Misperceptions of the intentions and capabilities of third states can have a similar effect. The most common tendencies are to exaggerate the likelihood that one's potential friends will intervene on one's behalf and the likelihood that one's potential enemies will stay neutral and to overestimate the military benefits of the former and underestimate the military costs of the latter, all of which reinforce military overconfidence.

CONCLUSION

I have reviewed some of the leading theories of international conflict, noted their key variables and the causal paths by which they lead to war or peace, acknowledged the great power bias of many of these theories, and suggested the extent to which key hypotheses might also be applicable to the kinds of regional and ethno-national wars that are likely to define international conflict in the early years of the twenty-first century. I have also described the levels-of-analysis framework that has shaped much of the intellectual debate about the sources of international conflict and that, with some modifications, structures the organization of essays in part I of this volume.

It is difficult to reach definitive conclusions regarding the causal importance of different levels of explanatory variables for international conflict in the recent past or in coming decades. First, an assessment of the relative impact of different variables at different levels is an empirical as well as a theoretical question, and space constraints have precluded me from assessing the weight of the empirical evidence in any detail. More important, theories of international conflict have increasingly begun to incorporate variables from several different levels of analysis. This means that an evaluation of the validity of a particular theory is not necessarily congruent with the evaluation of the importance of a particular level of analysis. A focus on the relative importance of different levels of analysis distracts attention from the more important task of understanding how variables at different levels of analysis interact and the contextual conditions that affect those interactions.

In addition, theories serve multiple purposes, and the utility of variables at different levels of analysis may be more useful for some theoretical purposes than for others. The trade-off between the analytic power and predictive utility of parsimonious theories and the descriptive richness of more complex theories is particularly salient. If we want a general theory that can provide maximum explanatory power across different temporal and spatial contexts and generate predictions, then theories based on international or domestic structures are likely to be particularly useful, whereas theories based on individual-level beliefs and psychological processes are less likely to be helpful because they are so demanding in terms of the detailed data required to apply them. But if we want a theory that can guide a more nuanced interpretation of a single historical case, or perhaps small number of cases, the additional descriptive accuracy provided by theories that incorporate individual and decision-making variables can be very useful.[73]

With these caveats in mind, let me offer some tentative comments about the relative importance of variables from different levels of analysis. This will vary depending on the "level" of the actors in question. Let us first consider the great powers. The decline in the frequency of great power war over time and the low likelihood of a great power war in the future is primarily the product of systemic-level developments in military technology that make the expected costs of war between nuclear powers far greater than any conceivable benefits from war.[74] Systemic-level unipolarity also reinforces the low probability of great power war, at least for the time being, but the eventual erosion of U.S. hegemony and the rise of new economic and military powers (China in particular) may create a source of great power crises and confrontations in the future.

Globalization, which increases economic interdependence and the economic benefits of the status quo, deters militarized conflict that might upset that status quo, and spreads a liberal ideology that reinforces the existing system, is an important but secondary factor reducing the likelihood of militarized conflict between the strongest states in the system. The same can be said for democracy, which independently reinforces peace between like-minded states. The declining utility of military force may increase the salience of economic competition among leading states in the system, but, as argued earlier, this is unlikely to lead to wars between the advanced industrial states. Individual-level variables play a relatively minor role at the great power level, though decisions regarding "humanitarian intervention" by the United States are likely to be influenced by the belief systems of particular presidents and key advisers but constrained by public attitudes.

At the regional level, global distributions of power will continue to be important in structuring the permissive conditions for war, at least in those areas in which the leading global powers have significant stakes. U.S. interventions in the wars over Kuwait and Kosovo would have been nearly impossible under Cold War bipolarity and Soviet objections, and continuing U.S. hegemony reduces the likelihood of certain kinds of regional wars because of U.S. interests in stability. Likely aggressors lack a great power ally who can provide ample quantities of modern armaments and who can minimize the downside risks of war by using its influence to stop a war before the costs become too great. In addition, regional states are increasingly interested in reaping the benefits of globalization through close ties with the West, a goal that would be seriously undermined by the initiation of an aggressive war. Among regional states themselves, balancing against primary threats and adjusting to changing power differentials through alliances and armaments will continue to be central themes in international relations.

The primary sources of interstate and internal conflicts in the Third World, however, are more likely to derive from internal rather than external variables. Systemic realist theories are too limited theoretically and too tied to the great power experience of the past to provide an adequate explanation of international conflict over the next several decades. The realist assumption that states have a hierarchy of goals and that external security needs dominate, while perhaps plausible for the great powers of the past, is more questionable in the contemporary Third World, which is characterized by constant resource shortages, threats to economic subsistence and social welfare, and political regimes of only tenuous legitimacy.

Third World political leaders not only give primacy to domestic interests over external security interests, but even conceive of security primarily in domestic terms, so that maintaining domestic political stability and their own positions of power often take precedence over all other interests.[75] Political leaders may prefer to achieve their goals by promoting economic development and perhaps democratization, but they have alternative strategies at their disposal. These include domestic repression, which sometimes increases the risks of civil war, and external scapegoating and predation.

Individual-level variables generally play a greater role in determining peace or war for regional and Third World states than for the great powers, at least for the period since World War II. The end of the Cold War, by destroying the relative simplicity of the bipolar order and increasing the complexity of world politics, has probably increased the importance of leaders' perceptions of their external environment and thereby increased the relative importance of individual-level variables. At the same time, the recent decline of authoritarian regimes has decreased somewhat the importance of the beliefs or psychology of any single decision maker by bringing more people into the decision-making process.

Much of this is speculation, of course. In the years leading up to 1914 many observers believed that war was impossible because its economic impact would be so devastating.[76] They were right about the premise but not about their hypothesized conclusion. In the 1980s few scholars predicted the end of the Cold War.[77] Forecasting the future in a more complex and chaotic world is an even more daunting task. But this makes it all the more important that our attempts to understand world politics be guided by well-developed theoretical frameworks that help to structure this complexity. I hope that this elaboration of the levels-of-analysis framework and survey of some of the leading theories of war has sensitized the reader to some of the critical factors influencing interstate and intrastate conflict and provided a framework for making sense of how they fit together.

NOTES

I thank Lori Gronich and Carmela Lutmar for helpful comments on this paper.

1. Jack S. Levy, Thomas C. Walker, and Martin S. Edwards, "Continuity and Change in the Evolution of War," in *War in a Changing World,* ed. Zeev Maoz and Azar Gat (Ann Arbor: University of Michigan Press, 2001); K. J. Holsti, *The State, War, and the State of War* (New York: Cambridge University Press, 1996); Peter Wallensteen and Margareta Sollenberg, "Armed Conflict, 1989–99," *Journal of Peace Research* 37, no. 5 (2000): 635–649; Mohammed Ayoob, chapter 9 in this volume.

2. Charles W. Kegley Jr., "The Neoidealist Moment in International Studies: Realist Myths and the New International Studies," *International Studies Quarterly* 37, no. 2 (June 1993): 141.

3. Thucydides, *History of the Peloponnesian War,* in *The Landmark Thucydides,* ed. Robert B. Strassler (New York: Free Press, 1996), 5.89, 352.

4. Kenneth N. Waltz, *Man, the State, and War* (New York: Columbia University Press, 1959). Waltz spoke of three "images" of war, but it is now common to speak in terms of "levels of analysis." See J. David Singer, "The Levels of Analysis Problem in International Relations," in *International Politics and Foreign Policy*, rev. ed., ed. James N. Rosenau (New York: Free Press, 1969), 20–29. This survey builds on Jack S. Levy, "The Causes of War and the Conditions of Peace," *Annual Review of Political Science* 1 (June 1998): 139–166.

5. Kenneth N. Waltz, *Theory of International Politics* (Reading, Mass.: Addison-Wesley, 1979); and Robert Jervis, *Perception and Misperception in International Politics* (Princeton, N.J.: Princeton University Press, 1976), chap. 1. It is sometimes useful to distinguish among global and regional systems, the dyadic (or bilateral) relations between a particular pair of states, and the external environment of an individual state (because states in different regions, and different states in the same region, each face a different external environment). Another way to think of levels of analysis is to focus on units of analysis rather than on levels of causation and to distinguish between relationships between states, between a state and an ethnic minority within the state, and between ethnic minorities within a state.

6. In this usage the statement that democracies go to war less frequently than do other states is a national-level hypothesis, whereas the statement that democracies rarely if ever fight each other is a dyadic-level hypothesis.

7. Ernest May, *Imperial Democracy* (New York: Harper and Row, 1961).

8. This does not necessarily mean that dyadic-level and systemic-level variables have a greater causal influence than do individual or domestic variables, only that they cannot be logically excluded from the analysis.

9. For hypotheses on the conditions under which threats of force tend to work to induce concessions, see Jervis, *Perception and Misperception,* chap. 3.

10. Waltz, *Man, the State, and War.*

11. The maximization of state interests is treated as a systemic-level or dyadic-level variable because it involves calculations of opportunities and constraints in the international system or in a particular relationship.

12. Waltz, *Theory of International Politics;* and Robert O. Keohane, ed., *Neorealism and Its Critics* (New York: Columbia University Press, 1986). Systemic power structures exert their influence by establishing "permissive conditions" for certain types of behavior as well as by more directly inducing behavior. The end of the Cold War and the collapse of bipolarity influenced the Persian Gulf War by allowing the United States and its allies to intervene without fear of Soviet intervention; if the Iraqi invasion of Kuwait had occurred a few years earlier, it is unlikely that an Arab coalition would have formed against Iraq or that the United States would have risked military intervention.

13. Jervis, *Perception and Misperception*, chap. 3.

14. This interpretation has been heatedly contested. See H. W. Koch, ed., *The Origins of the First World War*, 2d ed. (London: Macmillan, 1984); and Jack S. Levy, "Preferences, Constraints, and Choices in July 1914," *International Security* 15, no. 3 (winter 1990-91): 151–186.

15. Hans J. Morgenthau, *Politics among Nations*, 4th ed. (New York: Alfred A. Knopf, 1967); Edward V.

Gulick, *Europe's Classical Balance of Power* (Ithaca, N.Y.: Cornell University Press, 1955); Waltz, *Theory of International Politics*, chap. 6; and John Mearsheimer, "Back to the Future: Instability in Europe after the Cold War," *International Security* 15, no. 1 (summer 1990): 5–56.

16. One important difference between great power systems and regional systems is that the central assumption of anarchy is less valid for the latter, where powerful states outside the system can play a significant role. Consequently, some key balance-of-power propositions may need to be modified for regional systems.

17. This is illustrated by the Arab coalition against Iraq in 1991, in which Arab leaders indirectly aligned with their Israeli enemy to counter the more immediate threat posed by Saddam's Iraq, and by the constantly shifting coalitions in the war in Congo in the 1990s. It is true that long-standing ethnic rivalries often (but not always) prevent certain coalitions from forming, but so do rigid political ideologies in the international system. Balance-of-power theorists have long argued that by impeding effective alliance balancing, ideological rigidities undermine the conditions for stability and peace.

18. The Israeli strike against the Iraqi nuclear reactor in 1981 is the classic case of a preventive strike. See Jack S. Levy, "Declining Power and the Preventive Motivation for War," *World Politics* 40, no. 1 (October 1987): 82–107.

19. Robert Gilpin, *War and Change in World Politics* (New York: Cambridge University Press, 1981); and Jacek Kugler and Douglas Lemke, *Parity and War* (Ann Arbor: University of Michigan Press, 1996). Lemke's chapter applies power transition theory to regional systems.

20. The evidence is summarized in Kugler and Lemke, *Parity and War*. Note that the stabilizing effects of power preponderance at the dyadic level do not necessarily imply that imbalances of power are stabilizing at the systemic level, where balancing through alliances can create opportunities for war to restrict concentrations of power.

21. Roy Licklider, "The Consequences of Negotiated Settlements in Civil Wars, 1945–1993," *American Political Science Review* 89, no. 3 (September 1995): 681–690.

22. Chaim Kaufman, "Possible and Impossible Solutions to Ethnic Civil Wars," *International Security* 20, no. 4 (spring 1996): 136–175.

23. Barry R. Posen, "The Security Dilemma and Ethnic Conflict," *Survival* 35, no. 1 (spring 1993): 27–47; Jack Snyder and Robert Jervis, "Civil War and the Security Dilemma," in *Civil Wars, Insecurity, and Intervention,* ed. Barbara F. Walter and Jack Snyder (New York: Columbia University Press, 1999), 15–37; and James D. Fearon, "Commitment Problems and the Spread of Ethnic Conflict," in *The International Spread of Ethnic Conflict,* ed. David A. Lake and Donald Rothchild (Princeton, N.J.: Princeton University Press, 1998), 107–126.

24. Stephen Van Evera, "Hypotheses on Nationalism and War," *International Security* 18, no. 4 (spring 1994): 5–39; Donald Horowitz, "Irredentas and Secessions," in *Irredentism and International Politics,* ed. Naomi Chazan (Boulder, Colo.: Lynne Rienner, 1991), 9–22; and Benjamin Miller, "Explaining Variations in Regional Peace: Three Strategies for Peacemaking," *Cooperation and Conflict* 35, no. 2 (2000): 155–191.

25. The trade-promotes-peace hypothesis includes both systemic/dyadic and domestic causal variables; the democratic peace is domestic in nature; international institutions are systemic. Thus liberal theories of war and peace cannot be identified with a single level of analysis. On the development of liberal international theories, see Michael Doyle, *Ways of War and Peace* (New York: W. W. Norton, 1997). For an empirical analysis, see Bruce Russett and John R. Oneal, *Triangulating Peace: Democracy, Interdependence, and International Organization* (New York: W. W. Norton, 2001).

26. Institutionalist theories are usefully applied to the notion of collective security, including the Concert of Europe after the Congress of Vienna (1815). See Robert O. Keohane and Lisa L. Martin, "The Promise of Institutionalist Theory," *International Security* 20, no. 1 (summer 1995): 39–51; and Charles A. Kupchan and Clifford A. Kupchan, "Concerts, Collective Security, and the Future of Europe," *International Security* 16, no. 1 (summer 1991): 114–161.

27. The trade-promotes-peace hypothesis was implicit in the U.S. policy of détente toward the Soviet Union in the 1970s. U.S. leaders assumed that increased economic interdependence between the United States and the Soviet Union would increase Soviet incentives to cooperate on security issues and help deter uncooperative behavior, especially in the Third World.

28. It has been said that in prosperous trading states "people are too busy growing rich to have time for war." Geoffrey Blainey, *The Causes of War*, 3d ed. (New York: Free Press, 1988), 10. Note that other domestic groups may gain from protectionism rather than free trade and may attempt to influence state policy in that direction. This can lead to countermeasures and sometimes to trade wars that escalate.

29. Richard Rosecrance, *The Rise of the Trading State* (New York: Basic Books, 1986). The costs of territorial conquest have also increased with growing cultural self-assertiveness and nationalist opposition to political control, the incompatibility of political control with the liberal foundations of postindustrial economic innovation and productivity, the growth of antiwar attitudes in the West, increasingly powerful military capabilities of many medium-sized states, and the development of nuclear weapons.

30. Waltz, *Theory of International Politics;* and Joseph M. Grieco, *Cooperation among Nations* (Ithaca, N.Y.: Cornell University Press, 1990). As Joanne Gowa argues in *Allies, Adversaries, and International Trade* (Princeton, N.J.: Princeton University Press, 1994), concerns over relative gains or the "security externalities of trade" lead states to trade with friends but much less with adversaries or potential adversaries. This implies that states will not trade with their enemies during wartime. Trading with the enemy is an age-old phenomenon, however, and a pattern that runs contrary to common applications of both realist and liberal theories (recall that the liberal hypothesis that trade promotes peace is based on the assumption that the outbreak of war will seriously impede trade). See Katherine Barbieri and Jack S. Levy, "Sleeping with the Enemy: The Impact of War on Trade," *Journal of Peace Research* 36, no. 4 (July 1999): 463–479.

31. Soloman W. Polachek, "Conflict and Trade," *Journal of Conflict Resolution* 24, no. 1 (March 1980), 55–78; and Russett and Oneal, *Triangulating Peace.* For evidence that trade may promote conflict under some conditions, see Katherine Barbieri, "Economic Interdependence: A Path to Peace or Source of Interstate Conflict?" *Journal of Peace Research* 33, no. 1 (February 1996): 29–49; and Norrin M. Ripsman and Jean-Marc F. Blanchard, "Commercial Liberalism under Fire: Evidence from 1914 and 1936," *Security Studies* 6, no. 2 (winter 1996-97): 4–50.

32. Most empirical studies of the relationship between trade and conflict examine either the impact of trade on conflict or the impact of conflict on trade. But the true relationship is a reciprocal one, and the simultaneous and reciprocal effects of trade on war and war on trade need to be incorporated into a single model and tested in that form.

33. Samuel P. Huntington, "Why International Primacy Matters," *International Security* 17, no. 4 (spring 1993): 68–83.

34. A classic case of the militarization of commercial rivalries was the seventeenth-century Anglo-Dutch rivalry. Jack S. Levy and Salvatore Ali, "From Commercial Competition to Strategic Rivalry to War: The Evolution of the Anglo-Dutch Rivalry, 1609–1652," in *The Dynamics of Enduring Rivalries,* ed. Paul F. Diehl (Urbana/Champaign: University of Illinois Press, 1998), 29–63.

35. Paul Kennedy, *Preparing for the Twenty-First Century* (New York: Random House, 1993); and Robert D. Kaplan, *The Coming Anarchy* (New York: Random House, 2000).

36. The question of whether environmental change is a security issue, which has attracted considerable attention in the literature, is much broader than our question here—whether environmental change contributes to international conflict. Environmental change can threaten core values without involving violent international conflict. For discussions of environmental change as part of new conceptions of security, see Richard Ullman, "Redefining Security," *International Security* 8, no. 1 (summer 1983): 129–153. For critics of this connection, see Daniel Duedney, "The Case against Linking Environmental Degradation and National Security," *Millennium* 19, no. 3 (winter 1990); and Marc A. Levy, "Is the Environment a National Security Issue?" *International Security* 20, no. 2 (fall 1995): 35–62. See also Nils Petter Gleditsch's chapter (chapter 4) in this volume.

37. Thomas F. Homer-Dixon, "Environmental Scarcities and Violent Conflict: Evidence from Cases," in *Theories of War and Peace,* ed. Michael E. Brown et al. (Cambridge, Mass.: MIT Press, 1998), 501–536; Peter H. Gleick, "Water and Conflict: Fresh Water Resources and International Security," and Miriam R. Lowi, "Bridging the Divide: Transboundary Resource Disputes and the Case of West Bank Water," in *Global Dangers*, ed. Lynn-Jones and Miller (Cambridge, Mass.: MIT Press, 1995), 84–117, 118–143.

38. Although the 1979 "Soccer War" between El Salvador and Honduras is often described as a simple scarcity conflict driven by environmental pressures and famine, scapegoating and other governmental responses to those systemic pressures played a key role in the conflict. William H. Durham, *Scarcity and Survival in Central America: Ecological Origins of the Soccer War* (Stanford, Calif.: Stanford University Press, 1979).

39. It is true, however, that domestic demographic and economic variables clearly shape the differential rates of national growth that determine the distribution of power in the system, and that domestic economic structures and processes affect the degree of governmental support for international trade.

40. I focus here on the societal and individual levels but not the bureaucratic/organizational level. International relations theorists have demonstrated that bureaucratic/organizational factors influence levels of military spending, military doctrine and planning, and the conduct of war but have given less attention to their impact on the causes of war. See Graham T. Allison and Philip Zelikow, *Essence of Decision: Explaining the Cuban Missile Crisis,* rev. ed. (New York: Addison Wesley Longman, 1999); Barry R. Posen, *The Sources of Military Doctrine* (Ithaca, N.Y.: Cornell University Press, 1984); and Elizabeth Kier, *Imagining War: French and British Military Doctrine between the Wars* (Princeton, N.J.: Princeton University Press, 1997).

41. Marxist-Leninist theories of imperialism and war have always attracted some attention among international relations theorists, but that attention has declined with the end of the Cold War and the collapse of communist political systems in the Soviet Union and the Soviet bloc. Marxist-Leninist theory focuses on the domestic economic structure of capitalist societies and posits that the inequitable distribution of wealth generates "underconsumption," inadequate domestic investment, and stagnant economies. This leads to expansionist and imperialist foreign policies to secure external markets for surplus products, external investment opportunities for surplus capital, outlets for surplus population, and access to raw materials at stable prices, and also to high levels of military spending to stabilize and stimulate the economy. The result is arms races, conflict spirals, and war. Vladimir Ilyich Lenin, *Imperialism* (New York: International Publishers, 1939); and Bernard Semmel, ed., *Marxism and the Science of War* (New York: Oxford University Press, 1981). For summaries and critiques of Marxist-Leninist theories of imperialism and war, including its excessive economic determinism, see Anthony Brewer, *Marxist Theories of Imperialism*

(London: Routledge and Kegan Paul, 1980); and Raymond Aron, "War and Industrial Society," in *War,* ed. Leon Bramson and George W. Goethals (New York: Basic Books, 1958), 359–402.

42. Immanuel Kant, "Eternal Peace," in *The Philosophy of Kant,* ed. C. J. Friederich (New York: Modern Library, 1949), 430–476. Thomas Paine made a similar argument a few years before Kant. See Thomas C. Walker, "The Forgotten Prophet: Tom Paine's Cosmopolitanism and International Relations," *International Studies Quarterly* 44, no. 1 (March 2000): 51–72.

43. Jack S. Levy, "Domestic Politics and War," *Journal of Interdisciplinary History* 18, no. 4 (spring 1988): 662.

44. As a systemic theory, realism argues that state behavior is shaped by international pressures, not domestic structures or processes. This implies that, ceteris paribus, democratic dyads will go to war as often (proportionately) as any other pairs of states.

45. There is also substantial evidence that democratic dyads tend to engage in more peaceful processes of conflict resolution when they do get in disputes. Democracies also tend to win a disproportionate number of the wars they fight, suffer fewer casualties, and end their wars more quickly than other states. These patterns are summarized in James Lee Ray, *Democracy and International Conflict: An Evaluation of the Democratic Peace Proposition* (Columbia: University of South Carolina Press, 1995); Russett and Oneal, *Triangulating Peace;* and Bruce Bueno de Mesquita, James D. Morrow, Randolph M. Siverson, and Alastair Smith, "An Institutional Explanation of the Democratic Peace," *American Political Science Review* 93, no. 4 (December 1999): 791–808. Debate continues on the relative frequency of war involvement of democratic and nondemocratic states and of democratic war initiation, with some scholars now claiming that democracies really are more peaceful than authoritarian states. The differences are modest, however, in contrast to the extraordinarily strong relationship between democratic dyads and peace. See R. J. Rummel, "Democracies *Are* Less Warlike Than Other Regimes," *European Journal of International Relations* 1, no. 4 (December 1995): 457-479.

46. Criteria for war include a military conflict involving at least one thousand battle deaths, and criteria for democracy include regular fair elections, tolerance of opposition parties, and a parliament that at least shares powers with the executive. Possible exceptions to this "law" include the American Civil War and the Spanish-American War, among other cases. See Bruce Russett, *Grasping the Democratic Peace* (Princeton, N.J.: Princeton University Press, 1993); and Ray, *Democracy and International Conflict*. Note that it is democratic regime type, not similarity of regimes, that makes a difference, because authoritarian regimes often fight each other.

47. Kenneth A. Schultz, "Domestic Opposition and Signaling in International Crises," *American Political Science Review* 92, no. 4 (December 1998): 829–844.

48. See the chapter by Edward D. Mansfield and Jack Snyder (chapter 8) in this volume. Also Jack Snyder, *From Voting to Violence: Democratization and Nationalist Conflict* (New York: W. W. Norton, 2000).

49. Andrew J. Enterline, "Driving while Democratizing," *International Security* 20, no. 4 (spring 1996): 183–196; Michael D. Ward and Kristian S. Gleditsch, "Democratizing for Peace," *American Political Science Review* 92, no. 1 (March 1998): 51–61; Russett and Oneal, *Triangulating Peace;* and Edward D. Mansfield and Jack Snyder, "Democratic Transitions, Institutional Strength, and War" (unpublished paper, 2001).

50. Snyder, *From Voting to Violence;* V. P. Gagnon Jr., "Ethnic Nationalism and International Conflict: The Case of Serbia," *International Security* 19, no. 3 (winter 1994-95): 331–367.

51. Donald Kagan, *The Peace of Nicias and the Sicilian Expedition* (Ithaca, N.Y.: Cornell University Press, 1981); Jack S. Levy and Lily I. Vakili, "External Scapegoating in Authoritarian Regimes: Argentina in the Falklands/Malvinas Case," in *The Internationalization of Communal Strife,* ed. Manus I. Midlarsky (London: Routledge, 1992), 118–146.

52. Four centuries ago, for example, Jean Bodin argued that "the best way of preserving a state, and guaranteeing it against sedition, rebellion, and civil war is to . . . find an enemy against whom [the subjects] can make common cause." Cited in Jack S. Levy, "The Diversionary Theory of War," in *Handbook of War Studies,* ed. Manus I. Midlarsky (Boston: Unwin Hyman, 1989), 259.

53. Jack Snyder, *Myths of Empire: Domestic Politics and International Ambition* (Ithaca, N.Y.: Cornell University Press, 1991).

54. Christopher Gelpi, "Democratic Diversions: Governmental Structure and the Externalization of Domestic Conflict," *Journal of Conflict Resolution* 41,

no. 2 (April 1997): 255–282; and Ross Miller, "Regime Type, Strategic Interaction, and the Diversionary Use of Force," *Journal of Conflict Resolution* 43, no. 3 (June 1999): 388–402.

55. Bruce Bueno de Mesquita and Randolph M. Siverson, "War and the Survival of Political Leaders: A Comparative Study of Regime Types and Political Accountability," *American Political Science Review* 89, no. 4 (December 1995): 841–855. Although democratic political leaders are more likely than their authoritarian counterparts to be removed from office after a military defeat, the personal costs of removal are undoubtedly greater for many deposed authoritarian leaders, who have fewer legal protections.

56. A related hypothesis is that once involved in war, democracies extract more resources from society for the prosecution of the war effort than autocracies do. See Bueno de Mesquita et al., "An Institutional Explanation of the Democratic Peace." For some evidence that contradicts this, see Dan Reiter and Alan Stam III, *Democracies at War* (Princeton, N.J.: Princeton University Press, forthcoming 2002).

57. The evidence is not clear, but we do know that when democracies scapegoat against other democracies the ensuing conflict rarely, if ever, escalates to war.

58. An ethnic community is "a named human population with a myth of common ancestry, shared memories, and cultural elements; a link with a historic territory or homeland; and a measure of solidarity." Donald Horowitz, *Ethnic Groups in Conflict* (Berkeley: University of California Press, 1985), 55–92. Nationalism involves the devotion of the primary loyalties of group members to the ethnic or national community and the desire for their own independent state. Van Evera, "Hypotheses on Nationalism and War"; and Ted Robert Gurr, *Peoples versus States: Minorities at Risk in the New Century* (Washington, D.C.: United States Institute of Peace Press, 2000). See also the chapter by Roy Licklider (chapter 41) in this volume.

59. Samuel P. Huntington, "The Clash of Civilizations," *Foreign Affairs* 72, no. 3 (summer 1993): 22–49. This influential argument underestimates the importance of nationalism and other sources of division within broadly defined Islamic, Confucian, and Western civilizations.

60. Anthony D. Smith, *The Ethnic Origins of Nations* (New York: Basil Blackwell, 1986).

61. Serbs and Croats fought each other very little before this century, for example.

62. In the case of the disintegration of Yugoslavia and the war in Bosnia, for example, Milosevic promoted nationalist fervor both to mobilize the country for dealing with external security threats and opportunities and to increase his own popular appeal. V. P. Gagnon Jr., "Ethnic Nationalism and International Conflict," *International Security* 19, no. 3 (winter 1994-95): 331–367.

63. International migration may also be driven by economic and environmental factors. Substantial differentials in income and employment opportunities create economic incentives for people to migrate in search of economic security. In the contemporary era, the collapse of authoritarian regimes has removed some of the barriers to movements across borders and expanding global communication and transportation networks have created new opportunities for international migration. In addition, environmental degradation, droughts, floods, and famines generate large numbers of "environmental refugees," as noted earlier.

64. F. Stephen Larrabee, "Down and Out in Warsaw and Budapest: Eastern Europe and East-West Migration," *International Security* 16, no. 4 (spring 1992): 5–33. The framing of environmental issues in terms of "high politics" and national security may also serve a political strategy. The symbolism of national security increases the prospects that these issues may be put on the policy agenda and that research on these topics might gain funding from the government or foundations.

65. Myron Weiner, "Security, Stability, and International Migration," *International Security* 17, no. 3 (winter 1992-93): 91–126.

66. International migration does not always lead to social conflict. Migrants are often assimilated into the host country, particularly when they provide needed labor and skills and particularly when population movements take the form of gradual migrations (often in response to gradual changes in demography and economic incentives) rather than sudden displacements arising from ethnic conflicts or environmental disasters.

67. Weiner, "Security, Stability, and International Migration"; and Ronald R. Krebs and Jack S. Levy, "Demographic Change and the Sources of International Conflict," in *Demography and National Security,* ed. Myron Weiner and Sharon Stanton Russell (Providence, R.I.: Berghahn Books, 2001).

68. Homer-Dixon, "Environmental Scarcities," 157–159; and Duedney, "Environmental Degradation and National Security," 471.

69. Ole R. Holsti, "Cognitive Dynamics and Images of the Enemy," in *Image and Reality in World Politics,* ed. John Farrell and Asa Smith (New York: Columbia University Press, 1967), 16–39; and Alexander L. George, "The 'Operational Code': A Neglected Approach to the Study of Political Leaders and Decisionmaking," *International Studies Quarterly* 13, no. 2 (June 1969): 190–222. Variations in beliefs arise from differences in political socialization, personality, education, formative experiences and the lessons people learn from historical experience, and a host of other variables. See Jervis, *Perception and Misperception;* Richard Ned Lebow, *Between Peace and War* (Baltimore: Johns Hopkins University Press, 1981); and chapter 12, by Janice Gross Stein, in this volume.

70. Daniel Kahneman, Paul Slovic, and Amos Tversky, eds., *Judgment under Uncertainty: Heuristics and Biases* (Cambridge: Cambridge University Press, 1982); Richard Nisbett and Lee Ross, *Human Inference: Strategies and Shortcomings of Social Judgment* (Englewood Cliffs, N.J.: Prentice-Hall, 1980).

71. James D. Fearon, "Rationalist Explanations for War," *International Organization* 49, no. 3 (summer 1995): 379–414.

72. This builds on Jack S. Levy, "Misperception and the Causes of War: Theoretical Linkages and Analytical Problems," *World Politics* 36, no. 1 (October 1983): 76–99. See also Robert Jervis, "War and Misperception," *Journal of Interdisciplinary History* 18, no. 4 (spring 1988): 675–700. Each of these forms of misperceptions can also contribute to peace, though through different causal paths. Exaggeration of adversary capabilities, for example, may lead a state to reject a decision for preventive or preemptive war that might have been tempting under complete information.

73. On trade-offs between the generalizability of parsimonious models and the descriptive accuracy of more contextualized models, see Jack Snyder, "Richness, Rigor, and Relevance in the Study of Soviet Foreign Policy," *International Security* 9, no. 3 (winter 1984-85): 89–108; and Jack S. Levy, "Explaining Events and Testing Theories: History, Political Science, and the Analysis of International Relations," in

Bridges and Boundaries: Historians, Political Scientists, and the Study of International Relations, ed. Colin Elman and Miriam Fendius Elman (Cambridge, Mass.: MIT Press, 2000), 39–83.

74. On the pacifying effects of nuclear weapons, see John Lewis Gaddis, *The Long Peace* (New York: Oxford University Press, 1987); and Robert Jervis, *The Meaning of the Nuclear Revolution* (Ithaca, N.Y.: Cornell University Press, 1989).

75. Holsti, *The State, War, and the State of War;* Ayoob, chap. 9 in this volume; and Michael N. Bar-

nett and Jack S. Levy, "Domestic Sources of Alliances and Alignments: The Case of Egypt, 1962–1973," *International Organization* 9, no. 3 (summer 1991): 369–395.

76. Norman Angell, *The Great Illusion*, 4th ed. (New York: G. P. Putnam's Sons, 1913).

77. John Gaddis, "International Relations Theory and the End of the Cold War," *International Security* 17, no. 3 (winter 1992-93): 5–58.

2

The Causes of War

Michael Howard

NO ONE CAN DESCRIBE the topic that I have chosen to discuss as a neglected and understudied one. How much ink has been spilled about it, how many library shelves have been filled with works on the subject, since the days of Thucydides! How many scholars from how many specialities have applied their expertise to this intractable problem! Mathematicians, meteorologists, sociologists, anthropologists, geographers, physicists, political scientists, philosophers, theologians, and lawyers are only the most obvious of the categories that come to mind when one surveys the ranks of those who have sought some formula for perpetual peace, or who at least hoped to reduce the complexities of international conflict to some orderly structure, to develop a theory that will enable us to explain, to understand, and to control a phenomenon which, if we fail to abolish it, might well abolish us.

Yet it is not a problem that has aroused a great deal of interest in the historical profession. The causes of specific wars, yes: these provide unending material for analysis and interpretation, usually fuelled by plenty of documents and starkly conflicting prejudices on the part of the scholars themselves. But the phenomenon of war as a continuing activity within human society is one that as a profession we take very much for granted. The alternation of war and peace has been the very stuff of the past. War has been throughout history a normal way of conducting disputes between political groups. Few of us, probably, would go along with those socio-biologists who claim that this has been so because man is "innately aggressive." The calculations of advantage and risk, sometimes careful, sometimes crude, that statesmen make before committing their countries to war are very remotely linked, if at all, to the displays of tribal *machismo* that we witness today in football crowds. Since the use or threat of physical force is the most elementary way of asserting power and controlling one's environment, the fact that men have frequently had recourse to it does not cause the historian

29

a great deal of surprise. Force, or the threat of it, may not settle arguments, but it does play a considerable part in determining the structure of the world in which we live.

Indeed historians are usually less interested in the causes of war than they are in the causes of peace; in the way in which peaceful communities, controlled by legitimized authorities, have developed and sustained themselves at all. The great scholars who a hundred years ago gained the study of history its primacy of place in British universities, men such as Stubbs, Maitland, and Tout, devoted themselves to discovering how a society so peaceful and so law-abiding as that within which they lived had come into existence. They examined the interaction between power and consent, freedom and obligation, State and community, that has made possible the emergence of that humdrum condition of political life that we know as peace. In international affairs the occasions for rivalries, whether dynastic, religious, economic, political, or ideological, have been so self-evident that historians have found it more interesting to study the work of those statesmen whose skill *avoided* conflict—the Castlereaghs, the Cannings, the Salisburys, even the Palmerstons—than those whose ineptitude failed to prevent it. The breakdown of international order does not, on the whole, strike us as a pathological aberration from the norm. On the contrary, the maintenance of that order and its peaceful adjustment to changing circumstances appears as a task presenting a continuous challenge to human ingenuity, and our wonder, like Dr. Johnson's at women preaching, is not that it is done so imperfectly, but that it is under the circumstances ever done at all.

I spoke a moment ago about the multiplicity of books that have been written about the causes of war since the time of Thucydides. In fact I think we would find that the vast majority of them had been written since 1914, and that the degree of intellectual concern about the causes of war to which we have become accustomed has existed only since the First World War. In view of the damage which that war did to the social and political structure of Europe, this is understandable enough. But there has been a tendency to argue that because that war caused such great and lasting damage, because it destroyed three great empires and nearly beggared a fourth, it must have arisen from causes of peculiar complexity and profundity, from the neuroses of nations, from the widening class struggle, from a crisis in industrial society. I have argued this myself, taking issue with Mr. A. J. P. Taylor on the subject, but now I wonder whether on this, as on so many other matters, I was not wrong and he was not right.[1]

It is true, and it is important to bear in mind in examining the problems of that period, that before 1914 war was almost universally considered acceptable, perhaps an inevitable and for many people a desirable way of settling international differences, and that the war generally foreseen was expected to be, if not exactly *frisch und fröhlich,* then certainly brief; no longer, certainly, than the war of 1870 that was consciously or unconsciously taken by that generation as a model. Had it not been so generally felt that war was an acceptable and tolerable way of solving international disputes, statesmen and soldiers would no doubt have approached the crisis of 1914 in a very different fashion.

But there was nothing new about this attitude to war. Statesmen had always been able to assume that war would be acceptable at least to those sections of their populations whose opinion mattered to them, and in this respect the decision to go to war in 1914—for Continental statesmen at least—in no way differed from those taken by their predecessors of earlier generations. The causes of the Great War are thus in essence no more complex or profound than those of any previous European war, or indeed than those described by Thucydides as underlying the Peloponnesian War: "What made war inevitable was the growth of Athenian power and the fear this caused in Sparta."[2] In Central Europe there was the German fear that the disintegration of the

Habsburg Empire would result in an enormous enhancement of Russian power—power already becoming formidable as French-financed industries and railways put Russian manpower at the service of her military machine. In Western Europe there was the traditional British fear that Germany might establish a hegemony over Europe which, even more than that of Napoleon, would place at risk the security of Britain and her own possessions; a fear fueled by the knowledge that there was within Germany widespread determination to achieve a world status comparable with her latent power. Consideration of this kind had caused wars in Europe often enough before. Was there really anything different about 1914?

Ever since the eighteenth century, war had been blamed by intellectuals upon the stupidity or the self-interest of governing elites (as it is now blamed upon "military-industrial complexes"), with the implicit or explicit assumptions that if the control of state affairs was in the hands of sensible men—businessmen, as Cobden thought, the workers, as Jean Jaurès thought—then wars would be no more. By the twentieth century the growth of the social and biological sciences was producing alternative explanations. As Quincy Wright expressed it is his massive *Study of War,* "Scientific investigators . . . tended to attribute war to immaturities in social knowledge and control, as one might attribute epidemics to insufficient medical knowledge or to inadequate public health services."[3] The Social Darwinian acceptance of the inevitability of struggle, indeed of its desirability if mankind was to progress, the view, expressed by the elder Moltke but very widely shared at the turn of the century, that perpetual peace was a dream and not even a beautiful dream, did not even survive the Great War in those countries where the bourgeois-liberal culture was dominant, Britain and the United States. The failure of these nations to appreciate that such bellicist views, or variants of them, were still widespread in other areas of the world, those dominated by Fascism and by Marxism-Leninism, was to cause embarrassing misunderstandings, and possibly still does.

For liberal intellectuals war was so self-evidently a pathological aberration from the norm, at best a ghastly mistake, at worst a crime. Those who initiated wars must in their view have been criminal, or sick, or the victims of forces beyond their power to control. Those who were so accused disclaimed responsibility for the events of 1914, throwing it on others or saying the whole thing was a terrible mistake for which no one was to blame. None of them, with their societies in ruin around them and tens of millions dead, were prepared to say courageously: "We only acted as statesmen always have in the past. In the circumstances then prevailing, war seemed to us to be the best way of protecting or forwarding the national interests for which we were responsible. There was an element of risk, certainly, but the risk might have been greater had we postponed the issue. Our real guilt does not lie in the fact that we started the war. It lies in our mistaken belief that we could win it."

The trouble is that if we are to regard war as pathological and abnormal, then all conflict must be similarly regarded; for war is only a particular kind of conflict between a particular category of social groups, sovereign states. It is, as Clausewitz put it, "a clash between major interests that is resolved by bloodshed—that is the only way in which it differs from other conflicts."[4] If one had no sovereign states one would have no wars, as Rousseau rightly pointed out—but, as Hobbes equally rightly pointed out, we would probably have no peace either. As states acquire a monopoly of violence, war becomes the only remaining form of conflict that may legitimately be settled by physical force. The mechanism of legitimization of authority and of social control that makes it possible for the state to moderate or eliminate conflicts within its borders or at very least to ensure that these are not conducted by competitive violence—the mechanism to the study of which historians have quite properly devoted so much attention—makes possible the conduct of armed conflict with other states, and on occasion—if the state is to survive—it makes it necessary. These conflicts arise from conflicting claims, or interests, or ideologies, or perceptions; and these perceptions may indeed be fueled by social or psychological drives that we do not fully understand and that one day we may learn rather better how to control. But the problem is the control of social conflict *as such;* not simply of war. However inchoate or disreputable the motives for war may be, its initiation is almost by definition a deliberate and carefully considered act and its conduct, at least at the more advanced levels of social development, a matter of very precise central control. If history shows any record of "accidental" wars, I have yet to find them. Certainly statesmen have sometimes been surprised by the nature of the war they have unleashed, and it is reasonable to assume that in at least 50 percent of the cases they got a result they did not expect. But that is not the same as a war begun by mistake and continued with no political purpose.

Statesmen in fact go to war to achieve very specific ends, and the reasons for which states have fought one another have been categorized and recategorized innumerable times. Vattel the lawyer divided them into the necessary, the customary, the rational, and the capricious. Jomini the strategist identified ideological, economic, and popular wars, wars to defend the balance of power, wars to assist allies, wars to assert or to defend rights. Quincy Wright the political scientist divided them into the idealistic, the psychological, the political, and the juridical. Bernard Brodie in our own times has refused to discriminate: "Any theory of the causes of war in general or any war in particular that is not inherently eclectic and comprehensive," he stated, ". . . is bound for that very reason to be wrong."[5] Another contemporary analyst, Geoffrey Blainey, is on the contrary unashamedly reductionist. All war-aims, he

wrote, "are simply varieties of power. The vanity of nationalism, the will to spread an ideology, the protection of kinsmen in an adjacent land, the desire for more territory . . . all these represent power in different wrappings. The conflicting aims of rival nations are always conflicts of power."[6]

In principle I am sure that Bernard Brodie was right: no single explanation for conflict between states, any more than for conflict between any other social groups, is likely to stand up to critical examination. But Blainey is right as well. Quincy Wright provided us with a useful indicator when he suggested that "while animal war is a function of instinct and primitive war of the *mores,* civilized war is primarily a function of state politics."[7] Medievalists will perhaps bridle at the application of the term "primitive" to the sophisticated and subtle societies of the Middle Ages, for whom war was also a "function of the mores," a way of life that often demanded only the most banal of justifications. As a way of life it persisted in Europe well into the seventeenth century, if no later. For Louis XIV and his court war was, in his early years at least, little more than a seasonal variation on hunting. But by the eighteenth century the mood had changed. For Frederick the Great war was to be preeminently a function of *Staatspolitik,* and so it has remained ever since. And although statesmen can be as emotional or as prejudiced in their judgements as any other group of human beings, it is very seldom that their attitudes, their perceptions and their decisions are not related, however remotely, to the fundamental issues of power, that capacity to control their environment on which the independent existence of their states and often the cultural values of their societies depend.

And here perhaps we do find a factor that sets interstate conflict somewhat apart from other forms of social rivalry. States may fight —indeed as often as not they do fight—not over any specific issue such as might otherwise have been resolved by peaceful means, but in order to acquire, to enhance or to preserve their capacity to function as independent actors in the international system at all. "The stakes of war," as Raymond Aron has reminded us, "are the existence, the creation or the elimination of States."[8] It is a sombre analysis, but one which the historical record very amply bears out.

It is here that those analysts who come to the study of war from the disciplines of the natural sciences, particularly the biological sciences, tend, it seems to me, to go astray. The conflicts between states which have usually led to war have normally arisen, not from any irrational and emotive drives, but from almost a super-abundance of analytic rationality. Sophisticated communities (one hesitates to apply to them Quincy Wright's word, "civilized") do not react simply to immediate threats. Their intelligence (and I use the term in its double sense) enables them to assess the implications that any event taking place anywhere in the world, however remote, may have for their own capacity, immediately to exert influence, ultimately perhaps to survive. In the later Middle Ages and the Early Modern period every child born to every prince anywhere in Europe was registered on the delicate seismographs that monitored the shifts in dynastic power. Every marriage was a diplomatic triumph or disaster. Every stillbirth, as Henry VIII knew, could presage political catastrophe. Today the key events may be different, the pattern remains the same. A malfunction in the political mechanism of some remote African community, a coup d'état in a miniscule Caribbean republic, an insurrection deep in the hinterland of Southeast Asia, an assassination in some emirate in the Middle East—all these will be subjected to the kind of anxious examination and calculation that was devoted a hundred years ago to the news of comparable events in the Balkans: an insurrection in Philippopolis, a coup d'état in Constantinople, an assassination in Belgrade. To whose advantage will this ultimately redound, asked the worried diplomats, ours or

theirs? Little enough in itself, perhaps, but will it not precipitate or strengthen a trend, set in motion a tide whose melancholy withdrawing roar will strip us of our friends and influence and leave us isolated in a world dominated by adversaries deeply hostile to us and all that we stand for?

There have certainly been occasions when states have gone to war in a mood of ideological fervor like the French in 1792; or of swaggering aggression like the Americans against Spain in 1898 or the British against the Boers a year later; or to make more money, as did the British in the War of Jenkins' Ear in 1739; or in a generous desire to help peoples of similar creed or race, as perhaps the Russians did in 1877 and the British dominions certainly did in 1914 and 1939. But in general men have fought during the past two hundred years neither because they are aggressive nor because they are acquisitive animals, but because they are reasoning ones: because they discern, or believe that they can discern, dangers before they become immediate, the possibility of threats before they are made.

The Habsburg Monarchy might have shattered into a dozen pieces, the Russian railway system might have linked every corner of the empire with rapid transit communications, without a single Bavarian farmer or Ruhr factory-hand necessarily having his way of life disturbed. But were German statesmen and soldiers being totally paranoid in their fear that, in a Europe where the Russians could deploy so vast a superiority of military power and were supported not only by France but by a string of client Slav successor states in the Balkans, those farmers and factory-hands would indeed be very seriously at risk? And if our answer is that they were indeed being paranoid, and that that paranoia was induced, as many historians would now have us believe, by internal social tensions, what are we to say about British perceptions of German power in the 1930s? Why should the British people of that generation have felt disturbed by the revival of German military capabilities and the extension of their hegemony over Eastern Europe when German leaders were at the time quite sincerely disclaiming any intention of threatening either Britain herself or her control over her empire? Was this also paranoia? Those historians who have suggested that it was are not popular with their colleagues. But be this as it may, in 1914 many of the German people, and in 1939 nearly all the British, felt justified in going to war, not over any specific issue that could have been settled by negotiation, but *to maintain their power;* and to do so while it was still possible, before they found themselves so isolated, so impotent, that they had no power left to maintain and had to accept a subordinate position within an international system dominated by their adversaries. "What made war inevitable was the growth of Athenian power and the fear that this caused in Sparta." Or, to quote another grimly apt passage from Thucydides:

> The Athenians made their Empire more and more strong . . . [until] finally the point was reached when Athenian strength attained a peak plain for all to see and the Athenians began to encroach upon Sparta's allies. It was at this point that Sparta felt the position to be no longer tolerable and decided by starting the present war to employ all her energies in attacking and if possible destroying the power of Athens.[9]

You can vary the names of the actors, but the model remains a valid one for the purposes of our analysis. I am rather afraid that it still does.

Something that has changed since the time of Thucydides, however, is the nature of the power that appears so threatening. From the time of Thucydides until that of Louis XIV there was basically only one source of political and military power—control of territory, with all the resources in wealth and manpower that this provided. This control might come through conquest, or through alliance, or through marriage, or through purchase, but the power of

princes could be very exactly computed in terms of the extent of their territories and the number of men they could put under arms.

In seventeenth-century Europe this began to change. Extent of territory remained important, but no less important was the effectiveness with which the resources of that territory could be exploited. Initially there were the bureaucratic and fiscal mechanisms that transformed loose coagulations of territorial authority into highly structured centralized states whose armed forces, though not necessarily large, were permanent, disciplined and paid. Then came the political transformations of the revolutionary era which made available to these state-systems the entire manpower of their country; or at least as much of it as the administrators were able to handle. And finally came the revolution in transport, the railways of the nineteenth century that turned the revolutionary ideal of the "Nation in Arms" into a reality. By the early twentieth century military power —on the Continent of Europe, at least—was seen as a simple combination of military manpower and railways. The quality of armaments was of secondary importance, and political intentions were virtually excluded from account. The growth of power was measured in terms of the growth of populations and of communications; of the number of men who could be put under arms and transported to the battlefield to make their weight felt in the initial and presumably decisive battles. It was the mutual perception of threat in those terms that turned Europe before 1914 into an armed camp, and it was their calculations within this framework that reduced German staff officers increasingly to despair and launched their leaders on their catastrophic gamble in 1914.

But already the development of weapon technology had introduced yet another element into the international power calculus, one that has in our own age become dominant. It was only in the course of the nineteenth century that technology began to produce weapons-systems—initially in the form of naval vessels —that could be seen as likely in themselves to prove decisive, through their qualitative and quantitative superiority, in the event of conflict. But as war became increasingly a matter of competing technologies, rather than competing armies, so there developed that escalatory process known as the "arms race." As a title the phrase, like so many coined by journalists to catch the eye, is misleading. "Arms races" are in fact continuing and open-ended attempts to match power for power. They are as much means of achieving stable or, if possible, favorable power balances as were the dynastic marriage policies of Valois and Habsburg. To suggest that they in themselves are causes of war implies a naive if not totally mistaken view of the relationship between the two phenomena. The causes of war remain rooted, as much as they were in the pre-industrial age, in perceptions by statesmen of the growth of hostile power and the fears for the restriction, if not the extinction, of their own. The threat, or rather the fear, has not changed, whether it comes from aggregations of territory or from dreadnoughts, from the numbers of men under arms or from missile systems. The means which states employ to sustain or to extend their power may have been transformed, but their objectives and preoccupations remain the same.

"Arms races" can no more be isolated than wars themselves from the political circumstances that give rise to them, and like wars they will take as many different forms as political circumstances dictate. They may be no more than a process of competitive modernization, or maintaining a status quo that commands general support but in which no participant wishes, whether from reasons of pride or of prudence, to fall behind in keeping his armory up to date. If there are no political causes for fear or rivalry this process need not in itself be a destabilizing factor in international relations. But they may on the other hand be the result of a quite deliberate assertion of an intention to *change* the status quo, as was, for example, the German naval challenge to Britain at the beginning of this century.

This challenge was an explicit attempt by Tirpitz and his associates to destroy the hegemonial position at sea which Britain saw as essential to her security, and, not inconceivably, to replace it with one of their own. As British and indeed German diplomats repeatedly explained to the German government, it was not the German naval program in itself that gave rise to so much alarm in Britain. It was the intention that lay behind it. If the status quo was to be maintained, the German challenge had to be met.

The naval race could quite easily have been ended on one of two conditions. Either the Germans could have abandoned their challenge, as had the French in the previous century, and acquiesced in British naval supremacy; or the British could have yielded as gracefully as they did, a decade or so later, to the United States, and abandoned a status they no longer had the capacity, or the will, to maintain. As it was, they saw the German challenge as one to which they could and should respond, and their power position as one which they were prepared if necessary to use force to preserve. The British naval program was thus, like that of the Germans, a signal of political intent; and that intent, that refusal to acquiesce in a fundamental transformation of the power balance, was indeed a major element among the causes of the war. The naval competition provided rivalries and tensions, but it did not cause them; nor could it have been abated unless the rivalries themselves had been abandoned.

It was the general perception of the growth of German power that was awakened by the naval challenge, and the fear that a German hegemony on the Continent would be the first step to a challenge to her own hegemony on the oceans, that led Britain to involve herself in the continental conflict on the side of France and Russia. "What made war inevitable was the growth of *Spartan* power," to paraphrase Thucydides, "and the fear which this caused in *Athens*." In the Great War that followed, Germany was defeated, but survived with none of her latent power destroyed. A "false hegemony" of Britain and France was established in Europe that could last only so long as Germany did not again mobilize her resources to challenge it. German rearmament in the 1930s did not of itself mean that Hitler wanted war (though one has to ignore his entire philosophy if one is to believe that he did not); but it did mean that he was determined, with a great deal of popular support, to obtain a free hand on the international scene, *so oder so,* as he was in the habit of saying. With that free hand he intended to establish German power on an irreversible basis; this was the message conveyed by his armament program. The armament program which the British reluctantly adopted in reply was intended to show that, rather than submit to the hegemonial aspirations they feared from such a revival of German power, they would fight to preserve their own freedom of action. Once again to paraphrase Thucydides:

> Finally the point was reached when German strength attained a peak plain for all to see, and the Germans began to encroach upon Britain's allies. It was at this point that Britain felt the position to be no longer tolerable and decided by starting this present war to employ all her energies in attacking and if possible destroying the power of Germany.

What the Second World War established was not a new British hegemony, but a Soviet hegemony over the Euroasian land mass from the Elbe to Vladivostok; and what was seen, at least from Moscow, as an American hegemony over the rest of the world; one freely accepted in Western Europe as a preferable alternative to being absorbed by the rival hegemony. Rival armaments were developed to define and preserve the new territorial boundaries, and the present arms competition began. But in considering the present situation, historical experience suggests that we must ask the fundamental question: *what kind of competition is it*? Is it one between powers that accept the status quo, are satisfied with the existing power-relationship, and are concerned simply to modernize their armaments in order to preserve it? Or does it reflect an underlying instability in the system?

My own perception, I am afraid, is that it is the latter. There was period for a decade after the war when the Soviet Union was probably a status quo power but the West was not; that is, the Russians were not seriously concerned to challenge the American global hegemony, but the West did not accept that of the Russians in Eastern Europe. Then there was a decade of relative mutual acceptance between 1955 and 1965; and it was no accident that this was the heyday of disarmament/arms-control negotiations. But thereafter the Soviet Union has shown itself increasingly unwilling to accept the Western global hegemony, if only because many other peoples in the world have been unwilling to do so either. Reaction against Western dominance has brought the Soviet Union some allies and many opportunities in the global arena, and she has developed naval power to be able to assist the former and exploit the latter. She has aspired in fact to global power status, as did Germany before 1914; and if the West complains, as did Britain about Germany, that the Russians do not *need* a navy for defense purposes, the Soviet Union can retort, as did Germany, that she needs it to make clear to the world the status to which she aspires; that is, so that she can operate on the world scene by virtue of her own power and not by permission of anyone else. Like Germany, she is determined to be treated as an equal, and armed strength has appeared the only way to achieve that status.

The trouble is that what is seen by one party as the breaking of alien hegemony and the establishment of equal status will be seen by the incumbent powers as a striving for the establishment of an alternative hegemony, and they are not necessarily wrong. In international politics, the appetite often comes with eating; and there really may be no way to check an aspiring rival except by the mobilization of stronger military power. An arms race then becomes almost a necessary surrogate for war, a test of national will and strength; and arms control becomes possible only when the underlying power balance has been mutually agreed.

We would be blind therefore if we did not recognize that the causes which have produced war in the past are operating in our own day as powerfully as at any time in history. It is by no means impossible that a thousand years hence a historian will write—if any historians survive, and there are any records for them to write history from—"What made war inevitable was the growth of Soviet power and the fear which this caused in the United States." But times *have* changed since Thucydides. They have changed even since 1914. These were, as we have seen, bellicist societies in which war was a normal, acceptable, even a desirable way of settling differences. The question that arises today is, how widely and evenly spread is that intense revulsion against war that at present characterizes our own society? For if war is indeed now *universally* seen as being unacceptable as an instrument of policy, then all analogies drawn from the past are misleading, and although power struggles may continue, they will be diverted into other channels. But if that revulsion is not evenly spread, societies which continue to see armed force as an acceptable means for attaining their political ends are likely to establish a dominance over those which do not. Indeed they will not necessarily have to fight for it.

My second and concluding point is this. Whatever may be the underlying causes of international conflict, even if we accept the role of atavistic militarism or of military-industrial complexes or of socio-biological drives or of domestic tensions in fueling it, wars begin with conscious and reasoned decisions based on the calculation, made by *both* parties, that they can achieve more by going to war than by remaining at peace.[10] Even in the most bellicist of societies this kind of calculation has to be made and it has never even for them been an easy one. When the decision to go to war involves the likelihood, if not the certainty, that the conflict will take the form of an exchange of nuclear weapons from which one's own territory cannot be immune, then even for the most bellicist of leaders, even for those most insulated from the pressures of public opinion, the calculation that they have more to gain from going to war than by remaining at peace and pursuing their policies by other means will, to put it mildly, not be self-evident. The odds against such a course benefiting their state or themselves or their cause will be greater, and more *evidently* greater, than in any situation that history has ever to record. Society may have accepted killing as a legitimate instrument of state policy, but not, as yet, suicide. For that reason I find it hard to believe that the abolition of nuclear weapons, even if it were possible, would be an unmixed blessing. Nothing that makes it easier for statesmen to regard war as a feasible instrument of state policy, one from which they stand to gain rather than lose, is likely to contribute to a lasting peace.

NOTES

This chapter is reprinted from Michael Howard, *The Causes of War and Other Essays* (Cambridge, Mass.: Harvard University Press, 1983), 7–22.

This article was written in 1981—twenty years ago. Readers must use their own judgment as to whether its conclusions remain valid, but they should bear in mind that it was conceived at a particularly tense moment in the Cold War. The combination of the Soviet invasion of Afghanistan in 1979; the humiliating failure of the Carter administration to rescue the American diplomats held hostage in Iran the following year; the Soviet arms buildup, including the installation of SS20 missiles targeted on Western Europe; the advent to office of President Reagan with his denunciations of "the evil Empire": all had contributed to the collapse of "détente" between the superpowers and the opening of a new and dangerous phase in the Cold War. These events certainly influenced my thinking, but I trust that they did not distort it.

1. See "Reflections on the First World War," in my *Studies in War and Peace* (Temple Smith, 1970), 99.

2. *History of the Peloponnesian War,* trans. Rex Warner (Penguin, 1954), 25.

3. Quincy Wright, *A Study of War* (Chicago: 1941), vol. 2, 733.

4. Karl von Clausewitz, *On War* (Princeton University Press, 1976), 149.

5. Bernard Brodie, *War and Politics* (Macmillan, New York, 1973), 339.

6. Geoffrey Blainey, *The Causes of War* (London, 1973), 149.

7. Wright, *Study of War,* vol. 2, 144.

8. Raymond Aron, *Peace and War: A Theory of International Relations* (London, 1966), 7.

9. Thucydides, *History of the Peloponnesian War,* 77.

10. See Blainey, *Causes of War,* 128.

3

Empires and Geopolitical Competition

Gone for Good?

Charles A. Kupchan

LOOKING BACK

Empires have dominated the international landscape for much of recorded history. Even as technology, polity, and society have changed over the centuries, empires have risen and fallen with remarkable continuity. It was not until the delegitimation of imperial conquest and rule during the twentieth century that the prevalence of formal empire came to an end.

Empires have been such a recurring feature of the international landscape because they rest on a simple and durable geopolitical logic.[1] Imperial formations are based upon power asymmetry between a core state and a surrounding periphery. Order devolves naturally through the hierarchy that stems from power asymmetry. This hierarchy is usually strengthened over time as the core extracts wealth and manpower from the periphery and seeks to draw peripheral states into a stable political formation. Whether through the Roman practice of Romanization, the Byzantine reliance on religious conversion, or the Ottoman *millet* system (which set up local government along religious lines), cores regularly seek to draw the periphery toward the center through persuasion, co-optation, and incentive, not only through coercion.

The demise of an empire usually occurs when one imperial power is challenged by another. The resulting contest for hegemony requires the exceptional extraction of resources and usually degrades the internal cohesion of empires. Peripheral states take advantage of the opportunity to distance themselves from the core. And core states, weakened and exhausted by the demands of war, often lose the political will to maintain their imperial reach. The result is the dismantling of far-flung empires and the end of the core state's position atop the international hierarchy. The ascent of one empire followed by its eventual eclipse by the next in line has led to a recurring historical pattern of the rise and fall of great powers.[2]

The international spread of principles of democratic governance and self-determination has effectively brought to an end the long heyday of formal empire. The international community no longer deems it legitimate for strong states to colonize weaker ones. And the rise of nationalism—the doctrine asserting that the boundaries of states should coincide with the boundaries of nations—has meant the breakup of multiethnic empires into separate national states. Although the end of the imperial era and the rise of nationalism in some places have led to the formation of stable national states, elsewhere they have had less auspicious consequences. Many contemporary conflicts in the Balkans, the Middle East, Africa, and Asia have their roots in the dismantling of large, multiethnic empires and the drawing of new borders that cut across religious and ethnic boundaries.

The systemic forces that lie behind the rise and decline of great empires have thus left an indelible mark on the course of history. On the one hand, empires have frequently served as sources of order and stability as well as vehicles for the transmission of knowledge, religion, and culture. On the other hand, they have repeatedly caused major wars and served as vehicles of coercion and repression. Furthermore, the imperial age has left behind deep and lasting scars. The Middle East is still coping with political tensions left over from British and French colonialism. The violent breakup of Yugoslavia during the 1990s and the ongoing tension between Greece and Turkey have clear links to the remnants of the Ottoman empire. African Americans and American Indians still suffer from the long-term social consequences of America's colonial era. And in large swaths of the developing world, the experience of imperial rule and decolonization continue to spawn ethnic conflict, income inequalities, and territorial disputes.

LOOKING AHEAD

The collapse of the Soviet Union represented the demise of the last major empire of the twentieth century—and perhaps the last empire in history. Although formal empire may now be a historical artifact, the concept is still of much relevance to contemporary international politics. Indeed, the current unipolar structure of the international system operates according to a geopolitical logic quite similar to that of an empire. The United States enjoys a marked preponderance of power, with other major states arrayed around it in a hub-spoke pattern. Order and stability devolve from this natural hierarchy. There is no balancing among competing poles of power in large part because the power asymmetry between the United States and others is too stark. The stability engendered by unipolarity is thus quite similar to the stability engendered by an imperial formation.[3]

The notion of *consensual empire* offers one way of conceiving of the current international order. The United States, because of its preponderant resources, is able to set up and underwrite the rules of the international system. Other states abide by these rules and enter the U.S.-led order because they want to, not because they are coerced into doing so. The lure of attracting international investment, the disciplining effects of economic reform on politics, the spread of shared democratic values and practices—these have replaced colonial governors and direct rule as the main source of centripetal force pulling the periphery toward the core. In this sense, contemporary geopolitics resemble what came to be called the "informal empire" of Britain during the nineteenth century.[4] Informal governance through local elites and private business proved cheaper and more durable than direct intervention, which often provoked resistance from the periphery. Britain's hegemony was long lived and far reaching in part because reliance on informal means of governance reduced the costs of empire. In this sense, today's international system exhibits more continuity with the past than meets the eye.

This perspective raises critical questions about the future. If the stability of the current international system stems at least in part from its unipolar structure, what geopolitical consequences are likely to accompany the end of unipolarity? Will other states balance against the United States as the preponderant power, or will the informal, consensual, and multilateral nature of America's international governance prevent the formation of opposing coalitions and preserve stability?[5] Will a more equal distribution of global power bring with it the return of geopolitical competition among core areas, or will globalization, the spread of democracy, and the decreasing incentives to engage in predatory conquest prevent the return of traditional security rivalries?

The thrust of this essay is that traditional power politics and geopolitical competition are by no means gone for good. Democracy, international institutions, and the globalization of markets for trade, finance, and information do have powerful peace-causing effects. But these sources of stability may well be contingent upon the existence of a unipolar setting. Take away unipolarity, and globalization may do more to transmit global shocks than to engender convergence of values and domestic regimes. Had the United States not intervened in 1998 to stop the reverberations of the Asian financial crisis, a global economic crisis may well have ensued.[6] Accordingly, there is little room for complacency about the ability of the United States and other major states to manage peacefully systemic change. The record of imperial rise and fall and the catastrophic clashes that have occurred between ascending and fading empires provide adequate cause for sobriety and caution in thinking through the geopolitical future.

In the next section, I examine the causes of systemic change and explain why America's unipolar moment is not likely to last long. The United States will for decades to come continue to enjoy a stark military and economic superiority over other countries, but America's willingness to remain the globe's protector of last resort will gradually diminish. I then discuss the prospects for renewed competition among emerging poles of power, weighing the sources

of stability against those of rivalry. In doing so, I distinguish between those areas of the globe that already constitute a *security community*—a zone within which states have stable expectations of peaceful change—and those that continue to play by more traditional rules of geopolitics.[7] The Atlantic democracies, for example, after years of close cooperation, no longer threaten one another; war among them has become essentially unthinkable. From this perspective, a more equal distribution of global power will have more muted strategic consequences for the security community constituted by North America and Europe than for other parts of the globe. Whether a security community forms within East Asia, and between East Asia and the Atlantic democracies, will also play an important role in determining the consequences of systemic change. I therefore consider how to go about promoting peace within regions as well as preventing rivalry among them.

THE SOURCES OF SYSTEMIC CHANGE

Most analysts of international politics trace change in the distribution of power to two sources: the secular diffusion over time and space of productive capabilities and material resources; and the balancing against concentrations of power motivated by the search for security and prestige. Today's great powers will become tomorrow's has-beens as nodes of innovation and efficiency move from the core to the periphery of the international system. In addition, reigning hegemons threaten rising secondary states and thereby provoke the formation of countervailing coalitions. Taken together, these dynamics drive the cyclical pattern of the rise and fall of great powers.[8]

In contrast to this historical pattern, neither the diffusion of power nor balancing against the United States will be an important factor driving the coming transition in the international system. It will be decades before any single state can match the United States in terms of either military or economic capability. Current power asymmetries are by historical standards extreme. The United States spends more on defense than all other great powers combined and more on defense R&D than the rest of the world combined. Its gross economic output dwarfs that of most other countries and its expenditure on R&D points to a growing qualitative edge in a global economy increasingly dominated by high-technology sectors.[9]

Nor is balancing against American power likely to provoke a countervailing coalition. The United States is separated from both Europe and Asia by large expanses of water, making American power less threatening. Furthermore, it is hard to imagine that the United States would engage in behavior sufficiently aggressive to provoke opposing alliances. Even in the wake of NATO's air campaign against Yugoslavia, U.S. forces are for the most part welcomed by local powers in Europe and East Asia. Despite sporadic comments from French, Russian, and Chinese officials about America's overbearing behavior, the United States is generally viewed as a benign power, not as a predatory hegemon.[10] To be sure, the preponderance of American power and the dominance of U.S. culture will continue to engender resentment abroad. But this resentment is likely to manifest itself in terms of sporadic outbursts—both rhetorical and more substantive in nature (terrorism)—rather than through the systematic formation of a coalition aimed at serving as a counterweight to the United States.

The waning of unipolarity is therefore likely to stem from two novel sources: regional amalgamation in Europe and shrinking internationalism in the United States. Europe is in the midst of a long-term process of political and economic integration that is gradually eliminating the importance of borders and centralizing authority and resources. To be sure, the European Union is not yet an amalgamated polity with a single center of authority. Nor

does Europe have a military capability commensurate with its economic resources. But trend lines do indicate that Europe is heading in the direction of becoming a new pole of power. Now that its single market has been accompanied by a single currency, Europe has a collective weight on matters of trade and finance rivaling that of the United States. The aggregate wealth of the European Union's fifteen members is already roughly equal to America's, and the coming entry of a host of new members will tilt the balance in Europe's favor. Europe has recently embarked on efforts to forge a common defense policy and to acquire the military wherewithal to operate independently of U.S. forces. The European Union has appointed its first-ever high representative for foreign and security policy (Javier Solana, NATO's former secretary general), established bodies to provide political and military oversight, and embarked on efforts to create a rapid reaction force capable of deploying without U.S. assistance. It will be decades, if ever, before the European Union becomes a unitary state, especially in light of its impending enlargement to the east. But as its resources grow and its decision making becomes more centralized, power and influence will become more equally distributed between the two sides of the Atlantic. A more balanced strategic relationship is likely to follow.

The continuing rise of Europe and its leveling effect on the global distribution of power will occur gradually. Of more immediate impact will be a diminishing appetite for robust internationalism in the United States. Today's unipolar landscape is a function not just of America's dominating resources, but also of its willingness to use them to underwrite international order. Accordingly, should the will of the body politic to bear the costs and risks of international leadership decline, so too will America's position of global primacy.

On the face of it, the appetite of the American polity for internationalism has diminished little, if at all, since the collapse of the Soviet

Union. Both George Bush's and Bill Clinton's administrations pursued ambitious and activist foreign policies. The United States has taken the lead in building an open international economy and promoting financial stability, and it has repeatedly deployed its forces to trouble spots around the globe. But American internationalism may have reached a high-water mark and, for four compelling reasons, it will be dissipating in the years ahead.

First, the scope of America's commitments in Europe is not in equilibrium with the continent's new strategic landscape. The demise of the Soviet Union and the disappearance of the threat that gave rise to NATO should have lightened America's load in Europe. Instead, America's strategic commitments on the European continent have increased markedly over the course of the past decade. NATO admitted Poland, Hungary, and the Czech Republic in 1999, extending American defense guarantees into Central Europe. In addition, Bosnia, Kosovo, Macedonia, and Albania have effectively become NATO protectorates, and Estonia, Latvia, Lithuania, Slovakia, Slovenia, Croatia, Romania, and Bulgaria are now readying themselves to qualify for NATO membership. The prospect of these new commitments will force the United States to reconsider its strategic position in Europe. And absent a transcendent threat, the United States is likely to gravitate toward a strategic role in Europe that is less onerous and ambitious than during the Cold War. An American internationalism that is sustainable over the long term will entail fewer, not more, commitments. From this geopolitical perspective, the 1990s promise to be an aberration, not a precedent for the future.

Second, the internationalism of the 1990s has been sustained by a period of unprecedented economic growth in the United States. A booming stock market, an expanding economy, and substantial budget surpluses created a political atmosphere conducive to trade liberalization, expenditure on the military, and repeated engagement in solving problems in less

fortunate parts of the globe. And even under these auspicious conditions, the internationalist agenda showed signs of faltering. Congress, for example, has mustered only a fickle enthusiasm for free trade, approving NAFTA in 1993 and the Uruguay Round in 1994 but then denying President Clinton fast-track negotiating authority in 1997. Congress was also skeptical of America's interventions in Bosnia and Kosovo, tolerating them, but little more. In a period of stock market decline and stalled growth, these inward-looking currents will grow much stronger. The little support for free trade that still exists will dwindle. And such stinginess is likely to spread into the security realm, intensifying the domestic debate over burden-sharing and calls within Congress for America's regional partners to shoulder increased defense responsibilities. These trends appear to be more than hypothetical. In the presidential campaign and during his first few months in office, George W. Bush indicated that he plans to pursue a more restrained and selective brand of internationalism.

Third, although the United States has pursued a very activist defense policy during the 1990s, it has done so on the cheap. Clinton repeatedly authorized the use of force in the Balkans and in the Middle East. But he relied almost exclusively on air power, successfully avoiding the casualties likely to accompany the introduction of ground troops in combat. In Somalia, the one case in which U.S. ground troops suffered significant losses, Clinton ordered the withdrawal of U.S. forces from the operation. In NATO's campaign against Yugoslavia, week after week of bombing only intensified the humanitarian crisis and increased the likelihood of a southward spread of the conflict. Nevertheless, the United States blocked the use of ground forces and insisted that aircraft bomb from 15,000 feet to avoid being shot down.

Congress revolted despite these operational constraints minimizing the risks to U.S. personnel. A month into the campaign, the U.S.

House of Representatives voted 249 to 180 to refuse funding for sending U.S. ground troops to Yugoslavia without congressional permission. Even a resolution that merely endorsed the bombing campaign failed to win approval (the vote was 213 to 213). In short, the American polity appears to have near zero-tolerance for accepting casualties. The illusion that internationalism can be maintained with no or minimal loss of life will likely come back to haunt the United States in the years ahead, limiting its ability to use force in the appropriate manner when necessary.

Fourth, generational change is likely to take a toll on the character and scope of U.S. engagement abroad. The younger Americans already rising to positions of influence in the public and private sectors have not lived through the formative experiences—World War II, the rebuilding of Europe, the Cold War—that serve as historical anchors of internationalism. Individuals schooled in the 1990s and now entering the work force will have come of age after the fall of the Berlin Wall and its potent geopolitical symbolism. These Americans will not necessarily be isolationist, but they will certainly be less interested in and knowledgeable about foreign affairs than their older colleagues—a pattern already becoming apparent in Congress. In the absence of a manifest threat to American national security, making the case for engagement and sacrifice abroad thus promises to grow increasingly difficult with time. These political trend lines clearly point to a turning inward and a nation tiring of carrying the burdens of global leadership.

The coming decades thus promise to bring with them a transition from unipolarity to a more multipolar setting. Europe is the near-term challenger to America's current position of global dominance, although it is by no means clear what type of pole the European Union will constitute or what the scope of its ambition will be. Japan, although a world-class economic power, is likely to remain averse to geopolitical leadership for the foreseeable future. Over

time, China will rise to a position of global prominence. In the near term, China's rise raises the prospect of intraregional competition within East Asia, especially if America's role as extraregional balancer wanes. In the long term, Asia's ascendance will raise the prospect of interregional competition among North America, a collective Europe, and an East Asia whose internal landscape remains uncertain. Will the return of multipolarity lead to competition among power centers? Is the imperial rivalry of the past destined to return? Or has international politics entered a new era, suggesting that coming systemic change will occur peacefully?

RELATIONS AMONG POLES: WILL THE FUTURE RESEMBLE THE PAST?

Changes in the nature of power and in the nature of the polities that wield power mean that a coming shift in the structure of the system may take place in a new international environment. The advent of nuclear weapons, globalization, the spread of democracy, changes in the sources of wealth—these are all developments that could profoundly alter the process and the consequences of systemic change. What constitutes a pole could be undergoing transformation as well as the forces that will shape relations between poles.

In this section, I reflect on the nature of contemporary systemic change and evaluate the extent to which the lessons of the past speak to the challenges of the future. I begin by looking at how changes in material factors are likely to affect systemic change and relations among future poles. I then examine the impact of the relatively benign character of the current hegemon—the United States—on relations with rising challengers. In the nature of its polity and in the practice of its policies, the United States represents a departure from the past. Thereafter, I discuss the implications of the emergence of security communities for systemic change. In light of the fact that North America and Europe have carved out a zone of stable peace and virtually eliminated security competition between themselves, will a more equal balance of power across the Atlantic have limited geopolitical effects? How can existing security communities be protected against unraveling? How can they be enlarged? The answers to these questions will shed light on the nature of contemporary systemic change and help guide policymakers seeking to avoid the return of geopolitical competition among centers of power. I consider each of these claims in turn.

Changes in Material Conditions

NUCLEAR WEAPONS. There are sound reasons for believing that changes in military technology and the sources of wealth may dampen security competition and make systemic change easier to manage peacefully than in the past. Nuclear weapons breed caution and may succeed in limiting the intensity of strategic rivalry between poles of power. Predatory conquest and control over land and labor no longer represent the best pathway to economic and military supremacy; the great powers of today and tomorrow may be able to attain the wealth and influence they desire without aggression. Furthermore, contemporary globalization, more far reaching in both quantity and quality than ever before, may help encourage multiple power centers to pursue joint gains rather than seek individual advantage.

Nuclear weapons do decrease the chances that systemic change will be accompanied by major war. The prospect of nuclear devastation may well be sufficient to prevent reigning hegemon and rising challenger from engaging in the great contests for primacy that usually accompany the decline of one great power and the rise of another. At the same time, the nuclear revolution may make systemic change more precarious for three distinct reasons. First, if nuclear weapons do not succeed in deterring conflict among contenders for primacy, the resultant conflict among nuclear-armed power centers will be catastrophic. History makes clear that systemic change brings with it powerful war-causing forces. That these forces will be unleashed during the nuclear age warrants considerable thought about how best to dampen the possibility of hegemonic war. Furthermore, nuclear weapons in the hands of third parties increase the chances that systemic instability, even if not accompanied in the first instance by conflict among power centers, could have very dangerous consequences.

Second, nuclear weapons may embolden contenders for primacy and make them less willing to compromise to find a mutually acceptable order and new hierarchy.[11] Even if nuclear weapons do restrain parties from going to war, they may also make them less pliant partners because of the bargaining strength associated with nuclear capability. A declining hegemon may hold its ground because of its ability to threaten nuclear retaliation; despite the loss of its material superiority, it may seek to cling to its position in the global hierarchy. A rising challenger may be equally obstinate because of its nuclear capability.

Third, even if nuclear weapons prevent contenders for primacy from engaging in outright war, they may do little to facilitate rapprochement among leading power centers—and indeed may stand in the way of such rapprochement for the reasons just cited. A multipolar world in which stability is maintained by mutual nuclear deterrence is far preferable to war, but far less preferable than a multipolar world in which stability is maintained through cooperation. In this sense, scholars and analysts alike need to address how to bring about a systemic transition that leads to a warm, rather than cold, peace.

STATE POWER. Changes in the sources of state power may act to moderate the war-causing potential of systemic transition. Territorial conquest pays less than it used to; economic primacy is now rooted in technological innovation and communication, not land and labor. Globalization may also contribute to stability through several different pathways. High levels of international trade and investment and the globalization of production increase the costs of geopolitical rivalry. As Thomas Friedman has persuasively argued, the global marketplace is also imposing a "golden straightjacket" on states that enter it, leading to a convergence of domestic structures and ideology.[12] If states want to have access to international capital and the global market for goods and services, Friedman argues, they have to adhere to a relatively constraining set of political dictums and business practices. This domestic convergence may in turn reduce the likelihood of conflicts of interest.

While it is plausible, if not likely, that major powers will, for utilitarian reasons, engage in less predatory behavior than their imperial predecessors, a world in which power centers regularly engage in strategic restraint is not necessarily a stable world. Strategic restraint, while reducing direct rivalry between contenders for primacy, could result in the underprovision of security in third areas. Rather than compete for market access and strategic influence in developing areas, major powers may seek to cordon themselves off. The result could be an incremental return to disorder in the periphery, which ultimately would have the potential to undermine order in core areas. Imagine what might have happened in the Balkans had both the European Union and the United States refrained from military engagement throughout the 1990s. Conflict may well have spread throughout the Balkan peninsula, ultimately threatening the broader European and Atlantic security order. The ongoing proliferation of weapons of mass destruction also raises the stakes of instability in other areas.

It is also possible that contenders for primacy, even if they do not initially clash over territory, will engage in status competition.[13] Systemic change, after all, upsets the existing hierarchy, creating demands by rising powers for more voice and influence. A direct conflict of interest may therefore not be necessary for rivalry to begin and escalate. The sources of World War I, for example, lay not in disputes over borders or territory, but in Germany's desire for a level of influence in Europe commensurate with its economic capability. Status competition thus has the potential to escalate into geopolitical competition.

GLOBALIZATION. Parsing out the consequences of globalization for systemic change is complicated by the fact that "globalization" is itself an ambiguous and elusive term. If taken to be the global diffusion of trade, investment, production, and communication, then the phenomenon has both positive and negative effects on the prospects for peaceful systemic change. To be sure, high levels of cross-border trade and investment are encouraging leading states to pursue mutual advantage. The global diffusion of production sites is of particular importance because they constitute a more durable—and less easily moved—asset than equity investment. In addition, most of the world's wealthier states and those aspiring to such wealth are converging around a core set of capitalist values and practices, decreasing the likelihood of diverging interests. All of these features of a globalized economy may promote stability amid structural change.

But globalization also brings with it forces that could magnify the destabilizing effects of transition. Should sectoral or regional economic shocks take place, a fast, interdependent market will transmit such shocks globally. The 1930s made clear the extent to which spreading economic crisis can lead to geopolitical instability. Globalization may well widen the bandwidth within which market disturbances can occur without destabilizing the broader system. But once a certain threshold has been crossed, disturbances may spread with a vengeance.

The domestic convergence engendered by globalization also has negative as well as positive consequences for systemic stability. Developing states are converging around a common set of values and practices in order to encourage foreign investment and participate fully in the global economy. But strict adherence to economic principles imposed from outside can also have powerful backlashes if such adherence does not pay off. States buffeted by the international economy at times fight back, fostering the authoritarian tendencies that can in turn trigger external ambition and geopolitical rivalries. In *The Great Transformation,* Karl Polanyi linked twentieth-century fascism to excessive adherence to market principles and the gold standard.[14] His analysis has cautionary implications for today's global economy and the discipline of Friedman's golden straightjacket.

In sum, material conditions provide cause for both optimism and pessimism about the prospects for managing systemic change peacefully. At a minimum, this analysis suggests that there is little room for complacency in confronting the geopolitical consequences of a return to multipolarity.

Changes in Polity and Practice

One of the most puzzling aspects of the current strategic landscape is the absence of balancing against the United States. France, Russia, and China may cavil against what they see as America's overbearing, imperial behavior. But behind the scenes, they quietly welcome the presence of U.S. troops in Europe and Asia and the stability they engender. Far from balancing against the United States, most countries of the world behave as if they cannot get enough of American power and purpose.

This unusual absence of balancing against the hegemon is the product of three factors. First, America's location, with large expanses of water to its east and west, limits the threat it poses to major powers in Europe and Asia.

Were a country of the size and power of the United States to be located on the Eurasian landmass, it would be far more likely to trigger balancing. America's direct neighbors, Canada and Mexico, simply do not have the option of balancing because of stark power asymmetries.

Second, the scope of the power gap between America and potential rivals calls into question the feasibility and desirability of attempting to balance against the United States. With U.S. military spending roughly equal to that of the next five powers combined, no single state could realistically seek to act as a counterweight to U.S. power. Furthermore, with the United States underwriting and effectively fashioning the key multilateral institutions and practices in both the security and economic realms, challenging American dominance would bring with it considerable costs. To be sure, were coalitions of major states to form against the United States, those coalitions would have the wherewithal to act as counterweights to U.S. power. However, such coalitions simply are not taking shape. Europe is gradually emerging as a collective entity equal to the United States in economic terms. But the European project is being fueled primarily by efforts to escape national rivalry within Europe, not to balance against the United States.

That coalitions are not forming against the United States bring us to the third reason that balancing is not taking place: the character of American power. Were the United States engaging in predatory behavior—regularly invading other states and pursuing exploitative policies—balancing coalitions would no doubt form. Instead, the United States engages in policies that succeed, for the most part, in reassuring other states about its intentions. Put differently, because of the nature of its polity and its practice, other states attribute to the United States a benign character.[15]

Democratic government partially explains this perception of the United States. The American polity is transparent and porous. The vagaries of partisan politics are in plain view, as are the self-checking mechanisms associated with three competing branches of government. That the United States regularly engages in both self-binding (unilateral restraint) and co-binding (multilateral restraint) further reassures others about U.S. intentions. And as more countries become democratic and share a sense of affinity and commonality, they are likely to join the grouping of states within which security competition has been muted, if not eliminated.

A key question for the future is whether the absence of balancing against the United States will continue even as global power becomes more equally distributed. The stability and durability of traditional empires stemmed in large part from the core's material preponderance. When the core lost its power advantage, either to the periphery or to another rising core, competition and imperial demise followed. Will American policy change and become more aggressive when the United States is confronted with more capable rivals? Will a more self-possessed Europe engage in strategic rivalry with the United States, or will democratic values and institutions override the increased competitiveness that will accompany a more equal balance of power across the Atlantic? To address these questions, I turn to the role that security communities are likely to play in preserving order and facilitating peaceful change. If systemic change is on the horizon, a key determinant of its geopolitical consequences will be whether the security community formed across the Atlantic will withstand a new balance of power. It is equally important to speculate about how existing security communities can be enlarged or new ones created in order to incorporate rising powers such as China and Russia.

THE UNITED STATES AND EUROPE: SECURITY COMMUNITY OR RIVALRY?

Europe over the course of the next decade is likely to become a much more influential and independent actor. This evolution in Europe's international position is both desirable and inevitable. It is desirable because Europe's current level of strategic dependence on the United States is simply unsustainable over the long term; Americans will not indefinitely foot the bill for European stability. It is inevitable because as Europe deepens its collective governance and becomes a more formidable economic entity, it will aspire to a level of influence commensurate with its power.

The critical question for the future is thus not whether Europe will rise as an independent power center, but what effect a self-possessed Europe will have on the character of relations across the Atlantic. History suggests that a more equal distribution of power and influence between Europe and the United States will bring with it renewed geopolitical competition. The emergence of rivalry among poles of power is, after all, one of the few recurring truths of international politics.

Whether relative parity will indeed trigger rivalry between Europe and the United States depends in large part on what it is that now keeps the Atlantic relationship in such good shape. If, on the one hand, it is American dominance that now holds competition in abeyance, then the rise of Europe promises to trigger geopolitical competition. From this perspective, Europe is following America's lead because it does not have the power to do otherwise. When the power asymmetry comes to an end, so will European acquiescence. If, on the other hand, a shared commitment to democratic values and a common vision of an open, multilateral order are the foundation of the transatlantic community, then the West should easily weather a more equal distribution of power across the Atlantic. From this perspective, democratic norms and multilateral institutions will overwhelm the incentives on both sides of the Atlantic to engage in power balancing.[16]

My own assessment is that power asymmetry and shared norms and institutions are working together to produce the current durability and cohesiveness of the transatlantic community. Europe has been following America's lead in part because of U.S. preponderance, but also because it welcomes the particular brand of international order that the United States has crafted. As Europe matures and its aspirations broaden, more competition with the United States will follow. But this competition is likely to be muted and restricted largely to the economic realm. Such optimism that geopolitical rivalry between North America and Europe is not on the horizon stems from the following considerations.

The Atlantic democracies are far more than allies of convenience. They have succeeded in carving out a unique political space—a security community—in which the rules of anarchic competition no longer apply. These states enjoy unprecedented levels of trust and reciprocity. It is hard to imagine that their interests would diverge sufficiently to trigger strategic rivalry. Indeed, armed conflict among the members of the Atlantic community has become unthinkable. These attributes of the Atlantic community are deeply rooted in the democratic character of its members and in the thick network of institutions they have erected to regulate their relations. The benign quality of the relationship between North America and Europe is very unlikely to be threatened even by a quantitative shift in the balance of power.

The character of the emerging European polity also minimizes the potential for security competition between Europe and the United States. The European Union is primarily an instrument for managing the power of its member states, not for amassing and projecting it. Furthermore, even as integration proceeds, cultural and linguistic barriers are likely to prevent Europe from amalgamating into a single pole of power under a central authority. The decentralized nature of the emerging Europe will limit its willingness and ability to project power externally, further diminishing the risk of geopolitical competition with the United States.[17]

Despite the low probability that Europe's rise will lead to estrangement from the United States, some preventive measures are in order. Washington should ensure that it makes room for and encourages a stronger and more independent Europe. American efforts to resist Europe's ascent as a power center would only alienate Europeans and increase the chances of balancing and geopolitical rivalry. The United States and its European partners should also strengthen multilateral practices and institutions. When Washington is no longer able to call the shots, it will have no choice but to rely more heavily on consensual governance and multilateral institutions to manage international order.

THE REST AGAINST THE WEST?

The formation of a security community among the Atlantic democracies took decades. The threat posed by the Soviet Union provided critical impetus. The prospects of mutual economic gain helped bind states together and institutionalize cooperative behavior. And the cultural and historical affinity that exists between North America and Western Europe was an important facilitating condition. The durability of the political space occupied by the Atlantic democracies has been manifested not just in its continued existence, but also in its efforts to expand. Both NATO and the European Union have embarked on ambitious plans of enlargement, seeking to integrate the new democracies of Central Europe into the Atlantic community.

A key unknown of this process of enlargement is its consequences for Russia and for East Asia. Russia could balance against Europe, especially if NATO and the European Union exclude Russia in their plans for enlargement. At the same time, depending on politics in Moscow and in Western capitals, Russia could ultimately be included in a broader Europe. Should Russia end up being excluded from the European space, the potential is high for a return of competitive geopolitics to Eurasia. For reasons of both security and status, Russia would likely seek to reconstitute itself as an independent power center, increasing the chances that Moscow would try to reassert control over its immediate neighbors. Exclusion from Europe would also affect Russian identity, encouraging Russians to see Europe as the other, not the self. As Russia comes back on line as a major player, it is therefore important to ensure that its power, influence, and identity are arrayed with, rather than against, a power center in Western Europe. NATO and the European Union should therefore make a top priority the drawing westward of Russia and its embrace in the Atlantic security community.[18]

Mapping out a geopolitical trajectory for East Asia is far more complicated. East Asia is unlikely to become part of an Atlantic security community. None of the conditions that brought together the United States and Europe pertain. The Atlantic community and states in East Asia do not face a common threat. They do not share a cultural affinity. And they are at different stages of economic and political development. Furthermore, deep political cleavages still exist in East Asia, meaning that the states of the region will for the foreseeable future be preoccupied with one another, rather than with their collective relations with Europe or North America. The risk in the near term is the return of intraregional balancing and rivalry, especially if American internationalism wanes and the United States seeks to reduce the scope of its commitments in East Asia. From this perspective, facilitating cooperation and rapprochement among proximate poles of power *within* East Asia is a far more immediate and important challenge than fashioning East Asia's relations with other regions. Forming a security community within East Asia is thus a necessary condition for drawing the region into a broader zone of peace.

Regional reconciliation and rapprochement depend first and foremost on improving rela-

tions between China and Japan. Efforts to build a stable regional order will falter if East Asia's two major states remain estranged. Just as reconciliation between France and Germany was the critical ingredient in building a stable zone of peace in Europe, so too is Sino-Japanese rapprochement the sine qua non of a stable peace in East Asia.

Primary responsibility for improving Sino-Japanese ties lies with Japan. With an economy and political system much more developed than China's, Japan has far more latitude in exploring openings in the relationship. Japan can also make a major step forward by finally acknowledging and formally apologizing for its behavior during World War II. The United States can further this process by welcoming and helping to facilitate overtures between Tokyo and Beijing. Washington should also help dislodge the inertia that pervades politics in Tokyo by making clear to the Japanese that they cannot indefinitely rely on American guarantees to ensure their security. Japan therefore needs to take advantage of America's protective umbrella while it lasts, pursuing the policies of reconciliation and integration essential to constructing a regional security order resting on cooperation rather than deterrence.

If overtures from Tokyo succeed in reducing tensions between China and Japan, the United States will be able to play a less prominent role in the region, making possible an improvement in its own relations with China. As it buys time for Sino-Japanese rapprochement to get off the ground, the United States should avoid rhetoric and policies that might induce China to intensify its efforts to balance against Japan and the United States. Talk of an impending Chinese military threat is both counterproductive and misguided; the Chinese military is nowhere near world-class.[19] The United States should also avoid provocative moves, such as deploying antimissile defenses in the theater or supporting a Taiwanese policy of moving toward formal independence. China can do its part to strengthen its relationship with the United States by containing saber rattling over Taiwan, halting the export of weapons to rogue states, and avoiding actions and rhetoric that could inflame territorial disputes in the region.

CONCLUSIONS

As the next century progresses, unipolarity will give way to a world of multiple centers of power. This transition will take place in the near term both because of the rise of Europe and because American internationalism will gradually wane. Over the longer term, the rise of China and the East Asia region as a whole will ensure the emergence of a multipolar global landscape. The stability that unipolarity has engendered will be compromised as renewed competition accompanies the return of a global landscape inhabited by multiple poles. Relations between the United States and Europe will grow more difficult as the power balance between them equalizes. But there are sound reasons to be confident that such competition will not result in direct security rivalry. Multipolarity promises to have more dangerous consequences for East Asia, largely because the region has yet to go through the process of political and economic integration that brought peace to Europe.

An ultimate vision for the future is the construction of a concertlike directorate of the major powers in North America, Europe, and East Asia. These major powers would together manage developments and regulate relations both within and among their respective regions. Such regional centers also hold promise for the gradual incorporation of developing nations into global flows of trade, information, and values. Strong and vibrant regional centers, for reasons of both proximity and culture, often have the strongest incentives to promote prosperity and stability in their immediate peripheries. North America might therefore focus on Latin America; Europe on Russia, the Middle East, and Africa; and East Asia on South Asia and Southeast Asia.

Power will remain an inescapable determinant of international life. The aim should not be to negate it, but to channel it toward peaceful ends. It is far wiser and safer to get ahead of the curve and shape structural change by design than to find unipolarity giving way to a chaotic multipolarity by default. It will take a decade, if not two, for a new international system to evolve. But the decisions made during the early years of the twenty-first century will play a critical role in determining whether multipolarity reemerges peacefully or brings with it the competitive jockeying that has so frequently been the precursor to the great imperial clashes of the past.

NOTES

1. For an anatomy of empires, see Michael Doyle, *Empires* (Ithaca, N.Y.: Cornell University Press, 1986).

2. See Robert Gilpin, *War and Change in World Politics* (Cambridge: Cambridge University Press, 1981); Paul Kennedy, *The Rise and Fall of the Great Powers* (New York: Random House, 1987).

3. On the stability of unipolarity, see William C. Wohlforth, "The Stability of a Unipolar World," *International Security* 24, no. 1 (summer 1999).

4. See John Gallagher and Ronald Robinson, "The Imperialism of Free Trade," *Economic History Review*, 2d ser., 6, no. 1 (1953).

5. See John Ikenberry, "Institutions, Strategic Restraint, and the Persistence of American Postwar Order," *International Security* 23, no. 3 (winter 1998-99).

6. *Economic Report of the President* (Washington, D.C.: U.S. Government Printing Office, 1999), 235; available at w3.access.gpo.gov/usbudget/fy2000/pdf/erp.pdf.

7. See Karl Deutsch et al., *Political Community and the North Atlantic Area* (Princeton, N.J.: Princeton University Press, 1957); and Emanuel Adler and Michael Barnett, *Security Communities* (Cambridge: Cambridge University Press, 1998).

8. See Gilpin, *War and Change*; Kennedy, *Rise and Fall of the Great Powers*; and Christopher Layne,

"The Unipolar Illusion: Why New Great Powers Will Rise," *International Security* 17, no. 4 (spring 1993).

9. Wohlforth, "Stability of a Unipolar World," 10–22.

10. On the concept of benign power, see Charles Kupchan, "After Pax Americana: Benign Power, Regional Integration, and the Sources of a Stable Multipolarity," *International Security* 23, no. 2 (fall 1998). The qualities that endow American power with its benign character are discussed later.

11. See Gilpin, *War and Change.*

12. Thomas Friedman, *The Lexus and the Olive Tree* (New York: Farrar, Straus, and Giroux, 1999).

13. Randall Schweller, "Realism and the Present Great Power System: Growth and Positional Conflict over Scarce Resources," in *Unipolar Politics,* ed. Michael Mastanduno and Ethan Kapstein (New York: Columbia University Press, 1999)

14. See Karl Polanyi, *The Great Transformation* (New York: Octagon Books, 1975).

15. The proposition that the peoples of most countries attribute to the United States a benign character is admittedly controversial. Especially in countries whose populations have suffered because of direct or indirect military intervention by the United States, anti-American sentiment runs strong. At the same time, I would contend that the United States is far less predatory and exploitative than most other great powers in history. The best testimony to such qualities is the absence of balancing against the United States despite its stark material preponderance.

16. Ikenberry, "Institutions, Strategic Restraint, and the Persistence of American Postwar Order."

17. Fareed Zakaria has shown that centralization and a strong state were necessary conditions for ambitious external policies in the United States. See *From Wealth to Power: The Unusual Origins of America's World Role* (Princeton, N.J.: Princeton University Press, 1998).

18. See Charles Kupchan, "Rethinking Europe," *National Interest,* no. 56 (summer 1999).

19. See Bates Gill and Michael O'Hanlon, "China's Hollow Military," *National Interest,* no. 56 (summer 1999).

4

Environmental Change, Security, and Conflict

Nils Petter Gleditsch

AN EXTENDED CONCEPT OF SECURITY?

Since the emergence of the two great totalitarian movements in Europe in the 1920s and the repeated defeats for liberal internationalism, the realist school of thought has been dominant in international relations. Realism has emphasized the struggle for territory and resources with patterns of conflict and cooperation forming mainly on the basis of the struggle for power—military, economic, and political. A country can strengthen its position through conquest or alliance building and will tend to do so unless checked by countervailing power. The international system is anarchic, with unclear norms and weak institutions that cannot prevent aggression from states that challenge the established order. Security is mainly a zero-sum game in which a gain for one state is a loss for another.

The field of international relations has never universally accepted a pure realist notion of security, and in the past few decades alternative notions of security have gained ground. After the end of the Cold War, in particular, the notion of security has been subjected to intense scrutiny.

In one of the first challenges to the traditional security concept, the Palme Commission (Palme et al. 1982) launched the slogan *common security*, a positive-sum notion in which the greater security of one state was seen to be mutually reinforcing with that of another. A more radical challenge was put forward with the notion of *comprehensive security* (Westing 1989), which widened the scope of the traditional concerns. In modern parlance, *human security* is the buzzword, commonly defined as "safety from chronic threats such as hunger, disease, and oppression, and protection from the sudden and hurtful impact in the patterns of everyday life" (Lonergan 1999, 23; United Nations Development Programme 1994, 23).

The wider notions of security vary somewhat in the aspects they include. A comprehensive list might include

- *political security*, defined as the freedom from dictatorship and other arbitrary government,
- *economic and social security*, defined as the freedom from poverty and want,
- *cultural security*, defined as the freedom from ethnic or religious domination, and
- *environmental security*, defined as the freedom from environmental destruction and resource scarcity.

This list corresponds to the wide notion of human rights championed by many human rights activists, in which "the first generation of rights" encompasses political and civil rights, the second generation social and economic rights, and the third generation matters such as solidarity and environmental sustainability.

The wider concept of security was promoted in part by those who wanted to undermine the influence of power-political thinking on international relations. Recently, this idea has become more widely accepted, even to the point that it might be seen as the dominant paradigm. Military organizations and national security establishments in the West have embraced the broad concept of security, perhaps as a way of defining a new role for themselves in a world that has robbed them of their main enemy. NATO acknowledged the political, economic, and environmental roots of security in its redrafted Alliance Strategic Concept in 1991 (Stub 1997, 4). But in part it was seen as a response to a set of new challenges in the international relations of the post–Cold War period.

A comprehensive notion of security is not unproblematic. There is a danger of labeling any problem or strain an "insecurity." We may take heed from the discussion about an extended concept of violence in the late 1960s and early 1970s. The concept of "structural violence," originally a precise notion applied to deaths caused by maldistribution of resources, became so diluted that almost any perceived injustice could be defined as violence. Structural violence became a political slogan and eventually self-destructed. The term "insecurity"

should be reserved for major threats to human life. With this caveat in mind, we turn to the environmental component of the notion of comprehensive security.[1]

ENVIRONMENTAL SECURITY

An extensive literature has emerged on the conceptual problem of how to define security so that it includes environmental concerns (Buzan, Wæver, and de Wilde 1998; Westing 1989). From this literature we may discern three particularly important concerns:

- *to prevent war and armed conflict* resulting from resource scarcity and environmental degradation,
- *to prevent disasters other than war* resulting from such scarcity and degradation, and
- *to prevent the erosion of the earth's carrying capacity* resulting in the loss of environmental sustainability in the future.

All three are deliberately phrased in anthropocentric terms. Even more radical notions of environmental security can be found in the literature. Proponents of "deep ecology" advocate a biocentric view that gives equal weight to the rights of animals, trees, and even inanimate objects of nature such as mountains. Since none of these can speak for themselves, such rights must nevertheless be formulated and advocated by human beings.

The three anthropocentric goals of environmental security will be discussed in the next three sections of the article, in a slightly different order than shown in the list. But first we need to clarify the relationship between resource scarcity, environmental degradation, and insecurity.

The concern for how environmental degradation may lead to insecurity is at the core a question of the scarcity of resources. Robert Malthus ([1798, 1803] 1992) suggested that hunger was inevitable because human population grows exponentially while food production could be made to grow only in linear fashion. Thus, at some point the available food per capita would fall below the minimum needed to sustain the population, and a crisis would result. Neo-Malthusian thinking follows the same general logic but applies it to a wide range of resources. Thus, numerous writers have commented on future shortages of freshwater, based on finite amounts of available freshwater to be shared by an increasing number of people. In the mid-1970s, following the oil embargo organized by Arab oil-producing countries, great concern arose that the supply of minerals and energy sources might soon become deficient.

While resource scarcity is usually assumed to arise when population growth exhausts the available resources, scarcity may also coexist with resource abundance, if the distribution is skewed. Thomas Homer-Dixon, one of the most prominent proponents of the view that environmental factors play an important role in generating and exacerbating armed conflict, distinguishes among three forms of resource scarcity:[2]

- *demand-induced scarcity,* which results from population growth,
- *supply-induced scarcity,* which results from the depletion or degradation of a resource, and
- *structural scarcity,* which refers to the distribution of the resource.

The classical Malthusian model lies in the intersection of demand-induced and supply-induced scarcity, when the supply of the resource can no longer keep pace with the growth of the population. Many neo-Malthusians, particularly those on the political left, put at least equal emphasis on the distributional issues.

Resource scarcity can occur without environmental degradation, simply because a non-renewable source can run dry or demand can exceed what a renewable source can supply. In the event of environmental degradation—usually conceived of as a man-made disturbance of the ecosystem—the supply of the resource

will become insufficient more quickly. Any form of environmental degradation can be translated into a problem of resource supply. Pollution of freshwater resources reduces the supply of water that can be used for drinking, food production, and so on. Air pollution reduces the supply of fresh air.

One consequence of such a view is that all environmental problems can be interpreted as resource problems, but not vice versa. We follow standard terminology in talking about "environmental security," but it might have been preferable to talk about "resource security."

Environmental Insecurity from Armed Conflict

Despite the recent flurry of interest, the idea that resource constraints may lead to conflict is not new.[3] In fact, it is one of the oldest ideas in research on conflict and peace. Indeed, in one of the modern classics of the scientific study of war and peace, *A Study of War,* Quincy Wright devoted a long chapter to the relationship between war and resource use (Wright [1942] 1965, 1146–1197). Similarly, in *Statistics of Deadly Quarrels* Lewis F. Richardson (1960, 205–210) discussed economic causes of war, including the desire to acquire territory and the control of "sources of essential commodities."

Above all, the struggle over territory is generally recognized to be the most pervasive form of conflict. Wright (1965, 76) noted that "practically all primitive people will fight to defend their territory, if necessary." Kalevi J. Holsti (1991, 307) concluded that among interstate wars in the period 1648–1989, territory was by far the most important issue. In his earliest period, the issue figured in about half the wars, declining to about one-third in the post–World War II period. In a reanalysis, John Vasquez (1993, 130; 1995, 284) found that between 79 percent and 93 percent of all wars during Holsti's five time periods involved territory-related issues. Paul Huth (1996, 5), in a study of territorial disputes from 1950 to

1990, characterized this issue as "one of the enduring features of international politics." This holds for interstate as well as intrastate conflict. Peter Wallensteen and Margareta Sollenberg (2000) find that of the 110 conflicts in seventy-three countries in the first post–Cold War decade (all but 9 of these were internal conflicts) more than half were over territory, the rest over government. The territorial explanation for war is also consistent with the finding that wars occur most frequently between neighbors (Bremer 1992) or between proximate countries (Gleditsch 1995). It is still in dispute whether wars between neighbors occur mainly because they fight over territory, because they generate disagreements in their day-to-day interaction, or because they are more easily available for fights—but Vasquez (1995) presents a strong case for the territorial explanation.

A variety of territorial conflict concerns the exclusive economic zones (EEZs) on the continental shelf. While the symbolism of underwater territory is not as potent as that of "the soil of our fathers," the value in economic and strategic terms may be enormous. In the 1960s the unilateral declaration of 200-nautical-mile fishery zones by several Latin American coastal states provoked conflict with several states with oceangoing fishing vessels. At about the same time, deep-sea drilling for oil and natural gas and the prospects of harvesting minerals on the ocean floor led to increased interest in exploiting the extended coastal zones beyond the fisheries. This further increased the conflict of interest between coastal states and states with a regional or global reach in their commercial activities. After a long-drawn-out process, a compromise was reached in the form of the United Nations Convention on the Law of the Sea (UNCLOS) in 1982. UNCLOS did not enter into force until 1994 and still has not been ratified by the United States, but its provisions are generally respected. As a result, an area comprising one-third of the total world ocean surface and almost as great as the world's total land area had been added to the territory of individual nations (Bailey 1997, 217–222).

In addition to territory itself, several other resources are commonly seen as worth fighting for. The first is *strategic raw materials.* President Dwight D. Eisenhower—in the statement that made famous the "domino theory"—justified the strategic importance of Indochina in the 1950s by referring to the region's supply of raw materials such as tin, tungsten, and rubber.[4] Another is *sources of energy,* the most obvious example being oil supplies from the Persian Gulf, a factor in the 1990–91 Gulf War and other conflicts. A third resource is *shared water,* which could give rise to conflicts over water use or navigation rights. There are over 250 major river systems shared by two or more countries, and many of them are subject to unresolved disputes (Wolf et al. 1999). A fourth resource arguably worth fighting for is *food.* Disagreements about shared fishery resources have occasioned many confrontations between fishing vessels and armed vessels of coastal states (Soroos 1997), even in the North Atlantic, where most conflicts are solved peacefully. Increasing food prices have frequently given rise to violent domestic riots (de Soysa and Gleditsch 1999, 79 f), and in Indonesia in 1998 rising food prices were thought to have contributed to the downfall of the Suharto regime.

In view of the widespread concern for the environment and about the consequences of environmental disruption, it is surprising that there is not more systematic research about these issues. In recent years, a number of case studies have examined environmental factors in individual conflicts. The most numerous and best known are the studies by Thomas Homer-Dixon and his associates in Toronto (Homer-Dixon 1999; Homer-Dixon and Blitt 1998) and those carried out by the various projects of the Swiss Peace Foundation (Bächler 1999). Many of these case studies are built on elaborate theoretical models and contain detailed empirical descriptions. Their main problem is that they are often selected without any variation on the dependent variable. Homer-Dixon, in particular, has been criticized for studying only cases in which there was armed conflict as well as environmental destruction. He does not provide any systematic comparison with cases in which armed conflict did not erupt—even though they may have also suffered from environmental degradation. Thus, it is difficult to draw any general conclusions about causes of violence from his work. Such case studies may supply persuasive post-facto explanations for why things went wrong in Chiapas, or even horribly wrong in Rwanda, but their value in terms of predicting future conflict is rather limited.[5]

Environmental degradation may be seen as an independent cause of conflict. But environmental degradation can also be interpreted as a symptom of societal failure, which generates conflict. Authoritarian rule, lack of international cooperation, poverty, excessive consumption in rich countries, globalization of the economy—these are among the factors that are frequently blamed for environmental problems. The very same phenomena are linked to armed conflict.

Wenche Hauge and Tanja Ellingsen (1998) have integrated environmental degradation into a more general model of civil war and tested it on data from the 1990s. More specifically, they looked at soil erosion, deforestation, and lack of clean freshwater and concluded that environmental degradation *does* stimulate the incidence of conflict, but less so than political, economic, and cultural factors or previous conflict history. They also found that the severity of armed domestic conflict is better accounted for by high levels of military spending. Phase II of the State Failure project (Esty et al. 1998) found weaker evidence for a direct influence of environmental degradation. However, the results are not directly comparable since the State Failure project uses a more complex dependent variable.

In a study of deserts and conflict, Turi Saltnes (1998) found that there was indeed a relationship between the spread of deserts and internal armed conflict in the period 1980–90. But this relationship largely evaporated when she controlled for political and economic variables.

Finally, in an effort to test the rhetoric about the conflict implications of shared rivers, a recent empirical study found that where two countries share a river (along a border or across one) the probability of a militarized interstate dispute between them was indeed found to increase. This factor is much less conflict inducing (by an order of magnitude) than the neighbor effect itself, but roughly comparable to the effect of standard political and economic predictors of interstate conflict. And the probability of conflict between two countries sharing a river is lower if the countries are both democracies, highly developed, allied to each other, and so on (Toset, Gleditsch, and Hegre 2000). Aaron Wolf (1999c) has scrutinized the 412 international crises identified by Brecher and Wilkenfeld (1997) for the period 1918–94. He indicates that only in a small number of such crises "water was at least partially a cause." In half of them, not a single shot was fired, and none of the others were violent enough to qualify as wars. Many scholars have pointed to the Middle East as an area where water is a source of considerable tension (Lowi 1993). But conflicts between Israel and its neighbors and between Arab states are motivated by a host of ideological and political issues and by the issue of occupied land territory. Water can, at best, be viewed as one of several conflict issues in the region. In fact, Wolf (1999c, 254) argues categorically that "water was neither a cause nor a goal of any Arab-Israeli warfare."

Environmental Insecurity from Disasters Other than War

Armed conflict is direct violence between two or more organized parties. But environmental stresses and strains can kill in very different ways. Scarcity of freshwater, while probably not a major source of armed conflict, is a major source of disease in poor countries. Wolf (1999b, 1) asserts that more than a billion people lack access to safe freshwater, that almost 3 billion do not have access to fresh sanitation, and that more than 5 million people die every year from water-related diseases or inadequate sanitation. While these numbers are probably rough estimates, they do indicate that the current loss of life from such slow environmental disasters is likely to be far greater than that from war. Only very major wars, like the two world wars, can cause comparable numbers of deaths. In addition to its direct effects on human health, water shortage is a major threat to food security in dry areas that are too poor to compensate for crop failures with food imports.

While the scarcity of clear freshwater and the lack of proper sanitation facilities may be the biggest environmental problems of our time, many other environmental problems also pose a threat to human security. The accident at a chemical factory in Bhopal, India, in 1984 is reported to have killed more than two thousand residents in the area and to have permanently disabled many more. A number of other industrial accidents have also claimed more lives than most armed conflicts, in addition to impairing future living conditions.[6] The partial disappearance of the Aral Sea, one of the most dramatic man-made environmental disasters in this century, is seriously degrading the lives of thousands of people. As Murray Feshbach and Albert Friendly (1992) have shown, this is just one in a series of environmental catastrophes resulting from Soviet policies that gave priority to rapid industrial development at the expense of the environment and with little regard for human life. Vaclav Smil (1993) has reported in similar terms about Chinese environmental policies. Clearly, environmental strains can expose human beings to very serious risks whether or not armed conflict within or between nations results. Of course war also has long-term environmental effects that are entirely incidental to the war

effort but can claim a large number of lives. The nuclear bombings of Hiroshima and Nagasaki in 1945 provide a clear example.

Environmental Insecurity from the Erosion of the Carrying Capacity

Environmental *degradation* is not a new phenomenon, as is well known to anyone who has read descriptions of streets with running sewers in ancient Rome or of conditions in nineteenth-century industrial cities in Britain. But environmental *concern* is much greater today, and there is also a feeling that at the current very high level of general consumption, we are straining the global limits in an unprecedented way.

Examples can be found showing how environmental damage to nature has long-term—or even more or less permanent—effects. The Central Plateau of Spain and the Highlands of Scotland are unlikely to regain the forests that were wrecked by shipbuilding and overgrazing. If the more pessimistic views of the annual loss of species are anywhere near correct, humankind stands to lose not only the aesthetic value of many exotic species but, much more important, genetic variability that may prove valuable in medical research.[7]

The most serious challenge to the future sustainability of human civilization is undoubtedly global warming. If the sea level rises by several feet and the Gulf Stream is reversed, to take two of the more dramatic possibilities, life will become virtually impossible in low-lying areas of Bangladesh or the Maldive Islands, as well as in northern Europe.

With considerable justification, cornucopians point to the failure of many past predictions of gloom, such as the periodic warnings of global hunger issued by biologists like Paul Ehrlich (1968) and environmentalists like Lester Brown (annual). Negative news, even of future events that may never happen, seems to get more publicity than the slow but steady improvements in agricultural productivity reported by the Food and Agriculture Organization (FAO) or the encouraging decline in the population growth. Predictions of future disasters cannot be ignored, but neither can they be taken for granted without critical scrutiny.

CONDITIONS OF ENVIRONMENTAL INSECURITY

While resource and environmental factors may well play a significant role in human insecurity, this relationship is modified by other variables associated with insecurity. In other words, the resource and environmental bases of conflict must be viewed in the context of a multifaceted view of armed conflict. The next four sections look at some of the factors that must be part of such a broader view.

Politics

Democratic politics may influence the relationship between the environment and conflict through its effect on environmental policy and practice, but also through its effect on the way environmental conflicts are handled.[8]

Well-established political democracies are likely, everything else being equal, to demonstrate more enlightened environmental policies.[9] Democracies tend to be more open to trial and error, they are more responsive to the victims of environmental degradation, they participate more in international organizations, and they conclude agreements to alleviate environmental problems. Environmental activists in democratic countries frequently have considerable disagreements with the environmental policies of their own countries. These very complaints form an essential part of the self-adjusting political processes in democracies. This point was brought home with particular force following the exposure of the vast environmental disasters caused by the governments of the former Soviet Union and communist China, committed in complete disregard for the welfare of their citizens and not held in check by any organized opposition. Democracies are much less likely to let environmental problems deteriorate far enough for armed conflict to become a real risk.

The relationship between environmental degradation and conflict is also influenced by the phenomenon known as the democratic peace (Gleditsch and Hegre 1997; Raknerud and Hegre 1997). Democracies rarely if ever fight one another. Even minor resource conflicts like the "cod wars," the "turbot wars," and other fishery clashes in the North Atlantic are regarded with great embarrassment by the democracies involved. Thus, they make great efforts to settle such conflicts before anyone gets killed. Of course, if democracies rarely fight each other for any reason, it is not very likely that they will fight over resource or environmental matters. The same goes for civil wars: democracies rarely if ever experience serious levels of internal violence for any reason (Hegre et al. 1999).

Economics

Economic development also has a double influence on environmental behavior. First, wealth has a strong effect on environmental sustainability. Early economic progress in general, and industrialization in particular, is intimately associated with unhealthy working conditions, smog, acid rain, and pollution of freshwater resources. This has led many environmentalists to adopt the view that economic development, and capitalism in particular, is intrinsically harmful to the environment.

But at an advanced stage of industrialization, and even more so in postindustrial societies, the trend is reversed. An affluent society can afford to invest in new technologies to clean up pollution in industry, agriculture, and waste disposal. Such a society places a higher value on human resources and takes care to avoid the incapacitation or death of its highly educated labor force. In an economically advanced economy, several traditional indicators of environmental degradation—such as the lack of clean water, unhealthy sanitation, deforestation, and air pollution in the cities—have started to decline. Many forms of environmental degradation are primarily poverty problems. For instance, the three environmental problems studied by Hauge and Ellingsen (1998) —deforestation, soil erosion, and the lack of freshwater—are all negatively correlated with economic development; that is, the higher the economic development, the lower the degree of environmental deterioration. (For other empirical illustrations of this point, see Lomborg 1998, 159–160.) Early industrialization reinforces some of the environmental problems in poor rural societies and creates additional forms of environmental degradation, such as urban and industrial pollution, during a period when economic growth takes precedence over all other concerns. This gives rise to an inverted U-shaped relationship between economic development and environmental degradation, sometimes called an environmental Kuznets curve.

Environmental disasters that may seem, on the surface, to result from economic conditions are frequently an outcome of economic policy decisions. As Amartya Sen (1994) has pointed out, India has not suffered any major famines since independence, in spite of frequent crop failures and endemic starvation. He attributes this to the policies of the Indian government, operating under the constraints of political democracy and a free press. These constraints were much weaker under colonial rule, when India experienced several major famines. Similarly, the Chinese government was unable or unwilling to prevent the disaster in the agricultural sector resulting from the Great Leap Forward policy in 1958–60, and as a result tens of millions of people died. The North Korean famine in the 1990s is also more a result of economic policy than of environmental misfortune. At the same time, economic policy cannot provide a short-term cure for the poverty that is irrevocably interwined with large-scale undernourishment and poor health. To root out these problems requires long-term economic growth and technological progress.

Not all environmental problems are poverty problems. High emissions of greenhouse gases, for example, are particularly characteristic of the most highly developed countries. But the main reason for this is probably that such problems have not yet been fully recognized as true environmental concerns. Once they are, it seems very likely that the richest countries will be the ones in a position to deal with them most effectively, with new (and initially very expensive) technology, international agreements and trade in emission quotas, and so on.

Economic development is also likely to have a restraining influence on violent behavior in environmental conflict, since wealth is negatively associated with armed conflict, interstate (Hegre 2000) as well as intrastate (Hegre et al. 1999). Wealthy individuals and groups stand to lose more if war breaks out. Widespread wealth is likely to act as a general deterrent to participation in major violence. Rich countries trade more, and trade also seems to promote peaceful relations, a phenomenon usually called the "liberal peace" (Oneal and Russett 1999).

Cultural Factors

Many countries are seriously divided between ethnic and religious groups fighting for dominance or to secede from a national state. Several studies have found ethnic fragmentation to be related to domestic conflict, although less strongly than political or economic variables (Ellingsen 2000). Most of the cases studied by Homer-Dixon and his colleagues (Chiapas, South Africa, Rwanda, Gaza) concern highly divided or even segregated societies. Although environmental factors may have contributed to conflict in South Africa, Valery Percival and Homer-Dixon (2001) recognize that the racial basis of the conflict should not be overlooked. Where ethnic groups manage to cooperate, the prospects for negotiated and cooperative solutions to environmental problems are good.

Where ethnic groups do not, environmental factors will add to the problems created by the cultural conflict.

Conflict History

One of the strongest factors in accounting for current armed conflict, internal and external, is a history of armed conflict (Raknerud and Hegre 1997; Hegre et al. 1999). Armed conflict can have very destructive effects on the environment, as shown by the wars in Vietnam, Afghanistan, and elsewhere (Westing 1985, 1989). Human and material destruction of the environment at a vast scale in turn increases the scarcity of resources, possibly to the point at which violent conflict over scarce resources is a real possibility. The environmental effects of war are not the same as the effects of environmental destruction on the incidence of armed conflict. But countries may possibly move into a vicious cycle of poverty, authoritarian rule, environmental degradation, and violence. War leads to environmental destruction, which in turn—mixed with poor government and poverty—fuels new conflict.

ENVIRONMENTAL CHANGE AND RESOURCE SCARCITY

Environmental change is always taking place as a result of processes that are still well beyond the control of humans. Periods of global warming and cooling have come and gone long before human activity became so pervasive and widespread that it could influence such basic global processes.

In the environmental debate, neo-Malthusian doomsayers regularly clash with cornucopian prophets of environmental optimism.[10] "The Earth is rich. If there is poverty, it is because of human betrayal," wrote the Norwegian poet Nordahl Grieg in 1936 (Grieg 1947, 133), at a time when socialists still held to technological optimism. Today, radical environmentalists

tend to prefer the image of "Spaceship Earth," a repository of limited resources that capitalism is rapidly squandering. The international bestseller *The Limits to Growth* (Meadows et al. 1972) was a prime example of this line of thinking, predicting scarcities in a number of strategic minerals and other raw materials. A similar line was taken by Georg Borgström (1972) and others who predicted worldwide food shortages. More recently the center stage has been occupied by Lester Brown and the WorldWatch Institute (Brown et al. annual), who point to the impending crises that will occur if and when China joins the company of the affluent and its citizens adopt Western-style nutritional habits (Brown 1995). At the same time, writers such as John Maddox (1972), Julian Simon (1996), and Bjørn Lomborg (1998, 2001) have argued that improved technology and human ingenuity will once again enable humankind to overcome material scarcity, particularly when we make use of the market mechanism to set appropriate prices for scarce resources. In the mid-1970s the oil crisis was seen as the precursor to a series of similar crises in strategic minerals, such as copper. Today, the environmental optimists point out, most of these minerals are available in abundant quantities, raw material prices have been falling, and developing countries dependent on the exports of raw materials (such as Zambia in the case of copper) have suffered economically. Most international experts in agriculture, whether associated with the FAO (1998, 1999) or the international agricultural research institutes, have a relatively optimistic view of the productive capacity of global agriculture. Current UN projections for world population are believed not to exceed the numbers that can be fed even at the present levels of agricultural technology (Bie 1998; Lomborg 2001).

This debate has obvious implications for conflict scenarios. If the optimists are correct, resources are not generally scarce and predictions of increased global strife over resources are unlikely to come true. On the other hand, if the environmental pessimists are correct, we are constantly eroding the carrying capacity of the global environment and our resource use is already beyond sustainable levels. Then we should expect the competition for resources to get ever more fierce, eventually to the point that it may break the norms of nonviolent behavior, perhaps even within and between democracies.

In the debate about the total volume of global resources, the environmental optimists now appear to have the upper hand. But for the purpose of analyzing conflict behavior, the question of the availability of the resources is more important. While *global* resources may be abundant, *local* resources may not be sufficient. In other words, the key to avoiding serious and increasing resource scarcities lies in the question of *distribution,* within and between nations. This takes us back to those questions of economic and political structure. If people cannot afford to buy food or other basic necessities, or if authoritarian political structures prevent them from making use of available resources, overall abundance will not help. In such cases we will have starvation amid plenty. Thousands will continue to die from unclean freshwater while others are drinking bottled mineral water at $1,000 per cubic meter (Beaumont 1997).

GREED OR GRIEVANCE?

A perspective on civil war recently adopted by many economists is that such conflicts are motivated by "greed" rather than by "grievance." This perspective does see resources as relevant to the conflict, but it turns the neo-Malthusian perspective on its head: abundant natural resources are likely to hinder rather than promote growth and to stimulate authoritarian government. Economic development is usually associated with the emergence of democratic institutions. But countries whose wealth has been built quickly on oil and other raw materials,

notably many countries in North Africa and the Middle East, tend to lag behind other countries at the same level of wealth in the development of their political institutions. Resource abundance may also lead to conflict, not only because politically obsolete structures refuse to give way, but also because control over some or all of the resources can be captured by opposition groups that use them to fund their rebel movements. This is illustrated by the diamond-smuggling rebels in Angola and drug-funded rebels in Colombia and Peru (Collier 2000; de Soysa 2000).

THE ROLE OF POPULATION PRESSURE

High resource consumption and rapid population growth are the twin pillars of neo-Malthusian scenarios of future resource scarcities. But is population pressure increasing? The 1998 revised medium population projection of the United Nations indicates a world population of 9.7 billion in 2150, up 40 percent from the fall 1999 figure, but down 1.1 billion from the 1996 revision (United Nations 1999). Even the high-population scenario, which is not widely believed, yields a world population of 24.8 billion in 2150, less than what many food specialists see as the long-run global potential for food production. The main reason that global population projections are being revised downward is that many developing countries have followed industrialized countries in fertility reduction more rapidly and more widely that what had previously been believed. By 1995 no less than 44 percent of the world population lived in countries with fertility below replacement level (2.1 children per woman). While Islamic countries and Africa (despite AIDS) will continue to have high population growth for some time to come, the global specter of overpopulation is largely removed from the debate. Instead, the concern is with particular Third World countries that combine rapid population growth with poor development. In the rest of the world, the greater worry is now the "graying" of the population.

There has been relatively little systematic research on population pressure and violent conflict. Hauge and Ellingsen (1998) found a modest but significant effect of population density on internal armed conflict. They did not study the effect of population growth. Jaroslav Tir and Paul Diehl (1998) studied the effect of both types of population pressure on interstate conflict but found no significant relationship between population density and interstate conflict. They did find a modest but significant effect of population growth on interstate conflict, but there was little or no evidence that population growth increased the probability of states initiating conflict or escalating the conflict to war. These findings strengthen the notion that population pressure is unlikely to be a significant global factor in conflict in the future, although it may well be an important local factor in certain areas.

Even if population pressure is not likely to have a major influence on armed conflict at the global level, it could be important in stimulating conflict in very poor areas, particularly where there is resource competition between different ethnic groups.

Some have extrapolated from studies of rats and other animals in very crowded conditions and have foreseen friction and conflict in human beings living under similar conditions. However, in order for such studies to be relevant, population densities would have to be a great deal higher, and the freedom of movement a great deal lower, than what obtains in most human settlements. Indeed, the most crowded states in the world, city-states like Singapore and Hong Kong, are rather peaceful internally and externally as far as group conflicts are concerned. Individual conflict, such as crime, tends to be higher in urban areas, but this can be accounted for just as easily by greater opportunity and more anonymity as by greater resource conflict. In fact, individual crime in cities would seem to fit the "greed" model of conflict much better than the "grievance" model.

ENVIRONMENTAL COOPERATION

Environmental insecurity does not as a general rule involve dramatic events such as armed struggle, mass starvation, or extensive and serious degradation. Resource and environmental problems are frequently handled by piecemeal reform and peaceful conflict resolution. Indeed, a conflict of interest may stimulate increased collaboration, in order to regulate the use of the contested resource. The enormous "privatization" of sea territory that was completed with the Law of the Sea Treaty proceeded remarkably peacefully (Bailey 1997, 222). Countries with shared rivers need not fight about the water resources; they may conclude agreements and set up institutions for the joint administration of the available resources, as is the case with the countries along the Danube and the Rhine, or between Portugal and Spain. Even in the Middle East, countries that were at "hot war" several times during the Cold War have been able to work out agreements relating to the use of water (Libiszewski 1997; Lonergan 1997). In the early 1960s, in the middle of the Cold War, Norway and the Soviet Union were able to agree on a large scheme for the joint exploitation of the Pasvik River for hydroelectric power. Apart from the Soviet-Turkish border, the 200-kilometer border between Norway and the Soviet Union in the High North was the only place where a NATO country bordered directly on the Soviet Union. One might have expected this joint river to be the subject of considerable strife. On the contrary, it turned out to be the location of one of the largest collaborative projects between the two countries during the Cold War. The construction of large dams necessitated the revision of the border, but this process proceeded fairly smoothly and with no hint of a militarized dispute. Even where the peacebuilding factor of joint democracy is absent, then, countries with sustained economic growth may be reasonably satisfied with the outcome of a resource conflict that gives both of them a share of the resource. They will be less concerned about the precise distribution. On that basis, they can conclude cooperative agreements to resolve resource and environmental issues.

Wolf (1999a) has compiled a database for electronic searching of 150 water-related treaties, domestic and international. His skepticism about the prospects for future "water wars" is matched by an optimism about the peaceful resolution of conflicts over water, at least where the conditions for peaceful conflict resolution more generally are present. He records thirty-six hundred such treaties since A.D. 805 (1999c, 160).

ENVIRONMENTAL INSECURITY?

Few, if any, conflicts justify single-issue labels like "environmental conflict" or "ethnic conflict." We can always relate conflict to several issue dimensions, and the influence of one issue is usually modified by the influence of another. Resource and environmental issues do play a role in conflict, but the relationship between these issues and armed conflict is modified by the general political, economic, and cultural factors at work in armed conflict generally. In many cases, environmental degradation may more appropriately be seen as an intervening variable between poverty and poor governance on the one hand and armed conflict on the other. In this sense, environmental degradation may be seen more as a symptom that something has gone wrong than as a cause of the world's ills.

For policymakers, as well as NGOs and grassroots activists, a crucial question is at what point in the causal chain one can intervene to change things for the better. Political institutions are perhaps the most suitable short-term

intervention points because they can be changed relatively abruptly. In the long term, moving from poverty to wealth is probably the most effective means of improving human security. In this perspective, the most important function of the environmental indicators is that they can serve very effectively as warning lights, particularly in a world of growing environmental consciousness.

NOTES

1. My work has been supported by the United States Institute of Peace and the Research Council of Norway. This chapter draws on Gleditsch (1997, 1998, 2001). I am grateful for help and comments from Jesse Hammer, Aaron T. Wolf, Arthur Westing, and the editors of this volume, none of whom are responsible for whatever errors remain in the text. This is a publication from the Oslo Project Office of the Global Environmental Change and Human Security (GECHS) programs.

2. Homer-Dixon specifically refers to scarcity of renewable resources, which he calls "environmental scarcity." But the general argument applies equally to nonrenewable resources.

3. In this section I deal with interstate as well as intrastate conflict. Resource and environmental issues are relevant to both. As I argue later, the political, economic, and other factors that mediate between environmental factors and armed conflict are also very similar for the two types of conflict. For these reasons I have chosen to deal with them in parallel fashion.

4. For empirical examinations of the relationship between raw materials and armed conflict, see Hammarström (1986, 1997) and de Soysa (2000).

5. For a more detailed critique along these lines, see Gleditsch (1998, 391–392). For a response, see Schwartz et al. (2001).

6. For a discussion of such accidents and particularly how they are exacerbated by war or war preparations, see Westing (1990).

7. Myers (Myers and Simon 1994) argues that the loss of animal species runs into thousands every year. At the same time, Julian Simon (Myers and Simon 1994) and Lomborg (1998, 2001) argue that very few cases of species extinction are documented.

8. The views discussed here are formulated at greater length in Gleditsch (1997a).

9. See Gleditsch and Sverdrup (1996) and Payne (1995). For a different view, see Midlarsky (1998).

10. For a pointed confrontation, see Myers and Simon (1994). For a recent interpretation of the current environmental debate in Malthusian terms, see Ohlsson (1999).

REFERENCES

Bächler, Günther. 1999. *Violence through Environmental Discrimination.* Dordrecht: Kluwer Academic.

Bailey, Jennifer. 1997. "States, Stocks, and Sovereignty: High Seas Fishing and the Expansion of State Sovereignty." In Gleditsch, ed., 1997b, 215–234.

Beaumont, Peter. 1997. "Water and Armed Conflict in the Middle East—Fantasy or Reality?" In Gleditsch, ed., 1997b, 355–374.

Bie, Stein. 1998. "Food and Conflict." Paper presented at the Norwegian Foreign Ministry workshop, "Environmental Conflict and Preventive Action," November 23–24, Lysebu, Oslo.

Borgström, Georg. 1972. *The Hungry Planet: The Modern World at the Edge of Famine.* 2d rev. ed. New York: Macmillan.

Brecher, Michael, and Jonathan Wilkenfeld. 1997. *A Study of Crisis.* Ann Arbor: University of Michigan Press.

Bremer, Stuart. 1992. "Dangerous Dyads: Conditions Affecting the Likelihood of Interstate War, 1816–1965." *Journal of Conflict Resolution* 36, no. 2: 309–341.

Brown, Lester. 1995. *Who Will Feed China: Wake-Up Call for a Small Planet.* Environmental Alert Series. Washington, D.C.: WorldWatch Institute.

Brown, Lester, et al. Annual. *The State of the World.* Washington, D.C.: WorldWatch Institute.

Buzan, Barry, Ole Wæver, and Jaap de Wilde. 1998. *Security: A New Framework for Analysis.* Boulder, Colo.: Lynne Rienner.

Collier, Paul. 2000. "Doing Well Out of War: An Economic Perspective." In *Greed or Grievance: Economic Agendas in Civil Wars*, ed. Mats Berdal and David Malone. Boulder, Colo.: Lynne Rienner, 91–111.

Diehl, Paul F., and Nils Petter Gleditsch, eds. 2001. *Environmental Conflict.* Boulder, Colo.: Westview Press.

Ehrlich, Paul R. 1968. *The Population Bomb.* New York: Ballantine.

Ellingsen, Tanja. 2000. "Colorful Community or Ethnic Witches' Brew? Multiethnicity and Domestic Conflict during and after the Cold War." *Journal of Conflict Resolution* 44, no. 2: 228–249.

Esty, Daniel, et al. 1998. *State Failure Task Force Report: Phase II.* Washington, D.C.: State Failure Task Force.

FAO. Annual. *The State of Food and Agriculture.* Rome: Food and Agriculture Organization.

———. Annual. *The State of World Fisheries and Aquaculture.* Rome: Food and Agriculture Organization. 1999 edition available at http://www.fao.org/docrep/w9900e/.

Feshbach, Murray, and Albert Friendly, Jr. 1992. *Ecocide in the USSR: Health and Nature under Siege.* New York: Basic Books.

Gleditsch, Nils Petter. 1995. "Geography, Democracy, and Peace." *International Interactions* 20, no. 4: 297–323.

———. 1997a. "Environmental Conflict and the Democratic Peace." In Gleditsch, ed., 1997b, 91–106.

———. 1998. "Armed Conflict and the Environment: A Critique of the Literature." *Journal of Peace Research* 35, no. 3: 381–400. Reprinted as chap. 12 in Diehl and Gleditsch, eds., 2001.

———. 2001. "Resource and Environmental Conflict: The State of the Art." In *Responding to Environmental Conflicts: Implications for Theory and Practice*, ed. Alexander Carius. Dordrecht: Kluwer Academic.

Gleditsch, Nils Petter, ed. 1997b. *Conflict and the Environment.* Dordrecht: Kluwer Academic.

Gleditsch, Nils Petter, and Håvard Hegre. 1997. "Peace and Democracy: Three Levels of Analysis." *Journal of Conflict Resolution* 41, no. 2: 283–310.

Gleditsch, Nils Petter, and Bjørn Otto Sverdrup. 1996. "Democracy and the Environment." Paper presented at the Fourth National Conference in Political Science, January 8–9, Geilo, Norway.

Grieg, Nordahl. 1947. *Samlede dikt* (Collected Poems). Oslo: Gyldendal.

Hammarström, Mats. 1986. *Securing Resources by Force: The Need for Raw Materials and Military Intervention by Major Powers in Less Developed Countries.* Report no. 27. Uppsala, Sweden: Department of Peace and Conflict Research, Uppsala University.

———. 1997. "Military Conflict and Mineral Supplies: Results Relevant to Wider Resource Issues." In Gleditsch, ed., 1997b, 127–136.

Hauge, Wenche, and Tanja Ellingsen. 1998. "Beyond Environmental Security: Causal Pathways to Conflict." *Journal of Peace Research* 35, no. 3: 299–317. Reprinted as chap. 12 in Diehl and Gleditsch, eds., 2001.

Hegre, Håvard. 2000. "Development and the Liberal Peace: What Does It Take to Be a Trading State?" *Journal of Peace Research* 27, no. 1: 5–30.

Hegre, Håvard, Tanja Ellingsen, Nils Petter Gleditsch, and Scott Gates. 1999. "Towards a Democratic Civil Peace: Opportunity, Grievance, and Civil War, 1834–1992." Paper presented to the launch conference of the World Bank project on "Civil War, Crime, and Violence in the Third World," February 22–23. Available at http://www. worldbank.org/research/conflict/papers.htm. Shorter version in press in *American Political Science Review*, March 2001.

Holsti, Kalevi J. 1991. *Peace and War: Armed Conflicts and International Order, 1648–1989.* Cambridge: Cambridge University Press.

Homer-Dixon, Thomas. 1999. *Environment, Scarcity, and Violence.* Princeton, N.J.: Princeton University Press.

Homer-Dixon, Thomas, and Jessica Blitt, eds. 1998. *Ecoviolence: Links among Environment, Population, and Security.* Oxford: Rowman and Littlefield.

Huth, Paul K. 1996. *Standing Your Ground: Territorial Disputes and International Conflict.* Ann Arbor: University of Michigan Press.

Libiszewski, Stephan. 1997. "Integrating Political and Technical Approaches: Lessons from the Israeli-Jordanian Water Negotiations." In Gleditsch, ed., 1997b, 385–402.

Lodgaard, Sverre. 1992. "Environmental Security, World Order, and Environmental Conflict Resolution." In *Conversion and the Environment*, ed. Nils Petter Gleditsch. Proceedings of a Seminar in Perm,

Russia, November 24–27, 1991. PRIO Report, no. 2 (May): 115–136.

Lomborg, Bjørn. 1998. *Verdens Sande Tilstand* (The True State of the World). Copenhagen: Centrum. (Revised edition in English to be published by Cambridge University Press, 2001.)

———. 2001. "Resource Constraints or Abundance?" Chap. 6 in Diehl and Gleditsch, eds., 2001.

Lonergan, Steve. 1997. "Water Resources and Conflict: Examples from the Middle East." In Gleditsch, ed., 1997b, 375–384.

———, ed. 1999. *Environmental Change, Adaptation, and Security.* Dordrecht: Kluwer Academic.

Lonergan, Steve, and GECHS Scientific Planning Committee. 1999. *GECHS Science Plan.* IHDP Report no. 11. Bonn: International Human Dimensions Program on Global Environmental Change, for Global Environmental Change and Human Security Project.

Lowi, Miriam R. 1993. *Water and Power: The Politics of a Scarce Resource in the Jordan River Basin.* Cambridge: Cambridge University Press.

Maddox, John. 1972. *The Doomsday Syndrome.* New York: McGraw-Hill.

Malthus, Thomas Robert. [1798, 1803] 1992. *An Essay on the Principle of Population: Or a View of Its Past and Present Effects on Human Happiness: With an Inquiry into our Prospects Respecting the Future Removal or Mitigation of the Evils which It Occasions.* Reprint, Cambridge: Cambridge University Press.

Meadows, Donella H., et al. 1972. *The Limits to Growth: A Report for the Club of Rome's Project on the Predicament of Mankind.* New York: Universe.

Midlarsky, Manus. 1998. "Democracy and the Environment: An Empirical Assessment." *Journal of Peace Research* 35, no. 3: 341–361. Reprinted as chap. 8 in Diehl and Gleditsch, eds., 2001.

Myers, Norman, and Julian Simon. 1994. *Scarcity or Abundance? A Debate on the Environment.* New York and London: Norton.

Ohlsson, Leif. 1999. "Environment, Scarcity, and Conflict: A Study of Malthusian Concerns." Ph.D. diss. Department of Peace and Development Research, Göteborg University, Göteborg, Sweden.

Oneal, John R., and Bruce Russett. 1999. "Assessing the Liberal Peace with Alternative Specifications: Extending the Trade-Conflict Model." *Journal of Peace Research* 36, no. 4: 423–442.

Palme, Olof, et al. 1982. *Common Security: A Blueprint for Survival*. New York: Simon and Schuster, for Independent Commission on Disarmament and Security Issues.

Payne, Rodger A. 1995. "Freedom and the Environment." *Journal of Democracy* 6, no. 3: 41–55.

Percival, Valery, and Thomas Homer-Dixon. 1998. "Environmental Scarcity and Violent Conflict: The Case of South Africa." *Journal of Peace Research* 35, no. 3: 279–298. Reprinted as chap. 2 in Diehl and Gleditsch, eds., 2001.

Raknerud, Arvid, and Håvard Hegre. 1997. "The Hazard of War: Reassessing the Evidence for the Democratic Peace." *Journal of Peace Research* 34, no. 4: 385–404.

Richardson, Lewis F. 1960. *Statistics of Deadly Quarrels*, ed. Quincy Wright and C. C. Lienau. Pittsburgh: Boxwood; Chicago: Quadrangle Books.

Rogers, Katrina S. 1997. "Pre-empting Violent Conflict: Learning from Environmental Cooperation." In Gleditsch, ed., 1997b, 503–518.

Saltnes, Turi. 1998. *Forørkning—en konfliktskapende faktor? En kvantitativ analyse av forholdet mellom miljø og borgerkrig* (Desertification and Conflict: A Quantitative Analysis of the Relationship between the Environment and Civil War). Thesis for the Cand. polit. degree, Norwegian University of Science and Technology, Trondheim.

Schwartz, Daniel M., Tom Deligiannis, and Thomas Homer-Dixon. 2001. "The Environment and Violent Conflict." Chap. 13 in Diehl and Gleditsch, eds., 2001.

Sen, Amartya. 1994. "Liberty and Poverty: Political Rights and Economics." *New Republic,* January 10, 31–37.

Simon, Julian L. 1996. *The Ultimate Resource 2*. Princeton, N.J.: Princeton University Press.

Smil, Vaclav. 1993. *China's Environmental Crisis: An Inquiry into the Limits of National Development*. Armonk, N.Y.: Sharpe.

Soroos, Marvin S. 1997. "The Turbot War: Resolution of an International Fishery Dispute." In Gleditsch, ed., 1997b, 235–252.

Soysa, Indra de. 2000. "The Resource Curse: Are Civil Wars Driven by Rapacity or Paucity?" In *Greed or Grievance: Economic Agendas in Civil Wars*, ed. Mats Berdal and David Malone, 113–135. Boulder, Colo.: Lynne Rienner.

Soysa, Indra de, and Nils Petter Gleditsch, with Michael Gibson, Margareta Sollenberg, and Arthur Westing. 1999. *To Cultivate Peace: Agriculture in a World of Conflict*. PRIO Report no. 1. Oslo: International Peace Research Institute; Oslo and Washington, D.C.: Future Harvest. Available in electronic form at http://www.future-harvest.org.

Stub, Sverre. 1997. "Our Future—Common, or None at All." In Gleditsch, ed., 1997b, 3–14.

Tir, Jaroslav, and Paul F. Diehl. 1998. "Demographic Pressure and Interstate Conflict: Linking Population Growth and Density to Militarized Disputes and Wars, 1930–89." *Journal of Peace Research* 35, no. 3: 319–339. Reprinted as chap. 4 in Diehl and Gleditsch, eds., 2001.

Toset, Hans Petter Wollebæk, Nils Petter Gleditsch, and Håvard Hegre. 2000. "Shared Rivers and Interstate Conflict." *Political Geography* 19: 971–996.

United Nations. Population Division, Department of Economic and Social Affairs. 1999. *Long-Range World Population Projections: Based on the 1998 Revisions*. ESA/P/WP.153. Extracts available at http://www.popin.org/longrange. New York.

United Nations Development Programme. 1994. *Human Development Report*. Oxford: Oxford University Press, for United Nations Development Programme.

Vasquez, John A. 1993. *The War Puzzle*. Cambridge: Cambridge University Press.

———. 1995. "Why Do Neighbors Fight? Proximity, Interaction, or Territoriality?" *Journal of Peace Research* 32, no. 3: 277–293.

Wallensteen, Peter, and Margareta Sollenberg. 2000. "Armed Conflict, 1989–99." *Journal of Peace Research* 37, no. 5: 635–649.

Westing, Arthur. 1985. *Explosive Remnants of War: Mitigating the Environmental Effects*. London: Taylor and Francis, for Stockholm International Peace Research Institute.

———. 1989. "Environmental Component of Comprehensive Security." *Bulletin of Peace Proposals* 20, no. 2: 129–134.

Westing, Arthur H., ed. 1990. *Environmental Hazards of War: Releasing Dangerous Forces in an Industrialized World*. London: SAGE, for PRIO and UNEP.

Wolf, Aaron T. 1999a. "The Transboundary Freshwater Dispute Database Project." *Water International* 24, no. 2: 160–163. For the database, see http://terra.geo.terra.geo.orst.edu/users/tfdd/.

———. 1999b. "Water and Human Security." *AVISO: An Information Bulletin on Global Environmental Change and Human Security* 3.

———. 1999c. "'Water Wars' and Water Reality: Conflict and Cooperation along International Waterways." In Lonergan 1999, 251–265.

Wolf, Aaron T., et al. 1999. "International River Basins of the World." *Water Resources Development* 15, no. 4: 387–427.

Wright, Quincy. [1942] 1965. *A Study of War. Second edition, with a Commentary on War since 1942.* Chicago: University of Chicago Press.

5

Military Technology and Conflict

Geoffrey Kemp

THE RELATIONSHIP BETWEEN military technology and conflict is definitely a chicken-and-egg affair. The existence of military technology in a conflict region reflects the need for countries to defend themselves against adversaries or to redress grievances. Yet arms competition between adversaries can itself become a source of conflict or even a precursor for war. As a result, there are many different hypotheses concerning this relationship. While many believe that arms races result in wars, it is not easy to demonstrate a simple cause and effect. The real issues are the impact of weapons acquisitions on the stability of military balances and the relationship between these balances and other factors that contribute to conflict.

Likewise, it is difficult to identify specific weapons that contribute to an increase or decrease in the potential for armed conflict. Weapons, including weapons of mass destruction, do not cause wars or ensure peace by themselves —any more than handguns alone are responsible for murders or reduced crime in U.S. cities.

The critical factor is the politico-military environment into which the weapons are introduced. If the environment is inherently unstable and adversaries have a record of resolving disputes by force, new weaponry may heighten the perceptions of threat, providing a catalyst for war. However, if the environment is stable and the prevailing climate is one of reconciliation and peaceful dialogue or, alternatively, if both adversaries anticipate unacceptable casualties in a war, the impact of new weapons may be less dangerous and could even contribute to stability. Thus, weapons that may be considered destabilizing in one region may be deemed stabilizing in another.

In this essay I argue that there is no general theory of the relationship between arms and conflict, that cases can be found to fit many hypotheses, and that recent dramatic changes in technology have made it increasingly difficult to predict the effects of those charges.[1] Before we confront some of the future issues, I will provide some useful background information.

Throughout history the possession and production of arms has largely been a monopoly of the dominant political authority in a particular country or region. Until recently, most such authorities were oligopolies, if not outright dictatorships; the right of ordinary citizens to manufacture and own arms is not a universal right. Thus, one of the enduring beliefs of the National Rifle Association is that the constitutional right of U.S. citizens to bear arms is a unique and special right and is the most reliable way to ensure that the citizenry is not left defenseless against authorities who traditionally have a monopoly of organized military force at their disposal. While this prerogative is uniquely American and highly controversial, the sentiments it reflects have been shared by many of the subject peoples of the world, ancient and modern, who have been systematically denied access to arms and are inherently suspicious of arms control. For instance, during the nineteenth century an international initiative was launched by the European powers to ban the transfer of breech-loading rifles to sub-Saharan Africa on the grounds that such arms in the hands of natives would be a source of instability. If the colonial powers had far superior arms with which to rule over their subjects, small forces of militia could control vast areas of territory. This line of reasoning was summarized by the British satirist Hilaire Belloc, "Whatever happens / We have got / The Maxim gun / And they have not."

As long as military technology is a monopoly of the state or the colonial power, civil unrest and uprisings are controllable. However, once those who wish to change the status quo gain access to modern military technology—by covert purchase, mutiny, or rebellion—a more even distribution of power results, which often leads to civil war and revolution. Therefore, in considering the long-term perspectives on arms and conflict it is worth remembering the origins of the American Revolution and the important role that arms, both locally produced and procured from overseas (especially France), had

on the course of the war. Without this access to arms, American revolutionaries could not have fought against Britain. As it was, they were able to sustain their confrontation and eventually wear down an initially far superior power.

In recent years, a different set of questions has emerged in the context of arms and international relations. Three are especially important: (1) the relationship between developments in nuclear technology and the potential for conflict among the superpowers; (2) the relationship between the transfer of military technology from the great powers, who have traditionally been the major producers of arms, and the propensity of the recipients to engage in armed conflict; and (3) the impact on regional security of recent changes in the international system and new developments in military technology.

THE COLD WAR, THE CENTRAL ARMS RACE, AND THE BREAKUP OF THE SOVIET UNION

Since the early 1950s the debate about the impact of military technology on the international system has focused on two events: the central arms race between NATO and the Warsaw Pact countries and the proliferation of weapons technology to conflict regions in the rest of the world. Throughout the Cold War, there was ongoing controversy concerning the stability of the central arms race.

There were two very limiting arguments. Pessimists argued that constant changes in nuclear weapons technology and the momentum of the arms race made the balance of power delicate and therefore inherently unstable and dangerous. This group included many of the advocates of unilateral arms control and arms reductions. The Campaign for Nuclear Disarmament (CND), launched in the 1950s, and the nuclear freeze movement that gained momentum in the 1980s are two prominent examples of this line of thinking. Optimists held that the peace in Europe and between the superpowers was secure precisely because the horrors of war were too dreadful to contemplate. This was the view of most Western governments that subscribed to the principles of deterrence and supported investments in nuclear force modernization as the best way to ensure stability and a balance of power between NATO and the Warsaw Pact forces. Both schools concurred that one effect of the central balance of power, be it delicate or stable, was to export the Cold War to regional conflict areas, which, in turn, led to an accelerated regional arms buildup. However, there was much disagreement about whether regional arms races themselves made local conflict more or less likely.

Parallel to the arguments concerning the balance of power, a secondary set of issues concerned the economics of the various arms races. Again, pessimists argued that both the central and regional arms races were spurred by the desire of the military-industrial complex in the advanced countries to promote arms sales. Others made a very different case, namely that the spread of weapons of mass destruction to regional conflicts was stimulated by the reluctance of the industrial powers to provide adequate conventional arms. Examples of this reaction would be the decisions made at different times by Israel, South Africa, and Pakistan to develop nuclear weapons after being subject to arms embargoes by the key industrial states. It is clear that both the Republic of Korea and Taiwan came close to going nuclear for the same reasons and were persuaded from doing so only by extremely vigorous U.S. diplomatic intervention and increased support for their conventional armed forces.

Most modern theories of the arms race evolved during the Cold War. The primary focus was the impact of thermonuclear weapons on the balance of power and the propensity for conflict. In view of the enormous, quantifiable destruction potential of nuclear weapons, the relatively small number of them in inventories (as compared with conventional weapons), and the assumption that an all-out thermonuclear war would be of short duration, it was possible to articulate mathematical models of nuclear war. These models led most observers to believe that as long as there was proximate symmetry between the parties, a balance of terror would deter any side from risking war.

Although it remains unclear whether nuclear deterrence during this era was inherently stable or unstable, there is no doubt that for the past thirty years the Warsaw Pact and NATO countries enjoyed a nominally stable, but putatively dangerous, relationship. This stability resulted from several conditions:

- the awesome destructive capacity of thermonuclear weapons,
- the total integration of nuclear weapons into the force structures and military doctrines of the opposing alliances,
- clearly demarcated and accepted borders separating the forces,
- explicit policies regarding the use of force should either side invade the other,
- virtual consensus that there could be no victor in the event of full-scale war,
- an understanding that escalation to nuclear war would be highly likely if war broke out,
- clear lines of communication between adversaries,
- clear acceptance of Soviet and American dominance among the Warsaw Pact and NATO members,
- the ability of the adversaries to contain their competition in regional conflicts outside the central theater and to resist military intervention in the conflicts within the alliances, and
- stable regimes in both of the opposing camps.

The relationship between military technology and the most spectacular event of modern times—the breakup of the Soviet Union—is less clear. Between 1989 and 1991, the largest and possibly the most authoritarian and tightly controlled empire the world has ever seen collapsed. Comparable in scope to the dissolution of the Austro-Hungarian and Ottoman Empires at the end of World War I and the defeat of the Axis powers in 1945, the Soviet collapse will have a profound and lasting impact on the international system for decades to come. However, unlike the situations in 1919 and 1945, when the victorious military powers were able to impose some sort of order on the reemerging political boundaries, the events following the Soviet Union's demise have been anarchic.

The Soviet Union imploded. It was not defeated in a classic military encounter whereby the victors could dictate terms to the vanquished. New countries sprang up so fast that mapmakers could scarcely keep pace with the new names and new boundaries that spread across the Eurasian landmass. The Iron Curtain was shattered, and in its place hundreds of new borders came into being.

Although the breakup did not happen because of war, there is debate about how much the burden of war preparations contributed to the outcome. Some have argued that the United States' decision in the 1980s to deploy the extremely sophisticated Pershing II missile in Europe and to develop a space-based anti-missile defense system was the last straw that convinced Mikhail Gorbachev that the Soviet Union had no option but to abandon the arms race with the richer Western countries and to reform the Soviet economy. Once he made this decision, a floodgate of change opened that he was unable to control.

There was hope that a new world order would emerge reflecting the basic Western ideals that were upheld in the fight against communism. Peace, democracy, and economic development were to be the triumvirate of the future. The cornerstone of the new world order would be a more cooperative security environment, in which the traditional trappings of power politics—with major military alliances armed and prepared to fight each other—would be replaced by a mutually reinforcing defense

concept, an expanded NATO without the Warsaw Pact as an enemy. Each participant would contribute to overall security and the body itself would agree on rules of engagement to resist movement of aggressor countries that deviated from the norm. A new emphasis on the United Nations and other international organizations would be paralleled by a new focus on economic competition and cooperation as the key ingredients for global growth and political stability. The close relationship between military technology and security would be a thing of the past. But this hope was not to be fulfilled. The clearest legacy of the Soviet Union's demise has been chaos and regional conflict.

In sum, the breakup of the Soviet Union has undermined one of the key elements of the Cold War balance of power—stable borders and stable regimes—and has encouraged the further proliferation of weapons and the spread of new forms of extremely violent terrorism. The implications of this trend are considered later in this essay.

THE TRANSFER OF MILITARY TECHNOLOGY AND CONFLICT

Since the late nineteenth century, the transfer (either by sale, loan, or gift) of military technology from industrial to less industrial countries has been an important influence on international relations. Today, a revolution in military technology poses a new set of challenges and issues.

Over the decades, most industrial powers have regarded arms transfers as a necessary adjunct of national policy and strategic doctrine. In the case of the United States, it can certainly be argued that, on balance, arms sales and military assistance programs have benefited U.S. strategic interests. U.S. military supplies to allies were instrumental in winning the three critical wars of this century: World War I, World War II, and the Cold War. Other examples can be cited. U.S. arms have been essential to assuring Israel a qualitative edge and denying Arab coalitions any prospect of military victory. U.S. supplies to Saudi Arabia during the 1970s and 1980s permitted the United States and the Saudis to develop one of the most elaborate and modern logistical bases in the world, which was crucial to allied victory in Operation Desert Storm.

Critics of U.S. arms transfers argue that these policies have often led to disastrous, entangling confrontations, including the Vietnam War and the Iran-Contra scandal. Critics also argue that the United States should not provide arms to countries battling countries deemed as "bigger threats" because those countries may eventually become threats as well. For example, the U.S. supply of surface-to-air missiles such as Stingers to Afghanistan resistance fighters to defeat Soviet troops is now a threat to that region, including U.S. forces. Moreover, critics continue, peacetime arms sales to undemocratic countries strengthen corrupt dictators, promote aggressive behavior, and siphon off scarce economic resources that could be used more productively and humanely on other endeavors.

In the early 1970s a new phenomenon occurred, namely, the emergence of very rich oil-producing countries of the Middle East that had purchasing power but few skills to produce arms. The rapid buildup of arms in the Middle East and Persian Gulf area strengthened the argument that regional arms races were dangerous and that the recipients would have difficulty in absorbing, maintaining, and operating their advanced equipment without continued intense support from their suppliers. The classic example of this relationship existed between the United States and Iran from 1971 to 1979 and culminated in the deposition of the shah and attempts by the Khomeini government to sell military equipment back to the United States.[2]

Arms transfers are important tests of friendship. Nuclear weapons and their related delivery systems are the most sophisticated weapons. The only recipients of U.S. strategic nuclear delivery systems or support systems and technical knowledge have been Great Britain and France, which have also been the closest U.S. allies. Britain, in particular, has had an extremely close nuclear relationship with the United States. Most recipients of U.S. arms have not been permitted the full array of frontline equipment and key subsystems, even when able to pay full market prices. It may therefore be possible to rank the intimacy of relations between states according to the quality of the arms and other military support that have been provided.

American arms sales to close allies such as Britain are rarely criticized, because they are seen to be part of the NATO alliance and the need to integrate military doctrines and force capabilities to serve common goals. Equally relevant, arms transfers carry important messages in relations between major powers and minor powers. U.S.-Soviet rivalry in the Third World was built around competitive arms supply relationships with a long list of countries, large and small. Soviet arms supplies to Egypt in 1955 opened the way for more assertive Soviet diplomacy in the region. Seventeen years later, the United States used arms aid to bring Egypt back into the Western fold when President Anwar Sadat terminated his military relations with the Russians in 1972. In 1985–86, when Iraq and Iran were desperately fighting for survival in their brutal war, both relied on supplies from the outside to keep them going. The effectiveness of the U.S. arms embargo against Iran was a key reason the Ayatollah Khomeini gave instructions to obtain U.S. arms, even if it meant doing business with the United States and the hated Israelis. The White House thought it could use the supply of arms to cajole or tempt Iran into a better relationship and at the same time obtain the release of hostages; the Israelis thought that by supplying arms they could protract the war or, alternatively, ingratiate themselves with those members of the regime who might be favorably disposed to have a relationship with Israel once Khomeini left the scene.

The end of the Cold War has had two profound effects on arms transfers activities. First, it has led to a massive reduction in military aid from the superpowers, which has had the most impact on former Soviet clients. Syria's decision to join the Middle East peace process was directly related to Gorbachev's decision to end military aid. Second, the withdrawal of the superpowers from regional rivalries in Africa, Latin America, and South and Southeast Asia has had very different outcomes. In Africa, chaos and conflict continue but with less immediate international interest. South and Southeast Asia are steadily building up their military inventories (India and Pakistan both have nuclear weapons). In Latin America, more democratic regimes have emerged and the arms race is less a burden than it used to be.

RECENT WARS AND ATTITUDES AND BEHAVIORS TOWARD MILITARY TECHNOLOGY

In the decade since the breakup of the Soviet Union, a number of violent conflicts have been fought that require new thinking about the relationship between military technology and conflict. Several examples are noteworthy because they reflect very different lessons. These conflicts include the 1991 Persian Gulf War, the 1992–93 civil war in Somalia, the 1994 civil war and genocide in Rwanda, and the 1999 war in Kosovo. The Gulf War and Kosovo are important because of the extraordinary use the allies made of advanced technology, especially air power, and the remarkably few casualties the victors suffered. The wars in Africa reflect a different trend: the persistence of widespread violence with huge numbers of casualties on both sides caused mainly by old-fashioned weaponry.

The Gulf War has had an important effect on thinking about modern warfare and the global demand for advanced arms and related technologies.[3] The war revealed the vulnerability of the infrastructure in modern societies to precision bombardment. High technology improved both the precision and the survivability

of strike aircraft and cruise missiles. The global positioning system provided precise navigational information that enabled highly accurate artillery placement, logistical resupply, and battlefield mapping. Thermal sensors and night vision equipment on U.S. tanks and helicopters enabled them to target the enemy at night and through the thick smoke of oil well fires. The advanced Joint Surveillance and Attack Radar System (JSTARS) enabled U.S. forces to detect and track slow-moving ground targets against a cluttered background. This system, which is orders of magnitude more powerful than the older Airborne Warning and Control System (AWACS), was used to guide missiles in flight.

The industrial states, especially the ones that already possess a nuclear arsenal, saw the war as further proof of the need to restrict the proliferation of weapons of mass destruction, especially in the nuclear field. Yet some weaker states interpreted the U.S.-led technological onslaught in an entirely different manner. Nuclear weapons (and perhaps other weapons of mass destruction) are the only tools smaller, less technologically equipped countries can hope to acquire and deploy in the face of U.S. stealth aircraft, precision-guided munitions, and advanced command, control, communications, and intelligence (C3I).

One lesson of the Gulf and Kosovo conflicts was that offensive air power is a decisive factor in modern warfare and that unless countries invest billions of dollars in advanced air defense systems, they will become increasingly vulnerable to precision interdiction by the air forces of the major Western powers, especially the United States. However, another lesson, learned by the democratic countries that participated in these conflicts, was that modern warfare can and should result in a relatively low number of casualties for the predominant force. The Gulf War reinforced the notion that weapons of mass destruction may be needed as an equalizer between the high-tech U.S. forces and smaller states resisting U.S. and Western directives. While the Gulf War highlighted the impact of such high-tech arms, fiscal realities restrain many states and may force some to consider a shortcut, the less expensive option of developing certain types of weapons of mass destruction, especially chemical and biological weapons.

The response of specific countries to the Gulf War has varied. In Russia, which over the years has provided many of Iraq's arms, several schools of thought developed about the Gulf War. Some saw Iraqi ineptness as the cause for the poor performance of Soviet equipment. Others did not see any revolutionary change brought about by the use of advanced technology in the war, but they did think that the war confirmed the Soviet vision of a military-technical revolution. In that sense, the war reaffirmed the importance of developing new and improved military technology. Another approach suggests that the war was the beginning of a different type of conflict, in which the central issue becomes troop control. Through coordinated fire, maneuver, and radio-electronic combat, each side will seek to inhibit enemy troop control (and protect its own). In this scenario, ground troops become less important as new technology is used to destroy enemy C3I and combat systems.

The People's Republic of China (PRC) did not radically alter its view of military technology because of the Gulf War. The PRC was already modernizing, and the war merely reinforced that trend. The local and conventional context of the war also fit with the PRC's projections for its own forces. Elements of the Chinese leadership that believed human factors could offset a military-technological edge did not suffer a setback in the Gulf War. Overall, however, the Chinese continue to view the improvement of their military equipment as one aspect of the larger drive for economic modernization.

India was credited with providing one of the larger lessons of the war after a retired Indian army chief of staff said the results of the war suggest that adversaries should not fight the Americans without nuclear weapons. In Israel, the war highlighted a number of continuing security concerns. Iraq's surprise attack on Kuwait, a surprise to most officials around the world, reminded Israelis that even highly advanced intelligence has limits; technical measures do not eliminate the threat of surprise attack. U.S. weaponry reinforced Israel's emphasis on air power, electronic warfare, and precision-guided missiles.

Located next to the theater of operations, Iran recognized the power and speed of allied forces in the defeat of a former military adversary. Iranian leaders, accustomed to such bungled U.S. operations as the hostage rescue attempt in 1980, gained a new respect for U.S. military capabilities. Saudi Arabia moved in two directions as a result of the Gulf War. The Saudis rushed to purchase the latest aircraft, missiles, and other advanced weaponry, yet Saudi Arabia does not intend to develop an autonomous ability to repel aggressors, especially given its small population. Instead, the high-tech hardware is meant to delay a future aggressor until international (or U.S.) help arrives. High-tech weaponry cannot eliminate the need for alliances, especially against Iraq or Iran. Thus, even as Saudi Arabia bolstered its arsenal, it also worked to develop quiet but close military and security relations with the United States and other Western powers.

The Gulf War also generated new thinking about the nature of future combat. U.S. attempts to limit Iraqi civilian and even military casualties during the Gulf War have fanned interest in a new class of nonlethal weapons for future warfare. These include chemical agents that cause metal fatigue in enemy machinery, destroy their optical systems, choke engines, or "glue" equipment. Increased global deployment of electronically controlled weapons systems makes military equipment susceptible to high-power jamming and to nonnuclear electromagnetic pulses that destroy and paralyze electronic systems or systems connected to antennae or batteries. Infrasound generators (at very low frequencies) could be tuned to incapacitate humans temporarily, causing disorientation, vomiting, or bowel spasms.

The continuing information and communication revolutions have had a profound effect on how armed forces may wage war. While technological advances have vastly improved the efficiency and effectiveness of modern weapons systems, they have also opened up areas where the military is extremely vulnerable. This has led to the concept of cyberwar, pioneered by the RAND Corporation, which targets the central information systems of the modern war machine.[4] This novel approach to future warfare advocates conducting (and preparing to conduct) military operations according to information-related principles. Its techniques include destroying enemy information and communications systems, thus winning the "balance of information and knowledge," especially when the enemy has numerical superiority. It prevents the enemy from "knowing itself": who it is, where it is, what it can do when, why it is fighting, which threats to counter first. The Apache helicopter strike against Iraqi air defense controls at the outset of the Gulf War and the deception practiced by a relatively small number of Marines to lead the Iraqi army astray embody some principles of this approach.

As a result, the most effective weaponry and tactics of today may be outdated as the technological and information revolutions continue. The new emphasis focuses even more attention on intelligence, computers, and information. Meanwhile, while many countries saw the Gulf War as a justification for the purchase of advanced aircraft, missiles, and other high-tech military equipment, it remains to be seen which of these arms will be important in future wars.

NEW MILITARY TECHNOLOGY AND REGIONAL POWER BALANCES

The fact that Saddam Hussein was able to target Tel Aviv with SCUD missiles during the Gulf War demonstrated in the most vivid way possible the important role that missile technology plays in perceptions of geography and military power in the Middle East. As missile and aircraft ranges become longer and longer, as power can be projected over wider and wider regions, and as there is an increasing possibility that weapons of mass destruction may be developed, the former tight strategic circles that defined the military balance among various regional enemies in the Middle East will have to be expanded. Israel's strategic reach for both offense and defense now has to include concern about Iran and Iraq and possibly even Pakistan, as they all get missiles and capabilities that could reach Israel. Alternatively, as Israel's reach extends, those countries, too, will be worried about their vulnerability to Israeli power-projection capabilities. Similar types of cross-border strategic threat concerns are growing in other areas.

This phenomenon has important implications for regional security regimes in the Middle East and elsewhere. Participation in such a regime has always been a difficult issue in the context of European arms control, and it is even more difficult in the case of the Middle East. Thus, even if Israel reaches a military agreement with Syria, Jordan, Egypt, Lebanon, and the Palestinians, it would not let its guard down as long as the Gulf Cooperation Council (GCC) countries, Iran, and Iraq were outside the process. Since they have to be part of the process, and since there is a close relationship among Pakistan, the GCC countries, Iran, and Iraq, it is inevitable that Pakistan's capabilities will be included in Israeli calculus. The same logic applies to countries like Pakistan that worry about Israel.

In many respects, Desert Storm was a highly misleading military encounter because it was so one-sided. One clear lesson, however, is that modern conventional munitions bear absolutely no resemblance to those used in most previous conventional confrontations. The long range and high accuracy achieved by aircraft and missiles and the new real-time reconnaissance capabilities will revolutionize future warfare.

More accurate lethal weapons and better reconnaissance by themselves constitute a revolution. It is important, however, to juxtapose the new conventional capabilities of modern weapons with the dramatically changing target structures in regions such as the Persian Gulf. If one compares a map of infrastructure in the Gulf from 1970 with one from 1990 and then projects forward to 2010, it is clear that there has been and will continue to be an enormous change in the physical appearance of the region, putting an increased reliance on high-tech systems to ensure the wealth and day-to-day operation of these desert countries. The combination of a highly intricate and sophisticated oil infrastructure, an increasing dependence on desalinization and other water-distributing systems, and a very elaborate electrical grid system throughout the region points to a highly vulnerable target profile. One lesson of the Gulf War was that small numbers of munitions, accurately delivered against utility systems (such as the Iraqi electrical grid), can have a devastating impact in a very short period of time. Thus, it is not out of the question that a future Gulf War adversary, equipped with the type of technology the United States had as a monopoly in 1990–91, would be able to cripple the entire economic-industrial infrastructure of a country like Kuwait or the United Arab Emirates in a matter of hours, and in two or three days do devastating damage to Saudi Arabia's vast facilities.

In the coming decade, the ability of states in the Middle East to upgrade their military forces with some of the technologies used by the allies in 1991 will improve. If Iran and Iraq are able to purchase arms and technologies on the open market with few restrictions, they should be able to procure the types of forces that could pose a major threat to the economic well-being of their neighbors. In particular, they —or any other regional power such as Saudi Arabia or Israel—should be able to target high-value economic installations that have fixed coordinates and thus inflict great damage.

However, their capacity to destroy high-value military targets that are either security protected (hardened) or mobile will be far more limited. It is doubtful, for instance, that they will be able to duplicate the sort of military operation conducted by the allies during the Gulf War. While the strike component of regional powers may improve dramatically if they get access to high technology, the reconnaissance component will, in all likelihood, remain beyond their means. During the Gulf War, the United States relied on an extraordinary array of advanced sensors and early warning systems, including AWACS, JSTARS, and a satellite-based communications system that could relay real-time information to the battlefield.

This suggests that the military balance of power in the region will remain in the hands of the United States as long as it maintains a strong forward presence and continues to upgrade the reconnaissance component of its armed forces. While some regional conflicts might eventually be able to obtain some of the reconnaissance capabilities presently available only to the United States, it is unlikely that they will be able to match the latest systems that are being developed for the U.S. armed forces. Israel, with its own satellite-launching capability, is likely to come nearest to achieving this level of sophistication, though in theory a new Iraqi regime might have the funds to purchase space systems from China or Russia.

What are the strategic implications of this continuing gap between countervalue and counterforce targeting? It suggests that all sides will have a major stake in developing military forces and installations that are mobile, redundant, and hardened. Fixed, vulnerable targets are likely to become hostage targets in the way that U.S. and Soviet cities were hostage to nuclear blackmail during the Cold War. It also suggests that if both sides have the capability to destroy each other's civilian infrastructure, they will either be deterred from war or be encouraged to seek a preemptive military capability if they calculate that a surprise attack could destroy the adversary's ability to manage its forces.

PROLIFERATION AND ASYMMETRICAL WARFARE

It would be supreme irony if one effect of the improvement of nonnuclear weapons is to make chemical, biological, and nuclear (CBN) weapons the "poor war" alternatives to a high-cost "conventional" force. There is no doubt that both Iran and Iraq regard CBN weapons as force equalizers when considering conflict with the United States.

The lessons learned from the Gulf War and, later, Kosovo, prompted greater interest in the development of asymmetrical strategies that would allow smaller and poorer countries to deter the major powers. If you cannot afford to match the advanced powers' technology, you must use whatever capabilities you have to threaten the one component of the West's formidable arsenal that is vulnerable—its low tolerance for military casualties.

There are basically two ways to threaten the West's Achilles' heel. These are state-sponsored terrorism and the development of weapons of mass destruction (WMD) that can be either used directly against Western forces or provided to terrorist groups to conduct covert operations against Western military and civilian targets. While the technical superiority of the Western military forces has gone from strength to strength over the past decade, the parallel concerns about the vulnerability of Western societies to terrorism and WMD have grown. The use of the phrase "rogue states" by the United States government to describe countries capable of this type of strategy became commonplace in the latter half of the 1990s. Concern was motivated by the actions of countries such as North Korea, Iraq, Iran, and Libya, and, to a lesser extent, Syria and Cuba. The first four countries have demonstrated a willingness to support international terrorism against Western targets as well as a capacity to develop chemical, biological, and nuclear weapons and surface-to-surface missiles as a means of delivery. As a consequence, the United States has developed a number of very elaborate counterproliferation strategies designed to prevent and, if necessary, offset these developments. Some efforts have been more successful than others. As weapons, including those of mass destruction, continue to proliferate in extreme conflict regions such as the Persian Gulf and South and East Asia, there are increasing expectations and pressure for the development and deployment of theater missile defense systems that can protect forward U.S. forces against attack. But can modern technology protect against terrorists?

The World Trade Center bombing on February 26, 1993, was a dramatic portent of things to come. Six people died in this attack, but according to the presiding judge at the trial, the attack was meant to topple one tower onto the other tower in a cloud of cyanide gas; tens of thousands of Americans would have died. The gas crystals were supposed to vaporize in the explosion; instead, the gas burned up.[5] In 1995 in Tokyo, fanatics released the nerve gas sarin in the subway. We now know that their plans, too, went astray. Had the gas attack worked as originally planned, thousands of Tokyo citizens would have died, and it is not difficult to anticipate the chaos and horror that would have followed. In Russia, Chechen rebels have taken thousands of hostages in their struggle for independence against Moscow. They call for greater and more devastating acts against the Russian state, including targeting Moscow itself. Given their determination and success to date, we should not ignore what they say.

Megaterrorism is primarily associated with attempts to kill or take hostage thousands rather than hundreds of people. Yet it is not the only new forum of terrorism of which we must be aware. The growth of the Internet, the development of cyberspace as means of communicating with people around the world, and the extraordinary sensitivity of world financial markets to derivatives and other highly technical stock speculations raise the possibility of cyberterrorism on a vast scale that could collapse financial institutions and sow chaos throughout military communications systems. What used to be in the realm of science fiction is now becoming, unfortunately, a potential reality.

The vulnerability of modern societies to such terrorist acts may not be new, but the willingness of groups to engage in such acts probably is. While there have been numerous speculations about nuclear terrorists, the control of nuclear weapons has so far proved to be relatively successful. This is not the case with chemical or biological weapons, and certainly not with the Internet and cyberspace. Also, as the Oklahoma terrorist bombing in May 1995 demonstrated, high technology may not be necessary to create devastating results for unwary targets. So far, the radical Palestinian terrorists have killed many Israeli civilians by conducting suicide attacks with conventional explosives strapped to their bodies. It does not take much imagination to see that if they were strapped to some other device containing biological or chemical weapons the effects on Israeli society could be a thousand times worse.

Fortunately, the most blatant attempts at megaterrorism, the World Trade Center and the Tokyo subway, were failures. But this is not cause for complacency. The United States and the international community need to treat these threats as high priority. However, advocating a blueprint for greater vigilance is not easy, since the sources of terrorism are so diffuse and the motives of perpetrators so varied. Clearly, one priority must be to work closely with the countries of the former Soviet Union to prevent the covert export of materials that can be used to fabricate weapons of mass destruction, especially nuclear weapons.

The potential danger of "nuclear leakage" is so great that unless urgent practical steps are taken to help the former Soviet republics, including Russia, get better control of these resources, a disaster is probable. This will require much more engagement by the White House and the U.S. Congress. Specifically, it means that more money will have to be spent to expand and accelerate the U.S. purchase of highly enriched Russian uranium and excess plutonium and to help the Russians implement enhanced security systems, which must include better inventory control, site protection, and environmental controls. More elaborate proposals for an international plutonium bank and a "nuclear Interpol" should be considered immediately.[6]

As for containing the risks of other forms of terrorism, one fundamental step for the United States is to improve the cooperation among U.S. government agencies monitoring the activities of terrorist groups. In the case of the World Trade Center bombing, there was virtually no liaison or follow-up between the domestic agencies responsible for law enforcement (the FBI and the Department of Justice) and the intelligence agencies with expertise in dealing with state-sponsored terrorism.

CASUALTY AVERSION

The hypothesis that the advanced democratic countries are unwilling to accept significant casualties in the event of military conflict is based on mixed empirical data and a number of questionable propositions that have been advanced as a result of interpretation of the data. Four military conflicts are usually cited to make the argument. First, the high casualties suffered by the United States in Southeast Asia during the Vietnam War, including more than fifty thousand deaths of U.S. servicemen, resulted in a national trauma that made a new generation of U.S. military and political leaders unwilling to put American lives on the line absent a crisis that directly threatens vital U.S. interests. The Gulf War was such an occasion, and despite predictions of thousands of U.S. casualties, the net result was fewer than three hundred American deaths and many of those were attributable to "friendly fire." As a result, the belief grew that modern wars could be fought with low casualties if correct preparations were made and a strategy of using "overwhelming force" was applied.

The United States' low tolerance for casualties was reinforced in 1993. The U.S. intervention in Somalia undertaken in late 1992 as a humanitarian mission to save the starving people of that war-torn society turned into a mission designed to remove the key warlords who were fighting one another and the outside forces, including the United States and the United Nations. In one such encounter on October 3, 1993, eighteen U.S. servicemen were killed in a clash with Somali warlords and the body of one airman was dragged through the streets of Mogadishu for all the world to see. All U.S. troops were withdrawn at the end of March 1994 owing to the fierce political backlash in the United States against the operation.

The Kosovo case is even more illuminating since no one on the allied side died from enemy action. It was understood from the beginning of the air war against Yugoslavia that a high number of allied casualties was politically unacceptable. This put two significant constraints on the operation. The allied leaders ruled out the use of ground forces, thereby encouraging the Yugoslavs to believe they could outlast the allies if they could tolerate the air assaults. Second, it put a premium on caution when flying allied airplanes over Yugoslavia. This led to high-altitude bombing and probably a number of unnecessary civilian casualties from inaccurate targeting.

Despite these examples, there is no consensus whether or not the Western democracies will be prepared to sacrifice large numbers of casualties for a matter of vital interest. The most likely prediction is that while there will be reluctance to ever again engage in full-scale "undeclared wars" like Vietnam or unstructured local wars like Somalia, if another Gulf crisis occurred the democracies would probably be prepared to go to war again provided there was strong political leadership and an overwhelming preponderance of force available to win the conflict.

Much will depend upon the nature of future threats. Interestingly, by mid-2000 the term "rogue states" was officially dropped by the United States government, in part because of new political developments in North Korea and Iran that suggested that both governments, for different reasons, have decided to modify their revolutionary and belligerent attitudes toward the West and show more interest in cooperation than confrontation. However, Iraq remains a serious problem in the absence of UN weapons inspectors in the country. The United States government and the first two UN arms inspectors (Rolf Ekeus and Richard Butler) believe that Saddam Hussein still seeks to develop weapons of mass destruction.

Compounding the global proliferation problem were the dramatic events of May 1998, when first India and then Pakistan tested a number of nuclear devices and proclaimed that they were now nuclear weapons states. The Pakistani action was particularly troubling in view of Pakistan's own domestic instability and its close ties with the ultraradical Taliban leadership in Afghanistan. The Taliban has provided sanctuary to Osama bin Laden, the Saudi Islamic extremist who is believed to be responsible for two terrorist bombings of U.S. embassies in Kenya and Tanzania in 1998 that resulted in 224 deaths, including 12 U.S. citizens. The U.S. response to these attacks was to launch a cruise missile attack on bin Laden's headquarters in Afghanistan and against a pharmaceutical factory in Sudan believed to be funded by bin Laden to produce chemical weapons. Whatever the merits of these attacks, they heralded a new form of gunboat diplomacy whereby cruise missiles can be launched at virtually any target in the world by U.S. aircraft and warships.

At the other extreme we have the example of wars fought in Africa during the 1990s that were not characterized by the use of high-technology weapons as weapons of mass destruction but rather primitive weaponry, including machetes and spears as well as small arms and automatic handheld weapons. Yet the casualties suffered in these wars have been high and the nature of the fighting brutal. However, when the outside powers have felt compelled to intervene they have had to rely heavily on the United States for military logistics. No other country or group of countries has the necessary air- or sea-lift capacity to deploy forces in large numbers to remote regions of the world such as Rwanda or, for that matter, Kosovo. It was the embarrassment in Europe with the overwhelming predominance of U.S. forces during the Kosovo war that has nudged the European Union to begin plans to develop a European defense force capable of sustaining similar types of operations without having to rely so heavily on the United States.

CONCLUSION

The next century is likely to witness a continued debate about the relationship between military technology and conflict. While the prospects for nuclear apocalypse involving the superpowers have receded, the probabilities for the use of weapons of mass destruction in regional wars or acts of terror have increased. This trend, together with new advanced conventional munitions and the willingness of radical groups to resort to megaterrorism, suggests that the subject at hand will continue to be a central and highly dangerous element of international relations.

Over the past several hundred years, many dramatic technological changes have directly influenced the conduct of war and peace; at the time of their introduction these were not fully understood. Gunpowder, the steamship, the railway, the internal combustion engine, machine guns, radio, tanks, airplanes, and nuclear weapons fall into this category. Our generation is struggling with the implications of an information revolution that will change the nature of international relations and the role of force in ways we cannot yet foresee. The one clear lesson from history is that new technology has the capacity to be used both to provoke and to restrain conflict, depending upon the prevailing environment in which it is introduced. Until we have a clearer sense of how the revolution in military affairs relates to the other far-reaching structural and social changes brought about by the semiconductor chips, speculation about the future will be just that.[7]

NOTES

1. Some of the themes developed in this essay are examined in more detail in two studies by the author: *The Control of the Middle East Arms Race* (Washington, D.C.: Carnegie Endowment for International Peace, 1991); and "The Continuing Debate over U.S. Arms Sales: Strategic Needs and the Quest for Arms Limitations," in *The Arms Trade: Problems and Prospects in the Post-Cold War World*, ed. Robert E. Harkavy and Stephanie G. Neumann (Thousand Oaks, Calif.: Annals of the American Academy of Political and Social Science, September 1994).

2. The Khomeini government canceled $10.6 billion worth of outstanding arms orders. In addition, it wanted to sell back to the United States seventy-eight F-14 aircraft purchased by the shah. "Proposed Arms Sales for Countries in the Middle East," hearing before the Subcommittee on Europe and the Middle East, 96th Cong., 1st sess., August 1, 1979, 32, 34. Cited in Shahram Chubin, *Iran's National Security Policy: Capabilities, Intentions, and Impact* (Washington, D.C.: Carnegie Endowment for International Peace, 1994).

3. For more details, see Patrick J. Garrity, *Why the Gulf War Still Matters: Foreign Perspectives on the War and the Future of International Security*, Report no. 16 (Los Alamos, N.M.: Center for National Security Studies, Los Alamos National Laboratory, July 1993).

4. John Arquilla and David Ronfeldt, *Cyberwar Is Coming*, RAND Report P-7791 (Santa Monica, Calif.: RAND Corporation, 1992).

5. See Laurie Mylroie, "The World Trade Center Bomb: Who Is Ramzi Yousef? And Why It Matters," *National Interest* (winter 1995–96): 3–15.

6. For a comprehensive review of the nuclear leakage problem, see Graham T. Allison, Owen R. Cote, Jr., Richard A. Falkenrath, and Steven E. Miller, *Avoiding Nuclear Anarchy: Containing the Threat of Loose Russian Nuclear Weapons and Fissile Material,* Center for Science and International Affairs Studies in International Security, no. 12 (Cambridge, Mass.: MIT Press, 1996).

7. For more reading on the impact of the information revolution on warfare and conflict, see, among others, Department of Defense, *Conduct of the Persian Gulf War: Final Report to Congress,* Pursuant to Title V of the Persian Gulf Conflict Supplemental Authorization and Personnel Benefits Act of 1991 (Public Law 102-25) (Washington, D.C., April 1992); Andrew Krepinevich, "Cavalry to Computer," *National Interest* 37 (fall 1994): 30–42; Michael J. Mazaar, Jeffrey Shaffer, and Benjamin Ederington, *The Military Technical Revolution: A Structural Framework* (Washington, D.C.: Center for Strategic and International Studies, March 1993); and Alvin Toffler and Heidi Toffler, *War and Anti-War* (Boston: Little, Brown, 1993). See also Winn Schwartau, *Information Warfare* (New York: Thunder's Mouth Press, 1994); Martin C. Libicki, "What Is Information Warfare?" *Strategic Forum* 28 (May 1995): 1–4; William J. Perry, "Desert Storm and Deterrence," *Foreign Affairs* 70, no. 4 (fall 1991): 66–82; and Eliot A. Cohen, "A Revolution in Warfare," *Foreign Affairs* 75, no. 2 (March-April 1996): 37–54.

6

The Impact of Globalization on Strategy

Jean-Marie Guehenno

GLOBALIZATION DOES NOT SEEM so new to the world of strategy. The twentieth century has witnessed two world wars, which suggests that globalization was a strategic reality well before the word became fashionable. The invention of intercontinental missiles during the Cold War made the world an even smaller place. Strategy could no longer be compartmentalized by geography, since nowhere on earth was immune to the global reach of these missiles. Nonetheless, there is a perception that the art of strategy in the post–Cold War world will be substantially different from what has gone before.

Does "globalization" describe a new state of affairs that forces us to rethink strategy? That there is as yet no accepted definition of the word is probably a symptom of the conceptual uncertainties of the late twentieth century. We know what we have left but are still unclear as to the characteristics of the world we are entering. We use either negative definitions, such as the "post–Cold War order," or vague concepts, such as "globalization." Practitioners and analysts

of "traditional" diplomacy seem to fall into two main categories when confronted with the embryonic concept of globalization:

- Those who deny its importance and argue that, as far as strategy is concerned, nothing has changed. States are more resilient than the "globalizers" would have us believe.
- Those who argue that, although globalization brings a fundamental change of *scale*, it does not alter the *nature* of international relations. They expect existing institutions and actors to adjust to this new context, and they apply traditional strategic concepts. Some welcome the prospect of the United States acting as a benign hegemon; for others, globalization is merely "Americanization" in disguise, a new ideology legitimizing the supremacy of a particular power. According to the latter argument, the key strategic goal is to resist globalization. Depending on where they live, they expect existing international institutions—notably the European Union

83

(EU)—or their own nation-states to act as bulwarks against the anonymous, or not so anonymous, forces of globalization and to create a new "balance."

This article makes the case that the impact of globalization on international strategy is more fundamental than either of these "traditionalist" schools would lead us to believe. The convenient separation between domestic and international affairs is collapsing; "globalization" is the best word we have to describe that phenomenon, the consequences of which we can only begin to assess. It is a process that deeply challenges our traditional definition of strategy.

Assessing the impact of globalization on strategy is therefore tantamount to defining globalization itself. What is the meaning of national interest if human communities become more fluid and if local interests cannot be isolated from more global concerns? What is the meaning of balance of power if "powers" are no longer sovereign actors but interdependent players caught in a network of transnational interactions? What is the meaning of hegemony if the dominant power of our time, the United States, is itself a "reluctant sheriff," whose power, even if it is backed by the traditional instruments of military might, often seems to depend more on "soft power" and on the autonomous decisions of nonstate actors who project American economic and cultural influence?[1]

GLOBALIZATION PAST AND PRESENT

The present is sometimes compared with the period before the First World War, when the gold standard was uncontested, international capital flows reached historic highs, and international trade grew quickly.[2] This apparent "globalization" did not prevent a world war, nor did it render obsolete centuries-old rules of strategy. The absence of balance between competing powers and their conflicting claims

resulted in devastating conflict. Formally, that conflict ended with the treaties of 1919–21; in reality, it endured until the settlement of the "German issue." This took place, not with the end of the Second World War in 1945, but with the unification in 1990. It could even be argued that, as the EU enters a new phase with the creation of the Euro, this "ending" is still being fashioned.

These are the realities on which the perception that a historical cycle is coming to an end and that we are entering a new phase is based. But is it sufficient simply to suggest that globalization as it existed before 1914 is returning and that the world will be shaped by it in the same powerful and precarious way? While the analogies are striking, the differences, upon closer examination, are substantial. The process of integration and disintegration at the end of the twentieth century goes much deeper than that of the pre–First World War period. Before 1914, integration as well as disintegration was driven by the idea of the "state." Nation-states were seen as the key agents of change. The old empires were under threat precisely because nationalism was perceived to be a positive force: sovereignty was a legitimate goal, and statehood its instrument. The nationalisms of the prewar period were self-confident and aggressive; states harbored global ambitions free from the need to consider "globalization"— the word did not exist—as a force to be reckoned with. Capital markets, Russian bonds, for example, were politically driven, while national perceptions followed a national logic, which strengthened a sense of one's identity.

Today's world is different. The disintegration of the colonial empires and of the Soviet Union and the multiplication of states that followed and continues to this day have not strengthened states; on the contrary, they have quickly revealed the limits of statehood. It is noticeable that the post–Cold War nationalisms are strongest in the weakest countries; they are defensive in nature and reflect a lack of self-confidence rather than the dynamism of powerful nations competing for the spoils of decaying empires. Nationalism has remained a very strong force, but nation-states find it more and more difficult to consolidate state institutions. "Globalization" has become the convenient word to describe the many forces that seem to threaten such consolidation.

Both democracies and authoritarian regimes have lost their monopoly on international relations and now must compete with—and may unwittingly be changed by—transnational actors such as multinational corporations, financial institutions, the news media, and nongovernmental organizations (NGOs). The state's role has changed, as has the "international system," which can no longer be adequately described simply as an interstate arrangement.

For "traditionalists," these changes are limited to the financial and economic sphere; even there, they argue, state power should not be underestimated. While both the Bank of England and former Indonesian president Suharto have felt the power of financial markets, states remain the prime movers. Even if full financial sovereignty no longer exists, markets function properly only within a legal framework enforced by state authorities; self-regulating independent authorities exist, but the state remains the enforcer of last resort. Ultimately, political legitimacy remains in the state's hands, and it is a dangerous illusion to expect the forces of globalization to eliminate domestic political debates. In fact, globalization can actually strengthen traditional nationalism by fostering a sense of "us" against "them," as demonstrations in Seoul and Jakarta have shown. National communities may rise against the perceived diktats of foreigners.

If this "traditional" analysis is correct, globalization is not such a radical change. New actors have indeed emerged, but states should confront them in the same way as they have past threats to their power. Although globalization may be characterized by the increasing role of nonstate actors, traditional rules of strategy still apply: one should analyze motives

and interests, assess the balance of power, and, if necessary, try to change it by making alliances and exploiting contradictions. Neither George Soros nor the International Monetary Fund (IMF) need be more formidable challengers than the more traditional threats of the past.

However, the flaw in this analysis is to imagine that globalization can be understood wholly in terms of financial markets and to ignore the political issue of legitimacy. It is more than a purely economic phenomenon; it affects not only the movement of goods and capital, but also the circulation of people and ideas—and therefore all aspects of our lives. Globalization is a process that changes not only the external context within which states operate, but also the very nature of states and political communities. The idea of autonomous human communities, democratically or nondemocratically pursuing their own interest, is put into question.

The distinction between domestic and international affairs is being blurred as transnational solidarities appear, shaping perceptions and sometimes policies, without being mitigated by a potent counterweight such as the Cold War's strategic threat. Nationalism itself has begun to assume transnational proportions as extreme right-wing movements from France to Russia build links and try to coordinate their activities. Large Muslim minorities in European countries transform the "foreign" issue of Algerian civil war into a domestic problem. The presence of a sizable Turkish population in Germany overshadows dialogue between Turkey and the EU, while influential domestic lobbies in the United States have partly shaped Washington's attitude to NATO enlargement and the Middle East peace process. This was true throughout the Cold War. The alleged support of Chinese businesspeople for U.S. president Bill Clinton's candidacy in the 1996 presidential campaign reveals the controversies that can arise when communities become more fluid. If we accept that democracy is the institutionalization of the clash of interests, on which basis can these interests legitimately be part of the democratic debate?

More issues now have a global dimension: the environmental policies of China, the health situation in Africa, nuclear safety in Russia, and water management in the Middle East will affect the lives of millions of people who are not citizens of the countries that will make the decisions. A de facto interdependence calls into question the legitimacy of the traditional model of sovereignty. Moreover, the globalization of news, of which the Cable News Network (CNN) has become the symbol, transforms local events into world news and creates a global awareness even if it does not create a global community. With few exceptions, natural as well as man-made disasters are made public almost as they happen: in the democratic—and richer—parts of the world, the gap between our abstract sense of belonging to a global human community and concrete and emotional sense of solidarity with a much narrower community is thus made more tangible. While the human communities of the past could find some comfort in the narrow sense of their own identity, the identities of particular communities in a globalized world are constantly challenged by issues as well as perceptions from elsewhere.

This globalization does not create a homogeneous world community. It could be argued that the Cold War provided a unifying threat that made the world strategically coherent. With this threat removed, one can now speak of the "unbundling" of strategy, as well as of states. The EU's Nordic members are concerned about the evolution of the Baltic states; its Mediterranean members see the Maghreb as a priority.

Today's very different world thus combines greater integration with increased fragmentation. At the global level, specialized organizations or frameworks become the only way to deal with an ever-increasing complexity. There is no global community, but there are global issues, which are managed in issue-specific frameworks. At the local level, the more functional the world becomes, the more people feel the need to identify with a particular community based on values rather than utility. Fragmentation is not a remnant of the past, bound to disappear with globalization; on the contrary, it is a product of globalization. As we move from inherited communities, rooted in geography and history, to communities of choice, we find that communities of choice, because they are more precarious and do not enjoy the self-evidence of the territorial communities of the past, are more demanding; they want strong commitments from their members. This reaction to globalization, or more accurately this characteristic of globalization, can take several forms, ranging from nationalism and ethnicity to religious revival and sects.

The common theme of these reactions is the assertion of values. The more we feel that globalization is shaping our lives and that our future is not shaped within the boundaries of our particular political community, the more pressing the issue of legitimacy becomes. What is a legitimate power? Is it right to infer from a global market for goods, a global capital market, and from a global capital market, a global "political market" in which the interaction of millions of individual decisions would shape our future without the mediation of political institutions? The Asian crisis has already reinforced those who believe that the benefits of the free movement of capital are not as self-evident as those of the free trade in goods. The outburst of nationalist demonstrations against the IMF and foreign powers is a revealing sign of the growing importance of the issue of legitimacy.

This debate reveals the key feature that makes today's globalization so different from the period before 1914. Today's process is not just the global interaction of existing political entities, nor is it just the emergence of new actors that would compete with those entities. It is characterized by the weakening of existing mediating institutions, public and private, and the direct confrontation of individuals with global forces. "Disintermediation," to use a term from the financial world, is coming to the political sphere. This evolution calls into question the role of political institutions: their power and relevance seem to recede at the very moment when they are expected to meet the increased demand for identity.

GLOBAL THREATS

What is the meaning and purpose of strategy in this new context? Political communities were first developed to ensure the survival of their members. In ancient times, defeat meant slavery for the people of the defeated city, and one could say that the oldest and most fundamental requirement of any strategy was to protect a given community from that terrible threat. To this day, independence has remained a fundamental goal, and the right to self-determination is still one of the most powerful appeals that exists. The most important goal of a national strategy remains to prevent a given community from falling under the domination of another.

Yet what happens when the pursuit of independence reveals sovereignty's elusive character? What happens if political communities become less relevant, are eroded from below as well as from above? Globalization's first consequence for strategy is that it changes the nature of the threats to be faced. In a nonglobalized world, political communities both guaranteed their members' security and posed the main threat to the security of other communities. For a political community, being a threat as well as being threatened was a fact of life, and strategy meant finding the right balance that would ensure one's own security without provoking enemy coalitions. "Oderint dum metuant," as the Romans used to say ("they may hate us provided they fear us"). There was a certain continuum between the defense and the offense, and one could say that this ambivalence of human communities—guarantors of themselves as well as threats to others—was a self-reinforcing condition: each community was strengthened

by the perception of the threats emanating from outside.

The situation radically changes if the threat is no longer another competing community, but rather the internal weakening of communities. The right to self-determination becomes the right to secede, thus threatening the survival of existing states. This evolution, particularly if it is combined with the proliferation of weapons of mass destruction (WMD), may force us to rethink our strategic concepts. Two particular threats stand out: civil conflict and the new potency of international terrorism.

THE STRATEGIC IMPLICATIONS OF CIVIL CONFLICT

The distinction between civil and international conflict has been eroded. Civil wars have been the most vicious conflicts of recent years, yet the traditional great powers have been slow to appreciate their increasing strategic implications.

At first, the major powers, applying the traditional perspectives of strategy, could not see how civil conflict could represent a strategic threat. These conflicts—in Yugoslavia, Africa, and the former Soviet Union—did not disrupt any balance of power, and they were not taking place in strategically important areas. It took some time to become aware that these conflicts could be threatening not because they would create any surplus of power for the benefit of a particular country or group of countries, but because they eroded international standards and opened a "black hole" into which other countries would be sucked. Nations that were not directly involved in the conflict found that they could face neither their indifference nor their impotence.

But defining strategic goals in the absence of a clearly defined threat was difficult. There was no convenient yardstick by which one could measure the appropriate degree of engagement. Cynics might conclude that it was enough to manage public perceptions and that the best policy was the one that would minimize risks while giving the impression that something was being done. The ascendance of a humanitarian view of foreign policy reflected the temptation of governments to "do something" without, in the end, doing very much. Eventually, however, it became clear that isolating chaos with a cordon sanitaire was not a realistic option in a world in which the movement not only of people but also of information could not be stopped. It was not increasingly organized within an elaborate, global framework of legal standards, in which ethical norms would remain a purely national concern. The commitment to a system of law that is deemed necessary for the efficient management of a global economy cannot be sustained on a purely technical basis; it requires a sense of global values that may not be enough to create a global community, but that must at least create common ground between different communities.

Upholding international moral standards could become a strategic goal. However, the provisional nature of the Dayton accords of 1995 reveals the limited depth of the West's commitment to such standards. Although the West was moved to act by moral pressure as much as by more traditional strategic considerations, the solution found at Dayton was of a traditional nature. Rather than deploy sufficient forces to uphold international standards of behavior, the United States and its European allies created a balance of forces on the ground between the Muslim-Croat federation and the Serbs. The horrors of the Muslim-Croat war were conveniently forgotten and the Serbs contained, but Bosnia's de facto division through ethnic cleansing was accepted, and no side could claim the moral high ground. The war was at least temporarily ended; it is, however, unclear whether peace was made.

The undeclared "gray wars" of our age are thus unpleasant reminders of our ambivalence. We belong to particular communities, we identify with particular interests, we make a distinction between remote conflicts and threats that could directly affect our "homeland." Yet, we know that we can no longer ignore what happens in faraway countries of which we know nothing. We recognize that we have to define a scale of interest; but the "duty to interfere" does not give us a strategic yardstick to define the degree of involvement. Globalization does not allow a retreat behind physical or moral borders. We are at once more demanding in our expectation of what the international order should be and more flexible in our understanding of our own values: compromise and ambiguity are becoming the conditions that have been imposed upon us by globalization.

THE STRATEGIC IMPLICATIONS OF WMD TERRORISM

The evolution of terrorism is the second issue that may become a strategic threat characterizing the age of globalization. Terrorism is not a new phenomenon in international affairs, and although some terrorist acts, such as the Sarajevo assassination of 1914, have occasionally been the causes of historic events, the consensus among historians is that terrorism has never had much strategic significance. It is a weapon of the weak.

Terrorists' use of WMD may change this assessment. It has proved more difficult than expected for terrorists to acquire the knowledge needed to build and use these weapons. However, they may find it easier to do so as globalization erodes the distinction between state and nonstate actors. The rich countries of the Northern Hemisphere may face a range of new situations, from WMD terrorism supported by the technological know-how of a particular state to acts by autonomous groups benefiting from a state's collapse and the "privatization" of its capabilities. A "gray area" is taking shape, blurring the distinction between internal and external security issues, and between criminal and strategic threats.[3]

As this happens, the strategic concepts that were developed in the first forty years of the nuclear age will no longer apply. The strategic dialogue that nuclear deterrence forced upon states might be seen, in retrospect, as the ultimate rationalization of traditional strategy. The extreme centralization of nuclear decision making fitted well with the concept of states acting as unified rational actors, whose strategic value could be quantified and balanced against the risks of nuclear holocaust. The use of nuclear weapons or other WMD by nonstate actors, or their threat to use them (although we should continue to make a distinction between the various classes of WMD), would not allow for such a dialogue because of the nonterritorial nature of a nonstate actor that cannot be unequivocally linked to any state.

The stability achieved through deterrence would then have to be replaced by preventive, and sometimes preemptive, action. And the operational requirements of such actions may increase the pressure on states to develop their information-gathering capabilities and to take advantage of their remaining superiority in that domain. Such an evolution raises fundamental questions for democracies, which have always made a distinction between what they allow themselves to do "abroad" and what they are permitted to do domestically. If there is no "abroad," if each citizen is a potential enemy, the balance between the requirements imposed to safeguard the collective security of a group and the requirements of individual freedom may be upset at the expense of the latter.

Finally, WMD proliferation could give apparently local crises a global dimension that cannot be ignored; on the other hand, it could increase the West's reluctance to interfere by raising the risks of doing so. In that sense, the risk of proliferation is emblematic of the new threats associated with globalization. Fragmentation is the unexpected product of integration. Global war resulting from a confrontation of wills between competing communities seems less likely, but global chaos resulting from a general loss of political control over events, with similarly devastating consequences, does not seem impossible. Globalization will not dissipate Clausewitz's "fog of war"; rather, it will extend it to the political sphere.

GLOBAL OPPORTUNITIES

Globalization creates new threats, but it also provides strategy with new options. The perception that the dangers are greater than the opportunities may be partly reversed if strategy is able to take advantage of this new context. States should see nonstate actors not simply as competitors: they also can become indirect instruments of policy and, sometimes, partners. States may gain in influence what they lose in direct control. As they lose their monopoly on interstate relations, their natural response is to try to restore it by using nonstate agencies under their control; the Soviet Union used such agencies as "front organizations," for example. Private organizations, ranging from Islamic foundations to companies run by retired U.S. military officers, supplied arms and military advice to parties to the Yugoslav conflict, opening up a range of fresh options for Western policymakers. The activities of these organizations followed the traditional logic of covert action and can be considered as indirect state involvement.[4]

Democratic states can go further, however, and recognize the benefits of the autonomous action of nonstate actors that they do not control. German political foundations, some major U.S. foundations, and some French humanitarian organizations have built their independence, yet their strategic goals are in harmony with the objectives of the democratic community of which they are an expression. Their tactics may sometimes differ, creating problems for traditional diplomacy, but the benefits outweigh this risk. The fact that states have lost their monopoly of international relations also means that they do not have to carry the full burden of tensions and antagonisms that arise in the normal course of relations between states. And democracies, because their strength is based on their diversity, are particularly well placed to take advantage of this situation. For example, the United States would have less leverage over Beijing if it did not have to take into account the pressure of NGOs fighting for human rights in China.

Globalization provides states with another important opportunity: instead of operating in a system in which diplomacy was the single most important point of entry, the weakening of state structures and the resulting disintermediation make it easier for states to conduct indirect strategies. There is a much larger segment of the population whose horizons are not purely domestic, whether because of business connections, education, or the freer flow of information. Some have argued that this puts democracies at a disadvantage, because unaccountable dictators can afford to ignore those indirect actions, while democracies, because they have to live with diversity, are much more adept at sorting information and at integrating various pressures without being submerged by them. Dictators, because their power destroys the integrity of the information that is provided to them, are much more likely to be destabilized by the free flow of information. They face a dilemma: either they try to keep full control of the information coming into their country and thereby run the risk of being unable to understand the world they live in—as in the case of North Korea—or they accept some degree of openness and soon discover that one cannot be half-open in the age of information.

Globalization, because it extends to the sphere of international relations the methods and techniques that characterize contemporary democracies, gives a clear advantage to those nations that, for better and worse, have been most adept at manipulating perceptions without ever controlling them. In no sense does this imply the creation of a global democracy. In the international marketplace of ideas and clichés, however, those countries that have been trained in the disciplines of domestic political marketing may enjoy a strategic advantage.

STRATEGY AS MARKETING

In this new context, characterized by new threats but also new opportunities, can strategy still have a meaning? The word has traditionally had ambitious implications; as opposed to tactics, it suggests a capability to put one's actions in a longer time frame, to identify the factors that will be relevant for the future, and eventually to shape that future. In the age of globalization, such an ambition may be close to hubris. The interdependent world looks more and more like the weather system described by chaos theory; influenced by millions of variables, its causality does not follow a linear model, and consequences are not proportionate to causes. Thus it is a futile exercise to pretend to isolate key determinants. The meteorologist does build global models; his aim is only to identify sequences of events rather than to uncover a unifying rationality of the system.

The strategist of tomorrow may well look more like a meteorologist. He may have to change his goals as well as his methods. The idea that an individual or a human community could determine long-term goals and develop a strategy to attain them may become increasingly unrealistic: too many factors are beyond our control, and there are too many unknowns. Assessing the capabilities and resources of a few actors, calculating their potential courses of action so as to define policy options, was possible when a few states, which could be identified with their rulers, defined the game. Today, it is often as difficult to keep to one's own course of action as it is to predict that of others.

A successful *strategy* may become no more than a series of successful *tactics*. Under these circumstances, strategy's goal becomes, not identifying the best outcome and finding the means to attain it, but keeping as many options open for as long as possible to provide maximum tactical flexibility. The intrinsic value of having the option to make or not make a decision, long recognized in the financial world, may increasingly become part of politics. Several successful contemporary leaders seem to fit this pattern. They are often criticized by pundits for their lack of "vision." Their policy agenda is vague, and while they may define their objectives in very broad terms, their identity and goals are more accurately described as a style than as a program.

That does not mean that these leaders have abandoned all strategic ambitions. Rather, the framework in which they make their decisions has changed. They try to take advantage of the benefits of a short-term horizon; the fragmentation of time partly compensates for the integration of space and usefully puts a limit on the number of factors to be considered. Each new situation is managed as an independent play because, in the globalized world, there are many issues that have global implications, but there is usually only one issue at a time that catches the attention and is considered to be of global interest. Strategy then is no more than a pattern of action, linking together situations that are otherwise disjointed. That pattern is useful because it enhances predictability and helps to build a sense of identity in a particular community. Just as corporations compete to create "brands," political actors try to establish a "style."

This more limited definition of strategy reflects the weakening of the political institutions that embody particular human communities. A sovereign, or a nation well aware of its identity, could pursue a strategy that projected into the future its past memories and ambitions. When human communities become more precarious, the horizon shortens. Strategy then is as much about keeping a particular community together, with a sense of its own identity and collective interests, as about taking into account the actions of other international players. This shift in the goal of strategy has consequences for

the methods to be used: managing public perceptions becomes a key priority, because it is both what connects the various actors and what brings a human community together. In such situations, the most strategic decision becomes the shaping of the message.

MANAGING THE TRANSITION

This minimalist definition of the scope of strategy—if it can still be called strategy—applies to the many situations in which globalization has effectively diluted power and weakened the traditional actors of international relations. But globalization's impact is uneven, and different players have different definitions of strategy. The Gulf War of 1990–91 pitted Iraq—a traditional actor in which power was highly concentrated and which was keen to increase it by grabbing another's territory—against a coalition of countries that had to take into account globalization's constraints. The West's confrontation with Yugoslav president Slobodan Milosevic has brought into conflict two sets of strategic logic. In China's case, deciding what can be interpreted according to globalization's logic and what follows more traditional patterns is itself a problem of strategic importance.

The most difficult period to manage may be that which we are entering: globalization already has a strong impact but has not diluted political power to the point where traditional strategic assessments have lost their relevance. This period combines classic balance-of-power calculations with elements of a different world, in which security is built on a balance of dependence and in which the boundaries between communities are blurred and power is diluted. The methods used to ensure security in one context are precisely those that undermine it in another.

The question then arises whether international relations are manageable because of globalization, or in spite of it. It can be argued that, because the United States remains in many respects a "traditional" power, it has been uniquely able to manage crises. Iraqi territorial aggression—a threat of the most traditional kind—was met by the traditional instruments of power according to the rules of traditional strategy. However, neither Iraq's defeat nor the conclusion of the Dayton accords means that the challenge of managing a world whose component parts have reached different stages of development has been definitively met.

Several courses of action remain open. One practical answer is to entrust the United States with the task of managing that difficult transition. As long as political power matters, and as long as the process of dilution of power has not been completed, the United States could remain as the "reluctant" but "efficient sheriff" of a world in transition.[5] According to this view, hard American power will provide the umbrella under which more benign forms of power may be allowed to flourish. The United States is seen as the ultimate enforcer, a benevolent cop under whose auspices a world of norms and regulations can be progressively consolidated. The EU may excel at managing soft power, but it has shown its limits in the management of hard power and cannot provide the required reassurance. If that view is right, the only challenges raised by globalization are challenges to American power. The transition toward a truly global world will be jeopardized if other powers make the task of the benevolent cop in Washington more difficult, or if the U.S. government is itself paralyzed by the domestic impact of globalization.

How realistic is this American solution? The United States is certainly not immune to the powerful forces of globalization. On the contrary, the country is a laboratory of globalization, and it is doubtful whether such imperial power is sustainable in the long run in a democratic context. The process of fragmentation into narrowly focused communities is all the more powerful in the United States as its people

have to face the challenges of global integration, and it creates limits to the use of American power that are already skillfully exploited by those countries that do not want to be bullied by the United States. Globalization makes the definition of U.S. national interest ever more elusive, and lobbies can take advantage of that difficulty to promote their own agendas, at the expense of a more coherent and comprehensive strategy.[6] Internationally, the obstacles to U.S. leadership are no less significant. The power of the United States creates its own countervailing forces, and several countries contest the legitimacy of the privileged role that the United States sometimes seems to have assigned itself. In a world in which the issue of legitimacy is becoming more important, how can one particular country, benevolent though it may be, legitimately decide for the rest of the world and at the same time claim that legitimacy rests on democratic consent, not force? In many developing countries, that contradiction increases the suspicion that globalization is essentially an ideology designed to give intellectual legitimacy to U.S. claims to global power by undermining the political institutions of other countries while safeguarding the American government's authority.

Such suspicions, combined with Americans' own doubts over their country's role as global policeman, raise questions over the sustainability of the "benevolent sheriff" option. In addition, there are objective limits to American power, as exemplified by America's lack of control over much smaller actors such as Israel and Serbia and by the rise of new powers such as China.

An alternative may be to welcome the emergence of a multipolar world.[7] The strategic answer to globalization is thus to encourage a change of scale of political institutions. The EU and China are potential candidates for managing a transition in which continental states would structure global integration on a regional basis. The power of the United States would be more acceptable because it would be balanced by others, and the process of dilution of power and globalization of norms would be controlled and mediated by a few major political actors. A small number of superpowers would act as a "management board," agreeing on the rules and regulations that would create the best framework for the free, transnational interaction of individuals, corporations, and NGOs. Other countries would have no choice but to accept these norms.

However, this model assumes not only that second-tier players would acquiesce to such an arrangement, but also that a limited number of participants at the negotiating table will more easily reach agreement. There is, however, an ambiguity in the role attributed to these new continental superpowers: are they expected to be political powers in the traditional sense, and to take part in a concert of continental states that would follow the same logic as the ill-fated nineteenth-century European concert of nation-states? Such a prospect is not reassuring considering what eventually happened to the "Concert of Europe." Democratic passions eventually destroyed the moderation that was a prerequisite for the concert's continued success. The combination of secret diplomacy and public posturing proved fatal to peace in 1914. "Wilsonians" would claim that less secrecy would have preserved peace and that today's world would avoid making the same mistakes because it is more transparent. It can be argued, however, that the complexity that has replaced secrecy as a necessary tool of diplomacy raises the same risks. In many countries, people complain that deals are being made by technocrats behind their backs. A concert of continental states would quickly face the dilemmas that destroyed Europe's earlier concert of nations: too complex for global political packages and too political for compromise, it would oscillate between paralysis and crisis. In addition, the increased size of political institutions envisaged would strain relations between the few actors

entrusted with global management. It is unlikely that weakened political institutions, presiding over the destinies of ever-more diverse communities, would have the strength to produce the compromises necessary for the system's continued success. On the contrary, weak political actors would be tempted to pursue independence as a way to assert a precarious identity. In an interdependent world, this would most likely result in confrontation.

Whether the EU fits that model and is the most visible sign of an emerging multipolar world is still an open question, which will find an answer as the political nature of European integration is eventually defined. The EU does indeed seek to provide a balance against U.S. hegemony, and some U.S. reactions to the Euro reflect a fear of a potentially more independent Europe.[8] Moreover, the goals agreed to at Maastricht, a single currency and Common Foreign and Security Policy (CFSP), seem to suggest that the ultimate ambition of the EU is sovereignty in the most traditional sense. However, the institutional framework that made that agreement possible—an independent central bank—as well as the assertion that the CFSP must be compatible with the NATO membership of several EU members, shows that the aims of European integration may be more complex and less traditional.

One may argue that the EU is actually trying to invent a third model based neither on indefinite U.S. supremacy nor on the pursuit of independence and sovereignty. The EU's pooling of sovereignties does not aim to create a sovereign Europe that could afford to neglect other powers, including the United States. Rather, it seeks to prevent any country, including the United States, from adopting such a position. It aims to be an institutional and political response to interdependence. Such institutional interdependence will be manageable only if the adjustments necessary to reconcile several political entities of continental size are made on a functional basis, in separate, issue-related fora rather than through unwieldy global political packages. Negotiations should be fragmented and issues settled on their merits, thereby combining transparency with efficiency. This will be possible only if strong, specialized multilateral institutions provide the framework within which negotiations between states can take place and nongovernmental views can be considered. Eventually, common legal principles can be defined. These do not create a utopian "world law," but they do help to make different legal systems compatible and provide a basis for settling differences. The role of the World Trade Organization (WTO) in managing difficult U.S.-EU trade relations is a good example in this respect.

This method should not be confined to economic matters, and it has implications for politics; the creation of an international criminal court may in the future be seen as a significant first step and an important milestone. For the first time, an enforceable legal procedure that is not subject to the veto of a particular state is being created on a worldwide basis. Its aim is to establish standards of conduct that cut across national sovereignties, and it begins to create, in a concrete and realistic way, common ethical ground that transcends national borders while preserving the role of existing political entities.

Global institutions are not a substitute for nations. However, in a world characterized by a fast-growing network of transnational links complementing more traditional international ones, they can provide the framework within which states can interact with their new competitors and adjust to the "disintermediation of politics" without being submerged by it.

This third model faces as many obstacles as the previous two. It will be resisted by the United States, which will see the obstacles it puts in the way of the unilateral use of power. On the European side, some countries may find it easier to delegate responsibilities to the United States, while others will find the ambition of a fully independent Europe politically

more appealing. Political entities, even when their aim is to encourage a more modest view of politics, need slogans that catch the imagination, and "interdependence" is not the most exciting one. In the rest of the world, which has not experienced to the same degree as the Europeans the disasters of nationalism and which often puts less emphasis on institutions, the task of establishing the right mix of transnational and international institutions may look even more formidable. It also may be perceived as a Eurocentric approach. No other continent has institutions comparable to the EU, even if Latin America seems to be making progress in that direction. In Asia, international and transnational organizations remain weak.

CONCLUSION

When we consider the three scenarios envisaged here, only one conclusion can be drawn with certainty: our future will not conform to any one of them, but it will most likely borrow some elements of each. The indefinite supremacy of the United States is as unlikely as a return, on a larger scale and with even more dramatic consequences, to the confrontation of states. The more complex scenario of institutionalized interdependence is desirable and probably most sustainable once its foundations have been laid. However, the transition from a classic interstate system to organized interdependence is an uncertain process, and we are left with a big unanswered question. Now that the century that has witnessed the two most devastating wars in history has come to an end, does globalization make global war more or less likely?

The answer probably lies in the competition between the diffusion of power that creates its own system of checks and balances and the multiplying effect of modern technology on power in an interdependent world. The combination of highly concentrated power and the perception of global interests triggered both world wars. The global leaders of today have probably more power and less control over it than their predecessors. This may make them less ambitious and more prudent. It can also, however, lead to unpredictable chain reactions. "Traditional powers" may help to control the scope of events that escape the traditional patterns of an interstate system; on the other hand, they may dramatically increase the impact of these events should they become involved. As governance becomes ever more challenging, we may have to navigate between the twin risks of living in chaos or slipping unwittingly into global war.

The purpose of strategy in the age of globalization should be to avoid such outcomes. But a successful strategy will require different, almost contradictory, qualities: a good understanding of the world that we are leaving as well as of that which we may be entering; a talent for leadership combined with an opportunistic sense of adaptation to the diffusion of power; an ability to concentrate power and quickly make important decisions tempered by a willingness to allow most decisions to be made in an incremental and decentralized way; and an understanding of cold balance-of-forces calculations combined with a universalist sense of ethics.

NOTES

This chapter first appeared in *Survival* 40, no. 4 (winter 1998–99): 5–19. It has been edited for stylistic conformity with other chapters in this volume.

1. See Richard N. Haass, *The Reluctant Sheriff: The United States after the Cold War* (New York: Council on Foreign Relations, 1997); and Joseph S. Nye, *Bound to Lead: The Changing Nature of American Power* (New York: Basic Books, 1990).

2. See Paul Wolfowitz, "Bridging the Centuries," *National Interest*, no. 47 (spring): 1997.

3. See Richard Falkenrath, "Confronting Nuclear, Biological, and Chemical Terrorism," *Survival* 40, no. 4 (autumn 1998): 43–65.

4. On, for example, the activities of private military companies in Africa and the former Yugoslavia, see David Shearer, *Private Armies and Military Intervention*, Adelphi Paper no. 316 (Oxford: Oxford University Press for the IISS, 1997).

5. See Haass, *Reluctant Sheriff*.

6. Samuel P. Huntington, *The Clash of Civilizations and the Remaking of the World Order* (New York: Simon and Schuster, 1996).

7. Multipolarity has been a constant theme of French diplomacy, and the concept has found support in many developing countries.

8. Martin Feldstein, "EMU and International Conflict," *Foreign Affairs* 76, no. 6 (November-December 1997): 60–73.

7

Transnational Criminal Enterprises, Conflict, and Instability

Phil Williams

TRANSNATIONAL CRIMINAL ENTERPRISES are contributors to and beneficiaries of conflict and instability at both the domestic and the international levels. The growth of these organizations is a symptom of various underlying problems, such as state weakness, ethnic tensions, and regional rivalries; yet transnational criminal organizations also perpetuate and exacerbate these security problems, making them more difficult to contain or resolve. Transnational criminal enterprises use corruption as an instrument of influence, undermining the rule of law, corroding political behavior and political institutions, infiltrating financial institutions, and weakening civil society. They also use violence and intimidation to extort money from licit businesses, to eliminate rivals, and to contain or stifle government efforts to put them out of business. On occasion, organized crime groups help to supply the weapons that fuel ethnic conflicts or civil wars. Moreover, when these conflicts are ended, some of the belligerents transform themselves into transnational criminal

enterprises, providing expertise in violence and an additional degree of ruthlessness that facilitates their domination of criminal markets.

In a few cases, links do exist between transnational criminal enterprises and terrorist organizations, although those links do not amount to a systematic organized crime–terrorism nexus.[1] In some instances, organized crime groups use terror tactics; more often, terrorist organizations use organized crime activities to fund their political and military campaigns. Each type of group, in effect, appropriates the strategies and tactics of the other when necessary or expedient.[2] Yet this does not necessarily mean that there is a convergence of organized crime and terrorism. In many areas of the world, the distinctions between organized crime—which is essentially profit driven—and terrorism—which is about the pursuit of political change through the use of violence—remain clear and distinct. In other areas, however, such as parts of Africa, Central Asia, and the Balkans, and in specific countries, such as Afghanistan, Burma, and Colombia, the traditional distinctions between politically motivated organizations and those seeking financial gain have become blurred amid a complex mixture of insurgency, factionalism, warlordism, terrorism, crime, and corruption that is extremely difficult to disentangle, let alone manage. In Tajikistan during the 1990s, for example, there was a civil war that was partly an extension of old clan rivalries and traditional power struggles, partly a religious and ideological conflict, and partly a struggle for control of opium and heroin trafficking. In cases such as this, the major players are new forms of hybrid organizations that are part criminal organization, part terrorist, part mercenary, part political faction, and part warlord. They use violence against one another in a struggle for power in which the state is the prize and the spoils are control over an array of criminal markets and illegal activities.

Against this background, this chapter seeks to do several things. First, it explores the relationship between transnational criminal enterprises on the one hand and state weakness on the other. It looks initially at the conditions that give rise to transnational organized crime in particular countries and regions, and then considers the impact of organized crime in undermining the legitimacy and integrity of state structures. The discussion subsequently focuses more specifically on the relationship between organized crime and political and military instability, looking initially at ethnic conflict and civil war and then at rogue or pariah states. It suggests that an important factor in the continuation of ethnic conflicts or insurgencies is the capacity of the warring parties to use criminal activities to fund the struggle. This is particularly important where there is a diaspora linked to an ethnic faction or insurgent group. Elements of the diaspora engage in organized crime activities and contribute at least some of the proceeds to the cause. The link between criminal activities and conflict, however, varies from case to case. Some terrorist organizations, ethnic factions, or insurgents embrace crime

wholeheartedly; in other cases, however, the degree of criminal involvement varies throughout the organization, depending on local and personal decisions. Moreover, while criminal activities typically help to finance the struggle and, therefore, to perpetuate the conflict, there are important exceptions to this pattern. In Burma, for example, the government's willingness to tolerate drug trafficking by insurgent groups encouraged these groups to end the insurgency, while in Afghanistan it was the imposition of control by the Taliban rather than the conflict per se that facilitated a large increase in opium production. As far as pariah states are concerned, there does seem to be an emerging pattern in which the state apparatus itself engages in criminal activities to maintain itself (and to enrich the elite) in the face of international isolation.

STATE WEAKNESS AND THE RISE OF TRANSNATIONAL CRIMINAL ENTERPRISES

Although the demise of the nation-state has been long predicted, states retain their dominant position as the major organizational and structural mechanism for governing societies. In many states, however, there has been a reduction in both internal cohesion and the capacity to govern. During the 1990s the collapse of totalitarian forms of government in the former Soviet Union, the removal of dictators in several African states, the end of the apartheid system in South Africa, and the growth of broader forms of political participation in much of Latin America were all hailed as victories for democracy and freedom. Yet, in some cases at least, the collapse of the old regime brought with it a collapse of social controls. One of the major beneficiaries of this collapse was organized crime, which in many cases succeeded in hijacking or derailing the political and economic transitions toward democracy and the free market. This is not to suggest that organized crime developed overnight. Indeed, as Roy Godson has noted, strong authoritarian states encourage the development of a "political criminal nexus."[3] In the Soviet Union, for example, the nomenklatura used black-market criminals for their own enrichment at the same time that strong social control mechanisms imposed strict limits on the activities and power of criminal enterprises. It was only when the strong state collapsed that organized crime really began to flourish without restraint and became far more extensive and significant. Similarly, in Mexico the PRI traditionally used criminal organizations for its own purposes but essentially limited their power and influence. With the challenge to the PRI's monopoly of power, however, and the influx of massive amounts of money from drug trafficking, the situation changed dramatically—and organized crime increased immensely in scope, power, and pervasiveness. In both cases the symbiotic relationship between the state and organized crime continued, but the balance of power within the relationship tilted significantly in favor of the criminals. Organized crime was no longer the junior partner at the service of the state, but was an equal or even dominant partner using the state as the ultimate front for criminal activities.

A similar upsurge of organized crime occurred in South Africa, where the collapse of the apartheid state did not bring the political violence predicted by many observers but facilitated a massive increase in criminal violence, both organized and disorganized. The transition to the postapartheid state brought a government with much greater legitimacy than its predecessors, but law enforcement agencies still had very low status and limited resources. Indeed, it appears that the security and law enforcement agencies that emerged from the South African transition were ill suited to their new tasks. The policing agencies and security forces developed to uphold apartheid often had the wrong people and the wrong mandate to meet the new challenge of developing a strong, legitimate state in which the criminal justice system is efficient, fair, and respected. At the same time, the broadening of these forces has also brought problems that are linked in large part to the continuing inequalities in the society. Police are often tempted by bribery and on numerous occasions have formed criminal gangs of their own, engaging in armed robberies of banks and armored cars transporting currency.

Limited economic opportunities for the majority black population and the disparities of wealth and power have also ensured that organized crime groups and less sophisticated gangs such as those in the Western Cape always have plenty of recruits. In addition to facilitating the growth of indigenous organized crime, the South African transition has encouraged the influx of transnational criminal enterprises, including Nigerian organizations that not only control both the drug trade and prostitution in significant parts of Johannesburg, but also are spreading their activities to other cities and are increasingly willing to resort to violence.[4] Other criminal enterprises active in South Africa include Russians and Ukrainians, who have established small aviation services and are suspected of trafficking in arms and diamonds, the Italian Mafia, with Vita Palazollo as a key figure, and Chinese networks trafficking in endangered species.

A state in transition is particularly vulnerable to both indigenous and transnational criminal organizations because it is characterized by the collapse of state structures (which take considerable time and effort to reestablish, therefore allowing organized crime to operate with a low level of risk), major shifts in the principles underlying economic management (which lead to economic dislocation and large-scale migration from a poorly functioning legal economy to a more vibrant illegal economy), and a reorientation of relationships with the outside world, usually involving an opening of the economy and the society (which allows criminal groups from elsewhere to operate within the state). These vulnerabilities are all the more dramatic because of the suddenness with which they come into existence. As well as being the result of a sudden collapse of an old regime, though, state weakness can reflect a more long-term failure to develop viable, legitimate, and effective institutions and well-functioning legal and economic systems. In much of Africa, in particular, the problem has been the endemic weakness of the African state, stemming from a lack of congruence between state on the one side and ethnic, clan, and national loyalties on the other. Furthermore, few African countries have succeeded in developing a state capacity that facilitates effective policy interventions in the economy and society.

Whatever the short- or long-term causes of weakness, weak states share certain characteristics: a low level of state legitimacy, weak border controls, ineffective rules and laws, little economic or social provision for the citizenry, lack of regulation and protection for business, and the absence of social control through a fair and efficient criminal justice system. Normal state functions are rarely implemented efficiently or effectively. Not surprisingly, these weaknesses provide a greenhouse effect for organized crime. They can best be understood in terms of capacity gaps (i.e., gaps in state capacity) that lead inexorably to functional holes (that is, a failure of the state to fulfill certain basic functions that are normally associated with states and that are expected by the citizenry). Functional holes, in turn, are exploited by criminal organizations in one of two ways —either by taking advantage of the room for maneuver that they provide or by filling them, thereby substituting or compensating for the state's inadequacies.

The exploitation is most obvious with respect to weak criminal justice systems. The functional holes in this domain mean that organized crime can operate with a high level of impunity or, at the very least, a minimum of risk. In Russia, for example, few major organized crime figures have been arrested and incarcerated. The substitution has also been evident in Russia, where the failure of the state to provide an adequate regulatory framework for business provided a major windfall for organized crime. The lack of legal recourse for debt collection and the absence of legal mechanisms for arbitration meant that there was neither protection nor contract enforcement for business. Organized crime stepped into the breach, becoming a surrogate for government.[5] It provided a roof, or *krysha,* for businesses that in other circumstances would have relied on the legal and regulatory system.

If state weakness is a necessary condition for the growth of domestic organized crime and the influx of transnational criminal enterprises, it is not a sufficient condition. Some very weak African states, for example, have not yet attracted organized crime. The reason is clear—they offer few opportunities for the generation of criminal profits. Low risk is most attractive when accompanied by prospects for large profits. This explains why South Africa has become a magnet for transnational criminal enterprises in a way that other African states have not. For all its weaknesses, the South African state is more powerful than most other states in Africa and consequently would appear to be less attractive to criminals concerned with avoiding risks. Any additional risk incurred from operating in South Africa, however, is more than outweighed by the benefits and opportunities stemming from the country's well-developed infrastructure, its connections to the rest of the world (which make it an ideal transshipment country for all sorts of illicit goods), and its sophisticated financial system (which provides opportunities for money laundering). Such caveats notwithstanding, it is clear that many weak states provide attractive targets for criminal organizations, offering safe havens in which and from which these organizations can operate with a maximum of safety and a minimum of interference. Not surprisingly, therefore, organized crime seeks to ensure that such conditions continue by systematically perpetuating the weakness of state structures.

THE IMPACT OF TRANSNATIONAL CRIMINAL ENTERPRISES ON STATES AND SOCIETIES

As well as combating and undermining any effort to strengthen state structures, organized crime has other adverse consequences for the home state and society. At the same time, it has to be acknowledged—even if rather grudgingly—that organized crime and drug trafficking can have beneficial economic consequences for some countries. Colombia, for example, during the 1980s and 1990s avoided much of the economic volatility that characterized most of its Latin American neighbors. Its foreign exchange earnings were certainly given a boost by the export of cocaine and increasingly heroin, and sectors of the population also benefited from the import of cheap contraband goods that became part of the black-market peso exchange system—a method of brokering money and returning the profits to Colombia partly in the form of manufactured goods. These benefits, though, were almost certainly outweighed by the costs of narco-violence, the loss of government legitimacy as a result of drug-related corruption scandals, and the gradual deterioration of public order in Colombia as drug trafficking helped to fuel the struggle between the state, paramilitaries, and guerrilla forces.

More generally, transnational criminal enterprises can be understood as the AIDS of the contemporary state—parasitically breaking down the immune system or defenses of the body politic and creating a wide variety of pathologies in society. One of the most important means of doing this is corruption, which is typically used by both domestic and transnational criminal organizations to nullify the authority of the state and to neutralize its punitive powers. When individuals or groups within government benefit directly as a result of organized crime, then the capacity and the will of the state apparatus to inhibit criminal activities and to interfere with or destroy the organizations that engage in them are likely to be minimal.

There are many targets for corruption, including the police and the military (to undermine control and enforcement efforts), the judiciary (to ensure favorable verdicts or, at the very least, lenient penalties), the legislature (to inhibit the passage of effective and stringent laws), and the executive branch (to obtain protection and support). In some cases, the use of corruption goes beyond neutralization and, in effect, captures the state.

This has occurred in Russia, for example, where organized crime corruption networks have become pervasive in both political and economic life. Exploiting capacity gaps and functional holes in Russia, criminal organizations have made enormous use of corruption, often finding targets that were only too willing to comply with their demands. Organized crime has undermined efforts to establish the rule of law, robbed the judicial system of any credibility it might have developed, and eroded hopes for fair, efficient, and effective government. It has facilitated the concentration of illegal power rather than the creation of effective authority. At best, organized crime and corruption have retarded the transition to democracy and the free market; at worst, they have derailed the process, turning Russia into what some observers have termed a "mafiocracy" in which honest politicians and bureaucrats are immediately suspect and honest businesspeople are placed at an enormous competitive disadvantage. Not surprisingly, the result has been the emergence of an "iron triangle" in which politicians and government officials, businesspeople, and criminals are bound together in complex relationships that serve to undermine faith in the transition and in democratic government. The seamless web between these three groups has facilitated the looting of the state, stifled legitimate entrepreneurial activity, and undermined the prospects for replacing the rule of the party by the rule of law. One well-informed observer has even suggested that in Russia the transition from communism has led not to the democracy and free market eagerly anticipated by most Westerners but to a "new authoritarianism" of organized crime.[6] As with most forms of authoritarianism, significant reliance is placed on violence or the threat of violence to deal with those who oppose or challenge the power structure. Indeed, in Russia the extensive corruption has been buttressed by violence—during the 1990s there were on average between five hundred and six hundred contract killings each year. Moreover, the importance of contract killings was far greater than their number suggests: they were targeted at anyone—investigative journalist, political reformer, bank manager, businessperson—who in any way threatened, challenged, or obstructed organized crime.[7]

This is typical. Organized crime and drug trafficking generally bring with them an atmosphere of violence and intimidation. Powerful trafficking groups in Mexico, for example, have killed police chiefs, attorneys, judges, and journalists as well as politicians. When combined with drug money that took corruption in Mexico to new heights, the results have been far reaching. As one Mexican journalist described it: "Since the middle of the 1980s, the social fabric of Mexico has been ripped to shreds. We have changed from a tightly controlled and law abiding country to a land of violence, corruption and impunity. As never before, Mexicans are victims of an unprecedented growth in violence, led by the growth of narco-trafficking and organized crime which tends to undermine law enforcement. Slowly but inexorably, Mexico has become No Man's Land."[8] Violence and corruption are especially great on Mexico's border with the United States and in some instances have spilled over into the United States itself.

The growth of violence associated with organized crime, of course, is not a new phenomenon. In the 1980s and early 1990s in Colombia and Italy, criminal and drug trafficking enterprises initiated campaigns of violence against state structures. In both countries this was in large part a defensive measure. In Colombia the campaign of violence directed by Pablo Escobar targeted the policy of extraditing drug traffickers to the United States. In Italy the campaign was a response to what was seen by the Mafia as a betrayal by the Christian Democrats, with whom it had long had a collusive and mutually beneficial relationship. Ironically, in both cases the campaigns of violence led to a backlash that ultimately hurt the criminals. In Colombia the forces of the state, with U.S. encouragement and support, initiated a major offensive against the drug traffickers, dismantling not only the Medellín trafficking organizations led by Escobar but also the rival organizations from Cali. In Italy the killing of judges Giovanni Falcone and Paolo Borsellino provoked popular outrage and led eventually to a serious and concerted campaign to disrupt Italy's major criminal organizations, especially the Sicilian Mafia. Some successes were achieved, with major Mafia leaders arrested and incarcerated. In both cases, however, there were inadvertent and unforeseen consequences. In the Colombian case, there has been a flattening of the drug-trafficking industry, with the ten to fifteen major groups associated with Medellín and Cali being replaced by an estimated two hundred or so smaller groups and a concomitant shift in power toward Mexican trafficking organizations. For its part, the weakening of Italian organized crime groups has facilitated an influx of Albanian organized crime groups into Italy, sometimes challenging and sometimes cooperating with Italian criminal organizations. Even success has its costs.

In many ways Colombia and Italy are the exceptions in that the state was galvanized into fighting back. In other cases acquiescence is the norm as corruption ensures congeniality and the maintenance of the symbiosis between organized crime and state structures and personnel. Moreover, there is also a contagion-like effect from drug trafficking that can have massive impact on both contiguous states and transshipment states. The spillover effects from drug trafficking and the corruption and the violence that usually accompany it are increasingly obvious. In Latin America, for example, drug- and organized crime–related corruption have spread to Brazil, Venezuela, and Argentina, while the Caribbean states have increasingly witnessed the corruption and co-option of their governments by drug traffickers anxious to use the facilities in various Caribbean islands for the transshipment of drugs and, in some cases, illegal aliens to the United States.[9]

In the long term, corruption has an insidious and profoundly corrosive impact on the legitimacy and authority of states. From the perspective of the criminal organizations themselves, however, it is the preferable instrument for maintaining a desirable operating environment. Corruption payments are simply the cost of doing business—and regularizing such arrangements provides a degree of predictability that is helpful to smooth business transactions. Indeed, for transnational criminal enterprises, there is probably an optimum level of instability, above which they would prefer not to go. It is still clear in Mexico, for example, who the targets of corruption need to be and which law enforcement officials need to be intimidated or eliminated. If the process of social disintegration goes too far, it can be a hindrance or even a deterrent to transnational organized crime. This is not to deny that transnational criminal enterprises can benefit, on occasion, from ethnic conflicts, insurgencies, or even the activities of terrorist groups. The relationship between transnational criminal enterprises and various forms of conflict is discussed more fully in the next section.

TRANSNATIONAL CRIMINAL ENTERPRISES, ETHNIC CONFLICTS, AND INSURGENCIES

It is not entirely coincidental that what one observer described as the "retribalization of large swaths of humankind by war and bloodshed" coincided with an upsurge of transnational organized crime.[10] Yet, in some cases, conflict can complicate criminal activities. The Balkan conflicts in the 1990s compelled heroin traffickers from Turkey to find alternative routes to Western Europe. Similarly, excessive instability means that costs and risks outweigh the prospective gains of involvement in a particular country. This has probably been the case in parts of Africa. The situation in Somalia, for example, retarded the entry of large-scale transnational criminal organizations, which almost certainly would have found it difficult to establish a foothold in the clan-based chaos that dominated the country through much of the 1990s. In other cases, though, civil wars, ethnic conflicts, national liberation struggles, and terrorist campaigns can provide lucrative business opportunities for transnational criminal enterprises. As Thomas Naylor has acknowledged, "any insurgency using the international black market to finance its activities inevitably forms mutually profitable and likely quite durable relations with international criminal groups."[11] In this connection, there have been numerous reports of Russian organized crime groups supplying arms to Colombian traffickers and rebels in exchange for drugs.[12] Clearly, some conflicts are easy to exploit.

Moreover, in cases in which there is an international embargo or the imposition of sanctions, the profits that can be made from supplying prohibited goods, whether arms or other strategic necessities such as oil, are particularly alluring, offering incentives for transnational organized crime to take on a major role as supplier of embargoed goods. Linkages between warring parties and criminal organizations willing to take the risks of dealing with them can be mutually beneficial. At the same time the role of formal criminal organizations should not be exaggerated. Embargo busting appeals to a wide variety of actors who collaborate with the targets in circumventing the restrictions.[13] Consequently, supplying the belligerents or a state subject to sanctions can rapidly become a very crowded and competitive activity in which states, intelligence agencies, commercial enterprises, arms dealers, and criminal enterprises vie for profits.

Moreover, in some ethnic conflicts and civil wars, the belligerents, rather than relying on transnational organized crime for cooperation and supplies, simply go into business for themselves, thereby marginalizing the criminal enterprises. This phenomenon, described by one journalist as "fighters-turned-felons," has grown, as ethnic factions, insurgency movements, and terrorist groups have found it more difficult to obtain state sponsorship for their activities.[14] Criminal endeavors provide a substitute that enables these groups to finance and sustain their political struggles. This is particularly attractive when the ethnic group in question has strong transnational dimensions, developed through migration overseas. Diasporas generally provide support for ethnic and nationalist struggles back in the homeland.

One of the best-documented examples of this tendency has been the efforts of Tamil communities overseas to raise funds to support the military and political struggle carried out by the Liberation Tigers of Tamil Eelam (LTTE). Indeed, the LTTE itself has reportedly established cells in as many as thirty-eight countries, in Europe, the Middle East, and North America.[15] Generally the LTTE cells obtain financial support from the Tamil communities, through either voluntary contributions or intimidation and extortion. They also engage in a wide variety of criminal activities that extend well beyond the Tamil community. The Tamil drug connection, for example, became evident during the 1980s. In many respects, it was not surprising. The opportunities for drug trafficking by members of the LTTE are very considerable because of Sri Lanka's proximity to the Golden Triangle of Burma, Thailand, and Laos and to Pakistan and the Golden Crescent. Furthermore, the presence of LTTE representatives or supporters in Thailand—where they have reportedly been procuring arms and possibly heroin—also provides an excellent opportunity for entry into the business.[16] At the other end of the drug supply chain, Tamil refugees in Western Europe provided ready outlets for drug sales. Evidence of Tamil involvement in heroin trafficking began to emerge in the mid-1980s when several members of the LTTE were arrested for heroin trafficking in Italy in 1984.[17] Indeed, during the 1980s Tamil traffickers were responsible for one-fifth of the heroin seized in Switzerland, leading Swiss authorities to dub the problem the "Tamil connection."[18] More recent reports point to heroin traffickers using Colombo as a major transshipment point for heroin destined for the United States and Europe.[19]

Tamil networks have gone beyond drug trafficking, becoming involved in a wider range of criminal activities. They have become adept at credit card fraud in Britain and Canada, extortion in Germany, and social security fraud in France.[20] Tamils have also engaged in the counterfeiting of currency in several European countries and Australia. Furthermore, in a number of cases, there is evidence of a direct link between organized crime activities and the Tamil campaign in Sri Lanka. In a report completed in 1999, for example, the Royal Canadian Mounted Police claimed to have "clear evidence" that Tamil street gangs in Toronto and another Canadian city were sending the proceeds from bank and casino fraud, immigration fraud, drug smuggling, and trafficking in weapons to the LTTE to support terrorist activities.[21]

Although the criminal activities of Tamil supporters overseas have made it possible for the LTTE to continue its struggle for independence, criminal activities have also been used in Sri Lanka itself—and in its territorial waters, where the organization has engaged in both piracy and maritime terrorism. According to the Sri Lankan government, the head of the Tamil Tigers' finance division, R. Visendrarajan, who owns two shipping companies, runs an alien smuggling business that in 1999 alone moved seventeen thousand people to eleven countries.[22] Reportedly this business earned $340 million. The government concluded that the operation was "one of the LTTE's major fund-raising devices for its ongoing war with Sri Lankan government troops."[23] It also alleged that Visendrarajan's ships were used for gun-running and drug trafficking.

Significantly, there has also been a growth in both organized and disorganized crime in Sri Lanka. Deserters from the army have engaged in robberies, kidnapping, and murder, all of which have compelled the government to draft legislation to make membership in a criminal organization punishable, to allow the confiscation of property from criminals, and to impose stricter controls on bail and more severe sentencing, including possible reimposition of the death penalty.[24] This broader decline into more chaotic modes of crime and violence—accompanied by efforts of many Sri Lankans to emigrate—is a reflection of the political degeneration caused by both the LTTE's military struggle and its use of criminal activities to fund the insurgency.

Two countries where the links between conflict and drug trafficking are even stronger than those in Sri Lanka are Burma and Afghanistan, both of which are major producers of opium and heroin. In Burma there has long been a complex nexus between ethnic conflict and separatism on the one side and involvement in drug trafficking on the other. It was often alleged, for example, that Khun Sa's Shan United Army (SUA) was far more interested in the profits from drug trafficking than in establishing an independent Shan state. Even if this was not the case, the SUA managed to fund its military and political campaigns through the proceeds of drug cultivation and drug trafficking. The same was true of the many other ethnic factions that also demanded autonomy from the government of Burma. If drug trafficking initially perpetuated the civil strife in Burma, however, during the 1990s, somewhat ironically, it also contributed to a lessening of the conflict as the government "negotiated cease-fire

agreements with most of the drug-trafficking groups . . . offering them limited autonomy and development assistance in exchange for ending their insurgencies" and in effect permitting them to maintain their involvement in the drug business.[25] Critics, such as the U.S. government, have even suggested that the "cease-fire agreements have had the practical effect of condoning money laundering, as the government encouraged these groups to invest in 'legitimate' businesses as an alternative to trafficking."[26] Nevertheless, the de facto "legitimization" of the trafficking business has brought a semblance of peace and stability to a country that remains enormously factionalized and fragile.

The situation in Afghanistan bears some similarities to developments in Burma—although without any positive developments. During the 1980s the cultivation of opium and the sale of heroin were indispensable to the continuation of the mujahideen's campaign to eject Soviet military forces from Afghanistan—but were ignored by U.S. supporters intent only on inflicting losses on the Soviet Union. With the Soviet withdrawal and the subsequent chaos in Afghanistan through most of the 1990s, there was growing concern in the West about the increasing importance of Afghanistan as a heroin producer. Ironically, though, it was the relative stability subsequently imposed by the Taliban that proved to be "an immense boon to opium farming" and led to major increases in opium cultivation.[27] The Taliban, while suppressing the growing and consumption of hashish, has rationalized its tolerance for poppy cultivation on the grounds that opium and heroin are consumed primarily by unbelievers in the West.[28] It also imposes an Islamic tax called zakat on opium dealers, taking as much as 20 percent of the value of the opium.[29] In addition, individual commanders and provincial governors impose taxes and in some cases have gone into the business themselves.[30] Because of the importance of heroin to the Taliban's finances, the area under cultivation has been expanded and production has increased significantly. In its report on international narcotics in 1999 the U.S. Department of State noted that "these factions, especially the Taliban, who control 97 percent of the territory where poppy is grown, promote poppy cultivation to finance their war machines. Those in positions of authority have made proclamations against poppy production but otherwise evinced no political will to fight narcotics. Rather, they are in active collusion with smugglers and criminal elements to manufacture and export heroin."[31] Although the Taliban in 1997 formally banned the cultivation of opium poppy, the ban has not been enforced. On the contrary, the result of the taxation process, as one observer has pointed out, has been the legitimization of opium cultivation in Afghanistan.[32] Indeed, the Afghan experience suggests a particularly important pattern where drug cultivation is concerned—cultivation can grow amid chaos and conflict but can grow even more when the dominant party that emerges has a vested interest in the continuation or even intensification of the trade. It is not surprising, when considered from this perspective, that the Taliban has developed and exploited transnational connections with drug traffickers and organized crime networks from Russia and elsewhere in the former Soviet Union, links that in some cases can be traced back to the Soviet occupation.[33]

The other dimension of the heroin connection in Afghanistan concerns the spillover consequences, both short and long term. Central Asia, which became particularly important for transshipment after Pakistani authorities clamped down on the booming heroin trade in and through Pakistan, has borne the brunt of these consequences. In the short term the civil war that raged in Tajikistan from 1992 to 1997 was partly about control over the opium trade, with opium sales used by some of the factions to fund their bid for power. The long-term consequences are less dramatic but could ultimately prove even more destabilizing. As one close observer of the region has noted, "The heroin explosion from Afghanistan is now

affecting the politics and economics of the entire region. It is crippling societies, distorting the economies of already fragile states, and creating a new narco-elite which is at odds with the ever-increasing poverty of the population."[34] When mixed with other factors such as the simmering ethnic conflict in the Fergana valley, the weakness of government in Kyrgyzstan, and the drug-related government corruption in Turkmenistan, it is clear that the heroin trade provides added potential for regional instability.

This pattern of drug cultivation and trafficking within a broader military and political struggle for control is also evident in Colombia, where close relationships have been forged between criminal organizations and revolutionary or guerrilla movements. Ideological antipathies have been no barrier to alliances of convenience. There are very different views, however, about the role of the major insurgency groups, the Revolutionary Armed Forces of Colombia (FARC) and the National Liberation Army (ELN), in the drug business. On the one side are those like Rand Beers, assistant secretary for International Narcotics and Law Enforcement in the Clinton administration, who claim there is evidence of direct involvement of the FARC and the ELN in the drug trade. In Beer's assessment, their involvement goes beyond protection of drug cultivation areas and laboratories to include the transportation of drugs and chemical precursors and direct control of their own laboratories. He also claims that the FARC and the ELN "are receiving pure cocaine in payment for services provided to the drug traffic, and reselling it" to Brazilian criminal organizations in return for armaments.[35] In a similar vein, the U.S. drug czar, former general Barry McCaffrey, has claimed that the war in Colombia is simply "struggling over money out of drug production."[36] This interpretation is supported by the prevalence of trafficking among all factions. It is not only the left-wing guerrillas who use drug trafficking, either directly or indirectly, to fund their political and military activities; the same is true of at least some of the paramilitary groups, and it has frequently been alleged that Castano, one of the leaders of the Peasant Self-Defense Forces of Cordoba and Uraba (ACCU), is himself a major drug trafficker. In its annual narcotics report, the State Department in March 2000 noted that "like the guerrillas, the paramilitaries are involved in the drug trade and are competing for an ever-greater share."[37]

To see the Colombian conflict wholly in terms of greed and profit, however, ignores several considerations. First, the drug cultivators and producers—in response to declining coca production in Peru and Bolivia—moved into areas controlled by the guerrillas rather than the other way around. These areas were attractive because they held little risk of government interference. For the guerrillas, the influx provided a welcome and lucrative opportunity. At the same time, the FARC insists that its relationship with drug traffickers is strictly business. As Paul Reyes, a high-ranking official of the FARC, noted: "We charge them a tax. We don't do them any favors, and they don't do us any. . . . Where the economic base is coca . . . that's what we tax—not the traffickers directly, but their intermediaries. In other regions . . . we tax the cattle ranchers, the sugar growers, the businesses."[38] For drug traffickers, the tax has been variously estimated at 10 percent and 15 percent of the value of a kilo of cocaine. A leading member of the ELN has made a similar point about the limited nature of cooperation, albeit in relation to arms purchases. In an interview with a São Paulo newspaper, Domingos Bernardes of the ELN acknowledged that the organization sometimes buys weapons from drug traffickers. The logic and the rationale are simple: "Drug traffickers receive the same treatment as any corporation. You buy arms from whoever has them."[39]

Second, focusing only on the profit aspect ignores the political dimension of the insurgency, which continues to have an explicit political agenda that includes land redistribution

and other reforms. The insurgents benefit from links with drug traffickers, but they do so simply as a means of funding a struggle that is still predominantly political. Third, the guerrilla movements are not monolithic. There are numerous combat fronts, and local commanders enjoy considerable autonomy in how they acquire the resources both to run their own operations and to make the necessary contributions to central funds. In some cases, this is done through kidnapping for ransom; in others, funding is obtained through taxing traffickers or even engaging in trafficking. A representative of the UN Drug Control Program in Colombia, for example, has noted that in some areas FARC units are more intimately involved with cocaine processing and export than the leadership admits. "It's far from general, but we've seen it. . . . The local fronts are quite autonomous. But in some areas, they're not involved at all. And in others, they actively tell the farmers not to grow [coca]."[40]

The critical point in all this, however, is that the narcotics linkages of the guerrillas and paramilitaries continue to help fund the struggle, thereby making it more difficult for the negotiations between the guerrillas and the Colombian government to make substantial progress. The consequence of the drug linkage is to make the conflict less ripe for resolution. Resolution often depends on the physical exhaustion of the belligerents and the depletion of the resources they have available to continue pursuing their goals through violence. As long as the funds are available for the guerrillas to continue the armed struggle, the prospects for a peaceful resolution are limited. In this connection, the State Department's conclusion that "in 2000, the foremost obstacle to curbing narcotics trafficking in Colombia will still be guerrillas who depend heavily on the drug trade for their substantial annual income" could equally well be turned around.[41] The foremost obstacle to ending the insurgency in Colombia is the capacity of the guerrillas to continue funding themselves through criminal activities including taxing and, in some cases, direct participation in drug trafficking.

This issue of the precise nature of the involvement of political insurgents in drug trafficking is also evident in the context of other conflicts. The Turkish government, for example, has long claimed that the Kurdistan Workers Party (PKK), the Kurdish separatist organization in Turkey, is heavily involved in the processing of opium into heroin and subsequently in trafficking the heroin into Eastern and Western Europe. The situation is in fact more complicated. While there is clearly some involvement of PKK members and PKK units in heroin trafficking, it is not clear that the PKK as an organization is as directly involved as the Turkish government claims. An authoritative study of organized crime in the Netherlands, for example, noted the involvement in the heroin trade of "classic mafia-type organizations" from Turkey, of drug traffickers linked to the right-wing paramilitary Grey Wolves and the Nationalist Movement Party (MHP), "the ultra-nationalist movement that propagates the ideas of the Grey Wolves," and of "small left-wing parties, but not the PKK."[42] The study acknowledged, however, that "the PKK does . . . play an indirect role because of its extortion practices with businessmen, which definitely extend to include rich drug dealers."[43] This more complex assessment is also supported in a report by Alessandro Pansa, director of the Italian police force's Central Operations Service, who has concluded that "about 30 percent of the laboratories for the refining of heroin scattered around Turkish territory are currently in the hands of the PKK Kurdish rebels; the remainder, on the other hand, is allegedly run by the Turkish mafia."[44] The implication is that although the PKK does not have the monopoly on heroin trafficking through and from Turkey that the Turkish government claims, funds from drug trafficking in one way or another feed into its political struggle for a Kurdish homeland.

Drug trafficking has also been seen as a major source of funding for the Kosovo Liberation Army (KLA). Once again, however, it is not clear whether involvement is by the organization as a whole, particular units, or just individuals. Moreover, there is sometimes a tendency—especially in the propaganda war carried out by the Milosevic government—to automatically assume that Albanian drug trafficking and criminal organizations are closely linked to the KLA. In fact, it is important to distinguish between Albanian drug traffickers, Kosovar Albanian drug traffickers, and drug traffickers who are members of the KLA. Equally important is distinguishing between direct involvement in trafficking to fund a military struggle and the acceptance of financial support from trafficking organizations, which also happen to have some sympathy for the political cause of the Kosovars.

All this is not to deny that there has been some KLA involvement in drug trafficking. Nor is it to ignore the fact that since NATO forces were sent into Kosovo as peacekeepers, it has become an increasing center of criminal activity. Indeed, the same happened in Bosnia, where peacekeeping forces, in an effort to encourage contacts between the ethnic communities, created a zone for commerce that quickly became a hub for black-market activities. Black markets and other criminal activities sometimes make strange bedfellows as enemies find that they have a common interest in avoiding the authorities and developing mutually lucrative criminal enterprises that allow them to carry on their struggle against each other. In Northern Ireland, for example, there has on occasion been a degree of connivance and collusion between the IRA and Protestant paramilitaries running scams on building sites in order to swell their respective war chests.

The use of organized crime and drug trafficking by ethnic factions or insurgency groups is not the only kind of intersection between political life and organized crime. The other important aspect of organized crime and black markets is that they become the preserve of what can legitimately be termed criminal states.

CRIMINAL STATES

One concern in countries such as Russia and Mexico is that organized crime, in effect, either has taken over or is in the process of taking over at least parts of the state apparatus, resulting in what was described earlier as a captured state. Yet the converse of this is also possible, in which the state itself—or, more accurately, the regime—takes over crime. There are two reasons for this. One is that the political leaders themselves are, in effect, the criminal kingpins, benefiting directly from criminal activities that they control and manage and are not simply the beneficiary of corruption payments. Another is that involvement in criminal activities provides the state with a source of income that contributes to its wealth and even its survival as an independent state. Nigeria under the Abacha dictatorship is a good example of a criminal state in which the motive was predominantly financial gain for the elite and fits the first variant very well. Sani Abacha himself accumulated $645 million in Swiss bank accounts and $600 million in Luxembourg bank accounts.

The second variant can be found in North Korea, where the state has become virtually a continuing criminal enterprise. This has occurred not because state structures have been captured by criminal organizations but because the official apparatus itself has encouraged criminal activities as a means of providing funding for a state that is almost bankrupt.[45] With all other avenues blocked by North Korea's pariah status and its international isolation, organized criminal activities have become a temporary salvation. "North Korean officials in countries from Romania to Zambia are accused of using embassies and front companies to smuggle a mind-boggling array of goods, including untaxed cigarettes, bootleg CDs, fake antiques, and endangered species parts."[46] Furthermore, North Korean farmers, with state approval, have been cultivating opium for some years; there is also increasing evidence of North Korean involvement in methamphetamine trafficking. Production of counterfeit dollars and gem smuggling also form part of what has become a broad criminal portfolio. The emergence of a criminal state in North Korea is primarily a result of its authoritarian domestic structure and its international isolation and can be understood as an attempt to maintain this structure in the face of isolation and international pressure. Some observers have gone even further and suggested that the proceeds from criminal activity could be used to finance North Korea's nuclear program. If this is the case, then the criminal activities would appear to contribute to the threat of instability on the Korean peninsula. On the other hand, the funding generated by the criminal activities could also act as an important safety valve for avoiding the implosion of the North Korean state and a possible last-ditch aggression against South Korea.

There is also, of course, a third possibility, in which personal enrichment and state survival become so closely bound that they are impossible to separate. Serbia provides an excellent example of this variant of the criminal state. Indeed, involvement in organized crime and the black market provides the political leadership with control over resources that facilitates its continued control over the state, and it provides opportunities for the generation of wealth that the members of the elite do not want to relinquish. According to Duska Jovanic, a journalist specializing in the Mafia, criminals in the early 1990s were astounded by the way in which the communists not only took over their trade but also perverted it. As they noted: "When we were robbing banks in the West, we were taking money from Switzerland to Yugoslavia.

Now the Communists are taking money from here back to Switzerland."[47] More recently, a Western journalist described Serbia as a "thug-ocracy" that merged the political realm and the underworld.[48] Among the many activities of the Serbian criminal state was cigarette trafficking. Indeed, the conflict over Kosovo, while having complex roots, could be all too easily caricatured as a struggle between drug traffickers on the one side and cigarette smugglers on the other. One dimension of this activity concerned cigarettes that came into Yugoslavia as duty-free items and were then reexported to European Union states, including Italy, where they were sold in the retail trade. It has long been alleged that Marko Milosevic, son of the former president, was a major player in this market and many others.

Ironically, at the same time that the black market and the underground economy circumvented the sanctions imposed on Serbia, sanctions benefited the regime of President Slobodan Milosevic in several ways. First, government ministers holding monopolies exploited shortages of goods for personal enrichment through their control of smuggling channels. Second, and conversely, the sanctions hurt domestic opponents of the Milosevic government much more than the government itself and, for some time at least, weakened the social and economic bases for opposition to the regime. In Serbia transnational criminal activity helped the regime stay in power longer than might have been expected; in North Korea it continues to prop up the regime.

CONCLUSION

It is clear from all this that transnational criminal organizations typically complicate and exacerbate state weakness. When one considers ethnic conflicts and civil wars, however, the assessment is more complex. Transnational criminal enterprises are all too willing to take on the role of supplier of arms either for money or in exchange for drugs. In this sense there is a naturally symbiotic relationship between conflict processes and transnational criminal enterprises. Although there are obvious examples of this phenomenon, however, it is not as prevalent as is sometimes suggested. In some ethnic conflicts or civil wars, the various factions themselves tend to engage in organized crime as a method of financing. In effect, they become the functional equivalents of organized crime while retaining their fundamentally political character and purpose.

Whether the belligerents cooperate with criminal enterprises or simply co-opt their methods, the result is generally—although not invariably—to intensify and perpetuate the conflict. It is trite but true to note that conflicts come to an end when the belligerents are too exhausted and their resources too depleted to carry on the armed struggle. From this perspective, the criminal dimension of insurgent activities can be regarded as something that intensifies and prolongs conflicts, helping to maintain an incentive structure in which continued struggle is preferable to peace. The implication is that efforts at conflict management and attempts to achieve a resolution or cessation of the violence need to be accompanied by systematic efforts to eliminate the sources of funding. There are two difficulties here. The first is in coordinating diplomatic and law enforcement efforts in ways that would send a clear message to the belligerents about the advantages of peace. The second is that efforts to disrupt criminal activities are extremely difficult—a clampdown in one place usually leads to an increase elsewhere—with the result that the flow of funds contributing to the military effort is very difficult to staunch. An alternative approach is the one that appeared to work in Burma—where a government tacitly accepted the continuation of criminal activities (in that case, drug trafficking) in return for a cessation of insurgent wars. The difficulty with this, of course, is that it provides a solution to the conflict but perpetuates and even intensifies criminal activities such as drug trafficking. In short, there are no easy solutions. Criminal activities have become so woven into the fabric of post–Cold War conflicts that disentangling them is an enormously complex task.

Similarly, organized crime activities have been used by a few rogue or pariah states as a means of financing themselves and ensuring their survival in the face of economic sanctions and international isolation. In effect, the more typical process of organized crime capturing the state is reversed and the state employs organized criminality for its own purposes. In some ways, the phenomenon of organized crime activities being appropriated by ethnic factions, insurgency, and terrorist movements as well as some states is as disturbing as the rise of transnational organized crime itself. When added to the corrosive impact of organized crime and corruption on weak states, these developments suggest that the challenges to governance, at both the domestic and international levels, will become more rather than less prevalent and that conflicts will become even more resistant to resolution.

NOTES

1. See Phil Williams, "Terrorism and Organized Crime," in *Hype or Reality: The "New Terrorism" and Mass Casualty Attacks*, ed. Brad Roberts (Alexandria, Va.: Chemical and Biological Arms Control Institute, 2000).

2. I am grateful to Elizabeth Joyce for this formulation.

3. See "Political-Criminal Nexus: Overview," *Trends in Organized Crime* 3, no. 1 (fall 1997): 4–7.

4. Peter Gastrow, "An International Link to Organised Crime," *South Africa: Business Day*, January 21, 2000.

5. Diego Gambetta explores this theme in *The Sicilian Mafia: The Business of Private Protection* (Cambridge, Mass.: Harvard University Press, 1993). Federico Varese has applied the theme to Russia in a very insightful manner.

6. Louise Shelley, "Post-Soviet Organized Crime: A New Form of Authoritarianism," in *Russian Organized Crime: The New Threat*, ed. Phil Williams (London: Cass, 1997).

7. The analysis here draws on a large database of Russian contract killings created by Gregory O'Hayon and William Cook at the University of Pittsburgh's Ridgway Center.

8. Juan Ruiz Healy, "Mexican Violence: The Result of Our Fragile Government?" *Novedades*, reproduced in *The News (Mexico City)*, March 10, 2000.

9. I am grateful to Pablo Dreyfus for the point about spillover.

10. Benjamin R. Barber, *Jihad vs. McWorld* (New York: Random House, 1995).

11. R. Thomas Naylor, "The Insurgent Economy: Black Market Operations of Guerilla Organizations," *Crime, Law, and Social Change* 20 (1993): 13–51 at 23.

12. Sue Lackey, "Russian Mob Trading Arms for Cocaine with Colombia Rebels," MSNBC, April 9, 2000 (http:// www.msnbc.com/news/391623.asp).

13. See the superb analysis in R. Thomas Naylor, *Patriots and Profiteers* (Toronto: McClelland and Stewart, 1999).

14. Charles Hanley, "Increasingly Guerrillas Financed by Drugs," *Toronto Star*, December 29, 1994, A19.

15. This section draws on an unpublished paper by Jason Collins, University of Pittsburgh, April 2000; and on a Mackenzie Institute report, *Funding Terror: The Liberation Tigers of Tamil Eelam and Their Criminal Activities in Canada and the Western World* (Toronto: Mackenzie Institute, 1996).

16. Don Pathan, "Thailand, Tamil Tiger Foothold Shows Security Flaws," *Nation*, March 31, 2000.

17. Mackenzie Institute, *Funding Terror*.

18. Ibid.

19. "Sri Lanka Seen as Important Drug Conduit," Colombo, Sri Lanka, UPI, March 10, 2000.

20. Mackenzie Institute, *Funding Terror*.

21. Amran Abocar, "Canada: Canada Police Say Tamil Gangs Funding Rebels," Reuters, March 28, 2000.

22. "Sri Lanka's Rebels Involved in Trafficking Human Cargo," report from Colombo, Xinhua News Agency, April 7, 2000.

23. Ibid.

24. "Sri Lanka: War-Torn Sri Lanka Prepares to Battle Rising Crime," *Reuters*, March 22, 2000.

25. U.S. Department of State, Bureau for International Narcotics and Law Enforcement Affairs, *International Narcotics Control Strategy Report, 1999* (Washington, D.C.: Government Printing Office, March 2000).

26. Ibid.

27. Ahmed Rashid, *Taliban: Militant Islam, Oil, and Fundamentalism in Central Asia* (New Haven, Conn.: Yale University Press, 2000), 116.

28. Ibid., 118.

29. Ibid.

30. Ibid.

31. U.S. Department of State, *International Narcotics Control Strategy Report*.

32. Rashid, *Taliban*.

33. Ibid.

34. Ibid., 123.

35. "Brazil: Mafia Said Receiving Drugs from Colombian Rebels," *Isto E* (São Paulo), October 27, 1999, BBC Monitoring Service (in Portuguese).

36. General Barry McCaffrey, quoted in Karen DeYoung, "For Rebels It's Not a Drug War," *Washington Post*, April 10, 2000.

37. U.S. Department of State, *International Narcotics Control Strategy Report*.

38. DeYoung, "For Rebels It's Not a Drug War."

39. "Brazil: Guerrillas Say ELN Buys Arms from Drug Traffickers," Agency EFE, distributed via Comtex, March 26, 2000.

40. Klaus Nyholm, quoted in DeYoung, "For Rebels It's Not a Drug War."

41. U.S. Department of State, *International Narcotics Control Strategy Report*.

42. Cyrille Fijnaut et al., *Organized Crime in the Netherlands* (The Hague: Kluwer Law International, 1998), 83.

43. Ibid.

44. Marco Ventura, "It Is the PKK That Brings Heroin to Italy," *Il Giornale* (Milan), December 15, 1998.

45. David E. Kaplan, "The Wiseguy Regime: North Korea Has Embarked on a Global Crime Spree," *U.S. News and World Report*, February 15, 1999, 36–39.

46. Ibid., 36.

47. Chandler Rosenberger, "The Milosevic Mafia," *National Review* 46, no. 2 (February 1994): 28.

48. Tom Hundley, "Milosevic, Gangsters Bond in 'Thugocracy,'" *Chicago Tribune*, March 28, 2000.

8

Democratic Transitions and War

From Napoleon to the Millennium's End

*Edward D. Mansfield
and Jack Snyder*

DANGERS OF TRANSITION

The idea that democracies never fight wars against each other has become an axiom for many scholars. It is, as one scholar puts it, "as close as anything we have to an empirical law in international relations."[1] This "law" is invoked by U.S. statesmen to justify a foreign policy that encourages democratization abroad. In his 1994 State of the Union address, President Bill Clinton asserted that no two democracies had ever gone to war with each other, thus explaining why promoting democracy abroad was a pillar of his foreign policy.

It is probably true that a world in which more countries were mature, stable democracies would be safer and preferable for the United States. But countries do not become mature democracies overnight. They usually go through a rocky transition in which mass politics mixes with authoritarian elite politics in a volatile way. Statistical evidence covering the past two centuries shows that in this transitional phase of democratization, countries become more aggressive and war prone, not less, and they do fight wars with democratic states. In fact, states undergoing regime change in a democratic direction are about twice as likely to fight wars soon thereafter as are states that are not undergoing a regime change. Also, democratizing states are more prone to fight wars than are states undergoing regime change in an autocratic direction.

The 1990s bore out this historical pattern of democratization, nationalism, and war. In the decade following the collapse of the Berlin Wall, armed violence was intense in a number of regions that had just begun to experiment with electoral democracy and increased pluralism of public debate, including such hotbeds of ethnic warfare as the former Yugoslavia, the post-Soviet Caucasus, and Burundi in Central Africa.[2] At the close of the millennium, this trend was still going strong. Ethiopia and Eritrea, both adopting electoral forms of government in the 1990s, fought a bloody border war in 1999–2000.[3] The nuclear-armed, elected regimes of India and Pakistan fought a war in 1999 in the mountainous borderlands of Kashmir. Prime Minister Vladimir Putin ascended to the presidency of Russia's shaky new democracy by riding the popularity of his war in 1999–2000 against the unruly autonomous region of Chechnya.[4] After the fall of the Suharto dictatorship in Indonesia, elections and referenda led quickly to violence and international intervention in the province of East Timor, a former Portuguese colony seeking national independence in 1999, and to ethnic mayhem elsewhere in Indonesia.

The following evidence, which has been updated from an article we published in *Foreign Affairs* in 1995, should raise questions about the U.S. policy of promoting peace by promoting democratization.[5] The expectation that the spread of democracy will probably contribute to peace in the long run, once new democracies mature, provides little comfort to those who may face a heightened risk of war in the short run. Pushing nuclear-armed great powers like Russia or China toward democratization is like spinning a roulette wheel: Many of the outcomes are undesirable. Of course, in most cases the initial steps on the road to democratization will not be produced by any conscious policy of the United States. The roulette wheel is already spinning for Russia and perhaps will be soon for China. Washington and the international community need to think not so much about encouraging or discouraging democratization as about helping to smooth the transition in ways that minimize its risks.

THE EVIDENCE

In earlier research we conducted some preliminary statistical tests of the relationship between democratization and war.[6] Since then, the data and measures of regime type on which we relied have been updated and extended.[7] Here, we use these more recent data and measures to reevaluate the argument that democratic transitions promote war.

Our statistical analysis relies on the classifications of regimes and wars from 1811 to 1992 used by most scholars studying the democratic peace. Starting with these standard data, we classify each state as a democracy, an autocracy, or a mixed regime—that is, a state with both democratic and autocratic features. Initially, this classification is based on a composite index developed by Keith Jaggers and Ted Robert Gurr that emphasizes the constitutional constraints on the chief executive, the competitiveness of domestic politics, the openness of the process for selecting the chief executive, and the strength of the rules governing participation in politics.[8] However, we also break down the classification of each state's regime type into three of the components that make up this index: the openness of the process for selecting the head of state, the extent of the constraints on the chief executive, and the competitiveness of political participation.[9] In the following tests we analyze separately Jaggers and Gurr's composite index and each of the three component factors just mentioned.

Democratizing states are those that made any change in a democratic direction—that is, from autocracy to democracy, from a mixed regime to democracy, or from autocracy to a mixed regime. Because we view democratization as a gradual process rather than a sudden change, we test whether a transition toward democracy occurring over a five-year period is associated with the outbreak of an international war (that is, a war between nation-states) during the subsequent five years.[10] More specifically, we compare the regime type of each state in the first and last years of every non-overlapping five-year period beginning in 1811 to determine whether a democratic transition took place. We then determine whether each state became embroiled in an interstate war during the following five-year interval.

While our focus is on democratization, it is also important to assess the effects of autoc-

Figure 1. Regime Change and Probability of War: Composite Index

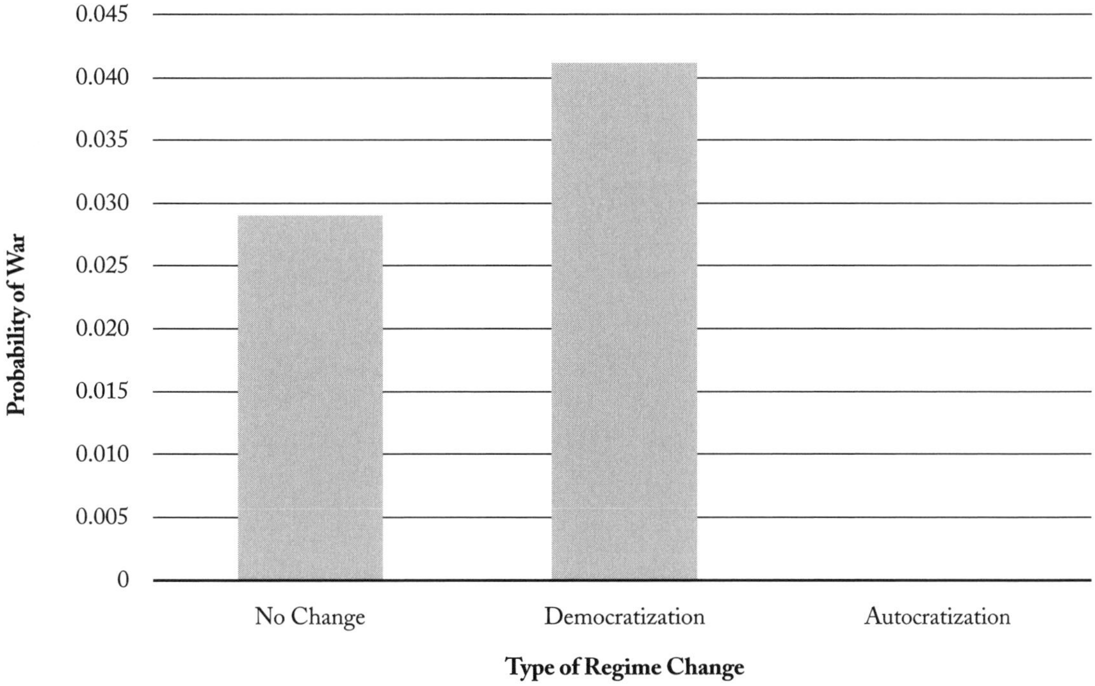

Note: The composite index measures the constitutional constraints on the chief executive, the competitiveness of domestic politics, the openness of the process for selecting the chief executive, and the strength of the rules governing political participation. See Jaggers and Gurr, "Tracking Democracy's Third Wave with the Polity III Data," *Journal of Peace Research* 32, no. 4 (1995): 469–482. Note that our analyses based on the composite index yield no case where autocratization led to the outbreak of an international war.

ratization on war. It is only through such an analysis that we can determine whether the effect of democratization on war reflects a more general tendency for *any* regime change, whether in a democratic or an autocratic direction, to promote belligerence. We therefore code states as autocratizing if they made a change in an autocratic direction during any five-year period analyzed here—that is, a change from democracy to autocracy, from a mixed regime to autocracy, or from democracy to a mixed regime.

To assess the strength of the relationship between democratization and war, we construct a series of contingency tables. Based on these tables, we compare the probability that a democratizing state will go to war with the proba-

bilities of war for states in transition toward autocracy and for states undergoing no regime change. The results of all of these tests—which are presented in figures 1–4—show that *democratizing states were more likely to fight wars than were states that had undergone no change in regime.* Given the rarity with which wars break out, it is not surprising that the observed probabilities of war are small. Nonetheless, states experiencing a democratic transition have been about 40 percent more likely to become involved in hostilities than states experiencing no regime change, if we focus on the composite index. Democratizing countries have been roughly twice as likely to become embroiled in belligerence than stable regimes, if we code

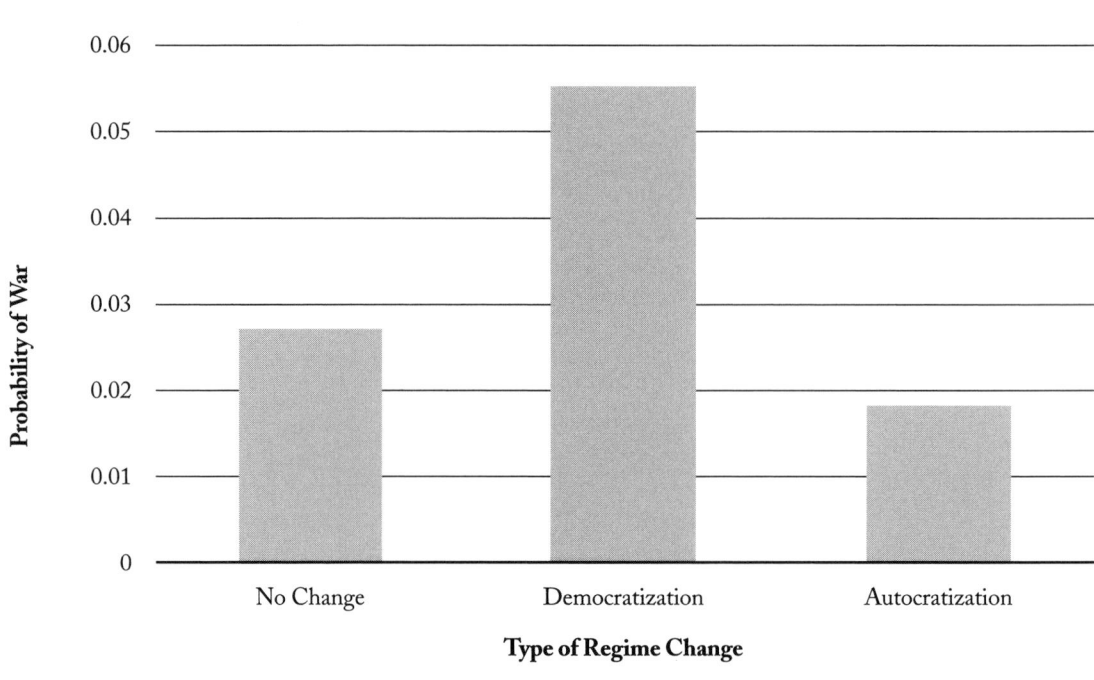

Figure 2. Regime Change and Probability of War: Openness of Selection of the Chief Executive

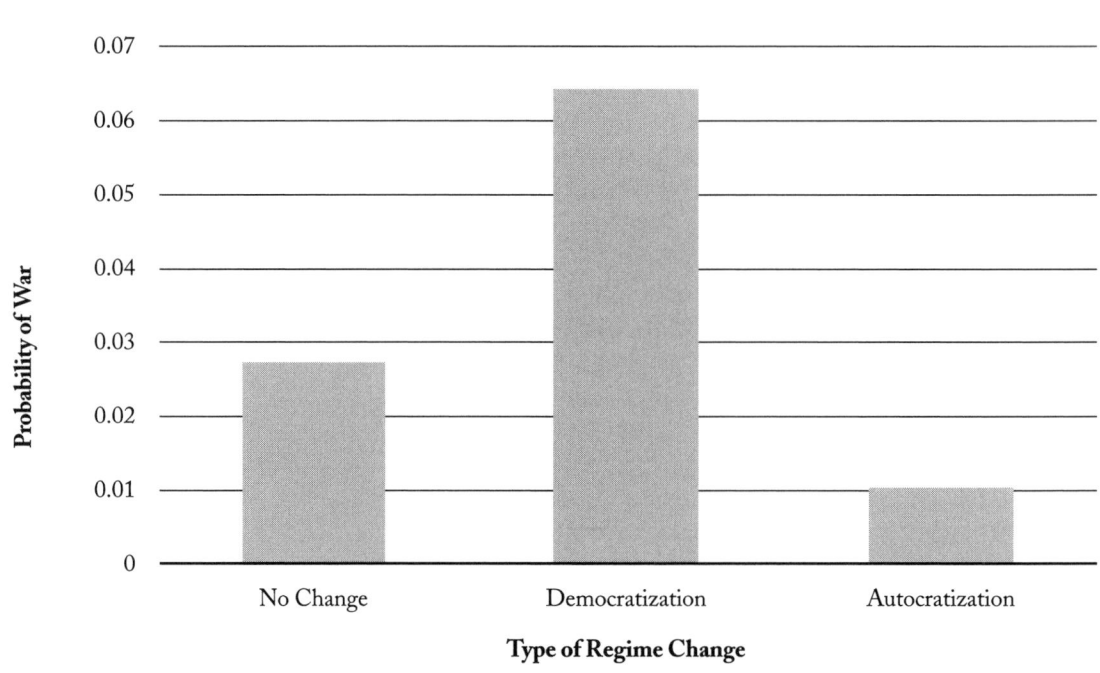

Figure 3. Regime Change and Probability of War: Constraints on the Chief Executive

Figure 4. Regime Change and Probability of War: Competitiveness of Political Participation

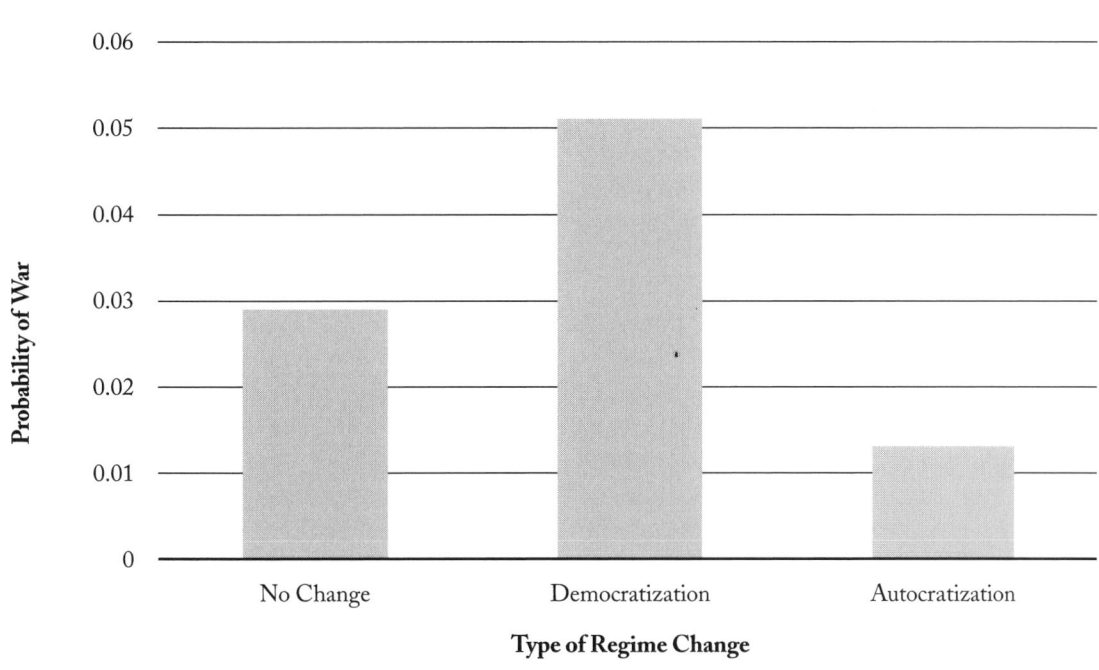

regimes using the openness of the process for selecting the head of state, the extent of the constraints on the chief executive, or the competitiveness of political participation.

Furthermore, the effects of democratization on war do not stem from a more general tendency for regime change to stimulate antagonism. As shown in figures 1–4, autocratizing countries are even less likely to engage in war than stable regimes, regardless of which variable is used to measure regime type. Thus, while the roughness of this simple statistical analysis is obvious, our results continue to indicate that democratization has precipitated war during the nineteenth and twentieth centuries.[11]

NATIONALISM AND DEMOCRATIZATION

The connection between democratization and nationalism is striking in both the historical record and today's headlines. We did not measure nationalism directly in our statistical tests. Nonetheless, historical and contemporary evidence strongly suggests that rising nationalism often goes hand in hand with rising democracy. It is no accident that the end of the Cold War brought both a wave of democratization and a revival of nationalist sentiment in the former communist states.

In eighteenth-century Britain and France, when nationalism first emerged as an explicit political doctrine, it meant self-rule by the people. It was the rallying cry of commoners and rising commercial classes against rule by aristocratic elites, who were charged with the sin of ruling in their own interests rather than those of the nation. Indeed, dynastic rulers and imperial courts had hardly been interested in promoting nationalism as a banner of solidarity in their realms. They typically ruled over a linguistically and culturally diverse conglomeration of subjects and claimed to govern by divine right, not in the interest of the nation. Often, these rulers were more closely tied by kinship, language, or culture to elites in other states than to their own subjects. The position of the communist ruling class was strikingly similar: a transnational elite that ruled over an amalgamation of peoples and claimed legitimacy from the Communist Party's role as the vanguard of history, not from the consent of the governed. Popular forces challenging either traditional dynastic rulers or communist elites naturally tended to combine demands for national self-determination and democratic rule.

This concoction of nationalism and incipient democratization has been an intoxicating brew, leading in case after case to ill-conceived wars of expansion. The earliest instance remains one of the most dramatic. During the French Revolution the radical Brissotin parliamentary faction polarized politics by harping on the king's slow response to the threat of war with other dynastic states. In the ensuing wars of the French Revolution, citizens flocked to join the revolutionary armies to defend popular self-rule and the French nation. Even after the revolution turned profoundly antidemocratic, Napoleon was able to harness this popular nationalism to the task of conquering Europe, substituting the popularity of empire for the substance of democratic rule.

After this experience, Europe's ruling elites decided to band together in 1815 in the Concert of Europe to contain the twin evils of nationalism and democratization. In this scheme, Europe's crowned heads tried to unite in squelching demands for constitutions, electoral and social democracy, and national self-determination. For a time nationalism and democratization were both held back, and Europe enjoyed a period of relative peace.

But in the long run, the strategy failed in the face of the economic changes strengthening popular forces in Western and Central Europe. British and French politicians soon saw that they would have to rule by co-opting nationalist and democratic demands rather than suppressing them. Once the specter of revolution returned to Europe in 1848, this reversal of political tactics was complete, and it led quickly to the Crimean War. British foreign secretary Lord Palmerston and French emperor Napoleon III both tried to manage the clamor for a broader political arena by giving democrats what they wanted in foreign affairs —a "liberal" war to free imprisoned nations from autocratic rule and to expand commerce.

But this was just the dress rehearsal for history's most potent combination of mass politics and rising nationalism, which occurred in Germany around the turn of the twentieth century. Chancellor Otto von Bismarck, counting on the conservative votes of a docile peasantry, granted universal suffrage in the newly unified Reich after 1870, but in foreign and military affairs, he kept the elected Reichstag subordinate to the cabinet appointed by the kaiser. Like the sorcerer's apprentice, however, Bismarck underestimated the forces he was unleashing. With the rise of an industrial society, Bismarck's successors could not control this truncated democracy, in which over 90 percent of the population voted. Everyone was highly politicized, yet no faction could achieve its aims through the limited powers of the Reichstag. As a result, people organized direct pressure groups outside electoral party politics. Some of these clamored for economic benefits, but many of them found it tactically useful to cloak their narrow interests in a broader vision of the nation's interests. This mass nationalist sentiment exerted constant pressure on German diplomacy in the Wilhelmine years before 1914 and pushed its vacillating elites toward war.

Democratization and nationalism also became linked in Japan on the eve of the Manchurian invasion in 1931. During the 1920s Japan expanded its suffrage and experimented with two-party electoral competition, though a council of elder military statesmen still made the ultimate decisions about who would govern. These semielected governments of the 1920s supported free trade, favored naval arms control, and usually tried to rein in the Japanese army's schemes to undermine the Open Door policy in China. Young Turks in the army developed a populist, nationalist doctrine featuring a centrally planned economy within an autarkic, industrialized, expanded empire while scapegoating Japan's alleged internal and external enemies, including leftist workers, rich capitalists, liberals, democrats, Americans, and Russians. After the economic crash of the late 1920s, this nationalist formula became persuasive, and the Japanese military had little trouble gaining popular support for imperial expansion and the emasculation of democracy. As in so many previous cases, nationalism proved to be a way for militarist elite groups to appear populist in a democratizing society while obstructing the advance to full democracy.

The interconnection among nationalism, democratization, and war was likewise present among some of the postcommunist states in the 1990s. Shortly after the breakup of the Soviet Union, one-quarter of Russia's voters, disgruntled by economic distress, backed the tough-talking nationalist party of the anti-Semite Vladimir Zhirinovsky in the 1993 parliamentary elections. Commentators were calling it "Weimar Russia." In this climate ostensible liberals like Russian president Boris Yeltsin and his Western-oriented foreign minister, Andrei Kozyrev, found themselves on the defensive on ethnic and foreign policy issues. Partly for this reason, Yeltsin decided to use military force to try to prevent secession from the Russian Federation by the ethnic Chechen rebels. As it turned out, Russian public opinion opposed the military intervention in Chechnya, which was characterized by Russia's relatively free press as a brutal, costly, and incompetent debacle. To help his reelection bid in 1996, Yeltsin promised to end the war. Nonetheless,

a chronic undercurrent of nationalism and loathing of the Chechens in the political discourse of Russia's shaky democracy left public opinion primed and ready for manipulation on this issue. Following a series of mysterious terrorist bombings in Moscow, which were attributed to "Chechens," and Chechen bandit raids into Russian territory in the summer of 1999, Yeltsin's new prime minister, Vladimir Putin, used a popular renewal of the military intervention in Chechnya to position himself as Yeltsin's successor. Although the label "Weimar Russia" proved to be an exaggeration, warlike nationalism was nonetheless intertwined with the fundamental workings of Russia's incipient democracy in the 1990s.

In the post-Soviet Caucasus, the new country of Armenia moved quite far in the direction of electoral democracy in the early 1990s while at the same time supporting an invasion of its ethnic foes in the neighboring state of Azerbaijan. The Azeris have been less successful in sustaining momentum toward democracy. However, in Azerbaijan's one relatively free and fair presidential election, the winner, Abulfez Elchibey, attacked the incumbent for being insufficiently nationalist and populist. Elchibey's platform emphasized Turkic identity and the strengthening of the Azeri nation-state to try to mount a counteroffensive against the Armenians.

The early stages of democratization were also implicated in the violent breakup of communist Yugoslavia. Especially in Serbia the political and military elites of the old regime, facing pressure for democratization, cynically but successfully created a new basis for popular legitimacy through nationalist propaganda in the mass media they controlled. In the climate of opinion that this manipulation fostered, Serbian elections in the late 1980s and 1990s became contests among different varieties of nationalists, each trying to outbid the others to claim the mantle of the true defenders of Serbdom against its ethnic foes.

THE SORCERER'S APPRENTICE

Although democratization often leads to war, that does not mean that the average voter wants war. Public opinion in democratizing states often starts off highly averse to the costs and risks of war. In that sense the public opinion polls taken in Russia in early 1994 were typical. Respondents said, for example, that Russian policy should make sure the rights of Russians in neighboring states were not infringed, but not at the cost of military intervention. Notwithstanding the ambivalence of the Russian public's view of the Chechen problem during the 1990s, by 1999 the Russians had been primed by inflammatory media coverage and the Putin government's military faits accompli to adopt a more belligerent stance toward the perennially troublesome Chechens.

Numerous historical and recent cases point to the effectiveness of calculated elite efforts to whip up belligerent nationalism among an initially pacific population during the earliest stages of a democratic transition. For example, Napoleon III successfully exploited the domestic prestige from France's share of the victory in the Crimean War to consolidate his rule, despite the popular reluctance and war weariness that had accompanied the war. Having learned this lesson well, Napoleon tried this tactic again in 1859. On the eve of his military intervention in the Italian struggle with Austria, he admitted to his ministers that "on the domestic front, the war will at first awaken great fears; traders and speculators of every stripe will shriek, but national sentiment will [banish] this domestic fright; the nation will be put to the test once more in a struggle that will stir many a heart, recall the memory of heroic times, and bring together under the mantle of glory the parties that are steadily drifting away from one another day after day."[12] Napoleon was trying not just to follow opinion but to make opinion bellicose, in order to stir a national feeling that would enhance the state's ability to govern a split and stalemated political arena.

Much the same has happened in contemporary Serbia. Despite the memories of Ustashe atrocities in World War II, intermarriage rates between Croats and Serbs living in Croatia were as high as one in three during the 1980s. Opinion was made bellicose by propaganda campaigns in state-controlled media that, for example, carried purely invented reports of rapes of Serbian women in Kosovo and even more so by the fait accompli of launching the war itself.

In short, democratizing states are war prone not because war is popular with the mass public, but because domestic pressures create incentives for elites to drum up nationalist sentiment.

THE CAUSES OF DEMOCRATIC WARS

Democratization typically creates a syndrome of weak central authority, unstable domestic coalitions, and high-energy mass politics. It brings new social groups and classes onto the political stage. Political leaders, finding no way to reconcile incompatible interests, resort to shortsighted bargains or reckless gambles in order to maintain their governing coalitions. Elites need to gain mass allies to defend their weakened positions. Both the newly ambitious elites and the embattled old ruling groups often use appeals to nationalism to stay astride their unmanageable political coalitions.

Needing public support, such elites rouse the masses with nationalist propaganda but find that their mass allies, once mobilized by passionate appeals, are difficult to control. So are the powerful remnants of the old order —the military, for example—which promote militarism because it strengthens them institutionally. This is particularly true because democratization weakens the central government's ability to keep policy coherent and consistent. Governing a society that is democratizing is like driving a car while throwing away the steering wheel, stepping on the gas, and fighting over which passenger will be in the driver's seat. The result, often, is war.

Political Stalemate and Imperialist Coalitions

Democratization creates a wider spectrum of politically significant groups with diverse and incompatible interests. In the period when the great powers were first democratizing, kings, aristocrats, peasants, and artisans shared the historical stage with industrialists, an urban working class, and a middle-class intelligentsia. Similarly, in the postcommunist world former party apparatchiks, atavistic heavy industrialists, and downwardly mobile military officers share the stage with populist demagogues, free-market entrepreneurs, disgruntled workers, and newly mobilized ethnic groups. In principle, mature democratic institutions can integrate even the widest spectrum of interests through competition for the favor of the average voter. But where political parties and representative institutions are still in their infancy, the diversity of interests may make political coalitions difficult to maintain. Often the solution is a belligerent nationalist coalition.

In Britain during the period leading up to the Crimean War, neither the Whigs nor the Tories could form a lasting governing coalition because so many groups refused to enter stable political alliances. None of the old elites would coalesce with the parliamentary bloc of radicals elected by urban middle-class and Irish voters. Moreover, protectionist Tories would not unite with free-trading Whigs and Peelite Tories. The social and political mid-Victorian equipoise between traditional and modern Britain created a temporary political stalemate. Lord Palmerston's pseudoliberal imperialism turned out to be the only successful formula for creating a durable ruling coalition during this transitional period of democratization.

The stalemate in German electoral politics in the Wilhelmine era was even more serious. In principle, coalitions of the left and the right might have formed a two-party system to vie for the favor of the average voter, thus moderating policy. In fact, both left and right were too internally divided to mount effective coalitions with internally consistent policies. Progressives dreamed of a bloc extending "from Bassermann to Bebel," from the liberal-democratic middle classes through the marxist working classes, but the differences between labor and capital chronically barred this development. Conservatives had more success in forging a "marriage of iron and rye," but fundamental differences between military-feudal Junkers and Ruhr industrialists over issues ranging from the distribution of tax burdens to military strategy made their policies incoherent. Germany wound up with plans for a big army and a costly navy, and nobody willing to pay for it.

In more recent times incipient democratization has likewise caused political impasses by widening the political spectrum to include too many irreconcilable political forces. In the final days of Yugoslavia, efforts by moderates such as former prime minister Ante Markovic to promote a federalist, democratic, economic reformist platform were hindered not only by ethnic divisions but also by the cleavage between market-oriented business interests on the one hand and party bosses and military officers on the other. Similarly, in Russia the difficulty of reconciling liberal, neocommunist, and nationalist political platforms and the social interests behind them led in the early 1990s to parliamentary stalemate, attempts to break the stalemate by presidential decree, tanks in the streets, and the resort to freelancing by breakaway regions, the military, and spontaneous privatizers of state property. One interpretation of Yeltsin's decision to use force in Chechnya is that he felt it necessary to show that he could act decisively to prevent the unraveling of central authority, with respect not only to ethnic separatists but also to other ungovernable groups in a democratizing society. Chechnya, it was hoped, would allow Yeltsin to demonstrate his ability to coerce Russian society while at the same time exploiting a potentially popular nationalist issue.

Inflexible Interests and Short Time Horizons

Groups threatened by social change and democratization, including still-powerful elites, are often compelled to take an inflexible view of their interests, especially when their assets cannot be readily adapted to changing political and economic conditions. In extreme cases there may be only one solution that will maintain the social position of the group. For Prussian landowners, it was agricultural protection in a nondemocratic state; for the Japanese military, it was organizational autonomy in an autarkic empire; for the Serbian military and party elites, it was a Serbian nationalist state. Since military bureaucracies and imperial interest groups occupied key positions in many authoritarian great powers, whether monarchal or communist, most interests threatened by democratization have been bound up with military programs and the state's international mission. Compromises that may lead down the slippery slope to social extinction or irrelevance have little appeal to such groups. This adds to the difficulty of finding an exit from the domestic political impasse and may make powerful domestic groups impervious to the international risks of their strategies.

Competing for Popular Support

The trouble intensifies when elites in a democratizing society try to recruit mass allies to their cause. Threatened elite groups have an overwhelming incentive to mobilize mass backers on the elites' terms, using whatever special resources they might retain. These resources have included monopolies of information (the Wilhelmine navy's unique "expertise" in making strategic assessments), propaganda assets (the Japanese army's public relations blitz justifying the invasion of Manchuria), patronage (Lord Palmerston's gifts of foreign service postings to the sons of cooperative journalists), wealth (the Krupp steel company's bankrolling of mass nationalist and militarist leagues), organizational skills and networks (the Japanese army's exploitation of rural reservist organizations to build a social base), and the ability to use the control of traditional political institutions to shape the political agenda and structure the terms of political bargains (the Wilhelmine ruling elite's agreement to eliminate anti-Catholic legislation in exchange for Catholic support in the Reichstag on the naval budget).

This elite mobilization of mass groups takes place in a highly competitive setting. Elite groups mobilize mass support to neutralize mass threats (for instance, creating patriotic leagues to counter workers' movements) and counter other elite groups' successful efforts at mass mobilization (such as the German Navy League, a political counterweight to the Junker-backed Agrarian League). The elites' resources allow them to influence the direction of mass political participation, but the imperative to compete for mass favor makes it difficult for a single elite group to control the outcome of this process. For example, mass groups that gain access to politics through elite-supported nationalist organizations often try to outbid their erstwhile sponsors. By 1911 German popular nationalist lobbies were in a position to claim that if Germany's foreign foes were really as threatening as the ruling elites had portrayed them, then the government had sold out German interests in reaching a compromise with France over the Moroccan dispute. In this way, elite mobilization of the masses adds to the ungovernability and political impasse of democratizing states.

Ideology takes on particular significance in the competition for mass support. New entrants to the political process, lacking established habits and good information, may be uncertain where their political interests lie. Ideology can yield big payoffs, particularly when there is no efficient free marketplace of ideas to counter false claims with reliable facts. Elites try out all sorts of ideological appeals depending on the social position they are defending, the nature of the mass group they want to recruit, and the kinds of appeals that seem politically plausible. A nearly universal element of these ideological appeals, however, is nationalism, which has the advantage of positing a community of interest uniting elites and masses. This distracts attention from class cleavages that divide elites from the masses they are trying to recruit.

The Weakening of Central Authority

The political impasse and recklessness of democratizing states are deepened by the weakening of the state's authority. The autocrat can no longer dictate to elite interest groups or mass groups. Meanwhile, democratic institutions lack the strength to integrate these contending interests and views. Parties are weak and lack mass loyalty. Elections are rigged or intermittent. Institutions of public political participation are distrusted because they are subject to manipulation by elites and arbitrary constraints imposed by the state, which fears the outcome of unfettered competition.

Among the great powers, the problem was not excessive authoritarian power at the center but the opposite. The Aberdeen coalition that brought Britain into the Crimean War was a makeshift cabinet headed by a weak leader with no substantial constituency. Likewise, on the eve of the Franco-Prussian War, Napoleon III's regime was in the process of caving in to its liberal opponents, who dominated the parliament elected in 1869. As Europe's armies prepared to hurtle from their starting gates in July 1914, Austrian leaders, perplexed by the contradictions between the German chancellor's policy and that of the German military, asked, "Who rules in Berlin?" Similarly, the 1931 Manchurian incident was a fait accompli by the local Japanese military; Tokyo was not even informed. The return to imperial thinking in Moscow was the result of Yeltsin's weakness,

not his strength. As the well-informed Moscow analyst Sergei Karaganov recently argued, the breakdown of the Leninist state "has created an environment where elite interests influence [foreign] policy directly."[13]

In each of these cases, the weak central leadership resorts to the same strategies as do the more parochial elite interests, using nationalist ideological appeals and special-interest payoffs to maintain their short-run viability, despite the long-run risks that these strategies may unleash.

Prestige Strategies

One of the simplest but riskiest strategies for a hard-pressed regime in a democratizing country is to shore up its prestige at home by seeking victories abroad. During the Chechen intervention newspaper commentators in Moscow and the West were reminded of Russian interior minister Viacheslav Plehve's fateful remark in 1904, on the eve of the disastrous Russo-Japanese War, that what the tsar needed was "a short, victorious war" to boost his prestige. Though this strategy often backfires, it is a perennial temptation as a means for coping with the political strains of democratization. German chancellor Johannes Miquel, who revitalized the imperialist-protectionist "coalition of iron and rye" at the turn of the century, told his colleagues that "successes in foreign policy would make a good impression in the Reichstag debates, and political divisions would thus be moderated."[14] The targets of such strategies often share this analysis. Richard Cobden, for example, argued in 1854 that military victories abroad would confer enough prestige on the military-feudal landed elite to allow them to raise food tariffs and snuff out democracy: "Let John Bull have a great military triumph, and we shall have to take off our hats as we pass the Horse Guards for the rest of our lives."[15]

Prestige strategies make the country vulnerable to slights to its reputation. Napoleon III, for example, was easily goaded into a full declaration of war in 1870 by Bismarck's insulting editorial work on a leaked telegram from the kaiser. For those who want to avoid such diplomatic provocations, the lesson is to make sure that compromises forced on the leaders of democratizing states do not take away the fig leaves needed to sustain their domestic prestige.

MANAGING THE DANGERS

Though mature democratic states have virtually never fought wars against each other, promoting democracy may not promote peace because states are especially war prone during the transition toward democracy. This does not mean, however, that democratization should be squelched in the interests of peace. Many states are now democratizing or on the verge of it, and stemming that turbulent tide, even if it were desirable, may not be possible. Consequently, the task is to draw on an understanding of the process of democratization to keep its unwanted side effects to a minimum.

Of course, democratization does not always lead to extreme forms of aggressive nationalism, just as it does not always lead to war. But it makes those outcomes more likely. Cases in which states democratized without triggering a nationalist mobilization are particularly interesting, since they may hold clues about how to prevent such unwanted side effects. Among the great powers, the obvious successes were the democratization of Germany and Japan after 1945, owing to occupation by liberal democracies and the favorable international setting provided by the Marshall Plan, the Bretton Woods economic system, and the democratic military alliance against the Soviet threat. More recently, numerous Latin American states have democratized without nationalism or war. Border skirmishes between Peru and Ecuador, however, coincided with democratizing trends in both states and a nationalist turn in Ecuadoran political discourse. Moreover, all three

previous wars between that pair over the past two centuries occurred in periods of partial democratization.

In such cases, however, the cure is probably more democracy, not less. In "Wilhelmine Argentina," the Falkland Islands/Malvinas War came when the military junta needed a nationalist victory to stave off pressure for the return of democracy; the arrival of full democracy has produced more pacific policies. Among the Eastern European states, nationalist politics has been unsuccessful in the most fully democratic ones—Poland, the Czech Republic, and Hungary—as protest votes have gone to former communists. Nationalism has figured more prominently in the politics of the less democratic formerly communist states that are nonetheless partially democratizing. States like Turkmenistan that remain outright autocracies have no nationalist mobilization—indeed no political mobilization of any kind. The rule seems to be: Go fully democratic, or don't go at all.

In any given case, other factors may override the relative bellicosity of democratizing states. These might include the power of the democratizing state, the strength of the potential deterrent coalition of states constraining it, the attractiveness of more peaceful options available to the democratizing state, and the nature of the groups making up its ruling coalition. What is needed is to identify the conditions that lead to relatively peaceful democratization and try to create those circumstances.

One of the major findings of scholarship on democratization in Latin America is that the process goes most smoothly when elites threatened by the transition—especially the military—are given a golden parachute. Above all, they need a guarantee that they will not wind up in jail if they relinquish power. The history of the democratizing great powers broadens this insight. Democratization was least likely to lead to war when the old elites saw a reasonably bright future for themselves in the new social order. British aristocrats, for example, had more of their wealth invested in commerce and industry than in agriculture, so they had many interests in common with the rising middle classes. They could face democratization with relative equanimity. In contrast, Prussia's capital-starved, small-scale Junker landholders had no choice but to rely on agricultural protection and military careers.

In today's context one of the most pressing threats to the elites of potentially democratizing authoritarian states stems from international efforts to prosecute them for crimes they committed under the old regime. In Rwanda and Burundi, for example, this was one of the factors that created an incentive for hard-liners to gamble on playing the ethnic conflict card as a way to hang on to power. In some transitional countries from the 1980s to the mid-1990s, such as Chile and South Africa, immunity deals encouraged old elites to relinquish their positions of power. More recently, however, international organizations, courts, and activist groups have been arguing that immunity arrangements do not apply to perpetrators of war crimes, genocide, torture, and other crimes against humanity. By indicting still-powerful figures like then Serbian president Slobodan Milosevic and by retroactively stripping immunity from former dictators like Chile's Augusto Pinochet, this new practice makes it difficult to offer credible golden parachutes to thugs who might in the future act as implacable spoilers of a democratic transition.

The transition to democracy proceeds more peacefully when the institutions needed for the functioning of a democratic society are already partially in place before mass-suffrage elections are held. South Africa, for example, experienced a relatively successful transition because of the legacy of well-developed, whites-only civic institutions that it inherited from the apartheid regime and expanded to include the whole population after the transition: a rationalized state bureaucracy, the rule of law, elections, a parliament, political parties, schools, and a professionalized media. In contrast,

Burundi, which had elections abruptly pressed upon its ethnic Tutsi minority dictatorship by international donors in 1993, had none of these institutions to build upon; as a result, within months of the elections, over one hundred thousand people were killed in ethnic strife. Wherever possible, the patient building of the institutional preconditions of democracy should precede the unleashing of competitive mass electoral politics.

Another top priority must be creating a free, competitive, and responsible marketplace of ideas in the newly democratizing states. Most of the war-prone democratizing great powers had pluralistic public debates, but the debates were skewed to favor groups with money, privileged access to the media, and proprietary control over information ranging from archives to intelligence about the military balance. Pluralism is not enough. Without a level playing field, pluralism simply creates the incentive and opportunity for privileged groups to propound self-serving myths, which historically have often taken a nationalist turn. One of the rays of hope in the Chechen affair was the alacrity with which Russian journalists exposed the costs of the fighting and the lies of the government and the military. Though elites should get a golden parachute regarding their pecuniary interests, they should be given no quarter on the battlefield of ideas. Mythmaking should be held up to the utmost scrutiny by aggressive journalists who maintain their credibility by scrupulously distinguishing fact from opinion and tirelessly verifying their sources. Promoting this kind of journalistic infrastructure is probably the most highly leveraged investment the West can make in a peaceful democratic transition.

Finally, the kind of ruling coalition that emerges in the course of democratization depends a great deal on the incentives created by the international environment. Both Germany and Japan started on the path toward liberal, stable democratization in the mid-1920s, encouraged by abundant opportunities for trade with and investment by the advanced democracies and by credible security treaties that defused nationalist scaremongering in domestic politics. When the international supports for free trade and democracy were yanked out in the late 1920s, their liberal coalitions collapsed. For China, whose democratization may occur in the context of expanding economic ties with the West, a steady Western commercial partnership and security presence is likely to play a major role in shaping the incentives of proto-democratic coalition politics.

In the long run the enlargement of the zone of stable democracy will probably enhance prospects for peace. In the short run much work remains to be done to minimize the dangers of the turbulent transition.

NOTES

1. Jack S. Levy, "Domestic Politics and War," *Journal of Interdisciplinary History* 18, no. 4 (spring 1988): 662.

2. Jack Snyder, *From Voting to Violence: Democratization and Nationalist Conflict* (New York: Norton, 2000), chaps. 5 and 6.

3. Ted Robert Gurr, *Peoples versus States: Minorities at Risk in the New Century* (Washington, D.C.: United States Institute of Peace Press, 2000), 293. Gurr considers Ethiopia as making a transition to "anocracy" (a partially democratic, mixed regime) in 1994. On Eritrea, see Ruth Iyob, "The Eritrean Experiment: A Cautious Pragmatism?" *Journal of Modern African Studies* 35, no. 4 (December 1997): 647–673.

4. Michael R. Gordon, "Russia Votes, Like It or Not: Chechnya War Fever Gives Pause in the West," *New York Times*, December 21, 1999, A1, A22.

5. Edward D. Mansfield and Jack Snyder, "Democratization and War," *Foreign Affairs* 74, no. 3

(May-June 1995): 79–97. As noted later, we have updated the statistical findings and commentary on contemporary events, but the historical and conceptual discussion here remains largely unchanged from that article.

6. See Edward D. Mansfield and Jack Snyder, "Democratization and the Danger of War," *International Security* 20, no. 1 (summer 1995): 5–38; and Mansfield and Snyder, "Democratization and War."

7. See Keith Jaggers and Ted Robert Gurr, "Tracking Democracy's Third Wave with the Polity III Data," *Journal of Peace Research* 32, no. 4 (1995): 469–482.

8. Ibid.

9. For the procedures used to code these variables, see Mansfield and Snyder, "Democratization and the Danger of War."

10. On the definition of and data on international wars, see Melvin Small and J. David Singer, *Resort to Arms: International and Civil Wars, 1816–1980* (Beverly Hills, Calif.: Sage Publications, 1982); and Singer and Small, "Correlates of War Project: International and Civil Wars Data, 1816–1992" (data set, stored at the Inter-University Consortium for Political and Social Research, Ann Arbor, Michigan, 1994).

11. For additional evidence on this score, see Edward D. Mansfield and Jack Snyder, "Democratic Transitions, Institutional Strength, and War" (typescript).

12. Alain Plessis, *The Rise and Fall of the Second Empire, 1852–1871* (Cambridge: Cambridge University Press, 1985), 146–147.

13. Sergei Karaganov, "Russia's Elites," in *Damage Limitation*, ed. Robert Blackwill and Sergei Karaganov (Berkeley: University of California Press, 1967), 250.

14. J. C. G. Rohl, *Germany without Bismarck* (Berkeley: University of California Press, 1967), 250.

15. Richard Cobden, letter to John Bright, October 1, 1854, quoted in John Morley, *The Life of Richard Cobden*, abridged ed. (London: Thomas Nelson), 311–312.

9

State Making, State Breaking, and State Failure

Mohammed Ayoob

TWO SIGNIFICANT REALITIES of the current international scene must form the backdrop to any discussion of the failure and disintegration of states and the problem of international order and governance in the last decade of the twentieth century. The first is the incontrovertible fact that the overwhelming majority of conflicts since the end of World War II have been located in the Third World. The second is the equally unassailable fact that most conflicts in the Third World either have been primarily intrastate in character or have possessed a substantial intrastate dimension, even if they appear to the outside observer to be interstate conflicts. This means that problems of international and domestic order have become inextricably intertwined during the current era and are likely to remain enmeshed well into the foreseeable future.

The validity of both these assertions is borne out by tabulations of wars and conflicts made by several scholars, including Kalevi J. Holsti and Evan Luard.[1] That these two trends—

concentration of conflicts in the Third World and the primacy of domestic sources of conflict —continued during the 1990s is confirmed by the figures presented in the *SIPRI Yearbook 1999,* which demonstrate that of the major armed conflicts that were waged in twenty-seven locations around the world in 1998, all but two were intrastate in character. The two exceptions, namely, the conflict between India and Pakistan over Kashmir and the border war between Ethiopia and Eritrea, are also intimately linked to the process of state and nation building in the countries concerned. This is especially true of the India-Pakistan case, where the Kashmir issue is inextricably tied to domestic political and security concerns. Almost all of these conflicts were located in the old or new Third World.[2] The new Third World refers to states in Central Asia, the Caucasus, and the Balkans that have emerged out of the disintegration of the Soviet Union and the dismemberment of Yugoslavia. There are abundant data, therefore, to support the conclusion that the overwhelming majority of conflicts in the international system since 1945 have been "a ubiquitous corollary of the birth, formation, and fracturing of Third World states."[3]

The end of the Cold War has led not to the irrelevance of the Third World as an explanatory category, but to its expansion as new states have emerged following the breakup of the Soviet Union and of Yugoslavia and as ethnic antagonisms that had been forced underground by the twin forces of Russian imperialism and Leninist ideology have resurfaced with a vengeance. In terms of their colonial background, the arbitrary construction of their boundaries by external powers, the lack of societal cohesion, their recent emergence into juridical statehood, and their stage of economic and political development, the states of the Caucasus and Central Asia and of the Balkans demonstrate political, economic, and social characteristics that are in many ways akin to those of the Asian, African, and Latin American states that have been traditionally considered as constituting the Third World. This is demonstrated above all by the developments in the 1990s in such disparate places as Kosovo and Chechnya.

STATE MAKING IN THE THIRD WORLD

The events of the past few years, by removing the Second World from the international equation, have helped present the dichotomy between the global core and the global periphery —the First World and the Third World—in very stark terms.[4] By removing the Cold War overlay from Third World conflicts and thus exposing their fundamental local dynamics, the end of bipolarity has also demonstrated the close linkage between these conflicts and the dynamics of state making (and its obverse, state breaking and state failure) currently under way in the global periphery.

However, the dichotomous representation of the First and Third Worlds that is currently fashionable hides the essential similarity in their process of state making, which has been (and is) crucial in determining the political trajectories of states. This point becomes clear if one compares the current situation in the Third World not with that prevailing within and among the industrial democracies today, but with the situation from the sixteenth to eighteenth centuries in Western Europe, when the earliest of the modern sovereign states were at a stage of state making that corresponded with the stage in which most Third World states find themselves today.[5]

The process of state making has been most succinctly defined by Youssef Cohen and colleagues in a seminal article published in 1981 as "primitive central state power accumulation."[6] Thus defined, state making must include the following:

- the expansion and consolidation of the territorial and demographic domain under a political authority, including the imposition of order on contested territorial and demographic space (war);
- the maintenance of order in the territory where, and over the population on whom, such order has been already imposed (policing); and
- the extraction of resources from the territory and the population under the control of the state, resources essential not only to support the war-making and policing activities undertaken by the state but also to maintain the apparatuses of state necessary to carry on routine administration, deepen the state's penetration of society, and serve symbolic purposes (taxation).[7]

All three broad categories of activities, however, depend on the state's success in monopolizing and concentrating the means of coercion in its own hands in the territory and among the population it controls. That is why the accumulation of power becomes so crucial to the state-making enterprise; the more primitive the stage of state building, the more primitive and, therefore, the more coercive the strategies employed to accumulate and concentrate power in the hands of the agents of the state. Cohen and colleagues stated in 1981: "The extent to which an expansion of state power will generate collective violence depends on the *level* of state power prior to that expansion. . . . The lower the initial level of state power, the stronger the relationship between the *rate* of state expansion and collective violence."[8] One needs to be reminded that the violence generated during the process of state making is the result of actions undertaken both by the state and by recalcitrant elements within the population that forcefully resist the state's attempt to impose order.

The inherent similarity in the logic of the state-building process provides us explanations for the current replication by Third World states of several dimensions of the early modern European experience of state making. Simultaneously, the difference in the pace at which state building has to be undertaken and completed in the Third World and the dramatically changed international environment in which Third World state making has to proceed explain the divergence in other dimensions from the earlier European model of state building. The similarities and the differences are equally important, as is the bearing they have on problems of authority and governance within Third World states.

It should be noted that in most of Europe, state making usually antedated the emergence of nations and nation-states by a couple of centuries. This is why it is essential not to confuse the building of modern sovereign states with the emergence of nation-states in the nineteenth and twentieth centuries. Charles Tilly has highlighted the distinction between modern sovereign (or, as he would call them, "national") states and nation-states. Tilly defines the former as "relatively centralized, differentiated, and autonomous organizations successfully claiming priority in the use of force within large, contiguous, and clearly bounded territories." Nation-states, on the other hand, are those "whose peoples share a strong linguistic, religious, and symbolic identity."[9] Nationalism, the necessary condition for the establishment of nation-states, although not of sovereign states, has been defined by Ernest Gellner as "primarily a principle which holds that the political and the national unit should be congruent."[10]

Sovereign and relatively centralized states that have performed successfully over a long period of time—and have therefore knit their people together in terms of historical memories, legal codes, language, religion, and so forth—may evolve into nation-states or at least provide the necessary conditions for the emergence of nation-states, but they are not synonymous with the latter. Historical evidence has convincingly demonstrated that in almost all cases in Europe, with the exception of the Balkans (an exception that may provide the clue to the current violence and strife in that region), the emergence of the modern sovereign state was the precondition for the formation of the nation.[11]

This generalization applied as much to latecomers such as Germany as to the earliest examples of modern states such as England and France. Without the central role performed by the Prussian state, Germany would probably have remained nothing more than a geographic or cultural expression. The similarity between the German experience on the one hand and the French experience on the other has been summed up well by Cornelia Navari: "When Hegel insisted that it was the state that created the nation, he was looking backwards to the history of France, not forward to the history of Germany. When Germany was unified 'from above' in 1870 and the Reich was formed, this way of proceeding did not appear to most Germans to be at variance with the experience of their Western neighbors—a substitution of Union 'by force' for the 'organic growth' of France and England. It appeared to be a repetition of it, differing only in that it was less bloody. Here, as there, the state was moving outwards into diverse feudal remnants of the old order, dissolving them, making all obedient to the same law."[12]

The chronological sequence of the establishment of the sovereign state and the evolution of nationalism in the Third World bears very close resemblance to that of modern Europe, with the state taking clear historical precedence over the nation. As Anthony Smith has put it very succinctly, "the western model is essentially a 'state system' rather than a 'nation system'; and this has been its fateful legacy to Africa and Asia." Smith goes on to point out that despite the differences in geopolitical and cultural terms between Europe and the Third World, "the central point . . . of the western experience for contemporary African and Asian social and political change has been the primacy and dominance of the specialized, territorially defined, and coercively monopolistic state, operating within a broader system of similar states bent on fulfilling their dual functions of internal regulation and external defence (or aggression)."[13]

In this context, it is instructive to note Tilly's point that "the building of states in Western Europe cost tremendously in death, suffering, loss of rights, and unwilling surrender of land, goods, or labor. . . . The fundamental reason for the high cost of European state building was its beginning in the midst of a decentralized, largely peasant social structure. Building differentiated, autonomous, centralized organizations with effective control of territories entailed eliminating or subordinating thousands of semiautonomous authorities. . . . Most of the European population resisted each phase of the creation of strong states."[14] Tilly's description of conditions in Europe at the birth of modern sovereign states has an uncanny resemblance to present conditions in many Third World societies. It thus helps to explain why if one arranges the current state-building strategies employed in the Third World on a continuum ranging from coercion to persuasion

(with the two ends representing ideal types), even those states like India that fall relatively close to the persuasive end of the continuum are forced to rely on significant amounts of coercion —as witnessed in Punjab, Kashmir, and the northeastern states—to entrench and consolidate the authority of the state in regions where it faces, or has faced, major challenges.

In order to replicate the process by which relatively centralized modern states are created, Third World state makers need above all two things: lots of time and a relatively free hand to persuade, cajole, and coerce the disparate populations under their nominal rule to accept the legitimacy of state boundaries and institutions, to accept the right of the state to extract resources from them, and to let the state regulate the more important aspects of their lives. Unfortunately for Third World state elites, neither of these two commodities is available to them in adequate measure.

Our point regarding the availability of time becomes clear if we examine the amount of time it took for the states of Western Europe to emerge as full-fledged sovereign states, enjoying the habitual obedience of their populations, basically secure in the legitimacy of their borders and institutions, and, therefore, in a position where they could respond positively to societal demands, since these demands no longer ran counter to the logic of state building and the accumulation of power in the hands of the state.

It was not until the beginning of the twentieth century that the states of Western Europe and its offshoots in North America emerged as the responsive and representative modern states that we know them to be today—the end products of the state-making process that had unfolded for at least three hundred or four hundred years. Although leading historians of state building in Europe differ about the exact dating of the origins, in the sense of beginnings, of the modern sovereign state, there is little argument about the fact that "it took four to five centuries for European states to overcome their weaknesses, to remedy their administrative deficiencies, and to bring lukewarm loyalty up to the white heat of nationalism."[15]

Unfortunately for Third World state makers, their states cannot afford the luxury of prolonging the traumatic and costly experience of state making over hundreds of years à la Europe. The demands of competition with established modern states and the demonstration effect of the existence of socially cohesive, politically responsive, and administratively effective states in the industrialized world make it almost obligatory for Third World states to reach their goal within the shortest time possible or risk international ridicule and permanent peripherality within the system of states. In this context it is valuable to point out that there was no dearth of "Somalias" and "Liberias" in seventeenth- and eighteenth-century Europe.

The pioneers of European state making (although not the latecomers such as Germany and Italy) were remarkably free from systemic pressures and demonstration effects, because all the leading contenders for statehood—England, France, Spain, Holland—were basically in the same boat, trying to navigate the same uncharted sea. Where European states did not have this opportunity and had to telescope together some of the sequential phases that constituted the process of state building, they suffered from a "cumulation of crises."[16] This applied particularly to the states of Germany and Italy, which emerged as unified sovereign entities only in the closing decades of the nineteenth century and were immediately faced with the pressures of mass politics. In fact, it can be argued that the emergence of Italian fascism and German Nazism was a result of the Italian and German state elites' inability in the first two decades of the twentieth century to respond successfully, in a context of mass politics, to the accumulated crises threatening their respective states.[17]

If this was the case with Germany, which had the well-established Prussian state at its core, one can well imagine the enormity of the challenge faced by the postcolonial states of the Third World. The latter's problems have been compounded by the fact that they are under pressure to demonstrate adequate statehood quickly; to perform the task of state making in a humane, civilized, and consensual fashion; and to do all this in an era of mass politics. The inadequacy of the time element and the consequent fact that several sequential phases involved in the state-making process have had to be collapsed or telescoped together into one mammoth state-building enterprise go a long way toward explaining the problems of authority and governance faced by the Third World states today.[18] Furthermore, the demand for humane treatment of subject populations during the early stages of state building has made that task in the Third World enormously difficult and complicated.

Given the short time at the disposal of state makers in the Third World and the consequent acceleration in their state-making efforts necessary to demonstrate that they are moving speedily toward effective statehood, crises erupt simultaneously, become unmanageable as the load they put on the political system outruns the political and military capabilities of the state, and lead to an accumulation of crises, which further erodes the legitimacy of the already fragile postcolonial state.

INTERNATIONAL NORMS OF STATEHOOD AND HUMAN RIGHTS

In addition to these internal factors, the workings of the international system, especially the policies adopted by the superpowers during the Cold War era, have complicated the process of state making in the Third World. By exporting superpower rivalry to the Third World in the form of proxy wars, both interstate and intrastate, and by transferring weapons to governments and insurgents in fragile polities in volatile regional environments, the bipolar global balance during the Cold War era greatly accentuated the insecurities and instabilities in the Third World.[19]

Even more important, certain international norms that have crystallized relatively recently have also had mixed effects on the security and stability of Third World states. Some of these new norms were actually adopted as a result of the entry of the postcolonial states into the international system and because of the pressure generated by the Third World majority, both within international forums like the United Nations General Assembly and outside.

The first of these norms relates to the inalienability of juridical sovereignty or statehood once conferred by international law and symbolized by membership in the United Nations. The sanctity of the borders of postcolonial states forms the logical corollary of this norm. While this international norm has done much to preserve the existence of several Third World states that may have otherwise been inviable, it has also, paradoxically, added to the security predicament of the Third World state. This point can best be understood by recalling that the elimination of states considered inviable, either because of their internal contradictions or because their existence did not suit great power aspirations, was perfectly acceptable to the European international community virtually through the end of World War I.

The international consensus on the alienability of juridical statehood began to change during the interwar period and crystallized after World War II in the context of the decolonization of Asia and Africa. Colonies, once granted independence, acquired the right to exist as sovereign entities, even if many of them (especially in Africa) did not possess "much in the way of empirical statehood, disclosed by a capacity for effective and civil government."[20] This change has meant that while this international norm, which crystallized after World War II, has protected the legal existence of postcolonial states without regard to their internal cohesiveness or the effectiveness of their domestic control, it has been unable to solve the security problems that such states face as a result of the contradictions present within their boundaries and inherent in their state-making process.

It is worth noting here that this guarantee encompassing juridical statehood and territorial integrity has begun to weaken in the post–Cold War era. This has been witnessed in a wide array of cases ranging from northern Iraq to Kosovo where the international community, led by the major Western powers, has intervened in contravention of the principles of state sovereignty and the territorial integrity of established states. However, this change in international norms, if consolidated, is unlikely to alleviate the Third World's security predicament. In fact, it is likely to worsen that situation considerably and to add to the prevalent instability and disorder in the Third World, because it has become linked to the issue of the right of ethnic groups to self-determination. It appears, therefore, that the Third World is caught in a no-win situation as far as this set of international norms is concerned.

A second set of international norms that has affected the security of the Third World is related to the issue of human rights, with primary emphasis on civil and political rights. While the modern conception of human rights can be traced to the natural law approach developed in eighteenth-century Europe, the recent normative force that human rights have acquired in the international arena is the result of the acceptance by the vast majority of states of the existence and the validity of such rights for all human beings, irrespective of their status as citizens of particular states.[21]

The changing attitude toward human rights as a legitimate concern of the international community has meant that they needed to be brought within the ambit of international law and rescued from their status as the exclusive preserve of sovereign states in relation to their own citizens. This led to their inclusion in the Preamble and Article 1 of the United Nations Charter and to their codification in the

Universal Declaration of Human Rights, adopted in 1948, and the two International Covenants on Human Rights that were opened for signature and ratification in 1966 and became operative in 1976.

This was a major development in the evolution of norms that govern the international system, for it acknowledged more clearly than ever before that individuals, as well as states, could now be considered subjects of international law. It also signified the international acceptance of the principle that individuals and groups have rights that are independent of their membership of individual states and that derive not from their national status but from their status as members of the human species.

The major problem with the implementation of human rights in the Third World is the fact that the concept of human rights owes its empirical validity to the existence and successful functioning of the industrialized, representative, and responsive states of Western Europe and North America. These states set the standards for effective statehood, as well as for the humane and civilized treatment of their citizens. They do so by their demonstrated success in simultaneously meeting the basic needs of the large majority of their populations, protecting their human rights, and promoting and guaranteeing political participation. But these states have, by and large, successfully completed their state-building process, are politically satiated and economically affluent, and possess unconditional legitimacy in the eyes of the overwhelming majority of their populations. They can therefore afford to adopt liberal standards of state behavior in relation to their populations, because they are reasonably secure in the knowledge that societal demands will not run counter to state interests and will not put state structures and institutions in any grave jeopardy.

What are currently considered in the West to be norms of civilized state behavior—including those pertaining to human rights of individuals and groups—are, in the Third World, often in contradiction with the imperatives of state making. These imperatives, as has been pointed out more than once, not only sanction but frequently require the use of violent means against recalcitrant domestic groups and individual citizens. Furthermore, the international norm upholding human rights runs directly counter to the norm that prescribes the inalienability of juridical statehood for Third World states.[22] While the latter is uncompromising in upholding the legality of the existence of Third World states within their colonially constructed boundaries, the former undermines the political legitimacy of these same states by prescribing standards and yardsticks in terms that most Third World states, struggling to perform the minimum tasks of maintaining political order, will be incapable of meeting for many decades to come.

Moreover, the simultaneous but contradictory operation of the two norms contributes to the creation and augmentation of internal discontent within Third World states. It does so by, on the one hand, forcing all the diverse and dissatisfied elements within Third World states to remain within their postcolonial boundaries and, on the other, encouraging these very elements to make political, administrative, and economic demands on the states that the states cannot respond to either because they lack the capabilities to do so or because doing so could seriously jeopardize their territorial integrity.

One can make the argument on behalf of Third World states, still struggling to translate their juridical statehood into empirical statehood, that the case for human rights (whether of individuals or groups) and against the state's use of violent means to impose order is not as morally unassailable as it may appear at first sight. This point can be made most effectively in the context of the failed states phenomenon, in which state structures have completely collapsed.[23] In these cases it can be demonstrated that in the absence of even rudimentarily effective states to provide a minimum degree of political order—as in Lebanon for the fifteen years of civil war, or as currently in Somalia, Liberia, or Sierra Leone, to mention just a few examples—the concept of human rights remains nothing more than a pure abstraction. In such a context the human rights ideal is impossible to implement even minimally, because in the absence of the sovereign a truly Hobbesian state of nature prevails, and the very survival of large segments of populations cannot be ensured.

These comments should not be taken as an apologia for authoritarian regimes in the Third World that ostensibly emphasize order at the expense of both justice and political participation. Authoritarian regimes often contribute a great deal to the creation and augmentation of disorder in Third World states despite paying lip service to the objective of maintaining and promoting order. Iran under the shah, the Philippines under Marcos, Zaire under Mobutu, and Nicaragua under Somoza—to cite but a few instances—all provide good examples of this tendency.

It is also true that most regimes in the Third World—especially authoritarian ones, but not excluding such democratic governments as that in India under Indira Gandhi in the mid-1970s—attempt to portray threats to their regimes as threats to the state. Discerning analysts, therefore, must carefully distinguish between issues of regime security and those of state security. However, in many cases, given the lack of unconditional legitimacy both of the regime and of the state structure in the Third World and the close perceptual connection between regime and state as far as the majority of the state's population is concerned, the line between regime security and state security becomes so thin, and the interplay between the two so dense, that it is virtually impossible to disentangle one from the other. As one perceptive scholar pointed out in connection with the Middle East, "those who rule must attempt to encourage loyalty to the state, of which they hope themselves to be the chief beneficiaries,

while at the same time seeking to disguise the fact that their system of power, and thus the identity of the political structure itself, frequently owes more to the old ties of sectarian and tribal loyalty."[24] In many such countries the fall of the regime is likely to signal the failure of the state as well; any student of Tudor England or Bourbon France will find this phenomenon very familiar.

ETHNONATIONAL SELF-DETERMINATION

The human rights issue raises a further problem. Given the multiethnic nature of most Third World states, if human rights are interpreted as group rights and, therefore, are seen to include the right to ethnonational self-determination, they are likely to pose grave threats to the territorial integrity and juridical statehood of postcolonial states, once again pitting one set of international norms against another. The renewed legitimation of the notion of ethnonational self-determination following the end of the Cold War—especially in Europe, symbolized by the prompt recognition accorded to the successor states to the Soviet Union and Yugoslavia and the separation of Slovakia from the Czech Republic—is likely to give a fillip to demands for ethnic separatism in the Third World.

Given the latent tensions between ethnicity and state-defined nationalism even in functioning federal polities such as India and the clear contradiction between ethnonationalism and state-defined nationalism in much of the Third World, any development anywhere in the international arena that may encourage ethnic separatist demands in the context of state and regime fragilities prevalent in the Third World is bound to add to the great strains already existing within these polities.[25] The veracity of this assertion is borne out by the fact that "under the banner of self-determination, there are active movements in more than sixty countries—one-third of the total roster of nations—to achieve full sovereignty or some lesser degree of 'minority' rights. A number of these movements have developed into ongoing civil wars."[26]

In this context, the international community's (and especially the major powers') endorsement of the doctrine of ethnonational self-determination—even if limited to exceptional cases as in the Balkans, the former Soviet Union, and the former Czechoslovakia—is bound to augment the challenge to the legitimacy of the principle that postcolonial states in their present form are territorially inviolable. The effects of such a contagion spreading have been summed up in a Council on Foreign Relations study that concluded that "while the creation of some new states may be necessary or inevitable, the fragmentation of international society into hundreds of independent territorial entities is a recipe for an even more dangerous and anarchic world."[27]

A major problem with ethnonational self-determination relates to the definition of the ethnic self seeking to determine its future. The self-perception and self-definition of ethnicity is usually subject to change, depending on the context in which it operates at any point in time. This is what Crawford Young has referred to as "the dynamic and changing character of contemporary ethnicity: Far from representing a fixed and immutable set of static social facts, cultural pluralism is itself evolving in crucial ways and is in major respects contextual, situational, and circumstantial."[28] Therefore, to link such a potent ideology as that of self-determination to a malleable idea like that of ethnicity—and then to legitimize this combination by reference to the principle of human rights of groups—is bound to introduce even greater disorder in the Third World than is already present, because it endows the demands of every disgruntled ethnic group with the legitimacy of the ideal of national self-determination. The danger is that this is exactly what the renewed popularity of the idea

of ethnonational self-determination may end up achieving, to the great detriment of both order and justice in the Third World.

The problem is further confounded by the fact that given the ethnic mixtures of populations in most countries, hardly any pure ethnic homelands still exist. This fact contradicts the ethnonationalists' assumption that "the earth's entire population, or most of it, divides into a finite number of distinct, homogeneous peoples. It follows that the world's ideal condition consists of that finite number of nation-states."[29] Attempts at ethnonational self-determination are, therefore, bound to run into resistance from ethnic minorities in presumed ethnic homelands. As William Pfaff has succinctly put it: "The ethnic state is a product of the political imagination; it does not exist in reality. . . . The idea of the ethnic nation thus is a permanent provocation to war."[30] Such conflict is expected to result either in virulent forms of ethnic cleansing or in the carving out of microstates from the ministates established on the basis of ethnic nationalism, or both.

QUASI-STATES AND FAILED STATES

Related to the issue of ethnonational self-determination is the failed-states phenomenon. Jack Snyder has described the link between the two by describing ethnic nationalism as "the default option." According to Snyder, ethnic nationalism "predominates when institutions collapse, when existing institutions are not fulfilling people's basic needs, and when satisfactory alternative structures are not readily available."[31] While this may not provide the total explanation for the revival of ethnonationalism, it does capture a very major ingredient that has contributed to the recent popularity of the ethnonationalist ideology, namely, the lack of effective statehood. This is true not only in the case of the components of the former Soviet Union and of the former Yugoslavia, but also in many parts of the Third World.

The lack of effective statehood was responsible for the emergence of what Robert Jackson has termed "quasi-states" in the Third World.[32] These quasi-states can now clearly be seen as precursors of failed states in the global South.

The end of the Cold War has had an important impact on the transformation of some of these quasi-states into failed states. This is especially true in those states that had witnessed high levels of superpower involvement in the military sphere, including the arena of arms transfers, during the Cold War. At the height of the Cold War, the superpowers attempted to strengthen client governments in internally fragmented states, often seeking to maintain a semblance of stability within countries that were allied with one superpower or the other. One major instrument of such support was the transfer of large quantities of relatively sophisticated arms to friendly regimes. In several instances such arms transfers led to countervailing transfers of weaponry by the rival superpower to forces opposed to the central authorities. Afghanistan during the 1980s came to epitomize this action-reaction phenomenon.[33]

Past superpower policies of pouring arms into fragmented polities have, however, become a major source of instability and disorder in the post–Cold War period. The presence of large quantities of relatively sophisticated weaponry (ranging from AK-47s to Stinger missiles) and the withdrawal of superpower support to weak and vulnerable regimes—support that was essential to prevent the central authorities from being overwhelmed by domestic rivals who, in turn, were divided among themselves—created near-total anarchy in countries such as Afghanistan and Somalia, where central authority completely collapsed, thereby turning these quasi-states into failed states.

Furthermore, the failure of the international community, principally the major powers and international organizations, to prevent and control the flow of small arms, which are responsible for the majority of deaths in current conflicts, is exploited by private arms dealers and transnational criminal cartels as well as states interested in making fast money in this murky area of arms trade. This unregulated arms bazaar not only adds to the misery of the populace but also undermines state authority in countries and regions most vulnerable to internal conflicts.[34]

The relationship between state failure and internal conflict is, however, not a one-way street with the former inevitably leading to the latter. The relationship is in many cases circular, with the two phenomena feeding upon each other and state weakness providing the political space for the intensification of conflicts among political factions and/or ethnic groups, and the latter in turn further eroding the capacity of the state to maintain order and provide security to its citizens. Suffering from acute insecurity, individuals often turn to political factions, ethnic groups, or even criminal gangs (and sometimes it is difficult to distinguish among the three categories) to provide them with protection in exchange for their loyalty and contribution—financial, physical, or both—to the "war effort."

There is another dimension of state failure that has a major impact upon the level of conflict within societies. Alex de Waal has pointed this out with great clarity in relation to Africa. He has argued that economic crisis in Africa has meant that "governments find it more difficult to sustain and control armies, which then turn to local sources of provisioning. These include requisitioning, looting and taxing populations, involvement in commerce, and diverting humanitarian aid. Though the causes of war in Africa and the aims of the combatants are still almost exclusively phrased in terms of achieving state power and affecting constitutional change, the realities on the ground reflect more intense predatory behaviour by soldiers."[35] This search for "survival" on the part of unpaid or poorly paid soldiers, who command great coercive power in relation to the rest of the population, contributes to the reality and perception of state failure while serving a "rational" purpose for those engaged in it.

Finally, state failure, like state making, must be viewed as a process, not an event. In William Zartman's words, it is akin to "a long-term degenerative disease"[36] rather than something that occurs at a particular point in time. Such an understanding of state failure will help one comprehend the fact that, as the Lebanese example demonstrates, the process is not irreversible. Furthermore, it will help one to understand why this process is usually accompanied by prolonged "uncivil wars" during which political factions fight over what they presume to be the state's carcass and the state attempts to revive itself by drawing upon its residual capacity and legitimacy. If one faction succeeds in by and large subjugating the others, it usually dons the mantle of the state in order to legitimize the concentration of coercive power in its hands.

Similarly, if one views conflict and war as process and not merely in terms of final outcomes, one has to conclude that there are usually groups, factions, and individuals that benefit economically, as well as politically, from the prolongation of such wars. They come to acquire a vested interest in perpetuating such conflicts. This is why "conflict entrepreneurs, as well as conflict victims, must be part of any analytical framework" devised to study what has been termed "complex political emergencies."[37] Such a perspective can help unravel the "rationality" behind what appear to the outside observer to be totally irrational conflicts.

DEMOCRATIZATION IN THE THIRD WORLD

Many state elites in the Third World seem to have realized during the past decade that the only way to prevent state making from being transformed into state failure is to grant greater political participation to those sectors of society —whether ethnic or socioeconomic—that were heretofore excluded from the exercise of political power. The recent wave of democratization in the Third World is in substantial part the result of the realization among the ruling elites in the developing countries that the survival of their states and regimes is crucially dependent upon defusing the severe crisis of legitimacy that they face in the contemporary context.

It would be too naive to suggest, however, that democratization—defined in terms of increasing guarantees for the exercise of civil and political liberties and in terms of political participation through the medium of competitive electoral politics—by itself, and in all contexts, will succeed in neutralizing ethnic separatism.[38] The success of the democratic experiment in defusing ethnic tensions will, therefore, depend on a number of factors, identified by Renée de Nevers as including "the speed with which ethnic issues are recognized; the level of ethnic tension when the democratization process begins; the size and power of different ethnic groups within the state; the ethnic composition of the previous regime and its opposition; the political positions of the leaders of the main ethnic groups; the presence or absence of external ethnic allies; and the ethnic composition of the military."[39]

There is, however, another side to the democratization coin. The demands of state building and democratization can be reconciled only if the democratizing state in the Third World is able to monopolize the instruments of violence within its territories, thus preventing dissident groups from attempting to change the state's boundaries when political controls are relaxed. This monopoly over instruments of violence is essential because "often the first act of forces liberated by the introduction of democracy is to seek some permanent escape from the state they see as having oppressed them."[40]

This is where the most severe problems are likely to arise, even if democratic political systems become the norm rather than the exception in the Third World. Democratic and (even more important) democratizing regimes cannot afford to be seen as weak when confronted by separatist challenges and, in the final analysis, cannot give up their right to lay down and enforce the rules (even if some of these have been negotiated with the opponents of the state) by which the game of politics is to be played within the boundaries of states over which they preside. Otherwise, the "democratic center may be questioned for its inefficiency in creating or its weakness in handling the secessionist crisis, opening the way for military intervention."[41]

This point is inadequately understood by most proponents of democratization in the Third World, who tend to equate democratic states with weak states on the assumption that strong states are bound to be autocratic by nature.[42] By making this assumption they fail to learn from the European experience that democracy emerged as the final stage of the state-building process and not at the expense of state building. Even in today's context, when democratization cannot wait until state building is completed, it cannot thrive in the absence of the political order that only a strongly entrenched state can provide.

Democratization, therefore, must complement rather than contradict the process of state making; without the political order that can be provided only by effective states, the gains of democratization cannot be sustained. Anarchies —as the examples of Lebanon, Somalia, Liberia, and Afghanistan clearly demonstrate—are no respecters of democratic values.

However, the reconciliation of the two imperatives of the consolidation of state power and democratization is not, and will not be, an easy task even if tremendous goodwill is present on all sides. Major tensions are bound to arise between state elites and their ethnic and political opponents who would like to put significant curbs on the power of the central state. In addition, where separatist insurgencies are already under way, major problems between separatists and democratizing central governments are likely to center around two basic

questions: What is the guarantee that groups espousing separatism will indeed surrender all arms and reconcile themselves to autonomous or semiautonomous status that will continue to be essentially dependent upon the good faith and the continuing political sagacity of the central government? What is the guarantee that central authorities, after persuading separatist ethnic groups to lay down their arms and thus overcoming immediate internal security crises, will continue to abide by their commitment to popular political participation, the constitutional protection of minority rights, and regional autonomy?

The answers provided to both questions by the Third World's historical record do not leave much room for optimism. Furthermore, if one goes by the earlier European experience, one is likely to conclude that the historical juncture at which most Third World states find themselves today is unlikely to permit a great deal of ethnic accommodation and political participation. These two processes usually run counter to the overriding imperative of consolidating state power and fashioning a state that is sovereign, not merely juridically but also empirically. However, one can make an effective argument that the late-twentieth-century context is so dramatically different from the late-eighteenth- or even the late-nineteenth-century context that radically new solutions must be found for this dilemma.

In other words, the problem of reconciling the demands of state making with those of democratization and human rights—as well as with demands for regional autonomy, devolution of powers, and protection of minority group rights—will have to be addressed much more creatively, and mutually acceptable solutions will have to be found, if the twin specters of failed states and destructive ethnonationalism are to be kept at bay. Above all, this means that the trajectories of democratization (including the preservation of group rights and local autonomy for substate units), on the one hand, and of the consolidation of coercive power and concentration of legitimate authority under the control of the state, on the other, must not diverge radically. In fact, they should ideally become mutually legitimizing agents, with democratization legitimizing the greater concentration of authority in the hands of the state and the concentration of centralized power legitimizing and facilitating the loosening of political controls and the guaranteeing of political and civil rights to the citizenry.

Most important, the two processes should not be allowed to become the polar opposites of each other. Faced with a stark choice between the territorial integrity of the state and democratization, state elites are invariably bound to opt for territorial integrity over democratization. Where the processes of territorial integrity and democracy collide, democratization cannot prevail without the disintegration of the state. Therefore, in order for the strategy of democratization to work successfully without threatening the disintegration of states, the state elites' decision to democratize must be firmly linked to the negotiated surrender of separatist groups where they exist. The disarming of such groups should proceed in tandem with the implementation of any plans for autonomy or devolution of powers that may have been negotiated between the parties.

THE ROLE OF THE INTERNATIONAL COMMUNITY IN DEMOCRATIZATION

The international community, working through the United Nations, can play a constructive role in encouraging reconciliation between state building and democratization. It can do so if it adopts a restrictive approach toward recognizing new political entities that attempt to break away from established states in the Third World. A too-permissive approach to state breaking, as witnessed in the early 1990s in the case of the former Yugoslavia, will add to conflict and anarchy rather than preserve international order. Colonially imposed state boundaries may be an iniquitous way of delineating the borders of Third World states, but every other alternative appears to be infinitely worse.

The United Nations must not fall into the trap of giving legitimacy to demands for secession from member-states unless the terms have been peacefully negotiated with the parent state. Exceptions like Eritrea, East Timor, or Kosovo must not influence, let alone determine, the norms of international behavior. Eritrea was a special case because its separation was negotiated with the post-Mengistu regime in Ethiopia. Furthermore, Eritrea regained the colonially crafted political identity within the colonial boundaries that had been compromised in 1952 by the internationally sponsored merger of the former Italian colony with the Ethiopian empire and the subsequent flagrant violation by Addis Ababa of Eritrean autonomy that had formed an integral part of the merger agreement. However, despite its peaceful separation from Ethiopia in the early 1990s, by the late 1990s Eritrea's relations with Ethiopia had deteriorated once again to such an extent that the two countries fought a bloody border war that has had tremendous adverse consequences for the economies of both states.

East Timor was also not a part of the Indonesian postcolonial state. Unlike the rest of Indonesia, which had been a Dutch colony, East Timor was a Portuguese colony that was forcibly annexed by Indonesia in 1975 when Portugal withdrew from the territory. Although it took twenty-five years for East Timor to regain its independence within its erstwhile colonial borders, the episode demonstrated the deep impact of colonial structures on shaping postcolonial national identities.

Kosovo is an unfinished business from the disintegration of Yugoslavia. The division of Yugoslavia into ethnically defined states led on the one hand to major civil conflict in Bosnia and on the other to the assertion of Kosovo's ethnic nationalism. The latter assertion, legitimized by the ethnic division of Yugoslavia, became particularly intense in the context of the Serbian attempt to marginalize politically and economically the large Kosovar Albanian majority in the province by reneging on its autonomous status. This forced the Albanians, who formed 90 percent of the population, to live in subordination both to the Serb minority in Kosovo and to the Serbian government in Belgrade. Had the multiethnic Yugoslav federation not been dismantled, the world would not have been faced with the ethnic cleansing in Bosnia, the Serb atrocities on the Kosovar Albanians, and the international intervention to prevent the repetition of ethnic cleansing in Kosovo.

All these cases also clearly demonstrate that self-determination turns into secession when democratic rights are denied to the people. The political systems of Ethiopia, Indonesia, and Serbia were all authoritarian in character during the periods relevant to this discussion. This factor seems to have contributed substantially in forcing the disaffected elements into armed rebellion in the absence of legitimate avenues for the expression of their grievances. Democratic governance, because of its inherent capacity to empower individuals and groups even in the most imperfect of circumstances, has the potential to act as a safety valve, often, although not always, successfully preventing the demand for self-determination from being transformed into one of secession.

To conclude, international norms and the policies of international actors—primarily great powers and international institutions—can play a crucial role in preserving international order by persuading domestic protagonists to make deals without violating the sovereignty of existing states. Above all, the international community can strengthen the juridical status and bolster the political authority of Third World states by refusing to countenance secessionist demands while trying to persuade all parties to accept the notion that self-determination must be delinked from secession and should be defined in terms

of empowering those segments of the population that have been denied access to political and economic power. In other words, self-determination should be perceived as synonymous with democratization (and its attendant power-sharing arrangements) rather than with the breakup of existing states.

This attitude will send clear signals to all concerned that the sovereign existence of post-colonial states is an essential prerequisite for the creation and maintenance of both domestic and international order. It will also signal that regimes that do not demonstrate a willingness to democratize must be ready to face international opprobrium, pariah status, and even sanctions. Such a stance on the part of the international community is necessary to prevent the Third World from sliding into greater anarchy. For, above all, it must be recognized that the problem of order in the Third World cannot be tackled by trying to transcend the Westphalian model (a world made up of sovereign states) but by attempting to strengthen it. The root cause of disorder in the Third World is linked to the inadequacy of state authority and not to the excessive use of state power. The augmentation of authority usually leads to a decrease in the reliance on force by the state because, as Robert Jackman has argued, power without force is the true measure of the political capacity of states.[43]

NOTES

1. Kalevi J. Holsti, *Peace and War: Armed Conflicts and International Order, 1648–1989* (Cambridge: Cambridge University Press, 1991), table 11.1, 274–278; and Evan Luard, *War in International Society: A Study in International Sociology* (London: I. B. Tauris, 1986), appendix 5, 442–446.

2. Margareta Sollenberg, Peter Wallensteen, and Andres Jato, "Major Armed Conflicts," in *SIPRI [Stockholm International Peace Research Institute] Yearbook 1999: World Armaments and Disarmament* (Oxford: Oxford University Press, 1999), 15.

3. Kalevi J. Holsti, "International Theory and War in the Third World," in *The Insecurity Dilemma: National Security of Third World States,* ed. Brian L. Job (Boulder, Colo.: Lynne Rienner, 1992), 38.

4. Shahram Chubin has made a similar argument forcefully in "The South and the New World Order," *Washington Quarterly* 16, no. 4 (autumn 1993): 87–107.

5. For greater detail on this argument, see Mohammed Ayoob, "The Security Predicament of the Third World State: Reflections on State Making in a Comparative Perspective," in *Insecurity Dilemma,* 63–80.

6. Youssef Cohen, Brian R. Brown, and A. F. K. Organski, "The Paradoxical Nature of State Making: The Violent Creation of Order," *American Political Science Review* 75, no. 4 (1981): 902.

7. For expanded discussions of the process of state making and its relationship to organized violence, see Keith Jaggers, "War and the Three Faces of Power: War Making and State Making in Europe and the Americas," *Comparative Political Studies* 25, no. 1 (April 1992): 26–62; and Charles Tilly, "War Making and State Making as Organized Crime," in *Bringing the State Back In*, ed. Peter B. Evans, Dietrich Rueschemeyer, and Theda Skocpol (New York: Cambridge University Press, 1985), 169–191.

8. Cohen et al., "Paradoxical Nature of State Making," 905 (emphasis in the original).

9. Charles Tilly, *Coercion, Capital, and European States, AD 990–1990* (Cambridge, Mass.: Basil Blackwell, 1990), 43.

10. Ernest Gellner, *Nations and Nationalism* (Ithaca, N.Y.: Cornell University Press, 1983), 1.

11. For details of this argument and the data on which it is based, see Charles Tilly, ed., *The Formation of National States in Western Europe* (Princeton, N.J.: Princeton University Press, 1975). See also Cornelia Navari, "The Origins of the Nation-State," in *The Nation-State: The Formation of Modern Politics,* ed. Leonard Tivey (Oxford: Martin Robertson, 1981), 13–38.

12. Navari, "Origins of the Nation-State," 34.

13. Anthony D. Smith, *State and Nation in the Third World* (New York: St. Martin's Press, 1983), 11, 17.

14. Charles Tilly, "Reflections on the History of European State Making," in *Formation of National States in Western Europe,* 71.

15. Joseph R. Strayer, *On the Medieval Origins of the Modern State* (Princeton, N.J.: Princeton University Press, 1970), 57.

16. Stein Rokkan, "Dimensions of State Formation and Nation Building: A Possible Paradigm for Research on Variations within Europe," in *Formation of National States in Western Europe,* 586.

17. For theoretically informed accounts of the "cumulation of crises" in Italy and Germany, see the chapters on Italy and Germany by Raymond Grew and John R. Gillis, respectively, in *Crises of Political Development in Europe and the United States,* ed. Raymond Grew (Princeton, N.J.: Princeton University Press, 1978).

18. The earliest modern states of Western Europe were able to complete their state-making process in three near-distinct phases: (1) establishing the centralized, "absolutist" state at the expense of a feudal order that had begun to lose much of its economic and political utility; (2) welding together the subjects of the centralized monarchy into a people with a common history, legal system, language, and, often, religion (in the sense of Christian schisms), thus leading to the evolution of a national identity and the transformation of the centralized monarchical state into a nation-state and; (3) gradually extending representative institutions (dictated by the necessity to co-opt into the power structure new and powerful social forces that emerged as a result of the industrial revolution), over decades if not centuries. Above all, as Stein Rokkan has pointed out, "what is important is that the western nation-states were given a chance to solve some of the worst problems of state building before they had to face the ordeals of mass politics" ("Dimensions of State Formation and Nation Building," in *Formation of National States in Western Europe,* 598).

19. For details of this argument, see Mohammed Ayoob, *The Third World Security Predicament: State Making, Regional Conflict, and the International System* (Boulder, Colo.: Lynne Rienner, 1995), chap. 5.

20. Robert H. Jackson, "Quasi-States, Dual Regimes, and Neoclassical Theory: International Jurisprudence and the Third World," *International Organization* 41, no. 4 (autumn 1987): 529.

21. R. J. Vincent, *Human Rights and International Relations* (Cambridge: Cambridge University Press, 1986), 19–36.

22. As Seyom Brown has pointed out, the intellectual position that "servicing . . . basic human rights is the principal task of human polities—and that the worth of any polity is a function of how well it performs this task—has put the legitimacy of all extant polities up for grabs, so to speak. Whether particular nation-states, and the prevailing territorial demarcations, do indeed merit the badge of political legitimacy is, according to this view, subject to continuing assessment; accordingly, neither today's governments nor today's borders are sacrosanct." *International Relations in a Changing Global System: Toward a Theory of the World Polity* (Boulder, Colo.: Westview Press, 1992), 126.

23. For a discussion of failed states, see I. William Zartman, *Collapsed States: The Disintegration and Restoration of Legitimate Authority* (Boulder, Colo.: Lynne Rienner, 1995).

24. Charles Tripp, "Near East," in *Superpower Competition and Security in the Third World,* ed. Robert S. Litwak and Samuel F. Wells, Jr. (Cambridge, Mass.: Ballinger, 1988), 113.

25. For an incisive discussion of the difference between ethnicity and ethnonationalism, see Ashutosh Varshney, "Contested Meanings: India's National Identity, Hindu Nationalism, and the Politics of Anxiety," *Daedalus* 122, no. 3 (summer 1993): 230.

26. Lloyd N. Cutler, foreword to *Self-Determination in the New World Order*, by Morton H. Halperin and David J. Scheffer with Patricia L. Small (Washington, D.C.: Carnegie Endowment for International Peace, 1992), xi.

27. Gidon Gottlieb, *Nation against State: A New Approach to Ethnic Conflicts and the Decline of Sovereignty* (New York: Council on Foreign Relations, 1993), 2.

28. Crawford Young, "The Temple of Ethnicity," *World Politics* 35, no. 4 (July 1983): 659.

29. Charles Tilly, "National Self-Determination as a Problem for All of Us," *Daedalus* 122, no. 3 (summer 1993): 30.

30. William Pfaff, "Invitation to War," *Foreign Affairs* 72, no. 3 (summer 1993): 99, 101.

31. Jack Snyder, "Nationalism and the Crisis of the Post-Soviet State," *Survival* 35, no. 1 (spring 1993): 12.

32. Robert H. Jackson, *Quasi-States: Sovereignty, International Relations and the Third World* (Cambridge: Cambridge University Press, 1990).

33. For details of Afghanistan in the 1980s during the height of superpower involvement in that country's civil war, see Olivier Roy, *Islam and Resistance in Afghanistan,* 2d ed. (Cambridge: Cambridge University Press, 1990).

34. Michael Renner, *Small Arms, Big Impact: The Next Challenge of Disarmament* (Washington, D.C.: Worldwatch Institute, 1997). See also British American Security Information Council, *Stopping the Spread of Small Arms: International Initiatives,* report of a seminar held at the United Nations, New York, September 25, 1998.

35. Alex de Waal, "Contemporary Warfare in Africa: Changing Context, Changing Strategies," *IDS Bulletin* 27, no. 3 (1996): 6.

36. I. William Zartman, "Introduction: Posing the Problem of State Collapse," in *Collapsed States*, 8.

37. Jonathan Goodhand and David Hulme, "From Wars to Complex Political Emergencies: Understanding Conflict and Peace-Building in the New World Disorder," *Third World Quarterly* 20, no. 1 (February 1999): 19. The authors provide examples from Sudan, Liberia, and Afghanistan to demonstrate that conflict entrepreneurs benefit from internal war and thus possess a vested interest in their indefinite continuation.

38. Democratization is used in the sense of movement toward democracy; the latter is perceived as the desired goal, while the former is the process through which this goal is achieved or at least approximated.

39. Renée de Nevers, "Democratization and Ethnic Conflict," *Survival* 35, no. 2 (summer 1993): 31–32.

40. John Chipman, "Managing the Politics of Parochialism," *Survival* 35, no. 1 (spring 1993): 168.

41. Larry Diamond, Juan J. Linz, and Seymour Martin Lipset, "Introduction: Comparing Experiences with Democracy," in *Politics in Developing Countries: Comparing Experiences with Democracy,* ed. Larry Diamond, Juan J. Linz, and Seymour Martin Lipset (Boulder, Colo.: Lynne Rienner, 1990), 29.

42. For example, Rajni Kothari, *State against Democracy: In Search of Humane Governance* (Delhi, India: Ajanta Publications, 1988).

43. Robert W. Jackman, *Power without Force: The Political Capacity of Nation-States* (Ann Arbor: University of Michigan Press, 1993).

10

Economic Causes of Civil Conflict and Their Implications for Policy

Paul Collier

THIS CHAPTER PRESENTS an economic perspective on the causes of civil war, based on empirical patterns globally over the period 1965–99. During this period, the risk of civil war has been systematically related to a few economic conditions, such as dependence upon primary commodity exports and low national income. Conversely, and astonishingly, objective measures of social grievance, such as inequality, a lack of democracy, and ethnic and religious divisions, have had no systematic effect on risk. I argue that this is because civil wars occur where rebel organizations are financially viable. The Michigan Militia was unable to grow beyond a handful of part-time volunteers, whereas the FARC in Colombia has grown to employ around twelve thousand people. The factors that account for this difference between failure and success are to be found not in the "causes" that these two rebel organizations claim to espouse, but in their radically different opportunities to raise revenue. The FARC earns around $700 million

per year from drugs and kidnapping, whereas the Michigan Militia is probably broke.

The central importance of the financial viability of the rebel organization as the cause of civil war is why civil wars are so unlike international wars. Governments can always finance an army out of taxation, and so governments can always fight each other. The circumstances in which a rebel organization can finance an army are unusual. This is why my analysis is confined to civil war: what I have to say has little or no bearing on intergovernment war. Because the results are so counterintuitive, I start by arguing why social scientists should be distrustful of the loud public discourse on conflict. I then turn to the evidence, describing each of the risk factors in civil war. I then try to explain the observed pattern, focusing on the circumstances in which rebel organizations are viable. Finally, I turn to the policy implications. I argue that because the economic dimensions of civil war have been largely neglected, both governments and the international community have missed substantial opportunities for promoting peace.

GREED OR GRIEVANCE? WHY WE CAN'T TRUST THE DISCOURSE

There is a profound gap between popular perceptions of the causes of conflict and the results from recent economic analysis. Popular perceptions see rebellion as a protest motivated by genuine and extreme grievance; rebels are public-spirited heroes fighting against injustice. Economic analysis sees rebellion as more like a form of organized crime. Either economists are being excessively cynical or popular perceptions are badly misled. I first want to suggest why popular perceptions may indeed be wrong.

Popular perceptions are shaped by the discourse that conflicts themselves generate. The parties to a civil war do not stay silent: they are not white mice observed by scientists. They offer explanations for their actions. Indeed, both parties to a conflict will make a major effort to have good public relations. The larger rebel organizations will hire professional public relations firms to promote their explanation, and the governments that they are opposing will routinely hire rival public relations firms.

Imagine, for a moment, that you are the leader of a rebel organization, needing to offer an explanation of your goals. What are the likely elements? Most surely, they will be a litany of grievances against the government, for its oppression, unfairness, and perhaps victimization of some part of the population that your organization claims to represent. That is, your language will be the language of protest. You will style your rebellion as a protest movement driven to the extremity of violence by the extremity of the conditions that "your" people face. Almost certainly, the government will have responded to your insurgency with an incompetent counterinsurgency campaign.

"Almost certainly" because counterinsurgency is extremely difficult.

The most obvious difficulty that a government faces in counterinsurgency is getting its army to fight. People prefer not to risk getting killed. Governments try various economic incentives to overcome this problem. For example, in one recent African conflict the government decided to pay its soldiers a premium if they were in a combat zone. Shortly after this incentive was introduced, the war appeared to spread alarmingly. In previously safe areas rebel groups set off explosions near barracks. It transpired that government soldiers were probably planting these bombs themselves. However, the more serious problems occur when the government succeeds in persuading its army to fight but then lacks the means to control the behavior of soldiers on the ground. From Vietnam onward, the result has been atrocities. Rebel groups may even hope for government atrocities because the atrocities then fuel the grievances. This discourse of grievance is how most people understand the causes of conflict. A thorough analysis of the causes of a conflict then becomes a matter of tracing back the grievances and countergrievances in the history of protest.

An economist views conflict rather differently. Economists who have studied rebellions tend to think of them not as the ultimate protest movements, but as the ultimate manifestation of organized crime. As Herschel Grossman (1999, 269) states, "in such insurrections the insurgents are indistinguishable from bandits or pirates." Rebellion is large-scale predation of productive economic activities. I will shortly set out why economists see rebellion in this way and the rather powerful evidence for it. However, their view is so at odds with the popular discourse on conflict that there is a temptation to dismiss it as fanciful. The techniques of economics do not help its arguments: compared with the compelling historical detail produced by histories of protest, the economist's approach seems arcane and technocratic. So, before I explain why economists see rebellion as they do, I want to show why the discourse on conflict cannot be taken at face value.

For a few moments, suspend disbelief and suppose that most rebel movements are pretty close to being large-scale variants of organized crime. *The discourse would be exactly the same as if they were protest movements.* Unlike organized crime, rebel movements need good international public relations and they need to motivate their recruits to kill. They need good international public relations because most of them are partially dependent upon international financial support. They need to motivate their recruits to kill because, unlike a mafia, a predatory rebel organization is periodically going to have to fight for its survival against government forces. A rebel organization simply cannot afford to be regarded as criminal: it is not good publicity and it is not sufficiently motivating. Rebel organizations have to develop a discourse of grievance in order to function. Grievance is to a rebel organization what image is to a business. In each case the organization will devote advertising resources to promote it. In the economist's view of conflict, grievance will turn out to be neither a cause of conflict nor an accidental by-product of it. Rather, a sense of grievance is deliberately generated by rebel organizations. The sense of grievance may be based upon some objective grounds for complaint, or it may be conjured up by massaging prejudices. However, while this distinction is morally interesting to observers—is the cause just?—it is of no practical importance. The organization simply needs to generate a sense of grievance; otherwise it will fail as an organization and so tend to fade away.

This interpretation of conflict is obviously not shared by rebel organizations or by the people who honestly support them: the justice of the struggle seems central to success. By contrast, the economic theory of conflict argues that the motivation of conflict is unimportant; what matters is whether the organization can

sustain itself financially. It is this, rather than any objective grounds for grievance, that determines whether a country will experience civil war. The rebel organization can be motivated by a whole range of considerations. It may be motivated by perceived grievances, or it may simply want the power conferred by becoming the government. Regardless of why the organization is fighting, it can fight only if it is financially viable during the conflict. War cannot be fought just on hopes or hatreds. Predatory behavior during the conflict may not be the objective of the rebel organization, but it is the organization's means of financing the conflict. By predatory behavior I mean the use of force to extort goods or money from their legitimate owners.

The economic theory of conflict, then, assumes that perceived grievances and the lust for power are found more or less equally in all societies. Groups are capable of perceiving that they have grievances more or less regardless of their objective circumstances, a social phenomenon known as relative deprivation. Some people will have a lust for power more or less regardless of the objective benefits conferred by power. In this case, *it is the feasibility of predation that determines the risk of conflict.* Predation may be just a regrettable necessity on the road to perceived justice or power, but it is the conditions for predation that are decisive. Whether conflict is motivated by predation or simply made possible by it, these two accounts come to the same conclusion: rebellion is unrelated to objective circumstances of grievance while being caused by the feasibility of predation.

On the most cynical variant of the predation theory, rebellion is motivated by greed, so that it occurs when rebels can do well out of war. On the power-seeking variant of the predation theory, rebels are motivated by a lust for power, but rebellion occurs only when rebels can do well out of war. On the subjective grievance variant of the predation theory, rebels are motivated by grievances, imagined or real, but rebellion occurs only when rebels can do well out of war. These three variants have in common the implications that rebels are not necessarily heroes struggling for a particularly worthwhile cause and that the feasibility of predation explains conflict. They can thus be grouped together in contrast to the objective grievance theory of conflict, in which rebels are indeed heroes struggling for a worthwhile cause, with the intensity of objective grievances explaining the occurrence of conflict.

Economists would argue that it is not really necessary to distinguish between the three variants of the predation theory. It does not really matter whether rebels are motivated by greed, by a lust for power, or by grievance, as long as what causes conflict is the feasibility of predation. Indeed, economists tend to set little credence on the explanations that people give for their behavior. Economists prefer to work by "revealed preference": people gradually reveal their true motivation by the pattern of their behavior, even if they choose to disguise the painful truth from themselves. Rebel leaders may come to believe their own propaganda much of the time, but if their words are decried by their behavior, then their words have little explanatory power.

There is less reason to doubt that those who support rebellion from afar are genuinely committed to the cause of grievance redressal. However, such supporters may simply have been duped. Rebel leaders have always sought outside supporters—"useful idiots," in Lenin's telling phrase. Among the people who are most susceptible to the discourse of grievance are those who care most passionately about oppression, inequality, and injustice. In short, if rebellion presents itself as the ultimate protest movement, it will attract as noncombatant supporters those who normally support protest movements. The economic theory of conflict argues that these people have been taken in by accepting the discourse at face value. As a proposition in social science this theory of conflict is a case of modern economics meeting

old marxism. As in Marx, the underlying cause of conflict is economic: in this case, the rebel organization is predatory upon certain parts of the economy. As in Marx, the "superstructure" is a set of beliefs that are false. The difference is simply that it is the *rebel* supporters who have the "false consciousness": they are gulled into believing the discourse that self-interested rebel leaders promote.

So, "greed or grievance"?—we can't tell from the discourse. Occasionally the discourse is rather blatantly at variance with the behavior. Take the recently settled conflict in Sierra Leone. A rebel organization built itself into around twenty thousand recruits and opposed the government. The rebel organization produced the usual litany of grievances, and its very scale suggested that it had widespread support. Sierra Leone is, however, a major exporter of diamonds, and there was considerable evidence that the rebel organization was involved in this business on a large scale. During peace negotiations the rebel leader was offered and accepted the vice presidency of the country. This, we might imagine, would be a good basis for addressing rebel grievances. However, the offer was not sufficient to persuade the rebel leader to accept the peace settlement. He had one further demand, which, once acceded to, produced a (temporary) settlement. His demand was to be the minister of mining. Cases such as this are at least suggestive that something other than grievance may be going on beneath the surface of the discourse. It is to this hidden structure of rebellion that I now turn.

THE EVIDENCE

Modern economics has two powerful tools: statistics and theory. People who are not economists are seldom convinced simply by economic theory, so I will begin with the statistical evidence. Anke Hoeffler and I have analyzed the pattern of conflict using a large new database on civil wars during the period from 1965 to 1999 (Collier and Hoeffler 2000). Following the political science convention, we classify a civil war as an internal conflict with at least one thousand battle-related deaths. During 1960–99 there were seventy-four civil wars globally. We analyzed why these wars occurred among the 161 countries in our sample. We divided the period into seven five-year subperiods and attempted to predict the occurrence of war during a subperiod by examining the characteristics at its start. The statistical techniques we used were logit and probit regressions. In practice, some civil wars occur in countries for which there are virtually no other data. We know that the country had a war, but we do not know enough of its other characteristics to include it in our analysis. This reduces our sample to forty-four civil wars. However, this number is still sufficient to find some strong patterns. The forty-four wars are listed (with asterisks) in table 1.

In order to get some feel for how important different risk factors are, it is useful to think of a baseline country. I will take as a baseline a country whose characteristics were all at the mean of our sample. By construction then, this is an extraordinarily ordinary country. These characteristics give it a risk of civil conflict of around 14 percent in any particular five-year period. Now, one by one, I will vary some of the more important risk factors.

The most powerful risk factor is a high level of primary commodity dependence. Countries that have a substantial share of their income (GDP) coming from the export of primary commodities are radically more at risk for conflict. The most dangerous level of primary commodity dependence is 26 percent of GDP. At this level the otherwise ordinary country has a risk of conflict of 23 percent. By contrast, if it had no primary commodity exports (but was otherwise the same, with characteristics still at the mean of the sample), its risk would fall to only one half of 1 percent. Thus, without primary commodity exports, ordinary countries

are pretty safe from internal conflict. When such exports are substantial, countries are in danger. Primary commodities are thus a major part of the conflict story. What else matters?

Both geography and history matter. Geography matters because if the population is highly geographically dispersed, the country is harder for the government to control than if everyone lives in the same small area. The geography of the Democratic Republic of the Congo (DRC, formerly Zaire) makes it unusually hard for government forces to control the country because the population lives around the fringes of a huge area, with the three main cities in the extreme west, extreme southeast, and extreme north. By comparison, Singapore would be a nightmare for a rebellion. In this city-state there is nowhere to hide, and government forces could be anywhere in the country within an hour. With Congo-like geographic dispersion our otherwise ordinary country has a risk of conflict of around 50 percent, whereas with Singapore-like concentration its risk falls to around 3 percent.

History matters because if a country has recently had a civil war its risk of further war is much higher. Immediately after the end of hostilities there is a 40 percent chance of further conflict. This risk then falls around one percentage point for each year of peace. However, how much history matters depends upon the size of the diaspora. For example, some countries have very large diasporas in the United States relative to their remaining resident population, whereas others do not. Suppose that our otherwise ordinary country has ended a civil war five years ago and now wants to know what its chances are for peace during the next five years. If the country has an unusually large U.S. diaspora, its chances of conflict are 36 percent. If it has an unusually small diaspora, its chances of conflict are only 6 percent. So, diasporas appear to make life for those left behind much more dangerous in postconflict situations.

Economic opportunities also matter. Conflict is concentrated in countries with little

Table 1. Major Armed Conflicts, 1960–99

An asterisk indicates inclusion in the statistical analysis.

Country	Start of the War	End of the War	Country	Start of the War	End of the War
Afghanistan	04/78	02/92	Mozambique	10/64	11/75
Afghanistan	05/92	ongoing	*Mozambique	07/76	10/92
Algeria	07/62	12/62	Myanmar/Burma	1968	10/80
*Algeria	05/91	ongoing	*Myanmar/Burma	02/83	07/95
Angola	02/61	11/75	*Nicaragua	10/78	07/79
*Angola	11/75	05/91	*Nicaragua	03/82	04/90
Angola	09/92	ongoing	*Nigeria	01/66	01/70
Azerbaijan	04/91	10/94	*Nigeria	12/80	08/84
Bosnia	03/92	11/95	*Pakistan	03/71	12/71
*Burundi	04/72	12/73	Pakistan	07/73	07/77
*Burundi	08/88	08/88	*Peru	03/82	12/96
Burundi	11/91	ongoing	*Philippines	09/72	12/96
Cambodia	03/70	10/91	*Romania	12/89	12/89
*Chad	03/80	08/88	Russia	12/94	08/96
*Colombia	04/84	ongoing	Russia	09/99	ongoing
*Cyprus	7/74	8/74	Rwanda	11/63	02/64
*Dominica	04/65	09/65	*Rwanda	10/90	07/94
*El Salvador	10/79	01/92	*Somalia	04/82	05/88
*Ethiopia	07/74	05/91	*Somalia	05/88	12/92
Georgia	06/91	12/93	*Sri Lanka	04/71	05/71
*Guatemala	07/66	07/72	*Sri Lanka	07/83	ongoing
*Guatemala	04/84	03/94	Sudan	10/63	02/72
Guinea–Bissau	12/62	12/74	*Sudan	07/83	ongoing
*India	08/65	08/65	Tajikistan	04/92	12/94
India	1984	1994	*Turkey	07/91	ongoing
*Indonesia	06/75	09/82	*Uganda	05/66	06/66
*Iran	03/74	03/75	*Uganda	10/80	04/88
*Iran	09/78	12/79	Vietnam	01/60	04/75
*Iran	06/81	05/82	Yemen	05/90	10/94
*Iraq	07/74	03/75	Yemen Arab Republic	11/62	09/69
*Iraq	01/85	12/92	Yemen People's Republic	01/86	01/86
*Jordan	09/71	09/71	Yugoslavia	04/90	01/92
Laos	07/60	02/73	Yugoslavia	10/98	04/99
Lebanon	05/75	09/92	Zaire/DRC	07/60	09/65
*Liberia	12/89	11/91	*Zaire/DRC	09/91	12/96
Liberia	10/92	11/96	*Zaire/DRC	09/97	09/99
*Morocco	10/75	11/89	*Zimbabwe	12/72	12/79

education. The average country in our sample had only 45 percent of its young males in secondary education. A country that has ten percentage points more of its youth in schools—say 55 percent instead of 45 percent—cuts its risk of conflict from 14 percent to around 10 percent. Conflict is more likely in countries with fast population growth: each percentage point on the rate of population growth raises the risk of conflict by around 2.5 percentage points. Conflict is also more likely in countries in economic decline. Each percentage point off the growth rate of per capita income raises the risk of conflict by around one percentage point.

The ethnic and religious composition of the country matters. If there is one dominant ethnic group that constitutes between 45 percent and 90 percent of the population—enough to give it control, but not enough to make discrimination against a minority pointless—the risk of conflict doubles. For example, in Sri Lanka the Tamils are a minority of around 12 percent of the population, and in Rwanda the Tutsis are around 10 percent to 15 percent of the population. Of course, in Sri Lanka the Tamils are a weak minority, whereas in Rwanda the Tutsis are a strong minority, controlling the government. However, clearly, in Rwanda, the Tutsi minority is too scared of being subject to ethnic dominance to hand over power. While ethnic dominance is a problem, ethnic and religious diversity does not make a society more dangerous—in fact, it makes it safer. A country that is ethnically and religiously homogeneous is surprisingly dangerous—the risk is 23 percent. By comparison, a country with ethnic and religious diversity equal to the maximum we find in our sample has a risk of only around 3 percent. Other than in the cases in which the largest ethnic group makes up between 45 percent and 90 percent of the population, diversity makes a society much safer.

Finally, some good news. Since 1990 the world has been significantly safer from civil conflict. If we add a dummy variable for the period since the end of the Cold War, it is statistically significant with a large effect. If we hold the causes of conflict constant at the average, we find that the risk of conflict was only half as great during the 1990s as during the Cold War. Of course, some of the other causes of conflict also changed during the 1990s—on average, per capita incomes rose faster than during the 1980s, which also reduced the risk of conflict. However, some countries became more dependent upon primary commodity exports or their economies collapsed, and these countries became more prone to conflict. As of 1995, the country with the highest risk of civil conflict according to our analysis was Zaire, with a three-in-four chance of conflict occurring within the next five years. Sadly, our model predicted this all too accurately.

This has been the statistical pattern of civil conflict since 1960. It is interesting both for what is important and for what is not. Clearly, there are some powerful dangers coming from primary commodities and diasporas, and there used to be risks from the Cold War. However, equally striking is what does *not* appear to affect conflict risk. Inequality, whether of incomes or of assets, has no discernible effect. Unequal societies are not more prone to conflict. A lack of democratic rights appears to have no significant effect. Ethnic and religious diversity, as noted, far from increasing the risk of conflict, actually reduces it. These are all obvious proxies for objective grievances. Unequal, ethnically divided societies whose members have few political rights may sound exactly like the sort of places that would be most prone to rebellion. They are surely the sort of places most in need of protest. And yet, such places, as far as we can tell, have no higher risk of violent conflict than anywhere else—indeed, thanks to their ethnic diversity, they are somewhat safer. The only protest-type variable that matters is a society characterized by ethnic dominance. This may be because we are not measuring objective grievances well enough. However, we have made an honest effort to utilize all the available comparable indices of objective grievance, of which there are now a number. At least as a working hypothesis, civil war is much more strongly related to the economic and geographic variables I have discussed than it is to objective grievances.

There are thus two surprises to be explained: Why is rebellion so unrelated to the objective need for protest, and why is it so strongly related to primary commodities and diasporas?

WHY IS REBELLION NOT LIKE PROTEST?

According to economists who have studied the dynamics of protest (Kuran 1989), the first problem with getting a protest going is that it is a "public good." That is, even if the protest succeeds in securing justice, everyone will benefit whether or not they bother to take part in the protest. Always, public goods face collective action problems: it makes more individual sense to free-ride on the efforts of others, and if everyone free-rides, nothing happens. This is a problem in a protest because the government might punish people who take part, unless there are so many people that there is safety in numbers. Further, in order to protest, most people will lose a day of income. This is one reason why such a high proportion of protesters are often students. The temptation to free-ride on a justice-seeking *rebellion* is very much stronger than the temptation to free-ride on a justice-seeking *protest*. A protest costs little, risks little, and offers a sense of citizenship. In effect, protestors are forcing an open election on an issue. Rebellion is a full-time commitment, and it is dangerous. Economists would predict that the collective action problem for a justice-seeking rebellion would usually be insuperable.

In analyzing the dynamics of protest, Kuran saw that a successful protest is one that escalates and that this depends upon a cascade of participation, drawing in increasingly lukewarm supporters. Suppose the potential supporters of a protest are ranked in order of their willingness to take personal risk. The most ardent supporters join the protest first, at the stage when, because the protest is small, it is easy for the government to victimize participants. Each time an additional supporter joins the protest, the risks of punishment for participation go down. The cascade depends upon the reduction in this risk inducing enough people to change their minds and join the protest that the risk falls further, inducing another group of people to change their minds. If the cascade works, then when a few committed people create an initial spark, it turns into a prairie fire. Could the rebellions we observe be failed protest movements, cases where a brave few hundred created the spark, but the rest of the society failed to ignite, leaving the brave core to turn into guerrilla fighters against the government? Are rebels just heroes who have been let down by the mass of cowards and so driven into more violent actions to protect themselves? Well, if they were, we would observe a clear pattern in rebellion.

Kuran suggests that the cascade is more likely to work in fairly homogeneous societies. In such societies there will be a dense continuum of opinion. Many people will be on the margin of changing their minds and so will be swung into action as the risks of government punishment start to fall. By contrast, if the society is split up into many different groups who see the concerns of other groups as irrelevant to their own, instead of a continuum of opinion there will be clusters broken by gaps. As soon as the cascade reaches the first gap it stops. One implication of this insight is that the societies in which protest will get stuck are those that are diverse. That is, if rebellions are the stuff of heroes let down by cowards, we should expect to find more of them in diverse societies. Recall that in fact we find precisely the opposite. Diverse societies have a much lower risk of rebellion than do homogeneous societies. Of course, if we scour history sufficiently thoroughly we will find examples of protest movements that aborted into rebellion. If we scour history we can find anything. However, the image of the rebel band as that part of the population that is the most dedicated and self-sacrificing is difficult to reconcile with the facts. Rebellion is not generally linked to the objective grievances—inequality, political repression, diversity—which are repeatedly used in rebel discourse. Nor is its incidence high in societies where we would expect protest movements to face the most difficulties. The sole exception to this is that in situations of ethnic dominance—with or without democracy—minorities (or majorities) may take to the gun. Other than this, the modern rebel appears truly to have been a "rebel without a cause."

WHAT CONDITIONS MAKE PREDATORY REBELLIONS PROFITABLE?

Empirically, the risk of rebellion is strongly linked to three economic conditions: dependence upon primary commodity exports, low average income of the country, and slow growth. I now suggest why this is the case.

Primary commodity exports are the most lootable of all economic activities. An economy that is dependent upon them thus offers plenty of opportunities for predatory rebellion. (For a formal model of loot-seeking rebellion, see Collier 2000b.) One indication that primary commodity exports are highly lootable is that they are also the most heavily taxed activity—the same characteristics that make it easy for governments to tax them make it easy for rebels to loot them. Indeed, rebel predation is just illegal taxation. Conversely, in some countries government has been described as legalized predation in which primary commodities are heavily taxed in order to finance the government elite. In the worst cases, those

who are the victims of such predation may not discriminate much between the behavior of the rebel organization and that of the government. This does not, however, mean that the rebels are "no worse" than the government. The presence of a rebel organization plunges the society into civil war, and the costs of war are likely to outweigh the costs of government predation.

Primary commodity exports are especially vulnerable to looting and taxation because their production relies heavily on long-lasting and immobile assets. A mine shaft that has been sunk is worth exploiting even if much of the anticipated profits are lost to rebels. Coffee trees that have been planted are worth harvesting even if much of the coffee has to be surrendered. Thus, rebel predation does not kill the activity off or shift it elsewhere as would happen were manufacturing the target. Further, because the produce is exported, it has to be transported to the port. Along the way there are many geographic "choke points" where rebels can extract a tribute if they control the choke points, even if only spasmodically. The government can be presumed to control the best choke point of all—the port itself. This behavior makes a rebel group somewhat like organized crime. However, it is organized crime with a difference. The government will try to defend the choke points from rebel attacks—it is, after all, defending its own revenue. Hence, unlike a mafia, the rebel group must expect sometimes to confront substantial government forces and so will need to protect itself. Rebel groups therefore need to be much larger than mafias. Typically, rebel organizations have five hundred to five thousand fighters, whereas mafias number generally in the range of twenty to five hundred. It is because rebel organizations need to be large and to confront government forces in order to function as predators that conflicts can produce cumulative mortality in excess of one thousand and so qualify empirically as civil wars.

Why is the risk of conflict much higher in countries where incomes are low? The explanation that jumps to mind is that when people are poor they have little to lose from joining a rebel group, so that rebel organizations find recruitment cheap. There may be something in this, but if young men can be recruited cheaply for the rebel organization, they can also be recruited cheaply by the government. Hence, low income does not automatically give rebellion an advantage. However, indirectly, low income does advantage the rebels. Around the world, the share of income that accrues to the government as tax revenue rises with income. For example, most OECD governments get around 40 percent of national income as tax revenue. In the really poor economies, like Ghana and Uganda in the early 1980s, the government was only raising around 6 percent of national income as taxation. This reduces the capacity of the government to spend on defense, and so makes rebel predation easier. Indeed, in low-income economies, governments will typically derive about half of their revenue from taxes on primary commodity exports (directly or indirectly), so that their revenue base is similar to that of the rebels. At higher income levels the government supplements these revenues with revenues from taxes on other economic activities. Thus, poor countries have a high incidence of conflict because governments cannot afford to supply either adequate defense or other public services to the population. Of course, there may be other reasons why poverty makes it easier for rebels. Poverty can make people desperate or angry. However, if this was an important effect we would expect to find that inequality makes conflict more likely: for a given level of average income, the more unequal the income distribution, the more severe the poverty of the poorest. In fact, inequality does not seem to effect the risk of conflict. Rebellion seems not to be the rage of the poor.

Indeed, if anything, rebellion seems to be the rage of the rich. One way in which rebel groups can lock in to predation of primary commodity exports is if they can secede with the land on which the primary commodities are produced. Such attempted secessions by rich regions are common. The Katangan secession movement in Zaire was based in the copper-mining region; the Biafran secession movement in Nigeria was based in the oil-producing region; the Aceh secession movement in Indonesia is based in an oil-producing region with per capita GDP three times the national average; the successful Eritrean secession was of a region with double the per capita income of the rest of Ethiopia. To the extent that the rebel group is not just benefiting itself through predation, but is fighting a political cause, that cause is the grievance of a rich minority at paying taxes to the poor majority. Such rebellions may have more in common with the politics of Staten Island (where a rich suburb is trying to secede from the tax jurisdiction of New York) than those of Robin Hood.

Slow economic growth and rapid population growth both make rebellion more likely. Presumably, they assist rebel recruitment. The rebel organization needs to build itself up fairly fast in order to survive against the army. Hence, for a given level of income, if there are few job opportunities, few schooling opportunities, and many young people needing work, the rebel organization has an easier task.

So, the observed pattern of rebellion is intelligible. High primary commodity exports, low income, and slow growth are a cocktail that makes predatory rebellions more financially viable. In such circumstances rebels can do well out of war.

WHY DOES ETHNIC DIVERSITY MAKE A SOCIETY SAFER, NOT MORE DANGEROUS?

One of the most striking empirical regularities is that societies that are diverse in terms of ethnicity and religion are significantly safer than societies that are homogeneous. If ethnic and religious hatreds were an important cause of conflict, the pattern would be the reverse, since in homogeneous societies there would be nobody to hate. Evidently, conflict is not being generated by such hatreds. However, it is less evident why diversity makes a society considerably safer, instead of simply having no effect.

I think that diversity makes a society safer because it makes rebellion more difficult. This is because, first and foremost, a rebel organization is neither a mafia nor a protest movement, but an army. Armies face huge problems of organizational cohesion and motivation. To fight effectively, soldiers must overcome their individual instincts to avoid danger and must take risks to help other members of their team. Military history abounds in stories of small groups defeating larger groups because they were better fighting units. The government army also faces these problems, but it has the advantage of already having had a long time to deal with them. By contrast, the rebel organization cannot usually afford to take years to build up its morale before it starts operations: it must recruit from scratch and rapidly start fighting. One simple principle is to keep the recruits as alike one another as possible. The more social ties there are within the organization—the same kin group, or at least same ethnic group, language group, and religion—the easier it will be to build a fighting force. This may be especially true of the officer core. The easiest way for a government to defeat a rebellion may be to buy off some of the officers. The more "social capital" there is within the group, the more cohesive it is likely to be.

This principle implies that in ethnically diverse societies rebellions will tend to be ethnically particular. This has two important corollaries. First, the more that the society is divided into a patchwork of different ethnic and religious groups, the more difficult it will be to recruit a force of a sufficient scale to be viable. For example, in Africa the average ethnolinguistic group has only around two hundred fifty thousand people, of whom around

twenty-five thousand will be young males. Thus, even before we allow for any further divisions of religion, an organization of five thousand fighters would need to recruit 20 percent of the age group. Diversity in the society thus makes the rebel task more difficult and so makes rebellion less likely.

The second corollary is that where conflict does take place in ethnically diverse societies it will take the form of some particular ethnic group rebelling against the government. As in any army, recruits will be motivated to kill the enemy by basic indoctrination in why the enemy deserves to be killed. Indeed, the simple Leninist theory of the rebel organization, which many rebel movements adopt even if they do not adopt marxist ideology, is that people are initially so oppressed that they do not realize they are oppressed. *It is a key task of the rebel organization to make people realize that they are the victims of injustice.* The economic theory of rebellion accepts this proposition and makes one simple but reasonable extension: the rebel organization can inculcate a subjective sense of injustice whether or not this is objectively justified. The rebel organization needs to inculcate a sense of injustice and will work to create it. From this follows a hatred of the enemy and a willingness to fight.

The inculcation of grievance is not a frivolous activity; it is vital for an effective fighting force. Take, for example, the Eritrean People's Liberation Front (EPLF), which staged probably the most effective rebellion in recent history. Its recruitment base was barely 2 million people and it had little foreign government support, yet it defeated an Ethiopian army of over four hundred thousand men that was supported by Russia. Its success obviously depended upon having its much smaller army well motivated. The EPLF deliberately built this motivation by routinely withdrawing its recruits from the front for six months to send them on indoctrination courses. If the society in which the rebellion occurs is ethnically diverse, the rebel organization will nevertheless be ethnically homogeneous to assist cohesion. Since the rebels will therefore be ethnically different from most of the rest of society, the obvious discourse for the rebel leadership to adopt with its recruits is that of ethnic grievance. Hence, ethnic grievance is actively manufactured by the rebel organization as a necessary way of motivating its forces. As a result, where conflicts occur in ethnically diverse societies, they will look and sound as though they were caused by ethnic hatreds.

A more remarkable example is the conflict in Somalia. Somalia is one of the most ethnically homogeneous societies in the world although, as in all traditional societies, within the single ethnic group are many lineage or kin groups. In the initial postindependence period, political power had been shared reasonably comfortably among these clan groups. However, in the instability following a dictatorship, a political opportunist, Mohammed Farah Aideed, induced the group living around the national arsenal to seize its considerable contents. The group then proceeded to build an army around these armaments. Building an army fast, Aideed based recruitment on his clan and its proximate lineage groups—in the absence of ethnic distinctions, clan membership was the only basis for creating cohesion in a fighting force. The excluded clans naturally felt threatened by this bid for power and so armed themselves in response. The resulting violent conflict in effect turned what had been a patchwork of closely related clusters of people into large rival groupings that hated one another. The conflict created the equivalent of interethnic hatred in an ethnically unified society.

A surprisingly similar example is the recent conflict in the Democratic Republic of the Congo (DRC). The DRC, a society that is highly ethnically diverse, is at the opposite end of the spectrum from Somalia. When President Laurent Kabila fell out with his Tutsi military support, he needed to build an army to oppose it. Because the DRC was so ethnically divided, this was difficult. Kabila needed

to recruit across ethnic boundaries in order to build a sufficient fighting force. He therefore manufactured an encompassing ethnic grouping, of which all groups other than the Tutsis were members. Just as Aideed had forged several clans in Somalia into a common fighting group distinct from the excluded clans, so Kabila hoped to forge several ethnic groups into a common fighting group. In both cases, the conflict created a need to manufacture intergroup hatred, but the basic conditions for it—a society divided into two large groups—did not exist. In both cases military necessity led to the invention not just of the grievances but of the groupings themselves. Conflict is not caused by divisions; rather, it actively needs to create them.

When such conflicts are viewed during or after the event, the observer sees ethnic hatred. The parties to the conflict have used the discourse of group hatred to build fighting organizations. It is natural for observers to interpret such conflicts as being caused by ethnic hatred. Instead, the conflicts have caused the intergroup hatred and may even, as in Somalia, have created the groups.

If the rebel organization succeeds in generating group grievance, perhaps by manufacturing both the grievance and the group, the resulting civil war becomes defined in terms of political conflict. However, it is the military needs of the rebel organization that have created this political conflict rather than objective grievances. Analysts often reason back from the political discourse during conflict and deduce that the war was the consequence of particularly intense political conflict, in turn based upon particularly strong reasons for grievance. Yet the intensity of objective grievance does not predict civil war. Many societies sustain intense political conflict for many years without this developing into war. Political conflict is universal, whereas civil war is rare. My argument is that where rebellions happen to be financially viable, wars will occur. As part of the process of war, the rebel organization must generate group grievance for military effectiveness. The generation of group grievance politicizes the war. Thus, the war produces the intense political conflict, not the intense political conflict the war.

IF DIVERSITY INCREASES SAFETY, WHY IS ETHNIC DOMINANCE SO DANGEROUS?

The one exception to the rule that homogeneous societies are more dangerous than diverse societies is ethnic dominance. By ethnic dominance I mean a society in which the largest single ethnic group makes up somewhere between 45 percent and 90 percent of the population. It is not difficult to see why such societies are dangerous. Having 45 percent or more of the population is sufficient in a democracy to give the group permanent control, or what political scientists call a stable winning coalition. Having less than 90 percent of the population suggests that it may be worth exploiting this power by transferring resources from the minority. If the minority is much smaller than 10 percent of the population, there is normally so little to be gained by exploiting it that the gain may be more than swallowed up in the costs of the transfer system.

Thus, in societies characterized by ethnic dominance, the majority probably has both the power to exploit the minority and an interest in doing so. The minority may become sufficiently fearful of permanent exploitation that it decides to fight. This is the exception to the absence of objective grievance effects, and a reason for it may be that democracy can offer no prospect of redress. In diverse societies not characterized by ethnic dominance, small groups that are excluded from power can hope at some stage to bid themselves into a winning coalition. Even dictators do not last forever. Thus, for example, in Kenya, where no tribe has close to a majority, the fifteen years of President Jomo Kenyatta's rule strongly favored his own large

tribe, the Kikuyu. However, Kenyatta had chosen as his vice president someone from a very minor tribe. On the death of Kenyatta, the vice president, Daniel arap Moi, succeeded to the presidency and has managed since 1978 to hold together a winning coalition of small tribes, excluding both the Kikuyu and the Luo, the two largest tribal groups. The small tribes in Kenyatta's Kenya were thus right to hope for eventual redress through the political, rather than the military, process. By contrast, in societies characterized by ethnic dominance, the minority has little to hope for through the political process. Thus, it is possible that rebellion in societies with ethnic dominance is the behavior of despair. Note that it makes little difference whether it is the majority or the minority that is in power. Even if the minority is in power, it dare not trust democracy because it does not trust the majority. This is perhaps the case with the Tutsi-dominated governments of Rwanda and Burundi, and perhaps even of the minority Tigrean-dominated government of Ethiopia.

WHY ARE DIASPORAS SO DANGEROUS?

Recall that empirically if a country that has recently ended a conflict has a large diaspora living in the United States, its risk that the conflict will resume is sharply increased.

There is little mystery about this effect. Diasporas sometimes harbor rather romanticized attachments to their group of origin and may nurse grievances as a form of asserting continued belonging. They are much richer than the people in their country of origin and so can afford to finance vengeance. Above all, they do not have to suffer any of the awful consequences of renewed conflict because they are not living in the country. Hence, they are a ready market for rebel groups touting vengeance and so are a source of finance for renewed conflict. They are also a source of pressure for secession. For example, the (peaceful) secession of Slovakia from the then Czechoslovakia was initiated not in Czechoslovakia itself, but in the Czechoslovak diaspora organizations in North America. City by city in North America, the diaspora organization divorced.[1] The reductio ad absurdum of such a trend would be for immigrant populations of the United States and the European Union to split their countries of origin into tiny "ethnic theme parks" while themselves enjoying the advantages of living in nations with scale and diversity.

Another source of foreign finance is governments that are enemies of the incumbent government. During the Cold War each of the superpowers offered inducements for Third World governments to align with it. Once a government had done this, it became the potential target of destabilization efforts from the other superpower. One means of destabilization was to fund rebel groups. Once the Cold War ended, the need for such destabilization ended, and so the external finance for rebel organizations declined, which perhaps explains why the risk of civil conflict was lower during the 1990s.

So What Can Be Done?

I have spent a long time on the diagnosis of the problem because different diagnoses lead to radically different policy solutions.

If you accept the conventional grievance account of conflict, then the appropriate policy interventions are to address the possible objective causes of grievance. On this account, countries should reduce inequality and increase political rights. These noble objectives are desirable on many grounds, but if the objective is civil peace, then on my analysis they will be ineffective.

A further policy, if you accept the grievance account, may be to redraw borders, split countries, and even move populations so as to achieve greater ethnic homogeneity. By contrast, if you accept that diversity makes coun-

tries safer, then this is the road to increased civil conflict and presumably also to increased international conflict. Perhaps a recent example of such an eventuality is the breakup of Yugoslavia. In the old Yugoslavia there was a sufficiently high degree of diversity that no one group constituted a majority—the society was not characterized by ethnic dominance. First, Slovenia, the richest region of Yugoslavia, seceded in what could be interpreted as an instance of the "rage of the rich," although there were most surely other motivations. Then Croatia, the next richest region, also seceded. Owing to these two secessions, the residual Yugoslavia was characterized by ethnic dominance. Civil and international war followed.

Hence, the policies that proceed from the grievance diagnosis are variously ineffective and counterproductive if you accept the predation diagnosis. What policies would work if this alternative interpretation of conflict is in fact correct? First, we need to distinguish between conflict prevention and postconflict situations. Before conflict, the approach implied by the predation analysis is to work through the major risk factors, identifying how to reduce them. Note that this approach is radically different from the more traditional approach, which attempts to identify grievances and redress them. The new approach is basically one of making it harder for rebel organizations to get established, and addressing objective grievances is not usually an effective way to achieve this goal. Postconflict, the problem is rather different. Rebel organizations have forced themselves onto the political landscape and have generated group grievance. Although both the grievances and the groups may be manufactured, they now exist and postconflict policy must address them. Hence, whereas conflict prevention should not be built around the reduction of objective grievances, the construction of sustainable peace in postconflict societies will have to address the subjective grievances of the parties to the conflict. I therefore consider the policies for conflict prevention and postconflict peace-building separately.

POLICIES FOR CONFLICT PREVENTION

Each society is different. The overall risk of conflict in a society is built up from a series of risk factors, and the balance of risk factors will differ from one country to another. Hence, the first step in conflict prevention is to decompose the overall risk into its constituent components and then put the most effort into reducing those risks that are the most important and the most amenable to policy. I take the potential risk factors in turn.

Economies with around a quarter of GDP coming from natural resource exports are acutely at risk of civil conflict. Four strategies may reduce this risk. First, the government can facilitate diversification of the economy away from dependence upon primary commodities. Better economic policy promotes diversification. In a really poor policy environment, the only export activities that survive are those with high location-specific rents. The World Bank's annual measure of policy (the Country Policy and Institutional Assessment) is significant in explaining the extent of primary commodity dependence. Policy improvement, sustained over a five-year period, reduces dependence in the next five-year period.

Second, the international donor community can target aid to these societies. Aid reinforces the effect of good policies in reducing primary commodity dependence.

Third, a government can try to make loot-seeking rebels unpopular by transparently using the revenue from primary commodity exports to fund effective basic service delivery. If the population sees government funding primary education and rural health care centers rather than Swiss bank accounts, then the population is going to be more hostile to rebels. There are, however, limits to the effectiveness of

community support for the government as a check on rebellion. For example, many of the youths who fought for the rebel movement in Sierra Leone are so unpopular that they dare not return to their communities, but this unpopularity did not stop them from joining a rebellion. The rebels deliberately targeted drug addicts and children for recruitment and so had an unusually dependent labor force.

Fourth, the international community can make it more difficult for rebel groups to sell the commodities they loot. Most of the international markets in commodities are, at some point along the marketing chain, fairly narrow, in the sense that there are not many market participants. Although primary commodities are more difficult to identify than branded manufactured goods, they differ in quality, and so markets can usually identify the origin of the commodity in the process of determining its quality. For example, at the stage at which diamonds are cut, their provenance can be established with reasonable accuracy, and diamond cutting is a highly skilled activity that can potentially be subject to a degree of international regulation. Of course, it will never be possible to drive illegal supplies out of the market, but it should be possible to drive them to the fringes of the market, where the goods can be sold only at a deep discount. Rebel predation would then become less lucrative.

Low income and economic decline are further risk factors. There is no quick fix for low income. However, within a single generation it is now possible for most poverty-stricken societies to lift themselves out of poverty. In a single generation South Korea managed to grow from a per capita income of $300 a year to $10,000 a year. Most very poor countries have poor economic policies. Changing these policies is often politically difficult because in the short term vested interests lose, but many societies have faced down these interests and transformed themselves. In such situations international aid has been shown to be effective in accelerating growth. For example, during the 1990s Uganda transformed its economic policies and, with the help of the international donor community, sustained a 7 percent annual growth rate. It is on track to realize the government objective of overcoming poverty within a generation. Within Uganda, a rebel group called the AFL recruits by offering the unemployed 200,000 shillings per month (around $150). Rapid growth will gradually make recruitment harder.

A further risk factor is ethnic dominance. If a society has a single ethnic group that is large enough to dominate democratic institutions, then democracy itself is not sufficient to reassure minorities. Ethnic dominance is a difficult problem. The most realistic approach is to entrench minority rights in the constitution. This can be done by explicitly legislating either group rights or strong individual rights. If all individuals are secure from discrimination, then individuals in minority groups are secure. The scope for this approach depends upon the credibility of the checks and balances that the state can erect upon government power. Usually, state institutions are not strong enough for this degree of trust, and so they can usefully be reinforced by international or regional commitments. For example, the European Union is requiring that the many Eastern European countries hoping to join it treat their minorities equally. Latvia moderated its policies toward its Russian minority in response to this requirement.

If governments and the international community can defuse the risk from primary commodity exports, generate rapid growth, and provide credible guarantees to minorities, then they can radically reduce the risk of conflict. They can achieve conflict prevention through large effort on a few risk factors.

POLICIES FOR POSTCONFLICT PEACEBUILDING

All the policies that are appropriate for conflict prevention are also appropriate for postconflict peacebuilding. However, they are unlikely to be sufficient. In the first decade of postconflict peace, societies face roughly double the risk of conflict predicted by the preconflict risk factors. Postconflict societies are thus at substantial additional risk because of what has happened to them during conflict.

Several factors may account for this increase in risk. A rebel organization has built an effective military capability, in part by the manufacture of group grievance, and in part by the accumulation of armaments, money, and military skills. People have become used to violence, so that the norms that inhibit political violence in most societies will have been eroded. People's political allegiance may have polarized, so that, as in Somalia, ethnic dominance has been created by the conflict even if the society was initially either diverse or homogeneous.

Many societies have severe objective group grievances that sustain intense political conflict, without getting close to civil war. Group grievance and intense political conflict are not in themselves dangerous: they are indeed the normal stuff of democratic politics. However, in postconflict societies, civil war has first built intense political conflict and then conducted that conflict through violence. Whereas most of the societies that have group grievances have no tradition of conducting their political conflict by means of violence, postconflict societies may have no tradition of conducting their political conflict nonviolently.

The rebel organization usually maintains its effectiveness during the postconflict period. Compared with a preconflict society with the same risk factors, the postconflict society is therefore much better prepared for war. The rebel organization has already recruited, motivated, armed, and saved. For example, Jonas Savimbi, the head of the Angolan rebel organization UNITA, was reputed to have accumulated over $4 billion in financial assets during the first war, some of which he then used to finance the start of the second.

Peace requires either that the intense political conflict continue but that the military option of conducting it be made infeasible, or that the political conflict itself be resolved. Each of these is difficult. To remove the military option requires demilitarizing the rebel organization, turning it into a conventional political party. This can happen. For example, Renamo, once a rebel military organization in Mozambique, is now a successful political party. Renamo was willing to demobilize, whereas UNITA was not. Mozambique was a postconflict success, whereas Angola was a failure, partly because Angola had diamonds and Mozambique did not. Aid donors were able to come up with a moderate financial package for Renamo, which made peaceful political contest an attractive option. Diamonds had made UNITA so rich that nothing donors could offer mattered, while renewed predation offered massive rewards. UNITA is believed to have earned around $2 billion from diamond mining in the first two years of renewed war. The massive importance of aid donors to the Mozambique economy may also have made the maintenance of a democratic system in which Renamo would have a fair chance more credible. In Angola the government did not need the donors and so had no means of reassuring UNITA that democratic rights of political contest would be maintained. Even when the rebel group demobilizes, the precedent of violent conflict is fresh in people's minds. This is perhaps why time itself improves the prospects of peace: the habits of peaceful conflict replace those of violent conflict.

The alternative to continuing the political contest but making the military option infeasible is to resolve the political contest itself. This requires at a minimum that grievances be addressed, even if though on average they are not objectively any more serious than those in peaceful societies. If, indeed, group grievance has been manufactured by rebel indoctrination, it can potentially be deflated by political gestures. While grievances may need to be addressed objectively, the main purpose of addressing them is probably for their value in changing perceptions.

The task of dealing with conflict that lacks proper boundaries between the political and the violent is difficult whether the approach is to restore boundaries or resolve the political conflict. However, the attitudes of the domestic population appear not to be the main reason why postconflict societies have a risk of further conflict that is not much greater than implied by their inherited risk factors. Recall that the main risk comes from diasporas living in rich countries. What can be done to reduce this risk? One approach is to build the diaspora into the peace process. For example, it is evident that the Irish American diaspora has played a major part in financing violence in the conflict in Northern Ireland. Protestant and Catholic rebel military organizations have actively raised funds in North America, and a number of the guns used in shootings turn out to have come (indirectly, it is hoped) from the Boston police department. When the peace faction within the IRA initiated the peace process, its leader went to Boston, and the British and Irish governments chose a U.S. senator to head the peace negotiations.

An extension of this approach is to target campaigns at the diaspora that emphasize that the domestic population wants to maintain peace because the costs of violence are so high. Diasporas bear none of these costs, and so they need to be reminded that others do. Governments can go much further. Diasporas are potentially major assets for the development process, with skills and business connections. The diaspora organizations can be given explicit tasks in promoting economic recovery, facing them with a choice between a constructive role and a destructive one. A complementary policy is for the governments of the countries in which these diasporas are resident to put clear limits on the activities of the diaspora organizations. Political support for violent rebel organizations is legitimate, but supplying material aid is not. For example, U.S. efforts to prevent countries such as Libya, Sudan, and Afghanistan from harboring terrorists who have killed U.S. citizens would have greater prospects of success were they to be put in the context of an international policy to set limits on the conduct of diasporas.

Dependence upon primary commodity exports turns out to be even more important as a risk factor in postconflict societies than in preconflict societies: the same level of dependence generates a significantly higher risk. One policy for mitigating the risks from primary commodities is open to postconflict governments that is not available preconflict: the government might decide to share the revenues peacefully and legally with the rebel organization. The rebels then do not need to fight in order to get what they want. This is, perhaps, what the government of Sierra Leone decided to do when it brought the rebel leader into government as minister of mining. The government attempted to give the rebels a greater interest in peace. There are, however, limits to this policy. If it is profitable for one rebel group to be predatory on primary commodity exports, once the rebels have been bought off, it will probably be profitable for another group to replace them.

While a postconflict government has more options for dealing with primary commodity dependence, it has fewer options for dealing with ethnic dominance. The provision of constitutional guarantees for ethnic minorities is unlikely to cut much ice in the low-trust environment that follows years of mutual hatred and killing. In such situations one option is for the international community to provide reassurance through an extended phase of military presence and its own guarantees. This is the solution currently being attempted in Bosnia and Kosovo. A further possibility is to determine that the country as constituted is inviable. However, rather than ethnic cleansing, a better solution may be federation with a neighboring country in which no ethnic group is dominant.

As in conflict prevention, rapid growth will assist peace. However, the task of achieving rapid growth requires somewhat different policies in postconflict societies. After a long war, economies tend to bounce back: they are so far below their productive potential. For example, in the first five years of peace after a fifteen-year war, economies on average grow at 6 percent a year (Collier 1999). Mozambique suffered an even longer war than this and recovered even more rapidly. One of the casualties of civil war is trust. Because life is so uncertain, people shorten their time horizons and are less concerned about building a reputation for honesty. Some people find it more profitable to behave opportunistically. As this behavior becomes more commonplace, the society switches into a low-level equilibrium of mutual suspicion and widespread opportunism. This raises the cost of all sorts of business transactions. For example, in Kampala, Uganda, a manufacturer of mattresses sold them wholesale on credit to agents who went up-country to sell them retail. One of the agents claimed that his entire consignment had been stolen by northern rebels. The manufacturer had to accept this alibi and forfeit the money. On the grapevine, he heard that the agent had invented the story, but he could not be sure what to believe.

Once a society has suffered a collapse into low trust, it takes concerted action to change expectations. Meanwhile, many functions that governments can normally rely upon simply do not work. The tax collection system, the courts, accountants, and doctors may all have been corrupted by opportunistic behavior. The government can respond to this problem by creating coordinated changes in expectations, institution by institution. For example, one common approach has been to close the old revenue-collecting part of the civil service and establish a new, independent institution to which people are freshly recruited. In return for better pay they are subjected to more rigorous checks for honest conduct. Being a new institution it is to some extent able to shed the burden of bad expectations that the old institutions carry.

The combination of primary commodity predation and opportunism implies that some people do well out of war (Collier 2000a). Although most people lose, others have an interest in war restarting. Hence, when wars do restart, they are not necessarily simply an outpouring of irrational hatred or deep fears. Indeed, both hatreds and fears can be played upon by those who expect to gain materially. One way in which a postconflict government can defend the peace against such manipulation is to publicize self-interest for what it is. Society at large needs to recognize that some groups have an interest in a return to conflict.

A corollary of this analysis is that rebel organizations, existing or prospective, can be viewed as rational economic agents. This has both a hopeful and a cautionary implication. The hopeful implication is that rebel organizations are likely to respond to incentives. For example, were the UN Security Council to introduce sanctions that made the economic and military circumstances of rebellion more difficult, the incidence of rebellion would decline. The cautionary implication is that it may be of little avail to buy off rebel groups. In countries where the objective conditions make rebellion financially feasible, if one group is bought off, others are likely to occupy the "market" opportunity for the generation of grievance.

CONCLUSION

Popular perceptions of the causes of civil conflict take at face value the discourse of the rebel organization. Civil war appears as an intense political contest, fueled by grievances that are so severe as to have burst the banks of normal political channels. Rebellions are thus interpreted as the ultimate protest movements, their cadres being self-sacrificing heroes struggling against oppression. In fact, most rebellions cannot be like this. When the main grievances

—inequality, political repression, and ethnic and religious divisions—are measured objectively, they provide no explanatory power in predicting rebellion. These objective grievances and hatreds simply cannot usually be the cause of violent conflict. They may well generate intense political conflict, but such conflict does not usually escalate to violent conflict.

By contrast, economic characteristics—dependence on primary commodity exports, low average incomes, slow growth, and large diasporas—are all significant and powerful predictors of civil war. Rebellions either have the objective of natural resource predation or are critically dependent upon natural resource predation to pursue other objectives. These, rather than objective grievances, are the risk factors that conflict prevention must reduce if it is to be successful. Since to date conflict prevention has paid scant attention to these causes of conflict, there is probably considerable scope for policy, both domestic and international, to prevent civil conflict more effectively.

While objective grievances do not generate violent conflict, violent conflict generates subjective grievances. This is not just a by-product of conflict, but an essential activity of a rebel organization. Rebel military success depends upon motivating its soldiers to kill the enemy, and this—as in the classic Leninist theory of rebel organizations—requires indoctrination. Hence, by the end of a civil war, there is intense intergroup hatred based upon perceived grievances. A conflict has been generated that has no boundaries between political and violent actions. The task in postconflict societies is partly, as in preconflict societies, to reduce the objective risk factors. However, because of this legacy of induced polarizing grievance, postconflict societies are much more at risk than is implied by the inherited risk factors. Either boundaries must be reestablished between the political contest and violence or the political contest must be resolved. Neither of these is easy, which is why, once a civil war has occurred, the chances of further conflict are so high.

NOTES

The findings, interpretations, and conclusions expressed in this paper are entirely those of the author. They do not necessarily represent the views of the World Bank, its executive directors, or the countries they represent.

1. I would like to thank Professor Frederick Prior of Swarthmore College for this information.

REFERENCES

Collier, Paul. 1999. "On the Economic Consequences of Civil War." *Oxford Economic Papers* 51: 168–183.

———. 2000a. "Doing Well Out of War." In *Greed and Grievance: Economic Agendas in Civil Wars*, ed. Mats Berdal and David Malone. Boulder, Colo.: Lynne Rienner.

———. 2000b. "Rebellion as a Quasi-Criminal Activity." *Journal of Conflict Resolution*.

Collier, Paul, and Anke Hoeffler. 1998. "On the Economic Causes of Civil War." *Oxford Economic Papers* 50: 563–573.

———. 2000. "Greed and Grievance in Civil War." World Bank, Policy Research Working Paper 2355.

Grossman, Herschel I. 1999. "Kleptocracy and Revolutions." *Oxford Economic Papers* 51: 267–283.

Kuran, Timur. 1989. "Sparks and Prairie Fires: A Theory of 'Unanticipated Political Revolution.'" *Public Choice* 61: 41–74.

11

Minorities and Nationalists

Managing Ethnopolitical Conflict in the New Century

Ted Robert Gurr

EFFECTIVE MANAGEMENT of ethnic and separatist conflicts by civil and international authorities presupposes an understanding of their nature, causes, and the outcomes of past efforts at accommodation. This chapter surveys some current evidence and analyses of *ethnopolitical conflicts*. These are conflicts in which groups such as the Mayans of Chiapas and the Bosnian Serbs who define themselves using ethnic or national criteria make claims on behalf of their collective interests against the state or against other political actors. The following general points need to be kept in mind:

- The "ethnic criteria" used by these groups to define themselves usually include common descent, shared historical experiences, and valued cultural traits. There is no warrant for assuming that any one basis for ethnic or cultural identity, such as religion, language, race, or a common homeland, is inherently more important or more likely to cause conflict than others.

- The claims made by ethnopolitical groups include material and political demands as well as claims arising from cultural and religious concerns. One cannot explain away the significance of cultural identity by arguing that what "really" motivates such groups is the quest for well-being or power. What is important is that ethnopolitical groups organize around their shared identity and seek gains for members of their group. It is misleading to interpret the Zapatistas as just a militant peasants' movement or the Bosnian Serbs as the equivalent of a political party: they draw their strength from cultural and historical bonds, not associational ones.

- Ethnopolitical groups are highly diverse. *National peoples* are regionally concentrated cultural groups, usually with a history of separate political existence, who want to protect or reestablish some degree of politically separate existence from the states that govern them. The Mayans of Chiapas and the Bosnian Serbs illustrate two different types: the

Mayans are indigenous peoples; the Bosnian Serbs are ethnonationalists. *Minority peoples* are culturally distinct groups in plural societies who seek equal rights, opportunities, and access to power within existing political communities. The Arab citizens of Israel are one example; others include African Americans in the United States and Brazil.

- The claims and political strategies of ethnopolitical groups vary according to their type and circumstances. National peoples usually seek *exit,* a goal that often leads to separatist wars and state repression. Minority peoples want *access,* a goal usually pursued by conventional political action and protest campaigns. In political systems that are open and responsive to ethnopolitical claims, leaders of ethnopolitical groups usually choose to work toward both kinds of objectives by nonviolent strategies. In states that suppress or ignore such claims, leaders are likely to follow strategies of violence that often escalate into protracted ethnic warfare. These are the conflicts that pose the greatest threat to regional and international security and are most likely to attract efforts at prevention, mediation, and negotiated settlement.

HOW SERIOUS IS THE ETHNOPOLITICAL CHALLENGE TO GLOBAL SECURITY?

Ethnopolitical conflict has been the world's most common source of warfare, insecurity, and loss of life for several decades.[1] The following evidence comes mainly from the Minorities at Risk project, an ongoing global study of the status, grievances, and conflicts of politically active ethnic groups:[2]

- Nearly one hundred national and minority peoples took part in serious, violent conflicts at some time between 1945 and 1990. Of these, sixty were protracted ethnonational conflicts; that is, they were fought over issues of group autonomy and lasted at least a decade.

- At the beginning of 1999 there were fifty-nine armed ethnically based rebellions under way, at least one of them in every world region. About twenty of these were large scale, such as those in Kashmir, Kosovo, and the eastern Congo.

- Since 1945, according to research by Barbara Harff, nearly fifty ethnic and religious minorities have been targeted in episodes of genocide and mass political murder that killed at least 6 million and as many as 10 million noncombatants.[3]

- In 1999 there were 11.5 million internationally recognized refugees and an estimated 7.5 million who were internally displaced. Most of these people were fleeing from civil wars, interethnic rivalries, and campaigns of mass murder and ethnic cleansing.[4]

The alarmist interpretation of these data is that the world is on the downward slope to anarchy within and among states, and to polarization of societies and continents along lines of religious and cultural cleavage. Evidence on trends during the 1990s suggests a more optimistic outlook:

- Of the fifty-nine armed ethnopolitical conflicts being fought in early 1999, seven were escalating and twenty-nine were stable, whereas twenty-three were de-escalating, either because of military defeats or as a result of negotiations and government-initiated reforms. The latter include a number of long-term and supposedly "intractable" conflicts that were on the verge of enduring settlement: for example, the Palestinian-Israeli conflict and the Naga rebellion in India.

- Most new ethnic rebellions of the late twentieth century began near the end of the Cold War and few have begun since then. More precisely, an average of eight new rebellions began each year between 1989 and 1992; since 1992 the average has fallen to two per year.

Table 1. Minorities at Risk in the 1990s by World Region

World Region (number of countries with populations over 500,000)	Number of Countries with Minorities at Risk	Number of Minorities at Risk	Population of Minorities at Risk (1998 estimates)	
			Total (in 000s)	Percentage of Regional Population
Western democracies and Japan (21)	15	30	99,453	11.7
Eastern Europe and the newly independent states (27)	23	59	57,058	13.9
East, Southeast, and South Asia (24)	20	59	428,976	13.4
North Africa and the Middle East (20)	13	28	101,538	26.0
Africa south of the Sahara (45)	27	67	221,079	35.7
Latin America and the Caribbean (24)	18	32	124,028	25.8
Total countries (161)	116	275	1,032,132	17.5

Note: This table tallies politically significant national and minority peoples greater than one hundred thousand or 1 percent of country population in countries with 1998 populations greater than five hundred thousand. The table is based on current research by the Minorities at Risk project, Center for International Development and Conflict Management, University of Maryland. Changing political circumstances and new information lead to periodic updates in the inclusion and exclusion of groups under observation. The number of countries above the five-hundred-thousand threshold in 1998 are shown in parentheses in the "World Region" column. The population figures for national and minority peoples usually are approximations. They are listed in appendix D to *Peoples versus States* (note 2). Population percentages are calculated from 1998 estimates for all countries in each region.

The Western democracies include Canada, the United States, Australia, New Zealand, and Japan, in addition to Western Europe. The Middle East includes North Africa, the Arab states, Turkey, Cyprus, Iran, and Israel. Asia includes Afghanistan, the Indian subcontinent, Southeast Asia, and Pacific Asia. Africa includes South Africa but excludes North Africa. Latin America includes Central America and the Caribbean.

- The number of new campaigns of ethnic protest traces the same pattern, from an average of twelve per year in the early 1990s to three per year since 1993. This decline foreshadows a continued decline in new ethnic rebellions. The recent historical record shows that a median span of ten years of nonviolent political action preceded new ethnic rebellions. Since the number of new ethnically based protest campaigns is declining, the pool of potential future rebellions also is shrinking.[5]

- One-sixth, at most, of the world's population identifies with politically active cultural groups. The Minorities at Risk project's current survey identifies 275 politically significant national and minority peoples in the world's 161 largest countries. The outer bounds of potential supporters for these ethnopolitical movements is slightly over 1 billion, or 17 percent of the global population. These groups are much more numerous in some regions than in others, as shown in table 1; the proportions in the Western democracies, the postcommunist states, and Asia are below the world mean. And more than half these 275 peoples are minorities who seek recognition and rights within existing societies, not a redrawing of international boundaries.[6] Other ethnic groups may make new claims in the future, but we probably have already heard from most of those that have serious grievances.

MODERNIZATION AND ETHNOPOLITICAL CONFLICT

The upward trend in ethnopolitical conflict that captured world attention at the beginning of the 1990s began in the 1960s before it stabilized and began to decline. The end of the Cold War made such conflicts more visible. Some were provoked by contention for power in postcommunist states; others were responses to democratic transitions in Africa. But neither the Cold War nor its passing "created" the cultural identities, animosities, or aspirations that have sparked these conflicts. Rather, the long-term trend is best understood as an indirect consequence of global processes of modernization.

Modernization refers to three large and interdependent changes that have reshaped the world in the past half century: the growth of the modern state and the state system, the development of a global economic system, and the communications revolution.[7] The processes of modernization are not new, but their pace and reach since 1950 have no historical precedent. And in combination they have vastly increased interaction and competition among cultural groups, and contention between cultural groups and the state.

The Growth of the Modern State

Virtually all new and postrevolutionary states of the past half century have been committed to consolidating and expanding their powers, emulating the precedents established by the successful states of the industrial North. This objective dictates, among other things, that states subordinate the special interests and relative autonomy of hundreds of ethnic groups to state elites' conception of national identity and interest. State building almost everywhere in the Third World has meant policies aimed at assimilating national and minority peoples, restraining their historical autonomy, and extracting their resources, revenues, and labor for the use of the state. The building of new communist states in Eastern Europe after 1945 had the same implications and consequences.

Some minority peoples, including most Chinese communities in Southeast Asia, have been able to share power and prosperity at the center of new states. Others—especially in Africa, where the reach of state power is limited—have been able to hold on to de facto local autonomy and sometimes to regain it when central authority collapsed. Eritrea gained independence after the overthrow of Ethiopia's marxist military regime in the early 1990s and Somaliland (northern Somalia) has had an effective government and de facto independence since the collapse of the Mogadishu government. But the net effect of state building in most parts of the world has been to substantially increase grievances of most culturally distinct groups, those that have been unable either to protect their autonomy or to participate meaningfully in power at the center.

The Development of a Global Economic System

The worldwide impetus to industrialize and to exploit underutilized human and natural resources has benefited some cultural groups and harmed others. Ethnoclasses in developing societies have often gained from expanding economic opportunities; some also have mobilized in efforts to overcome discriminatory barriers that restricted their access to new wealth. Indigenous peoples have been most adversely affected. Whether they like it or not, their resources and labor are being absorbed into national and international networks of economic activity. Indigenous peoples are almost always disadvantaged by the terms of their incorporation. Their reactions have been especially sharp in response to the alienation of the lands, forests, and natural resources on which they are culturally as well as materially dependent.[8]

The Communications Revolution

The spread of the mass media and the ready availability of electronic forms of communication facilitate or enhance every stage in the conflict process. Rapid and dense communication networks make cultural groups more aware of their identities and shared interests. They bring them into close contact with supporters and sources of inspiration elsewhere. And they give leaders powerful means to mobilize mass followings and coordinate their political actions. Virtually every new communication technique has been adapted by ethnopolitical groups for their own purposes. Islamic activists have used audiocassettes to spread their gospel of renewal and revolution since the 1970s. The Miskito Indians of Nicaragua used the radiophones of Moravian churches to coordinate their resistance to the Sandinistas in the early 1980s. And a great many ethnic activist organizations now are on the World Wide Web, with the GreenNet especially favored by activists.

THE POLITICAL MOBILIZATION OF ETHNIC GRIEVANCES: OR, WHY MINORITIES REBEL

The question here is why and how culturally distinct groups become engaged in protest and rebellion against the state. Modernization sets the larger context. The specifics of each group's situation determine how it acts within that context. Four general factors determine the nature, intensity, and persistence of their actions. They are

- the *salience of ethnocultural identity* for members and leaders of the group,
- the extent to which the group has collective *incentives* for ethnopolitical action,
- the extent of the group's *capacities* for collective action, and
- the availability of *opportunities* in the group's political environment that increase its chances of attaining group objectives through political action.

Propositions about these four factors are derived from existing theories of collective action and are central to explaining political action by any kind of identity group.[9] The key to analyzing the origins of ethnopolitical conflict is to show how each factor is activated by the characteristics and circumstances of communal identity groups.

The Salience of Ethnocultural Identity

The first general proposition is that the greater the salience of ethnocultural identity for people who share common descent, cultural traits, and historical experiences, the more likely they are to define their interests in ethnocultural terms and the easier it is for leaders to mobilize them for collective action. I assume that cultural identities—those based on common descent, experience, language, and belief—tend to be stronger and more enduring than most civic and associational identities. Nonetheless, the salience of cultural identity varies widely among and within groups and is subject to change over time. The descriptive question is, How salient is ethnocultural identity at any point in time? The analytic question is, What determines the salience of a group's identity?

Scholars recognize that communal identities are multidimensional. There is no warrant for assuming that any one basis for ethnic identity, such as race, language, religion, or a common homeland, is intrinsically more important than another. Some traits, though, are associated with particularly strong and durable collective identities. In multiracial societies, shared physical attributes ("race") are almost always primary markers of group identity. Religion also is a strong source of group cohesion, except in societies where its force has been eroded by secularism. A group's language is another key marker of identity, a source of group cohesion, and a recurring issue of contention among groups in heterogeneous societies. But I agree with David Laitin that language disputes alone are not a common source of deadly rivalries, because language differences are subject to individual and collective compromises. Individuals in heterogeneous societies can and ordinarily do speak several languages, but they cannot be both black and white or both Hindu and Muslim.[10]

If cultural factors are variable, does salience originate in a people's material interests, as marxists have argued? It is true enough that claims made by ethnopolitical groups include material and political demands as well as claims based on their ethnocultural interests. But it is not reasonable to explain away the significance of cultural identity by arguing that what "really" motivates the leaders and members of such groups is the quest for material benefits or power. The decisive factor is that ethnopolitical groups organize around their shared identity and seek gains or redress of grievances for the collectivity. It is a commonplace that manipulative leaders such as Slobodan Milosevic and Franjo Tudjman use appeals to Serbian and Croatian nationalism as a means to advance their personal political agendas. It is equally important to recognize that most people who follow them do so because they think their collective interests are best served by militant nationalists.

The general proposition is that the salience of ethnocultural identity depends on how much difference it makes in people's lives. If an ethnic group is treated differently, by denial or privilege, its members will become more self-conscious about their common bonds and interests. Minimize differences, and ethnic identity becomes less significant as a unifying principle.

Three more specific propositions are suggested. First, the greater a people's dissimilarity from groups with which they interact regularly, the more salient their identity is likely to be. Second, ethnocultural identity is important when it contributes to a group psychology of comparative advantage or disadvantage. Groups in heterogeneous states make comparisons of relative worth based on their collective experiences and myths. Advantaged groups often feel superior because they share a belief that they are the original people of a place (the Malay claim to be "sons of the soil") or that they have exceptional skills (the European claim to a civilizing mission toward colonial peoples) or that they have overcome adversity and hostile challengers (the basis of Afrikaners' sense of superiority over black Africans).[11] The belief in comparative superiority helps to explain ethnic domination and the resistance of advantaged groups to ethnopolitical challenges. It also motivates some separatist movements by relatively advantaged peoples, for example, the Catalans of Spain.

Comparative superiority is the other side of the coin of what Vamik D. Volkan calls the "chosen traumas" of disadvantaged peoples, their beliefs about their victimization.[12] The ethnocultural identity of disadvantaged and victimized groups is salient because it is the source of invidious distinctions—the inequalities in status, economic well-being, and access to political power that are maintained by advantaged groups. Insofar as a people's race, culture, or beliefs provide others with grounds for discriminating against them, the salience of their ethnocultural identity is likely to be high.

Third, open conflict with the state and rival groups sharpens the salience of group identity. Many of the appeals used by ethnopolitical leaders aim at increasing the salience of group identity by invoking historical memories and symbols of victimization. Serious episodes of conflict leave bitter residues in people's memories and for a long time afterward can be used by leaders to justify political action. Serbian nationalists, for example, made effective use of fifty-year-old memories about atrocities committed by the Croatian Ustashi to mobilize Serbian support for their 1991–92 war with the newly independent state of Croatia. Labeling helps: Serb leaders referred to Croats as Ustashi.

Incentives for Ethnopolitical Action

The second general proposition is that the greater the shared incentives among members of an ethnocultural identity group, the more likely they are to support and participate in ethnopolitical action. *Ethnopolitical action* refers to any organized activity in pursuit of the group's objectives, beginning with mobilization, the process by which people are recruited into movements. Once people are mobilized, participation can take diverse forms, depending on the group's political environment and the strategic and tactical decisions of its leaders. The range of actions includes conventional politics, collective action (strikes, demonstrations, nonviolent direct action), and rebellion (terrorism, armed uprisings, guerrilla wars, civil wars).

Three types of incentives prompt political action by identity groups: resentment about losses suffered in the past, fear of future losses, and hopes for relative gains. The relative importance of each of these incentives depends on a group's changing position in relation to other groups and to the state. The general proposition builds on familiar arguments about the causes of relative deprivation. People who have lost ground relative to what they had in the past are said to experience decremental deprivation and are motivated to seek redress for what was lost. Those who anticipate losses, especially reversal of an improving trend, ex-

perience progressive deprivation that disposes them to support movements that defend and promote the group's present status and attainments. Groups in which nationalist or revolutionary expectations have taken hold are motivated to seek a fundamental change in their political status.

The incentives of ethnopolitical groups are not inherently nonrational nor do they necessarily dispose people to ethnopolitical violence. Instead they constitute a potential for goal-directed political action. They are analogous to what Charles Tilly characterizes as the collective interests that form the basis for group mobilization.[13] But incentives for ethnopolitical groups are different from Tilly's calculated "collective interests" because they have an intrinsic affective component. Members of identity groups usually resent their disadvantages and seek redress not only, or even necessarily, with self-interest in mind, but also with passion, self-righteousness, and solidarity with their kindred.[14]

Comparative and case studies point to four general conditions that strongly affect group incentives for collective action. The four are collective disadvantages, loss of political autonomy, repression, and the "frames," or cognitive understandings, they have of their situation.

COLLECTIVE DISADVANTAGES. First, the greater a group's collective disadvantages vis-à-vis other groups, the greater the incentives for action. *Disadvantage* means socially derived inequalities in material well-being, political access, or cultural status by comparison with other social groups. Inequalities provide incentives for remedial action. If inequalities are maintained by overtly discriminatory policies, the minorities affected have powerful incentives for action because their resentment is easily focused on the agents of discrimination. All but 33 of the 275 groups in the Minorities at Risk survey were subject to one or several kinds of discrimination in the mid-1990s.[15]

Economic discrimination

- 113 groups experienced active economic discrimination due to contemporary social practice or public policies.
- 66 groups were economically disadvantaged because of past discrimination or neglect.
- 92 groups experienced no economic discrimination.

Political discrimination

- 135 groups experienced active political discrimination due to contemporary social practice or public policies.
- 65 groups were politically disadvantaged because of past discrimination or neglect.
- 74 groups experienced no political discrimination.

Cultural discrimination

- 65 groups experienced substantial cultural restrictions, for example, with respect to language use, religious practice, practice of group customs, and formation of cultural organizations.
- 51 groups experienced limited cultural restrictions.
- 158 groups experienced no cultural restrictions.

THE LOSS OF POLITICAL AUTONOMY. Regaining political autonomy is a second major incentive. Virtually all ethnonationalists, national minorities, and indigenous peoples either were once independent of external control or were part of political entities other than the states that now govern them. The U.S. conspiracy that deposed the last ruling monarch of independent Hawaii in 1893, the fragmentation of the Hungarian nation into a half-dozen segments in 1919, and the conquest of Tibet in 1951 are historical facts that give rise to persistent grievances and hopes for restoration. They are potent symbols for political entrepreneurs whose projects are to restore indigenous rights or regain national autonomy. The greater the loss of autonomy, and the more recently it occurred, the greater the likely effect of such appeals.

REPRESSION. Repressive control of an ethnopolitical group is a third major incentive for collective action. The general principle is that the use of force against people who think it is unjust may inspire fear and caution in the short run but provokes resentment and enduring incentives to resist and retaliate in the longer run. White supremacy in the American South was maintained until the early 1960s by legal repression and extralegal violence. Long before the Russians' first invasion of secessionist Chechnya in December 1994, Russian governments had used force to establish and maintain control of the region. In both cases repression left enduring legacies of anger and resentment, which in the United States animated a decade of direct action and violent protest by African Americans and in Chechnya motivated widespread, intransigent resistance to Russian attacks in 1994–95 and 1999–2000.

FRAMES FOR ETHNOPOLITICAL ACTION. Empowering ideas about national self-determination and collective rights of minorities also give impetus to ethnopolitical movements because they provide justifications for action. Theorists of social movements describe these kinds of orienting ideas as "frames," or cognitive understandings. In Sidney Tarrow's summary, "Inscribing grievances in overall frames that identify an injustice, attribute the responsibility for it to others and propose solutions to it, is a central activity of social movements."[16] The most effective frames for identity groups are those that fit their cultural predispositions and immediate circumstances. Three doctrines that have been widely used as frames by contemporary ethnopolitical movements are the principle of national self-determination, the doctrine of indigenous rights, and international declarations that guarantee the rights of religious and cultural minorities.

Is it plausible to think that frames derived from these empowering doctrines are an independent source of incentives for collective action by identity groups? Perhaps they are for intellectuals and aspiring leaders. For collectivities, though, the effect of these doctrines probably is contingent on other kinds of incentives and on how closely they identify with the group. People are more likely to frame their situation and actions as a struggle for group rights or self-determination if they already have a sense of injustice about disadvantages and repression. And group identifiers are more likely to accept these doctrines if they learn of them through networks of communication within the group and from credible leaders.

The Dynamics of Protracted Conflict

The foregoing theoretical argument incorporates some strong feedback effects. The salience of group identity and the incentives for collective action are based partly on repression and disadvantages imposed on the group because the group resisted in the past. It is precisely this mutually reinforcing dynamic that generates protracted ethnopolitical conflicts such as those between Catholics and Protestants in Northern Ireland, Hutus and Tutsis, Palestinians and Israelis, Tamils and Sinhalese. Historical analysis should pinpoint the particular conjunction and sequence of conditions that set off a given episode. Once these conflicts have gone through several cycles, however, they tend to become self-generating. The general approach to the chicken-and-egg problem of which came first, grievances or political action, is to examine the consequences of each episode of protracted conflict. If an ethnic group in conflict is subject to repression and its disadvantages persist without any compensatory gains, then we should expect to see a resentful reinforcement of group identity and a disposition (incentives) to wait and work for future opportunities to rebel.

The Capacity for Ethnopolitical Action

The third general proposition is that the greater the cohesion and mobilization of an ethnocultural identity group, the more frequent and sustained its participation in political action. And, we can add, the more likely it is to gain concessions and greater access to power. Cohesive groups are those held together by dense networks of communication and interaction. *Mobilization as process* refers to the ways in which members of ethnopolitical organizations are recruited and motivated. *Mobilization as variable* signifies the extent to which group members commit their energies and resources to collective action in pursuit of shared interests.

A sense of collective identity and some awareness of common interests (salience of identity and collective incentives, analyzed previously) are necessary preconditions for mobilization. A widely used strategy of ethnopolitical organizations is to build a sense of common interest by employing frames that incorporate symbols of shared identity and grievance. But commitment to ethnopolitical organizations cannot be constructed or maintained from nothing. If a people's cultural identity and incentives for joint action are weak, they seldom can be mobilized by any leaders in response to any new threat or opportunity. On the other hand, the conjunction of shared incentives and a strong sense of group identity —a conjunction found among black opponents of apartheid in South Africa and among Shi'is and Kurds in Iraq after the Gulf War— provides highly combustible material that fuels what may appear to be spontaneous action in response to new opportunities.

Four traits, in addition to shared identity and incentives, shape a group's capacity for sustained and effective political action: its territorial concentration, its preexisting organization, its formation of coalitions, and the authenticity of its leaders.

TERRITORIAL CONCENTRATION. Rebellion is feasible for groups that have a territorial base but very difficult to organize for dispersed and urban groups. Recent empirical studies have used large-*n* comparisons in conjunction with case study materials to test these effects. Monica Duffy Toft examined seventy-two ethnic-based civil wars since 1945 and found that 88 percent involved groups that were regionally concentrated compared with only 6 percent that were dispersed. A reanalysis of the Minorities at Risk data set by James Fearon and David Laitin confirms Toft's results and observes that geographic concentration predicts rebellion in all world regions. By contrast, the groups least likely to rebel are those concentrated in urban areas.[17]

PREEXISTING ORGANIZATION. The cohesion of an identity group depends on high and sustained levels of interaction among its members. Speaking a common language and sharing home ground both promote interaction. So does preexisting social organization. Cohesion is high among people who practice a common religion (Shi'is in Iraq, Saudi Arabia, and Bahrain), share an economic niche (Chinese entrepreneurs in Southeast Asia), or dominate a political establishment (Hausa-Fulani in the Nigerian officer corps, Mende in Sierra Leone's government ministries). The organizational basis for the U.S. civil rights movement came from black southern churches, colleges, and the NAACP, all of which expanded rapidly from 1930 to the mid-1950s.[18]

Moreover, established political institutions usually are more cohesive than new political movements and can mobilize members at lower cost. For example, the capacity for collective action is relatively high in groups whose traditional authorities still command respect, as is the case among the Afars in Ethiopia and Hazaris in Afghanistan. The same is true of groups that control an autonomous regional government. The constituent republics of the USSR provided the institutional framework within which nationalists in the Baltic, the Caucasus, and Ukraine built independence movements in the late 1980s. I am not suggesting that all regional political entities, such as states in India or organized tribes in the United States, are inherently disposed to ethnorebellion. The point is that, given incentives and opportunities, it is easier to build ethnopolitical movements among people who have significant cohesion due to frequent and routine interaction as members of an existing institution. In the language of collective action theory, cohesion reduces the costs of organizing collective action.

FORMATION OF COALITIONS. In addition, the capacity for ethnopolitical action depends on overcoming narrower loyalties to clans, classes, and communities. Identity groups are heterogeneous and their boundaries often are fluid. The effective boundaries of an ethnopolitical group may depend more on coalition formation than on the objective scope of group identity. Palestinians, for example, are dispersed throughout the Middle East, include adherents of two major religions, are stratified by class, and support competing political organizations. The effectiveness of the Palestinian national movement, now on the verge of statehood, is due to the incorporation of most of these elements into the Palestine Liberation Organization (PLO). If the aspiring leaders of ethnopolitical groups fail to build inclusive coalitions, then mobilization and joint action are impeded, resources are deflected into factional fighting, and it is easier for states to co-opt and deflect ethnopolitical opponents. Kurdish nationalism offers a counterpoint to the Palestinian example. From the 1920s to the 1990s Kurds in Turkey, Iraq, and Iran fought a series of ethnonational rebellions seeking autonomy or independence. But Kurdish leaders have rarely coordinated political action across state boundaries and most of their rebellions have been crippled by rifts among the rebels themselves. If the Kurds had coalesced in a coherent and durable transnational movement, they might not now be the Middle East's largest nation—numbering 20 million to 30 million people—without a state.

AUTHENTICITY OF LEADERSHIP. Leadership is central to the process of mobilizing and overcoming divisions within groups. "Leadership" refers to a set of skills whose effectiveness in identity groups depends on context, not a manual of organizational behavior or a body of nationalist doctrine. Authenticity of leaders may be the most critical factor. The concept is analogous to legitimacy in the arena of conventional politics. Ethnopolitical leaders are authentic if they are seen as representing the most essential values and aspirations of the group and if their actions are thought to be in the common interest.

Authenticity is a matter of degree and can be gained or lost. Established leaders usually have authenticity by virtue of their position. They control resources, command preexisting loyalties, symbolize group identity, articulate group interests and demands, and manage coalitions. Thus they have ample means for overcoming the collective action problem, that is, the reluctance of most individuals to commit to the risky enterprise of protest and rebellion. But they can lose authenticity by wrong words and deeds. Alternative leaders are quick to capitalize on errors by their established counterparts. Entrepreneurial leaders—those who aim to build new ethnopolitical movements—face greater obstacles than the leaders of established organizations. They control fewer resources and depend more on symbolic skills and personal example. Entrepreneurial leaders also are more likely to articulate "frames" that give people a new sense of hope and power. Often they are risk takers who help convince and attract followers by dramatic personal acts of resistance. And they are especially likely to appeal to supporters who are dissatisfied with established leaders and organizations.

■ ■ ■

To summarize the argument thus far, an ethnopolitical group's capacity for political action depends, first of all, on the salience of group identity and shared incentives. Capacity is enhanced if the group has preexisting organizational networks and authentic leaders who can bridge internal divisions, whether by coalition building or by other means. And it is easier to build ethnopolitical movements and sustain campaigns of political action if most of the group shares a common homeland.

The theory sketched here also incorporates a response to writers who attribute ethnopolitical violence to "bad leaders." There are many instances of leaders who have led their people into devastating conflicts by playing on communal antagonisms, and sometimes they have done so in the service of personal ambition. Chechens, Serbs, and Rwandan Hutus all suffered grievously in the 1990s from the failed policies of militantly nationalistic and opportunistic leaders. The counterpoint is that people get the leaders they deserve, or more precisely they get the leaders they are prepared to follow. Skillful leaders can strengthen existing group ties and provide a greater awareness of shared interests, but they cannot create them. Given the existence of identity and interest, ethnic entrepreneurs can build militant political movements, but only within limits of group members' expectations about what objectives and actions are acceptable.[19]

Opportunities and Choices

The ways in which identity, incentives, and capacity are translated into ethnopolitical action depend on aspects of political and cultural context that are difficult to summarize in general propositions. Some actions are spontaneous and reactive, such as racially motivated riots in Los Angeles in 1965 and 1992, each of which was provoked directly or indirectly when police used force against individuals resisting arrest. But most ethnopolitical action, including all sustained campaigns of protest and rebellion, is shaped by strategic assessments and tactical decisions of the leaders and activists of politically mobilized communal groups.

OPPORTUNITY STRUCTURES. The concept of *political opportunity* refers to factors external to a group that influence its decisions about how to pursue ethnopolitical objectives. *Durable opportunity factors* include the political character of the state, its resources, and whether an ethnopolitical group has long-term alliances with other groups in the domestic political arena. These durable factors shape the ways in which groups organize and affect their long-term choices about strategies. Changes in the structure of a group's political environment are *transient opportunity factors.* Examples include changes in political institutions, turnover of elites, shifts in government policy, and the emergence of new political allies. Transient factors can give a boost to mobilization and morale, enhance the credibility of some leaders and frames, and lead to shifts in group claims and strategies. They also help determine the targets and timing of political action.[20]

The impact of transnational structures and actions on ethnopolitics has become so pervasive since the 1980s that we need to extend the concept of political opportunities from the domestic to the international level. The role of external support for ethnopolitical groups has long been recognized, especially the political and material assistance that external patrons provide for separatist movements. Deepa Khosla has examined the range of political, material, and military support given by foreign states to ethnopolitical minorities in the Third World in the 1990s. Slightly more than half (95 of 179 minorities in her study) received foreign support. All but 2 of 23 ethnonationalist groups benefited from foreign support, and so did half of communal contenders (32 of 64) and nearly half of indigenous peoples (24 of 52). Communal contenders and ethnonationalists both received more military than non-military support.[21]

The *international political opportunity structure* encompasses an ethnopolitical group's international allies and opponents, its kindred groups, and regional and international orga-

nizations. Recent studies of transnational networks show that they also have patterned effects on political mobilization and strategies of some kinds of ethnopolitical groups. For example, indigenous groups in Latin America have developed durable transnational links among one another, with global indigenous movements, and with some environmental NGOs.[22]

THE STATE CONTEXT OF ETHNOPOLITICAL ACTION: EFFECTS OF STATE POWER AND DEMOCRACY. The state's political institutions and capabilities structure ethnopolitical groups' choices about the objectives to pursue and the means to do so. First, the resources and administrative capabilities of the state set limits on what groups may obtain. Second, the openness of the political system affects group leaders' choices about whether to participate, protest, or rebel. Evidence from the Minorities at Risk study points to the special significance of three factors: *the scope of state power,* the political values and practices of *institutionalized democracy,* and the transient effects of *democratization.*

Scope of state power. State power is a durable opportunity factor. Strong states are those that have ample resources and the administrative and political capacity to control or regulate most economic, social, and political activity. The strongest states in the late twentieth century have included most of the advanced industrial democracies, China, and, until the 1980s, some Soviet bloc states. Postcolonial and postrevolutionary leaders throughout this century have sought to build strong states on the Western or Soviet model. The expansion of state power is likely to have crosscutting effects on national and minority peoples. State strategies of subordination and assimilation almost invariably increase collective grievances: administrative restraints are imposed, lifeways are altered, traditional cultures are denigrated or marginalized. At the same time the potential costs of collective action increase because the agents of an expanding state are usually intrusive and vigilant. On the other hand, groups whose leaders have countervailing resources, or low-cost access to decision-making processes, may be able to maintain group autonomy and secure payoffs for cooperating with dominant groups. All such statements are fraught with "maybes" because they depend on the dominant state's ideology and on the abilities of group leaders to obstruct, to adapt, and to acquire and deploy influential allies. In Lenin's USSR the Communist Party recognized the principle of national self-determination for non-Russians, and Stalin accepted the more limited principle of cultural-national autonomy. In Ataturk's Turkey, however, no political or cultural alternatives to Turkish identity were tolerated. The People's Republic of China follows the principle of cultural autonomy for minority peoples but adamantly opposes "splittists," such as Tibetan and Muslim Uigher nationalists who want political autonomy.

The outcomes of minority peoples' resistance to state building are problematic. Strong, resource-rich states have the capacity either to accommodate or to suppress national peoples and minorities at relatively low cost, depending on the preferences of state elites. Gains are most likely to be won by identity-based movements that maintain sustained, nonviolent campaigns for reforms that do not threaten state security. Rulers of weaker states face more stark, zero-sum choices when confronted by ethnopolitical challenges. They can expand the governing coalition at risk to their own positions, or they can devote scarce resources to all-out warfare against communal rivals. The Tutsi-dominated government of Burundi was under international pressure during the 1980s and early 1990s to incorporate the Hutu majority and, to its credit, attempted to do so by democratic means. The plan foundered in a coup and a welter of killings by militant Tutsis who rejected sharing power with Hutu leaders who won the 1993 elections.[23] In Rwanda, by contrast, the Hutu elite in the early 1990s faced pressures from international actors to accommodate Tutsi rebels but chose genocide rather than compromise.

A third alternative to incorporation or warfare is to negotiate independence or autonomy with ethnonationalists. The nonviolent deconstruction of the USSR, a powerful but declining state, provided a strong precedent. In 1993 Czechoslovakia fissioned peacefully into two independent republics. Candidates for political fragmentation at the onset of the twenty-first century include Canada, Belgium, South Africa, Russia, Serbia-Montenegro, Iraq, Sri Lanka, Pakistan, Ethiopia, Burma, Sudan, and the Democratic Republic of the Congo (formerly Zaire).

The connection between state strength and opportunities for successful ethnonational rebellion at the end of the twentieth century probably is curvilinear. Secession or autonomy is most likely to be gained in either relatively strong or very weak states: in strong states such as Canada and Belgium because democratic elites may be persuaded that peaceful divorce is less costly than civil war, and in weak states such as Moldova and Somalia because they lack the means to reclaim secessionist regions by force or inducements. Between these extremes are states with enough will and resources to wage war with ethnonational rebels but not the means to bury them or buy them out. These are the states most at risk of protracted ethnopolitical wars.

Institutionalized democracies. Democratic institutions and elites are the other durable opportunity factor that weighs heavily in the strategic calculus of ethnonationalists. Western European democracies and India afford more than a dozen illustrations in the past twenty-five years of the principle that democratic elites can be persuaded to extend autonomy when enough political resources are brought to bear by communal leaders. Ethnonationalists have used a mix of conventional and violent tactics in these conflicts, but with a couple of Indian exceptions—Nagas, Tripuras, Mizos—the winners have been ethnically based movements that relied on sustained mobilization and participation in conventional politics and protest, not armed rebellion. The practice of *democratic accommodation under pressure* is evident in the ways democratic governments process other kinds of ethnopolitical demands.

Managing ethnopolitical conflicts in institutionalized democracies depends most fundamentally on two principles. The first is implementing universalistic norms of equal rights and opportunities for all citizens, including ethnoclasses. The second is pluralistic accommodation of indigenous and regional peoples' desires for separate collective status. Although the application of these norms to national and minority peoples is relatively new and imperfect, empirical comparisons made in the Minorities at Risk study show that national and minority peoples in contemporary industrial democracies face few political barriers to participation and are more likely to use the tactics of protest than of rebellion.[24] The reasons are inherent in the political cultures and policies of modern democratic societies. In the past half century most political leaders of these societies have become more responsive to the interests of politicized ethnic groups, in particular to groups able to mobilize large constituencies and allies in persistent campaigns of protest—another example of the principle of *democratic accommodation under pressure* at work. Groups using violent protest and terrorism, by contrast, have risked backlash and loss of public support. Thus, the calculus for ethnopolitical action in democracies favors protest over rebellion.

Transitions to democracy. The process by which many former autocracies in the Second and Third Worlds have sought to establish more participatory and responsive political systems has problematic consequences for ethnic mobilization and conflict. Successful democratization means the establishment of regimes in which ethnic and other interests are accommodated by peaceful means. But the *process* of transition creates threatening uncertainties for some groups and opens up a range of transitory political opportunities for ethnic entrepreneurs.[25]

Postcommunist regimes relaxed coercive restraints on nationalism and interethnic rivalries at a time when the institutionalized means for their expression and accommodation did not yet exist or were fragile and distrusted. The problem of postrevolutionary communist states was diagnosed by Milovan Djilas, the Yugoslav revolutionary turned critic, in an essay written shortly before his death in 1995: "When revolutions occur, ethnic identities get hammered down, only to bounce back with elemental force unless precisely defined relationships have developed in a society: democratic institutions, a free economy, a middle class. In this regard communism left behind it a desert."[26] The result, in Yugoslavia and elsewhere, was a resurgence of communal activism, both protest and rebellion. Similar consequences can be expected to follow from democratization in multiethnic Third World autocracies. The most dubious expectation of all is that authoritarian states such as Sudan, Iraq, Burma, and Burundi may be able to defuse ethnopolitical wars by moving toward democracy. Democratic institutions in societies riven by ethnic rivalries are more likely to increase incentives and opportunities for more fighting than to provide pathways to peaceful accommodation.

To summarize, in established democracies the opportunities for ethnic mobilization are substantial and so are potential gains—for cohesive groups that rely largely on nonviolent tactics. The proposition is that institutionalized democracy facilitates nonviolent ethnopolitical action and inhibits ethnic rebellion. This tendency is reinforced in strong states, those that have ample power and resources to respond to pluralist interests.

In democratizing autocracies, by contrast, national and minority peoples ordinarily feel a loss of security simultaneously with a transient increase in opportunities for mobilization and action. New democratic regimes usually lack the resources or institutional means to make and guarantee the kinds of accommodations that typify the established democracies. There-fore, democratization in its early stages facili-tates both ethnically based protest and rebellion. The worst-case scenario is that accommoda-tion is rejected by all contenders, leading to civil war and the reimposition of autocratic rule by the strongest faction.[27]

It is worth repeating that both the USSR and the Federal Republic of Yugoslavia faced such conditions in 1990–91. The majority of Soviet and Russian leaders chose democracy and decentralization. They accepted the inde-pendent statehood of fourteen constituent re-publics of the USSR and subsequently negoti-ated autonomy arrangements with a number of regional entities within the Russian Federa-tion whose leaders were toying with secession. Serbian nationalists chose to fight rather than switch, with devastating consequences that persist into the twenty-first century.

THE INTERNATIONAL CONTEXT OF ETHNOPOLITICAL ACTION

A great many international factors help shape the aspirations, opportunities, and strategies of ethnopolitical groups. They also affect state policies toward minorities. Moreover, the nature of international engagement is a major deter-minant of whether ethnopolitical conflicts are of short duration or long and whether they end in negotiated settlements or humanitarian disasters.

Foreign Support for Contenders

Foreign sympathizers can contribute substan-tially to an ethnopolitical group's cohesion and political mobilization by providing material, political, and moral support. Indigenous rights organizations such as the American Indian Movement (in the 1970s) and the World Council of Indigenous Peoples (in the 1980s and 1990s) have promoted the establishment of numerous indigenous peoples' movements,

provided strategic guidance for their leaders, and pressured governments to respond posi-tively. In the 1970s and 1980s the PLO or-ganized and supported opposition activity by Palestinians in Jordan, Lebanon, and Israel's Occupied Territories. External support for ethnonational groups often provokes responses that offset opportunities. Weak regimes facing ethnopolitical challengers frequently seek bi-lateral military assistance and political support that enhance their capacity to counter ethno-political challenges. The most tragic and de-structive consequences occur when competing powers support different sides in ethnopolitical wars. Such proxy wars are usually protracted and very deadly, and they are not likely to end in negotiated settlements unless and until it is in the interest of the external powers.

Withdrawal of external support may open up possibilities for settlement, as happened in Afghanistan and Angola in the early 1990s. In both these instances, however, international efforts at settlement failed, quickly in Afghani-stan and slowly in Angola, because one or more contenders could not be persuaded that partic-ipation in coalition governments was preferable to fighting for complete victory. In Afghani-stan the cessation of Russian and U.S. support in 1991 led to a new phase of civil war, fought this time not between marxists and Islamists but among communal rivals for power. Despite UN-led support for a succession of coalition governments, the country was rent by another seven years of armed conflict among political movements based on Tajiks, Uzbeks, Hazaris, and Pushtuns. The Taliban Islamist move-ment, which consolidated control in 1998, de-rived its support almost exclusively from the Pushtuns. More exactly, the Taliban repre-sents the political and religious interests of mullahs from Qandahar, in southern Afghani-stan. Thus the Taliban is a vehicle by which one element of the Pushtuns has reestablished the group's historic hegemony.[28]

The resumption of protracted ethnopolitical conflict, despite international efforts to broker a political settlement, is another manifestation of what James Fearon analyzes as a commitment problem.[29] Angola affords a clear example. The Angolan government's main challenger since 1975 has been the National Union for the Total Independence of Angola (UNITA), based mainly on the Ovimbundu people of southern Angola. During the Cold War the United States and South Africa gave UNITA ample material and political assistance in a proxy war against the Cuban-supported government in Luanda. Near the end of the Cold War, after Cuban troops had withdrawn and the government had shed its marxist trappings, an internationally brokered peace plan led to multiparty parliamentary and presidential elections in 1992. In the absence of mutual trust and international guarantees, neither party acted in good faith. UNITA rejected the election results and many UNITA supporters in the capital were massacred. Another round of international pressure led in 1997 to formation of a coalition government with UNITA's Jonas Savimbi as head of the now-legal opposition. But UNITA did not demobilize its fighters and continued to acquire new arms from old friends. The government expelled some of the UNITA parliamentarians and prompted the others to establish a new, "tame," UNITA. While politicos maneuvered in the capital, UNITA expanded its military control, and by 1998 a full-fledged civil war again was being fought. By late 1999 the government finally had the upper hand, which prompted renewed international efforts to isolate Savimbi and his supporters.[30]

In summary, external military support for contenders in ethnopolitical wars increases group capacities and opportunities for action but also makes it likely that conflicts will be protracted, deadly, and highly resistant to settlement. In the 1990s the international emphasis has shifted to constructive engagement like that practiced by the United States toward South Africa (and Namibia) in the 1980s. The essential strategy of constructive engagement

is the use of political pressure and incentives to push adversaries toward negotiated settlements. Constructive engagement is most likely to succeed when used in coordinated fashion by major powers and regional and international organizations. But of course it sometimes fails, as shown by the Angola example.

International Spillover of Ethnopolitical Conflict

Group incentives, capacities, and opportunities are amplified by the contagious example of successful political action elsewhere and by diffusion of ethnopolitical conflict from nearby regions.

Contagion and communication refer to the processes by which one group's actions provide inspiration and guidance, both strategic and tactical, for groups elsewhere. Though some observers have argued that civil or ethnic conflict is in general contagious, a closer reading of the evidence suggests that the strongest contagion effects occur within networks of similar groups. Informal connections and influences have long existed among disadvantaged peoples, so that, for example, one finds Australian Aborigines in the early 1960s organizing freedom rides in rural New South Wales, and Dayaks in northern Borneo in the 1980s resisting commercial logging of their forests with rhetoric and tactics remarkably like those used by native Canadian peoples in the early 1990s. By century's end thickening webs of connections among like-minded groups were in place.

More precisely, networks of communication, political support, and material assistance have developed among similar groups that face similar circumstances. The two densest networks at the beginning of the twenty-first century link Islamic communities and indigenous peoples, respectively. Their connectivity depends on international conferences, transcontinental travel by activists, and fax, phone, and Internet exchanges. Organizations in these networks gain access to expertise on leadership, communications, and mobilization. Their appeals gain plausibility because they resonate with sentiments held by similar peoples elsewhere. Equally important, groups in the networks benefit from the inspiration of successful movements elsewhere, successes that provide the images and moral incentives that help motivate activists.

Contagion effects are not automatic. First, as suggested in the discussion of empowering ideas, frames and victories are contagious only for people who have a preexisting sense of collective identity and some notion of common interests. Second, contagion presupposes some degree of leadership and networks of communication within the group, not just images and rhetoric from outside. Stephen M. Saideman makes a persuasive argument that contagion is most likely to affect groups whose economic and political circumstances are similar to those of ethnonational groups that initiate a successful movement, especially other groups in the same country.[31]

Diffusion refers to the direct "spillover" of conflict from one region to another, either within or across international boundaries. The contagion of conflict is indirect; diffusion is direct. For example, more than twenty national peoples in the Caucasus have been caught up in ethnopolitical tumult in the 1990s through the diffusion (and contagion) of proactive and reactive nationalism. The Association of the Peoples of the Caucasus, which represents most of the peoples of the north Caucasus, was founded after riots between Georgians and Abkhazians in July 1989 to help Abkhazians and other north Caucasus peoples provide assistance to threatened kindred. Since then activists and fighters have moved fluidly from one regional conflict to another and so have arms and supplies.[32] Governments also are active players: in the early 1990s Russians promoted the Abkhaz war of independence and North Ossetia (in the Russian Federation) supported autonomy-minded South Ossetians

(in Georgia). The most intense and complex spillover effects in ethnopolitical conflict happen among groups like these that straddle international boundaries—intense and complex because they draw in a multiplicity of ethnic and state actors. Of the 275 groups currently in the Minorities at Risk study, nearly two-thirds have kindred in one or more adjacent countries. Political activists in one country often find sanctuary with and get support from their transnational kindred. Generations of Kurdish leaders and *peshmergas* (warriors) in Turkey, Syria, Iraq, and Iran have provided safe havens for one another's political movements.

Diasporas also are a substantial and growing source of external support for ethnonationalists. Since the 1970s Kurdish rebels in Turkey have raised substantial funds from Kurdish workers in Western Europe. Chechen communities in the Middle East, descendants of exiles and political refugees from past conflicts, in the 1990s sent fighters and material support to their rebellious cousins in the Caucasus.

These observations suggest three general propositions about contagion and diffusion effects. First, an ethnopolitical group's incentives for political action are increased by successful mobilization and political action by similar groups elsewhere. Contagion effects are strongest among similar groups (e.g., ethnonationalists) in the same country, weaker in adjoining countries, and weakest for more distant kindred. Contagion is enhanced by the existence of transnational networks linking similar groups. Second, a group's capabilities for political action are increased by political and material support from segments of the group elsewhere, especially from segments that are mobilized (whether as disadvantaged minorities or as a dominant group in control of the state). Political, material, and military assistance from foreign countries also increases capabilities but is likely to prompt the challenged state to seek offsetting support from its own allies. Third, a group's opportunities for rebellion are increased by the number of segments of the group in adjoining countries and by their proximity to open conflict (including civil and interstate war). They also are enhanced by power transitions in regional and global alliance structures.

INTERNATIONAL GOOD PRACTICE FOR MANAGING ETHNOPOLITICAL CONFLICT

Since the end of the Cold War there has been a distinct shift in international orientations toward ethnopolitical conflict, away from sponsoring proxy wars and toward promoting the accommodation of contending interests. Efforts at international management of ethnopolitical conflict have reinforced domestic efforts at reducing ethnic tensions. The Minorities at Risk study provides two telling bodies of evidence. First is an analysis of the outcomes of fifty-seven wars of self-determination fought between 1960 and 1999, wars such as those of East Timor, Tamil Nadu, southern Sudan, and Nagorno-Karabakh. These wars, whose protagonists claim the right to their own communally based state or autonomous region, are among the most deadly and protracted of all ethnopolitical conflicts. *Between 1993 and the beginning of 2000 wars of self-determination have been halved.* During the 1990s sixteen separatist wars were settled by negotiated peace agreements and ten others were checked by cease-fires and ongoing negotiations. Fewer separatist wars are being fought now—eighteen by our count—than at any time since the early 1970s. This steep decline helps put the rebellion of Kosovar Albanians in perspective. The armed conflict that began with a few bombings and ambushes by the Kosovo Liberation Army in late 1997 was the only new ethnic war in Europe after 1994.[33]

Less visible than the shift toward settlement of separatist wars is a parallel trend toward accommodation of ethnic demands that have not yet escalated into armed conflict. Leaders of ethnopolitical movements almost always seek support by appealing to minority peoples' resentment about their lack of political participation, material inequality, and cultural recognition and justify such claims by referring to international standards of individual and group rights. Looking past the rhetoric of justice denied, we find substantial evidence of changes in minority group status that undercut the effectiveness of these appeals. Discrimination eased for more than one-third of the groups monitored by the Minorities at Risk project between 1990 and 1998, mainly because governments formally recognized and guaranteed their political and cultural rights.

There was no "invisible hand" guiding the global decline in serious ethnic conflict or the improvement in minority status during the 1990s. These trends are the result of concerted efforts by a great many people and organizations, including domestic and international peacemakers and some of the protagonists themselves. Relations between ethnic groups and governments have changed in the 1990s because of the evolution of a new doctrine of international good practice for managing ethnic conflict that has six essential principles.[34]

1. *Recognize and promote group political, cultural, and economic rights.*

   The first and most basic principle is the recognition and active protection of the rights of minority peoples. This means freedom from discrimination based on race, national origin, language, or religion that is complemented by institutional means by which organized ethnic groups can protect and promote their collective cultural and political interests. Western democracies have taken the lead in articulating, promoting, and implementing such policies. During the early 1990s the emphasis of Western advocates of human rights shifted from individual rights to protection of collective rights of national minorities. The effect of standard-setting texts adopted in 1990–95 by the Organization for Security and Cooperation in Europe (OSCE) and the Council of Europe was to establish principles for protection of minorities in European countries. The texts prohibit forced assimilation and population transfer, endorse autonomy for minority communities within existing states, and acknowledge that national minority questions are legitimate subjects of international relations both at the United Nations and within European regional organizations.[35]

Virtually all European democracies have implemented these principles. In the first stage of democratization in postcommunist Europe, some ethnonational leaders manipulated the democratic process to serve nationalist interests at the expense of minorities such as the Russian residents of the Baltic states, the Hungarians in Slovakia and Romania, and the Serbs in Croatia. In most of these countries a combination of diplomatic engagement by European institutions and the democratic electoral process checked the implementation of new discriminatory policies.

2. Recognize the right of regional minorities to substate autonomy.

A corollary principle is the right of national peoples to exercise some degree of autonomy within existing states to govern their own affairs. This is a logical consequence of the first principle. That is, it follows that if minorities who constitute a majority in one region of a heterogeneous democratic state have the right to protect and promote their collective interests, then they should have the right to local or regional self-governance. Federal political systems provide a "one-size-fits-all" approach to regional autonomy. In 1980 the new democratic government of Spain established a countrywide federal system in a largely successful effort to satisfy the separatist ambitions of Basques, Catalans, and Galicians. An alternative is *asymmetrical* federalism, in which some units have greater self-governing powers than others. The United States successfully uses both: federalism with limited powers for the fifty states, quasi sovereignty and more extensive powers to meet the distinctive political interests of organized Native American tribes and the Commonwealth of Puerto Rico.[36]

The principle of substate autonomy for national minorities is difficult to implement in centralized states for several reasons. One is the inherent resistance of most governing elites to devolution of central authority, especially in response to open challenges. Second is the fear that granting autonomy to rebels will lead to outright secession and provide a precedent for other groups. Third is the necessity to negotiate situation-specific arrangements that satisfy both parties. International examples and encouragement can help overcome elite resistance to devolution, especially if it is clear that international actors oppose complete separation and are willing to provide security guarantees to all parties.[37] The second fear is not supported by facts on the ground. There are very few contemporary instances in which negotiated autonomy led to independence. Sometimes an autonomous regional government pushes hard for greater authority, as the Basques have done in Spain. But the ethnic statelets that won de facto independence in the 1990s—Somaliland, Abkhazia, the TransDniester Republic (between Moldova and Ukraine), and the "federated state" of Kurdistan in northern Iraq—did so because states refused to negotiate autonomy arrangements, not because they did so.

With reference to autonomy agreements, there is now a large set of models to draw upon. The best-known autonomy agreements have been reached through negotiated settlements of wars of self-determination, such as the Oslo Accords and Northern Ireland's Easter Accords. Less well known but equally effective are conflict-containing agreements that established a federal state for India's Mizos in 1986, an autonomous republic for the Gagauz in Moldova in 1994, and regional autonomy for the Chakma people in Bangladesh's Chittagong Hills in 1997.

3. *Democratic institutions and power sharing are preferred means for protecting group rights.*
Recognition and protection of collective rights are two of the domestic elements of the preferred strategy for managing ethnic heterogeneity. Political democracy is a third. It provides the institutional means by which national peoples and minorities in most societies secure their rights and pursue collective interests. There are other institutional mechanisms for the protection of communal groups' interests, for example, the hegemonic exchange system (Donald Rothchild's term for communal power-sharing arrangements in which one group dominates) found in many nondemocratic African states. Nonetheless, democracy, in one of its European variants, is widely held to be the most reliable guarantee of minority rights. It is inherent in the logic of democratic politics that all peoples in heterogeneous societies should have equal civil and political rights.

There is near-conclusive evidence that modern democracies rarely fight one another and are tempered in their use of repression against internal opponents. Before-and-after comparisons of national and minority peoples in new democracies, carried out using the Minorities at Risk data, show that their political and cultural status usually improve substantially during democratic transitions. The new democracies of Europe, Asia, and Latin America were especially likely to provide legal and institutional means for protecting and promoting minority rights.[38] Authoritarian governments were not immune to this trend either, especially in Asia. The Vietnamese and Indonesian governments both lifted some restrictions on their Chinese minorities, though for reasons that had more to do with improving relations with the People's Republic and maintaining access to Chinese capital than in response to doctrines of group rights.

4. *Mutual accommodation is the preferred strategy for managing civil conflicts.*
The fourth principle is that disputes between states and national and minority peoples are best settled by negotiation and mutual accommodation. One remarkable but little-noticed achievement of democratic Russia has been its negotiation of power-sharing agreements with Tatarstan, Bashkiria, and some forty other regions in the Russian Federation (only some of which have non-Russian nationalities). The agreement between the Russian Federation and Tatarstan went the greatest symbolic distance by treating the parties as equals: It refers to the mutual delegation of power. It could have and should have been a model for settling the dispute between the Russian Federation and Chechnya. However much the Russians may have been willing to compromise before embarking on their winter 1994–95 campaign, Chechen nationalists wanted nothing short of total independence, and the conflict continues.

The preference for accommodation is evident in the outcomes of most recent wars of self-determination. Armed conflict usually begins with demands for complete independence—and ends with negotiated or de facto autonomy within the state. There are many reasons why most ethnonational leaders are willing to settle for fifty cents (or less) on the dollar, but it usually comes down to the fact that they are strategically and politically overmatched. Nationalists willing to continue fighting for total independence, such as rebel leaders in Chechnya and East Timor, are rare. Governments, on the other hand, tend with increasing frequency to the calculation that it is less costly to negotiate an agreement for regional and cultural autonomy and to redistribute development funds than it is to fight endless insurgencies—all the more so because other states and international organizations are encouraging them to negotiate. The Turkish government's obdurate resistance to organized Kurdish participation in conventional politics has become an anachronism.

If the parties to separatist conflicts recognize that the costs of accommodation are probably less than the costs of prolonged conflict, then it is only a short step to mutually deciding that it is more advantageous to work toward a negotiated settlement early, after an initial show of resolve and force, rather than after prolonged warfare. Gagauz and Moldovan nationalists came to such a conclusion in 1992, as did Tuareg rebels and the governments of Mali and Niger in the mid-1990s.

5. *International engagement to promote negotiated settlements of ethnopolitical conflicts.*
The principle that serious ethnic disputes should be settled by mutual accommodation is backed by the active engagement of major powers, the United Nations, and regional organizations such as the OSCE and the Organization for African Unity (OAU). Efforts at international management of ethnopolitical conflict take many forms. The European Union has used the carrot of candidate membership in the union to dissuade the Baltic states from imposing draconian restrictions on their Russian residents and to induce Turkey to check human rights abuses against the Kurds.

International actors have compelling reasons for seeking the resolution of ethnic conflicts at an early stage. One is to avoid the regional insecurity that accompanies civil warfare and the breakup of existing states. The scary lessons of regional insecurity in the Balkans and the Caucasus in the early 1990s had a galvanizing effect on international opinion and commitment to early and constructive engagement. A second reason is economic: trade and investment in the burgeoning international economy are dependent on political stability both within and among countries. Humanitarian considerations come in a strong third among the compelling reasons: informed Western publics and activist NGOs lobby ever more effectively for international responses to impending humanitarian crises.

Preventive diplomacy has great current popularity not only because early engagement is potentially cheaper than belated responses to ethnic and other internal disputes, but also because it has become the preferred instrument of the new doctrine for managing threats to regional security. The OSCE has relied extensively and effectively on observer missions and discrete diplomacy to help resolve ethnic disputes. The Organization of the Islamic Conference, not usually recognized as a peacemaker, played a decisive role in promoting negotiations in the 1970s and 1980s aimed at ending hostilities between Moro nationalists and the government of the Philippines. The United States used diplomatic and economic levers throughout the 1990s to prompt the Israeli government and the PLO to engage in meaningful negotiations.

It is important to recognize and encourage the participation of NGOs and private individuals as intermediaries and mediators in situations of ethnic conflict. The World Council of Churches played a crucial role in brokering the 1972 agreement that ended the first phase of Sudan's civil war. Former president Jimmy Carter, working from the Carter Center at Emory University, helped broker a 1999 agreement by which the governments of Sudan and Uganda agreed to end support for ethnic insurgents operating in one another's territories. Former senator George Mitchell has played a similar role in securing the implementation of the Easter Accords in Northern Ireland. Such organizations and individuals function effectively in part because they are trusted by parties to conflict—and they are trusted because they are seen as operating independently of big-power political interests.

6. *Coercive intervention is a necessary response to gross violations of human rights.*
   Most current UN peacekeeping operations aim at separating the contenders in ethnopolitical conflicts. What has happened in the 1990s is growing acceptance of the principle that preemptive action—so-called peacemaking or peace enforcement missions —is sometimes necessary and justifiable. Coercive intervention, as in Serbia and East Timor, is the international system's response of last resort to gross violations of human rights and to ethnic wars whose spillover effects threaten regional security. Nationalist Serbia was the pariah state and bombing range of Europe in 1999 precisely because it had refused throughout the 1990s to make any significant concessions to the Kosovars and, most immediately, because it blatantly violated principles about group rights accepted elsewhere in the region.

A WORK IN PROGRESS

Some parts of the world will continue to experience ethnic warfare and repression by states and ethnopolitical movements that reject these six principles for managing conflict in heterogeneous societies. Few states in the Islamic world are prepared to grant full political and cultural rights to religious minorities. The Chinese government adamantly refuses to consider real autonomy as a solution for separatist demands by Tibetans, Uighers, or Mongols. A number of protracted ethnopolitical conflicts are highly resistant to regional and international influence. Wars in Afghanistan and

Sudan seem intractable unless and until one party or coalition wins a decisive victory. Odds are against durable settlements for ethnic wars between Kurdish nationalists and governments in Iraq and Turkey, or between militant Tamils and the Sri Lankan government. The greatest challenges to international practice for containing ethnic conflicts are in Africa. A vast conflict zone extends from Sudan and Ethiopia through the Great Lakes region to the Congo basin and the Angola highlands. Interstate rivalries interact in extraordinarily complex ways with communal rivalries throughout the region.

These examples highlight situations of ethnic conflict that should have the highest priority for remedial and preventive action. By whom and how? The answers depend on which actors have the will, the political leverage, and the resources to act. Kosovo, East Timor, and Chechnya illustrate that the reach of the new doctrine and practice of managing ethnic conflict depends on whether the principles are accepted by those whose conflicts are to be managed, and equally on the will and ability of regional and international organizations to implement them. International and regional organizations are most likely to pursue effective preventive strategies in areas where the Western powers have vital interests, which means Europe, Latin America, and the Middle East. African and Asian conflicts are more remote and resistant to external influence. The strategy here should be to encourage and assist regional organizations, especially the OAU, and to hope (and quietly encourage) the Association of Southeast Asian Nations to engage in informal diplomacy on issues other than regional economic policy. When preventive strategies fail or are not pursued in the first place, the international challenges are different: how to provide humanitarian aid and how to contain the regional dispersion of conflict.

NOTES

1. See the latest annual survey by Peter Wallensteen and Margareta Sollenberg, "Armed Conflict, 1989–98," *Journal of Peace Research* 36, no. 5 (1999): 593–606. During the 1990s about three-quarters of the conflicts identified, which includes those wars between as well as within states, were wars between politically organized communal groups and governments.

2. The Minorities at Risk (MAR) project was begun by the author in 1986 and since 1988 has been based at the University of Maryland's Center for International Development and Conflict Management. Funding for work summarized in this chapter has been provided by the United States Institute of Peace, the National Science Foundation, and the Hewlitt Foundation. For detailed reports on findings, see Ted Robert Gurr, *Minorities at Risk: A Global View of Ethnopolitical Conflicts* (Washington, D.C.: United States Institute of Peace Press, 1993); and Ted Robert Gurr, *Peoples versus States: Minorities at Risk in the New Century* (Washington, D.C.: United States Institute of Peace Press, 2000). For documentation on all groups in the study, see the project's Web site at http://www.bsos.umd.edu/cidcm/mar.

3. Tabulated from information on communal targets of genocides and politicides from 1945 to 1999, as reported in Barbara Harff and Ted Robert Gurr, "Genocide and Politicide in Global Perspective: The Historical Record and Future Risks," in *Just War and Genocide: A Symposium*, ed. Stan Windass (London: Macmillan, for the Foundation for International Security, 2001).

4. Early 1999 estimates are from the UN High Commission for Refugees, http://www.unchr.ch. Also see the annual *World Refugee Survey* (Washington, D.C.: U.S. Committee for Refugees, 1999), which suggests that internally displaced persons number at least 15 million.

5. Documentation on this and the preceding two points is provided in Gurr, *Peoples versus States*, chap. 2.

6. Ibid., chap. 1. This chapter describes the criteria used to identify ethnopolitical groups and also discusses differences among such groups by region and type.

7. The foundation of modernization theory was laid down by Karl Deutsch, *Nationalism and Social Communication* (Cambridge, Mass.: MIT Press, 1953). For an early reappraisal of what modernization means for ethnic identities, see Walker Connor, "Nation-Building or Nation-Destroying?" *World Politics* 26 (April 1972): 319–355. For important recent assessments, see Jonathan Friedman, *Cultural Identity and Global Process* (London: Sage Publications, 1994); Fred W. Riggs, "The Modernity of Ethnic Identity and Conflict," *International Political Science Review* 19 (July 1998): 269–288; and Susan Olzak and Kiyoteru Tsutsui, "Status in the World System and Ethnic Mobilization," *Journal of Conflict Resolution* 42 (December 1998): 691–720.

8. Two important comparative studies are Franke Wilmer, *The Indigenous Voice in World Politics: Since Time Immemorial* (Newbury Park, Calif.: Sage Publications, 1993); and George Psacharopoulos and Harry Anthony Patrinos, eds., *Indigenous People and Poverty in Latin America: An Empirical Analysis* (Washington, D.C.: World Bank, 1994).

9. Evidence about the salience of group identity can be found in many sources; my thinking about them has been especially influenced by Donald L. Horowitz, *Ethnic Groups in Conflict* (Berkeley: University of California Press, 1985). The concept of incentives incorporates arguments about the motivating forces of relative deprivation, from my *Why Men Rebel* (Princeton, N.J.: Princeton University Press, 1970), and of rational goal-seeking. The notion of capacity is analogous to Charles Tilly's concept of mobilization as developed in *From Mobilization to Revolution* (Reading, Mass.: Addison-Wesley, 1978), 69–90. The significance of opportunities external to the group is central to theoretical models developed by Doug McAdam, *Political Process and the Development of Black Insurgency, 1930–1970* (Chicago: University of Chicago Press, 1982); and Sidney Tarrow, *Power in Movement: Social Movements and Contentious Politics*, 2d ed. (Cambridge and New York: Cambridge University Press, 1998). Milton J. Esman gives political opportunity a prominent role in his comparative analysis of ethnic political movements, *Ethnic Politics* (Ithaca, N.Y.: Cornell University Press, 1994). The process by which groups organize for and sustain collective action is assumed to be fundamentally a rational one, as analyzed by Mark Irving Lichbach in *The Rebel's Dilemma* (Ann Arbor: University of Michigan Press, 1995).

10. Contention about language in heterogeneous societies is the topic of extensive comparative research; see, for example, Horowitz, *Ethnic Groups in Conflict*, and the writings of David D. Laitin, most recently his *Identity in Formation* (Ithaca, N.Y.: Cornell University Press, 1998).

11. Horowitz, *Ethnic Groups in Conflict*, 141–185. Also see articles on Israelis, Afrikaners, and Hindus in "Chosen Peoples," special issue of *Nations and Nationalism* 5, no. 3 (1999): 331–430.

12. See Vamik D. Volkan, "On Chosen Trauma," *Mind and Human Interaction* 4 (1991): 3–19; and Volkan, *Bloodlines: From Ethnic Pride to Ethnic Terrorism* (New York: Farrar, Straus, and Giroux, 1997).

13. For patterns of relative deprivation and the conditions under which it leads to political violence, see Gurr, *Why Men Rebel*, chap. 2. On group interests and mobilization, see Tilly, *From Mobilization to Revolution*, 69–90.

14. For a sensitive analysis of minority group members' nonmaterial incentives for taking part in collective action, see Dennis Chong, *Collective Action and the Civil Rights Movement* (Chicago: University of Chicago Press, 1991).

15. For definitions, coding procedures, and a detailed summary of the data, see Gurr, *Peoples versus States*, chap. 4. For empirical evidence on the correlation of discrimination with ethnopolitical action, see Ryan Dudley and Ross A. Miller, "Group Rebellion in the 1980s," *Journal of Conflict Resolution* 42 (February 1998): 77–96; and Ted Robert Gurr, "Why Minorities Rebel: A Cross-National Analysis of Communal Mobilization and Conflict since 1945," *International Political Science Review* 14, no. 2 (1993): 161–201.

16. Tarrow, *Power in Movement*, 123. The frame concept is derived from the work of Erving Goffman, *Frame Analysis: An Essay on the Organization of Experience* (Cambridge, Mass.: Harvard University Press, 1974).

17. See Monica Duffy Toft, "Do Settlement Patterns Matter?" (unpublished paper, Center for Science and International Affairs, Harvard University, Cambridge, Mass., 1998); and James D. Fearon and David D. Laitin, "Weak States, Rough Terrain and Large-Scale Ethnic Violence since 1945" (paper presented at the annual meeting of the American Political Science Association, Atlanta, September 1999). Similar results are reported by Erik Melander, *Anarchy Within: The Security Dilemma between Ethnic Groups in Emerging Anarchy*, Research Report 52 (Uppsala, Sweden: Department of Peace and Conflict Research, Uppsala University, 1999).

18. Tarrow develops a general argument that social networks and preexisting institutions provide the basis for mobilization for social movements; see his *Power in Movement*. The institutional origins of civil rights protest are documented by McAdam in *Political Process and the Development of Black Insurgency, 1930–1970*. For an analysis of the role of religious institutions in facilitating the political opposition of 105 religiously distinct minorities, see Jonathan Fox, "Do Religious Institutions Support Violence or the Status Quo?" *Studies in Conflict & Terrorism* 22, no. 2 (1999): 119–139. Fox finds that these institutions support opposition only when religious institutions feel they are threatened or when the religious minority has a nonreligious political agenda.

19. On the role of leadership rivalries in the Chechen conflict, see Valery Tishkov, *Ethnicity, Nationalism and Conflict in and after the Soviet Union: The Mind Aflame* (London and Thousand Oaks, Calif.: Sage Publications, 1997), 216–219. On the former Yugoslavia, see, for example, V. P. Gagnon, Jr., "Ethnic Nationalism and International Conflict: The Case of Serbia," *International Security* 19, no. 3 (1994–95): 130–166; and Susan Woodward, *Balkan Tragedy: Chaos and Dissolution after the Cold War* (Washington, D.C.: Brookings Institution, 1995). A comparative analysis of the manipulation of communal identities is Human Rights Watch, *Playing the "Communal Card": Communal Violence and Human Rights* (New York: Human Rights Watch, 1995).

20. The concept of political opportunity is widely used in analyses of the origins and dynamics of social movements; see, for example, Tilly, *From Mobilization to Revolution;* McAdam, *Political Process and the Development of Black Insurgency, 1930–1970;* and Tarrow, *Power in Movement*. The discussion here follows from Tarrow's definition of political opportunity structure as "the dimensions of the political environment that provide incentives for people to undertake collective action by affecting their expectation for success or failure" (p. 85). The distinction between durable and transient opportunity factors is mine.

21. Deepa Khosla, "Third World States as Intervenors in Ethnic Conflict: Implications for Regional and International Security," *Third World Quarterly* 20, no. 6 (1999): 1143–1156. Her analysis uses coded data on international support from the Minorities at Risk project.

22. Pamela Burke illustrates this point in her detailed study of the transnational allies of indigenous peoples in the Peruvian Amazon, "The Globalization of Contentious Politics: The Amazonian Indigenous Rights Movement" (Ph.D. diss., University of Maryland, 1999).

23. See Michael S. Lund, Barnett R. Rubin, and Fabienne Hara, "Learning from Burundi's Failed Democratic Transition, 1993–96: Did International Initiatives Match the Problem?" in *Cases and Strategies for Preventive Action*, ed. Barnett R. Rubin, Preventive Action Reports, vol. 2 (New York: Century Foundation Press, 1998), 47–92.

24. For a detailed analysis of strategies of ethnic political action in established democracies, transitional democracies, and autocracies, see Gurr, *Peoples versus States*, chap. 5.

25. On the problematic consequences of the recent wave of democratization, see Samuel P. Huntington, "Democracy's Third Wave," *Journal of Democracy* 2 (spring 1991): 12–34. On its implications for ethnopolitical conflict, see Larry Diamond and Marc F. Plattner, eds., *Nationalism, Ethnic Conflict, and Democracy* (Baltimore: Johns Hopkins University Press, 1994); and Amy L. Chua, "Markets, Democracy, and Ethnicity: Toward a New Paradigm for Law and Development," *Yale Law Journal* 108 (October 1998): 1–107.

26. From Milovan Djilas, *Fall of the New Class: A History of Communism's Self-Destruction* (New York: Alfred A. Knopf, 1998), quoted in Michael Ignatieff, "Prophet in the Ruins," *New York Review*, March 4, 1999, 30.

27. Detailed comparative evidence on the impact of democratic transitions in the 1980s and 1990s on minority group rights and conflicts is reported in Gurr, *Peoples versus States*, chap. 5.

28. See Barnett R. Rubin, *The Fragmentation of Afghanistan* (New Haven, Conn.: Yale University Press, 1995); and his article "Afghanistan under the Taliban," *Current History* 98 (February 1999): 81.

29. James D. Fearon, "Commitment Problems and the Spread of Ethnic Conflict," in *The International Spread of Conflict: Fear, Diffusion, and Escalation*, ed. David A. Lake and Donald Rothchild,

(Princeton, N.J.: Princeton University Press, 1998), 107–126.

30. Donald Rothchild interprets the breakdown of settlements in Angola as a commitment problem in *Managing Ethnic Conflict in Africa: Pressures and Incentives for Cooperation* (Washington, D.C.: Brookings Institution, 1997), chap. 5. For a useful comparative analysis of the interplay between warfare and political maneuvering in attempts to settle southern African conflicts, including Angola, see Thomas Ohlson and Stephen John Steman with Robert Davies, *The New Is Not Yet Born: Conflict Resolution in Southern Africa* (Washington, D.C.: Brookings Institution, 1994).

31. Stephen M. Saideman, "Is Pandora's Box Half-Empty or Half-Full? The Limited Virulence of Secessionism and the Domestic Sources of Disintegration," in *International Spread of Ethnic Conflict*, 127–150.

32. See Paula Garb, "Ethnicity, Alliance Building, and the Limited Spread of Ethnic Conflict in the Caucasus," in *International Spread of Ethnic Conflict*, 185–199.

33. The fifty-seven wars and their outcomes are listed and analyzed in Gurr, *Peoples versus States*, chap. 6. For a more detailed analysis that is updated through October 2000, see Ted Robert Gurr, Monty G. Marshall, and Deepa Khosla, *Peace and Conflict 2000: A Global Survey of Armed Conflicts, Self-Determination Movements, and Democracy*, Report from the Integrated Network for Societal Conflict Research (College Park, Md.: Center for International Development and Conflict Management, University of Maryland, 2000).

34. Elsewhere I have referred to this as a new regime of managed ethnic heterogeneity. See *Peoples versus States*, chap. 7.

35. See, for example, Hugh Miall, ed., *Minority Rights in Europe: Prospects for a Transnational Regime* (New York: Council on Foreign Relations Press, 1994); and Jennifer Jackson Preece, "National Minority Rights vs. State Sovereignty in Europe: Changing Norms in International Relations?" *Nations and Nationalism* 3, no. 3 (1997): 345–364.

36. There are a great many variants of federalism; see, for example, contributions to Gunther Bächler, ed., *Federalism against Ethnicity? Institutional, Legal, and Democratic Instruments to Prevent Violent*

Minority Conflicts (Zurich: Verlag Rügger for the Swiss Academy of Human and Social Sciences, 1997).

37. On the importance of security guarantees for ensuring that negotiated settlements hold, see Barbara F. Walter, "The Critical Barrier to Civil War Settlement," in *Civil Wars, Insecurity, and Intervention*, ed. Barbara F. Walter and Jack Snyder (New York: Columbia University Press, 1999), 38–69.

38. Gurr, *Peoples versus States*, chap. 5.

12

LEADERSHIP AND HUMAN AGENCY

Image, Identity, and the Resolution of Violent Conflict

Janice Gross Stein

IN BOTH ENDURING interstate rivalries and bitter ethnic conflict, interests are shaped by images that in turn are partially shaped by identity. What we see as a threat is a function in large part of the way we see the world and who we think we are. Embedded enemy images and collective beliefs are a serious obstacle to conflict management, routinization, reduction, or resolution. Once formed, enemy images tend to become deeply rooted and resistant to change, even when one adversary attempts to signal a change in intent. The images themselves then contribute autonomously to the perpetuation and to the intensification of conflict.

Prospects for reducing and resolving violent conflict are not as grim, however, as this analysis suggests. I argue that the identities that shape images are not given but are socially reconstructed as interactions develop and contexts evolve over the trajectory of a conflict. Change in identity can reshape images, and changing images can provoke a reconstruction of identity. If they are to be effective, peacemakers who confront bitter civil wars or enduring state rivalries must address interests in the broader context of images and identity.

At least two important bodies of scholarship challenge the importance of intergroup differences and embedded images as significant contributors to violent conflict. Structural explanations of conflict generally give little attention to the processes that mediate between attributes of the environment and behavior. Explanations that focus on competition for scarce resources or changes in patterns of alignment assume that conflict can be explained independently of the images of its participants and their perceptions of threat. Yet modern psychology has demonstrated repeatedly that stimulus-response models are inaccurate representations of human behavior. Insofar as the same stimulus is interpreted differently by different individuals or groups, beliefs matter.

A second body of scholarship uses rational choice models to explain the resort to violence as an optimal response to collective fears of the future.[1] As groups begin to fear for their safety, strategic dilemmas arise that are exacerbated by information failures and problems of credible commitment, and, fueled by political entrepreneurs, conflict explodes into violence. Violence becomes a rational response to strategic dilemmas fueled by fear. These explanations are compatible with psychological explanations insofar as they develop the intervening mechanisms that can transform fear into violence. David Lake and Donald Rothchild argue, for example, that ethnic activists deliberately play on fears of collective insecurity, which are in turn magnified by political memories and anxieties.

Cognitive and social psychology addresses the origins of and triggers to the collective fears that prepare the ground for violence. Who individuals and groups think they are determines in part how they see the world, and the way people see the world shapes how and when they perceive threat and how they formulate their goals, assess the constraints, process information, and choose strategies. Individuals are not passive receptors of environmental stimuli; they actively construct representations of their environment. The extent of individual and group variation in interpretation suggests that structural explanations of political behavior are rarely determining.

Images of an enemy can form as a response to the persistently aggressive actions of another state or group. A conflict generated by aggressive or militant leaders with vested interests in escalating conflict is generally not amenable to reduction unless intentions change. These kinds of individual and group images are not the subject of this chapter. Rather, I focus on conflict generated by images and fears that form when the intent of the other is not hostile, but action is ambiguous in an unstructured environment; or conflict generated by images that were once accurate but no longer reflect the intentions of one or more parties. Under these conditions, social-psychological analysis is important both in the explanation of

conflict and in generating prescriptions to reduce its intensity.

This chapter examines the roles of leaders, elites, and publics to assess the still only partially understood social-psychological processes of the creation, retention, and revision of enemy images by individuals and by groups. In this connection, I pay particular attention to the impact of group identity. This chapter first examines the psychological, social, and political processes that create and reinforce hostile images. The second part of the chapter explores the conditions under which adversarial images are likely to change. To explain the changes in enemy images that facilitate conflict management, routinization, reduction, and resolution, I draw on propositions from social psychology to develop a concept of "trial-and-error learning" from failure and look particularly at the strategies one adversary can use to promote change of image by another.

IDENTITY AND THE CREATION OF ENEMY IMAGES

An image refers to a set of beliefs or to the hypotheses and theories that an individual or group is convinced are valid. An image includes both experience-based knowledge and values, or beliefs about desirable behavior.[2] When these individual images are shared within a group and defined in opposition to another group, they become stereotyped.[3] A stereotyped image is a group belief about another group or state that includes descriptive, affective, and normative components. Stereotyped enemy images, generally simple in structure, set the political context in which action takes place and decisions are made. Converging streams of evidence from social psychology, cultural anthropology, international relations, and comparative politics suggest that individuals and groups are motivated to form and maintain images of an enemy even in the absence of solid, confirming evidence of hostile intentions.

Enemy images can be a product of the need for identity and the dynamics of group behavior. People have a fundamental human need for identity. Identity is the way in which a person is or wishes to be known by others; it is a conception of self in relation to others. An effective identity includes beliefs and scripts for action in relation to others. An individual almost always holds more than one identity and generally moves freely among these identities depending on the situation. I am, for example, a mother with my sons, a daughter-in-law with my in-laws, a teacher with my students, and a scholar with my university colleagues. Individual identity is highly situational and relational.

One important component of individual identity is social identity, or the part of an individual's self-concept that derives from knowledge of his or her membership in a social group or groups, together with the value and emotional significance attached to that membership.[4] Social psychologists suggest that people satisfy their need for positive self-identity, status, or reduction of uncertainty by identifying with a group.[5] These needs then require bolstering and favorable comparison of the "in-group" with "out-groups."[6] Membership in a group leads to systematic comparison, differentiation, and derogation of other groups through processes of categorization and social comparison.

The most striking finding of social psychologists is that social differentiation occurs even in the absence of material bases for conflict. This need for collective as well as individual identity leads people to differentiate between "we" and "they," to distinguish between "insiders" and "outsiders," even when scarcity or gain is not at issue. In an effort to establish or defend group identity, groups and their leaders identify their distinctive attributes as virtues and label the distinctiveness of others as vices. This kind of "labeling" responds to deep social-psychological needs and can lead to the creation of enemy stereotypes and culminate in conflict.

An examination of massive state repression leading to group extinction, for example, concluded that genocides and politicides are extreme attempts to maintain the security of one's "identity group" at the expense of other groups.[7] Ethnocentrism, or strong feelings of self-group centrality and superiority, does not necessarily culminate in extreme or violent behavior. However, it does draw on myths that are central to group or national culture and breeds stereotyping and a misplaced suspicion of others' intentions.[8]

Common cognitive biases can also contribute to the creation of enemy images and the sharpening of polarization. The egocentric bias leads people to overestimate the extent to which they are the target of others' actions. Leaders are then likely to see their group or state as the target of the hostility of others even when they are not. The fundamental attribution error leads people to exaggerate systematically the importance of others' dispositions or fixed attributes in explaining their undesired behavior. Leaders are, therefore, likely to attribute undesirable behavior to the "character" of other groups or states rather than to the difficulties they face in their environment.[9] President Hafiz al-Assad of Syria rarely drew a distinction between Israel's leaders, ignored differences among political parties, explained Israel's behavior as a consequence of its Zionist character, and dismissed the impact of public opinion on the policy of a democratically elected leadership. He consistently exaggerated the "disposition" of Israel's leaders at the expense of the situation they confronted.

Social identity and differentiation, however, do not lead inevitably to violent conflict through stereotypical enemy images.[10] If they did, conflict would occur at all times, under all conditions. Differentiated identities and cognitive biases are necessary but insufficient explanations of the formation of enemy images. If they were sufficient, individuals, groups, and states would have strong enemy images all the time. This is clearly not the case. The critical variables are the kinds of environments in which individuals and groups seek to satisfy their needs and the norms that they generate and accept. Certain kinds of international and domestic conditions mediate and facilitate the formation of enemy images.[11]

MEDIATING FACTORS: THE DOMESTIC CONTEXT

Several important qualifications are necessary before we can address the relationship between identity and violence. First, personal and social identity are often in tension with each other as people seek both individuation and inclusion. By identifying strongly with a group, people inevitably de-emphasize their individual identity, and those with a strong sense of individual identity give less weight to their group identities. Human rights activists, for example, characteristically identify less with a particular group and more with norms of individual responsibility.

People also generally identify with several groups. I am a Torontonian at home, an Ontarian when I travel in Canada, and a Canadian when I travel abroad. People typically identify with a group whose importance is most salient in a given situation.[12] Which group identity is activated is situationally specific.

The critical question is under what conditions identity and violent conflict are related. Why are relationships among some groups so much more competitive—and violent—than among others?[13] Hutus and Tutsis have engaged in violent conflict six times since 1962, while Québecois and Anglophones in Canada, despite their important and deep differences, have not fought for over two hundred years. Moreover, substantial numbers of Québecois share multiple identities, including strong and positive identification with Canada. What mediating conditions explain why strong group identity precipitates violent conflict only in some situations?

The answer lies at least in part in the variability of identity. Social identity is not given; it can be chosen freely by an individual, imposed

by others who have the authority and resources to do so, or socially constructed through interaction with others.[14] The patterns of identity formation and mapping are critical. Conflict does not develop when the sources of identities or the identities themselves are compatible. I experience no conflict, for example, among my multiple identities as a Torontonian, an Ontarian, and a Canadian. When the identity an individual chooses is incompatible with the identity imposed by others or the social context in which the identity is constantly being re-created, conflict can develop. Muslims living in Bosnia and Herzegovina, for example, defined themselves as Serbs or Croats until the 1970s, when the Serb and Croat identities began to be re-created to exclude Muslims. Only then did they begin to define themselves as Bosnian Muslims with a distinct political identity. Even then, however, incompatible political identities may not be sufficient to create violent conflict. To return to the Canadian example, some Québecois see fundamental incompatibilities between being a Quebecker and being a Canadian, but do not consider a resort to force. They do not because they are committed to norms of fairness and due process, and they expect that these commitments are reciprocated by their counterparts in English Canada.[15]

Several important mediating conditions have been identified that sharpen identity and prepare the terrain for violent conflict. The first set of factors operates between groups within incompatible identities, while the second set is internal to the groups. Ethnic or national identity intensifies during periods of social, economic, or political crisis, when uncertainty grows and the mechanisms in place to protect one group from another lose their credibility.[16] Barry Posen argues that as central authority declines in the context of socioeconomic or political crisis, fears about physical security grow, and groups invest in measures to protect themselves, making the violence they fear more likely.[17] State weakness, its perceived incapacity to protect one group from the anticipated violence of another, is an important trigger of violence among groups with incompatible identities.

Identity conflict is often a competition for ownership of the state and control of its resources. States can stand above and attempt to mediate conflict—by, for example, giving representation to different groups, as in Belgium —or be the creature and the instrument of one exclusive group, as in Nigeria, where the Hausa historically dominated military regimes.[18] The expropriation of the identity, symbols, and resources of the state by one group to the exclusion of others is a strong predictor of the likelihood of violence.

Conflict can trigger violence among groups under conditions of scarcity. Some evidence suggests that culturally and physically similar groups can generate hostility and aggression toward one another due to competition for scarce resources.[19] Analyses of civil violence similarly conclude that relative deprivation is the most important condition for participants in collective violence.[20] As the gap grows between material expectations and assets, aggression toward those perceived as the cause of relative deprivation will grow and intensify. The competition for scarce resources is exacerbated when the state actively controls the distribution of important resources. In the former Yugoslavia, for example, Slovenes and Croats actively resented federal redistribution of resources to poorer regions of the country. Loss aversion is likely to intensify when groups compete for scarce resources in a context of decline: When expectations remain stable, but capabilities decline, people who are experiencing a decline in their assets, or "loss," are especially likely to make risky choices.[21] Yet the Czechs and the Slovaks competed for scarce resources and divided assets without a resort to violence. Competition for resources and relative deprivation, a sharpened version of competition, cannot fully account for violence among groups with differentiated and competing identities.[22]

Conflicts of identity are likely to escalate to violence when group members consider that recognition of another's identity can compromise their own, when they perceive the granting of rights to the other as an abdication of their own identity, and when they fear that the other group may move preemptively to make gains at their expense. Throughout much of its history, the Israeli-Palestinian conflict has been this kind of existential conflict; because both identities are tied to the same territory, leaders on both sides long felt that acknowledgment of the other's identity would fundamentally compromise their own.[23] When one or the other group has attempted, for example, to seize territory and establish a presence on contested ground, violence has resulted. When the state is too weak or unwilling to constrain preemptive action by one group, the other group becomes more fearful, loses confidence in institutional arrangements, deepens the perception of the hostility of its ethnic rival, and prepares for violence. Leaders of ethnic groups manipulate group fears to solidify their positions within their own ethnic community. Ethnic activists, with a strong need to identify with their ethnic group, manipulate identities and fears to produce a rapid and spontaneous process of social polarization that magnifies hostility and fear among groups.[24] As polarization proceeds, members of an ethnic group are pressured by their leaders—and by the reciprocal intensification of hostility in the other group—to identify only with their ethnic group and to break any crosscutting ties. In the former Yugoslavia, for example, despite a high degree of social integration among Croats and Serbs, ethnic activists were able to initiate a process that broke apart families and forced members to self-identify with a single group. In a related process, "political entrepreneurs," who see opportunities for political gain, may take advantage of a process of social polarization to achieve political ends. They deliberately reinterpret histories and traditions to sharpen ethnic differentiation, heighten grievance, and increase fear.[25] Slobodan Milosevic was both an ethnic activist and a political entrepreneur: he exaggerated Croatian violence against Croatian Serbs and the Muslim threat to Serbia in Kosovo as a pretext to consolidate and expand the political power of the Serbs when the state structure of Yugoslavia weakened following Tito's death.

"Spoilers," or militant ethnic activists, have also fomented social polarization when new political arrangements that would cut across ethnic cleavages seem likely.[26] After the moderate Hutu and Tutsi reached a painful compromise on new arrangements for political leadership in Rwanda, the militant Hutus, anticipating their exclusion from political power and marginalization, deliberately planned the assassination of the moderate Hutu leadership and a genocidal campaign of violence against Tutsis. The Rwandan genocide is often mistakenly explained as the result of competition for scarce resources or the weakening of the state structures or as a primordial rivalry between the two dominant ethnic groups. None of these is a sufficient explanation for the outburst of genocidal violence. Militant leaders who feared marginalization and loss from institutional arrangements that would have dampened polarization chose to execute others rather than to accept a diminished political status. They were able to mobilize support for genocidal action because they expertly played on long-standing ethnic fears.

Entrepreneurial leaders or elites whose domestic support is uncertain or threatened can manipulate identities and create myths to bolster political loyalty.[27] To gain public support, parochial interest groups that benefit from militarist or imperialist policies create strategic rationalizations, or "myths." Over time, some elites come to believe the myths that they have learned, making these images extraordinarily resistant to change. A process of mythmaking that perpetuates hostile imagery is most likely when concentrated interest groups trade and logroll.[28]

The salience and the intensity of identity are tied closely to the perceived stakes of ethnic relations.[29] The greater the gap between expectations and capabilities, the more important the values that are endangered by declining capabilities, and the smaller the range of other satisfactions that can compensate for the loss in assets, the more receptive populations are to elite attempts to manipulate identities to create and sustain enemy images.[30]

Differences in domestic political conditions make some kinds of populations more receptive to elite manipulation than others.[31] In controlled political regimes, leaders and elites who dominate the instruments of communication can more easily manipulate identities and mass images. Not only the kind of regime but also the organization of society has an impact on the creation of hostile imagery. The hallmark of a deeply divided society, one that is likely to sustain significant hostile imagery and experience violent conflict, is the presence of separate structures, organized on the basis of identity, that infuse every aspect of society. In Lebanon, for example, political office from the center to local levels traditionally has been allocated on the basis of religious identity. In these kinds of societies, creation and maintenance of ethnic stereotypes and enemy images is easily done.

This analysis suggests that differentiated identities are not themselves a cause of violent conflict. Even when incompatible identities are present, violence is likely only when triggered by the exclusionary acts of leaders, either monopolizing the resources of the state against groups within their own societies or pressing claims against those within others. Leaders and elites evoke threats to political identity that then provoke stereotyping and contribute to violence.

MEDIATING FACTORS: THE INTERNATIONAL CONTEXT

The international environment of states can create conditions in which identity or cognitive biases trigger the creation of enemy images, even in the absence of aggressive behavior by others. The distinguishing characteristic of the well-known "security dilemma" is that behavior perceived by one group or state as threatening and aggressive is a defensive response to an inhospitable strategic environment. To enhance their security, leaders take measures that simultaneously diminish the security of others.[32] For forty years, leaders in the Soviet Union and the United States saw their own behavior as a defensive response to the aggressive intentions and actions of the other.[33] The U.S. proposal to build a limited antimissile defense system to protect against "rogue" states appears obviously defensive to proponents in Washington yet is widely understood in Europe and Asia as an exercise in U.S. hegemony and a trigger to a new arms race. The interpretation of a defensive action by one as offensive by another can feed and fuel an image of an enemy that is then reinforced over time in a spiraling process of interaction. As we have seen, security dilemmas can operate between groups inside the state or between states. Common to both levels is an unjustified fear arising from the inherent ambiguity of actions, which culminates in a self-fulfilling prophecy and a spiral to violence.

The regional and global environments can also contribute to the escalation of a conflict to violence. Ethnic conflict can spill across borders when one of the ethnic groups can draw on support, either from "kin" across the state border or from governments that feel threatened by the intensifying conflict. Resources from outside can be mobilized to prepare for violence and to shift the power among ethnic communities within a state under stress. When ethnic conflict in Rwanda spilled across the border into eastern Zaire, Hutus from Rwanda quickly established control over refugee camps and used the camps as bases for recruitment and training. The presence of a large number of Hutus disturbed the fragile ethnic balance and alarmed the Banyamulenge, the Tutsi community living in the eastern region of Zaire. Facing an unprecedented number of Hutus in their region, and doubtful of the protection they would receive from President Mobutu Sese Seko, the Banyamulenge gave their support to

Laurent Kabila as he moved to challenge the existing regime.

Within a year, the newly established government of the Democratic Republic of the Congo quickly found its territories in the east under attack by its erstwhile allies, the militia forces supported by the Tutsi governments of Rwanda and Burundi, in large part because President Kabila did not satisfy their demands for protection from Hutu exiles. He in turn asked for and received support from the neighboring states of Zimbabwe and Angola. Congo found itself at the vortex of a widening regional war that engulfed neighboring states and culminated in a wide intraregional war with devastating social and economic consequences. After a lengthy process of negotiation, the parties to the conflict, both states and militias, signed a cease-fire in Lusaka, but the cease-fire was broken almost as soon as it was signed and the United Nations has been unable to persuade all the parties to stop the fighting. The ethnic match lit by Hutus in Rwanda struck a tinderbox of fragile regimes and multiethnic societies and ignited the widest regional conflagration in modern African history.

The Israeli-Palestinian conflict similarly embroiled all of Israel's neighbors and sparked wider regional wars as the Arab states supported the Palestinians in three full-scale wars. Even when the wider conflict was defused between Egypt and Israel, the fighting moved to Lebanon, where regional powers fought a proxy war for fifteen years. Only after more than forty years of fighting did the identity conflict between Israelis and Palestinians return to the top of the agenda and its spillover effects begin to diminish.

THE PERSISTENCE OF ENEMY IMAGES

Once stereotyped images are in place, they are extraordinarily difficult to change. In the first instance, because enemy images contain an emotional dimension of strong dislike, there is a strong desire to maintain the existing image and little incentive to seek new information about a foe.[34] Stereotyped images also generate behavior that is hostile and confrontational and increase the likelihood, therefore, that an adversary will respond with hostile action. A cycle of reciprocal behavior then reinforces adversary images by providing allegedly confirming evidence of hostile intentions. Enemy images tend to become self-fulfilling and self-reinforcing.[35]

Enemy images are also the product of deeply rooted social and psychological needs and frequently serve the interests of important groups and elites. Consequently they become central to and well embedded within larger belief systems. Research has established at least three different schemas of enemies: imperials, barbarians, and degenerates.[36] Throughout the Cold War, the Soviet leadership saw the United States as an "imperial" enemy, Chinese leaders have at times stereotyped others as "barbarians," and the Ayatollah Khomeini in Iran described Western leaders as "degenerates."

Cognitive processes tend to support stereotypical images and biases once they are established. People make heavy use of social stereotype in predicting one another's personal characteristics and behavior. Drawing on stereotypes, they also tend to make social predictions with greater subjective certainty or confidence than can be justified by their objective accuracy.[37] Behavioral memory retrieval processes operate differently when judging in-group and out-group members, contributing to a perpetuation of social biases and implicit theories of others that are linked to individual differences in evaluative processing.[38] Attribution processes also influence judgments of discriminatory behavior.[39]

Theories of cognitive consistency expect that the least central parts of a belief system, that is, those with the fewest interdependent cognitions, will change first. Central beliefs are generally most resistant to change. People tend to modify at the margin and to change peripheral beliefs first.[40] In the process of making inferences, people also seek to maintain their beliefs by reducing the challenge of discrepant information. The well-established tendency to discount inconsistent information contributes significantly to the persistence of stereotypes.[41] When people receive discrepant information, they generally make the smallest possible change in their beliefs; they will change their beliefs incrementally, allow a large number of exceptions and special cases, and make superficial alterations rather than change their central beliefs. Indeed, exposure to contradictory information frequently results in the strengthening of beliefs.[42] People also tend to actively seek and interpret information that confirms the negative image.[43]

Cognitive psychology has identified a number of heuristics, or mental rules of thumb, that can make enemy images resistant to change even in the face of discrepant information.[44] They describe how individuals process information using convenient shortcuts. Two of the best documented heuristics are availability and representativeness.[45] The availability heuristic refers to people's tendency to interpret present information in terms of what is most easily available in their cognitive repertoire.[46] An enemy image is usually easily available and salient. The heuristic of representativeness refers to people's proclivity to exaggerate similarities between one event and a prior class of events.[47] When action is ambiguous, people tend to treat it as representative of earlier hostile behavior.

IMAGE CHANGE

Stability in enemy images is the default and change the exception. Yet conservatism does not hold unconditionally. Belief systems and schemata, the active reconstruction of experience at a higher level of abstraction, also change, at times dramatically. Psychological, social, and political variables affect the propensity of change in enemy images.

Change in images is in part a function of the rate at which discrepant information occurs. Cognitive psychologists identify several factors that facilitate change. They suggest that important beliefs can change dramatically when there is no other way to account for "large" amounts of contradictory data.[48] Greater change will occur when information arrives in large batches, rather than bit by bit. President George Bush, for example, did not change his image of Mikhail Gorbachev in 1988–89 even though the Soviet leader made a series of unilateral gestures to the United States and spoke often of the changing Soviet identity. Only when information about large changes arrived in a rush, after the fall of the Berlin Wall in 1989, did Bush finally alter his well-established image of the Soviet leader.

Significant change in beliefs about others also occurs when people are exposed to inconsistent information and are persuaded that the behavior is not an arbitrary response to their environment but reflects the "nature" of the others. Croatian and Muslim leaders did not change their image of Serbs because they attributed the change in Serbian policy to their military setback by the Croatian forces in Krajina. The social and political conditions that promote uncharacteristic attributions to "dispositional" rather than "situational" factors have not been fully identified.[49]

Images can also change incrementally over time. As people consider information about an adversary inconsistent with their previous knowledge, they incorporate into their belief the conditions under which the image does not hold. This kind of process permits gradual change and adjustment.[50] When controlled political systems become more open or as leaders and elites receive new information about their rival, their image of the "other" can change incrementally.

Cognitive explanations of image change pay insufficient attention to the emotional factors that can motivate—or inhibit—change. Not only "cold" cognition but also "hot" emotions affect the likelihood of image change. The less the intensity of an emotional commitment to an identity and its associated images, the less resistant these images are to change in the face of disconfirming information.[51]

Theories of social cognition do not adequately specify the external conditions or mediating causes of any of these changes.[52] Critics rightly contend that the neglect of context is disturbing; the social in "social" cognition research is largely absent.[53] Theories of social cognition do not model explicitly the processes that link changes in the environment to cognitive constructs and explain how images change. Political and historical analyses must supplement theories of social cognition with careful examination of the political and social interests with a stake in change and explore the social configurations that promote change in group images.

LEADERS AND POLITICAL LEARNING

Conflict between groups or states that is fueled by embedded images or competing identities is particularly difficult to resolve. The issues are not simply distributive, subject to bargaining, trade-off, and logrolling, but far deeper, tied to political constructions of self and other that create fear and hostility. Confidence-building measures, institutional arrangements to protect the security and rights of minorities, guaranteed autonomy through federal and confederal political structures, power sharing, and mutual recognition are all helpful and necessary political instruments in the tool kit of conflict reduction and resolution.[54] In addition, truth commissions and war crimes tribunals work at the deeper levels of grievance, fear, and distrust that fuel and sustain identity conflict.

To begin a process of conflict reduction when images are deeply embedded requires leadership. How do leaders develop and accept new ideas, ideas that are inconsistent with embedded images and incompatible identities? Social learning theory suggests that emotional responses are not natural but learned and reinforced through social interactions, and that emotional and behavioral responses can be influenced by changes in cognitive constructs; they can be relearned.[55] I examine leadership and draw on propositions from social psychology to develop a concept of "trial-and-error learning" from failure.

The role of leadership in helping to resolve multilateral issues in complex international negotiations is widely recognized. "Structural" leaders facilitate cooperation by using resources effectively to build coalitions and persuade others to change their positions. These kinds of leaders are almost always representative of the most powerful states or groups in the conflict and can use their advantage in resources to change the terms of the bargain. Informal "entrepreneurs" help the parties to help themselves by brokering deals and to dissolve familiar collective action problems associated with complex negotiations. They are especially important when groups or states have incorrect or uncertain assessments of the other's preferences and when good information is either scarce or expensive. "Intellectual" leaders provide new ideas, information, and, at times, legitimacy that is essential to concluding a negotiated agreement.[56]

Although the context of complex multilateral international negotiation is very different from that of identity conflict at the group or state levels, all three types of leadership are valuable in the reduction and resolution of identity conflict. Powerful leaders who are influenced by new ideas can provide more accurate information at a lower cost and can commit resources to change the terms of the bargain. These resources are important not only in crafting new kinds of settlements but in carrying constituencies with them. Critical to a process of conflict resolution is learning by leaders. Here I pay particular attention to evidence from social learning theory of how people learn from failure.

Learning from failure is consistent with evidence that embedded identity conflict is susceptible to reduction when the parties confront a mutually hurting stalemate and see no alternative but compromise. When violence has failed —often repeatedly—leaders are most receptive to information that challenges embedded images and are more open to new ideas.

There is as yet no unified theory of learning, and psychology has not identified the conditions or thresholds that predict when different forms of learning are likely to occur. Most psychological theories of learning are not very useful in specifying the dynamics of learning, in large part because they analyze learning within highly structured environments. Learning theories in educational and experimental psychology are associationist: they treat learning as a change in the probability of a specified response in the face of changing reward contingencies.[57] This concept of learning is not helpful in social and political environments where appropriate responses are unknown or disputed.

Political psychologists distinguish between simple and complex learning. Learning is simple when means are better adjusted to ends. Complex learning occurs when people develop more differentiated images and when these images are integrated into higher-order structures that highlight difficult trade-offs.[58] Complex learning, at its highest level, may lead to a reordering or a redefinition of goals. From this perspective, learning must include the development of more complex structures as well as changes in content.[59]

These concepts of learning are a useful first cut at explaining changes in hostile images that then shape or permit new directions in policy, but they fail to distinguish change from learning. Without some evaluative criteria, any cognitive change can be considered learning, and the concept of learning becomes redundant. Change in cognitive content or structure does not always constitute the "learning" that is necessary for conflict reduction. For example, in the year preceding his decision to invade Kuwait,

Saddam Hussein simplified his schema and concluded that the United States was engaged in a conspiracy to undermine his regime.[60] Although these changes in Saddam's schema do provide a powerful explanation of his foreign policy behavior, they cannot be considered learning.[61] A concept of political learning must include an evaluation of the structure and content of cognitive change.[62] These kinds of evaluative judgments inevitably are and will be essentially contested.

More helpful are several strands of social-psychological theory and research that examine the liabilities of success and the benefits of failure in promoting organizational learning.[63] When failure challenges the status quo, it can draw attention to problems and stimulate the search for solutions. Only certain kinds of failures promote learning—highly predictable failures provide no new information, but unanticipated failures that challenge old ways of representing problems are more likely to stimulate new formulations. When Bosnian Serb forces suffered an unexpected and humiliating military defeat at the hands of Croatia, Slobodan Milosevic moved vigorously to push a reformulated policy in Bosnia and Herzegovina. Similarly, the United Nations Security Council, learning from its previous failure in Somalia, has refused to dispatch observers and supporting troops to the Democratic Republic of the Congo until all parties have agreed to observe the Lusaka Protocol. Responding to failure, leaders "learn through experimentation" rather than through more traditional patterns of avoidance.[64]

Learning through failure can provoke a series of sequential experiments that generate quick feedback and allow for a new round of trial-and-error experimentation.[65] This kind of trial-and-error model of learning captures the dynamics of social cognition far more effectively than cognitive theories that model as the perceiver a "passive onlooker, who . . . doesn't *do* anything—doesn't mix it up with the folks he's watching, never tests his judgments in

action or interaction."[66] It does not represent learning as a neat linear process with clear causal antecedents, but as a messy, dynamic, interactive social, organizational, and political process.

First I examine the internal conditions that can promote learning by one adversary. For the purposes of this chapter, I define learning as changes in images and identity that promote conflict routinization, reduction, and resolution. I then explore the strategies that leaders or groups can use to promote the kinds of changes in their adversary's image of themselves that can lead to a reduction in conflict. The distinction between internal and external stimuli to learning and change in image and identity is artificial, since the process is usually highly interactive, but it is convenient for analytic purposes.

President Anwar Sadat of Egypt demonstrated political learning through trial and error. He developed a far more complex and differentiated image of Egypt's adversary and initiated a series of actions that triggered a process of conflict reduction.[67] Changes in the image of Israel led to changes in behavior that in turn provoked further change in enemy images. Learning accelerated in the doing.

To develop a satisfactory explanation of image change through political learning, we need to identify the conditions and strategies that promote learning. One obvious explanation is the change in the international distribution of capabilities—a relative decline in Egyptian capabilities in relation to Israel, for instance. If changes in Egyptian enemy images were a straightforward response to structural changes in the international system, then the analysis of political dynamics and image change is unnecessary. If, on the other hand, there were important divisions within the Egyptian leadership, and interpretations of the environment were contested, then structural factors alone cannot provide a sufficient explanation of the change in Sadat's concepts. In Egypt in the mid-1970s there were deep divisions within the leadership and new, bitterly contested interpretations. It is therefore unsatisfying to explain the changes in Sadat's images of Israel as a rational adaptation to unambiguous feedback from the environments.[68]

Social and political factors can also be important triggers of image change and political learning.[69] Shifting political coalitions can be a powerful explanation of image change if new leaders are chosen primarily because of the content of their beliefs. The evidence is clear that almost all of Sadat's advisers opposed change and that Arab allies threatened sanctions and expulsions. The Egyptian president acted alone, against all advice, confident that he would ultimately persuade the Egyptian public and Arab allies.[70]

Political succession and domestic politics are helpful in explaining whose images prevail under what set of political conditions. Shifts in social structure and political power determine whether leaders can implement policies based on changed images. They do not and cannot address the important question of why, for instance, Sadat began to "think" differently about conflict and how and why he changed his images and developed new concepts and new policies toward Israel.

WHY LEADERS LEARN

The changes in Sadat's images suggest two conditions that motivated political learning.[71] The first condition was the importance of domestic reform. After the Ramadan War in October 1973, Sadat attached new importance to the role of the private and the foreign sectors, which were expected to provide both finance and technology. The new economic strategy of quasi-liberal experimentation was consistent with Sadat's strategy of conflict reduction; stabilization of Egypt's security environment was essential if the capital and investment necessary to push the economy forward were to flow into Egypt.

A second factor is the prior experience of the failure of alternatives to accommodation.

Sadat, as well as Egyptian generals, recognized that Egypt had fought the war in 1973 under optimal conditions; a military alliance with Syria had permitted a coordinated two-front attack for the first time, Arab oil producers had joined in the accompanying diplomatic offensive, and Egypt had the strategic advantage of surprise. Yet even under those conditions, Egypt had come perilously close to a serious military defeat after important initial military successes in crossing the Suez Canal. In the years following the October War, Sadat had expanded the gains he had made through a process of phased disengagement with Israel. In this context, he was reluctant to risk the limited gains he had achieved in renewed warfare. Failure of earlier policies underlined asymmetric capabilities and unfavorable trends.

The evidence suggests that Sadat was highly motivated to learn. He searched for new information through intermediaries and then through secret meetings between high-level Egyptian and Israeli leaders. He was receptive to the information that he received in large part because he was motivated to change existing images and policies. Sadat began with a small change in image, moved tentatively to small actions, was receptive to feedback, learned, and initiated a new series of actions that generated further feedback and change.[72] Sadat ultimately developed confidence that acts of reassurance would be reciprocated by Israel. Learning was not orderly and linear but experimental, through trial and error; enemy images changed as a result of a complex interactive relationship between political learning and action that provided quick feedback.

Sadat was motivated to change a deeply embedded enemy image by his interest in freeing resources for domestic reform and the earlier failure of alternatives to accommodation. These two stimuli to learning are not easily manipulated from the outside by others. They were the cumulative result of long-standing trends in Egyptian domestic and foreign policy. Although this kind of fundamental learning is not necessary for crisis management or the routinization of conflict, it is an essential precondition of conflict reduction and resolution. Fundamental learning encouraged Sadat to use strategies of reassurance to initiate a process of conflict reduction.

STRATEGIES OF CONFLICT MANAGEMENT AND REDUCTION

Hostile imagery must change if conflict is to be reduced and resolved. Interstate conflict has been managed and routinized without modification in elite, much less public, images, but civil violence as well as interstate conflict cannot be resolved unless images change and leaders and publics learn. The process must also be reciprocated. Once leaders or groups begin to change their image of their adversary and are interested in attempting to resolve their conflict, they must change the image their adversary has of them if conflict reduction is to make any progress.

When leaders recognize that misperception and stereotyping govern their adversary's judgments as well as their own, they can try, by making an irrevocable commitment, to reassure their adversary of their benign intentions and to create incentives for conflict reduction.[73] This is precisely the strategy adopted by President Sadat in 1977.[74]

Dissatisfied with the progress of negotiations in the autumn of 1977, yet unprepared to accept the status quo, Sadat searched for a dramatic move that would both reduce the tension and distrust between Egypt and Israel and induce Israel to make major concessions to reduce the conflict. It was the distrust built up over decades, he argued, that constrained the attempt to negotiate the issues at stake and fueled the cycle of wars. Sadat began with secret negotiations between Egypt's deputy prime minister and Israel's foreign minister in Morocco, where each agreed to make a critical concession—Israel indicated its willingness to return most of the Sinai peninsula to Egyptian sovereignty, and Egypt agreed to peace and the establishment of diplomatic relations with Israel.[75] Although these proposals were not fully satisfactory to either party, both sides were assured that their concessions would be reciprocated rather than exploited. Shortly thereafter, Sadat came to Jerusalem and spoke to the Knesset of the Egyptian terms for peace. Egyptian demands were unchanged, but Israel's leaders and public paid attention to the irreversible deed rather than to the content of the words. In large part through this single, dramatic act of reassurance, Sadat changed the trajectory of the conflict by changing his image among both the elite and the public in Israel.

Sadat's arrival in Jerusalem challenged the most important set of beliefs about Arab goals among Israel's leadership and public. His visit provided the dramatic evidence that was needed to overcome deeply entrenched enemy images. A broad spectrum of Israelis had assumed that Arab leaders were unrelentingly hostile, so much so that they were unprepared to meet Israel's leaders face to face. Once these core beliefs were shaken and Israel's identity was acknowledged, it became easier for Israelis to begin to revise associated assumptions and expectations.

President Sadat spoke over the heads of Israel's leadership directly to Israel's public. With his flair for the dramatic, he created the psychological and political symbols that would mobilize public opinion to press their more cautious and restrained leaders. In so doing, he removed a constraint on Israel's leaders and created a political inducement to action. Public learning, far more than elite learning, seems to require a dramatic and irrevocable demonstration of an adversary's benign intentions. Elites are more likely to learn incrementally as they focus their attention on changing information over time. The public only selectively focuses its attention and is likely to be more resistant to gradual learning. Public opinion did change in Israel in response to a highly visible, unexpected, dramatic action.

Under this very special set of conditions, reassurance through irrevocable commitment succeeded brilliantly. The two critical components that make an irrevocable commitment reassuring to an adversary are its obviously high cost to the leaders who issue the commitment and its irreversibility. The strategy has been used so infrequently in part because it is often very difficult and very risky to design a commitment that is both high in cost and irreversible.[76] Leaders frequently have neither the resources nor the information necessary to make irrevocable commitments. In attempting to change an adversary's image through a self-binding commitment, leaders face a difficult trade-off; they are more likely to make offers that are reversible and less costly, but reversible, low-cost offers are far less likely to provoke fundamental change in an adversary's image.

Reassurance through irrevocable commitment also requires a degree of freedom from domestic political and bureaucratic constraints. In Egypt after the October War, Sadat had great autonomy in decision making and, indeed, could withstand the resignation of his foreign minister. Even under such circumstances, the making of an irrevocable commitment to leaders long identified as antagonists can be difficult to justify to the public. Yet it is the public nature of the commitment that contributes to its irreversibility and credibility.[77] For all these reasons, the making of self-binding commitments to jolt an adversary to change its image and learn is likely to be difficult.

When a strategy of irrevocable commitment is impossible, one strategy that builds in some opportunity for learning is an adapted version of graduated reciprocation in tension-reduction (GRIT).[78] The initiator announces in advance that it is beginning a series of conciliatory actions designed to reduce conflict and then implements these actions whether or not the other side reciprocates. The actions, moreover, should be easily verifiable. As each step is implemented, the initiator invites its adversary to reciprocate but does not specify the appropriate response. Further, a reciprocal response by an adversary should be rewarded by a somewhat more conciliatory action. These actions, however, should not impair the defensive capacity of the initiator. If the other side attempts to exploit the concession, the initiator should respond with an appropriate action, but only to the degree necessary to restore the status quo.

Experimental studies concur that strategies like GRIT, which build in a series of conciliatory initiatives taken independently of the other's actions, are more effective than strategies that reciprocate directly and immediately.[79] Moreover, they were as effective among players who were judged generally competitive by their previous actions as they were among those who were generally cooperative. A second variant that is also effective is a reciprocal strategy that is slow to retaliate and slow to return to conciliation; this variant of reciprocity allows for initial misperception and modest learning.[80]

The experimental evidence may be overoptimistic when action occurs outside the laboratory. The general secretary of the Soviet Union, Mikhail Gorbachev, went far beyond a graduated strategy of reciprocity as he attempted to change U.S. images. In 1985 he initiated a series of unilateral conciliatory actions and persisted even when they were not reciprocated.[81] Despite this series of unilateral Soviet actions, many in Washington resisted change in their image of the Soviet Union and remained skeptical of Gorbachev's intentions.[82] Paradoxically, it was Gorbachev who "learnt by doing" in a complex interactive relationship between beliefs and behavior—action led to further change in his beliefs as he made inferences from his behavior about his convictions.[83] Large and significant amounts of discrepant information were necessary before U.S. leaders changed their image of the Soviet Union. It took Soviet tolerance of the destruction of the Berlin Wall, a dramatic and irreversible signal, to change U.S. images and provoke fundamental learning.

CONCLUSION

Strategies of conflict resolution that focus only on competing interests will likely not be sufficient to provoke the learning that is fundamental to the change of hostile imagery and identity conflict. In both enduring interstate rivalries and bitter ethnic conflict, interests are shaped by images that in turn are partially shaped by identity. What we see as a threat is a function in large part of the way we see the world and who we think we are. Serbian memories of Croatian attacks during World War II and "betrayal" by the great powers—their identity as victims in a hostile world—shaped the way leaders defined their interests and helped to explain the continuing support by Serbs for leaders and policies that imposed terrible costs.

If threatened identities facilitate the creation of hostile imagery and contribute to violent conflict, then securing these identities must be a fundamental component of conflict resolution. If they are to be effective, peacemakers who confront bitter civil wars or enduring state rivalries must address interests in the broader context of images and identity. In the former Yugoslavia, the conflict could best be managed temporarily by territorial partition and safe havens. The conflict can be resolved only if the parties recognize the legitimacy and the permanence of the others' identities. President Sadat's recognition of Israel's legitimacy was the critical key that unlocked the long and difficult peace process that culminated in mutual recognition by Israel and the Palestinians of the legitimacy of the other's identity.

In conflict between states, reciprocal recognition of legitimacy and renunciation of the use of force can most directly secure threatened identities and reshape interests. In civil conflicts, the challenge is the same, but the strategies are necessarily somewhat different. Fractured states can be reconstructed through political separation and mutual recognition

of competing identities, through a "consociational" or group building-block approach, where elite leaders accommodate and groups remain distinct with constitutional guarantees, or through an integrative approach, which seeks to forge multiethnic coalitions with crosscutting ties.[84]

Prime Minister Yitzhak Rabin recognized in the last years of his life that there could be no military solution to the conflict between Israelis and Palestinians and made the fundamental decision to recognize the political identity of Palestinians. He first experimented with negotiation with Palestinian leaders drawn from the West Bank and Gaza but concluded that they did not have sufficient authority to make peace. He was reluctant to negotiate with Yasir Arafat, chairman of the Palestine Liberation Organization (PLO), because he was pessimistic that the two could find an acceptable settlement. Rabin nevertheless allowed his foreign minister, Shimon Peres, to explore through a private channel the possibility that Arafat would agree to a gradual, incremental process that would allow Israel to test the intentions of the PLO in exchange for recognition of the political identity of the Palestinians and the creation of the Palestine National Authority. Critical to the process was mutual recognition of identity and political separation of the two peoples. Over time, secured identities should reshape images and interests as the two peoples disengage and redefine their political, economic, and national frontiers.

Mutual recognition and political separation is the most far-reaching strategy of conflict reduction. In 1989, after a brutal civil war that lasted over a decade, leaders of Lebanese religious groups modified the fundamentals of their prewar consociational bargain. Instead of privileging the Maronite Christian community, Muslims and Christians now share power equally. The bargain still provides for a Maronite Christian president, a Sunni Muslim prime minister, and a Shiite president of the

National Assembly. Political decisions are still made by leaders at the top and their communities remain distinct.

The forging of multiethnic coalitions with crosscutting ties is yet another strategy. This was the principal demand of the Muslim leadership of Bosnia and Herzegovina. The agreement reached in Dayton honors a multiethnic Bosnia in principle, but in its political arrangements provides for de facto separation of Bosnian Serbs from Muslims and Croats. Kosovo simmers unresolved as Kosovars press for formal independence and Serbia insists on integration.

In all these cases, conflict reduction required more than reciprocation of small concessions in a gradually building process. The core of the solution lies in the often difficult decision by senior leaders to acknowledge, respect, and accommodate different identities and share political power. Informal track-two diplomacy can facilitate the discussion of deep identity issues in parallel with the more formal negotiation of interests that are gradually redefined after identities are recognized. The international community can facilitate power-sharing arrangements by tying progress in conflict resolution to the broader basket of issues that flows from membership in good standing in the global community.

All these strategies assume that identities are fixed and that they must be accommodated as they are. Such a pessimistic assumption is unwarranted. I have argued that identity is not given, but that it is socially reconstructed as interactions develop and contexts evolve. In his brilliant analysis, Benedict Anderson observed that nations, unlike families and clans, where individuals can know the others, are "imagined communities," whose past, tradition, and connections are interpreted and reinterpreted through time.[85] Political identities similarly depend on imagined communities whose traditions are constructed and reinterpreted. Identities can consequently be reshaped and reconfigured as leaders and communities restructure their relationships.

Identities are complex structures, with components that emphasize shared communitarian traditions and norms that usually include emphasis on protection of the weak, social responsibility, generosity, fairness, and reciprocity as well as honor, reputation, and vengeance. Emphasis given to these different norms varies with the situation. Skilled mediators can emphasize the positive values of responsibility, fairness, and compassion as important elements of honor and reputation. Appeal to the "best" in the tradition of an identity may shift the emphasis within an "imagined community" to create the space for fairness and reciprocity that can ultimately change images, reshape interests, and culminate in tolerance and recognition of others' identities.

Threatened identities are conducive to hostile imagery, incompatible definitions of interest, and violent conflict. Often, violent conflict escalates to a painful level of destruction before serious attempts at conflict management, much less conflict resolution, begin. Yet defeat and destruction are extraordinarily expensive teaching tools. In their wake, deep enmity can preclude the fundamental learning that is necessary for image change and tolerance of the identities of others. Only after repeated failures do the parties begin to negotiate the issues, and then usually at a superficial level. The challenge for peacemaking in the twenty-first century is to engage the parties earlier and at a deeper level so that the identities of some can be stretched to tolerate the identities of others.

NOTES

1. David A. Lake and Donald Rothchild, "Containing Fear: The Origins and Management of Ethnic Conflict," *International Security* 21, no. 2 (fall 1996): 41–75; and Barry R. Posen, "The Security Dilemma and Ethnic Conflict," in *Ethnic Conflict and International Security*, ed. Michael E. Brown (Princeton, N.J.: Princeton University Press, 1993), 103–124.

2. Milton Rokeach, *The Nature of Human Values* (New York: Free Press, 1973), 5; and Yaacov Vertzberger, *The World in Their Minds: Information Processing, Cognition, and Perception in Foreign Policy Decisionmaking* (Stanford, Calif.: Stanford University Press, 1990), 114–127.

3. Daniel Druckman, "Nationalism, Patriotism, and Group Loyalty: A Social Psychological Perspective," *Mershon International Studies Review* 38 (1994): 43–68 at 50.

4. Henri Tajfel, *Human Groups and Social Categories* (Cambridge: Cambridge University Press, 1981), 255.

5. Michael Hogg and Dominic Abrams, "Toward a Single-Process Uncertainty-Reduction Model of Social Motivation in Groups," in *Group Motivation: Social Psychological Perspectives* (London: Harvester Wheatsheaf, 1993), 173–190 at 173.

6. Henri Tajfel, *Social Identity and Intergroup Relations* (New York: Cambridge University Press, 1982); Henri Tajfel and John C. Turner, "The Social Identity Theory of Intergroup Behavior," in *Psychology of Intergroup Relations*, 2d ed., ed. Stephen Worchel and William G. Austin (Chicago: Nelson-Hall, 1986), 7–24; Michael Hogg, *The Social Psychology of Group Cohesiveness: From Attraction to Social Identity* (New York: New York University Press, 1992); Marilyn B. Brewer and Sherry K. Schneider, "Social Identity and Social Dilemmas: A Double-Edged Sword," in *Social Identity Theory: Constructive and Critical Advances*, ed. Michael Hogg and Dominic Abrams (London: Harvester Wheatsheaf, 1990), 169–184; and David Messick and Diane Mackie, "Intergroup Relations," *Annual Review of Psychology* 40 (1989): 45–81.

7. Barbara Harff and Ted Robert Gurr, "Toward Empirical Theory of Genocides and Politicides: Identification and Measurement of Cases since 1945," *International Studies Quarterly* 32, no. 3 (September 1988): 359–371.

8. Kenneth Booth, *Strategy and Ethnocentrism* (London: Croom Helm, 1979).

9. Susan T. Fiske and Shelley E. Taylor, *Social Cognition* (Reading, Mass.: Addison-Wesley, 1984), 72–99.

10. Jonathan Mercer ("Anarchy and Identity," *International Organization* 49, no. 2 [spring 1995]: 229–252), argues that social identity theory confirms the neorealist argument that an anarchic international environment produces self-help behavior. Mercer does acknowledge, however, that the impact of

differentiation on military conflict will depend on political, economic, and historical factors.

11. D. M. Taylor and F. M. Moghaddam, *Theories of Intergroup Relations: International and Social Psychological Perspectives* (New York: Praeger, 1987).

12. John C. Turner et al., *Rediscovering the Social Group: A Self-Categorization Theory* (Oxford: Basil Blackwell, 1987).

13. For an excellent discussion of this issue, see James M. Goldgeier, "The Role of Political Psychology in Rethinking Security Studies" (unpublished paper, Washington, D.C., 1997).

14. Ted Hopf, "Russian Identity and Foreign Policy in Estonia and Uzbekistan" (unpublished paper, Ohio State University, Columbus, Ohio, 1997).

15. For a discussion of how moral norms and obligations that prevail in primary groups are reinterpreted at the national level, see Paul Stern, "Why Do People Sacrifice for Their Nations?" *Political Psychology* 16, no. 2 (1995): 217–235.

16. Lake and Rothchild, "Containing Fear," 43.

17. Posen, "The Security Dilemma and Ethnic Conflict."

18. Paul Brass, ed., *Ethnic Groups and the State* (Totowa, N.J.: Barnes and Noble Books, 1995); and Ted Robert Gurr, *Minorities at Risk: A Global View of Ethnopolitical Conflict* (Washington, D.C.: United States Institute of Peace Press, 1993).

19. Muzafer Sherif, *In Common Predicament: Social Psychology of Intergroup Conflict and Cooperation* (Boston: Houghton Mifflin, 1966). The impact of "relative deprivation," or a context in which groups stand to lose but some groups stand to lose more than others, is disputed.

20. Ted Robert Gurr, *Why Men Rebel* (Princeton, N.J.: Princeton University Press, 1970), 12–13.

21. Ibid., 46–50. For a discussion of loss aversion and its impact on cooperation, see Janice Gross Stein and Louis Pauly, eds., *Choosing to Cooperate: How States Avoid Loss* (Baltimore: Johns Hopkins University Press, 1989).

22. In "Containing Fear," Lake and Rothchild identify three mediating variables—information failures, incredible commitments, and the security dilemma—as the catalysts to violence in a context of incompatible identities and mutual fear.

23. Herbert C. Kelman, "Creating the Conditions for Israeli-Palestinian Negotiations," *Journal of*

Conflict Resolution 26, no. 1 (March 1982): 39–76 at 61.

24. Timur Kuran, "Ethnic Dissimilation and Its International Diffusion," in *The International Spread of Ethnic Conflict*, ed. David A. Lake and Donald Rothchild (Princeton, N.J.: Princeton University Press, 1998), 35–60.

25. T. Ranger, *The Invention of Tradition* (Cambridge: Cambridge University Press, 1983).

26. Stephen Stedman, "Spoilers in Peace Processes," in *New Challenges to International Conflict Resolution*, ed. Paul Stern (Washington, D.C.: National Academy Press, 2000).

27. Human Rights Watch, in its report issued in 1995, concluded that "time after time, a proximate cause of violence is governmental exploitation of communal differences. . . . The 'communal card' is frequently played, for example, when a government is losing popularity or legitimacy, and finds it convenient to wrap itself in the cloak of ethnic, racial, or religious rhetoric." *Playing the Communal Card: Communal Violence and Human Rights* (New York: Human Rights Watch, 1995), viii.

28. Jack Snyder, *Myths of Empire: Domestic Politics and International Ambition* (Ithaca, N.Y.: Cornell University Press, 1991), 2–6, 31–49.

29. Milton J. Esman, *Ethnic Politics* (Ithaca, N.Y.: Cornell University Press, 1994); and Milton J. Esman, "Ethnic Politics and Economic Power," *Comparative Politics* 19, no. 4 (1986): 395–418.

30. Gurr, *Why Men Rebel*, 59.

31. In "The Role of Political Psychology in Rethinking Security Studies," Goldgeier incisively reviews the social-psychological literature on this question.

32. They are likely to do so when geography is harsh and provides no buffer zone or margin for error; when offensive and defensive technology are difficult to distinguish; and when the relative power balance between adversaries is changing so that for at least one of the two, the advantages of striking first are substantial. See Robert Jervis, "Cooperation under the Security Dilemma," *World Politics* 30 (1978): 167–214.

33. Richard Ned Lebow and Janice Gross Stein, *We All Lost the Cold War* (Princeton, N.J.: Princeton University Press, 1994).

34. Druckman, "Nationalism, Patriotism, and Group Loyalty," 63.

35. Dean G. Pruitt and Jeffrey Z. Rubin, *Social Conflict* (New York: McGraw-Hill, 1986), 117–118; and Mark Chen and John A. Bargh, "Nonconscious Behavioral Confirmation Processes: The Self-Fulfilling Consequences of Automatic Stereotype Activation," *Journal of Experimental Social Psychology* 33, no. 5 (September 1997): 541–560.

36. Richard W. Cottam, *Foreign Policy Motivations: A General Theory and a Case Study* (Pittsburgh: University of Pittsburgh Press, 1977); Richard Herrmann, *Perceptions and Behavior in Soviet Foreign Policy* (Pittsburgh: University of Pittsburgh Press, 1985); Richard Herrmann, "The Empirical Challenge of the Cognitive Revolution: A Strategy for Drawing Inferences about Perceptions," *International Studies Quarterly* 32 (1988): 175–203; and Richard Herrmann and Michael P. Fischerkeller, "Beyond the Enemy Image and Spiral Model: Cognitive-Strategic Research after the Cold War," *International Organization* 49, no. 3 (summer 1995): 415–450.

37. Susan E. Brodt and Lee D. Ross, "The Role of Stereotyping in Overconfident Social Prediction," *Social Cognition* 16, no. 2 (summer 1998): 225–252.

38. Jeffrey W. Sherman et al., "Intergroup Bias in Group Judgment Processes: The Role of Behavioral Memories," *Journal of Experimental Social Psychology* 34, no. 1 (January 1998): 51–65; and Ying-yi Hong et al., "Implicit Theories and Evaluative Processes in Person Cognition," *Journal of Experimental Social Psychology* 33, no. 3 (May 1997): 296–323.

39. Diana Burgess and Eugene Borgida, "Refining Sex-Role Spillover Theory: The Role of Gender Subtypes and Harasser Attributions," *Social Cognition* 15, no. 3 (fall 1999): 332–365.

40. J. R. Anderson, *The Architecture of Cognition* (Cambridge, Mass.: Harvard University Press, 1982).

41. L. Ross, M. R. Lepper, and M. Hubbard, "Perseverance in Self-Perception and Social Perception: Biased Attributional Processes in the Debriefing Paradigm," *Journal of Personality and Social Psychology* 32 (1975): 880–892.

42. E. R. Hirt and S. J. Sherman, "The Role of Prior Knowledge in Explaining Hypothetical Events," *Journal of Experimental and Social Psychology* 21 (1985): 519–543.

43. Pruitt and Rubin, *Social Conflict*, 112–119.

44. "Heuristics" refers to the rules leaders use to test the propositions embedded in their beliefs. See

D. von Winterfeldt and E. Edwards, *Decision Analysis and Behavioral Research* (New York: Cambridge University Press, 1986).

45. The heuristic of anchoring refers to the estimation of the magnitude or degree of the same phenomenon by picking an "available" initial value as a reference point and making a comparison. See Fiske and Taylor, *Social Cognition*, 250–256, 268–275.

46. Michael Ross and Fiore Sicoly, "Egocentric Biases in Availability and Attribution," *Journal of Personality and Social Psychology* 37 (1979): 322–336.

47. Daniel Kahneman and Amos Tversky, "On the Psychology of Prediction," *Psychological Review* 80 (1973): 237–251.

48. Robert Jervis, *Perception and Misperception in International Politics* (Princeton, N.J.: Princeton University Press, 1976), 288–318; and Jennifer Crocker, Darlene B. Hannah, and Renée Weber, "Person Memory and Causal Attributions," *Journal of Personality and Social Psychology* 44, no. 1 (1983): 55–66 at 65.

49. Lee Ross, "The Intuitive Psychologist and His Shortcomings: Distortions in the Attribution Process," in *Advances in Experimental and Social Psychology* 10, ed. L. Berkowitz (New York: Academic Press, 1977).

50. E. T. Higgins and J. A. Bargh, "Social Cognition and Social Perception," in *Annual Review of Psychology* 38, ed. M. R. Rosenzweig and L. W. Porter (Palo Alto, Calif.: Annual Reviews, 1987), 369–425 at 386.

51. Vertzberger, *The World in Their Minds*, 136.

52. An exception is Ralph Erber and Susan T. Fiske, "Outcome Dependency and Attention to Inconsistent Information," *Journal of Personality and Social Psychology* 47 (1984): 709–726.

53. James H. Kuklinski, Robert C. Luskin, and John Bolland, "Where Is the Schema? Going Beyond the 'S' Word in Political Psychology," *American Political Science Review* 85, no. 4 (December 1991): 1341–1380 at 1346.

54. Lake and Rothchild, "Containing Fear," 53–64.

55. Albert Bandura, *Aggression: A Social Learning Analysis* (Englewood Cliffs, N.J.: Prentice-Hall, 1973); Neta A. Crawford, "The Passion of World Politics: Propositions on Emotion and Emotional Relationships," *International Security* 24, no. 4 (spring 2000): 116–156 at 128; and Rom Harre, ed., *The Social Construction of Emotions* (Oxford: Basil Blackwell, 1986).

56. Oran Young, "Political Leadership and Regime Formation: On the Development of Institutions in International Society," *International Organization* 45, no. 3 (1991): 281–308; and Oran Young, "Comment on Andrew Moravcsik, 'A New Statecraft? Supranational Entrepreneurs and International Cooperation,'" *International Organization* 53, no. 4 (autumn 1999): 805–809. For a discussion of entrepreneurial leadership, see Abram Chayes and Antonia Handler Chayes, *The New Sovereignty: Compliance with International Regulatory Agreements* (Cambridge, Mass.: Harvard University Press, 1995); Michael Barnett and Martha Finnemore, "The Politics, Power, and Pathologies of International Organizations," *International Organization* 53, no. 4 (autumn 1999): 699–732. For a critical perspective, see Andrew Moravcsik, "A New Statecraft? Supranational Entrepreneurs and International Cooperation," *International Organization* 53, no. 2 (spring 1999): 267–306.

57. T. L. Good and J. E. Brophy, *Educational Psychology: A Realistic Approach* (New York: Longman, 1990).

58. Ernest Haas, *When Knowledge Is Power: Three Models of Change in International Organizations* (Berkeley: University of California Press, 1990), 84.

59. Ibid.

60. In an effort to deal with the problem of evaluation, analysts refer to pathological learning, or changes that impede future cognitive growth. See James Clay Moltz, "Divergent Learning and the Failed Politics of Soviet Economic Reform," *World Politics* 45, no. 2 (January 1993): 301–325 at 303.

61. See Janice Gross Stein, "Deterrence and Compellence in the Gulf: A Failed or Impossible Task?" *International Security* 17, no. 2 (fall 1992): 147–179.

62. For a similar argument, see George W. Breslauer, "What Have We Learned about Learning?" in *Learning in U.S. and Soviet Foreign Policy*, ed. George W. Breslauer and Philip E. Tetlock (Boulder, Colo.: Westview Press, 1991), 825–856.

63. Sim B. Sitkin, "Learning through Failure: The Strategy of Small Losses," *Research in Organizational Behavior* 14 (1992): 231–266.

64. D. T. Campbell, "Reform as Experiments," *American Psychologist* 24 (1969): 409–429.

65. See C. Argyis and D. A. Schon, *Organizational Learning* (Reading, Mass.: Addison-Wesley, 1978).

66. Ulric Neisser, "On 'Social Knowing,'" *Personality and Social Psychology Bulletin* 6 (1980): 601–605 at 603–604, cited in Kuklinski, Luskin, and Bolland, "Where Is the Schema?" 1341–1356 at 1346.

67. I detail the scope of political learning in "The Political Economy of Strategic Agreements: The Linked Costs of Failure at Camp David," in *Double-Edged Diplomacy: International Bargaining and Domestic Politics*, ed. Peter Evans, Harold Jacobsen, and Robert Putnam (Berkeley: University of California Press, 1993), 77–103. See also my "Political Learning by Doing: Gorbachev as an Uncommitted Thinker and Motivated Learner," in *International Relations Theory and the Transformation of the International System*, ed. Richard Ned Lebow and Thomas Risse-Kappen (New York: Columbia University Press, 1995).

68. Steven Weber, "Interactive Learning in U.S.-Soviet Arms Control," in *Learning in U.S. and Soviet Foreign Policy*, ed. George W. Breslauer and Philip E. Tetlock (Boulder, Colo.: Westview Press, 1991), 784–824.

69. Haas, *When Knowledge Is Power*.

70. Generational change and political succession can also explain a fundamental change in leaders' images; the source of change is not individual learning but a change in elites. Generational change was irrelevant in Egypt: Sadat was of the same generation of Gamal Abdel Nasser and he learned after he had been president for several years.

71. Richard Ned Lebow, "When Does Conciliation Succeed?" in *International Relations Theory and the Transformation of the International System*, ed. Lebow and Risse-Kappen.

72. See my "The Political Economy of Strategic Agreements" and my "Political Learning by Doing."

73. Dean G. Pruitt and Peter J. Carnevale (*Negotiation in Social Conflict* [London: Open University Press, 1992], 146) term this kind of strategy "unilateral conciliatory initiatives."

74. Z. Maoz and D. S. Felsenthal, "Self-Binding Commitments, the Inducement of Trust, Social Choice, and the Theory of International Cooperation," *International Studies Quarterly* 31 (1987): 177–200.

75. Moshe Dayan, *Breakthrough: A Personal Account of the Egypt-Israel Peace Negotiations* (New York: Alfred A. Knopf, 1981), 44–52.

76. Maoz and Felsenthal, "Self-Binding Commitments," 198.

77. Ibid., 191–192.

78. Charles Osgood, *An Alternative to War or Surrender* (Urbana: University of Illinois Press, 1962).

79. S. Lindskold, P. S. Walters, and H. Koutsourais, "Cooperators, Competitors, and Response to GRIT," *Journal of Conflict Resolution* 27 (1983): 521–532.

80. D. G. Pruitt and M. J. Kimmel, "Twenty Years of Experimental Gaming," *Annual Review of Psychology* 28 (1977): 363–392.

81. In 1985 Gorbachev announced the suspension of Soviet countermeasures in response to the deployment of intermediate-range nuclear forces (INF) by NATO, and a moratorium on further deployments of SS-20s. That same year he proclaimed a unilateral moratorium on nuclear testing. In October 1985 the Soviet Union also paid its back dues to the United Nations for peacekeeping, began to cooperate with the International Atomic Energy Agency, and reworked its position in the Strategic Arms Reduction Talks (START). In January 1986 Gorbachev urged a program of complete nuclear disarmament to be achieved in three stages by the year 2000. In 1987 the Soviet Union agreed to intrusive on-site verification inspections as part of the INF agreement and announced its decision to withdraw from Afghanistan. In December 1988, at the UN General Assembly, Gorbachev also announced the unilateral reduction of active Soviet military forces by 15 percent and the withdrawal of more than 40 percent of Soviet tank divisions from Eastern Europe, together with 50 percent of Soviet tanks.

82. Policy Planning Staff and National Security Council Staff, interviews by author, Washington, D.C., February 1989.

83. M. P. Zanna, J. M. Olson, and R. H. Fazio, "Attitude-Behavior Consistency: An Individual Difference Perspective," *Journal of Personality and Social Psychology* 38 (1980): 432–440.

84. Timothy D. Sisk, *Living Together: International Mediation to Promote Power Sharing in Ethnic Conflicts* (New York: Carnegie Commission on Preventing Deadly Conflict, 1995).

85. Benedict Anderson, *Imagined Communities*, 2d ed. (London: Verso, 1991).

13

Ethnic and Internal Conflicts

Causes and Implications

Michael E. Brown

MANY POLICYMAKERS AND JOURNALISTS believe that the causes of ethnic and internal conflicts are simple and straightforward.[1] The driving forces behind these violent conflicts, it is said, are the "ancient hatreds" that many ethnic and religious groups have for each other. In Eastern Europe, the former Soviet Union, and elsewhere, these deep-seated animosities were held in check for years by authoritarian rule. The collapse of authoritarian rule, it is argued, has taken the "lid" off these ancient rivalries, allowing long-suppressed grievances to come to the surface and escalate into armed conflict. U.S. president George Bush, for example, maintained that the war in Bosnia among Serbs, Croats, and Muslims grew out of "age-old animosities."[2] His successor, Bill Clinton, argued that the end of the Cold War "lifted the lid from a cauldron of long-simmering hatreds. Now, the entire global terrain is bloody with such conflicts."[3] Writing about the Balkans, the U.S. political commentator Richard Cohen declared: "Bosnia is a formidable, scary place of high mountains, brutish people, and tribal grievances rooted in history and myth born of boozy nights by the fire. It's the place where World War I began and where the wars of Europe persist, an ember of hate still glowing for reasons that defy reason itself."[4]

Most scholars reject this explanation of ethnic and internal conflicts.[5] This simple but widely held view cannot explain why violent conflicts have broken out in some places but not in others, and it cannot explain why some disputes are more violent and harder to resolve than others. It is undeniably true that Serbs, Croats, and Muslims have many historical grievances against one another and that these grievances have played a role in the Balkan conflicts that raged in the 1990s. But it is also true that other groups—Czechs and Slovaks, Ukrainians and Russians, French-speaking and English-speaking Canadians—have historical grievances that have not led to violent conflict in the post–Cold War era. This single-factor explanation cannot account for the variation we see in the incidence and intensity of ethnic and internal conflicts.

In this chapter I will review scholarly thinking about the causes of ethnic and internal conflicts, developing four main arguments along the way. First, I submit that scholars have identified four main sets of underlying factors that make some situations more predisposed to violence than others: structural factors, political factors, economic/social factors, and cultural/perceptual factors. Second, I contend that the catalytic factors or triggers of ethnic and internal conflicts have received far less attention from scholars and that conflicts can be triggered in several different ways. Third, I argue that scholars have not paid enough attention, in particular, to the roles played by domestic elites in transforming potentially violent situations into deadly confrontations. The actions of domestic elites trigger many internal conflicts. They merit special attention. Fourth, I maintain that these distinctions have important real-world implications. No single set of factors is responsible for every type of violent conflict; different forces operate in different cases. It follows that no single set of policy responses will work everywhere, all the time. Different kinds of problems call for different kinds of responses. The challenge for scholars is to identify and analyze the different sets of factors that bring about different kinds of conflicts. The challenge for policymakers is to develop effective responses to these different types of problems.

DEFINITIONS

We must begin with some definitions. Policymakers, journalists, and scholars often use the terms "ethnic conflict," "internal conflict," "civil war," and "regional conflict" interchangeably. This is a mistake. It is important for us to be precise because if we mischaracterize the nature of a conflict and the driving forces behind a conflict, our policy responses are more likely to be misguided.

Ethnic Conflict

The term "ethnic conflict" is often used loosely, to describe a wide range of intrastate conflicts that are not, in fact, ethnic in character. The conflict in Somalia, for example, is occasionally referred to as an ethnic conflict even though Somalia is the most ethnically homogeneous country in Africa. The conflict in Somalia is not between rival ethnic groups, but between rival gangs, clans, and warlords, almost all of whom belong to the same Somali ethnic group.

According to Anthony Smith, an "ethnic community" is "a named human population with a myth of common ancestry, shared memories, and cultural elements; a link with a historic territory or homeland; and a measure of solidarity."[6] Six criteria must be met, therefore, before a group can be called an ethnic community. First, the group must have a name for itself. This is not trivial; a lack of a name reflects an insufficiently developed collective identity. Second, the people in the group must believe in a common ancestry. This is more important than genetic ties, which may exist but are not essential. Third, the members of the group must believe that they have shared historical experiences. These beliefs often come in the form of myths or legends passed from generation to generation by word of mouth. Fourth, the group must have a shared culture, which is generally based on a combination of language, religion, laws, customs, institutions, dress, music, crafts, architecture, even food. Language and religion are especially powerful ethnic markers. Fifth, the group must feel an attachment to a specific piece of territory, which it may or may not actually inhabit. Sixth and last, the people in a group have to think of themselves as a group in order to constitute an ethnic community; that is, they must have a sense of their common ethnicity. The group must be self-aware.[7]

Scholars disagree about the origins and dynamics of ethnic identities. The debate is usually characterized as a dispute between "primordialists" and "instrumentalists."[8] The heart of the debate is a difference of opinion about two things: (1) whether or not ethnic identities have deep historical roots and (2) whether or not ethnic identities change significantly over time. Primordialists contend that ethnic identities have deep historical roots and change little over time. John Stack explains: "For primordialists, a sense of peoplehood forms the essence of ethnic identity. Ethnicity becomes an expression of basic group identity, basic in that fundamental group attributes are passed down from one generation to the next."[9] Instrumentalists maintain that ethnic identities are often recent constructs and that they change dramatically with the passage of time. Paul Brass elaborates: "Ethnic communities are created and transformed by particular elites in modernizing and in post-industrial societies undergoing dramatic social change. This process invariably involves competition and conflict for political power, economic benefits, and social status between competing elite, class, and leadership groups both within and among different ethnic categories."[10] In short, instrumentalists contend that political elites play decisive roles in constructing and shaping ethnic identities and that their actions are driven largely, if not entirely, by their political and economic self-interests.

My view is that it is highly problematic to make sweeping generalizations about very different kinds of groups. Estimates of the number of ethnic groups in the world vary widely, depending on whether the researchers making the estimates are interested in simple ethnolinguistic distinctiveness or politically active groups. Those who are interested in the former estimate that there are between three thousand and nine thousand ethnic communities in the world.[11] Those who focus on the latter find that at least two hundred groups merit attention.[12] Estimates aside, I would suggest that (1) some groups have deep historical roots, while others do not, and (2) some groups have fairly static identities, while others are dynamic.

In short, there is a lot of variation along both of these dimensions. The best approach, as Milton Esman argues, is to draw on both the primordialist and instrumentalist positions:

> Ethnicity cannot be politicized unless an underlying core of memories, experience, or meaning moves people to collective action. This common foundation may include historical experiences, such as struggles against outsiders for possession of a homeland, or cultural markers, especially language, religion, and legal institutions that set one community apart from others. Ethnic identities are also contextual, adaptable to and activated by unexpected threats and new opportunities; they can be oriented to fresh goals, and they can be infused with new content. Historical myths can be shaped from imagined pasts to legitimate current goals; boundaries can expand and contract. Thus every ethnic collectivity and solidarity can be located on a spectrum between (primordial) historical continuities and (instrumental) opportunistic adaptations.[13]

We can therefore define an "ethnic conflict" as a dispute about political, economic, social, cultural, or territorial issues between two or more ethnic communities. Two points should be kept in mind about this phenomenon.

First, ethnic conflict is inherent in multiethnic societies. Groups will inevitably disagree about political, economic, and social issues, and in multiethnic countries the fault lines will often be defined in ethnic terms. Ethnic problems are likely to be widespread, moreover, because fewer than 20 of the more than 185 states that exist today are ethnically homogeneous (with ethnic minorities constituting less than 5 percent of the population).[14]

Second, ethnic conflicts are not necessarily violent conflicts. A case in point is the struggle between French Canadians in Quebec who seek more political autonomy or outright independence from the Canadian government and those who want to maintain the status quo. Czechoslovakia's "velvet divorce" is another. Tragically, other ethnic conflicts generate unspeakable levels of savagery, as we have seen in Bosnia, Rwanda, and elsewhere. The challenge for well-intentioned policymakers is to keep ethnic problems from becoming violent conflicts. Once the violence threshold is crossed, ethnic relations become more volatile and coexistence becomes more problematic.

Internal Conflict

Although Smith's conception of ethnic communities is broad—it would include groups defined in religious terms, for example—many internal conflicts are not ethnic in character. Internal conflicts are violent political disputes whose origins can be traced primarily to intrastate rather than interstate factors; armed violence takes place (or threatens to take place) primarily within the borders of a single state.[15] Types of internal conflicts include power struggles involving civilian or military leaders, challenges by criminal organizations to state sovereignty, and ideological struggles, as well as ethnic conflicts and secessionist campaigns. Many internal conflicts are nonviolent and are resolved through established political, economic, and social mechanisms. In violent conflicts the level of violence can range from low-level terrorist campaigns to sustained guerrilla insurgencies to all-out civil war or genocide. In most internal conflicts the key actors are governments and rebel groups, but when state structures are weak or nonexistent, groups fight between and among themselves in a Hobbesian universe of their own.[16]

Analysis of these conflicts is complicated by the fact that some countries have to contend with two or more different conflicts at the same time. A further complication is that some internal conflicts are driven by a combination of ideological, criminal, political, and ethnic motivations, and some conflicts mutate over time. Most power struggles, moreover, are characterized by the protagonists in politically convenient ethnic or ideological terms. These complications make analysis difficult but not impossible.

For example, the problems that Georgia experienced in the 1990s with Abkhazian and South Ossetian separatists were ethnic in nature; the struggle for power among political factions in Tbilisi was not. The Burmese military's repression of Karen, Naga, and Rohingya insurgents has produced several ethnic conflicts; its suppression of the democracy movement in the country as a whole has other political motivations. The leaders of the Sendero Luminoso and Tupac Amaru movements in Peru were initially motivated by ideological agendas they sought to advance, but they later placed more and more emphasis on the plight of indigenous peoples. This conflict, therefore, evolved from an ideological struggle into a hybrid.

Civil War

Although many internal conflicts become violent, only some should be classified as true civil wars. Scholars and analysts generally begin calling violent conflicts "wars" after one thousand people have been killed.[17] This is a reasonable benchmark for distinguishing between low-level and high-level violence, but two more criteria should be added to the equation. First, for an internal conflict to be classified as a civil war, the protagonists must have group identities and organizational capacities. Civil wars are fought between self-aware, defined groups that have organizational capacities to plan and carry out military operations in support of political goals.[18] Spontaneous, spasmodic riots, therefore, are not civil wars because they do not have organizational infrastructures. The communal rioting between Hindus and Muslims in India in the 1990s was horrific and deadly, but it was not a civil war because much of the violence was spontaneous and fueled by mass agitation. Second, internal conflicts have to be sustained over time to be called civil wars. It is difficult to draw a precise line between internal conflicts and civil wars in this regard, but civil wars (unlike riots) last more than a few hours or a few days. As discussed, the protagonists have organizational capacities for sustained military campaigns in support of their goals.

Regional Conflict

Many ethnic conflicts, internal conflicts, and civil wars start out as intrastate disputes, but they become regional, interstate crises when outside powers become involved.

Many policymakers and journalists have simplistic and mechanistic views of how this comes about: They frequently rely on crude analogies to diseases, fires, floods, and other forces of nature. For example, in explaining why the United States needed to send troops to Bosnia as part of the NATO peacekeeping mission there, President Bill Clinton commented that if the United States failed to act, "the conflict that already has claimed so many people could spread like poison throughout the entire region."[19] His secretary of state at the time, Warren Christopher, argued that "if this best hope for peace fails, the war will re-ignite and spread."[20] Earlier in the war, Christopher explained why it was important for the United States to become "actively engaged" in Bosnia: if the West failed to stop the fighting there, he argued, "you may well have the entire Balkans involved . . . it could draw in Greece and Turkey . . . the United States has a stake in preventing the world from going up in flames."[21] Many think of conflicts "spilling over" from one place to another in hydraulic fashion. Writing about Bosnia, for example, the journalist Misha Glenny worried about "the spillover of this struggle into the Aegean Sea."[22] Scholars can get caught up in this kind of thinking as well. Indeed, there is a sizable scholarly literature that views the regionalization of internal conflict as a "contagion" problem.[23]

This way of thinking about the regional dimensions of internal conflicts is both simplistic and mechanistic. It is simplistic because it sees things moving in one direction only: from the place where the conflict began to neighboring states, which are characterized as the passive, innocent victims of epidemics, firestorms, floods, and rivers of refugees. This way of thinking is mechanistic, moreover, because it sees things happening in an uncontrolled and uncontrollable fashion. Problems are blamed on forces of nature or "conflict" itself rather than on the decisions and acts of individuals, groups, and governments. "No-fault" history is the result. The policy implication that flows from this line of reasoning is that little can be done to control these inanimate forces.

We can develop a more sophisticated understanding of this problem by distinguishing between the effects of internal conflicts on neighboring states and the actions that neighboring states take with respect to these conflicts. The effects of internal conflicts on neighboring states fall into five main categories: (1) refugee problems, (2) economic problems, (3) military entanglements, (4) instability problems, and (5) full-blown war. We also need to distinguish between and among the different kinds of actions that neighboring states take with respect to internal conflicts. The most useful way to analyze this problem is to dissect the different motivations that neighboring states have in these situations. One can therefore distinguish among (1) comparatively benign, humanitarian interventions aimed at relieving suffering and restoring regional peace and security; (2) defensive interventions aimed at safeguarding national security interests; (3) protective interventions designed to protect ethnic brethren who are being persecuted; (4) opportunistic meddling designed to further political, economic, or military interests; and (5) opportunistic invasions. Many interventions are of course driven by a combination of considerations, and states always try to characterize their actions in benign terms, regardless of their true motivations.[24]

In sum, there are many different ways neighboring states can be affected by and become involved in internal conflicts. Although neighboring states can be the passive victims of turmoil in their regions, they are often active contributors to military escalation and regional instability: opportunistic interventions are common. It is therefore a mistake to think of internal conflicts "spilling over" from one place

Table 1. Underlying Causes of Ethnic and Internal Conflicts

Structural Factors	Economic/Social Factors
Weak states	Economic problems
Intrastate security concerns	Discriminatory economic systems
Ethnic geography	Economic development and modernization
Political Factors	**Cultural/Perceptual Factors**
Discriminatory political institutions	Patterns of cultural discrimination
Exclusionary national ideologies	Problematic group histories
Intergroup politics	
Elite politics	

to another through a process that is always beyond human control. Many—perhaps most —regional conflicts are the products of discrete decisions made by identifiable individuals, groups, and governments that are not necessarily immune to international pressure. This is important, because another critical threshold is crossed when internal conflicts begin to involve neighboring states. Violence then becomes much more difficult to control and resolve.

THE UNDERLYING CAUSES OF ETHNIC AND INTERNAL CONFLICTS

Scholarly literature on ethnic and internal conflict has tended to focus on the underlying factors that make some places and some situations more prone to violence than others. More specifically, scholars have identified four main clusters of factors that make some places more predisposed to violence than others: structural factors, political factors, economic/social factors, and cultural/perceptual factors (see table 1).

Structural Factors

Three structural factors have been identified as important precursors of ethnic and internal conflict: weak states, intrastate security concerns, and ethnic geography.

Weak states are the starting point for many analyses of ethnic and internal conflict.[25] Some states are born weak. Many of the states that were carved out of colonial empires in Africa and Southeast Asia, for example, were artificial constructs. They lacked political legitimacy, politically sensible borders, and political institutions capable of exercising meaningful control over the territory placed under their nominal supervision. The same can be said of many of the states created out of the rubble of the Soviet Union. The vast majority of these new entities came into existence with only the most rudimentary political institutions in place.

In many parts of the world, sub-Saharan Africa perhaps most notably, states have become weaker over time. In some cases, external developments such as reductions in foreign aid from major powers and international financial institutions and drops in commodity prices have played key roles in bringing about institutional decline. In other cases, states have been weakened by internal problems such as corruption, administrative incompetence, and an inability to promote economic development. Many countries have suffered from several of these problems at the same time.

When state structures weaken, violent conflict often follows. Power struggles between and among politicians and would-be leaders intensify. Provincial leaders become increasingly independent and, should they consolidate control over military assets, virtual warlords. Ethnic groups that had been oppressed by the center are more able to assert themselves politically, perhaps in the form of more administrative autonomy or their own states. Ethnic groups that had been protected by the center or had exercised power through the state find themselves more vulnerable. Criminal organizations become more powerful and pervasive, as we have seen in the Caucasus and elsewhere. Borders are controlled less effectively. Cross-border movements of militia, arms, drugs, smuggled goods, refugees, and migrants therefore increase. Massive humanitarian problems, such as famines and epidemics, can develop. The state in question might ultimately fragment or simply cease to exist as a political entity.

When states are weak, individual groups within these states develop *security concerns:* groups worry that other groups may pose security threats, and many feel compelled to provide for their own defense.[26] If the state in question is very weak or if it is expected to become weaker with time, the incentives for groups to make independent military preparations can be very powerful. The problem is that, in taking steps to defend themselves, groups often threaten the security of others. This can lead neighboring groups to take steps to provide for their own security, which in turn diminishes the security of those who first started down this path: this is the security dilemma. These problems are especially acute when empires or multiethnic states collapse and ethnic groups suddenly have to provide for their own security. One group's rush to deploy defensive forces will appear threatening to other groups. Moreover, the kinds of forces most commonly deployed— militia and infantry equipped with light arms —have inherent offensive capabilities even if they are mobilized for defensive purposes; this inevitably intensifies the security concerns of neighboring groups.

The third structural factor that can contribute to instability is *ethnic geography.*[27] More specifically, states with ethnic minorities are more prone to conflict than others, and certain kinds of ethnic demographics are more problematic than others. Some states are ethnically homogeneous and therefore face few problems on this score. However, as noted, fewer than 20 of the more than 185 states in existence today are ethnically homogeneous.[28] Some of these states, such as Japan and Sweden, have had a uniform ethnic composition for some time. Others—contemporary Poland, Hungary, the Czech Republic—have few minorities today because of the population transfers and the genocide that took place during World War II and the way in which borders were drawn after the war. It is important to note, however, that ethnic homogeneity is no guarantee of internal harmony: Somalia is one of the most ethnically homogeneous states in sub-Saharan Africa, yet it has been riven by clan warfare and a competition for power between and among local warlords.

In some states with ethnic minorities, ethnic groups are intermingled; in others, minorities tend to live in separate provinces or regions of the country. Countries with different kinds of ethnic geography are likely to experience different kinds of internal problems.[29] Countries with highly intermingled populations are less likely to face secessionist demands because ethnic groups are not distributed in ways that lend themselves to partition. However, if secessionist demands develop in countries with intermingled populations, ethnic groups will seek to establish control over specific tracts of territory. Direct attacks on civilians, intense guerrilla warfare, forced expulsion, and genocide may result. Countries with groups distributed along regional lines are more likely to face secessionist demands, but warfare, if it develops, will generally be more conventional in character.

Most states, particularly those carved out of former empires, have complex ethnic demographics and face serious ethnic problems of one kind or another. In Africa, for example, arbitrary borders have divided some ethnic groups and left them in two or more countries. Most African countries contain large numbers of ethnic groups, some of which are historic enemies.[30] Many of the states of the former Soviet Union inherited borders that were deliberately designed to maximize ethnic complications and cripple the political effectiveness of local leaders.[31] In short, ethnic geography can play an important role in the stability equation.

Political Factors

Four main political factors have attracted attention in scholarly analysis of ethnic and internal conflict: discriminatory political institutions, exclusionary national ideologies, intergroup politics, and elite politics.

First, many argue that the prospects for conflict in a country depend to a significant degree on the type and fairness of its *political institutions.* Closed, authoritarian systems are likely to generate considerable resentment over time, especially if the interests of some ethnic groups are served while others are trampled. Even in more democratic settings, resentment can build if some groups are inadequately represented in government, the courts, the military, the police, political parties, and other state and political institutions. The legitimacy of the system as a whole can, over time, fall into question. Violent conflict is especially likely if oppression and violence are commonly employed by the state or if a political transition is under way. The latter can take many forms, including democratization, which can be destabilizing in the short run even if it promises stability in the long run.[32]

Second, much depends on the nature of the prevailing *national ideology* in the country in question. In some places nationalism and citizenship are based on ethnic distinctions rather than on the idea that everyone who lives in a country is entitled to the same rights and privileges. Although the existence of civic conceptions of nationalism is no guarantee of stability —civic nationalism prevails in Indonesia— conflict is more likely when ethnic conceptions

of nationalism predominate. Under what conditions are these two conceptions of nationalism likely to emerge? According to Jack Snyder:

> Civic nationalism normally appears in well institutionalized democracies. Ethnic nationalism, in contrast, appears spontaneously when an institutional vacuum occurs. By its nature, nationalism based on equal and universal citizenship rights within a territory depends on a supporting framework of laws to guarantee those rights, as well as effective institutions to allow citizens to give voice to their views. Ethnic nationalism, in contrast, depends not on institutions, but on culture. Therefore, ethnic nationalism is the default option: it predominates when institutions collapse, when existing institutions are not fulfilling people's basic needs, and when satisfactory alternative structures are not readily available.[33]

It is not surprising, therefore, that there are strong currents of ethnic nationalism in parts of the Balkans, Eastern and Central Europe, and the former Soviet Union, where state structures and political institutions have diminished capacities, and in those parts of the developing world where state structures and political institutions are weak.

It is important to keep in mind that exclusionary national ideologies do not have to be based on ethnicity. Religious fundamentalists committed to establishing theocratic states divide societies into two groups: those who subscribe to a theologically derived political, economic, and social order and those who do not.

Third, many scholars argue that the prospects for violence in a country depend to a significant degree on the dynamics of domestic, *intergroup politics.*[34] The prospects for violence are great, it is said, if groups—whether they are based on political, ideological, religious, or ethnic affinities—have ambitious objectives, strong senses of identity, and confrontational strategies. Conflict is especially likely if objectives are incompatible, groups are strong and determined, action is feasible, success is possible, and intergroup comparisons lead to competition, anxiety, and fears of being dominated.

The emergence of new groups and changes in the intergroup balance of power can be particularly destabilizing.

Fourth, some scholars have emphasized *elite politics* and, more specifically, the tactics employed by desperate and opportunistic politicians in times of political and economic turmoil. According to this line of thinking, ethnic conflict is often provoked by elites in times of political and economic turmoil in order to fend off domestic challengers. Ethnic bashing and scapegoating are tools of the trade, and the mass media are employed in partisan and propagandistic ways that further aggravate interethnic tensions. The actions of Slobodan Milosevic in Serbia and Franjo Tudjman in Croatia stand out as cases in point.[35]

Economic/Social Factors

Three broad economic and social factors have been identified as potential sources of ethnic and internal conflict: economic problems, discriminatory economic systems, and the trials and tribulations of economic development and modernization.

First, most countries experience *economic problems* of one kind or another sooner or later, and these problems can contribute to intrastate tensions. In the industrialized world, problems can emerge even if a country's economy is growing—if it is not growing as fast as it once was or fast enough to keep pace with societal demands. In Eastern Europe, the former Soviet Union, parts of Africa, and elsewhere, transitions from centrally planned to market-based economic systems have created a host of economic problems, ranging from historically high levels of unemployment to rampant inflation. Many countries in what we would like to think of as the developing world seem to be in a semipermanent state of economic shambles. Others are in an economic free fall. Unemployment, inflation, and resource competition contribute to societal frustrations and tensions and can provide the breeding ground for conflict.

Economic reforms do not always help and can contribute to the problem in the short term, especially if economic shocks are severe and state subsidies for staples, services, and social welfare are cut. In short, economic slowdowns, stagnation, deterioration, and collapse can be deeply destabilizing.[36]

Second, *discriminatory economic systems,* whether they discriminate on a class basis or an ethnic basis, can generate feelings of resentment and levels of frustration prone to the generation of violence.[37] Unequal economic opportunities, unequal access to resources such as land and capital, and vast differences in standards of living are all signs of economic systems that disadvantaged members of society will see as unfair and perhaps illegitimate. This has certainly been the case in Sri Lanka, for example, where the Sinhalese majority has discriminated against Tamils in recent decades. Economic development is not necessarily the solution. Indeed, it can aggravate the situation: economic growth always benefits some individuals, groups, and regions more than others, and those who are on top to begin with are likely to be in a better position to take advantage of new economic opportunities than the downtrodden. Even if a country's overall economic picture is improving, growing inequities and gaps can aggravate intrastate tensions.

Third, many scholars have pointed to *economic development and modernization* as taproots of instability and internal conflict.[38] The process of economic development, the advent of industrialization, and the introduction of new technologies, it is said, bring about a wide variety of profound social changes: migration and urbanization disrupt existing family and social systems and undermine traditional political institutions; better education, higher literacy rates, and improved access to growing mass media raise awareness of where different people stand in society. At a minimum, this places strains on existing social and political systems.[39] It also raises economic and political expectations and can lead to mounting frustration when these expectations are not met. This can be particularly problematic in the political realm, because demands for political participation usually outpace the ability of the system to respond. According to Samuel Huntington, "The result is instability and disorder. The primary problem . . . is the lag in the development of political institutions behind social and economic change."[40]

Cultural/Perceptual Factors

Two main cultural and perceptual factors have been identified by scholars as sources of ethnic and internal conflict. The first is *cultural discrimination* against minorities. Problems include inequitable educational opportunities, legal and political constraints on the use and teaching of minority languages, and constraints on religious freedom. In extreme cases draconian efforts to assimilate minority populations combined with programs to bring large numbers of other ethnic groups into minority areas constitute a form of cultural genocide. Aggressive forms of these policies were implemented by Joseph Stalin in the Soviet Union in the 1930s and 1940s, particularly in the Caucasus. Similar policies have been pursued by China in Tibet since the 1950s. Somewhat less vicious forms of assimilationist policies have been pursued in Bulgaria with respect to ethnic Turks, in Slovakia with respect to ethnic Hungarians, and in Thailand with respect to members of northern and western hill tribes, for example.[41]

The second factor that falls under this broad heading has to do with *group histories and group perceptions* of themselves and others.[42] It is certainly true that many groups have legitimate grievances against others for crimes of one kind or another committed at some point in the distant or recent past. Some "ancient hatreds" have legitimate historical bases. However, it is also true that groups tend to whitewash and glorify their own histories, and they often demonize their neighbors, rivals, and adversaries. Explaining away the Hutu slaughter

of eight hundred thousand to one million Tutsi in Rwanda in 1994, one Hutu who had been training for the priesthood insisted, "It wasn't genocide. It was self-defense."[43] Stories that are passed down from generation to generation by word of mouth become part of a group's lore. They often become distorted and exaggerated with time and are treated as received wisdom by group members.

These ethnic mythologies are particularly problematic if rival groups have mirror images of each other, which is often the case. Serbs, for example, see themselves as heroic defenders of Europe and Croats as fascist, genocidal thugs. Croats see themselves as valiant victims of Serbian hegemonic aggression. When two groups in proximity have mutually exclusive, incendiary perceptions of each other, the slightest provocation on either side confirms deeply held beliefs and provides the justification for a retaliatory response. Under such conditions, conflict is hard to avoid and even harder to limit once started.

THE PROXIMATE CAUSES OF ETHNIC AND INTERNAL CONFLICTS

Scholars have done a commendable job of surveying the underlying factors that make some situations particularly prone to violence, but they have devoted less effort to analyzing the catalytic factors—the triggers or proximate causes—of ethnic and internal conflicts. As James Rule put it in his review of the literature on civil violence, "We know a lot of things that are true about civil violence, but we do not know when they are going to be true."[44] The result is that we know a lot less about the causes of ethnic and internal conflicts than one would guess from looking at the rather massive literature on the subject.

A useful way to analyze the proximate causes of ethnic and internal conflicts is to distinguish between conflicts that are triggered by (1) elite-

Table 2. Proximate Causes of Ethnic and Internal Conflicts

	Internally Driven	**Externally Driven**
Elite Level	Bad leaders	Bad neighbors
Mass Level	Bad domestic problems	Bad neighborhoods

level as opposed to mass-level factors and (2) internal as opposed to external developments.[45] Conflicts can therefore be triggered by four different combinations of factors—by internal, mass-level factors (bad domestic problems); by external, mass-level factors (bad neighborhoods); by external, elite-level factors (bad neighbors); and by internal, elite-level factors (bad leaders). These combinations can be depicted in a two-by-two matrix (see table 2). Put another way, these different sets of problems generate four different kinds of conflicts.

First, conflicts can be triggered by internal, mass-level phenomena, such as rapid economic development, modernization, and internal migration. To put it more prosaically, they can be caused by "bad domestic problems." Modernization, migration, and urbanization have generated stability problems in many parts of the developing world, including Indonesia, Mexico, Nigeria, and Pakistan, for example.

The proximate causes of a second set of conflicts are mass level but external in character: swarms of refugees or fighters crashing across borders, bringing turmoil and violence with them, or radicalized politics sweeping through regions. These are conflicts caused by the "contagion," "diffusion," and "spillover" effects to which many policymakers, analysts, and scholars give much credence.[46] One could say that such conflicts are caused by "bad neighborhoods." A devastating example of this problem unfolded in Central Africa in the mid-1990s. The genocide in Rwanda in the spring and summer of 1994 led millions of people to flee the country. Vast numbers of Hutu—soldiers, militia members, and civilians—fled to eastern Zaire after the Tutsi established control over

Rwanda in July 1994. The Hutu refugee camps in Zaire became bases of operations for Hutu militia strikes into Rwanda. The Rwandan government, supported by Uganda and allies in Zaire, invaded Zaire in 1996, leading to the overthrow of the Mobutu regime in 1997 and yet another intervention in 1998. As the decade came to a close, at least half a dozen external actors were involved in the continuing conflict in the newly named Democratic Republic of the Congo. A peace accord was signed in 1999, but central authority in the country had been shattered.[47]

The proximate causes of a third set of conflicts are external but elite level in character: they are the results of discrete, deliberate decisions by governments to trigger conflicts in nearby states for political, economic, or ideological purposes of their own. This only works, one must note, when the permissive conditions for conflict already exist in the target country; outsiders are generally unable to foment trouble in stable, just societies. Such conflicts, one could say, are caused by "bad neighbors." Examples include the Soviet Union's meddling in and subsequent 1979 invasion of Afghanistan, which has yet to emerge from chaos, and Russian meddling in Georgia and Moldova in the 1990s.[48] Another example is Rhodesia's establishment of Renamo in 1976 to undermine the new government in Mozambique.[49]

The proximate causes of the fourth and final type of conflict are internal and elite level in character. Variations include power struggles involving civilian (Georgia) or military (Nigeria) leaders; ideological contests over how a country's political, economic, social, and religious affairs should be organized

(Algeria, Peru); and criminal assaults on the state (Colombia). To put it in prosaic terms, such conflicts are triggered and driven by "bad leaders."

THE IMPORTANCE OF DOMESTIC ELITES

Scholars have paid comparatively little attention to the roles played by domestic elites in instigating ethnic and internal conflicts. The result is "no-fault" history that leaves out the pernicious effects of influential individuals—an important set of factors in the overall equation.

Although mass-level factors are clearly important underlying conditions that make some places more predisposed to violence than others, and although neighboring states routinely meddle in the internal affairs of others, the decisions and actions of domestic elites often determine whether political disputes veer toward war or peace. Leaving elite decisions and actions out of the equation, as many social scientists do, is analytically misguided. It also has important policy implications: underappreciating the import of elite decisions and actions hinders conflict management efforts and fails to place blame where blame is due.

The proximate causes of many internal conflicts are the decisions and actions of domestic elites, but these conflicts are not all driven by the same domestic forces. There are three main variations: ideological struggles, which are driven by the ideological convictions of various individuals; criminal assaults on state sovereignty, which are driven primarily by the economic motivations of drug traffickers; and power struggles between and among competing elites, which are driven by personal political motivations. Admittedly, these compartments are not watertight. It is nonetheless important to make these distinctions, however rough they may be: there are several distinct motivational forces at work here—several identifiable proximate causes of internal violence. It is important to

have an appreciation of the multifaceted nature of the problem, particularly if one is interested in enhancing international efforts to prevent, manage, and resolve internal conflicts.

Ideological Conflicts

Some internally driven, elite-triggered conflicts are ideological struggles over the organization of political, economic, and social affairs in a country. Some ideological struggles are defined in economic or class terms; others are fundamentalist religious crusades guided by theological frameworks. Ideological struggles over how political, economic, and social affairs should be organized have not gone away with the end of the Cold War, but they have tended to take on new forms. Class-based movements with marxist agendas have faded from the scene in many parts of the world, including Southeast Asia, the Middle East, Africa, and Latin America, although some rebels in Colombia have remained largely true to form. Some rebel movements—in Guatemala and Peru, for example—have mutated and taken on the political agendas of indigenous peoples and ethnic minorities. In many places—Afghanistan, Algeria, Egypt, India, Iran, Sudan—conflicts have formed around new secularist-fundamentalist fault lines. These ethnic and fundamentalist movements draw on many of the same sources that impelled class-based movements in the Cold War era—patterns of political, economic, and cultural discrimination, and widespread dissatisfaction with the pace and equitability of economic development—but they are channeled in different directions. In other words, many of the underlying causes of these conflicts are the same, but their proximate causes have changed.

Criminal Assaults on State Sovereignty

Some internally driven, elite-triggered conflicts are in effect criminal assaults on state sovereignty. In several countries in Asia and Latin

America, in particular, drug cartels have accumulated enough power to challenge state control over large tracts of territory. This has been a problem at various times in Afghanistan, Burma, Colombia, Mexico, Pakistan, and Tajikistan, for example. In Colombia, most notably, state sovereignty has been directly challenged by drug barons and their criminal organizations.[50] This problem shows no sign of abating. A related problem is that, with the end of the Cold War and reductions in financial support from Moscow and Washington, many ethnic groups and political movements have turned to drug trafficking to finance their activities. This is true, for example, of various groups in Colombia and Peru.[51] In addition to its other pernicious effects, drug trafficking complicates the nature of the conflicts in question and makes conflict management more difficult.

Power Struggles

Many conflicts are fundamentally power struggles between and among competing elites. Of the three types of internally driven, elite-triggered conflicts outlined here, personal power struggles are probably the most common. Some are sustained government campaigns to repress ethnic minorities and democratic activists. This would seem to be a fair characterization of the conflicts in Burma and Iraq, for example.

One type of power struggle is particularly prominent and particularly pernicious: it accounts for much of the slaughter in the former Yugoslavia and Rwanda, and it has played a role in the conflicts in Azerbaijan, Burundi, Chechnya, Georgia, India, Kenya, Nigeria, Romania, Sri Lanka, Sudan, and elsewhere.[52] The starting point is a lack of elite legitimacy, which leads to elite vulnerability. Vulnerabilities can be brought about by weakening state structures, political transitions, pressures for political reform, and economic problems. Those who are in power are determined to fend off emerging political challengers and anxious to shift blame for whatever economic and political

setbacks their countries may be experiencing. In cases in which ideological justifications for staying in power have been overtaken by events, those in power need to devise new formulas for legitimizing their rule. Entrenched politicians and aspiring leaders alike have powerful incentives to play the "ethnic card," embracing ethnic identities and proclaiming themselves the champions of ethnic groups.[53]

This produces a shift in the terms of public discourse from civic nationalism to ethnic nationalism and to increasingly virulent forms of the latter. Ethnic minorities are often singled out and blamed for the country's problems: ethnic scapegoating and ethnic bashing become the order of the day. When power struggles are fierce, politicians portray other ethnic groups in threatening terms and inflate these threats to bolster group solidarity and their own political positions; perceived threats are extremely powerful unifying devices.[54] When leaders have control over the national media, these kinds of campaigns are particularly effective; a relentless drumbeat of ethnic propaganda can distort political discourse quickly and dramatically. Political campaigns such as these undermine stability and push countries toward violence by dividing and radicalizing groups along ethnic fault lines. In the former Yugoslavia, Serbian leader Slobodan Milosevic and Croatian leader Franjo Tudjman rose to power by polarizing their societies even though Serbs and Croats had coexisted peacefully for decades.

Why Do Followers Follow?

It is easy to understand why desperate and opportunistic politicians in the midst of power struggles would resort to ethnic appeals. For many politicians, tearing their countries apart and causing thousands of people to be killed are small prices to pay for getting or staying in power. The more intriguing question is: Why do followers follow?[55] Given that politicians all over the world employ ethnic appeals of one kind or another, why do these appeals resonate in some places but not others? Why do large numbers of people follow the ethnic flag in some places at some times, but not others?

Two factors are particularly important in this regard: the existence of antagonistic group histories and mounting economic problems. If groups have bad histories of each other and especially if they see themselves as victims of other, aggressive communities, ethnic bashing and inflated threats seem plausible. If economic problems such as unemployment and inflation are mounting and resource competition is intensifying, ethnic scapegoating is more likely to resonate and more people are likely to accept a radical change in a country's political course, including armed confrontation. In short, the emergence of elite competition may be the proximate cause of conflicts in places such as the former Yugoslavia and Rwanda, but hostilities escalate because of the existence of underlying problems—problematic group histories and economic problems—and a combustible setting.

POLICY IMPLICATIONS

This discussion of the causes of ethnic and internal conflict has three main policy implications. First, if it is useful to distinguish among the underlying conditions and proximate causes of ethnic and internal conflict, it follows that those interested in conflict management should have a two-track strategy. One track should be a series of sustained, long-term efforts focused on the underlying problems that make violence likely. Particular attention should be paid to economic problems, distorted group histories, and patterns of political, economic, and cultural discrimination. The other track should be a series of more aggressive efforts focused on the proximate causes of ethnic and internal conflicts—the triggers that turn potentially violent situations into armed confrontations.

Both tracks need to be pursued. Long-term efforts to address the permissive conditions of ethnic and internal conflicts are relatively low-cost, low-risk undertakings, but they tend to be neglected by policymakers in distant capitals and international organizations who are inevitably preoccupied with the crisis du jour. At the same time, the catalytic factors responsible for triggering violence—often in places where bloodshed could be avoided—merit careful attention and vigorous action.

Second, conflict management efforts need to take into account the fact that ethnic and internal conflicts can be triggered by four sets of proximate causes: internal, mass-level forces; external, mass-level forces; external, elite-level forces; and internal, elite-level forces. Different kinds of conflict management efforts will be needed in each case. No single set of actions will suffice across the board.

Third, conflict management efforts should focus aggressively on the decisions and actions of domestic elites, who are often responsible for sparking ethnic and internal conflicts. Conflicts triggered by power struggles between opportunistic and desperate politicians are common and should therefore receive special international attention. Since economic problems make escalation and violence more likely, emergency economic relief packages should be part of the equation when tensions rise and danger looms. Cynical campaigns to mobilize ethnic support, polarize ethnic differences, and blame other ethnic groups for whatever troubles a country may be experiencing are often responsible for inciting violence and leading countries into all-out civil wars. It follows that international actors interested in preventing these conflicts from becoming violent and escalating out of control should endeavor to neutralize hatemongers and their propaganda. At a minimum, this means launching international information campaigns and antipropaganda efforts to ensure that reasoned voices can be heard and alternative sources of information are available in political debates. In more extreme cases, when leaders call for the extermination of their adversaries or entire ethnic groups, as in Rwanda in 1994, more forceful measures will be called for. Radio and television stations can be jammed or destroyed, and leaders can be captured by international military forces and brought before international tribunals. Taking coercive action is a big step, but some situations—such as calls to commit genocide—should lead to forceful international action.

Many ethnic and internal conflicts are triggered by self-obsessed leaders who will do anything to get and keep power. They often incite ethnic violence of the most horrific kind for their own political ends. If the international community is serious about preventing ethnic and internal conflicts, it needs to think more carefully about the kinds of political behavior that should be proscribed and the kinds of actions it will be willing to take to steer or even seize control of domestic political debates. These are extremely difficult problems, both intellectually and politically, but they have to be confronted if international actors are to prevent or limit these conflicts.

One of the implications of this analysis is that distant powers and the international community in general are not as helpless as the conventional wisdom might lead us to believe. Ethnic and internal conflicts are often triggered by the decisions and actions of domestic elites, not by mass unrest or some uncontrollable form of domestic or regional mass hysteria. Bad leaders and bad behavior are discrete problems that can be identified and targeted for action. These decisions and acts are not necessarily immune to international pressure. To the contrary, they mark moments when distant international powers can use their leverage and influence the course of events.

NOTES

1. This chapter is based on Michael E. Brown, introduction and "The Causes and Regional Dimensions of Internal Conflict," in *The International Di-*mensions of Internal Conflict*, ed. Michael E. Brown (Cambridge, Mass.: MIT Press, 1996), 1–31, 571–601.

2. George Bush, quoted in Jack Snyder, "Nationalism and the Crisis of the Post-Soviet State," in *Ethnic Conflict and International Security*, ed. Michael E. Brown (Princeton, N.J.: Princeton University Press, 1993), 79–101 at 79.

3. Bill Clinton, quoted in Ann Devroy, "President Cautions Congress on 'Simplistic Ideas' in Foreign Policy," *Washington Post*, May 26, 1994.

4. Richard Cohen, "Send in the Troops," *Washington Post*, November 28, 1995.

5. See, for example, Snyder, "Nationalism and the Crisis of the Post-Soviet State"; Barry Posen, "The Security Dilemma and Ethnic Conflict," in *Ethnic Conflict and International Security*, 103–124; and Susanne Hoeber Rudolph and Lloyd I. Rudolph, "Modern Hate," *New Republic*, March 22, 1993, 24–29.

6. See Anthony Smith, "The Ethnic Sources of Nationalism," in *Ethnic Conflict and International Security*, 27–41 at 28–29.

7. This discussion is based on ibid., 28–31.

8. For an excellent overview of this debate, see Milton J. Esman, *Ethnic Politics* (Ithaca, N.Y.: Cornell University Press, 1994), 10–16. See also James McKay, "An Exploratory Synthesis of Primordial and Mobilizationist Approaches to Ethnic Phenomena," *Ethnic and Racial Studies* 5, no. 4 (October 1982): 395–420; and George M. Scott, "A Resynthesis of the Primordial and Circumstantial Approaches to Ethnic Group Solidarity: Towards an Explanatory Model," *Ethnic and Racial Studies* 13, no. 2 (April 1990): 147–171.

9. John F. Stack, Jr., "Ethnic Mobilization in World Politics: The Primordial Perspective," in *The Primordial Challenge: Ethnicity in the Modern World*, ed. John F. Stack, Jr. (New York: Greenwood Press, 1986), 1–11 at 1. See also Harold R. Isaacs, *Idols of the Tribe: Group Identity and Political Change* (Cambridge, Mass.: Harvard University Press, 1975), 38–45.

10. Paul R. Brass, *Ethnicity and Nationalism: Theory and Comparison* (Newbury Park, Calif.: Sage Publications, 1991), 25. See also Benedict Anderson, *Imagined Communities: Reflections on the Origins and Spread of Nationalism*, 2d ed. (London: Verso, 1991).

11. See James Minahan, *Nations without States: A Historical Dictionary of Contemporary National Movements* (Westport, Conn.: Greenwood Press, 1996), xvi; and Bernard Nietschmann, "The Third World War,"

Cultural Survival Quarterly 11, no. 3 (September 1987): 1–16.

12. One wide-ranging study estimates that 233 minority groups either have experienced systematic discriminatory treatment or have taken political action in support of collective interests; see Ted Robert Gurr, *Minorities at Risk: A Global View of Ethnopolitical Conflicts* (Washington, D.C.: United States Institute of Peace Press, 1993), 5–11. Another survey identifies 210 groups that have mobilized in pursuit of political self-determination; see Minahan, *Nations without States*, xvi–xvii.

13. Esman, *Ethnic Politics*, 14.

14. See David Welsh, "Domestic Politics and Ethnic Conflict," in *Ethnic Conflict and International Security*, 43–60 at 45.

15. Conflict is of course a fact of life in every society and political system. Our concern, however, is with violent conflict.

16. For a thoughtful discussion of definitional conundrums, see Harry Eckstein, "Introduction: Toward the Theoretical Study of Internal War," in *Internal War: Problems and Approaches*, ed. Harry Eckstein (New York: Free Press, 1964), especially 8–21. See also James B. Rule, *Theories of Civil Violence* (Berkeley: University of California Press, 1988), 9–13; and Lori Fisler Damrosch, introduction to *Enforcing Restraint: Collective Intervention in Internal Conflicts*, ed. Lori Fisler Damrosch (New York: Council on Foreign Relations Press, 1993), 4–5.

17. See Melvin Small and J. David Singer, *Resort to Arms: International and Civil Wars, 1816–1980* (Beverly Hills, Calif.: Sage Publications, 1982).

18. As noted in the discussion of internal conflicts, the key actors in these struggles are usually governments and rebel groups, but in some cases nongovernmental groups and militias fight between and among themselves.

19. Bill Clinton, quoted in "Clinton's Words: 'The Promise of Peace,'" *New York Times*, November 22, 1995.

20. Warren Christopher, "No Troops, No Peace," *New York Times*, November 27, 1995.

21. Warren Christopher, quoted in Mats R. Berdal, "Fateful Encounter: The United States and UN Peacekeeping," *Survival* 36, no. 1 (spring 1994): 30–50 at 36–37.

22. Misha Glenny, "Heading Off War in the South Balkans," *Foreign Affairs* 74, no. 3 (May-June 1995): 98–108 at 103.

23. See, for example, John A. Vasquez, "Factors Related to the Contagion and Diffusion of International Violence," in *The Internationalization of Communal Strife*, ed. Manus I. Midlarsky (London: Routledge, 1992), 149–172; and Gurr, *Minorities at Risk*, 132–135. For an excellent overview of this literature, see Stuart Hill and Donald Rothchild, "The Contagion of Political Conflict in Africa and the World," *Journal of Conflict Resolution* 30, no. 4 (December 1986): 716–735.

24. For more discussion, see Brown, "The Causes and Regional Dimensions of Internal Conflict," 590–599.

25. See I. William Zartman, "Introduction: Posing the Problem of State Collapse," in *Collapsed States: The Disintegration and Restoration of Legitimate Authority*, ed. I. William Zartman (Boulder, Colo.: Lynne Rienner, 1995), 1–11; and Gerald B. Helman and Steven R. Ratner, "Saving Failed States," *Foreign Policy*, no. 89 (winter 1992–93): 3–20.

26. See Posen, "The Security Dilemma and Ethnic Conflict." See also Esman, *Ethnic Politics*, 244–245.

27. See Stephen Van Evera, "Hypotheses on Nationalism and War," *International Security* 18, no. 4 (spring 1994): 5–39; and Posen, "The Security Dilemma and Ethnic Conflict."

28. See Welsh, "Domestic Politics and Ethnic Conflict," 45.

29. See Alicia Levine, "Political Accommodation and the Prevention of Secessionist Violence," in *International Dimensions of Internal Conflict*, 311–340.

30. See Stephen John Stedman, "Conflict and Conciliation in Sub-Saharan Africa," in *International Dimensions of Internal Conflict*, 235–265.

31. See Matthew Evangelista, "Historical Legacies and the Politics of Intervention in the Former Soviet Union," in *International Dimensions of Internal Conflict*, 107–140.

32. See, for example, Ted Robert Gurr and Barbara Harff, *Ethnic Conflict and World Politics* (Boulder, Colo.: Westview Press, 1994), chap. 5; Arend Lijphart, *Democracy in Plural Societies* (New Haven, Conn.: Yale University Press, 1977); and Edward D. Mansfield and Jack Snyder, "Democratization and the Danger of War," *International Security* 20, no. 1 (summer 1995): 5–38.

33. Snyder, "Nationalism and the Crisis of the Post-Soviet State," 86. See also William Pfaff, "Revive Secular Citizenship above 'Ethnic' Nationality," *International Herald Tribune*, July 20, 1993.

34. See Joseph Rothschild, *Ethnopolitics: A Conceptual Framework* (New York: Columbia University Press, 1981); Donald L. Horowitz, *Ethnic Groups in Conflict* (Berkeley: University of California Press, 1985); Charles Tilly, *From Mobilization to Revolution* (Reading, Mass.: Addison-Wesley, 1978); Charles Tilly, "Does Modernization Breed Revolution?" *Comparative Politics* 5, no. 3 (April 1973): 425–447; Lewis Coser, *The Functions of Social Conflict* (Glencoe, Ill.: Free Press, 1956); Gurr and Harff, *Ethnic Conflict and World Politics;* and Van Evera, "Hypotheses on Nationalism and War." For an overview, see Saul Newman, "Does Modernization Breed Ethnic Conflict?" *World Politics* 43, no. 3 (April 1991): 451–478; and Jack A. Goldstone, "Theories of Revolution: The Third Generation," *World Politics* 32, no. 3 (April 1980): 425–453.

35. See V. P. Gagnon, Jr., "Ethnic Nationalism and International Conflict: The Case of Serbia," *International Security* 19, no. 3 (winter 1994–95): 130–166; Human Rights Watch, *Playing the "Communal Card": Communal Violence and Human Rights* (New York: Human Rights Watch, 1995); and Warren Zimmermann, "The Last Ambassador: A Memoir of the Collapse of Yugoslavia," *Foreign Affairs* 74, no. 2 (March-April 1995): 2–20. See also Michael E. Brown, "The Impact of Government Policies on Ethnic Relations," in *Government Policies and Ethnic Relations in Asia and the Pacific*, ed. Michael E. Brown and Sumit Ganguly (Cambridge, Mass.: MIT Press, 1997), 511–575.

36. For a general discussion and several case studies, see S. W. R. de A. Samarasinghe and Reed Coughlan, eds., *Economic Dimensions of Ethnic Conflict* (London: Pinter Publishers, 1991). For a detailed discussion of the economic roots of the wars in the former Yugoslavia, see Susan L. Woodward, *Balkan Tragedy: Chaos and Dissolution after the Cold War* (Washington, D.C.: Brookings Institution, 1995), especially chap. 3. For a discussion of the economic sources of turmoil in South Asia, see Sandy Gordon, "Resources and Instability in South Asia," *Survival* 35, no. 2 (summer 1993): 66–87.

37. For an overview of Marx on this question, see Rule, *Theories of Civil Violence*, chap. 2; and A. S. Cohan, *Theories of Revolution* (New York: John Wiley, 1975), chaps. 4–5. For a discussion of how this applies to the developing world in particular, see Gordon, "Resources and Instability in South Asia."

38. See Samuel P. Huntington, *Political Order in Changing Societies* (New Haven, Conn.: Yale University Press, 1968); Samuel P. Huntington, "Civil Violence and the Process of Development," in *Civil Violence and the International System*, Adelphi Paper no. 83 (London: International Institute for Strategic Studies, 1971), 1–15; Ted Robert Gurr, *Why Men Rebel* (Princeton, N.J.: Princeton University Press, 1970); Walker Conner, "Nation-Building or Nation-Destroying?" *World Politics* 24, no. 3 (April 1972): 319–355; and Walker Conner, *Ethnonationalism: The Quest for Understanding* (Princeton, N.J.: Princeton University Press, 1994). For an overview of this literature, see Newman, "Does Modernization Breed Ethnic Conflict?" For critiques of this approach, see Rod Aya, "Theories of Revolution Reconsidered: Contrasting Models of Collective Violence," *Theory and Society* 8, no. 1 (July 1979): 1–38; and Tilly, "Does Modernization Breed Revolution?"

39. See Chalmers Johnson, *Revolutionary Change* (Boston: Little, Brown, 1966); and Mark Hagopian, *The Phenomenon of Revolution* (New York: Dodd, Mead, 1974). For an overview, see Cohan, *Theories of Revolution*, chap. 6; and Goldstone, "Theories of Revolution," 425–434.

40. Huntington, *Political Order in Changing Societies*, 5.

41. Many argue that formal, minority rights safeguards are the solution. See, for example, Jonathan Eyal, "Eastern Europe: What about the Minorities?" *World Today* 45, no. 12 (December 1989): 205–208; Wiktor Osiatynski, "Needed Now: Bills of Rights," *Time*, December 24, 1990; L. Michael Hager, "To Get More Peace, Try More Justice," *International Herald Tribune*, July 30, 1992; and Stephen S. Rosenfeld, "Serbs Are the Problem, Minority Rights the Solution," *International Herald Tribune*, September 26–27, 1992.

42. See Van Evera, "Hypotheses on Nationalism and War"; Posen, "The Security Dilemma and Ethnic Conflict," 107; Snyder, "Nationalism and the Crisis of the Post-Soviet State," 92–93; and Donald Rothchild and Alexander J. Groth, "Pathological Dimensions of

Domestic and International Ethnicity," *Political Science Quarterly* 110, no. 1 (spring 1995): 69–82.

43. Hutu apologist quoted in "You're Saying We Did It?" *Economist*, June 3, 1995, 38.

44. Rule, *Theories of Civil Violence*, 265.

45. Similar distinctions have been made by others. See Renée de Nevers, *The Soviet Union and Eastern Europe: The End of an Era*, Adelphi Paper no. 249 (London: International Institute for Strategic Studies, 1990), 27–29; and Stuart J. Kaufman, "An 'International' Theory of Inter-Ethnic War," *Review of International Studies* 22, no. 2 (April 1996): 149–171.

46. See note 23.

47. For an excellent overview of the crisis in Central Africa, see David Shearer, "Africa's Great War," *Survival* 41, no. 2 (summer 1999): 89–106.

48. On Afghanistan, see Sumit Ganguly, "Conflict and Crisis in South and Southwest Asia," in *International Dimensions of Internal Conflict*, 141–172. On Moldova and Georgia, see Evangelista, "Historical Legacies and the Politics of Intervention in the Former Soviet Union."

49. This observation comes from Stephen Stedman.

50. For a detailed discussion of drug-related problems in Latin America, see Marc Chernick, "Peacemaking and Violence in Latin America," in *International Dimensions of Internal Conflict*, 267–307.

51. Ibid.

52. See Human Rights Watch, *Playing the "Communal Card."* See also Stedman, "Conflict and Conciliation in Sub-Saharan Africa."

53. See Human Rights Watch, *Playing the "Communal Card."*

54. See Esman, *Ethnic Politics*, 244.

55. See Horowitz, *Ethnic Groups in Conflict*, 140.

PART II
INTERVENTION STRATEGIES AND THEIR CONSEQUENCES

14

Intervention

Toward Best Practices and a Holistic View

Chester A. Crocker

IT IS A SIGN OF THE TIMES that there is renewed interest in studying the lessons we have learned from intervention in foreign conflicts. Lacking an agreed-upon strategic paradigm, decision makers find themselves needing both a conceptual compass and a means for relating different types of "threat" to the kinds of power that may be relevant in addressing them. All too often, the intervention debate has been handled as if the only real issue is military intervention, as distinguished from other types of third-party-assisted processes by a range of "external" actors. One-dimensional debates about interventionism and unilateralism miss a richer reality revolving around the central issues of context, timing, sequencing, the link between force and diplomacy, and deciding what works where.

The premise of this chapter is that the majority of contemporary conflicts will require some form of third-party intervention if they are to be brought under control and settled. This chapter discusses a variety of conflict types and situations in which third parties inter-

vened. The purpose is to illustrate selectively certain principles of "best practice" in third-party interventions (1) by different sets of actors, (2) using different instruments and techniques, (3) in distinct types of societies, and (4) at various points in the conflict life cycle. The term "intervention" is intended to convey the full range of methods and tools whereby a variety of external parties—for instance, the United States, other major powers, the United Nations, and nongovernmental organizations (NGOs)—may become involved in attempts to cope with conflict. In addition to looking at the full spectrum of nonmilitary as well as military forms of intervention, the chapter considers the question of conflict preemption and then focuses on some lessons learned at both the strategic or policy level and the operational level in the field. Its purpose is not to advocate or critique intervention as such, but to advance a basis for prudent thinking on the topic.

A starting place is to recognize that the question of engagement in the management and resolution of conflicts is not one that can be answered by slogans or hasty reference to moral imperatives. Students and practitioners alike have to do their homework case by case while remaining cautious about abstract formulas and relearning the value of apparently pedestrian notions such as good judgment, operational competence, enhanced attention to coordination of diverse efforts, awareness of the vital importance of the implementation phase in peacemaking, and—not least—the centrality of leadership. If we can learn from the bittersweet experience of the 1990s as well as earlier decades, the current state of strategic disorientation may pass.

VARIETIES OF CONFLICT

The post-1945 period has witnessed a rapid decline in traditional interstate conflict and a comparable rise in internal strife: civil wars, anticolonial and anti-imperial wars, ethnic-religious conflicts, wars over regime legitimacy, wars to overthrow foreign or minority rule and other repressive systems, wars of governmental and territorial fragmentation (secession, imperial collapse), and wars over who fills the void in failed states. This trend appears to be holding. It is reflected in the distribution of UN peace operations: nine of the fourteen operations mounted between 1945 and 1987 involved essentially interstate conflict, whereas only six of the twenty-two operations begun between 1988 and 1994 were at least partially interstate in character (Afghanistan-Pakistan, Iran-Iraq, Cuban withdrawal from Angola, Central America, Chad-Libya, and Iraq-Kuwait).[1] Significantly, none of this latter group involved substantial numbers of UN troops (blue helmets). Of some twenty UN peace operations initiated between 1994 and mid-2000, only the United Nations Mission in the Democratic Republic of the Congo (MONUC, 1999–) and the United Nations Preventive Deployment Force to Macedonia (UNPREDEP,

1995–99) could be termed substantially interstate in character: the former because of the central role of foreign intervention in the conflict and foreign troop withdrawal in the notional agreement on which MONUC is based; the latter because of its intended deterrent role vis-à-vis Belgrade. All but two of the twenty-seven major armed conflicts identified by a leading European research center in 1999 were internal, even if a number of them (e.g., Sierra Leone, the Democratic Republic of the Congo, Tajikistan, Kosovo) featured regional triggers or other external factors.[2]

With the collapse of the Soviet Union and Yugoslavia, the zone of actual or potential conflict has expanded. Much of this conflict potential is also of the internal variety. In regions where traditional interstate conflicts continue—notably, the Middle East and South Asia—conflict tends to be embedded in regional security complexes reflecting ethnic and sectarian divisions. Pure cases of classic interstate rivalries (e.g., China and the Spratly Islands, Iran-Iraq, Iraq-Kuwait, Peru-Ecuador) are harder to find. However, the traditional type of conflict and associated UN role have not died out completely, as the recently agreed-to UN cease-fire monitoring role between Ethiopia and Eritrea illustrates.

This prevalence of internal conflict is the main reason why third-party intervention—especially direct military action—is so often fraught with difficulty and controversy. After all, it is common knowledge that it is hard for outsiders to manage internal conflicts. They tend to be brutal and bloody: familiarity of the sort acquired by combatants in civil wars appears to breed a special contempt for the enemy and to create a heightened incentive for aggressive tactics against "enemy" civilians. When states and empires fall apart, the lesson learned by affected communities is to strike first or pay the price. In other words, the security dilemma is particularly acute in such conflicts.[3]

The superficial implication for outsiders is to steer clear of trying to manage such affairs.

When protracted social conflicts or ethnic wars are hot, they may become too hard to handle. Better to let them ripen, say some observers; to wait until the parties reach the point of mutual exhaustion or until one side capitulates. Outsiders, some argue, are best advised to wait until there is a peace to make—or, better yet, to keep—before becoming engaged. Moreover, some research suggests that victories rather than negotiated settlements may be the most durable way to solve internal wars in any case.[4] Under this logic, the choices facing outsiders are very stark indeed: (1) intervene to hasten victory by one side while acting simultaneously to mitigate the conflict's human consequences; (2) intervene to stop the bloodshed, stabilize the lines between the sides, and work for conflict transformation, an approach that may require long-term occupation of the country concerned —as NATO nations have discovered in their Balkan protectorates; or (3) stay out in order to "give war a chance" to resolve the dispute once and for all, the way things used to happen in premodern times.[5]

Another argument against intervention in internal wars is our vestigial uneasiness about crossing the sovereignty line and getting into other people's business. Not only are outsiders not necessarily best equipped to do these things; they have no self-evident mandate to do them. Nation building, that optimistic term from the early 1960s, was discredited in Vietnam and has hardly been rehabilitated in Somalia. Americans, one might add, have particular handicaps as intervenors in domestic conflicts abroad: our moralistic political culture and historic aversion to entanglements with dubious partners clash with real-world conditions beyond our shores. For all these reasons, we have come to believe that the practical impact of intervening in civil wars and nationalist revolutions can be likened to the impact of walking in front of a moving train.

For a time in the mid-1990s arguments like these were marshaled as reasons why the United States and its Western allies could not have been expected to do much about the Bosnias, Rwandas, and Somalias of the post–Cold War era. The lesson, presumably, was to avoid them, eschew the idealistic enthusiasms of the early 1990s (e.g., "assertive multilateralism"), and lower our risks. Accordingly, UN peace operations were sharply curtailed and detailed analyses were undertaken to derive lessons learned. Yet even then it was clear that the world's leading and most successful nations could not simply walk away from internal wars. After all, three years of dithering in Bosnia left Western leaders no honorable way to avoid asserting themselves multilaterally in order to reshape the battlefield; this, of course, is what they eventually did when they decided on the military steps which created the road to the 1995 Dayton accords. The political and moral price of inaction had become too high. Nor was this rethink confined to southeastern Europe, where NATO's belated intervention did, if nothing else, stop the fighting. Soon, people began to recall that successful intervention in internal conflicts was indeed possible. Surely, it was not a mistake for the United Nations and the major powers to authorize military and civilian oversight of the decolonization of Namibia (1989–90), supervise the Cambodian settlement and elections (1991–93), monitor the Salvadoran settlement of 1991, and authorize the substantial military and civilian effort to implement the complex Mozambican peace accords of 1992 that led to UN-supervised elections in 1994. These successes contrasted sharply with mounting international unease and a crescendo of apologies over the failure to act decisively to stop the Rwandan genocide in 1994.

As the first post–Cold War decade progressed, the military intervention pendulum began to swing back, albeit hesitantly, as seen in abortive efforts to dispatch UN or "coalition-of-the-willing" forces to Central Africa (1996); in the Italian-led, UN-blessed intervention in Albania (1997) followed by NATO's Kosovo war (1999); and in the post-Kosovo decisions to place UN-mandated or -led forces in East Timor and Sierra Leone (2000) and even to consider a substantial expansion of the UN presence in the Democratic Republic of the Congo. This return of the pendulum reflected the realization that walking away was not really a strategy. The real strategic issues revolved around the questions of (1) overcommitment—how to avoid excessive strains on the finite military resources of the major "security-exporting" nations; (2) what kinds of intervention work best (is military intervention the proper response and, if so, under what circumstances?); and (3) capability—how to adapt to the reality that although some conflicts require nonconsensual, peace enforcement measures, neither the United Nations nor the great majority of regional security organizations have the necessary military capabilities to take such measures. Inevitably, these issues remain at the center of debate since they are fundamentally about definitions of national interest and the relative priority attached to doing something about internal wars in distant places of little obvious strategic importance.[6]

These debates are sometimes construed as an argument between an interest-based and a value-based policy. That misses the point. The real issue in the post–Cold War intervention cases that turned sour has less to do with abstract principles (i.e., interests versus values) and more to do with learning how to intervene competently. This is why a sharpened focus on best practices in third-party intervention is urgently required. Moreover, from an American angle, it is simply not politically sustainable for the world's leading nation to ignore a significant moral and humanitarian challenge when that challenge can be met at an acceptable cost without undercutting other significant national interests. To be sure, there will be times when an internal conflict is beyond reach for reasons of physical access or geopolitical or cultural reality. But it is nonsense to argue that Western nations must not act in the Balkans or Central Africa unless they are prepared to intervene everywhere—including in Sudan, Tibet, and

Chechnya. Global leadership entails a level of concern for international law and order, including the rules by which states and governments (and rebels in some cases) conduct themselves. It does not mean universal, global governance.

Moreover, it is increasingly difficult to argue that local, internal wars will—if left alone—simply burn themselves out and produce a stable outcome without impacting the broader regional environment in which the conflict occurs. All too often, we have seen internal wars—in Colombia, Liberia, Afghanistan, Bosnia, Rwanda, and Congo—metastasize into regional conflicts and regionalized vested interests in continued warfare. In the post–Cold War era, even the remotest conflicts are readily internationalized through diaspora networks, information technology, and the geometric expansion of nongovernmental activism on behalf of perceived underdogs and victims. Losers no longer lose definitively, and winners find it ever harder to achieve decisive victory.[7]

In these circumstances, we are nonetheless called upon to identify the major differences among the plethora of current and recent cases and to indicate where to draw the lines on intervention. What conflicts are we correct to avoid and which ones warrant some form of intervention? First, there are many kinds and levels of conflict, and we should not be frightened into uttering a pessimistic, one-dimensional mantra after watching a few bad days of CNN. The payoff and the price of successful intervention depend on what phenomena we are responding to. Yes, we probably should avoid military entanglement in nationalist revolutions and civil wars pitting whole groups and classes against one another or against foreign control—unless there are overarching strategic reasons that demand intervention, as in the case of the United States in Afghanistan, but not in the case of the United States in Vietnam. Equally, the record shows that intervention in some types of internal conflict can be effective when there are important stakes and high confidence in the possibility of shaping an acceptable outcome at a reasonable price. Examples include the United States and United Nations in El Salvador, the United Nations in Mozambique and Namibia, France in Chad and Zaire, the United States in Grenada, and Great Britain during the terminal colonial phase in Malaya, Rhodesia/Zimbabwe, Swaziland, and East Africa. Looking even further back, one could argue that the U.S. military action in the Philippines in 1899–1902 served its purpose.[8]

It may be that internal wars based on seemingly primordial sentiments tend toward zero-sum thinking and the progressive elimination of neutral or common ground. Military intervention in cases of this sort (e.g., Kosovo and Sudan) may require the intervenor to occupy the country and suppress the fighting. There are few volunteers for open-ended imperial policing today, apart, perhaps, from the Russians along their southern flanks and the Chinese in Tibet.

Equally important, however, there are few pure cases of ethnic conflict in the sense of a spontaneous mass eruption of ethnic antagonisms. A strong argument can be made that an apparently pure case such as Rwanda was in part an ersatz creation of ambitious, ethnic entrepreneurs. Perhaps the purest of such cases are, in fact, nationalist rejections of alien, minority, or foreign rule—as happened in Afghanistan, Dutch East Indies/Indonesia in 1945–49, South Africa, Namibia, Algeria in 1954–62, Rhodesia/ Zimbabwe, and Vietnam. But even in such ostensibly clear cases, the struggles had a complex history and their outcome was influenced by many local and external factors.

When reviewing contemporary conflicts such as Bosnia, Liberia, Sri Lanka, and Rwanda, great care should be taken with the sweeping label "ethnic conflict."[9] In these cases, as in so many others over the past fifty years, reality is shaped decisively by such factors as

- the actions and inactions of foreigners,
- the case-specific balance of forces and the possibilities of asserting external leverage on the parties,

- the goals and ambitions of individual leaders and the opportunities presented to them for achieving those goals, and
- the availability of military hardware and its relevance to the specific circumstances of local conflict.

Upon close inspection, we will find that the much-advertised syndrome labeled "ethnic conflict" has its roots in a mix of special situations and concrete local factors: the collapse of central institutions, structural and political uncertainties at times of rapid change, the holding of ill-prepared elections, the emergence of entrepreneurial politicians who use ethnicity as a platform and a tool, the splintering of armies and the rise of warlords, unrestrained arms transfers, and the availability of natural and financial resources (legal or criminal) to fuel the descent into violence. In sum, we should be looking beyond the general notion of ethnicity to draw lessons about the sorts of situations that serve as tinder for the fires we associate with the post–Cold War era.

THE VARIETIES OF INTERVENTION

There is a vast range of intervention options between doing nothing and sending in the marines. In any given situation, the spectrum of intervention options depends on several key variables. It varies, first, with the stage of the conflict—that is, its status, form, and "ripeness." Closely related to these factors is the character of the society or societies in which the conflict occurs and the nature of the parties to the conflict and of their decision-making systems —in other words, their "accessibility" to various forms of outside intervention. But intervention options also depend upon the character of potential third parties—their capabilities, leverage, and linkage to (or "fit" with) the parties, their level of interest, and the sustainability of their potential commitment to the intervention role. These latter variables underscore the role of political will and leadership in sustaining the intervention for the time required to complete it effectively.

An interstate conflict situation may demand an immediate military response, akin to a police action, to uphold the law or maintain collective security, as was the case in Operation Desert Storm, a U.S.-led, UN-blessed coalition effort. Military intervention, however, can take many forms: unilateral action by individual governments (the United Kingdom in Sierra Leone in 2000, the United States in the Dominican Republic in 1965); ad hoc coalitions of the willing (the Western allies in Lebanon in the early 1980s); UN peace operations to keep and implement an agreed-upon peace plan (Mozambique in the early 1990s); regional peacekeeping or peace enforcement led by a regional security organization (ECOWAS in Liberia, NATO in the Balkans, both in the 1990s); UN-mandated actions led by an indispensable regional or global power (Italy in Albania, the United States in Haiti, Australia in East Timor).

Similarly, diplomatic intervention for conflict management can take several forms. When it is sustained and becomes a central feature of policy toward a region or country—as in the U.S. mediation initiatives in the Middle East and southern Africa over the past twenty-five years or so—it makes sense to describe such diplomatic intervention as strategic. In these examples, conflict management and resolution have become the essence of U.S. regional strategy, and its requirements affect all other regional policies regarding issues such as arms transfers, covert action, trade and sanctions, and human rights.

Such interventions—based on a coherent diplomatic strategy sustained over long periods of time—have successfully advanced U.S. interests by using U.S. influence to push the parties toward agreements.[10] Where direct U.S. leverage is limited, we have had to borrow that of others, as in southern Africa, where American diplomacy, up until the mid-1990s, was tightly integrated with British efforts in a series

of productive initiatives to settle conflicts in Zimbabwe, Namibia, Angola, Mozambique, and South Africa. This example and the sustained, decades-long Middle East peace process are among the few cases of such strategic engagement in peacemaking today, by the United States or anyone else. The U.S.–NATO–European Union initiatives toward Bosnia from the early days of the Vance-Owen plan through the Kosovo war in 1999 qualify only at the margin, given the lack of unified diplomatic vision and of effective linkage to and control over the parallel peacekeeping and peace enforcement operation on the ground. The 1995 decision to use U.S. and NATO force to change the military balance on the ground was a step forward in creating the leverage needed to support an activist diplomacy. But while these elements produced the Dayton accords and a dubious Kosovo victory, alliance diplomacy has been fitful and unsteady in developing a clearly communicated "end state" for the Balkan region and its constituent parts.

Episodic diplomatic intervention in stubborn, unripened cases, such as in Cyprus and Kashmir, and crisis-driven intervention when fighting flares up, as conducted by Jordan and Egypt when Yemen's fragile unity was shattered by secessionist moves in 1994, are more common than long-term strategic commitment to peacemaking. Unlike the latter, the episodic and crisis-driven types offer little chance for outsiders to develop substantial leverage apart from the leverage inherent in the balance of forces on the ground. (Sometimes, of course, it may take some changes in the military situation to bolster the arm of the negotiators and create fresh openings for settlement. However, this usually works much better when there already exists an active negotiating framework within which the parties and the intervenor operate.)

In the case of crises, formulas for settlement may amount to little more than cease-fires that continue to break down until a fresh military status quo emerges. Such interventions represent limited (albeit vital) efforts to suppress or contain the fighting, but they may have little to do with real settlement or resolution.

Periodic negotiation initiatives of the Cyprus type represent exploratory probes to test the parties' temperature, try out fresh ideas, or convey frustration over the gridlock. Such efforts may move the process along, but actual settlement must await a significant change in the underlying situation affecting the parties. Meanwhile, the de facto division of the local communities may harden attitudes and raise the price of a deal.

The range of potential intervenors has expanded dramatically in the post–Cold War period—in part due to the increasingly evident limits on the capacity and willingness of governments and intergovernmental bodies to engage promptly and effectively in many situations and in part due to the sharply reduced "barriers to entry" by unofficial groups in conflict arenas. Increasingly, NGOs of all sorts are intervening abroad and playing a role in conflict situations. Professional groups, media, specialized civil society and conflict resolution groups, humanitarian relief and development organizations, religious bodies, and human rights advocacy groups all belong on this list.[11] Their actual and potential contributions are difficult to quantify, but they are often underestimated by governmental bodies, just as they are typically overestimated by the NGO community itself. The phenomenon of NGO activism in conflict arenas has clearly come of age when practitioners and commentators alike focus on potential pitfalls and unintended consequences —as well as benefits—of such activity.[12] In one exceptionally well documented account of lessons learned from the case of Burundi (1993–95), former UN special representative Ahmedou Ould-Abdallah draws hard-hitting conclusions about the need for enhanced communication and coordination between NGOs and governmental and intergovernmental actors. The envoy pushes strongly for the concept of an international "lead actor" in such cases and urges the adoption of a "code of conduct"

covering the duties and responsibilities of all foreign actors intervening in conflict situations.[13] At the same time, this veteran observer is at pains to underscore the important contributions to peace made by experienced private actors (such as Search for Common Ground and International Alert in the Burundi case).

The lead role of the Sant'Egidio community, a Catholic lay group, in initiating a mediation exercise in Mozambique's civil war in the early 1990s is an example of the nongovernmental sector filling a temporary vacuum. The Mozambique case exemplifies success, although credit must be shared with several governments, including Italy, Britain, Portugal, the United States, Zimbabwe, Botswana, Kenya, and South Africa, as well as with private individuals and UN officials. All of these actors played a role in getting the parties to agree to and then to implement the 1992 settlement.[14] In a more recent example, the Geneva-based Henry Dunant Centre for Humanitarian Dialogue played a discreet and skilled behind-the-scenes role in encouraging the government of Indonesia and the Free Aceh Movement to agree in May 2000 on the adoption of a "humanitarian pause" in order to facilitate a dialogue between the central authorities and Achinese rebels.

Some types of political or mediatory interventions are probably best conducted by governments or groups of governments, while others can and should be left to international economic or humanitarian institutions, creative individuals, nongovernmental agencies, and other actors. Once again, the key variables are timing (stage and status of the conflict) and characteristics of the affected society and of the parties themselves.[15] The kinds of interventions appropriate to the preconflict and prenegotiation phases of an impending conflict will be quite distinct from interventions undertaken at the height of a hot conflict—and from actions that should be taken to support an agreement once the parties have progressed that far. To take the last of these examples, support for peace implementation and peacebuilding may involve foreign governments sharing with the signatories of a peace accord intelligence data in support of confidence-building measures; NGOs observing and monitoring human rights commitments; military agencies or private security companies assisting in demining operations in conflict zones to facilitate the deployment of peace operations personnel; third-party militaries helping to retrain and demobilize local forces; international financial institutions coordinating bilateral and multilateral assistance and postwar reconstruction programs; publicly funded experts advising on how to strengthen judicial systems and assist divided societies in coping with past injustice or humanitarian crimes; and NGOs providing programs to spread skills in intergroup relations, conflict resolution, religious reconciliation, and democracy building. As this brief list suggests, there is a bewildering range of activities and actors that may be relevant to the postsettlement phase of conflict management. This variety underscores the importance of coordinating among them and of developing a sense of responsibility for maintaining "best practices" so as to make the overall effort successful.[16] A basic interdependence exists between the "harder" and "softer" forms of intervention—and an awareness of what they all share is the beginning of wisdom.

SOME REFLECTIONS ON CONFLICT PREVENTION AND PREEMPTIVE ACTION

In case after case of intervention during the turbulent post–Cold War years, the lesson to be learned is the great benefit of preemptive engagement in promoting negotiated alternatives to continued repression or expanding violence and upheaval. Western diplomacy has been based on this goal of conflict prevention and containment in places such as Indonesia in the 1940s, the Middle East for the past thirty years, and southern Africa in the 1970s and 1980s. These undertakings have entailed costs and risks, and success has never been easy or guaranteed. But it is simply wrong to claim that all such conflicts are beyond reach and that a forward "engagement" policy is doomed to fail.

Moreover, proponents of a hands-off, nonintervention stance have an obligation to measure the price of doing nothing at all and to compare it to the "least bad" forms of preemptive intervention. Experience in such places as Afghanistan, the former Yugoslavia, Rwanda, and Liberia suggests that it is too easy for decision makers to adopt a narrow view of the choices before them and thereby overlook the political and economic consequences of inaction. At root, this is a political question: How to encourage bureaucratic and political structures to measure the known price of sticking their necks out and doing something against the less tangible and measurable costs—human casualties, loss of political prestige, famine and refugee relief, economic reconstruction, and peacekeeping—associated with having to pick up the pieces later?

Once we recognize the importance of preemption, how do we recognize the tinder that can fuel intractable internal strife, and what can we do about it? One answer is to underscore the fundamental importance of the process by which politicized conflicts become militarized. (This may or may not have much to do with ethnicity; more likely, it relates to such variables as arms supplies and the strength of governmental institutions.) Once domestic political conflict becomes militarized, the task of conflict resolution is immeasurably complicated, since the special character and requirements of military hierarchies must be factored into the settlement. To turn this point around, the price of inaction rises dramatically once the political-military threshold is crossed and constituencies with a vested interest in warfare, weapons procurement, and military resource mobilization become entrenched.

Examples of preemptive action to control the tinder include the following.

- *Deferring elections in societies not yet prepared to hold them and likely to become more polarized and fragile as a result of an election.* A poorly prepared and inadequately supervised election in Angola in 1992 led directly to escalated warfare. Separate elections in the republics of the former Yugoslavia in the earlier 1990s empowered ethnic nationalists and paved the way for the wars of disintegration. Ironically, elections at the federal (i.e., Yugoslav) level could have strengthened the legitimacy of Yugoslavia's reformist premier Ante Markovic, whereas republican elections had the opposite effect. (Timely Western financial support for Markovic could have had a parallel effect.) This points to the importance of strategic, results-oriented thinking by third parties. Yet, even with the example of prewar Bosnia before them, Western leaders repeated the error by precipitous scheduling of the next round of elections immediately after the 1995 Dayton accords. Outsiders should be wary of mechanistic policy formulas for elections. Unless a political culture rooted in democratic practice has been built up, elections are as likely to exacerbate conflict as they are to moderate it. That is why outside parties should encourage creative thinking about power-sharing formulas to accompany elections and provide the losers of those elections with a "safety net" that will encourage them to respect the voters' choice. To be sure, there is a natural tension between peacemaking and democratization: in a crunch, the former should come first, as the South Africans showed the world during their 1990–94 negotiated transition.

- *Encouraging incumbents who prefer to retain a measure of control over the process to act preemptively to promote political solutions and thus engineer a face-saving exit.* Examples include Gorbachev in Afghanistan, de Gaulle in Algeria, and de Klerk in South Africa. Farsighted incumbents thereby obviate the need for third-party, external intervention. Sometimes, however, they need a little third-party "help" to recognize the merits of acting preemptively. Outsiders can play a decisive role in encouraging the departure of doomed despots and opening the way toward soft landings that preempt drawn-out bloodshed (as Reagan did in the Philippines and Clinton did in Haiti) or dramatic showdowns (as Thatcher did in Zimbabwe and Bush did in Ethiopia).

- *Allocating real, timely resources, energy, and political capital to the tasks of disarming, retraining, and reintegrating former combatants into civil society.* Much more could be done to create tailored, multilateral programs for these purposes, so that political leaders and military commanders can make peace and then can live up to their commitments. Once again, Angola in 1991–92 showed how not to do it: Inadequate resources were made available for programs to attract soldiers and fighters to the encampment sites and keep them there, a weakness that spawned distrust, cheating, and an early return to battle. Problems with demobilization and reintegration of combatants also helped reignite fighting in Afghanistan, Cambodia, and Nicaragua. These issues were handled far more skillfully in the El Salvador settlement and in Mozambique, where soldiers actually protested in hopes of being demobilized more rapidly, due to the fact that the inducements offered were more attractive than the poor conditions of military service. Stopping a war requires preemptive action such as reintegrating, channeling, and supporting marginalized groups that are good at causing mayhem and living by the gun.

- *Resisting calls for secession and territorial fragmentation as "solutions" to internal strife.* It is probably too early to draw sweeping lessons from the three most prominent post–Cold War examples of territorial fragmentation: Ethiopia-Eritrea, USSR–former Soviet Union, and the former Yugoslavia. But we are entitled at a minimum to note that the Eritreans earned their autonomy on the battlefield only after more than thirty years of struggle and only after they negotiated a formula for separation and future relations with the Ethiopians. This is more than a question of procedural niceties, as the Bosnian tragedy illustrates. Warren Zimmermann reminds us that Yugoslavia's breakup was identified as the worst possible contingency in U.S. embassy analyses of the early 1990s, a forecast supported at the time by Bosnian leader Alija Izetbegovic, who viewed Yugoslavia's survival in some form as essential to Bosnia's own survival.[17] Western disarray and collapse on the principle of negotiated separation led directly to war. We should think twice about calling for the breakup of more states. If events seem to be headed that way, we should underscore the central importance of a negotiated outcome (as happened in Czechoslovakia). If violence looms even after a negotiated breakup —as it did between Eritrea and Ethiopia just a few years after their negotiated parting in the early 1990s—external parties may need to intervene with massive diplomatic force (that is, threatening denial of all forms of international status) to insist on respect for legitimate norms of conduct, something the West and the Organization of African Unity failed to do in 1998–99.

STRATEGIC CONDITIONS FOR SUCCESS

It is important to underscore that success in most endeavors, including foreign policy, is an inherently relative notion. Policymakers too easily allow excessive expectations to cloud public debate and media coverage. In some circumstances, success can legitimately be defined as the avoidance of major setbacks or disasters. In others, success may mean a marginal improvement in stabilizing, containing, and checking the human price and territorial spread of a volatile struggle. Or, success may mean the creation of building blocks for a settlement or even obtaining a fully implemented one, complete with resolution of the underlying issues. The short answer to the question of what connotes success is that it depends.

Those who decide to intervene (in whatever manner) have an obligation to develop their own definition of success and to keep it firmly in mind while laboring to avoid making things worse. Success is unlikely unless the intervenor has a commitment to succeed, a willingness to take on critics and challengers, a readiness to take the lead so that others can follow, and sufficient belief in the project to have a chance of shaping the terms of public debate. The intervenor who fails to establish publicly some standard of success may become the victim of others' standards.

Experience suggests that most conflicts in the modern, post-1945, era do not resolve themselves. To bring them under control, some type of external, third-party initiative is usually required. To be sure, only the local actors are capable of creating the institutions and inclusive habits of governance that inhibit civil wars. But it is external parties that typically have the capacity to shape, directly and indirectly, the environment in which these dramas play out and—once a conflict spiral has begun—to influence the options available and the choices made by local actors. Admittedly, in a few places a home- grown process of peacemaking and reconciliation may prove successful. But even the South African case illustrates a significant pattern of outside influences supporting the locally controlled negotiation that produced the settlement and transition of 1993–94. It is striking how few conflict-torn societies possess anything approaching the wealth of civil society institutions, the extent of mediation and negotiation skills, and the depth of leadership found in the South Africa of the 1980s and 1990s. These resources for peacemaking do not exist in Tajikistan, Bosnia, Yemen, Burundi, Haiti, or most other troubled lands. They may have only recently begun to emerge in Sri Lanka,

Indonesia, and Northern Ireland and among Israelis and Palestinians. And we should have no illusion that the process of acquiring indigenous capacity for solving conflict will be quick.

Outsiders will be needed for the foreseeable future to move peacemaking forward—by undertaking direct actions and diplomatic initiatives, defining the parameters of tolerable behavior, and legitimizing principles for settlement and for membership of the global system. Often, as in Mozambique during the 1992–94 settlement process, they are needed to translate a "ripening" situation into the essential building blocks of the transition from war to peace. Without outsiders to provide many of the pressures, ideas, concepts, resources, deadlines, and inducements, there would have been no settlement in that war-torn land. Without outsiders to sustain the settlement through several arduous years of implementation, the underlying agreements would have quickly collapsed.

This is not to advocate intervention by elements of the international community at all times, in every conflict. The U.S. government cannot play such a role everywhere. Nor can any combination of major powers set themselves up as world policemen. There is a limit to how many conflict situations can be managed or settled successfully, even with the most determined leadership and skillful personnel. Some conflict situations—and the people who reside there—are probably doomed to remain in the triage ward of the global system. Nonetheless, the international community can certainly do better than it has during the first post–Cold War decade, an experimental period that featured wild swings of the interventionist pendulum—from excessive enthusiasm to severe risk avoidance—and an abundance of learning the hard way. This was perhaps most evident in the performance of the permanent and nonpermanent members of the Security Council, who have the dominant role in UN peacekeeping decisions.

The good news as of early 2001 is that there is now a substantial and impressive body of

case studies from which lessons are being learned and certain principles developed. As discussed in depth elsewhere in this volume,[18] the United Nations' experience in the 1990s painfully demonstrates the limits on UN capability for the muscular, peace enforcement form of military intervention. Political leaders have begun to learn that it does no service to the cause of international security to thrust the United Nations forward in a hypocritical attempt to be seen "doing something" about a conflict, unless there is a basis for potential success. In practical terms that means that the mandate approved by the Security Council and the Secretariat must be accompanied by adequate military and financial resources to carry it out.

In this regard, it is heartening to see the widespread support expressed for the Brahimi report of August 2000, named after Algerian diplomat Lakhdar Brahimi, the chairman of the Panel on United Nations Peace Operations appointed by Secretary-General Kofi Annan.[19] This plain-speaking document strips away much of the hypocrisy and buck-passing argumentation surrounding UN peace operations. It also points the spotlight on the Security Council members' bad habit of approving peacekeeping mandates without making available the quality and quantity of financial and manpower resources required to meet the security challenges likely to arise in the field. If implemented in a serious manner, the Brahimi report could point the way toward best practice in UN peace operations by curtailing ill-considered and inadequately supported interventions, encouraging the greater use of career military officers to assess requirements, and fostering greater willingness to make resources and political support available so that the United Nations can do those jobs it is asked to do.

The bad news is that old habits of inept Security Council decision making under pressure of public and media opinion continue, as witnessed most clearly in the poor management of the United Nations' Sierra Leone operation in the early months of 2000. Almost every peacekeeping lesson from the 1990s was ignored by the council and the Secretariat in this ill-conceived venture, which would have become a complete disaster were it not for the skilled rescue mission launched by British paratroopers operating bilaterally—that is, outside the United Nations Mission in Sierra Leone (UNAMSIL).[20] At least three peacekeeping lessons were ignored in Sierra Leone: One, if a peace deal includes a known bad actor who could become a "spoiler," be prepared with adequately trained, led, and equipped forces and a mandate to enforce compliance if necessary. Two, in an uncertain and dangerous environment with a significant risk that UN goals will be contested or resisted, do not bluff with inadequate forces; rather, have the means available from the outset to establish dominance on the ground. And three, in such environments, the intervening authority must have the mandate, rules of engagement, and command, control, communications, and intelligence arrangements required to make recalcitrant parties behave, not ones that tempt the parties to test the authority's manhood at every opportunity.

Even the Brahimi report understates the critical importance of identifying precisely who will marshal those tactical, operational capabilities—real-time military intelligence; meticulous tactical planning; seamless internal, interservice, and interallied communication—that a rapid reaction or expeditionary force must possess to be effective even in limited operations. Yet, these ingredients may spell the difference between smooth operations and total fiascos.[21] The implication of these sobering thoughts may, in practice, be that the United Nations should no longer attempt this sort of muscular peacekeeping in dangerous environments, since it finds it difficult to recruit a competent core of well-trained and properly equipped forces to serve within a UN-commanded force of varying quality and capability. Instead, the United Nations may have to focus on those missions it can handle—traditional peacekeeping (e.g., the

operations in Cyprus, Ethiopia-Eritrea, and the Golan Heights) and "expanded," or "second-generation," peacekeeping involving political transitions backed by a negotiated settlement (e.g., the missions in Mozambique and El Salvador). This leaves peace enforcement to those capable of doing it—UN-mandated coalitions led by a strong global power or a regional lead nation. This is the model that in varying degrees proved successful in the end in Bosnia, Kosovo, Haiti, East Timor, Albania, and Somalia (during the Unified Task Force [UNITAF] phase of the operation, not during the United Nations Operation in Somalia [UNOSOM] phase). Debate continues on whether there may be an intermediate category of peacekeeping somewhere between peace enforcement (as in the cases of Desert Storm and Bosnia after Dayton—operations universally recognized to be beyond the capacity of the United Nations) and expanded, or second-generation, peacekeeping. There is also a range of views on whether such a middle option is within or beyond the reach of UN-led forces. This intermediate category could consist of UN-led peace operations based on the principles of "enhanced consent" using some coercive capacity when parties breach the mandate or the underlying peace accord,[22] or it could be based on the principles of "coercive inducement" that also entail tailored and proportionate uses of coercion by UN-mandated but not UN-commanded coalitions.[23]

It is interesting to reflect on the fact that something like an intermediate option was tried once before, some forty years ago in central Africa. The United Nations Operation in the Congo (ONUC, 1960–64), not UNOSOM, was the first time the international system decided "to paint a country blue." It did so by deploying nearly twenty thousand troops plus a large civilian element to central Africa for four years at a cost of some $2 billion (1991 dollars). The effort succeeded in holding together a vast land facing huge internal and external challenges. It checked the further intrusion of the Cold War into central Africa and warded off unknown scenarios of disorder and instability affecting much of the region. ONUC did these things against great odds: divisions within the Security Council and in Africa and the absence of either a clear and agreed-upon mandate or an agreed-upon political framework. Enforcement was used (though without Chapter VII blessing). ONUC's success reflects the determined leadership of the key civilian and military people who ran it both in the field and in New York; the consistent availability of major military units from key states, especially India; and the continuous assurance of U.S. logistical and financial backing (Washington paid nearly 50 percent of the military costs and 70 percent of the bill for civilian elements).[24]

Forty years after ONUC, we may forget how divisive and controversial the operation was at the time—not in the United States, where the importance of the UN role was understood, but internationally, where ONUC's "can-do," improvised operating procedures and purposeful but expensive conduct cost it the support of both Moscow and Paris. ONUC had a chilling impact on peace operations generally and especially in Africa, but it helped stabilize a region and, in this sense, worked. It is remarkable how readily nations forget their accomplishments and their habits of prevailing against the odds.

Intervention fatigue and the real price tag of sustaining military deployments in conflicted societies have encouraged growing attention to the possibilities (and limits) of intervention by regional and subregional actors. System overload at the global, great-power level reached a culminating point in 1994 in Rwanda, whose trauma was tolerated by world leaders who would subsequently find it necessary to apologize for their earlier inaction. When big powers and the "international community" disengage, they create regional or subregional vacuums. Under some circumstances, this leads to a transitional "law of the jungle" that features no ultimate safety nets and an international security structure that has little to offer to regions of

"low priority." Security leadership by dominant regional powers (sometimes called "hegemons") can work in some circumstances—that is, where there is a militarily and diplomatically competent nation to volunteer for the role, where that role is generally welcomed, and where there is some form of authorizing or mandating process (through the United Nations or some other, agreed-upon mechanism) to legitimize actions taken. But there are no easy panaceas in this trial-and-error phase of global transition; few regional powers or regional security organizations apart from NATO can meet the kinds of criteria just mentioned, and even NATO runs into difficulty with the third criterion if the Security Council is divided, as we have seen in Kosovo. In short, the "regional option" exists only in the imagination in a majority of cases.[25] At present there is no substitute for coherent, coordinated intervention by global powers.

The striking aspect of the best assessments of post–Cold War peacekeeping is their emphasis on the relationship between the level of difficulty of a specific conflict case and the resources made available to carry out a successful mission.[26] We have learned that a central strategic condition for successful intervention is to meet the challenges of implementation after an agreement has been reached and a peace operation decided upon. Just as conflicts seldom resolve themselves, peaceful settlements do not implement themselves. The role of foreign intervenors cannot end on the day that agreements are signed. Implementing mechanisms are essential to keep things on track, to sustain the political chemistry that produced the deal, and to maintain the linkages and pressures that led to the breakthrough. As in other fields of endeavor such as law or business, statecraft in zones of conflict illustrates the maxim that the real negotiation begins after the agreements are signed. Outsiders who orphan the settlements they have helped produce will watch them collapse.[27]

These observations are especially pertinent at the military level, where it is vital to obtain and sustain the right balance between challenges on the ground and security mechanisms for responding to them. But this is above all a political and strategic issue, relating to every aspect of an intervention during the implementation phase. Intervenors need an explicit implementation strategy to carry things forward from the point of agreement to that of successfully implemented settlement. While each case differs, some core questions arise in many cases. How will the signatory parties remain in communication after the ink is dry? Who will run the overall implementation process, including all elements of the settlement (e.g., cease-fire monitoring, refugee returns, encampment of rival forces, elections preparation and organization, human rights monitoring, troop withdrawals or redeployments)? Who will define success and declare that the implementation phase has been completed? How will the intervening powers coordinate with one another, with local authorities, and with regional or international organizations? Whose task is it to see that parties carry out their commitments? What mechanisms and safety nets are available to rescue the process if it goes off the rails? What roles can outsiders play to observe, monitor, verify, guarantee, and, if appropriate, enforce compliance? How will the various military, political, humanitarian, and economic tracks of a settlement be coordinated, and who will make certain that this happens? How will external civilian, military, and NGO leaders coordinate their actions with one another and with local counterparts?

In any implementation process, there is a central role for imaginative improvisation and swift resolution of problems large and small that are certain to arise. This is why top-flight leadership is essential in complex, political-military undertakings. Similarly, a well-led implementation can have a transforming effect on the climate that develops among the parties, making possible compromises and deals that would have been unthinkable before the settlement. But everything hinges on taking the

implementation phase seriously. A good test of how well the implementation process will work is to identify who, ultimately, is responsible for making sure that the whole complex operation works. Unless the buck stops somewhere, implementation will be rocky. Waging peace, like waging war, is a full-time job for dedicated professionals who are prepared to work around the clock, seven days a week, and who conduct themselves according to the highest standards of personal responsibility. Successful practitioners bring both pride and passion to this demanding work.

Another strategic lesson learned from past cases of intervention is that success depends on understanding the connection between military power and diplomatic strategy. Third-party diplomatic intervention (e.g., mediation) is seldom effective unless it either reflects a favorable, underlying balance of forces or is backed by actors with the power and leverage to affect that balance. The complex international and regional diplomacy leading up to the July 1999 Lusaka Accords on the Congo crisis illustrate the point. Fluid military conditions on the ground and untested levels of political will and commitment within the rival alliances provided a poor environment for negotiated agreement. Diplomacy never developed the traction required to manage the conflict because there was no "hurting stalemate" between the parties and no unified application of external pressures and incentives on them to make peace.

Military interventions have a much higher chance of producing a durable result when they are linked either to a political settlement or to an ongoing political process for obtaining one. In fact, military action without a clear political context is of little use: pressure requires diplomacy to have an impact, just as diplomacy needs an element of pressure to be effective. In this connection, a special word is in order about humanitarian interventions. Success in these undertakings can be measured at two levels: saving lives, and creating a political basis for resolving the issues that put lives at risk in the first place. The absence of strong prospects for the second level of success should not become an excuse for doing nothing to protect people when something can be done at an acceptable cost to the intervenors (even if this requires ongoing effort, as in Iraq). But humanitarian action makes so much more sense when conceived as a bridge to a political process that can provide the best basis for a successful exit. This was one of the missing ingredients that undercut the impact of U.S. and UN intervention in Somalia. In Kosovo, the absence of an agreed-upon "end state " or of a negotiating mechanism for clarifying the ultimate status of this occupied province of the former Yugoslavia is one of the most debilitating challenges facing the NATO-UN intervention presence there.

Recent history is replete with examples illustrating this military-political nexus. A clear political context was lacking for the second Lebanon intervention of 1983. The U.S. covert war in Nicaragua in the 1980s lacked a political context until the Central American presidents provided one. The brief resumption of the United States' clandestine support for the National Union for the Total Independence of Angola (UNITA) after 1985 was effective because it was linked to, and supportive of, an ongoing negotiation process leading to the 1988 Namibia-Angola settlement. The U.S.-UN intervention in Haiti in 1994 derived essential strength from the political framework surrounding the action, a framework based on the United Nations and the Organization of American States (OAS). It is not an accident that many of the United Nations' successes in peace operations have occurred in cases involving the implementation of a negotiated settlement plan: for example, El Salvador, Cambodia, Mozambique, and Namibia.

By contrast, the thirty-year-old UN peace-keeping presence on Cyprus has played a useful role of the traditional blue-helmet variety through confidence building, cease-fire monitoring, and violence reduction. But its success in these terms has, if anything, reduced the pressures among the parties and the Western powers to push for a real settlement. Viewed another way, the UN operation has helped to stabilize the island's de facto partition, which was not the operation's originally intended purpose.

A final strategic condition for success in post–Cold War intervention is the need for coherence—an overall unity of effort and purpose—among the intervening actors. When outside parties do not agree in their analysis of a conflict or of what should be done to move a peace process forward, the effect can all too easily be to confuse the parties or, worse, encourage them to engage in maneuvering, shop for the most sympathetic outsiders, or simply play for time. Achieving coherence of third-party action has become increasingly complex as the range and diversity of intervenors has multiplied in recent years.[28] For this very reason, the importance of striving for coherence is more notable than in simpler times.

The issue of coherence arises at both the strategic and the operational levels. The presence or absence of coherence affects the chances for success of all sorts of interventions. Military professionals understand that this point is central to the effectiveness of war-fighting and joint operations in contingencies ranging from peace enforcement to UN-led peacekeeping. Strategic unity of purpose is as essential in peace operations as it is in traditional warfare. Experience during the 1990s has shed a bright spotlight on the high cost of disunity, confusion, or divided loyalties in the chain of command. It takes sustained and regularized effort for alliances and coalitions to work well together because there are so many gaps and differences to be overcome: issues of doctrine, language, technological levels, training and leadership caliber, national pride and prestige, and interoperability and compatibility of systems. These issues can be overcome only by integrated operational planning and regular intelligence exchanges as well as practical experience in running joint commands. Unless a coalition or alliance is prepared to devote the time and resources to "jointness" and has a core of compatible military units, it is unlikely to achieve desired results in the field. In a sophisticated military alliance such as NATO, this requires a strategic commitment in principle to work together on a host of doctrinal, structural, training, and operational issues.[29]

But this point about coherence is not limited to the domain of military affairs. Multinational diplomatic interventions such as mediation and joint political strategies such as peace implementation require imaginative leadership to motivate and induce diverse actors to work together. Governments are unlikely to be successful in these efforts unless they are capable of hammering out joint strategies and concerted actions, not only with one another but also with international organizations, nongovernmental organizations, humanitarian agencies, and other bodies. As with military actions, a host of obstacles stand in the way of achieving such coordination and coherence: issues of pride and status; divergent national or organizational agendas; differences in the "culture" and style of various actors; and above all the question of deciding who leads, who coordinates whom, and who speaks for a multiparty coalition. In an effort to overcome such problems, national leaders and international civil servants (especially special representatives of the UN secretary-general and of intergovernmental groups such as the European Union and the OAS) have adopted the practice of establishing contact groups or groups of "friends" to work regularly to shepherd along a mediation effort or to provide support to a fragile peace process. Typically, such groups comprise like-minded major powers, a regional leadership grouping, a group of interested donors and cooperation partners, or a collection of nations that witnessed or "guaranteed" earlier phases of a peace process and continue to have an interest in supporting it.[30]

It is not difficult to identify cases where the absence of political-diplomatic coherence has spelled failure of third-party efforts to promote peace in regional conflicts: Bosnia (1992–94),[31] Burundi (1993–99),[32] and Nagorno-Karabakh (1992–95).[33] Failures of peacemaking efforts in Sudan, Congo, and Afghanistan have many roots, but not least has been an utter lack of coherence among external actors with interests in the conflict area and influence on the warring parties.

The lesson we are learning from all these cases is that the starting place in external efforts to influence the parties to a conflict is to assess the possibilities for achieving coherence, the chances for developing a common script and a joint strategy, and the obstacles to recruiting or co-opting all relevant players onto a united team. A lead nation or grouping that wishes to shape events through some mixture of military and political intervention will ignore at its peril the necessity of achieving strategic unity and of neutralizing or marginalizing those who have reasons to stand in the way.

OPERATIONAL CONDITIONS FOR SUCCESSFUL INTERVENTION

An intervenor must have the capacity for effective and prompt decision making. Whether intervention is military or nonmilitary (but especially when it is the former), there is no excuse for getting involved in other peoples' conflicts incompetently. Dual-key decision systems, elaborate committees, and multiple vetoes do not work in highly complex, distant, and dangerous situations. If the job of intervention is to be done well, someone must be placed in charge, held accountable, given the requisite mandate and resources, and steadily supported or else replaced.

Interventions should be viewed as full-time work for those in charge. They should be run like a task force on an around-the-clock basis. This principle of coherent and clear intervention management is valid on an intergovernmental basis as well as within individual governments; similarly, it is valid for both diplomatic and military interventions. One study of the 1992–94 Somalia operation concluded: "The three chains of [military] command running during UNOSOM II underline the importance of a lesson that should be adapted from Murphy's Laws of Combat: If it takes more than ten seconds to explain the command arrangements, they probably won't work."[34] The problems posed by unclear command structures are compounded when political decision makers and military commanders interact.

Prospective intervenors must be on guard for scenarios that risk converting intervention forces into targets or hostages. No armed forces of any kind (UN blue helmets or national units) should be deployed as tokens, symbols, or tripwires in the absence of either previous political agreements and "a peace to keep" or a firm and clear determination to punish severely anyone who harms or threatens to harm them. When power projection becomes overwhelmed by the rigors of force protection, the balance shifts against the outsiders. This is not a new lesson. The British learned it before agreeing to pull out of the Suez Canal Zone (1954) and before abandoning their facilities in Aden (1968); the French learned it at Dienbienphu (1953–54) and did not repeat such errors in Algeria; the United States learned it in Lebanon in 1983; UNOSOM II learned it in south Mogadishu (May to October 1993); and the permanent members of the UN Security Council relearned it in Bosnia (1992–95).

Intervenors should never lose the political initiative, never allow themselves to give away vetoes, and never lose control of the clock. An early lesson in decisive interventionism came from London in late January 1964: With the approval of African civilian leaders, a combined-arms force of some five thousand men intervened at six places in three countries (Tanganyika, Kenya, and Uganda) to reverse mutinies, deter coups, and restore civilian control. The operations succeeded with minimal casualties. French forces based regionally and in the metropole have repeatedly conducted such operations in former African colonies, again with minimal loss of life. A very different example was provided by the United Nations Transitional Authority in Cambodia (UNTAC) in 1991–93, which achieved some of its key goals because it retained the united support of the main external actors, sidestepped the Khmer Rouge's noncooperation on military issues, and proceeded with elections despite the Khmer Rouge's boycott. The result: no gratuitous vetoes were issued and UNTAC achieved a 90 percent voter turnout in the May 1993 elections.

In April 1989, the South West African People's Organization (SWAPO), the Namibian nationalist movement, mounted an incursion from Angola into Namibia in hopes of acquiring by force the internal bases it had never obtained at the negotiating table. This gambit was thwarted militarily by the South Africans and politically by the united stand taken by the United Nations' field leadership, the British, Americans, Cubans, Russians, and several neighboring African states. The Namibian independence process was put back on track. During the UNITAF phase of intervention in Somalia (December 1992–April 1993), the U.S. leadership defined the military agenda, preemptively engaged both warlords and civilian constituencies, and jump-started a process of political dialogue. These gains quickly eroded when one warlord seized the initiative a few months later, after UNOSOM II took over from UNITAF. By October of that year, Washington was imposing withdrawal deadlines upon itself, a sure sign of the collapse of political will.

The old saying about not changing horses midstream applies well to intervention. It would be difficult to imagine—with hindsight—a more poorly executed and ill-timed "handoff" than the UNITAF–UNOSOM II transition in 1993 in Somalia. Within a mere four months of mounting the initial intervention, that intervention's leadership, doctrine, reporting channels and oversight, available resources, and mission mandate were transformed. Worse, the new mandate was significantly more ambitious, while the military resources available to support it were cut back severely. The collapse of continuity and institutional memory coincided with a shift in the power balance, inviting a test of strength. Somalia, of course, offers many lessons. But the seemingly casual handling of the transition guaranteed a subsequent foreign policy failure, even if the intervention was successful in saving hundreds of thousands of lives.[35] The 1995 U.S.-UN transfer in Haiti proceeded far better, suggesting that lessons can be learned fast.

When a great nation decides to engage in the affairs of distant regions, it should first make sure that the necessary homework has been done and that the right people are on the policy team, including people who know something about the place in which the intervention is to occur. Former president George Bush understood this when he selected the team to plan and lead the U.S. effort in Somalia. Had senior people in key capitals known more about the true circumstances that spawned Rwanda's tragedy of 1994–95, we might have been less blinded by our Somalia backlash and more prepared to take an early stand against the butchery. Had the Russians done their homework on Afghanistan (and Ethiopia and Angola) in the late 1970s, they might have averted what Gorbachev later identified as the "bleeding wound" that forced Moscow to dump its ramshackle Third World empire.

A final operational condition for success relates to the special importance of key people and particular nations and their military forces. The specific personal, professional, and political qualities of the intervenors can make an enormous difference. At one level, this point appears self-evident. But when analyzing vast and complex subjects, it is easy to slip into abstract generalizations that overlook the most important variables. Just as it is hard to imagine Operation Desert Storm without the U.S. armed forces, it is important to identify the factors that have

contributed to success in less dramatic and smaller-scale interventions.

UN interventions that have worked are those that have enjoyed steady hands on the tiller and reliable and around-the-clock support in key local embassies and their home capitals. The United Nations Angola Verification Mission (UNAVEM II, 1991–92) did not have these things. The United Nations Operation in Mozambique (ONUMOZ) benefited from both of them. UNTAC enjoyed solid political support from major powers; this ingredient was lost in UNOSOM II. People make a difference; the Namibian transition unquestionably gained from the leadership of an outstanding team of UN civilian and military people.

CONCLUSION

This chapter has underscored the variety of contemporary conflicts and the vast menu of potential responses for dealing with these conflicts. Understanding the global disorders of the 1990s requires looking behind the labels, slogans, and abstractions so commonly used to describe events and define our options. This close, case-by-case inspection permits us to appreciate the tremendous range of possible intervening actors in the contemporary global system and to appreciate the potential for selective global engagement by the United States, without automatically falling victim to the dangers of overcommitment.

The historic record makes clear that interventions can succeed as well as fail, and it offers a range of strategic and operational lessons from specific cases. Some of the most interesting examples revolve around seemingly pedestrian notions that have long been at the core of effective statecraft: political will and staying power, continuity of policy management in complex undertakings, operational competence and sound judgment in negotiating and implementing settlements, seizing and keeping the initiative, the interdependence of military power and diplomacy, the vital importance of focusing on how negotiated agreements are to be implemented, the imperative of achieving coherence among intervening actors, and the role of top-flight leadership. Intervention in the affairs of others is a serious business. It is not an arena for mere posturing or for being seen as "doing something." It should be attempted only with the most talented, most committed, and most tenacious people and pursued with a relentless intensity.

NOTES

1. One of the best overviews of trends in UN peace operations is Pamela L. Reed, J. Matthew Vaccaro, and William J. Durch, *Handbook on United Nations Peace Operations* (Washington, D.C.: Henry L. Stimson Center, April 1995).

2. SIPRI (Stockholm International Peace Research Institute), *SIPRI Yearbook 2000: Armaments, Disarmament, and International Security* (Oxford: Oxford University Press, 2000).

3. One of the best illustrations of the problem is in Barry Posen, "The Security Dilemma and Ethnic Conflict," *Survival* (spring 1993). See also Barbara F. Walter and Jack Snyder, eds., *Civil Wars, Insecurity, and Intervention* (New York: Columbia University Press, 1999), esp. 1–69.

4. Roy Licklider, "The Consequences of Negotiated Settlements in Civil Wars, 1945–1993," *American Political Science Review* 89, no. 3 (September 1995).

5. See Edward Luttwak's chapter in this volume (chapter 16).

6. See Joseph Nye, "Redefining the National Interest," *Foreign Affairs* 78, no. 4 (July-August 1999); and the author's comment "A Poor Case for Quitting," *Foreign Affairs* 79, no. 1 (January-February 2000).

7. See Luttwak's chapter in this volume and the author's rejoinder to an earlier version that appeared in *Foreign Affairs,* "Give War a Chance," 78, no. 4 (July-August 1999).

8. This argument is made by Max Boot in his review of Brian McAllister Linn's *The Philippine War, 1899–1902* (Lawrence, Kans.: University of Kansas Press, 2000) in *The National Interest* (summer 2000).

9. The literature on ethnic conflict is too vast to summarize here. In addition to Ted Robert Gurr's chapter in this volume (chapter 11), see Stephen Van Evera, "Hypotheses on Nationalism and War," *International Security* 18, no. 4 (spring 1994): 5–39; Milton J. Esman, "Political and Psychological Factors in Ethnic Conflict," in *Conflict and Peacemaking in Multiethnic Societies,* ed. Joseph V. Montville (Lexington, Mass.: Lexington Books, 1990); Anthony D. Smith, *Myths and Memories of the Nation* (New York: Oxford University Press, 1999); and Walter and Snyder, eds., *Civil Wars, Insecurity, and Intervention.*

10. For a sustained discussion of the history and potential of such engagements in American policy, see Alan K. Henrikson, "Constructive Containment," *Fletcher Forum of World Affairs* 19, no. 2 (summer-fall 1995): 1–17.

11. See Pamela Aall's chapter in this volume (chapter 23).

12. See Mary Anderson's chapter in this volume (chapter 37).

13. Ahmedou Ould-Abdallah, *Burundi on the Brink: A UN Special Envoy Reflects on Preventive Diplomacy* (Washington, D.C.: United States Institute of Peace Press, 2000), 113–115.

14. For detailed discussion of the presettlement and postsettlement phases of this diplomacy, see the chapters by Andrea Bartoli, "Mediating Peace in Mozambique: The Role of the Community of Sant'Egidio," and Aldo Ajello, "Mozambique: Implementation of the 1992 Peace Agreement," in *Herding Cats: Multiparty Mediation in a Complex World,* ed. Chester A. Crocker, Fen Osler Hampson, and Pamela Aall (Washington, D.C.: United States Institute of Peace Press, 1999).

15. For a more detailed discussion of gaining access and comparative advantages of various actors, see Crocker, Hampson, and Aall, "Multiparty Mediation and the Conflict Cycle," in *Herding Cats.*

16. See Nicole Ball's chapter in this volume (chapter 42).

17. Warren Zimmermann, "The Last Ambassador: A Memoir of the Collapse of Yugoslavia," *Foreign Affairs* 74, no. 2 (March-April 1995): 6.

18. See chapters 32, 31, and 43 by Michael Doyle, Rolf Ekeus, and Stephen Stedman, respectively, in this volume.

19. "Report of the Panel on United Nations Peace Operations," United Nations General Assembly/Security Council A/55/305-G/2000/809, dated August 21, 2000.

20. See Blaine Harden, "In Africa, a Lesson in How Not to Keep the Peace," *Washington Post,* May 14, 2000; and Robert Oakley, "Self-Delusion in Bringing Peace," *Washington Times,* May 23, 2000.

21. For a critical assessment of the Brahimi report, see John Mackinlay, "Mission Failure," *World Today,* November 2000; for a chilling account of the extraordinary high price of communication barriers and lack of unity of command even within the U.S. forces deployed in Somalia—let alone between them and other elements of the UNOSOM II mission—see Mark Bowden, *Black Hawk Down: A Story of Modern War* (New York: Atlantic Monthly Press, 1999); and Kenneth Allard, *Somalia Operations: Lessons Learned* (Washington, D.C.: National Defense University Press, 1995), 55–61.

22. See Michael Doyle's chapter in this volume (chapter 32).

23. See the arguments for this approach in Donald C. F. Daniel and Bradd C. Hayes with Chantal de Jonge Oudraat, *Coercive Inducement and the Containment of International Crises* (Washington, D.C.: United States Institute of Peace Press, 1999).

24. This discussion draws upon the analysis in William J. Durch, "The UN Operation in the Congo, 1960–1964," in *The Evolution of UN Peacekeeping: Case Studies and Comparative Analysis,* ed. William J. Durch (New York: St. Martin's Press for the Henry L. Stimson Center, 1993), 315–352.

25. See the discussions of regionalism in chapters 33 and 34 by Connie Peck and David Yost, respectively, in this volume.

26. See the Brahimi report cited in note 19 and Stephen Stedman's chapter in this volume (chapter 43).

27. The best sustained treatment of the implementation phase in peacemaking is in Fen Osler Hampson, *Nurturing Peace: Why Peace Settlements Succeed or Fail* (Washington, D.C.: United States Institute of Peace Press, 1996).

28. See the chapter by Chester A. Crocker, Fen Osler Hampson, and Pamela Aall in this volume (chapter 30).

29. See James P. Thomas, *The Military Challenges of Transatlantic Coalitions,* Adelphi Papers no. 333 (London: IISS, 2000), 56–57 and 79–82.

30. For examples of such groups in action, see the chapters on Cambodia, Namibia, El Salvador, Mozambique, and Peru-Ecuador by Richard H. Solomon, Chester A. Crocker, Alvaro de Soto, Aldo Ajello, and Luigi Einaudi, respectively, in *Herding Cats,* ed. Crocker, Hampson, and Aall.

31. Susan L. Woodward, "Bosnia and Herzegovina: How Not to End Civil War," in *Civil Wars, Insecurity, and Intervention,* ed. Walter and Snyder.

32. Fabienne Hara, "Burundi: A Case of Parallel Diplomacy," in *Herding Cats,* ed. Crocker, Hampson, and Aall.

33. John J. Maresca, "Resolving the Conflict over Nagorno-Karabakh: Lost Opportunities for International Conflict Resolution," in *Managing Global Chaos: Sources of and Responses to International Conflict,* ed. Chester A. Crocker and Fen Osler Hampson with Pamela Aall (Washington, D.C.: United States Institute of Peace Press, 1996).

34. Allard, *Somalia Operations: Lessons Learned,* 9.

35. For an elaboration of the lessons of Somalia, see Chester A. Crocker, "The Lessons of Somalia," *Foreign Affairs* 74, no. 3 (1995).

15

Preventive Statecraft

A Realist Strategy for the Post–Cold War Era

Bruce W. Jentleson

ONE OF THE MOST OFTEN HEARD CRITICISMS of conflict prevention is that it is unrealistic.[1] Self-styled "realists" do not dispute the desirability of preventing ethnic cleansing, genocide, and other deadly conflicts, but they question both the viability and the value of priority efforts to do so. Aren't many of these conflicts just the playing out of history—of "Balkan ghosts" that still haunt the region, of precolonial African tribal hatreds, of other deeply historical animosities? Is it sufficiently in the interests of major powers such as the United States that they should run the risks of trying to prevent conflict? Why not just wait and see and, if needed, resort to later-stage conflict management?

For all its self-styled realism, this line of argument is flawed even on its own terms. It is wrong about both the viability and the value of conflict prevention. It underestimates the interests at stake and overestimates the costs and risks, especially compared with the costs and risks incurred by waiting or not acting. There is a realism, not just idealism, to preventive statecraft.

I intentionally use the term "preventive statecraft" as a shift from "preventive diplomacy." I have come to prefer "preventive statecraft" because it better conveys the importance of thinking in terms of "mixed strategies"; it is not just confined to negotiation and other classical forms of diplomacy but also encompasses preventive threats and uses of military force and other more coercive components. I should add that while long-term approaches to prevention (what the Carnegie Commission on Preventing Deadly Conflict called "structural" prevention) are essential in their own right, my focus is more on the short- to medium-term onset of potential crises ("operational" prevention in the Carnegie Commission distinction).[2]

THE VIABILITY OF PREVENTIVE STATECRAFT

The question of the viability of preventive statecraft in its essence is a debate over historical determinism. The assumption of an overwhelming inevitability to these conflicts that is inherent in their characterization as a playing out of history is indicative of what is called the "primordialist view," in which ethnic conflicts are seen primarily as manifestations of fixed, inherited, deeply antagonistic historical identities.[3] In this analysis the end of the Cold War stripped away the constraining effects of the strategic overlay of bipolar geopolitics, releasing the "Balkan ghosts" and other historical hatreds to their "natural" states of conflict.

If the primordialist theory were valid, then it truly would be hard to hold out much prospect for preventive statecraft. Yet as a number of studies have shown, ethnic identities are much less fixed over time, and the frequency and intensity of ethnic conflict much more varying over both time and place, than the primordialist theory would have it. The point is made, albeit with some hyperbole, in a statement by a Bosnian Muslim schoolteacher that "we never, until the war, thought of ourselves as Muslims. We were Yugoslavs. But when we began to be murdered because we are Muslims things changed. The definition of who we are today has been determined by our killing."[4]

Michael Brown delineates other variables such as political institutions and socioeconomic factors that are less historically deterministic but are still possible "underlying" sources of ethnic as well as other internal conflicts.[5] However, while these underlying factors are helpful in identifying dispositions toward political instability, they almost always end up both overdetermined and underdetermined in their explanations of the fundamental reasons why violence actually occurs in any particular case.[6]

The optimal analytic approach both for avoiding the historical determinism fallacy and for getting beyond underlying factors to proximate, violence-triggering factors is through a "purposive" view of what the key sources of deadly conflict are. This approach acknowledges the deep-seated nature of ethnic identifications and the corresponding intergroup tensions, animosities, and unfinished agendas

of vengeance and retribution that carry forward as historical legacies. But it takes a much less deterministic view of how, why, and if these identity-rooted tensions become deadly conflicts. The dominant dynamic is not the playing out of historical inevitability but rather the consequences of calculations by parties to the conflict of the purposes served by political violence. It is in seeking to influence this calculus that preventive statecraft has its potential viability.

In all of the cases in the Carnegie Commission study I led (see note 1) there were specific and identifiable opportunities for the international community to limit, if not prevent, the conflicts. For example, in the Somalia case Ken Menkhaus and Louis Ortmayer acknowledge that "no amount of preventive diplomacy could have completely preempted some level of conflict," but they trace "a virtual litany of missed opportunities," presenting solid evidence "that timely diplomatic interventions at several key junctures might have significantly reduced, defused and contained that violence." In the Rwanda case Astri Suhrke and Bruce Jones also are able to substantiate a series of missed opportunities, making a number of points in this regard, including that "a more determined international response against the extremists would have found allies" in the military.[7] As for Croatia and Bosnia and Herzegovina, Susan Woodward is clear that "there are few, if any, deadly conflicts in recent history that have provided more opportunity for prevention than the wars that engulfed the Balkan peninsula with the disintegration of Yugoslavia in 1991." In these and other cases in our study the assessment of missed opportunities is made conscious of and consistent with the caveats concerning counterfactual analysis. Although one can never be entirely confident in the conclusions drawn from what-might-have-been scenarios, one's confidence certainly increases in proportion to the rigor and empirical grounding of their analyses and arguments.[8]

Another important conclusion is that notwithstanding claims to neutrality or noninvolvement, there is no nonposition for international actors. While international actors may profess neutrality, be it limiting their involvement to humanitarian rescue or simply staying out, there is no "nonposition" for the international community in the sense of no impact one way or the other. If one party to the conflict assesses that it has the advantage in military and other means of violence over the other, as long as the other cannot count on international assistance to balance and buttress, it should be no wonder that it chooses war. In some instances the choice of war is at least in part a preemptive one, made less out of outright aggressive intentions than as a manifestation of the "security dilemma," in which warfare breaks out from mutual insecurities and fears of vulnerabilities, which credible international action could have assuaged. In this regard, to cite two other cases from the Carnegie study, Gail Lapidus stresses that Boris Yeltsin still had "a considerable repertoire of tools and strategies" for Chechnya in 1994 other than military intervention but made his choices in part based on knowing that the United States and others in the international community were not going to impose significant costs for using force. William Zartman shows how the conflicting parties in Congo-Brazzaville in 1997 exploited the unwillingness of the international community to get involved in any serious way.

In sum, there is ample basis for arguing for the viability of preventive statecraft. Conflict prevention is, to be sure, a formidable undertaking; but it is possible. A sense for both the differences and the possibilities is integral to a genuine realism. The claims are not that some policy X surely would have prevented ethnic cleansing in Bosnia, or some policy Y smoothly rebuilt the Somali state, or some policy Z prevented genocide in Rwanda. But we also should not accept the assertion that nothing else could have been done, that no more or

nothing different was viable than the policies as pursued.

THE STRATEGIC VALUE OF PREVENTION

Another charge leveled by realist critics of preventive statecraft is that it involves low interests but high risks and costs. This is to ask the hardheaded question of whether preventive statecraft is worth doing, even if it is doable. It may be viable, but does it have sufficient value to international actors for them to run the risks and incur the costs of undertaking it? Why not just wait and see, kick the problem down the road? These are among the widely accepted saws premised on the ostensible pragmatic preferability of later-stage conflict management to early-stage conflict prevention.

The counterargument here is twofold: first, this basic calculus needs to be reassessed; second, the dynamics of these conflicts contradict the assumed preferability of waiting to see if concerted action is necessary.

Reassessing the Interests/Costs Calculus

The low interests/high costs calculus so often cited as the realist argument against conflict prevention underestimates the interests at stake for the international community and overestimates the cost differential between acting early and acting late. Indeed even though many of the 1990s conflicts did not involve inherently strategic locales, the damage to major power and other international interests proved greater than anticipated.

The very terms "ethnic cleansing" and "genocide" leave no doubt about the severity of the escalation of the conflicts in Croatia, in Bosnia and Herzegovina, and in Rwanda. Had these conflicts stayed at relatively low levels of violence, perhaps the realist calculus of limited interests would have held. But they did not, and so it did not. Nor does it necessarily matter in this regard whether one puts the miscalculation in underestimating the likelihood of escalation or in foreseeing this as a possibility but still holding to a limited interests assessment. Where the interests assessment went wrong was in sticking too much to standard measures like locale ("not strategic real estate") and resource endowments ("no oil"), and not taking into account how conflicts even in such places can have disproportionate impacts on interests when violence escalates to such extreme levels.

If it were the case that the fires of ethnic conflicts, however intense, would just burn upon themselves and not have significant potential to spread regionally or destabilize more systematically, or if the options for later action had the presumed pragmatic preferability, then in strict realist terms one could argue that major powers could afford to just let these conflicts be. But that is not always or even frequently the case. As numerous cases have shown and as much of the literature substantiates, spread is much more common than self-containment. This occurs through various combinations of direct "contagion" through the actual physical movement of refugees and weapons to other countries in the region, "demonstration effects" that even without direct contact activate and escalate other conflicts, and other modes of conflict diffusion.[9] Consequently, when there is no prevention, the real estate in question risks getting bigger. Whether because the conflict then takes in areas that are more strategic or simply because a larger area is in crisis, outside powers can find their interests much more at risk.

The Rwanda case became virtually a classic example of this, in terms of the direct and intense interconnection of the consequences of the Rwandan conflict and the precipitants of the Zairean one. This is not to ignore the much deeper causes of Mobutu's fall. Nor is it in any way to imply that the end of the Mobutu kleptocratic dictatorship was a bad thing. But the conflict diffusion point is about how violence begat violence.

This is not to totally reverse the assessment of interests. It is not the case that preventive statecraft always has an interests-based rationale for outside powers. Some conflicts may not escalate to ethnic cleansing or genocide. Not all conflicts have the same likelihood of diffusion. There is some logic to giving greater weight to other factors in relations with a major power, especially when the conflict in question embodies an asymmetry of motivations that leans toward that state's interests, a qualifying point that Lapidus makes in the Chechnya case. The central point, though, is that *these are assessments to be made, not assumptions to be set.*

A related point concerns the basic fallacy in the dichotomy so often drawn between realism and idealism. In the most fundamental sense "the distinction between interests and values," as Stanley Hoffmann argues, "is largely fallacious . . . a great power has an interest in world order that goes beyond strict national security concerns and its definition of world order is largely shaped by its values."[10] Moreover, it is worth pondering whether in such a globalist age we want to become a people that does not feel a moral imperative to seek to prevent genocide and other mass violence and destruction just because it may be on a geopolitically unimportant piece of real estate. This too is both a moral question and a pragmatic one, as it bears upon how such hardening can affect domestic intersocietal relations.

Furthermore, whereas the costs of waiting tend to be assumed to be less than the costs of acting early, they have proven to be much greater than expected and arguably more than those for preventive action would have been. One study estimated that the costs of conflict prevention to outside powers in the Bosnia case would have been $33.3 billion, compared with the estimated $53.7 billion that it actually cost. Similar disproportions were extrapolated for other cases: for example, $5 billion costs for the Haiti conflict compared with $2.3 billion estimate for conflict prevention; $7.3 billion compared with $1.5 billion for Somalia; and in a case of successful prevention, Macedonia, $0.3 billion costs in the 1990s for prevention compared with $15 billion had the conflict even reached intermediate intensity, let alone higher, levels.[11]

Still, though, one can see why, like people in general, policymakers put greater weight on immediate costs compared with anticipated ones. It always seems easier to pay tomorrow rather than today—thus the success of credit cards, thus the failures of preventive statecraft. There is the added probability calculus that perhaps the costs won't have to be paid, the bill won't come due, if the issue peters out or at least self-limits. But we see that the bills did come due, and when they did it was with the equivalent of exorbitant interest and late fees.

The less quantifiable aspect of costs is the credibility of major powers and international institutions. There is a point to be made that credibility is not just about resolve but also about judgment and the capacity to discern when major interests are at stake and when they are not. But so too does credibility incur costs when international actors appear to lack the judgment to discern that their interests are at stake and/or to lack the will to act when their interests are at stake.

Conflict Dynamics

The other set of reasons for the realism of preventive statecraft concerns the dynamics of the conflict itself. As difficult as conflict prevention is, the onset of mass violence transforms the nature of a conflict. A Rubicon is crossed, on the other side of which resolution and even limitation of the conflict become much more difficult.

A former Croatian militiaman who later turned himself in reflected on his own killing of seventy-two civilians and command of a death camp. "The most difficult thing is to ignite a house or kill a man for the first time," he stated, "but afterwards even this becomes routine."[12] The addition of revenge and retribution to other sources of tension plunges a conflict down to a fundamentally different and more difficult depth. Certain international strategies that might have been effective at lower levels of conflict are less likely to be so amid intensified violence. Preventing the spread of conflict within Bosnia never was going to be easy, but after all the killings, the rapes, and the other war crimes, the task was vastly harder.[13] So too in Rwanda, Somalia, and elsewhere where mass violence was not prevented. In contrast, a major factor in the success of preventive statecraft in Congo-Brazzaville in 1993 was that international action came relatively early, before levels of violence grew too high.

One key reason for these deteriorating dynamics lies in the "conflict constituencies" concept Menkhaus and Ortmayer develop.[14] Prevention is more difficult when the interests of major domestic actors are served more by perpetuation and intensification of the conflict than by its resolution. The capacity of leaders who see their interests well served by the conflict to expand and maintain constituencies is that much greater when they have retribution and revenge to invoke. Similarly, leaders pushing nonviolence and cooperation have a harder time maintaining support. At minimum the security dilemma gets exacerbated as more and more people feel they have little choice even from a defensive perspective but to mobilize for warfare. Moreover, the offense has the advantage as it is easier militarily to attack than to hold, feeding the incentive to act preemptively.[15] It is not a simple algorithm of the more deaths, the stronger the conflict constituencies, but the push in this direction is evident.

Another aspect is that certain international strategies that may have been effective at lower levels of conflict are less likely to be so amid intensified violence.[16] Part of this is the classic problem for statecraft that the more extensive the objectives, the greater and usually more coercive are the strategies needed to achieve them. Consistent with both Thomas Schelling's deterrence/compellence distinction and

Alexander George's work on coercive diplomacy, preventing a conflict from escalating to violence is a more limited objective than ending violence once it has begun.[17] This is a key reason why, for example, Susan Woodward concludes that certain European Community strategies "might have been very effective . . . had they been applied earlier." It is also why John Maresca argues that "the most promising opportunities for conflict resolution by the international community may occur at the very beginning of an outside intervention while it [the outside intervention] is still credible and before it bogs down." Comparable arguments are made in other cases.[18]

It is in this very crucial sense that options do *not* necessarily stay open over time, that a problem can get harder down that road to where it has been kicked, that when you wait you may end up seeing a much more difficult problem than you first saw. Other related literature shows a similar dynamic. Jacob Bercovitch and Jeffrey Langley, in their study of ninety-seven disputes of various types involving 364 separate mediation attempts, found a declining success rate for mediation as fatalities increased. David Carment shows a much greater chance for third parties to help achieve "definitive" rather than "ambiguous" outcomes to civil wars and other internal conflicts when they intervene at an early rather than a middle stage. In a later and larger study on ethnic conflict, Carment and Patrick James acknowledge that "while there are no guarantees that early action will be successful, the prospects for success decrease over time." David Smock, surveying a number of African cases, simply and clearly concludes that "starting early is better than starting late." Roy Licklider goes further, arguing that once civil wars get going a military victory tends to be a more stable "solution" than a negotiated settlement.[19] While each of these studies has its own way of trying to identify where the Rubicon is, as do the cases in our Carnegie study, the specifics are less important than the basic pattern of mass violence

marking a Rubicon on the other side of which resolution and even limitation of the conflict become much more difficult.

This also has implications for the important and powerful theory of "ripeness," developed by Zartman and others.[20] The central idea is that there are points in the life cycle of conflicts that are more conducive to possible resolution than others. When a situation is not "ripe," as determined in large part by the extent to which the parties to the conflict are disposed to seriously consider an agreement, international strategies have much less chance of succeeding than others. But while ripeness theory is helpful in counseling prudent assessments of when and where to engage so as not to overestimate the chances of success, it sometimes gets interpreted and applied in ways that underestimate the risks and costs of waiting. Natural processes do not work only in one direction; they can move toward ripening but also toward "rotting." The crops can be left in the fields too long as well as harvested too early; the conflict may be intervened in too early, but it also can deteriorate over time, grow worse, become too far gone.

Moreover, putting such severely shattered societies back together again is enormously difficult, hugely expensive, very risky—and, very possibly, just not possible. One of the key tenets of the argument for not acting early has been that when the time comes what is needed to be done can be done. Yet in practice the international community has discovered that ending the conflict has been one thing, putting these societies back together quite another. It is a problem, to draw again on work by Zartman, of "putting humpty-dumpty together again."[21] Even providing humanitarian aid to societies once they are war torn has been difficult and dangerous.

One of the more controversial debates in the conflict resolution literature has been over proposals for partition and mass population transfers as the optimal approach in cases of particularly deadly conflicts involving peoples deeply divided along ethnic and other lines of identity.

The rationale, as Chaim Kaufmann puts it, is that we need to acknowledge that some of the solutions to ethnic conflicts that may be desirable are "impossible," while those such as partition and mass population transfers that we reactively dismiss are the only ones that really are "possible."[22] The aim here is not to resolve this debate. But the very fact that such far-reaching proposals are on the table is further reason why prevention is so important. A world that gives up on the values of social integration and societal heterogeneity would be headed in a dangerous direction. The key is to avoid ending up in situations in which the choice is between a bad option and a worse option, especially when that which is desirable is impossible and that which is possible is not very desirable.

POLICY RECOMMENDATIONS

My intent here is to make a few key points; greater detail and argument are elaborated elsewhere.[23]

Integrating Force and Diplomacy

Other studies have provided comprehensive inventories of the range of diplomatic strategies that can be used for conflict prevention.[24] One of the points I want to emphasize is the importance of mixed strategies, combining both inducements and coercive measures, offering carrots and wielding sticks. This is never strictly a reflexive Skinnerian combination, but the general point is the need to avoid the dichotomies that so often get drawn between coercive, threat-based strategies on the one hand and positively inducing strategies of cooperation on the other. A "viable theory of deterrence," as Alexander George and Richard Smoke argued back in the 1970s in the Cold War context, requires less of an "exclusive preoccupation with threats of punishment" as the sole means for influencing an adversary's behavior, and more of "a broader theory of processes by which

nations influence each other, one that encompasses the utility of positive inducements as well as, or in lieu of, threats of negative sanctions."[25] Similarly, post–Cold War theories of cooperation that focus exclusively on positive inducements and fail to encompass the utility that threats and negative action can have on facilitating cooperation also lack the necessary complexity and dynamism.[26]

Thus, more often than not, the diplomatic components of a preventive strategy need to be backed by a credible threat of military force or other coercive strategies. As a matter of deterrence, given the purposive nature of these conflicts and the deliberate calculations made by certain parties that they can prevail militarily at acceptable cost, the credibility of the international community's threat to respond coercively is a crucial factor. As a matter of reassurance, with regard to the ways in which the parties may be driven to military action less out of strict aggression than out of the uncertainty inherent in the security dilemma and "commitment" problem, the protection that only international actors can provide is key for the parties to feel secure in restraint and agreements.

The guiding requisites for seeking this balance should be along the lines of a *fair-but-firm strategy*. On the one hand the parties to the conflict must have confidence in the fairness of international third parties, with fairness defined as a fundamental commitment to peaceful and just resolution of the conflict rather than partisanship for or sponsorship of one or the other party to the conflict. But fairness is not necessarily to be equated with impartiality if the latter is defined as strict neutrality even if one side engages in gross and wanton acts of violence or other violations of efforts to prevent the intensification or spread of the conflict. The parties to the conflict must know both that cooperation has its benefits and that those benefits will be fully equitable; the parties must also know that noncooperation has its consequences and that the international parties are prepared to enforce those consequences differentially as warranted by who does and does not do what. In this regard fairness and firmness go together symmetrically.

Macedonia is the most often cited example of a successful preventive deployment. First as a division of UNPROFOR (United Nations Protection Force, as already deployed in Croatia and Bosnia) and then with its own mandate and moniker as UNPREDEP (United Nations Preventive Deployment Force), these troops were on the ground at a very early stage in the conflict cycle. Their size and mission were limited, but their presence was felt. The Nordic countries and Canada took on the bulk of the burden for this operation, but the U.S. troops, despite being small in number and confined to low-risk duties, were disproportionately important as "a signal to all those who want to destabilize the region," as stressed by Macedonian president Kiro Gligorov.[27]

Like all cases, though, the generalizability of the Macedonia case must be conditional. Different situations always have to be assessed on whether preventive military action or the threat thereof is likely to have positive deterrence and/or reassurance effects or to exacerbate the conflict. However, the usual assumption of using force only as a last resort does need to be questioned. "Preserving force as a last resort implies a lockstep sequencing of the means to achieve foreign policy objectives," Jane Holl argues, "that is unduly inflexible and relegates the use of force to *in extremis* efforts to salvage a faltering foreign policy."[28] Force rarely, if ever, should be a first resort, but it often needs to be more of an early resort.

Any preventive military forces must be given a robust mission and appropriate training, equipment, and organization to carry out their mission. Their mandate should include the authority to use force if necessary, not just for the troops' self-protection but consistent with the objectives being pursued and the reality of the conflict. The number of troops must be sufficiently large to make this mandate credible and doable. They must be adequately armed

to fulfill their mandate. There must be a unified command. There must be effective coordination with other diplomatic and political actors and initiatives including with nongovernmental organizations (NGOs).

The characterization of many interventions undertaken in recent years as humanitarian accurately describes the consequences of the conflicts more than their causes. In April 1991, after a deadly cyclone hit Bangladesh, killing 139,000 people and causing $2 billion worth of damage to this already impoverished country, the U.S. military forces that were sent to help provide relief and reconstruction were on a genuine humanitarian mission. But the starvation in Somalia and the massive refugee flows in Rwanda, Croatia, and Bosnia and Herzegovina were all politically precipitated humanitarian crises. To be successful, and indeed to be credible, given the nature of the instability, military action needed to have been sufficiently strong and assertive in terms of the scope of the mandate authorizing military action, the size of the forces, and the rules of engagement to overcome the reluctance of the target to comply.

U.S. policy has only begun to address these issues. The Pentagon's 1997 Quadrennial Defense Review (QDR) included "smaller-scale contingency operations" (SSC) in its "full spectrum of crises." SSC were defined as "operations [that] encompass the full range of joint military operations beyond peacetime engagement but short of major theater warfare, and include: show-of-force operations, interventions, limited strikes, noncombatant evacuation operations, no-fly zone enforcement, peace enforcement, maritime sanctions enforcement, counterterrorism operations, peacekeeping, humanitarian assistance and disaster relief."[29] Follow-on Pentagon reports have built somewhat on this, but still not nearly to the extent that doctrine and strategy have been developed at the conventional and strategic levels. The new Bush administration came into office with limited interest in these issues. On the other hand, a number of defense strategists have been pushing to give greater centrality to ethnic and related conflicts in force structure planning and the setting of overall strategy.

UN capabilities tend to be better suited for genuine situations of peacekeeping—that is, when the parties have come to agreement and mostly require a third party to secure the peace they have made—than in "peace operations" when peace is still to be made. It was successes of the former type that garnered the 1988 Nobel Peace Prize for the UN peacekeeping forces (e.g., Afghanistan, Iran-Iraq war). It was failures of the latter type (e.g., the former Yugoslavia) that so decimated the UN peacekeeping reputation. The United Nations definitely can enhance its peace operations capabilities, and Secretary-General Kofi Annan has made this a high priority. The mid-2000 Report of the Panel on UN Peace Operations (the "Brahimi report") makes a number of proposals in this regard.[30] While the proposals have been well received, doubts persist about whether they will be implemented.

Regional multilateral organizations (RMOs) also are taking on increasingly important roles. This is indicative of the shifting geopolitical dynamics of the post–Cold War era by which the sources of instability tend to be more regionally rooted than globally transmitted. There also is increasing recognition of the link between regional security and the peaceful resolution of ethnic and other internal conflicts. In this general pattern we see varying manifestations, both among different RMOs—for example, the Organization for Security and Cooperation in Europe (OSCE) being more active than the Organization of African Unity (OAU) —and within an RMO—for example, the OSCE being much more successful in the Baltics and Macedonia than in Nagorno-Karabakh or Croatia and Bosnia.

When it comes to the use of force, we have such cases as NATO's role in Kosovo in particular and also in Bosnia. We also see shifts in post–Cold War NATO doctrine, explicitly recognizing that security threats are less likely to come from "calculated aggression against the territory of its Allies" than from risks of "the adverse consequences that may arise from serious economic, social and political difficulties, including ethnic rivalries and territorial disputes, which are faced by many countries in Central and Eastern Europe." Africa is the region other than Europe where there has been the most effort to develop regional capacity for preventive military intervention, especially through ECOMOG (Economic Community of West African States Cease-Fire Monitoring Group), with regional power Nigeria in the lead. Results have been mixed at best, as evidenced in Liberia, Ivory Coast, and Sierra Leone.

In sum, the difficulties in establishing the modes and mechanisms for integrating force and diplomacy must not be underestimated. But unless these difficulties can be better managed and overcome, preventive statecraft will lack the combination of inducement and coercion essential to success in most cases.

Establishing the Norm of Sovereignty as Responsibility

The importance of norms in international affairs is too often underestimated. Although they "do not determine action," as Martha Finnemore argues, they "create permissive conditions for action."[31] Norms provide an internationally recognized standard against which policies are measured and to which behavior is held. They legitimize action against states or other offenders whose actions violate that standard. Although this always has been true to some extent, it is especially true in our current era. Questions of legitimacy seem to be more prevalent than during the Cold War, when so much ultimately came down to the dynamics of superpower dominance and competition. Cold War superpower intervention exemplified what Stephen Krasner calls the "organized hypocrisy" by which powerful states have generally abided by international legal sovereignty, meaning the juridical recognition of sovereign legal status and rights for all states, but have not let this stand in the way of their practice of realpolitik.[32] In this post–Cold War era, though, being able to claim the rightness of an action is more of an issue and as such makes normative considerations not just a matter of ideals but also an increasingly important calculation for power and influence.

The crucial normative issue is the tension between conceptions of sovereignty as, on the one hand, the rights of states and, on the other hand, the responsibilities of states. The sovereignty-as-rights norm recognizes each state as having its own jurisdictional exclusivity and giving very limited and narrowly construed bases of legitimacy for some other actor, whether another state or an international institution, to seek to insert itself in the domestic affairs of a state. "No agency exists above the individual states," as Robert Art and Robert Jervis write, "with authority and power to make laws and settle disputes."[33]

Strict sovereignty-as-rights constructionists are quick to cite Article 2 (7) of the UN Charter: "Nothing contained in the present Charter shall authorize the United Nations to intervene in matters which are essentially within the domestic jurisdiction of any state." Yet numerous other portions of the UN Charter provide normative and legal basis for the individual as the "right and duty bearing unit" in international society. Article 3 affirms that "everyone has the right to life, liberty and the security of person"; Article 55 commits the United Nations to "promote . . . universal respect for, and observance of, human rights and fundamental freedoms"; Article 56 pledges all members "to take joint and separate action" toward this end. Further affirmations of the inalienability of basic human rights are ensconced in the Genocide Convention, the Universal Declaration of Human Rights, and other international covenants that make no distinction on whether the offender is a foreign invader or one's own government. Indeed UN secretary-general Kofi Annan affirms that "the [UN] Charter was issued in

the name of 'the peoples,' not the governments of the United Nations. . . . The Charter protects the sovereignty of peoples. It was never meant as a license for governments to trample on human rights and human dignity. Sovereignty implies responsibility, not just power."[34] Annan goes on to stress the legitimacy of interventions based on the Chapter VII provision for preserving international peace and security even when the locus of the conflict is intrastate. Even Article 2 (7) is qualified with "the important rider that this principle shall not prejudice the application of enforcement measures under Chapter VII." In other words, even national sovereignty can be set aside if it stands in the way of the Security Council's overriding duty to preserve international peace and security.[35]

Francis Deng, Bill Zartman, Don Rothchild, and colleagues present the conception of responsible sovereignty as states "at the very least ensuring a certain level of protection for and providing the basic needs of the people."[36] Neither Deng et al., nor Secretary-General Annan, nor others are necessarily arguing for international trusteeships, protectorates, or other such extreme measures. The concept of sovereignty, as James Rosenau argues, allows for gradations, conditionalities, and other combinations.[37] Moreover, any abridgments on state sovereignty would need to avoid becoming guises for power politics and maintain the utmost consistency with their normative bases. But the key point is that the scope of a state's right to sovereign authority is not unconditional or normatively superior to the right to security of the polity.

To the extent that the norm of sovereignty as responsibility is recognized, the question remains of who can claim legitimacy to intervene, especially militarily. Secretary-General Annan has been careful to link his support for the sovereignty-as-responsibility norm to the role of the United Nations as the principal if not exclusive international actor to claim legitimacy for such interventions. In criticizing the U.S.-NATO action in Kosovo, he strongly asserted his view that the UN Security Council is "the sole source of legitimacy on the use of force." Yet he also acknowledged the failings of the Security Council to act as it should have in this crisis, noting that it failed to "unite around the aim of confronting massive human rights violations and crimes against humanity on the scale of Kosovo" and as such was risking "betray[ing] the very ideals that inspired the founding of the United Nations."[38] The two aspects of this statement bring out both the strength and the weakness of answering "the United Nations and only the United Nations" to the question of who can intervene.

As the world's only multilaterally universal political body, the United Nations possesses a unique role in providing collective legitimization. No other body or international actor can claim comparable legitimacy for establishing global norms and for authorizing action in its name. Yet by its very nature the United Nations also is susceptible to being unable to act in ways that best serve those norms. It was not just in the Kosovo case that some UN members invoked the sovereignty-as-rights norm as the articulated basis for opposing an intrastate interventionary action when in fact this position was much more based on particularistic national interests. The unarticulated concern has been about precedents that might later be used to challenge certain of their own practices that need to be protected by claims of the sanctity of sovereignty as rights because they are profoundly inconsistent with sovereignty as responsibility. This is altogether natural positioning for any self-interested state to take, but the garb of principle needs to be stripped away, especially when the state involved is a permanent member of the Security Council with veto power.

In fact, in the 1990s interventions authorized by the Security Council have set some important precedents. For example, UNSC 688 (1991), authorizing a peacekeeping mission protecting the Kurds in northern Iraq, and the "all necessary means" authorization (1994) of

the U.S. military intervention in Haiti marked significant shifts from strict conceptions of sovereignty as states' rights. Most cases, though, have been to protect refugees and for other humanitarian purposes. Indeed the doctrines of refugee protection and other humanitarian intervention have been taking on increasing legitimacy.[39]

However, with regard to preventive statecraft, the norm remains much weaker. In cases such as the Baltics, as well as Macedonia and Congo in 1993, the international involvement was at the invitation of the host government and thus the normative constraint was more avoided than overcome. Requiring an invitation, however, also means that such an invitation often will not come, with the consequence that intrastate conflicts will be "protected" from international action. The norm of sovereignty as responsibility as it pertains to preventing intrastate violence needs to be strengthened sufficiently to legitimize early action to prevent, and not just respond to, genocides and other deadly violence and humanitarian crises.

When major powers claim intervention legitimacy, as the United States and NATO did in Kosovo, the concern is raised that normative claims are being used as guises for power politics. To be sure, we cannot go so far as to convey or imply open-ended or even overly elastic normative justification for unilateral or mini-multilateral interventions by the United States, NATO, or any other major power or powers. But we also must confront the consequences of limiting normative legitimacy only to the United Nations. Concerns about precedent and order are serious ones, but they can leave the international community unable to uphold the very norms of peace, justice, and human rights that it claims to value.

In sum, however the "who" question is worked out, given the intrastate nature in whole or in part of the vast majority of major post–Cold War conflicts, the central point is the need for a conception of sovereignty that also reflects the responsibilities that come with the rights. The scope of a state's right to sovereign authority is not unconditional or normatively superior to the right to security of the polity. Unless this conception of sovereignty as responsibility gains greater international legitimacy, international conflict prevention strategies will continue more often than not to be too little, too late.[40]

THE DILEMMA OF POLITICAL WILL: HOW FIXED, HOW FLEXIBLE THE POLITICAL CONSTRAINTS?

Almost every study of conflict prevention concludes that when all is said and done, the main obstacle is the lack of political will. As an explanatory statement this is largely true. The United States and other governments have not acted because they have not had the political will to do so. If the domestic constraints that make this so are unchangeable and fixed, then that is the end of the story. Prevention will continue to be sporadic and mostly too little, too late. There is reason to argue, though, that the domestic constraints are not necessarily all that fixed, that they have greater potential malleability than typically is presumed.

In my Peaceworks study, in which I go into greater detail, I focus especially on public opinion and its ostensible "casualty phobia."[41] Poll after poll shows the U.S. public to be much more internationalist than isolationist. This does not mean that it will support every international commitment made, but it does mean that there is a basic understanding of the need and desirability of maintaining an active role in the world. Moreover, my own studies of public opinion on the use of military force show a "pretty prudent public" that is neither gun-shy nor trigger-happy but rather makes distinctions according to the principal purposes military force is to serve and supports or opposes it accordingly.[42] The tolerance for casualties is not very high, but it is not as low as often is

assumed, especially when the Somalia political firestorm is the case from which generalizations are made. Data for Kosovo, showing a willingness to support the use of ground troops and to sustain support amid anticipated casualties, reinforce the pattern as evidenced in other cases.

A related misconception is the attribution of exaggerated power over public opinion to the "CNN effect." One of the most insightful analyses of this dynamic is Warren Strobel's article in *Managing Global Chaos*. Strobel's main point, based on the Somalia and Bosnia cases, is that while "it is true that U.S. government policies and actions regarding international conflict are subject to more open public review than previously in history. . . . When policy is well grounded, it is less likely that the media will be able to shift officials' focus. When policy is clear, reasonably constant, and well communicated, the news media follow officials rather than lead them."[43]

As for Congress, its constraints also should not be taken, as they so often are, to be so fixed as to be largely prohibitive. On issues of use of force Congress often stops short of going so far as to explicitly block the president from acting. It often criticizes the action, seeks to condition and limit it, condemns it rhetorically —but rarely does Congress go so far as to try to flatly prohibit the president from using force when he has decided to do so. Moreover, as the preceding analyses show, the underlying politics also have some play in them. This is consistent with the study by Steve Kull and Mac Destler on how Congress has been "misreading" the public in many respects on foreign policy since the end of the Cold War.[44]

CONCLUSION

One of the main reasons why leaders have been so reluctant to take on preventive statecraft is that they have held to the conventional wisdom critique of its lack of realism: that the costs to be borne and the risks to be run are too high and the interests at stake too low. In challenging this conventional wisdom and showing the realism of preventive statecraft as a strategic calculation, we address this crucial aspect of the political will question on its own terms. We also have shown that political will is not an insurmountable problem, that political constraints have a degree of malleability. This is not just inveighing against inaction on moral grounds. It is not just trying to place policy over politics. Rather, it is to argue that politics and policy are more complementary than assumed, that the reason for arguing that there can and should be political will for preventive statecraft is that political and policy interests both are better served.

All this speaks to what is possible. Whether it becomes actual requires sustained efforts both intellectual and political. As we undertake such efforts, we should bear in mind some other lessons to be learned from the early post–World War II era. When Bernard Brodie and other leading thinkers of the early Cold War period first began developing the theories on which the dominant deterrence paradigm was to be based, the basic idea was relatively simple and straightforward: Preserve the peace through fear of retaliation. That core idea was further developed, refined, elaborated, modified, adapted, extended—indeed it became a major component of an entire paradigm that dominated U.S. foreign policy and most of international affairs for a generation. So too, here in the post–Cold War era do we need to work with the core idea of preventive statecraft: Act early to stop disputes from escalating or problems from worsening. Reduce tensions that if intensified could lead to war. Deal with today's conflicts before they become tomorrow's crises. Much more development, refinement, elaboration, modification, adaptation, and extension are needed. For if we know one thing for sure, it is that the need for prevention is not going to subside any time soon.

NOTES

1. This paper is based on a project I led for the Carnegie Commission on Preventing Deadly Conflict and the resulting book I edited, *Opportunities Missed, Opportunities Seized: Preventive Diplomacy in the Post–Cold War World* (Lanham, Md.: Rowman and Littlefield, 1999). The book includes ten case studies from the 1990s: Croatia-Bosnia, Rwanda, Somalia, Nagorno-Karabakh, Chechnya, Macedonia, Congo-Brazzaville, Russia-Latvia/Estonia, Russia-Ukraine, and North Korea. These represent different types of conflicts that characterize the post–Cold War world as well as a mix of successes and failures—that is, opportunities missed and opportunities seized. Each case study was written by a noted expert. There also are chapters by Alexander George and Jane Holl on the problem of the "warning-response gap" and by this author laying out a conceptual and analytic framework and then drawing analytic conclusions and policy lessons. It is from these latter chapters that this paper is drawn.

2. For some of the definitions of preventive diplomacy, see Michael S. Lund, *Preventing Violent Conflicts: A Strategy for Preventive Diplomacy* (Washington, D.C.: United States Institute of Peace Press, 1996); and Carnegie Commission on Preventing Deadly Conflict, *Preventing Deadly Conflict* (Washington, D.C.: Carnegie Commission on Preventing Deadly Conflict, 1997).

3. Crawford Young, ed., *The Rising Tide of Cultural Pluralism: The Nation-State at Bay?* (Madison: University of Wisconsin Press, 1993); David A. Lake and Donald Rothchild, eds., "Spreading Fear: The Genesis of Transnational Ethnic Conflict," in *The International Spread of Ethnic Conflict: Fear, Diffusion, and Escalation* (Princeton, N.J.: Princeton University Press, 1998), 5–7; Harold Isaacs, *Idols of the Tribe: Group Identity and Political Change* (New York: Harper and Row, 1975); and Robert D. Kaplan, *Balkan Ghosts: A Journey through History* (New York: St. Martin's Press, 1993).

4. Chris Hedges, "War Turns Sarajevo Away from Europe," *New York Times*, July 29, 1995.

5. Michael E. Brown, "The Causes of Internal Conflict: An Overview," in *Nationalism and Ethnic Conflict*, ed. Michael E. Brown, Owen R. Cote Jr., Sean M. Lynn-Jones, and Steven E. Miller

(Cambridge, Mass.: MIT Press, 1997), 4–12. See also I. William Zartman, ed., *Collapsed States: The Disintegration and Restoration of Legitimate Authority* (Boulder, Colo.: Lynne Rienner, 1995); Michael E. Brown, ed., *Ethnic Conflict and International Security* (Princeton, N.J.: Princeton University Press, 1993); Samuel P. Huntington, *Political Order in Changing Societies* (New Haven, Conn.: Yale University Press, 1968); and Ted Robert Gurr, *Why Men Rebel* (Princeton, N.J.: Princeton University Press, 1970).

6. See also David Carment, "The Ethnic Dimension in World Politics: Theory, Policy, and Early Warning," *Third World Quarterly*, no. 4 (1994): 557.

7. See also the study convened by the Carnegie Commission, the Georgetown University Institute for the Study of Diplomacy, and the United States Army involving an international panel of senior military leaders that, while stressing the requisites such a force would have had to meet, generally concurred: Scott R. Feil, *Preventing Genocide: How the Early Use of Force Might Have Succeeded in Rwanda* (Washington, D.C.: Carnegie Commission on Preventing Deadly Conflict, 1998). See also reports on General Romeo Dallaire's testimony to the UN International Criminal Tribunal for Rwanda, such as Stephen Buckley, "Mass Slaughter Was Avoidable, General Says," *Washington Post*, February 26, 1998, A17, A22.

8. Five key methodological criteria for counterfactual analysis—specificity, minimal historical rewrite, plausible causal logic, knowability, doability—are elaborated in Jentleson, *Opportunities Missed, Opportunities Seized,* chap. 1. See also Philip E. Tetlock and Aaron Belkin, eds., *Counterfactual Thought Experiments in World Politics: Logical, Methodological, and Psychological Perspectives* (Princeton, N.J.: Princeton University Press, 1997).

9. Stuart Hill and Donald Rothchild, "The Contagion of Political Conflict in Africa and the World," *Journal of Conflict Resolution* 30 (December 1986): 716–735; Stuart Hill, Donald Rothchild, and Colin Cameron, "Tactical Information and the Diffusion of Peaceful Protests," in *International Spread of Ethnic Conflict,* ed. Lake and Rothchild, 61–88.

10. Stanley Hoffmann, "In Defense of Mother Teresa: Morality in Foreign Policy," *Foreign Affairs* 75 (March-April 1994): 172; see also Stanley Hoffmann, "The Politics and Ethics of Military Intervention," *Survival* (winter 1995-96): 29–51.

11. Michael E. Brown and Richard N. Rosecrance, eds., *The Costs of Conflict: Prevention and Cure in the Global Arena* (Lanham, Md.: Rowman and Littlefield, 1999), 225.

12. Chris Hedges, "Croatian's Confession Describes Torture and Killing on a Vast Scale," *New York Times*, September 5, 1997, A1.

13. For further discussion of this point, see Vamik Volkan, *Blood Lines: From Ethnic Pride to Ethnic Terrorism* (New York: Farrar, Straus and Giroux, 1997).

14. For another analysis of these conflict dynamics, see Stephen John Stedman, "Spoiler Problems in Peace Processes," *International Security* (fall 1997); Timur Kuran, "Ethnic Dissimilation and Its International Diffusion," and Stephen M. Saidemann, "Is Pandora's Box Half Empty or Half Full? The Limited Virulence of Secessionism and the Domestic Sources of Integration," in *International Spread of Ethnic Conflict,* ed. Lake and Rothchild.

15. Barry Posen, "Military Responses to Refugee Disasters," *International Security* 21 (summer 1996): 342–343.

16. For example, Timothy Sisk concludes that power sharing is more likely to work if it is done early in the conflict cycle than if it is done late; *Power Sharing and International Mediation in Ethnic Conflicts* (Washington, D.C.: United States Institute of Peace Press, 1996).

17. Thomas C. Schelling, *Arms and Influence* (New Haven, Conn.: Yale University Press, 1966), 69–74; Alexander L. George and William E. Simons, eds., *The Limits of Coercive Diplomacy,* 2d ed. (Boulder, Colo.: Westview Press, 1994); Alexander L. George, *Forceful Persuasion* (Washington, D.C.: United States Institute of Peace Press, 1992).

18. See the chapters by Woodward and Maresca in *Opportunities Missed, Opportunities Seized,* ed. Jentleson.

19. Jacob Bercovitch and Jeffrey Langley, "The Nature of the Dispute and the Effectiveness of International Mediation," *Journal of Conflict Resolution* 37 (1993): 670–691; David B. Carment, "The Effectiveness of Third-Party Mediation to End Civil Wars" (paper presented to the 18th World Congress of the International Political Science Association, Seoul, Korea, August 1997), 3; David B. Carment and Patrick James, eds., *Peace in the Midst of Wars: Preventing and Managing International Ethnic Conflicts* (Columbia:

University of South Carolina Press, 1998); David R. Smock, ed., *Creative Approaches to Managing Conflict in Africa: Findings from USIP-Funded Projects*, Peaceworks no. 15 (Washington, D.C.: United States Institute of Peace, 1997), 1–4; and Roy Licklider, *Stopping the Killing: How Civil Wars End* (New York: New York University Press, 1993).

20. I. William Zartman, *Ripe for Resolution: Conflict and Intervention in Africa* (New York: Oxford University Press, 1989); and Richard N. Haass, *Conflicts Unending: The United States and Regional Disputes* (New Haven, Conn.: Yale University Press, 1992).

21. I. William Zartman, "Putting Humpty-Dumpty Together Again," in *International Spread of Ethnic Conflict*, ed. Lake and Rothchild.

22. Chaim Kaufmann, "Possible and Impossible Solutions to Ethnic Civil Wars," *International Security* 20 (spring 1996): 136–175.

23. Jentleson, *Opportunities Missed, Opportunities Seized;* Bruce W. Jentleson, *Coercive Prevention: Normative, Political, and Policy Dilemmas*, Peaceworks no. 35 (Washington, D.C.: United States Institute of Peace Press, 2000); and Bruce W. Jentleson, "How to Intervene: Challenges for Ethnic Conflict Deterrence and Humanitarian Interventions" (paper presented at the conference "Military Intervention: Issues for the Next Presidential Administration," Bush School for Government and Public Service, Texas A&M University, College Station, Tex., November 30–December 1, 2000).

24. Lund, *Preventing Violent Conflicts;* and Carnegie Commission, *Preventing Deadly Conflict.*

25. Alexander George and Richard Smoke, "Deterrence and Foreign Policy," *World Politics* 41 (January 1989): 182; and their award-winning study *Deterrence in American Foreign Policy: Theory and Practice* (New York: Columbia University Press, 1974), esp. chap. 21.

26. For a similar argument, see Bruce W. Jentleson, *With Friends Like These: Reagan, Bush, and Saddam, 1982–1990* (New York: W. W. Norton, 1994), esp. chap. 5.

27. Michael G. Roskin, "Macedonia and Albania: The Missing Alliance," *Parameters* (winter 1993-94): 98; Carnegie Commission on Preventing Deadly Conflict, *Final Report* (Washington, D.C.: Carnegie Commission on Preventing Deadly Conflict, 1997), 64.

28. Jane E. Holl, "We the People Here Don't Want No War: Executive Branch Perspectives on the Use of Force," in Aspen Strategy Group, *The United States and the Use of Force in the Post-Cold War Era* (Washington, D.C.: Aspen Institute, 1995), 124 and passim.

29. U.S. Department of Defense, *Quadrennial Defense Review*, 1997, http://www.defenselink.mil:80/pubs/qdr/sec3.html, 6.

30. United Nations, *Report of the Panel on United Nations Peace Operations*, August 2000, http://www.un.org/peace/reports/peace_operations/docs/recommend.htm.

31. Martha Finnemore, "Constructing Norms of Humanitarian Intervention," in *The Culture of National Security*, ed. Peter J. Katzenstein (New York: Columbia University Press), 158. See also Martha Finnemore, *National Interests in International Society* (Ithaca, N.Y.: Cornell University Press, 1996).

32. Stephen D. Krasner, *Sovereignty: Organized Hypocrisy* (Princeton, N.J.: Princeton University Press, 1999).

33. Robert J. Art and Robert Jervis, *International Politics: Enduring Concepts and Contemporary Issues* (New York: HarperCollins, 1992), 2.

34. Kofi Annan, "Intervention," Ditchley Foundation Lecture 35, 1998, 2. See also Kofi Annan, *Report of the Secretary-General on the Work of the Organization*, United Nations General Assembly, Official Records, Fifty-Fourth Session, supplement no. 1 (A/54/1), September 1999.

35. Ibid.

36. Francis M. Deng et al., *Sovereignty as Responsibility: Conflict Management in Africa* (Washington, D.C.: Brookings Institution, 1998), 28.

37. James N. Rosenau, "Sovereignty in a Turbulent World," in *Beyond Westphalia: State Sovereignty and International Intervention*, ed. Gene M. Lyons and Michael Mastanduno (Baltimore: Johns Hopkins University Press, 1995), 195.

38. "Secretary-General Says Renewal of Effectiveness and Relevance of Security Council Must Be Cornerstone of Efforts to Promote International Peace in Next Century," United Nations Press Release SG/SM/6997, May 18, 1999.

39. See, for example, Jarat Chopra and Thomas G. Weiss, "Sovereignty Is No Longer Sacrosanct: Codifying Humanitarian Intervention," *Ethics and International Affairs* 6 (1992): 95–117.

40. For views that concur on some points with my discussion here and disagree on others, see the papers from the Pugwash Study Group on Intervention, Sovereignty and International Security (Pugwash Meeting no. 252, December 1999), available at http://www.pugwash.org.

41. Jentleson, *Coercive Prevention.*

42. Bruce W. Jentleson and Rebecca Britton, "Still Pretty Prudent: Post–Cold War American Public Opinion on the Use of Military Force," *Journal of Conflict Resolution* 42 (August 1998): 395–417; and Bruce W. Jentleson, "The Pretty Prudent Public: Post Post-Vietnam American Opinion on the Use of Military Force," *International Studies Quarterly* 36 (March 1992): 49–74.

43. Warren P. Strobel, "The Media and U.S. Policies toward Intervention: A Closer Look at the 'CNN Effect,'" in *Managing Global Chaos: Sources of and Responses to International Conflict,* ed. Chester A. Crocker and Fen Osler Hampson with Pamela Aall (Washington, D.C.: United States Institute of Peace Press, 1996), 358, 374. A revised version appears as chapter 40 in this volume.

44. Steven Kull and I. M. Destler, *Misreading the Public: The Myth of a New Isolationism* (Washington, D.C.: Brookings Institution Press, 1999).

16

The Curse of Inconclusive Intervention

Edward N. Luttwak

WAR IS THE GREAT EVIL, but it does have a great virtue: unlike poverty, for example, it is not self-perpetuating, but is, on the contrary, self-destroying. By consuming and destroying the material and moral resources needed to keep fighting, war itself prevents its own continuation. Moreover, as with any other phenomenon within the paradoxical realm of strategy, war must eventually turn into its opposite after exceeding its culminating point of maximum destruction. That is why, absent compelling reasons, wars should not be interrupted by outsiders, blocking their process of transformation. True, the opposite of war may only be a becalmed passivity, not more than an unrecognized state of nonwar rather than a negotiated peace, an armistice, or even a temporary cease-fire. And whatever nonwar it is, that result may not be reached for a very long time, because the speed with which war destroys itself obviously depends on its intensity and scale.

In many civil wars, the intensity of the fighting is low or else its scale is limited, with the violence mostly confined to specific areas within a wider environment that the fighting might affect only marginally, if at all. The power that controls the unaffected areas can therefore continue to extract human and material resources to keep fighting indefinitely.

In Sri Lanka, for example, an especially violent separatist war focused on the Jaffna peninsula has afflicted the northern part of the island, while the central and southern parts of the country have remained largely unaffected, except for spectacular but very sporadic terrorist attacks; in most years, foreign tourists have continued to frequent tranquil southern beaches. Sri Lankan governments have therefore been able to continue fighting with their own resources against Tamil separatists sustained by contributions from the Tamil diaspora and from India's Tamil Nadu across the water.

In Sudan, likewise, the fighting has been limited to the south; it has mostly been of very low intensity and also seasonal, with the government's dry-season offensives followed by rainy-season retreats. Sudanese governments have therefore been able to use unaffected northern resources to continue fighting in the south, while the separatists have sustained their own very limited combat operations with the meager external aid they have received.

Elsewhere in Africa, notably in Angola, Congo (formerly Zaire), Liberia, and Sierra Leone, internal wars have been widely destructive of civilian infrastructures and civilian lives *without* thereby extinguishing themselves. There are two ready explanations for these apparent deviations from the rule.

First, while there has been much looting, destruction, and violence perpetrated against unarmed civilians incapable of defending themselves, there has been in toto very little combat, that is, two-sided fighting by armed elements. Normally, if one side advances after building up its strength, the other side runs away—if there is no flight, there is no advance. Artillery —the great killer in most wars—is rarely present and more rarely employed because logistic resupply is scant or nonexistent. Even the use of small arms is usually very restricted, because armed groups mostly depend on the ammunition they can carry on their backs, or on meager in-unit transport. Moreover, such shooting and occasional artillery shelling as take place tend to be mostly in the form of unaimed fires, which cause very few casualties on either side, though they often harm civilian lives and property in between. In other words, armed Africans rarely kill each other, so that the war-terminating phenomenon of combat attrition is mostly absent.

Second, the wars of sub-Saharan Africa have not been supplied by the generic economic production of civil societies that generic wartime destruction diminishes pro rata, but rather by revenues obtained from foreign purchases of oil, gold, and diamonds. All three are typically extracted by totally self-contained operations unaffected by the destruction of power supplies, communications, and transport infrastructures. Any party that controls and can protect such revenue flows can continue fighting indefinitely, even if the country as a whole is reduced to utter ruin—and that is exactly what all parties have been doing in these African civil wars. In that regard, the logic of strategy asserts itself as an almost physical process. Had World War II been fought only by fits and starts during dry seasons, only in secondary theaters far from Germany or Japan, and only by troops mostly unwilling to fight each other, it too would continue still.

War can become the origin of peace by the total victory of one side or another, by the sheer exhaustion of all sides, or—more often —because the conflict of aims that originally caused the war is resolved by the political transformations that war itself brings about. As the fighting continues, the worth of whatever was to be gained or defended is reconsidered against its costs in blood, treasure, and agony, eventually diminishing or nullifying the ambitions that motivated war in the first place.

That is not, however, a straightforward process, because the political commitment to go to war is self-strengthening. Having started the fight hoping to gain something of value at acceptable cost, the attacker who collides with unexpectedly strong resistance might persist even if his gains cannot possibly compensate for what he has already lost in blood, treasure, tranquillity, and prestige. Having started to fight by another's choice, the defender will also have framed some initial purpose for his resistance—a purpose deemed worthy of sacrifice, before the full extent of that sacrifice could be known. Even when the original hopes of attack or defense are disappointed, as so often happens, success may yet seem tantalizingly near, perhaps to be won with just one more fight, a few more casualties, a little more wealth expended after so many casualties suffered and after so much wealth consumed (the asymmetrical position of those who face the loss of everything in defeat obviously strengthens their resistance). It may have been the prospect of gaining much for little that originally made war attractive. But if the costs of war are unexpectedly large, their very magnitude will be an incentive to persist during an intermediate stage: the greater the sacrifice already made, the greater the need to justify it by finally achieving the aim.

During that stage, the behavior of belligerents is conditioned by the political stance of the original war party or war leaders, whose fortunes will depend on how their past responsibility for having started the war is viewed—which in turn depends on the present view of the future outcome. The incentive to sustain the *hope* of victory is then very strong.

But as the war continues, perspectives eventually shift. The results originally hoped for are increasingly compared not with the sacrifices already made, but rather with the further sacrifices that seem likely if the fighting does not end. Even if the original war party or war leaders remain in power, their ambitions can then be diminished or even extinguished, to the point where they may give up all hope of gain, being content to moderate their loss. As that process unfolds, hostilities can eventually come to an end as the aims of each side become congruent instead of being mutually exclusive. Even the Pacific war, a most peculiar struggle between Japanese aggressors with large but defined aims and their erstwhile American victims at Pearl Harbor and in the Philippines who demanded all—unconditional surrender —came to an end only when the Americans tacitly accepted the Japanese demand for the continuity of the imperial institution.

War fully achieved, with forces fought out and every promising expedient tried, with much destruction suffered and inflicted, with hopes of greater success finally spent, may lead to a peace that *can* be stable and lasting. But if war is interrupted before its self-destruction is achieved, no peace need ensue at all. So it was in Europe's past when wars were still fought intermittently during spring and summer campaigning seasons, each time coming to an end with the arrival of winter—only to resume afresh in the spring. And so it has been again ever since the establishment of the United Nations and the formalization of great-power politics in its Security Council.

Since 1945 wars among lesser powers have rarely been allowed to follow their natural course. Instead, they have typically been interrupted very early, long before they could exhaust and destroy the energies of war to establish the preconditions of peace.

It has become the fixed routine of the permanent members of the UN Security Council to abruptly stop the combat of lesser powers by ordering cease-fires. Unless further diplomatic interventions directly ensue to impose peace negotiations as well, cease-fires merely relieve war-induced exhaustion, favoring the reconstitution and rearming of the belligerents, thus intensifying and prolonging the fighting once the cease-fire comes to an end. That was true, for example, of the Arab-Israeli war of 1948–49, which might have ended in a matter of weeks by sheer exhaustion, if two successive cease-fires ordained by the UN Security Council had not allowed the belligerents to recuperate until they were ready to resume fighting. It was so again after the disintegration of Yugoslavia in 1991. Dozens of imposed UN cease-fires interrupted the fighting between Serbs and Croats in the Krajina borderlands, between the forces of the Serb-Montenegrin federation and the Croat army, and among the Serbs, Croats, and Muslims of Bosnia. Each time, the belligerents exploited the pause to recruit, train, and equip additional forces for further combat. Indeed, it was under the protection of successive cease-fires that both the Croats and the Bosnian Muslims were able to build up their own armed forces to confront the well-armed Serbs. That is an outcome that many may have found desirable, but the overall effect was to greatly prolong the war and widen the scope of its killings, atrocities, and destructions.

It has also become routine to interrupt wars in more lasting fashion by imposing armistices. Again, unless directly followed by successful peace negotiations, armistices perpetuate the state of war indefinitely because they shield the weaker side from the consequences of refusing the concessions needed for peace. Fearing no further defeats or territorial losses behind the indirect protection of the great powers that guarantee the armistice, the losing side can deny peace to the winning side and even attack its lands in deniable ways by infiltrating raiders and guerrillas. An armistice is not therefore half a peace or a halfway station to peace, but merely a frozen war. Armistices therefore provide the strongest possible incentive to prolong competitive arms races indefinitely, as in the case of India and Pakistan and of the two Koreas.

Nevertheless, as long as the Cold War persisted, cease-fires and armistices imposed by the United States and the Soviet Union acting in concert had a compelling justification. At a time when both were greatly inclined to intervene in the wars of lesser powers to avert the defeat of their respective clients, U.S. and Soviet leaders prudently preferred to act jointly to stop the fighting in many cases. That made competitive interventions unnecessary, avoiding the eventual danger of a direct clash between U.S. and Soviet forces that could escalate to the nuclear level. While the imposed cease-fires of the Cold War years ultimately increased the sum total of warfare among the lesser powers themselves, and armistices did perpetuate the state of war among them, both were clearly the lesser evil from a global point of view, as compared with the possibility of a catastrophic Soviet-U.S. war caused by reciprocal interventions.

By contrast, after the Cold War neither the United States nor the Russian Federation had any inclination to intervene *competitively* in the wars of lesser powers. The United States acted with many allies to reverse Iraq's conquest of Kuwait of August 1990. The Russian Federation for its part has sent combat forces as well as weapons in support of one side or the other in Caucasian and Central Asian wars and insurgencies. Neither, however, has acted

specifically to thwart the other, and neither now seems ready to contemplate armed interventions against the other. And the same is true of such other great powers as can still be said to exist. It follows that the evil consequences of interrupting war still persist in full, while no greater danger is being averted.

In the absence of anything resembling a classic great-power competition, cease-fires and armistices are now generally imposed on lesser powers multilaterally, for essentially disinterested motives—often indeed for no better reason than assuaging the revulsion of television audiences exposed to harrowing scenes of war. Of course, the result is to ensure that there will be many more such scenes.

It is well known that disinterested behavior, not guided by self-interested calculations, randomizes outcomes. What is now happening, however, is typically much worse than a scattering of random outcomes, because cease-fires and armistices imposed on warring lesser powers *systematically* prevent the transformation of war into peace. The Dayton accords of November 1995 are typical of the kind: they condemn Bosnia to remain divided into three rival armed camps, with combat suspended among the Croats, Muslims, and Serbs, but with the state of war indefinitely prolonged. Because no side is threatened by defeat and loss, no side has a sufficient incentive to negotiate peace; because no path to peace is even visible, the dominant priority is to prepare for another war rather than to reconstruct devastated economies and ravaged societies. The outcome of uninterrupted war would certainly have been unjust from one perspective or another but would eventually have imposed some sort of peace, allowing people to rebuild their lives and communities.

In addition to the United Nations, there is now a proliferation of multilateral organizations that make it their business to intervene in other people's wars. Their common inherent characteristic is that they insert themselves in war situations while refusing to engage in combat. That greatly adds to the damage.

It is certainly the absolute priority of UN "peacekeeping" contingents to avoid casualties to their own personnel. Their unit commanders therefore habitually appease the *locally* stronger belligerent, accepting its dictates, tolerating its abuses. If the totality of UN peacekeeping forces in a given context would appease the stronger side, for example, the Bosnian Serbs in the early stages of the Bosnia fighting, the result could be very conducive to peace. For in that case, the UN presence would actually enhance the peacemaking potential of war by helping the strong to defeat the weak that much faster and more decisively. Unfortunately, the appeasement that is inevitable when forces that do not want to fight are thrust into war situations is neither homogeneous nor strategically purposeful. Instead, it merely reflects the determination of each UN contingent to avoid confrontations and casualties to itself. As each unit appeases the locally stronger side, the overall result is to prevent the emergence of any coherent *im*balance of strength capable of ending the fighting.

Nor can UN contingents whose absolute priority is to avoid combat protect civilians caught up in the fighting or deliberately attacked. UN peacekeeping forces have been passive spectators of violence against civilians and even outright massacre, as in Rwanda and Bosnia. Sometimes their presence is worse than useless in protecting civilians: in the Srebrenica enclave in July 1995, the Dutch contingent not only failed to fight to protect the civilians in their care as military honor would have required, but also unwittingly assisted in subsequent massacre by helping the Bosnian Serbs to separate the men of military age—very broadly defined—from women and children. Almost all the men were promptly murdered.

At the same time, the very presence of UN forces inhibits the normal remedy of endangered civilians, which is to escape from the combat zone. Deluded into thinking that they will be protected, civilians in danger remain in place until it is too late to flee. Moreover,

prospective host countries deny war refugee status to civilians coming from areas where UN troops are supposedly keeping the peace—even though they are entirely failing to shield civilians under attack. In the specific case of the siege of Sarajevo in 1992–94, appeasement interacted with the pretense of protection in an especially perverse way: UN personnel strictly inspected outgoing flights to prevent the escape of Sarajevo civilians in obedience to a cease-fire agreement negotiated with the locally dominant Bosnian Serbs, who habitually violated that cease-fire.

Multilateral institutions such as the European Union, the former Western European Union, and the Organization of Security and Cooperation in Europe lack even the United Nations' rudimentary command structure and have no assigned, let alone organic, military forces of their own. Yet they too now seek to intervene in warlike situations, with predictable consequences. Bereft of forces even theoretically capable of combat, they satisfy interventionist urges mandated by member-states, or even motivated by their own institutional ambitions, by sending lightly armed or unarmed policemen, gendarmes, or simply "observers." All of the latter must necessarily act as UN peacekeeping troops habitually do, only more so, by accommodating the wishes of the locally stronger side. And of course they cannot even try to protect endangered civilians, while their presence again inhibits the private remedy of flight.

Warlike organizations such as NATO and the ECOWAS Cease-Fire Monitoring Group (ECOMOG), which presided over the chaos of Liberia and Sierra Leone, are theoretically capable of stopping wars. Their interventions too must have destructive consequences by prolonging the state of war but should at least be able to protect civilians from the consequences of the wars they are prolonging. Even that fails to happen, however. National forces engaged in multinational interventions avoid combat risks at all costs, and not much can be done to protect civilians without acceptance of some combat risks. That is true of African and most other Third World forces, whose assignment to the United Nations is largely a matter of gaining very generous monetary compensation for poorly armed, poorly trained, and poorly paid soldiers (who often recoup themselves by looting, collecting bribes, and black-market trafficking). But it is also true of the best-trained and best-paid forces of the most ambitious armies. When U.S. troops arrived in Bosnia in the wake of the 1995 Dayton accords, they were under strict orders to avoid armed clashes, and it was under those orders that they failed to arrest known war criminals passing through their checkpoints. In Kosovo, too, U.S. generals have made sure that U.S. soldiers would not be placed in harm's way. The chairman of the U.S. Joint Chiefs of Staff, General Henry H. Shelton, intervened before the Kosovo war to ensure that U.S. troops would not be endangered by ground combat, during the war to ensure that forty-eight Apache helicopter aircrew would not be endangered by flying combat missions, and after the war to ensure that U.S. troops would not be endangered by actually patrolling their sector.

More broadly, because no differences in troop performance can be admitted, multinational commands are institutionally incapable of exercising quality control over the troops offered by member-states, and neither can they impose uniform standards of tactical or ethical conduct. Deliberately risk-minimizing strategies aside, the conjoined deployment of both potentially combat-capable and hopelessly ineffectual troops tends to reduce the performance of all troops involved to the lowest common denominator. That was true even of otherwise fine British troops in Bosnia before 1995, and of the otherwise vigorous Nigerian marines in Sierra Leone. Soon even quasi-elite troops adopt passive self-protective tactics that prevent them from actually keeping the peace or protecting civilians.

The phenomenon of "multinationally induced troop degradation" can rarely be documented as such, though its consequences have been abundantly visible in the litter of the dead, mutilated, raped, and tortured that attends UN interventions. But sometimes the true state of affairs is powerfully illuminated by the rare exception, such as the vigorous Danish tank company in Bosnia that promptly replied to each episode of firing against it in 1993–94, quickly stopping all attacks against it. If the pattern of degradation into ineffectual passivity were not so normal, such a case of combat troops acting as combat troops would not have attracted attention. The record of the ECOMOG troops in Sierra Leone has by contrast included over the years frequent routs at the hands of small bands of rebel child soldiers, many episodes of organized looting directed by unit commanders themselves, countless rapes, and some summary executions.

The most disinterested of all interventions in other people's wars are humanitarian relief activities. They are also the most destructive.

The largest and most protracted, and still continuing, humanitarian intervention in all of human history is the United Nations Relief and Works Agency (UNRWA). On the model of its predecessor, the United Nations Relief and Rehabilitation Agency (UNRRA), which was then still operating displaced persons' camps in Europe, UNRWA was originally established during the 1948–49 Arab-Israeli war to feed, shelter, educate, and provide health services to Arab refugees who had fled from Israeli zones in the former territory of Palestine to other parts of Palestine under Egyptian or Jordanian control, to the Gaza Strip and the West Bank, or to Lebanon, Syria, and Trans-Jordan, as it then was.

By keeping refugees alive in Spartan conditions that encouraged their rapid emigration or local resettlement, UNRRA's camps in Europe served to absorb postwar resentments. By policy, nationalities were mixed, to prevent the emergence of groups bent on revenge under wartime leaders, many of them inevitably ex-collaborators with the Germans. UNRWA camps, however, provided a higher standard of living than most Arab villagers had previously enjoyed, with an assured and more varied diet, organized schooling, infinitely superior medical care, and no backbreaking labor in stony fields. As a result, they instantly became desirable homes rather than eagerly abandoned transit camps. They thus turned escaping civilians into lifelong refugees who gave birth to refugee children who grew up in turn to have refugee children of their own.

During more than a half century of its operation to date, UNRWA has thus perpetuated a Palestinian refugee nation, perfectly preserving its resentments in as fresh a condition as in 1948, keeping the first bloom of vengeful emotions intact. The young were not allowed to find their own way to new lives; instead they were kept under the control of their defeated elders, to be taught their duties of revenge and reconquest in UNRWA-financed schools from the earliest childhood. By its very existence, UNRWA dissuades integration into local societies and inhibits emigration, but in addition, the mere concentration of Palestinians in the camps has always facilitated the voluntary or forced enlistment of refugee youths by armed organizations that have fought both Israel and one another. In these different ways, UNWRA has greatly contributed to half a century of Arab-Israeli violence and still now powerfully retards the advent of peace.

Had each European war been attended by its own postwar UNRWA, equipped to provide a higher standard of living than the ambient, today's Europe would be filled with giant camps for tens of millions of descendants of uprooted Gallo Romans, abandoned Vandals, defeated Burgundians, and misplaced Visigoths —not to speak of more recent refugee nations such as post-1945 Sudeten Germans. Europe would have remained a purely geographic expression, a mosaic of warring tribes undigested and unreconciled in their separate feeding camps. And the number of unresolved conflicts would roughly correspond to the total number of wars ever fought.

UNRWA is not unique, having had various counterparts elsewhere, such as the Cambodian refugee camps along the Thai border that incidentally provided safe bases for the mass-murdering Khmer Rouge. But because UN activities are mercifully limited by ungenerous national contributions to its treasury, their sabotage of peace is at least localized. That is not true of the proliferation of feverishly competitive nongovernmental organizations (NGOs) that nowadays seek war refugees to help. The absolute, existential priority of NGOs is to keep attracting charitable contributions. Their principal means of doing so is to be seen to be as active as possible in high-visibility situations. Only the most dramatic natural disasters attract any significant mass-media attention, and that too only briefly. After an earthquake or flood, the cameras soon depart to record the next disaster. War refugees, by contrast, can attract sustained mass-media attention if kept conveniently concentrated in reasonably accessible camps. Because regular forms of warfare among well-organized belligerents in more developed areas offer very few opportunities for NGOs, they naturally focus their efforts elsewhere, aiding war refugees in the poorest parts of the world, especially in Africa. That more or less ensures that the feeding, shelter, and health care offered, while perhaps abysmal by global standards, are sufficient to keep refugees in place perpetually. The consequences are entirely predictable. Among many lesser examples, the huge refugee camps established along the Congo/Zaire border with Rwanda in the wake of the 1994 genocide of Tutsis by the Hutus, which was followed by the Tutsi conquest of Rwanda, stand out as a particularly egregious case. NGOs that answer to no authority sustained a Hutu nation in exile that would otherwise have dispersed to find a myriad of private destinies in the vastness of Zaire. The presence of a million or so Hutus still under their genocidal leaders made the consolidation of Rwanda impossible. Armed Hutu activists, fed by NGOs along with everyone else, kept the other refugees under oppressive control, enlisting, training, and arming their young to continually raid across the Rwanda border to kill more Tutsis.

To keep refugee nations in existence forever, to fuel unending conflict by artificially preserved resentments, is bad enough. But to insert material aid into combat situations is even worse. Many NGOs that operate in an odor of sanctity routinely supply the logistics of war. Themselves defenseless, they cannot exclude active warriors from their feeding stations, clinics, and such shelter as they provide. Refugees are presumptively on the losing side, the warriors among them in retreat. By intervening to help them, NGOs systematically impede the progress of their enemies toward a decisive victory that can bring war to an end. Impartial to a fault, NGOs sometimes help both sides, thus also sabotaging the transformation of war into peace by mutual exhaustion.

When especially threatened, moreover, as in Somalia through the 1990s but less visibly in other places too, NGOs purchase security from local war bands, often the very same bands that threaten them. No recondite strategic calculation is needed to uncover the result: unless the totality of their payments is insignificantly small—definitely not true of Somalia—NGOs themselves prolong the warfare whose consequences they seek to mitigate.

Almost all wars nowadays become endemic conflicts that never end because the transformative effects of both decisive victories and exhaustion are blocked by outside interventions of one kind or another. Thus the evils of war persist, but without eventually compelling peace.

That the paradoxical logic of strategy cannot exceed its limits is no excuse for the current practice of systematically sabotaging war's peacemaking potential by outside interventions that are disinterested and therefore both arbitrary and usually inconclusive. Nor is it an excuse for UN and NGO refugee assistance by permanent encampment, instead of immediate humanitarian relief followed by natural dispersion when quick repatriation is impossible. That guarantees the perpetuation of refugee polities whose only possible ideology is revanchist, which in turn guarantees perpetual war—as in Rwanda's case of late. Again, had the United Nations and today's plague of irresponsible, self-seeking NGOs existed in Europe's past, the continent would contain no stable states but only vast camps of unreconciled refugee nations, still battling their ancient enemies.

17

The Debate about Intervention

Stanley Hoffmann

THE TRAGIC SERIES of disintegrating states racked by ethnic conflicts, sectarian quarrels, gang warfare, or huge human rights violations has, in the past decade, replaced the more traditional interstate Cold War as the most salient aspect of the "diplomatic-strategic" arena of international relations. I have reviewed elsewhere the political and ethical issues raised by humanitarian interventions, especially those of a collective nature, and I have in particular examined the Yugoslav conflicts.[1] My purpose here is to reflect on the arguments for and against such interventions, which have multiplied over the years. After a brief review of the opinions of theorists, I will first examine the arguments that defend them and then turn to the criticisms of intervention, before concluding in favor of the former despite the strength of the critics' points.

TRADITIONAL VIEWS OF INTERVENTION

It is often useful to return to the pronouncements of political philosophers about issues that recurrently plague statesmen and affect ordinary citizens. However, on our subject the wisdom of the theorists tends to fall short. Realists, as analysts, look at interventions, unilateral or collective, as ordinary manifestations of power in an anarchic milieu; normatively, they do not go much beyond advocating prudence and moderation. Neorealism focuses on the determining role of the international system's structure; as most of the internal conflicts take place in states of limited importance, or else in states of sufficient power to deter outside interventions, these conflicts are not deemed significant enough to affect the structure; as for collective interventions, they are seen as little more than fleeting coalitions of powers rather than as manifestations of any autonomous role of international institutions.[2] The policy advice that follows from this is for states to avoid interventions unless vital issues of state security and survival are at stake for them in an internal crisis elsewhere.

Liberal political philosophy has had to deal more forthrightly with foreign military interventions. It has been caught between the different implications of two related conceptions.

One was its vision of a more harmonious world in which representative regimes running states with powers sharply limited by national and transnational civil society would have fewer reasons to fight and compelling reasons to settle conflicts peacefully. Liberalism also stated its conviction that such a world could come into existence only if nondemocratic regimes were displaced and replaced by democratic ones. The vision entailed a defense of state sovereignty and a condemnation of outside interventions, especially if they use force. The conviction suggested that achieving the vision might require such interventions against obnoxious regimes—both when they commit aggression against neighbors (hence the theory of collective security) and when they massacre or oppress their people.

Immanuel Kant came down on the side of nonintervention "in the constitution and government of another state." The exception he mentions—the case of a state "split into two parts" by dissension between two sides "which, while constituting a separate state," "lay claim to the whole"—turns out not to be really an exception, because "as long as this inner strife was not decided, the interference of outside powers would be a trespass on the rights of an independent people struggling only with its inner weakness," "an actual offense which would tend to render the autonomy of all states insecure."[3]

John Stuart Mill's position was more complex and elaborate but not as profoundly different from Kant's as one might think. He justifies forcible intervention in two cases. One is "the case in which one of the parties is of a high and the other of a very low grade of social improvement," for the same international customs and rules of international morality that exist between civilized nations do not exist "between civilized nations and barbarians." (Liberalism and imperialism were thus seen as perfectly compatible.) The other case, among civilized states, is that of "a people struggling against a foreign yoke, or against a native tyranny upheld by foreign arms." Thus, outside intervention by force is admissible on behalf of self-

determination—but not for self-government: intervention to help a people set up free institutions (rather than its own state) is rejected because it cannot be proven that "it would be for the good of the people themselves."[4] In contemporary terms, this would mean Bosnia, Kosovo, and East Timor, yes; Haiti, Somalia, and Rwanda, no.

Michael Walzer, a century later, adopted Mill's distinction and encased it, so to speak, in his "legalist paradigm"—his conception of "an international society of independent states" endowed with "the rights of territorial integrity and political sovereignty." In this society "only aggression can justify war," but helping a nation secede and obtain, through self-determination, its own independent state is legitimate; intervention in a civil war whose stake is the control of the central government is not, because each nation has a right to resolve the problem of who should govern it by itself, without outside interference. However, Walzer added to the short list of justified military interventions humanitarian ones, when they are "a response (with reasonable expectation of success) to acts that shock the moral conscience of mankind," because "government armies engaged in massacres are readily identified as criminal" (his example is Pakistan in what was to become Bangladesh).[5]

Most recently, John Rawls's *Law of Peoples* exemplifies another liberal tension—this time between the notion of a society of "peoples" bound by a series of principles that are those of modern interstate law (so that they are divided into two categories: decent peoples, democratic and "hierarchical," who respect those norms, and "outlaw states" that do not) and the more contemporary international law that grants certain rights (and obligations) directly to individuals. Rawls resolves this tension by including in his list of principles to be observed by "peoples" the respect of human rights. This allows him to qualify his principle number four—"peoples are to observe a duty of nonintervention"—in the case of "outlaw states" that commit "grave violations of human rights." What is striking in Rawls's conception is that he moves away both from the rigid distinction between self-determination and self-government Mill and Walzer advocated and from the tight embrace of the former. "No people has a right of self-determination, or a right to secession, at the expense of subjugating another people"; conversely, coercive interventions are allowed in "grave cases," when "domestic institutions violate human rights" or "limit the rights of minorities living among them." The question left open is how to bring outlaw states to honor the law of peoples in cases other than the "grave violations of human rights" that justify intervention. Rawls tells us that it is a question of foreign policy, political wisdom—and luck; he suggests economic and diplomatic pressures depending on "a political assessment of the likely consequences of various policies."[6] The shift from a license for intervention in defense of national self-determination to a justification for intervention in defense of human rights is part of the gradual shift from a liberalism of nation-states endowed by international law with rights and duties to a liberalism of rights and duties for both states and individuals, the rights of the states—including the right to sovereignty—being increasingly subordinated to their respect and promotion of the rights of the individuals.

COLLECTIVE, FORCIBLE INTERVENTIONS

We turn now to the contemporary debate and to the arguments in favor of collective, forcible interventions—or even unilateral ones in "egregious" cases (to use Rawls's adjective), when collective institutions are paralyzed or passive (we can think of India in Bangladesh or Tanzania against Idi Amin).

One argument is conspicuously absent, or subdued: it is that of the need to help national self-determination when it is being resisted.

Even in the case of East Timor, the clamor for an external military interference was based on the atrocities committed by Indonesian military and paramilitary forces after the UN-sponsored referendum on independence rather than on a duty to enforce the results of this referendum given Indonesia's noncompliance. In Kosovo the Rambouillet document promised a referendum on the status of the territory after three years, but the agreement that put an end to the war in June 1999 referred only to an ill-defined autonomy. The focus throughout was on Serb atrocities, not on Kosovar demands for independence. (This had already been the case when the Security Council ordered Saddam Hussein to stop the massacres of Kurds and Shiites—there was no promise of self-determination for the Kurds.)

The Catholic doctrine of just war has been the traditional middle ground between Christian pacifism and theories justifying holy war to propagate a faith. It has developed in the context of interstate conflicts, but we find that today most of the justifications for interventions in domestic conflicts fall in the traditional categories of the *jus ad bellum*. These deal with just causes—self-defense and the vindication of rights; proportionality of values—the values destroyed should not exceed those that are being upheld; proper authority—who can legitimately decide the resort to force; reasonable chance of success; and last resort—the exhaustion of all efforts to save peace. The causes deemed important enough to require intervention can be divided into two categories. The first is the properly humanitarian one: the disinterested duty to put an end to or to reduce human suffering. This is the argument of Joelle Tanguy, speaking as an official of Doctors Without Borders. She makes a case for impartial aid agencies providing assistance to all the victims of humanitarian disasters and against linking it to "the kind of intervention carried out by political and military bodies," which condones the use of force. The latter will add to the suffering. "Both approaches are necessary, but in order to serve their purposes, we believe that they must be carried out independently."[7] In her view, politicizing humanitarian assistance makes it the hostage of political calculations and military priorities. Interference, yes; force, no. This is, obviously, the position of an NGO.

The second category of arguments addresses the right of states to use force inside the borders of other states. Usually, the "just cause" that is invoked is the defense of human rights when there are massive violations of them—in cases of genocide, brutal ethnic cleansing, or monstrous brutalities committed by rebel or rival gangs (as in Liberia or Sierra Leone). This is both clear enough and vague enough to leave room for argument: Was the level of violence in Kosovo before March 1999 high enough to vindicate military action? Was the latter justified, rather, by the violation of past agreements Milosevic had signed and the anticipation of further ethnic cleansing?

An elegant formulation comes from Kofi Annan: The UN Charter is "a living document, whose . . . very letter and spirit are the affirmation of . . . fundamental human rights," whereas sovereignty is being "redefined by the forces of globalization and international cooperation."[8] Less diplomatically, David Luban argues that "there is nothing regrettable about violating the statist order in order to protect human rights; the justice and injustice of war should be assessed along the dimension of human rights protection, not state sovereignty protection, and the social ontology that places states above individuals is indefensible."[9]

To the argument made by realists, that the pursuit of such altruistic aims contradicts the very logic of international relations—a logic of selfishness—and that the promotion of such values is not in the nature of "the game," which aims at promoting state interests, the advocates of a new international law reply that these are false distinctions, because the toleration of shocking or egregious atrocities is likely to lead either to chaos spreading through imitation or to regional destabilization through

arms smuggling, massive flows of refugees, and self-interested interventions in support of feuding parties. (Of course, this does not address cases when such effects are not visible; paradoxically, East Timor was one such case. But here it could be argued that upholding the result of a UN-sponsored referendum was indeed both value and interest driven.)

The limitation, however vague, of causes of forcible intervention to particularly serious violations of rights is a way of dealing with the proportionality between values saved by force and values destroyed by it. Defenders of the war in Kosovo have replied to critics of the way in which it was waged—against civilian installations more than against Serb forces—by arguing that the damage was necessary to put an end to, and less horrendous than, the continuation of the ethnic cleansing of the Albanians.

On proper authority, the "intervenors" have been, on the whole, champions of the United Nations. But on the one hand they have become aware of its limitations (about which more will be said) and on the other they have deemed the cause more important than the procedure of the UN Charter, the substance more compelling than the formalities. This is why many (but not all) did defend the bypassing of the Security Council in the case of Kosovo, and the transformation of NATO from a military alliance (last used as a UN agent in Bosnia) into a regional organization, a "principal," substituting for a veto-ridden Security Council. Others would have preferred a resort to the council, followed by a resort to NATO or to a "coalition of the willing" if the council had been paralyzed by a Russian and/or a Chinese veto.

It is because of both proportionality and the need for a reasonable chance of success that the defenders do not seem bothered by the contrast between action against Serbia, or in Haiti, and inaction against Russia over Chechnya. Reasonable chance of success is, of course, a very iffy notion. Those who went beyond a purely humanitarian delivery of food and medicines in Somalia thought they had a good chance of eliminating the warlord Mohammed Farah Aideed; many believed that there was little chance of stopping the genocide in Rwanda after it began in the summer of 1994, despite later vehement arguments to the contrary. A reasonable chance of success requires a willingness to bear certain costs and to launch an effort sufficient to have such a chance. The United States had no such willingness in Somalia and in Rwanda; and despite British and Nigerian attempts, nobody was ready for a sufficient effort in Sierra Leone.

No less controversial is the last condition of *jus ad bellum:* that force be used only as a last resort. Not only can one think of cases in which force was used too late to save many victims (Bosnia, Haiti) and would, if used early, probably have been less destructive of "enemy" lives than protracted sanctions that hit innocent civilians over many years, but opponents of military intervention, it seems, will never be satisfied that all hopes for a peaceful resolution had been extinguished before force was used or that the efforts presented by officials as honest attempts at reaching an agreement had not been designed to be rejected. Defenders of NATO's actions in Kosovo insist that even after Rambouillet the Serbs refused any plan that would have allowed international forces into Kosovo. Critics point to provisions of the Rambouillet agreement (especially the right of NATO forces to move from Hungary to the disputed area) that, in their view, no self-respecting Serb government could have accepted. But if it could not accept this and yet was willing to accept outside "peacekeepers," Serbia surely could have made it clear.

The key, for the defenders of forcible intervention for humanitarian goals, is the vision of an international order in which state sovereignty is not an absolute but a set of attributes that can be curtailed when essential human rights are being violated, and in which the ban on aggression that has limited sovereignty since the Covenant of the League of Nations is completed by a ban on such internal atrocities as ethnic cleansing and systematic massacres of "enemies of the state." As in the Wilsonian view, or in that of Hans Kelsen, war is either a crime or a sanction enforced by the international society; but what constitutes a crime is no longer limited to transgressions across borders.

CRITICISMS OF INTERVENTION

The opponents or critics of intervention have deployed a formidable arsenal of arguments. Many of them raise questions about the "justness" of defending human rights abroad. The most sweeping attacks are of two kinds. One is legalistic, the other political. The legalistic stance proclaims the sanctity of the principle of national sovereignty as the cornerstone of the post-Westphalian world order and of its corollary, the principle of nonintervention. The latter is seen as protecting not only the state against outside interference and subversion, but also its citizens, for whom the state is the precondition of order and the focus of social identity. It is this crucial role of the state, even in an age of economic and technological globalization, which the World Court recognized when it gave an advisory opinion that refused to declare nuclear weapons illegal because of the right of states to defend themselves.

The political attack comes from the realists. They look at international relations from the viewpoint of the states and argue that a sound foreign policy is one that protects and promotes their essential interests. When they are in question, states need no human rights or humanitarian arguments to justify their interventions. When such interests are not involved, and even if one could argue in legal terms that there may be a right to intervene, say, against genocide— something, it must be added, these critics are not ready to concede—a distinction would still have to be made between such a right and an obligation to intervene. For military action to be an obligation, essential interests need to be at stake—as in the case of aggression. Risking lives "in the absence of any definable national interest" can only lead to overcommitment, to serious damage to relations with other, often far more important, governments, and to an erosion of domestic support.[10] There are too many dogs fighting in the world arena, and the United States has no dogs in most of those fights. Indeed, the truly vital interests—the protection of national security from foreign aggression, the preservation of U.S. world status and economic resources from challengers—are threatened by the external policies of rivals or rogues, not by their internal actions (which may be impossible, or far too risky, to try to stop).

A specifically military variant of this position, well stated by General Colin Powell, stresses that the purpose of U.S. armed forces is to fight and defeat enemies. The "other new missions that are coming along" are peripheral and must remain so.[11] Otherwise U.S. forces will be depleted by marginal operations and made unavailable and unfit for the real lurking dangers.

The neorealists, who look at international relations from the viewpoint of the system and of its stability, see internal wars as potentially destabilizing, at worst, when outsiders interfere and especially insofar as external intrusions can be interpreted as acts of disguised imperialism committed by a small coterie of Western powers, and, at best, as insignificant for structural change.

Thus, while the defenders of intervention are moved by a nightmare of human suffering spreading chaos if each state is left, so to speak, in possession of the people under its jurisdiction, the opponents are inspired by a nightmare of interstate chaos if the pillars of state sovereignty and nonintervention are torn down. They are also upset by the kinds of selectivity and inconsistency that crusades for good causes are bound to lead to. Responding to every "egregious" violation of human rights being physically and politically impossible, any criterion of choice other than the defense of essential na-

tional interests is likely to be morally shocking and politically embarrassing. Small states will be the targets but not the main powers; allies (such as the Turks) will be protected from "their" Kurds, but Iraq's Kurds will be favored. The Croats and the Bosnians will be allowed to have their states, but the Serbs will be barred from extending their control over Serbs in Croatia and in Bosnia. Kosovo will be encouraged to secede de facto, but Katanga's attempt to secede from Congo in the early 1960s was crushed. Ethnic atrocities in Europe will rouse to action states that will be far more indifferent to horrors in Sudan, or Rwanda, or Sri Lanka.

Selectivity and inconsistency in choosing whom to attack are not the only inevitable effects of the moralistic approach; there will also be constant doubt and debate about what rights are to be protected. What constitutes a genocide? (Remember the State Department's reluctance to call what happened in Rwanda genocide.) Do random massacres and mutilations on a grand scale amount to genocide? Are deliberate policies aimed at starving opponents as "egregious" as massacres? What acts can be seen as barbaric? (Many in Europe believe that U.S. capital punishment is uncivilized.) Is there any consensus on what constitutes an attack on human dignity? Is political persecution always less obnoxious than atrocities and group persecutions, because it attacks people for choices they have made or actions they have undertaken?

The conclusion is obvious: Get out of this morass and return to the verities of realism. There is only one problem with this: the definition of the national interest. A mild form of realism would recognize that all powers must heed the *imperatives* of physical and economic security, but also that many have sufficient resources to promote and protect *preferences*, especially about the kind of international milieu they would like to operate in; and among these preferences, the elimination of certain kinds of unacceptable behavior has every right to figure. Moving further away from orthodox realism, we might argue that certain important values constitute interests, both because, as moral persons, we have ethical interests about human behavior and because, as political persons, we have an interest in a certain kind of order that can no longer be limited to interstate relations, given the porousness of borders and the speed of communication and of communicable diseases, among which violence is one. Is risking lives to save others abroad less essential than risking them for the defense of unessential bases or redundant resources? Are inconsistencies and selectivity on a global scale any worse than those one finds in the application of domestic punishments, tax laws, or educational policies?

Another criticism of the cause for which intervention occurs is that it presupposes a clear distinction between oppressors and victims, whereas in reality the victims of terror may themselves have practiced terrorism and engaged in provocations. This charge has been leveled particularly against the Kosovars and their Liberation Army and (by the Russians) against the Chechens. In a world of few angels, it remains nevertheless necessary to distinguish between mere sinners and true devils. There is little doubt that Bosnian Muslims were more often the victims of Serbs and Croats than the instigators of terror against them, or that Kosovars, since the revocation of their autonomy, had been grievously mistreated. War is often a contest between pure evil and part evil, as Arthur Koestler recognized about World War II. Indeed, this problem is not different from that of identifying an aggressor in interstate affairs.

Next comes the issue of the proper authority to wage a war of intervention. Here, the critics point out a dilemma. If—in true realist fashion—it is the United States that takes the lead (either unilaterally or as shaper of a coalition in the United Nations or NATO or the Organization of American States), it will risk both dissipating its resources and fomenting considerable resentment abroad, among foes, rivals, and even allies with little sympathy for the self-proclaimed "indispensable nation" and for the burdens borne by the "only superpower." If, in order to avoid all this, the United States turns the mess over to the United Nations, there is a grave risk of throwing away the required "chance of success," given the bureaucratic inefficiency of the organization (painfully evident in Bosnia) as well as its dependence on the political support of and guidance by a number of states with divergent concerns, different designs for the UN mission, and a tendency to dump on it more responsibilities than it can handle or to give it mandates that are unrealistic (such as the protection of free havens in Bosnia or the establishment of peace among armed factions in Cambodia, Angola, Somalia, and Sierra Leone).[12] Many of the critics conclude that the least objectionable formula would be entrusting the task to a regional organization. The problem, however, is that the Organization of African Unity, in the most troubled of continents, has shown itself both too divided and too devoid of resources to take the lead—hence its passivity vis-à-vis Sudan and its failure in Rwanda and the Democratic Republic of the Congo. The Organization of American States remains dominated by the United States, and the European Union has not reached the stage of strategic-diplomatic action so far. In the successful case of East Timor, where no intervenors used force, it was a combination of U.S. diplomatic and economic pressures and of a "coalition of the willing" led by Australia that obliged Indonesia to retreat. Thus there is indeed something Sisyphean about the problem of authorization.

Critics also question whether military interventions respect the principle of proportionality of values. They emphasize the very high costs the intervenors often impose on the supposed beneficiaries. In the case of Kosovo, the immediate effect of the bombing operation was the massive expulsion of the Kosovars whose protection was the objective of the war, and the U.S. preference for the immunity of their combatants increased casualties among noncombatants, both Serbs and Kosovars. Conversely, in Bosnia the limits put by the Security

Council on the mandate of the United Nations Protection Force (UNPROFOR) left the "safe havens" unprotected and Srebrenica at the mercy of its genocidal conquerors. These were two opposite ways of violating the old rule "Do no harm."

Another set of criticisms concerns the principle of last resort. Waiting too long in the hope that diplomacy will work and is not just used by the "guilty" party as a delaying tactic can allow the party to consolidate its forces and to begin to carry out its murderous designs. It can be argued persuasively that the United States should have intervened in Haiti when thugs opposed the arrival of U.S. ships, which turned around and left, or in Kosovo just after Milosevic's violation of the deal he had made with Richard Holbrooke in October 1998. In Bosnia's case it took more than three years to get to the "last resort." Critics point out that given the dangers of such delays, and the human costs of military intervention, preventive action would be preferable. There was practically none undertaken in Yugoslavia in the spring of 1991. In both Somalia and Rwanda, the UN presence had been withdrawn before the tragedies that hit those countries, whereas in Macedonia, where observers have been stationed for many years, peace has been preserved. The case for prevention has, however, one major flaw. Unless the Security Council decides under Chapter VII that a situation creates a threat to peace and security and orders a country to accept the stationing of an international force, the need for that country's consent can thwart the effort at prevention—as we saw in Kosovo; and not all countries are likely to obey UN "commands."

The most impressive critiques concern the "reasonable chance of success." In interstate wars the definition of success is the defeat of one side's forces and the acceptance by the loser of the conditions set by the winner (for instance, the restoration of Kuwait's independence and integrity in the Persian Gulf War, and that of South Korea's sovereignty over its territory in the Korean War). In internal wars

defeating the violator of human rights is only the beginning of a long ordeal that often requires more from international society than it is willing to devote to areas that are not strategically or economically important. For what is at stake after military victory is, in these cases, the rebuilding or the building of a state, from the outside and by outsiders. The long experience of the United Nations in Cambodia has shown how difficult this is. Often the United Nations has not had the mandate and the means to disarm factions that can thus continue to make trouble, as in Angola, or else the mandate exists, but the members lack the will to carry it out, as in Somalia. When the objective of the operation is the establishment of democracy in a place that has not practiced it and where most of the preconditions for it are missing, the outsider has a choice between, so to speak, reducing democracy to a mere free election and actively and gradually setting up the institutions and inculcating the values and the procedures that breed democratic government. The former may be too little, and the latter is likely to provoke charges of neocolonialism. What the United States, Britain, and France did in post-1945 Germany was not done by the United States in Haiti after the return of President Jean-Bertrand Aristide. It is too soon to say whether a new, stable, Bosnia will emerge from the Dayton accords. This is because success has been defined, both there and in Kosovo, as the establishment of a peaceful multiethnic society—that is, the organized coexistence of ethnic groups that have just gone through traumatic violence. There seems to be an unhappy choice between trying to reach what, in the short term, is an unreasonable objective (whose lack of realism, as in Kosovo, fuels endemic violence against the remaining Serbs) and a partition that may look, so to speak, surgically sound now but would be likely to create new territorial claims, to reward the ethnic cleansers, and above all to promote balkanization. When, as in Kosovo, the hatreds are still incandescent, even the minimal objective—the elimination of ethnic violence—may require more of a military and of a policy presence than states are willing to contribute.

Thus, success after war requires the international fire brigade to spend a disproportionate amount of its resources on tasks that are unpleasant and difficult, in areas that, to quote John Kenneth Galbraith on Vietnam, ought to be allowed to return to the obscurity they so richly deserve. And success requires the outsiders to make extremely difficult choices: how far to go in enlisting the local political forces, whose objectives may be far different from those of the "liberators" or occupiers (as in Kosovo), versus how far to go in becoming the de facto rulers of a country, at the cost of fostering deep resentments and of perpetuating external tutelage. Another difficult choice is between encouraging a reconciliation of the previously warring factions or parties and insisting on the punishment of those guilty of war crimes and crimes against humanity. Such punishment turns out, in fact, to be a necessary prelude to reconciliation, but in the short run it may have the opposite effect, and it may be beyond the capacity of the outside intervenors to locate and detain the criminals.

A final charge needs to be mentioned. It is in the realm of the *jus in bello* and concerns the proportionality of the means used by the intervenors to their ends. In interstate wars often the military means have been excessive and violated the immunity of noncombatants. In internal conflicts the means have tended to be both insufficient and inadequate. Yugoslavia in 1992–94 is a clear case of insufficiency—Serbs and Croats pushed around and aside the hapless UN forces repeatedly. Somalia was another such case. Kosovo was a case of inadequacy: the "American way of war" ruled out ground forces for far too long and resulted in high-altitude bombing that inflicted little punishment on the Serb forces that were driving the Kosovars out of the country.

The essence of the critique of intervention in internal conflicts is the argument that the present nature of international society dooms such enterprises or ambitions. By having to concentrate on cases that do not involve the domestic turbulence in major powers, they oblige states to devote to secondary or inessential areas resources and attention that they are reluctant to provide, thus almost guaranteeing fiascoes: peacekeepers with no mandate to use force if the parties resume fighting (Angola, Cambodia, and Croatia in the spring of 1995), peacemakers who are far better at fighting than at the "social work" required after victory. States have to concentrate on essentials, for domestic as well as for geopolitical reasons, and international or regional organizations have neither sufficient autonomy (political and military) nor sufficient competence to be useful actors rather than parts of the problem.

TOWARD A GLOBAL SOCIETY?

If one recognizes that the traditionalist critique is often pitilessly correct, one is left with a fundamental choice.

One may conclude that, the world being as it is, military interventions in domestic crises represent "a bridge too far"; that they should be undertaken only in exceptional circumstances: the atrocities committed amount to genocide, the effects of intervention will not be worse than those of inaction, and there is a broad consensus among civilized nations, domestic support in those that will have to provide the bulk of the forces, and the willingness to stay the course for postwar rehabilitation and reconstruction. Paradoxically enough, Rwanda should have been such a case—but only the first condition was met. If one accepts this point of view, one does not thereby dismiss the importance of human rights, but one considers them as above all a domestic responsibility, and in the innumerable instances in which there are serious violations because of the nature of the regimes, outside prodding should be prudently limited to cases in which no vital interest would have to be sacrificed to the cause of human rights abroad, and to methods of diplomatic and, exceptionally, economic pressure.[13]

However, if one believes that the toleration of, so to speak, fragmented chaos and bloodshed is dangerous even though the victims live in areas that realists tell us "don't matter" because they're poor and strategically insignificant—dangerous because murder and misery spread, refugees multiply, warlords and terror cross borders, and rich and powerful countries, unlike the wealthy in the United States, cannot live as gated communities—then the realist prescriptions appear neither moral nor politically sophisticated. If one believes that a world of sovereign states and of international institutions tightly dependent on and controlled by them is both increasingly unrealistic politically, given the effects of globalization and the need for better international governance, and morally unacceptable when states fall into murderous chaos or regimes massively violate essential human rights, then one has to choose the path of reform of the international system, so that it can begin to cope adequately with the protection of these rights.

This means, on the one hand, that the states that are concerned should prepare adequately for interventions when the violations and atrocities are sufficiently or very likely to be "egregious," adopt strategies that are capable of success yet minimize civilian casualties and suffering, and be ready to engage in protracted enterprises of state building or rebuilding. Given the hostility of the U.S. military to what other nations have often considered perfectly valid peacekeeping tasks for its soldiers, the United States might consider forming a special police force separate from the army. Given the reluctance of U.S. elites and of a large fraction of the U.S. public to bear the main part of the burden, other states or groupings need to be enlisted. The recent decisions of the European Union to create an adequate common

security policy that would allow for such interventions are encouraging.

On the other hand, international and regional organizations must be given the capabilities they lack in this domain. The United Nations needs "a UN-legion-type force" in order to eliminate the problems of command and control that have plagued past efforts, when national forces put at the disposal of the United Nations often received contradictory instructions from their governments and the United Nations. This "legion" could be either the kind of UN volunteer force Brian Urquhart has repeatedly advocated or a force composed of contingents in readiness put at the United Nations' disposal by national governments. It would be paid for on the UN budget. The United Nations should also revive the notion of trusteeships, established for a limited duration (but for as long as necessary) in order to restore and consolidate failed or new and shaky states.

The reason why the second option is preferable is a doubly normative one. It is ethically normative because it is morally imperative to shift the balance from the states to the human beings and to curtail the sovereignty of the former whenever it is exerted at the expense of the latter. (In my view, the crucial determinant of the state's rights is not the consent of the citizens: there are too many instances of majority consent to measures of discrimination, racism, or xenophobia; it is the respect of human rights.) There is also a politically normative component: the states, even when they are as powerful as the United States, are increasingly incapable of solving their problems unilaterally, and the global economic system in a world of accelerated technological progress poses rising social and environmental problems that cannot be solved in the Westphalian legal framework or in the realist theoretical one. We are moving from an interstate "anarchical society" to a global society, which ought to be at the service of human beings.

NOTES

1. See Stanley Hoffmann, *World Disorders* (Lanham, Md.: Rowman and Littlefield, 1998), chap. 11; and *The Ethics and Politics of Humanitarian Intervention* (South Bend, Ind.: University of Notre Dame Press, 1996).

2. Cf. Kenneth Waltz, "Structural Realism after the Cold War," *International Security* (summer 2000): 5–41.

3. C. J. Friedrich, ed., *The Philosophy of Kant* (New York: Modern Library, 1949), 434.

4. John Stuart Mill, in *The Anglo-American Tradition in Foreign Affairs*, ed. Arnold Wolfers and Laurence W. Martin (New Haven, Conn.: Yale University Press, 1956), 213, 215.

5. Michael Walzer, *Just and Unjust Wars* (New York: Basic Books, 1977), 61, 106.

6. John Rawls, *Law of Peoples* (Cambridge, Mass.: Harvard University Press, 1999), esp. 37 and 81, 93.

7. Berkeley Institute of Governmental Studies, *Public Affairs Report* (January 2000): 1.

8. Kofi Annan, Secretary-General's Report to the General Assembly, UN Press Release SG/SM7136, GA/9596, September 20, 1999.

9. David Luban, "Intervention and Civilization" (unpublished paper), 10.

10. Henry Kissinger quoted in Ivo H. Daalder, "Knowing When to Say No: The Development of UN Policies for Peace-Keeping," in *UN Peace-Keeping, American Policy, and the Uncivil Wars of the 1990s*, ed. William J. Durch (New York: St. Martin's Press, 1996), 50.

11. Colin Powell quoted in ibid., 41.

12. Kissinger (quoted in ibid., 50) put it this way: "[I]f international consensus is the prerequisite for the employment of American power, the result may be ineffective dithering. If . . . international machinery can commit U.S. forces, the risk is American involvement in issues of no fundamental national interest."

13. Economic sanctions usually harm civilians, including those whose rights one tries to protect from abroad; the exceptional case is South Africa, where the representatives of the black majority approved of Western sanctions against apartheid.

18

The Delusion of Impartial Intervention

Richard K. Betts

THE UNITED STATES, the United Nations, and the North Atlantic Treaty Organization (NATO) have had rocky experiences in humanitarian interventions in civil conflicts in the decade since the Cold War ended. Disastrous mistakes and shaky successes have outnumbered jobs solidly well done. By the end of the 1990s there was some evidence of learning from earlier errors, but not enough. The biggest such intervention—the war over Kosovo—will remain a subject of hot debate for many reasons, not least because there is no agreement about whether it should be counted a success or a failure.[1] NATO's strategy in Kosovo did not make one of the two mistakes emphasized later in this chapter (it was not impartial), but it did make the other (it was limited). In another big case—Bosnia—NATO intervention helped to put over a provisional peace settlement after the UN effort proved bankrupt. This was only achieved, however, by stipulating contradictory terms in the Dayton Peace Accords (in principle, reunification of three parts

of the country, but in practice, partition). It is doubtful that this anomalous arrangement can last longer than the NATO occupation that papers over the contradiction. Despite some learning, many humanitarian interventionists still don't get it. This chapter focuses on the misconceptions evident in the first half of the 1990s that still infect thinking among many who seek to use military instruments to relieve suffering and injustice in benighted countries.

Physicians have a motto that peacemakers would do well to adopt: "First, do no harm." Neither the United States nor the United Nations quite grasped this for most of the 1990s. After the end of the Cold War unleashed them to intervene in civil conflicts around the world, they did reasonably well in some cases, but in others they unwittingly prolonged suffering where they meant to relieve it.

How did this happen? By following a principle that sounds like common sense: Intervention should be both limited and impartial, because weighing in on one side of a local struggle undermines the legitimacy and effectiveness of outside involvement. This Olympian presumption resonates with respect for law and international cooperation. It has the ring of prudence, fairness, and restraint. It makes sense in old-fashioned UN peacekeeping operations, where the outsiders' role is not to make peace, but to bless and monitor a cease-fire that all parties have decided to accept. But it becomes a destructive misconception when carried over to the messier realm of "peace enforcement," where the belligerents have yet to decide that they have nothing more to gain by fighting.

Limited intervention may end a war if the intervenor takes sides, tilts the local balance of power, and helps one of the rivals to win—that is, if it is not impartial. Impartial intervention may end a war if the outsiders take complete command of the situation, overawe all the local competitors, and impose a peace settlement—that is, if it is not limited. Trying to have it both ways (limited *and* impartial) usually blocks peace by doing enough to keep either side from defeating the other, but not enough to make them stop trying. And the attempt to have it both ways brought the United Nations and the United States—and those whom they sought to help—to varying degrees of grief in Bosnia, Somalia, and Haiti.

WHO RULES?

Wars have many causes, and each war is unique and complicated, but the root issue is always the same: Who rules when the fighting stops? In wars between countries, the issue may be sovereignty over disputed territory, or suzerainty over third parties, or influence over international transactions. In wars within countries the issue may be which group will control the government, or how the country should be divided so that adversaries can have separate governments. When political groups resort to war, it is because they cannot agree on who gets to call the tune in peace.

A war will not begin unless both sides in a dispute would rather fight than concede. After all, it is not hard to avert war if either party cares primarily about peace—all it has to do is let the other side have what it claims is its due. A war will not end until both sides agree who will control whatever is in dispute.

Is all this utterly obvious? Not to those enthusiasts for international peace enforcement who are imbued with hope for global governance, unsympathetic to thinking of security in terms of sovereignty, or viscerally sure that war is not a rational political act. They cannot bring themselves to deal forthrightly in the currency of war. They assume instead that outsiders' good offices can pull the scales from the eyes of fighting factions, make them realize that resorting to violence was a blunder, and substitute peaceful negotiation for force. But wars are rarely accidents, and it is no accident that belligerents often continue to kill each other while they negotiate, or that the terms of diplomatic settlements usually reflect results on the battlefield.

Others sometimes proceed from muddled assumptions about what force should be expected to accomplish. For instance, in a bizarre sequence of statements in spring 1994 (before the NATO intervention the following year), President Clinton threatened air strikes against the Bosnian Serbs and then said, "The United States is not, and should not, become involved as a partisan in a war." Next he declared that the United States should lead other Western nations in ending ethnic cleansing in Bosnia, only to say a moment later, "That does not mean that the United States or the United Nations can enter a war, in effect, to redraw the lines . . . within what was Yugoslavia."

This profoundly confused policy, promulgated with the best of lawyerly intentions, inevitably cost lives on all sides in Bosnia. For what legitimate purpose can military forces be directed to kill people and break things, if not to take the side of their opponents? If the use of deadly force is to be legitimate killing rather than senseless killing, it must serve the purpose of settling the war—which means determining who rules, which means leaving someone in power at the end of the day.

How is this done without taking someone's side? And how can outside powers pretend to stop ethnic cleansing without allocating territory—that is, drawing lines? Yet for several years Clinton and UN secretary-general Boutros Boutros-Ghali made threats not in order to protect recognized or viable borders, but to enforce naturally unstable truce lines that made no sense as a permanent territorial arrangement. In the early 1990s such confusion made intervention an accessory to stalemate, punishing either side for advancing too far, but not settling the issue that fueled the war.

Some see a method in the madness. There are two ways to stop a war: either one side imposes its will after defeating the other on the battlefield, or both sides accept a negotiated compromise. The hope for a compromise solution accounts for a misconceived impartiality. This is not to say that compromise never works. Indeed, after the turning point of 1995 in Bosnia, the Dayton accords emerged as a compromise, but one that embedded instability in the settlement, for reasons discussed later. To work, compromise must first be possible, and then it must prove durable.

When is compromise probable? When both sides believe that they have more to lose than to gain from fighting. Because leaders are often sensible, this usually happens before a war starts, which is why most crises are resolved by diplomacy rather than combat. But peaceful compromise has to seem impossible to the opponents for a war to start, and once it begins, compromise becomes even harder. Emotions intensify, sunk costs grow, demands for recompense escalate. If compromise was not tolerable enough to avert war in the first place, it becomes even less attractive once large amounts of blood and treasure have been invested in the cause.

If neither side manages to pound the other into submission and a stalemate emerges, does a compromise peace become more practical? Not for a long time, and not until many more lives have been invested in the contending quests for victory. Stalemates rarely seem solid to those with a strong stake in overcoming them. Belligerents conjure up one set of military stratagems and schemes after another to gain the upper hand, or they hope for shifts in alliances or outside assistance to tilt the balance of power, or they gamble that their adversary will be the first to lose heart and crack. Such developments often do break stalemates. In World War I, for example, trench warfare in France ebbed and flowed inconclusively for four years until the Russian capitulation. This allowed the Germans to move armies from the east and achieve a breakthrough that unglued the Western Front and almost brought them victory in the spring of 1918. Then the Allies rebounded, turned the tables with newly arrived American armies, and won the war six months later.

Stalemate is likely to yield to negotiated compromise only after it lasts so long that a military solution appears hopeless to both sides. In the Iran-Iraq War, where UN mediation was useful, the two sides had fought ferociously but inconclusively for eight years. The United Nations smoothed the way for both sides to lay down their arms, but it is hard to credit that diplomatic intervention with as much effect in bringing peace as the simple exhaustion and despair of war makers in Tehran and Baghdad. Mediation is useful, but it helps peacemaking most where peacemaking needs help least.

In Bosnia, war among the Serb, Croat, and Muslim populations went on for nearly four years until the shocking disgrace at Srebrenica laid bare the bankruptcy of UN efforts. After the Security Council declared Srebrenica to be a "safe area" but refused to back up the declaration with the means to enforce it, the Dutch UN contingent stood by as the Serbs conquered the city, rounded up thousands of Muslims, and murdered them. NATO entered the fray, tilted decisively against the Serbs, bombed heavily in the "Deliberate Force" campaign, and stood by as the Croatian ground offensive cleansed the Krajina region of Serbs. Thus external intervention became more effective when it switched to being much less impartial and much less limited. But why did it take outside powers so long to get to that point?

COMPROMISES THAT KILL

If there is any place where peacemaking needed help most, and failed most abjectly, it was Bosnia in the early 1990s. There, the West's attempt at limited but impartial involvement abetted slow-motion savagery. The effort wound up doing things that helped one side and counterbalancing them with actions that helped the other. This alienated both sides and enabled them to keep fighting.

The United Nations tried to prevent the Serbs from consolidating their victory, but without going all the way to provide consistent military support for the Muslims and the Croats. The main UN mission was humanitarian delivery of food and medicine to besieged communities, but this amounted to breaking the sieges—a military and political effect. It is hardly surprising that the Serbs interfered when they could get away with it. In line with the humanitarian rationale, the United Nations supported "safe areas"—pockets of Muslims and Croats hanging on in areas conquered by the Serbs. Apart from such limited action to frustrate the last phase of territorial rearrangement by force, UN and U.S. attempts to settle the war were limited to diplomatic mediation, an arms embargo, a "no-fly zone," and economic sanctions on Belgrade.

For over a year, the UN presence inhibited forceful reaction to Bosnian Serb provocations because French, British, and other units on the ground were hostage to retaliation. U.S. and UN threats were not just weak and hesitant; by trying to be both forceful and neutral, they worked at cross-purposes. First, after much dancing around and wringing of hands, the United Nations and NATO used force on behalf of the Bosnian government, albeit with only a few symbolic "pinprick" air raids against Serb positions. But the outside powers did this while refusing to let those they were defending buy arms to defend themselves. Given the awkward multilateral politics of the arms embargo, this may have been understandable; but as strategy, it was irrational, plain and simple.

Impartiality compounded the absurdity in August 1994, when the UN military commander also threatened the Bosnian government with attack if it violated the weapons exclusion zone around Sarajevo. UN strategy thus bounced between unwillingness to undertake any combat at all and a commitment to fight on two fronts against both belligerents. Such lofty evenhandedness may make sense for a judge in a court that can enforce its writ, but hardly for a general wielding a small stick in a bitter war.

Overall, UN pressures maintained a teetering balance of power between the belligerents; the intervenors refused to let either side win. Economic sanctions worked against the Serbs, while the arms embargo worked against the Muslims. The rationale was that evenhandedness would encourage a negotiated settlement. The result, however, was not peace or an end to the killing, but years of military stalemate, slow bleeding, and delusionary diplomatic haggling.

The desire for impartiality and fairness led outside diplomats to promote territorial compromises that made no strategic sense. The Vance-Owen plan mimicked the unrealistic 1947 UN partition plan for Palestine: a geographic patchwork of noncontiguous territories, vulnerable corridors and supply lines, exposed communities, and indefensible borders. If ever accepted, such a plan would have created a territorial tinderbox and a perpetual temptation to renew the conflict. Yet Washington said it was willing to thrust tens of thousands of American troops into the Bosnian tangle to enforce just such an accord.

As it turned out, the Dayton accords did not rest on a Vance-Owen-type patchwork. The agreement accepted a de facto three-way partition, where most of the territory controlled by each of the three factions was connected. At the same time the agreement embraced the principle that Bosnia should be a unitary, reintegrated state. As long as outside forces continue to occupy Bosnia, this contradiction between integration in principle and partition in practice can function and paper over the failure of the intervenors to establish a peace that the locals can make final on their own.

In Somalia in 1992–93, the United States succeeded laudably in relieving starvation. Then, fearful that food supply would fall apart again after withdrawal, Washington took on the mission of restoring civil order. This was less limited and more ambitious than the outside powers' "strategy" in Bosnia, but it stopped short of taking charge and imposing a settlement on the warring factions.

Incongruously, the international operation in Somalia worked at throwing together a local court and police organization before establishing the other essential elements of government, an executive and a legislature. Then U.S. forces set out to arrest General Mohammed Farah Aideed—who was not just a troublemaker but one of the prime claimants to governing authority—without championing any other contender. The U.S. attempts failed but killed a large number of Somalis and further roiled the political waters in Mogadishu. Stung by casualties to U.S. forces, Washington pulled out and left UN troops from other countries holding the bag, maintaining an indecisive presence, and taking casualties of their own.

It may have been wise to avoid embroilment in the chaos of conflict among Somali clans. But it was then naive to think that intervention could help to end the local anarchy. As Michael Maren asked, "If the peacekeepers aren't keeping the peace, what are they doing?"—especially after the cost of the intervention topped $1.5 billion. Not only was the UN operation indecisive, Maren argued, but it fueled the fighting by letting the feuding factions compete for UN jobs, contracts, and cash. In areas where UN forces were absent, the parties reached accommodation in order to reestablish commerce rather than jockey for UN resources.[2]

After early forceful rhetoric by President Clinton had raised expectations about U.S. action, experiences in Bosnia and Somalia helped to brake enthusiasm in New York and Washington for taking on other peace operations. It is indeed wise to be more selective than in the heady days of hope for collective security that followed the end of the Cold War, but it will be unfortunate if the Western powers and the United Nations abandon such missions altogether. Indeed, bad conscience over the failure to step in to stop genocide in Rwanda, and reinvigorated confidence from pseudo-success in Bosnia and Kosovo, has kept multilateral intervention alive into the twenty-first century. Without full recognition of the misconceptions of the early post–Cold War period, the same problem—attempts to bring peace turning out to postpone peace—can arise again.

Of course, not all problems are due to impartiality. In Haiti, for example, the United States and the United Nations clearly did choose sides, supporting the exiled president, Jean-Bertrand Aristide; eventually the unmistakable U.S. willingness to invade forced the junta in Port-au-Prince to back down. Even there, however, suffering was prolonged by the initially limited character of the intervention.

For over a year after the junta reneged on the Governors Island Agreement, Washington relied on economic sanctions against Haiti, a "trickle-up" strategy of coercion that was bound to hurt the innocent long before it touched the guilty. The blockade gradually devastated the health and welfare of the country's masses, who were powerless to make the policy changes demanded by Washington and on whose behalf the sanctions were supposedly being applied. Yet sanctions offered no incentive to Haiti's kleptocratic elites to cut their own throats, and sanctions were not what made the generals sign the accord brokered by former president Jimmy Carter. (The U.S. invasion force did that.) Instead, the many months during which sanctions were left to work were used by the junta to track down and murder Aristide supporters at a steady pace.

Meddling in the tragic saga of Haitian misgovernment was a dubious gamble for the United States, considering the formidable durability of Haiti's predatory political culture. While the relatively peaceful entry of the occupying U.S. forces was welcome, the fledgling Haitian experiment in democracy looked shaky, to say the least, when U.S. troops departed. The best that can be said is that, as of early 2000, things had turned out better than it appeared they might at the beginning of the occupation. The September 1994 agreement did not disband the Haitian military or even completely purge its officer corps, whose corruption and terror tactics had long been most of the problem. Even worse, the accord hinted that —for the first time in the crisis—Washington might have erred on the side of impartiality. American leaders spoke of the generals' "military honor," U.S. troops were ordered to cooperate with the usurpers' security forces, and many of the anti-Aristide gangsters were left free to plot to regain power. Deciding whether to intervene in Haiti was agonizing. Once that was done, however, picking a side was certainly wise. But that choice was weakened by dithering too long with sanctions and then appearing to waver in support for the chosen side when U.S. military force was finally applied.

Impartiality nonetheless remains a norm in many other cases. It has worked in cases that lie beyond traditional peacekeeping, such as the cease-fire mediation between Iran and Iraq or the political receivership of the United Nations Transitional Authority in Cambodia (UNTAC). When looking at the reasons for these successes, however, it becomes apparent that impartiality works best where intervention is needed least, where wars have played themselves out and the fighting factions need only the good offices of mediators to lay down their arms. Impartiality is likely to work against peace in the more challenging cases—where intervention must make the peace, rather than just preside over it—because it reflects deeper confusion over what war is about.

IMPERIAL IMPARTIALITY

If outsiders such as the United States, the United Nations, or NATO are faced with demands for peace in wars where passions have not burned out, they can avoid the costs and risks that go with entanglement by refusing the mandate—staying aloof and letting the locals fight it out. Or they can jump in and help one of the contenders defeat the other. But can they bring peace sooner than exhaustion from prolonged carnage would, if they remain impartial? Not with a gentle, restrained impartiality, but with an active, harsh impartiality that overpowers both sides: an imperial impartiality. This is a tall order, seldom with many supporters, and it is hard to think of cases where it has actually worked.

The closest thing to a good example of imperial impartiality is the UN operation in Cambodia—a grand-scale takeover of much of the administrative authority in the country and a program for establishing a new government through supervised elections and a constituent assembly. Despite great obstacles, tenuous results, and eventual unraveling, UNTAC fulfilled most of its mandate; the final unraveling also left the country better off than it had been before the UNTAC operation. This success should be given its due. As a model to rescue the ideal of limited and impartial intervention, however, it falls short.

First, the United Nations did not nip a horrible war in the bud; as was the case with Iran and Iraq, it capitalized on fifteen years of exhaustion and bloody stalemate. The outside powers recognized that the main order of business was to determine who rules, but they did not act before the local factions were weary enough to agree on a procedure for doing so.

Second, UN intervention was limited only in one sense: it avoided direct enforcement of the transition agreement when local contenders proved recalcitrant. Luckily, such incidents were manageable, or the whole experiment would have been a fiasco. In other respects, the scale of involvement was too huge to provide a model. Apart from the wars in Korea and Kuwait, UNTAC was the most massive intervention in UN history. It involved thousands of personnel from a host of countries and billions of dollars in expenditures. The Cambodia operation proved so expensive, at a time when other demands on the United Nations were escalating dramatically, that it cannot be repeated much more than once in a blue moon. (The occupation of Kosovo is the next blue moon.)

Third, although UNTAC should count as a success—especially after the election it conducted against all odds in 1993—the operation's results were unstable. Despite a tremendous UN presence, the terms of the transition agreement were never faithfully followed by all the local combatants and continued to erode after UNTAC's departure. For example, because the Khmer Rouge reneged, none of the Cambodian factions disarmed to the degree stipulated in the agreement; after the election, the constituent assembly never seriously debated a constitution but more or less rubber-stamped King Norodom Sihanouk's demands; and sporadic fighting between the Khmer Rouge and other parties continued before and after UNTAC left.

Fourth, and more to the point, the UN success in Cambodia was linked with impartiality only in principle, not in effect. The real success of the transition overseen by UNTAC was not in fostering a final peaceful compromise among the parties in Cambodia, but in altering the balance of power among them and marginalizing the worst one. The transition did not compel an end to violent strife, but it did facilitate the realignment of parties and military forces that might bring it about. The old Cold War alignment of Sihanouk, Son Sann, and the Khmer Rouge against the Vietnamese-installed government in Phnom Penh was transformed into a new coalition of everyone against the Khmer Rouge. Any peace Cambodia could achieve had to come from a new balance of power. Ultimately the revised balance that facilitated the peace accord shifted altogether, as the Khmer Rouge was eliminated completely, and then the Hun Sen forces suppressed moderate opposition and took firm control of the country.

The least impartial and most imperial example of post–Cold War intervention was NATO's war against Serbian Yugoslavia for the purpose of protecting the Albanians of Kosovo. One may question that intervention on many grounds: the justification for starting the war (since greater crimes against humanitarian values were being perpetrated elsewhere, in places such as Sudan or Sierra Leone, without prompting such forceful intervention); or whether NATO's attack exacerbated the problem it was meant to cure (Belgrade did not begin mass expulsions of Albanians until after NATO bombing began); or whether NATO's insistence on limiting the military effort to aerial attack delayed resolution of the conflict and increased Albanian suffering; or whether the result represents a huge net improvement on the prewar situation (in effect, ethnic cleansing of the Albanian majority by the Serb minority was traded for the reverse after Belgrade surrendered control of the territory); or whether the strategic costs in damage to relations with great powers—Russia and China—were outweighed by the humanitarian benefits; or whether there is any legitimate way that NATO can ever end its occupation of Kosovo (to get Yugoslavia to surrender, NATO promised that Kosovo would remain under Belgrade's sovereignty, but this principle can never be turned into practice again without betraying the Kosovar Albanians). The fact remains, however, that the intervention did succeed in its primary purpose: removing Kosovo's Albanians from the oppression of the Serb central government. NATO did so by supporting unambiguously one side in the civil war and by executing military operations that, while not unlimited, were massively destructive.

MEDDLING WITHOUT MUDDLING

The "peacekeeping" that has been the United Nations' forte can help fortify peace, but it does not create peace as "peace enforcement" is supposed to do. During the decade after the Cold War, the United States and the United Nations stumbled into several imbroglios where it was not clear which of the two missions they were pursuing, and there was much head scratching about the gray area between operations under Chapters VI and VII of the UN Charter. Washington and New York responded to rough experiences by remaining mired in indecision and hamstrung by half-measures (Bosnia to 1995), facing failure and bailing out (Somalia), acting only after a long period of limited and misdirected pressure (Haiti), or holding back from action where more awesome disaster than anywhere else called for it (Rwanda). UN performance was so frequently disappointing that great powers turned to another multilateral organization—NATO—when they wanted to use force effectively in Bosnia and Kosovo. In Kosovo, NATO almost avoided the delusion of impartiality. Indeed, it initiated a war against Belgrade explicitly on behalf of the Kosovar Albanians. NATO could not bring itself to own up to the logic of what it was doing, however, because it refused to

endorse independence for the group for which it was fighting. This illogic may have eased the way for Slobodan Milosevic to capitulate, but it left the intervenors with no honorable way out of indefinite occupation of Kosovo.

If intervention is not to be foresworn and is not to be undertaken arbitrarily, what is the alternative? To do better in picking and choosing, it would help to be clearer about how military means should be marshaled for political ends. The following points should be kept in mind.

Recognize that to make peace is to decide who rules. Making peace means determining how the war ends. If U.S. or UN forces are going to intervene to make peace, they will often have to kill people and break things in the process. If they choose to do this, they should do so only after they have decided who will rule afterward.

If claims or capabilities in the local fracas are not clear enough to make this judgment, then they are not clear enough for intervention to bring peace. By the same token, international forces should not mix in the dangerous business of determining who governs without expecting deadly opposition. An intervention that can be stopped in its tracks by a few dozen fatalities, as the U.S. operation in Somalia was, is one that should never begin.

Avoid half-measures. If the United States or the United Nations wishes to bring peace to violent places before tragedy unfolds in full, gruesome detail, they should act decisively by either lending their military weight to one side or forcing both sides to compromise. In either case, leaders or outside powers should avoid what the natural instincts of successful politicians and bureaucrats tell them is sensible: a middle course.

Half-measures often make sense in domestic politics, but that is precisely because peace already exists. Contending interests accept compromises negotiated in legislatures, adjudicated in courts, and enforced by executives because the state has a monopoly on organized force; the question of who rules is settled. That is the premise of politics in peace; in war, that premise is what the fighting is all about. A middle course in intervention—especially a gradual and symbolic use of force—is likely to do little but muddy both sides' calculations, fuel their hopes of victory, or kill people for principles only indirectly related to the purpose of the war. If deadly force is to make a direct contribution to peace, it must engage the purposes most directly related to war—the determination of borders and the distribution of political power. (NATO used force less hesitantly and abstemiously in Bosnia in 1995 and Kosovo and Serbia in 1999 and, aided by ground action from Croatia in the first case and the Kosovo Liberation Army in the second, succeeded in defeating Serb forces. In neither of these later cases, however, did NATO go all the way to settling the terms of local government. It embraced the fantasy of re-creating integral multiethnic states, rather than reinforcing permanent partitions.)

Do not confuse peace with justice. If outside powers want to do the right thing but do not want to do it in a big way, they should recognize that they are placing a higher premium on legitimacy than on peace. Most international interventions since the end of the Cold War were not driven by the material interests of the outside powers but by their moral interests: securing peace and justice. Peace and justice, however, are not natural allies, unless right just happens to coincide with might.

Outside intervention in a civil war usually becomes an issue when the sides are closely enough matched that neither can defeat the other quickly. When material interests are not directly involved, it is impractical to expect great powers or the United Nations to expend the resources for an overwhelming and decisive military action. So if peace should take precedence, intervention should support the mightiest of the rivals, irrespective of their legitimacy. If the United Nations had weighed in on the side of the Serbs when they were dominant in Bosnia in the early 1990s or had

helped Aideed take control in Mogadishu rather than trying to jail him, there might well have been peace in Bosnia and Somalia much earlier. If justice takes precedence, however, limited intervention may well lengthen a conflict. Perhaps putting an end to killing should not be the first priority in peacemaking, but interventionists should admit that any intervention involves such a choice.

Tension between peace and justice also arises in assessing territorial divisions like those proposed for Bosnia. If the aim is to reduce violent eruptions, borders should be drawn not to minimize the transfer of populations and property, but to make the borders coherent, congruent with political solidarity, and defensible. This, unfortunately, makes ethnic cleansing the solution to ethnic cleansing. Also, it will not guarantee against later outbreaks of revanchism, but it can make war less constant.

Do not confuse balance with peace or justice. Preventing either side from gaining a military advantage prevents ending the war by military means. Countries that are not losing a war are likely to keep fighting until prolonged indecision makes winning seem hopeless. Outsiders who want to make peace but do not want to take sides or take control themselves try to avoid favoritism by keeping either side from overturning an indecisive balance on the battlefield. This supports the military stalemate, lengthens the war, and costs more lives.

Make humanitarian intervention militarily rational. Sometimes the imperative to stop the slaughter or save the starving should be too much even for the most hard-boiled realists, and intervention may be warranted even if it does not aim to secure peace. This was a motive in Bosnia and Somalia in the early 1990s, but intervention there involved presence in battle areas, constant friction with combatants or local political factions, and skirmishes that escalated without any sensible strategic plan. Bad experiences in those cases prevented rapid multilateral intervention in the butchery in Rwanda, intervention that could have saved many more lives.

Operation Provide Comfort, the U.S. humanitarian intervention in northern Iraq, and the unilateral French action in Rwanda provide better models. In these cases, the intervening forces carved out lines within which they could take command without fighting, but which they could defend if necessary—areas within which the intervenors themselves would rule temporarily. Then they got on with ministering to the needy populations and protecting them from assault. Such action is a stopgap, not a solution, but it is less likely to make the war worse.

In Bosnia, by contrast, the "safe areas," weapons exclusion zones, and towns supplied by American airdrops in the early 1990s were islands surrounded by hostile forces and represented messy territorial anomalies in what was effectively, at that point, a Serb conquest. It was no surprise that the Serbs would hover, waiting to pounce whenever they thought they might get away with it, probing and testing the resolve of the outsiders to fight, waiting for the international community to tire of the effort to keep the enclaves on life support.

Calling attention to mistakes, confusions, and uncomfortable choices is not intended to discredit intervention altogether. It is meant to argue for caution, because confusion about what is at issue can make such undertakings cause conflict rather than cure it. Doing it right is not impossible. The United States and the United Nations have collaborated successfully in peacemaking in the past, most notably in the wars over Korea and Kuwait. Enthusiasm for widespread involvement in local conflicts in the early 1990s was based on expectations that it would require a small proportion of the effort of those two huge enterprises. Unfortunately, this was probably true in some cases

where the United Nations held back, as in Rwanda, and untrue in some cases where it jumped in, as in Bosnia. Peacemaking will not always cost as much as it did in Korea and Kuwait. The underlying issues, however, are much the same—who is in charge, and in what pieces of territory, after a war ends. Intervention that proceeds as if the issues are different —and can be settled by action toward the belligerents that is both evenhanded in intent and weak in capability—will more likely prevent peace than enforce it.

Scarcely better, if at all, are interventions that learn this lesson halfway and use ample force and diplomatic legerdemain to secure peace agreements that do not really settle the question of who rules. This is what happened in Bosnia in 1995 and in Kosovo in 1999. Such interventions step up to the delusion of impartiality when they apply force but then back away in the diplomatic aftermath. By pretending not to side decisively with one side against the other in a peace settlement, and pretending to support the reintegration of hopelessly riven polities, such interventions purchase peace at the price of an indefinite liberal, multilateral imperium.

NOTES

1. See Michael Mandelbaum's masterfully scathing criticism, "A Perfect Failure: NATO's War against Yugoslavia," *Foreign Affairs* 78, no. 5 (September-October 1999); and the Clinton administration's rebuttal, James Steinberg, "A Perfect Polemic: Blind to Reality on Kosovo," *Foreign Affairs* 78, no. 6 (November-December 1999).

2. Michael Maren, "Leave Somalia Alone," *New York Times*, July 6, 1994, A19.

19

Using Force

Lessons and Choices for U.S. Foreign Policy

Richard N. Haass

THE QUESTION OF WHETHER and, if so, how to intervene with military force is always controversial for any political system, if only because of the potential costs—both human and economic—of such a decision. When the United States faces this decision, however, the stakes are different: Because of its status and strength, what the United States chooses to do—and not to do—with the military instrument of foreign policy can have an extraordinary impact on events and on the evolution of international relations in the post–Cold War world.[1]

Intervention can mean different things. Military interventions differ from one another in scale, composition, duration, intensity, authority, and, above all, objective. They need not involve shooting; shooting is actually only one way to use military force. The distinction that is generally not useful is the most common, that is, "offensive versus defensive." Not only is this distinction primarily in the eyes of the beholder, but it also breaks down in the real world. The same weapon system can be used both ways; moreover, one can have tactical offensive operations taking place within an overall defensive strategy, and tactical defensive efforts within the context of an overall offensive strategy.

Military interventions can, however, be usefully classified by other purposes: deterrence, prevention (to destroy or hobble an emerging capability of an adversary, something similar to but not the same as preemption, which is better understood as attacking an adversary just prior to it attacking or using some specific weapon), coercion, punishment (punitive actions), peacekeeping, war fighting, peacemaking, nation building, interdiction, humanitarian goals, and rescue missions. In addition, there is the indirect option of providing military assistance to a party to a dispute, which some would term an intervention.

It is important to use these terms with precision, not simply for reasons of analysis, but also for communication. Two in particular merit some explanation. *Peacekeeping* is used here to refer to operations carried out in a consensual environment. Such operations are more political than military and are carried out by modestly armed forces interposed between local parties. In some cases, the mission will take on additional tasks, such as disarming or demobilizing military and paramilitary forces and/or monitoring elections or troop withdrawals. But the key is the neutrality of the mission and the readiness of the local parties to accept a foreign role.

Peacemaking, on the other hand, is very different. The term is used here not as it often is, to refer to all efforts meant to promote conciliation, diplomatic and military alike. Used so broadly, the term is difficult to distinguish from foreign policy or diplomacy. Rather, peacemaking refers to those military operations that take place in "uncertain" environments and where (unlike with peacekeeping) at least one of the local parties is prepared to use force to promote its aims.[2] At the same time, peacemaking is normally something less than war fighting, given the military restraint exercised (out of political choice) and the limited strength of the opposition. (The word "normally" is instructive, as on occasion—for example, the 1999 Kosovo campaign—peacemaking has come to be all but indistinguishable from war fighting.) It is sometimes referred to as "aggravated peacekeeping," a term that should only be used guardedly: great harm has been done (and great tragedy has ensued) in undertaking peacekeeping missions when the reality proved to be something much more demanding and dangerous.[3]

Another concept, not discussed here, is *peace enforcement.* This is a legal term, not a military one. It normally refers to actions undertaken pursuant to Chapter VII of the UN Charter. The fact that such actions can range from naval interdiction in support of sanctions to intense war fighting—Desert Storm was a peace enforcement operation—renders the term too broad to be useful.

Terminology aside, it is most important to recognize that intervening everywhere is not an option, even for a great power or superpower like the United States. There will always be more reasons to intervene than resources available or than the body politic is prepared to support. The need to choose is critical.

The good news is that it is possible to make the policymaking process more manageable by examining past experiences. It is essential to appreciate that interests alone do not solve the question of whether and how to intervene. That something is perceived as vital does not mean that military force provides the best or even a viable alternative for policymakers. At the same time, that an interest is less than vital should not rule out the use of military force as a policy. The United States can sustain high-interest, high-cost interventions as well as low-interest, low-cost efforts. What it cannot sustain are interventions that promise to be (or turn out to be) low interest but high cost.

More generally, any intervention must pass three basic tests:

- The intervention must have potential to succeed; that is, it must be possible to see how military force can be employed in a way that will protect or promote the interest in question.
- The likely benefits of intervening should outweigh the likely costs once the projected responses of allies and adversaries are factored in.
- The likely ratio of benefits to costs should also compare favorably with that of other choices, including using other tools of policy (diplomacy, sanctions, incentives, covert action, and humanitarian or military assistance) or doing nothing at all.

CLASSIC SCENARIOS

How do these principles apply? The two most demanding scenarios for the use of force by the United States in the foreseeable future are also the most straightforward. The first scenario is an imminent or actual North Korean invasion of the Republic of Korea. The second is an imminent or actual attack by Iran or Iraq upon Kuwait, Saudi Arabia, or any of several other Gulf states. In both these situations, the decision to respond with force would be almost automatic, given the mix of stakes and commitments. Not surprisingly, these are two theaters in which the United States has fought major military engagements in the post–World War II era, in both cases with considerable assistance from others and with formal international endorsement.

A third demanding scenario requiring the potential use of force raises greater problems: protecting Taiwan against China. It is possible to imagine China attacking or blockading Taiwan should the latter declare independence or make additional movement in that direction. In such a situation, the United States would almost certainly use air and naval forces to defend Taiwan, a course of action suggested by the U.S. decision (in 1996) to dispatch an additional carrier battle group to this region in the aftermath of Chinese missile tests designed to intimidate Taiwan on the eve of an election there. What makes all this extremely complicated and dangerous is that any U.S. use of force would want to be adequate to protect Taiwan yet limited (at least in its application) so as not to provoke an all-out war with China.

All these potential scenarios have a traditional, interstate character. At issue are both specific interests and what is still the basic organizing principle of international society, that is, defending state sovereignty against external aggression. Each of these cases involves borders and clear divisions between the territory of the attacking state and the attacked. There is a status quo that can be restored and maintained. Such conflicts can normally best be fought with massive force used decisively from the outset to destroy the adversary's abil-

ity to project military power; such conflicts can best be deterred (prevented) by maintaining capable forces in the area and by leaving no doubt about U.S. willingness to intervene decisively if U.S. interests are challenged.

Another kind of scenario involves more limited potential interventions that are smaller in scope and shorter in duration but that nevertheless have a clear and important purpose. They include hostage rescues, limited punitive reprisals against terrorists or states supporting them, and interdiction on behalf of sanctions, narcotics policy, or immigration regulation. These potential military interventions can be readily defined and carried out with high expectations of military success, as well as with domestic and international support. Such interventions are more likely to prove successful if they are kept narrow in purpose, involve ample force, and are conducted decisively.

Far more difficult (yet still easy to foresee) are possible calls for military intervention in complex and controversial circumstances. One set of scenarios involves launching preventive strikes on unconventional military capabilities. A second set involves intervening in the internal affairs of others for either humanitarian or political purposes. Both kinds of situations have already been the subject of considerable debate; both are likely to provide the United States with some of its most difficult foreign policy choices in the years to come.

PREVENTIVE INTERVENTIONS

Preventive uses of force are reactive in the sense that they respond to developments perceived as threats, but they are—and are likely to be viewed as—proactive in every other sense. The temptation to undertake preventive attacks mounts as an emerging threat materializes and the likelihood of conflict grows. Preventive attacks become more attractive if conflict is seen as increasingly probable on decreasingly favorable terms.

Preventive strikes are most likely against two types of targets. The first is terrorist capabilities. The August 1998 cruise missile strikes against terrorist camps in Afghanistan are one example. The problem with these is that the targets are often "soft" and easily moved or re-created. The second and more likely set of targets is those facilities central to the development of unconventional weapons. Here there can be a problem stemming from a lack of knowledge, as was the case in August 1998 when the United States attacked a pharmaceutical facility in Sudan that was alleged to be associated with chemical weapons but that may not have been. In other situations, it may well prove impossible to destroy the target because of protective measures. Also, preventive attacks can lead to a larger conflict; for example, a limited attack on North Korean nuclear facilities could trigger a massive Korean conflict, possibly including the use by North Korea of capabilities not eliminated in a preventive strike.

There are also diplomatic problems to consider. The notion of preventive self-defense—"legitimate anticipation" in the words of one legal scholar—is not universally accepted in principle and is difficult to apply in the specific.[4] The international community has long embraced the norm of the right of self-defense and is beginning to recognize a second norm of humanitarian intervention. It is, however, a long way from accepting preventive strikes to destroy the nascent unconventional weapons capabilities of states deemed by some to be "rogues" as a third norm.[5]

The net result is that the preventive use of force is an attractive option only in rare circumstances. Defensive measures and punitive attacks against state sponsors of terror are more effective responses to terrorists, while proliferation concerns can normally be better addressed by a mix of nonproliferation strategies, deterrence, tactical adjustments, and defensive measures. But preventive attacks may be the best option against the emergence of a militarily significant unconventional capability if

diplomacy (or diplomacy buttressed by sanctions and/or incentives) fails to place an acceptable ceiling on the threat, if effective defense is not available, and if war seems likely. Indeed, such circumstances could well arise in both northeast Asia and the Gulf region at any time.

INTERNAL INTERVENTIONS

One of the few clear aspects of the post–Cold War world is the prevalence of strife within countries or between those just made independent. Sometimes the fighting is between groups defined by ethnicity or tribe; in other situations, the government (or the lack thereof) is the main problem. The result is conflict that bears many of the characteristics of civil war: the absence of a clear battlefield, no sharp line between combatant and civilian, multiple parties with uneven discipline, and deep emotions that make ending the fighting nearly impossible.

Too many recent examples come to mind: Somalia, Rwanda, Haiti, Bosnia, Kosovo, East Timor, Chechnya.[6] In such situations, the United States tends to have stakes that are humanitarian and possibly economic and strategic. But generally the size of these stakes is modest or less than vital. Neither U.S. security nor American prosperity will be undermined if many people die and many more are left homeless. Still, depending on the specific circumstances, U.S. security may be affected; and, regardless of the details, this country's sense of decency and morality is offended by what it sees or knows is going on.[7] The result is pressure to do something, often with military force.

Direct military involvement in the internal affairs of another state tends to be for one of three purposes: nation building (recasting the institutions of the society), humanitarian relief (providing protection and the basic necessities of life, often through the establishment of safe havens), or coercion or peacemaking (bolstering an arrangement in the absence of local consent or tilting the balance in favor of a contending individual or group). The question is when to choose one or another of these approaches and when to do nothing at all.[8]

Answering the question of whether to intervene will be extremely difficult because of the need for selectivity. The impossibility of responding to all such situations cannot be rationale for inaction—just because the United States cannot intervene everywhere does not mean it ought not intervene anywhere—but it does highlight the need to explain and defend decisions to intervene (as well as not to intervene) if domestic and international support is to be forthcoming. As a rule of thumb, the case for intervention grows stronger the worse the humanitarian disaster, the greater the degree to which other interests will be promoted or at least not adversely affected by acting, and the more costs can be kept down, either through the design of the operation or the participation of others.

NATION-BUILDING INTERVENTIONS

Like humanitarian intervention, nation-building intervention can be motivated by how a state treats its own people. It can also be motivated by a desire to transform a state's foreign policy so that it does not again resort to force against neighbors. But nation building is a far more ambitious enterprise than humanitarian intervention, which is limited in means and ends. Interventions designed to make a country secure and stable require replacing the existing political authority (or creating one where none exists), so that local people can lead relatively normal lives. Nation building normally requires defeating and disarming any local opposition and establishing a political authority that enjoys a monopoly or near monopoly of control over the legitimate use of force.

Successful nation building can involve first going to war, as in the case of both Japan and Germany. In both cases, nation building required years of occupation. Nation building can also result from efforts to assert authority and provide order amid chaos. Regardless, to succeed, nation building sometimes must seek to do nothing less than remake a political culture. It is more demanding in the near term than humanitarian intervention, but potentially less so over the very long term. It is highly intrusive, as even the limited nation-building efforts in Panama, Grenada, and Somalia all demonstrate.

Opportunities for successful nation building are rare. Few regimes are that dangerous, and even when they are, not many outsiders will want to pay the price. Also, it is impossible to be confident that the values the United States seeks to promote will take root. Neither the United States nor the world is likely to support for a second time the sort of methods—and the time they require—imposed on Germany and Japan after World War II. North Korea appears to be a prime exception because of its demonstrated aggression and the availability of South Koreans to undertake an occupation.

In recent times, for example, the United States shied away from attempting nation building in Iraq out of concern that it would take years, be opposed by both the American people and the Arab members of the coalition, result in many casualties, lead to Iraq's breakup, and in the end fail because of authoritarian and nationalist traditions in Iraq. In Somalia, nation building was not given a fair chance; it was never preceded by the necessary (and expensive) peacemaking. But even if those measures had been taken, there is no guarantee that nation building would have worked—or would have been worth the cost, since a more limited humanitarian alternative was under way. Where nation building was somewhat successful, in Grenada and Panama, the United States enjoyed conditions not easily replicated. Grenada proved receptive in part because of its modest size and population. Panama was accustomed to an intrusive U.S. presence and already had a democratically elected government supported by the majority of the people (although it was prevented from taking office).

Haiti is proving to be a major test case. The political and military weakness of the existing regime and the absence of civil strife meant that an intervention could gain control of the country with relative ease; the major challenge is in nation building, a task that the United States has shared with others but that is proving difficult and of long duration. What is more, the effort may still fail because of Haiti's political culture. Military occupation can provide only a context for nation building; it is up to other tools of foreign policy, including economic assistance and direct support of civil society, to actually carry out the enterprise.

SAFE HAVENS

Safe havens can be created as a magnet for people or they can be established where the endangered people already are, if they happen to be concentrated in one or only a few places. A modest number of ground forces and significant air support are required to protect the humanitarian area or areas, that is, to make the safe haven safe. The area is protected further by enforcing a weapons-exclusion zone around it and a no-fly zone over it. In addition, air forces must be ready to carry out disproportionately large punitive attacks on those who violate the area in any way.

This is essentially what the French did for a time in Rwanda and what the United States did at first in Somalia and is still doing in northern Iraq. The no-fly zone over Bosnia-Herzegovina and the exclusion zone around Sarajevo and five other designated cities might have been additional examples, but the effectiveness of the policy was undermined by the delay in introducing it and by the absence of will to carry out meaningful punitive action. As a result, all six cities designated "safe" by the United Nations were attacked for years, and two fell to hostile forces.

This approach has some obvious costs and drawbacks. Safe havens are open ended, offering no guaranteed exit date for those who maintain them. (Kosovo, effectively transformed into a large safe haven, could well require NATO troops for decades given the nature of the regime in Belgrade and the unwillingness of local Serbs and Albanians to live in peace with one another.) Some pilots and ground troops are likely to be lost in establishing and maintaining the safe haven. Except in situations where an endangered population already is concentrated in one area, establishing such zones can either fail to protect some people or force them to migrate to safety, thereby rewarding the aggressor. Most of all, safe havens are limited in what they can accomplish directly. Humanitarian interventions should not be confused with more ambitious interventions, especially peacemaking and nation building.

Still, safe havens offer an attractive policy option. They are designed to provide a respite from the problem at an affordable cost, not a solution.[9] They are needed until the politics of the situation evolve. Safe havens thus not only keep people safe but also buy time for other approaches to work, such as implementing sanctions, providing arms, and engaging in diplomacy or covert action. The utility of safe havens for future Somalias, Rwandas, or even Bosnias is obvious.

PEACEMAKING AND COERCIVE INTERVENTIONS

Opportunities for successful peacemaking and coercive intervention—that is, the uses of force to affect the course of events directly by turning the United States into a limited protagonist in a struggle—are likely to be rare. Lebanon demonstrated that peacemaking is extremely demanding militarily and difficult to sustain politically, both at home (because of the high costs and uncertain prospects for success) and in the target country (where nationalist pressures, the difficulties of working with disorganized internal forces, and the need to act with great restraint in order not to alienate neutral parties must be considered). It can, however, be carried out successfully, as Grenada and Panama demonstrate. (Haiti was a potential peacemaking effort that proved unnecessary when the overwhelming U.S. force was able to enter without opposition.)

Bosnia became an example of peacemaking when NATO aircraft in the summer of 1995 attacked Bosnian Serb positions in order to weaken them and their hold on territory and to increase their willingness to enter into a negotiated agreement.[10] So, too, did Kosovo, when in early 1999 NATO aircraft and cruise missiles attacked Serbian positions in Serbia as well as in Kosovo itself for eleven weeks in order to coerce Serbia's leadership into accepting a package in which it would cease all acts of aggression in Kosovo, withdraw the bulk of its armed presence from the province, allow a NATO-dominated peacekeeping force into the province, and allow Kosovo a large degree of political autonomy.[11]

Still, very few situations will involve interests of sufficient importance to justify the inevitable costs of direct American military participation on the side of one of the local parties. Coercive actions—limited uses of force designed to affect the behavior of the targeted party—are easier to mount than peacemaking operations; the problem is what to do if they do not succeed. (In Kosovo the reality turned out even worse, in that the costs of the air campaign were enormous even though in the end it did succeed.) The choice then tends to be between escalating to peacemaking or backing away from direct military intervention and choosing some other policy instrument, either arming the favored faction (an indirect military option) or pursuing another realm of policy, such as sanctions, diplomacy, or covert action.

Air power can accomplish many things, but not everything. Six weeks of intense bombing of Iraq and Iraqi forces could not liberate Kuwait during the 1990–91 Persian Gulf conflict; it also took one hundred hours of ground warfare. Air power can prepare a battlefield, but it cannot control it. Kosovo underscored a related limitation; although aerial bombardment over the course of some eleven weeks did help persuade Slobodan Milosevic to agree to NATO terms, it seems apparent that the threat of introducing ground forces made a greater impact. Regardless, terrible things happened to civilians on the ground when only air power was employed: thousands of innocent people lost their lives and hundreds of thousands lost their homes and became internally displaced or refugees. In the end, Kosovo was not one but two wars: an air war dominated by NATO and a ground war dominated by Serbian military and paramilitary forces.

UNILATERALISM VERSUS MULTILATERALISM

Much of the American debate over the use of military force has focused on the choice between acting alone and acting with others. In reality, the choice is less stark, as the opportunities for purely unilateral action will be few. In most situations, intervention will be partly multilateral, involving other countries in addition to the United States. The United States will need one or more forms of assistance, including base rights, overflight, intelligence, combat forces, economic help, and political support. Two questions are worth asking: In which situations will the United States want to marginalize or even eliminate the involvement of others? In those situations where the involvement of others is deemed either necessary or desirable, in what form should it come?

These are difficult questions, for multilateralism has both positive and negative aspects. On the positive side, multilateralism is closely tied to international legitimacy. Arab force contributions in the Gulf War were critical, for political more than for military reasons, just as the support of the Organization of Eastern Caribbean States was useful during the Grenada action. Foreign involvement also helps at home, where resentment is all but certain to undermine support for a costly and extended intervention if the United States bears most or all of the economic, military, and human burdens of the endeavor.

But multilateralism is not without costs. Such costs transcend the economic price of the United States assuming its share of an operation. Keeping the Gulf coalition intact required going to the United Nations, which in turn slowed down the use of force, most notably early in the crisis when ships entering or leaving Iraqi ports were interdicted. Multilateralism can also translate into a loss of control over the situation on the ground. For example, in Somalia, the United States encountered problems over both strategy and operations because it shared responsibility with the United Nations and other countries that were contributing troops. In Bosnia, European governments cited humanitarian operations to justify opposing the more aggressive policies suggested by the United States. The Bosnia experience also illustrated the problems that can stem from a cumbersome chain of command, which involved political and military officials (both on-site and at headquarters) representing the United States, NATO, and the United Nations. Many of the same issues surfaced during the Kosovo campaign.

There are a number of approaches to multilateralism: loose collaboration among concerned nations; coalitions of the willing; standing regional organizations; international forces organized by and under the United Nations for specific tasks; or the creation of a standing UN army. A policy based on unilateralism combined with modest forms of multilateralism (informal coalitions) seems best. Such a policy offers flexibility and does not require gaining the support of those opposed to a specific undertaking.

The other approaches appear more problematic. Loose collaborations lack the integration and coordination needed for larger undertakings. Strengthening regional organizations ought to be a goal, but it will require years for it to come to fruition. Such organizations tend to lack the consensus to take on missions removed from their core purpose. NATO is a partial exception here, although both Bosnia and Kosovo revealed the difficulty it has in tackling new missions. The United Nations appears most attractive as a legitimizer for war fighting and as an organizer of peacekeeping. Anything more ambitious seems both impractical and arguably unwise, given the divisions in the Security Council and the organization's lack of military capability.[12] There is a diplomatic price to be paid for acting without Security Council endorsement—U.S. relations with both Russia and China suffered in the aftermath of the Kosovo operation that was mounted with NATO but not UN support—but it can be a price worth paying depending on the interests at stake.

Despite the need for a degree of multilateralism, the United States needs to maintain a unilateral military option. It cannot plan its forces on the assumption that others will be willing or able to bear the burdens of major military undertakings. Nor does the United States want to give others a veto when it decides to intervene with force. Indeed, in some cases, such as large-scale combat or war, multilateralism will be mostly supportive of the United States. In other cases—such as preventive and punitive actions, rescue efforts, or interventions in places where there are special interests (such as Panama, the Philippines, or the Middle East)—U.S. leaders may want or need to act alone.

As a rule, interventions calculated to be modest and short term lend themselves to unilateralism (or modest forms of multilateralism). Unilateral uses of force maximize speed and the secrecy of decision making and implementation, and they also heighten political and military freedom of action. This was the case in the Philippines, Libya, and Panama, as well as with the Iran hostage rescue effort. It was also true in June 1993 when the United States launched cruise missile strikes on Iraq. Unilateralism can also be helpful when deterrence or coercion is called for; it avoids the time-consuming debates of joint efforts and does not require building a broad consensus. Much the same thinking explains the unilateral attacks carried out against Sudan and Afghanistan during the summer of 1998.

But acting alone has its costs and drawbacks. As already noted, it is hard to execute most interventions without some form of help from others. Acting unilaterally can be expensive; it risks domestic support if Congress and the American people ask why the United States is bearing burdens that no one else is. It can also be controversial internationally, as questions of legality and legitimacy inevitably arise. U.S. unilateralism also runs the risk of triggering unilateral actions by others. In any event, the United States will simply not have adequate forces to come close to meeting all the claims on it. It will have to do some things with others or delegate them entirely. Thus, unilateralism can become unsustainable over time if costs begin to mount.

There is little reason for U.S. involvement in traditional peacekeeping, a mission that many countries can readily undertake, unless it is expressly sought by the protagonists and is in an area where U.S. interests justify the contribution, such as the Middle East. Similarly, the United States normally should stay outside, or minimize its role in, peacemaking and nation building. These missions do not exploit the unique capabilities of U.S. forces for high-intensity combat. They are time-consuming and tie down U.S. troops that could be used elsewhere. They are also inherently costly, whether measured in terms of dollars or casualties and lives. Where appropriate, the United States would be wise to advocate and participate in safe havens as an alternative. If, however, peacemaking or nation building is deemed desirable and feasible, such missions should almost always be undertaken by coalitions, either recognized regional organizations or less formal arrangements. Furthermore, the United States should insist that in return for its support, the mission be designed with an adequate appreciation of the risks and costs, a consideration that will often support the modest aim of separating rather than reintegrating hostile populations.

U.S. participation in multinational peacemaking and nation building raises special questions. Experiences in Lebanon and Somalia suggest that direct U.S. involvement can be counterproductive, as it can stimulate opposition and aggressive action against the effort; in many settings, taking on the United States and demonstrating an ability to kill or capture soldiers of the world's only superpower has political value. The comparative advantages of the United States in such situations are in the realms of intelligence, transportation, and logistical support. However, the United States will find it difficult to assume leadership if it is unwilling to share the risks; as a result, in situations that meet U.S. criteria, some combat participation may be required if other countries are to be persuaded to join the effort. In these cases, the United States must be aware of the risks and use sufficient force.

U.S. willingness to operate under the command of others should depend upon the circumstances. As a rule of thumb, the greater the stakes and the greater the U.S. role, the more that U.S. forces should act under U.S. commanders. But where U.S. forces are only a small part of an overall effort, there is no reason to preclude non-American command, particularly if the operation is designed so that U.S. forces enjoy considerable autonomy within the area or mission they are assigned. Here, the NATO parallel comes to mind: essential self-command of U.S. forces in the field, even if overall direction of the operation is shared or held by others. In addition, UN or non-American command poses little problem if the operation is true peacekeeping (and not something more) in a context that is truly consensual. The bigger issue in such cases is not the command arrangements, but whether U.S. forces ought to be involved at all.

CONCLUSIONS

The prospects for the United States intervening effectively with military force—in particular, in those circumstances involving real or imminent aggression by states against their neighbors—have improved. A number of factors—the emergence of a new generation of advanced conventional weapons, the end of the Cold War risk of escalation to global war, the fact that many adversaries find themselves lacking superpower support—support the ability of the United States to use military force effectively on the battlefield. This potential will only be realized, however, if it uses ample force early and decisively.

Three other developments, however, are less encouraging. First, the United States will see its interests challenged more directly and will face humanitarian problems more often in the future. Second, some of these challenges will probably include unconventional weaponry; if the United States is not to be deterred from acting for fear of large-scale casualties, it must develop tactics, strategies, and weapons that will reduce the chance and costs of escalation to chemical, biological, or nuclear arms. Third, there is declining popular and congressional support for military interventions. The proper response is not to bow to this mood, but to take it into account. Sustaining interventions will require substantial political effort from the most senior levels of government. The greater the costs, the greater the effort that will be required.

The potential for intervening effectively with military means for other purposes, particularly internal conflicts, is less clear-cut. The advantages of modern technology that are useful on the open battlefield are often irrelevant in civil conflicts that take place in heavily congested areas where friend cannot be distinguished from foe. Television pictures may increase our desire to act when we see innocent people suffering because of government policy or inaction, and new ways of thinking may provide a legal basis for intervention; but intervening in internal situations can prove difficult and dangerous for an outsider—even one who possesses great power—if the local protagonists are prepared to fight to the end.

The dangers of a more interventionist bias are manifest. Using military force to intervene on behalf of a people against their government or nongovernmental forces is a complicated undertaking that can place the intervening party squarely in the middle of another nation's politics. Moreover, a norm tolerant of intervention can easily be abused by others looking for a pretext to intervene. Even if there is a real reason to intervene, it can quickly lead to counterinterventions by additional outside parties. Indeed, it is precisely these concerns that helped create the norm in favor of state sovereignty and against outside intervention.

This does not argue for always staying out of such situations. What makes a great power great is, in part, a willingness to intervene militarily on behalf of interests that are less than vital. Military force cannot substitute for political and economic efforts, but it can provide a context in which they are more likely to succeed. Sometimes it is desirable to act—when the need is great and it is possible to use force to improve matters at a cost that is commensurate with the stakes. In such cases, the United States may want to consider options that create safe havens, providing long-term relief at a cost it and others can sustain, rather than taking on the more ambitious enterprises of peacemaking or nation building. In other situations, the approach that makes the most sense may be a form of peacekeeping that accepts the separation of formerly warring parties rather than attempts the more ambitious and costly approach of trying to bring about and maintain social reintegration.

The United States will also want to identify a desirable and sustainable division of labor among itself, regional organizations, and the United Nations. However, the presumption should be in favor of continued U.S. leadership, at times alone, more often in informal coalitions. There are limits to how much the United States can and should seek to devolve formal responsibility to other organizations (including NATO) and the United Nations in particular given the lack of political consensus and military capacity.

Generally, multilateralism can be a useful or necessary military or political precondition to U.S. intervention; at the same time, it can prove cumbersome or an obstacle. It is not, however, an alternative to U.S. leadership. Multilateralism is most likely to be effective if the United States takes the lead in making the case for a collective response and contributing to the common effort. (The 1999 crisis in East Timor, when Australia took the lead in forming an international force, was something of an exception.) The more ambitious the undertaking, the more U.S. leadership and participation will be necessary and the more likely the United States will want to act in a loosely structured fashion. The more uncertain the stakes, or the greater the gap between stakes and likely costs, the more careful the United States ought to be about lending support, much less direct involvement, to an effort.

This chapter argues not only for selectivity, but also for what might be described as tailoring; the "how" of the intervention becomes as important as the "whether." This, in turn, suggests a need to consider emphasizing (without exaggerating) air power, arming local protagonists, and, above all, creating safe havens or limiting one's aim to separating hostile factions in the sort of internal conflicts that have come to characterize the post–Cold War world. It argues for political leadership, both to make the case to others to work with us and to persuade the American people and Congress to give their support. It also argues for fashioning

"coalitions of the willing and able" to undertake these missions. Last, history argues for not ignoring other tools of foreign policy, including economic and military assistance, sanctions, incentives, diplomacy, and covert action. This last point is critical: the military is but one policy instrument, and, however important or even decisive it may be in some contexts, it cannot be expected to carry the full burden of America's world role.

NOTES

1. For a discussion of the U.S. debate, see Richard N. Haass, *Intervention: The Use of American Military Force in the Post–Cold War World,* rev. ed. (Washington, D.C.: Brookings Institution Press, 1999); Richard K. Betts, "The Delusion of Impartial Intervention," *Foreign Affairs* 73, no. 6 (November–December 1994): 21–33; Michael Mandelbaum, "The Reluctance to Intervene," *Foreign Policy* 95 (summer 1994): 3–18; Fareed Zakaria, "The Core versus the Periphery," *Commentary* 96, no. 6 (December 1993): 25–29; and Richard Falk, "Hard Choices and Tragic Dilemmas," *Nation,* December 20, 1993, 755–764.

2. The Joint Chiefs of Staff define situations as permissive, uncertain, or hostile. Permissive contexts tend to call for peacekeeping; uncertain environments for peacemaking; and hostile conditions for war fighting.

3. For a different approach to terminology, see Boutros Boutros-Ghali, *An Agenda for Peace* (New York: United Nations, 1992). For a broader discussion of these issues, see Laurence Martin, "Peacekeeping as a Growth Industry," *National Interest* 32 (summer 1993): 7. For another skeptical view of the wisdom of intervening in internal conflicts, at least until they have burned themselves out, see S. J. Stedman, "The New Interventionists," *Foreign Affairs* 72, no. 1 (winter 1992–93): 1–16. Also see Robert Cooper and Mats Berdal, "Outside Intervention in Ethnic Conflicts," *Survival* 35, no. 1 (spring 1993): 138; William J. Durch, *The Evolution of UN Peacekeeping: Case Studies and Comparative Analysis* (New York: St. Martin's Press, 1993); *The Blue Helmets: A Review of United Nations Peacekeeping* (New York: United

Nations, 1990); Marrack Goulding, "The Evolution of UN Peacekeeping," *International Affairs* 69, no. 3 (July 1993): 451–464; Mats R. Berdal, *Whither U.N. Peacekeeping?* (London: International Institute for Strategic Studies, 1993); and Dick Kirschten, "Missions Impossible," *National Journal,* October 30, 1993, 2576–2580.

4. See Michael Walzer, *Just and Unjust Wars: A Moral Argument with Historical Illustrations* (New York: Basic Books, 1977), 74–85.

5. Indeed, there is not even agreement on what constitutes a "rogue state" or on whether the term itself is of use. For a valuable discussion of this set of issues, see Robert S. Litwak, *Rogue States and U.S. Foreign Policy: Containment after the Cold War* (Baltimore: Johns Hopkins University Press, 2000). For a discussion of various approaches to dealing with "countries of concern" (i.e., the states formerly known as "rogues"), see Richard N. Haass and Megham L. O'Sullivan, eds., *Honey and Vinegar: Incentives, Sanctions, and Foreign Policy* (Washington, D.C.: Brookings Institution Press, 2000).

6. Three recent volumes that assess many of these cases as well as others are Richard N. Haass, *Intervention: The Use of American Military Force in the Post–Cold War World,* rev. ed. (Washington, D.C.: Brookings Institution Press, 1999); Donald C. F. Daniel and Bradd C. Hayes with Chantal de Jonge Oudraat, *Coercive Inducement and the Containment of International Crises* (Washington, D.C.: United States Institute of Peace Press, 1999); and Demetrios James Caraley, ed., *The New American Interventionism: Lessons from Success and Failures* (New York: Columbia University Press, 1999).

7. See David Fisher, "The Ethics of Intervention," *Survival* 36, no. 1 (spring 1994): 54. This is an important article that finds in the just war criteria grounds for using military force in many instances where intervention has been delayed or ruled out. See also Jonathan Moore, ed., *Hard Choices: Moral Dilemmas in Humanitarian Intervention* (New York: Rowman and Littlefield, 1998).

8. For a sampling of the large literature devoted to this question, see Laura W. Reed and Carl Kayson, eds., *Emerging Norms of Justified Intervention* (Cambridge, Mass.: American Academy of Arts and Sciences, 1993); *Right versus Might: International Law and the Use of Force* (New York: Council on Foreign Relations, 1991); Christopher Greenwood, "Is There a Right of Humanitarian Intervention?" *World Today* 49, no. 2 (February 1993): 34–40; Louis Henkin, "Notes from the President: The Mythology of Sovereignty," *American Society of International Law Newsletter* (March-May 1993): 1, 6–7; Barbara Harff, "Bosnia and Somalia: Strategic, Legal, and Moral Dimensions of Humanitarian Intervention," *Philosophy and Public Policy* 12, no. 3/4 (summer-fall 1992): 1–7; and David J. Scheffer, Richard N. Gardner, and Gerald B. Helman, *Three Views on the Issue of Humanitarian Intervention* (Washington, D.C.: United States Institute of Peace, 1992). For more cautionary or skeptical views, see the chapters by Michael Akehurst and Hedley Bull in *Intervention in World Politics,* ed. Hedley Bull (Oxford: Clarendon Press, 1984); Joshua Muravchik, "Beyond Self-Defense," *Commentary* 96, no. 6 (December 1993): 19–24; Peter Rodman, "Intervention and Its Discontents," *National Review,* March 29, 1993, 28–29; Dimitri K. Simes, "When Good Deeds Make Bad Policy," *Washington Post,* August 29, 1993, C1–2; Adam Roberts, "The Road to Hell: A Critique of Humanitarian Intervention," *Harvard International Review* 16, no. 1 (fall 1993): 10–13, 63; Edward N. Luttwak, "Give War a Chance," *Foreign Affairs* 78, no. 4 (July-August 1999): 36-44; and Alan F. Kupperman, "Rwanda in Retrospect," *Foreign Affairs* 79, no. 1 (January-February 2000): 94-118. For a brief primer, see Raymond W. Copson, *The Use of Force in Civil Conflicts for Humanitarian Purposes: Prospects for the Post–Cold War Era* (Washington, D.C.: Congressional Research Service, 1992).

9. On the larger issue of the increasing need to design a lower-risk approach to intervention, see Edward N. Luttwak, "Toward Post-Heroic Warfare," *Foreign Affairs* 74, no. 3 (May-June 1995): 109–122.

10. See Ivo Daalder, *Getting to Dayton: The Making of America's Bosnia Policy* (Washington, D.C.: Brookings Institution Press, 2000).

11. See Ivo Daalder and Michael O'Hanlon, *Winning Ugly: NATO's War to Save Kosovo* (Washington, D.C.: Brookings Institution Press, 2000).

12. A contrary view, one sympathetic to a greater UN role, is Richard N. Gardner, "Collective Security and the 'New World Order': What Role for the United Nations?" in *Two Views on the Issue of Collective Security* (Washington, D.C.: United States Institute of Peace, 1992), 1–17; Gregory Harper, "Creating a U.N. Peace Enforcement Force: A Case for U.S.

Leadership," *Fletcher Forum of World Affairs* 18, no. 1 (winter–spring 1994): 49–63; and *Defining Purpose: The U.N. and the Health of Nations* (Washington, D.C.: United States Commission on Improving the Effectiveness of the United Nations, September 1993). The latter report also favors creating a 5,000- to 10,000-person standing UN force. Other proposals for a UN legion include Brian Urquhart, "For a U.N. Volunteer Military Force," *New York Review of Books,* June 10, 1993, 3–4; and Edward Luttwak, "Unconventional Force," *New Republic,* January 25, 1993, 22–23. Also see exchanges on the issue (subsequent to the Urquhart piece) in *New York Review of Books,* June 24, 1993, and July 15, 1993. See also Urquhart's "Whose Fight Is It?" *New York Times,* May 22, 1994, 15. For a self-critical view of the performance of the United Nations and the international community writ large, see *Report of the Independent Inquiry into the Actions of the United Nations during the 1994 Genocide in Rwanda,* December 15, 1999 (http://www.un.org/News/ossg/rwanda_report.htm).

20

Interventionist Strategies and the Changing Use of Force

Lawrence Freedman

WAR IS INHERENTLY CONFUSING, messy, wasteful, inefficient, and uncertain. One reason for this is that war involves a number of actors who are each pursuing distinctive and conflicting goals, often based on particular worldviews and with their own convictions about their areas of comparative strategic advantage. Another is that war invokes, in prospect and practice, the rawest human emotions, including almost always fear and chronic insecurity, as well as greed and protectiveness toward others, heroism, and cruelty. Plans may be hatched by the cool and the calculating, but they are likely to be implemented by the passionate and the unpredictable. Because Western liberal societies recoil at these inherent characteristics of war, they have recoiled at war itself, but when war is unavoidable they have sought to adapt war to render it more rational and controllable. It is in this light that new technologies are habitually viewed, as a means of turning war against its own nature.

TWO REVOLUTIONS

This view of the potential of new technologies was even true as the prevailing technological trends appeared to be taking war ever further away from serving as a rational instrument of policy. In the 1950s the trend was assumed to point toward ever increasing destructive power directed against whole societies, exemplified by thermonuclear weapons in combination with long-range ballistic missiles. So significant was this development that Soviet strategists dubbed it a "revolution in military affairs" (RMA). The logic of this revolution pointed to nonnuclear victims being terrorized into submission; victory against a nuclear opponent, however, was much more uncertain and required gambling everything on a surprise attack or on the conduct of a complex psychological game. The only way such a war could be controlled was by not fighting it at all, but the only way that a nuclear arsenal could then serve as an instrument of policy was by leaving open the possibility that in certain, stressed conditions control would be lost and a nuclear war might begin regardless. Out of this came elaborate theories of deterrence, which developed strategies based on the most rigorous assumptions of rationality and calculability.[1]

In recent years another "revolution in military affairs" has been proclaimed, but this time for contrary trends, still stressing long ranges, but now allowing for discrete targets to be chosen and attacked with ever greater care and precision under ever more reliable command and control.[2] This RMA is offered as a means of pulling the conduct of war back from mass slaughter to something more contained and discriminate, geared to disabling an enemy's military establishment with the minimum necessary force. It depends on control not through deterrence but rather through the most cost-effective modes of fighting.

There is no reason to doubt the assumption behind this new RMA that the extraordinary developments in computer power and the ability to manipulate and move information with speed and accuracy will continue, just as few queried the probability that nuclear weapons once launched would inflict awesome damage, no matter how untested their systems. The new RMA, like the old, will allow firepower to be deployed with speed and accuracy, often over considerable distances. Weapons will become easier to use, smaller, more portable, and effective over longer ranges. Some policymakers may worry that already too much critical information is reaching them in a vast, undifferentiated flow, but they will not argue for less in the form of widening intelligence gaps or slower communications. Instead policymakers will argue for improved filters, trackers, and forms of presentation.

Although it is always necessary to be cautious about the claims made for advanced systems, it would be unwise to assume that these systems will probably fail the practical test of war. Until 1991 the best arguments seemed to

be with the skeptics, who warned of how the most conceptually brilliant systems would be brought down low by exceedingly complex designs, inept maintenance, incompetent operators, or simply employment in climatic or topographical settings for which they were not intended. Look back at the pre–Desert Storm debate in the United States for many worries about the effects of sand and desert sun on U.S. equipment, or predictions of high casualties due to blue-on-blue attacks. One of the most impressive aspects of Desert Storm was that sufficient equipment worked as advertised to bamboozle Iraqi forces.[3]

JUST AND EFFICIENT WARS

More contestable is the presumption behind much RMA advocacy in the United States that the new technologies almost dictate types of strategy that meet particular and demanding standards of military efficiency. These standards require that no more resources be expended or assets ruined than absolutely necessary to achieve specified political goals. Most important, as little human blood as possible must be shed. These standards are particularly demanding with regard to land forces. Navies and air forces have shown how firepower can be directed against defined target sets over long ranges and with high accuracy, but armies have traditionally sought to occupy territory and not just eliminate items on it. RMA advocacy argues that even as they take land, armies can manage without having their own firepower beside them, for defensive as well as offensive purposes. Instead, they can operate with artillery and aircraft deployed well to their rear. Relieved of the need to travel accompanied by heavy armor and artillery, they should then be far lighter and more mobile, and able to dispense with a long logistics tail. With more kept to the rear, less is at risk.

The attraction of such a force structure is obvious. Reduced risk taking is critical to easing the political constraints on Western war making. Since the later stages of the Vietnam War it has been taken for granted that popular tolerance is low for high casualty rates in any conflict that falls short of an existential struggle for national survival. If any use of force for limited purposes is to be deemed legitimate, then its effects must also be limited. In this respect, therefore, the strategic choices apparently mandated by the new RMA are not so much slavishly following a line of technological development as adhering to a line of political expectation and of ethical thinking in Western societies, based on the Christian "just war" tradition. As exemplified by the Kosovo war, the discourse surrounding all Western military activities these days has a high moral content. Questions of justice and proportionality in warfare have come to the fore.[4] It is realpolitik and the pursuit of the national interest whatever the costs to others that now appear outdated.

The just war tradition insists on respect for the distinction between combatants and noncombatants and demands that force be proportionate to the task at hand. Whereas nuclear strategies that kept the peace through preparations for mass destruction under the first RMA strained at this tradition and threatened it with irrelevance, wars rationalized by reference to the pursuit of basic human values and conducted with regard for the safety of innocent civilians fit snugly. The RMA appears to meet the standards by posing minimal risk to friendly forces, with firepower concentrated as far as possible on enemy forces and military infrastructure rather than on civil society.

The RMA has another political advantage in allowing military operations to be limited in time as well as contained in space. By taking full advantage of information technologies, the concentration of firepower should be so quick, accurate, and lethal that the opponent will be left shocked and disabled before its own forces are fully mobilized. Wars that drag on and fail to reach a decisive conclusion can suffer an erosion of public support as well as encounter mounting calls from the international community for a political settlement.

RMAs in Conflict

There are a number of reasons for caution before this view of future war is embraced. If this were a true revolution in military affairs, then the new technologies would point strongly to specific forms of exploitation, so that all countries would come to structure their armed forces in similar ways to prepare for some rather standardized encounters. Yet access to the new technology is unlikely to be uniform. In past conflicts between advanced states it was presumed that while variations between individual weapons types could make a difference, there would be broad symmetries between the belligerents, thus placing an even greater premium on numbers, training, and tactics. During the Cold War the notion of a possibly decisive technological breakthrough was nurtured, but once the nuclear arms race reached a certain point, the ideas became more fanciful. Meanwhile, through a combination of decolonization and the arms trade, the gap in equipment between the advanced and the developing world started to narrow. This past convergence may hide some growing divergences, for there is still a lot of Cold War weaponry about, and it is likely to be the mainstay of battles for some time to come. Nonetheless, to the extent that the focus is on conventional war, the evidence suggests that the United States is pulling ahead technically in advanced systems from even its closest allies and certainly its old enemies.[5]

There is one important qualification to this. Many of the means of information collection, interpretation, and dissemination are spin-offs from widely available commercial systems. Ordinary individuals around the world can now take advantage of the Internet, locate their position with the Global Positioning Satellite (GPS), undertake complex analyses on a laptop computer, and talk across continents on mobile phones. In many cases military and civilians alike, from different countries, are using the same systems—for example, satellite communications. So the information environment is becoming steadily more democratic even while there may be a growing hierarchy in firepower.

The general understanding of the strategic possibilities of the new technologies has been shaped by a decade of conflict following the end of the Cold War and Iraq's occupation of Kuwait. The Gulf War caused a sea change in attitudes because it appeared to vindicate not only the line of technological development but also the associated Western way of precision warfare. However, one reason for the impressive performance was Saddam Hussein's ignorance of this potential. So the vindication carried its own refutation. Future opponents would take more care when inviting battle with the United States given the proven vulnerability of second-rate conventional forces to attacks by the first-rate.

Those who are almost bound to lose wars fought on Western terms have every incentive to adopt alternative strategies that play to their advantage. If the promise of precision warfare lies in keeping casualties and economic damage down on both sides and confining them largely to the military sphere, the same logic encourages those seeking to discourage Western military action to adopt tactics and weapons that make widespread death and destruction more rather than less likely. This may be the case even when the opponent has comparable equipment. The systems associated with the RMA do not preclude the adoption of strategies that allow for forms of warfare that are vicious and cruel in their effects. There may be less excuse for crude and indiscriminate modes of war fighting on the grounds that nothing better is possible, as, for example, with strategic bombing during World War II. But there are now also opportunities for those who seek to target civil society with deliberation. One side

may boast that the accuracy of its weapons allows it to avoid nuclear power plants, hospitals, and apartment blocks. Another may be pleased to use the same accuracy to score direct hits on these targets so as to maximize rather than minimize human suffering.

Nor do the new technologies displace established means of causing terrible destructiveness. Russia has made clear that it expects to rely on nuclear weapons to balance the conventional advantages of the NATO countries, just as in the past NATO adopted a nuclear strategy to compensate for its alleged conventional weakness.[6] The first RMA, the thermonuclear revolution, has yet to run its course. The capability to destroy hundreds of thousands of human beings in a nuclear flash is still part of our everyday reality and, despite the cumulative efforts of the abolitionists, is likely to remain so for the foreseeable future.[7] So too will chemical weapons, which first made their presence felt during World War I. There may, of course, be other technologies that are still in their infancy but that may have startling effects. The biotechnologies, for example, have so far been less conspicuous in their conventional military applications than the electronic. They appear more in predictions of grotesque and malign types of weapons.

If we postulate a contest between the first and second RMAs, it is by no means clear which would win. The attempt to develop credible first-strike capabilities against nuclear missiles was undermined years ago as soon as they were deployed on submarines, and even primitive nuclear powers appreciate the need to hide their weapons. Experience from almost a decade of attempts to deal with Iraq's weapons of mass destruction by air strikes rather than authorized destruction by UN inspectors is not encouraging.[8] Key facilities have often been revealed only by defectors; components are mobile and readily concealed; chemical stocks if attacked might create lethal clouds of toxic materials. There is an understandable interest in exploring what technology could provide to support defenses against attacks by mass destruction weapons.

The United States may decide to deploy a National Missile Defense system as soon as it becomes feasible, designed to provide protection against the limited missile attacks from rogue states, of which the most frequently mentioned is North Korea, which are supposedly desperate to construct intercontinental ballistic missiles. The proposed system is much more modest than President Ronald Reagan's strategic defense initiative of the 1980s, which was undone by its ambition after promising to protect the American people from a Soviet attack through a variety of space-based means. Even against unsophisticated opponents the defensive task is awesome. The attacker can choose targets and can expect to achieve surprise. The defender has to be on constant alert with comprehensive coverage. An incoming missile has to be detected and then accurately tracked before it can be successfully intercepted. The interceptor may find itself chasing a decoy rather than an actual warhead. Faced with a barrage of offensive missiles, the consequences of even one getting through can be horrendous. If it remains difficult to defeat a nuclear strategy with conventional weapons, then those vulnerable will continue to look to deterrence through the threat of retaliation in kind.

For all these reasons, the main threat to the RMA is now assumed to be responses based on maximizing pain, possibly through weapons of mass destruction or less drastic means of spreading a conflict to take in civilian populations. These responses are now described as asymmetrical strategies.[9] At one level an asymmetrical strategy is unexceptional. If an enemy cannot fight as you can, then he has to fight differently. At another level an asymmetrical strategy can be said to indicate a natural incentive to opt for weapons of mass destruction and terrorism (possibly in a horrifying conjunction) as a response to the West's preference for more people-friendly forms of warfare. The Iraqi example gave this fear credibility,

and it may work well for regional powers that want to exert hegemony without any opportunistic Western intervention (as with Russia and Chechnya). Reference to a nuclear arsenal constitutes a convincing argument in itself.

This formulation may be too simple. There are very good reasons why nuclear weapons and other instruments of mass destruction will be a last resort even for the most roguish states. There are, furthermore, still very few countries for whom using such weapons is an option and it is by no means clear that the numbers will inexorably grow. This is an area where prophecies have been notoriously pessimistic. Use of nuclear weapons carries the highest risks. If the West is pushed too far, strong responses to acts of terror cannot be precluded.

A more relevant form of asymmetry may lie in the assumed Western preference for quick and clean wars. The technologies associated with the RMA appear to work best in open spaces and are less appropriate for urban warfare, where it is much easier to conceal forces and harder to fix on targets and destroy them with any discrimination, and where fighting may be for bridges and apartment blocks. Preparations for battles against distinct military formations can be of little value when it becomes necessary to separate out combatants from noncombatants in situations where the opponent takes the form of a militia that easily merges into civil society. The relevance of this particular asymmetry is that it arises in types of operations that are becoming commonplace.

CAUSES OF CONFLICT

The RMA model as elaborated by U.S. advocates appears geared toward a great-power war in which both sides have eschewed nuclear escalation. One criticism of RMA proponents is that they have often shown little interest in or patience with the types of wars in which Western forces find themselves increasingly engaged, as if these lesser events distract from the true vocation of the military establishments of great powers, which is to prepare for climacteric confrontations with other great powers.[10] By preparing to defeat a "peer competitor," the U.S. military has become vulnerable to accusations of preparing to fight the wrong war. There is no prospective enemy in sight that would be a real match in a conventional military encounter.

The great-power era, when the international system was shaped by competition and rivalry among a set of large states able to project their military strength well beyond their own borders, may be over. During this era grand strategy was set by reference to the prevailing balance of power. By the Cold War this had settled down into a contest between two ideological blocs, each led by a superpower. After the collapse of communism, the United States was suddenly transformed from a superpower into a lonely "hyperpower" with no equals. It has been argued that this transformation cannot last and that novel great-power challenges are bound to emerge. Russian military strength may revive; China is on the ascendant. The gloomier schools of international relations have refused to preclude the possibility of Germany and Japan reacting to the new order by returning to their bad old ways as aggressive and radical powers. Yet despite these prognostications, during the decade since the end of the Cold War the gap between the United States and all others has widened rather than narrowed, especially in light of the remarkable strength of the U.S. economy. While direct great-power conflicts cannot be ruled out, even less so in Asia than in Europe, they are for now among the least likely future wars. Western countries are now remarkably at peace with themselves, so that even the remaining disputes (normally about trade) among them appear trivial in comparison with disputes of the past.

This does not mean that balance-of-power thinking has become obsolescent. Rather, the international system contains regional balances of power that sometimes overlap. The old great powers, including the United States, can become part of these regional balances, but their objectives tend to differ from those of earlier periods. This is because of the proliferation of states since the end of World War II. As a result of decolonization, which saw all the old European empires dismantled, and then the intensifying pressures on multinational states to fragment, the number of constitutionally independent entities in the international system has grown dramatically. The old great powers have shown no interest in recolonization, and this in itself limits their potential future rivalry. In addition, attitudes to regional conflicts are no longer influenced by the Cold War, which once provided grounds for intervention in the need to prevent a local victory by an ally of the ideological opponent, or grounds for restraint in the risk of escalation into a great-power war. The dangers now seen result less from the emergence of radical strong states and more from the weakness of so many new states. Poor economic development, profound social cleavages, and feeble political institutions can make these weak states vulnerable to internal conflicts, often ferocious, and to predatory neighbors.

The orderly parts of the world may look on the disorderly with sadness or contempt but at the same time judge that it is neither necessary nor possible to do anything about it, beyond a certain amount of charity. This is the equivalent of the response of prosperous suburbs to destitute and desperate parts of the inner city. Yet most Western governments would be uncomfortable with the thought that they can dismiss a large section of the world's population as having nothing to do with them. They have developed an interest in regulating the generality of international conflict for a variety of reasons—to uphold the norm of nonaggression, thwart gross violations of human rights, prevent resort to weapons of mass destruction, impede the expansion of conflict into neighboring states, and provide disaster relief.

Other motives for intervention include concern for the fate of expatriate communities and anxieties that continued violence may induce a sense of spreading instability, dislocate the international economy (for example, by affecting commodity prices), or prompt refugee flows. Oil has traditionally been a factor guaranteed to capture the attention of large energy consumers, and it has ensured continuing interest in the affairs of the Persian Gulf. This has taken the form of rivalry for privileged access to oil production and reserves or possible collective action to deny a producer monopoly power. It is oil that now summons the West to attend to the Caucasus, because of the presumed desirability of a pipeline from Azerbaijan taking in Georgia and Turkey rather than Iran or Russia. The pipeline battle, and the need for regional stability, has been one factor in Russia's battle to hold on to Chechnya.

Some commentators postulate the emergence of new threats arising from Third World turbulence, inspired perhaps by fundamentalist Islam, romantic nationalism, or something more visceral, taking over governments or operating as transnational freelancers, seeking access to weapons of mass destruction, or just relying on crude terrorist devices.[11] There are undoubtedly militants around the world who can give substance to these fears, who are able to tap seething resentments against the West, and whose access to a variety of means could inflict real hurt. For all these reasons Western governments and their intelligence agencies have to watch out for the Osama bin Ladens as well as the Saddam Husseins. But it remains hard to see how these factors could combine in such a way so as to pose a decisive threat to the Western way of life.

Out of these concerns has emerged a class of operations, of which there are now a number of examples that essentially involve Western forces intervening in local political struggles. Forms of intervention must necessarily vary to take account of not only those basic factors of location, topography, and climate that always determine what is militarily practical, but also substantial differences in the regional political context, the sponsoring multilateral organization (if any), and the origins of the local conflict. Intervention may not move beyond a period of coercion in which the threat of action is used to produce agreement among the belligerents, including provisions for the consensual deployment of external forces. During this stage the legal/moral framework for any later action against enemy resistance can be established. Once, in the next stage, any resistance has been broken, the final stage will address issues of reconstruction and reconciliation as responsibility is taken for what may be a shattered and deeply divided country. This may turn out to be a prolonged but largely low-level version of the previous stage.

THE WESTERN WAY

Before we consider whether these interventions can be made to conform to Western preferences with regard to low-cost, low-pain warfare, it is important to assess the validity of the starting assumptions. For example, have Western societies now entered a postheroic age that cannot tolerate battlefield casualties?[12] Past ages were not always that heroic, except in an involuntary sense, while in recent years Western countries have been prepared to accept substantial casualties in order to reverse aggression or stop the slaughter of innocents. Few anticipated the modest casualties resulting directly from Desert Storm. Experience suggests that the real intolerance is of sacrifice for no purpose or up to a level completely out of proportion to the stakes in the conflict. Such limits are rarely approached these days, and when the risk of the combination of casualty and futility appears high, governments have been quick to extricate themselves. As with charitable giving, there are limits to the burdens gladly accepted in the conduct of altruistic wars. Abrupt withdrawals characterized U.S. policy after setbacks were suffered in Beirut and Somalia. In both cases there were explanations for withdrawal other than the absolute level of casualties.[13] It is also worth noting that most European countries seem to have been less affected by casualties than the United States. France took casualties in Lebanon and Bosnia regularly without evidently flinching, while Britain, with years of steady losses in Northern Ireland, made the case for taking the risk of a ground offensive in Kosovo. The issue in the U.S. military may be more a question of a culture that discourages risk taking in general. The presumption of casualty intolerance may therefore be no more than a hypothesis that has not yet been put to a severe test. Nonetheless, if the hypothesis has implanted itself in the minds of Western leaders, then it is likely to influence the conduct of future operations. Even if European politicians are more ready to risk combat, their freedom of maneuver will be limited, because in all probability the U.S. military will carry the burden disproportionately. This is one reason why there is an attempt to create a European capacity for combat that is independent of the United States.[14]

The hypothesis that Western populations are extremely concerned about casualties imposed in their name also needs to be treated with care. Led by President Bill Clinton, NATO made a clear choice in Kosovo. It was prepared to accept the risk of imposing real pain on Serbian society, rather than just Serb forces, as a means of keeping down the risk to its own forces. When the air campaign initially failed to get results, it was made more extensive and intensive, to the point where the damage to the Serb economic—as much as the military—infrastructure probably contributed to Belgrade's decision to agree to terms. NATO did so fully aware that its own media would scrutinize the causes of every civilian casualty and of every evident blunder, of which there were a number. Public opinion often appeared uncomfortable with the results of NATO's bombing but still recognized that terrible things

happen in war through accident as well as by design and, critically, took the view that those who initiate violence should not be surprised if it comes to engulf their societies.

At both ends of the 1990s Iraq and Serbia saw an opportunity in Western promises of low collateral damage. They almost dared attacking air forces to take the risk of causing high civilian casualties by placing key military assets, such as tanks or aircraft, next to schools, hospitals, and religious sites. There was certainly an expectation that Western forces would not engage in gratuitous cruelty, that military actions would be clearly linked to a realizable political purpose, and that the wider international community would judge the application of force by high standards and would expect that every effort would be made to keep all casualties to a minimum. Western governments at times appeared caught by the unrealistic expectations they had encouraged about avoiding collateral damage (itself an unfortunate phrase). Great attention was paid by the media to "blunders." Once exacting standards for precision are set, the routine tragedies of past wars can appear as outrages that threaten to invalidate the whole purpose of a modern war. As appropriate targets may well lie in the gray area between the strictly military and the civil, Western countries will inevitably fall short of these standards. As this point appeared more widely understood than credited by Western politicians and the media, in the future there might be more candor from the start of an operation about the risks to all concerned, even while every effort is made to minimize those risks.

This candor will be particularly important if there is continual reliance on air power as the military instrument of choice. The evident comparative advantage of the West here means that this has appeared as a virtually risk-free military option. It is notable that air—or cruise missile—strikes are now often invoked as the first tough measures to be taken after diplomatic isolation and economic sanctions have been perceived to fail. It is almost the military equivalent of breaking diplomatic relations—something that is relatively painless for the instigator to do though it may not actually be very helpful. There are, however, dangers in using armed force for political symbolism in crisis management, unless something very real is being symbolized.

The limits to air power were illustrated by the war in Kosovo, where air power was relied on to the exclusion of land power. Unfortunately the air threat posed to Serbia and its armed forces up to late March 1999 was large enough to signal an interest but insufficient to compel the target to change behavior. It was reasonable for the Serbs to assume that they would have to face little more than four days of raids on air defense sites and command centers. Once its bluff was called, NATO had to implement this inadequate threat with initially inadequate results. The level of air strikes was raised in a hurry, increasing the risk not so much of casualty but of blunder and moving to what was by necessity, in practice, a punitive campaign.

The fact that this campaign eventually helped to compel a change in Belgrade's policy was later taken as some sort of vindication of air power acting alone.[15] Yet the war in Kosovo was partly won on the ground—but not by NATO. The hints that NATO was actually contemplating an eventual land invasion may well have been instrumental in persuading Belgrade to withdraw, but more important was probably the growing strength of the Kosovo Liberation Army (KLA). The whole objective of the Serb campaign was to defeat the KLA and deprive it of the population base required for sustained operations. But the ability of the KLA to grow in strength and confidence must have indicated to President Slobodan Milosevic that in the end he would lose Kosovo and that there was little point in taking even more pain from NATO air power.

Furthermore, the unwillingness or inability to commit NATO troops had two important political consequences. First, it gave the Serbs the time and the space for "ethnic cleansing," which was largely carried out by units barely inhibited by NATO aircraft. Second, as NATO forces effectively followed it into Kosovo, the KLA acquired far more political clout and prestige than was commensurate with the alliance's prewar Western political goals. This added to the demands on the postwar peacekeeping force, which soon looked set for a long stay.

Another challenge from Kosovo to contemporary air power theory was in questioning the value of striking the "centers of gravity" upon which the whole of the enemy's military effort is supposed to depend. In practice this tends to mean attacking sources of power and communications that are relevant to both civilian and military spheres. The evidence of Kosovo suggests that it was the impact on the civilian sphere that made the most difference, as the quality of life in Serbia steadily deteriorated under the impact of NATO's air bombardment. There is no evidence that the American people found the bombing of Serbia particularly uncomfortable, but it is clear that President Clinton doubted that even a few casualties would be acceptable for this particular cause. Given a choice between a principled defeat and a barely legitimate victory, most governments will choose the latter.

In Bosnia and Kosovo, Serb forces were in the end defeated by local forces working in concert with, if not actually coordinated by, Western air forces. In both cases Western political influence depended on the speedy insertion of substantial ground forces. There they can provide "aid to the civil power" from putting down food riots to calming intercommunal tensions to dealing with organized crime and vigilantes. These roles differ from those of traditional UN blue-helmeted peacekeepers, who were geared to monitoring agreed cease-fire lines. Indeed, when forces configured as traditional peacekeepers were put into ongoing conflicts, without any peace to keep, as in Bosnia, the result was that their vulnerability inhibited sterner actions by the donor governments.

The conclusion drawn from the Balkan experience, backed up now by East Timor and a whole range of African contingencies, is that these interventions put a premium on rough-and-ready soldiering, whether in "permissive" (that is, with the notional consent of all parties) or "nonpermissive" environments. There will always be a reluctance to insert light forces in dangerous situations, even in more accessible locales than Kosovo, unless the forces are confident that they can defend themselves and will be backed up quickly if necessary.

LOGISTICS AND MULTILATERALISM

Although the risk of severe casualties contributed to caution regarding the use of land forces in Kosovo, logistical factors were even more important. Kosovo is one of the most inaccessible places in Europe, and many of the states on the access routes, such as Greece and Macedonia, were nervous about any association with a NATO offensive. Albania was much more sympathetic, but its facilities were primitive. In studies of contemporary military operations, logistics is often considered a rather dull and secondary subject, yet it often sets the parameters within which operations take place. Once a significant amount of air- or sea-lift is required, then important time constraints are introduced. Governments earmark forces for "rapid" deployments, but in contrast to the growing expectations of "real-time" intelligence and immediate communication, no logistician has yet found the secret of real-time deployment. To move a significant force requires weeks, and sometimes months. Because of the lack of awareness of these issues, logistics is more likely than other areas to cause misunderstanding and vexation between military and political elites. Civilians become frustrated by how long everything takes. Military personnel believe that they are asked to take unnecessary risks with inadequate resources and preparation under the pressure for quick results. Once

in place the force has to be sustained. If it becomes necessary to maintain units for extended periods in particular locations, then new stresses are created in the whole military system, as issues of tours of duty and supplies have to be addressed.

Again the realities of contemporary operations contradict the hopes of theorists, in this case the requirement that all operations be geared toward achieving a decisive result. The experience of the past decade is that it is unwise for countries to expect to exit a vicious local conflict and assume everything will stay settled after they have forcefully altered the local power structure. Insisting on an "exit strategy" at the point of entry is something of a give-away, encouraging the opponent to threaten an interminable conflict, in which the fighting is long term and mean, even if also spasmodic and at a low level. Once Western countries accept that they have interests in and responsibilities to parts of the world susceptible to political turbulence, then they must also accept that a prolonged effort will be required from all concerned, as well as major changes in the attitudes and behavior of international organizations and individual states.

The logic of regular interventions is therefore that Western states will leave military deposits around the globe, asserting interests in stability and high standards of political behavior, and supporting the proconsuls appointed by international organizations. Continuing political influence will depend on sustaining a physical presence. Each deposit reduces the spare military capital for future interventions. At some point, if this process continues, a collection of Western protectorates will have been acquired, but without further investment, their forces will be so stretched that they will be unable to cope with yet another emergency, no matter how worthy the cause. To avoid this situation governments will need to be not only careful and selective in the interventions they undertake, but also imaginative in preparations for postwar reconstruction. Specialized forces, perhaps drawing heavily on reservists to make up the numbers, will be required to perform roles that are more akin to high-intensity policing than war fighting as normally understood.

Another way to avoid overstretch is to involve as many countries as possible in these operations. Multilateralism also has the merit of adding legitimacy. By and large major powers confine unilateral interventions to their immediate neighborhood, as, for example, did the Americans in Grenada, Panama, and Haiti and the Russians in their "near abroad." However, even here there is always a preference for involving other smaller, local countries to demonstrate that more than narrow national interests are being served. Whether multilateralism is for political effect or to make up the numbers, once this path is followed, the rationale must have a broad appeal, sufficient for a consensus within the sponsoring organization. This can shape the political goals of an intervention. When a coalition has to be put together, further time is inevitably lost in the processes of consensus building. Suitable allies and their potential contributions have to be identified, their particular sensitivities ascertained, hostilities in the United Nations Security Council addressed, perhaps economic sanctions tried first, and ambassadors of peace allowed to flit hither and thither to find the peaceful resolution to a crisis.

CONCLUSION

These various aspects of contemporary operations have important consequences. Their special logistical and political requirements mean that the gap between recognizing a problem and acting to do something about it will allow the opponent sufficient time either to complete the activity that rang alarm bells in the first place or at least to prepare for the intervening force. They place heavy demands on land forces, probably to ensure military victory but almost certainly to sustain a tolerable peace.

How do these requirements fit in with the models of conflict surrounding the "revolution in military affairs" and the desire to reduce the pain of war through exercising greater control over its conduct and ensuring a quick and decisive result? Certainly many of the technologies associated with the RMA are suitable for these types of operations. Political storms at home and abroad can be avoided if casualties are kept down on all sides. Good tactical intelligence is vital, although working with unfamiliar societies requires a grasp of local culture and political complexities as much as vivid images on visual display units. Excellent communications can nip developing problems in the bud and allow for efficient use of available forces. They may not, however, require the most sophisticated forms of battle management, while notions of a digitized battlefield are likely to remain wide of the mark. Almost all conflicts these days appear to have an Internet dimension, whether this be sending spoof messages or overloading target sites or passing instructions to networks of activists, but these are generally secondary activities, often morale boosting in nature. They are not going to provide substitutes for the basic military capabilities that allow for territory to be held and political influence exerted.

There are therefore some real choices to be made between procuring the most advanced capabilities, which may be essential only in major war contingencies that for the moment seem remote, and maintaining sufficient force levels to be able to cope with the more regular contingencies. To the extent that the United States judges that it must incline toward the most advanced lest it be caught out in some future great-power confrontation, it will still probably be able to cope with most of the more short-term demands on its forces. That may not prove to be so straightforward for allies of the United States, which must accept a certain investment in the more advanced systems if only to stay in touch and feel able to operate alongside U.S. forces. With a limited budget, however, there is a risk that this effort could jeopardize investment in more basic capabilities that may be essential to core tasks.

The critical issue is not so much capabilities as expectations. Sophisticated systems can alleviate but never eliminate the essential vulgarity of war. Most contemporary conflicts take the form not of epic encounters for great-power dominance to be decided through the test of set-piece battles but of brutish, protracted contests that are often confusing to outsiders. Outsiders tend to recoil from these struggles, precisely because they do not lend themselves to the straightforward imposition of political will through dominant force. Rather, they require outsiders to accept long-term responsibility for distressed parts of the world and their associated onerous and complicated military demands. Unfortunately, responsible Western governments cannot simply choose the wars that are easy to fight and win; they must also act where a failure to do so will result in chronic instability, with even greater distress to those directly involved and deleterious consequences for the wider community.

NOTES

1. See in particular T. Schelling, *The Strategy of Conflict* (New York: Oxford University Press, 1963). The various strategies are discussed in L. Freedman, *The Evolution of Nuclear Strategy* (London: Macmillan, 1989), chap. 12.

2. For definitions of the RMA, see A. Krepinevich, "Cavalry to Computer: The Pattern of Military Revolutions," *National Interest* 37 (fall 1994); A. W. Owens, "The Emerging System of Systems," *U.S. Naval Institute Proceedings* (May 1995): 35–39; and E. Cohen, "A Revolution in Warfare," *Foreign Affairs* 75, no. 2 (March-April 1996). My views on the RMA are developed at length in L. Freedman, *The Revolution in Strategic Affairs* (London: Oxford University Press for the International Institute for Strategic Studies, 1998).

3. A. H. Cordesman and A. R. Wagner, *The Lessons of Modern War*, vol. 2, *The Gulf War* (Boulder, Colo.: Westview Press, 1996).

4. See J. T. Johnson, *Morality and Contemporary Warfare* (New Haven, Conn.: Yale University Press, 1999).

5. For a balanced assessment of the ability of U.S. allies to follow the U.S. lead in the RMA, see A. Richter, "The American Revolution? The Response of Advanced Western States to the Revolution in Military Affairs," *National Security Studies Quarterly* 4, no. 4 (1999): 1–28.

6. For an alarming analysis of contemporary Russian attitudes on nuclear strategy, see P. V. Pry, *War Scare: Russia and America on the Nuclear Brink* (Westport, Conn.: Praeger, 1999).

7. The various views on the future role of nuclear weapons can be found in the contributions to J. Baylis and R. O'Neill, eds., *Alternative Nuclear Futures: The Role of Nuclear Weapons in the Post–Cold War World* (Oxford: Oxford University Press, 1999).

8. A. Cordesman, *The Lessons of Desert Fox: A Preliminary Analysis* (Washington, D.C.: Center for Strategic and International Studies, 1999).

9. D. Lovelace, *The Evolution of Military Affairs: Shaping the Future U.S. Armed Forces* (Washington, D.C.: National Defense University, 1997).

10. D. Macgregor, *Breaking the Phalanx: A New Design for Landpower in the Twenty-First Century* (Westport, Conn.: Praeger, 1997).

11. G. Cameron, *Nuclear Terrorism: A Threat Assessment for the Twenty-First Century* (London: Macmillan, 1999).

12. E. Luttwak, "Towards Post-Heroic Warfare," *Foreign Affairs* 74, no. 3 (May-June 1995): 109–122.

13. J. Burk, "Public Support for Peacekeeping in Lebanon and Somalia: Assessing the Casualties Hypothesis," *Political Science Quarterly* 114, no. 1 (1999): 53–78.

14. Presidency Conclusions, *Common European Policy on Security and Defence*, Helsinki, December 10 and 11, 1999. On the difficulties of formulating a common European foreign and security policy, see J. Zielonka, *Explaining Euro-Paralysis: Why Europe Is Unable to Act in International Politics* (London: Macmillan, 1998).

15. J. Keegan, "So the Bomber Got Through After All," *Daily Telegraph*, June 4, 1999. For a skeptical view, see E. H. Tilford, "Operation Allied Force and the Role of Air Power," *Parameters* (winter 1999–2000). For assessments of the war, see T. Judah, *Kosovo: War and Revenge* (New Haven, Conn.: Yale University Press, 2000); and A. Schnabel and R. Thakur, eds., *Kosovo and the Challenge of Humanitarian Intervention* (Tokyo: United Nations University Press, 2000). On the issues of humanitarian intervention, see A. Roberts, "NATO's 'Humanitarian War' over Kosovo," *Survival* 41, no. 3 (autumn 1999): 102–123.

UN Sanction Regimes and Violent Conflict

Chantal de Jonge Oudraat

THIS CHAPTER EXAMINES the effectiveness of multilateral economic sanctions in preventing, managing, or resolving violent conflict.[1] Since the end of the Cold War, the United Nations Security Council has increasingly used economic sanctions for this purpose. Indeed, since 1989 the UN Security Council has imposed economic sanctions sixteen times—compared with twice in the period from 1945 to 1988 (see table 1). In eleven of these sixteen cases, sanctions were imposed to contain or to stop internal conflicts. In one case, sanctions were imposed to restore international peace and security and to force Iraq to end its occupation of Kuwait.[2] In another case, an arms embargo was imposed to stop the war between Eritrea and Ethiopia. In the other three cases, sanctions were imposed to force Afghanistan, Libya, and Sudan to extradite individuals suspected of terrorist attacks.

The political effectiveness of many of these sanction regimes has been limited. They have often imposed tremendous economic costs on the target countries, but they have not always changed the political behavior of the leaders of those countries. Moreover, the economic impact on the countries in question has had many unintended social and humanitarian effects, leading many commentators to question the morality of economic sanctions as a policy instrument.[3]

Notwithstanding the weak track record of economic sanction regimes, the imposition of economic sanctions remains for many policy-makers an attractive—seemingly inexpensive and low-risk—way of showing concern and taking action. They generally hope that the decision to impose economic sanctions will eliminate the need to take more assertive action, such as using or threatening to use military force. Moreover, unlike with the use of force, there is no international legal impediment to the imposition of sanctions.[4] In sum, because sanctions continue to be a popular policy instrument, it is important to develop a better understanding of the way sanctions work in order to increase their effectiveness and limit their harmful humanitarian effects.

The scholarly literature on sanctions is massive.[5] Most scholars and analysts are pessimistic about the effectiveness of economic sanctions. In part, this is because analysts have paid too much attention to the outcomes of sanction regimes and too little attention to the conditions under which the imposition of sanctions can be effective in bringing about changes in political behavior. They have neglected to develop sanction strategies and ways to implement them. Sanction analysts have also tended to study economic sanctions in isolation, independent of other coercive policy instruments such as the use of force.

I argue that economic sanctions can be effective policy instruments if they are part of comprehensive coercive strategies that include the use of force and if they are implemented properly. Many sanction regimes in the 1990s failed because they did not meet these two key conditions—they were not integrated into comprehensive coercive strategies and they were not properly implemented.

That said, sanctions are no panacea. In some cases, it is best to forgo economic sanctions; they are blunt instruments and should be imposed only when outside powers are willing to use the whole array of coercive instruments available to them—that is, if they are willing to use military force. When outside powers have limited objectives, they may want to use targeted economic sanctions. These types of sanctions generally have limited economic impacts and, like diplomatic or cultural sanctions, have mainly symbolic value; their effectiveness in bringing about changes in political behavior is limited.

In this chapter, I do five things. First, I define economic sanctions and examine different types of sanctions. Second, I briefly review the track record of the multilateral sanction regimes of the 1990s. Third, I outline the elements of a sanctions strategy—that is, a strategy that will suggest when and how sanctions should be imposed. Fourth, I examine implementation and third-party compliance issues. Fifth, I develop some policy recommendations.

DEFINITIONS AND TYPES OF ECONOMIC SANCTIONS

Economic sanctions are nonmilitary measures that restrict or arrest normal international economic exchanges with a state or a nongovernmental group, with the purpose of changing the political or military behavior of the government or group in question. Economic sanctions are different from trade wars, in which governments restrict or stop international economic exchanges in order to gain more favorable terms of trade. Underlying the theory of sanctions is the expectation that economic costs will translate into political effects—that economic deprivation will produce public anger and politically significant protest, which in turn will lead to changes in the political behavior of troublemaking elites or their removal from power.

Economic sanctions can be comprehensive or partial. They may encompass a multitude of services and goods or they may be limited to specific services and strategic goods, such as air traffic or oil. They may limit and ban exports —embargoes—or they may limit and ban imports—boycotts.

Targeted sanctions—that is, measures that target corporations or people—became the subject of much research in the latter half of the 1990s.[6] These sanctions hold out the promise of avoiding costs to neighboring countries, as well as to innocent people in the countries in question. Targeted economic or financial sanctions consist of freezing designated corporate or individual overseas assets and prohibiting international financial transactions with such corporations or individuals.

Arms embargoes are a special kind of economic sanction. Unlike with regular economic sanctions, their primary objective is not to inflict economic pain but to deny access. Indeed, arms embargoes are imposed to restrict military capabilities and, thereby, to induce military stalemates and to prevent conflicts from escalating. They are also imposed to limit third-party involvement in conflicts.

The objective of sanctions imposed by the UN Security Council under Chapter VII of the UN Charter is "to maintain or restore international peace and security." The council has tremendous latitude in defining threats to "international peace and security" and it has shown great creativity in the post–Cold War era in defining these threats. Indeed, it has increasingly deemed internal conflicts and gross violations of human rights to be justifications for international action.[7]

Economic sanctions imposed by the UN Security Council are coercive measures. They are intended to deter parties from engaging in certain types of behavior or to compel parties to undo or reverse certain political or military acts. The yardstick of a successful UN sanction regime is an observable change in behavior.[8]

A decision to impose mandatory sanctions needs affirmative votes from nine members of the UN Security Council, including the votes of China, France, Russia, the United Kingdom, and the United States—the five permanent members of the council. Once the council has decided to impose economic sanctions under Chapter VII of the charter, all UN member-states are required to carry out these measures.[9] Indeed, when states join the United Nations they agree to carry out the decisions of the Security Council. The council, however, has no way of forcing recalcitrant states to adhere to sanction regimes unless it imposes sanctions on these states as well.[10] Building and maintaining strong international political support for sanction regimes is therefore essential.

THE TRACK RECORD OF MULTILATERAL SANCTION REGIMES

Since the end of the Cold War comprehensive economic sanction regimes have been adopted four times. Partial economic sanctions have been adopted eight times. Targeted financial sanctions have been imposed twice. Arms embargoes have been imposed eleven times. (See table 1.) A brief review of these sanction regimes follows.[11]

Comprehensive Economic Sanctions

Comprehensive economic sanction regimes were adopted against Iraq in 1990, against the Federal Republic of Yugoslavia (FRY) in 1992; against the military junta in Haiti in 1994; and, again in 1994, against the Bosnian Serbs.

IRAQ. Sanctions against Iraq were imposed because of its invasion and illegal occupation of Kuwait in August 1990.[12] However, sanctions failed to have the desired effect—Iraqi withdrawal from Kuwait—so in January 1991 a coalition of states led by the United States used military force and expelled Iraq from Kuwait. Subsequently sanctions remained in place to force Iraqi compliance with the so-called cease-fire resolution—in particular, its disarmament provisions.[13]

In economic terms, Iraq was a good candidate for sanctions. Its economy was weak following Iraq's eight-year war with Iran. Moreover, Iraq was highly dependent on trade; oil exports accounted for more than 95 percent of Iraq's foreign currency exchange receipts and represented 60 percent of its GDP. In addition, Iraq's foreign debt was high. In political terms, however, Iraq was less vulnerable to sanctions. Its mainly rural population lived under a strict and very repressive authoritarian regime, which did not tolerate political opposition. That Saddam Hussein, the Iraqi leader, had little regard for the country's population had been

Table 1. UN Security Council Sanctions Imposed under Chapter VII of the UN Charter (1945–2000)

Target	Date Imposed	Comprehensive Economic Sanctions	Partial Economic Sanctions	Targeted Financial Sanctions	Arms Embargoes	Enabling UNSC Date Lifted	Resolution
Southern Rhodesia	Dec. 16, 1966	▓				Dec. 21, 1979	232 (1966) 460 (1979)
South Africa	Nov. 4, 1977				▓	May 25, 1994	418 (1977) 919 (1994)
Iraq	Aug. 6, 1990	▓					661 (1990)[a]
Republics of the Former Yugoslavia	Sept. 25, 1991				▓	June 18, 1996	713 (1991)[b] 1021 (1995)
Federal Republic of Yugoslavia	May 30, 1992	▓				Nov. 22, 1995	757 (1992)[c] 1022 (1995)[d]
	March 31, 1998				▓		1160 (1998)
Bosnian Serbs	Sept. 23, 1994	▓				Oct. 1, 1996	942 (1994) 1074 (1996)
Somalia	Jan. 23, 1992				▓		733 (1992)
Libya	March 31, 1992		▓		▓	April 5, 1999	748 (1992)[e]
Liberia	Nov. 19, 1992				▓		788 (1992)
Haiti	June 16, 1993		▓		▓	Aug. 27, 1993	841 (1993) 861 (1993)
	Oct. 18, 1993		▓				873 (1993)
	May 21, 1994	▓				Oct. 16, 1994	917 (1994) 944 (1994)

UNITA (Angola)	Sept. 15, 1993		864 (1993)[f]
	June 12, 1998		1173 (1998)
Rwanda	May 17, 1994	Aug. 16, 1995	918 (1994)[g] 1011 (1995)[h]
Sudan	May 10, 1996		1054 (1996)[i]
Sierra Leone	Oct. 8, 1997	June 5, 1998	1132 (1997) 1171 (1998)[j]
	July 15, 2000		1306 (2000)
Taliban (Afghanistan)	Nov. 15, 1999		1267 (1999)
Eritrea and Ethiopia	May 17, 2000		1298 (2000)

a. For subsequent resolutions, see Office of the Spokesman for the Secretary-General (OSSG), *Use of Sanctions under Chapter VII of the UN Charter*, at http://www.un.org/News/ossg/sanction.htm.

b. See also UNSC Resolution 727 (1992), January 8, 1992, which reaffirms that the arms embargo applies to all republics of the former Yugoslavia.

c. See also UNSC Resolution 787 (1992), November 16, 1992, and UNSC Resolution 820 (1993), April 17, 1993, which strengthened the sanction regime. UNSC 943 (1994), September 23, 1994, suspended certain sanctions on the FRY.

d. Sanctions were suspended in November 1995. They were lifted on October 1, 1996. See UNSC Resolution 1074, October 1, 1996.

e. See also UNSC Resolution 883 (1993), November 11, 1993, which tightened sanctions on Libya. Sanctions were suspended on April 5, 1999. *See UN Security Council Presidential Statement*, S/PRST/1999/10.

f. See also UNSC Resolution 1127 (1997), August 28, 1997, and UNSC Resolution 1130 (1997), September 29, 1997, which strengthened the sanction regime.

g. See also UNSC Resolution 997 (1995), June 9, 1995, which affirmed that the prohibition on the sale and supplies of arms for use in Rwanda also applied to persons in the states neighboring Rwanda. The sale and supply of arms to nongovernmental forces for use in Rwanda remained prohibited.

h.

i. See also UNSC Resolution 1070 (1996), August 16, 1996, which foreshadowed an air embargo on Sudan. This embargo never went into effect because of the expected humanitarian consequences.

j. The arms embargo remained in place for members of the former military junta and Revolutionary United Front.

Source: United Nations, Office of the Spokesman for the Secretary-General, *Use of Sanctions under Chapter VII of the UN Charter*, March 31, 2000; http://www.un.org/News/ossg/sanction.htm.

demonstrated dramatically in March 1988, when he attacked Halabjah, a town 160 miles northeast of Baghdad, with chemical weapons. Over five thousand people were killed and many more seriously injured in the attack.[14]

Given these conditions it became clear to U.S. president George Bush early in the crisis that economic sanctions alone would not be sufficient to dislodge Iraq from Kuwait.[15] Bush consequently began a massive deployment of military forces in Saudi Arabia and elsewhere in the Persian Gulf.[16]

Postwar sanctions have been in effect for over ten years. As with the prewar sanctions, implementation of this regime has been relatively good. Postwar sanctions have also been very effective in terms of their economic impact on Iraq. Iraq's GDP in 1993, at $10 billion, was close to 1960s levels. The annual value of imports fell from $11.5 billion in 1980 to $0.5 billion in 1996, and over the same period exports plummeted from $28.3 billion to $0.5 billion.[17] However, the sanction regime has been less effective from a political point of view—Saddam Hussein remains in charge in Baghdad and he has not given up on plans to develop weapons of mass destruction. Moreover, the sanction regime has had grave humanitarian consequences in Iraq. This undercut the legitimacy of sanctions and made the sanctioners look like the bad guys.

Indeed, humanitarian exemptions to the sanction regime did not prevent the Iraqi people from suffering great hardship.[18] Recognizing their predicament, the UN Security Council adopted the Oil for Food Program in August 1991. Under the terms of this program, revenue from the sale of Iraqi oil could be used to pay for food and medicines.[19] However, implementation of the program has been troubled. Indeed, a major structural flaw of the program is that it can be effective only if it has the full cooperation of the Iraqi government. It took until December 1996 to obtain such cooperation from Baghdad. For more than five years Saddam Hussein refused to accept

the conditions under which Iraqi oil revenues could be spent. Moreover, the Iraqi government, unconcerned about the welfare of its population, would frequently order insufficient supplies of food and medicines, stock up supplies in warehouses, illegally reexport humanitarian supplies, or simply stop oil exports.[20] By increasing the plight of the Iraqi people, the Iraqi leadership hoped to put moral pressure on the members of the Security Council to lift sanctions altogether.

By the end of 1999, this Iraqi counterpressure produced some results. Calls for the lifting of sanctions were increasingly heard at the Security Council. France, Russia, and China, in particular, lobbied for a sanction exit strategy. In December 1999 the council committed itself to suspending sanctions if Iraq accepted a new weapons monitoring and verification system.[21] Little headway was made in the months that followed and negotiations on such a system were stalled.

Meanwhile, the humanitarian situation in Iraq continued to deteriorate, and UN secretary-general Kofi Annan warned the members of the Security Council that they were losing the propaganda war about who was responsible for the situation in Iraq—Saddam Hussein or the United Nations. Annan also acknowledged that the Oil for Food Program had not met the essential needs of the Iraqi people.[22]

The postwar sanctions, unlike their prewar counterparts, were not integrated into a comprehensive coercive strategy. After the war, outside powers were not willing to escalate and mount a sustained military operation.[23] By limiting their options in this manner, outside powers may have managed to keep Iraq from developing new weapons programs, but this came at heavy moral costs and at the expense of the health of the Iraqi population.

FRY AND BOSNIAN SERBS. Economic sanctions against the FRY were imposed because of its involvement in the war in Bosnia.[24] First imposed in May 1992, sanctions were strengthened in November 1992 and again in April 1993.[25] Sanctions were imposed on the Bosnian Serbs in September 1994, after they refused to accept the peace plan presented by the Western powers and their allies.[26] Western powers stepped up their coercive effort in Bosnia in July 1995, and a two-week bombing campaign was carried out against the Bosnian Serbs in August and September 1995. Sanctions were suspended later in the year, following the negotiation of the Dayton Peace Accords.[27]

The FRY had a very vulnerable economy from a sanctions standpoint. In the early 1990s the Yugoslav economy was in the midst of a difficult transition from centralized to market-based arrangements. Unemployment and inflation had been on the rise since 1981. At the same time, foreign borrowing had become more difficult and had been made conditional on the implementation of domestic economic reforms. Finally, the dissolution of Yugoslavia in 1991 imposed heavy costs on the FRY economy. The former republics of Yugoslavia had been economically interdependent; in particular, they had relied heavily on one another for food, energy supplies, and manufactures. Moreover, Serbia and Montenegro produced only 20 percent of the fuel they needed; they depended on imports from China, Russia, Iran, and Romania for most of the rest.[28] Balancing against this, FRY citizens had substantial foreign currency reserves. This helped mitigate the effect of sanctions initially.[29]

The political conditions for imposing sanctions were less than ideal. The communist apparatus was still largely in place in the FRY. Slobodan Milosevic, the Serbian leader, controlled the country's police forces and the media. The army was loyal to him, and the political opposition was weak. Finally, Serbia is a predominantly rural state that had been the home to strong nationalist appeals and ethnic scapegoating since the late 1980s. The rallying-around-the-flag effect turned out to be strong in the FRY. Milosevic was not swept away in a popular uprising.

Most scholars agree that after 1993 implementation of the sanction regime was good. Indeed, the sanctions against the FRY benefited from unprecedented international arrangements designed to assist states—in particular, neighboring states—to implement and enforce the measures decreed by the UN Security Council.[30] That said, there is little scholarly consensus with respect to the political effectiveness of the economic sanctions imposed on the FRY. Some scholars credit sanctions with remarkable success; others believe that the sanctions had no impact whatsoever.[31]

I argue that the FRY case is one of missed opportunities. Had the threat of more stringent sanctions in 1993 and 1994 been supported by a credible threat of military action, as well as a unified front by the Western allies, the war in Bosnia might have ended at those junctures, and outside powers might have avoided resorting to the use of military force.

The sanctions that were imposed in May 1992 had little effect on the war in Bosnia; indeed, during the summer of 1992, the eastern, northern, and northwestern parts of Bosnia experienced systematic forced expulsions of civilian populations. In November 1992 the UN Security Council, in response to numerous sanction violation reports, decided to strengthen the sanction regime. In addition, the European Union (EU) and the Conference on Security and Cooperation in Europe (CSCE) had started a program to help neighboring states implement, monitor, and enforce the sanction regimes.[32] Meanwhile, diplomatic efforts to negotiate a truce made some headway when the UN and EU negotiators—Cyrus Vance and David Owen—presented a comprehensive peace plan in January 1993 that might have been acceptable to all of the concerned parties. Although U.S. support for the peace plan was slow to materialize, the UN Security Council formally endorsed the plan on April 17 and threatened the FRY with tougher sanctions if the plan was not accepted by all parties within nine days.

Negotiations between Owen and Milo-
sevic ensued. The latter endorsed the plan on
April 25. However, the Bosnian Serbs opposed
the plan and sanctions went into effect on
April 26. In a last-ditch effort to save the plan
Owen convened a meeting of all parties on
May 2, 1993, in Athens. At that time Radovan
Karadzic, the Bosnian Serb leader, agreed to put
the plan to a popular vote on May 16.

Owen was convinced that Milosevic had
given up the idea of forming a greater Serbia
and that he consequently supported a settlement. Owen believed that the threat of more
stringent sanctions had managed to split the
Serbs. Moreover, Owen believed that the
threat of the use of force had been instrumental in bringing about a change in Milosevic's
position. Indeed, at the time Owen had hinted
repeatedly at the consequences of Serbian intransigence: if the Serbs did not accept the plan,
Western powers would contemplate the use
of force. The fact that the sanction resolution
had explicitly authorized states to use force to
enforce the sanction regime gave some credibility to these threats. Owen believed that Belgrade would not have voiced any objections if
the Vance-Owen plan had been imposed on the
Bosnian Serbs militarily.[33] However, the inde-
cisiveness of the Clinton administration and
dissent among the Western allies made such a
course impossible.[34]

Indeed, the United States was never enthusiastic about the Vance-Owen plan. Washington had made it clear that U.S. troops would
be available only if all parties consented to the
agreement; U.S. troops would not be available
to impose the agreement on the warring factions. European powers were unwilling to impose the plan on the Bosnian Serbs without
U.S. support. The timid Western reaction to
the Serb assaults on Srebrenica in April 1993
drove this point home.[35] In addition, U.S. secretary of state Warren Christopher's maiden
trip to Europe in early May 1993 and the subsequent debate between the United States and
Europeans over "lift and strike" showed the

Bosnian Serbs that none of the Western powers had much stomach for forceful military
action.[36] Not surprisingly, the Bosnian Serbs rejected the plan on May 16, 1993; they thought
that they could ride out the storm. Disagreements among the Western allies had undercut
the threat of more stringent economic sanctions as well as the threat of the use of force.[37]

Ultimately, the effect of the sanctions helped
to harden Milosevic's position, and he quickly
reestablished full relations with the Bosnian
Serbs.[38] Indeed, given Milosevic's domestic
political position, he could not abandon the
Bosnian Serbs—this would have led to trouble
in Serbia with the extremist right. The latter
had done surprisingly well in the December
1992 Serbian parliamentary elections and had
challenged Milosevic's support of the Vance-
Owen plan. Only direct military action against
the Bosnian Serbs by outside powers could
have shielded Milosevic from a domestic political backlash.

The second missed opportunity for the effective use of sanctions came in 1994. In July
the Contact Group took the diplomatic initiative and presented a new peace plan that was
linked to a partial lifting of UN sanctions.[39]
Again Milosevic gave his support to the Contact Group's peace plan and threatened to sever
political and economic ties with the Bosnian
Serbs if they rejected the plan. The promise of
a partial lifting of the sanctions was alluring to
Milosevic. Moreover, the Western powers had
foreshadowed the possible use of military
force. The active involvement of the United
States in the Contact Group made the use of
force a real possibility. Finally, the creation of
the Bosnian/Muslim-Croat Federation had
changed the balance of forces in Bosnia. Even
so, the Bosnian Serbs rejected the plan. The
following day, Milosevic, as he had promised,
broke off economic and political relations
with the Bosnian Serbs. Milosevic's reward for
this gesture was limited, however.[40] The subsequent sanctions imposed by the UN Security
Council on the Bosnian Serbs made Bosnian

Serb leaders virtual prisoners in the Bosnian areas they controlled. Yet these sanctions had little effect in terms of changing the behavior of Bosnian Serb leaders. In addition, the FRY blockade was not watertight and Milosevic continued to support Ratko Mladic, the Bosnian Serb military leader.[41]

Moreover, the Western allies soon revealed themselves to be as feeble as ever. The United States backpedaled on its threats to launch military strikes, and before long the Western coalition was again at loggerheads over the U.S. proposal to lift the arms embargo on the Bosnian government and to strike Bosnian Serb targets from the air—an issue that had divided the allies since 1993.

Again, Milosevic was thrust back into the arms of the Bosnian Serbs. This episode begs the question of whether a more substantial sanction suspension package would have led Milosevic to be firmer with the Bosnian Serbs. Such a strategy may have seemed morally repugnant in the face of the atrocities committed by the Serbs, yet such a strategy, coupled with direct military action against the Bosnian Serbs, was adopted by the United States and the international community in 1995.

Indeed, in August 1995, after the fall of Srebrenica, the international community finally decided to stop the war in Bosnia. For the first time, the United States engaged in direct talks with Milosevic. U.S. interlocutors convinced Milosevic that he had no choice but to agree with the plan that they had laid on the table. Milosevic knew that the United States was willing to use military force to achieve its objectives. This, rather than the effect of the sanctions, seems to have been the reason why Milosevic in turn put pressure on the Bosnian Serbs.

In sum, the threat of economic sanctions combined with the threat of military force—rather than the long-term effects of sanctions—was the key to changing Milosevic's behavior. The international community failed to bring about such changes in 1993 and 1994; these were missed opportunities for peace. The

dissent among the members of the UN Security Council—most notably, the United States and its European allies—made the development of an all-encompassing coercive strategy toward the FRY and the Bosnian Serbs impossible for most of the 1992–95 period.

HAITI. The UN Security Council threatened Haiti with an oil and arms embargo in June 1993. Its goal was to return to power the democratically elected Haitian president, Jean-Bertrand Aristide, who had been ousted by a military coup in September 1991.[42] All economic indicators, including Haiti's extreme dependency on outside oil supplies and on the United States for most of its trade, led many to believe that the Haitian junta would quickly agree to negotiations.[43] And indeed, two days before sanctions were to take effect, the military junta agreed to enter into negotiations with Aristide. These negotiations, under joint UN-OAS chairmanship, were successful in producing an agreement that included the creation of a new government, the deployment of UN peacekeepers, and the return of Aristide. Sanctions would be lifted once a new prime minister was nominated, but before the deployment of UN peacekeepers and before the return of Aristide.[44]

Implementation of the agreement was slow: it took one month to nominate a new prime minister and suspend sanctions.[45] Delays also occurred on the UN side: the Security Council did not authorize the peacekeeping mission until the end of September 1993. Meanwhile, the situation in Haiti had considerably deteriorated and violence was on the rise. Members of the United Nations failed to respond to these dangerous developments. By the time the first batch of UN peacekeepers arrived in Haiti in October 1993, the Haitian military and its supporters had stocked up on supplies and mustered enough confidence to stage an unfriendly reception in the harbor of Port-au-Prince that prevented the peacekeepers from disembarking.[46]

In response to this act of deviance, sanctions were reimposed on Haiti and UN member-states were authorized to enforce the embargo with a naval blockade.[47] Moreover, in December 1993 the Security Council presented the Haitian military with an ultimatum —implement the July 1993 agreement or face stronger sanctions. The Security Council's deadline of January 15, 1994, came and went without any action being taken.

The members of the Security Council were deeply divided over how to handle the Haitian situation.[48] France wanted to expand the sanctions on Haiti. This was opposed by the United States, which feared that stronger sanctions would lead to a surge in Haitian refugees coming to Florida. Washington proposed financial measures targeted at specific individuals. Finally, China, piqued by Aristide's support for the Taiwanese demand to become a member of the United Nations, blocked all decisions on Haiti.

It would take an unprecedented new wave of Haitian refugees trying to find shelter in the United States and the subsequent mobilization of the U.S. congressional Black Caucus and other Democratic Party interest groups in Washington to stir the U.S. government into action and have it take the lead in developing a more forceful and coherent policy toward Haiti.

In May 1994 the UN Security Council approved the imposition of a total trade ban on Haiti, except for medical supplies and foodstuffs. It also imposed travel restrictions on the Haitian military and police and urged UN member-states to freeze the financial assets of these individuals. However, the freezing of assets was a nonmandatory sanction left to the discretion of member-states. Sanctions would be lifted only after the resignation of the military junta and after the deployment of UN peacekeepers. At the same time, measures were taken to tackle sanction-busting efforts.[49]

The strengthened sanction package had little effect. The ill-advised retreat of the USS *Harlan County* made the United Nations and the United States appear weak. Moreover, with little else to lose, the Haitian military and its collaborators seemed to harden rather than soften their positions. In the summer of 1994, they threw all UN officers out of the country. Faced with this new act of hostility, the Security Council authorized a military operation to depose the junta.[50] U.S. troops landed in Haiti on September 19, 1994. Aristide was returned to power on October 15, 1994, and UN sanctions were lifted soon after that.[51] Since then, Haiti has struggled to keep violence under wraps, install a democratic regime, and resuscitate its economy.

The Haitian case is instructive in several respects. First, like the FRY case, Haiti is a case of missed opportunities. The weak reaction from the international community to the rise of violence in the summer and fall of 1993 made the Haitian military confident that they could defy the international community.[52] Failure to deploy UN peacekeepers at that time added to the junta's confidence and was probably one of the most ill advised decisions the United States made. It prolonged the life of the junta and the suffering of the Haitian people.

Second, although Haiti's economy was vulnerable to sanctions, the predatory nature of the country's military regime should have instilled caution in outside actors. The suffering of the Haitian poor was of no concern to the junta.

Third, as in the Iraqi case, the humanitarian effects of the sanction regime were considerable and could have been easily foreseen. Haiti is the poorest country in the Western Hemisphere.[53] Over 70 percent of the Haitian population live in abject poverty and have no ready access to safe drinking water or medical care. The UN sanctions, even if they were not very well implemented, accelerated the decline of the Haitian economy. Between 1992 and 1993 the country's GDP fell by almost 20 percent. By 1994 over thirty thousand people had lost their jobs, and unemployment ranged between 65 percent and 80 percent. Meanwhile, the production of food crops declined and food prices soared. These economic effects led to an unexpected "rallying-around-Aristide" effect that produced an increase in Haitian refugees trying to seek shelter in the United States.[54] This, of course, was something the United States was keen to avoid.

Fourth, as is often the case in internal conflicts, sanctions had asymmetrical effects. In this case, Aristide and his supporters—the good guys—were more vulnerable to sanctions than the Haitian ruling elites—the bad guys.

Fifth, implementation of the sanction regime was poor. The Haitian military and the ruling elite managed to obtain most basic—and many not-so-basic—goods. Many states considered the implementation and enforcement of the sanction regime to be a U.S. problem. Putting a naval blockade into place or closing the Haitian-Dominican border presented few technical or resource problems for the United States. It did, however, pose political problems, and it was only in May 1994 that Haiti's border with the Dominican Republic was sealed. This, however, came too late and had no political impact on the Haitian military. Moreover, early suspension of the sanction regime in 1993 gave the ruling elite opportunities to set up alternative supply routes. Indeed, members of the junta cornered the drug traffic and other illegal trade in contraband.

Finally, the Haiti case shows that credible threats of economic sanctions can be effective. The credibility of such threats is strengthened if all coercive options—including the use of military force—remain on the table.[55] Once the credibility of outside powers is undercut, threats to use sanctions are no longer sufficient. At that point, sanctions have to be followed and they have to be followed by real action.

Partial Economic Sanctions

Partial economic sanctions were adopted against Libya in 1992, Haiti in 1993 (twice), UNITA in 1993, Sudan in 1996, Sierra Leone in 1997 and in 2000, and the Taliban in 1999. In all of these cases, the UN Security Council characterized the situations as "threats to international peace and security." The Libyan, Sudanese, and Afghan cases nonetheless differed from the others in that they involved compliance with a very specific council demand—the extradition of alleged terrorists.[56] The cases of Angola and Sierra Leone had a more general objective—stopping civil strife. I examine only the latter two cases because my focus is on the problems associated with violent conflict.

UNITA (Angola). An oil and arms embargo was imposed on Jonas Savimbi's National Union for the Total Independence of Angola (UNITA) after Savimbi refused to honor the results of the UN-supervised elections in 1991 and after UNITA resumed fighting.[57] Subsequently, the UN Security Council repeatedly threatened to impose additional sanctions on UNITA. However, it failed to follow through on these threats, for fear that additional sanctions might disrupt and prevent direct negotiations between the parties.[58]

In 1997 the military situation in Angola deteriorated considerably. It became clear at that point that UNITA was not negotiating in good faith. UNITA, moreover, refused to demobilize its military forces. The Security Council, responding to increased pressure from UN member-states to take more forceful action, imposed travel and diplomatic sanctions on UNITA in August 1997.[59] These sanctions were postponed twice, but they finally took effect on October 30, 1997.[60] They had, however, little impact on Savimbi's forces, and fighting escalated in 1998.

The Security Council again responded by strengthening its sanctions on UNITA. It decided in June 1998 to freeze UNITA's financial assets, ban all financial transactions with UNITA, and prohibit the trade of Angolan diamonds not certified by the Angolan government. Travel restrictions on UNITA officials were also tightened.[61] Again, sanctions had little effect. UNITA continued to sell diamonds and procure the arms and supplies it needed for its war effort. UNITA officials also continued to travel, and many "unofficial" offices and representatives operated in capitals around the world.[62]

Implementation and enforcement of this sanction regime were dismal. Poor implementation was due in part to the fact that nongovernmental groups are often difficult to isolate economically. Moreover, guerrilla groups such as UNITA are not particularly vulnerable to normal trade sanctions, mainly because they do not engage in normal trade. In addition, independent rebel groups generally withstand economic or political pressures well: they have a high pain threshold and their members are generally highly motivated. Finally, UNITA had access to diamonds, which enabled it to keep its military campaign alive. Estimates of UNITA's diamond sales from January 1993 to December 1998 vary between $2.3 billion and $3.7 billion.[63] This enabled UNITA to build a highly mobile and well-armed army of thirty-five thousand soldiers. Since 1998 UNITA's diamond sales have gone down sharply. That said, it still has many millions of dollars' worth of diamonds with which to finance its war machine.[64] Moreover, neighboring countries such as Burkina Faso, Namibia, Rwanda, South Africa, and Zambia help UNITA smuggle its diamonds out of Angola and provide safe havens for UNITA diamond transactions.[65]

Given the ineffectiveness of trying to change UNITA's behavior, the UN Security Council decided in 1999 to change tack and adopt a different strategy. Instead of focusing on UNITA it shifted its attention to the sanction busters. It commissioned a report on sanction violations and hoped to induce better third-party compliance through a "naming-and-shaming" campaign. This report, published in March 2000, broke with a holy UN practice and openly accused people, including acting and former heads of state, of violating the sanction regime.[66] Whether this "naming-and-shaming" campaign will have results remains to

be seen. Within the United Nations the report received a reserved welcome. The report, according to one diplomat, was a very "rough diamond," and many argued that the accusations had not been sufficiently substantiated.[67]

SIERRA LEONE. In May 1997 the Armed Forces Revolutionary Council (AFRC) overthrew the newly elected civilian government of Ahmed Kabbah.[68] Five months later the UN Security Council imposed a UN oil and arms embargo on Sierra Leone as well as travel restrictions on members of the junta.[69] The council also authorized the Military Observer Group (ECOMOG) of the Economic Community of West African States (ECOWAS) to enforce the sanction regime, using military force if necessary. The aim of the sanction effort, as in Haiti, was to restore a civilian government to power.[70]

Sanctions seemed to have an initial positive effect. Only fifteen days after they were imposed the Conakry agreement was signed. This agreement called for the restoration of the elected civilian government within six months and the demobilization of Sierra Leone's armed forces and rebel groups.

However, as in Haiti, junta leaders failed to implement the agreement. In February 1998 Nigerian-led ECOMOG troops removed the junta from power. Kabbah was returned to office, and UN sanctions were lifted.[71] Sanctions remained in force against members of the military junta and the Revolutionary United Front (RUF), a rebel group that had sided with the AFRC junta.[72]

The situation in Sierra Leone remained fragile. In October 1998 RUF forces launched a major offensive. They seized control of Freetown, the capital of Sierra Leone, in January 1999. Although ECOMOG troops retook the capital and reinstalled the civilian government later that month, much of the country remained in the hands of the rebels.

The Nigerian government, wary of the war in Sierra Leone that was costing it $1 million per day and the lives of hundreds of its soldiers, realized that it was in no position to win. Under international pressure, from the United States in particular, Kabbah and RUF leader Foday Sankoh started negotiations.[73] These talks began in May 1999 and resulted in the Lomé agreement in July 1999. A government of national unity was established. The rebels were given amnesty, and the United Nations was invited to oversee implementation of the agreement and deploy a six-thousand-strong international force.[74]

The Lomé agreement unraveled in May 2000. Like Savimbi in Angola, Sankoh had cornered a substantial part of Sierra Leone's diamond trade. Some have estimated that Sierra Leone was losing $200 million to $300 million annually to smuggling, mainly by the RUF.[75] Until his arrest in May, Sankoh had secured the cooperation of Liberian president Charles Taylor, and most of the RUF "conflict diamonds" passed through Liberia, which sold false certificates to hide their origin. Liberia has exported since the mid-1990s some 31 million carats—more than two hundred years' worth of Liberia's national capacity.[76]

In July 2000, after several hundred UN peacekeepers had been taken hostage, the Security Council imposed a boycott on rough diamonds from Sierra Leone.[77] But without monitoring and enforcement mechanisms, these sanctions are likely to have little effect.

Partial sanctions in Angola and Sierra Leone failed because they were stand-alone measures, not part of a coercive strategy, and because of poor implementation. An energetic response to the first signs of defiance may well have led to very different outcomes in both countries. Half measures, however, stood no chance of success.

Targeted Financial Sanctions

The UN Security Council adopted mandatory targeted financial sanctions twice in the 1990s—against UNITA, its senior officials, and their family members in 1998, and against the Taliban, its senior officials, and their family members in 1999.[78] Given the limited amount of overseas funds held by the latter, these sanctions were mainly symbolic.

Targeted financial sanctions against UNITA had little effect on UNITA's ability to fund its war effort. The bulk of UNITA's financial assets were in the form of rough diamonds, which were sold as needed. Moreover, UNITA made significant amounts of money in the form of landing fees for aircraft bringing in food, medicines, and other commodities. In 1996–97, when commercial activity in Angola was at its peak, UNITA may have earned as much as $5 million per month.[79] The UN expert report on violations of the Angolan sanction regime concluded that UNITA managed to use a network of sanction-busting banks, financial institutions, and money managers for a number of important financial transactions.[80]

The cases show that targeted financial sanctions have serious implementation problems. The many ways in which true ownership of assets can be concealed, the speed by which financial assets can be transferred, and the fact that many countries have neither the technology nor the domestic legislation to monitor financial transactions are some of the implementation problems associated with these types of sanctions. Moreover, Internet banking has opened up new ways to move money around —ways that sanction and money-laundering experts have only started to analyze. Many of the techniques to make targeted financial sanctions work borrow from traditional money-laundering detection techniques. Such techniques are progressing, yet the possibilities for laundering money remain huge.

In sum, targeted financial sanctions, while attractive in theory, remain extremely problematic to implement. They require monitoring and enforcement capabilities that most countries do not possess. Moreover, setting up such mechanisms may well be too expensive for many countries. The imposition of targeted financial sanctions remains thus mainly symbolic, and changes in political behavior will be limited.

Arms Embargoes

Arms embargoes were imposed eleven times since the beginning of the 1990s—on the republics of the former Yugoslavia, 1991; Somalia, 1992; Libya, 1992; Liberia, 1992; Haiti, 1993 (twice); UNITA (Angola), 1993; Rwanda, 1994; Sierra Leone, 1997; FRY, 1998; and Eritrea and Ethiopia, 2000. In most of these cases, arms embargoes were part of larger economic sanction regimes.

Only in the cases of Somalia, Liberia, Rwanda, the FRY, and Ethiopia and Eritrea did the UN Security Council impose stand-alone arms embargoes. The dismal economic situations in most of these countries made outside powers wary of imposing additional economic sanctions. In the case of Rwanda, the arms embargo was an utterly inappropriate response to the unfolding genocide.

Third-party compliance with arms embargoes has generally been very poor. Internal conflicts are usually fought with small arms and light weapons—mortars, machine guns, rifles, machetes, and the like. The international trade in light weapons such as these is extremely difficult to regulate, especially since much of this trade is conducted on the black market.[81]

Imposing arms embargoes when violent conflicts are active is often seen as a logical first step toward halting violence. However, the Bosnia case has made the council more attentive to the unintended effects of arms embargoes, particularly in cases of internal conflict. Indeed, in these cases, arms embargoes tend to favor the warring factions that have access to governmental military stockpiles and industries, and undermine the abilities of others to organize and defend themselves. Arms embargoes can thus favor one side over the other and may permit one side to win, rather than pushing both sides toward a military stalemate and a political settlement.[82] This explains why the council did not impose an arms embargo on Sudan and Burundi in 1996 or on Afghanistan in 1999.

SANCTION STRATEGIES: WHEN AND HOW TO IMPOSE SANCTIONS

A sanction strategy should provide guidance about when and how to impose sanctions. It should also provide guidance about when and how to lift sanctions. Properly assessing the strengths and vulnerabilities of targets is essential. Indeed, the effectiveness of coercive efforts, including the imposition of sanctions, is determined to a large extent by the economic and political characteristics of the target. They will tell us whether the target is able to withstand economic pressures and devise counterthreats and actions that could neutralize the effects of sanctions. Once the target's strengths and weaknesses are properly assessed, outside powers should decide which sanction tactics are likely to be most effective: a swift and crushing blow or a gradual tightening of the screws. Finally, outside powers should formulate the conditions under which sanctions should be lifted or abandoned.

Assessing the Target

When outside powers consider imposing sanctions, they should carefully examine the economic and political characteristics of the target (see table 2).[83] Three economic characteristics of the target are particularly important: the nature and general health of the economy, including its level of development;[84] export and import dependencies; and the volume of overseas assets. The economic impact of sanctions depends on how quickly the target economy can adjust. Adjustment rates differ from one economic system to the next. Market economies are generally more vulnerable to economic sanctions than are centrally planned

Table 2. Economic and Political Characteristics of the Target: Making Targets More or Less Vulnerable to Sanctions

Economic Characteristics	
More Vulnerable	**Less Vulnerable**
Nature of the Economy	
Market economy	Centralized economy
Highly developed economy	Weakly developed economy
Weak economy	Healthy economy
Export and Import Dependency	
Strong dependency	Weak dependency
International Capital Market Dependency	
Strong dependency	Weak dependency

Political Characteristics	
More Vulnerable	**Less Vulnerable**
Type of Society	
Industrial	Rural
Ethnically mixed	Ethnically homogeneous
Nature of the Political Regime	
Democratic	Authoritarian
Political Opposition	
Strong	Weak

economies, because in market economies the allocation and distribution of resources is dependent on external price signals, instead of decisions by central authorities. For example, in the FRY Milosevic could weaken the impact of sanctions by instructing state enterprises to keep workers on the payroll and to continue to pay wages and pensions. Developing and rural economies, because they are generally more labor-intensive than capital-intensive, are

also less vulnerable to sanctions. Depressed economies and those in recession are more vulnerable to boycotts or embargoes of services and goods than are robust and expansionist economies. That said, outside powers should be careful about imposing sanctions on developing or troubled economies. Sanctions aggravate existing developmental problems and may easily result in the creation of humanitarian crises. Moreover, the imposition of sanctions in cases such as these may give political elites easy excuses for the dire state of their economies—they can blame sanctions for the economic problems the country is experiencing.

Foreign trade is another good indicator of economic vulnerability. Countries that are highly reliant on trade with a limited number of partners are especially vulnerable to economic sanctions. Haiti, because of its extreme dependence on the United States, was hence considered to be a "good" candidate for sanctions. This vulnerability increases if exports or imports consist of raw materials or industrial goods, as opposed to small consumer goods. The former are more important to keep economies going. Moreover, raw materials, except diamonds, are more difficult to smuggle across borders than small consumer goods. The presence of strategic resources, such as oil or gas, may make targets less vulnerable to sanctions, particularly if the targets are relatively self-reliant in other sectors of the economy. But if the export of strategic resources is their main source of income, the targets may be very vulnerable. For example, Iraq, because of its dependency on oil exports—60 percent of its GDP—was extremely vulnerable to sanctions.

Finally, it is important to measure the volume of the target's overseas assets. A heavy reliance on foreign banks or international financial institutions makes a country more vulnerable to financial sanctions. The importance of foreign investment and remittances from nationals abroad is also a good indicator of economic vulnerability. If financial transactions like remittances are not covered by a sanction regime, they may enable targeted countries to weather the impact of a sanction regime, as has happened in the case of the FRY.

The social and political characteristics of a target that are key for the effectiveness of sanctions are the type of society, including the internal cohesiveness and ethnic and religious makeup of a society; the nature of the political regime; and the strength of the political opposi-

tion. The type of society in the target country has a major impact on the effectiveness of sanctions. Industrialized societies, which have sizable middle classes of businesspeople and retailers, are more sensitive to the pressure of economic sanctions than are rural societies. Indeed, these middle classes are likely to push for negotiations and compromise. Moreover, group cohesion tends to be weaker in industrialized societies than in rural societies. Hence, the emergence of a rallying-around-the-flag effect is less likely in industrialized countries.[85] The level of cohesiveness of a society is also influenced by its ethnic and religious makeup. An ethnically or religiously homogeneous country will have stronger cohesiveness than countries that are ethnically or religiously mixed. It is thus important for those imposing sanctions to have a good understanding of the ethnic politics of a country.

The nature of the regime will also influence the prospects for sanctions. Authoritarian regimes are generally less vulnerable to sanctions than are democratic regimes, because the former are usually better able to control their political opponents. The existence of a political opposition is often cited as one of the critical conditions for the success of sanctions. One of the main premises of sanction theory is that sanctions will bolster political opposition to a regime. However, the FRY case suggests that the imposition of comprehensive sanctions once the opposition is weak is counterproductive. Indeed, the effects of sanctions may ruin their chances to build up a following. In cases such as these, ruling elites will depict their political opponents as traitors and thereby provoke a rallying-around-the-flag effect. Ruling elites will consequently draw strength from their deviance to the outside world.

When a country is in the midst of a civil war, sanctions will often have asymmetrical effects, because different groups will almost always have different vulnerabilities. Identifying the different strengths and weaknesses of these groups, including the different effects sanctions may have on them, is essential to avoid hurting the good guys, as has happened in Haiti.[86] In some cases it will be difficult to isolate these groups economically, and sanctions in such cases may not be the best way to go. If a country's political system has completely collapsed, as was the case in Somalia, it will be hard to identify a target for sanctions and their use will therefore be more problematic.

In sum, sanctions can be expected to be most effective when dealing with healthy market economies, which are highly dependent on trade and international capital markets. Similarly, industrialized, democratic countries with a preexisting strong political opposition can be expected to respond more quickly to economic pressures. Most UN sanction cases would score high—in terms of sanction vulnerability—on trade and international capital market dependencies and low on the structural economic factors. On the political factors they would almost all score low. The poor results of the UN sanction regimes should thus not have come as a surprise.

Sanction Tactics

Once outside powers have determined that sanctions can be used effectively to bring about political change in a target country, they have to decide how to impose sanctions.

Two schools of thought dominate the debate over how to impose sanctions. One school of thought maintains that sanctions are most effective when they are imposed immediately and comprehensively. Those who subscribe to this line of thinking argue that the gradual imposition of sanctions gives the target time to take steps to make sanctions less effective, such as stockpiling supplies, finding alternate trade routes and partners, and moving financial assets.[87]

The other school of thought contends that sanctions are most effective when they are partial and imposed incrementally. They argue that comprehensive sanction regimes are the equivalent of wars by attrition and that they will almost always trigger rallying-around-the-flag effects. Moreover, they argue that sanctions should be used to bring parties to the negotiating table. Comprehensive sanctions may have a greater impact on the economy of the target, but this does not necessarily translate into changes in political behavior; on the contrary, it may harden the target's positions.[88] Indeed, they argue that too much embargo may kill an embargo.

I believe that both schools of thought are right some of the time—different problems and situations may call for different strategies. Some cases warrant swift and comprehensive sanctions, while others call for a more gradual approach. The political and economic characteristics of a target are the keys to determining which road to choose.

Partial economic sanctions may be sufficient when targets score high in terms of sanction vulnerability. For example, gradual and partial sanctions may be sufficient when sanctioners are dealing with targets that have market economies and strong trade and international capital market dependencies. Partial sanctions like oil embargoes may also be sufficient when countries are highly dependent on outside energy resources. In addition, partial sanctions may be indicated when dealing with weak economies and economies with structural development problems. Indeed, in such cases the imposition of comprehensive sanctions may easily lead to a humanitarian emergency. Finally, partial and gradual sanctions may be sufficient when sanctioners are dealing with democratic regimes, strong political oppositions, and industrialized, atomized types of societies. Conversely, centralized economies, authoritarian regimes, rural societies, and countries with weak political oppositions and no trade or capital market dependencies should probably be hit immediately with comprehensive sanctions. Outside powers should also consider the threat of the use of force in such cases.

In determining whether to strike quick and hard or slow and soft, outside powers may also want to consider the seriousness of the situation at hand. In principle, all UN sanction cases have as an objective to "restore or maintain international peace and security." That said, some situations may be more serious than others. Sanctions should be proportionate to the objective to be achieved: the more ambitious the goal, the stronger the sanction regime. When outside powers are faced with gross violations of human rights or genocide, they may want to forgo the imposition of sanctions and intervene militarily. In all cases the threat of the use of force should remain on the table.

Sanction Exit Strategies

Good sanction strategies should also provide guidelines about when and how to lift sanctions. These exit strategies should not be confused with exit schedules. True exit strategies will identify the conditions under which sanctions can be lifted. Sanctions may be lifted either because the behavior that led to the imposition of sanctions has changed or because sanctions have failed to bring about a change in behavior.[89]

Comprehensive sanction regimes often have devastating humanitarian implications and are difficult to maintain over time. Therefore, they should not remain in place for too long. International experience with comprehensive sanction regimes in the 1990s—against Iraq, Yugoslavia, and Haiti—indicates that keeping sanctions in place for several years is highly problematic. Sanctions tend to lose their effectiveness over time. The target has time to take adaptive measures, which increases its self-sufficiency and reduces its dependency on the outside world. It may also develop new links with states not fully participating in the sanction regime. Finally, the humanitarian situation in a targeted country may become explosive, which may make the continuation of sanctions difficult to justify.

If sanctions fail to have the desired political effects, two alternative strategies should be considered soon thereafter. First, one can promise rewards in the form of sanction relief if the target engages in "good" behavior. That said, the lifting of sanctions before all conditions are met may be tricky, as was shown in the Haiti case. Indeed, the Security Council decided to lift sanctions against Haiti after certain terms of the Governors Island Agreement had been met, but before Jean-Bertrand Aristide, the democratically elected president, was restored to power. The Haitian military, which signed the agreement in bad faith, took advantage of this window of opportunity and rapidly stocked up on strategic goods. Once its stockpiles were replenished, it continued to defy the UN Security Council. Unfortunately, the UN Security Council did not react immediately to these challenges, and the Governors Island Agreement fell apart. In sum, a carrot-and-stick approach requires accurate assessments of the target's aspirations and intentions. It also requires vigilance by outside powers and immediate reactions if the target gets off course.

Second, one can increase pressure on targets by threatening the use of military force. The threat to use force may have to be made early on if the target is not particularly vulnerable economically or politically. The Haiti and FRY cases suggest that the threat to use force will enhance the coercive effect of sanctions. Indeed, it will add credibility to the coercive effort and demonstrate the seriousness of outside powers.

In sum, a sanction strategy provides guidance about when and how to impose sanctions. It also specifies when to step up the pressure and/or lift sanctions. One of the keys to having an effective sanction strategy is having detailed knowledge of the target. Once a strategy is decided on, outside powers must make sure that sanctions are implemented effectively. Clearly one should not impose sanctions if one lacks the means to implement or enforce these measures. Nonimplemented sanctions undermine the credibility of sanctions in general as well as the credibility of those imposing sanctions.

Implementation and Third-Party Compliance

Third-party compliance with sanction regimes is critical. There is little disagreement about this point in the scholarly and analytical literature on the subject. Every sanction regime has nonetheless suffered from implementation problems. More specifically, three problems have plagued the implementation of sanction regimes.

First, states have interpreted sanction regimes differently. Although UN sanctions are supposed to be imposed collectively following decisions of the UN Security Council, the implementation of sanction regimes is left to individual states. Once a UN sanction resolution is adopted, most states have to adopt national legislation to implement these UN measures. The language of UN sanction resolutions is often the result of compromise formulations with vague and ambiguous wording.[90] Hence, the interpretation of sanction resolutions will often vary from state to state, which in turn leads to uneven implementation of sanction regimes.

Although most UN sanction regimes have established sanctions committees, which have the task of examining and promulgating guidelines to facilitate implementation, such interpretive guidance is not binding on UN members. Since sanctions have become a commonly used instrument, it is important to ensure that compliance is effective. The uncertain legal nature of these committees' rulings has led some authors to suggest that sanction resolutions should contain explicit mandates that allow sanctions committees to interpret sanction resolutions.[91]

Giving the committees interpretive authority could enhance the implementation of sanction regimes. Proposals to create a single sanctions committee, which would deal with all UN sanction regimes, are based on the same logic.[92]

Second, states monitor and enforce sanctions differently. Few states have the expertise or resources needed to establish or maintain efficient monitoring and enforcement mechanisms.[93] Moreover, targeted states may engage in countermeasures and make the cost of compliance too high for third parties.[94] For example, the FRY frequently threatened neighboring countries with military action. The fear that enforcement of sanctions could lead to military conflict made these neighboring countries extremely wary of enforcing the sanction regime.

A sanction regime that does not investigate violations and consequently deal with violators is a regime that will ultimately lose its credibility. Handling these noncompliance problems is generally left to individual states, however. Sanction resolutions rarely include provisions that call for reactions to sanction violations. Hence, there is no uniformity when it comes to dealing with noncompliance. Streamlining national legislation in this domain would reinforce sanction regimes and prevent individual and corporate sanction busters from simply moving from one country to another in order to avoid prosecution and punishment. Experience with recent sanction regimes has also pointed to the desirability of establishing national sanction implementation offices, which would coordinate monitoring and enforcement activities at the national and international levels.[95] This is particularly important with respect to targeted financial sanctions.

International organizations can be very helpful when it comes to monitoring sanction regimes. The efforts by the European Union in monitoring the sanctions against the FRY and Bosnia were very effective in this regard. Most UN sanctions committees have been authorized to carry out investigations into alleged violations of the regimes in question.

However, their activities in this domain have been limited and ineffective. In general, these committees do not have the resources they need to effectively monitor sanction regimes. Unlike the European Union, the United Nations is not able to deploy several hundred people in the field. Plans to strengthen the UN capacities in this area regularly surface. Most of these proposals and initiatives are dead letters because the United Nations has not been provided with sufficient resources to address these problems.[96]

Once different organizations get involved in monitoring and enforcement activities, it is important to ensure coordination between them and to define the exact responsibilities of each organization so that they do not work at cross-purposes. An effective sanction regime requires coordinated efforts at the national, regional, and international levels.

Third, the costs of sanctions are often distributed unequally across states. Sanctions often have unintended negative effects on third states, and some states are harder hit than others. Without assistance from the international community, these states may not be sufficiently motivated to implement and enforce the regime in question. This issue came to the fore when sanctions were imposed on Iraq and, even more important, in the case of the international sanctions against the FRY.

Article 50 of the UN Charter gives states the right to consult with the Security Council if they suffer unduly from sanctions imposed on other countries. Until 1990, the council received only four such requests and took action in only two of them.[97] However, the Iraqi sanction regime imposed in 1990 triggered requests for assistance from twenty-one states, which estimated their total losses at more than $30 billion.[98] This prompted Boutros Boutros-Ghali, the newly elected UN secretary-general, to urge the Security Council to address this issue and devise a set of measures that could be put in place to insulate states from the unintended negative effects of sanction

regimes.[99] He subsequently proposed the establishment of a body that would assess the likely impact of sanctions on both the target country and other countries before sanctions are imposed; monitor implementation of economic sanctions; measure the effects of sanctions, which would enable the Security Council to adjust them and maximize their impact while minimizing collateral damage; ensure the delivery of humanitarian assistance to vulnerable groups; and evaluate claims submitted by states under Article 50 of the charter.[100]

Many countries opposed the plan on the grounds that the UN Security Council would become paralyzed if it had to make sure that it had enough resources to compensate states for collateral damage before deciding on sanctions.[101] Moreover, they argued, in situations where the maintenance or restoration of international peace and security were at stake, the council had to be able to act swiftly. This would make prior consultations difficult, if not impossible.[102] Opponents of the plan also raised questions about the methodology that was to be employed to assess the losses of affected countries.

Ideally, the issue of compensating and assisting third parties that suffer collateral damage from sanction regimes would be dealt with collectively. Since decisions to impose sanctions are made collectively, the costs of sanctions should also be borne collectively, just as the costs of peacekeeping activities are borne by all UN member-states.[103] In practice, compensation of third parties has been dealt with on an ad hoc and case-by-case basis.[104] This will probably continue.

Implementation and third-party compliance are essential for the effectiveness of sanction efforts. They require the building of an international political consensus, the establishment of monitoring and enforcement mechanisms, and the provision of financial resources to address burden-sharing problems. Contrary to popular belief, economic sanctions are not cost-free.

CONCLUSIONS AND RECOMMENDATIONS

The track record of UN sanction regimes has been mixed. Comprehensive and partial sanction regimes have been unsuccessful in stopping civil strife. This is due in part to the fact that many of these sanction regimes were stand-alone measures and not part of concerted coercive efforts to stop the violence. In addition, little attention was given to implementation and third-party compliance problems. The misapplication of this policy instrument in the 1990s should not lead us to drop this policy instrument from our policy repertoire.

Indeed, the missed opportunities in, for example, Haiti and the FRY show that under certain conditions sanctions can be effective in bringing about political change. First, sanctions need to be part of a comprehensive coercive strategy that includes the threat and use of military force. The coercive potential of economic sanctions is greatly enhanced when they are coupled to the threat to use military force: this indicates that outside powers are serious. Sanctions should be seen as part of a coercive continuum. A good coercive strategy will tell outside powers when and how to impose sanctions and when and how to step up coercive pressure and change instruments. Knowledge of the target is essential in this regard.

Second, sanctions need to be implemented and complied with by third parties. Monitoring and enforcement mechanisms need to be put into place. The experiences in the FRY case are particularly illuminating in this regard. Imposing sanctions is not a cost-free policy. Like the use of force, it requires resources. Neighboring countries may need compensation for economic losses and they may need assistance in setting up monitoring and enforcement mechanisms. Finally, to ensure third-party compliance, a broad international consensus on the use of coercive action needs to be built. Someone has to take the lead in defining and keeping the relevant international actors focused on the precise objectives that are to be achieved. In the case of Iraq, the United States played such a role. In the cases of the FRY and Haiti, the United States hesitated and the sanction efforts faltered.

Targeted sanctions caught the fancy of many in the international community in the late 1990s. The effectiveness of targeted financial measures, however, is limited. Indeed, very few states possess the technical means and domestic legislation to monitor financial transactions.

Because of their potential serious social and economic effects, sanctions should not stay in place for long periods of time. Even partial or selective sanctions—that is, sanctions that are limited to a certain commodity—may have secondary and unintended consequences. For example, arms embargoes may keep victims defenseless. Similarly, air traffic controls may impede the delivery of humanitarian relief. The UN Security Council has recognized this problem and now frequently requests the UN Secretariat to prepare assessment reports.

If outside powers are not willing to consider the use of military force, they should not contemplate the imposition of economic sanctions. The imposition of sanctions should be considered only if the problem is serious enough to ultimately warrant the use of force. Coercion is serious business, especially when it has devastating humanitarian consequences—as economic sanctions generally do. International powers should go down this road only if they are prepared to pay the multiple costs of coercion and if they are determined to see the process through.

NOTES

1. The focus of this chapter is limited to mandatory multilateral UN sanctions; that is, sanctions adopted under Chapter VII of the UN Charter. This chapter does not examine sanctions adopted by

regional organizations or one or more states—for example, the sanctions imposed by the Organization of American States (OAS) on Haiti in 1991, or those imposed by a group of African countries on Burundi in 1996. On unilateral U.S. sanctions see, for example, Douglas Johnston and Sidney Weintraub, *Altering U.S. Sanctions Policy: Final Report of the CSIS Project on Unilateral Economic Sanctions* (Washington, D.C.: Center for Strategic and International Studies, February 1999); and Ernest H. Preeg, *Feeling Good or Doing Good with Sanctions: Unilateral Economic Sanctions and the U.S. National Interest* (Washington, D.C.: Center for Strategic and International Studies, 1999). See also George E. Shambaugh, *States, Firms, Power: Successful Sanctions in United States Foreign Policy* (Albany: State University of New York Press, 1999); and Gary Clyde Hufbauer, Jeffrey J. Schott, and Kimberly Ann Elliot, *Economic Sanctions Reconsidered: History and Current Policy*, 3d ed. (Washington, D.C.: Institute for International Economics, 2000).

2. Sanctions remained in place even after the Western coalition drove Iraq out of Kuwait. In April 1991 the lifting of sanctions became dependent on Iraqi implementation of UN Security Council (UNSC) Resolution 687 (1991) of April 3, 1991, including compliance with far-reaching disarmament and inspection provisions.

3. See, for example, Joy Gordon, "A Peaceful, Silent, Deadly Remedy: The Ethics of Economic Sanctions," *Ethics and International Affairs* 13 (1999): 123–150; John Mueller and Karl Mueller, "Sanctions of Mass Destruction," *Foreign Affairs* 78, no. 3 (May-June 1999): 43–53; Thomas G. Weiss, David Cortright, George Lopez, and Larry Minear, *Political Gain and Civilian Pain: Humanitarian Impacts of Economic Sanctions* (Lanham, Md.: Rowman and Littlefield, 1997); and Patrick Clawson, "Sanctions as Punishment, Enforcement, and Prelude to Further Action," *Ethics and International Affairs* 7 (1993): 17–37.

4. Unlike with the use of force, the UN Charter does not contain a specific prohibition on the use of economic sanctions. It does not prohibit states from imposing sanctions unilaterally if they so wish.

5. See, for example, David Cortright and George A. Lopez, *The Sanctions Decade: Assessing UN Strategies in the 1990s* (Boulder, Colo.: Lynne Rienner, 2000); Hufbauer, Schott, and Elliot, *Economic Sanctions Reconsidered;* Margaret Doxey, *United Sanctions: Current Policy Issues* (Halifax, N.S.: Centre for Foreign

Policy Studies, Dalhousie University, June 1999); Richard N. Haass, ed., *Economic Sanctions and American Diplomacy* (New York: Council on Foreign Relations, 1998); and Robert Pape, "Why Economic Sanctions Do Not Work," *International Security* 22, no. 2 (fall 1997): 90–136. See also the rebuttals by Kimberly Ann Elliot, "The Sanctions Glass: Half Full or Completely Empty," and Robert A. Pape, "Why Economic Sanctions Still Do Not Work," *International Security* 23, no. 1 (summer 1998): 5–65, 66–77; Jonathan Kirshner, "The Microfoundations of Economic Sanctions," *Security Studies* 6, no. 3 (spring 1997): 32–64; John Stremlau, *Sharpening International Sanctions: Toward a Stronger Role for the United Nations* (New York: Carnegie Corporation of New York, November 1996); Margaret Doxey, *International Sanctions in Contemporary Perspective* (New York: St. Martin's Press, 1996); Elizabeth Rogers, "Economic Sanctions and Internal Conflicts," in *The International Dimensions of Internal Conflict*, ed. Michael E. Brown (Cambridge, Mass.: MIT Press, 1996), 411–434; Peter van Bergereijk, *Economic Diplomacy, Trade and Commercial Policy: Positive and Negative Sanctions in a New World Order* (Brookfield, Vt.: Edward Elagar, 1994); Lisa L. Martin, *Coercive Cooperation: Explaining Multilateral Economic Sanctions* (Princeton, N.J.: Princeton University Press, 1992); David Baldwin, *Economic Statecraft* (Princeton N.J.: Princeton University Press, 1985); and David Baldwin, "The Sanctions Debate and the Logic of Choice," *International Security* 24, no. 3 (winter 1999-2000): 80–107.

6. Targeted sanctions are also called smart sanctions. In the literature, individual travel restrictions are generally also referred to as targeted or smart sanctions. That said, individual travel bans are more like diplomatic sanctions, which are not treated in this chapter. On targeted and smart sanctions, see the proceedings of the Interlaken seminars organized by the Swiss government at www.smartsanctions.ch/start.html. See also the proceedings of the first expert seminar on smart sanctions organized by the Bonn International Center for Conversion and the Foreign Office of the Federal Republic of Germany, Bonn, November 21–23, 1999, at www.bicc.de./general/events/unsanc/papers.html.

7. Some states resist this tendency to broaden the definition of what constitutes a "threat to international peace and security." They would like the UN Security Council to adhere to a strict interpretation of the UN Charter and not meddle in the internal affairs of states. Yet in an era of globalization, communal strife and gross violations of human rights are difficult to ignore and often pose threats to regional and international peace and security. Indeed, they often produce huge flows of refugees and cross-border military activities.

8. UN sanctions are not intended to punish targets. Indeed, sanctions imposed by the Security Council are political, not legal, instruments. They are discretionary measures decided upon by the council outside any legal or disciplinary context. As such they are unlike sanctions that enforce international or national law. See Serge Sur, *Security Council Resolution 687 of 3 April 1991 in the Gulf Affair: Problems of Restoring and Safeguarding Peace*, UNIDIR Research Papers, no. 12 (New York: United Nations, 1992), 15–16. See also Vera Gowlland-Debbas, *Collective Responses to Illegal Acts in International Law: United Nations Action in the Question of Southern Rhodesia* (Dordrecht, the Netherlands: Martinus Nijhoff, 1990), 461–485.

9. See United Nations Charter Articles 41, 25, and 27.

10. Nor has the Security Council much to offer in terms of positive incentives that could induce parties to comply with sanction regimes.

11. For a more detailed examination of these regimes, see Cortright and Lopez, *Sanctions Decade*.

12. Iraq invaded Kuwait on August 2, 1990. The UN Security Council voted on multilateral sanctions on August 6, 1990. It barred all imports from and exports to Iraq, excepting only medical supplies, foodstuffs, and other items of humanitarian need. See UNSC Resolution 661 (1990). See also UNSC Resolution 665 (1991) of August 25, 1991, which authorized enforcement of Resolution 661 (1990) in the form of a naval blockade.

13. See UNSC Resolution 687 (1991) of April 3, 1991.

14. Saddam Hussein's human rights record was abominable. He also deported many thousands of Iraqi Shiites to Iran during the 1970s and 1980s.

15. See George Bush and Brent Scowcroft, *A World Transformed* (New York: Alfred A. Knopf, 1998), 302–333. See also Eric D. K. Melby, "Iraq," in *Economic Sanctions and American Diplomacy*, 111.

16. By the middle of September the number of U.S. troops in the region reached one hundred fifty

thousand, including a formidable array of air power. These first troop deployments were primarily intended to deter Iraq from invading Saudi Arabia. In November Bush proposed to double U.S. deployments in the region. This signaled the offensive character of U.S. troop deployments. By January 1991 five hundred thousand foreign troops were stationed in the region. For details, see Lawrence Freedman and Efraim Karsh, *The Gulf Conflict 1990–1991: Diplomacy and War in the New World Order* (Princeton, N.J.: Princeton University Press, 1993), 203, 209.

17. See Sarah Graham-Brown, *Sanctioning Saddam: The Politics of Intervention in Iraq* (London, New York: IB Tauris Publishers, 1999), 161.

18. In August, when it first imposed sanctions, the Security Council had exempted medical supplies, foodstuffs, and other items of humanitarian need. See UNSC Resolution 660 (1990) of August 6, 1990.

19. See UNSC Resolution 706 (1991) of August 15, 1991. See also UNSC Resolution 712 (1991) of September 19, 1991; UNSC Resolution 778 (1992) of October 2, 1992; and UNSC Resolution 986 (1995) of April 14, 1995. The latter established new modalities for the Oil for Food Program and authorized the sale of up to $1 billion of Iraqi oil every three months. In February 1998 this amount was raised to $5.25 billion every six months. See UNSC Resolution 1153 (1998) of February 20, 1998. In December 1999 the ceiling on oil exports was lifted. See UNSC Resolution 1284 (1999) of December 17, 1999.

20. The Iraqi government is able to do so because distribution of humanitarian relief in the center and south of the country is controlled by the Iraqi government. In the north—the Kurdish part of Iraq—the distribution of humanitarian supplies is in the hands of the United Nations. Consequently, the humanitarian situation is much better in that part of the country. See, for example, the Report of the UN Secretary-General S/2000/208, March 10, 2000.

21. See UNSC Resolution 1284 (1999) of December 17, 1999. This resolution established the United Nations Monitoring, Verification and Inspection Commission (UNMOVIC) and lifted the ceiling on oil exports.

22. See United Nations Press Release SC/6833, March 24, 2000. Annan's report to the council is contained in the Report of the UN Secretary-General S/2000/208, March 10, 2000.

23. The United States would regularly launch limited military air strikes against Iraq, yet these strikes stopped short of a sustained military campaign and were only partially supported by its allies.

24. The FRY and the other former republics of Yugoslavia were struck with an arms embargo in September 1991. See UNSC Resolution 713 (1991) of September 25, 1991. This embargo stayed in place until June 1996. See UNSC Resolution 1021 (1995) of November 22, 1995.

25. In May 1992 the council decided on full trade sanctions, a freeze on the financial assets of the government of the FRY, a ban on maritime and air traffic, and a ban on participation in sporting and cultural events. Belgrade's diplomatic representation abroad was also reduced. See UNSC Resolution 757 (1992) of May 30, 1992. In November 1992 the council decreed that the transshipment through the FRY of petroleum, coal, steel, and other products was prohibited. See UNSC Resolution 787 (1992) of November 16, 1992. In April 1993 the council strengthened the transshipment bans through the FRY and decided to freeze funds held by the government of the FRY and by FRY commercial, industrial, and public companies. This freeze did not cover personal bank accounts. See UNSC Resolution 820 (1993) of April 17, 1993.

26. The council decided that all economic contact with Bosnian Serbs was prohibited, including all river traffic. It also ordered UN member-states to block all Bosnian Serb financial assets. Moreover, the council decided that states should refrain from having talks with the Bosnian Serb leadership as long as the latter refused to accept the proposed peace plan. See UNSC Resolution 942 (1994) of September 23, 1994.

27. See UNSC Resolution 1022 (1995) of November 22, 1995. The sanctions imposed on the Bosnian Serbs were suspended in February 1996. Sanctions were officially terminated in October 1996. See UNSC Resolution 1074 (1996) of October 1, 1996.

28. For details, see Susan L. Woodward, *Balkan Tragedy: Chaos and Dissolution after the Cold War* (Washington, D.C.: Brookings Institution, 1995); and Carol J. Williams, "Defiant Serbia Moves to Avert Gas Shortages," *Los Angeles Times*, June 2, 1992, A4.

29. It was estimated that the National Bank of Yugoslavia had between $1.8 billion and $2.2 billion in overseas assets. Private assets held in different offshore banking centers were believed to total between $3.3 billion and $5 billion. See Vojin Dimitrijevic and

Jelena Pejic, "UN Sanctions against Yugoslavia: Two Years Later," in *The United Nations in the New World Order: The World Organization at Fifty*, ed. Dimitris Bourantonis and Jarrod Wiener (New York: St. Martin's Press, 1995), 146.

30. These arrangements involved a variety of international organizations—the United Nations, the Organization for Security and Cooperation in Europe (OSCE), the European Union (EU), the North Atlantic Treaty Organization (NATO), the West European Union (WEU), and the International Conference on the Former Yugoslavia (ICFY). They covered maritime traffic, land border control posts, and riverine traffic.

31. For example, Stremlau *(Sharpening International Sanctions)* believes they were effective, while Woodward *(Balkan Tragedy)* believes they were not effective. Julia Devin and Jaleh Dashti-Gibson ("Sanctions in the Former Yugoslavia: Convoluted Goals and Complicated Consequences," in *Political Gain and Civilian Pain*, ed. Thomas Weiss et al. [New York: Rowman and Littlefield, 1997], 182) believe that they were somewhat effective.

32. Sanction Assistance Missions (SAMs) were set up in October 1992 in Hungary, Romania, and Bulgaria. Macedonia got a SAM in November 1992. Croatia, Ukraine, and Albania received SAMs in early 1993.

33. See David Owen, *Balkan Odyssey* (New York: Harcourt Brace, 1995), 159.

34. On U.S. policy, see, for example, Bert Wayne, *The Reluctant Superpower: United States' Policy in Bosnia, 1991–95* (New York: St. Martin's Press, 1997).

35. In response to persistent Bosnian Serb attacks on the Muslim enclave of Srebrenica, Western powers decided to make Srebrenica a safe area. However, they would not deploy sufficient military forces to make this a real safe area. See UNSC Resolution 819 (1993) of April 16, 1993. On May 6, 1993, other Muslim enclaves—Bihac, Gorazde, Sarajevo, Tuzla, and Zepa—were also declared safe areas. See UNSC Resolution 824 (1993) of May 6, 1993.

36. In May 1993 the United States proposed to lift the arms embargo on the Bosnian government and to strike Bosnian targets from the air. Europeans who by that time had many thousands of troops on the ground were fiercely opposed to this "lift-and-strike" strategy. They feared increased fighting and casualties.

37. It is possible that Owen was too gullible and that Milosevic did not sign on to the Vance-Owen plan in good faith. Indeed, Milosevic and Karadzic might have been using "good cop–bad cop" tactics. The lack of unity among Western powers enabled them to play such a game. That said, bad faith on the part of Milosevic would have been an additional reason for the Western powers to threaten to escalate.

38. Owen believed that Milosevic had been insufficiently rewarded when he threw his support behind the Vance-Owen plan. According to Owen, that lack of international encouragement made him renege on his promise to cut off the Bosnian Serbs in May 1993. See Owen, *Balkan Odyssey*, 297–298.

39. The Contact Group was created in April 1994 and was composed of France, Germany, Russia, the United Kingdom, and the United States.

40. The rewards consisted of a lifting of the ban on all civilian flights to and from Belgrade, the reintroduction of a ferry service to Italy, and the lifting of the ban on participation in sports and cultural exchanges. See UNSC 943 (1994) of September 14, 1994.

41. Owen had negotiated the deployment of a civilian monitoring mission along the borders of the FRY and the Bosnian Serb–controlled territory. It reported many violations. Moreover, the border between the Bosnian Serb–controlled territory and Croatia was not covered by the monitoring arrangement. Indeed, that part of Croatia was controlled by the Croat Serbs, who refused to cooperate with international monitors.

42. See UNSC Resolution 841 (1993) of June 16, 1993. Initial efforts, including a call for sanctions, by the OAS to restore Aristide to power failed.

43. The United States was Haiti's main trading partner: 75 percent of Haitian exports went to the United States and 60 percent of Haitian imports came from the United States.

44. For details on the agreement, see James Morell, *The Governors Island Accord on Haiti*, International Policy Report (Washington, D.C.: Washington Center for International Policy, September 1993).

45. Sanctions were suspended by UNSC Resolution 861 (1993) of August 27, 1993.

46. Banners warned that the deployment of UN troops would result in another Somalia, where days earlier U.S. soldiers had been killed. Following those killings, President Bill Clinton announced that all U.S.

troops would withdraw from Somalia. The Haitian military evidently hoped to scare off the United States. When Clinton ordered the USS *Harlan County*—the ship transporting the first two hundred UN (U.S.) peacekeepers—to withdraw, the Haitian military took this to be a great victory. It encouraged them to pull out of the agreement so painstakingly negotiated in July 1993.

47. See UNSC Resolution 873 (1993) of October 13, 1993, and UNSC Resolution 875 (1993) of October 16, 1993.

48. More generally, relations in the UN Security Council were tense, and U.S. fumbling in Somalia and Bosnia undercut American attempts to create a powerful international coalition to solve the Haitian crisis.

49. See UNSC Resolution 917 (1994) of May 6, 1994. Sanctions went into effect on May 21, 1994.

50. See UNSC Resolution 940 (1994) of July 31, 1994.

51. See UNSC Resolution 944 (1994) of September 29, 1994.

52. It may be recalled that within the United States support for Aristide was lukewarm. Aristide's populist rhetoric was much disliked in Washington. Moreover, certain parts of the U.S. government had longstanding relations with the Haitian military and its paramilitary supporters.

53. It had the lowest life expectancy rate (forty-eight years), the highest infant mortality rate (124 per 1,000), and the highest illiteracy rate (between 63 percent and 90 percent). Some 70 percent of Haitian children suffered from malnutrition and 35 percent were seriously malnourished.

54. Those who fled Haiti did so not only for economic reasons or to avoid political persecution but also to show support for Aristide.

55. Some analysts have argued that sanctions in Haiti were a failure because they were not comprehensive and because they were imposed gradually. See, for example, Elizabeth Rogers, "Economic Sanctions and Internal Conflict," in *The International Dimensions of Internal Conflict*, ed. Michael E. Brown (Cambridge, Mass.: MIT Press, 1996), 424. I believe that the track record in Haiti was uneven because outside powers—the United States, in particular—were not clear about what they wanted to achieve. As time went by, they lost credibility.

56. Partial economic sanctions were imposed on Libya because of its alleged support to terrorist groups and its refusal to extradite individuals accused of carrying out terrorist attacks on two passenger planes—the Lockerbie attack on December 21, 1988, and the UTA DC10 bombing on September 19, 1989. Sanctions on Libya curtailed air traffic and the activities of its diplomatic and consular missions. The UN Security Council also imposed an arms embargo on Libya. See UNSC Resolution 748 (1992) of March 31, 1992. In 1993 sanctions were broadened to include certain types of equipment used at oil transport terminals and refineries. The air embargo was also tightened. In addition, the council decided to freeze some governmental financial assets. See UNSC Resolution 883 (1993) of November 11, 1993. Sanctions were lifted in April 1999, when the Libyans agreed to turn over the individuals in question to a specially appointed court in the Netherlands. Sanctions had modest economic effects in this case, but they were sufficiently onerous to push the Libyans toward a negotiated solution.

In the case of Sudan, sanctions were imposed after Sudan refused to extradite three individuals suspected of having attempted to assassinate Egyptian president Hosni Mubarak on June 25, 1995. Sanctions consisted of a reduction of Sudanese diplomatic and consular staff abroad. The United Nations also imposed travel restrictions on Sudanese staff, as well as on Sudanese military and government officials. See UNSC Resolution 1054 (1996) of April 26, 1996. In August 1996 the council threatened to impose an air embargo. See UNSC Resolution 1070 (1996) of August 16, 1996. This embargo never went into effect. Alarmed by the humanitarian effects of economic sanctions in Iraq and Haiti, many states, including Egypt, opposed tougher economic sanctions on Sudan. Moreover, a UN assessment team concluded that the proposed aviation sanctions could have serious effects on the flow of foodstuffs and medicines, as well as the humanitarian operation Operation Lifeline Sudan. This was the first time the United Nations prepared a humanitarian assessment report before the actual imposition of sanctions.

Sanctions on the Taliban were imposed because of its refusal to hand over Osama bin Laden and his associates. They were believed to be responsible for the terrorist attacks on the U.S. embassies in Kenya and Tanzania. Sanctions went into effect on November 15, 1999. They consisted of a freeze of financial assets and a boycott of Taliban-owned aircraft. See UNSC Resolution 1267 (1999) of October 15, 1999. However, given the limited amount of funds abroad and the limited scope of Taliban-controlled air traffic, these sanctions have had little impact.

57. See UNSC Resolution 864 (1993) of September 15, 1993.

58. See UNSC Resolution 890 (1993) of December 15, 1993, and UNSC Resolution 1075 (1996) of October 1996, which threatened additional sanctions. See also Stephen John Stedman, "Spoiler Problems in Peace Processes," *International Security* 22, no. 2 (fall 1997): 39–40.

59. See UNSC Resolution 1127 (1997) of August 28, 1997.

60. See UNSC Resolution 1130 (1997) of September 29, 1997, and UNSC Resolution 1135 (1997) of October 29, 1997.

61. See UNSC Resolution 1173 (1998) of June 12, 1998. See also UNSC Resolution 1149 (1998) of January 27, 1998; UNSC Resolution 1157 (1998) of March 20, 1998; and UNSC Resolution 1164 (1998) of April 29, 1998.

62. See *Report of the Panel of Experts on Violations of Security Council Sanctions against UNITA*, UN document S/2000/203, March 10, 2000.

63. See "Angola II, Deadly Diamonds: UNITA's New Armour Financed by a Web of Deals from Luzamba to Antwerp," *Africa Confidential* 40, no. 8 (April 16, 1999). See also Blaine Harden, "Africa's Gems: Warfare's Best Friend," *New York Times*, April 6, 2000.

64. It has been estimated that in February 1999 alone UNITA sold $32 million worth of diamonds. See "Angola II, Deadly Diamonds."

65. See *Report of the Panel of Experts on Violations of Security Council Sanctions against UNITA*.

66. Ibid.

67. See James Bone, "UN Notebook: Has Angola Sanctions Panel 'Gone Awry'?" *UN Wire*, April 11, 2000 (www.unfoundation.org). See also "Angola/UN Name and Shame," *Africa Confidential* 41, no. 6 (March 17, 2000): 8. On April 18, 2000, the Security Council established a monitoring mechanism in order to collect information, investigate leads, and verify information provided by all sources concerning violations of the council's previous sanction resolutions against UNITA. See UNSC Resolution 1295 (2000) of April 18, 2000.

68. The Kabbah government was elected in February 1996.

69. See UNSC Resolution 1132 (1997) of October 8, 1997. In August 1997, the Economic Community of West African States (ECOWAS) had imposed comprehensive economic sanctions.

70. Although Sierra Leone's economy was vulnerable to sanctions, UN economic pressure was expected not to have much effect on the political behavior of the rebels. In fact, sanctions were expected to turn the humanitarian situation in Sierra Leone into a disaster —Sierra Leone is one of the poorest and least developed countries in the world. The council realized this and imposed a restricted sanction regime only after being prodded to do so by ECOWAS. Moreover, shortly after sanctions were imposed, the United Nations sent an assessment team to Sierra Leone to measure the humanitarian effects of sanctions. See UN Office for the Coordination of Humanitarian Affairs (OCHA), *Inter-Agency Assessment Mission to Sierra Leone: Interim Report*, February 1998. Since the mid-1990s the United Nations had become more cognizant of the humanitarian effect of sanctions. For example, despite insistent requests from neighboring countries, the UN Security Council did not impose sanctions on Burundi when Major Pierre Buyoya took power in a military coup in July 1996. The council feared the humanitarian consequences of such action. Similarly, it decided against the imposition of economic sanctions against Sudan because of the potential humanitarian consequences.

71. See UNSC Resolution 1156 (1998) of March 16, 1998.

72. See UNSC Resolution 1171 (1998) of June 5, 1998.

73. See "Sierra Leone Talks Peace," *Economist*, June 5, 1999; and "Waking from Sierra Leone's Long Nightmare," *Economist*, July 3, 1999. See also Ryan Lizza, "Where Angels Fear to Tread: Telling One's Truth," *New Republic*, July 24, 2000, 22–27.

74. See UNSC Resolution 1270 (1999) of October 22, 1999. Troop strength was increased to 11,100 in February 2000. See UNSC Resolution 1289 (2000) of February 7, 2000.

75. See Douglas Farah, "Diamonds Are a Rebel's Best Friend: Mining of Gems Helps Sierra Leone Militia Stall Peace Process," *Washington Post*, April 17, 2000.

76. See Harden, "Africa's Gems."

77. See UNSC Resolution 1306 (2000) of July 5, 2000.

78. See UNSC Resolution 1173 (1998) of June 12, 1998 (UNITA); and UNSC Resolution 1267 (1999) of October 15, 1999 (Taliban). The financial measures aimed at the Haitian military were voluntary —states were only "urged" to adopt such measures. See UNSC Resolution 917 (1994) of May 6, 1994. In the case of the financial sanctions imposed on the Bosnian Serbs, the UN Security Council Sanctions Committee never designated specific corporations or individuals. Implementation of this provision of the resolutions was thus very much left to the judgment of individual states.

79. See *Report of the Panel of Experts on Violations of Security Council Sanctions against UNITA*.

80. Ibid.

81. See Joanna Spear, "Arms Limitations, Confidence Building Measures, and Internal Conflict," in *The International Dimensions of Internal Conflict*, 377–410.

82. Ibid., 393.

83. The effectiveness of sanctions imposed on "nongovernmental" groups is in large part related to the degree that those groups can be isolated economically and politically.

84. The level of development of a country can be measured in different ways. Economic indicators include per capita income, growth rate, and the size of the manufacturing, services, and agricultural sectors. Social indicators include life expectancy, infant mortality, and access to health services and potable water.

85. Lewis Coser has argued that when the degree of group cohesion is strong, external pressure reinforces cohesiveness and willingness to resist such pressure. When group cohesion is weak, external pressure leads to apathy and group disintegration, and hence a diminished capacity to resist outside pressure. See Lewis Coser, *The Functions of Social Conflict* (New York, London: Free Press, Macmillan, 1964), 87–94.

86. Jonathan Kirshner also emphasizes the importance of disaggregating the target. See Jonathan Kirshner, "The Microfoundations of Economic Sanctions," *Security Studies* 6, no. 3 (spring 1997): 32–64.

87. See, for example, Hufbauer, Schott, and Elliot, *Economic Sanctions Reconsidered;* Kimberly Ann Elliot,

"Factors Affecting the Success of Sanctions," in *Economic Sanctions: Panacea or Peacebuilding in a Post–Cold War World?* ed. David Cortright and George Lopez (Boulder, Colo.: Westview Press, 1995), 51–60; Elizabeth Rogers, "Economic Sanctions and Internal Conflicts," in *The International Dimensions of Internal Conflict*, 413; Carnegie Commission on Preventing Deadly Conflict, *Preventing Deadly Conflict: Final Report* (New York: Carnegie Corporation of New York, December 1997), 54; U.S. Department of State, Inter-Agency Task Force on Serbian Sanctions, "UN Sanctions against Belgrade: Lessons Learned for Future Regimes," in *The Report of the Copenhagen Round Table on UN Sanctions: The Case of the Former Yugoslavia, Copenhagen, 24–25 June 1996 and Annexes* (Brussels: SAMCOMM, European Commission, 1996), 327.

88. See, for example, Ivan Eland, "Think Small," *Bulletin of Atomic Scientists* (November 1993): 36–40; Ivan Eland, "Economic Sanctions as Tools of Foreign Policy," in *Economic Sanctions*, 29–42; James McDermott, Ivan Eland, and Bruce Kutnick, *Economic Sanctions' Effectiveness as Tools of Foreign Policy*, GAO/NSIAD-92-106 (Washington, D.C.: U.S. General Accounting Office, February 1992). See also Cortright and Lopez, *Sanctions Decade*.

89. The importance of exit, or termination, strategies has been recognized within the UN community. However, in practice such strategies have not been adopted. See, for example, *United Nations Sanctions as a Tool of Peaceful Settlement of Disputes: Non-Paper Submitted by Australia and the Netherlands*, A/50/322, August 3, 1995.

90. Many authors have argued that the UN Security Council should adopt standardized texts for its sanctions resolutions. This would also facilitate efforts to develop national legislation for sanction regimes. See Cortright and Lopez, *Sanctions Decade*, 234.

91. See *United Nations Sanctions as a Tool of Peaceful Settlement of Disputes: Non-Paper Submitted by Australia and the Netherlands;* and Michael P. Scharf and Joshua L. Dorosin, "Interpreting UN Sanctions: The Rulings and Role of the Yugoslavia Sanctions Committee," *Brooklyn Journal of International Law* 19 (1993): 771–827.

92. Scharf and Dorosin ("Interpreting UN Sanctions," 826) called for the creation of a single comprehensive sanctions committee, which would deal with all UN sanction regimes and be composed of legal experts chosen by the council members for fixed periods. They also propose that the committee make its decision by vote rather than by consensus and authorize oral and written presentations for purposes of interpretation by states other than council members. See also the proposal by Lloyd (Jeff) Dumas, who suggests the creation of a UN Council on Economic Sanctions and Peacekeeping (CESP), in "A Proposal for a New United Nations Council on Economic Sanctions," in *Economic Sanctions*, 187–199.

93. Cortright and Lopez (*Sanctions Decade*, 234) report that only twelve countries have laws enabling them to enforce financial sanctions.

94. Indeed, the enforcement of a sanction regime may entail the use of force. Naval blockades are the most common sanction enforcement mechanism.

95. See, for example, Final Report of the Commission of Inquiry on the Rwandan Arms Embargo, S/1996/195, March 14, 1996, par. 77–79. See also *Report of the Panel of Experts on Violations of Security Council Sanctions against UNITA*.

96. In April 2000 the UN Security Council decided to set up, independently of the UN Sanctions Committee, a dedicated mechanism that would collect information and investigate leads concerning violations of the sanction regime imposed on UNITA (Angola). It will be interesting to see whether this group of five experts will be endowed with sufficient resources to carry out its job effectively. See UNSC Resolution 1295 (2000) of April 18, 2000.

97. For details, see *Report of the UN Secretary-General on the Question of Special Economic Problems of States as a Result of Sanctions Imposed under Chapter VII of the United Nations*, S/26705 or A/48/573, November 8, 1993, par. 5–23.

98. Ibid., par. 24–25.

99. See *Report of the UN Secretary-General: An Agenda for Peace*, S/24111 or A/47/277, June 17, 1992, par. 41.

100. See *Position Paper of the UN Secretary-General on the Occasion of the Fiftieth Anniversary of the United Nations: Supplement to an Agenda for Peace*, S/1995/1 or A/50/60, January 3, 1995, par. 73–76.

101. See *Report of the UN Secretary-General on the Question of Special Economic Problems of States as a Result of Sanctions Imposed under Chapter VII of the United Nations*, S/26705 or A/48/573, November 8, 1993, par. 140.

102. See *Report of the Special Committee on the Charter of the UN on Implementation of the Provisions of the Charter of the United Nations Related to Assistance to Third States Affected by the Application of Sanctions under Chapter VII of the Charter*, A/50/361, August 22, 1995, par. 7.

103. This argument is developed in *Position Paper of the UN Secretary-General on the Occasion of the Fiftieth Anniversary of the United Nations;* and *Report of the Special Committee on the Charter of the UN on Implementation of the Provisions of the Charter of the United Nations Related to Assistance to Third States Affected by the Application of Sanctions under Chapter VII of the Charter.*

104. Cortright and Lopez (*Sanctions Decade*, 230) suggest the organization of special donor conferences when imposing sanctions.

22

Soft Power and Conflict Management in the Information Age

Joseph S. Nye, Jr.

AN INFORMATION REVOLUTION is strongly affecting the relations of states, economies, and civil societies in the twenty-first century. By information revolution, I refer to the rapid technological advances in computers, communications, and software that have led to dramatic decreases in the cost of information. As with steam at the end of the eighteenth century and electricity at the end of the nineteenth, there have been lags in productivity growth as society learns to utilize the new technologies. Although many industries and firms have been undergoing rapid structural changes since the 1980s, the economic transformation is far from complete. It is generally agreed that we are still in the early stages of the information revolution.[1]

As information becomes more plentiful and cheap, it is more available to small states, private firms, nongovernmental actors, and ordinary citizens. Barriers to entry are lowered, and some economies of scale are reduced. In the past, it was costly to own a printing press or to communicate to distant parts of the globe.

Now anyone with a computer is a desktop publisher, and anyone with a modem and access to the Internet can communicate over great distances at trivial costs compared with the past. Of course, not everyone has a computer. Computers are far more prevalent in some countries and socioeconomic classes than others, and 70 percent of the world's people do not own a telephone, much less a modem. Satellite communications may help some countries and regions to leapfrog over the stage of stringing phone lines, but major inequalities will persist for a long time to come.

Nonetheless, the effects of the information revolution are already significant. Private corporations are able to implement global production strategies that can switch economic activities around the world. Nearly half of world manufacturing takes place in such widely distributed domains. Nongovernmental actors can organize transnationally around various issues at very low transaction costs. Not only have nongovernmental actors pressed governments successfully on issues such as the environment and land mines, but they have done so by reaching across borders to significant constituencies within states, thus blurring the distinction between domestic and international politics. Many of these organizations are more like networks than bureaucratic hierarchies.

Some theorists see the reversal of the dominance of the modern centralized state that has characterized international relations for the past three and a half centuries.[2] While the Westphalian system of sovereign states is still the dominant pattern in international relations and will remain so for a long time to come, one can begin to discern a pattern of crosscutting communities and governance that bears some resemblance to the situation before 1648. The power of the state will increasingly be supplemented by that of other actors.

Of course the information revolution is not the only powerful trend undermining the Westphalian system. Globalization and marketization also have powerful effects. Both are related to the information revolution, but they also have independent roots. Globalization has ancient origins, and its current phase dates back to American strategy after World War II and the desire to create an open international economy to forestall another depression and to contain communism. The institutional framework and political pressures for opening markets were a product of American policy, but they were reinforced by developments in the technology of transportation and communications that made it increasingly costly for states to turn away from global market forces.

Like globalization, the development of markets also has been strongly affected by the information revolution. At a macrolevel, the failure of the Soviet planned economy to respond adequately to the information revolution led to the collapse of Soviet power and the end of bipolarity. At the microlevel, information is central to effective markets, and the growth and diffusion of information has lowered transaction costs and made all types of contracting much easier. Thus the information revolution is not the sole cause of the current changes in international relations, but it has accentuated other causes as well as produced its own independent effects. One of the most important of these effects has been to increase the role of soft power.

POWER AMONG STATES

Power is like love—easy to feel but hard to define. A basic distinction is between behavioral power—the ability to obtain outcomes you want—and resource power—or the possession of the resources that are usually associated with the ability to get the outcomes you want. Behavioral power, in turn, can be divided into hard power and soft power.

Hard power is the ability to get others to do what they otherwise would not do through threat of punishment or promise of reward. Whether by economic carrots or military sticks, the ability to coax or coerce has long been the central element of hard power. Military prowess has always been important, and economic threats and sanctions have been commonly used instruments. In addition, hard power is often found in relationships characterized by asymmetrical interdependence. The less vulnerable party is able to manipulate or escape the constraints of an interdependent relationship at low cost and thus gain the upper hand. In the context of hard power, asymmetries of information can greatly strengthen the less vulnerable party.

Soft power, on the other hand, is the ability to achieve desired outcomes though attraction rather than coercion, because others want what you want. It works by convincing others to follow you or getting them to agree to norms and institutions that produce the desired behavior. Soft power can rest on the appeal of one's ideas or culture or the ability to set the agenda in ways that shape the preferences of others. If a state can make its power legitimate in the perception of others and establish international institutions that encourage others to define their interests in compatible ways, it may not need to expend as many of its costly traditional economic or military resources.[3]

Hard power and soft power are related, but they are not the same. Samuel Huntington is correct when he says that material success makes a culture and ideology attractive and that decreases in economic and military success lead to self-doubt and crises of identity. He is wrong, however, when he argues that "soft power is power only when it rests on a foundation of hard power."[4] The soft power of the Vatican did not wane as the size of the Papal States diminished. Canada, Sweden, and the Netherlands, which often champion popular issues, tend to have more influence than some other states with equivalent economic or military capability. The Soviet Union had considerable soft power in Europe after World War II but squandered it with the invasions of Hungary and Czechoslovakia, even at a time when Soviet economic and military power were still continuing to grow. Similarly, collapse of the American economy or deterioration of its political culture would erode American soft power.

Soft power varies over time and different domains. America's popular culture, with its commercial, libertarian, and egalitarian currents, dominates film, television, and electronic communications in the world today. However, not all aspects of that culture are attractive to all others; for example, American soft power is limited in conservative Muslim cultures. Nonetheless, the spread of information and American popular culture has generally increased global awareness of and openness to American ideas and values. To some extent this reflects deliberate policies, but more often soft power is an inadvertent by-product.

American soft power comes from several sources. One is values. For example, to the extent that the United States is seen as a beacon of liberty, human rights, and democracy, others are attracted to follow the American lead. To the extent that the United States fails to live up to its proclaimed standards and is seen as a hypocrite, others are less willing to follow. Thus the quality of U.S. domestic life—prosperity, social safety nets, equal access to justice, democratic elections—has a strong impact on America's international position. President Kennedy, for example, recognized during the Cold War that racial segregation at home undercut American foreign policy and moved to remedy the situation.

Another source of American soft power is education. Every year, half a million students come from all over the world to study in American colleges and universities. Not all students go home satisfied, but most have a more realistic and positive opinion of the United States than they had before they arrived. For example, a number of children of Chinese leaders study in the United States. In 1999, when Chinese government propaganda was lambasting America, a former student who was the son of a high official published a book suffused with positive descriptions of the United States that was widely read in Beijing.[5]

Cultural exports are a third source of American soft power. American films and television programs dominate popular culture, and American art and academic writing are influential in high culture. The rapidly spreading Internet includes a preponderant American content. Soft power derived from U.S. popular culture is sometimes enhanced unintentionally by its very detractors. Some Iranian officials, for example, say that to understand what they mean by "the great Satan," one need merely watch MTV. But that is exactly what many young Iranians want to do.

Soft power also works through involvement in international organizations. To the extent that institutions such as the International Monetary Fund, NATO, and the InterAmerican Human Rights Commission shape the agenda of choices for other countries in ways that are compatible with American interests, they enhance American soft power. When the United States is seen as living within frameworks of agreed rules taking into account the opinions of others, its power is legitimized. Legitimacy is a power reality. If the United States can legitimate its power in the eyes of other countries and maintain institutions that encourage others to define their interests in congruent ways, then the United States need not expend as much on traditional economic or military sources of power. This does not mean that hard power and soft power are perfect substitutes, for example, in conflict management. The ability of NATO forces to overawe contending parties through preponderant military force is essential to keeping the peace in situations like those in Bosnia or Kosovo. But the fact that NATO forces come from countries with attractive values helps ease their acceptance and facilitate their task.

It is not enough for the United States to merely proclaim that it is right. Others must see it that way too. On the contrary, when the United States is seen as a unilateralist ignoring the views of others, it loses some of its soft power.

As was noted, the United States is not the only country with soft power. It just happens to have the largest sources of soft power at this stage in history. As other countries set attractive examples, educate foreign students, export appealing cultural products, or use international institutions to draw others to their agenda, they are also investing in soft power.

INFORMATION AND POWER

In the eighteenth-century European balance of power, territory, population, and agriculture provided the basis for infantry, which was a crucial power resource, and France was a principal beneficiary. In the nineteenth century, industrial capacity provided the crucial resources that enabled Britain and, later, Germany to gain

dominance. By the mid-twentieth century, science, and particularly nuclear physics, contributed crucial power resources to the United States and the Soviet Union. In the twenty-first century, information technology broadly defined is likely to be the most crucial power resource, and here again the United States is in the lead.

The new conventional wisdom is that the information revolution has a decentralizing and leveling effect. As it reduces costs, economies of scale, and barriers of entry to markets, it should also reduce the power of large states and enhance the power of small states and non-state actors. In practice, however, international relations are more complex than the technological determinism of the new conventional wisdom suggests. Some aspects of the information revolution help the small, but others help the already large and powerful.[6] There are several reasons why.

First, important barriers to entry and economies of scale remain in some aspects of power that are related to information. For example, soft power is strongly affected by the cultural content of what is broadcast or appears in movies and television programs. Large established entertainment industries often enjoy considerable economies of scale in content production and distribution. The dominant American market share in films and television programs in world markets is a case in point.

Second, even where it is now cheap to disseminate existing information, the collection and production of new information often require major costly investments. In many competitive situations, it is the newness of information at the margin that counts more than the average cost of all information. Intelligence collection is a good example. States like America, Britain, and France have capabilities for collection and production that dwarf those of other nations. In some commercial situations, a fast follower can do better than a first mover, but in terms of power among states, it is usually better to be a first mover than a fast follower.

Third, first movers are often the creators of the standards and architecture of information systems. The path-dependent development of such systems reflects the advantage of the first mover. The use of the English language and top-level domain names on the Internet is a case in point. Partly because of the transformation of the American economy in the 1980s and partly because of large investments driven by the Cold War military competition, the United States was often the first mover and still enjoys a lead in the application of a wide variety of information technologies.

Fourth, military power remains important in some critical domains of international relations. Information technology has some effects on the use of force that benefit the small and some that favor the already powerful. The off-the-shelf commercial availability of what used to be costly military technologies benefits small states and nonstate actors, and the vulnerability of large states' information systems offers lucrative targets for terrorist (including state-sponsored) groups.

Other trends, however, strengthen the already powerful. Many military analysts refer to a "revolution in military affairs" that has been produced by the application of information technology. Space-based sensors, direct broadcasting, high-speed computers, and complex software provide the ability to gather, sort, process, transfer, and disseminate information about highly complex events that occur in wide geographic areas. This dominant battlespace awareness combined with precision force provides a powerful advantage. As the Gulf War showed, traditional assessments of balances of weapons platforms such as tanks or planes become irrelevant, unless they include the ability to integrate information with those weapons. Many of the relevant technologies are available in commercial markets, and weaker states can be expected to have many of them. The

key, however, will not be the possession of fancy hardware or advanced systems, but the ability to integrate a system of systems. In this dimension, the United States is likely to keep its lead, and in terms of information warfare, a small edge makes all the difference.

One of the most interesting aspects of power in relation to increasing flows of information might be called the "paradox of plenty."[7] A plenitude of information leads to a poverty of attention. Attention becomes the scarce resource, and those who can distinguish valuable signal from white noise gain power. Editors, filters, and cue givers become more in demand, and this is a source of power. Power does not necessarily flow to those who can produce or withhold information, but to those who can certify it.

Among editors and cue givers, credibility is the crucial source of power. Reputation becomes even more important than in the past, and political struggles occur over the creation and destruction of credibility. Communities tend to cluster around credible cue givers, and, in turn, perceived credibility tends to reinforce communities. Governments compete for credibility not only with other governments, but with a broad range of alternatives including news media, corporations, nongovernmental organizations, intergovernmental organizations, and networks. It is impossible, for example, to understand the politics of global warming without including the role of an epistemic community like the Intergovernmental Panel on Climate Change. If we think counterfactually, Iraq might have found it easier to have won acceptance for its view of the invasion of Kuwait as a postcolonial vindication, analogous to India's 1975 capture of Goa, if CNN had framed the issue from Baghdad rather than from Atlanta (from which Saddam was portrayed as analogous to Hitler in the 1930s). Soft power allowed the United States to frame the issue. The Gulf War was won by the hard power of military force, but the Gulf War coalition (and the enabling UN resolutions) owed a lot to soft power.

Politics then becomes a politics of competitive credibility. Governments compete with one another and with other organizations to enhance their own credibility and weaken that of their opponents—witness the struggle between Serbia and NATO to interpret events in Kosovo in 1999. Reputation has always mattered in world politics, but the role of asymmetrical credibility becomes an even more important power resource because of the paradox of plenitude in an information age. The BBC, for example, was an important soft power resource for Britain in Eastern Europe during the Cold War. Now it (and other government broadcasts) has more competitors, but to the extent that it maintains credibility in an era of white noise, its value as a power resource may increase. It is not merely a Cold War relic.

One implication of the increasing importance of editors and cue givers in an information age is that soft power will become more important relative to hard power. Countries that are well placed in terms of soft power will make relative gains. Of course, as argued earlier, soft power varies with the targeted audience. Thus American individualism may be popular in Latin America at the same time that it appears as offensive libertinism in some Middle Eastern countries. Moreover, governments can gain and lose soft power depending on their performance at home. With those caveats taken into account, the states that are likely to gain soft power in an information age are (1) those whose dominant culture and ideas are closer to prevailing global norms (which now emphasize liberalism, pluralism, and autonomy); (2) those with the most access to multiple channels of communication and thus more influence over how issues are framed; and (3) those whose credibility is enhanced by domestic and international performance that conforms with their political and economic ideas. The first two aspects favor the United States, and the third depends on what policies are pursued at home and abroad.

THE POWER OF NONSTATE ACTORS

Two and a half decades ago, Robert Keohane and I asked what the world would look like if one reversed the critical assumptions (unified states use force to pursue security) of the realist model that had previously dominated most portrayals of international politics.[8] Doing so led us to posit an ideal type called "complex interdependence" with three conditions: (1) a minor role of military force, (2) absence of hierarchy among issues, and (3) multiple channels of contact among societies. To what extent has the world moved in the direction of those conditions?

The approximation of complex interdependence varies by region. In regard to the realist assumptions about the role of military force and hierarchy of issues, Europe has changed significantly, while Africa and the Middle East have not. Globally, change is greatest in multiple channels of contact among societies. Here one can see an order of magnitude shift as a result of the Internet. In the 1970s, transnational contacts were growing, but the people involved were relatively small numbers of elites involved in multinational corporations, scientific groups, and academic institutions. Now the Internet is creating low costs of transnational communications for many millions of people.

There has been not only a great increase in the number of transnational and transgovernmental contacts compared with what we described two decades ago, but also a change in type. Earlier transnational flows were heavily controlled by large bureaucratic organizations, like multinational corporations or the Catholic Church, which could profit from economies of scale. Such organizations remain important, but the lower costs have now opened the field to loosely structured network organizations, and even individuals. These nongovernmental organizations can develop a soft power of their own. Their ideas and values are often attractive transnationally. Their networks are particularly effective in penetrating states without regard to borders and using domestic constituencies for agenda setting. The 1997 Landmine Conference was an interesting coalition of network organizations working with middle-power governments such as Canada and some individual politicians and celebrities; this grouping was able to capture attention and set the agenda in a way that overcame resistance by the U.S. government. The role of NGOs was also important as a channel of communication across delegations in negotiations over global warming. In 1999 a transnational coalition of NGOs disrupted the meetings of the World Trade Organization in Seattle, a feat that was repeated in April 2000 against the World Bank in Washington, D.C.

Another type of transnational network is the epistemic community of like-minded experts. By framing issues in which knowledge is important, epistemic communities become influential in forming coalitions and in bargaining processes. By creating knowledge, they can provide the basis for effective cooperation. The Montreal Convention on ozone is an example. While not entirely new, epistemic communities have grown as a result of the lowered costs of communications and sometimes with the support of governments. To the extent that they produce a transnational consensus, they lessen the degrees of difference among parties and reduce the intensity of conflict.

Whatever the future effects of interactivity and virtual communities, one political effect of increased information flows through multiple channels is already clear: states have lost much of their control over information about their own societies. States that seek to develop economically need foreign capital and the technology and organization that go with it. Increasingly, foreign capital demands transparency, as was seen in the Asian financial crisis. Governments that are not transparent are not credible, since the information they offer is seen as biased and selective. NGOs and other actors in civil society that promote attractive values and act in a manner that maintains their credibility have more opportunities to build international consensus in an information age than ever before.

IMPLICATIONS FOR FOREIGN POLICY

Because massive flows of cheap information have expanded the number of transnational channels of contacts across national borders, and global markets and nongovernmental actors are playing a larger role, states are more easily penetrated by outside influences and less like the classic realist model of solid billiard balls bouncing off each other. As a result, political leaders find it more difficult to maintain a coherent set of priorities in foreign policy issues and more difficult to articulate a single national interest. Although the coherence of U.S. government policies may diminish because of these transnational penetrations, our institutions, because they are democratic, will be attractive, and the openness of our society will enhance credibility, which is a crucial resource in an information age. Thus we will be better placed to make use of soft power. At the same time, the soft power that comes from being a "city on the hill" does not provide the coercive capability that hard power does. Alone, it does not support a very venturesome foreign policy.

Different aspects of the information age cut in different directions in terms of American national interests. On the one hand, a good case can be made that the information revolution will have long-term effects that benefit democracies. Democratic societies can create credible information because they are not threatened by it. Authoritarian states will have more trouble. Governments can limit their citizens' access to the Internet and global markets, but they will pay a high price if they do so. Singapore and China, for example, are currently wrestling with this problem. Moreover, transparency is becoming a key asset for countries seeking investments. Governments that want rapid development will have to give up some of the barriers to information flows that were typical in the past. Such trends are favorable to the long-term interests of the United States in a more open and democratic world.

On the other hand, some aspects of the information age are less benign. The free flow of broadcast information in open societies has always had an impact on public opinion and the formulation of foreign policy, but now the flows have increased and the shortened news cycles have reduced the time for deliberation. By focusing on certain conflicts and human rights problems, broadcasts pressure politicians, directly and indirectly, to respond to some foreign problems and not others—for example, Somalia rather than the southern Sudan in 1992. The so-called CNN effect makes it harder to keep some items off the top of the public agenda that might otherwise warrant a lower priority. Now, with the added interactivity of activist groups on the Internet, it will be harder than ever to maintain a consistent agenda of priorities.

Also problematic is the effect of transnational information flows on the stability of national communities. Marshall McLuhan once prophesied that communications technologies would turn the world into a global village.[9] Instead of a single cosmopolitan village, they may be producing a congeries of global "villages," with all the parochial perspectives that the word implies, but also with greater awareness of global inequalities. Global economic forces are disrupting traditional lifestyles, and the effects are to increase economic integration and communal disintegration at the same time. This is particularly true of weak states left in the aftermath of the collapse of the Soviet empire and the old European empires in Africa. Political entrepreneurs use inexpensive information channels to mobilize some of the discontented to identify with subnational tribal communities, some with repressive nationalism, and some with transnational ethnic and religious communities. This in turn leads to increased demands for self-determination, increased violence, and violation of human rights—all in the presence of television cameras and the Internet. The result is a difficult set of issues on the foreign policy agenda.

SOFT POWER AND CONFLICT MANAGEMENT

Soft power can play a role in managing such conflicts, but one must not oversell it. For one thing, soft power is difficult to use directly. Much of it is produced and controlled by civil society outside the control of government. To some extent, national soft power in the form of values is almost an inadvertent by-product of domestic political life, and popular American cultural exports are controlled more by Hollywood than by Washington. Even in countries with more central political control than in the United States, the importance of credibility limits the extent to which governments can manipulate their soft power in an information age. Moreover, as mentioned earlier, setting an example does not provide power unless others choose to follow it. Sometimes examples are ignored; and sometimes when cultural values differ dramatically, examples can be counterproductive. Thus soft power is not simply another "tool" to be added to the peacekeeper's "toolkit" like an additional battalion of troops. But attraction to the values for which peacekeepers stand can facilitate their tasks.

Hard power and soft power should not be seen as opposed to each other in policy contexts. They work best when they reinforce each other. At the beginning of the twenty-first century, the position of the United States is a stronger version of that occupied by Britain in the late nineteenth century. America is preponderant, but not dominant in the sense of being able to control the world. At best it can hope to shape the environment of global politics. That includes not only protecting its national interests narrowly defined, but also realizing that if the largest country in the system does not attend to the production of public goods like international order, no smaller country will be able to do so. Thus the American national interest must include systemic values as well as more particular interests. For nineteenth-century Britain, these included maintaining the balance of power so there were no temptations to wage aggressive war, promoting an open international economy so that all countries can prosper, and maintaining access for all to the international commons (which in that period meant freedom of the seas). As updated and added to in table 1, these systemic goals are appropriate for the United States. To the extent that the largest country pursues such systemic goals, it will prevent crises and reduce the prospects of conflict—indirectly through the first four roles and directly through the fifth role. A combination of hard power and soft power is the best way to accomplish these systemic goals. Obviously the hard-power resources of military and economic clout are essential. But if the United States stands for attractive values and lives up to them in its domestic and international behavior, then the American military and economic presence will be welcome and more effective. And the acceptability of that presence will help when the United States turns to the direct role of convenor and mediator.

We can derive five maxims or rules of thumb for policymakers to follow in using soft power to avoid and manage conflicts. First, and perhaps most important, is to use hard power to structure situations so that soft power can be more effective. Europe provides a good example. With the collapse of the Soviet empire at the end of the Cold War, there were a number of paths that Eastern European nations could take. Some, like Yugoslavia, collapsed into bitter ethnic conflicts. Others such as Romania, Hungary, and Slovakia could have succumbed to such tensions. One of the reasons that they did not was that the headquarters of both

Table 1. Key Roles of a Preponderant But Not Dominant Power

1. Maintain the balance of power among major states (most notably, Russia, China, Japan, and the European Union)

2. Promote an open international economy (in areas such as money, trade, services, and energy)

3. Keep international commons open (oceans, outer space, global climate, plant and animal species, cyberspace)

4. Support international rules and institutions (in such areas as arms proliferation, peacekeeping, economic cooperation, environmental protection, humanitarian issues, and human rights)

5. Act as convener and mediator (as, for instance, in the cases of the Middle East, Northern Ireland, and Greece and Turkey)

NATO and the European Union in Brussels provided magnets of attraction. The two institutions also provided a vision of a positive future that had a powerful effect in dampening conflict well in advance of the dates that the Eastern European countries hoped to enter the Western clubs. In doing so, NATO and the European Union offered incentives in Eastern European domestic politics to eschew the easy path of arousing and riding ethnic hatred. American and West European officials made clear that such a path would preclude entry into those organizations and rule out the attractive future that they represented.

At a broader level, promotion of democracy and human rights is an important part of a foreign policy that tries to shape a less conflictual future environment. Such values cannot be the sole goal of a foreign policy. Survival is a logically prior value, and strategic stability is thus a vital interest. Moreover, it is not clear that we know how to promote democracy where economic and social preconditions do not yet exist. There is considerable evidence, however, that democratic countries are less likely to fight one another, and that countries that respect the rights of their citizens are less likely to fight other liberal societies. Thus the use by the United States of hard and soft power to foster democracy and human rights can be an important part of conflict prevention.

A second maxim is to invest in soft power when possible. Even though much soft power is an inadvertent societal by-product, policy decisions can have some effect in increasing it. For one thing, Americans should be clear when their domestic policies weaken the power of their attractive example, as racial segregation did in the past. Promoting racial and other forms of social justice remains crucial for the United States. Immigration policy is also important, both as a symbol of a multiethnic society and because many immigrants provide crucial avenues of communication with their former countries. Visa policies and education exchange programs are important in maintaining the flow of international students into our educational institutions. And while most American broadcast and communications exports will come from the private sector, it will still be worthwhile to invest in government cultural centers and radio programs. Some areas are too small or too powerful for the private sector to handle alone—for instance, Bosnia and China (where market considerations led some companies to self-censor).

Third, it will be important for Western policymakers to find ways to include the right nongovernmental organizations in their planning. NGOs today provide more aid than the entire UN system.[10] Some, such as the Red Cross or Médecins Sans Frontières, have unique access to areas of conflict. Often they can provide crucial information. Many are effective observers and promoters of human rights. Some organizations are explicitly devoted to conflict prevention and resolution. By engaging new institutions, we can spread the risks and resource base. We can benefit from, and reinforce, the soft power of these institutions of civil society. Conversely, it will be necessary

not to reinforce the soft power of the wrong type of nongovernmental actors. In some areas, terrorist networks like that of Osama bin Laden are seen as attractive. If we overdramatize their threat, we build up their heroic stature and increase their malevolent soft power.

Fourth, the United States should use its position in the world to play the role of peacemaker and conciliator for the systemic reasons stated earlier and because doing so is an investment in soft power (which in turn can increase our effectiveness as a conflict manager). When the United States helps to mediate conflicts in the Middle East, Northern Ireland, or the Aegean, it develops a reputation for being what Secretary of State Madeleine Albright called, in another context, an indispensable nation. This capacity works better in some situations and regions than in others. In Ulster, both Ireland and Britain had strong ties to the United States, and Senator George Mitchell was seen as an impartial arbiter. In the Israeli-Palestinian conflict, the United States was clearly more aligned with Israel, but its influence in Israel and it efforts to play an even-handed role made it an indispensable part of the negotiating process. In the Aegean, the United States was an attractive interlocutor to both its Greek and Turkish NATO allies and managed to stave off a number of dangerous incidents. On the other hand, in South Asia, India has mistrusted the United States (and everyone else) on the difficult issue of Kashmir, and in the Russia-Japan dispute over the Kuril Islands, the United States is allied with Japan and unable to solve the problem with Russia. A reputation for evenhandedness and intelligence in all senses of the word and generally attractive values can enhance conflict mediation. In turn, a reputation for success in conflict mediation contributes to future attractiveness in that domain. Successful mediation is not only good per se but also a wise way to build soft power.

Finally, it will be important for American policymakers (and congressional leaders) to resist unilateralist temptations. The United States has a general interest in multilateral regimes of laws and institutions to organize international actions to deal with issues such as trade, finance, the environment, proliferation of weapons of mass destruction, peacekeeping, human rights, and so on. Americans give up some portion of their freedom of action in order to constrain other countries. That is the price of living with global interdependence. Those who denigrate the importance of multilateral law and institutions forget that legitimacy is a power reality. When the United States acts as a bully that extends its laws (for example, on trade with Iran or Cuba) into the jurisdiction of other countries, or when it casually rejects a multilateral framework, it diminishes its soft power. The German journalist Josef Joffe points out that historically, when one country is preponderant, the desire of others to balance its power leads them to team up against it. He asks why this has not yet happened to the United States. One of the reasons he cites is American soft power. Most others do not see the United States as a threat, but rather as an attraction. Succumbing to unilateralism would rapidly squander this soft power.[11]

In conclusion, soft power is not some new panacea that will solve the problems of conflict management, but an instrument that will be of increasing importance in an information age. It is not easy to use, but it is too important to be ignored. Combined wisely with hard power, it can serve the purpose of preventing and managing conflicts and creating a more peaceful world.

NOTES

1. Elaine Ciulla Kamarck and Joseph S. Nye, Jr., eds., *democracy.com? Governance in a Networked World* (Hollis, N.H.: Hollis, 1999), chap. 1.

2. See, for example, Alvin Toffler, *The Third Wave* (New York: William Morrow, 1980), 342–343; Susan Strange, *The Retreat of the State* (Cambridge: Cambridge University Press, 1996); Jessica Mathews, "Power Shift," *Foreign Affairs* 76, no. 1 (January-February 1997).

3. Joseph S. Nye, Jr., *Bound to Lead: The Changing Nature of American Power* (New York: Basic Books, 1990), chaps. 1 and 6.

4. Samuel P. Huntington, *The Clash of Civilizations and the Remaking of World Order* (New York: Simon and Schuster, 1996), 92.

5. Qian Ning, *A Foreign Student in America: A Contemporary Story* (in Chinese) (Beijing, 1999).

6. Robert Keohane and Joseph S. Nye, Jr., "Power and Interdependence in the Information Age," *Foreign Affairs* 77, no. 5 (September-October 1998).

7. Herbert A. Simon, "Information 101: It's Not What You Know, It's How You Know It," *Journal for Quality and Participation* 21, no. 4 (July-August 1998): 30–33.

8. Robert O. Keohane and Joseph S. Nye, Jr., *Power and Interdependence: World Politics in Transition* (Boston: Little, Brown, 1977).

9. See, for example, Marshall McLuhan, *Understanding Media: The Extensions of Man* (New York: McGraw-Hill, 1964).

10. "The Non-Governmental Order: Will NGOs Democratise, or Merely Disrupt, Global Governance?" *Economist*, December 11, 1999.

11. Josef Joffe, "How America Does It," *Foreign Affairs* 76, no. 5 (September-October 1997): 13–27.

23

What Do NGOs Bring to Peacemaking?

Pamela Aall

THE DEBATE ON INTERVENTION—whether or not we should intervene, what is the best mechanism for intervention, who should authorize it, who should do it—involves a fundamental question: do we have an obligation to intervene to protect human rights and lives threatened by conflict?[1] The "we" referred to in this debate is an ever-shifting set of entities—the United Nations, the United States, France, Australia, the European Union, the Organization of African Unity, the Organization for Security and Cooperation in Europe, the "international community"—in other words, the full array of official institutions from individual states to intergovernmental organizations. In this debate, nongovernmental organizations (NGOs) are usually mentioned only as an afterthought. Yet, nonofficial institutions—private humanitarian agencies, charity organizations, church groups, human rights advocates, and even individuals—are active in these operations, answering what they see as a humanitarian imperative to save lives and protect the powerless.

In their desire to help the vulnerable, these organizations have responded to conflict throughout the world, sometimes as a function of their mission to bring humanitarian relief or to protect human rights, and sometimes as a deliberate attempt to intervene in the conflict.[2] As representatives of civil society, many commentators argue, NGOs are important components of the peacemaking process, capable of promoting sustained reconciliation at the grassroots level in societies split by civil war and ethnic and religious strife. Their presence in conflict situations and increasingly active role have affected the whole spectrum of international responses to conflict, bringing more actors into peacemaking, peacekeeping, and peacebuilding and creating the conditions for private people and institutions to intervene as third parties.[3]

These activities raise the question of whether these independent entities help or hurt peace efforts. In situations in which conditions are deteriorating rapidly or violence has already erupted, these organizations may be intensifying the confusion and raising the noise level in an already tense environment. Their activities—unintentionally or otherwise—may exacerbate conflict in war zones, as some have documented.[4] On the other hand, as the award of the 1999 Nobel Peace Prize to Médicins Sans Frontières indicates, there is also evidence that they make essential contributions to conflict prevention and resolution, contributions that are just now being recognized.

Given that the presence of NGOs is a feature of almost all international interventions, it is important to understand the nature of NGO intervention. What is special about track-two work—a term for nonofficial peacemaking efforts—that differentiates it from track-one, or official, intervention? When are NGOs effective and when should they be cautious about becoming involved? When NGOs do engage in peacemaking, do they have attributes that give them a special edge? Does their nonofficial status give them credibility with the parties to a conflict or prevent them from operating in the highly charged, high-stakes environment of peacemaking? Finally, there is the issue of relating to the broader peacemaking picture. The current international response to conflict is a study in complexity, involving many different types of institutions, mandates, rules of engagement, decision-making structures, and capabilities. This complexity can itself become a factor determining the failure or success of an outside intervention, depending on whether these institutions launch competing initiatives or establish some means to support one another's efforts. Where do private nonprofit organizations fit into this framework, and how do they interact with the other third-party actors?

This chapter looks at three aspects of NGO activity in conflict. First, it reviews three types of NGOs—humanitarian, human rights, and conflict resolution organizations—and examines their interaction with conflict situations. Here, the focus is on NGOs as they carry out their principal missions, more or less independently of other third-party institutions, and

on their abilities to contribute to or to impede conflict management. Second, it looks at some of the resources that allow NGOs to play a constructive role despite their relative lack of power and material strength. Third, it examines how NGOs interact with other institutions, looking at challenges of coordination and coherence arising from NGOs' presence in conflict zones at the same time that other external third parties are actively engaged in conflict management.

Although local NGOs play a critical role in conflict management, the review concentrates on international NGOs, in part because of the kinds of third-party roles they play in conflicts and in part because of their relationships to the other third-party peacemakers.[5] This chapter argues that the impact of NGOs on peacemaking varies: some of their activities inhibit conflict management, whereas others support it—both directly and indirectly. Different types of NGOs can contribute to conflict resolution, playing important roles in the international response to conflict and using several types of power in order to do so. Their effectiveness depends not least on their relationship with other third parties, on how well they coordinate their efforts with the official peace process and how are they accepted by the official third-party actors.

NGOs AND THEIR CAPACITY FOR CONFLICT MANAGEMENT

NGOs are relatively new and very independent players in the array of third-party institutions that respond to conflict, making it difficult to gauge with certainty how their actions affect the international response. This difficulty is intensified by an understandable tendency on the part of casual observers to group all NGOs together, as if a common set of mandates and institutional structures governed them all. Here, we differentiate among three major types of NGOs—humanitarian, human rights, and conflict resolution entities—that operate in conflict situations and explore their strengths and weaknesses in conflict management.

One of the many problems of examining NGOs is determining what an NGO is.[6] For our purposes, NGOs are defined as private, self-governing, not-for-profit institutions dedicated to alleviating human suffering; or to promoting education, health, economic development, environmental protection, human rights, and conflict resolution; or to encouraging the establishment of democratic institutions and civil society. This broad definition covers a wide spectrum of institutions, from humanitarian organizations to human rights activists to church groups to thinly disguised political parties.

In discussing these organizations, it is important to distinguish between international NGOs, which operate in more than one country, and local, or indigenous, organizations, which confine their operations to one country, region, or village. Although both international and local NGOs are affected by the political environment, laws, and security procedures of the host government, local NGOs are more vulnerable to state harassment in cases where NGO activity is seen as a threat to the prevailing power structures. International NGOs generally have more resources than do local NGOs; local NGOs generally have more connection to the people and problems at hand.[7]

A more ambiguous distinction is between secular and religious NGOs. Some religious NGOs have missionary mandates, making religion a cornerstone of their activities; others acknowledge the religious community from which they spring but do not make religion a salient element of their work. Others, such as the Quakers and the Mennonites, act from deeply held religious beliefs but do not include religious components in their conflict resolution work. As with the field as a whole, the diversity of religious-based NGOs defies easy generalizations about how they resemble or differ from secular institutions; it is simply another factor to keep in mind.

A distinct characteristic of the NGO world is its growth over the past twenty-five years, as illustrated by the fact that most of the 160-plus members of Inter*Action*, an umbrella organization for major American relief and development NGOs, were founded after 1975.[8] Pinning down the number of NGOs—local and international—active around the world is not easy. For example, using relatively strict criteria for identifying NGOs, the Union of International Associations estimated that in 1996–97 the number of NGOs was somewhat over 38,000.[9] However, two years earlier, a leader in the NGO field had guessed that there were approximately 24,000 indigenous NGOs in the Indian province of Tamil-Nadu alone—a number, if accurate, that would account for more than 60 percent of the Union of International Associations figure.[10] Part of the difficulty lies in defining what constitutes an NGO; part reflects the absence of a universal clearinghouse or registry of these independent and independently minded organizations. What is clear, however, is that in recent years NGOs have proliferated rapidly.

NGO management structures differ around the world. For instance, most British, Canadian, and American NGOs are governed by boards of trustees according to the institution's bylaws. Board members are legally accountable for the NGO's operations and responsible for the fulfillment of its mission and financial obligations. NGOs in other parts of the world have sprung up according to (or sometimes in opposition to) their own national laws and traditions. Some are similar to American NGOs; some are quasi-governmental structures, fully funded and essentially managed by the state; some are effectively opposition parties and highly political in nature; some are locally organized cooperatives that depend on the energy and influence of one or two individuals.

NGOs have budgets ranging from next to nothing to over a billion dollars. As one of the largest international NGOs, the American Red Cross has a budget of $2.4 billion (1999).

CARE, Médicins Sans Frontières, Catholic Relief Service, and World Vision have annual budgets of between $300 million and $400 million. Funding comes from both public and private sources, with many organizations relying purely on private philanthropy. For others, public funding has become a significant part of their budgets. Working in partnership with government organizations or as private contractors to deliver services for government agencies, NGOs received $8 billion, or 10 percent of public development aid given globally, in 1994.[11]

In terms of staffing, some international NGOs operate with a mix of nationalities, with top management provided by the nationals of the NGO's country of origin and many operational staff positions filled by local employees. A number of international NGOs consist almost entirely of teams of outside experts who work with indigenous groups in a capacity-building arrangement. Some international human rights groups employ individuals from around the world but hesitate to involve local people in monitoring human rights for fear of jeopardizing their safety. At the same time, these international human rights organizations often work closely with local human rights groups, bringing international attention to the findings of these small organizations.

This review of the institutional structures of NGOs is much too short to convey the great variations in staffing, organization, management, funding, mission, activities, and culture within the NGO community and serves mainly to point out the institutional differences that exist not only between NGOs with different missions but also among NGOs that share the same mission. However, it is worth emphasizing a few characteristics that these institutions share:

- they have no official, governmental status;
- they often serve as a bridge between the official world and the grassroots level, sometimes as advocates for the grassroots,

sometimes as implementers of government (or international organization) policy;
- they are independent organizations and place great value on their independence; and
- they generally enjoy few of the traditional sources of leverage available to governments and intergovernmental organizations.

This last point is key to understanding their capacities and limitations in conflict management.

Humanitarian NGOs

Within the international NGO community, humanitarian organizations are the most numerous group and include some of the largest agencies, including the American Red Cross, CARE, Oxfam, International Rescue Committee, World Vision, Médicins Sans Frontières, and Catholic Relief Services.[12] Some of these organizations specialize in responding to humanitarian crises, while others divide their efforts and resources between relief and development efforts. Although the division between relief work and development work is breaking down—and much attention, especially with regard to conflict, is currently focused on emphasizing the relief-to-development continuum—these two activities are still carried out, by and large, by different staffs.

Development involves long-term projects aimed at helping communities build sustainable social, economic, and political structures. The assistance focuses on the development of vital components of society—agriculture, education, infrastructure, employment, and so forth—and is deemed a success when continued aid becomes unnecessary because a society has become self-sufficient. Development work, which can have a significant effect on conflict management within a society, usually ceases at times of mass violence. International development staff depart and return only when the conflict is over; during a crisis, they are replaced by relief staff whose area of expertise is responding to emergency situations wherever they may occur.

Relief is characterized by short-term, emergency service in the face of a disaster, whether natural or man-made. These operations include airlifting food, clean water, and sanitation equipment to distressed populations; establishing shelter for homeless victims; repairing salvageable structures; and preventing, containing, and treating life-threatening diseases. There is a strong connection between relief and development work—the ways in which humanitarian crises are addressed may have profound effects on the development conditions —and this has its parallels in conflict management terms. If an NGO favors one group or area during a crisis, it may find that its ability to play a mediating role in a later dispute—even after the conflict is settled—will be hampered by its earlier action. Recognition that humanitarian action takes place on a long continuum is breaking down the distinction between relief and development, but for the purpose of understanding NGOs in conflict, it is still useful to consider them separate activities.

The focus in relief work is on saving lives, not managing conflict. However, according to John Prendergast, a practitioner with long experience in conflict-related relief work, these life-saving measures can sometimes exacerbate conflict and fuel the misery that the humanitarian NGO is trying to relieve.[13] The contrast between the intention to do good and the inability to prevent the bad is most starkly illustrated by the experience of humanitarian NGOs in refugee work in civil conflicts in the 1990s. The internal conflicts of this decade produced enormous numbers of refugees (people who flee across international borders) and internally displaced people (those who flee their homes but do not cross an international border).

In 1999 the Office of the United Nations High Commissioner for Refugees (UNHCR) estimated that approximately 40–50 million people were living as refugees or internally displaced persons, having been forced from their homes by hostile forces. Refugee NGOs provide many specialized services, including components with strong conflict management potential. Refugee assistance ranges from supplying basic human needs during mass migrations of displaced persons to protecting the rights of individual asylum seekers. In the initial phase of a migration, which is typically accompanied by starvation, disease, and death on a large scale, the urgent need is for relief—for water, food, and shelter for a frightened and exhausted population. Over the longer term, relief organizations provide education, health care training, and community-building skills to displaced populations; strengthen local relief and health services; reunite families; and encourage self-sufficiency through training in agriculture and job skills, income generation, and the production of relief supplies.

Protection of displaced populations is an equally important part of the work of refugee NGOs. It is this aspect of their activity that came under siege in the civil conflicts of the 1990s.[14] Confronted by massive numbers of refugees, the relief agencies could not screen individuals seeking refuge in camps, most of who were legitimate refugees but some of whom had committed atrocities and participated in genocide. By helping the innocent, the agencies thus unintentionally supported those responsible for the conflict and endangered the security of both genuine refugees and relief officials. The humanitarian agencies' dilemma was heightened by the fact that in these messy conflicts, the warlords and militia controlled food supply lines to the camps and imposed control over the refugees, setting themselves up as legitimate, representative governing bodies within the refugee camps. NGOs were faced with a horrible choice: either house and feed the entire refugee population, including the warmongers, or withdraw completely, leaving the refugees to fend for themselves.

Repatriation became highly problematic. The humanitarian community had to cope with a repatriation situation over which they had little control: spontaneous Rwandan repatriation from the Zaire camps; less-than-voluntary repatriation from Tanzania; refusal to repatriate in Bosnia; and over-eager refugees returning to unsafe conditions in Kosovo. Besides the militia intimidation of refugee camps, humanitarian agencies had to deal with refugee fatigue or outright hostility in receiving countries; deep-seated fears among refugees about their safety after repatriation or, contrarily, a disregard for personal safety in their eagerness to return home; and political matters over which they had no control, such as internationally mandated election schedules that drove repatriation timetables.

These failures to protect the innocent have driven wedges between different sections of the humanitarian community: NGOs, international organizations, and states. In 1997 Amnesty International, a major human rights NGO, publicly criticized UNHCR for failing to protect refugees' lives and human rights in Tanzania and Rwanda.[15] In another case, Médecins Sans Frontières pulled out of Eastern Zaire in protest at the unsafe conditions of the refugee camps, only to be replaced by other humanitarian organizations as soon as it left. In addition, humanitarian agencies complain that they are being used by the major political powers, first as substitutes for political response and then as scapegoats for failures when humanitarian efforts go wrong.

These recent experiences in working with refugees have challenged the humanitarian field's tradition of neutrality and forced humanitarians to grapple with the question of whether a policy of neutrality is still possible or whether, in the face of intimidation by a militia or other organized efforts that target vulnerable groups, humanitarian NGOs should take action to bring the warmongers to justice or at least to exclude them from the relief programs.

These factors weaken humanitarian agencies' capacity for conflict management in these situations and undermine their ability to carry out their humanitarian mission. Well aware of the dilemmas confronting it, the humanitarian community has attempted to address them, in part by establishing codes of conduct and in part by some intensive soul-searching about the nature and limitations of humanitarian action.[16] Mary Anderson set the stage for this self-examination by developing the notion that humanitarian NGOs should at least subscribe to a Hippocratic oath that they will "first do no harm" in the course of their work.[17] Anderson and others have taken this concept of "no harm" much further, suggesting ways in which humanitarian aid can help ameliorate conflict.[18] These suggestions range from protective measures to prevent theft of humanitarian food supplies and other goods by warring parties to wholesale incorporation of conflict management and resolution techniques into the planning and implementation of humanitarian activities. CARE, for instance, instituted conflict resolution training for its staff working in the Great Lakes region of Africa, and Catholic Relief Services has launched a program that combines peacebuilding, development, and reconstruction work in Bosnia and Herzegovina, Burundi, India, and the Federal Republic of Yugoslavia.[19] The readiness of humanitarian NGOs to adopt procedures to prevent or counteract the negative effects of their work will determine how effective these organizations will be, not only in conflict management and peace operations but in humanitarian action in general.

Human Rights NGOs

The mission of human rights NGOs such as Amnesty International and Human Rights Watch is to define and promote the basic rights of all people and to prevent political and economic repression. Protection of the rights of the individual has a long history in many countries but is still contentious in others—and not only in states with repressive regimes but also in those with governments or societies whose religious or cultural values are at odds with the principles of individual rights.[20] Although international human rights NGOs have monitored conflicts for decades, in the past ten years they have increasingly brought to international attention numerous atrocities spawned by civil war in such places as Cambodia, Bosnia, and Rwanda.

The goal of organizations active in human rights is to seek out, research, and address specific and general situations where repression occurs. In gathering information, the staff, volunteers, and members of NGOs visit vulnerable areas as observers; interview local NGOs, churches, community groups, activists, and professionals; and seek relevant official documentation. On the basis of this research, they mount systematic campaigns to alert the public and officials to the plight of particular victims, whether individuals or entire populations. Campaigns consist of testifying before government committees, international organizations, and other influential policymaking and lawmaking bodies and reporting abuses to the world press, thereby not only educating officials and the public but also exerting pressure on institutions to condemn offending parties, a process known as "shaming."[21] Organizations such as Peace Brigades International may also provide unarmed protection to vulnerable groups, accompanying them in hostile situations to enhance their safety.[22] Many human rights organizations do not accept funding from government sources in order to avoid creating the impression of a conflict of interest in their work.

The assessment of how effective human rights organizations are in conflict management depends in part on the position of the assessor. Specialists in conflict management disagree on the place of human rights accountability within the conflict management process.[23] Some believe that peacemaking and peacebuilding must involve all important parties to the conflict, even if some of those parties have abused human rights. Without the essential cooperation of these groups, any peace agreement will be vulnerable to the actions of a disaffected or antagonized combatant. The early hesitation of the international community to pursue indicted war criminals in Bosnia reflected not only a deep caution about further military engagement but also a reluctance to drive Serbian president Slobodan Milosevic away from the Dayton agreement.[24]

On the other side of the argument, human rights activists claim that enduring peace can be established only after some sort of recognition of suffering and reckoning for abuses has occurred.[25] These efforts can have a punitive component, such as imprisonment or exile, but they can also involve a grant of amnesty: the simple act of acknowledgment—of telling one's story, of hearing others' stories, of admitting guilt, of accepting that admission of guilt—can contribute to healing after a conflict. Bodies such as the Truth and Reconciliation Commission in South Africa and the Commission on the Truth for El Salvador have helped to establish the basis for national reconciliation after civil strife. Without a commitment to individual accountability, say human rights activists, a peace process may collapse under the weight of resentments, which target whole populations and cause permanent societal fractures.

No matter which argument one accepts, it is clear that the work of human rights NGOs is not always a stabilizing factor in a conflict situation and can run counter, at least in the short term, to peacekeeping efforts. In their direct condemnation of human rights abusers, NGOs may complicate the peace process by further antagonizing parties within a conflict. In the long run, however, their contribution to the development of the concept of individual human rights, good governance, and civil society may be key to the viability of a peace process. In carrying out their mission, therefore, they may both bolster and undermine the conflict management process. Their increasing sophistication and proven ability to carry out their primary mission ensure that they will remain important players in conflict and postconflict situations. Their contribution to conflict management will depend in part on their ability to influence and their willingness to work with other peacemakers, and the extent of this cooperation may help to determine the future success of any international effort in conflict mediation.

Conflict Resolution NGOs

The Carter Center's 1995 *International Guide to NGO Activities in Conflict Prevention and Resolution* listed eighty-three organizations devoted to conflict management.[26] These organizations are dedicated to averting crises through preventive measures or to acting as intermediaries in an active conflict. They work with opposing parties, facilitate negotiations, and help to uphold accepted solutions. In some cases they initiate and catalyze dialogue between parties; in others, they monitor and expedite it.

The field of conflict resolution has many sources, including the academic disciplines of political science, international relations, psychology, sociology, anthropology, biology, economics, mathematics, and law. Other seedbeds include the long history of domestic labor-management disputes and negotiation; the civil rights movement and various efforts to resolve racial, community, and domestic ethnic conflict; the emergence of social activism in the 1960s and 1970s, including the antiwar, feminist, and environmental movements; the development of alternative dispute settlement mechanisms —such as arbitration and mediation—which take place outside of the domestic court system; the work of NGOs dedicated to nonviolence, such as the Quakers and the Mennonites; and policymakers and diplomats whose practice of negotiation, mediation, and conflict resolution on a national and multilateral basis has long provided insights for the field.[27] As can be seen from these varied sources, the understanding and practice of conflict resolution evolved largely outside of governmental structures; in the international sphere, conflict resolution has been developed to complement or substitute for official third-party intervention.[28] Most of the organizations involved in conflict resolution represent one specific approach.

Many conflict resolution approaches seek to make the participants aware of their own role in a conflict and to give them tools to resolve or at least ameliorate the situation. Beneath this broad canopy lie many different programs in conflict management, ranging from courses to improve negotiation skills to strategies for identifying and resolving the underlying causes of conflict.[29]

Using these and other conflict resolution techniques, conflict resolution NGOs focus on different levels of society and different groups. Some concentrate almost entirely at the grassroots level while others focus on opinion leaders or on potentially explosive elements in a society. For instance, the Washington-based Strategic Initiatives of Women teaches Somali women conflict management skills and trains them to develop peacebuilding networks and increase their political participation.[30] In Bosnia, the Center for Strategic and International Studies' program on preventive diplomacy holds training sessions that bring together clergy and laity from the Serbian Orthodox Church, the Roman Catholic Church, the Muslim and Jewish communities, and various Protestant churches. The London-based organization International Alert operates in West Africa, the Great Lakes region, the former Soviet Union, and Sri Lanka to support peacemaking and peacebuilding efforts, working with official and nonofficial groups to increase institutional capacity and to offer parties to conflicts a chance to discuss issues and to establish relationships in an informal setting.

In addition, some of the large relief and development NGOs have added a conflict resolution component to their work, recognizing that development itself can create new tensions and alter existing relationships. As long-term and community-level participants in strife-ridden areas, these NGOs are well placed to help foster the development of civil society and of relationships that can underpin an enduring peace. The United Methodist Committee on Relief created a program in Bosnia to set up a multicultural conflict resolution center at Sarajevo University, establish forums and training programs for local police, and create centers where conflict resolution can be institutionalized. Catholic Relief Services has peacebuilding programs in thirty-eight conflict-prone countries, with activities ranging from conflict resolution workshops to peace and justice commissions to training in advocacy and citizen diplomacy.

Many conflict resolution organizations focus on transforming how individuals perceive conflict. The institutions that engage in this time-consuming and labor-intensive work are often small and depend heavily on the skills and expertise of a few individuals, characteristics that can limit the effectiveness of these NGOs. One commonly voiced criticism of conflict resolution work is that it is sporadic, consisting of one-time programs that focus on developing conflict resolution skills or bringing contending parties together for discussion or workshops. These programs, claim their detractors, lack the long-term commitment that would allow conflict resolution activities to build on one another. In a simplistic characterization of this behavior, these organizations have been accused of "parachuting" into a conflict, introducing some foreign problem-solving techniques based on Western principles and values, and then leaving rapidly to parachute into yet another conflict.[31]

This criticism is often unfair, as many NGOs work closely with local groups to build on indigenous methods of conflict resolution and to build up capacity for peacebuilding within the society in conflict. In addition, many of these institutions are committed to long-term programs but have to scramble for resources to fund that work. Fund-raising is not an easy task. The field of conflict resolution is not only young but also—in the eyes of many potential funders—unproven; much skepticism exists about whether it is possible to promote reconciliation in entrenched conflicts, especially conflicts based on ethnic or religious schisms. Unlike humanitarian NGOs, which can point to physical reconstruction as proof of their effectiveness, conflict resolution NGOs can only point to the dog that did not bark—to the conflict that did not re-ignite—as proof of their success. Few funders are willing to take the risk that the slow, difficult work of conflict resolution will bear fruit. Without long-term funding, conflict resolution NGOs are hobbled in the kinds of programs they can conduct.

In addition, conflict resolution institutions can also represent a threat to existing power structures and provoke the hostility of host governments and other authorities. Individuals working on conflict resolution in Bosnia tell stories of being thrown out of officials' offices simply for using the word "reconciliation."[32] Without the substantial resources of humanitarian NGOs or the protective cover enjoyed by large UN institutions such as UNHCR, these NGOs can be easily intimidated or shut down by antipathetic governments.

THE NATURE OF NONOFFICIAL POWER

The above review of NGOs in conflict situations focuses on their *potential* capacity to promote or hinder conflict resolution as an outgrowth of their work, alone or in collaboration with others. The question remains, however, whether NGOs can realize that potential and provide third-party assistance to antagonists locked in a violent conflict or stalemated negotiation. At first glance, the answer to this question may seem self-evident. History and common sense tell us that mediation is generally the province of individual states or international organizations that have the power—whether moral or material—to influence the parties, that can produce positive and negative inducements to promote settlement. NGOs, by and large, do not have this kind of power. There are, however, a number of cases in which NGOs have played an active role in mediation: the Community of Sant'Egidio in Mozambique, the Norwegian Institute for Applied Social Science (FAFO) in the Oslo Accords, the South China Sea Informal Working Group, the Dartmouth Conference Regional Conflicts Task Force in Tajikistan, and interventions by Jimmy Carter and the Carter Center in Haiti, North Korea, Bosnia, and the Great Lakes region. With the exception of former president Carter, whose prestige outweighs that of many current national office-holders, these organizations are relatively powerless: they have few material resources, small staffs, and low profiles, even in their countries of origin. What has allowed these organizations to gain entry as third parties into conflicts and, once in, to play an effective role?

The issue of entry is often one of preexisting relationships, of contacts and trust built up over a period of time.[33] FAFO was able to engage both Palestinians and Israelis because its long-term work on social conditions in the West Bank and Gaza had allowed it to establish a reputation for professionalism and evenhandedness among influential leaders in both government and academia. Sant'Egidio's close relationship with a Mozambican bishop allowed this organization to engage on a gradual basis with the government and the rebels. Other factors can also lead to NGO involvement in third-party conflict intervention. The very fact that the parties perceive these NGOs to be powerless may increase their attractiveness to the antagonists: if the attempt to open dialogue fails, the parties lose little by way of reputation or potential inducements to settle. The South China Sea Informal Working Group—a nonofficial attempt to build confidence and constructive multilateral relations among states with interests in the South China Sea through focusing on concrete, solvable problems—presents a low-risk option for dialogue among the claimant countries around the South China

Sea. If some practical issues, such as navigational safety, were resolved in this forum, it would benefit the whole region. If the hard issues, such as demarcation of sovereign rights, remained unsettled and even undiscussed, the nonofficial and consultative nature of the working group exercise protects the participant states from being held accountable for the lack of progress.

Whether and how NGOs affect negotiations once they are under way involves a different set of questions. Effective mediation involves a complex interweaving of circumstances and attributes: Does the mediator have the resources to commit for the long haul? Is it able to discern and reframe the underlying interests and needs of disputants? Can it help to create conditions that make settlement possible? Mediation often entails strategic and tactical ploys on the part of the mediator, such as the use of timing, deadlines, sequencing, enlightening (or disillusioning), legitimizing, persuading (sometimes to the point of coercion), and protecting. If mediators are to employ these tactics successfully, they need both power and sources of leverage. Although a number of NGOs have been able to bring some of these talents to their peacemaking efforts, international organizations and individual states clearly retain the comparative advantage in mediation.[34] NGOs, however, are not powerless. What sorts of resources do these institutions bring to conflict situations? What do they bring to the table in terms of legitimacy and leverage?

In chapter 22 of this book, Joseph Nye differentiates between "hard" and "soft" varieties in his analysis of the current dynamics of power. According to his definition, hard power "is the ability to get others to do what they otherwise would not do through threat of punishment or promise of reward." Soft power, on the other hand, "is the ability to get desired outcomes because others want what you want, rather than do what you make them do. It is the ability to achieve desired outcomes through attraction rather than coercion."[35]

Jeffrey Z. Rubin has suggested that there are several different kinds of resources and influence that mediators can bring to the negotiating table and that these are related to six different bases of power. Two of these—reward and coercive power—derive from a mediator's ability to offer incentives and disincentives in order to change the conflict parties' calculations of the costs and benefits of remaining at war. Four of these powers, however, are based on more intangible attributes: *legitimate power* derives from the parties' perception that the mediator brings legitimacy and authority to the proceedings; *referent power* is based on the relationship between the mediator and the parties and is a power that results from the value that the parties put on this relationship; *expert power* flows from the mediator's knowledge and experience with certain issues; and *informational power* involves the information that the mediator conveys, as in cases when the mediator acts as a go-between or message carrier.[36]

These last four categories of power are quite different from traditional views of power that focus on material resources and military force, or carrots and sticks.[37] Both Rubin's and Nye's definitions create space for intangible sources of influence: expertise, legitimation, relationships, moral exemplars, and the elusive concept of "attraction." This is certainly the sphere that NGOs inhabit.[38] The question remains, however, as to whether NGOs also need, have access to, and can employ more coercive forms of force in their peacemaking efforts.

The example of Mozambique points the way toward an answer.[39] Although framed by the Cold War in ideological terms, the Mozambican civil war was fought between the hardline socialist government of Frelimo and the rebel force Renamo and was essentially a power clash between two groups to determine who would guide Mozambique's future. The civil war, which started in 1977, continued for fifteen years, inflicting hundreds of thousands of casualties and creating millions of displaced people. Remarkably, the peace agreement between the two factions that was signed in 1992 and that brought an end to the fighting was brokered by a lay Catholic organization established to help the poor. How did this happen?

First of all, the organization, the Community of Sant'Egidio, established some credibility with Renamo and Frelimo by virtue of its long relationship with a Mozambican peacemaker, the bishop of Beira. Besides representing a powerful and respected moral force, the community also benefited from the intercession of Enrico Berlinguer, the head of the Communist Party in Italy. Through its own relationships, through moral authority enhanced by good relations with the Vatican, and through its access to authoritative figures, the community exercised referent, expert, legitimate, and informational power—or, in Joseph Nye's terms, soft power.

However, Sant'Egidio also made allies among states that could provide leverage. It worked closely with the Italian government, which hosted the two years of peace talks in Rome. Italy provided financial support and a role model of a democracy built on contending forces. Sant'Egidio kept the U.S. government informed about what it was doing. U.S. support for the effort was important, but it was also helpful that the United States was willing to take a back seat. For its part, the U.S. government offered lots of technical expertise on military, legal, economic, and institutional issues in the negotiations. Mozambique's neighbors, Zimbabwe and Kenya, and the Vatican also provided support for the process.

Through these strategic alliances, the Community of Sant'Egidio was able to borrow the power to reward and to coerce. Whether it would ever have asked for this hard power to be exercised and, if asked, whether the states involved would ever have acceded to the request is another question. What is important for this analysis, however, is that far from being a powerless institution, the NGO was endowed with substantial intangible resources and was backed by allies that had the ability to supply or withhold incentives for the parties to settle.

PULLING IN THE SAME DIRECTION: TOWARD A COHERENT PEACEMAKING STRATEGY

The previous sections looked at NGOs as sole actors in situations of conflict. But NGOs rarely act alone in these situations. In any given conflict, multiple mediators may be active, as well as other third parties such as peacekeeping forces, UN representatives, refugee and development agencies, and other NGOs. Such a profusion of actors makes peacekeeping efforts messy and sometimes chaotic, a characteristic that compounds the ethical and practical challenges NGOs face in conflict management by testing their ability to engage or collaborate with the other third parties.

Coordination among all third-party institutions in conflict has been the subject of much attention on the part of the United Nations, individual governments, militaries, and NGOs since the first post–Cold War major complex emergency, Operation Provide Comfort, brought these institutions together in 1991.[40] Although consultation between NGOs and official structures has increased greatly since the early 1990s, significant problems still exist in areas such as information sharing. Indeed, collaboration with other types of organizations is still hard to achieve, especially in a fast-moving, turbulent, and complex emergency or conflict situation.[41]

Traditionally, NGOs have acted independently, with little coordination either among themselves or with the intergovernmental organizations and the military forces active in a peace operation. With the proliferation in the 1990s of NGOs and of relief operations involving military personnel, coordination between NGOs and the military became a major concern for participants in multilateral peace operations. These organizations have perceived their roles to be distinct and nonoverlapping. Many NGO staff felt uneasy working with military forces, whether from their own countries or from the country receiving assistance. NGOs, conscious of the need to preserve their neutrality and the protection that vulnerability affords them, have sometimes felt themselves to be endangered by a close association with the military. In addition, some NGO staff and local people may see peacekeeping and peace enforcement missions as repressive rather than protective in nature. For their part, military leaders have tended to regard NGOs as undisciplined and their operations as uncoordinated and disjointed.

In operations in Iraq and Somalia, the establishment of closer working relationships between NGOs and the military contributed to the successful delivery of humanitarian assistance within an extremely volatile and dangerous environment. These same operations, however, also underlined the importance of establishing better and more rapid communications among the international actors responding to the conflict and a clearer comprehension of the mission's overall objectives. While they enjoyed a high level of cooperation in the Somalia operations, the military and NGOs had different interpretations of the mission's objectives. The military's concern with avoiding "mission creep" accentuated its desire to go in, fix the problem, and get out quickly. Conversely, the NGO perspective during this crisis was long term, aimed as much at addressing the root causes of the crisis as at delivering relief.[42]

Barriers to cooperation and mutual support are not posed solely by differences in mandates, objectives, and capabilities. Organizational culture is also a barrier to collaboration.[43] In a number of areas—patterns of decision making, attitudes toward authority, attitudes toward the population they are aiding, educational background, philosophical grounding—marked differences exist between the two communities. Most NGOs do not have an elaborate hierarchical structure; instead, they are decentralized and relatively flat in their authority structures, with an informal managerial style that operates through personal engagement. The military, by contrast, has a strong hierarchical structure in which the lines of authority are clear and duties well defined. In this structure, mission objectives are generally articulated before an operation begins and rules of engagement guide all parts of the structure, from senior decision makers to the soldiers on the ground. Planning and preparation are highly valued; militaries spend considerable time preparing for all sorts of conditions and contingencies, anticipating worst-case scenarios and simulating real conditions in their training programs.

In a tumultuous situation, the decentralized, flexible approach to management embedded in most NGOs can be a great asset. The willingness to act when speed is essential and detailed planning is impossible makes these organizations among the best equipped to respond to sudden challenges. But this ability to turn on a dime—to change strategies, shift resources, quickly expand or shut down operations—can appear chaotic to the military, whose operations involve large numbers of people and resources and which values detailed planning and preparation.

Recent experience in Kosovo, East Timor, and Sierra Leone argue for a close relationship between NGOs and the international military peacekeeping forces, and attitudes on both sides have certainly begun to change. Exposure to each other's strengths and capabilities has served to increase the military's respect for the innovation and dedication of NGOs and to foster an appreciation among NGOs for the unsurpassed logistical capacity of the military. Both sides recognize the benefits of a closer relationship, and the military has been particularly assiduous in including the NGO perspective in its training sessions. It has been so effective, in fact, that members of the humanitarian community have complained that they do not have the personnel to meet the military's demand for authentic NGO or UNHCR voices in their programs.[44]

Militaries have sought to improve their collaboration with NGOs by creating civil-military operations centers (CMOCs) and other mechanisms that bring together military, NGO, and international organization personnel to advance mutual goals. These operations centers not only allow the three groups to share information and views but also provide a venue for practical matters such as briefings by the military on land mines or security conditions. They do not serve, however, as coordinating mechanisms.

Even when NGOs and international military peacekeeping forces are ready to forge a close relationship, other factors may frustrate that ambition. For instance, in Bosnia the rules of engagement that governed action by the U.S. military stipulated that staff travel only in convoys of four or more vehicles, which could be better protected than smaller groups. The ability to move quickly around the country, however, was important to the work of international NGO staff. American NGO workers, therefore, often traveled by themselves in private cars or hitched rides in armored vehicles with officials of the Organization for Security and Cooperation in Europe or UNHCR, rather than wait for a U.S. military convoy to be formed.

Problems of coherence and coordination in the military-NGO relationship often revolve around operational matters; solving those problems involves identifying how each side can help the other and how they can avoid tripping each other up. Both sides must also recognize that although they rarely engage in the same kind of work, the success of one is critical to the success of the other. NGOs cannot function in a hostile, volatile environment and must depend on security forces to protect their staff and resources. Peacekeeping forces can only withdraw once NGOs and other civilian agencies have begun the tasks of consolidating the peace and moving toward reconstruction and reconciliation.

Coherence is equally important to the success of NGO participation in active mediation or conflict facilitation. As noted, in most conflict zones numerous political or humanitarian actors are active on the ground, including the United Nations, UNHCR, representatives of various states, and NGOs. Nonofficial organizations—even those involved in peace talks—generally play a supporting role when a negotiation process is under way. Through workshops, facilitations, consultations, and other means they can broaden support for the official negotiations or provide a seedbed for ideas that can be fed into the official process. Good communication between NGOs and the principal negotiators or mediators makes these goals easier to obtain and serves the needs of both parties.

The Inter-Tajik Dialogue, a long-term process to foster peace in Tajikistan through discussion among influential members of the country's nascent, almost nonexistent, civil society, was effective in part because the organizers—a Russian-American team—kept in close touch with the official UN peace talks.[45] However, keeping in touch is a complicated matter, likely more dependent on the initiative of the NGO rather than on that of the official institution. Experience in Northern Ireland with a track-two effort to allow parties to the conflict to test ideas and build relationships in private workshops shows how complicated the matter can be. In this case, the track-two effort made no concerted attempt to keep the British government informed of its progress. Consequently, the British government remained unaware of the workshops until it too wished to launch a similar project. "The result," says one of the organizers of the track-two effort, "was a minor diplomatic frisson and a salutary lesson in the pitfalls of complex mediation. In an ideal world there should be strong lines of communication between all points on the mediation chain."[46]

Collaboration in these circumstances involves more than keeping other parties informed. It calls for agreeing on methods and goals and exercising a good deal of discipline in order to allow other, more appropriate, institutions take the lead when the situation demands.

The Community of Sant'Egidio succeeded in Mozambique because the more powerful states —the United States, Italy—and the United Nations allowed it to proceed without interference but provided support as needed. The story of former president Jimmy Carter's private intervention in Bosnia in late 1994, however, is more ambiguous as it was not necessarily coordinated with the on-going peacemaking efforts. His intervention resulted in a four-month cease-fire—a welcome respite from fighting but one that may have served to give the parties to the conflict time to regroup and prepare for renewed conflict rather than to allow peace to take hold.

Consideration of the willingness to collaborate and confer with other institutions leads naturally to a discussion of accountability.[47] Accountability is a key issue for all NGOs, especially those active in conflict situations. Whether they become involved in conflict through mediation efforts or through humanitarian work, they are changing the situation through their own activities.[48] In addition, in a number of crisis situations, NGOs have come to assume responsibilities that far exceed their original missions. For instance, in both Rwanda and Somalia, NGOs moved into the vacuum caused by the collapse of central authority, undertaking many of the basic municipal services usually provided by the local governments. In the process, these NGOs effectively replaced the state. The NGOs' ability to swiftly initiate and improvise alternative services certainly benefited the local people, but it also raised a critical issue: to whom or to what is an NGO accountable—the local people, other third-party institutions, the international community, the government of the country in which it is headquartered, its board of trustees, its funders, or all of the above?[49] It is not the good intentions of the NGOs that are in question. Rather, concern focuses on the unintended consequences of an international NGO's pursuit of its mission to help, protect, empower, or bring peace.

Another set of concerns revolve around the traditional independence of these private voluntary organizations. NGOs have no obligation to enter a situation of conflict, no obligation—once in—to remain committed, and no obligation to pull out if other third parties disengage. Therefore, NGOs contribute to the unpredictability of the international community and to its seeming inability to coordinate an effective response to conflict, as the competing efforts in Burundi point out.[50] This independence of action is complicated by these institutions' fungibility. A real strength of the NGO sector is that so many actors, so many organizations are willing to play a role in helping. This embarrassment of riches means that NGOs can respond quickly to specific situations, tailoring programs to fit local needs. But it also means that for every NGO that is willing and able to respond, others are willing and able to take its place if it withdraws, as the case of Médecins Sans Frontières in Zaire illustrates.

Funding also affects long-term commitment. Outside of the United States, governments are often the principal funders of NGOs, a situation that blurs the line between public and private sectors. NGO work will reflect this relationship. The Norwegian government, for instance, has established a special fund for responding to conflict that allows the government —and the NGOs it supports—to remain engaged over time. In countries where government support for NGOs is more sporadic, smaller organizations find it harder to maintain operations. The U.S. situation is complicated by the fact that most American humanitarian NGOs receive a combination of public and private funding. NGOs in the United States have been accused of using images of human suffering in their fund-raising campaigns. These campaigns seek to demonstrate an NGO's worth, and an excellent way of doing this is to show the NGO actively responding to the most newsworthy calamity of the day. But there is another side to this story. Often NGOs are working in the field before a crisis breaks out and remain there long after the height of the crisis is over. Money may pour into these crises while television cameras and international reporters are documenting suffering, but it dries up when the international attention recedes. While larger NGOs can make up the difference by drawing on other funds, smaller ones are obliged to leave the scene of the crisis or curtail their activities there. Managing commitment in the face of financial uncertainty adds to the complexity of establishing effective partnerships among official and nonofficial third parties in a conflict situation.

CONCLUSION

The difficulty of assessing the effectiveness of NGOs in conflict management is compounded by the long-term nature of conflict management work. As NGOs operate principally at the grassroots level, their contribution to any kind of societal reconciliation is hard to determine. By the time a conflict is resolved, many different factors and actors will have played a role, making it almost impossible to determine whether the actions of any one NGO or group of NGOs made a difference. Nonetheless, despite this uncertainty, it is apparent that NGOs can successfully perform a great variety of conflict management roles. They can provide early warning of impending conflict, act as channels of communication between parties in conflict, serve as mediators or facilitators in nonofficial—and occasionally in official— negotiations, work at the grassroots level to effect reconciliation at the local level, and train postconflict administrators in the intricacies of civil society.[51] They can serve as seedbeds for developing new ideas on effective conflict management strategies. Their ability to respond quickly to changing circumstances and their extensive knowledge of the societies in which they operate enable them to design appropriate programs and to change direction or priorities to meet the challenges of working in conflict. Their access to multiple sources of nontraditional power allows them to bring resources to a peacemaking effort that official organizations usually do not employ.

How effective NGOs are in managing conflict depends in part upon how the term "conflict management" is defined. If conflict management is defined to include a broad array of actions to prevent, mitigate, and resolve conflict, then NGOs are central to conflict management at every phase of the conflict cycle. Acting alone or in concert, they can affect behavior at many levels of society and are especially potent in states struggling to rebuild their social, economic, and political infrastructure after a civil war. However, if the definition includes an ability to mobilize international resources and political will, to impose a settlement, and to offer incentives and threats to opposing parties to change their behavior, then NGOs often operate at the margins. They can prompt the principals from behind the curtain and on occasion can briefly enter onto the stage, but they are dependent on the stars of the production—individual states or international organizations—to carry the action forward and bring the drama to some conclusion. Only in unusual cases, such as the Oslo and Mozambique peace processes, do they play leading roles.

The lessons of the 1990s make it clear that peacemaking is a long-term process that embraces both the broad and the narrow definitions of conflict management. Sustaining peace depends on mutually supportive actions and collaborative efforts of multiple third parties, each of which brings special expertise or resources to the process. NGOs are particularly effective at saving lives, promoting development, drawing attention to inequities and abuses, peacebuilding at the grassroots level, building support for peace, and—on very rare occasions—acting as a mediator between parties to the conflict. They are also very important to developing a culture of peace, to creating wider support—and, at times, much-needed

momentum—for an official peace process. They can provide a valuable service by promoting understanding and contact between antagonists through facilitation and dialogue and can do this in quiet settings away from the spotlight of official negotiations. As essential as they are to the overall international response to conflict, however, their activities cannot provide a substitute for concerted action on the part of the major states, whether acting by themselves or in support of the United Nations. In the complex environment of peacemaking, where everyone may have a part to play but no one can play all the parts, there is still a lot of work to do to determine which organization is best suited to intervene, under what circumstances, and at which point. Understanding better the nature of NGO intervention and clarifying the role that NGOs can play, alone or in collaboration with state- or UN-sponsored peace initiatives, will be an important step in designing effective long-term international responses to violent conflict.

NOTES

1. Portions of this chapter appeared in Pamela Aall, "NGOs, Conflict Management, and Peacekeeping," in *Peacekeeping and Conflict Resolution*, ed. Tom Woodhouse and Oliver Ramsbotham (London and Portland, Ore.: Frank Cass, 2000), 121–141.

2. These activities have altered NGO roles. See, for instance, Mark Duffield, "NGO Relief in War Zones: Towards an Analysis of the New Aid Paradigm," *Third World Quarterly* 18, no. 3 (1997): 527–542.

3. Boutros Boutros-Ghali, *An Agenda for Peace: Preventive Diplomacy, Peacemaking, Peacekeeping*, Report of the Secretary-General, June 17, 1992 (New York: United Nations).

4. See David R. Smock, *Humanitarian Assistance and Conflict in Africa* (Washington, D.C.: United States Institute of Peace Press, 1996); and Mary Anderson, *Do No Harm: How Aid Can Support Peace—or War* (Boulder, Colo.: Lynne Rienner, 1999).

5. For examples of local NGO activity in peacemaking, see David Smock, *Private Peacemaking,*

Peaceworks no. 20 (Washington, D.C.: United States Institute of Peace, 1998); Steven M. Riskin, *Three Dimensions of Peacebuilding in Bosnia,* Peaceworks no. 32 (Washington, D.C.: United States Institute of Peace, 1999); and Donna Ramsay Marshall, *Women in War and Peace,* Peaceworks no. 34 (Washington, D.C.: United States Institute of Peace, 2000). For instances of local women's groups playing critical roles in conflict management and peacemaking, see Sanam Naraghi Anderlini, *Women at the Peace Table* (New York: UN Development Fund for Women, 2000).

6. Some definitions focus on functions. The World Bank defines NGOs as "private organizations that pursue activities to relieve suffering, promote the interests of the poor, protect the environment, provide basic social services, or undertake community development." See Carmela Malena, *Working with NGOs: A Practical Guide to Operational Collaboration between the World Bank and Non-governmental Organizations* (Washington, D.C.: Operation Policy Department, World Bank, March 1995), 13. Others define NGOs by what they are not, especially in relation to government and private business and industry. Lester Salamon talks about "a global third sector . . . not dedicated to distributing profits to shareholders or directors, pursuing public purposes outside the formal apparatus of the state." See Lester M. Salamon, "The Rise of the Non-profit Sector," *Foreign Affairs* 73, no. 4 (July–August 1994): 109. A good, although slightly dated, explanation of NGOs' relationship to the United Nations in conflict work appears in Andrew Natsios, "NGOs and the UN System in Complex Humanitarian Emergencies: Conflict or Cooperation?" *Third World Quarterly* 16, no. 3 (1995): 405–419.

7. Local and international NGOs do not always agree on how to improve conditions in a particular area. In Chad, for example, local NGOs hoped that a proposed oil pipeline would bring economic benefits to a poor country, while international NGOs focused on the environmental damage the pipeline might cause and the revenues it might generate for a government they accused of human rights violations. See Douglas Farah and David B. Ottaway, "Watchdog Groups Rein in Government in Chad Oil Deal," *Washington Post,* January 4, 2001, 14.

8. Figures taken from Tracy Geoghegan and Kirsten Allen, eds., *InterAction Members Profiles, 1995–1996* (Washington, D.C.: InterAction, 1995).

9. Union of International Associations, *Yearbook of International Organizations* (Brussels: Union of International Associations, 1996).

10. Julia Taft, president of Inter*Action,* speaking at the United States Institute of Peace conference on *Managing Chaos,* Washington, D.C., November 30, 1994.

11. Leon Gordenker and Thomas G. Weiss, "Pluralizing Global Governance: Analytical Approaches and Dimension," in *NGOs, the UN, and Global Governance,* ed. Thomas G. Weiss and Leon Gordenker (Boulder, Colo.: Lynne Rienner, 1996), 25.

12. For an excellent analysis of the experience of the humanitarian community in the early 1990s, see Larry Minear and Thomas G. Weiss, *Mercy under Fire: War and the Global Humanitarian Community* (Boulder, Colo.: Westview Press, 1995). See also Thomas G. Weiss and Cindy Collins, *Humanitarian Challenges and Intervention: World Politics and the Dilemmas of Help,* 2d ed. (Boulder, Colo.: Westview Press, 2000).

13. See John Prendergast, *Frontline Diplomacy: Humanitarian Aid and Conflict in Africa* (Boulder, Colo.: Lynne Rienner, 1996).

14. This topic was the focus of a meeting held at the United States Institute of Peace in March 1997 with UNHCR and NGO officials. I am particularly grateful to Iain Guest for his insights on the dilemmas of humanitarian response.

15. Amnesty International–USA press release, "International Community Failing to Provide Solutions for Massive Human Rights Violations in 1996," June 18, 1997; also Amnesty International–USA press release, "Tanzania/Rwanda: International Cooperation in Forcing Refugees Back from Tanzania," December 6, 1996 (www.amnestyusa.org).

16. See, for instance, the code of conduct for the International Red Cross and Red Crescent Movement and NGOs in disaster relief, sponsored by the International Committee of the Red Cross plus a number of NGOs, including Caritas International, Catholic Relief Services, the International Federation of Red Cross and Red Crescent Societies, Save the Children, the Lutheran World Federation, Oxfam, and the World Council of Churches.

17. Anderson, *Do No Harm.*

18. See also Prendergast, *Frontline Diplomacy;* John Paul Lederach, *Building Peace: Sustained Reconciliation in Divided Societies* (Washington, D.C.: United States Institute of Peace Press, 1997); Lisa A. Mullins,

Disaster Response: When Good Intentions Aren't Enough (Washington, D.C.: Inter*Action*, 1990).

19. Catholic Relief Services, "Peacebuilding Activities" (unpublished report of the Catholic Relief Service, 2000).

20. Arie Bloed, *Monitoring Human Rights in Europe: Comparing International Procedures and Mechanisms* (Norwell, Mass.: M. Nijhoff in cooperation with the International Helsinki Foundation for Human Rights, 1993).

21. See, for instance, the regular reports of Human Rights Watch and the annual review issued by Amnesty International.

22. Liam Mahoney and Luis Enrique Eguren, *Unarmed Bodyguards: International Accompaniment for the Protection of Human Rights* (West Hartford, Conn.: Kumarian Press, 1997); and Sylvia Alexander, *A Handbook of Practical Strategies for Local Human Rights Groups* (New York: Human Rights Program of the Fund for Peace, 1999), 19–20.

23. See Pauline H. Baker's chapter (chapter 44) in this volume.

24. Milosevic was indicted by the International War Crimes Tribunal in The Hague on May 27, 1999, in the midst of the NATO campaign against Serbia. Whether this indictment represents a shift in great-power thinking about the balance between accountability and peacemaking remains to be seen. That the indictment occurred only after Serbia had entered into a state of war with the Western alliance seems to indicate that European and North American governments are still cautious about mixing the two objectives.

25. For a comprehensive survey and analysis of the issues surrounding accountability, see Neil Kritz, ed., *Transitional Justice: How Emerging Democracies Reckon with Former Regimes* (Washington, D.C.: United States Institute of Peace Press, 1995).

26. Carter Center, *International Guide to NGO Activities in Conflict Prevention and Resolution* (Atlanta: Carter Center, December 1995).

27. Excellent summaries of the field include Martha Harty and John Modell, "The First Conflict Resolution Movement, 1956–1971: An Attempt to Institutionalize Applied Interdisciplinary Social Science," *Journal of Conflict Resolution* 35, no. 4 (December 1991): 720–758; Louis Kriesberg, "The Development of the Conflict Resolution Field," in *Peacemaking in International Conflict: Methods and Techniques,* ed.

I. William Zartman and J. Lewis Rasmussen (Washington, D.C.: United States Institute of Peace Press, 1997), an updated version of which appears in this volume as chapter 25; and James H. Laue, "Contributions to the Emerging Field of Conflict Resolution," in *Approaches to Peace: An Intellectual Map,* ed. W. Scott Thompson and Kenneth M. Jensen with Richard N. Smith and Kimber M. Schraub (Washington, D.C.: United States Institute of Peace Press, 1992).

28. Christopher Mitchell and Michael Banks, *Handbook of Conflict Resolution: The Analytical Problem-Solving Approach* (London and New York: Pinter, 1996).

29. For an idea of the variety of approaches organizations and conflict resolution experts take to conflict resolution see Louis Kriesberg's chapter in this volume (chapter 25); Roger Fisher, William Ury, and Bruce Patton, *Getting to Yes: Negotiating Agreement without Giving In* (New York: Penguin, 1991); Lederach, *Building Peace;* and Herbert C. Kelman, "The Interactive Problem-Solving Approach," in *Managing Global Chaos: Sources of and Responses to International Conflict,* ed. Chester A. Crocker and Fen Osler Hampson with Pamela Aall (Washington, D.C.: United States Institute of Peace Press, 1996), 501–519. See also Eileen F. Babbitt, "The Contribution of Training to Conflict Resolution," in *Peacemaking in International Conflict,* ed. Zartman and Rasmussen.

30. See David Smock, ed., *Creative Approaches to Managing Conflict in Africa,* Peaceworks no. 15 (Washington, D.C.: United States Institute of Peace, 1997) for a summary of this and other conflict management projects, some involving NGOs, in Africa; and Smock, ed., *Private Peacemaking.*

31. See, for example, Irving Kristol, "Conflicts That Can't Be Resolved," *Wall Street Journal*, September 5, 1997; and the thoughtful criticisms by Gunnar M. Sorbo, Joanna Macrae, and Lennart Wohlegemuth in *NGOs in Conflict: An Evaluation of International Alert* (Bergen: Chr. Michelsen Institute, 1997).

32. Based on interviews with international NGO staff, Sarajevo, May 1996.

33. Chester A. Crocker, Fen Osler Hampson, and Pamela Aall, eds., *Herding Cats: Multiparty Mediation in a Complex World* (Washington, D.C.: United States Institute of Peace Press, 1999), 47–62, 678–686.

34. Ibid., 19–45.

35. Joseph S. Nye, Jr., "Soft Power and Conflict Management in the Information Age," chapter 22 of this volume.

36. Jeffrey Z. Rubin, "International Mediation in Context," in *Mediation in International Relations: Multiple Approaches to Conflict Management,* ed. Jacob Bercovitch and Jeffrey Z. Rubin (New York: St. Martin's Press, 1992).

37. Joseph S. Nye Jr., *Bound to Lead: The Changing Nature of American Power* (New York: Basic Books, 1990).

38. Outside of the conflict management field, NGOs have long used these softer forms of power, as in the campaigns of Amnesty International and other human rights organizations. However, the development of information technologies has allowed NGOs to organize campaigns for political change on many issues. For a very interesting examination of six cases (including the international campaign to ban land mines) of successful transnational advocacy by NGOs showing the use of moral authority and the power of persuasion to change official policy on significant issues, see Ann M. Florini, ed., *The Third Force: The Rise of Transnational Civil Society* (Tokyo and Washington, D.C.: Japan Center for International Exchange and the Carnegie Endowment for International Peace, 2000).

39. Andrea Bartoli, "Mediating Peace in Mozambique: The Role of the Community of Sant'Egidio," in *Herding Cats*, ed. Crocker, Hampson, and Aall, 245–274.

40. See, for instance, Andrew Natsios, "NGOs and the UN System in Complex Humanitarian Emergencies: Conflict or Cooperation?" in *NGOs, the UN, and Global Governance,* ed. Weiss and Gordenker, 67–81.

41. See *Managing Communications: Lessons from Interventions in Africa,* a summary of the proceedings of a conference sponsored by the United States Institute of Peace and the National Defense University, June 20, 1996 (Washington, D.C.: United States Institute of Peace, March 1997).

42. Pamela Aall, "Nongovernmental Organizations and Peacemaking," in *Managing Global Chaos,* ed. Crocker and Hampson with Aall, 433–443.

43. Pamela Aall, Dan Miltenberger, and Thomas G. Weiss, *A Guide to IGOs, NGOs, and the Military in Peace and Relief Operations* (Washington, D.C.: United States Institute of Peace Press, 2000).

44. The U.S. military has explored its relationship to NGOs in such diverse settings as the Army peacekeeping simulations at Fort Polk; the Marines' annual Emerald Express exercises; and a symposium at the National Defense University on "Beyond Jointness," which examined civil-military relations in peace operations.

45. See Harold Saunders, "The Multilevel Peace Process in Tajikistan," in *Herding Cats,* ed. Crocker, Hampson, and Aall, 161–179.

46. Paul Arthur, "Multiparty Mediation in Northern Ireland," in *Herding Cats,* ed. Crocker, Hampson, and Aall, 469–501.

47. See P. J. Simmons, "Learning to Live with NGOs," *Foreign Policy* (fall 1998): 82–96.

48. For further discussion of this point, see the chapters by Richard Betts (chapter 18) and Mary Anderson (chapter 37) in this volume.

49. Several works have tackled the complexities of NGO accountability, including Michael Edwards and David Hulme, eds., *Beyond the Magic Bullet: NGO Performance and Accountability in the Post–Cold War World* (West Hartford, Conn.: Kumarian Press, 1996).

50. See Fabienne Hara, "Burundi: A Case of Parallel Diplomacy," in *Herding Cats,* ed. Crocker, Hampson, and Aall, 135–158.

51. For an in-depth review of NGO work in early warning and conflict resolution in Guatemala, Macedonia, Sir Lanka, Nigeria, Sudan, Rwanda, and Burundi, see Robert I. Rotberg, ed., *Vigilance and Vengeance: NGOs Preventing Ethnic Conflict in Divided Societies* (Washington, D.C.: Brookings Institution Press, 1996).

PART III
NEGOTIATION, MEDIATION, AND OTHER POLITICAL INSTRUMENTS

24

Parent, Midwife, or Accidental Executioner?

The Role of Third Parties in Ending Violent Conflict

Fen Osler Hampson

THERE HAS BEEN MUCH RECENT DISCUSSION about the requirements for successful peacebuilding and the construction of durable political settlements to end violent conflict in societies that have experienced prolonged civil strife as a result of communal cleavages of ethnic, religious, or other kinds.[1] This debate is marked by a growing sense of pessimism about the ability of external third parties not only to influence the process of negotiation but also to assist with the implementation of a settlement once a peace agreement is reached. Many commentators accept the argument that implacable "ancient hatreds" fuel these civil conflicts and believe that coercive or noncoercive interventions by external actors to end violent conflict are likely to be marginal at best and counterproductive at worst.[2]

In contrast to this viewpoint, a second school of thought (what might be termed the "interventionist school") believes that a variety of coercive and noncoercive measures can be used to affect the course of a conflict and bring the parties, if not to the negotiating table, at least to some other form of political accommodation that will end violence.[3] These approaches stress the moral obligation to intervene in civil conflicts, especially when civilians are threatened and egregious human rights violations are taking place or have taken place. They look to cases where international interventions helped to end military hostilities, defuse tensions, and lay the groundwork for peace, as in Namibia, Mozambique, El Salvador, Cambodia, Nicaragua, Bosnia, and even Kosovo.

Among those who believe that intervention can make a difference, however, there is little consensus about the requirements for successful intervention or the appropriate methods and means to end violent conflict. Not only is there no consensus about who the intervenors should be, but also there is little apparent consensus about what the political aims of such interventions should be. Should the aim be to separate parties? To arm them in an effort to achieve a balance of power? To negotiate a cease-fire so that parties can begin a process of negotiation to resolve their differences? To mediate an end to conflict but leave the implementation of the settlement up to the parties themselves? To assist with the implementation of the settlement? Or to assist with the establishment of new governance structures and democracy itself? Some of these differences reflect differing assumptions about the fundamental nature of intercommunal conflict and the social, political, and military dynamics of conflict processes. Others, however, are based on competing assessments about the appropriate timing of interventions and the comparative strengths and weaknesses of different potential third-party intervenors. Generally, the approaches suffer from a lack of specificity about the relationship between the conditions that lead to conflict and the independent impact or effect (positive and negative) of third-party interventions on conflict itself. There is also little consensus about what constitutes "success" in managing or resolving conflict.

This chapter has two goals. First, it will undertake a comparative assessment of the key assumptions—both about conflict and about third-party roles—underlying the different schools of thought on intervention. The chapter will argue that there is in fact a close relationship between the way third-party roles are defined, on the one hand, and the treatment of causes of intercommunal conflict by scholars and policy analysts, on the other.[4] These schools are classified accordingly as *"hard"* and *"soft"* realist approaches, which have a state-security orientation; *social-psychological* approaches, which have a societal or human security-based orientation; and *governance-based* approaches, which focus on state-society linkages and third-party roles in developing, strengthening, or transforming those linkages.

Second, the chapter will argue that although these four different schools or approaches to third-party intervention—which are, to some extent, rooted in different disciplinary perspec-

tives—often present themselves as mutually exclusive alternatives, they should not be viewed as such. Each approach contains elements that complement aspects of the other approaches, and we should not be wedded to a narrow view about either the causes of intercommunal conflict or the potential intervention strategies available to a wide range of third parties to manage, settle, or resolve such conflicts.

CONTRASTING APPROACHES TO THIRD-PARTY INTERVENTION

Among political scientists, the debate about appropriate intervention strategies can be characterized as a debate between "realist" and "liberal" interpretations of the sources of intercommunal conflict. Even so, within these competing paradigms there are different schools of thought about what intervention strategies are desirable or warranted. "Hard" realists argue for a narrow range of intervention strategies that largely revolve around the use of force (threatened or actual) to restore order. "Soft" realists contemplate a wide range of policy options that include diplomacy and mediation as intervention strategies for changing the cost-benefit calculus of warring parties in favor of a negotiated political settlement. Both hard and soft realists, however, eschew the much more comprehensive kinds of intervention strategies envisaged in liberal approaches, which have a different interpretation about the sources of conflict and the requirements for political order. In contrast, governance-based and social-psychological approaches to conflict management and third-party intervention stress the role of societal actors in peacebuilding and the creation of new norms—at both the psychological and the institutional levels—that transform attitudes and lead to a process of reconciliation. This is because the sources of conflict are seen as psychological and rooted in perceptions of injustice and victimization.

Hard Realism

Hard realism takes as its point of departure neorealist international relations theory as propounded by Kenneth Waltz and his students, some of whom have turned to studying intercommunal conflict processes in recent years.[5] Hard realism is of the view that the dynamics of ethnic conflict are not all that different from the dynamics of interstate relations in an anarchic international system. Not only do ethnic communities experience the same kind of security dilemma as states when the domestic political order breaks down as a result of state failure, but also the same kind of offense-defense escalatory spiral (where one side misinterprets the other's "defensive" actions as being provocative) can occur as ethnic groups misinterpret the strategic intentions of other groups, thus intensifying the pressure to raise mass armies.[6] According to some hard realists such as Steven Van Evera, the risks of war become greater if different nationalities become more densely intermingled with one another, populations become stateless, and borders become seen by the parties to the conflict as illegitimate and indefensible. If the boundaries of emerging states are compatible with ethnic boundaries, the risks of war will be correspondingly lower. The incentives to annex neighboring territories, however, will increase if there are diaspora populations in those territories. Elites who do not enjoy political legitimacy may also become purveyors of various nationalist myths in their efforts to consolidate power, further raising the risks of conflict.[7]

For hard realists, the use of force and the balance of power play key roles in the resolution of ethnic and intercommunal disputes. If ethnic groups are not to annihilate one another in their struggle for supremacy and control of the state, particularly if one side is militarily stronger than the others, then a new balance of forces has to be created, either by denying arms and resources to the stronger sides or by providing arms and resources to the weaker sides to compensate for their militarily inferior position (or by some combination of the two). In some instances, direct military intervention by outside third parties may also be warranted to redress the balance and/or defend the weaker parties. Although the role of force is central to hard realists' assessments of interethnic struggles, so too is the notion of parity or symmetry in military capabilities as a way of bringing violent conflict to an end among rival ethnic groups.

For hard realists, only great powers such as the United States have the resources and capacity to intervene or influence the course of events in such conflicts. The incentives for great powers to intervene, however, will be limited because relatively few situations justify the costs associated with great-power intervention. Richard Haass, for example, argues:

> Coercive actions—limited uses of force designed to affect the behavior of the targeted party—are easier to mount than peacemaking operations; the problem is what to do if they do not succeed. The choice then tends to be between escalating to peacemaking or backing away from direct military intervention and choosing some other policy instrument, either arming the favored faction (an indirect military option) or pursuing another realm of policy such as sanctions, diplomacy, or covert action.[8]

One of the most forceful advocates of hard realism is Chaim Kaufmann.[9] Kaufmann argues that so-called ethnic wars are the result of the processes of political mobilization, hypernationalism, and intercommunal security dilemmas that engender "ethnic cleansing." As tensions rise and conflict escalates, "populations come increasingly to hold enemy images of the other groups, either because of deliberate efforts by elites to create such images or because of increasingly real threats."[10] Even ostensibly defensive measures will be seen as threatening, leading to a spiral of escalating hostilities.

The only way to address the intercommunal security dilemma is through a process of what Kaufmann calls "ethnic unmixing"; that is, the forcible expulsion or emigration of rival ethnic groups, as occurred in Greece and Turkey, Cyprus, India, Israel, Nagorno-Karabakh, Nigeria, and the former Yugoslavia. Kaufmann and others believe that partition and ethnic separation are the only real solutions to ethnic conflict, given that—in the realists' view—power sharing and other attempts to pool sovereignty have poor track records.[11]

Hard realists such as Kaufmann do not rule out international intervention to end ethnic and intercommunal wars. However, they believe that intervention should be limited to sanctions, military aid, and direct military intervention to redress the military balance of power, particularly if the weaker side is the aggrieved party, so that clear territorial boundaries allowing for the creation of new sovereign entities can be established and maintained. The role of the third-party intervenor is that of "balancer"—to use the language of Waltz and Stephen Walt—where the goal of intervention is territorial partition along interethnic lines, rather than the search for political accommodation, intercommunal reconciliation, or some other integrative formula.[12] The means of intervention are also military and largely coercive. This model offers little room for the third-party mediator who tries to negotiate a new set of political arrangements—other than partition—among the warring parties or factions. Equally, the model assumes that ethnic identities are fixed and immutable. Once beliefs, images, and attitudes toward other communities have hardened, they are difficult to change either by the parties themselves or through the assistance of third-party intervenors.

This argument carries with it a number of difficulties, not the least of which is its reification of the concept of ethnicity and the relationship between conflict and ethnicity. As many scholars argue, political identities, including ethnicity, are mutable and can soften or harden over time.[13] The track record of power sharing or federalism is not all bad.

Multiethnic states such as Belgium, Canada, India, Malaysia, South Africa, and Switzerland have managed interethnic competition with varying degrees of success through formulas such as power sharing, federalism, and consociational democracy.[14]

Perhaps the most serious objection to partition-based "solutions" is the notion that interethnic disputes are amenable to a "fair" territorial solution. Different communal groups are often in fierce competition over the same bits of territory and may, therefore, be unwilling to grant concessions that allow for a division of territorial spoils; that is, competition is truly zero-sum. Consider, for example, the competing claims of Israelis and Palestinians over the status of Jerusalem, or the difficulties the Greek and Turkish Cypriot communities have experienced in redrawing communal boundaries in UN-mediated, intercommunal negotiations.[15] Even in Bosnia, in the aftermath of successive rounds of ethnic cleansing and the 1995 Dayton peace agreements, which ratified the territorial status quo, borders remain contested.[16] NATO's difficulties with withdrawing from Kosovo also reveal the unintended consequences of humanitarian interventions that lead to de facto partition and that strengthen demands among those seeking to achieve their independence.[17] Rather than resolving interethnic conflict, partition may simply sow the seeds for more conflict if parties cannot agree where the lines should be drawn, whose historical claims to territory are legitimate, and what kinds of restitution should be offered to those who have lost homes and property.[18]

Soft Realism

Soft realism is distinguished from hard realism is a number of key ways. Like hard realism, it sees the security dilemma as one of the main causes of intercommunal conflict giving rise to "collective fears of the future," in the words of David Lake and Donald Rothchild.[19] While ethnic "activists" and political entrepreneurs will exploit communal insecurities and contribute to the polarization of society—particularly if the state is not strong enough to protect the security needs and interests of minorities—these activists and entrepreneurs are secondary, rather than primary, "causes" of conflict. Like hard realism, soft realism believes that conflict can be understood as a rational political process—driven by strategic behavior on the part of ethnic entrepreneurs—in which the costs of civil war and violence are deemed to be lower than any of the political alternatives. Political myths and emotions may feed into this process, but strategic dilemmas lie at the heart of it. However, unlike hard realism, soft realism believes that there is a role for the exercise of soft power—that is, mediation, exchanges of information, and negotiation—in the management of ethnic conflict. Third-party interventions do not have to be coercive in order to be effective, but they do have to be sensitive to the dynamics and structure of conflict if they are to affect its course.[20]

Soft realism contemplates a wider range of state actors and international organizations in the mediation and management of intrastate conflicts. However, because mediation leverage depends upon persuasion, extraction, termination, manipulation, and the ability to offer side payments and/or withhold resources from the parties, great powers such as the United States tend to be both more active and more effective mediators than small or medium-sized powers.[21] Although the end of the Cold War freed international organizations from their bipolar constraints and allowed them to play a greater role in mediation and conflict management, soft realists argue that international organizations have been overwhelmed by the task.[22]

Unlike hard realism, soft realism offers room for nonterritorial, politically based solutions in the management of interethnic and communal conflicts. Soft realism, for instance, envisages a major role for the power-sharing provisions in any politically negotiated settlement. Arend

Lijphart defines power sharing as the "participation of the representatives of all significant groups in the government of the country and the high degree of autonomy for these groups."[23] Additionally, power sharing can include proportionality in political representation and in public service appointments, as well as the minority veto. Others view political relations as "negotiable" through institutions such as political parties and mechanisms such as vote pooling and the formation of multiethnic coalitions. Donald Horowitz argues that these kinds of institutional mechanisms have alleviated some of the strains in ethnically and religiously divided societies.[24] However, the solid basis for a political settlement in the eyes of both Lijphart and Horowitz is an agreement that contains power-sharing provisions for winners and losers, even in the aftermath of political elections. From a negotiating standpoint, power sharing also means that all parties should have a seat at the negotiating table. Power sharing has a greater potential for laying the groundwork for democratic practices and institutions when it is embraced by moderate political leaders who are flexible and adaptable in addressing conflicts between contending communal interests.[25] One of the main challenges of mediation is to create the right mix of inducements (positive and negative) so that potential "spoilers" in the peace process have fewer incentives to defect and wreck a settlement later on.[26]

Effective mediation also depends on timing and careful attention to the dynamics of the conflict itself.[27] In order for third-party interventions such as mediation to be effective, a conflict has to reach a plateau or the level of a "hurting stalemate." At this point, the parties no longer feel they can use force to gain a unilateral advantage and, therefore, become willing to consider other options. At this point, the conflict—to use William Zartman's phrase—is "ripe for resolution," insofar as the parties perceive the costs and prospects of continued confrontation to be more burdensome than the costs and prospects of a settlement.[28] In addition to shifting power balances and the emergence of a hurting stalemate, additional requirements for ripeness may include (1) redefinition by the parties of their interests because of changes, for example, in leadership or constituency pressures; (2) replacement of previous or existing norms and patterns of behavior by new ones that increase the possibility of compromise; (3) shared perceptions among the parties about the desirability of an accord; (4) agreement between the parties on a new, common bridging formula to settle their differences; and/or (5) availability of a formula allowing for compromise and a negotiated settlement.[29]

The importance that soft realists give to the concept of ripeness suggests that third parties are only one element in the overall peacemaking-peacebuilding process. What many conflicts lack, therefore, is not so much a shortage of skilled third parties as the ripeness of the conflict itself. That said, what exactly are third parties supposed to provide the peace process at the point that a hurting stalemate has been reached?

According to Lake and Rothchild, third parties can reduce the security dilemma generated by intercommunal conflict by providing confidence-building measures that "reassure ethnic peoples about their future."[30] In their strategic interaction model, confidence-building measures serve a function similar to that of international regimes in the neoliberal theories of Robert Keohane and others.[31] That is to say, confidence-building measures promote exchanges of information and increase transparency, thus reducing the incentives to defect from negotiated political commitments. Such measures include power-sharing systems, elections, and specific electoral rules to guarantee minority rights, regional autonomy, and federalism, all of which can be promoted and developed with the assistance of third parties who help to "alter the internal balance of ethnic power" and to provide "guarantees for new ethnic contracts between the warring parties."[32]

However, many of the same criticisms leveled at regime theory apply to the institutionalist arguments offered by Lake and Rothchild.[33] Just as international regimes involve different forms and structures, confidence-building measures intended to reduce the likelihood and/or scope of interethnic conflict can involve these as well. Strategic interaction models cannot explain what kinds of institutional arrangements work best, when, and where. For example, these models cannot explain whether power sharing is preferable to formal federalism or to certain kinds of confederal arrangements, nor can they explain under what circumstances and conditions power sharing might be preferable. The argument that "institutions matter" may be less compelling than arguments that address the relative utility and efficacy of particular kinds of institutional arrangements under clearly specified conditions.

A second criticism of soft realism is that it is highly state-centric. It offers little guidance regarding the problems of confidence building at the societal and psychological levels. If we have learned one thing from contemporary intercommunal conflicts, it is that they have the potential to mobilize and victimize whole societies, engulfing cities and suburbs, town and countryside, profoundly affecting the lives of all. Civil wars and the atrocities carried out by the perpetrators of ethnic cleansing and other human rights abuses leave deep psychological wounds. These scars do not heal easily and, if left to fester, can lead to renewed outbreaks of violence as victims seek revenge.[34]

Governance-Based Approaches

In contrast to hard and soft realism, governance-based approaches see ethnic and communal conflicts less in terms of strategic security dilemmas and more in terms of a set of causal relationships in which the key variables are the denial of human rights, of due process of law, and of liberal pluralist forms of democracy.[35] Human rights violations are seen as underpinning the security dilemma and as key contributing factors to conflict-escalation processes. As Paul LaRose-Edwards argues, "fear of [human rights] violations engenders self-defence and creates the security dilemma that drives escalation."[36] Civic intolerance in the form of the denial of minority communal and religious rights may also be a major cause of conflict, as in the case of Sri Lanka, where, according to David Little, the Sinhalese Buddhist majority "have asserted their claims to cultural and political preeminence over the Tamil, and mainly Hindu, minority by means of violence . . . [but also] politically, according to the system instituted by the British before they relinquished colonial control in 1948."[37]

This view of conflict management is anchored in a Kantian model of liberal democracy that stresses the rule of law and liberal norms as key ingredients in the establishment of a "just" political order.[38] Accordingly, it has its own unique view about what third parties should be called upon to contribute to the peace process. In contrast to hard realism (which sees a continuing role for force and the balance of power in the management of communal or ethnic conflict) or soft realism (which contemplates a need for confidence-building structures and power sharing), governance-based approaches see the challenge of peacebuilding and third-party involvement largely in terms of the creation of participatory governance structures, the development of new social norms, and the establishment of the rule of law and democracy. Governance is defined

> as the exercise of political, economic, and administrative authority to manage a nation's affairs. It is the complex mechanisms, processes, relationships, and institutions through which the citizens and groups articulate their interests, exercise their rights and obligations, and mediate their differences. . . . Effective democratic forms of governance rely on public participation, accountability, and transparency.[39]

In stressing the importance of domestic political institutions, governance-based approaches

to peacebuilding have something in common with soft realism. However, whereas soft realism is state-centric and oriented to power sharing at the national level, governance-based approaches emphasize the importance of creating democratic political institutions and participatory governance structures at the societal level in an attempt to restore civil society. Thus,

> strengthening the enabling environment for sustainable human development depends not only on a state that governs well and on a private sector that provides jobs and income, but also on civil society organizations that facilitate political and social interaction and that mobilize various groups in society that participate in economic, social, and political activities. They provide checks and balances on government power and on the private sector, but they can also contribute to, and strengthen, both of the other domains.[40]

The concept of governance, therefore, relates to a complex system that includes aspects of the legal and judiciary system, the public service, the private sector, and the interactions among these institutions and the organizations of civil society. What this means for peacebuilding, however, is that democracy and human rights are priorities because they are the preconditions to securing a lasting peace. Power-sharing settlements with weak democratic foundations are more prone to failure because they rest on the goodwill of the parties rather than on secure legal and democratic foundations. According to Pauline Baker, examples of settlements based on the power-sharing model (i.e., soft realism) are Angola, Cambodia, and Mozambique. In contrast,

> conflicts settled along the lines of the democratizers' model are South Africa, Namibia, and El Salvador, where real political change included measures to ensure moral accountability and justice in the long term. Indeed, in these conflicts, recognition that the crises were basically human rights struggles, rather than mere power grabs by disgruntled interests, enabled real power sharing to go forward.[41]

Baker notes that outside mediators and intervenors cannot be morally neutral but must take sides, "supporting those who stand for democracy and human rights."[42] Nonetheless, the obvious risk in taking sides is that this may compromise the neutrality and effectiveness of the third-party mediator.

Good governance, therefore, depends on the active promulgation of new norms and codes of conduct, particularly in the area of human rights.[43] Since atrocities and violations of human rights are among the main characteristics of civil wars, the security institutions of the state—the armed forces and police—are usually suspect because they can be seen as instruments of coercion by the state against its people. Reform of these institutions is fundamental to the peace process and the consolidation of democratic reforms. International tribunals and truth commissions are necessary to bring the element of impartiality required to restore faith in the judicial process and the rule of law.[44]

From a governance standpoint, third parties —particularly international organizations such as the United Nations and its affiliated agencies, as well as nongovernmental organizations— are the key actors that may be required to perform a wide range of roles and services in the interests of restoring or establishing democracy and good governance practices. Some of these activities are considered in Boutros Boutros-Ghali's *Agenda for Peace*, where the former UN secretary-general defines "peacebuilding" as a broad set of activities that

> tend to consolidate the peace and advance a sense of confidence and well-being among the people. . . . [The list of peacebuilding activities includes] disarming the previously warring parties and the restoration of order, the custody and possible destruction of weapons, repatriating refugees, advisory and training support for security personnel, monitoring elections, advancing efforts to protect human rights, reforming or strengthening governmental institutions and promoting formal and informal processes of political participation.[45]

Although Boutros-Ghali suggests that the "United Nations has an obligation to develop and provide . . . support for the transformation of deficient national structures and capabilities, and for the strengthening of democratic institutions," he also recognizes that the "authority of the United Nations system to act in this field would rest on the consensus that social peace is as important as strategic or political peace."[46] Questions of exactly how the United Nations and international society should go about achieving a "social consensus," and where such a consensus might come from, remain unanswered.

From a traditional realist or neorealist perspective, governance-based approaches to intervention raise delicate questions about state sovereignty and how far local actors are prepared to allow outsiders to shape domestic institutions and political practices, and where, indeed, international society is prepared to give its blessing to such efforts.[47] A second potential objection is that in asserting categorically that a stable political order must necessarily be a "just" one, governance-based approaches underestimate the difficulties of democratization and the unstable political forces that may be unleashed by democratic institutions and processes in societies unaccustomed to democracy and the rule of law.

As Samuel P. Huntington noted many years ago, and as Edward D. Mansfield and Jack Snyder reaffirm in their chapter in this volume, in the unstable social, economic, and political environment of societies that are coming out of a civil war, a shift to democracy that is too rapid may actually prove counterproductive if pressures for political participation cannot be accommodated by the newly created political institutions.[48] The result may be greater levels of political instability and with it the increased likelihood of intercommunal violence and war.

Democratization efforts (either those sponsored externally or those promoted indigenously), such as holding elections, need not have calamitous results. However, attention has to be paid to timing and to pairing elections with power-sharing formulas that provide a safety net for minorities and ensure that politics does not become a zero-sum game. Unless there is some form of compensation, those who lose at the ballot box will have a strong incentive to take up arms and resort to force to achieve their political objectives.[49] The lack of a power-sharing arrangement is one reason why the 1991 Bicesse Accords in Angola fell apart. In contrast, power sharing was conducive to a peaceful transition in South Africa, where the parties recognized early on that a coalition government was necessary to appease rival factions and advance the process of national reconciliation.[50]

Even if the choices between democracy and power sharing are not as stark as those portrayed by some adherents of governance-oriented peacebuilding, a third problem with this approach is determining how to prioritize among the very long list of peacebuilding tasks when resources are scarce and potential donors or would-be peacebuilders are overstretched and reluctant to assume new burdens. Beyond keeping the peace itself, the list of tasks includes reconstructing civil society at both the national and the local levels; reintegrating displaced populations into society and the economy; redefining the role of the military and police forces in the maintenance of law and order; building communities and allowing them to survive by bridging the gap between emergency assistance and development; rebuilding micro-enterprises and instituting macroeconomic reforms; and addressing the needs of particularly vulnerable groups in society, such as women and children.[51]

Furthermore, different donors often bring their own priorities to peacebuilding, greatly complicating the job of coordinating their efforts. Scholars and practitioners are paying growing attention to the role of the international development community in the tasks of postconflict rebuilding and reconstruction. Various proposals have been offered to strengthen the coordination of donors' efforts.[52] There is also a growing consensus among scholars and policymakers that political leadership is a vital ingredient in social and economic reconstruc-

tion and that resources must be channeled into those areas where they can have the greatest impact. However, it still remains an open question whether democracy and the rule of law can be fostered from the outside, and what kinds of intervention by outside actors are most likely to contribute not just to national reconciliation but also to a democratic peace.[53]

Social-Psychological Approaches

Much of the above discussion is confined to what political scientists, legal scholars, and practitioners have to say about intercommunal conflict management processes. With few exceptions, these approaches do not stray far from their disciplinary foundations. For example, although both realist approaches to conflict management are based on a model of conflict —the security dilemma—that is, in essence, psychological, the means and methods that both types of realists identify to manage conflict and restore political order are not. Therefore, none of these three approaches has much to say about how to tackle the psychological origins of conflict and the "embedded enemy images"—a phrase used by political psychologist Janice Gross Stein in her chapter in this volume—which are a serious obstacle to managing conflict and reducing tensions.

The work of psychologists and sociologists in the field of conflict management and resolution focuses on the question of reconciliation and the role of third parties in initiating and advancing intercommunal reconciliation processes. As we see in Harold Saunders's contribution to this volume, there is also a growing literature by practitioners who are directly involved in intercommunal conflict resolution and training in protracted conflicts.[54] These practitioners typically argue that peacebuilding is about changing attitudes and that attitudinal change requires a change in the procedures, roles, and structures of the disputing parties, including the development of institutional capacity at the local or communal level for dealing with conflict. Attitudinal change can be fostered through special problem-solving workshops, training in conflict resolution, and/or third-party assistance in developing and designing other kinds of dispute resolution systems that are compatible with local culture and norms and are directed at elites at different levels (top, middle range, and grassroots) in society.

The specific approach that problem solving should take is a matter of contention. According to Joseph Montville, any attempt at reconciliation must first come to grips with the acute sense of victimization felt by those who have been involved in ethnic or sectarian violence. Victimization, according to Montville, typically has three components: "It is the personal experience of stunning violence. . . . [T]here is no way that the violence can be seen as just and deserved; and the threat of violence continues into the future."[55] Montville argues that the process of mourning is essential to the healing process. For this to occur, however, the victimizers have to "accept responsibility for their acts and those of their predecessor governments and people, recognize the injustice done, and in some way ask forgiveness of the victims."[56] Just how this is to be achieved is unclear, as is the role of third parties interested in seeking justice and getting the victimizers to accept formal responsibility for their acts.

The problem-solving workshop, pioneered by John Burton and Herbert Kelman, is based on the assumption that conflict is a subjective, phenomenological, and social process.[57] It takes issue with the ripeness thesis about hurting stalemates on the grounds that, because conflict is essentially a matter of perceptions, third parties have to work on changing the perceptions, attitudes, values, and behaviors of the parties to a conflict. Ripeness, in other words, does not emerge automatically. It has to be cultivated with the assistance of third parties who help the conflicting parties to reach a better understanding of the dimensions of the conflict and the joint strategies required for a mutually acceptable solution.

The problem-solving workshop organized by the scholar-practitioner attempts to change the process of interaction among conflicting parties. Problem solving seeks to open channels of communication between the parties, allowing both sides to see their respective intentions more clearly and to be more aware of their own reactions to the conflict. Workshops are aimed at cultivating respect and objectivity so that the parties develop a mutual commitment to cooperation in their relationship. Based on the work on group processes, which shows that individuals are more disposed to cooperate in small, informal, intergroup activities, the problem-solving workshop helps to de-escalate the conflict. The approach seems to work best if individuals are drawn from middle-range elites (e.g., academics, advisers, ex-officials, retired politicians) and can influence policy but are not accountable for decisions themselves. By helping to establish communications between parties at the subelite level and typically at the prenegotiation stage, these workshops undermine the "we-they" image of conflict, begin a discussion of framework solutions, identify steps that will break the impasse, and create some understanding of the processes that will lead the parties out of the conflict.[58]

The problem-solving workshop should not be confused with third-party assistance with negotiations. It should also not be confused with conflict resolution training and assistance in the design and development of conflict management systems, structures, procedures, and skills for different groups—such as middle-range or grassroots leaders—of the kind described by Hal Saunders. As he explains,

> negotiation around the table is only a later part of a larger political process in which conflicts are resolved by peaceful means. That larger political process is the peace process—a mixture of politics, diplomacy, changing relationships, negotiation, mediation, and dialogue in both official and unofficial arenas.[59]

Saunders calls the larger political process "the public peace process," or circum-negotiation;

that is, a dialogue that takes place at a quasi-official level around or prior to the formal peace process. These dialogues are directed at local leaders, leaders of indigenous nongovernmental organizations, community developers, health officials, refugee camp leaders, intellectuals, and humanitarian leaders. As John Paul Lederach discusses in his chapter in this volume, this dialogue process can be helped by specialized training programs that explore ways of establishing and building relationships; by procedural assistance in facilitation, mediation, and brokering; and by substantive assistance in tasks such as data collection, fact finding, establishment of dispute and arbitration panels, and other kinds of cooperative decision making or dispute resolution between or within different national, ethnic, religious, or racial groups. (Among the pioneers in developing these new approaches to conflict resolution at the community and grassroots levels are groups such as the Mennonite Central Committee and the Quakers.)[60]

In contrast to the state-centered approaches of hard and soft realism, these approaches focus on societal relations and the development of dispute resolution systems at the local, as opposed to the national, level. Third parties are supposed to play a neutral and facilitating role in these kinds of activities, guiding rather than directing the parties to mutually acceptable approaches to problem solving. Private scholar-practitioners and nongovernmental organizations are the preferred third-party candidates for this kind of mediation or facilitation role, because they enjoy expert and reputational authority that makes them acceptable to the parties to the conflict.

Societal-based approaches to conflict resolution and reconciliation present a number of difficulties. The first is an access problem. Outsiders offering problem-solving skills and dispute resolution training may not be acceptable to the parties or may not be taken seriously. If they have special contacts or connections with particular groups in society, they may be viewed by other groups as biased or partisan.

A second problem is the dissemination of the results of problem-solving workshops and dispute resolution training programs. Unless elites and decision makers are carefully selected and targeted for such programs, the programs themselves will have limited or no impact in changing attitudes and behaviors in society as a whole. It may also be difficult to offer such programs in areas of acute conflict, where they are needed most, because of the physical risks to both trainer and trainees.

Third, there is the problem of re-entry. Individuals may be willing to cast off their prejudices and to reverse roles in the classroom or training setting, but once they return to their jobs and positions in society the temptation to revert to old patterns of behavior will be strong because of the pressures of the workplace and the immediate social environment.

Finally, it is difficult to measure the results of problem-solving workshops and conflict resolution facilitation and training programs. There is a great deal yet to be learned about whether such programs do, in fact, lead to a fundamental change in attitudes and to the acquisition and development of new skills for resolving conflict. Although there may be an immediate and discernible change in behaviors that is measurable at the local project level, the wider social impact may be difficult to measure because the effects of these programs are so diffuse.

ASSESSING THE FOUR APPROACHES

Each of the four approaches discussed contains different insights into the causes of ethnic and sectarian violence and the strategies and approaches to intervention (see table 1). Hard and soft realism stress the role of security dilemmas and strategic factors in ethnic and intercommunal conflict. Governance-based and social-psychological approaches emphasize human rights violations and perceptions of victimization as sources of communal conflict

Table 1. Contending Approaches to Conflict Management

Intervention School	Assumptions about Causes of Conflict	Conflict Management Strategies[1]	Third-Party Intervenor
Hard Realism	Domestic anarchy; security dilemmas fueled by hypernationalism and political mobilization, strategic behavior, and miscalculation	• Do nothing and avoid intervention (default position) • Partition • Containment • Change power balances via military and resource transfers or boycotts and sanctions	Great powers
Soft Realism	Domestic anarchy; security dilemmas fueled by hypernationalism and political mobilization, strategic behavior, and miscalculation	• Mediation and coercive diplomacy • Peacekeeping and other confidence-building measures that reduce incentives to defect from negotiated agreements • Power sharing and political accommodation • Isolation/containment of spoilers	Great powers and middle powers; international and regional organizations
Governance-Based Approaches	Sources of conflict lie in the denial of human rights, due process of law, and absence of democratic institutions	• Restoration of rule of law • Elections • Democratic institution building (e.g., support for political parties) • Power-sharing and participatory governance arrangements among different social and communal groups • Restoration of civil society	International and regional organizations; nongovernmental organizations; other groups in civil society
Social-Psychological Approaches	Sources of conflict are primarily psychological and based on embedded enemy images and feelings of victimization	• Perpetrators must accept responsibility for previous acts of violence • Forgiveness and reconciliation • Problem-solving workshops • Circum-negotiation • Training in dispute resolution	Scholar-practitioners; conflict resolution NGOs; religious groups

1. It should be noted that not all conflict management strategies within a given school are necessarily compatible. Depending on the political situation and level of violence, different intervention strategies may be required.

and escalation. Assessments about which intervention strategies work best, when, and where are dictated by these differing assumptions about the sources of conflict.

Each approach offers unique insights into both the causes and the dynamics of intercommunal conflict. However, methods of social research that stress parsimony and single causes (e.g., the security dilemma) or simple resolving formulas (e.g., partition) are frequently at odds with the complexities of real life. Conflicts are shaped by many factors, such as the collapse of central institutions; the holding of ill-prepared elections; the emergence of opportunistic politicians who use ethnicity as a platform; the splintering of armies and the rise of warlords; the logic of preemptive military moves creating a chain reaction of violence; arms transfers; the availability of natural and financial resources, legal and criminal, to fuel the descent into violence; and perceptions of victimization.[61]

The list of causes for intercommunal conflict is long, and different third-party intervenors may enjoy different kinds of comparative advantages, depending on the specific issues that lie at the heart of a particular dispute and on where a particular conflict stands on the rungs of the escalatory/de-escalatory ladder. Timing is also important. Some situations may be more ripe for certain kinds of intervention than others, depending on who does the intervening. We need to acquire a better understanding of the comparative advantages of third parties in conflict management, as well as which instruments or techniques used in conflict management (e.g., the use of force versus mediation) work best, when, where, and under what conditions.

MULTIPLE INTERVENTION AND SEQUENCING STRATEGIES

The fact that numerous factors are at play in any given conflict argues against an intervention strategy that is directed at a single cause or at alleviating only one set of social or political pressures. As Loraleigh Keashly and Ronald Fisher observe, protracted or intercommunal conflicts contain a large number of constituencies with different demands, interests, and belief systems.

> With such a large number of elements, it seems unreasonable to expect that a single intervention strategy could deal with all of them. It seems more useful to envision intervention . . . as a *coordinated* series of concurrent and consecutive strategies directed towards the long-term goal of resolving the conflict.[62]

Such a sequencing strategy is premised on the notion that most conflicts—even protracted ones—have a life cycle of their own, characterized by various phases or stages.[63] These include a period of rising tensions between or among parties, followed by confrontation, the outbreak of violence, and the escalation of military hostilities. In the postagreement or post-settlement phase, a conflict may go through several de-escalatory phases as well, such as a cease-fire, followed by a formal settlement, rapprochement, and eventual reconciliation. There is, of course, an implied linearity to conflict processes in this model that should not be taken literally. Just as some conflicts may ripen, others may unripen or turn rotten. Many conflicts experience an ebb and flow and it is important to recognize that the conflict cycle can reverse itself.

Nonetheless, during the various phases or stages of a conflict the intensity of security dilemmas among rival groupings is likely to vary. Parties will tend to feel more secure in their relations with other groupings when the level of violence is low, when formal ties exist between different groups, and when institutionalized channels of communication, although perhaps frayed, are still available. If seemingly random acts of violence increase, different groups may start to arm themselves and factions may become increasingly aware of the power asymmetries that exist between themselves and other groups. The security dilemma will become more acute and the desire for peaceful and co-operative strategies of conflict will weaken.

The kinds of confidence-building measures that are required to alleviate the pressures of the security dilemma will vary accordingly from one setting to another depending on the intensity of those pressures. In some cases, peace-keeping and monitoring of cease-fires will be sufficient to reduce the potential for armed violence and a renewal of conflict. In others, where the security dilemma is much more acute, it may be necessary to generate a much more robust series of confidence-building measures than those initially implemented by external third parties to create incentives for collaboration.

The depth or intensity of the security dilemma also has implications for the cognitive and emotive elements of decision making by the parties to the conflict and for the third-party conflict manager that may be required to help reduce tensions and de-escalate the conflict. At the low end of the conflict spectrum, where violence is sporadic, the governance and psychological schools argue that parties may be able and willing to handle disputes on their own or to consider interventions by local entities or nonstate actors—i.e., track-two or multi-track diplomatic initiatives and interventions.[64] Parties may wish to keep international organizations and great powers out of the conflict because interventions by these actors may further complicate the issues and raise the stakes in ways that further polarize attitudes.

This is not to say that great-power intervention is undesirable or should be avoided at lower rungs on the escalatory ladder—sometimes a dramatic intervention is just what is needed to avert violent conflict—but there may well be resistance to intervention by the parties themselves. Outside actors, particularly great powers, may also not want to intervene because the costs and risks of intervention outweigh the potential political benefits.[65]

At the upper end of the conflict ladder, however, official track-one (or state-based) diplomacy and intervention by great powers may be required to bring the parties to the negotiating table—what is sometimes called "mediation with muscle."[66] This is because nonstate actors and other bodies often lack the requisite resources and leverage to change the cost-benefit calculus of warring parties in favor of a negotiated settlement.

Even so, the choices may not be quite so stark because second-track initiatives by small powers or nongovernmental organizations can assist with prenegotiation processes in situations where the parties are deadlocked or where the risks of formal communication are deemed to be too high, as in the case of the role that Norway played in the Oslo peace talks between Israelis and Palestinians.[67] Such premediated interventions may complement more formal diplomacy and "muscled" mediations. The use of force against recalcitrant elements or those intent on wrecking the peace process may also be critical to political interventions, as we have seen in the case of NATO air strikes in Bosnia, which helped to bring the parties to the negotiating table at Dayton.[68] In other circumstances, however, mediation is possible without resort to force, as illustrated in Namibia and El Salvador, where third-party mediators were able to get warring sides to the negotiating table through the use of political, as opposed to military, instruments.[69]

Interventions by third parties, however, can also have unintended negative consequences. With some notable exceptions, much of the scholarly and policy literature pays scant attention to the negative aggregate externalities of interventions, that is, the unintended by-products or "collective social and political bads" that may arise as a result of third-party intervention.[70]

Yet, these externalities should be calculated before any action is undertaken. For example, when different communal groups are badly splintered and dispersed over a wide geographical area, partition-based solutions can spark new demands that will be difficult to control once the initial partition has taken place. For example, the division of the Indian subcontinent into India and Pakistan at the time of independence from British rule was subsequently followed by the secession of East Pakistan (Bangladesh) from the rest of Pakistan and has also been followed more recently by various secessionist movements within India, such as in Kashmir and the Punjab.[71]

That said, it is also important to recognize that effective third-party intervention depends on the capabilities, leverage, and linkage of third parties to the conflict and the extent to which they see themselves as stakeholders. Third parties that are not stakeholders and have limited resources may have greater difficulty exercising leverage than those that can bring something to the table, such as great powers that can offer side payments in the form of aid, arms, and trade.[72]

Moreover, the availability of different entry points to the conflict may well be a function of where the conflict stands on the rungs of the escalatory/de-escalatory ladder. To the question, "What intervention strategy is most appropriate for managing intercommunal conflict?" the only honest answer is "It depends." Different tools and techniques are appropriate for different levels of violence and of escalation of the conflict, for different types of conflict, and for differences in the number of parties and issues to the dispute. It may also take several false starts to figure out what works, what does not work, and who has the most to offer as a third party.[73]

STAYING POWER AND SUCCESS

Whatever third parties do—and we have suggested that multiple strategies and entry points exist—they must also possess staying power. Viable peace processes—such as the ones that have taken place in El Salvador, Mozambique, and Namibia, and many of the other cases discussed by Michael Doyle in his chapter in this volume—can only come about if third parties

entrench themselves. Third parties must remain fully engaged during the negotiations that lead up to a settlement and during its implementation. Interventions that fail are typically associated with a lack of staying power or an inability to muster the resources needed to build a secure foundation for a settlement or some process of intercommunal reconciliation.[74]

Staying power must also be coupled with modest expectations about what is achievable and what constitutes success. The goals of intervention should be set neither too high—which leads to disappointment—nor too low—which invites cynicism and may be an excuse for disengagement and third-party withdrawal when the job is only half done. Success is inherently relative in any peacemaking or peacebuilding venture. It may be useful to link the notion of success to different phases of the peace process and not define it in terms of an unattainable end point, such as the creation or restoration of full-blown democracy.

The renunciation of violence by warring factions is clearly a necessary precondition for the restoration of political order. However, success in this sense is only partial. As governance-based approaches remind us, for a peace process to be durable, institutions and support structures at various societal levels must be put in place so that parties are discouraged from taking up arms again.

However, the transition to democracy often proves more destabilizing than stabilizing in war-shattered states, and it is preferable to work toward a more gradual process of democratization and political accommodation. Such a transition must include electoral arrangements that (1) reward political moderation, (2) are timed to reduce rather than exacerbate intercommunal tensions, and (3) are complemented by efforts to strengthen political institutions and governance arrangements at the national and local levels.

Even so, much of the burden of peacebuilding in this transitional period lies with the parties themselves and not with external actors, as we are reminded by both realist approaches. Realists also remind us that interventions can sometimes make the situation worse and further escalate conflict. Third parties must always be prudent and attentive to the potential unintentional consequences of their good intentions. Third parties must also recognize that they are not parents, but only midwives to the birthing process by which peace emerges. But as soft realists, governance-based approaches, and social-psychological schools underscore, third parties can help to produce some of the conditions that lead to peace. Intervention has a track record marked as much by success as by failure.

NOTES

1. This article is an updated and somewhat revised version of an earlier piece, "Third-Party Roles in the Termination of Intercommunal Conflict," which originally appeared in *Millennium: Journal of International Studies* 26, no. 3 (1997): 727–750.

2. See, for example, Robert D. Kaplan, *Balkan Ghosts: A Journey through History* (New York: Vintage, 1994). For skeptical views about the possibilities of successful intervention, see Edward N. Luttwak, "Give War a Chance," *Foreign Affairs* 78, no. 4 (July-August 1999): 36–44, and his chapter in this volume (chapter 16). Also see Richard K. Betts "The Delusion of Impartial Intervention," *Foreign Affairs* 73, no. 6 (1994): 20–33, as well as his chapter in this volume (chapter 18); Roy Licklider, "The Consequences of Negotiated Settlements in Civil Wars, 1945–1993," *American Political Science Review* 39, no. 3 (1995): 681–690; and Joseph R. Rudolf Jr., "Intervention in Communal Conflicts," *Orbis* 39, no. 2 (1995): 259–273.

3. The moral and political arguments for intervention are discussed in Stanley Hoffmann's chapter in this volume (chapter 17). Also see Thomas G. Weiss, ed., *Military-Civilian Interactions: Intervening in Humanitarian Crises* (Lanham, Md.: Rowman and Littlefield, 1999); William Shawcross, *Deliver Us from Evil* (New York: Simon and Schuster, 2000); Oliver Ramsbotham and Tom Wodehouse, *Humanitarian Intervention in Contemporary Conflict: A Reconceptualization* (London: Polity Press, 1996); Kofi Annan, "Two Concepts of Sovereignty," *Economist*, September 18, 1999; Kofi Annan, "'We the Peoples': The Role of the United Nations in the Twenty-First Century: Millennium Report of the Secretary-General of the United Nations* (New York: United Nations, 2000); Stanley Hoffmann, *The Ethics and Politics of Humanitarian Intervention* (Notre Dame: Indiana University Press, 1996); and United Nations, *Report of the Secretary-General to the Security Council on the Protection of Civilians in Armed Conflict,* UN Doc. no. S/199/957, September 8, 1999.

4. This article uses several terms to describe different types of civil conflict. "Ethnic conflict" refers to spontaneous mass eruptions of ethnic antagonisms within a state. "Sectarian conflict" refers to conflicts between narrow or partisan sects or factions. "Intercommunal conflict" refers to conflicts between communities that do not necessarily have ethnic roots, such as some religious or socio-economic conflicts.

5. Kenneth N. Waltz, *Theory of International Politics* (New York: McGraw-Hill, 1979). See, for example, the selections in *Neorealism and Its Critics,* ed. Robert O. Keohane (New York: Columbia University Press, 1986).

6. The interethnic offense-defense escalatory spiral is similar to Robert Jervis's "security dilemma" in international politics. See Robert Jervis, *Perception and Misperception in International Politics* (Princeton, N.J.: Princeton University Press, 1979), 58–116. On misinterpreting the strategic intentions of other groups and the raising of mass armies in response to this competition, see Barry R. Posen, "Nationalism, the Mass Army, and Military Power," *International Security* 18, no. 2 (1993): 80–124. Recent attempts to apply these concepts to a number of different case studies of civil conflict include Barbara F. Walter and Jack Snyder, eds., *Civil Wars, Insecurity, and Intervention* (New York: Columbia University Press, 1999); and David A. Lake and Donald Rothchild, eds., *The International Spread of Ethnic Conflict: Fear, Diffusion, and the Escalation Process* (Princeton, N.J.: Princeton University Press, 1998).

7. Stephen Van Evera, "Hypotheses on Nationalism and War," *International Security* 18, no. 4 (1994): 5–39.

8. Richard N. Haass, "Using Force: Lessons and Choices for U.S. Foreign Policy," in *Managing Global Chaos: Sources of and Responses to International Conflict,* ed. Chester A. Crocker and Fen Osler Hampson with Pamela Aall (Washington, D.C.: United States

Institute of Peace Press, 1996), 203. See also Richard N. Haass, *Intervention: The Use of American Military Force in the Post–Cold War World* (Washington, D.C.: Carnegie Endowment for International Peace, 1994).

9. Chaim Kaufmann, "Possible and Impossible Solutions to Ethnic Wars," *International Security* 20, no. 4 (1996): 136–175.

10. Ibid., 141 and 147.

11. See, for example, Robert A. Pape, "Partition: An Exit Strategy for Bosnia," *Survival* 39, no. 4 (1997–98): 25–28; and Andrew Bell-Fialkoff, *Ethnic Cleansing* (New York: St. Martin's Press, 1996). For interesting policy discussions about the implications of ethnic cleansing, see *Forced Migration in the Newly Independent States of the Former Soviet Union: Hearing before the Subcommittee on International Operations and Human Rights of the Committee on International Relations*, U.S. House of Representatives, 104th Cong., 2d sess., May 22, 1996 (Washington, D.C.: United States Government Printing Office, 1996); and *Bosnian Refugees: Hearings before the Subcommittee on International Operations and Human Rights of the Committee on International Relations*, U.S. House of Representatives, 104th Cong., 1st sess., September 28, 1995 (Washington, D.C.: United States Government Printing Office, 1995).

12. Waltz, *Theory of International Politics;* and Stephen M. Walt, *The Origins of Alliances* (Ithaca, N.Y.: Cornell University Press, 1987).

13. See, for example, Benedict Anderson, *Imagined Communities: Reflections on the Origin and Spread of Nationalism* (Ithaca, N.Y.: Cornell University Press, 1991); Ted Robert Gurr, *Minorities at Risk: A Global View of Ethnopolitical Conflicts* (Washington, D.C.: United States Institute of Peace Press, 1993); Ted Robert Gurr, *Peoples versus States: Minorities at Risk in the New Century* (Washington, D.C.: United States Institute of Peace Press, 2000); Ted Robert Gurr and Barbara Harff, *Ethnic Conflict in World Politics* (Boulder, Colo.: Westview Press); Taiser M. Ali and Robert O. Matthews, eds., *Civil Wars in Africa: Roots and Resolution* (Montreal and Kingston: McGill-Queen's University Press, 1999); Stephen R. David, "Internal War: Causes and Cures," *World Politics* 49, no. 4 (1997): 552–576; Milton J. Esman, *Ethnic Politics* (Ithaca, N.Y.: Cornell University Press, 1994); Ernest Gellner, *Nations and Nationalism* (Ithaca, N.Y.: Cornell University Press, 1993); and Michael Brown, ed., *Ethnic Conflict and International Security* (Princeton,

N.J.: Princeton University Press, 1993). On the immutability of ethnic identities, see Walker Connor, *Ethnonationalism: The Quest for Understanding* (Princeton, N.J.: Princeton University Press, 1994).

14. See Donald Horowitz, *Ethnic Groups in Conflict* (Berkeley: University of California Press, 1985); and Joseph Rothschild, *Ethnopolitics: A Conceptual Approach* (New York: Columbia University Press, 1981).

15. On competing Israeli and Palestinian claims, see, for example, Martin Gilbert, *Jerusalem in the Twentieth Century* (New York: John Wiley and Sons, 1996); and United Nations, *Jerusalem: Visions of Reconciliation—an Israeli-Palestinian Dialogue* (New York: United Nations, 1993). On the dispute over Cyprus, see Norma Salem, ed., *Cyprus: A Regional Conflict and Its Resolution* (New York: St. Martin's Press, 1992); and Monteagle Stearns, *Entangled Allies: U.S. Policy toward Greece, Turkey, and Cyprus* (New York: Council on Foreign Relations, 1992).

16. See James A. Schear, "Bosnia's Post-Dayton Traumas," *Foreign Policy*, no. 104 (1996): 87–101.

17. See, for example, Michael Ignatieff, *Virtual War: Kosovo and Beyond* (New York: Metropolitan Books, 2000); Tim Judah, *Kosovo: War and Revenge* (New Haven, Conn.: Yale University Press, 2000); and Ivo H. Daalder and Michael E. O'Hanlon, *Winning Ugly: NATO's War to Save Kosovo* (Washington, D.C.: Brookings Institution, 2000).

18. Radha Kumar, "The Troubled History of Partition," *Foreign Affairs* 76, no. 1 (1997): 22–35; and Nicholas Sambanis, "Partition as Solution to Ethnic War: An Empirical Analysis of the Theoretical Literature," *World Politics* 5, no. 3 (2000).

19. David A. Lake and Donald Rothchild, "Containing Fear: The Origins and Management of Ethnic Conflict," *International Security* 21, no. 2 (1996): 41.

20. See, for example, Chester A. Crocker, Fen Osler Hampson, and Pamela Aall, eds., *Herding Cats: Multiparty Mediation in a Complex World* (Washington, D.C.: United States Institute of Peace Press, 1999), esp. chaps. 1–3; Jacob Bercovitch, ed., *Resolving International Conflicts: The Theory and Practice of Mediation* (Boulder, Colo.: Lynne Rienner, 1996); Christopher R. Mitchell, "The Process and Stages of Mediation: Two Sudanese Cases," in *Making War and Waging Peace: Foreign Intervention in Africa*, ed. David R. Smock (Washington, D.C.: United States Institute of Peace Press, 1993), 139–159; and Thomas Princen,

Intermediaries in International Conflict (Princeton, N.J.: Princeton University Press, 1992).

21. See Saadia Touval, *The Peace Brokers* (Princeton, N.J.: Princeton University Press, 1982), and I. William Zartman, ed., *Elusive Peace: Negotiating an End to Civil Wars* (Washington, D.C.: Brookings Institution, 1995).

22. See Saadia Touval, "Why the UN Fails," *Foreign Affairs* 73, no. 5 (1994): 44–57. For other views on the role of the United Nations, see Thomas M. Franck, "Break It, Don't Fake It," *Foreign Affairs* 78, no. 44 (1999): 116–118; and Michael J. Glennon, "The New Interventionism," *Foreign Afairs* 78, no. 3 (1999): 2–7. On the potential role of regional organizations, see Connie Peck's chapter in this volume (chapter 33); and Ruth Wedgewood, "Regional and Subregional Organizations in International Conflict Management," in *Managing Global Chaos*, ed. Crocker and Hampson with Aall, 275–286.

23. Arend Lijphart, "The Power Sharing Approach," in *Conflict and Peacemaking in Multiethnic Societies*, ed. Joseph V. Montville (New York: Lexington Books, 1991), 494.

24. Donald L. Horowitz, "Making Moderation Pay: The Comparative Politics for Ethnic Conflict Management," in *Conflict and Peacemaking in Multiethnic Societies*, ed. Montville, 451–476.

25. See Timothy D. Sisk, *Power Sharing and International Mediation in Ethnic Conflicts* (Washington, D.C.: United States Institute of Peace Press, 1996).

26. See Stephen John Stedman, "Spoiler Problems in the Peace Process," *International Security* 22, no. 2 (1997): 5–53.

27. See I. William Zartman, *Ripe for Resolution: Conflict and Intervention in Africa* (New York: Oxford University Press, 1985); and I. William Zartman, "Ripening Conflict, Ripe Moment, Formula, and Mediation," in *Perspectives on Negotiation*, ed. Diane B. Bendahmane and John W. McDonald Jr. (Washington, D.C.: Foreign Service Institute, U.S. Department of State, 1986), 217–218. Among the various adherents to Zartman's concept of ripeness, see Richard N. Haass, *Conflict Unending: The United States and Regional Disputes* (New Haven, Conn.: Yale University Press, 1990); and Donald K. Rothchild, *Managing Ethnic Conflict in Africa: Pressures and Incentives for Cooperation* (Washington, D.C.: Brookings Institution, 1997).

28. Haass, *Conflict Unending*, 27–28.

29. See Janice Gross Stein, "Getting to the Table: Triggers, Stages, Functions, and Consequences of Prenegotiation," *International Journal* 42, no. 2 (1989): 475–502; and Brian Tomlin and Brian S. Mandell, "Mediation in the Development of Norms to Manage Conflict: Kissinger in the Middle East," *Journal of Peace Research* 28, no. 1 (1991): 43–55.

30. Lake and Rothchild, "Containing Fear," 57.

31. See Robert O. Keohane, *After Hegemony: Cooperation and Discord in the World Economy* (Princeton, N.J.: Princeton University Press, 1984); and Stephen D. Krasner, ed., *International Regimes* (Ithaca, N.Y.: Cornell University Press, 1983).

32. Lake and Rothchild, "Containing Fear," 66–67.

33. See Stephan Haggard and Beth Simmons, "Theories of International Regimes," *International Organization* 41, no. 3 (1987): 491–517; and Volker Rittberger, ed., *Regime Theory and International Relations* (Oxford: Oxford University Press, 1995).

34. See the chapter by Neil J. Kritz in this volume (chapter 47).

35. See, for example, International IDEA, *Democracy and Deep-Rooted Conflict: Options for Negotiators* (Stockholm: International IDEA, 1997); and International IDEA, *Democracy and Global Cooperation at the United Nations: Towards Peace, Development, and Democratization* (Stockholm: International IDEA, 2000).

36. Paul LaRose-Edwards, *UN Human Rights Operations: Principles and Practice in United Nations Field Operations* (Ottawa: Human Rights and Justice Division, Department of Foreign Affairs and International Trade, 1996), 10.

37. David Little, "Religious Militancy," in *Managing Global Chaos*, ed. Crocker and Hampson with Aall, 84.

38. On various approaches to liberalism, see Michael W. Doyle, *Ways of War and Peace: Realism, Liberalism, and Socialism* (New York: W. W. Norton, 1997).

39. United Nations Development Programme, *Reconceptualizing Governance*, Discussion Paper no. 2 (New York: United Nations, 1997), 9.

40. Ibid., 17.

41. Pauline H. Baker, "Conflict Resolution versus Democratic Governance: Divergent Paths to Peace?"

in *Managing Global Chaos,* ed. Crocker and Hampson with Aall, 568.

42. Ibid.

43. On the potential role of international norms in defusing ethnic conflict, see David Little, *Sri Lanka: The Invention of Enmity* (Washington, D.C.: United States Institute of Peace Press, 1994).

44. Neil J. Kritz, ed., *Transitional Justice: How Emerging Democracies Reckon with Former Regimes,* vol. 1 (Washington, D.C.: United States Institute of Peace Press, 1995), 82–103, 292–334, and 375–438; and Alexandre S. Kamarotos, "Building Peace, Democracy, and Human Rights: International Civilian Missions at the End of the Millennium," *International Peacekeeping* 2, no. 4 (1995): 483–509.

45. Boutros Boutros-Ghali, "An Agenda for Peace," in *United Nations, Divided World: The UN's Role in International Relations,* ed. Adam Roberts and Benedict Kingsbury, 2d ed. (Oxford: Clarendon Press, 1992), 488.

46. Ibid., 489.

47. On this debate, see, for example, Michael Mandelbaum, "Foreign Policy as Social Work," *Foreign Affairs* 75, no. 1 (1996): 16–32; and Stanley Hoffmann, "In Defense of Mother Theresa," *Foreign Affairs* 75, no. 2 (1996): 172–175.

48. See Samuel P. Huntington, *Political Order in Changing Societies* (New Haven, Conn.: Yale University Press, 1969). See also Edward D. Mansfield and Jack Snyder, "Democratization and the Danger of War," *International Security* 20, no. 1 (1995): 5–38.

49. Elections can also be a sham for genuine democracy. See Fareed Zakaria, "The Rise of Illiberal Democracy," *Foreign Affairs* 76, no. 6 (1997).

50. See Fen Osler Hampson, *Nurturing Peace: Why Peace Settlements Succeed or Fail* (Washington, D.C.: United States Institute of Peace Press, 1996), 87–128; and Timothy D. Sisk, *Democratization in South Africa: The Elusive Social Contract* (Princeton, N.J.: Princeton University Press, 1995).

51. On these priorities, see Nicole Ball's chapter in this volume (chapter 42); Nicole Ball with Timothy Halevy, *Making Peace Work: The Role of the International Development Community* (Baltimore: Johns Hopkins University Press, 1996), 81–102; Nicole Ball, "The Challenge of Rebuilding War-Torn Societies," in *Managing Global Chaos,* ed. Crocker and Hampson with Aall, 607–622; Nat J. Colletta, Markus

Kostner, and Ingo Wiederhofer, *The Transition from War to Peace in Sub-Saharan Africa* (Washington, D.C.: World Bank, 1995), 1–43; Jonathan Moore, *The UN and Complex Emergencies: Rehabilitation in Third World Transitions* (Geneva: United Nations Research Institute for Social Development, 1996), 1–41; and James K. Boyce, *Economic Policy for Building Peace: The Lessons of El Salvador* (Boulder, Colo.: Lynne Rienner, 1996), 1–18, 73–106, and 107–154.

52. See, for example, Development Assistance Committee, Organization for Economic Cooperation and Development, *Task Force on Conflict, Peace, and Development Cooperation: DAC Policy Guidelines for Development Cooperation in Conflict-Prevention and Post-Conflict Recovery,* Document CD.C./DAC(96)31/REV1 (Paris: Organization for Economic Cooperation and Development, February 1997); and Antonia Handler Chayes, Abram Chayes, and George Raach, "Beyond Reform: Restructuring for More Effective Conflict Intervention," *Global Governance* 3, no. 2 (1997): 117–146.

53. For a skeptical viewpoint, see Roland Paris's chapter in this volume (chapter 45); and Roland Paris, "Peacebuilding and the Limits of Liberal Internationalism," *International Security* 22, no. 2 (1977): 54–89.

54. Also see, for example, I. William Zartman and J. Lewis Rasmussen, eds., *Peacemaking in International Conflict: Methods and Techniques* (Washington, D.C.: United States Institute of Peace Press, 1997), esp. 23–80.

55. Joseph V. Montville, "Epilogue: The Human Factor Revisited," in *Conflict and Peacemaking,* ed. Montville, 538.

56. Ibid.

57. See, for example, John W. Burton, *Conflict and Communication: The Use of Controlled Communication in International Relations* (London: Macmillan, 1969); Herbert C. Kelman, "Informal Mediation by the Scholar/Practitioner," in *Mediation in International Relations: Multiple Approaches to Conflict Management,* ed. Jacob Bercovitch and Jeffrey Z. Rubin (New York: St. Martin's Press, 1992), 64–96; and Ronald J. Fisher, "Prenegotiation Problem-Solving Discussions: Enhancing the Potential for Successful Negotiations," in *Getting to the Table: The Processes of International Prenegotiation,* ed. Janice Gross Stein (Baltimore: Johns Hopkins University Press, 1989), 206–238.

58. See Herbert C. Kelman, "Social-Psychological Dimensions of International Conflict," in *Peacemaking in International Conflict,* ed. Zartman and Rasmussen, eds., 191–238; and Ronald J. Fisher, "Interactive Conflict Resolution," in the same volume, 239–272.

59. Harold H. Saunders, "Prenegotiation and Circum-negotiation: Arenas of the Peace Process," in *Managing Global Chaos,* ed. Crocker and Hampson with Aall, 419.

60. See John Paul Lederach, *Building Peace: Sustainable Reconciliation in Divided Societies* (Washington, D.C.: United States Institute of Peace Press, 1995); and Mike C. H. Yarrow, *Quaker Experiences in International Conciliation* (New Haven, Conn.: Yale University Press, 1978).

61. Some of these multiple causes of conflict are considered in Brown, ed., *Ethnic Conflict and International Security;* and Gurr, *Minorities at Risk* and *Peoples versus States.*

62. Loraleigh Keashly and Ronald J. Fisher, "Towards a Contingency Approach to Third-Party Intervention in Regional Conflicts: A Cyprus Illustration," *International Journal* 45, no. 2 (1990): 424 (emphasis in original).

63. See Michael S. Lund, *Preventing Violent Conflicts: A Strategy for Preventive Diplomacy* (Washington, D.C.: United States Institute of Peace Press, 1996), 38.

64. See James Notter and Louis Diamond, *Building Peace and Transforming Conflict: Multi-Track Diplomacy in Practice,* Occasional Paper no. 7 (Washington, D.C.: Institute for Multi-Track Diplomacy, 1996).

65. On how to overcome some of these challenges, see the Carnegie Commission on Preventing Deadly Conflict, *Preventing Deadly Conflict: Final Report* (New York: Carnegie Corporation of New York, December 1997), esp. 25–38.

66. I. William Zartman and Sandra Touval, "International Mediation: Conflict Resolution and Power Politics," *Journal of Social Issues* 41, no. 2 (1985): 27–45.

67. Jane Corbin, *The Norway Channel: The Secret Talks That Led to the Middle East Peace Accords* (New York: Atlantic Monthly Press, 1994); and Abdel Monem Said Aly, "The Road to Oslo and Beyond: Prospects for an Arab-Israeli Peace," *Security Dialogue* 25, no. 1 (1994): 37–51.

68. See James Gow, *Triumph of the Lack of Will: International Diplomacy and the Yugoslav War* (London: Hurst and Company, 1997), 276–279.

69. See Hampson, *Nurturing Peace,* 53–86 and 129–170.

70. For these exceptions, see, for example, Betts, "Delusion of Impartial Intervention"; and Mary B. Anderson, "Humanitarian NGOs in Conflict Resolution," in *Managing Global Chaos,* ed. Crocker and Hampson with Aall, 333–354.

71. See Kumar Rupesinghe and Khawar Mumtaz, eds., *Internal Conflict in South Asia* (London: Sage, 1996); and Ralph Premdas, S.W.R. de A. Samarasinghe, and Alan B. Anderson, eds., *Secessionist Movements in Comparative Perspective* (London: Pinter, 1990).

72. On mediator motivations, see C. R. Mitchell, "The Motives for Mediation," in *New Approaches to International Mediation,* ed. C.R. Mitchell and Keith Webb (New York: Greenwood Press, 1988), 29–51.

73. For an in-depth discussion analysis of these and other aspects of third-party mediation and intervention in the "conflict cycle," see Crocker, Hampson, and Aall, *Herding Cats,* esp. chaps. 2 and 3.

74. In addition to my own earlier work on this subject in *Nurturing Peace,* where I make this argument in some detail, see Barbara F. Walter, "A Critical Barrier to Civil War Settlement," *International Organization* 51, no. 3 (1997): 335–364; and Barbara F. Walter, "Designing Transitions from Civil War: Demobilization, Democratization, and Commitments to Peace," *International Security* 24, no. 1 (1999): 127–155, who offers similar observations.

25

The Growth of the Conflict Resolution Field

Louis Kriesberg

THE FIELD OF CONFLICT RESOLUTION (CR) is oriented toward changing conflicts so that they can be conducted constructively, even creatively, in the sense that violence is minimized, antagonism between adversaries is overcome, outcomes are mutually acceptable to the opponents, and settlements are enduring. CR includes long-term strategies, short-term tactics, and actions by adversaries as well as by mediators. It is based on the work of academic analysts and official and nonofficial practitioners. As such, the rapidly expanding CR field is not a narrowly defined discipline but is a general approach.

The first part of this chapter examines the major phases in the growth of the CR approach, particularly as it relates to international relations. The second part of the chapter discusses the current status of the field and likely future developments.

PHASES IN THE GROWTH OF CONFLICT RESOLUTION

Conflict resolution is a complex field of endeavor, with many interdependent kinds of activities. This is the natural consequence of the many tasks its practitioners seek to accomplish and the diverse sources of its development. This section discusses the contributions made by scholars, practitioners, and organizations within four periods: 1914–45, when ideas and actions prepared the way for the emergence of the CR field; 1946–69, a period of early efforts and basic research; 1970–85, a period of crystallization and expansion; and 1986–present, a time of differentiation and institutionalization.

The periods are not discrete; events and developments in later years have antecedents in earlier periods, and what begins in one period stretches into later years. The sequence in which matters are discussed indicates their relative salience, not their origins. For a chronological listing of major publications and events in the field, see the appendix. Developments in the United States are given particular attention for many reasons, including the central role they have played in what is becoming an increasingly global endeavor.

1914–45: Precursors

The outbreak of World War I greatly undermined liberal optimism that spreading democracy and economic expansion would produce a relatively harmonious world in the near future. Wilsonian idealism briefly revived such expectations in the postwar era, but they were short-lived. The Great Depression, the rise of fascism, and the horrors and devastation of World War II further undermined faith in the attainment of enduring peace. These developments provided the context for efforts that contributed to the beginnings of modern conflict resolution.

One major body of work that helped lay the foundation for CR's growth encompassed analyses of the eruption of large-scale conflicts. This included studies of class-based struggles, particularly revolutions, as exemplified in the work of Crane Brinton (1938). Case studies examined the outbreak of wars and quantitative analyses were made of the incidence of wars, notably in Quincy Wright's monumental study (1942). Another major subject in this period was the analysis of conflicts within organizations, particularly labor-management conflicts. In this regard, the work of Mary Parker Follett (1942) notably helped lay the groundwork for contemporary CR.

The importance of nonrational sources in the outbreak of revolutions and wars was a major theme in some of this work. Thus, research on these matters examined scapegoating and other kinds of displaced feelings, susceptibility to propaganda, and personal attributes of leaders manipulating powerful political symbols (Lasswell 1930). These phenomena were evident in various social movements and their attendant conflicts. For some analysts, the rise of Nazism in Germany seemed to exemplify many aspects of these developments.

In addition to analyzing the causes of intense conflicts, some work was done on ways in which conflicts can be managed and their destructive escalation avoided. First appearing in the 1930s, these analyses of social-psychological and group processes in ethnic, industrial, family, and other conflicts left a legacy of methods and issues upon which CR scholars have built (Lewin 1948).

To some extent, the nonrational aspects of many conflicts made them amenable to management, since they were not based entirely on a clash of objective interests. The human relations approach to industrial conflict built on this assumption (Roethlisberger and Dickson 1943). Other research about industrial organizations stressed the way struggles based on differences of interests could be controlled by norms and structures, if asymmetries in power were not too large. The experience with regulated collective bargaining provided a model for this possibility.

1946–69: Early Efforts and Basic Research

In the 1950s and 1960s, rapid growth in many CR-relevant scholarly and practitioner activities provided the foundations for further CR research. Some of the work was spurred by the specter of nuclear annihilation that the Cold War evoked, but many other components of CR had independent origins. Basic research in many academic disciplines helped establish a solid base for the later applications of CR. An early locus for such work was the University of Michigan, where the *Journal of Conflict Resolution* began publication in 1957 and the Center for Research on Conflict Resolution was established in 1959 (Harty and Modell 1991). The International Peace Research Institute in Oslo (PRIO) was also founded in 1959.

Obviously, social context profoundly affects the course of social conflicts and the way analysts and partisans think about them. For many years after the end of World War II, people were preoccupied with economic reconstruction and growth. This was followed by an era largely distinguished by concerns about justice, autonomy, and equality. In the 1960s national liberation struggles emerged in European colonies in Africa and Asia; the United States was the scene of mass social unrest over civil rights and the country's involvement in Vietnam; and student demonstrations and national revolutions seemed to engulf the world's political landscape. Many analysts as well as activists viewed these struggles as based on valid grievances and worthy of support.

The Cold War profoundly structured world politics and the ways analysts thought about conflict resolution for over four decades, but its character changed significantly over that time. The 1962 Cuban Missile Crisis was followed by a brief thaw in the Cold War. A longer-lasting transformation began in 1969, aided by three changes. First, the antagonism between the Soviet Union and the People's Republic of China had become especially intense, as revealed in the bloody skirmishes along their border. Second, the Social Democratic Party came to power in West Germany and instituted its policy of accommodation with Eastern Europe and the Soviet Union *(Ostpolitik)*. Third, Richard Nixon became president of the United States and, partly as a way to end U.S. engagement in the war in Vietnam, undertook a policy of détente with the Soviet Union.

Spurred by concerns about the possible eruption of nuclear as well as non-nuclear wars, an important body of scholarly work based on quantitative methods flourished from the onset of the Cold War. Systematic data began to be collected in an effort to examine the incidence and correlates of wars (Richardson 1960; Singer 1972). In addition, quantitative data on conflicting and cooperative interactions among nations began to be collected. These data continue to be analyzed, testing CR as well as traditional international relations concepts (McClelland 1968; Isard 1988; Leng 1993; Vasquez 1993).

Another important body of work focused on the ways cooperative activities and institutions provide a basis for increasing international integration that lessens the possibility of destructive conflict. Much of this work consisted of examining variations in the levels of integration and cooperation among countries, and found that highly integrated countries formed communities with little likelihood of war, as documented in the work of Karl Deutsch and others (1957). An important strand of thought argued that functional integration among countries would help create the reality of a common interest in peace (Mitrany 1943). Ernst B. Haas (1958) analyzed how this occurred in the case of the European Coal and Steel Community, established in 1951, which evolved into the present-day European Union.

Game theory also has influenced the development of CR. It has helped analysts think about the conflict implications of various payoff matrices and the strategies chosen by interacting players (Rapoport and Chammah 1965). The prisoner's dilemma payoff matrix especially has been the basis of much study. Rather than assuming a zero-sum game, in which one side wins what the other loses, the variable-sum or mixed-motive game of the prisoner's dilemma type has been the subject of considerable research. In the prisoner's dilemma game, each side can choose to cooperate or to defect (and seek unilateral advantage). In the payoff matrix, if one side cooperates and the other does not, the player who cooperates loses a great deal and the defecting player gains a great deal. If they both cooperate, they both gain a considerable amount; if they both defect, they both lose much. From the perspective of each party, with no additional information about what the other side will do, the best strategy is to defect; but if both sides do that, they both lose. Many experiments have been conducted to discern what factors affect the likelihood that people will follow one strategy or the other. Thomas Schelling's influential work (1960), also drawing from game theory, examined the logic of bargaining.

During this period traditional diplomacy was also subjected to careful analysis, with researchers inferring principles of practice that could be used to create policy in a nuclear age (Iklé 1964). The increasing attention to the new conditions of international politics created by nuclear weapons, especially for the purpose of deterrence, stimulated growing interest in the subjective and nonrational components in foreign policy decision making and crisis behavior (Jervis 1976; Jervis, Lebow, and Stein 1985; Janis 1972).

Considerable research was done in the 1950s and 1960s on factors affecting the relations between potentially contending groups and how overt struggle can be prevented or, failing that, waged constructively and resolved amicably. Research methods included public opinion surveys, field observations, and small-group experimentation. For example, research on race and ethnic relations produced the well-documented finding that equal-status interaction among members of different ethnic groups reduces prejudice and antagonistic behavior among them. Another relevant finding is that the development of superordinate goals can bring contending groups into a cooperative relationship (Sherif 1966). Morton Deutsch (1973) conducted a variety of experiments on constructive and destructive conflict processes, helping to set the agenda for much subsequent work.

Also during this period many sociologists analyzed the processes of industrial, community, ethnic, and other kinds of conflicts (Coleman 1957). Moreover, some analyses treated social conflicts as a generic phenomenon, noting similarities as well as differences among them (Coser 1956). Recognizing the ubiquity of conflicts, many sociologists directed their attention to the functions of conflicts and how conflicts were waged and settled. Some anthropologists studied dispute settlement processes in societies with and without formal legal systems (Nader 1965; Gulliver 1979).

The analysis of nonviolent action provided another significant contribution to the development of CR (Sharp 1973). As articulated by some leaders of nonviolent campaigns, committing violence made future negotiation and reconciliation much more difficult. Instead, they argued, waging a nonviolent struggle enhanced the likelihood of later attaining an enduring and mutually acceptable outcome.

An additional influence in the growth of CR has been the diverse field of peace research

(Stephenson 1989), which makes several kinds of contributions. It draws attention to how people in different cultures and roles are socialized to believe that certain ways of waging conflicts are proper and others are not. Peace research also examines the social and institutional bases of war, including the military-industrial complex and other vested interests influencing the decision to pursue external conflicts; in so doing, this school of research contributes to the demystification of large-scale conflicts. The peace research community's examination of how protracted conflicts may be de-escalated is particularly germane to CR. For example, the idea underlying Graduated Reciprocation in Tension-Reduction (GRIT) is that de-escalation of tensions between adversaries can occur if one side announces it is undertaking conciliatory actions, invites reciprocation, and persists in conciliatory moves even when there is no immediate reciprocation (Osgood 1962). This idea has been influential in the CR field, and there is evidence that GRIT has been an effective instrument in peacemaking, under certain conditions when applied to protracted international conflicts (Etzioni 1967; Goldstein and Freeman 1990).

While much work was being done on the academic front, actual CR practice underwent significant change during 1946–69, when unofficial diplomacy became increasingly important in international affairs. For example, in 1957 nuclear physicists and others engaged in analyzing the possible use of nuclear weapons from the United States, Great Britain, and the Soviet Union began meeting to exchange ideas about reducing the chances that nuclear weapons would be used again (Pentz and Slovo 1981). The first meetings were held at the summer home of Cyrus Eaton in Pugwash, Nova Scotia, and developed into what have come to be called the Pugwash Conferences on Science and World Affairs. From the 1950s through the 1970s, the discussions at these meetings contributed to the signing of the Partial Test-Ban Treaty, the Nuclear Nonproliferation Treaty, the Biological Weapons Convention, and the Antiballistic Missile Treaty. In 1995 the Pugwash Conferences and Joseph Rotblat, their executive director, won the Nobel Peace Prize.

Other regular, nonofficial meetings between well-connected persons from adversarial parties also were significant in opening up new channels of communication to discuss solutions for contentious issues. One important international example is the Dartmouth Conference (Chufrin and Saunders 1993). At the urging of President Dwight D. Eisenhower, Norman Cousins, then editor of the *Saturday Review*, brought together a group of prominent U.S. and Soviet citizens as another communications channel when official relations were especially strained. The first of many such meetings was at Dartmouth College in 1960.

Practice was also changing in the domestic sphere. Thus, lines of communication among diverse community groups are sustained by ongoing interethnic and interreligious councils or dialogue groups. More particularly, in the United States the civil rights struggle gave new salience to the power of nonviolent action. In response to these actions and to the outbreaks of violence, efforts to mitigate the civil strife associated with the protests and demonstrations included commissions of inquiry and also quiet mediation carried out by the U.S. Justice Department.

1970–85: Crystallization and Expansion

During this period, the practice of CR flourished. As new fields of CR activity were cultivated and grew, publications disseminated CR ideas, and reports of experience with more and more types of mediation were published. Academic and nonacademic institutions added training in negotiation and mediation to their programs.

A consensus on many of the core ideas of CR crystallized during this period. Part of this consensus included the idea that conflicts often could be restructured and reframed so that partisans would regard the conflict as a shared problem that had mutually acceptable solutions. The consensus did not preclude the option of coercive struggle to help bring about such change. Another core idea is that intermediaries provide many services that assist adversaries to construct mutually acceptable agreements to settle and ultimately resolve their conflicts. Furthermore, the consensus included the idea that negotiators and mediators could learn how to improve their skills to manage and settle disputes in ways that would enhance the adversaries' relationships.

The rapid expansion of CR in the United States was in many ways a social movement, whose origins could be traced to the convergence of several other social movements, including the post-1960s appeal of local self-government and community activism (Adler 1987; Scimecca 1991). CR as a social movement was also fostered by the peacemaking and mediation activities of religious organizations, particularly those associated with the Society of Friends (Quakers) and the Mennonites. In addition, the expansion was furthered by the growth of the legal profession, litigation, and the ensuing congestion of the American court system. The emerging alternative dispute resolution (ADR) movement seemed attractive to some lawyers and many nonlawyers as an alternative to adversarial proceedings and an attractive option to some of the judiciary as a way to reduce the burden on the courts (Ray 1982). Also, CR seemed to offer peace movement members, whose numbers soared in the early 1980s, a practical alternative to the nation's reliance on military options (Lofland 1993). Finally, CR ideas arising from research and theory provided a theoretical basis and intellectual justification for CR practices.

During this period the Cold War underwent profound changes as well. Official détente began to crumble in the mid-1970s and collapsed by the end of the decade. The Cold War intensified again, spurred on by the rhetoric and policies of the Reagan administration. But the growing integration of the world economy undermined the premises of the superpower rivalry. Suffering economic stagnation, the Soviet Union began a radical course of reform with the accession to power of Mikhail Gorbachev in 1985, which would lead quickly to the end of the Cold War.

One important development in CR during the 1970–85 period was the great expansion of CR work throughout the world. Notable contributions to theory and practice emerged from European peace research. In Germany several peace and conflict research institutes were established after the Social Democratic Party came to power in 1969. Ideas about nonoffensive defense and how military defense could be structured so that the other side was not threatened spread across the continent; such ideas included a new generation of possible confidence-building measures. Finally, the earlier work of Gene Sharp on nonviolent action evolved into the idea of a civilian-based defense.

Feminist theory and research were another source of ideas in the development of CR. Feminist thought provided a critique and an alternative to the prevailing emphasis on hierarchy and coercive power as the essential mode of decision making in social life, including the international realm (Harris and King 1989). The feminist critique, viewing the traditional perspective largely as a product of men's socialization and dominance, sought to emphasize the importance of nonhierarchical social relations and the possibility of reaching integrative agreements through relatively consensual decision-making processes. Feminist theory also highlighted the many contributions of women in public as well as private life, even in a patriarchal world. In many ways these feminist ideas were congenial with CR and contributed to its growth.

Additional contributions during this period stemmed from further scholarly investigations of game theory. For example, Snyder and Diesing (1977) analyzed international crises and found that the variation in representative payoff matrices of the crises helped explain their outcomes. Another body of work was based on the payoff matrix for the prisoner's dilemma game. Computer simulations and other evidence indicated that cooperation would result if one party followed a tit-for-tat strategy in an extended series of reiterated games (Axelrod 1984). In an analysis of interactions among the Soviet Union, the United States, and the People's Republic of China, however, the GRIT model seemed to provide a better fit with movement toward de-escalation and cooperation than did tit-for-tat (Goldstein and Freeman 1990).

An extensive body of social-psychological theory and research also has made important contributions to CR. Testing a variety of theories pertaining to cognition, interaction, and personality, among others, the research methodology has been predominantly small-group experimentation. Some work, for example, focused on how entrapment (persisting in behavior because of previous investment in the behavior) contributes to escalating conflicts and how the process can be interrupted (Brockner and Rubin 1985). A great deal of work in many disciplines during this period focused on the negotiation process (Druckman 1977; Zartman 1978).

Another important contribution to the growth of CR is the considerable research and theorizing about social movements (Tilly 1978; Toch 1965). The influential resource-mobilization approach stresses not only the importance of grievances as a source of social movement activity, but the belief that such grievances can be redressed. The emergence and transformation of large-scale conflicts, therefore, can be regarded as a function of the apparent strength of the opposition, the capabilities of the social movement's members, and the leaders' formulation of credible goals.

Peace movement actions during the period 1970–85 manifested themselves in traditional ways, such as mass public demonstrations, but they also took on new forms, such as innovative kinds of civil disobedience. The anti–Vietnam War demonstrations and resistance ended as U.S. military forces were withdrawn from Vietnam. After years of quiescence, peace movement actions were renewed in the early 1980s, with new goals and different forms, including demonstrations and political mobilization in the United States in favor of a bilateral freeze on the production, testing, and deployment of nuclear weapons (Marullo and Lofland 1990; Meyer 1990). In many Western European countries, protest demonstrations and political pressure were directed at preventing the deployment of NATO's cruise and Pershing II missiles against the Soviet Union. In addition, a groundswell of people-to-people diplomacy occurred during this period, as large numbers of U.S. citizens visited the Soviet Union and U.S. cities developed ties with Soviet counterparts (Lofland 1993).

Also during this period, interactive problem-solving workshops became increasingly popular. In this method of conflict resolution, a convenor (in most cases, an academic) brings together a few members of a conflict's opposing sides to guide and facilitate their discussions about the conflict (Kelman 1992). The participants typically have ties to the leadership of their respective sides or have the potential to become members of the leadership in the future. The workshops usually go on for several days, moving through several distinct stages.

John Burton, Leonard Doob, Herbert Kelman, Edward Azar, Ronald Fisher, and others are responsible for developing the workshop concept as a method of conflict resolution (Fisher 1996). Workshops typically have been held in relation to protracted internal and international conflicts, such as those in Northern Ireland, Cyprus, and the Middle East.

The workshops' participants themselves sometimes become quasi mediators upon returning to their adversary group, but as workshop participants, they do not attempt to negotiate agreements (Kriesberg 1995). Sometimes they later become negotiators, as was the case in the negotiations between the Palestine Liberation Organization (PLO) and the Israeli government in the early 1990s (Kelman 1995).

Problem-solving workshops are one channel of what is often referred to as track-two diplomacy in international relations (Montville 1991). Track one consists of the mediation, negotiations, and other official exchanges between governmental representatives. Track two includes more than problem-solving workshops and is best viewed as multitrack (McDonald 1991). Among the many unofficial channels are transnational organizations within which members of adversarial parties meet and discuss matters pertaining to the work of their common organizations. Another track includes ongoing dialogue groups, with members from the adversary parties discussing contentious issues between their respective countries (or communities or organizations).

Finally, the practice of ADR also greatly expanded during this period, as community dispute resolution centers were established in many parts of the United States. CR was also increasingly used in public disputes over environmental issues, such as disposal of radioactive waste, water usage, and landfills (Susskind and Cruikshank 1988).

1986–Present: Differentiation and Institutionalization

Since the mid-1980s, the nature and the context of large-scale conflicts have changed in significant ways. The ending of the Cold War at the close of the 1980s profoundly transformed the international system and also greatly affected intrastate conflicts. For example, conflicts among groups identifying themselves in terms of ethnicity, religion, language, and similar attributes, rather than ideology, became more salient (Gurr 2000). The globalization of the world due to technological advances and the increased integration of the global market has also transformed international and intrastate conflicts, for example, by raising the likelihood of external intervention into large-scale domestic as well as international conflicts.

All these changes have affected CR ideas and practices. The rise of complex communal, environmental, and socioeconomic conflicts—often without clear right and wrong sides—has enhanced the pertinence of the CR approach to find and maximize mutual benefits for all groups who find themselves in conflict with one another. Moreover, some of these conflicts, particularly those involving ethnic differences, have been especially brutal and destructive. These developments have also directed increased attention to cultural attributes as the source of communally based conflicts and their management (Rubinstein and Foster 1988; Cohen 1991; Faure and Rubin 1993; Ross 1993; Lederach 1995; Zartman 1996; Avruch 1998; Salem 1997; Gopin 2000).

In addition, recent developments have renewed attention to the emotional factors in conflicts and their resolution (Scheff 1994). Memories of past atrocities and humiliations often evoke feelings of revenge to regain lost honor and ease emotional traumas. Several academics and practitioners have developed CR methods that incorporate alternative ways of addressing such feelings (Volkan 1988).

CR research has continued to be directed at the use and effects of various kinds of mediation in international and other types of conflicts (Mitchell and Webb 1988; Kressel and Pruitt 1989; Princen 1992; Bercovitch 1996). Research examining the conditions that lead to de-escalating efforts, whether mediated or not, has also expanded. Many elements must converge for conflicts to undergo a transition to de-escalation, including the adversaries' belief that they cannot gain what they want unilaterally or that efforts to do so would be too painful. Another important element is the possibility of an agreement among the adversaries, offering a mutually acceptable alternative (Touval and Zartman 1985). Policy-relevant research is often framed in terms of discerning the right time to undertake various kinds of

de-escalating strategies (Zartman 1989; Kriesberg and Thorson 1991).

In addition to mediation and negotiation, CR analysts and practitioners have expanded their work to include more and more phases of conflicts. Thus, increasing attention has been devoted to the prenegotiation phase, or the process of getting adversaries to the table (Stein 1989). Work at even earlier phases, before a conflict escalates, is also gaining attention, as is work in the post-settlement phase, involving the development of stable political structures and methods of reconciliation between the conflict's adversaries. All this is part of viewing conflicts in a long-term perspective, including the avoidance of conflicts becoming intractable, the transformation of protracted conflicts into tractable ones, and the establishment of a stable peace, and perhaps reconciliation, between former adversaries.

The expansion in CR activities has increased differentiation in two ways: by the kind of conflict and by the stage of conflict. From the outset, interpersonal and intergroup conflicts were distinguished, as were domestic and international conflicts. However, more and more arenas of CR work have emerged that address conflicts varying according to the context, the issues at stake, the nature of the adversaries, and the CR methods employed. For instance, CR research and practice may focus on school settings, family relations, public disputes over environmental issues, ethnic relations, interreligious struggles, interstate border disputes, and fights about the allocation of scarce resources.

Significantly, too, specialization is now developing according to the phase of a conflict that is the focus of CR work. Thus, a great deal of attention is being given to early warning and preventing the eruption of large-scale violence within and between states, often emphasizing the efforts of official and nonofficial intervenors (Ackerman 2000; Lund 1996; Carnegie 1997). Various CR practitioners have also begun to pay more attention to institutional arrangements for managing recurrent conflicts before they become protracted and destructive. Their work applies in a variety of conflict-prone venues, ranging from large industrial enterprises to multiethnic societies (Ury, Brett, and Goldberg 1988).

Other practitioners and analysts focus on ways to stop the escalation of a conflict, for example, by managing crises (Brecher 1993), by initiating de-escalation (Kriesberg 1992; Mitchell 2000), by peacekeeping interventions, and by applying sanctions (Brecher 1993; Cortright 2000). Finally, CR work is giving increasing attention to post-hostilities peacebuilding, including research into sustaining peace agreements, promoting reconciliation, and developing cultures of peace (Hampson 1996; Boulding 2000; Weiner 1998; Kacowicz 2000).

In addition to becoming increasingly differentiated, CR is becoming more institutionalized. In the United States its practice is legislatively mandated in certain circumstances, for example, in the development of certain federal regulations and in child custody cases in some jurisdictions. Institutionalization is also evident in the establishment of many research centers, several of the more prominent ones being based at universities and originally funded by the William and Flora Hewlett Foundation. In addition, many universities provide graduate training in conflict analysis and resolution, including certificate programs within professional schools and graduate degree programs, as well as M.A. and Ph.D. programs in conflict resolution. Many independent and university-based centers also provide training and consulting services in conflict resolution and mediation. Training and practice in mediation are increasingly finding their way in all levels of education, in private corporations, and in government agencies. CR techniques are also being introduced in more and more areas of the world—for example, in Eastern Europe and the former Soviet Union, as illustrated by the activities of Partners for Democratic Change, based in the United States. Finally, comprehensive syntheses of the field as it relates to

large-scale conflicts have been published (Kriesberg 1998; Miall 1999).

The practice of CR has continued to evolve. In the domestic arena applications have increased in areas relating to deeply rooted ethnic and other communal antagonisms, often exacerbated by immigration, and to deeply held value differences, such as those relating to abortion. These issues often require long-term strategies to build mutually respectful relations and legitimate institutionalized procedures to manage conflicts and to achieve a sense of justice for all parties involved.

In the international realm, the engagement of outside, unofficial intermediaries in the conflicts within and among countries has increased. This CR method requires considerable sensitivity to elicit and adapt local approaches rather than impose methods developed in another setting (Lederach 1995). This type of international response to conflict has been accompanied by a parallel increase in conventional interventions by international governmental organizations and individual governments into the internal affairs of other countries, particularly in cases of humanitarian crises and extreme violations of human rights. This was evident in Somalia, Iraq, Haiti, Rwanda, the former Yugoslavia, Indonesia, Sierra Leone, and elsewhere during the 1990s. Such governmental actions raise profound questions about the existence of shared standards and conceptions regarding sovereignty and human rights (Damrosch 1993; Deng et al. 1996).

CURRENT AND FUTURE ISSUES

Having considered the growth of the CR field, we can now examine areas of consensus and disagreement within the field. The remainder of the section will discuss how international relations theory and practice and CR are tending to converge and complement each other. The discussion will suggest how the diversity of CR activities provides opportunities for complementary work.

Consensus and Dissensus within the CR Field

As CR activities have evolved, crystallized, and become institutionalized, some elements of consensus have emerged among those working in the field. Yet the great variety of conflicts to which CR is applied and the wide range of sources of CR ideas make universal agreement on CR precepts and techniques unlikely.

MATTERS OF CONSENSUS. There is general agreement, at least in principle, that there are specific CR strategies and tactics for particular kinds of conflicts and conflict stages. Thus, long-term strategies that combine a variety of methods typically are required to prevent a conflict from escalating destructively. Attention has been devoted to the various methods that are appropriate for intermediaries trying to hasten de-escalation at different stages of a conflict, referred to as the "contingency approach" (Keashly and Fisher 1995; also see Kriesberg 1996).

Also, the CR community generally recognizes the important influence adversaries have on each other in both escalating and de-escalating a conflict. Partisans, however, frequently attribute the cause and course of a conflict to the other side's internally driven characteristics or to characteristics within the larger social system that cannot be affected (Jervis 1976; Kelley and Michela 1980). The CR approach stresses that both sides affect the relationship and focuses efforts on what each party can do to influence the course of a struggle (Kriesberg 1998).

Finally, there is growing recognition among CR practitioners that every social conflict involves many parties and issues (Putnam 1988; Kriesberg 1992). Viewed as such, social conflicts share certain elements and are thus interlocked. The changing salience of one conflict relative to another serves as a source of escalation and de-escalation; consequently, reframing a conflict so that its salience is reduced often promotes its settlement and resolution.

MATTERS OF DISSENSUS. CR analysts and practitioners and those outside the field have subjected many of its aspects to sharp critiques. The internal debates are emphasized here. CR workers differ in the emphasis they place on "conflicts" versus "disputes" and on their settlement, resolution, or transformation. *Dispute* sometimes refers to contestations over matters that are negotiable and contain the elements of compromise, while *conflict* is about issues that involve deep-rooted human needs (Burton 1990). According to this view, *conflict resolution* means solving the problems that led to the conflict, and *transformation* means changing the relationships between the parties to a conflict; *conflict settlement* refers to suppressing the conflict itself, without dealing with deeper causes and relations. Not all CR analysts and practitioners make such a sharp distinction; they generally regard some types of contestations as more limited than conflicts but recognize that disputes may also be episodes in a larger conflict. The settlement of disputes, then, may contribute to changes in the relationship between adversaries and the gradual transformation of their conflict. A related question persists: to what extent is attaining justice and satisfying basic needs for the contending parties crucial for an enduring peace?

CR analysts and practitioners also differ in the importance they accord to coercion and violence in the way conflicts are conducted and settled or resolved. Some analysts reason that any reliance on coercion is antithetical to a problem-solving resolution of a conflict. Traditional "realists," on the other hand, tend to assume that all conflicts are ultimately resolved by coercion. Many people working in the CR field, believing that power differentials are an inescapable fact of all relationships, take a middle ground. They stress the varieties of power, such as the ability to impose positive and negative sanctions, normative or persuasive inducements, and altruism and shared identity (Boulding 1989). They also emphasize how conflicts are reframed, and the parties' self-identity redefined, in the course of a struggle and efforts to resolve it.

Some observers argue that the dominant party in a conflict may use CR as an instrument of control. Without taking sides in this debate, we must concede that insofar as parties are unequal in status, power, or other resources, the weaker party tends to give up more in a mediated or negotiated agreement (Gulliver 1963; Nader 1991). But this is perhaps even more likely to be true if the dispute is settled by other procedures.

Finally, practitioners disagree about when various methods of conflict de-escalation and resolution may be appropriate (Laue and Cormick 1978). Some would not try to mediate or otherwise facilitate a settlement between parties in a highly asymmetrical relationship. Indeed, many feminists and others criticize CR practitioners for their tendency to ignore power differences in their haste to employ CR techniques (Taylor and Miller 1994). However, others in the field believe there is no alternative when seeking to mediate conflicts with power inequalities, since conflict parties rarely are equal in their resources and capabilities. These CR practitioners may even regard facilitating the adversaries' recognition and acceptance of the realities of their relationship as contributing to a settlement.

One way to resolve the dilemmas these views pose is to incorporate constructive methods of waging a struggle into the adversaries' strategic repertoire. Thus, some CR analysts and practitioners emphasize ways of redressing power imbalances without denying the grievances or interests of the opposition, which is the appeal of nonviolent action for many people (Wehr, Burgess, and Burgess 1994). However, CR also refers to strategies and tactics to help balance asymmetrical parties in negotiations

(Deutsch 1973; Zartman and Rubin 1996; Zartman 1987).

Convergence and Complementarity between Conflict Resolution and International Relations

The fields of CR and international relations overlap and are increasingly converging, in part because of the radically changing nature of the world and of social conflicts. Also, practitioners and academics in both fields, regardless of their approaches, have sought to build links to the other community. Professional associations, foundation-supported meetings, and the efforts of many academic and nonacademic institutions, such as the United States Institute of Peace, have facilitated interchanges and this convergence.

However, CR and conventional international relations (IR) theory and practice will and should remain somewhat divergent. Traditional IR thinking tends to be "realist" in its emphasis on sovereign states, the centrality of power seeking by political leaders, and the importance of military force. CR can provide a corrective to inappropriate reliance on these views (Galtung 2000). Even less-traditional IR thinking and practice are often distinguishable from many kinds of CR approaches, and those differences can provide a sound basis for complementary work.

CONVERGENCE. Many CR ideas have gone beyond the confines of academia to the general public and official and unofficial practitioners. One notable example is the idea that adversaries can achieve win-win outcomes. Thus, the transmission of German and other European peace researchers' ideas about nonoffensive defense to Soviet leaders in the early and mid-1980s played an important role in Gorbachev's "new thinking" and its acceptance within the Soviet foreign policy bureaucracy (Kriesberg 1992). Furthermore, a variety of CR practices have become widely accepted in coping with conflicts. These practices include establishing informal dialogue groups, incorporating brainstorming periods in negotiations, and using various intermediaries.

Innovative ideas and practices in international relations have contributed to some noteworthy CR developments, resulting in useful and enduring syntheses. For example, analyses of actual cases of mediation in international conflicts have broadened the concept of the mediator's role and mediation activities. When officials of major states serve as mediators, their access to economic, military, and status resources and their interests in the outcome of the mediation all contribute to the process (Princen 1992). Despite the widespread belief that mediators must strive for neutrality and minimize assertiveness, information about mediation in many arenas reveals that mediators are often highly active in shaping both the process used and the agreement reached (Kolb et al. 1994). The great variety of mediation activities that can be combined differently in manifold roles, and the diversity of persons who provide some of those services—inside as well as outside those roles—are increasingly being explored (Bercovitch 1996).

Another example of synthesis derives from the attention traditional international relations has devoted to the study of institutions. Recent analyses of normative regimes and an array of other formal and informal institutional arrangements that have been negotiated to resolve problems related to weapons, human rights, environmental protection, and many other issues enrich the repertoire of options adversaries can consider for various ways out of a destructive conflict. Increasingly, CR practitioners are focusing not only on the process of de-escalation and negotiation, but on the fairness and durability of the outcomes as well. Such a focus leads them to consider possible formulas that can not only settle a dispute, but also settle it in a way that makes it unlikely to recur.

Finally, the profound changes in the nature of the world system, noted at the outset of this chapter, have impelled convergence. This may be seen in the increasingly crucial role of nongovernmental agents as both partisans and intermediaries in many transnational conflicts (Chatfield, Pagnucco, and Smith 1996).

COMPLEMENTARITY. Peacemaking practices of CR and international relations often complement one another, whether sequentially or simultaneously. Many examples of sequential complementarity can be cited, usually when the CR practice involves nonofficial or track-two methods that precede the more traditional diplomatic approaches, since track-two diplomacy may prepare the groundwork for official negotiations. At other times, negotiations are initiated in a track-two channel and then handed off to an official negotiating forum. Sometimes, the traditional diplomatic channel reaches an impasse and a new track is opened informally. When progress is made, the negotiations are then transferred back to the official channel. This was the case in the 1993 negotiations between Israelis and PLO representatives conducted in Oslo, Norway (Kriesberg 2001).

Another example is the work deriving from one of the task forces established under the auspices of the Dartmouth Conference in 1982. Following the decline of U.S.-Soviet détente, members of the conference established task forces on (1) arms control and (2) regional conflicts to examine what had gone wrong. Reflection on the process and the phases of the conference's development provided the basis for two members of the regional conflicts task force, Gennady Chufrin and Harold Saunders, to co-chair the Inter-Tajik Dialogue (Saunders 1995). The dialogue brought together a wide range of Tajiks in 1993, following the first round of a vicious civil war that erupted after the Soviet Union dissolved and Soviet Tajikistan became independent. Meeting several times a year, the dialogue group's members moved back and forth across five distinct stages: (1) deciding to engage in dialogue to resolve mutually intolerable problems; (2) coming together to map out the elements of the problems and the relationships that perpetuate the problems; (3) uncovering the underlying dynamics of the relationships and beginning to see ways to change them; (4) planning steps together to change the relationships; and (5) devising ways to implement their plan. In practice, participants may remain at one stage for several meetings and even return to an earlier stage when circumstances change.

Some of the Tajiks from different factions participated in the official negotiations that began in 1994, after the Inter-Tajik Dialogue had met several times (Saunders 1999). Crucial to the conduct of the negotiations and to reaching the final agreement signed in 1997 were changes in the powers supporting the government, Russia, and the opposition, Iran, and the engagement of neighboring countries. In addition, the United Nations and the Organization for Security and Cooperation in Europe, in a subsidiary way, provided mediating services. The activities of all these parties and of the unofficial dialogue group were well coordinated (Saunders 1999; Iji 2001).

In some instances organizers of short-term problem-solving workshops have turned them into a series, constituting a continuing workshop with the same participants. This is the case with the continuing Israeli-Palestinian workshop organized by Rouhana and Kelman (1994). Meeting four times between November 1990 and July 1992, the workshops lasted three or four days and followed ground rules designed to facilitate analytical discussion of the issues that encouraged joint thinking about the conflict. The third-party facilitators, following an intervention model, steered the participants through two major phases: first, the presentation of concerns and needs; then, joint thinking about satisfying them and overcoming the barriers to doing so.

These and earlier workshops involving Israeli Jews and Palestinian Arabs contributed in several ways to the later official negotiations between the Israeli government and the PLO

(Kelman 1995). For example, the understandings about each other's points of views and concerns, and possible ways to reconcile them, provided the basis for officials on each side to believe a mutually acceptable formula could be found. However, the breakdown in negotiations in the fall of 2000 indicates that the support for the negotiations needed to be much wider and deeper, that the agreements previously reached needed to be more completely implemented, and that mutual reassurances about the needs of both being understood needed to be more clearly articulated.

CR efforts also sometimes complement relatively traditional international relations activities when they are carried out simultaneously. One way this occurs is when unofficial tracks parallel official negotiating tracks, as was the case in the Pugwash and Dartmouth meetings during the years of U.S.-Soviet negotiations regarding arms control.

The multiplicity of intermediary efforts, however, can also hamper effective de-escalation and the achievement of enduring, mutually acceptable agreements. This can occur in several ways. Too many uncoordinated efforts can undermine one another as they convey different messages to the adversaries about what different intermediaries have in mind regarding the future course of the conflict. Or one or more of the adversaries may try to play one intermediary against another. In addition, intermediaries may compete for attention and strain the capability of the adversaries' representatives to provide an adequate response.

Nevertheless, in large-scale conflicts various intermediaries and approaches generally need to be combined in order to be effective. If they are well coordinated, their effectiveness enhances the efforts of any one approach. Such coordination includes actions pursued simultaneously and sequentially, as exemplified in the 1989–92 peace process that ended Mozambique's war (Hume 1994). In the course of its missionary and humanitarian work in Mozambique, the Community of Sant'Egidio, a Catholic lay order based in Rome, had developed ties with both the government of Mozambique and the insurgent Mozambican National Resistance (Renamo) forces. Both sides found various possible international governmental organizations to be unacceptable mediators, even as they both began to consider ways of ending the war. Yet Sant'Egidio was accepted to act as a facilitative mediator. Since it was not a state actor, it could provide a setting for negotiations that did not raise issues about the status of the adversaries.

A four-person team acted as mediators: two members of Sant'Egidio, the archbishop of Beira, and a member of the Italian parliament who had previous foreign ministry service. During the negotiations, however, representatives of many governments assisted in the peace process. The Italian government helped with the arrangements and consulted with the negotiating parties. Representatives of the governments of France, Portugal, the United Kingdom, and the United States and representatives of the United Nations consulted with the mediators and with representatives of Renamo and the Mozambican government; in 1992 the representatives joined the formal negotiations as observers. In addition, the governments of neighboring countries contributed to the process. For example, President Robert Mugabe of Zimbabwe helped arrange the first meeting and handshake between President Joaquim Chissano of Mozambique and Renamo leader Afonso Dhlakama. In addition, nongovernmental organizations, including those providing humanitarian assistance, actively consulted during the negotiations. As the process evolved, the various intermediaries consulted with one another and coordinated their efforts. A peace agreement was signed in Rome on October 4, 1992.

CONCLUSION

Some disagreements about what can and should be done regarding specific conflicts usually arise from strongly held values. People assign different priorities to values, such as achieving and maintaining freedom or economic well-being and upholding the value of social justice or avoiding deadly violence. The priority given to such values affects preferences about the timing of de-escalation and peacemaking efforts, for example, whether to equalize the power differential between belligerents before trying to settle the conflict. Values also affect preferences about which parties should participate in negotiating a settlement; for example, in deciding whether to exclude especially hard-line factions on one or more sides.

At present, when so many peoples in the world seek to realize their own values, choices must be made among conflicting values. Such trade-offs inevitably pose moral dilemmas. For example, how much pain and suffering should be borne (and by whom) to continue fighting to perhaps gain a better settlement later? The CR approach cannot solve such moral dilemmas. However, CR tends to favor long-term processes and outcomes that take into account all sides of a conflict and that maximize the participation of the people directly affected.

CR is a vigorous, evolving field of endeavor, encompassing a great variety of perspectives and methods; its many advocates are familiar with interdisciplinary strife as well as cooperation. The diversity is natural and even beneficial, since no single perspective or method suits every conflict during every phase of its course. A familiarity with the many possible methods of CR is valuable, since proper policymaking in response to conflict requires a large repertoire of possible strategies and techniques. Some are suitable for one person or organization and not another, and rarely can any single person or group transform a conflict or resolve it. Many people contribute a bit, and in this new globalized era of relative political instability among and within nation-states, many more people must contribute if destructive conflicts and oppressive outcomes are to be avoided or reduced.

APPENDIX: SIGNIFICANT PUBLICATIONS AND EVENTS IN THE GROWTH OF CONFLICT RESOLUTION

1942 Mary Parker Follett, *Dynamic Administration*

Quincy Wright, *A Study of War*

National War Labor Board established

1947 Federal Mediation and Conciliation Service established as independent agency

1948 UN Educational, Scientific, and Cultural Organization initiates Project on Tensions Affecting International Understanding

1952 Elmore Jackson, *Meeting of Minds: A Way to Peace through Mediation*

1956 Lewis Coser, *The Functions of Social Conflict*

1957 *Journal of Conflict Resolution*, based at the University of Michigan, begins publication

Karl Deutsch et al., *Political Community and the North Atlantic Area*

Pugwash Conferences on Science and World Affairs holds first meeting

1959 Center for Research on Conflict Resolution established at the University of Michigan

International Peace Research Institute (PRIO) founded in Oslo, Norway

1960 Lewis Richardson, *Statistics of Deadly Quarrels*

Thomas Schelling, *The Strategy of Conflict*

1961 Theodore F. Lentz, *Towards a Science of Peace*

1962 Kenneth Boulding, *Conflict and Defense*

Charles E. Osgood, *An Alternative to War and Surrender*

1964 *Journal of Peace Research* begins publication, based at PRIO

International Peace Research Association founded

1965 Anatol Rapoport and A. Chammah, *The Prisoner's Dilemma*

John Burton and others organize a problem-solving workshop with representatives from Malaysia, Indonesia, and Singapore

1966 Muzafer Sherif, *In Common Predicament*

1969 John W. Burton, *Conflict and Communication: The Use of Controlled Communication in International Relations*

1970 Leonard W. Doob, *Resolving Conflict in Africa: The Fermeda Workshop*

Consortium on Peace Research, Education, and Development (COPRED) founded

Program on Nonviolent Conflict and Change established at Syracuse University

1971 Adam Curle, *Making Peace*

1972 J. David Singer and Melvin Small, *The Wages of War, 1816–1965*

1973 Department of Peace Studies, awarding graduate degrees, established at the University of Bradford, England

Morton Deutsch, *The Resolution of Conflict: Constructive and Destructive Processes*

Louis Kriesberg, *The Sociology of Social Conflicts* (*Social Conflicts*, 1982 rev. ed.)

Gene Sharp, *The Politics of Nonviolent Action*

Society of Professionals in Dispute Resolution (SPIDR) holds inaugural conference

1979 P. H. Gulliver, *Disputes and Negotiations: A Cross-Cultural Perspective*

1981 Roger Fisher and William Ury, *Getting to YES*

1983 National Conference on Peacemaking and Conflict Resolution (NCPCR) holds first meeting

1984 United States Institute of Peace founded

Robert Axelrod, *The Evolution of Cooperation*

The William and Flora Hewlett Foundation establishes a program to support work in conflict resolution theory and practice

1985 Saadia Touval and I. William Zartman, eds., *International Mediation in Theory and Practice*

I. William Zartman, *Ripe for Resolution: Conflict and Intervention in Africa*

The Network for Community Justice and Conflict Resolution established in Canada

1986   Christopher W. Moore, *The Mediation Process*

1987   Lawrence Susskind and Jeffrey Cruikshank, *Breaking the Impasse*

George Mason University begins offering a Ph.D. program in conflict resolution

1989   Kenneth Kressel and Dean G. Pruitt, eds., *Mediation Research*

Partners for Democratic Change founded, linking university-based national centers in Sofia, Prague, Bratislava, Budapest, Warsaw, and Moscow

1992   Instituto Peruano de Resolución de Conflictos, Negociación, y Mediación (IPREEECONM) established in Peru

1993   Marc Howard Ross, *The Management of Conflict: Interpretations and Interests in Comparative Perspective*

1994   Anita Taylor and Judi Beinstein Miller, eds., *Conflict and Gender*

1995   John Paul Lederach, *Preparing for Peace: Conflict Transformation across Cultures*

Organization for Security and Cooperation in Europe established as a primary instrument for early warning, conflict prevention, and crisis management

1996   South African Truth and Reconciliation Commission established

Fen Osler Hampson, *Nurturing Peace: Why Peace Settlements Succeed or Fail*

Michael S. Lund, *Preventing Violent Conflicts*

1998   Eugene Weiner, ed., *The Handbook of Interethnic Coexistence*

2000   Elise Boulding, *Cultures of Peace: The Hidden Side of History*

Johan Galtung, Carl G. Jacobsen, Kai Frithjof Brand-Jacobsen, and Finn Tschudi, *Searching for Peace*

REFERENCES

Ackermann, Alice. 2000. *Making Peace Prevail: Preventing Violent Conflict in Macedonia.* Syracuse, N.Y.: Syracuse University Press.

Adler, Peter S. 1987. "Is ADR a Social Movement?" *Negotiation Journal* 3, no. 1: 59–66.

Avruch, Kevin. 1998. *Culture and Conflict Resolution.* Washington, D.C.: United States Institute of Peace Press.

Axelrod, Robert. 1984. *The Evolution of Cooperation.* New York: Basic Books.

Bercovitch, Jacob, ed. 1996. *Resolving International Conflicts: The Theory and Practice of Mediation.* Boulder, Colo.: Lynne Rienner.

Boulding, Elise. 2000. *Cultures of Peace: The Hidden Side of History.* Syracuse, N.Y.: Syracuse University Press.

Boulding, Kenneth. 1962. *Conflict and Defense.* New York: Harper and Row.

———. 1989. *Three Faces of Power.* Beverly Hills, Calif.: Sage.

Brecher, Michael. 1993. *Crises in World Politics.* Oxford: Pergamon.

Brinton, Crane. 1938. *The Anatomy of Revolution.* New York: W. W. Norton.

Brockner, Joel, and Jeffrey Z. Rubin. 1985. *Entrapment in Escalating Conflicts.* New York: Springer-Verlag.

Burton, John. 1969. *Conflict and Communication: The Use of Controlled Communication in International Relations.* London: Macmillan.

———. 1990. *Conflict: Resolution and Provention.* New York: St. Martin's Press.

Carnegie Commission on Preventing Deadly Conflict. 1997. *Final Report of the Carnegie Commission on Preventing Deadly Conflict.* New York: Carnegie Corporation.

Chatfield, Charles, Ronald Pagnucco, and Jackie Smith, eds. 1996. *Solidarity beyond the State: The Dynamics of Transnational Social Movements.* Syracuse, N.Y.: Syracuse University Press.

Chufrin, Gennady I., and Harold H. Saunders. 1993. "A Public Peace Process." *Negotiation Journal* 9, no. 2: 155–177.

Cohen, Raymond. 1991. *Negotiating across Cultures.* Washington, D.C.: United States Institute of Peace Press. (Rev. ed., 1997.)

Coleman, James. 1957. *Community Conflict.* New York: Free Press.

Cortright, David, and George Lopez, with Richard W. Conroy, Jaleh Dashti-Gibson, and Julia Wagler. 2000. *The Sanctions Decade: Assessing UN Strategies* in the 1990s. Boulder, Colo., and London: Lynne Rienner.

Coser, Lewis. 1956. *The Functions of Social Conflict.* New York: Free Press.

Curle, Adam. 1971. *Making Peace.* London: Tavistock.

Dahrendorf, Ralf. 1959. *Class and Class Conflict in Industrial Society.* Stanford: Stanford University Press.

Damrosch, Lori F. 1993. *Enforcing Restraint: Collective Intervention in Internal Conflicts.* New York: Council on Foreign Relations.

Deng, Francis, et al. 1996. *Sovereignty as Responsibility.* Washington, D.C.: Brookings Institution.

Deutsch, Karl, et al. 1957. *Political Community and the North Atlantic Area.* Princeton, N.J.: Princeton University Press.

Deutsch, Morton, 1973. *The Resolution of Conflict: Constructive and Destructive Processes.* New Haven, Conn.: Yale University Press.

Doob, Leonard W., ed. 1970. *Resolving Conflict in Africa: The Fermeda Workshop.* New Haven, Conn.: Yale University Press.

Druckman, Daniel, ed. 1977. *Negotiations: Social-Psychological Perspectives.* Beverly Hills, Calif.: Sage.

Etzioni, Amitai. 1967. "The Kennedy Experiment." *Western Political Quarterly* 20 (June): 361–380.

Faure, Guy Olivier, and Jeffrey Z. Rubin, eds. 1993. *Culture and Negotiation.* Beverly Hills, Calif.: Sage.

Fisher, Roger, and William Ury. 1981. *Getting to YES: Negotiating Agreement without Giving In.* Boston: Houghton Mifflin.

Fisher, Ronald F. 1996. *Interactive Conflict Resolution: Pioneers, Potential, and Prospects.* Syracuse, N.Y.: Syracuse University Press.

Galtung, Johan, Carl G. Jacobsen, Kai Frithjof Brand-Jacobsen, and Finn Tschudi. 2000. *Searching for Peace.* London and Sterling, Va.: Pluto.

Goldstein, Joshua S., and John R. Freeman. 1990. *Three-Way Street: Strategic Reciprocity in World Politics.* Chicago: University of Chicago Press.

Gopin, Marc. 2000. *Between Eden and Armageddon: The Future of Religion, Violence, and Peacemaking.* New York and London: Oxford University Press.

Gulliver, P. H. 1979. *Disputes and Negotiations: A Cross-Cultural Perspective.* New York: Academic Press.

Gurr, Ted Robert. 2000. *Peoples versus States: Minorities at Risk in the New Century.* Washington, D.C.: United States Institute of Peace Press.

Haas, Ernst B. 1958. *The Uniting of Europe.* Stanford, Calif.: Stanford University Press.

Hampson, Fen Osler. 1996. *Nurturing Peace: Why Peace Settlements Succeed or Fail.* Washington, D.C.: United States Institute of Peace Press.

Harris, Adrienne, and Ynestra King, eds. 1989. *Rocking the Ship of State: Toward a Feminist Peace Politics.* Boulder, Colo.: Westview Press.

Harty, Martha, and John Modell. 1991. "The First Conflict Resolution Movement, 1956–1971: An Attempt to Institutionalize Applied Interdisciplinary Social Science." *Journal of Conflict Resolution* 35 no. 4: 720–758.

Hume, Cameron. 1994. *Ending Mozambique's War.* Washington, D.C.: United States Institute of Peace Press.

Iji, Tetsuro. 2001. "International Mediation in Tajikistan: The 1997 Peace Agreement." Paper presented at the annual convention of the International Studies Association, Chicago, February 22, 2001.

Iklé, Fred Charles. 1964. *How Nations Negotiate.* New York: Harper and Row.

Isard, Walter. 1988. *Arms Races, Arms Control, and Conflict Analysis: Contributions from Peace Science and Peace Economics.* New York: Cambridge University Press.

Jackson, Elmore. 1952. *Meeting of Minds: A Way to Peace through Mediation.* New York: McGraw-Hill.

Janis, Irving L. 1972. *Victims of Groupthink.* Boston: Houghton Mifflin.

Jervis, Robert. 1976. *Perception and Misperception in International Politics.* Princeton, N.J.: Princeton University Press.

Jervis, Robert, Richard Ned Lebow, and Janice Stein. 1985. *Psychology and Deterrence.* Baltimore: Johns Hopkins University Press.

Kacowicz, Arie M., Yaacov Bar-Siman Tove, Ole Elgstrom, and Magnus Jerneck, eds. 2000. *Stable Peace among Nations.* Lanham, Md.: Rowman and Littlefield.

Keashly, Loraleigh, and Ronald J. Fisher. 1995. "Complementarity and Coordination of Conflict Interventions: Taking a Contingency Perspective." In *Resolving International Conflicts,* ed. Jacob Bercovitch. Boulder, Colo.: Lynne Rienner.

Kelley, Harold, and John Michela. 1980. "Attribution Theory and Research." *Annual Review of Psychology* 31: 457–501.

Kelman, Herbert C. 1992. "Informal Mediation by the Scholar Practitioner." In *Mediation in International Relations,* ed. Jacob Bercovitch and Jeffrey Z. Rubin. New York: St. Martin's Press.

———. 1995. "Contributions of an Unofficial Conflict Resolution Effort to the Israeli-Palestinian Breakthrough." *Negotiation Journal* 11, no. 1: 19–27.

Kolb, Deborah M., et al. 1994. *When Talk Works: Profiles of Mediators.* San Francisco: Jossey-Bass.

Kressel, Kenneth, and Dean G. Pruitt, eds. 1989. *Mediation Research.* San Francisco: Jossey-Bass.

Kriesberg, Louis. 1973. *The Sociology of Social Conflicts.* Englewood Cliffs, N.J.: Prentice-Hall. (Rev. ed., *Social Conflicts,* 1982.)

———. 1992. *International Conflict Resolution: The U.S.-USSR and Middle East Cases.* New Haven, Conn.: Yale University Press.

———. 1995. "Varieties of Mediating Activities and of Mediators." In *Resolving International Conflicts,* ed. Jacob Bercovitch, 219–233. Boulder, Colo.: Lynne Rienner.

———. 1996. "Preventing and Resolving Destructive Communal Conflicts." In *The International Politics of Ethnic Conflict: Theory and Evidence,* ed. Patrick James and David Carment. Pittsburgh: University of Pittsburgh Press.

———. 1998. *Constructive Conflicts: From Escalation to Resolution.* Lanham, Md.: Rowman and Littlefield.

———. 2001. "Mediation and the Transformation of the Israeli-Palestinian Conflict." *Journal of Peace Research* 38 no. 3: 373–392.

Kriesberg, Louis, and Stuart J. Thorson. 1991. *Timing the De-Escalation of International Conflicts.* Syracuse, N.Y.: Syracuse University Press.

Lasswell, Harold D. 1930. *Psychology and Politics.* Chicago: University of Chicago Press.

Laue, James, and Gerald Cormick. 1978. "The Ethics of Intervention in Community Disputes." In *The Ethics of Social Intervention,* ed. Gordon Bermant, Herbert C. Kelman, and Donald P. Warwick. Washington, D.C.: Halsted.

Lederach, John Paul. 1995. *Preparing for Peace: Conflict Transformation across Cultures.* Syracuse, N.Y.: Syracuse University Press.

Leng, Russell J. 1993. *Interstate Crisis Behavior, 1816–1980.* New York: Cambridge University Press.

Lentz, Theodore F. 1961. *Towards a Science of Peace.* New York: Bookman Associates.

Lewin, Kurt. 1948. *Resolving Social Conflicts.* New York: Harper and Brothers.

Lofland, John. 1993. *Polite Protesters: The American Peace Movement of the 1980s.* Syracuse, N.Y.: Syracuse University Press.

Lund, Michael S. 1996. *Preventing Violent Conflicts: A Strategy for Preventive Diplomacy.* Washington, D.C.: United States Institute of Peace Press.

Marullo, Sam, and John Lofland, eds. 1990. *Peace Action in the Eighties.* New Brunswick, N.J.: Rutgers University Press.

McClelland, Charles A. 1983. "Let the User Beware." *International Studies Quarterly* 27: 169–178.

McDonald, John W. 1991. "Further Explorations in Track Two Diplomacy." In *Timing the De-Escalation of International Conflicts,* ed. Louis Kriesberg and Stuart J. Thorson. Syracuse, N.Y.: Syracuse University Press.

Meyer, David S. 1990. *A Winter of Discontent.* New York: Praeger.

Miall, Hugh, Oliver Ramsbotham, and Tom Woodhouse. 1999. *Contemporary Conflict Resolution.* Cambridge: Polity.

Mitchell, Christopher. 2000. *Gestures of Conciliation: Factors Contributing to Successful Olive Branches.* New York: St. Martin's Press.

Mitchell, Christopher R., and K. Webb. 1988. *New Approaches to International Mediation.* Westport, Conn.: Greenwood Press.

Mitrany, David. 1943. *A Working Peace System: An Argument for the Functional Development of International Organization.* New York: Oxford University Press. (Reprinted in 1966 as *A Working Peace System.* Chicago: Quadrangle Books.)

Montville, Joseph V. 1991. "Transnationalism and the Role of Track-Two Diplomacy." In *Approaches to Peace: An Intellectual Map,* ed. W. Scott Thompson and Kenneth M. Jensen. Washington, D.C.: United States Institute of Peace Press.

Nader, Laura, ed. 1965. "The Ethnography of the Law." Special issue of *American Anthropologist* 67, no. 6, part 2 (December).

———. 1991. "Harmony Models and the Construction of Law." In *Conflict Resolution: Cross-Cultural*

Perspectives, ed. Kevin Avruch, Peter W. Black, and Joseph A. Scimecca. New York: Greenwood Press.

Osgood, Charles, 1962. *An Alternative to War or Surrender.* Urbana: University of Illinois Press.

Pentz, Michael J., and Gillian Slovo. 1981. "The Political Significance of Pugwash." In *Knowledge and Power in a Global Society,* ed. Eilliam M. Evan. Beverly Hills, Calif.: Sage.

Princen, Thomas. 1992. *Intermediaries in International Conflict.* Princeton, N.J.: Princeton University Press.

Putnam, Robert. 1988. "Diplomacy and Domestic Politics: The Logic of Two-Level Games." *International Organization* 42 (summer): 427–453.

Rapoport, Anatol, and A. Chammah. 1965. *The Prisoner's Dilemma: A Study in Conflict and Cooperation.* Ann Arbor: University of Michigan Press.

Ray, Larry. 1982. "The Alternative Dispute Resolution Movement." *Peace and Change* 8 (summer): 117–128.

Richardson, Lewis. 1960. *Statistics of Deadly Quarrels.* Pittsburgh: Boxwood Press.

Roethlisberger, Fritz Jules, and William J. Dickson. 1943. *Management and the Worker.* Cambridge, Mass.: Harvard University Press.

Ross, Marc Howard. 1993. *The Management of Conflict: Interpretations and Interests in Comparative Perspective.* New Haven, Conn.: Yale University Press.

Rouhana, Nadim N. 1995. "The Dynamics of Joint Thinking between Adversaries in International Conflict: Phases of the Continuing Problem-Solving Workshop." *Political Psychology* 16, no. 2: 321–345.

Rouhana, Nadim N., and Herbert C. Kelman. 1994. "Promoting Joint Thinking in International Conflicts: An Israeli-Palestinian Continuing Workshop." *Journal of Social Issues* 50, no. 1: 157–178.

Rubenstein, Robert A., and Mary LeCron Foster, eds. 1988. *The Social Dynamics of Peace and Conflict.* Boulder, Colo.: Westview Press.

Salem, Paul, ed. 1997. *Conflict Resolution in the Arab World: Selected Essays.* Beirut: American University of Beirut.

Saunders, Harold H. 1995. "Sustained Dialogue on Tajikistan." *Mind and Human Interaction* 6: 123–135.

———. 1999. *A Public Peace Process: Sustained Dialogue to Transform Racial and Ethnic Conflicts.* New York: St. Martin's Press.

Scheff, Thomas J. 1994. *Bloody Revenge: Emotions, Nationalism, and War.* Boulder, Colo.: Westview Press.

Schelling, Thomas. 1960. *The Strategy of Conflict.* Cambridge, Mass.: Harvard University Press.

Scimecca, Joseph A. 1991. "Conflict Resolution in the United States: The Emergence of a Profession?" In *Conflict Resolution: Cross-Cultural Perspectives,* ed. Kevin Avruch, Peter W. Black, and Joseph A. Scimecca. New York: Greenwood Press.

Sharp, Gene. 1973. *The Politics of Nonviolent Action.* Boston: Porter Sargent.

Sherif, Muzafer. 1966. *In Common Predicament.* Boston: Houghton Mifflin.

Singer, J. David. 1972. "The Correlates of War Project: Interim Report." *World Politics* 24, no. 2: 243–270.

Snyder, G., and P. Diesing. 1977. *Conflict among Nations.* Princeton, N.J.: Princeton University Press.

Stein, Janice Gross, ed. 1989. *Getting to the Table.* Baltimore: Johns Hopkins University Press.

Stephenson, Carolyn M. 1989. "The Evolution of Peace Studies." In *Peace and World Order Studies: A Curriculum Guide,* ed. Michael Klare and Daniel C. Thomas. 5th ed. Boulder, Colo.: Westview Press.

Susskind, Lawrence, and Jeffrey Cruickshank. 1987. *Breaking the Impasse: Consensual Approaches to Resolving Public Disputes.* New York: Basic Books.

Taylor, Anita, and Judi Beinstein Miller, eds. 1994. *Conflict and Gender.* Cresskill, N.J.: Hampton Press.

Tilly, Charles. 1978. *From Mobilization to Revolution.* Reading, Mass.: Addison-Wesley.

Toch, Hans. 1965. *The Social Psychology of Social Movements.* 2d ed. New York: Bobbs Merrill.

Touval, Saadia, and I. William Zartman, eds. 1985. *International Mediation in Theory and Practice.* Boulder, Colo.: Westview Press.

Ury, William L., Jeanne M. Brett, and Stephen B. Goldberg. 1988. *Getting Disputes Resolved.* San Francisco: Jossey-Bass.

Vasquez, John A. 1993. *The War Puzzle.* New York: Cambridge University Press.

Volkan, Vamik D. 1988. *The Need to Have Enemies and Allies.* Northvale, N.J.: Jason Aronson.

Wehr, Paul, Heidi Burgess, and Guy Burgess. 1994. *Justice without Violence*. Boulder, Colo.: Lynne Rienner.

Weiner, Eugene, ed. 1998. *The Handbook of Interethnic Coexistence*. New York: Continuum.

Wright, Quincy. 1942. *A Study of War*. Chicago: University of Chicago Press.

Zartman, I. William. 1987. *Positive Sum: Improving North-South Negotiations*. New York: Transaction Publishers.

————. 1989. *Ripe for Resolution: Conflict and Intervention in Africa*. 2d ed. New York: Oxford University Press.

————, ed. 1978. *The Negotiation Process: Theories and Applications*. Beverly Hills, Calif.: Sage.

————, ed. 1996. *Elusive Peace: Negotiating an End to Civil Wars*. Washington, D.C.: Brookings Institution.

Zartman, I. William, and Jeffrey Z. Rubin. 1996. *Power and Asymmetry in International Negotiations*. Laxenburg, Austria: International Institute of Applied Systems Analysis.

26

International Mediation in the Post–Cold War Era

Saadia Touval and I. William Zartman

INTERNATIONAL CONFLICTS ARE FREQUENTLY the subject of third-party mediation. We do not know how common mediation was in earlier history, but studies of modern international relations indicate that it has been a frequent occurrence for at least two hundred years. It remains so in the present post–Cold War era. Although the end of the Cold War has brought about many changes in international politics, it has reduced neither the incidence of international conflicts nor the tendency of third parties to mediate those conflicts that they find especially troublesome.

"Conflict" here refers to politico-security issues. Typically, in international economic or environmental disputes, rival parties are not as forcefully competitive, nor are the means of conducting the dispute as violent as in politico-security conflicts. Conflicts over politico-security issues take place within a context of power politics, which has a major effect on international mediation. This premise provides the conceptual underpinning of our analysis of the participants' motives in mediation, the conditions that affect the performance and roles of mediators, and the keys to effective mediation of international conflicts. The term "international conflict" refers here both to interstate conflicts and to domestic ones that are affected by the involvement of external parties. When external parties provide political, economic, or military assistance or asylum and bases for actors involved in domestic struggles, domestic conflicts inevitably assume an international dimension.

Mediation is a form of third-party intervention in a conflict. It differs from other forms of third-party intervention in conflicts in that it is not based on the direct use of force and it is not aimed at helping one of the participants to win. Its purpose is to bring the conflict to a settlement that is acceptable to both sides and consistent with the third party's interests. Mediation is a political process with no advance commitment from the parties to accept the mediator's ideas. In this respect, it differs from arbitration, which employs judicial procedure and issues a verdict that the parties have committed themselves beforehand to accept. Mediation is best thought of as a mode of negotiation in which a third party helps the parties find a solution that they cannot find by themselves. To accomplish its purposes, mediation must be made acceptable to the adversaries in the conflict, who must in turn cooperate diplomatically with the intervenor. But mediators often meet initial rejection from the conflicting parties; thus their first diplomatic effort must be to convince the parties of the value of their services before the mediation process can get started.

THE MEDIATOR'S MOTIVES

States use mediation as a foreign policy instrument. Their intervention as mediators is legitimized by the goal of conflict reduction, which they typically proclaim. The desire to make peace, however, is intertwined with other motives best described within the context of power politics. To understand these motives it is most helpful to employ a rational-actor approach, using cost-benefit considerations. Mediators are players in the plot of relations surrounding a conflict, and so they have an interest in its outcome; otherwise, they would not mediate. In view of the considerable investment of political, moral, and material resources that mediation requires and the risks to which mediators expose themselves, motives for mediation must be found as much in domestic and international self-interest as in humanitarian impulses. Mediators are seldom indifferent to the terms being negotiated. Not surprisingly, they try to avoid terms not in accord with their own interests, even though mediators' interests usually allow for a wider range of acceptable outcomes than the interests of the parties. Self-interested motivation holds for superpowers, medium-sized powers, and international organizations.

Mediation by States

Mediating states are likely to seek terms that will increase the prospects of stability, deny their rivals opportunities for intervention, earn them the gratitude of one or both parties, or enable them to continue to have a role in future relations in the region. Both defensive and offensive goals can be promoted through mediation, and they often blend together. (For a further discussion of states' interest in managing conflict, see Udalov 1995 and Zartman 1995.) Mediators act defensively when a continuing conflict between others threatens the mediator's interests. An end to the conflict is therefore important to the mediator because of the conflict's effects on the mediator's relations with the disputing parties. For example, if two of the mediator's allies engage in a conflict, it can disrupt and weaken the alliance or strain the parties' relations with the third-party mediator. A conflict between two states may also upset a regional balance or provide opportunities for a rival power to increase its influence by intervening on one side of the conflict.

In some situations, a conflict may threaten to escalate and draw in additional parties. Actors who fear such escalation and expansion may seek to reduce the conflict to avoid becoming involved in hostilities. Mediation in such cases may involve one intervenor or it may be a collective endeavor by two or more states acting within or outside the framework of an international organization. For example, the efforts to mediate the various conflicts arising out of the dissolution of Yugoslavia involved the European Union, the Organization for Security and Cooperation in Europe, NATO, the United Nations, the informal "Contact Group," Russia, and the United States. Even rival powers, protecting their turf, are known to have cooperated and engaged in joint mediation when they feared that continuation of a particular conflict might endanger their security (for example, U.S.-Soviet cooperation on

Laos in 1961–62 and on the Arab-Israeli war in 1973).

The second self-interested motive for mediation is offensive: the desire to extend and increase influence. In this case, the solution of the conflict has no direct importance for the mediator and is only a vehicle for improving relations with one or both parties. A third party may hope to win the gratitude of one or both parties in a conflict, either by helping them out of the conflict or by aiding one of them to achieve better terms in a solution than would otherwise be obtainable. Although the mediator cannot throw its full weight behind one party, it can increase its influence by making the success of the negotiations depend on its involvement and by making each party depend on it to garner concessions from the other party. Mediators can also increase their presence and influence by becoming guarantors of any agreement, which necessarily includes risks and responsibilities.

A number of historical examples illustrate these interests. U.S. mediation in the Rhodesia/Zimbabwe conflict in 1976–79 and the Soviet mediation in 1966 and U.S. mediation in 1999 between India and Pakistan were inspired by a mixture of defensive and offensive motives. From a defensive vantage, the United States feared the Rhodesian conflict would provide opportunities for the Soviet Union to gain influence by supporting the African nationalists. But because the African groups concerned were already politically close to the Soviet Union and China, the U.S. mediation was also an attempt to improve relations with these groups and thus extend American influence.

Soviet mediation between India and Pakistan was partly inspired by the Soviet desire to improve relations with Pakistan, a country that had hitherto been on better terms with the United States and China. The Soviet Union also sought to build its prestige and establish a precedent that would justify future involvement in the affairs of the region. At the same time, there were important defensive motives for Soviet intervention. The Indo-Pakistan conflict provided China an opportunity to extend its influence into Pakistan and thus establish a presence close to the southern borders of the Soviet Union. With the conflict reduced, the opportunity for Chinese expansion would be diminished. U.S. mediation in the same area in 1999 followed the same interests in reverse, augmented by an interest in obtaining a signature to the Nuclear Nonproliferation Treaty from the parties.

The United States has been the most active mediator of international conflicts since 1945 (Touval 1992). This involvement is consistent with an interest-based explanation of mediators' motives. Because the United States feared that conflicts would provide the Soviet Union with opportunities to intervene and expand its influence, the United States often sought to dampen conflict, and mediation was an appropriate instrument to that end. In addition, without reference to the Soviet Union, U.S. help was sometimes solicited by smaller states engaged in conflict because of the United States' power and prestige. Pressed by its friends for support, and always fearful that support for one side in a local conflict would throw the other side into the Soviet embrace, the United States often found that the least risky course in such situations was to mediate between the disputants.

The patterns of interest prompting states to mediate have not changed since the end of the Cold War, although the readiness of third parties to become involved and the political geography of mediatory interventions have been modified. The United States seems less willing to mediate than in the past. Its reluctance to engage in mediation can best be explained by its perception that other peoples' conflicts now pose less of a threat to U.S. security than they did during the Cold War. Russia, on the other hand, has become somewhat more active in areas of the former Soviet

Union, notably in the Caucasus (Nagorno-Karabakh, Georgia-Ossetia). This has become an area where its influence is significant, its interests are predominant, and its security is endangered. A notable shift has been taking place in Western countries, where humanitarian concerns of public opinion have come to play a more important role in shaping foreign policies than in the past. The need to respond to domestic public opinion has sometimes led a government to intervene in foreign conflicts, including civil wars, even when they are not perceived as impinging on its security interests. Since mediation carries fewer costs for intervenors than military action, especially if pursued through international organizations, collective mediation seems to be on the increase. Examples include the mediations in Afghanistan, Haiti, Liberia, Sierra Leone, Angola, Mozambique, Congo, Rwanda, Burundi, Somalia, Sudan, and the former Yugoslavia.

Mediation by Small and Medium-Sized Powers

Mediation by small and medium-sized powers is also motivated by self-interest, some of which is related to domestic issues. Such concerns and interests include the possibility that a conflict may spill over into the mediator's territory; the fear that the local conflict may expand and draw in powerful external actors (India's mediation in Sri Lanka in 1986–87 prior to its military intervention is an example of both these concerns); the reluctance to take sides in a conflict between other nations (Saudi Arabia in many inter-Arab conflicts); the attempt to promote norms that tend to enhance the mediator's own security (the 1963 Ethiopian mediation between Algeria and Morocco concerning the validity of borders inherited from the colonial period); and the assertion of a mediation vocation to build a country's role in regional affairs (Libya's mediation in the Horn of Africa, Costa Rica's mediation in Central America).

Small and medium-sized powers may also wish to enhance their influence and prestige through mediation. Egypt's and Algeria's mediation between Iran and Iraq in 1975 was motivated by the desire to prove their usefulness to both belligerents, as well as to reduce intra-Islamic conflict. Algerian mediation between the United States and Iran on the issue of American hostages seems to have been inspired by the hope that mediation would generate goodwill from the U.S. public toward Algeria and thus help improve relations between Algeria and the United States. This hope was related to U.S. support for Algeria's adversary, Morocco, in the Western Sahara war against the Algerian-supported Polisario movement. Other cases in which states sought to enhance their international standing through mediation include India's attempt to mediate between the United States and the Soviet Union and China in the 1950s; Ghana's effort to mediate in the Vietnam War in 1965–66; and Romania's try at an intermediary role in that same conflict, in U.S.-Soviet relations, and in Arab-Israeli relations (notably in helping to arrange Egyptian president Anwar Sadat's visit to Jerusalem in 1977).

Small and medium states have few alternative foreign policy instruments at their disposal, and mediation increases their usefulness and independence in relation to their stronger allies. Moreover, when pressed to take sides in a conflict, they may seek to escape their predicament by assuming the role of a mediator in the conflict. In the post–Cold War era, small and medium states continue to have a role as mediators. Kenya and Zimbabwe attempted to mediate the Mozambique conflict; Zaire, the Angolan conflict; South Africa, the conflicts in Nigeria, Lesotho, and Swaziland; the Association of South East Asian Nations (ASEAN), the conflict in Cambodia; Norway, the Palestinian-Israeli conflict; and Saudi Arabia the conflicts in Yemen and Lebanon. Many states—including Tanzania, South Africa, Togo, Tunisia, Algeria, Saudi Arabia,

Costa Rica, and Colombia—consider mediation of the conflicts in their regions to be a major element of their foreign policy.

Mediation by International Organizations and NGOs

The motives of international organizations are somewhat more complex than those of states. Peacemaking is the raison d'être of several international organizations and is thus enshrined in their charters. Yet intergovernmental organizations are also subject to the particular policies and interests of their member-states. Accordingly, the United Nations was frequently paralyzed by the Cold War and engaged in peacemaking much less than its charter suggested it should. Some of the mediation efforts that it undertook were smoke screens to conceal the intensity of U.S. involvement (for example, in the Arab-Israeli conflict). Regional organizations were not hindered by the Cold War to the same extent as the United Nations. However, because mediation requires agreement among the organizations' most influential members, as well as acceptance by the parties directly involved, regional organizations were not as actively engaged in peacemaking as they might have been.

The end of the Cold War freed international organizations from their bipolar constraints, and they rushed into mediation and conflict management. As a result, their reputations and resources became overextended and their efforts were not rewarded with the expected quick success. In as short a time, member-states pulled back, blamed the organizations (which they ran), and greatly reduced their mediation activities. On his own, UN secretary-general Boutros Boutros-Ghali sent special representatives to conflict areas; the Organization of African Unity (OAU) added a section on conflict prevention, management, and resolution to the Secretariat; ASEAN took on new mediation roles; and the Inter-Governmental Agency on Drought and Development (IGADD) in

the Horn of Africa, the Southern African Development Community (SADC), the Economic Community of West African States (ECOWAS), and the West African Economic Community (CEAO) mediated conflicts in their midst. Thus, the post–Cold War era has seen new regional organization activity to fill the slack left by the United Nations, plus a gradual reevaluation of UN potential. The UN experiences in Somalia, Rwanda, and Cambodia have shown both the possibilities for mediation by the world organization and the difficulty in separating its role from the specific—indeed, narrow—interests and concerns of leading member-states in the Security Council.

Nonstate mediators, whose interests are not as apparent or suspect as those of the primary players of power politics, nevertheless share motives of self-interest. At the very least nonstate mediators have a role and a reputation to establish or defend and thus an interest in appearing as good and successful mediators. (The concerns of the World Council of Churches and the All-African Conference of Churches in launching their mediation of the Sudanese civil war in 1971 is an interesting example [Assefa 1987], as is the highly motivated work of the Vatican in 1978–84 in mediating the Beagle Channel dispute [Princen 1992] and of the Community of Sant'Egidio in mediating in Mozambique and Algeria [Johnston and Sampson 1994; Zartman, ed. 1995].) Often a nonstate actor's interest extends beyond mediation to establishing a presence and keeping the organization clean and ready for other functions. In this regard, nonstate mediators come very close to state mediators in the nature of their interests.

Concern for peace as a value in and of itself, suspicion of other interested mediators' motives, and perception of the inherent limitations on states' mediating roles have led a variety of nonstate actors to propose themselves as international mediators. Many of these are interested in a particular outcome, not because it affects them directly, but because they believe in its inherent desirability. Thus, the several private agencies striving for usefulness in the Rhodesian and Liberian civil wars were working to find an acceptable path to Zimbabwean independence and to a new political system in Liberia, respectively, not some other outcome. All nonstate actors have an interest in enhancing their positions as useful third parties, not out of any venal egotism but because they believe they have something to offer; furthermore, a reinforcement of their standing and reputation helps them do their job.

THE PARTIES' MOTIVES IN ACCEPTING MEDIATION

Opponents in a conflict face two interrelated questions: whether to accept mediation and, if so, whose offer of mediation to accept. Parties accept intervention because they, like mediators, expect it to work in favor of their interests. The most obvious motive is the expectation that mediation will gain an outcome more favorable than the outcome gained by continued conflict—that is, a way out. The parties also hope that mediation will produce a settlement when direct negotiation is not possible or will provide a more favorable settlement than can be achieved by direct negotiation. Although the adversary may not have a similar assessment, it may accept and cooperate with the mediator if it feels that rejection may cause even greater harm—for example, damaging relations with the would-be mediator, decreasing the chances for an acceptable negotiated outcome, or prolonging a costly conflict. Such considerations sometimes help to induce states to accept intervention even in domestic conflicts (for example, Sri Lanka's acceptance of India's mediation, and Angola's acceptance of U.S. mediation). The parties may also accept mediation in the hope that the intermediary will reduce some of the risks entailed in making concessions and the costs incurred in conflict, protecting their image and reputation as they move toward a compromise. They may also believe a mediator's involvement implies a guarantee for the final agreement, thus reducing the danger of violation by the adversary.

The acceptance of mediation by international organizations can also be premised on the ability of these organizations to bestow normative approval, rather than on their capacity to influence the adversary or arrange for a satisfactory compromise. This factor is present in the case of the United Nations but is perhaps clearest in the case of the International Committee of the Red Cross (ICRC). The ICRC's ability to offer an improved image to a fighting or detaining authority can be a powerful incentive for the parties to accept its presence and services and to accede to its proposals.

Partiality and Acceptability

If the acceptance of mediation is based on a cost-benefit calculation, then the assumption that mediators must be perceived as impartial needs to be revised (Touval 1982). The mediator's impartiality is not as important to the adversaries' decision to accept mediation as is their consideration of the consequences of accepting or rejecting mediation: How will their decision affect the prospects of achieving a favorable outcome? And how will it affect their future relations with the would-be mediator?

Initially, third parties are accepted as mediators only to the extent that they are seen as capable of bringing about acceptable outcomes; then, their subsequent meddling is tolerated because they are already part of the relationship. Although there is no necessary relationship between a mediator's past partiality and its future usefulness, good relations between it and one of the adversaries may in fact be an aid to communicating, to developing creative proposals, and to converging the two parties' positions. Closeness to one party implies the possibility of "delivering" it, thereby stimulating the other party's cooperation. Indeed, the implications of closeness can be carried one step further: since mediators are not likely to be successful (that is, attractive to the other party) if they are perceived as preferring a solution favoring the party to which they are close, a biased mediator's acceptability and success lies in the likelihood of its delivering the party toward which it is biased into an agreement.

Several examples illustrate these points. In the Rhodesia/Zimbabwe mediation in 1976–79, the Africans' belief that British and U.S. sympathies were with the white Rhodesians rendered British and U.S. mediation promising and stimulated African cooperation. In several mediations between Arab parties and Israel, the Arabs' belief that the close U.S.-Israeli ties would enable the United States to deliver Israeli concessions made American mediation attractive to them. In the Tashkent mediation in 1966, the Soviet Union was accepted as a mediator by Pakistan, despite its close relationship with India. Pakistan perceived the Soviet Union to be concerned enough about Pakistan's growing cooperation with China to want to improve its own relationship with Pakistan and close enough to India to bring it into an agreement. The United States accepted Algeria as a mediator in 1979–80 with Iran not because Algeria was considered impartial, but because its ability to gain access to and facilitate the agreement of people close to Khomeini held promise that it might help to release the hostages.

Although they cannot fully side with one party, mediators can allow themselves some latitude in their degree of partiality. This latitude may allow them to express their preference regarding the outcome of the negotiation. In the Zimbabwe and Namibia negotiations, the United States was not indifferent to the nature of the settlement: the outcome had to open the way for majority rule. Although this meant that the United States supported the essence of the African position and, by implication, sought to eliminate the white settlers as a sovereign political actor, the white settlers nevertheless accepted U.S. mediation as a means to get them out of a no-win situation.

An interest in specific outcomes is common in the mediations of international organizations. The United Nations, the OAU, the ICRC, and the Organization of American States (OAS) all have some general norms that they wish to uphold beyond the principle of peaceful settlement. They try to promote solutions that can be interpreted as compatible with the standards of the Geneva Conventions and of their charters and that protect their image as guardians of these standards. Indeed, they can formally condemn parties for deviating from these standards as a means of enforcing them. The European Community, trying to mediate a settlement of the disputes arising out of the dissolution of Yugoslavia in 1991 and concerned about the impending dissolution of the Soviet Union, enunciated the principle of inviolability of internal borders within states, equating their status to that of international borders. On the other hand, the OAU was so strongly attached to the principle of successor state integrity that it was incapable of mediating the Biafran or the Namibian conflict, so strongly attached to the principle of *uti possidetis* (legitimacy of inherited boundaries) that it was unable to mediate the Ogaden war, and so strongly attached to the principle of noninterference in internal affairs that it was unable even to constitute a commission to mediate the Sudanese and Rwandan civil wars.

Acceptance of mediation, whether the mediator is a state or an international organization, is not automatic (Crocker, Hampson, and Aall 1999; Maundi, Khadiagala, Nuameh, Touval, and Zartman 2000). It depends on the promise of attractive outcomes for the parties. When the OAU establishes an ad hoc commission to mediate a dispute, consultation procedures give the parties an implicit say in the composition of the commission. The result is often a balanced slate rather than an impartial commission, because members are likely to seek to protect the interests of their friends and not to form their views solely on the basis of abstract principles.

Independent nonstate agencies, such as the ICRC or the Community of Sant'Egidio, do not have partiality or composition problems. Nevertheless, their acceptance as a mediator is still not automatic. Conflicting parties are not concerned with whether the ICRC or Sant'-Egidio will perform humanitarian functions objectively, but whether the framework of its involvement will further their interests. Thus, states may deny that an armed conflict that would justify an ICRC intervention is occurring or has occurred or that a Sant'Egidio venue for dialogue is appropriate. Yet the legal framework is sometimes subject to negotiation, and the terms of involvement can be influenced by their perceived effect on the interests of the parties, rather than by the latter's perception of the mediator's impartiality.

Mediators must be perceived as having an interest in achieving an outcome acceptable to both sides and as being not so partial as to preclude such an achievement. Again, the question for the parties is not whether the mediator is objective, but whether it can provide an acceptable outcome.

TIMING OF MEDIATION

Since mediators are motivated by self-interest, they will not intervene automatically, but only when they believe a conflict threatens their interests or when they perceive an opportunity to advance their interests. Such threats and opportunities are unlikely to be noticed when there is a mild disagreement between parties. Usually it is only after the conflict escalates that its implications are perceived. By then, the parties are likely to have become committed to their positions and to a confrontational policy, ever reducing the common grounds on which mediation must proceed. For that mediation to succeed, the parties must be disposed to reevaluate their policies.

Two conditions are especially conducive to such reevaluation: mutually hurting stalemates and crises bounded by a deadline or, to use a metaphor, plateaus and precipices (Zartman 1989). A mutually hurting stalemate begins when one side realizes that it is unable to achieve its aims, resolve the problem, or win the conflict by itself; the stalemate is completed when the other side reaches a similar conclusion. Each party must begin to feel uncomfortable in the costly dead end that it has reached. Both sides must see this plateau not as a momentary resting ground, but as a flat, unpleasant terrain stretching into the future, providing no later possibilities for decisive escalation or graceful escape.

Mediation plays upon the parties' perceptions of having reached an intolerable situation. Without this perception, the mediator must depend on persuading the parties that breaking out of their deadlock is impossible. Indeed, the mediator may even be required to make it impossible. Thus, deadlock cannot be seen as a temporary stalemate, to be easily resolved in one's favor by a little effort, a big offensive, a gamble, or foreign assistance. Rather, each party must recognize its opponent's strength and its own inability to overcome that strength, as well as the cost of staying in the stalemate.

For the mediator, this means cultivating each side's perception that its unilateral policy option—to take action without negotiation—is a more expensive, less likely way of achieving an acceptable outcome than the policy of negotiation. A plateau is therefore as much a matter of perception as of reality for the parties and as much a subject of persuasion as of timing for the mediator. Successful exploitation of a plateau shifts both sides from a combative mentality to a conciliatory mentality.

A crisis, or precipice, represents the realization that matters are swiftly becoming worse. It implies impending catastrophe, such as probable military defeat or economic collapse. It may be accompanied by a policy dilemma that involves engaging in a major escalation, the outcome of which is unpredictable, or seeking a desperate compromise that threatens one side as much as the other. It may also be a catastrophe that has already taken place or has been narrowly avoided. Whatever its tense (because parties are bound to disagree about the inevitability of an impending event), it marks a time limit to the judgment that "things can't go on like this" (Zartman 1987, 285ff).

For the mediator, the crisis as precipice should reinforce the dangers of the plateau, lest the parties become accustomed to their uncomfortable deadlock. Mediators can manipulate stalemates and crises: they can use them and they can make them. If there is a recognized impending danger, mediators can use it as a warning and as an unpleasant alternative to a negotiated settlement. And if they do not agree that a crisis exists, mediators can work to implant a common perception that it or a mutually hurting stalemate does exist. In its most manipulative role, a mediator may have to create a plateau or a precipice, usually citing pressure from a fourth party. That is what the United States did in 1977 to get the Namibia negotiations started, citing irresistible pressure for sanctions if the sides did not start talking.

Plateau and precipice are precise but perceptional conditions, and they have governed the timing of successful mediation in most cases. They are not self-implementing: they must be seen and seized. Unfortunately, they depend on conflict and its escalation. It would be preferable if the need for a ripe moment could be combined with the desirability of treating conflict early, as sought in preventive diplomacy. To do this, mediators need to develop a perception of stalemate at a low level of conflict, or to develop a sense of responsibility on the part of a government to head off an impending conflict, or to develop an awareness of an opportunity for a better outcome made available through mediation. There are few examples, as yet, of mediators using such tactics successfully.

MODES OF MEDIATORS

Mediators use three modes to marshal the interests of all the involved parties toward a mutually acceptable solution to the conflict. The mediator uses communication, formulation, and manipulation, in that order. Since mediation is helping the parties to do what they cannot do by themselves, each of these three modes refers to a different level of obstacle to the conduct of direct negotiations.

When conflict has made direct contact between parties impossible, thereby preventing the parties from talking to each other and from making concessions without appearing weak or losing face, the mediator can serve as communicator. In this situation, mediators simply act as a conduit, opening contacts and carrying messages. They may be required to help the parties understand the meaning of messages through the distorting dust thrown up by the conflict or to gather the parties' concessions together into a package, without adding to the content. This role is completely procedural, with no substantive contribution by the mediator, and in its simplest form it is completely passive, only carrying out the parties' orders for the delivery of messages. Tact, wording, and sympathy, mixed in equal doses with accuracy and confidentiality, are necessary character traits of the mediator as communicator.

The second mode of mediation requires the mediator to enter into the substance of the negotiation. Since a conflict may not only impede communications between parties but be so encompassing that it prevents them from conceiving ways out of the dispute, the parties need a mediator as formulator. Formulas are the key to a negotiated solution to a conflict; they provide a common understanding of the problem and its solution or a shared notion of justice to govern an outcome. Just as the conflict often prevents the parties from finding imaginative ways out, it may also prevent them from seeing the value of the mediator's suggestions at first hearing. Therefore, the mediator as a formulator often needs to persuade the parties, as well as to suggest solutions to their disputes. Persuasion involves power and therefore requires greater involvement than mere communication. Not only does the mediator get involved in the substance of the issue, but it must also lean on the parties —albeit in the subtlest ways—to adopt its perceptions of a way out. Mediators as successful formulators must be capable of thinking of ways to unblock the thinking of the conflicting parties and to work out imaginative ways to skirt those commitments that constrain the parties.

The third mode requires the mediator to act as a manipulator. Here the mediator assumes the maximum degree of involvement, becoming a party to the solution if not to the dispute. As a manipulator, the mediator uses its power to bring the parties to an agreement, pushing and pulling them away from conflict and into resolution. When the obstacle to agreement is the seemingly paltry size of the outcome, the mediator must persuade the parties of its vision of a solution; it must then take measures to make that solution attractive, enhancing its value by adding benefits to its outcome and presenting it in such a way as to overcome imbalances that may have prevented one of the parties from subscribing to it. The mediator may have to go so far as to improve the absolute attractiveness of the resolution by increasing the unattractiveness of continued conflict, which may mean shoring up one side or condemning another, either of which actions strains the appearance of its own neutrality. This is the role of the "full participant," such as U.S. diplomats played in the 1970s Middle East peace process and in the 1980s Namibian-Angolan negotiations.

Mediation is a triangular relationship. When the mediator operates as a communicator, it operates as a bridge between two contestants, or as a pump on the conduit between them. As a formulator, the mediator assumes a position of greater activity, one which pressures and messages emanate from as well as pass through. As a manipulator, the mediator becomes so active that it calls into question the triangular relationship. It may even unite the two adversaries in opposition to the mediator; for example, in the Yemen civil war (1962–70) the two sides resolved their differences in order to oppose Egyptian interference, when Egypt was acting more as an intervenor than as a mediator. But the mediator, by throwing its weight around, threatens and is threatened by the possibility of turning the triangle into a dyad. The mediator's threat to side with one party may bring the other party around, for fear that mediation may end and with it any possibilities for a solution. As a threat to the mediator, each party may try to win the mediator over to its own side to increase its chances of winning rather than of having to come to terms. At the same time, of course, each party may regard the mediator with high suspicion as a potential ally of the other side. Although it makes the mediator's job more difficult, suspicion is good because it keeps the mediator honest.

POWER IN MEDIATION

Power—the ability to move a party in an intended direction—is often referred to in mediation as "leverage." Although leverage is the ticket to mediation, mediators tend to remain relatively powerless throughout the exercise. The extent of the mediator's power depends entirely on the parties, whose acceptance of a mediator depends on its likelihood (potential power) of producing an outcome agreeable to both sides. This circular relationship plagues every mediation exercise. Contrary to a common misperception, mediators are rarely "hired" by the parties; instead, they have to sell their services, based on the prospect of their usefulness and success. From the beginning, the mediator's leverage is at the mercy of the contestants. The parties, whose interest is in winning, view mediation as meddling, unless it produces a favorable outcome. They welcome mediation only to the extent that the mediator has leverage over the other party, and they berate the mediator for trying to exert leverage over them.

A mediator has six sources of leverage: first, persuasion, the ability to portray an alternative future as more favorable than the continuing conflict; second, extraction, the ability to produce an attractive position from each party; third, termination, the ability to withdraw from the mediation; fourth, limitation, the ability to close off parties' alternatives for winning or mediating the conflict; fifth, deprivation, the ability to withhold resources from one side or to shift them to the other; and sixth, gratification, the ability to add resources to the outcome. In every case the effectiveness of the mediator's leverage lies with the parties themselves and is underlain by their need for a solution, a characteristic that makes leverage in mediation difficult to achieve.

Using persuasion, the first source of leverage, the mediator in any mode must be able to point out the attractiveness of conciliation on available terms and the unattractiveness of continued conflict, a purely communicative exercise independent of any resources. Secretary of State Henry Kissinger, whose country was not devoid of resources or the willingness to use them, nevertheless spent long hours painting verbal pictures of the future with and without an agreement for Egyptian, Syrian, and Israeli audiences. His actions may not have been sufficient in the last rounds of the withdrawal negotiations, but they certainly were necessary. President Jimmy Carter's mediations at Camp David in September 1978 and in Cairo and Jerusalem in March 1979 bear the same characteristics of the power and limitations of persuasion.

Mediation is unwelcome until it can extract a proposal from one party that is viewed as favorable by the other. This second source of leverage is the most problematic, yet it is the basis of all mediation. The crucial moment in mediation comes when the mediator asks a party's permission to try for the other's agreement to a proposal; this exchange is the heart of the formulation mode. But its success depends on the parties' need for a way out of the impasse of conflict—demonstrating the importance of the mutually hurting stalemate as an element of the ripe moment. Assistant Secretary of State Chester A. Crocker and his team shuttled back and forth between Angola and South Africa in search of attractive proposals to carry to each side, but that exchange was not forthcoming until the conditions of 1988 made the stalemate intolerable to both sides.

The third source of leverage, termination, lies in the mediator's ability to withdraw and leave the parties to their own devices and their continuing conflict. Again, the impact of withdrawal is entirely in the hands of the disputing parties; they may be happy to see the mediator leave, but if the mutually hurting stalemate is present, they will be sensitive to the threat of leaving. However, if the mediator needs a solution more than the parties, it will be unable to threaten termination credibly. Secretary Kissinger brandished the threat in mediating the Golan Heights withdrawal in 1974 and activated it at the second Sinai withdrawal the following year. Another example comes from the 1995 Bosnia Peace Conference at Dayton. It was only after Secretary of State Warren Christopher told the delegations on November 20, the twentieth day of the conference, that in a few hours he would announce that the conference had failed, that the parties finally resolved their remaining differences, bringing the mediation to a successful conclusion. Yet again, Secretary of State James Baker (1999, p. 188) notes about the Madrid peace process the importance of "the threat to . . . lay the dead cat on their doorstep. No one wanted to accept the blame for scuttling the process. Sometimes this felt like the only leverage I had."

The fourth source is the opposite of the previous one and consists of the mediator's ability to block alternative avenues for the parties either to achieve victory or to find other sources of mediation. If the parties can look elsewhere to strengthen their positions or to provide more favorable mediation, the original mediator loses its hold on their attention and commitment to the process. Assistant Secretary of State Crocker kept repeating that his mediation efforts in the Angolan-Namibian conflict were "the only game in town" and, when South Africa tried an alternative route toward the end of the process, he made sure that it would lead nowhere. Eritrea and Ethiopia played off mediators and in the meanwhile secured massive quantities of arms in 1999 to defeat the mediation attempts. As long as the leaders who had seized the capitals of the two Congos in 1997 had the support of the Angolan and other armies, they had no interest in the various attempts to mediate their conflicts with their opposition parties.

The remaining sources of leverage use the conflict and the proposed solution as their fulcrums, thus making manipulation their primary mode of mediation. Leverage derives from the mediator's ability to tilt toward (gratification) or away from (deprivation) a party and thereby to affect the conditions of a stalemate or of movement out of it. The activity may be verbal, such as a vote of condemnation, or more tangible, such as visits, delivery of food aid, or arms shipments. The point of this leverage is to worsen the dilemma of parties rejecting mediation and to keep them in search of a solution.

The mediator may shift weight in order to prevent one party from losing the conflict because the other's victory would produce a less stable and hence less desirable situation. Such activity clearly brings the mediator very close to being a party in the conflict. Arms to Israel and Morocco, down payments on better relations with South Africa, and abstentions on UN votes are examples of U.S. shifts-in-weight during various mediation processes. The Soviet Union threatened to shift weight away from India in the Security Council debate on the Indo-Pakistan war, and Britain threatened to shift weight against the Patriotic Front in Rhodesia. Threats of this kind

are effective only to the degree that they are believed.

The specific form of gratification is the side payment, the subject to which the term "leverage" is usually applied. As weight shifts affect the continuing conflict, side payments may be needed to augment or enhance the outcome to one or more parties. Side payments require considerable resources and engagement from the mediators; thus, they are rarely made and certainly not the key to successful mediation. Yet when the outcome is not large enough to provide sufficient benefits for both parties or to outweigh the present or anticipated advantages of continued conflict, some source of additional benefits is needed. Side payments may be attached to the outcomes themselves, such as third-party guarantees of financial aid for accomplishing changes required by the agreement, or they may be unrelated to the outcome itself, simply additional benefits that make agreement more attractive. The graduated aid package attached to the Israeli and Egyptian agreement to disengage in the Sinai and then to sign a peace treaty is an example, which in turn gave rise to similar demands in the negotiations between Israel and Syria. Sometimes the demand for side payments by the parties may be as extraneous to agreement as is their supply.

Of all these, the principal element of leverage is persuasion—the ability of the mediator to reorient the parties' perceptions. As with any kind of persuasion, the mediator's ability depends on many different referents that are skillfully employed to make conciliation more attractive and continuing conflict less so. These referents may include matters of domestic welfare and political fortunes, risks and costs, prospects of continuing conflict and of moving out of it, reputations, solidity of allies' support, world opinion, and the verdict of history.

The other basic element in leverage is need—the parties' need for a solution that they cannot achieve by themselves, for additional support in regional or global relations, and for a larger package of payoffs to make a conciliatory outcome more attractive. Perception of this need can be enhanced by the mediator, but it cannot be created out of nothing. Side payments with no relation to the outcome of the conflict are effective only insofar as they respond to an overriding need that outweighs the deprivation of concessions on the issues of the conflict itself. Parties can be made aware of needs that they did not recognize before, particularly when the chances of assuaging them seem out of reach. The provision of Cuban troop withdrawal from Angola, which met South Africa's need for a countervailing reward, led to the South African troop and administration withdrawal from Namibia, yet this need was not formulated during the 1970s rounds of the mediation. Persuasion often depends on need, but then need often depends on persuasion.

What do these characteristics say about "powerful" and "powerless" mediators? The common distinction between "interested" and "disinterested" mediators is less solid than might appear. All mediators have interests, most mediators are interested in the conflict in some way, and "biased" mediators may even have an advantage in access to one or both of the parties. If mediation were only persuasion, or "pure" persuasion, it would not matter who practiced it, and entry into the practice would be equally open to any silver-tongued orator. But mediation is more than simple persuasion, and the basis of effective persuasion is the ability to fulfill both tangible and intangible needs of the parties. The mediator's leverage is based therefore on the parties' need for the solution it is able to produce and on its ability to produce attractive solutions from each party.

Although official mediators are usually needed to help conclude agreements between disputing parties, unofficial (that is, nonstate) mediators may be effective persuaders and may be useful in helping to reorient the perceptions of the parties' values and opportunities. If the required mode of mediation is low—limited to communication—and the felt need

for a solution is high in both parties, informal mediation may be all that is necessary to bring the parties to negotiation. However, the higher the required mode, the lower the felt needs, the more structural interests involving a third party, and the more the conflict involves states rather than nonstate actors, the less likely informal mediation can be an effective substitute for the official attention of states. Statesmen are not necessarily better mediators, but they can provide interest- and need-related services that informal mediators cannot handle.

Unofficial mediation in Africa provides a good illustration. Textbook cases of mediation were effected by the World Council of Churches and the All-African Conference of Churches in the southern Sudanese civil war in 1972, and the Community of Sant'Egidio in Mozambique in 1990–92 and Algeria after 1994. The church bodies widened the perceptions of opportunity among the parties and persuaded them to move to resolution. The mediators were not unbiased, having closer ties with the southern Sudanese and Mozambican rebels than with the government, and they were not without means of leverage, being able to threaten a resumption of supplies if the government broke off talks; in Algeria, all they could offer was a venue and encouragement. The stalemates that had been building over the years were reinforced by a mediator-induced perception of an attractive way out for the parties. The nonstate mediator played a major role and deserves credit for the operations; the subsequent collapse of the Sudanese agreement a decade later and the incompleteness of the Algerian démarche were due to other causes, not to a failed mediation. But behind the nonstate mediator in the Sudan stood an international organization—the assistant secretary general of the OAU, Mohamed Sahnoun—and behind him stood a mediator of last resort—the emperor of Ethiopia, Haile Selassie; and around the nonstate mediator in Mozambique stood an array of interested states—the United States, Russia, Italy, Portugal, Kenya,

Zimbabwe, and South Africa. At a number of telling points in the operation, state actors were needed because guarantees that only a state could provide were required. The loneliness of the nonstate mediator in Algeria in 1995 goes far to explain its limited success.

Nearly two decades after the Sudanese venture, a private mediation was attempted in 1990 in a related conflict between the Eritrean rebels and the Ethiopian government. The private mediator was a former head of state, Jimmy Carter, who was perceived in the field as carrying official backing. The démarche responded to an appeal elicited from the parties and was carried out with dedication and skill. It failed because there was no mutually hurting stalemate and because the nature of the conflict changed during the mediation. The success of the Tigrean rebellion caused any ripeness in the previous moment to dissipate. The mediator was unable to persuade the parties of their deadlock or of their need to find a way out or to respond to any of the parties' needs for solutions, support, or side payments. Carter was in contact with heads of state in the region and obtained their sympathy and interest, even their benevolent neutrality during the mediation. But only states could have supplied the missing elements of support and side payments, and even then there was no guarantee that they would have been any more successful than Carter was, especially given the absence of a ripe moment.

An example of a private mediation backed by a state was Carter's intervention in Haiti in 1994. When the ruling junta refused to give up power and transfer it to the elected president, Jean-Bertrand Aristide, as demanded by the United Nations, Carter went to Haiti, persuaded the junta leaders to withdraw, and negotiated the terms of their withdrawal. Carter succeeded this time mainly because his mediation took place hours before the scheduled launch of a U.S. military invasion intended to remove the junta by force and because political credibility was added by the participation of

Senator Sam Nunn, chairman of the Senate Armed Services Committee, and General Colin Powell, former chairman of the Joint Chiefs of Staff.

Many other mediations have benefited from a reversal of the roles portrayed in the Horn and in Haiti, that is, from informal support and assistance in a mediation performed by a state actor. In Zimbabwe, and more broadly in the Arab-Israeli dispute, many private efforts have helped strengthen the context and prepare the terrain for official mediation. Although any efforts to improve premediation conditions make a contribution, private efforts actually to mediate in the Northern Irish, Falklands, Cyprus, and current Arab-Israeli conflicts have been notorious failures. Ripe moments and leveraged buy-offs by state mediators are the necessary ingredients, and even they may not be sufficient.

ETHICAL DILEMMAS

Mediators often pursue the double goal of stopping a war and settling the issues in dispute. They will pursue both, trying to end the bloodshed and to devise a settlement that is perceived to be fair by the parties involved, and thus be acceptable and durable.

However, in trying to achieve these goals, mediators are often confronted with the realization that settling the conflict in a manner that is considered fair by the disputants is likely to take a long time. Mediators may therefore face a dilemma of whether or not to give priority to a cease-fire and postpone the settlement of the conflict for later. Viewed somewhat differently, the choice may be seen as one between order and justice; to be sure, the two objectives are closely related. A durable cessation of hostilities requires a peace settlement. Justice requires order, and order, to endure, must be just. But these are long-term historical perspectives. For mediators, the choice is immediate: What should they do next? Should they pursue both objectives simultaneously, or should they give priority to a cease-fire?

The ethical dilemma arises because the issue is not merely one of sequencing. The sequencing has consequences. As we have seen, warring parties are more likely to settle when the continuing confrontation hurts badly and produces grave risks. A cease-fire, ending the bloodshed, is likely to ease the pain and reduce the risks. It will create a tolerable stalemate, a situation that the disputants may find preferable to the alternative of granting the concessions necessary for a compromise settlement. But cease-fires tend to be unstable and are often punctuated by wars and additional bloodshed; examples include the cease-fires between Israel and various Arab parties, between India and Pakistan, between Greeks and Turks in Cyprus, among the rebel groups and governments in Liberia and in the two Congos, and between the warring parties in the former Yugoslavia.

Unfortunately, it is impossible to predict reliably which course of action will ultimately cost more—an early cease-fire that may collapse and be followed by more fighting because the conflict remains unresolved, or a continuation of a war while the search goes on for a definitive settlement of the conflict. An argument for giving priority to a cease-fire is that predictions of the near term are generally more reliable than those of the more distant future. The mediator can be certain that an ongoing war will produce casualties. The proposition that cease-fires break down, leading to the renewal of war and producing higher casualties over the long term, is far less certain. Nevertheless, the dilemma exists.

Another dilemma is whether to facilitate an attainable settlement that violates international norms or to hold out for one that is consistent with principles of justice adopted by the international community. One may argue that mediators of international conflicts should pursue terms that are attainable, even if they are attainable mainly because they reflect the balance of power between the adversaries,

rather than jointly held notions of justice. There are two important arguments against such a course of action. One is that such a settlement is unlikely to endure. One of the parties (sometimes both) will resent terms that it considers unjust and will seek to overturn them at the earliest opportunity. The other argument concerns the wider ramifications of such settlements for world order. A settlement that is inconsistent with international principles may tend to undermine their validity, creating uncertainties about the norms and thus weakening constraints upon international conduct. In other words, such settlements, while appearing to settle a particular conflict, may cause wider long-term damage by undermining the foundations of international peace and security.

Such a dilemma has been faced by the international community seeking to mediate the conflict in Bosnia. The choice there has been perceived as one between separating the warring parties through a partition and pursuing a settlement that will preserve the integrity of a multiethnic Republic of Bosnia and Herzegovina. Partition has been criticized as tantamount to legitimizing territorial conquests and the consequences of ethnic cleansing, and thus rewarding aggression. Insistence on a settlement respectful of the norm of preserving the integrity of the Bosnian state has been criticized for prolonging the war and thus costing tens of thousands of additional casualties (besides the argument that it is inconsistent with the reluctance of the international community to protect the integrity of the pre-1991 multiethnic Yugoslav state).

The dilemma facing mediators in such situations is stark. What comes first—striving to protect the norm of respect for the integrity of states, trying to teach members of warring ethnic groups (Serbs, Croats, and Bosnian Muslims; Greeks and Turks in Cyprus; southern and northern Sudanese; Armenians and Azeris in Mountainous Karabakh; Tajiks, Uzbeks, and Pushtuns in Afghanistan) to coexist in peace, or saving lives by separating the groups and postponing the search for justice until later?

A good answer would require prescience. It is possible that promoting a settlement that is perhaps attainable but inconsistent with international norms might cause serious long-term injury to international peace and security. Should mediators work for terms that seem attainable, provided they promise to stabilize a cease-fire, despite their corrosive long-term effects? Viewing norms as merely tentative and conditional propositions is destructive to order. But eschewing settlements that do not conform to established norms, even if doing so allows mutual slaughter to continue, is also destructive to peace and order. Such dilemmas are not new. But these and other ethical issues have become pressing for international mediators in recent years. Guidelines for resolving such dilemmas are not easy to come by.

for the parties to live together despite their dispute—it does not provide deep reconciliation or cancel the causes of the conflict. Left again to their own instincts, the parties may well fall out of their mediated settlement, and there are plenty of cases (often unstudied by analysts and practitioners focusing on the moment of mediation) in which the hard-bargained agreement has subsequently fallen apart under changed conditions or revived enmities. For this reason, although the mediator is often tempted to start a process and then slip away as it develops its own momentum, it may in fact be required to be more involved in the regional structure of relations after its mediation than before. Yet it must not be a crutch forever, lest it become a party to the conflict. This is the final challenge and dilemma for mediators: how to disengage from a mediating role without endangering the carefully brokered settlement.

CONCLUSION

More interest and less leverage is involved in third-party mediation than is commonly assumed. Adversarial parties and potential mediators all make an interest calculation that involves much more than the simple settlement of the dispute. Their calculations include relations among the conflicting parties and third parties and the costs and benefits of all of them in both conflict and conciliation. Leverage comes from harnessing those interests and from the third party's ability to play on perceptions of needs, above all on needs for a solution.

Mediation acts as a catalyst to negotiation. It facilitates the settlement of disputes that parties would be able to accomplish on their own, if they were not so absorbed in their conflict. Mediation becomes necessary when the conflict is twice dominant: providing the elements of the dispute and preventing parties from seeking and finding a way out. Even when it is successful, mediation can cut through only some of those layers, providing a means

REFERENCES

Assefa, Hizkias. 1987. *Mediation of Civil Wars.* Boulder, Colo.: Westview Press.

Baker, James A., III. 1999. "The Road to Madrid." In *Herding Cats*, ed. Crocker, Hampson, and Aall.

Chester A. Crocker, Fen Osler Hampson, and Pamela Aall, eds. 1999. *Herding Cats: Multiparty Mediation in a Complex World.* Washington, D.C.: United States Institute of Peace Press.

Johnston, Douglas, and Cynthia Sampson. 1994. *Religion: The Missing Dimension of Statecraft.* New York: Oxford University Press.

Maundi, Mohammed, Gilbert Khadiagala, Kwaku Nuameh, Saadia Touval, and I. William Zartman. 2000. "Entry into Mediation." Unpublished manuscript.

Princen, Thomas. 1992. *Intermediaries in International Conflict.* Princeton, N.J.: Princeton University Press.

Touval, Saadia. 1982. *The Peace Brokers.* Princeton, N.J.: Princeton University Press.

———. 1992. "The Superpowers as Mediators." In *Mediation in International Relations: Multiple Approaches to Conflict Management*, ed. Jacob

Bercovitch and Jeffrey Z. Rubin. New York: Macmillan/St. Martin's Press.

Udalov, Vadim. 1995. "National Interests and Conflict Reduction." In *Cooperative Security: Reducing Third World Wars*, ed. I. William Zartman and Victor Kremenyuk. Syracuse, N.Y.: Syracuse University Press.

Zartman, I. William. 1987. "The Middle East: Ripe Moment?" In *Conflict Management in the Middle East*, ed. G. Ben-Dor and D. Dewitt. Lexington, Mass.: D.C. Heath.

———. 1989. *Ripe for Resolution.* 2d ed. New York: Oxford University Press.

———. 1995. "Systems of World Order and Regional Conflict Reduction." In *Cooperative Security: Reducing Third World Wars*, ed. Zartman and Kremenyuk.

———, ed. 1995. *Elusive Peace: Negotiating an End to Civil Wars.* Washington, D.C.: Brookings Institution.

27

Bargaining and Problem Solving

Two Perspectives on International Negotiation

P. Terrence Hopmann

BARGAINING AND PROBLEM SOLVING: THEORETICAL FOUNDATIONS

The topic of international negotiation has been treated by scholars and practitioners of the diplomatic art for centuries, at least since François de Calières in 1716 and Fortune Barthélémy de Felice in 1778.[1] However, it has only been since about 1960 that the systematic study of negotiations has begun to push the analysis of this fundamental process in international relations beyond a set of ad hoc case studies or the presumption that diplomacy is no more than an art form. The underlying assumption of the traditional case approach is that every negotiation is unique and that no meaningful generalizations about the process can be derived. Others treat negotiations as an art to be mastered only by experienced diplomats who develop a subjective understanding of the process that cannot be conveyed in a meaningful way to those who are uninitiated

in the intricacies of the art form. Neither approach treats negotiations as a topic that can be analyzed in a systematic and generalizable fashion.

This all began to change with the advent of systematic theorizing about international negotiations, beginning with Thomas Schelling's *Strategy of Conflict* in 1960, Anatol Rapoport's *Fights, Games, and Debates* in 1960, and Fred Charles Iklé's *How Nations Negotiate* in 1964.[2] Reliance on formal game theory was more explicit and extensive in the work of both Schelling and Rapoport, whereas Iklé integrated this theoretical orientation with more traditional international relations theory and an extensive set of illustrative cases from the "real world" of international diplomacy. However, all of these early works had in common their foundation in the theory of non-zero-sum, or "mixed-motive," games, in which parties have both competitive and cooperative options available. Mixed-motive negotiations involve situations in which parties seek, in Iklé's classic phrase, "the realization of a common interest where conflicting interests are present."[3]

Even though these early works treated negotiation as a mixed-motive game, almost from the beginning they began to divide into approaches that emphasized the competitive nature of the negotiation process (namely, the effort to advance the interest of one state relative to its rivals) and those that highlighted the more cooperative effort to enlarge the joint interests of both parties simultaneously. Even though the theory of non-zero-sum games allowed for mutual benefits, the game theorists typically noted that parties have to protect themselves from being exploited by others.[4] The need to avoid exploitation means that each party needs to bargain in a competitive fashion in order not to convey the impression to its counterpart that it can easily be taken advantage of.

The key aspects of the negotiation process were characterized by *bargaining,* in which (1) initial offers are made by each party to the other, (2) commitments are made to certain positions in an effort to hold firm, (3) promises of rewards and threats of sanctions are issued to induce other parties to make concessions, (4) concessions are made as one party moves closer to the other, (5) retractions of previous offers and concessions are issued as parties draw apart, and (6) finally, if the dynamics of concession making overcome the pressures to diverge, the parties tend to converge upon agreement somewhere between their opening offers.[5] Alternatively, the centrifugal forces may prevail, producing either a stalemate or the breakdown of negotiations. As Iklé emphasized, at every point in a negotiation each party is confronted with a three-way choice: (1) accepting agreement, (2) continuing to negotiate in the hope of obtaining better terms, or (3) breaking off negotiations.[6] Even if agreement is reached, inequality of resources, of ability to exercise influence, and of bargaining skill may lead to asymmetrical outcomes, but in virtually all cases the outcome will constitute a compromise, falling somewhere between the opening positions of the parties. This process of bargaining has often been summarized as one that produces agreement through "concessions and convergence."[7]

This bargaining paradigm became the dominant approach to the topic of international negotiations in the 1960s and 1970s. It especially tended to become linked with realist interpretations of international politics more broadly, since realism emphasizes the essentially competitive nature of relations among sovereign nation-states in an anarchic international system. In this system, states are always confronted with a security dilemma: threats from other states require that they take defensive positions, which may in turn appear threatening to other parties, requiring them also to adopt defensive positions.[8] This cycle often leads to a spiraling of tensions and conflict among competitive states in a world in which no superior authority is able to guarantee the security of any state. Within the realist paradigm, bargaining offered an alternative to force as a means by which states could advance their national interests in an essentially hostile world.

An alternative to the bargaining framework for the study of international negotiations has also arisen in recent decades, in part associated with the renewed interest in the liberal paradigm in the field of international politics as a whole. Nonetheless, the roots of this new paradigm can also be traced to the early work of the game theorists, especially to Anatol Rapoport. Not being content to stop with a presentation of bargaining models, Rapoport concluded his 1960 book on game theoretic foundations for the analysis of conflict with the following important observation:

> At present game theory has, in my opinion, two important uses, neither of them related to games nor to conflict *directly.* First, game theory stimulates us to think *about* conflict in a novel way. Second, game theory leads to some genuine impasses, that is, to situations where its axiomatic base is shown to be insufficient

for dealing even theoretically with certain types of conflict situations. These impasses set up tensions in the minds of people who care. They must therefore look around for other frameworks into which conflict situations can be cast.[9]

Rapoport thus chose to go beyond formal games and to introduce the concept he called "debate," a joint search for "empathetic understanding" among individuals and for a "domain of validity" in which their interests and understandings overlap. In Rapoport's view, it is only through a process of developing mutual understanding and seeking mutual gains that fundamental conflicts among different belief systems can be resolved peacefully. Through this effort to go beyond bargaining theory and to introduce debate, Rapoport laid the foundations for a second perspective on international negotiations, which has frequently been identified as the *problem-solving* paradigm. Building on the basic assumptions of the traditional bargaining framework, this approach, however, stresses that states do not always have incompatible goals, but they often find themselves in situations where real or perceived conflicts of interest arise. Sometimes these may be due to real differences in goals, but at times they may also be a function of different perceptions or understandings of the issues with which they are grappling, and these sometimes create the *appearance* of implacable hostility. In this paradigm, the parties become trapped in a cycle of hostility that produces common threats to their collective security, and in situations such as these, their joint security can be ensured only by cooperative efforts to advance their common interests. In these instances, problem-solving theorists argue, negotiators ought to search for common ground that will enable them to solve their joint problem in ways that will be beneficial to all parties to a dispute.

In their 1965 book on labor-management negotiations, Richard Walton and Robert McKersie described these two paradigms as "distributive bargaining" and "integrative bargaining."[10] In a mixed-motive game, distributive bargaining refers to that aspect of bargaining in which the interests of the parties are in basic conflict and each party tries to win for itself the largest possible share of whatever value is being divided. By contrast, integrative bargaining refers to a situation in which the parties may jointly enlarge the benefits available to both, so that both may gain from creating a larger amount of "value" to be shared among themselves. Thus, this is sometimes referred to as "win-win" negotiations. This can be viewed through the economists' classic metaphor of a pie: the integrative bargainer emphasizes making the biggest and best possible pie with limited supplies, whereas the distributive bargainer is more concerned with how the pie will be divided after it is baked. In the same vein, James Sebenius has referred to these aspects of negotiations as "value creation," creating a larger supply of value to go around, and "value claiming," in which each individual claims the largest possible share of the values at stake for himself or herself.[11] In trade theory, this is the essential distinction between mercantilists who prefer protectionism to advance the economic interests of one's own state relative to its competitors and liberals who advocate free trade because of its propensity to produce greater welfare for most consumers in most countries participating in a free-trade regime.

The problem-solving perspective has blossomed into a major and distinctive approach to the study and analysis of international negotiations since about 1980, and it has increasingly played an important role in the actual conduct of international negotiations, especially since the end of the Cold War. Of particular significance for the enhanced influence of this paradigm is the work on "principled negotiations" of Roger Fisher, William Ury, and Bruce Patton,[12] which emphasizes basing negotiations on interests rather than on bargaining positions; the "diagnosis-formula-detail" perspective of William Zartman and Maureen Berman,[13] which stresses the importance of first under-standing a problem and then arriving at a general conceptual formula to guide bargaining about details; and the "problem-solving workshops" of John Burton and Herbert Kelman, which seek to facilitate the ability of actors to realize their basic needs and self-identity through informal interactions.[14]

This chapter seeks to compare and elucidate these two perspectives on negotiations.[15] Before we can proceed, however, some basic points need to be made about both the nature of models in general and commonalities shared by most theories of negotiations regardless of the dominant framework. First, the bargaining and problem-solving paradigms are social constructs that are intended to elucidate a much more complex reality. By highlighting certain features of the negotiation process, they necessarily emphasize differences rather than commonalities.

Second, these paradigms constitute what has long been described in the terminology of the nineteenth-century German sociologist Max Weber as "ideal types." As such, they represent pure forms at opposite ends of a continuum, whereas most reality falls somewhere between these two pure versions. Most practitioners of negotiations pick and choose from among the features of both. Nonetheless, they are useful if for no other reason than because certain types of negotiations tend to cluster in one or the other category, and the distinctions between them point to some differences that are both theoretically important and relevant to practitioners.

Third, the paradigm that will be best for negotiation depends largely on the nature of the parties, the issues being negotiated, and a wide range of contextual factors that cannot be discussed fully in a chapter of this length. It is important to emphasize, however, that no one paradigm fits all negotiations and thus adoption of a paradigm should be contingent upon the concrete situation of each particular negotiation. The models may be useful, nonetheless,

in revealing the logical consequences of choosing one paradigm over the other and in helping practitioners of the art of negotiation to be more reflective about the choices that they make in any given set of circumstances.

In addition, the bargaining and problem-solving paradigms share certain basic assumptions about the nature of negotiations. First, negotiation may be defined in both approaches as a dynamic process that occurs when two or more interdependent parties face a conflict of interest or a joint problem that they seek to settle by diplomatic rather than military means. The process by which the parties seek to convert these initial conditions into an agreed outcome (including an "agreement" not to agree and to break off negotiations) is the defining characteristic of negotiation theory. In essence, therefore, negotiation theories focus on the *process* of getting from a mixed-motive situation to an outcome of agreement, stalemate, or nonagreement. The debate between bargaining and problem-solving models focuses on the nature of this process.

Second, in the case of international negotiations, this process is normally carried out by certain individuals given various degrees of latitude to act as representatives of a particular nation-state or other actor on the international stage. States are abstract entities, and they are brought to life by the individuals who act in various capacities on their behalf. On the one hand, these individuals may be highly constrained by a tightly defined "national interest," or, on the other hand, they may have wide-ranging latitude to act as they think best. But in all cases their identity, needs, fears, and hopes as individuals interact with the institutional constraints imposed by the state and with the roles they are assigned as representatives of the state to account for their overall behavior.

Third, the focus in this chapter on negotiation process largely overlooks a number of other factors that may also influence significantly the outcome of negotiations. These factors include the history of the relationship between the parties (for example, whether they are traditional enemies or allies); the nature of the issues (for example, whether they concern issues such as trade or national security); the number of parties (whether bilateral, minilateral [a small number of states, greater than two but typically fewer than ten], or fully multilateral [as in large international organizations or regional and global forums]); the intensity of emotional involvement (for example, whether the very identity of the parties is at stake or if there are merely routine differences of interest).[16]

Fourth, all approaches share certain criteria for evaluating outcomes, and these criteria may be both empirical and normative. Empirically, one may investigate which approach best describes and explains how the negotiation process is actually conducted in international relations. Normatively, one may make claims about which negotiation process is likely to be most efficient and produce the best possible agreements under varying conditions. Thus all negotiations may be modeled in terms of three aspects: (1) the context that defines the conflict or problem that is to be negotiated, (2) the process of negotiating itself, and (3) the outcome, falling along a continuum from complete agreement to intensified conflict.

In order to evaluate the difference between these two approaches, therefore, we must also establish some criteria for evaluating negotiating outcomes against which we can judge the relative capacity of each negotiating approach, not only to produce an agreement, but also to increase the likelihood of arriving at a *desirable* outcome. In general, negotiation outcomes may be evaluated according to four criteria.[17]

1. *Agreement.* The first and most obvious criterion is whether or not the parties reach an agreement. As the subsequent criteria suggest, however, we should not assume that agreement is always good for its own sake; to be valuable, an agreement must leave all parties better off than they would be without an agreement. Iklé has also pointed out that

negotiations may not always be conducted with the primary goal of reaching agreement; they may be pursued instead for "side effects," such as satisfying domestic or international "public opinion."[18] However, I will not consider this issue here and shall instead focus solely on negotiations that ostensibly seek to arrive at a mutually acceptable outcome.

2. *Efficiency.* This refers to the extent to which the parties were able to reach the best possible agreement collectively given the constraints inherent in the situation. An agreement is considered to be inefficient or "suboptimal" if another agreement were possible in which all parties would have considered themselves to be better off. In terms of the economists' metaphor of the pie, this criterion asks whether or not the agreement results in making the largest and best pie possible with the available ingredients.

3. *Equity.* Equity refers to the degree to which the agreement is perceived by the parties as "fair" and "equitable." Of course, fairness is always a subjective concept. As Steven Suranovic suggests, it may include components such as the following: not discriminating in the treatment of the parties on the basis of some irrelevant criteria; distributional equity, in the sense that all parties benefit relatively equally in accordance with some agreed-on standard; universalistic, or "golden rule," considerations, in which each party is willing to be placed in the position of the other and abide by the agreement if he or she were in the other's shoes; and reciprocal fairness, in which all parties perceive that mutually beneficial steps taken by one party were reciprocated by the other parties.[19]

4. *Stability.* The durability of the agreement over time is also important. An agreement may be considered stable if no party has an incentive to defect from the terms of the agreement during its lifetime; indeed, it is most stable when all parties have an interest in seeing that the agreement is fully

implemented. This criterion thus follows from the previous ones in that an agreement will be stable to the extent that each party sees it as beneficial and fair and that it is in each party's interest to implement it fully and faithfully. This may also depend on the degree to which the agreement really resolves rather than papers over the issues underlying the conflict and promotes a more cooperative relationship among the parties over the long term, not only with regard to the issue under negotiation, but also in terms of the relationship itself.

Given these common objectives of any theory about negotiations, the purpose of this chapter is to explore the implications of two different paradigms—bargaining and problem solving—for the analysis of the *process* of international negotiations and to look at how they have found their way into the discourse of contemporary international diplomacy.

THE BARGAINING PARADIGM

The bargaining approach to negotiations focuses primarily on states as represented by a group of negotiators who have to achieve specific national interests. Generally these interests are assumed to be fixed and unitary, and the diplomat's task is to try to maximize those national interests through negotiation. Interests are mapped on the bargaining situation as "preferences," and the outcome of the negotiation may be evaluated according to the amount of "utility" produced for the state by the negotiation's outcome. Utility is generally expressed as falling along a linear continuum, ranked from the highest to lowest amount of value over which the parties are competing; since much of the theory derives from economics, it is not surprising that these models usually treat bargaining situations as if there were a continuous unit of value such as money that could be arrayed on a one-dimensional, linear scale.

Therefore, issues being negotiated fall along a continuum such as that depicted in the horizontal axis of figure 1. The preferences of both parties may then be represented as measures of the gains or losses that they would obtain as the result of a settlement at any point along that issue dimension. These gains and losses are expressed on the vertical axis, with the zero point being the location at which the parties are "indifferent" between agreement and nonagreement: that is, at this point, they see no net gains associated with agreement and no net losses associated with agreement and no net losses. Above this point, an agreement will provide them with positive payoffs, and below this point, they will suffer losses. Thus, the point at which each party's preference line crosses the level of indifference represents the point of minimum acceptable agreement for that actor, beyond which the agreement will produce negative value and thus be unacceptable. Put differently, beyond this point the negotiators believe that they have alternatives that are more attractive than reaching agreement, so they should reject any agreement in this area (to the right of A's minimum point and to the left of B's minimum point in figure 1). In this situation, no agreement is better for the negotiators than one that leaves them worse off, so that any proposal to agree at either end of the issue continuum should be rejected. Alternatively, when the parties' preferences fall above this line of indifference, agreement will be beneficial, and the further the preferences ascend above the line, the more beneficial an agreement will be. While parties naturally prefer the maximum possible benefit relative to the point of indifference, in fact any agreement above the minimum acceptable agreement offers an outcome that is preferable to nonagreement. Thus, in the final analysis, negotiators should be prepared to accept any agreement that leaves them better off than they would be with no agreement.

Furthermore, the space between the minimum acceptable points of the two parties constitutes a range of possible agreements that will

Figure 1. A Simple Model of Two-Party Bargaining

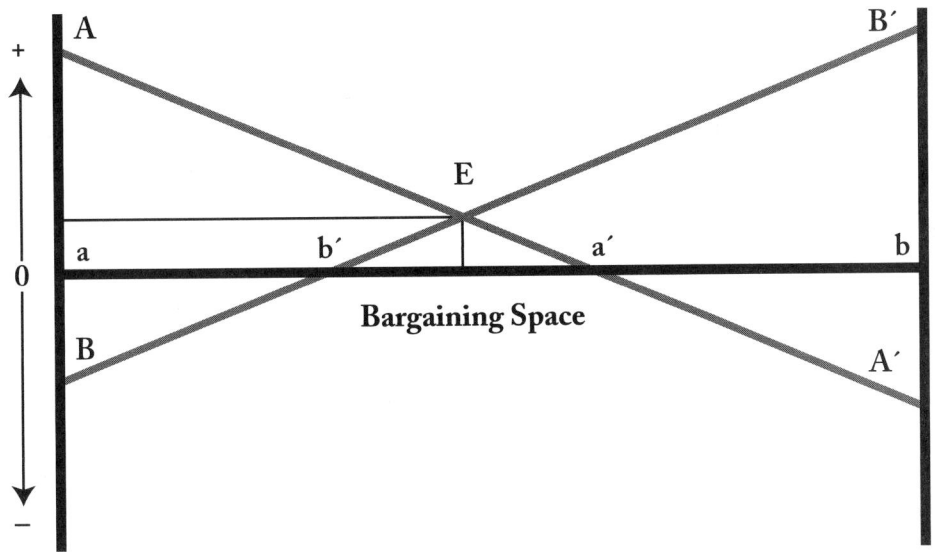

horizontal axis = issue dimension
vertical axis = gains (+) and losses (−) relative to
    nonagreement (0)
A—A′ = A's preference curve
B—B′ = B's preference curve
a = A's preferred outcome

a′ = A's minimum acceptable outcome
b = B's preferred outcome
b′ = B's minimum acceptable outcome
E = point of "equitable" solution, where gains of
      both parties relative to nonagreement are equal

be beneficial to both negotiators, often referred to as "bargaining space." However, in figure 1 the two parties have inverse preferences: party A prefers an agreement to the left end of the bargaining space, whereas party B prefers agreement toward the right; only somewhere in between, where the two preferences intersect, are their net benefits from the agreement equal. If the parties could somehow agree in principle that they wanted a "fair" settlement, and if they had full information, not only about their own preferences but about the other's as well, then they would settle at the point where their preference lines intersect, where gains relative to the points of minimum acceptable agreement are equal for both parties.

However, agreement on the principle of equity is often difficult to achieve, especially in international relations in which one party's

relative gains may put the other party at a long-term disadvantage, such as when the issue involves strategic relations between the parties. Furthermore, since preferences are seldom fully known, bargainers often have an incentive to be deceptive, making the other party believe that they have more attractive alternatives to agreement than they really do. And the party with more desirable alternatives to a negotiated agreement has a bargaining advantage since it can credibly threaten to walk away from the negotiation table without suffering disastrous consequences, whereas a party without good alternatives may feel it needs to bargain indefinitely even if it sees its gains being whittled away to the barest minimum. As Fisher, Ury, and Patton point out, however, no party should be left worse off than it would be by pursuing its "Best Alternative to a Negotiated

Agreement (BATNA)."[20] But this in no way ensures that the outcome will be "fair" or "equitable." Unequal alternatives will generally produce unequal outcomes; the party with better alternatives to a negotiated agreement will generally do better in distributive bargaining than a party with less desirable alternatives.

Finally, in the world of international relations, where resource differences often matter, parties may try to manipulate the preferences of others by threatening them with negative consequences if they do not agree or by promising them rewards if they do agree. Capabilities translate into bargaining power in several ways: first, parties with greater capabilities can generally make their threats and promises more credible to the other party; second, parties have different capacities to actually carry out rewards and punishments. When one country perceives that another has substantial capabilities to carry out punishing actions, for example, and when it also perceives that it has the will to implement its threats and actually invoke the punishments, then the fear of receiving a highly damaging punishment may be enough to make the weaker party concede to the demands of the stronger in order to avoid the punishment. Similarly, the stronger may induce the weaker to make concessions with promises of rewards. In either case, the different capabilities of states tend to translate fairly directly into asymmetrical outcomes favoring the stronger and disadvantaging the weaker.

In bargaining situations, parties often tend to be more concerned about relative gains than absolute gains. In a self-help world, they generally seek the maximum gains for themselves relative to their potential foes. Of course, if they become overly greedy and make demands on their counterparts that fall outside the range of bargaining space, where their opponent would receive negative value, then the counterpart is almost certainly going to reject their demands and may even break off negotiations. Unless they can coerce the other party into compliance, that party will usually opt out of

an unfavorable agreement. And if one party literally forces an agreement on an unwilling partner, then we are operating in the realm of coercive politics rather than negotiations; negotiations presuppose that all parties are at least formally free to accept or reject agreements according to whether or not they serve their own interests.

The goal of a competitive bargainer motivated to seek the highest possible relative gains is to reach agreement just inside the opponent's point of minimum acceptability, where their preferences overlap, but where one party gains a lot and the other gains relatively little. But in theory, as long as the weaker party is making some gains, no matter how small, accepting such an agreement ought to be preferable to walking away and forgoing even the modest benefits of agreement. On the other hand, awareness of the dilemmas of relative gains may make even the weaker party afraid of accepting an agreement that benefits the opponent even more. In this case, one party might forgo an agreement that would produce benefits greater than the status quo or the next best alternative to an agreement, if the party's potential competitors are perceived to be gaining more than they are from the agreement. If both parties are highly sensitive to relative gains, then the range of viable agreement may be reduced to those gains very near the intersection of the preference lines where the relative differences are negligible. The result is that even mutually beneficial agreements may be rejected, and the range of agreement may be narrowed greatly, making mutually acceptable agreements extremely hard to identify, much less consummate.

The process of negotiation is characterized in this approach largely by mutual concessions leading toward some convergence of positions within available bargaining space. The most general finding in research about this process is that it works best when concessions by one party are reciprocated by concessions by the other party. When a reciprocal cycle of mutual concessions is initiated, it may create a dynamic of mutual responsiveness that eventually produces an agreement. Yet, in most circumstances, one of the parties must take the risk of introducing the first concessions to get the cycle started, or else the parties may remain locked in a situation of reciprocal stalemate.[21]

However, parties may be reluctant to offer the first concession for fear that their flexibility will be interpreted by the others as a sign of weakness, so that the latter will try to exploit rather than to reciprocate the concession. If one party succeeds in remaining "firm" while the other behaves "flexibly," the concessions may be one-sided and lead to asymmetrical outcomes if the exploited party—the "sucker"—allows the process to continue until agreement is reached. Therefore, more often than not, a party that feels exploited will try to opt out of the process, resulting in stalemate.

Parties may also try to reinforce their position by making firm commitments to particular positions, attempting to convince the other that it is virtually impossible for them to offer concessions from their announced positions. They may do this by trying to deceive the other about their minimum acceptable point of agreement so as to move the range of possible agreements in a direction favorable to their interests. However, especially when both parties do this, they run the risk of creating a situation in which it "appears" that no range of mutually acceptable agreement exists. If the parties mistake this appearance for reality, they may give up efforts to solve the problem. If true preferences had been revealed, however, a mutually beneficial solution could have readily been found. Of course, a party engaging in deceptive behavior could change this appearance of stalemate by revealing the "truth," but generally negotiators are reluctant to do this since it reduces the credibility of all future bargaining moves.

Furthermore, negotiators who gain a reputation for bargaining in bad faith may undermine the confidence and trust the other party will have in their country's willingness to implement fully and fairly whatever agreement is reached. Parties may often be unwilling to sign an agreement that they know would be in their interest if it were fully implemented when they do not trust the other party to actually carry out its agreements. Mistrust generated by hard or misleading bargaining tactics may thus raise serious doubts about the willingness of deceptive bargainers to abide by whatever agreements they eventually conclude. Thus, for example, during the Cold War years the United States was sometimes reluctant to accept arms control agreements with the Soviet Union, not because those agreements were intrinsically harmful to U.S. interests, but because the U.S. negotiators did not trust their Soviet counterparts to implement fully agreements that they signed.

Negotiators may thus paint themselves into a corner from which they cannot readily escape by their efforts to "win" in the distributive bargaining game, only to discover that they have misjudged the other parties' preferences (or tenacity at deception) and thus created a situation in which no agreement can be achieved. They may find themselves caught between a rock and a hard place: to concede at this point reveals their deception, whereas to hold fast ensures that no agreement will be reached, even one that may have been beneficial. In this way, the desire by one party to get maximum benefit for itself may deprive that party of lesser but nonetheless substantial benefits that otherwise might have resulted had the parties negotiated on the basis of "real" rather than exaggerated preferences and points of minimum acceptable agreement.

On the other hand, if one party is successful in making its commitments credible to the other parties, then the others have only a choice between accepting agreement on the terms announced by the first or rejecting those terms and creating a stalemate. Under these circumstances, the first party may decide to abandon its commitments in order to get the process moving, but in so doing it also undermines the credibility not only of the abandoned commitments but of future commitments as well, with all of the negative consequences already noted. Therefore, parties are often unwilling to back down from their commitments once issued, and this aspect of bargaining can frequently produce stalemate, even though the objective situation would have permitted a wide range of mutually beneficial agreements.

One way of breaking stalemates in distributive bargaining situations is through the use of threats and promises. Threats and promises within the bargaining process are contingent statements by one party to try to get another party to modify its position and to make specific concessions desired by the first party. Specifically, one party may threaten another that it will punish the other or remove a reward if the other does not make the desired concession. Of course, the punishment is implemented only if the other does not comply. And compliance with the threat depends upon whether or not the threatened party perceives that the punishment (or reward forgone) will be more costly than the concession. Alternatively, one party may promise a reward to another if the latter makes a desired concession. In this case, the reward is contingent upon the concession being made, and it is withheld if no concession is forthcoming. Similar to a threat, a promise is effective in inducing concessions if the receiving party believes that the value of the reward will more than offset the costs associated with the concession.

Technically, rational parties should respond the same way to threats and promises. However, psychological theories suggest that promises of rewards or positive inducements are more likely to yield concessions than are threats, which often cause the threatened party to dig in its heels and to refuse to yield.[22] Furthermore, threats and promises may lead to counterthreats and counterpromises that, if they offset each other, may also increase the likelihood of deadlock in the negotiation process. Therefore,

there is no assurance that threats and promises can effectively break stalemates, and when they do, because they are usually one-sided, they increase the likelihood that the outcomes of the negotiation process will be asymmetrical and thus perceived as "unfair" by the party that was compelled to concede in the face of threats or promises.

Finally, stalemates may be broken when a third party intervenes to assist in the coordination of concessions. An effective third party may be able to create simultaneous concessions, so that neither party appears to be weak relative to the other. The third party may coordinate the concession and convergence process so that neither party fears exploitation; indeed, the reciprocity of the process may even be guaranteed by the third party. Thus bargaining is most likely to be effective in the presence of third-party mediators; yet, ironically, when bargaining processes are utilized in international disputes, more often than not there is little or no third-party involvement.

Therefore, commitments, threats, and promises in bargaining processes all run serious risks of creating stalemate. To be successful in reaching agreement, bargaining generally requires reciprocity. Yet reciprocity may be hard to generate when there is little or no trust and no assurance that concessions will be reciprocated more or less proportionately. And the fear of exploitation may induce caution in any party considering initiating concessions, thereby reducing the likelihood that agreement can be achieved. Furthermore, since all parties will seek to minimize their own concessions, outcomes from the bargaining process tend toward the "lowest common denominator" of agreement; in other words, they generally tend to be suboptimal since the caution induced by the process makes it difficult to discover and move toward more efficient, better agreements. This leads to results that approximate the standard of "satisficing" identified by Herbert Simon as a basis for decision making in complex organizations, where many diverse goals need to be accommodated simultaneously.[23]

Finally, since concession making may be asymmetrical—especially when the capabilities of the parties to make commitments, threats, and promises are unequal, often due to differences in power between the parties—the outcome of bargaining also is frequently asymmetrical, so that at least one of the parties may regard the agreement as "unfair." Indeed, bargaining processes generally make it difficult to locate "fair" outcomes. Fairness in bargaining is generally interpreted as "splitting the difference" between the two sides. But the critical question is, "The difference between what?" Naively, many assume that a fair outcome is equidistant between the opening offers of the two sides. But this obviously gives an advantage to the "hard" bargainer who makes the most extreme opening offer, to the disadvantage of a "soft" bargainer who is trying to make a "reasonable" initial offer; that can hardly be called "fair." Most game theorists would argue that a fair solution falls between the minimum acceptable positions of the two parties, where their gains relative to their next best alternative are equal. But in a real negotiation in which these values are unknown, the incentive for each party to exaggerate its alternatives is great. Again, the greater rewards go to the party that distorts its true preferences more, an outcome that would hardly be described as "fair." In short, the tactical maneuvering inherent in bargaining makes "fair" outcomes extremely difficult to discover.

There can be little doubt that the bargaining approach has tended to dominate in most actual international negotiations, especially in those involving issues in which the security and well-being of the state is at stake and bad agreements may undermine essential state interests. Obvious examples of U.S. officials known for their tough bargaining would include Secretary of State Henry Kissinger during the Vietnam peace negotiations in 1968–73 and Ambassador Richard Holbrooke

during the Dayton accords negotiations on Bosnia and Herzegovina in 1995; while both may have occasionally utilized problem-solving techniques, on balance their negotiation repertoire drew heavily from the bargaining tradition.

Furthermore, the fact that policymakers and diplomats from many countries around the world are more familiar with the earlier bargaining approaches to negotiations rather than with the newer alternatives means that different ways of negotiating are seldom considered seriously. Most individuals acting on behalf of states tend to perceive the world largely in realist terms, where negotiations are "won" or "lost" and where relative gains matter, so it should hardly be surprising that approaches reflecting these assumptions are frequently brought to the negotiation table by most experienced diplomats. Even in those cases in which realists adopt some techniques generally associated with problem solving, what most clearly distinguishes them from liberal problem solvers is that their efforts are principally guided by the goal of maximizing their own interests regardless of the needs and interests of others.

The likelihood that bargaining will prevail is also enhanced by an essential paradox of negotiation theory. There is little disagreement that, even within the bargaining framework, two conciliatory negotiators can more readily identify and settle upon mutually beneficial terms than can two competitive negotiators. On the other hand, a "soft" negotiator paired with a "hard" bargainer may be exploited by the latter.[24] And the fear of being exploited may drive even a cooperatively oriented negotiator to resort to "hard" bargaining tactics to parry the attacks of a tough counterpart. Thus the presence of one hard bargainer in a negotiation is often sufficient to drive the entire negotiation into a competitive exercise in which everyone is likely to end up worse off. Of course, even a party desiring a cooperative process and a mutually beneficial outcome may have to protect itself from being forced into an even worse position if the tough party got its way and was able to drive home a hard bargain that would produce a highly asymmetrical outcome. In distributive bargaining, conflictual behavior tends to drive out cooperation, to the detriment of everyone.

THE PROBLEM-SOLVING PARADIGM

The goal of negotiation from the problem-solving perspective is to solve common problems that the parties face in order to benefit everyone. Therefore, the issue under negotiation is best defined not as a conflict between the parties that must be *resolved* but rather as a common problem confronting all parties that must be *solved*. The goal of the problem-solving process is to find a solution to a generally costly problem that will make all parties better off. This means that a key aspect of the problem-solving approach involves the way in which the issue under negotiation is "framed." If the issue is initially conceived in competitive zero-sum terms, the first requirement of problem solving is that it be reframed; it should be treated instead as a problem that affects all parties and can thus be solved only when the parties agree to work together to produce a joint solution.

Roger Fisher has frequently distinguished problem solving from bargaining through reference to how the parties are seated at the negotiating table. In bargaining situations, the parties metaphorically face each other across the table, whereas in problem-solving situations they sit on the same side of the table facing a common enemy—the problem that needs to be solved.[25] This problem-oriented focus views security not as an isolated issue, but as one factor often intertwined with other political, economic, social, and cultural issues. Achieving security depends upon more than considerations of power. This approach emphasizes parties' intentions; it does not dismiss the importance of interests but assumes on the contrary that all parties' primary intention is to realize their interests. It also assumes that each party can be expected to accept and implement agreements that serve its interests, even if the agreements also serve the interests of others at the same time.

Problem solvers emphasize that negotiators should not be content just to divide up some "fixed pie" among themselves. Distributive bargaining is often inadequate for several reasons. First, as economic theory points out, it is "inefficient," producing "suboptimal" outcomes. In this approach, the parties take the value to be negotiated as a fixed commodity, to be divided among themselves. If one is dealing with a fixed amount of a commodity, valued identically by all parties, then there may be no alternative but to negotiate over dividing the pie. So if an estate having purely monetary value is to be divided among heirs, distributive bargaining may be unavoidable. But if there is more than money at stake, and if the heirs value money, property, heirlooms, personal mementos, and the like differently, then the very *differences* in preferences among the items may suggest a way to "enlarge" the value of the estate by seeing that each heir receives what he or she values relatively most highly.

Proponents of problem solving have often illustrated the basic concept using a simple parable in which two women are negotiating over the division of a dozen oranges. At first, the discussion focuses on dividing them equally between the two women, the classic "50 percent" solution. But a third party enters the scene and asks each woman why she wants the oranges. The first answers that she wants to make orange juice, whereas the second announces that she wants to make marmalade. Therefore, the third party proposes peeling all of the oranges and giving the pulp of all twelve oranges to the first woman and all of the peels to the second. This way, each woman gets the full value of all 12 oranges *in terms of her interests* and no one loses any value in the exchange, whereas if each had received six whole oranges and thrown away the peel or the insides, then half of the potential value of the oranges would have been lost. That is, the outcome would have been inefficient, or suboptimal. By taking into account the different value of the oranges for each of the women, the third party doubled the net value of the oranges, creating new value. The issue of the division of value became irrelevant. As Fisher, Ury, and Patton note: "People generally assume that differences between the two parties create the problem. Yet differences also lead to a solution."[26]

Of course, not all disputes have such neat solutions, but the problem-solving approach suggests that the parties should not settle automatically for the value as originally defined by the disputants. Instead, they ought to consider what is at stake for each of them in the dispute and then search for ways to fulfill their needs and interests to the greatest extent possible. While both parties seldom win everything simultaneously—that is, most of the time they need to settle for less than their maximum objectives—it is often possible for them to achieve simultaneously benefits that when aggregated exceed 100 percent of the original value.

The 1978 Camp David negotiations between Israel and Egypt, mediated by President Jimmy Carter of the United States, a good example of a negotiator who frequently adopted a problem-solving approach, may illustrate this point. The major issue under negotiation formally was the division of the Sinai Peninsula, captured by Israel from Egypt in the 1967 war and temporarily partitioned in negotiations brokered by Henry Kissinger in 1974. The maximum positions featured Egypt's claim for the full return of all lands captured by force, whereas Israel insisted on the right to control the Sinai to defend against future Egyptian attacks. However, when Carter asked both sides to explain their primary reasons for wanting the Sinai, there were distinct differences behind their irreconcilable preferences. Egypt wanted the return of the Sinai to restore its

territorial integrity, since it considered all of the Sinai to be part of sovereign Egyptian territory. Israel, by contrast, laid no claims to sovereignty over the Sinai. Israel argued instead that its control was necessary to provide security against terrorist attacks and future invasions from Egyptian military forces massing on Israel's borders in the vast Sinai desert. In the light of these different values, however, an "integrative" solution appeared. The Sinai could be returned to Egyptian sovereignty to restore its full territorial integrity, while it could also be demilitarized under international monitoring to ensure that it could not be used as a future base for either terrorists or Egyptian military units. Thus, an agreement could be fashioned that met the basic needs of both parties simultaneously; this is the essence of the problem-solving, integrative approach to international negotiations.

The process of problem solving also tends to be substantially different from that entailed in traditional bargaining. Its general outlines are more likely to follow a three-phase model proposed by Zartman and Berman: diagnosis, formula, and detail.[27] It is essential that problem solving begin with a diagnosis of the problem, before any positions are taken by the parties and before any solutions are proposed. This approach thus prevents the parties from becoming locked in to fixed, hard positions at the outset of the negotiation, which makes later concession making difficult to achieve. Instead, the parties should focus on the nature and causes of the problem, how it affects them all, and how they can jointly approach a solution. In the later stages of the diagnostic phase, the parties may begin to explore the general outlines of possible solutions without putting anything down in concrete. They may also define in greater detail the nature of the process that they hope to undertake throughout the remainder of the negotiations, since no one negotiation process works well for all problems; therefore, it is important to adapt the negotiation process itself to the nature of the problem. Consistent with the medical metaphor suggested by the term, diagnosis requires the parties to determine what is wrong before they begin to develop a solution; premature locking in on the "cure" may cause the parties to select a negotiation process that may in fact make the problem worse rather than better.

Once the parties have established a joint diagnosis of the problem, including their own interests and needs regarding its solution, they should begin to explore alternative "formulas" that may provide an overarching framework for a solution that takes account of their joint needs and interests. The parties should refrain from making individual proposals to solve the problem, starting with two divergent positions and then attempting to merge them. Instead, they should work together and search through a wide range of possible options that might solve their problem until they find the one best solution for all parties in terms of the criteria of efficiency, equity, and stability. This formula should upgrade rather than distribute the interests of the parties; it should raise the common denominator of agreement to the highest possible level; and it should create the greatest possible collective value. An integrative formula should thus meet the needs of *all* parties to the greatest extent possible. Only after a general formula has been discovered should the parties begin to negotiate over details. At times, however, disagreements about details may require that they return to reconsider the preliminary formula, but at least prior agreement upon a tentative formula provides guidance for the detail phase and assures the parties that their basic needs and interests will be incorporated into any final settlement.

Good formulas are seldom found through exchanging proposals and concessions. Instead they are generally discovered through processes of brainstorming, problem-centered working groups, "seminars" that bring together the disputants and recognized experts on the issues under dispute, and noncommittal explorations of possible options until one good option is found that satisfies everyone. This means that the process of developing formulas is generally best done in informal meetings, away from the glare of public attention. It generally means that negotiators should try to avoid having domestic constituencies eliminate options until they have had a chance to discuss the options with their counterparts informally. This is necessary so that the negotiators can avoid "painting themselves into a corner" by their own rhetoric, which may be picked up by domestic audiences who will then prevent the negotiators from changing their positions in ways that may appear to undermine their previously articulated positions.

Of course, negotiators may resist adopting a problem-solving approach at the outset of negotiations, so that they must often be persuaded to enter into a problem-solving mode. It is largely for this reason that problem-solving negotiations often begin with what is usually referred to as "track-two" diplomacy. Track-two negotiations are usually conducted by politically significant elites who nonetheless are not official agents of their government. As private citizens who are not able to commit their states to agreements, they can think about alternative ways of reframing the problems under negotiation and explore new options for solution that may not otherwise be permissible. The goal of track-two negotiations is to have the informal negotiations conducted by individuals of sufficient status, however, so that any formula for agreement that they discover in the process of brainstorming can then be conveyed to diplomats and political leaders and can thus enter into the more formal, "track-one" negotiations. The Oslo negotiations between Israelis and Palestinians serve as a good example of this kind of process, in which individuals from both countries negotiated informally near Oslo until they found sufficient common ground that could provide a basis for formal negotiations at the interstate level.

In addition to track-two diplomacy, the presence of third-party mediators may substantially increase the ability of parties to enter into a problem-solving process. Mediators may employ a wide range of methods to induce disputing parties to shift from a conflictual to a problem-solving mode. As relatively passive facilitators, they may guarantee both parties that the negotiations will be conducted according to appropriate rules to achieve a level playing field, assuring them that one party will not exploit their collective efforts to find mutually beneficial solutions to their mutual problems. Or they may become more active and attempt to encourage the parties to change their mindsets through using role-playing exercises, brainstorming sessions, or other devices intended to induce cognitive change. Finally, they may play an active and even manipulative role by offering "carrots" to the parties for abiding by the rules of the problem-solving game or threatening them with "sticks" if they try to take advantage of the process.

Even in the absence of track-two negotiations or an outside third party, one of the primary parties may simply insist on utilizing problem-solving techniques. The party may attempt to convince the counterparts that such techniques are in their joint interest, since they increase the likelihood of reaching an agreement that benefits both parties more than would be likely if they stuck to traditional, competitive bargaining with all the risks of suboptimal outcomes, stalemate, or even a break-off of negotiations associated with that approach. Problem-solving negotiations should also focus on serving the basic needs of the parties to a conflict rather than responding primarily to positions defined largely in terms of abstract national interests. Problem solving tends to assume that conflicts, especially those that lead to violence, usually involve more than just the clash of geopolitical interests. Rather, the basic human need for identity—the feeling of belonging to a national, ethnic, or kinship group —and for fundamental personal security in both a material and a spiritual sense underlies many international conflicts. Many of these needs are felt emotionally rather than rationally. Unless the negotiation process addresses these basic, underlying needs directly, it is not likely to produce enduring solutions to the problems at hand. In these kinds of deep-seated conflicts, only a problem-solving orientation is likely to be at all successful in resolving the underlying conflicts rather than simply papering them over.

Similarly, problem solving tends to emphasize that many conflicts contain significant elements of misperception and misunderstanding. Unless the negotiation process is able to get below the surface, unless it can begin to identify those elements of conflict based on misperception rather than on "real" conflicts of interest, it is likely to produce at best only partial or superficial solutions. Bargaining, in which interests are traded off against one another, is not likely to differentiate sufficiently between these varying sources of conflict, and thus its solutions are not likely to respond to the many layers of conflicts. A problem-solving approach thus attempts to distinguish between those aspects of conflicts based on misperception and those based on conflicts of identities or material interests. It requires the parties to empathize with the other parties, to see the world through the eyes of the others as well as through their own. It should encourage the parties to modify their images of one another and of the problem rather than just compromising over different positions as if the conflict were nothing but a contest between objectively different sets of interests.

Proponents of problem solving frequently assert that international regimes and organizations create a set of norms within which negotiations take place that facilitate an atmosphere of cooperation. These institutions may be called upon to mediate disputes or to assist in the collective implementation, verification, and enforcement of agreements. Thus the negotiating behavior of states may be constrained by the institutional context within which negotiations take place. So, for example, negotiations between the United States and Japan on trade issues within the context of the World Trade Organization (WTO) are conditioned by the history, set of prior agreements, and institutional structures already provided by the WTO system. These make it less likely that the two countries will treat their dispute solely as a bilateral conflict of interest, isolated from the institutional context that provides guidelines for resolving disputes of this kind. Contrary to the typical assumptions of bargaining models, states generally do not enter negotiations as unitary, independent, and autonomous actors. Rather, they are frequently participants in international institutions that create a normative context and set of broad understandings of the issues, limit their sovereignty, and constrain many aspects of their behavior, both in the negotiations themselves and in the implementation of negotiated agreements.

Finally, problem solving generally works best in the presence of a neutral third party. Mediators provide several key functions in problem-solving negotiations. First, they manage the process. They do this by setting the rules of the game and preventing the parties from sliding into hard bargaining behaviors or premature closure. They can set up procedures such as brainstorming, in which ideas are thrown out to be discussed in such a way that no one is committed to any particular idea until it has been fully discussed and accepted by all. They can encourage the adoption of procedures that build confidence, create empathy, instill the norm of reciprocity, and overcome misperceptions and misunderstandings. Second, they can be a catalyst for cognitive change, encouraging the parties to reframe the problem until it is defined in a way that makes sense to all parties. Third, they can assist the parties in the process of searching for new options to solve their problems. In some cases, mediators may even draft proposed agreements, submit them to the parties for criticism, and revise them until they meet collective approval.

In short, this analysis suggests that problem-solving approaches may generate agreements that are more efficient, equitable, and stable than is usually possible with traditional distributive bargaining. They can be more efficient because they encourage a search for agreements that strive to enlarge the range of possible solutions to include some possibilities that might advantage all parties simultaneously, rather than split the differences between initial positions. Outcomes are more likely to be perceived as equitable because in problem solving "fairness" is not defined primarily in terms of one's payoffs relative to the other parties, but according to one's own internal, absolute standards—whether all parties realize their basic needs and interests and perceive themselves to be better off with an agreement than they would be without one. This standard enables all parties to realize a satisfactory outcome, and an "equitable" agreement is one in which all parties are satisfied and invidious comparisons among parties are avoided.

Lastly, problem-solving negotiations may promote agreements that are usually more stable and enduring than the often asymmetrical outcomes of bargained agreements. This is in part a consequence of the fact that they are negotiated through a process that builds rather than undermines mutual confidence and trust among the parties. But it is also based on the assumption that parties have an incentive to implement agreements that they perceive to serve their interests. And since the criterion for a successful agreement in problem solving is that it serve the essential interests of all parties simultaneously, the incentives for dragging feet or even actively undermining an agreement are likely to be absent, and all parties should perceive that they have a stake in the successful implementation of whatever agreement has been struck. Thus, advocates of problem solving contend that it not only makes the probability of achieving an agreement greater but also tends to produce *better* agreements in terms of efficiency, equity, and stability.

Of course, problem-solving approaches may not be applicable to all situations in which international negotiations occur. And they face their most severe challenges when a negotiator seeks to employ a problem-solving approach when the counterpart cannot be persuaded to do likewise. Problem solving clearly works best when all parties agree to the basic "rules of the game," approach the issue from a similar perspective, and utilize compatible negotiating processes. Unfortunately, when one party insists on using tactics of hard, distributive bargaining, it may force all others either to adopt a hard bargaining approach or to risk being taken advantage of by the "hard" bargainer.

Proponents of problem solving such as Fisher, Ury, and Patton argue that the best response to a "hard" bargainer is to come back with unconditional cooperation, in an effort to convince the other party to reciprocate and engage in "principled" negotiation.[28] Although this makes a good deal of sense normatively, unfortunately there is very little empirical evidence to validate this assertion. Most research suggests that unconditional cooperation in the face of exploitative behavior produces asymmetrical agreements, almost always to the detriment of the cooperative party. By contrast, some degree of firmness is most likely to deter distributive bargainers from pushing their advantage too far. If parties that wish to search for a mutually beneficial solution can hold their ground in the face of tough bargaining, then there is some chance that they can convince the counterpart to adapt an approach that more closely approximates problem solving. And even if that effort fails, the firm response can guarantee the party an agreement that is at least marginally superior to a minimally acceptable agreement, even if it falls short of a more mutually beneficial outcome that might have been achieved had both parties engaged in problem solving rather than distributive bargaining.

Indeed, most of the research on negotiations has indicated that the dynamic that produces the greatest long-run cooperation is "tit-for-tat" reciprocity, in which cooperative behaviors by one party are immediately reciprocated by the other, and in which conflictual behavior is also immediately retaliated for by a tough response.[29] Of course, this form of reciprocity may cause mutual competition to become "locked in." In this case, it is necessary for one party to break the cycle of pure reciprocity by undertaking some "unilateral initiatives." These initiatives are likely to be successful in breaking the cycle of competition, however, only when they are also reciprocated more or less immediately.[30] Therefore, unconditional cooperativeness in the face of intransigence is likely to reinforce the intransigence, since it may seem to the party using it that "hard" bargaining is successful in extracting concessions from the other, conciliatory, party.

The value of reciprocity is largely due to its predictability, that is, the assurance it provides to each party that its behavior will be reciprocated by the other. By contrast, when a pattern of interactions becomes characterized by uncertainty and confusion, cooperation is likely to break down. One party may try against all odds to return to a cooperative pattern and be exploited by a competitive opponent, or both parties may fall back on a strategy of minimizing maximum losses through behaving competitively. One negotiator may take advantage of the confusion to enhance its relative gains at the expense of its opponent. Or both parties may assume the stance of "defensive positionalists" and both may lose as a consequence. The fundamental paradox of negotiation, therefore, is that the abandonment of problem solving by a cooperatively oriented party may sometimes force the parties not only into distributive bargaining, but also into an especially destructive form of hard bargaining that produces "lose-lose" outcomes.

RECONCILING BARGAINING AND PROBLEM-SOLVING APPROACHES TO NEGOTIATION

Can these competing paradigms be reconciled? Since they represent two rather different approaches to negotiation, at first sight this would seem to be a difficult task. It is evident that the two paradigms represent ends of a continuum between which most actual negotiations are likely to take place, borrowing some features from each in different mixes according to the circumstances. They do, nonetheless, depict fundamentally different "ideal types" of negotiating processes. At a conceptual level there are two ways to help both the analyst and the practitioner of negotiation choose between these two perspectives: the first is practical and the second is theoretical.

Practical Considerations

The practical issues faced by practitioners emphasize that the appropriate approach to negotiation depends on the nature of the issue under negotiation, the preexisting relationship among the parties, and other background factors that establish the context for negotiation. Therefore, the choice depends on fitting the negotiation method to the particular requirements of each different negotiation context rather than trying to apply one approach to many disparate cases. This approach to reconciling bargaining and problem solving takes an essentially pragmatic orientation. It assumes that the "best" method of negotiating is the one that "works" under a particular set of conditions and that no single method works well under all circumstances. The key task, therefore, is to identify those conditions under which a bargaining approach is more likely to be effective than problem solving and vice versa. Several factors are likely to be particularly significant.

Bargaining tends to be an appropriate model for negotiation when there are two or relatively few parties and a single or a few issues, which may more or less be arrayed along divisible continua. Many negotiable issues resemble the classic bargaining problem of a buyer and seller haggling over the price of any good, such as a used car, for example. Each party makes an opening bid and focuses on an undisclosed point of minimal acceptable agreement (BATNA). As long as the minimum points of the parties are not mutually exclusive, there exists between them a range of bargaining space. The primary tasks for the negotiators thus are twofold: (1) to identify the approximate range of bargaining space within which agreement may be reached, and (2) to engage in concession making (perhaps induced by various manipulative tactics) until the positions of the parties converge somewhere in the middle. Furthermore, since there is a range of possible agreements falling along a continuum, there are many possible points of compromise between the positions preferred by each party. In other words, payoffs are easily divided among the parties, and the nature of the problem may not present many options other than some division of value among them.

In cases such as these, bargaining techniques are generally necessary to prevent one party from being exploited because of its apparent flexibility. Prescriptive advice may be useful in assisting the parties to reach agreement by helping negotiators remain flexible in making new offers, in accepting offers of the other party, and in making concessions to the other, while avoiding impasses based on rigid commitments and retractions of previous offers. The major dilemma in these bargaining situations, as noted, derives from the fact that bargaining tactics designed to "win" a larger share of the good for one party may create a stalemate and thus detract from the ability of the parties even to reach agreement, whereas tactics designed to facilitate rapid and efficient consummation of agreements may cause the party using such tactics to receive a smaller share of the gains than might have otherwise been possible. Thus bargaining theory still has an important explanatory and prescriptive role to play: namely, to advise on how to juggle these competing demands of the bargaining situation not only to reach agreement, but to achieve results that the parties will consider reasonably "fair" or "equitable" in terms of some common standards of distributive justice.

Finally, bargaining may often be relevant when at least one of the parties pursues intransigent tactics and when power asymmetries constitute an important factor in the negotiation. In both cases, of course, the weaker or more flexible party should probably first try to persuade the counterpart to adopt a more problem-solving approach if power and hard bargaining tactics are less likely to influence the eventual outcome. Unfortunately, this is not always possible, and, as noted previously, the overwhelming majority of empirical research suggests that under these conditions flexibility and openness may lead to exploitation of the "sucker." In these cases, as Dean Pruitt and Jeffrey Rubin emphasize, a bargaining approach of "firm flexibility" may be preferred, in which one party is firm about its basic interests, refusing to consider agreements that would leave it worse off than without an agreement, while being flexible to explore solutions that are also responsive to the interests of the other.[31]

On the other hand, a great many negotiating problems are not readily susceptible to solution by this kind of bargaining. These kinds of problems tend to have several features that differentiate them from issues more amenable to solution through a concession-convergence process. Under the following conditions, a problem-solving approach to negotiations is more likely to produce favorable outcomes.

1. If there appears to be an absence of bargaining space, which can reflect either a "real" conflict of interest or "misperception" of the situation by one or more parties, then the parties must go beyond pure bargaining in order to open up negotiation space and "discover" options for agreement that may not be evident at first sight. This is particularly relevant in those deep-rooted conflicts that have endured for a long time and are considered intractable. Here integrative formulas must be created or discovered, since the problem as originally defined has long defied solution through standard bargaining techniques.

2. If multiple and complex issues are linked in such a way that they cannot readily be negotiated one by one, then something more than bargaining may be required. Of course, bargaining theory has long included the concept of trade-offs, in which several issues are combined, or "packaged," in such a way that one party "wins" on the issues of greater importance to itself, while the second "wins" on the issues that it considers to be of greater importance than its counterpart.[32] However, when the situation resembles what Robert Keohane and Joseph Nye refer to as "complex interdependence,"[33] resort to inventive exploration of options, brainstorming, logrolling, and the creation of "issue packages" may facilitate reaching agreement.

3. When there are multiple parties whose preferences are different and crosscutting rather than reinforcing, there is usually no well-defined and mutually agreed-on "issue dimension" along which bargaining may occur. Thus multilateral negotiations, especially those with large numbers of parties, have generally proven resistant to negotiation by pure bargaining. Typically, multilateral negotiations involve the creation of coalitions, which are enlarged by finding new supporters, until a consensus is achieved about a possible outcome. In these situations, a process that focuses more on holistic problem solving in the search for resolving formulas rather than bargaining about details is more likely to produce agreements that are perceived as efficient, equitable, and stable by the vast majority of participating states.

4. If there is intense emotional involvement by the parties, if mutual misperceptions are common, if tensions are high, and if the most fundamental needs, identities, and interests are threatened, then the parties' cognitive framing of the problem typically prevents the identification of a clear issue dimension or bargaining space. This requires a process that goes below the superficial treatment of issues as they were initially defined by the parties in order to explore the parties' more profound needs to locate solutions that will help resolve deep-seated conflicts.

Under any of these four conditions, generally some form of creative problem solving may facilitate arriving at good solutions to the issues under negotiation. This process typically includes such features as issue redefinition (aggregating issues or "packaging" trade-offs, disaggregating issues or "fractionating," and reframing issues through "role reversal," "brainstorming," or other "perspective-taking" techniques); basing the outcome on widely recognized principles that suggest mutually beneficial solutions rather than on the result of power-oriented tactics; utilizing third parties or mediators, playing roles ranging from fairly passive "good offices" to actively exerting "influence" on the main conflicting parties to assist them in reaching agreement; and task-oriented group behaviors, including the emergence of efficient leadership and the effective "management of complexity" by the group.[34] These kinds of behaviors may not only create a cooperative negotiating process and produce efficient and mutually beneficial agreements, but also improve the relationships among the parties over the long term, well beyond the duration of the actual negotiations.

Theoretical Considerations

In order to reconcile bargaining and problem solving theoretically, it is helpful to adopt a "metatheoretical" position that views both paradigms as the mental constructs of both theorists and practitioners. This position assumes that the parties themselves have it within their power to define the issues and context and therefore to create the conditions in which negotiations will take place. Since conflicts on the global stage exist almost entirely in the minds of actors, those agents create, or "construct," their own image of the negotiation context. The agents, therefore, adopt collectively an approach to conflict resolution that will work well for them. In short, this argument is consistent with "constructivist" interpretations of international politics. It asserts that both conflict and negotiations are socially constructed processes; the mental process by which actors create their images may be the determinative factor in deciding whether the bargaining or the problem-solving paradigm, or some third option not yet fully developed, is likely to emerge as the dominant view of negotiation.

While generally acknowledging the presence of an objective reality to international politics not dependent on the observer, constructivists also assert that what we make of that "reality" —how we interpret it—is socially constructed. Thus the theoretical debate between realism and liberalism about international politics is largely a question of whether the agents who engage in the day-to-day business of conducting international relations conceive of the world as essentially anarchic and conflictual or whether they see themselves acting within an international "society" based on broadly shared norms of behavior and accordingly act on the belief that cooperation among states is possible and desirable.[35] The fact that statesmen have for centuries acted in accordance with a socially constructed set of rules—the core tenets of realism—has in fact "created" a world that behaves very much as realists would predict. Thus, the empirical evidence that has been generated for decades by scholars to validate the realist model, for example, may do nothing more than confirm the dominant role played by realist ideas as a guide to the conduct of international diplomacy, among them the belief in the utility of bargaining as the basis for all international negotiations. It does not follow from this, however, that realism is inherently true, that it has uncovered a set of necessary or objective laws of international politics. Nor does it follow that the world is impervious to change when and if political actors believe in a different set of assumptions and rules about how to act in international politics.

Applied to negotiations, the constructivist approach suggests that bargaining and problem solving represent two different social constructions, neither of which describes or explains some underlying reality. Instead, the prevalence of bargaining in a large number of historical cases most likely reflects the beliefs of political actors, operating within a social milieu often referred to in shorthand as the "international community," about the nature of negotiations, and indeed about the nature of international politics altogether. The fact that a belief in the validity of the bargaining approach to negotiations, which tends to be associated with realism, has in the past been broadly accepted and internalized by diplomats actually engaged in the day-to-day process of negotiating may be the key to explaining its prevalence in the everyday world of international politics throughout much of recent history. However, this is not necessarily testimony for the general validity, much less the preferability, of this paradigm, and recent experience indicates that a new generation of diplomats, more often familiar with and sometimes trained in the use of problem-solving methods, has begun to have an increasing impact on the actual conduct of diplomacy.[36]

A self-fulfilling prophecy may be at work here. Since most senior diplomats were trained during the period when the realist paradigm was dominant in the field of international relations, it is likely that whatever theoretical analysis of negotiations they might have encountered would have been heavily laden with the content of bargaining theory. Believing it to be valid, along with the realist perspective

to which it is closely related conceptually, they have tended to negotiate *as if* bargaining constituted the only appropriate approach to international negotiations. And when most negotiators subscribe to and act in accordance with the expectations of a single paradigm, it should hardly be surprising that empirical analysis reveals evidence to support this paradigm. But this occurs not because this paradigm is inherently superior to all others, but because it is the only one that has been internalized within the belief systems of most relevant actors. Finding evidence to support the validity of the paradigm in their own behavior and in the behavior of those with whom they interact, they implicitly confirm the validity of the paradigm within their own minds and continue to act according to its precepts. As the prevailing ideas and paradigms about the negotiation process change, however, so the actual practice of diplomacy may eventually change as a direct consequence.

The constructivist critique does not imply, however, that the rules of realism or the tactics of positional bargaining can be ignored in the practice of diplomacy. On the contrary, when one party attempts to "buck the system" and follow a different set of rules of the game than the other actors in international politics, the fact that these rules did not constitute some underlying structural reality may be no consolation. The party that ignores the prevailing rules of the game may simply emerge as the loser in a world where everyone else plays according to those rules.

The constructivist approach also sensitizes us to the fact that the rules of the game are not immutable, since they are socially constructed rather than dictated by fixed structures over which political agents have no control. Realists note, of course, that the rules of the realist game have been around more or less for twenty-five centuries, at least since the writing of Thucydides in the fifth century B.C. But even that fact alone does not prevent human beings from "constructing" different social worlds, including ones in which power and violence no longer play a dominant role. Social norms *do* change: two hundred years ago, slavery was widely held as an inevitable part of human society as set down by "natural law," a view inherited from the world of the classical Greeks of the fifth century B.C. While slavery still exists in a few isolated locations in the year 2000, nowhere is it still regarded as "natural," "inevitable," "legitimate," or morally "right."

This constructivist view also suggests that assumptions about the presumed laws of international politics can also change, albeit gradually, and new paradigms may replace old ones as the dominant "social construction" or widely shared weltanschauung (worldview) held by actors within the international community. Especially since the end of the Cold War, liberal ideas have gained increasing currency in the regular practice of international politics, and in a closely related fashion, problem-solving approaches have gained widespread acceptance as a viable alternative to distributive bargaining as an approach to international negotiations. It will be interesting to observe in the years ahead what will happen if the problem-solving paradigm becomes even more widely accepted by the community of professional diplomats. A few individuals appear to have behaved in accordance with the problem-solving paradigm in approaching conflicts. One example is Jimmy Carter's actions during the Egyptian-Israeli negotiations at Camp David, to say nothing of his more recent forays into diplomacy in his efforts to apply problem solving to difficult conflicts involving North Korea, Haiti, and Bosnia and Herzegovina. Yet he and others like him are still regarded with suspicion by a majority of the professional diplomatic community who were socialized in a different paradigm. And it may require a generational shift before the process of resocializing a new cohort of diplomats and national leaders becomes fully reflected in the regular conduct of diplomacy.

Nonetheless, the larger community is beginning to recognize that there are many conflicts where the liberal, problem-solving perspective can generate solutions that could not be found through traditional bargaining processes. Only after this paradigm shift has been internalized and the new paradigm gains widespread acceptance in practice will we begin to evaluate fully the effectiveness of the newer perspectives. We must first build up sufficient empirical data from actual international negotiations in which problem-solving approaches have been attempted before we can evaluate systematically the utility of problem solving in comparison with bargaining. This additional evidence should help us to understand the much more subtle conditions under which each perspective may be useful at facilitating agreements to resolve different kinds of international conflicts.

When greater confidence in the problem-solving paradigm is established within the diplomatic community, it can be expected to provide guidance to negotiators seeking to develop a flexible approach to the resolution of international conflicts. In this perspective, diplomats should be sensitive to the need to foster long-term relationships with other states, in which the joint effort to find mutually beneficial solutions to common problems and to develop stable long-term relationships takes precedence over the attempt to gain short-term tactical advantages. Although bargaining will no doubt remain a significant part of international negotiations, its role will increasingly be relegated to those specific situations in which intense, mostly zero-sum conflicts of interest prevail. Since the vast majority of relationships among states in a complex, multipolar world are not of this type, however, bargaining approaches to negotiation should no longer retain their dominance in both the theory and the practice of international diplomacy. The effort of liberal theorists to expand the potential for resolving international conflicts and enhancing cooperation through the problem-solving orientation toward negotiation may thus become increasingly relevant in a substantial majority of relationships in the post–Cold War international system.

NOTES

1. See I. William Zartman, introduction to *The 50% Solution*, ed. I. William Zartman (Garden City, N.Y.: Doubleday Anchor, 1976), 29; and, in the same volume, Fortune Barthélémy de Felice, "Negotiations, or the Art of Negotiating," 47–65.

2. Thomas Schelling, *The Strategy of Conflict* (Cambridge, Mass.: Harvard University Press, 1960); Anatol Rapoport, *Fights, Games, and Debates* (Ann Arbor: University of Michigan Press, 1960); and Fred Charles Iklé, *How Nations Negotiate* (New York: Frederick A. Praeger, 1964).

3. Iklé, *How Nations Negotiate*, 3–4.

4. In such a situation, both parties have a mutually beneficial, joint solution to the game. However, each party can also maximize its individual interest at the expense of the other by playing competitively. Each party's fear that the other will behave in this way and leave it worse off causes both players to play competitively, producing an outcome in which both players typically "lose," at least in comparison with the mutually cooperative solution. See Rapoport, *Fights, Games and Debates*, 173–179.

5. These various bargaining behaviors have been operationalized in a coding system called Bargaining Process Analysis (BPA) by Charles E. Walcott and P. Terrence Hopmann, "Interaction Analysis and Bargaining Behavior," in *The Small Group in Political Science: The Last Two Decades of Development*, ed. Robert T. Golembiewski (Athens: University of Georgia Press, 1978).

6. Iklé, *How Nations Negotiate*, 59–60.

7. I. William Zartman, "Negotiation as a Joint Decision-Making Process," in *The Negotiation Process: Theories and Applications*, ed. I. William Zartman (Beverly Hills, Cailf.: Sage, 1978), 67–86.

8. The argument about realists as "defensive positionalists" is presented in Joseph M. Grieco, "Understanding the Problem of International Cooperation: The Limits of Neoliberal Institutionalism and the Future of Realist Theory," in *Neorealism and Neoliberalism: The Contemporary Debate*, ed. David Baldwin (New York: Columbia University Press, 1993), 303.

9. Rapoport, *Fights, Games, and Debates*, 242.

10. Richard E. Walton and Robert B. McKersie, *A Behavioral Theory of Labor Negotiations* (New York: McGraw-Hill, 1965), 4–5.

11. James K. Sebenius, "Negotiation Analysis," in *International Negotiation: Analysis, Approaches, Issues*, ed. Victor A. Kremenyuk (San Francisco: Jossey-Bass, 1991), 209–211.

12. Roger Fisher, William Ury, and Bruce Patton, *Getting to Yes: Negotiating Agreement without Giving In*, 2d ed. (New York: Penguin, 1991).

13. I. William Zartman and Maureen R. Berman, *The Practical Negotiator* (New Haven, Conn.: Yale University Press, 1982).

14. John W. Burton, *Resolving Deep-Rooted Conflict: A Handbook* (Lanham, Md.: University Press of America, 1987); John W. Burton, *Conflict: Resolution and Provention* (New York: St. Martin's Press, 1990); and Nadim N. Rouhana and Herbert C. Kelman, "Promoting Joint Thinking in International Conflicts: An Israeli-Palestinian Continuing Workshop," *Journal of Social Issues* 50, no. 1 (1994): 157–178.

15. This chapter represents a substantially revised and updated version of an earlier paper on this topic. See P. Terrence Hopmann, "Two Paradigms of Negotiation: Bargaining and Problem-Solving," *Annals of the American Academy of Political and Social Science* 542 (November 1995): 24–47.

16. Although I do not explore these other influences on the outcome of negotiations thoroughly in this chapter, I have tried to do so in my book, *The Negotiation Process and the Resolution of International Conflicts* (Columbia: University of South Carolina Press, 1996).

17. Ibid., 28–30.

18. Iklé, *How Nations Negotiate*.

19. Steven M. Suranovic, "A Positive Analysis of Fairness with Applications to International Trade," *World Economy* 23, no. 3 (March 2000): 283–307.

20. Fisher, Ury, and Patton, *Getting to Yes*, 97–106.

21. Hopmann, *Negotiation Process*, 184–188.

22. Ibid., 70–72.

23. Herbert Simon, *Models of Man: Social and Rational* (New York: John Wiley and Sons, 1957), 198.

24. A "hard" bargainer is generally defined as one who frequently makes threats and firm and uncompromising commitments and generally seeks to intimidate his or her counterpart into making concessions while seldom reciprocating concessions; by contrast, a "soft" bargainer usually initiates new proposals, makes frequent concessions, utilizes promises of rewards more than threats of punishment, and is quick to reciprocate concessions made by the other. See Hopmann, *Negotiation Process*, 71–72; and Fisher, Ury, and Patton, *Getting to Yes*.

25. Fisher, Ury, and Patton, *Getting to Yes*, 61.

26. Ibid., 73.

27. Zartman and Berman, *Practical Negotiator*.

28. Fisher, Ury, and Patton, *Getting to Yes*, 129–143.

29. See Robert Axelrod, *The Evolution of Cooperation* (New York: Basic Books, 1984).

30. For a summary of relevant research findings, see Daniel Druckman and P. Terrence Hopmann, "Behavioral Aspects of Negotiations on Mutual Security," in *Behavior, Society, and Nuclear War*, vol. 1, ed. Philip E. Tetlock, Jo L. Husbands, Robert Jervis, Paul C. Stern, and Charles Tilly (New York: Oxford University Press, 1989), 107–115.

31. Dean G. Pruitt and Jeffrey Z. Rubin, *Social Conflict: Escalation, Stalemate, and Settlement* (New York: McGraw-Hill, 1986), 153.

32. See Hopmann, *Negotiation Process*, 82–84.

33. Robert O. Keohane and Joseph S. Nye, *Power and Interdependence: World Politics in Transition* (Boston: Little, Brown, 1977), 24–25.

34. See Gilbert R. Winham, "Negotiation as a Management Process," *World Politics* 30, no. 1 (1977): 87–114; and Hopmann, *Negotiation Process*, 245–249.

35. See the classic article on this issue, Alex Wendt, "Anarchy Is What States Make of It: The Social Construction of Power Politics," *International Organization* 46 (spring 1992): 391–425.

36. For some useful examples, many of which illustrate the use of problem-solving techniques in recent international negotiations, see Chester A. Crocker, Fen Osler Hampson, and Pamela Aall, eds., *Herding Cats: Multiparty Mediation in a Complex World* (Washington, D.C.: United States Institute of Peace Press, 1999).

28

Negotiating across Cultures

Raymond Cohen

IT SHOULD BE ADMITTED from the outset that it is hard to gauge the precise influence of cultural factors on international negotiation. Negotiators tend to be more conscious of the impact of culture when talks fail than when they succeed (Hendriks 1991). Various factors clearly impinge on any negotiation, including system of government, individual psychology and belief, ideology, public opinion, and misperception. Thus, the decisive influence on the course and outcome of events in any single case is likely to be open to dispute. Moreover, the student of diplomatic negotiations cannot contrive the conditions of a laboratory experiment, in which different variables are modified in turn while the others are held constant. One can, however, observe phenomena that recur over time, even though the circumstances, cast of actors, and subject matter may change.

In autobiographical literature, U.S. diplomats frequently allude to the marked differences between American and "non-Western" (for want of a better term) approaches to negotiation and the impact of those differences on their work (e.g., Lewis 1989; Moser 1986; Quandt 1987; Solomon 1987). That this is not simply an American problem is confirmed by French, British, and Swedish experience, among others (Elgström 1990; Plantey 1982; Yahuda 1993).

Cross-cultural conundrums have been exemplified in recent years in such key diplomatic episodes as the Iran-Contra affair, the failures of diplomacy that preceded the Falkland Islands and Persian Gulf Wars, the debacle over renewing China's most-favored-nation status, the intervention in Somalia, and the ongoing saga of trade talks with Japan. Australian prime minister Paul Keating's contretemps with Malaysian leader Mahathir Mohamad (Cohen 1998), British governor of Hong Kong Chris Patten's botched talks over Hong Kong with Beijing (Yahuda 1993), and the long stalemate in Syrian-Israeli negotiations (Cohen 1994) are other cases in point.

There are many possible definitions of culture. Lately, culture has come to be seen as more

469

about software than hardware, about the operating instructions for group life and not simply about behavior or material artifacts. According to this view, culture is made up of meanings, conventions, and presuppositions, that is, the grammar that governs the creation and use of symbols and signs. It can also be thought of as the shared "common sense" or "local knowledge" underpinning a group's construction of reality (Geertz 1983). Indeed, culture molds the community, because without it communication, coordinated activity, and social life itself would be impossible.

Cross-cultural differences have been demonstrated to affect many kinds of human relationships and activities (e.g., Samovar and Porter 1994). If unencumbered discourse rests on harmonious expectations, then the encounter of incongruent conventions of meaning is likely to lead to confusion. International negotiators are no more immune to the projection of culturally inappropriate assumptions onto members of unfamiliar societies than are business people, exchange students, and tourists. Disputing this position, Zartman and Berman (1982) argue that "negotiation is a universal process . . . and that cultural differences are simply differences in style and language" (p. 226). However, birth, life, and death are also universal experiences, yet this has not prevented humankind, in its great cultural diversity, from evolving profoundly discrepant understandings of their significance.

LINGUISTIC DISSONANCE

One suggestive approach to intercultural dissonance rests on the perception of culture as a store of shared meanings. The body of implicit, received truth held by the group is reflected most revealingly in language. Every society can be observed to possess a specialized negotiating vocabulary loaded with affective and metaphorical connotations. When negotiation takes place across cultures, the ostensible point

at issue may be complicated by semantic and procedural discontinuities. Culturally grounded assumptions about negotiation (and about the subject in contention) can be uncovered, in the first instance, by lexical analysis. Comparison of the meaning (and also, as important, usage) of relevant terms across cultures reveals potential sources of both dissonance and reconciliation, which can then be checked against behavior.

Most theoretical writing on international negotiation presupposes the existence of a fixed linguistic and behavioral framework permitting the drawing of conclusions valid for all nations. Key concepts and categories of analysis such as "opening proposal," "concession," "compromise," "contract," and so on are taken to have the same weight and function across cultures. But reliance on a single language with its built-in cultural viewpoint imposes a misleadingly uniform structure and excludes deviant possibilities. For example, if modern English has no use for terms associated with group conciliation in a situation of endemic feuding or bargaining distinctions at different hierarchical levels, then the observer restricted to English may overlook relevant non-Anglo-Saxon dimensions of negotiating behavior. Negotiation possesses both universal and particular features reflecting local traditions and needs. Specific understanding of and approaches to it are embedded within given cultural settings. Imagine trying to describe the U.S. approach to law and governance in the language of a society unfamiliar with individual rights and the adversarial system—without once resorting to the English language. Just as such complex social phenomena as conflict resolution and human relationships are conceived differently across cultures, so too is negotiation.

Studies of Chinese negotiating style, for example, indicate the central role of *guanxi* (very loosely, personal connections) in the process of negotiation (Pye 1982; Solomon 1987). Lee Kuan Yew of Singapore goes so far as to explicitly offer the services of his country to outsiders as a privileged intermediary with the People's Republic of China because of Singapore's *guanxi* (Foreign Broadcast Information Service, March 1, 1994). But it would be restrictive to think of *guanxi* simply as a "bargaining chip," though it is easiest for Westerners to understand it this way. Rather, it should be seen as a way of doing business completely different from that customary in the West.

If long-term relationships and not the one-time "negotiation" are of the essence, then categories of analysis expressed by such English terms as "opening proposal" and "final agreement" lose the well-defined (and, for native English speakers, self-evident) significance that they possess in an American context. Cultivating friendship may be the first task to be performed when doing business with the Chinese, but it is not an opening proposal or even a move. Within a relationship-oriented rather than a deal-oriented context, informal contacts, tacit hints, and the reciprocal sensitivity of partners to each other's needs are of paramount importance. (Compare a successful marriage with a "brief encounter.") In these circumstances, there may be no formal "opening bid" at the "negotiating table" at all.

Study of Japanese negotiating style suggests a similar caveat. The English word "contract," for instance, the official document containing the authoritative and legally binding text of the mutual obligations agreed upon by the signatories, is usually translated into Japanese by the word *keiyaku*.

> Yet *keiyaku* has a narrower meaning than the word contract as it is used in the United States as a legal term. While contract is used in the United States to mean a legally enforceable promise or a set of promises with accompanying duties and rights, *keiyaku* implies just part of the process of negotiation, namely, the promissory stage, in which two parties agree to work together to create a mutually advantageous relationship. The implications of a transaction created by a *keiyaku* [are] unclear to Americans because much of the negotiation and most of the details of the transaction are intended

to be filled in later. (Zhang and Kuroda 1989, p. 206)

Negotiation, then, is more than a set of behavior patterns, though this may be what we first observe. Form is simply the outward expression of meaning. Societies have certain profound cultural needs and themes that language and behavior serve and reflect. *Musyawarah* is a Malay word meaning consensual decision making through discussion and consultation, in which elaborate and prolonged efforts are made to reach an agreed position while saving everyone's face and ensuring group harmony. The term and the activity are central to the politics of the Association of Southeast Asian Nations, because open disagreement and controversy are abhorred in the acutely face-salient cultures of Southeast Asia (Thambipillai and Saravanamuttu 1985). To decipher a society's mode of operation, one must penetrate the surface of behavior to reach the underlying stratum of culturally grounded meanings as revealed in the language.

Thus, linguistic analysis provides a good point of entry to the study of negotiation across cultures. The appearance of predicted semantic antinomies—contradictions of basic principles—in the form of incongruent behavior at the negotiating table can then be observed empirically. Although the examples given so far have related to procedure, an identical analysis can also be applied to issues of substance. In Arab-Israeli negotiations in recent years, for instance, much has hung on sometimes profound differences in the meaning and resonance of the equivalent Hebrew and Arabic terms for such concepts as "normalization," "withdrawal," "land," "water," and "peace."

HIGH-CONTEXT VERSUS LOW-CONTEXT COMMUNICATION

Along with the detailed lexical comparisons required to identify possible cross-cultural dissonance, another more general distinction found to be both descriptively and prescriptively useful is that between high-context and low-context cultures (Hall 1976; Ting-Toomey 1985). High-context communication is associated with key elements in the ethos of collectivistic societies: the requirements of maintaining face and group harmony. The high-context culture communicates allusively rather than directly. As important as the explicit content of a message is the context in which it occurs, that is, the surrounding nonverbal cues and nuances of meaning. People in cultures that put the group before the individual are acutely concerned about how they will appear in the eyes of others. Speech is therefore more about preserving and promoting social interests than transmitting information. High-context speakers must weigh their words carefully, for whatever they say will be scrutinized and taken to heart. Face-to-face conversations contain many emollient expressions of respect and courtesy. Directness and contradiction are greatly disliked. Speakers in this kind of culture feel acutely uncomfortable about delivering a blunt no. They want to please others and prefer inaccuracy and evasion to painful precision: the substantive element of a message, though elliptical and encoded, will be unmistakable to insiders.

It is hard for members of a collectivistic culture to deal with a stranger from outside their circle, and a personal relationship must be established before a frank exchange becomes possible. Timing is also important. Much probing and small talk will precede a request, because a rebuff causes great embarrassment. To the outsider, the high-context individual may appear insincere, suspicious, and devious, but these traits are simply part of the veneer of courtesy and indirection essential for preserving social harmony. Nor is mistrust a deviant characteristic, but the manifestation of an ingrained caution required for dealing with members of other groups. Collectivistic individuals, in their own society, are justifiably receptive to hidden meanings, always on the watch for subtle hints known from experience to be potentially

present in the tone of a conversation and the accompanying facial expressions and gestures —body language—of interlocutors.

The low-context culture, exemplified by the United States, reserves a different role for language. Very little meaning is implicit in the context of an articulation. On the contrary, what has to be said is stated explicitly. Indirect language is strongly disliked; "straight-from-the-shoulder" talk is admired. "Get to the point" is the heartfelt reaction to small talk and evasive formulations. One has little time or patience for "beating around the bush," but wishes to get down to business and move on to another problem. Why waste time on social irrelevancies? Doing business should not require interlocutors to be bosom friends. Clearly, this propensity is associated with an individualistic freedom from group constraints and niceties, an ability to distinguish between professional and social role-playing.

Language performs, then, an informational rather than socially lubricative function in low-context cultures. Accuracy and truthfulness are great virtues. Politeness does not dictate contrived formulas and verbal embellishments. Contradiction is not deemed offensive; indeed, society flourishes on debate, persuasion, and the hard sell. Subtlety and allusiveness in speech, if grasped at all, serve little purpose. Nor does face possess the crucial importance it has for the high-context culture. There is less sensitivity to what others say. Allusion and gesture are secondary to verbal content.

The depiction presented here of high- and low-context cultures is generalized and oversimplified; many outstanding American negotiators have departed markedly from the low-context model. No culture ever possessed precisely the features depicted by the two paradigms, which represent simplified ideal types. What is important for the purpose of this brief survey, however, is not the particular traits of a culture in isolation, but the chemistry that occurs when negotiators representing mutually discordant traditions come into contact. It is the relative gap between the protagonists that counts, not their respective idiosyncratic features. Should a cross-cultural divide exist, certain typical patterns of miscomprehension can be observed to recur. A final proviso to be noted is the effect of power. For example, in Israeli-Palestinian talks cultural dissonances have been marked, but given the power discrepancy, the Palestinians have had to take, in the final analysis, what has been offered.

DIPLOMATIC MISREADINGS

The contrasting uses of language by Americans and their high-context negotiating partners have provided fertile grounds for misunderstanding. The first lesson to learn in Egypt, one former ambassador remarked, is that "Egyptians hate to turn you down; they never say no." And again: "They don't say no, . . . but nothing happens" (Veliotes 1988). Another U.S. diplomat with long service in Mexico City notes that the Mexican habit was "not to say no, just never to say yes," which means that a negotiation might continue indefinitely and indeterminately (Wilcox 1989). How, then, is one to know whether consent is genuine or feigned? If one's antennae are sufficiently attuned to accompanying verbal and nonverbal signals, it may be possible to read between the lines. Otherwise, the true message becomes clear only in retrospect. If nothing happens, one has been the victim of the "social affirmative."

Since persistence, not taking no for an answer, is a familiar trait of U.S. diplomacy, the Mexican and Egyptian reluctance to disappoint their interlocutor may set the scene for mutual bafflement and frustration. William Quandt (1987), who participated in the Camp David negotiations, argues that drawn-out negotiations may be a "sign that the Egyptian side is not ready for a deal but does not want to bear the onus for breaking off negotiations" (p. 119).

This inconclusive pattern of behavior has repeated itself on several occasions in recent years, often in negotiations involving the U.S. Department of Defense. One negotiation that dragged on for almost a decade concerned the passage of nuclear-powered warships (NPWs) of the U.S. Sixth Fleet through the Suez Canal. There is no doubt that the Egyptian government was genuinely sensitive to the environmental risks, real or imagined, of nuclear power and of its possible effect on navigation through the canal. U.S. ambassador Hermann Eilts first raised the issue in the mid-1970s with President Anwar Sadat, who passed him on to Defense Minister Abd-el-Ghani Gamasy. The latter noted in turn that his authority did not extend to running the waterway and shuffled Eilts off onto the bureaucracy (Eilts 1988). Egyptian procrastination continued for an extended period without the U.S. Defense Department grasping that the Egyptians wished to let the matter drop. Eventually, some years later, President Hosni Mubarak was persuaded to agree, and in 1984 an NPW went through for the first time. But it was a pyrrhic victory; when news of the ship's passage was tactlessly leaked by Deputy National Security Adviser John Poindexter, the agreement, entered into by the Egyptian government reluctantly and against its better judgment, was immediately called off by the embarrassed Egyptians (Veliotes 1988).

High-context individuals always find it easier to agree than to disagree. Confronted with a persistent and undesirable request, the "social affirmative" is simply the line of least resistance in order to escape from an uncomfortable situation. The fault is not theirs, but that of their unobservant interlocutor, who has failed to draw the correct conclusions from the hesitancy and unenthusiastic nature of the reply. Not even the sophisticated and cosmopolitan John Kenneth Galbraith, President John Kennedy's appointee as ambassador to India, was immune from this lapse. During the first days of the 1962 Sino-Indian border war, the State Department (looking ahead to the postwar period and a possible resolution of the Indo-Pakistani

Kashmir dispute) decided that it would be helpful for Prime Minister Jawaharlal Nehru to request, through U.S. good offices, Pakistani assurances of nonintervention. Galbraith (1969) describes in painful detail his insensitive importuning of the Indian leader.

Galbraith first asked Nehru if the United States could inform Ayub Khan, the Pakistani president, that India would welcome Pakistani assurances. Nehru replied, lukewarmly, that "he would have no objection to our saying so." This was not good enough for the ambassador. Galbraith then "moved in very hard." Would Nehru say that he would *"warmly accept"* such assurances? Looking "a little stunned"—as well he might—Nehru consented, adding that such a gesture might be helpful for the future. Galbraith resolved to press home his advantage. Could Nehru *"assure"* him that he would respond to such assurances? Yes, "on some appropriate occasion he would," Nehru responded with telltale discomfort. Galbraith moved in for the kill. "This was a time for generosity, and he should be *immediately forthcoming.*" Pressed to the wall, Nehru agreed (p. 385, emphasis added). It was another ultimately counterproductive success. Nehru, under extreme duress, his army being pushed back by seemingly irresistible Chinese pressure, had no choice but to give his unwilling consent. But to beg a favor of Pakistan, a sectarian state that in Indian eyes stands for the antithesis of everything secular India represents, was humiliating. In the end, the mediation failed and the United States squandered most of the credit it had gained by helping India in its hour of need (Coon 1989).

To the dislike of confrontation and contradiction, high-context cultures add a related and characteristic propensity for indirect and understated formulations. The motive in both cases is the same: the wish to avoid an abrupt and abrasive presentation, to maintain harmony, and to save the face of the interlocutor. Meaning is imparted by hints and nuances. Set against the U.S. preference for "straight talk,"

subtlety and opacity may be taken for evasiveness and insincerity. However, this is to judge the habit from a culture-bound perspective. Protecting the feelings of one's interlocutor is very far from deliberate falsehood. Despite their professional skills, U.S. diplomats have often fallen into this pattern of error.

Nehru's "habit of understatement" posed, in its time, a conundrum for U.S. diplomats. A classic failure of understanding occurred in February 1954. In what was to be a watershed in U.S.-Indian relations, the Eisenhower administration had decided to grant military aid to Pakistan. This was a bitter moment for Nehru and the Indian government and marked the failure of a diplomatic campaign. In the Indian worldview, Pakistan was seen as the "enemy of the race," and its arming by the United States was a most alarming development. Before the public announcement of the deal, U.S. ambassador George Allen had been instructed to deliver a personal letter from President Dwight Eisenhower and to make clear that the American decision was not directed against India and that it was hoped that friendly relations between the two countries would in no way be impaired. If the aid were misused for aggression against India, the United States would take action both within and without the United Nations to thwart it. An Indian request for military aid would also be sympathetically considered.

Nehru carefully read through the letter and the text of the forthcoming announcement. When he had finished "he smiled, studied his cigarette for a few moments, then said in a pleasant and almost confidential tone, 'I have never at any moment, since the subject arose two or three months ago, had any thought whatsoever that the U.S. government, and least of all President Eisenhower, wished to do any damage to India.'" After expressing appreciation for the letter, Nehru proceeded to a judicious and calm explanation of his concerns. "What disturbed him was not American motives but the possible consequences of this action." He spoke of "small groups of extremists among the Indian Muslims who did not conceal their pleasure over Pakistan aid because they hoped it might lead to a renewal of Muslim domination of India." Communal violence in India and increased tension throughout India and Pakistan might follow. Moreover, although the government of Mohammed Ali in Pakistan was moderate, its political organization was weak, and some successor might depart on a reckless adventure.

For all the dignity and restraint of his manner, Nehru was, in fact, revealing his innermost fears. The American decision was a nightmare come true. Nehru had publicly expressed his opposition to military aid for Pakistan and the government of India had officially protested such a move. But Allen completely missed the true meaning of Nehru's words. The ambassador commented on how "surprisingly pleasant" the conversation had been and how Nehru had "made a conscious effort to be agreeable." In an extraordinary misjudgment, both of Nehru's reaction and of Nehru's policy of nonalignment, Allen concluded that Nehru "showed no adverse reaction to the President's offer to consider sympathetically any Indian request for military aid, and it is possible that he was rather pleased." The ambassador hoped that discussion on this subject would diminish after a few days. "I do not anticipate serious public demonstrations" (*Foreign Relations of the United States* 1985, pp. 1738–1739).

In fact, the subsequent Indian reaction was vehement: demonstrations, official protests, and an extended period of strained relations. Particularly offensive to the government of India were the cynical offer of military aid and the patronizing assurances that the deal was in no way directed against India, but that if necessary the United States would thwart any aggression. As one historian of U.S.-Indian relations concludes, to this day Indians complain about the 1954 episode: "It may have done more to complicate Indo-American relations than any other single development" (Palmer 1984, p. 24).

TEMPORAL DISCONTINUITIES

Besides linguistic dissonance, disparate concepts of time can also have an important impact on negotiations across cultures. In any negotiation, participants are obliged to make judgments on three key issues in which culturally grounded assumptions about the negotiating posture of the opposing side are of the essence: the relationship between its opening bid and the minimal outcome it will ultimately settle for; the most favorable timing of concessions, if any; and the optimal point at which to make a truly final offer. There are various ways in which low- and high-context expectations of bargaining could be contrasted. For instance, the U.S. propensity to view negotiation generally as an instrumental exercise in problem solving stands in marked contrast to the tendency of collectivistic cultures to distinguish between "normal" distributive bargaining and negotiation that entails a challenge to identity or test of honor. In the latter cases, special techniques of reconciliation and face saving may be more appropriate than "carpet trading" (see Quandt 1987, p. 120).

Contrasting high- and low-context assumptions about tempo and timing are particularly salient in negotiations across cultures. Not all high-context concepts of time can be condensed into a single ideal type, but the American view of the linear, sequential, and compartmentalized nature of time is sufficiently distinctive to be meaningfully juxtaposed against other variants.

Beliefs about the meaning and structure of history, the importance of the future, and the organization of the present are fundamental to a society's construction of reality (Hall 1973). From the point of view of negotiation, American temporal rigidity can be contrasted with high-context flexibility. In the context of the American "can-do" work ethic, time is viewed as a quantifiable, linear commodity that extends from the present into the future at an unchanging rate and is to be precisely divided up and allotted in advance. Planning is supposed to enable individuals and organizations to use their resources efficiently while reducing the element of future uncertainty to a minimum. Schedules are rigid, and tight deadlines are fixed so as to maintain work discipline and retain the sequential ordering of tasks. As E. T. Hall (1973) points out, "once set, the schedule is almost sacred, so that not only is it wrong, according to the formal dictates of our culture, to be late, but it is a violation of the informal patterns to keep changing schedules or appointments or to deviate from the agenda" (p. 157). Individuals are expected to accommodate themselves and their work to the time previously allotted, rather than the reverse.

The tight scheduling of American industrial culture has little meaning for societies closer to the rhythms of traditional rural life. Caught up in the cycle of the seasons and their timely tasks, the village dweller is indifferent to the arbitrary divisions of the clock. Every task has its due time; steadiness, not haste, is the cardinal virtue. The day is punctuated by concrete activities—prayer, food, work—but there is no sense of a uniform progression of time divided up into equal bits (Eickelman 1977). Furthermore, in "face-to-face" societies, in which relationships have priority over objects, the subjugation of man to calendar violates fundamental proprieties.

The competition between rigid and flexible concepts of time is unequal, for patience and perseverance stand the negotiator in better stead than habits of urgency. It is hard enough negotiating the issues; bargaining against an inner clock compounds the difficulty. Worse, U.S. negotiators join an instinctive impatience to an overwhelming obligation to succeed; U.S. culture—in the form of public opinion, career dictates, and governmental expectations—does not take kindly to inconclusive outcomes. In the contest of wills, as their opposite numbers are well aware, Americans are at a disadvantage. Whereas Americans must bring matters to a prompt conclusion, their opponents can

sit them out or, if necessary, credibly threaten to walk away from the bargaining table altogether. These are valuable tactical advantages.

The tendency of U.S. negotiators to give ground in the face of an obdurate rival was commented on years ago by the U.S. delegate to the Panmunjom armistice talks for ending the Korean War (see Young 1968). A similar asymmetrical propensity to concession emerged in the 1955 talks for the release of U.S. citizens kept in the People's Republic of China (PRC) against their will. The United States displayed a pattern of early, unreciprocated concession. At the second session of the negotiations, on August 2, Chinese delegate Wang seized the initiative and put forward a series of demands. Among other things, he called on the United States to supply a list of names of Chinese who had been issued exit visas. At the next session, two days later, U.S. ambassador Alexis Johnson spent the whole time responding to the Chinese position and handed Wang the requested list of seventy-six names. Far from thanking him, Wang "expressed dissatisfaction" and demanded a complete list of Chinese nationals in the United States. Other unreciprocated U.S. concessions followed in subsequent sessions.

By August 23 the negotiations had stuck on the Chinese refusal to agree to release all the Americans at the same time. Ambassador Johnson was reduced to appealing to Wang's sense of fair play by pointing out the "successive concessions" made by the American side. Not even a "definite promise" had been made in return. But the Chinese delegate tenaciously declined to accept either an explicit commitment or a deadline. By August 31 Johnson concluded that the Chinese position was intractable. Wang "showed no great sense of urgency." In its instructions of September 2, the State Department accepted Johnson's judgment that the immediate release of half the Americans was "as good as can be expected." The final agreement left many Americans in Chinese hands, where they were to languish for years

(*Foreign Relations of the United States* 1986, pp. 9, 14, 42, 52, 59, 62, 64, 73–74, 75, 85, 86).

It might be thought that the U.S. position was inherently weaker than that of China, in that U.S. nationals were being held under duress, while any Chinese resident in the United States was free to leave at any time. Actually, the United States had a very strong card to play, had its patience extended beyond the five weeks that marked the apparent limit of its endurance. The agenda of the talks, agreed to on August 1, contained two items. The first was the civilian repatriation issue; the second was "other practical matters at issue between the two sides," implying the U.S. economic blockade of China and the confrontation over Taiwan. The Chinese were really interested in this latter item, not the handful of unfortunate American civilians. Item one was simply the entry price for item two. However, Wang, with great poise, never revealed his interest in any other issue by the merest hint and simply ignored Johnson's threat not to proceed to anything else until the first item was settled.

The dysfunctional American propensity for self-induced deadlines was also evident in the 1978 normalization talks with the PRC (Bernstein 1988). It is now clear that the haste with which these negotiations were pursued by the Carter administration was particularly inappropriate because time was really working against Beijing. There were some tactical, but mostly scheduling, reasons that the United States wanted an agreement by the end of 1978—the forthcoming Senate debate over ratification of the Panama Canal treaties, the Strategic Arms Limitation Treaty (SALT) talks with the USSR, and ongoing involvement in the Egyptian-Israeli peace process— but none of these were insurmountable. China's need for a normalization of relations was, in fact, far more pressing. The establishment of full diplomatic relations between the two countries was the condition for a visit to the United States by Deng Xiaoping. This visit was vital to Deng to obtain the appearance of U.S.

complicity in the February 17, 1979, People's Liberation Army attack on Vietnam as a deterrent to feared Soviet intervention.

At a meeting of top U.S. officials on June 20, 1978, it was first decided to aim for completion of the normalization negotiations by December 15. Clearly, the Chinese were not supposed to be informed of this target date. Secretary of State Cyrus Vance argued that this deadline "would allow us to proceed with Peking at a reasonable pace and would have some negotiating advantages over a stretched-out process." However, National Security Adviser Zbigniew Brzezinski (1983) had already told Deng that President Jimmy Carter was prepared to move as quickly as possible, and in September Carter himself openly stressed to the head of the PRC liaison office in Washington the desirability of a quick normalization. While the Chinese remained firm on their insistence that the United States terminate its arms relationship with Taiwan, Brzezinski made little attempt to conceal his own sense of urgency. He "told the Chinese ambassador that if we missed this opportunity, we would have to delay normalization until far into 1979. The congressional schedule would be overloaded and we would have to move ahead on SALT and a possible meeting with Brezhnev" (p. 229).

The negotiating advantages to the Chinese of this artificially induced sense of urgency are obvious. It was made to appear, with no basis in the objective situation, that the United States was more eager than China for agreement. As might be anticipated, there was a price to be paid for U.S. impatience. Washington had early on reconciled itself to the Chinese refusal to renounce officially its right to use force to reunify Taiwan with the mainland. In lieu of an explicit Chinese concession, it was decided to settle for a U.S. statement of "interest in the peaceful resolution of the Taiwan issue," which would not be contradicted by a simultaneous Chinese statement. But on December 15, 1978, U.S. desires notwithstanding, Beijing went ahead with a statement that did reject the American position. The manner in which Taiwan would be brought "back to the embrace of the motherland," the PRC declared, "is entirely China's internal affair." It was a ringing slap in the face for Carter. To add insult to injury, in 1982 fresh negotiations on the problem of Taiwan produced a new agreement. In return for a remarkable U.S. commitment not to exceed past qualitative and quantitative levels of arms sales to Taiwan, China now pledged to seek a peaceful solution to unification. It had succeeded in selling the same horse twice.

INTERCULTURAL COMMUNICATION IN THE NEW GLOBAL DIPLOMACY

Classic diplomacy, as it evolved over centuries in the European states system, came to reflect the values and assumptions of an "international diplomatic culture." Coming from similar social backgrounds, grounded in common civilizational canons, educated to the same convictions, diplomats constituted something like a medieval guild. Formidable immunities and privileges protected their exclusive position. Thus, they could be assured of dealing with colleagues who had a shared loyalty to the profession and "spoke the same language" they did. Like other guilds, the diplomatic corps possessed a proprietary claim over its specialty, the conduct of negotiations. This meant not only that international negotiations rested on a common stock of technical procedures and terms, but also that understanding prevailed at a deeper, commonsense level about what the activity was all about. Martin Wight (1977) correctly pointed to the possession of a common culture as the prerequisite for the emergence of states systems, from the time of the ancient Greeks onward.

Over the course of the past half century, this situation has radically changed. For the first time in history a universal, inclusive diplomatic

system has come into existence, in which almost all states maintain relations with almost all other states. In the new dispensation, the West still enjoys certain marked advantages: the continuing preeminence of the United States, the centrality of Western cities, especially New York and Washington, and the dominance of the English language. But as the international system has accepted new members, the balance has gradually shifted toward other civilizations and economies. "The order that is now emerging," Henry Kissinger (1995) observes, "will have to be built by statesmen who represent vastly different cultures" (p. 27).

Only a generation ago cross-cultural dissonance was of little concern to a still exclusive, self-centered Western diplomacy. Treating Gamal Abdel Nasser like a supplicant in the 1956 Aswan Dam talks, U.S. secretary of state John Foster Dulles made little effort to broadcast on the same wavelength as the emerging Third World nations. Today, reflecting the altered agenda and makeup of the international community, the West necessarily conducts a greatly increased proportion of its business outside the former charmed circle. In the past, leaders like Leopoldo Galtieri (Argentine junta leader), Saddam Hussein, and the Ayatollah Khomeini would not have qualified as interlocutors; today, they negotiate as equals.

Cultural differences might remain marginal if professional diplomats still enjoyed an exclusive position at the negotiating table, but today they are no longer the only actors in international negotiations. In an age of "Concorde diplomacy," politicians, officials from domestic agencies, and figures from the private sector are just as likely to be involved in international negotiation. Ease of travel has particularly reduced the role of the resident embassy (Henderson 1994). Multilateral negotiation at international conferences is another feature of the shifting professional scene. As nondiplomats play an increasing role, narrow, culture-bound attitudes and habits, usually unmodified by diplomatic training, knowledge of languages, or experience of service abroad, risk overshadowing shared specialist skills.

What conclusions are to be drawn from the potential for discord suggested above? The first conclusion is linguistic: where possible, the problem of cultural-linguistic dissonance can be alleviated by using a common language, a *lingua franca,* almost inevitably English. In Israeli-Palestinian talks, English saved the day: "redeployment" sounds much more neutral and technical than its Hebrew and Arabic equivalents. Unfortunately, this solution is not always available to negotiators for prestige or technical reasons, and officials and leaders may be unwilling or unable to use English.

Nor should it be thought that reliance on English obviates all misunderstanding, as State Department interpreter Edmund Glenn argued (1966). Not everyone who speaks in English, thinks in English; disguised dissonances remain. It was essential that basic United Nations texts be published in French and other languages, one UN official explained, "because they translate lines of thought and outlooks different from an Anglo-Saxon vision and perspective" (Horovitz 1995). Expertise in the language and culture of one's interlocutor is still needed. This lesson was dramatically brought home by the fall of the shah of Iran. In 1979 the United States possessed few officers in Tehran who knew Farsi. This not only inhibited its capacity to gather intelligence, but also meant that officials from the two cultures often unwittingly talked past each other (Sick 1985). Foreign language is not just a medium of communication but also a means of penetrating beneath the surface of a society.

A second conclusion relates to the acquisition of professional skills. In comparison to the situation of only a few years ago, there has been an expansion in negotiation training, both for diplomats and for executives in the private sector. Here, though, the position is less favorable than it appears. Many of the courses in negotiation—often based on a culture-bound, can-do philosophy of "getting to yes"—pay insufficient attention to cross-cultural variation. This tendency can be readily observed in the work of Roger Fisher, an influential author, educator, and founder of the Program on Negotiation at Harvard Law School. His practical recommendations for international negotiators invariably underestimate cultural differences. In the 1990–91 Persian Gulf crisis, for example, Fisher repeatedly called for fair and sympathetic consideration of Saddam Hussein's legitimate needs and concerns. This "you win, I win" approach, doubtless appropriate to a domestic U.S. market, was strikingly unsuited to the requirements of compelling the Iraqi leader to withdraw his army of occupation from Kuwait; it merely repeated the initial error of assuming that Saddam Hussein was a reasonable statesman who would prefer a peaceful, compromise outcome to war (Baram 1994; Fisher 1990). Negotiation training, then, has to incorporate both a general sensitivity to cross-cultural differences and detailed coaching in individual national styles.

If my arguments in this chapter are accepted, a third, more general, conclusion can be drawn about the role of diplomacy. In a situation of increasing globalization it follows that a culturally informed diplomacy is peculiarly suited to act on the boundary between societies as an interpretive and conjunctive mechanism, facilitating comprehension and the smooth conduct of negotiation. Within governments, foreign ministries are uniquely well equipped not just to coordinate international delegations, but also to provide an authoritative cultural interpretation of the interlocutor and advice on negotiating strategies. In this vital area of expertise, this evolutionary niche, diplomats have an evident comparative advantage. No other agency, private or official, is in a better position to cultivate cross-cultural skills and foreign languages (and the long-term relationships that underpin business in high-context societies). Linguistic proficiency—the key to cross-cultural insight—and local knowledge have been valued attributes of the skilled diplomat since time immemorial (e.g., Henderson 1994). These traditional assets are more appropriate today than ever. By laying special emphasis on the attributes of cross-cultural negotiating competence, diplomats will be well placed to help their societies meet the challenges of globalization in the years ahead.

References

Baram, A. 1994. "The Iraqi Invasion of Kuwait: Decision Making in Baghdad." In *Iraq's Road to War*, ed. A. Baram, 5-6. New York: St. Martin's Press.

Bernstein, T. P. 1988. *The Negotiations to Normalize U.S.-China Relations*. Pew Case Studies no. 426. Pittsburgh: University of Pittsburgh, Graduate School of Public and International Affairs.

Brzezinski, Z. 1983. *Power and Principle: Memoirs of the National Security Adviser, 1977–1981*. London: Weidenfeld and Nicolson.

Cohen, R. 1994. "Culture Gets in the Way." *Middle East Quarterly* 1: 45–53.

———. 1998. "Conflict Resolution across Cultures: Bridging the Gap." In *Culture in World Politics*, ed. D. Jacquin-Berdal, A. Oros, and M. Verweij. London: Macmillan.

Coon, C. 1989. Interview of former ambassador to Nepal by author.

Eickelman, D. F. 1977. "Time in a Complex Society: A Moroccan Example." *Ethnology* 16: 39–55.

Eilts, H. 1988. Interview of former ambassador to Egypt by author.

Elgström, O. 1990. "Norms, Culture, and Cognitive Patterns in Foreign Aid Negotiations." *Negotiation Journal* 6: 147–159.

Fisher, R. 1990. "Getting to 'Yes' with Saddam: How Words Can Win." *Washington Post*, December 9, 1990.

Foreign Broadcast Information Service (FBIS), Southeast Asia, March 1, 1994, pp. 50–51.

Foreign Relations of the United States. 1985. Vol. 11, 1952–1954. Washington, D.C.: U.S. Government Printing Office.

Foreign Relations of the United States. 1986. Vol. 3, 1955–1957. Washington, D.C.: U.S. Government Printing Office.

Galbraith, J. K. 1969. *Ambassador's Journal: A Personal Account of the Kennedy Years*. Boston: Houghton Mifflin.

Geertz, C. 1983. *Local Knowledge*. New York: Basic Books.

Glenn, E. S. 1966. "Meaning and Behavior: Communication and Culture." *Journal of Communication* 16: 248–272.

Hall, E. T. 1973. *The Silent Language*. New York: Anchor Press.

———. 1976. *Beyond Culture*. New York: Anchor Press.

Henderson, N. 1994. *Mandarin*. London: Weidenfeld and Nicolson.

Hendriks, E. C. 1991. "Research on International Business Negotiations: An Introduction." In *Business Communication in Multilingual Europe: Supply and Demand*, ed. C. Braecke and H. Cuyckens, 169–186. Antwerp: ENCoDe/UFSIA.

Horovitz, N. 1995. "Frenchman, Speak English!" *Ha'aretz*, January 7, 1995.

Kissinger, H. A. 1995. *Diplomacy*. New York: Simon and Schuster.

Lewis, S. W. 1989. Interview in the *San Diego Union*, May 8.

Moser, L. J. 1986. "Negotiating Style: Americans and Japanese." In *Toward a Better Understanding: U.S.-Japanese Relations*, ed. D. B. Bendahmane and L. J. Moser, 43–51. Washington, D.C.: U.S. Department of State, Foreign Service Institute.

Palmer, N. D. 1984. *The United States and India: The Dimensions of Influence*. New York: Praeger.

Plantey, A. 1982. "A Cultural Approach to International Negotiation." *International Social Science Journal* 93: 535–544.

Pye, L. 1982. *Chinese Commercial Negotiating Style*. Cambridge, Mass.: Oelgeschlager, Gunn, and Hain.

Quandt, W. B. 1987. "Egypt: A Strong Sense of National Identity." In *National Negotiating Styles*, ed. H. Binnendijk, 105–124. Washington, D.C.: U.S. Department of State, Foreign Service Institute.

Samovar, L. A., and R. E. Porter. 1994. *Intercultural Communication: A Reader*. 7th ed. Belmont, Calif.: Wadsworth.

Sick, G. 1985. *All Fall Down: America's Fateful Encounter with Iran*. London: I. B. Tauris.

Solomon, R. H. 1987. "China: Friendship and Obligation in Chinese Negotiating Style." In *National Negotiating Styles*, ed. H. Binnendijk, 1–16. Washington, D.C.: U.S. Department of State, Foreign Service Institute.

Thambipillai, P., and J. Saravanamuttu. 1985. *ASEAN Negotiations: Two Insights*. Singapore: Institute of Southeast Asian Studies.

Ting-Toomey, S. 1985. "Toward a Theory of Conflict and Culture." *International and Intercultural Communication Annual* 9: 71–86.

Veliotes, N. 1988. Interview of former U.S. ambassador to Egypt by author.

Wight, M. 1977. *Systems of States*. Leicester, U.K.: Leicester University Press.

Wilcox, R. 1989. Interview of former U.S. official in Mexico City by author.

Yahuda, M. 1993. "Hong Kong's Future: Sino-British Negotiations, Perceptions, Organization, and Political Culture." *International Affairs* 69: 245–266.

Young, K. T. 1968. *Negotiating with the Chinese Communists: The United States Experience, 1953–1967*. New York: McGraw-Hill.

Zartman, I. W., and M. R. Berman. 1982. *The Practical Negotiator*. New Haven, Conn.: Yale University Press.

Zhang, D., and K. Kuroda. 1989. "Beware of Japanese Negotiation Style: How to Negotiate with Japanese Companies." *Northwest Journal of International Law and Business* 10: 195–212.

29

Prenegotiation and Circum-negotiation

Arenas of the Multilevel Peace Process

Harold H. Saunders

CRUCIAL AS IT IS, negotiation around the table is only a later part of a larger political process in which conflicts are resolved by peaceful means. That larger political process is the peace process—a mixture of politics, diplomacy, changing relationships, negotiation, mediation, and dialogue in both official and unofficial arenas. Work apart from negotiation is a significant part of that process because it deals with people, problems, and moments that are not yet ready for formal mediation and negotiation. But that work, like every other act of peacemaking and peacebuilding, must be understood as an intertwined part of an overall peace process.

In many cases, the process in which conflicting groups first contact one another, then talk, and eventually commit to an agreed settlement is even more complicated, time-consuming, and difficult than reaching agreement in negotiations. Those who try to resolve conflict peacefully need to consider the context of a larger political process that deals with the obstacles to negotiation as well as the hurdles in negotiation. We call that larger context the peace process, and only in that setting do we understand the fullest meaning of what has been called prenegotiation.[1]

Unless we enlarge our conceptual framework to understand why parties to a conflict will not talk and what might enable them to engage in dialogue, we are not constructing a theory of negotiation or of peacemaking that will give negotiation the greatest possibility of success. We must deal with questions such as these:

- What causes and enables individuals to conclude that they have "had enough"—that a situation hurts their interests so badly that they cannot let it continue?
- Why and how do they arrive at the conclusion that some kind of joint effort with other involved parties is both necessary and possible?
- Why is the relationship conflictual?

- What are the obstacles to change and the junctures at which the dynamics of the relationship might be changed?
- Why and how can parties to a conflict reach out to the other side?
- What are the possible ways of seeking a joint solution?

The responses to these questions and others like them shape the tasks that have been called prenegotiation. Approaches to these tasks may call on some of the skills of mediation and negotiation, but they also require the insights and the art of those who think deeply about why human beings fear, hate, kill, and change their relationships. These approaches draw on the varied capacities of the psychoanalyst, the psychologist, the politician, the lawyer, the teacher, the person of God, and the compassionate human being.

This work is done in the political arena, not in the negotiating room or its antechambers. Its challenge in today's world is that no single academic or professional discipline is designed to educate the whole human being to participate in this whole political process. The thinking required will not come from combining existing disciplines; it will emerge only from large new perspectives. It will be "supradisciplinary." The peace process as a human process for peacemaking and peacebuilding may offer such a perspective.

The concept of a multilevel peace process —with the work apart from negotiation woven continuously through its fabric—provides the largest possible framework both for creating opportunities to address these questions and for moving toward peace. Until we work within that large a conceptual context, we will not have adequate theories of conflict prevention, management, resolution, mediation, and negotiation. We need a concept large enough to allow us to draw on the broadest reservoirs of resources and insights from which to choose the most appropriate instrument for a particular problem.

At some moments in that process, participants may decide that negotiation provides a workable framework for their situation; at others, they may decide that a problem is too dangerous to ignore but is not ready for formal approaches. Many of today's deep-rooted human conflicts are not ready for formal mediation or negotiation. Human beings do not negotiate about their identities, fears, suspicions, anger, historic grievances, security, dignity, honor, justice, rejection, or acceptance.

Peace requires a process of building constructive relationships in a civil society—not just negotiating, signing, and ratifying a formal agreement, central as this may be in defining new relationships between groups or countries. That will increasingly be true of conflicts in the twenty-first century. The multilevel peace process provides a conceptual context within which to combine the fullest possible range of instruments for moving from violence to peace. The tasks of the peace process apart from negotiation provide an important framework for this movement.

CLARIFYING TERMS: PRENEGOTIATION AND CIRCUM-NEGOTIATION

The term "prenegotiation" can be confusing in at least three respects. Thus it is crucial to define my use of terms.

First, the prefix "pre" suggests a position in time before negotiation. We can more accurately say that this work is accomplished apart from negotiation. It can indeed pave the way for formal mediation and negotiation. But it can also take place during a negotiation, but apart from it, when negotiators are stuck and need a larger perspective, new formulations, or broader political support. It can even take place after one successful negotiation when parties move to tackle the next problem.

Second, the use of the word "negotiation" suggests that the problem is how to start a negotiation. The real problem is how to start a political process that can change relationships and lead to the end of violence, to peace, and to reconciliation. The methods used in that process may or may not include negotiation.

I once asked an academic colleague whether every conflict has a negotiated solution. He replied that he thought so. But as I reflected on my very different experience, I concluded that there must be solutions through means other than negotiation. Having worked for five presidents, I have heard leaders say, "This problem is too tough to negotiate, yet I must do something about it." I want leaders and citizens alike to have as many options for reframing issues or taking steps in the political arena to change conflictual relationships as they have options for getting people to the negotiating table.

Third, some scholars have defined prenegotiation as an exactly limited period of preparation for negotiation. "Prenegotiation begins," writes I. William Zartman, "when one or more parties considers negotiation as a policy option and communicates this intention to other parties. It ends when the parties agree to formal negotiations (an exchange of proposals designed to arrive at a mutually acceptable outcome in a situation of interdependent interests) or when one party abandons the consideration of negotiation as an option."[2] The important work of setting the agenda, staffing the negotiation, defining ground rules, and solving problems of the setting may more accurately be called negotiation preparation. Or perhaps this is the appropriate meaning of prenegotiation.

With these points made, we will now discuss the times and the tasks apart from negotiation that have the purpose of beginning, sustaining, and nourishing a peace process by changing relationships and paving the way for negotiation or other peaceful steps to resolve conflict. For this work, I prefer the term "circum-negotiation"—the work that goes on around negotiation.[3] The multilevel peace process embraces prenegotiation, negotiation, and circum-negotiation and involves citizens outside government with no authority to negotiate as well as officials with credentials to negotiate binding agreements.

THE MULTILEVEL PEACE PROCESS IN A CHANGING GLOBAL SETTING

Our changing world demands that we broaden our conceptual framework. For the past 350 years, we have tended to think of conflict in the context of the nation-state system. Attempts to resolve conflict have relied on the traditional instruments of statecraft—force, mediation, negotiation, propaganda, and economic sanctions and incentives. In this power-politics model for analyzing international relations, leaders of nation-states amass economic and military power to pursue objectively defined interests in zero-sum contests of material power against other nation-states.

Our increasing experience of the complex interdependence of today's world causes us to think beyond a system focused mainly on the nation-state. Relationships among countries today are increasingly a political process of continuous interaction among significant elements of whole bodies politic across permeable borders.

As normally defined, the state-centered concepts of the past do not embrace this relationship between whole bodies politic. Citizens outside as well as within government are both instigators and resolvers of conflict. There are some things that only governments can do, such as negotiate binding agreements; there are others that only citizens outside government can do, such as change human relationships. State borders no longer exclude a large range of interactions among citizens, and human beings have many identities—ethnic, racial, linguistic, regional, global, cultural, professional, avocational, religious, ideological, economic— many of them not defined or bounded by the nation-state.

I have settled on the concept of relationship to capture that dynamic political process of continuous interaction between whole bodies politic. Although the word "relationship" is unfamiliar in international relations, I intend to bring the human dimension into the study, teaching, and conduct of international relationships and into the prevention, management, and resolution of conflict. The term "relationship" suggests the need to study not only relations between states but the overall relationships among groups of human beings and whole bodies politic.

I focus not only on negotiating a division of material goods to settle a conflict between institutions but also on changing the conflictual relationships that gave rise to the struggle and that therefore must be changed in order to resolve the conflict. That is the work of whole human beings in whole bodies politic—citizens both in and out of government. That is the work of a multilevel peace process, involving all significant elements of a body politic.

Formal negotiation may evolve from preparations explicitly devoted to starting negotiation, or negotiations may become possible only after citizens who have no authority to prepare for negotiation decide in dialogue apart from negotiation that it is time to risk trying to live together in peace. In another circumstance, a new phase in negotiation may be blocked until a positive political environment has been created by citizens outside government. As they change relationships through their own interactions, the need for an entire phase in negotiation may be bypassed. The challenge is to understand how work in all of these arenas— including the work apart from negotiation— interacts to initiate and sustain movement from violence toward peace.

THE OVERALL PEACE PROCESS: FOUR ARENAS

Our understanding of the multilevel peace process has evolved since 1974. We now think of the process as operating in four interactive arenas. The work of prenegotiation can be accomplished in any of them. One is not superior to another; one may simply be more feasible or appropriate in a given situation. The important task is to understand how they can work together in complementary ways.

The Official Process

In the early months of Secretary of State Henry Kissinger's 1974 shuttle diplomacy in the Middle East, those of us flying with him first used the phrase "negotiating process" to describe our mediation of a series of interim agreements. Soon, however, we realized that the phrase was too narrow, because our stated purpose was for each interim agreement to change the surrounding political environment and make possible a further step. We coined the phrase "peace process" to capture the experience of this series of mediated agreements embedded in a larger political process. It was in that larger political process that relationships changed. Human interactions changed the attitudes in bodies politic that constrained governments or pressed them to move forward. At that time, we were focusing on how governments could reshape the political environment.

In the 1970s the Soviet-U.S. governmental effort called "détente" aimed to "move from confrontation to negotiation" as the heart of the relationship between the nuclear superpowers. A decade after détente foundered, Soviet president Mikhail Gorbachev recognized the need not just to negotiate arms control agreements but to address directly the deep distrust Americans felt toward the Soviet Union. His address to the United Nations General Assembly in December 1988 was essentially a speech to convince the U.S. people that the Cold War could end and that a new relationship was possible. Again, this was an official act. Similar official processes in El Salvador, Guatemala, South Africa, Northern Ireland, and the former Yugoslavia have yielded agreements that will require years to play out. Official as well as quasi-official and public peace processes are ongoing as of this writing in Israel and Palestine; Armenia, Azerbaijan, and Nagorno-Karabakh; and Georgia.

The Quasi-Official Process

Unofficial groups closely related to the official process have formed on a number of fronts. Although made up of citizens outside government, these groups consult with officials, feeding them ideas or formulations.

For example, in 1993 a small group of Israelis and Palestinians outside government began meeting with the informal acquiescence of officials; they graduated to talks moderated by the Norwegian foreign minister, with officials informed at each stage, and they finally produced an agreement that was formally adopted by the Israeli government and the Palestine Liberation Organization. As another example, the National Commission for the Consolidation of Peace (COPAZ) was created in El Salvador by the 1992 peace agreement between the government and guerrilla forces. Made up of representatives of all political parties in the Legislative Assembly, its mandate was to oversee implementation of the political aspects of the agreement. This required working out compromises on major legislative acts. Finally, the Soviet-U.S. Dartmouth Conference —the longest continuous bilateral exchange between U.S. and Soviet citizens, started in 1960 at the initiative of President Dwight Eisenhower with the approval of Chairman Nikita Khrushchev—fell partly into this category because Soviet participants normally spoke under the discipline or instruction of the Soviet Communist Party. Each group was briefed by officials before meetings and reported to them afterward.

A Public Peace Process: Sustained Dialogue

In today's world, many of the deep-rooted conflicts that command our attention have resulted from the breakdown of states or seem beyond the reach of governments. Many of these situations are not ready for negotiation; therefore, since the 1960s, citizens outside government have developed approaches built around sustained dialogue. These dialogues address the human causes of conflict. They engage representative citizens from the conflicting parties in designing steps to be taken in the political arena to change perceptions and stereotypes, to create a sense that peace may be possible, and to involve more and more of their compatriots. In 1991 some of us coined the phrase "public peace process" to name this work of citizens outside government.[4]

Israelis and Palestinians outside official bodies met in countless dialogues for almost two decades before official and quasi-official negotiations took place. These dialogues created a critical mass of people in each body politic who recognized the other group as persons with valid human needs and desires to fulfill their own legitimate aspirations. More important, the people decided they could risk trying to live at peace. The dialogues also produced many of the formulations and reassurances that made possible formal negotiations between Israel and the Palestine Liberation Organization.

In Tajikistan, parties to a civil war met in unofficial dialogue for thirteen months before UN-sponsored negotiations between the government and the opposition began.[5] In the public domain, the opposition created its own organization and put forward a platform that provided a basis for government agreement to negotiations. Two dialogue participants were signatories. The dialogue group wrote an unsolicited "Memorandum on a Negotiating Process for Tajikistan" before negotiators first met in April 1994. Three of those who produced that memorandum became delegates in the formal negotiations as citizens outside government. A year later, when the official negotiations were stalled over a mechanism to oversee a "process of national reconciliation," the dialogue group produced two memos on the subject—

one outlining options and a second fleshing out one option when leaders agreed on it. Although the dialogue group has sent memos to negotiators and is known by officials, it is not responsible in any way to official bodies, nor are participants instructed by them.

Civil Society

The fragmentation and the reconfiguration of civil society that underlie conflict and its resolution need to be considered when planning peacemaking and peacebuilding. Most thinking about preventing and resolving conflict has focused on the dynamics of conflict itself—its causes, escalation, stalemate, and settlement. A larger framework would include what happens in a civil society as violence breaks it down into warring units and as genuine peace rebuilds and reconnects them. Picture the following sequence of developments:

- *First:* A functioning society includes many relationships and networks of relationships. Whether in totalitarian societies or democracies, some span the fault lines that divide people and provide spaces where perceptions can change and differences can be handled peacefully. When a regime collapses, some of those organizations may be dismissed —especially if they were creations of the regime, as in the Soviet Union—and the vacuum is often filled by armed groups vying for control.
- *Second:* As a society fragments, whatever social units survive—tribal, clan, ethnic, or regional groupings; ideological movements; or criminal networks—coagulate into like-minded "alliances." Relationships between unlike groups that pursued shared interests across fault lines are severed. Violence is the medium of exchange.
- *Third:* Mediators help opposing factions reach agreement on ending the violence. They address tangible issues and interests and the division of power. But the agreements

they produce are like skeletons without the necessary ligaments, muscles, sinews, flesh, nerves, or blood vessels. They cannot change human relationships, and they do not normally think of the need to regenerate those groups and political processes that span the divisions in a peaceful civil society.
- *Fourth:* During a civil conflict, citizens outside government may begin dialogue across the lines of conflict. They create organizations to help refugees return home, restore local water systems, or re-create trading patterns. They begin to generate connections between the coagulations of warring groups forming the sinews of nascent cohesion in a society building peace. Those connections provide the first ingredients of economic recovery.[6]

This picture was drawn from the experience of Tajikistan's first four years of independence, but it could apply to other conflicts. The point is that work critical to implementing agreements is done apart from negotiations in this arena.

The purpose of identifying these four arenas in the multilevel peace process is not to give primacy to any one, but to underscore the importance of a comprehensive strategy developed around the complementarity in their interactions. The official process can be enabled, constrained, or impelled by work in the other arenas. The process may lead to negotiation, but sometimes, as the dynamics of relationships change in the larger political process, a whole phase in preparation for negotiations may be superseded. Key issues—for example, adversaries accepting each other as a legitimate negotiating partner—can be resolved in the public arena and not come to the negotiators' agenda except as a given. Sometimes, projects in the civil society bring together important elements of a whole body politic and build public support for official agreements—an approach crucial to implementing the Dayton accords on Bosnia, for example.

These arenas characterize collections of actors in the peace process, but these collections of actors alone are not the peace process. We must add the dimension of time. The peace process embraces the interactions of these collections of actors over time to change relationships. That is why the process is laid out in phases below.

A BRIEF WORD ABOUT THIRD PARTIES

Although they are not the main subject of this chapter, it is important to note that both governmental and nongovernmental third parties can work in each of these four arenas of the peace process—the official process, the quasi-official process, the public dialogue, and civil society. Each party may perform a different function.

The most creative thinking about third-party involvement focuses not on the role of a single actor but on the process through which a complex of functions is performed. One can identify, for example, the roles of instigator, communicator, persuader, organizer, precipitator, legitimizer, convenor, moderator, manager, funder, teacher, idea formulator—all played by different combinations of actors. The issue is not whether a bilateral initiative or a third-party role is the correct approach, but rather what mix of involvement is most appropriate at a particular time in a particular situation.[7]

When I was explaining the Dartmouth Conference—the bilateral dialogue between Soviet and U.S. citizens that involved no third party—a colleague asked, "But who performs the third-party role?" I replied, "One organization on each side organized and paid for the meetings. Co-moderators chaired meetings, set the agenda, jointly advanced it, and were stewards of the process." After the Cold War ended, the Dartmouth Conference Task Force on Regional Conflicts acted as a third-party team—perhaps the first Russian-U.S. citizens'

peacemaking team—to launch a dialogue among the factions from the civil war in Tajikistan. The role played depended simply on the needs to be met.

THE MULTILEVEL PEACE PROCESS

A peace process operates in different arenas over time—sometimes simultaneously, sometimes in sequence, sometimes in parallel, sometimes overlapping. Its purpose is to reconcile parties in conflict, seeking to understand how the interaction among those arenas over time helps prepare human beings to change conflictual relationships. For the sake of illustration, this chapter examines the interaction between two of these arenas—the public and the official—as parts of the multilevel peace process.

The chapter also examines that interaction in each of five phases of the peace process. The stages of both the public peace process, which is built around a process of sustained dialogue, and the official peace process, which is normally built around negotiation or mediation, have been described elsewhere.[8] I focus here on the interaction of arenas.

Use of the term "phases" in this chapter is simply a convenient way of focusing on who can do what at each point in the evolution of a peace process. Speaking of phases suggests precision and rigidity that do not exist in the real world. In reality, participants move back and forth between stages in a circular rather than linear fashion as they revisit assumptions or tackle new problems. But presenting the process in phases sharpens thought about the tasks that need to be performed at each step, and it adds the dimension of time to the process.

One example of the value of analyzing the peace process in phases comes from the Arab-Israeli experience. From 1974 through 1979 the world came to see the Egyptian-Israeli peace process as a series of negotiated agreements, culminating in the peace treaty of 1979.

When the focus shifted to the Israeli-Palestinian front, those two parties did not even recognize each other; the process was back in a period before negotiation, where the instruments of negotiation were useless. Attention needed to return to the task of bridging the deep human gulf between two peoples. Much of that work needed to be done by citizens outside government.

PHASE ONE: DEFINING THE PROBLEM AND DECIDING TO ENGAGE

Phase one is a time when those involved in a conflict—citizens both in and out of government—decide whether they can allow a situation to continue as it is or whether to reach out to the other side. Deciding how to act on those decisions is likely to be more complicated and to take longer for those inside than those outside government.

Some individuals both in and out of government are ready to say, "Enough!" and to risk working toward a solution. Policymakers recognize that they cannot get what they want by unilateral action and decide to explore whether negotiation—an effort with the other side to find a joint solution—may be possible. But their exploration may often have to be made unilaterally, because the symbolism of talking with an enemy may make direct talk taboo. Citizens outside government, on the other hand, have more freedom to talk to people on the other side to get a firsthand feel for what may be possible. Learning what brings people to this conclusion is crucial. Often it is stark recognition that the costs of continuing conflict have already become too high. Or some individuals may be far-sighted enough to recognize that the consequences of continuation will become intolerable at some future point.

Often individuals on the threshold of taking a step are reluctant or even fearful to reach out to the other side, with good reason. Some deny that a problem exists because they are not yet ready to face others' pain. Citizens in some situations risk assassination; governments risk vehement backlash; even in nonconflict situations, individuals are afraid to talk with people who they feel discriminate against them, do not care about them, or even hate or harm them.

Public Process

At this stage, before participants ever come face to face, they need to understand the nature, purpose, and ground rules of the dialogue. Four questions must be addressed: Who will take the initiative? Who will participate? How can resistance to meeting and talking with the adversary be overcome? Under whose auspices and where will the dialogue take place?

An individual or small group in one community may reach out directly to individuals on the other side, or a respected third party may find and communicate to each side that some of the opposition want to talk. Someone on each side or a third party carefully identifies a dialogue group of about a dozen members who reflect thinking in various sectors of each party and who are respected in their communities. Often, it is best to aim at the second and third levels in organizations because participants at those levels are freer to talk while still understanding their groups' needs. Some individuals may need to discuss their fears of meeting with the adversary. Finally, they agree to meet to listen to each other with respect and to speak to each other from the heart. They will meet in a place considered safe by both sides.

Official Process

Policymakers have a more complex task during phase one. After reaching personal decisions that they must reach out to the other side, they have to pave the way for bringing a government and a body politic along with that decision. Because of the time this will take, those in the public peace process (who can act on their individual decisions) may start talking long before officials are ready to move. In policy-making, how one defines a problem begins to determine what one will do about it. Heated national debate can focus on the definition of a problem. Disagreements can lead factions to kill one another. So the policymakers—probably consulting an ever-widening inner circle—work carefully to frame the issue.

Once policymakers in a small group have defined the problem, they must understand how nearly unified or divided their own side is, how they and the adversary differ, and what barriers must be overcome. As they bridge differences within their own group, they begin forming an internal base in the official and civic arenas. The steps they take become part of the larger political process that eventually surrounds a negotiation.

Where the gap between one party and another seems large, policymakers must consider—still among themselves—how their pictures of the problem can be brought into closer alignment. It is a milestone when one party includes the other's definition of the problem in its own. It is normal for each side to buttress its own position by ignoring the rights, the claims, or the pain of others. One condition for deciding to seek a joint solution is seeing that a problem is at least partly a shared problem and that the hopes, pains, needs, positions, and political base of each party suggest the possibility of mutual responsiveness.

Policymakers may decide not to go beyond this in-house deliberation because of conditions either within their own group or on the other side. One option is for them to suspend their efforts and watch a public process explore possibilities, change relationships, generate options, and build public support. This is what happened in the Israeli-Palestinian and Tajik-istani peace processes. Redefining a problem and changing relationships are often tasks for the public arena, and that public experience can contribute to the official assessment of the feasibility of negotiation.

PHASE TWO: MAPPING ISSUES AND RELATIONSHIPS

In this phase, both officials and citizens design an exploration of possibilities on the other side, but each group moves differently. Officials must be able to stop at any time. They need to estimate the chances of success in order to build political support for a commitment to negotiate, but they may have to do this without serious discussion with the other side. Citizens, on the other hand, begin face-to-face dialogue to develop a firsthand picture of how issues and priorities are defined and begin to judge the possibilities of working together.

Public Process

Coming together for the first time, participants "map," or draw a mental picture of, the main problems that affect their relationships and identify the significant relationships that are responsible for creating these problems and that would need to be changed to resolve them. The group has a dual agenda: concrete problems are the starting point, but the purpose is always to probe the dynamics of the relationships that underlie them.

This stage ends when the group identifies and gives priority to a few problems it feels it must address systematically, one at a time. What they learn during this process becomes the essence of an agenda for either negotiation or their own continuing work.

At this point, those in the public peace process are moving ahead of officials. They are hearing directly the positions of people on the other side, as well as the feelings and assumptions that lie behind those positions. They are also gradually learning to see those in their dialogue as human beings. In many cases, officials are still working from their perceptions (or misperceptions) of the other side's positions and motives unless they are in close touch with those in the public arena.

Official Process

Perhaps the most critical period in the official peace process comes when leaders are deciding whether to commit themselves to an attempt at a negotiated settlement. Crystallizing that commitment is a complex part of the official peace process, because it involves interrelated judgments both about constituents' views and about the adversary's. Leaders are engaged in a mapping exercise, but they are mapping both their own political terrain and possibilities and the elements of the relationship with the other side.

Before leaders will openly commit to negotiate, they have to answer four questions: Will a negotiated solution be better than continuing the present situation? Can a fair settlement be fashioned, one that would be politically manageable? Will leaders on the other side accept the settlement and survive politically? Will the balance of forces permit agreeing to such a settlement?

Before taking a new direction, officials have to be more open about testing the waters in their own body politic. Judgments of the highest political and human order—about how much damage or pain a people can suffer—are required. Also required are the courage and the foresight to try to persuade others that the current situation cannot continue. Judgments about where a course of action will lead over time will have to be convincing. Astute political judgments must be made about when a constituency is ready to move, and skill is needed to create the catalyst.

It is essential to understand the other side's human and political needs. Officials must estimate the likelihood of success as a basis for deciding whether to commit themselves to try negotiation, but they will often need to explore the other side's views only quietly and indirectly. While citizens outside government can make this determination in dialogue with the adversary, officials are normally constrained by their positions; sometimes, the mere act of shaking hands or meeting casually with an adversary carries symbolic significance. Even if they talk directly, they must be guarded. In such situations, a third party who can talk with both sides may help assure them that enough common ground exists as a basis for beginning negotiation. If policymakers judge that the two sides are close to a mutually acceptable agenda, they will open more formal communication to try to arrange a negotiation.

PHASE THREE: GENERATING THE WILL FOR A JOINT SOLUTION

In this phase, individuals in each arena will probe the main issues more deeply and determine whether there is a will to deal with them. The aim is the same in and out of government, but each group will pursue it differently. If those in the public dialogue decide to work together in a new way, they will move into the work of stage four without having to justify their decision publicly. Officials, on the other hand, will often be meeting directly and intensively to write terms of reference for negotiation. From that experience, they will agree to begin negotiation or suspend the effort; either choice will be a public act for which they will be accountable.

Public Process

Participants probe specific problems to uncover the dynamics of underlying relationships with three aims: to determine how badly present relationships hurt their interests, to begin seeing ways to change those relationships, and to decide whether to try implementing such changes.

The main purpose in this stage is to generate the will to change conflictual relationships in order to deal with the problems that face the group. The tasks are (1) to shift discourse from explanation of positions to real dialogue in which participants begin interacting constructively; (2) to probe the problems that participants have agreed need most work and to use that analysis as a vehicle for illuminating the dynamics of key relationships; and (3) to create conditions in which participants can muster the will to design ways of changing destructive relationships that block change by asking them to assess where the present relationships are leading.

This stage generates several results: (1) the experience of an increasingly probing dialogue that deepens and begins to change relationships within the group; (2) a new body of insight into the perceptions, feelings, and mind-sets of others; (3) a picture of how relationships between the parties need to change; and (4) above all, a judgment that the costs of continuing the situation and relationships outweigh the costs of trying to change them. The critical product—and stage three cannot end without it—is the will to change. If that will is present, the group will move to a significantly different mode of working together in stage four. Their rationale for moving on could influence a decision by officials to begin negotiation.

Official Process

Once the parties have decided to try to negotiate, the third phase of the official peace process turns to preparing for negotiation, substantively and logistically. Four kinds of issues will have to be addressed:

- Determining the larger strategy and character of the negotiations will require answering several questions. Will the negotiations aim at a series of interim steps or at a comprehensive final settlement? What can be accomplished at each step? Are secret exchanges possible, and, if so, how much should be attempted in secret? Can a third party help?
- A second issue will be the mechanics of the negotiation. Will there be direct or mediated negotiation? Where and when will negotiations take place?

- A third question is whether all needed factions are represented and whether they are represented by the right people.
- Finally, terms of reference must be developed to ascertain that the parties have compatible objectives in the negotiation and that similar principles will guide decisions on the elements of a settlement. Sometimes, terms of reference contain ambiguities that both conceal important differences and reveal common ground.

Officials will end this period with a design for negotiation and will decide whether to begin. A crucial purpose has been to accumulate evidence that the risk of negotiation is justified—that negotiation can succeed, that the outcome could improve the situation, and that failure would be manageable.

PHASE FOUR: SCENARIO BUILDING AND NEGOTIATION

Once parties have decided to work together toward a joint solution, citizens and officials will employ two different approaches, sustained dialogue and negotiation. They will also aim at two different but complementary products, each reflecting particular capacities and roles. Citizens will aim at a changed relationship that enables them to work together in agreed ways in the society at large. Officials will seek a formal, written agreement.

Public Process

The vehicle for deepening the group's work requires participants to design a scenario of interacting steps that can be taken in the political arena to change troublesome relationships. As a microcosm of the larger relationships involved, the group learns the process of change by experiencing it and experiences what the relationship would have to become if the desired changes were to be accomplished. Such a group goes through four steps:

- It lists obstacles to changing relationships in the ways needed; the obstacles may be physical or psychological.
- Once the group has developed a full list of obstacles, it develops a parallel list of steps that could help erode or remove those obstacles. Some of these may be official steps; most will be steps to be taken by citizens' groups.
- It lists those groups that can take the steps envisioned.
- To change a relationship, the steps must be arranged in a realistic, interactive sequence —a pattern of action, response, and further response. For instance, party A may be able to take step 1 only if assured that party B will respond with step 2; party B may agree, but only if party A will respond with step 3 or party C will make supportive moves.

The critical part of the scenario is not the action list, but the idea of reinforcing interactions. It is important because relationships change in the course of those interactions. This differs sharply from the normal government approach—that one will act and the other will react, usually with little consultation about the political process they should be trying to generate by working together.

Official Process

Negotiation may already have begun in stage three, as the parties worked toward a starting point for negotiation or as a third party sought common ground. But the negotiating process changes character when participants begin trying to reduce what they have only talked about to a written agreement that can withstand the judgment of bodies politic.

The negotiation phase in the official peace process has been described extensively elsewhere, so I will make only two comments. First, there is a sharp difference between working out formal solutions to concrete problems and changing the human relationships that create many of those problems. Governments must tackle the formal solutions, but they cannot decree changes in human relationships. That is the task of citizens outside government. Second, there is an equally sharp difference between agreed-upon steps to solve a problem and the process of new interactions between the parties that could be generated in the implementation. Formal negotiations normally pay little attention to the political processes in which relationships actually change; citizens do. Work in both arenas is complementary.

PHASE FIVE: ACTING TOGETHER TO IMPLEMENT AGREEMENTS

Implementing agreements is often thought of as a series of actions to be taken. It is less often thought of as part of a long-term political process for changing relationships, in which negotiation is but one event. Paradoxically, in a continuing peace process that involves a sequence of negotiated agreements, implementation of one agreement may become part of preparing the political setting for the next, as faithful implementation builds confidence in the process and in the other party. It was particularly true in the Arab-Israeli peace process, for instance; each agreement in the early years was explicitly seen as but one step in a "step-by-step" process in which each agreement's implementation paved the way for the next. The history-making Camp David accords changed nothing on the ground, but they provided a framework for at least five more negotiations, which themselves would become part of the process of implementation by laying down new directions for implementation. These new directions would grow out of both the preparation for new negotiations and the work apart from negotiation that takes place in the public and civic arenas.

Public Process

Participants devise practical ways to put their scenario into action. They need to ask specific questions: Do conditions in the body politic permit implementing this scenario? Does the capacity exist to carry it through? Who needs to take what steps? Whatever their action, it both differs from and supports actions that emerge from negotiation.

Official Process

Governments will carefully watch each other to ensure that agreements reached have been scrupulously carried out. The process of implementation may last a number of years. For the most part, the steps agreed on will be limited to changing juridical and physical arrangements; governments can also take steps to change perceptions in each body politic, but changing human relationships will still be primarily citizens' business.

In both arenas, implementation is one more phase in developing a long-term political relationship in a framework that recognizes the peace process as designed to change relationships over time. Plotting a course in which the official and public peace processes—along with work in the quasi-official arena and in civil society—can complement each other can lead to new partnerships between governments and their people, which in themselves offer new potential for preventing and resolving conflict.

PRENEGOTIATION, CIRCUM-NEGOTIATION, AND THE PEACE PROCESS

The work apart from negotiation and in negotiation that paves the way for the peaceful resolution of conflict can be most richly understood when placed in the context of a multi-level peace process and when each arena of that process is seen in interaction with others over time. Governments must organize both substantively and politically for formal negotiations to produce precise written agreements. The political environment for initiating and implementing those agreements—the changes in relationships essential to peacemaking and peacebuilding—may best be shaped by citizens outside government, often interacting in complementary ways with those inside. Today's deep-rooted human conflicts demand the largest possible framework for marshaling the full array of resources and instruments in the whole body politic. That framework is the multilevel peace process. The work we call circum-negotiation is often the critical human part of that process.

NOTES

1. I began to develop these thoughts in a progression of articles I wrote soon after leaving government work in 1981: "Getting to Negotiation," a review of Roger Fisher and William Ury's *Getting to Yes: Negotiating Agreement without Giving In* (Boston: Houghton Mifflin, 1981), published in *Harvard Law Review* 95, no. 6 (April 1982); a paper prepared for the Center for the Study of Foreign Affairs, U.S. Department of State, Washington, D.C., in June 1983, published by the center in 1984 as "The Prenegotiation Phase," in *International Negotiation: Art and Science*, ed. Diane B. Bendahmane and John W. McDonald, Jr.; and "We Need a Larger Theory of Negotiation: The Importance of Prenegotiating Phases," *Negotiation Journal* 1, no. 3 (July 1985). This chapter draws on that body of work and moves beyond to establish a larger conceptual framework.

2. I. William Zartman, "Prenegotiation: Phases and Functions," in *Getting to the Table: The Processes of International Prenegotiation*, ed. Janice Gross Stein (Baltimore: Johns Hopkins University Press, 1989), 1–17.

3. For the term "circum-negotiation," I am indebted to Carol E. Saunders.

4. I first used the phrase "public peace process" in 1991 in a paper titled "Framework for a Public Peace Process: Toward a Peaceful Israeli-Palestinian Relationship" that was produced by a dialogue among a group of nonofficial Israelis and Palestinians that I moderated. Held in July 1991, the dialogue was sponsored by the Beyond War Foundation (renamed Foundation for Global Community) in Palo Alto, California. It was next used in Gennady I. Chufrin and Harold H. Saunders, "A Public Peace Process," *Negotiation Journal* 9, no. 2 (April 1993): 155–177. In this article, I first put forward the notion of sustained dialogue as a five-stage process. The comprehensive statement of the conceptual framework and of the process of sustained dialogue is found in Harold H. Saunders, *A Public Peace Process: Sustained Dialogue to Transform Racial and Ethnic Conflicts* (New York: St. Martin's Press, 1999).

5. The Inter-Tajik Dialogue was convened in March 1993 under the auspices of the Dartmouth Conference Regional Task Force, cochaired by Gennady I. Chufrin and Harold H. Saunders. The dialogue had met twenty-six times by the end of 1999. It is funded by the William and Flora Hewlett and the Charles Stewart Mott Foundations. It is conducted within the framework of the five-stage public peace process of sustained dialogue laid out in the Chufrin-Saunders article cited in note 4. The Charles F. Kettering Foundation in the United States and the Russian Center for Strategic Research and International Relations in Moscow organized the process.

6. This section on civil society is drawn from a letter written in January 1996 by David Mathews, president of the Charles F. Kettering Foundation,

and Harold H. Saunders to Cyrus Vance and David Hamburg, cochairs of the Carnegie Commission on Preventing Deadly Conflict.

7. An excellent presentation of this thinking may be found in Christopher Mitchell, "The Process and Stages of Mediation," in *Making War and Waging Peace: Foreign Intervention in Africa,* ed. David R. Smock (Washington, D.C.: United States Institute of Peace Press, 1993), especially 139–160.

8. Sustained dialogue as part of the public peace process was first laid out in Harold H. Saunders, "Four Phases of Non-Official Diplomacy," *Mind and Human Interaction* 3, no. 1 (July 1991): 30. The global context and the need for a public peace process—now laid out in five stages—were presented in Chufrin and Saunders, "A Public Peace Process." The public peace process is developed in Randa Slim and Harold H. Saunders, "Dialogue to Change Conflictual Relationships," in *Higher Education Exchange* (Dayton, Ohio: Kettering Foundation, 1994), 43–56. A second Russian edition of the Chufrin-Saunders article was published in Dayton, Ohio, by the Charles F. Kettering Foundation in 1995. The process is described fully and placed in political and global context in Saunders, *A Public Peace Process.* A short version for use in ethnic conflicts in the United States and an organizer's and moderator's manual for conducting sustained dialogue appears in the appendix of that book.

For a study of the official peace process, see Harold H. Saunders, *The Other Walls: The Arab-Israeli Peace Process in a Global Perspective,* rev. ed. (Princeton, N.J.: Princeton University Press, 1991), chap. 2; the description of the official peace process in this chapter draws heavily on that source.

30

Is More Better?

The Pros and Cons of Multiparty Mediation

Chester A. Crocker,
Fen Osler Hampson,
and Pamela Aall

THE CHANGING ENVIRONMENT OF MEDIATION

Mediation has a long history in international relations.[1] As Thucydides' account of the Peloponnesian War reminds us, the Greeks frequently resorted to mediation to avert violent conflict.[2] So too did the Romans and the Italian city-states of Renaissance Italy. The Treaty of Westphalia (1648), which led to the origins of the modern state system, arguably increased the need for mediation because the anarchical nature of international society, based on autonomous sovereign states, produced disputes that were not easy to resolve using the relatively weak instruments of international law.[3]

The past fifty years have seen an increase in the demand for mediators, partly because the international system changed profoundly during that period: the end of World War II, the emergence of the bipolarity of the Cold War, the rapid decolonization of vast areas of the globe, and the shift to the post–Cold War era. During the Cold War, mediators were used to positive effect in a number of major international crises. Over the years, the United States played a key role in successive mediation attempts to end the conflict between Israel and its Arab neighbors[4] and in various regional crises around the globe, such as in southern Africa.[5] The Soviet Union was only sporadically involved in mediation, notably in Tashkent in 1966, when it attempted to broker a settlement between India and Pakistan over Kashmir.[6]

Representatives of international and regional organizations also used their "good offices" on occasion to mediate an end to various conflicts, as in the efforts of the secretary-general of the United Nations to mediate an end to the Iran-Iraq war or successive rounds of UN mediation in Cyprus.[7] Even middle powers such as Canada and Algeria had their moments as mediators on the world stage. Canada played an important intermediary role in the 1956 Suez crisis. Algerian representatives played a vital role in helping to mediate an end to the

U.S. hostage crisis in Iran.[8] But these instances of middle-power mediation tended to be the exception rather than the norm. At the same time, mediated interventions by the United Nations or regional organizations were hampered by the U.S.-Soviet rivalry.[9]

During the Cold War there were also various instances of mediation carried out by nongovernment officials or representatives of various religious or secular institutions. The Vatican, for example, played a key role in mediating an end to the century-long dispute between Argentina and Chile over the Beagle Channel.[10] The International Committee of the Red Cross (ICRC) and the Quakers were involved in various humanitarian mediations in Africa's civil wars in the 1960s and 1970s.[11] However, mediated interventions of this kind were rare and generally confined to humanitarian objectives such as negotiating a temporary cease-fire that would allow food and medicine to be ferried to those in need.

The nature of warfare in the 1990s changed radically from the earlier decades of the latter half of the twentieth century. The proxy battles —fought between armed troops—that characterized the Cold War gave way to bloody civil and intercommunal conflicts in Haiti, Somalia, Sudan, Rwanda, Zaire, Congo-Brazzaville, Liberia, Bosnia, and Central Asia. At the same time that these internecine conflicts increased in number, there seemed to be an increase in the appetite for a negotiated settlement, as witnessed in Northern Ireland, El Salvador, Guatemala, Haiti, South Africa, Namibia, and Mozambique. Taken together, these circumstances led to a growing role for the international community in peacekeeping and peacemaking, and especially in mediating political agreements in seemingly intractable conflicts.

Other important developments in international politics have changed both the content and the nature of international mediation. First, individual states—the United States in Bosnia, Norway in the Middle East, Australia in East Timor, Tanzania in the Great Lakes—have played important roles in responding to crises or fostering negotiations. These new ventures, however, are not always successful, as the Canadians discovered when they attempted in 1996 to spearhead a multistate peace mission to Zaire (now the Democratic Republic of the Congo) but were unable to muster support from their partners. In addition, the roles that traditional diplomacy played in this new world have changed. Representatives of governments struggled with both the meaning and the practice of sovereignty as both global and subnational forces challenged the status quo. Career diplomats at the U.S. State Department and other foreign ministries still participated in peacemaking, but the appointment of dozens of special envoys and special representatives by heads of state and the UN secretary-general brought a whole series of new actors, and a new dynamic, into the official diplomatic process.

Second, the end of the Cold War has freed to some extent international organizations from their bipolar constraints and allowed them to take on new roles in mediation and conflict management.[12] Regional organizations and coalitions of small and medium-sized powers have also become more active as mediators, facilitators, and conflict managers.[13] Even in those situations in which great powers have intervened as a result of domestic political pressure or threatened national interests, there is seemingly a greater willingness to share the costs of intervention—military and political—with other states and international actors.[14]

Third, the widespread presence of religious, humanitarian, and development nongovernmental organizations (NGOs) in countries and regions of conflict has created a third tier of actors beyond states and international organizations. NGOs not only seek to alleviate the plight of refugees and other victims of violent conflict but also see themselves as having the capacity, expertise, and knowledge to initiate a process of dialogue between warring parties and factions.[15] In some instances, outside governments, wishing to intervene politically to stop the fighting, are willing to support these groups because they offer an entry point into the conflict.

Fourth, the renewed interest in mediation as an instrument of conflict management is prompted by the recognition that civil or intercommunal conflict is not easily dealt with by other modes of conflict management, such as international legal tribunals, arbitration, or even the use of force, which is costly and has obvious limitations as an instrument of third-party intervention.[16] Mediation represents a relatively low-cost alternative between the choices of doing nothing and large-scale military intervention.[17]

Finally, it is arguably the case that international norms are changing. There does appear to be a growing sentiment that something must be done to prevent further eruptions of wide-scale intercommunal violence that threaten regional stability. Some of these sentiments are fueled by the media and the publicity given to the victims of genocide and civil war on television.[18] But there is also a growing sense of moral responsibility premised on the recognition that the international community has an interest in advancing human rights, democracy, and the rule of law because strengthening them will contribute to the development of a more peaceful and stable international order.[19]

THE ELUSIVE DEFINITION OF MEDIATION

Definitions of mediation are as various as mediators themselves. Most, however, include the idea of a process undertaken by an outside party to bring or maintain peace. Some concentrate on the negotiation process itself. I. William Zartman and Saadia Touval state that "mediation is best thought of as a mode of negotiation in which a third party helps the parties find a solution which they cannot find by themselves."[20] Richard Bilder differentiates between the relatively passive activity of providing good offices and the more proactive role of the mediator: "Good offices and mediation are techniques by which the parties, who are unable to resolve a dispute by negotiation, request or agree to limited intervention by a third party to help them break an impasse. In the case of good offices, the role of the third party is usually limited simply to bringing the parties into communication and facilitating their negotiations. In the case of mediation, the mediator usually plays a more active part in facilitating communication and negotiation between the parties and is sometimes permitted or expected to advance informal and nonbinding proposals of his or her own."[21]

In his attempt to define mediation, Jacob Bercovitch puts forward a wide interpretation while still linking it to the negotiation process: "Mediation is . . . a process of conflict management, related to but distinct from the parties' own negotiations, where those in conflict seek the assistance of, or accept an offer of help from, an outsider (whether an individual, an organization, a group, or a state) to change their perceptions or behavior, and to do so without resorting to physical force or invoking the authority of law."[22]

James Laue broadens the reach of the mediator to include assisting "the parties in their negotiations or other problem-solving interaction,"[23] a theme Christopher Mitchell takes up in his definition of mediation as "intermediary activity . . . undertaken by a third party with the primary intention of achieving some compromise settlement of the issues at stake between the parties, or at least ending disruptive conflict behavior."[24]

The same range of definition appears in discussions of negotiation, and the activities that lead to negotiation. I. William Zartman uses the term "prenegotiation" to describe the activities engaged in after one party has decided that negotiation is an option but before the actual negotiation takes place.[25] This term has the virtue of delimiting by time and activity actions directly relevant to a negotiation. It, however, does not capture all the practices undertaken before and after a negotiation by official and nonofficial bodies to bring parties to a realization that negotiation is an option and to keep them committed to the negotiated agreement after it has been reached. Harold Saunders's neologism "circum-negotiation," defined as "the tasks apart from negotiation that have the purpose of beginning, sustaining, and nourishing a process by changing relationships and paving the way for negotiation or other peaceful steps to resolve conflict,"[26] attempts to encompass these many practices. Many of the tasks he identifies ("instigator, communicator, persuader, organizer, precipitator, legitimizer, convenor, moderator, manager, funder, teacher, idea formulator")[27] are precisely those undertaken by third parties in order to support movement toward and commitment to a settlement.

DEFINING MULTIPARTY MEDIATION

One of the reasons that scholars continue to debate the definition of mediation and its range of activities is that the practice of mediation is evolving in response to changing circumstances. The increase in peacemaking efforts and in the variety of organizations and individuals who undertake them has stretched the meaning of mediation. A U.S. president appoints a special envoy for East Africa who may play a valuable role in preventing conflict by embodying both great-power and international interest in keeping the peace and by using that leverage to stop an escalation in violence. A humanitarian NGO, using a combination of education, persuasion, and focused deployment of resources, plays a pivotal role in inducing local agencies to implement portions of a peace treaty. While

these may not be examples of mediation in the narrow sense, they are political interventions between warring parties in support of political solutions to contested issues.

Along with an expansion in the numbers and activities of third-party intervenors in conflict, there has been a rise in what we call "multiparty mediation"—situations involving multiple mediators, whether sequential, simultaneous, or "composite" mediatory actors such as the United Nations or the Organization for Security and Cooperation in Europe. This aspect—the added layers of complexity for all the parties involved in a mediated negotiation —complicates any mediator's job, raising the question of who is in charge of the mediation and offering parties alternative venues for their lobbying. It can also, however, mean opportunity for moving a peace process forward, as using an alternative channel may allow stalled talks to restart or may serve to develop support for already negotiated options.

Multiparty mediation refers in this chapter to attempts by many third parties to assist peace negotiations in any given conflict. These attempts may occur sequentially—one institution at a time—over the life of the conflict or may occur simultaneously, involving many different mediators with various institutional bases on the ground at the same time, as happened in 1997 in Zaire. Diplomatic interventions by intergovernmental organizations or coalitions are in themselves multiparty mediations. In these circumstances, the mediation is on behalf of a number of sovereign states, each of which has its own objectives, interests, priorities, and domestic constraints.

Multiparty mediations may also refer to a number of attempts at mediation by different actors over the life cycle of the conflict. In the early stages of a conflict, for example, nonofficial groups may be the only third parties active in the attempt to bring groups together or alert the international community to the need for preventive diplomacy or some kind of action.

If the conflict has escalated to full-scale violence, however, mediation may be undertaken by an international organization or by a representative of a national government who has the necessary influence and ability to move the parties to the conflict toward a negotiated solution. After a conflict is over or a negotiated settlement has been reached, many outside organizations may be involved in a postconflict situation, sustaining implementation of agreements reached by the parties, as has been the case in Bosnia.

To recap, multiparty mediation may be undertaken by international or regional organizations, national governments, and nongovernmental organizations. It may also be undertaken by a collective body such as a coalition of states that represent more than one set of national interests.[28] The mediations undertaken by a range of institutions may occur simultaneously or sequentially and may involve a variety of mediators who intervene in the conflict at different times. Our definition of multiparty mediation therefore includes an important temporal component and is intended to suggest that more than one mediator may be involved in a conflict at any given point in time or over the total life cycle of the conflict itself. The concept of multiparty mediation refers to simultaneous interventions by more than one mediator in a conflict, interventions by composite actors such as regional organizations or contact groups, and sequential mediated interventions that again involve more than one party.

The term "multiparty," therefore, has a triple meaning, and we recognize that the range of issues associated with multiparty interventions in a sequential setting may well differ from those where various mediators intervene in the same conflict at the same time. That being so, we also recognize that some conflicts may include mediated interventions that comprise both components, that is, simultaneous and sequential interventions that occur during more than one phase of the conflict.

CHALLENGES OF MANAGING MULTIPARTY MEDIATION

The complexity of an international response that comprises multiple mediators as well as other third-party actors such as peacekeeping forces, development agencies, NGOs, and lone operators has made peacemaking efforts messy, difficult, and at times chaotic in a number of today's conflicts. The vicious nature of these conflicts, however, and the high costs for the international community of failing to prevent or end war make it critical to manage these third-party interventions—to understand current mediations, their consequences, and requirements for leadership and cooperation in these joint, or at least contiguous, ventures.

Management in these circumstances is not a matter of establishing a line of command and responsibility. Organizing the diverse third-party peacemaking entities is a lot like organizing cats. As anyone who has lived with them can tell you, cats cannot be organized. Independent beings, they will do what they choose to do, gazing at your efforts with mild curiosity or simply ignoring you. Gaining a cat's cooperation is a complicated matter of setting a course the cat might find reasonable and employing incentives (food often works) that persuade it at least to give your idea some thought. The challenge to any principal mediator entering into a conflict is how to make a cohesive whole out of the independent third-party peacemaking initiatives, building on the positive results of earlier mediations, keeping simultaneous interventions by different actors from canceling each other out, bringing along the many interests that lie behind the third-party endeavor, organizing the handoff to a successor. In this aspect of his or her work, the mediator faces an array of highly autonomous individuals and organizations, such as special representatives of powerful states or of the UN secretary-general, high-level politicians, and committed individuals who are privately funded and accountable to no government or international organizations. Like cats, these independent agents rarely feel an obligation, or even a desire, to cooperate and they retain the ability to walk away from the mediation or to launch competing initiatives. The mediator cannot force these other third parties to collaborate but must persuade them to enter into a working relationship that reinforces rather than undermines the peacemaking mediation.

The wealth of willing third parties may be a boon to international peacemaking, but it also raises serious management issues about how and why these multiparty interventions come about; whether and how they are coordinated; who provides leadership; what determines the level of commitment in terms of human and financial resources; and who is responsible for keeping an already mediated settlement on track and preventing the collapse of the agreement lest it become orphaned.

The presence or availability of different mediators at varying stages of a conflict raises another series of questions. Are some mediating agents particularly effective during one phase of the conflict and less effective during other phases? Do these mediation efforts during different phases of a conflict—assuming that there is more than one—build on one another? Or do they constitute a series of ad hoc attempts at peacemaking whose success depends not on any cumulative effort but on the effectiveness of the mediator or the weariness of the different warring factions?

As more countries and institutional actors become involved in mediation, a judicious assessment is required not only of their comparative institutional strengths and weaknesses, but also of how to encourage complementary efforts and how to coordinate the process when one actor or institution is handing off the responsibilities for mediation to others. In addition, we need to know more about the main obstacles to achieving coordination and coherence among different mediators in such settings and how to overcome the problems faced by

multiple mediators working without a common script in trying to mediate a negotiated resolution to conflict.

THE WARS IN THE BALKANS: AN ILLUSTRATION

The wars in the Balkans since 1991 illustrate some of the challenges of multiparty mediation: the difficulty of mediation when so many voices are speaking at the same time; the difficulty of keeping a multiparty mediation on track; the comparative advantage of different third-party institutions at different times during the conflict and the particular qualities a powerful state brings to the mediation process when disputants are at their most intractable.

The case of the conflict in the former Yugoslavia, especially the Serbian-Croatian war in 1991–92 and the Bosnian war in 1992–95, provides a good example of multiparty mediation in several senses of the definition. First, there were a number of third parties that offered their services or more or less compelled the parties to accept them as intermediaries: the United Nations, the European Community/European Union (EC/EU), the United States, and, in a private capacity, former president Jimmy Carter. These concerted interventions were by and large sequential: first the European Community (now the European Union), then the United Nations, then a joint UN-EU effort, the brief Carter-negotiated cease-fire in late 1994–early 1995, and then the United States. A number of the interventions also represented mediations by institutions—the United Nations and the European Union—that are composed of governments with high degrees of sovereignty in the foreign policy arena. Consequently, despite the European Union's attempt to create a common foreign policy among its member nations, both institutions are subject to strong, often contradictory, expressions of national interest among their memberships. As discussed earlier, these interventions by intergovernmental organizations are included in our definition of multiparty mediation because the mediator, whether UN special representative Yasushi Akashi or the Vance-Owen team, is subject to the multiple pressures of the organization's membership. And finally, some of the mediation efforts were simultaneous. Jimmy Carter's effort to arrange a cease-fire occurred while David Owen and Thorvald Stoltenberg were still active and the U.S. government, in the person of Robert Frasure, was negotiating with Slobodan Milosevic to end the sanctions in return for recognition of Bosnia.[29]

The conflict in the former Yugoslavia was in part a by-product of the end of the Cold War. The regime of Josip Broz Tito, who ruled over a unified Yugoslavia for thirty-five years, had repressed ethnic identification as part of a campaign to build a nation-state out of the disparate communities of Serbia, Macedonia, Montenegro, Bosnia, Slovenia, and Croatia. Even the traditional enmity between Serbs and Croats, intensified by the activities of the Croatian Ustashe and the Serbian Chetniks during World War II, seemed to fade into competition for political and economic power between the two largest Yugoslav states. Intermarriages among the ethnic groups became common, and when Bosnian Muslims mobilized in the 1960s and 1970s, it was as a political force in order to strengthen their position against the larger states of Serbia and Croatia rather than as a religious force.[30] Yugoslavia seemed to support several anomalies: an open communist system and a unified, ethnically diverse state. Unnoticed by the outer world, this model developed cracks along ethnic and political fault lines before Tito died in 1980 but really started to crumble after his death, especially after the fall of the Berlin Wall and the political transitions that overtook Eastern and Central Europe as a consequence. In the midst of this political transition in Yugoslavia, politicians such as Slobodan Milosevic and Franjo Tudjman began to use ethnic nationalism as a political platform to increase their own power base.

The Yugoslavian wars began in 1991 with the conflict first between Slovenia and Belgrade, and then between Croatia and Belgrade. The trigger for the latter's turn to mass violence was Croatia's declaration of independence. This declaration coincided with Slovenia's declaration of independence, provoked in both cases by a Serbian refusal to recognize a Croatian as head of the rotating federal presidency. Belgrade failed to subdue the Slovenians militarily and so turned to Croatia. Compared with the later Bosnian conflict, this was a short war. The Croats, poorly armed and vulnerable to the UN arms embargo on Yugoslavia, and the well-equipped and -trained Serbian federal army fought for four months. During this time, the Croats found ways around the arms embargo and were recognized internationally as a sovereign state. These changes strengthened the Croatian position against the Serbs and may have contributed to Serbs' understanding that this early conflict was headed for an impasse, a hurting stalemate that increased the parties' willingness to negotiate rather than continue military action.

The international response to this war and the later Bosnian war, which were simultaneously intrastate and interstate, was equally a product of the post–Cold War period. After its attempts to stop the dissolution of Yugoslavia had failed, the United States claimed that European institutions should take responsibility for this European conflict. The European Community agreed and stepped up to the challenge, first enlisting Henry Wijnaendts as the EC's envoy to Yugoslavia and later appointing Lord Peter Carrington, former British foreign secretary, to intervene on its behalf. The European Community then teamed up with the United Nations to negotiate a peace in the former Yugoslavia in 1991. Former U.S. secretary of state Cyrus Vance, acting for the United Nations, was successful in negotiating a cease-fire in Croatia, but the end to the war came about because of changes on the battlefield and in international recognition of Croatia's independence. Lord Carrington on behalf of the European Community had a more difficult time in getting the Yugoslav republics to negotiate a joint future, an effort undercut by the German recognition of Croatian independence.[31] From these first third-party attempts at intervention, the deleterious effects of multiple voices making conflicting statements was apparent in this complex case.

The problems caused by competition among the peacemakers were even more apparent in the diplomatic interventions in the war in Bosnia. In the spring and summer of 1992, the war in Bosnia began, sparked in part by the profoundly different political futures the three ethnic groups envisioned for Bosnia. Whereas the Croats and the Serbs wanted to carve Bosnia up along ethnic lines, the Muslims wanted to keep the nascent country together. Again the United Nations and the European Union were teamed as the agents of third-party intervention. A stronger duo is hard to imagine. Cyrus Vance again represented Secretary-General Boutros Boutros-Ghali, bringing with him years of experience and a gloss of U.S. involvement in addition to the moral authority of the United Nations. Former British foreign secretary David Owen was appointed as envoy on behalf of the European Union, representing the collective power of Yugoslavia's close neighbors and largest trading partners.

The joint mediating team painstakingly put together a proposal for the resolution of the conflict, a plan that involved recognizing Bosnia and Herzegovina as a decentralized state composed of ten provinces and the eventual demilitarization of the whole country. The proposal was accepted as a basis for negotiation by all three parties, although both Muslim and Serb authorities had strong reservations about it. Its reception in the United States, however, was mixed. *Time* magazine claimed that the plan clearly favored the Serbs and a critical opinion piece by Anthony Lewis in the *New York Times,* entitled "Beware of Munich,"

drew parallels between the Vance-Owen peace plan and Chamberlain's negotiations with Hitler in 1938.[32] While members of the departing Bush administration were cautiously supportive, the new secretary of state, Warren Christopher, expressed doubts on the day following Bill Clinton's inauguration that the plan would work.[33] His ambivalence developed into skepticism by mid-February and set the pattern for U.S. reluctance to engage with the European-UN mediation effort, a pattern that continued until the United States put its weight behind the creation of the Federation of Bosnia and Herzegovina in March 1994. This agreement ended the war between the Croats and the Muslims in Bosnia and was the result of an intensive effort by Charles Redman, appointed by Christopher as the Bosnian negotiator during this period. The agreement was important, although as Daniel Serwer (the U.S. special coordinator for the federation) notes, the State Department remained ambivalent about devoting the attention and resources needed to make the agreement a success.[34]

A private effort occurred in December 1994 when former president Jimmy Carter traveled to Pale and Sarajevo and managed to secure an agreement among the parties for a four-month cease-fire. How private this effort was is not clear. Certainly, in carrying out his initiative, Carter acted independently of the U.S. diplomatic corps. Nonetheless, he may have had White House backing—or at least tacit support—for his work. On the official side, the United States was becoming more involved in the peacemaking effort, principally through a quiet —and ultimately unsuccessful—series of negotiations between U.S. special envoy Frasure and Milosevic.[35]

As public criticism about U.S. unwillingness to play a role in ending the war in the former Yugoslavia increased, pressure mounted for the Clinton administration to do something. Rumors of a massacre at Srebrenica and the horrifying late August 1995 mortar attack on a Sarajevo market seemed to galvanize the administration.[36] NATO bombing of Serb positions around Sarajevo and then more generally around western and northern Bosnia started on August 30. At the same time a Croat-Muslim military advance, supported by the Muslim authorities and by the Croatian army, streamed into the Krajina region, pushing back Serb forces on the ground as the international community was pounding them from the sky. Changes in the military equation on the ground and in the third parties' willingness to use force quickly altered the reckoning for the Serbs. Ripening in this case occurred when the Serbs overplayed their hand and a previous military imbalance (favoring the Serbs) was transformed by the Croat-Muslim advance and the use of NATO air power. This created for the first time a mutually hurting stalemate that mediators could manipulate to bring the Bosnian Serbs and their patron, Slobodan Milosevic, to the table.

The Dayton accords that followed this changed understanding of the costs and benefits of continued fighting was an agreement imposed by the United States on three reluctant ethnic groups. The full engagement of the United States gave the U.S. mediator, Richard Holbrooke, a tremendous amount of leverage —both positive and negative—with which to impress upon the parties the absolute necessity of coming to settlement. The mediation took every ounce of leverage that the superpower could bring to bear, including the personal attention of the president and the offer of sixty thousand peacekeeping troops available for the implementation phase. The reemergence of the United States, however, changed this mediation from a diffuse multiparty peacemaking effort to a much more focused, single-party one. The Europeans were frozen out of the key decision-making processes and the United Nations was thrust to the background, replaced in the implementation by the almost nonexistent Organization for Security and Cooperation in Europe (OSCE) and the newly established Office of the High Representative (OHR).

As we look at the Bosnian case, what does it tell us about the complexities of multiparty mediation? The first and most costly lesson in terms of human lives is that the propensity of individuals and institutions to try to run the show themselves—as the Europeans did in the early years of the Yugoslav wars—works only if they have the necessary willingness, resources, and persuasiveness to back it up. The UN-EU mediation had resources in the member-states that compose the institutions but found it difficult to marshal them. Individual states, protecting and pursuing their own interests, effectively diluted the mediation effort, and the mechanism to compel them to act concordantly was lacking. Further, the failure to engage—or to convince—the United States meant the loss of valuable leverage for the UN-EU effort and meant that member-states added to their balance ledgers the possibility of antagonizing the United States: a minor cost to some but more significant to Germany and Britain.

On the U.S. side, it proved possible to muster both willingness and resources to gain entry and to impose a settlement—in one sense a measure of a high degree of effectiveness. The U.S. reluctance, however, to support the Vance-Owen plan undercut these early mediators and led to a long period of mutual recriminations, the Europeans blaming the United States for its unwillingness to commit troops on the ground and its propensity to criticize the European-UN plan without offering an alternative. The Americans blamed the Europeans for a failure of nerve and an incompetency that allowed the Serbs to commit atrocities under the noses of the peacekeepers.

Bosnia also presents some interesting reflections on when institutions—no matter which they are—can intervene effectively. During the long war, while the Serbs were winning on the battlefield, they were uninterested in considering the possibility of negotiating. This posture changed only when the combined force of the Croatian offensive and NATO bombing attacks changed the situation on the ground. Does this mean that the Bosnian war was ripe for resolution in the fall of 1995? In a sense, yes. The Serbs, the most aggressive party to the conflict at this late stage in the war, had to refigure in these new circumstances the costs and benefits of continuing to lose soldiers, territory, prestige, and the patronage of Slobodan Milosevic. At the same time, however, it seems that the Croats had more fight in them and were prepared to pursue a military victory. In addition, the Muslims became more eager to exploit the change in the military balance rather than to negotiate a deal. This is hardly the definition of a mutually hurting stalemate.

The role of the third-party intervenors in managing this situation, in changing the Serbs' perceptions, and in restraining the Croats was critical to developing a state of ripeness. The combination of the use of force and the figurative (and one wonders if it was at times literal) strong-arming of Milosevic to bring his clients to the negotiating table provide an extreme example of the use of leverage to change the parties' appreciation of costs. Only a very powerful state, capable of pulling along a military alliance such as NATO and of providing incentives and disincentives could have played this role in 1995. It does not mean that, given another constellation of circumstances—including a unity of purpose and coordination among the third-party actors—the EU-UN effort was incapable of bringing peace at an earlier stage. These efforts, however, were stymied as third parties looked for scapegoats among allied partners and undercut their own—and all other—efforts. And this raises a final point that this case illustrates: political will among the intervenors to end the conflict and to forge the necessary coordination and unity of purpose is an essential element of multiparty mediation success. Too often such political will is missing from joint international engagements.

THE COSTS AND BENEFITS OF MULTIPARTY MEDIATION

As the example of the Balkan conflicts shows, there are costs and benefits of multiparty mediation in today's conflicts. Keeping a number of independent third parties on target, or just keeping them informed, demands much time and energy on the part of the principal mediator. Balanced against the benefits of an internationally supported peace agreement, these costs may be well worth the capital they consume. In other cases, however, these costs outweigh the benefits and can actually set back the peacemaking process. Too many parties can cause confusion and dilute responsibility among the various peacemakers; just as important, this multiplicity of efforts can waste the resources of the already overtaxed third-party institutions that respond to conflict. In these cases, the multiparty aspect of the mediation effort becomes a liability.

Costs

SHARED ANALYSIS OF PROBLEMS AND SOLUTIONS. One of the first tasks facing an individual or institution undertaking a third-party intervention is to identify the causes of the conflict and, based on this analysis, construct possible solutions. This is not an easy exercise. As noted in the introduction to this volume, there is rarely, if ever, a single cause of a conflict. Disputes turn to mass violence for a variety of reasons, some deep-seated and structural, some more immediate, and some that serve principally as triggers when other circumstances are right. Even when there is open communication among the various third parties, disagreements about the relative importance of the identified causes can result in disagreements over the solution and lead to tensions and interagency disputes. Often, however, there is not open communication among third parties, shared analyses of problems and solutions never occur, and joint strategies are much more difficult to create. In other cases the lack of open communication may reflect an unacknowledged divergence of interests that inhibits cooperation and guarantees that third parties—despite a professed desire for peace—work at cross-purposes. This lack of common vision becomes a contributing factor to other costs of multiparty mediation, such as mixed messages, unnecessary duplication of efforts, and failure to manage transitions from one third-party agency to another. Such problems have bedeviled interallied diplomacy in the Balkans, Central Asia, Sudan, and Central Africa.

MIXED MESSAGES AND FORUM SHOPPING. An obvious set of problems has to do with having too many "cooks" involved in the collective mediation enterprise. If there is no shared analysis of the problem, and no sense of a common solution, different mediators can undermine each other when they talk to the parties. Some situations call for a clear delegation of authority for conducting negotiations, particularly when negotiations are being conducted on separate tracks and with different constituencies. The danger of sending mixed or confusing signals rises with an increase in the number of mediators, and the international community will undermine its own efforts if the parties perceive that they can exploit differences among mediators who are working at cross-purposes. The inclination of the parties to go "forum shopping" also grows, with the ever present hope of finding a mediator who is sympathetic to their own particular interests and agenda.

The Great Lakes crisis of the mid- to late 1990s produced all sorts of official mediations, particularly from the United Nations, the Organization of African Unity (OAU), the European Union, the Arusha group of states, the United States, and numerous NGOs. The sheer number of special envoys, each with his own special agenda and set of motivations, undermined official claims that the international community itself wanted peace. Many of these initiatives failed to solve the problems of communication gridlock and to some extent compounded the difficulties of reaching a settlement because they were too focused on narrow agendas without fully grasping the larger elements of the situation and the wide range of humanitarian, development, and human rights concerns that were central to it.[37] In such circumstances the parties' own divisions reinforce external confusion and rivalries among the external third parties purporting to help.

WASTING RESOURCES AND DROPPING THE BALL. Multiple third parties engaged simultaneously or sequentially produce challenges of management and coordination that go beyond the problems of mixed messages and forum shopping. Not only is there a waste of effort and resources that occurs when there is no clear leadership or delegation of authority in an intervention, but such management problems can also affect the fate of a peace agreement. Problems of handoff between one peacemaker and the next are all too frequently encountered when different mediators try to engage parties in negotiations over a prolonged period of time. These handoff problems are typically encountered in the transitional period between the successful negotiation of a peace settlement and its subsequent implementation. During this period, misunderstandings and conflicting interpretations about implementation are common. New problems may also surface that were not adequately addressed during the negotiation of the settlement or that arise from the competition for scarce resources in the post-conflict reconstruction of society and economy. The difficulties experienced by those responsible for implementing the settlement in question may be compounded by poorly defined mandates and inadequate resources for sustaining the peace process. Such issues have severely aggravated the problems encountered by external intervenors in Bosnia, Somalia, Rwanda, and Sierra Leone.

BUCK-PASSING AND BLAME AVOIDANCE. In any collective mediation undertaking of the composite or simultaneous variety there is always the danger that different mediators will duck the tough issues and try to pass the responsibility and blame when things go wrong. Just as there may be strong incentives to share the costs and risks of mediation and negotiation in the most problematic cases, there are also incentives to distance oneself from failures or the prospect of imminent failure. In the early years of the Balkan crisis, the United States was all too willing to stay clear of Yugoslavia and pass the buck to the Europeans after initial U.S. efforts to prevent the breakup of Yugoslavia had failed. It was only several years later, when public criticism of U.S. unwillingness to play a role intensified after the horrifying attack in August 1995 on a Sarajevo market, that the Clinton administration fully reengaged itself in the conflict, appointing Richard Holbrooke to serve as the U.S. mediator.

Benefits

Multiparty mediation can also bring to a peacemaking effort cumulative benefits that make the difference between success and failure. Third-party intervention in conflict is a delicate matter, needing tact and persuasion as much as boldness and persistence. In the complicated world of modern conflict, it is not always possible for one institution or country to fulfill these requirements, and often more than one third party is necessary to prepare and establish a way to peace. This burden sharing, even in circumstances in which the organizations do not fully collaborate, often provides the means to avoid conflict or cement a peace agreement. The ability to support each other's efforts is one clear benefit of multiparty mediation. There are many others.

GAINING ENTRY AT DIFFERENT STAGES. Individuals and institutions have different strengths and capabilities that, depending on the stage of the conflict, may be more appropriate to facilitating negotiations and establishing communications and dialogue among the parties. For instance, at the low end of the conflict curve, before the outbreak of major hostilities or large-scale violence, multitrack mediated interventions by nonofficial actors can be effective in defusing conflicts before they escalate. At the height of the conflict, engaging the antagonists becomes much more difficult; mediation at this point may require the kind of "muscle" that only states, individually or in coalition, can provide.[38] The implementation period, however, may require a combination of institutions: peacekeeping or peace enforcement forces, regional organizations, official aid agencies, and NGOs all play important roles in developing a sustainable peace.

At the early stages of a conflict, the antagonists may eschew high-level mediation by states or international organizations because they do not want to commit themselves to a formal dialogue with its attendant political costs and risks. In these circumstances multiparty mediation can help to prevent the escalation of stakes by creating a set of parallel tracks for informal dialogue and communication. As the parties talk to each other in an informal setting removed from the political limelight, these dialogues can reduce tensions and encourage the development of trust and working relationships.

For instance, the Informal Working Group on the South China Sea provides useful illustrations of multiparty mediation as an instrument of conflict prevention. The South China Sea project was conceived as a series of nonofficial workshops, organized by a joint team comprising an Indonesian diplomat and a Canadian academic, that was sequenced over a period of almost ten years to discuss a range of joint scientific, environmental, and legal issues in the South China Sea. These workshops complemented a series of ongoing bilateral negotiations at the official level between various states in the region, making this a case of multiparty mediation involving simultaneous and sequential negotiations on two parallel tracks.

Delegates, many of whom were government officials, participated in these nonofficial workshops in their individual capacities. The success of these workshops in fostering dialogue, developing ideas for joint cooperation, and reducing tensions by placing issues once considered taboo on the negotiating agenda is due largely to the informal nature of the discussion and the functional and problem-solving manner in which issues have been addressed.

A number of examples of the benefits of complex mediatory initiatives during the hot conflict stage can be found in Central America in the 1980s and early 1990s. For example, the layered, interactive relationships among Contadora states, the Contadora "support group," the Esquipulas process led by Central American leaders, the Organization of American States (OAS), the UN secretary-general and his special envoy, and "friends of the secretary-general" all helped produce momentum toward the resolution of regional, cross-border, and internal conflicts, especially in the cases of Nicaragua, El Salvador, and ultimately Guatemala. This division of effort between "outsider neutrals" and "insider partials" points to a pattern of particular relevance where regional (insider) sensitivities and special insights may be needed adjuncts of more distant and more powerful actors.[39]

The case of Mozambique offers an especially compelling illustration of the benefits of a well-orchestrated and diplomatically nuanced appreciation of the vital importance of having all external players pull on the oars together, during both the negotiation phase (1990–92) and the implementation phase (1992–94). During each phase, the lead actors worked assiduously to keep other, more powerful, actors both coordinated and well informed. As a result, at times of hard choices and real tests, the third parties were working basically from the same sheet of music and the Mozambican parties were induced to sustain the peace and adhere to their commitments.[40] The implementation of the Dayton accords saw the creation of one new mediatory institution, the OHR, and the sudden expansion of the responsibilities of another institution, the OSCE. Both institutions had a mixed record in promoting and facilitating the civilian implementation effort but, through their efforts, provided important lessons about the types of third-party institutions that are needed to provide leadership, direction, and coordination in a massive multiparty peace implementation exercise.

OPENING NEW AVENUES FOR DIALOGUE. When one avenue is blocked, the activities of another mediator or party providing "good offices" can create a new opening in the negotiation process. The process that led to the Oslo accord was a multiparty effort to provide a new opportunity to bring together Israelis and Palestinians. The Norwegians were able to open up a confidential back channel to the ongoing formal and public Washington-led negotiations that involved high-level, direct face-to-face negotiations between Israeli and Palestinian officials. The nongovernmental partner in these negotiations provided academic camouflage that gave the parties "their much-needed 'deniability,'" and the Norwegians' ability to deflect media attention allowed parties to take some risks without fear of exposure. It is worth noting that the Clinton administration gave its full backing to the Oslo peace process when an agreement was reached. A small country like Norway was able to play the role of third-party facilitator precisely because it was perceived by the parties as neutral and impartial; Norway did not assume the role of full-fledged "mediator" and did not seek the mandate to do so.[41]

CREATING LEVERAGE, ISOLATING SPOILERS, AND SHARING COSTS AND RISKS. Multiparty mediation, particularly when undertaken by a coalition or collective body, provides a critical mechanism not only for sharing the costs and risks of mediation but also for multiplying sources of leverage. In the Peru-Ecuador border conflict, for example, the four guarantor countries to the 1942 Rio Protocol between Peru and Ecuador were able to work together to help resolve the boundary dispute that escalated into full-scale warfare between the two countries in 1995. The guarantors were the only channel of communication between the two countries and no negotiation would have been possible without the guarantors. As the U.S. mediator noted, "because the four guarantor states were powerful and successful countries, this automatically put pressure on the parties at least to appear to be working toward a settlement." At the same time, the "legitimacy of their actions and recommendations" came from the original Rio Protocol, which not only provided a legal framework but also gave broader political legitimacy and coherence to the peace process.[42]

CATALYTIC ROLES IN PROMOTING SYSTEMIC CHANGE. In a number of cases, ongoing civil or "internal" conflicts are entangled in a wider complex of regional and/or great-power interests that sustain conflict processes and thwart the possibilities for a settlement. On such occasions, composite mediation efforts that involve key regional and/or global actors may be critical to restructuring relations at the wider subsystemic or even systemic level if there is to be any hope of reaching a negotiated settlement. Multiparty mediation efforts may serve as an important catalyst for advancing systemic change, particularly in those conflicts that threaten to spread across a region or strategic area. In the early 1990s, the five permanent members of the United Nations Security Council worked together in a multiparty effort to mediate the Comprehensive Peace Agreement for Cambodia. The Cambodian settlement became an agent of broader, systemic, change, serving to redefine relations between China and Vietnam, the United States and Russia, and the United States and all of Indochina. The mediators as parties to this wider process of structural transformation not only encouraged changes that were already beginning to occur but also acted as a catalytic force by providing a cover for Soviet disengagement from Vietnam and normalization of relations between Hanoi and Beijing. Other catalytic agents—the United Nations, the Association of Southeast Asian Nations (ASEAN), and Australia—were also important to moving the process forward and prompting the thaw in China-Vietnam relations that was critical to the settlement in Cambodia. This case points out that regional and international resources, when mobilized, can be critical factors in moving the conflict parties toward a negotiated settlement.[43]

In building support for the Madrid talks in the Middle East process, the United States tried to capitalize on the dramatic new realities and reshaping of interstate relations in the region as a result of the cooperative, allied effort in the Gulf War against Iraq, coupled with the rapid decline of Soviet influence in the region with the collapse of the Soviet Union.[44] Secretary of State James A. Baker realized that any new American initiative was condemned to failure if it simply resurrected the diplomatic status quo. The United States, therefore, in its traditional role as mediator and broker of Israel's relations with its neighbors, launched an ambitious new set of negotiations on two tracks: one that would lead to an Israeli-Palestinian dialogue (with all the difficulties that entailed) and the other in the form of direct talks between Israel and its Arab neighbors. This tactical decision, Baker noted, not only enhanced American credibility, but also gave the parties the necessary cover to change their long-standing policies toward each other. Looking back on Madrid and the events that followed, Baker observed that "like a phoenix, the Middle East peace process was reborn in Madrid out of the ashes of the collapse of communism and of Saddam's ill-conceived invasion of Kuwait."[45]

BUILDING SUPPORTIVE CONSTITUENCIES WITHIN SOCIETY. Just as it may be necessary to build support upward, there is a similar need to work downward from the national level to the community level in order to engage local constituencies in the peace process. A peace initiative in Tajikistan, which has helped to develop a complementary peace process on different tracks, provides an example of a multilevel effort. The nonofficial dialogue initiated under the auspices of a six-person U.S.-Russian team helped pave the way for negotiations at a time when there was no contact between the government and the opposition. These informal discussions helped build trust and develop the agenda for subsequent negotiations at the official level. As part of their activities, dialogue members and organizers briefed top leaders in the government and the opposition as well as the U.S. government and the United Nations. Once formal negotiations were under way, the dialogue shifted its efforts to working with various civic groups on developing intercommunal mediation and negotiation mechanisms that supported the process of national reconciliation. Harold Saunders describes the dialogue as a "mind at work in the middle of a country making itself."[46] Similar kinds of constituency building are also evident in the various initiatives on the Northern Ireland conflict.[47]

CONCLUSION

This account makes clear that complex or multiparty mediation is here to stay. This fact has direct and inescapable effects on the practice of diplomacy and third-party intervention in conflicts and so has specific implications for practitioners as well as students who seek to understand the new environment of mediation described here. The final reckoning of costs and benefits of multiparty mediation produces a somewhat mixed balance sheet: whereas more is not necessarily better, it is not necessarily worse. It is necessarily more complicated, and so much depends on the capacity of lead actors to work together, to recognize the temptations and pitfalls of a more "complex" environment, and to seize the opportunities for leadership

and adherence to standards of best practice. Much also depends on a recognition that an enduring peace needs the skills, talents, and commitment of all sorts of actors: official and nonofficial, state-based and UN-based, diplomats, lawyers, and humanitarians. And finally, much depends on an acknowledgment by all third parties that current conflicts place on them new burdens to open their eyes to the broader context in which they operate and to avoid the introverted preoccupations and interinstitutional competition that can bring more trouble than good to international efforts to foster peace.

NOTES

1. This chapter was drawn from the introductory chapters and the conclusion of the volume we edited in 1999, *Herding Cats: Multiparty Mediation in a Complex World* (Washington, D.C.: United States Institute of Peace Press, 1999). This book brings together cases written by the principal mediators of significant interstate and intrastate conflicts. Only some of the cases are referred to in this chapter, but all of them yield significant insights into the challenges of multiparty mediation.

2. Thucydides, *History of the Peloponnesian War*, trans. Thomas Hobbes (Chicago: University of Chicago Press, 1989).

3. Jacob Bercovitch, J. Theodore Anagnoson, and Donnette L. Willie, "Some Contextual Issues and Empirical Trends in the Study of Successful Mediation in International Relations," *Journal of Peace Research* 28, no. 1 (1991): 7–17.

4. Efraim Inbar, "Great Power Mediation: The USA and the May 1983 Israeli-Lebanese Agreement," *Journal of Peace Research* 28, no. 1 (1991): 71–84; Sidney Dawson Bailey, *Four Arab-Israeli Wars and the Peace Process* (London: Macmillan, 1990); Saadia Touval, *The Peace Brokers: Mediators in the Arab-Israeli Conflict, 1948–1979* (Princeton, N.J.: Princeton University Press, 1982); and Jeffrey Z. Rubin, ed., *Dynamics of Third-Party Intervention: Kissinger in the Middle East* (New York: Praeger, 1981).

5. Chester A. Crocker, *High Noon in Southern Africa* (New York: W. W. Norton, 1992); David R. Smock and Chester A. Crocker, eds., *African Conflict*

Resolution: The U.S. Role in Peacemaking (Washington, D.C.: United States Institute of Peace Press, 1995); and Stephen Chan and Vivienne Jabri, *Mediation in Southern Africa* (London: Macmillan, 1993).

6. Thomas Perry Thornton, "The Indo-Pakistani Conflict: Soviet Mediation in Tashkent, 1966," in *International Mediation in Theory and Practice*, ed. Saadia Touval and I. William Zartman (Boulder, Colo.: Westview Press, 1985), 141–171.

7. Diane Bendahmane and John MacDonald, eds., *Perspectives on Negotiation* (Washington, D.C.: Foreign Service Institute, 1986).

8. Bousetta Allouche, "La médiation des petits états: Retrospective et perspective," *Études Internationales*, no. 25 (June 1994): 213–236; Gary Sick, "The Partial Negotiator: Algeria and the U.S. Hostages in Iran," in *International Mediation in Theory and Practice*, 21–66; and Warren Christopher et al, *American Hostages in Iran: The Conduct of a Crisis* (New Haven, Conn.: Yale University Press, a Council on Foreign Relations Book, 1985).

9. Raimo Vayrynen, "The United Nations and the Resolution of International Conflicts," *Cooperation and Conflict* 20, no. 3 (1985): 141–171; Oran Young, *The Intermediaries: Third Parties in International Crises* (Princeton, N.J.: Princeton University Press, 1967).

10. Thomas Princen, *Intermediaries in International Conflict* (Princeton, N.J.: Princeton University Press, 1992).

11. C. H. Mike Yarrow, *Quaker Experiences in International Conciliation* (New Haven, Conn.: Yale University Press, 1978); and David P. Forsythe, "Humanitarian Mediation by the International Committee of the Red Cross," in *International Mediation in Theory and Practice*, 233–250.

12. Barry M. Blechman, "Emerging from the Intervention Dilemma," in *Managing Global Chaos: Sources of and Responses to International Conflict*, ed. Chester A. Crocker and Fen Osler Hampson with Pamela Aall (Washington, D.C.: United States Institute of Peace Press, 1996), 287–295; J. William Durch, ed., *The Evolution of UN Peacekeeping: Case Studies and Comparative Analysis* (New York: St. Martin's Press, 1993); J. William Durch, *UN Peacekeeping, American Policy, and the Uncivil Wars of the 1990s* (New York: St. Martin's Press, 1996); and Kjell Skjelsbaek, "The UN Secretary-General and the Mediation of

International Disputes," *Journal of Peace Research* 28, no. 1 (1991): 99–115.

13. Ruth Wedgwood, "Regional and Subregional Organizations in International Conflict Management," in *Managing Global Chaos*, ed. Crocker and Hampson with Aall, 275–285.

14. Amitai Etzioni, "Mediation as a World Role for the United States," *Washington Quarterly* 18, no. 2 (summer 1995): 75–87.

15. Thomas G. Weiss, *The United Nations and Civil Wars* (Boulder, Colo.: Lynne Rienner, 1996); Christopher Mitchell, "The Process and Stages of Mediation," in *Making War and Waging Peace: Foreign Intervention in Africa*, ed. David R. Smock (Washington, D.C.: United States Institute of Peace Press, 1994), 139–159; Hizkias Assefa, *Mediation of Civil Wars: Approaches and Strategies—The Sudan Conflict* (Boulder, Colo.: Westview Press, 1987); and I. William Zartman, ed., *Elusive Peace: Negotiating an End to Civil Wars* (Washington, D.C.: Brookings Institution, 1995).

16. Jacob Bercovitch and Allison Houston, "The Study of International Mediation: Theoretical Issues and Empirical Evidence," in *Resolving International Conflicts: The Theory and Practice of Mediation*, ed. Jacob Bercovitch (Boulder, Colo.: Lynne Rienner, 1996), 11–35; Richard B. Bilder, "Adjudication: International Tribunals and Courts," in *Resolving International Conflicts*, 155–190; and Michael Brown, *International Dimensions of Internal Conflict* (Cambridge, Mass.: MIT Press, 1996).

17. Jacob Bercovitch, *Social Conflicts and Third Parties: Strategies of Conflict Resolution* (Boulder, Colo.: Westview Press, 1984); and Jacob Bercovitch, "International Mediation: A Study of the Incidence, Strategies, and Conditions of Successful Outcomes," *Cooperation and Conflict* 21, no. 3 (1986): 155–168.

18. Warren P. Strobel, *Late-Breaking Foreign Policy: The News Media's Influence on Peace Operations* (Washington, D.C.: United States Institute of Peace Press, 1997).

19. David Cortright, *The Price of Peace: Incentives and International Conflict Prevention* (Lanham, Md.: Rowman and Littlefield, 1997); Lori Fisler Damrosch, *Enforcing Restraint: Collective Intervention in Internal Conflicts* (New York: Council on Foreign Relations, 1993); and Tom Hadden, "The Role of International Agencies in Conflict Resolution: Some Lessons from the Irish Experience," *Bulletin of Peace Proposals* 18, no. 4 (1987): 567–572.

20. I. William Zartman and Saadia Touval, "International Mediation in the Post–Cold War Era," in *Managing Global Chaos*, ed. Crocker and Hampson with Aall, 446; see also chapter 26 in this volume.

21. Richard Bilder, "International Third-Party Dispute Settlement," in *Approaches to Peace: An Intellectual Map*, ed. W. Scott Thompson and Kenneth M. Jensen, with Richard N. Smith and Kimber M. Schraub (Washington, D.C.: United States Institute of Peace Press, 1992), 198.

22. I. William Zartman and J. Lewis Rasmussen, eds., *Peacemaking in International Conflict: Methods and Techniques* (Washington, D.C.: United States Institute of Peace Press, 1997), 130.

23. James Laue, "Contributions of the Emerging Field of Conflict Resolution," in *Approaches to Peace*, ed. Thompson et al. 314.

24. Christopher Mitchell, *The Structure of International Conflict* (New York: St. Martin's Press, 1981), 287.

25. I. William Zartman, "Prenegotiation: Phases and Functions," in *Getting to the Table: The Processes of International Prenegotiation*, ed. Janice Gross Stein (Baltimore, Md.: Johns Hopkins University Press, 1989), 1–17.

26. Harold Saunders, "Prenegotiation and Circumnegotiation," in *Managing Global Chaos*, ed. Crocker and Hampson with Aall, 421.

27. Ibid., 425.

28. Clive Archer, "Conflict Prevention in Europe: The Case of the Nordic States and Macedonia," *Cooperation and Conflict*, no. 29 (December 1994): 367–386; and Victor H. Umbricht, *Multilateral Mediation: Practical Experiences and Lessons* (The Hague: Martinus Nijhoff Publishers, 1989).

29. Richard C. Holbrooke, *To End a War* (New York: Random House, 1998), 63.

30. Noel Malcolm, *Bosnia: A Short History* (New York: New York University Press, 1996), 202.

31. Warren Zimmerman, *Origins of a Catastrophe: Yugoslavia and Its Destroyers* (New York: Times Books, 1996), 161.

32. Bruce W. Nelan, "Serbia's Spite," *Time*, January 25, 1993, 48; and Anthony Lewis, "Beware of Munich," *New York Times*, January 8, 1993.

33. David Owen, *Balkan Odyssey* (New York: Harcourt Brace, 1996), 94–101.

34. Daniel Serwer, "A Bosnian Federation Memoir," in *Herding Cats*, 547–586.

35. Holbrooke, *To End a War*, 63.

36. Ibid., 74, 93.

37. Fabienne Hara, "Burundi: A Case of Parallel Diplomacy," in *Herding Cats*, 135–158.

38. Saadia Touval, *The Peace Brokers: Mediators in the Arab-Israeli Conflict, 1948–1979* (Princeton, N.J.: Princeton University Press, 1982).

39. See Paul Wehr and John Paul Lederach, "Mediating Conflict in Central America," in *Resolving International Conflicts*, ed. Bercovitch. See also Alvaro de Soto, "Ending Violent Conflict in El Salvador," in *Herding Cats*, 345–385.

40. Andrea Bartoli, "Mediating Peace in Mozambique: The Role of the Community of Sant'Egidio," and Aldo Ajello, "Mozambique: Implementation of the 1992 Peace Agreement," in *Herding Cats*, 245–273, 615–642.

41. Jan Egeland, "The Oslo Accord: Multiparty Facilitation through the Norwegian Channel," in *Herding Cats*, 527–546.

42. Luigi R. Einaudi, "The Ecuador-Peru Peace Process," in *Herding Cats*, 405–429.

43. Richard H. Solomon, "Bringing Peace to Cambodia," in *Herding Cats*, 275–323.

44. James A. Baker III, "The Road to Madrid," in *Herding Cats*, 183–205.

45. Ibid., 205.

46. Harold H. Saunders, "The Multilevel Peace Process in Tajikistan," in *Herding Cats*, 177.

47. Paul Arthur, "Multiparty Mediation in Northern Ireland," in *Herding Cats*, 469–501.

PART IV
INSTITUTIONS AND REGIMES OF SECURITY AND CONFLICT MANAGEMENT

31

New Challenges for the United Nations

Rolf Ekeus

AT THE TURN OF THE CENTURY the United Nations is facing a quartet of challenges that have grown out of events during the past decade. First there is a crisis of identity. The United Nations was originally conceived as a coalition of the nations that fought and won the war against Germany and Japan, but it soon became a battleground for the Cold War. The disintegration of the great wartime alliance required adjustments that were not foreseen when the United Nations Charter was drafted. A major portion of the membership adhered to ideologies or doctrines that nihilistically rejected fundamental human rights and subjected human beings to the absolute authority of state or party, thus compromising one of the fundamental tenets of the charter.

For four decades this dualism in world politics between the principles of human rights and the practices of their rejection molded the development of the United Nations and the charter. Charter values were marginalized. At the same time, a distinct third presence emerged in the form of the nonaligned movement. The Security Council, vested with extraordinary rights and powers, was reduced to the level of a debating society, while the UN General Assembly transformed itself into an arena for a political beauty contest between two ideological camps, wooing political favors from the nonaligned countries. The Secretariat envisioned by Dag Hammarskjöld, the second secretary-general, as an impartial international civil service in the tradition of the civil services of Britain and the Scandinavian countries, turned into a market for the exchange of posts. Political expediency and affiliation together with "geographical distribution" (the practice of making promotion and recruitment dependent upon nationality rather than merit) superseded the main charter rule that UN staff should be recruited according to the highest standards of efficiency, competence, and integrity. This prevailing culture, however, did not stop several secretaries-general from surrounding themselves with some selfless, honest, and hardworking private staff, who managed to keep the Secretariat afloat.

In spite of the virtual recasting of the original idea of the United Nations as a consequence of the Cold War, the United Nations made some significant contributions to international security during the same period. Pressures generated in the General Assembly had a decisive effect in speeding up the inevitable decolonization process. The repugnant apartheid policy came under constant attack from the UN system at a time when many individual countries preferred to support and cooperate with South Africa. The United Nations developed principles and practices of peacekeeping and peace-making that led to some spectacular successes. The political, economic, and social aspects of poverty in the Third World were identified and highlighted better in the context of the United Nations and its agencies than elsewhere. The United Nations also raised awareness of the importance of protecting the global environment.

After forty years of marginalization nothing was more earthshaking for the United Nations than the end of the Cold War. The important role that the United Nations and the Security Council played when the United States assembled the coalition to defeat Iraq and liberate Kuwait showed in a single moment that the Cold War was over. The coalition handed over to the Security Council the responsibility of formulating and implementing the cease-fire after the end of the Gulf War. U.S. President George Bush declared the dawn of a new international order and a central role for the United Nations in that order. The Security Council set up the United Nations Commission on Iraq (UNSCOM) to oversee the disarmament of Iraq. That organ worked initially with the strong mandate and united support of the council. Unfortunately, after some years that unity started to fray and, with weakened political support, UNSCOM ran into difficulties. Many of the old bad ways of the United Nations started to show. Secretary-General Boutros Boutros-Ghali embarked upon the thankless

task of reforming the Secretariat but did not, in spite of considerable efforts, muster enough enthusiasm in the Secretariat and among member-states to be effective against both internal resistance and governmental skepticism. The Security Council gave the Secretariat major operational tasks without providing it with resources for planning and preparation. After the first euphoric post–Cold War years, the permanent members slowly returned to their earlier habit of dictating the work of the council with veto or threats of veto even when their immediate security interests were not affected. This behavior effectively marginalized the role of the ten nonpermanent members. The actions and reactions of the Security Council members, after the short-lived cooperative approach of the early nineties, run the risk of reenacting Cold War practices.

The General Assembly, which built its collective philosophy on the principle of noninterference in the internal affairs of a member-state, has found the new times and the new challenges taxing. Witness the confused and contradictory reactions to the speech by Secretary-General Kofi Annan at the opening session of the General Assembly in September 1999. The secretary-general's observations about humanitarian intervention and the imperative to respect and protect human rights even at the cost of national sovereignty got a cool, if not hostile, reception by most nonaligned countries.

Such complex choices appear to make the majority long for the old heroic times of the General Assembly, when its foremost task was to fight colonialism and apartheid.

In sum, the United Nations, with one foot in a well-established and predictably routine past and another in an unknown future, is suffering from an acute identity crisis.

The second challenge facing the United Nations is a crisis of confidence that has appeared in the wake of a number of setbacks for operations mandated by the Security Council. UN operations in the context of the breakup of Yugoslavia have generally been seen as moderate failures. That this is a fair judgment with regard to operations in Bosnia can be questioned on two accounts. The UN operations in Bosnia came into play first after the European Union had unsuccessfully taken charge and the United Nations had to pick up the pieces. Furthermore, the failure of the UN leadership to decide whether to use the promised NATO air support for its entrenched peacekeeping forces on the ground was partly due to the concern of the British and French commanders that their soldiers would be exposed to retaliation from Serb forces if a bombing campaign were to take place. This together with poor staff work at the UN Headquarters in New York and the consequent lack of unity of command—the national contingents preferred to take their orders from their capitals —doomed the operation.

In Somalia, another operation aimed at restoring a collapsing society as part of a nation-building effort, became a public relations fiasco. Again, a serious lack of coordination and the unwillingness of local troop commanders —this time American—to work under a central command led to failure. The passivity of both the Secretariat Headquarters and Security Council members, despite strong warnings from the field that a genocide was imminent in Rwanda, brought the United Nations to a crisis of confidence, especially among African nations, when the genocide occurred as had been forewarned.

The aforementioned evolution during the nineties of the use in the Security Council of veto power has accentuated the loss of confidence in the Security Council and, as a consequence, in the United Nations.

The third challenge with which the United Nations must deal is a financial crisis. The refusal of the United States to pay its dues to the United Nations on time—specifying conditions unsupported by the UN Charter on eventual payments and unilaterally reducing its financial obligations, thus leaving others to pick up the tab—is undercutting any possibility for meaningful long-term resource planning. The disregard for the organization by its largest member-state weakens the authority of the United Nations in its efforts to represent the interests of the community of states when it tries to bring the ideas and principles of the United Nations to bear on international problems and crises.

The final challenge to the United Nations is presented by the rapid change in international relations brought on by globalization. If the organization cannot effectively deal with this fourth challenge, it will enter a crisis greater than dangers posed by the other three challenges. The United Nations—in spite of its name—is not an organization of states; its members are states represented through their governments. Information technology (IT) has added completely new meaning to communication and information. Expansion of the market economy has taken away control of the means of communication from governments and, with the IT revolution, has made it almost impossible for governments to regulate and manipulate information. Business dominates international economic activities, and governments have only marginal influence on the movements of international finance. Governments must give space to new international actors, especially business enterprises operating within the narrow motivations of market and profit. Market forces and networking of civil society influence the international agenda more than before. Furthermore, the spread of democracy and democratic ideals tends to focus attention on the needs of people rather than of states.

A consequence of all this is that, if the United Nations is to avoid exponential marginalization, the organization must find ways and means to function with a number of non-governmental actors that are not easily subordinated in traditional hierarchies under governmental command and control. It is worth pointing out, however, that both business and financial markets depend upon functioning legal structures and government regulations. Some international organizations are emerging, notably the European Union, that are structures above governments. These international actors have mostly a benevolent effect on international cooperation and do not operate against the principles of the United Nations. More problematic is the emergence of international actors working directly against the values of the UN Charter, namely, organized crime, narcotics syndicates, terrorist organizations, and regional warlords. These actors operate across international boundaries, thus posing an international, rather than national, problem.

Although the United Nations is shaken by its own shortcomings in facing the challenges of globalization and the complexities of modern security, it is evident that UN members will call upon the body to serve the international community and deal with these looming challenges. The new security threats reflect contradictions and tensions that embrace a wide range of political, economic, social, and religious issues. UN responses have to be multilateral and cooperative. Globalization of the world economy and of security threats obviously requires globalization of the tools with which to address them. No single state, not even the United States, and no limited group of states, such as the G-8, is capable of coming up with answers to these problems.

CONTRADICTIONS OF CULTURE AND VALUES

None of the challenges facing the United Nations is such that the United Nations could not meet it creatively. That does not necessarily mean that the United Nations of today would be able to accomplish the task. Nonetheless, the United Nations does possess certain characteristics, especially its almost complete universality, and potential capabilities that make it a natural recourse for the search for

solutions. The United Nations could hardly be given a more difficult task than to mitigate clashes between deeply antagonistic cultures, values, and religions. But no other framework is better equipped to address the harmful consequences of the divide between cultures and value systems. The UN Charter contains elements that have been accepted by states of all cultures. The values reflected in the charter constitute, even with differing interpretations, at least a modicum of understanding that could help or allow the United Nations to grow as a moral center. The organization should identify common values across national, ethnic, religious, and other boundaries to counter the political-cultural pessimism generated by recent theories of the inevitability of clashes between civilizations.

Furthermore, the United Nations must develop into an instrument of dialogue among peoples. UN agencies that deal with development cooperation and international assistance can help create a sense of solidarity that transcends the fault lines separating cultures. The basic concept for the United Nations must be that security is to be achieved by cooperation rather than by confrontation.

In addition, security in the twenty-first century must be defined within wide parameters. Security today is a reflection of social and economic conditions as well as of military dispositions. Security considerations must thus be integrated with economic, environmental, civil society, and demographic considerations. Neglect or ignorance of any of these parameters may adversely affect security in its conventional sense.

LESSONS OF KOSOVO AND HUMANITARIAN INTERVENTION

The Kosovo conflict was a confrontation between values and cultures rooted for centuries in two peoples, Serbs and Albanians, who claim sovereignty over the same territory. The brutal ethnic cleansing of Kosovo that began in the fall of 1998 and continued into the winter came only two years after the world had witnessed atrocities in Bosnia. After the near fiasco in Bosnia the United Nations was tested once again. This time the question was whether the Security Council would rise to the occasion. It turned out that two of the five veto powers threatened to block any action when the Yugoslav government did not heed the Security Council's request to halt the initiation of ethnic cleansing. China had only shortly before the outbreak of the Kosovo conflict vetoed an extension of the UN preventive deployment force in Macedonia (UNPREDEP), a small but highly successful operation to help Macedonia stay out of the emerging conflicts in the region. This happened at the same time that large numbers of refugees from Kosovo threatened the country's stability. China, obviously miffed by Macedonia's economic contacts with Taiwan, followed a pattern displayed in similar situations involving UN peacekeeping efforts in Guatemala and Haiti and blocked the continuation of UNPREDEP. No direct and vital Chinese security interests were threatened by the Macedonian operations, nor would they have been threatened by an operation in Kosovo. The declared Russian resolve to veto a Security Council decision to force Belgrade to end the destruction of Kosovo was likewise an exercise of veto power that was not prompted by a direct threat to vital security interests.

The decision by the NATO states to start their air campaign in March 1999 against the Republic of Yugoslavia without a mandate from the Security Council plunged the United Nations into a full-fledged constitutional crisis. The charter gives the Security Council alone the authority to enforce compliance with its resolutions. How should the organization react when the world is witnessing an overture to the massive and systematic destruction of Kosovo through the forceful removal of Kosovars from

their homeland and the destruction of their culture, of their social and economic identity, and of their property records (thus eradicating traces of a civilization)? It was already clear that the political expediency of referring to the Kosovo crisis as an internal matter had been exhausted. But should the United Nations resist an operation that was aimed at protecting a population from a massive violation of its human rights on the grounds that it had not been possible to muster support for the requisite mandate from the Security Council?

By stopping the ethnic cleansing and the crimes against humanity, NATO acted in conformity with the principle of humanitarian intervention. This should not necessarily be seen as a violation of the principles of the United Nations, because the charter obliges member-states to uphold, promote, and protect the human rights of every individual. As noted, Secretary-General Kofi Annan affirmed this principle in a statement in September 1999, when he declared that individual sovereignty is as important as national sovereignty.

It goes without saying that acceptance of the principle of humanitarian intervention will not go untested. The secretary-general's reminder to the membership of the significance of individual sovereignty is also a reminder that the charter is built upon the principle of respect for the dignity and worth of the human being. Nothing says that this principle is subordinate to the principle of noninterference, which is strongly embedded in the culture of the United Nations, especially its General Assembly. Most governments continue to rally around the principle of noninterference, and only determined efforts by the secretary-general and members of the Security Council could hope to modify it.

It is difficult to see how the contradiction between the principle of noninterference—so highly prized, especially by the smaller and less powerful states—and the notion of humanitarian intervention can be dealt with. This contradiction cannot, however, be ignored, as it has the potential to tear the organization to pieces. Ideally, the General Assembly would lay down the ground rules, but realistically it is difficult to see how the majority of the often politically, economically, and structurally weak states in the developing world could approve the limiting of state sovereignty. The best one could envision would be a commission of truly eminent persons set up by the General Assembly that thoroughly assesses the problem over time. This process would allow the General Assembly membership to become familiar with the imperative of including the idea of humanitarian intervention in international law. However, the Security Council is probably in a better position to consider how humanitarian emergencies could be acceptable grounds for the invocation of actions under Chapter VII of the charter. The problem will not disappear, and the council will be repeatedly faced with it. The council should be advised to lay down in advance the principles under which it would contemplate endorsement of humanitarian intervention. This would increase predictability and dispel some of the concerns that humanitarian intervention would pave the way for the international community to take arbitrary actions outside the scope of the charter against individual states.

THE MANDATE OF THE SECURITY COUNCIL

The experience of the almost frantic peacekeeping and crisis management activities during the nineties makes clear that the Secretariat has not been given adequate resources to plan and manage such operations. Instead of strengthening the capacity of the United Nations to take on added responsibilities in this field, the member governments have shown a marked preference for farming out tasks to regional organizations. Organizations such as NATO and other regional arrangements and coalitions of the willing have assumed important roles in carrying out crisis management or peacekeeping operations. However, in such cases it is the Security Council that provides the legal foundation—the mandate—for such action, in particular when the use of force is contemplated. Without such legal foundation, a clear risk of anarchy exists in international relations. It is not difficult to lay out scenarios in which operations without a Security Council mandate could have serious implications for the security of smaller states and for international peace, security, and stability in general.

However, as was noted in the case of the Security Council's decision making on Kosovo, the principle of the Security Council mandate cannot be absolute. When human life and dignity are threatened on a massive scale, a Security Council paralyzed by a veto would undermine the authority and the relevance of the United Nations. In such exceptional emergencies, the justification for humanitarian intervention without a UN mandate has to be assessed on a case-by-case basis, in light of the values at stake and whether all other means have been exhausted. It is especially important that the proportionate use of force and the effects on international law are considered.

Preferably, such situations should not be allowed to occur. Security Council members should make a much stronger effort than they have in previous years to negotiate in earnest, without the threat of veto, and to try to find ways and means to settle a problem or resolve a crisis. An emphasis on early action before a conflict has turned into destruction and tragedy could diminish the tendency to resort to threats of veto. Various proposals have been aired with regard to limiting the frequency of vetoes without changing the charter. One proposal is that the permanent Security Council members could reach an understanding not to cast a veto in cases in which their direct security interests are not at stake. Another idea is to convince the permanent members to limit their application of the veto only to such decisions as enforcement action in accordance with Chapter VII of the charter.

PREVENTION OF CONFLICT

Preventive diplomacy is often mentioned as an activity that the United Nations and the Security Council should undertake with new vigor. This, however, is easier said than done.

From the outset the United Nations was tasked to focus on prevention. The charter states in Article 1 that the purpose of the organization is to take effective collective measures for the prevention and removal of threats to peace. However, over the years the Security Council has been preoccupied with handling conflicts and wars and has had little opportunity to deal with international problems in a preventive mode. Therefore, the council has acquired little experience in prevention. One recent case was the establishment of the preventive force in Macedonia, UNPREDEP, which did well as long as it was allowed to operate. The council, however, did not fully distinguish itself as a champion for prevention as it failed to keep the force in place during the emerging Kosovo crisis, owing to China's veto. It is indeed difficult to see the council becoming a major tool for policies of prevention. Its culture corresponds much more to crisis management and to the idea of the council serving as a sort of political fire brigade to be brought into action after the outbreak of war.

DISARMAMENT AS PREVENTIVE DIPLOMACY

In January 1992 the Security Council met at the highest level (i.e., heads of state or government) and, in the wake of the Gulf War and disclosures about Iraq's weapons of mass destruction (WMD), declared that the proliferation of WMD constitutes a threat to international peace and security. Given the council's responsibilities in this respect, the declaration was a call for action.

However, since January 1992 the council has remained passive in the face of proliferation threats. This was illustrated by the council's tepid reaction to the setback for nonproliferation efforts when India and Pakistan in May 1998 declared themselves through nuclear tests to have acquired the status of nuclear weapons states.

With regard to WMD, a basic treaty and convention structure is in place through such multilateral agreements as the Nuclear Nonproliferation Treaty and the Biological and Chemical Weapons Convention. The United Nations therefore has an opportunity—and a responsibility—to enhance security against the threats posed by such weapons by implementing and, if necessary, enforcing obligations under the relevant treaties. Another high priority for the United Nations should be to develop practical strategies to prevent the proliferation of WMD and to control the means for their production and delivery. In a similar vein, the United Nations should find ways to limit the flow of small arms and other conventional weapons to troubled and conflict-ridden regions—an issue that the Security Council periodically addresses with respect to one or another country in crisis.

The urgency and complexity of these challenges have increased with the growing importance of nonstate actors. Regional warlords, criminal syndicates, and terrorist groups, which already traffic in huge quantities of conventional weapons, have recently shown interest in trading in and acquiring WMD, related components, and their means of production. These developments call for new thinking and new approaches from the United Nations.

It is difficult to see how any individual state or even a regional group of states could by itself tackle proliferation challenges, which come in many shapes and forms. Only a globally organized and coordinated approach could have an impact. The very complexity of proliferation pressures requires extraordinary and wide-ranging measures. Proliferation is a reflection of national or regional conflicts or tensions. It operates through the transfer of illicit materials and technology and can be traced through banks, financial transactions, and money trails, involving small and big, rich and poor states.

The United Nations, as an organization of states in which governments define the rules, should have a role in shaping a nonproliferation strategy. Problems of national security and law and order will remain within the domain of the state. It would be difficult, even in times of globalization and privatization, to find any international or national structure better placed than the United Nations to address such issues. However, the organization in practice appears to shy away from disarmament and nonproliferation in spite of the fact that they are among the original, basic objectives of the United Nations. The world-threatening destructive potential of nuclear and certain other weapons is such that disarmament could be seen as a natural and central concern for the United Nations.

The prevailing philosophy of the Secretariat, encouraged by the leading members of the Security Council, is to look upon weapons as a symptom of a political problem or dysfunction, not as a cause of a problem. The question for the future is whether the United Nations, as a state-based organization, is ready to shoulder responsibility for disarmament and arms regulation—so clearly within its mandate—or whether the international community should look for another institutional framework. A role for the United Nations would necessitate rethinking both inside the Secretariat and among member-states as well as considerable structural changes within the Secretariat, the most important of which would be the recruitment of personnel well versed in the complexities of weapons and arms control and disarmament. Such a cultural paradigm shift not only

would be significant for the organization's willingness and ability to deal with weapons of mass destruction, but also would open the door for preventive approaches to halting the illicit trafficking of small arms. This would help the United Nations live up to the charter's commandment regarding the prevention of conflict.

INSTITUTIONAL REFORMS

Although the problems facing the United Nations emanate from the actions and attitudes of the member governments, the organization itself needs reforms if it is to meet the challenges ahead. Institutional reform should aim at making the organization fit to deal with new tasks, particularly interacting with civil society, as well as focusing on weaknesses as regards structures, financing, and operations. The authority and significance of the Security Council would need to be strengthened, and this could be achieved through a measured enlargement of the number of members of the council. Adding more veto power and permanent members, however, is an idea that would not necessarily strengthen the council, given the performance of the council in recent years.

The nonpermanent members of the Security Council have consistently demonstrated a high degree of competence and responsibility. This stands in contrast to the difficulty of the permanent members in defining their new roles in the context of post–Cold War multilateral imperatives, a difficulty that is harming the influence and effectiveness of the council. The United States appears reluctant to concede political authority to the United Nations and the international community, whether the issue is over UN command of its peacekeeping units or adherence to multilateral treaties such as the Comprehensive Test Ban Treaty and the ban on land mines. The two European Union members, France and the United Kingdom, continue to insist on their national identity in the council, while elsewhere they are proponents of a European security and defense identity. This weakens the European Union as an actor in the United Nations on behalf of its membership. Russia frequently supports Belgrade and Baghdad, in spite of their challenges to the United Nations and repeated violations of human rights and international law. China appears to see the privileged position of a veto-empowered permanent member primarily as an opportunity to block any decision that could infringe upon even the narrowest of its interests.

The Secretariat would need a major overhaul. The policy of recruitment must emphasize efficiency, competence, and integrity, not only in theory but also in practice. The organizational structures should be tailored to the tasks entrusted to the Secretariat. Decision-making and management procedures must be changed, especially in the administrative and financial fields, in order to radically speed up decision making. The potential of large gains in efficiency made possible by the IT revolution should be realized. Higher mobility in the Secretariat should prevent organizational fiefdoms from appearing. The level of expertise should be raised by expanding the recruitment of staff with special skills and eliminating routine jobs as much as possible—and a lot is possible. That would mean that the tendency to nationally earmark positions in the Secretariat would disappear. Such a move would certainly elicit protest, but it would also raise the professionalism of the Secretariat and thus its ability to deal with new tasks.

It has been pointed out frequently that the United Nations does not offer a policymaking forum to deal with economic emergencies, commensurate with the Security Council on issues of international peace and security. One option might be to reform the existing Economic and Social Council (ECOSOC), but a more radical suggestion is to create a Security Council for Economic Affairs. Much speaks in favor of the idea of strengthening the UN role in economic affairs, particularly in regard to the problem of poverty. However, there are clear limits to this approach. Governments, especially in economically advanced countries, no longer control developments in this field, as the market economy and the theories surrounding it prevail. With nongovernmental actors dominating the world economy and the flow of financial resources, the best the United Nations could probably achieve would be to offer itself through ECOSOC as a forum for consultation between governments and the great financial and economic interests. This would be similar to the yearly World Economic Forum in Davos, but with the additional guarantee of systematic governmental participation.

Nongovernmental organizations (NGOs) and other members of civil society, helped by new technologies, can create influential networks that can give them considerable impact on questions on the UN agenda. It is not easy for the United Nations, an organization of states, to cohabit with civil society. Yet civil society often represents important idealistic and creative forces, whose strength and influence could be drawn on by the United Nations to promote the goals of the organization. Here the United Nations has a competitive advantage. The agendas of various NGOs tend to be highly focused, if not single-issue crusades. There is no better framework than that which the United Nations can offer to put these single issues in context and to make them components of the more comprehensive and strategic tasks of fighting poverty; promoting peace, security, prosperity, human rights, and social justice; and protecting the global environment. A priority for the United Nations should therefore be to establish intensive dialogue with civil society.

The information society can open up new prospects and possibilities for the United Nations, especially if computers can be distributed to all parts of the world, including developing countries. Via the Internet, data and information can be transmitted to schools in remote villages. The know-how and experience of the organization and its specialized agencies in medicine, agriculture, engineering, science, and education could, through the Internet, reach out to those most in need, offering critical help and advice, while minimizing bureaucratic delay.

THE ROOT CAUSES OF CONFLICT

In addition to an enlarged role in coordinating and overseeing various disarmament efforts such as the nonproliferation of WMD, the prevention of illicit small-arms trafficking, and the creation of transparency in the transfer of small arms, the UN system as a whole should pay particular attention to strengthening its own capacity for conflict prevention and to addressing root causes of conflict. Long-term security is closely linked to sustainable development, including the eradication of poverty.

During the past ten years the United Nations and the international community have devoted large and growing financial, technical, and personnel resources to humanitarian assistance. This has been a necessary investment, reflecting a spontaneous political will to react to complex emergencies. The United Nations has proved well suited to play a leading role in coordinating international humanitarian assistance, both governmental and nongovernmental in origin. The organization should uphold and develop this role further. But with the idea of prevention in mind, the international community must engage the United Nations in a systematic and radically new orientation to support sustainable development. Without diminishing the importance of emergency relief efforts, the organization should address long-term social and economic development. The United Nations must make a new commitment to developing the economies and societies of poor countries. The very nature of modern media, with their immediacy, their speed, and their audiences with ever shorter attention spans, makes it neither politically nor commercially attractive to focus on such complex and slow-moving issues as sustainable development for the eradication of poverty. With less media attention being devoted to long-term development, the role of leadership in promoting the cause of development becomes more important. Secretary-General Kofi Annan has initiated a process of strengthening coordination among relevant programs. Leaders of other UN-related institutions such as the World Bank and the United Nations Development Programme (UNDP) play important roles in this context.

The immediate problems are the meager resources available to the United Nations for developing cooperation and the difficulty in focusing donor interest on long-term approaches. Achieving long-term results in the area of development depends upon the donor community providing sufficient resources. However, at present only four countries—Denmark, Norway, Sweden, and the Netherlands—have met the UN target of 0.7 percent of gross national product being devoted to transfer of aid to developing countries.

Development requires an effective partnership among governments in order to generate sufficient external resources. But there is little hope of establishing sustainable development without thorough political, social, and economic reform. The United Nations has with considerable success taken the lead in establishing sustainable development as a guiding principle. But in pursuing this policy, the membership has limited the concept to focus almost exclusively on the rational use of national resources. This is both laudable and indispensable. But global poverty still remains the most serious and urgent problem for the international community. It is therefore important for the entire development cooperation community to recognize that the scope of sustainable development should be widened. To a considerable degree, the modest or nonexistent progress in energizing development stems from structural shortcomings of both political and social character.

It is obvious that these structures in the developing countries need reform.

THE ROLE OF DEMOCRACY

Lack of democracy is the most serious obstacle to sustainable development. It undermines rational and effective use and distribution of resources for development. The inherent functions of democracy—freedom of thought, of expression, of association, and of movement, as well as tolerance of all groups within society and equal opportunity for each person—all support an effective flow of relevant data in society and make possible rational decisions on the use and distribution of resources. In nondemocratic societies, where media are silenced and no freedom of expression exists, rational decisions cannot be reached because of the lack of reliable information. Corruption is likewise a deeply destructive element in the economic and social structures of poor countries. Only a democratic society can effectively deal with corruption. Thus, democracy is indispensable in the long-term fight against poverty.

The attainment of democracy was not an explicit goal of the United Nations when it was founded. The coalition of nations that defeated Germany and Japan contained democracies, yes, but it also encompassed various authoritarian regimes, including the hideous dictatorship of Stalin's Soviet Union. It was therefore obvious that democracy was not to become an element of the UN Charter. The democracies constituted a distinct minority in the newly founded United Nations and became an even smaller minority with the addition of new members, from the fifties through the seventies, because of decolonization.

However starved the UN Charter may be on explicit references to democracy, it does contain seed elements for democracy in the powerful language in its preamble, according to which the objective of the United Nations is to reaffirm faith in fundamental human rights, in the dignity and worth of human beings, and in equal rights for men and women.

With the collapse of the antidemocratic Soviet Union and the end of the Cold War, democracy has been given a chance to expand. Western, Eastern, and Central Europeans in the November 1990 Charter of Paris undertook to build, consolidate, and strengthen democracy as the only system of government for their nations. This was the first time that states in a major international instrument declared their commitment to democracy as a principle to be recognized by all states.

All UN member-states have accepted the Universal Declaration of Human Rights, which contains elements essential for democracy. The protection and promotion of these rights is the first responsibility of democratic government. But democracy is more than human rights. It is based on the will of the people, expressed regularly through free and fair elections. In today's United Nations, close to a majority of member-states do not even share the principle of free and fair elections. Furthermore, democracy is representative and pluralistic; entails accountability to the electorate and the obligation of public authorities to comply with the law and administer justice impartially; and is based on the fundamental idea that no one is above the law. These characteristics of democracy are the key components of a national structure that could support sustainable social and economic development and the uprooting of corruption.

The UN membership has a long way to go to make the organization a club of democratic states. A recognition of democracy as the only system of government by the member-states would constitute a genuine renewal and revitalization of the organization. Such recognition could be the bedrock of reform. No other single policy would have a more positive and far-reaching impact on development and the struggle against poverty. Some scholars and politicians insist that war is not possible between democracies. Even if this proposition overstates the case, it is a matter of record that armed conflicts between democracies are rare. Furthermore, experience and political logic strongly suggest that the probability of war in a world of expanding democracy would radically diminish. Thus democratic development among the nations would strengthen international peace and security.

It goes without saying that even if the United Nations could unite around a declaration of democracy as the only acceptable system of government, many of its members would not immediately become democracies. Even today the Universal Declaration of Human Rights of 1948 is not fully observed by several member-states. However, a declaration on democracy would mean a recognition of democracy and a commitment to strive for its establishment everywhere. Remember, it was the Soviet Union that signed on to the Charter of Paris in November 1990. It did not take long until the democratic (albeit imperfectly democratic) Russia emerged.

The significance of democracy for security, development, and the eradication of poverty challenges the United Nations and its membership to make democracy the centerpiece of its strategy for the new decade—indeed, for the next fifty years.

To increase the flow of technical and financial resources to the developing countries, a compact might be formed inside the United Nations between the member-states of the Organization for Economic Cooperation and Development (OECD) and the poorer countries. It would provide increased development assistance in return for a commitment to democracy. Such a compact would bring structural political, economic, and social reforms to the center of the development process. This would consolidate democracy inside the membership of the United Nations and constitute a major shift in the character of the organization, the first since its creation fifty years ago.

CONCLUSION

Today the United Nations is faced with a number of challenges. The organization has moved from the early years of idealism through the Cold War period of cynical self-service by its members, to a search for a new role in the contemporary political, economic, and social environment. There is a crisis of confidence in the organization following its marginalization and operational setbacks, a financial crisis, and a crisis of globalization, which has brought powerful new nonstate actors onto the international scene.

All challenges can be met, but that requires creativity and new approaches. Differences in cultural and religious values must be identified and dealt with through emphasis on common fundamental values. One basic concept could be the principle of common security and the recognition of common security interests and the understanding of a wider concept of security in today's environment of globalization. The Kosovo conflict tests the concept of humanitarian intervention and must be seen in the context of how veto power is used or abused. The United Nations must rethink its principles of absolute national sovereignty and give space to the humanitarian aspects of conflict. Although the prevention of conflict is declared as a policy objective, it is difficult to realize. A much more energetic approach by the United Nations toward nonproliferation and the control of small arms, however, would have a positive impact on the policies of conflict prevention.

The poverty of nations must be recognized in practice not only as an economic phenomenon but foremost as a reflection of political and social structures. Lack of democracy is the most serious obstacle to development. A strategy for peace and development must be based upon the acceptance and introduction of democracy everywhere. The UN Charter is based upon respect for human dignity and human worth. In the decades to come it should expand its scope to regard democracy as the only acceptable system of government.

32

War Making and Peace Making

The United Nations' Post–Cold War Record

Michael W. Doyle

SINCE THE END OF THE COLD WAR, the community of nations has experienced a near revolution in the relation between what is in the legitimate realm of state sovereignty and what is subject to legitimate international intervention. From 1990 through 1993 the UN Security Council adopted a strikingly intrusive interpretation of Chapter VII of the UN Charter, the enforcement provisions concerning international peace and security. Member-states then endorsed a radical expansion in the scope of collective intervention just as a series of ethnic and civil wars erupted across the globe. Unfulfilled commitments, on the one hand, and escalating use of force, on the other, soon provoked a severe crisis in this wide interpretation of "peace enforcement." In Bosnia and Somalia wide "peace enforcement" amounted to "war making" as the United Nations threatened to impose by force outcomes—ranging from disarmament and safe havens to "no-fly zones" and national borders—on armed factions that recognized no political authority superior to

their own.[1] Elsewhere, as in Rwanda, the UN record was a failure even to attempt to exercise enforcement as peace agreements fell apart. More than five hundred thousand Tutsis and moderate Hutus fell at the hands of genocidal extremists who had seized the government. The current balance sheet on UN "war making" thus suggests that while the United Nations has played an effective role in legitimizing enforcement coalitions for armed collective security (as in Korea and against Iraq), the organization has proved to be a very ineffective peace enforcer, or war maker, in the many civil conflicts that emerged in the post–Cold War world.

But that is only half the story. At the same time evidence from the peace operations in Namibia, El Salvador, Cambodia, Mozambique, and Eastern Slavonia (Croatia) suggests a seemingly contradictory but actually complementary conclusion. Drawing on the examples of these other UN operations, one can argue that the United Nations can succeed in fostering peace through consent, building on an enhancement of Chapter VI–based peace-making negotiations and a creative, multidimensional implementation of the transitional authority that the peace agreements provide. The United Nations' future as peace maker, however, has been under challenge in the U.S. Congress and elsewhere from those who fail to understand how successful the United Nations has been and can continue to be in a "peace-making" role.[2] The theme of this essay is simple: We should avoid "throwing the baby out with the bathwater."

THE UNITED NATIONS' EXPANDING AGENDA FOR PEACE

In the early 1990s, with the end of the Cold War, the UN agenda for peace and security rapidly expanded. At the request of the UN Security Council Summit of January 1992, Secretary-General Boutros Boutros-Ghali prepared the conceptual foundations of an ambitious UN role in peace and security in his seminal report, *An Agenda for Peace*.[3] The secretary-general outlined five interconnected roles that he hoped the United Nations would play in the fast-changing context of post–Cold War international politics:

- *Preventive diplomacy*, undertaken in order "to prevent disputes from arising between parties, to prevent existing disputes from escalating into conflicts and to limit the spread of the latter when they occur." Involving confidence-building measures, fact finding, early warning, and possibly "preventive deployment" of UN authorized forces, preventive diplomacy seeks to reduce the danger of violence and increase the prospects of peaceful settlement.
- *Peace enforcement*, authorized to act with or without the consent of the parties in order to ensure compliance with a cease-fire mandated by the Security Council. Acting under the authority of Chapter VII of the UN

Charter, these military forces are composed of heavily armed, national forces operating under the direction of the secretary-general.
- *Peace making*, designed "to bring hostile parties to agreement" through peaceful means such as those found in Chapter VI of the UN Charter. Drawing upon judicial settlement, mediation, and other forms of negotiation, UN peace-making initiatives seek to persuade parties to arrive at a peaceful settlement of their differences.
- *Peacekeeping*, established to deploy a "United Nations presence in the field, hitherto with the consent of all the parties concerned," as a confidence-building measure. UN peacekeepers monitor a truce between the parties while diplomats strive to negotiate a comprehensive peace or officials to implement an agreed peace.
- *Postconflict peacebuilding*, organized to foster economic and social cooperation with the purpose of building confidence among previously warring parties; developing the social, political, and economic infrastructure to prevent future violence; and laying the foundations for a durable peace.

Between 1987 and 1994 the Security Council quadrupled the number of resolutions it issued, tripled the peacekeeping operations it authorized, and increased from one to seven per year the number of economic sanctions it imposed. Military forces deployed in peacekeeping operations increased from fewer than ten thousand to more than seventy thousand. The annual peacekeeping budget accordingly skyrocketed from $230 million to $3.6 billion in the same period, thus reaching to about three times the regular UN operating budget of $1.2 billion.[4] The activities of the Security Council in preventive diplomacy and sanctions, the Secretariat's role in election monitoring, and above all the massive growth in peacekeeping and peace enforcement—all testified to the newly appreciated role the international community wanted the United Nations to perform.

These initiatives, peace enforcement most striking among them, also reflected significant shifts in the international legal and political environment in which the United Nations operated. Member-states of the United Nations subtly extended the acceptable scope of UN activity by altering the definition of what was once considered to be essentially sovereign, national activity. Matters once legally preserved from UN intervention such as civil conflicts and humanitarian emergencies within sovereign states now became legitimate issues of UN concern. Gross violations of global standards of human rights were seen to override domestic sovereignty, becoming a defining issue for what was a legitimate matter of international attention. Human rights then were increasingly claimed to be inherently global, a proposition endorsed by the Vienna Conference on Human Rights in June 1993.[5]

The Security Council also expanded the operational meaning of the UN Charter's Article 2(7) authority to override domestic sovereignty when a "threat to the peace, breach of the peace, or act of aggression" (Article 39) arose. The new interpretation of UN jurisdiction soon appeared to include a wide range of what were once seen as infringements of traditional sovereignty. Indeed, "threat to the peace, breach of the peace, or act of aggression" came to mean severe domestic violations of human rights, civil wars and humanitarian emergencies, and almost whatever a Security Council majority (absent a permanent-member veto) said they were.[6]

The reduction in the scope of sovereignty under Article 2(7) and the expansion in Security Council authority under Article 39 had roots in the striking changes in the international system that emerged at the end of the Cold War. A new spirit of multilateral cooperation from the USSR, beginning with President Mikhail Gorbachev's reforms, met a new spirit of tolerance from the United States. Together the two former adversaries broke the forty-year gridlock in the UN Security Council.

Post–Cold War cooperation meant that the Security Council was now functioning as the global guardian of peace and security. The Security Council had now become what it was supposed to have been since 1945—the continuation, incorporated in the design of the UN Charter, of the World War II Grand Alliance. At the same time there also emerged an ideological community of democratic values that gave specific content to the cooperative initiatives of these years. The Vienna Conference on Human Rights in 1993 and President Gorbachev's plea before the General Assembly for "global human values" signified that human rights were no longer merely a Western but rather a global principle of good governance.[7]

The two developments coincided with a temporary conjunction of power and will. Following the collapse of the USSR, the United States experienced a "unipolar moment" when its power eclipsed that of all other states. At the same time the international community, including the United States, adopted a strategy of "assertive multilateralism," which lasted from the Persian Gulf War in January 1991 to the disaster in Mogadishu, Somalia, on October 3, 1993. The five permanent members of the Security Council, led by the United States, provided a degree of commitment and resourceful leadership that the United Nations had rarely seen before. Eschewing the national role of "Globocop" in order to address a pressing domestic agenda, the Clinton administration encouraged Secretary-General Boutros Boutros-Ghali to take an ever more assertive role in international crises. The small dissenting minority in the Security Council—which included China on some occasions and Russia and others—was not prepared to resist the United States on issues that did not affect their paramount national interests. The successful reversal of Saddam Hussein's aggression in the Persian Gulf and the December 1992 U.S.-led rescue of segments of the Somali population from starvation heralded what appeared to be a remarkable partnership. The Security

Council decreed, the United States and its allies led, and—conveniently, for the while—many other states paid and supported.

Together, authority, will, and power made the new globalism feasible and legitimate. Collective intervention by the United Nations was morally, politically, and legally acceptable where unilateral intervention was not. Because it appeared more impartial and not self-serving, the UN community was perceived to be speaking for the whole community of nations. The traditional suspicion of intervention was thus allayed and the traditional moral, political, and legal restraints were lifted.

GENERATIONS OF
UN PEACE OPERATIONS

Peacekeeping operations have come to encompass three distinct activities that have evolved as "generations" of UN peace operations. They include not only the early activities of Chapter VI (or so-called 6 and $^1/_2$) "first-generation" peacekeeping, which call for the interposition of a force after a truce has been reached, but also a far more ambitious group of "second-generation" operations that focus on political reconstruction and that rely on the consent of parties and an even more ambitious group of "third-generation" operations that function with Chapter VII mandates and without a comprehensive agreement reflecting the acquiescence of the parties.[8] In today's circumstances, these operations involve less interstate conflict and more factions in domestic civil wars, not all of which are clearly identifiable—and few of which are stable negotiating parties. Current peace operations thus intrude into aspects of domestic sovereignty once thought to be beyond the purview of UN activity.

In traditional peacekeeping, or *first-generation peacekeeping*, unarmed or lightly armed UN forces were stationed between hostile parties to monitor a truce, troop withdrawal, or buffer zone while political negotiations went forward. As F. T. Liu, an eminent UN peacekeeping official, has noted, monitoring, consent, neutrality, nonuse of force, and unarmed peacekeepers constituted a stable and interdependent combination. Neutrality worked when parties consented to the monitoring and, because unarmed peacekeepers enjoyed consent, there was no need for the latter to use force.[9] The forces provided transparency—an impartial assurance that the other party was not violating the truce—and raised the costs of defecting from and the benefits of abiding by the agreement with the threat of exposure, the potential resistance of the peacekeeping force, and the legitimacy of UN mandates. The benefit was obvious: armed conflict was held at bay.[10] The price of first-generation mandates, as in the long Cyprus operation, was sometimes paid in conflicts delayed rather than resolved. Today these monitoring activities continue to play an important role on the Golan Heights between Israel and Syria, and on the border between Kuwait and Iraq.

The second category, *second-generation, multidimensional operations*, involves the implementation of complex, multidimensional peace agreements. In addition to the traditional military functions, the peacekeepers are often engaged in various police and civilian tasks, the goal of which is a long-term settlement of the underlying conflict. Taking a substantial step beyond first-generation operations, these operations are based on consent of the parties. But the nature of consent and the purposes for which it is granted are qualitatively different than in traditional peacekeeping.

In second-generation operations, the United Nations is typically involved in implementing peace agreements that go to the roots of the conflict, helping to build a long-term foundation for stable, legitimate government. As Secretary-General Boutros-Ghali observed in *An Agenda for Peace*, "peace-making and peace-keeping operations, to be truly successful, must come to include comprehensive efforts to identify and support structures which will tend to consolidate peace.... [T]hese may include disarming the previously warring parties and the restoration of order, the custody and possible destruction of weapons, repatriating refugees, advisory and training support for security personnel, monitoring elections, advancing efforts to protect human rights, reforming or strengthening governmental institutions and promoting formal and informal processes of political participation."[11]

The United Nations has a commendable record of success in second-generation, multi-dimensional peacekeeping and peacebuilding operations as diverse as those in Namibia (UNTAG), El Salvador (ONUSAL), Cambodia (UNTAC), Mozambique (ONUMOZ), and Eastern Slavonia (UNTAES).[12] The UN role in helping settle those conflicts has been fourfold. In the successful agreements the United Nations served as a peace maker facilitating a peace treaty among the parties; as a peacekeeper monitoring the cantonment and demobilization of military forces, resettling refugees, and supervising transitional civilian authorities; as a peacebuilder monitoring and in some cases organizing the implementation of human rights, national democratic elections, and economic rehabilitation; and in a very limited way as a peace enforcer when the agreements came unstuck.

In Secretary-General Boutros-Ghali's lexicon, "peace enforcing" missions—which in effect are war making—are *third-generation operations*, which extend from low-level military operations to protect the delivery of humanitarian assistance to the enforcement of cease-fires and, when necessary, authoritative assistance in the rebuilding of so-called failed states. Like Chapter VII UN enforcement action to roll back aggression, as in Korea in 1950 and against Iraq in the Gulf War, the defining characteristic of third-generation operations is the lack of consent by one or more of the parties to some or all of the UN mandate.[13] There is a crucial difference between wide enforcement in the absence of broad consent and focused enforcement in the context of an agreed-upon comprehensive peace, a distinction to which I will return.

With all of Minerva's usual sense of timing, insightful doctrine for these peace-enforcing operations appeared just as Somalia and Bosnia exposed their limitations. Recent studies have thoughtfully mapped out the logic of the strategic terrain between UN peacekeeping and UN enforcement action.[14] Militarily these operations seek to *deter, dissuade, and deny.*[15] By precluding an outcome based on the use of force by the parties, the United Nations instead uses collective force (if necessary) to persuade the parties to settle the conflict by negotiation. In the former Yugoslavia, for example, the United Nations following this strategy could have established strong points to deter attacks on key humanitarian corridors. (It did but the Serbs bypassed them.) Or it could have threatened air strikes, as was done successfully around Sarajevo in February 1994, to dissuade a continuation of the Serb shelling of the city. Or it could have denied (but did not) the Serb forces their attack on Dubrovnik in 1992 by countershelling from the sea or bombing from the air the batteries in the hills above the city.

Forcing a peace depends on achieving a complicated preponderance in which the forces (UN and local) supporting a settlement acceptable to the international community hold both a military predominance and a predominance of popular support, which together permit them to impose a peace on the local military forces and their popular supporters that oppose peace.

The result of these three generations operating together in the post–Cold War world was an unprecedented expansion of the UN role in the protection of world order and in the promotion of basic human rights in countries until recently torn by costly civil wars. Sovereignty was enhanced and a modicum of peace, rehabilitation, and self-sustaining self-determination was introduced in Namibia, Cambodia, El

Salvador, Mozambique, and Eastern Slavonia. Tens—perhaps, even hundreds—of thousands of lives were saved in Somalia and the former Yugoslavia. But in 1993 and 1994, the more ambitious elements of third-generation peace enforcement encountered many of the problems interventionist and imperial strategies have faced in the past and discovered fresh problems peculiar to the global character of the United Nations.

A CRISIS IN WAR MAKING

Somalia

The UN peace enforcement effort in the large part of Somalia outside General Mohammed Farah Aideed's stronghold in southern Mogadishu proceeded according to plan. By mid-1993 starvation was not an issue in the areas within the reach of UN protection. In contrast, three hundred thousand Somalis died in 1991–92 in a famine induced by the murderous competition of the Somali warlords. In 1993, with the protection of the United Nations Operation in Somalia (UNOSOM II), UNICEF was assisting forty thousand pupils. Thirty-two hospitals and 103 mobile vaccination teams were active (75 percent of the children under five received measles vaccine). Seventy thousand refugees returned from Kenya. Thirty-nine district councils and six regional councils were formed. UNOSOM had begun to recruit five thousand former Somali policemen to perform basic police functions.

Nonetheless, the disaster on October 3, 1993, involving the killing of eighteen U.S. soldiers (in which more than three hundred Somalis also died), the earlier crisis on June 5 in which twenty-four Pakistani peacekeepers were killed after they fired on a Somali crowd, and the fruitless effort to capture General Aideed over the preceding summer together exposed what had become a politically bankrupt attempt

to enforce law and order on an increasingly resistant population.

With the advantage of hindsight, we can identify policy mistakes, without which Somalia might look very different today.[16] A more thorough partnership with Somalia's regional neighbors in a mediation effort in 1991,[17] a more extensive mandate for the U.S.-led Unified Task Force (UNITAF) in December 1992 (when controlling the heavy and light weapons of the clans would have been easier), and above all a smoother political transition from UNITAF's partial successes in negotiating with the warlords to UNOSOM's more ambitious state-building agenda might have made a difference.

The fundamental problem was a famine induced by drought, by the ravages of the civil war that followed on the collapse of Major General Mohammed Siad Barre's dictatorship, and by the rapacious extortion of the Somali warlords who taxed relief convoys in order to fund their competition for power. Only a Somali "Leviathan" with a monopoly of violence or a "Superwarlord" capable of playing warlord against warlord could restore order and end the famine. UNOSOM I (the monitoring mission with five hundred Pakistani troops holed up in the port of Mogadishu) could do very little, not even prevent grain ships from being shelled from shore. The UN special representative, Mohammed Sahnoun, valiantly tried to negotiate a peace, appealing to the humanity of the very warlords who ran the famine. In December 1992 the U.S.-led UNITAF became the Somali "Leviathan," and the roads were opened and the famine broken.[18] UNITAF met almost no opposition because the mass of the people welcomed the relief, and the warlords knew it was temporary—no threat to their power.

In May 1993 UNOSOM II came face to face with the fundamental problems. Its mandate included the authority to disarm the factions—a disarmament to which, we should note, the faction leaders had agreed, on paper, at the Addis Ababa Conference in March 1993.[19] But this mandate, unlike UNITAF's, threatened the political existence of the warlords. It proposed the establishment of a Somali national authority that would be elected by the people and sustained by a police force trained by the United Nations. UNOSOM, however, was a paper tiger, lacking the capacity to enforce (or even bargain for compliance with) the agreement. Most of its troops were lightly armed, vulnerable to the weapons the warlords withdrew from the temporary UNITAF cantonment. UNOSOM's logistics were immobile, dependent on Mogadishu port facilities, which made the United Nations too dependent on Aideed to threaten a credible withdrawal from his zone. The rank-and-file faction fighters were required to disarm in May 1993; UNOSOM established an alternative employment program in January 1994. The entire force relied too much on the military and logistic backbone of the U.S. contingent, which was poorly coordinated with the overall UNOSOM force. UNOSOM survived casualties inflicted on the Pakistanis in June, but when Aideed attacked the Americans in October he struck UNOSOM's Achilles' heel.

Former Yugoslavia

The opposite of UNOSOM's aggressiveness emerged in the United Nations Protection Force (UNPROFOR) operation in the former Yugoslavia. There the United Nations was not doing what it had been criticized for doing in Somalia. The United Nations was committed to protecting the humanitarian convoys and the safe areas as well as maintaining an arms embargo over the entire area and an economic embargo against Serbia. But the failure to protect the Bosnian Muslims (and also the Croats and the Serbs), the relief convoys, and even the peacekeepers themselves left the UN force in a most equivocal position. In Bosnia alone, after the establishment of UNPROFOR, tens (perhaps even hundreds) of thousands of Muslims

and thousands of Serbs and Croats died, and more than a million Muslims and a quarter million Serbs had to flee their homes, according to the estimates of Thorvald Stoltenberg, the UN mediator.[20]

The protection dilemma was real. With more than half the population in the UN-designated Bosnian safe areas directly dependent on UN convoys for food and medicine, military action against the predominantly Serb aggressors would have been met by a complete cutoff of humanitarian assistance by those same Serbian forces, which controlled the access roads.[21]

None of UNPROFOR's military forces were prepared to undertake a massive military campaign designed to defeat the Bosnian Serb forces. The United States limited its contribution to air forces. Its once preferred strategy— "lift [the 1991 UN arms embargo] and strike [by air, against Serb gunners]"—was designed to level the playing field between Serb forces and the poorly equipped Bosnian forces. But the United States was never prepared to invest its own soldiers on the ground in a peace-enforcement operation or even to ship significant quantities of heavy weapons to Bosnia (presumably by airlift over the Croat and Serb lines) and train the Bosnians in their use.[22] Radical Muslim forces from Iran and the Palestine Liberation Organization were ready to come to Bosnia's aid, but they were rejected by Russia and, it seemed to many observers, would have merely widened the fighting to Kosovo, Macedonia, and even beyond. The resulting UNPROFOR strategy—"constrict [the level of violence] and contain"—was not without costs to its European proponents. UNPROFOR, with large contingents of British, French, and Canadian troops, sustained more than seventy fatalities. But the strategy had two great advantages: it was tolerated by the Russians and the killing was contained within Croatia and Bosnia.

Again, with the advantage of hindsight, we can see what appear to be mistakes, most of them occasioned by the Security Council's foisting mandates (without the means to implement them) on the UN forces in the field. Resolutions were issued that bore upon the Bosnian Serbs, yet the international community was not prepared to exert effective pressure. What pressure there was came from the indirect effects of the misery that the international economic embargo inflicted on the Serbian public. In retrospect, we can see that the UN Protected Areas in Croatia lacked adequate buffer zones and sufficient peacekeepers, providing the Serbs with excuses not to disarm and the Croats with the opportunity to engage in incursions.[23] In Bosnia the declared Safe Havens were never adequately provided with UN forces. They were too small, militarily vulnerable, and economically nonviable, and they lacked wide enough connecting corridors.[24]

The taproot of error was identified in Cyrus Vance's warnings in December 1991 not to recognize the independence of Croatia and Bosnia outside the framework of an overall settlement of Yugoslavia.[25] The only separable parts of Yugoslavia immediately recognizable as independent, sovereign nation-states were Slovenia and (arguably) Macedonia. For Serbs, the federal unity of "Yugoslavia" was what made "small" Serbia tolerable and the non-Serb governments of Croatia and Bosnia safe for their Serbs. For Croats, the inclusion of Bosnia in Yugoslavia was what made Bosnia safe for its Croats. For Bosnian Muslims, the inclusion of Croatia in Yugoslavia was what made the Bosnian republic safe in Yugoslavia, which otherwise would have been dominated by the Serbs. Croatia, some suggest, might have been partitioned between Croats and Serbs, but the ethnic mix was too intimate in Bosnia to allow a peaceable partition.

The wars came to a halt in the summer and fall of 1995. UNPROFOR and NATO had at last been provoked by the Bosnian Serbs to mount a full-scale bombing campaign. As important, Croatia "solved" its Krajina problem the old-fashioned way—with "blood and iron," ethnically cleansing the entire region of its

Serb inhabitants (except for Eastern Slavonia, which was peacefully reintegrated into Croatia by UNTAES from January 1996 to January 1998). The Bosnian Serbs had done the same to Srebrenica and Zepa, leaving Gorazde as the only safe area, apart from Sarajevo in the eastern region of the former Bosnia. Slowly and painfully, thus borders and ethnicities had begun to correspond in the former Yugoslavia. Peace efforts culminated in the Dayton accords. But the fighting in the region was far from over. President Slobodan Milosevic soon faced another insurgency in Kosovo, the overwhelmingly Albanian zone of Serbia, and he proceeded to try to resolve it the same way he had the movements for independence in Croatia and Bosnia.

The operations in Somalia and Bosnia saved hundreds of thousands of lives. The starvation probably would have continued in Somalia, resulting in the loss of a hundred thousand to perhaps a quarter million lives.[26] Only UNPROFOR prevented the complete ethnic cleansing of Bosnia by the Serbs and the Croats. Yet the political costs of strategic failure were high.

Both failures soon claimed victims elsewhere. Following the October 3 crisis in Somalia, U.S. senators clamored for immediate withdrawal of all U.S. forces from UNOSOM. The Clinton administration barely succeeded in holding out for a March 31, 1994, withdrawal date. Emboldened by the prospective U.S. withdrawal from Somalia, associates of the attachés terrorizing Haiti chased U.S.-UN advisers from the harbor of Port-au-Prince, wrecking the Governors Island peace plan and eventually forcing the administration to pursue the very risky decision (from the standpoint of U.S. domestic politics) to invade Haiti. Learning to say no, the United States led the Security Council's rejection of the request to protect thousands of displaced persons in Burundi fleeing the coup and slaughter of the government in October 1993. It also sought to limit the scope of UN engagement in massacre-torn Rwanda in April 1994, which resulted in the slaughter of hundreds of thousands and the displacement of even more into Tanzania and Zaire.

A Fantastic Gap

Time and again, UN "war making" (wide peace enforcement) provoked what General François Briquemont, the former commander of UNPROFOR, denounced as "the fantastic gap between the resolutions of the Security Council, the will to execute those resolutions and the means available to commanders in the field." The "fantastic gap" signals to some that borders are up for grabs and that massacres and ethnic cleansing will go unpunished. The United Nations thus showed itself to be ineffective in imposing order by force, whether to disarm factions in Somalia or provide humanitarian protection in Bosnia. Instead it became complicit in a record of inadequate protection, mission creep, seemingly unnecessary casualties, and Vietnam-like escalation, on the one hand, and 1930s-style appeasement, on the other. It is difficult to disagree with the conclusion that the United Nations is remarkably ill suited to war making. Indeed, Karl von Clausewitz's famous principles, ranging from the tactical to the political, seem to have been consistently honored in the breach.[27]

Clausewitz and Peacekeeping

Tactically, even at the high point of the violence associated with UNOSOM, UN forces lacked the heavy equipment, including in particular armored personnel carriers and tanks, that would have been needed to ensure the safety of UN forces and dominate the urban battlefield. UNPROFOR suffered from a lack of operationally relevant military information. Despite the escalating levels of violence, the missions in both Somalia and Bosnia remained defined as peacekeeping, not war fighting. The war that did occur was supposed to occur in the midst of a civilian population whose protection

was the first purpose of the operation. All this gave rise to what has become known as the Force Commander's Complaint: "If you order me to fight a war I will, but not in vehicles painted white!"

Strategically, force commanders lacked command and control, the classic requirement of unity of command. The first act of every peacekeeping battalion was to establish a communications and command link with its national command authority. Any proposed action involving the threat of violence would be referred to national authorities for approval.[28] Force commanders, by consequence, negotiated rather than directed their forces, which was part of the reason for the lack of support on both June 5, when the Pakistanis took twenty-four casualties, and October 3, when the U.S. Rangers (who operated independently of the UNOSOM command) experienced disaster.[29]

At the grand strategic, or political command, level the United Nations suffers from an irresponsible divorce between the Security Council and the UN operation in the field. At times the Security Council issued mandates, for example, for Bosnian safe areas, without providing the forces that military experts had argued were necessary to implement the mandates.[30] Delays also erode the effectiveness of UN peace operations, and delays in deployment of up to a year are not uncommon. At the political policy level that shapes all strategic implementation, UN war making suffers from severe disabilities: some a product of the incapacity of the organization; others due to the competing interests and limited support offered by member countries (particularly the five permanent members of the Security Council); and others a product of the kind of wars the United Nations has tried to address.

- The United Nations is particularly poorly suited to interventionist strategies involving the strategic employment of coercive force. The political roots of UN "command-and-control" problems are threefold. On the one hand, countries with battalions in UN peace operations are reluctant to see their (often lightly armed) troops engaged in combat under UN direction, doubting whether a UN force commander of any nationality other than their own will take due care to minimize risks. Countries with seats on the Security Council, on the other hand, pressured to achieve a response to civil war crises and unwilling to confront the United Nations' ongoing resource crisis, assign missions to UN peace operations without providing adequate means to achieve those missions. On top of this, the UN Secretariat lacks the skills and number of personnel needed to manage (i.e., coordinate) a large-scale armed enforcement operation. The Secretariat's traditional ideology (despite recent practice) is highly protective of national sovereignty and (to its credit) lacks the psychological distance required to order coercive punishment on political movements with even the smallest degree of popular support.[31] Having been used repeatedly as a scapegoat by its leading member-states, it also tends to be extremely risk averse and self-protective of the organization even when risk taking may be justified.

- Some have argued that effective intervention requires choosing sides. Richard Betts has argued that effective intervention tends to require nonimpartial and nonneutral use of force in order to economize on the use of force. The most economical intervention thus assists the strongest party in achieving effective sovereignty or assists the party whose interests are closest to those of the intervenor. Otherwise, the international actor finds itself caught in the middle, providing material support to each of the factions without the support of any of the factions.[32] Picking the winner makes considerable sense for unilateral interventions with national objectives. But the Security Council faces difficulties in directing any form of a strategic military campaign, and choosing sides

is even more difficult in any campaign short of one directed against international aggression or genocide because of the variety of national objectives that enters into the multilateral intervention. Each permanent member of the Security Council can use its veto to prevent a UN-endorsed intervention that would disadvantage its perceived client. Minimally equipped and with a mandate produced by a delicately negotiated least common denominator in the Security Council, neutrality tends to be the limit of UN peace operations. If the United Nations had at its disposal substantial forces, impartial enforcement would become more feasible but only in the service of genuinely multilateral goals.

- "Peace-enforcing fatigue" is also afflicting the United Nations' contributing countries, whether new or old. States are rarely willing to invest their resources or the lives of their soldiers in war other than for a vital interest (such as oil in the Persian Gulf). But if states have a vital national interest in a dispute, they are not likely to exercise the impartiality a UN peace operation requires. Nor are they likely to cede decision-making control or command of their forces over to the United Nations.

- The very act of intervention, even by the United Nations, can mobilize nationalist opposition against the foreign forces. Intervention contributed to a significant growth of support for Aideed's Somali National Alliance. Aideed's supporters soon roundly condemned UN "colonialism."[33] The strategic balance is not static. Military intervention tilts two local balances, improving the military correlation of forces but often at the cost of undermining the more important political balance.

- Coercively intervening for eventual self-determination, as John Stuart Mill noted over a century ago, is very often a self-contradictory enterprise.[34] If the local forces of freedom, self-determination, and human rights cannot achieve sovereignty without a foreign military intervention, then they are very unlikely to be able to hold on to power after the intervention force leaves. Either the installed forces of freedom will collapse or they themselves will employ those very coercive methods that provoked and justified the initial intervention.[35]

The United Nations thus presents an almost textbook case of multiple strategic incapacities produced by both institutional incapacity and lack of support from its member countries. Its failings as a war maker appear deeply structured in its multilateral character, which serves as an invitation to buck-passing and rhetorical solutions to substantive problems. Multilateral cooperation is far from impossible. It has been achieved numerous times, even under trying circumstances. The Combined Chiefs of Staff managed the World War II Grand Alliance. The International Monetary Fund, the World Bank, the World Trade Organization, and numerous multilateral regimes work, often with smaller coalitions of like-minded states in charge or through imaginative schemes of delegation.[36] But the UN Security Council is a special problem. It lacks the forced commonality of interests against the Axis that shaped the World War II Grand Alliance (the council's immediate ancestor). It usually lacks the cultural consensus or charismatic leadership that can bind other multilateral institutions. Yet its global security role is more strategically demanding—facing uncertainties absent a clear regime of norms or procedures, required to adjust flexible means to fluid ends—than that of the typical successful multilateral organizations. The fifteen-member Security Council, subject to the veto of the Permanent Five, looks much like the storied, eighteenth-century Polish Diet subject to its debilitating vetoes. Neither was/is suited for rational strategic action.

Nonetheless, encountering strategic problems while intervening in ethnic and civil wars is not unique to the United Nations. The Multinational Force in Lebanon created even larger catastrophes of misdirected, overly violent, and intrusive intervention in 1983. Even with national-quality command and control, the United States failed to impose peace in Vietnam in the 1960s; the Soviets failed in Afghanistan. Moreover, the United Nations is nothing more than the collective agent of its member-states. Some of the United Nations' organizational incapacities could be cured by additional resources from its member-states, which devote but a tiny fraction of the resources they spend on national security to collective action under the United Nations.

PEACE MAKING: STRATEGIES OF ENHANCED CONSENT

The United Nations' deficiencies as a war maker are offset by its often unappreciated successes as a peace maker. The United Nations has succeeded when it has negotiated and then implemented a consensual basis for a restoration of law and order and human rights. Second-generation, multidimensional operations have been based on consent of the parties. But the nature of consent and the purposes for which it has been granted are qualitatively different than in traditional, or first-generation, peacekeeping. UNTAC in Cambodia, for example, was based on the consent of the parties, as expressed in the Paris agreements, but it moved beyond monitoring the actions of the parties to the establishment of a transitional authority that actually implemented directly crucial components of the mandate. Moreover, its scale was vastly larger than that of all but the enforcement mandates and it found itself operating without the continuous (in the case of the Khmer Rouge) or complete (in the case of the other factions) cooperation of the factions.

The United Nations has a commendable record of success in second-generation, multidimensional peacekeeping operations as diverse as those in Namibia (UNTAG), El Salvador

(ONUSAL), Cambodia (UNTAC),[37] Mozambique (ONUMOZ), and Eastern Slavonia/Croatia (UNTAES). The UN role in helping settle those conflicts has been fourfold. It served as a *peace maker* facilitating a peace treaty among the parties; as a *peacekeeper* monitoring the cantonment and demobilization of military forces, resettling refugees, and supervising transitional civilian authorities; as a *peacebuilder* monitoring and in some cases organizing the implementation of human rights, national democratic elections, and economic rehabilitation; and in the last resort and in a discrete, carefully constrained, and impartial manner as a focused *peace enforcer*. Together these roles create new dimensions of *transitional authority* for the international community. Exercising those authorities well makes all the difference.

Though nonenforcing and consent based, these operations are far from harmonious. Consent is not a simple "bright line" demarcating the safe and acceptable from the dangerous and illegitimate. Each function requires an enhanced form of consent if the United Nations is to help make a peace in the contentious environment of civil strife. We need, therefore, to focus on new ways to design peace operations if the United Nations, in the face of likely resistance, is to avoid having to choose either comprehensive enforcement or complete withdrawal.[38]

Peace Making

Achieving the peace treaty itself will often require heavy persuasion by outside actors. In Cambodia the USSR and China are said to have let their respective clients in Phnom Penh and the Khmer Rouge know that ongoing levels of financial and military support would not be forthcoming if they resisted the terms of a peace treaty that their patrons found acceptable. Peace treaties may themselves depend on prior sanctions, threats of sanctions, or loss of aid provided by the international community.[39]

The construction of an agreed-upon peace is more than worth the effort. During the process of negotiation the contending factions can discover the acceptable parameters of peace that are particular to the conflict. Going beyond a mere truce, a comprehensive peace treaty addresses grievances and designs new institutions that test the true willingness of the parties to reconcile. Peace negotiations, furthermore, can mobilize the support of local factions and of the international community in support of implementing the peace. And a negotiated peace treaty can establish new entities committed to furthering peacekeeping and peacebuilding.[40]

The United Nations has developed a set of crucially important innovations that help manage the making of peace on a consensual basis. First among them is the diplomatic device that has come to be called the Friends of the Secretary-General. This brings multinational leverage to UN diplomacy to help make and manage peace. Composed of ad hoc, informal, multilateral diplomatic mechanisms that join together states in support of initiatives of the secretary-general, the Friends of the Secretary-General legitimates with the stamp of UN approval and supervision the pressures interested states can bring to bear to further the purposes of peace and the United Nations.

For Cambodia, the Core Group in New York and its counterpart, the Extended P-5, in Phnom Penh played a Friends role in the negotiation and the management of the peace process. Composed of representatives of the Security Council's Permanent Five (P-5)—the United States, France, Russia, China, and the United Kingdom—and "extended" to include Australia, Indonesia, Japan, and other concerned states, the Extended P-5 took the lead in the construction of the Paris agreements. It provided key support to UNTAC, both political and financial, and, led by Japan, it helped organize the International Committee on the Reconstruction of Cambodia (ICORC), which raised pledges for almost $1 billion while providing special funds for various projects. But the Extended P-5 lacked a fixed composition. It included, of course, the P-5 but then included or excluded others on an ad hoc basis, depending on the issue and topic covered and the "message" the group wished to send. For example, Thailand was excluded from certain meetings in order to send a signal of concern about its lack of support for the restrictions imposed on the Khmer Rouge. In Cambodia, moreover, there was not a sovereign government to monitor or support. Much of the Extended P-5's diplomacy was therefore directed at UNTAC itself, protecting, for example, the interests of national battalions. It also served as a back channel for the UNTAC special representative to communicate directly with the Security Council.[41]

In El Salvador the Four Friends of the Secretary-General were Venezuela, Mexico, Spain, and Colombia. Frequently joined by a "fifth friend"—the United States—they together played a crucial role in negotiating and implementing the peace accords.[42] So too did the Core Group in Mozambique. Hope for the former Yugoslavia centered on the Contact Group that included Russia, the United States, France, Germany, and the United Kingdom. Informal diplomatic support groups have also been active in Haiti, Namibia, Nicaragua, Georgia, Afghanistan, and Guatemala.[43]

Playing a crucial role in the secretary-general's peace-making and preventive diplomacy functions, these groupings serve four key functions. First, the limited influence of the secretary-general can be leveraged, multiplied, and complemented by the Friends. The United Nations' scarce attention and even scarcer resources can be supplemented by the diplomacy, finances, and clout of powerful, interested actors. Second, the very act of constituting themselves as a group, with the formal support of the secretary-general, lends legitimacy to the diplomatic activities of interested states that they might not otherwise have.[44] It allows for constructive diplomacy when accusations of special and particular national interest could taint bilateral efforts. The third function is coordination. The Friends mechanism provides transparency among the interested external parties, assuring them that they are all working for the same purposes and, when they are doing so, allowing them to pursue a division of labor that enhances their joint effort. It ensures that diplomats are not working at cross-purposes because they regularly meet and inform one another of their activities and encourage one another to undertake special tasks. And fourth, the Friends mechanism provides a politically balanced approach to the resolution of civil wars through negotiation. It often turns out that one particular "friend" can associate with one faction just as another associates with a second. In the Cambodian peace process, China backstopped the Khmer Rouge, just as France did Prince Norodom Sihanouk and Russia (with Vietnam) did the State of Cambodia. The Friends of the Secretary-General open more flexible channels of communication than a single UN mediator can provide. Members also advise and guide UN intermediaries in the peacekeeping and peacebuilding discussed later, although the process tends to work best when they support rather than move out in front of the United Nations.

While valuable, the Friends instrument can also disrupt the United Nations' effort to coordinate a peace process and, in effect, use the United Nations' multilateral credibility for partisan national purposes. In part this danger is the corresponding cost of the many advantages the Friends bring. One way to reduce the tendency toward runaway "Friends" is to have the UN's special representative chair the "Friends" meetings in the field and an assistant secretary-general from the Department of Politics Affairs do so in New York.

Multidimensional Peacekeeping

Even consent-based peace agreements fall apart. In the circumstances of partisan violence and "failed states," agreements tend to be fluid. In the new civil conflicts, parties cannot force policy on their followers and often lack the capacity or will to maintain a difficult process of reconciliation leading to a reestablishment of national sovereignty.[45]

Peace treaties and their peacekeeping mandates thus tend to be affected by two sets of contradictory tensions. First, in order to get an agreement, diplomats assume all parties are in good faith. But to implement a peacekeeping and peacebuilding operation, planners must assume the opposite—that the parties will not or cannot fulfill the agreement made. Moreover, diplomats, who design the peace treaty, tend to think in legal (authority, precedent) not strategic (power, incentives) categories. Treaties thus describe obligations; they tend to be unclear about incentives and capacities.

All these militate against clear and implementable mandates. Diplomats seek to incorporate in the treaty the most complete peace to which the parties will agree. UN officials seek to clarify the United Nations' obligations. Knowing that much of what was agreed to in the peace treaty will not be implementable in the field, the officials who write the secretary-general's report (which outlines the implementation of the agreement) contract or expand the mandate of the peace operation.[46] Confused mandates are an inevitable result of this tension.

A second tension also shapes the peacekeeping mandate. The mandate, like a natural resource contract, is an obsolescing bargain. When a country begins a negotiation with an oil company for the exploration of its territory, the company holds all the advantages. The costs of exploration are large while the possibility of oil is uncertain. The country must therefore cede generous terms. As soon as oil is discovered, the bargain shifts as discovered oil is easy to pump and any oil company can do it. The old bargain has suddenly obsolesced.[47]

So it is with a UN peacekeeping operation: the spirit of agreement is never more exalted than at the moment of the signing of the peace treaty; the authority of the United Nations is never again greater. Then the parties assume that the agreement will be achieved and that all are cooperating in good faith. They depend upon the United Nations to achieve their various hopes. Although the United Nations has put some of its diplomatic prestige on the line, it as yet has no investment in material resources. The United Nations, in short, holds most of the cards. But as soon as the United Nations begins its investment of money, personnel, and operational prestige, then the bargaining relationship alters its balance. The larger the UN investment—these multidimensional operations represent multibillion-dollar investments —the greater the independent UN interest in success is and the greater the influence of the parties becomes. Since the parties control an essential element in the success of the mandate, their bargaining power rapidly rises. So, in the late spring of 1993 as the crucial elections in Cambodia approached, UNTAC chief Yasushi Akashi acknowledged, "I cannot afford not to succeed."[48]

This dual tension in designing peacekeeping operations emphasizes that time is critical. The United Nations should be ready to implement the mandate as soon after the signing of a peace treaty as is practicable. UNTAC suffered a large decrease in authority in early 1992 as time passed and expectations of the factions and the Cambodian people were disappointed.

These tensions also explain how the ideal framework (both legal and political) of a treaty can dissolve in days or months, as the Cambodian peace agreements did. The provisions of peace accords become so general, ambiguous, or unworkable that many of the details have to be worked out in the implementation process. To be minimally effective under those circumstances, the United Nations must innovate.

The United Nations thus needs a flexible political strategy to win and keep popular support and create (not just enjoy) the support of local forces of order. In a failed state, as was the case in a society subject to colonial rule, what is most often missing is modern organization. This was what colonial imperial centers supplied, in their own self-interest, as they mobilized local resources to combat local opposition. Over the longer run indigenous forces such as the King's Own African Rifles in colonial West Africa and other locally recruited military battalions (not metropolitan troops) were the forces that made imperial rule effective, that preserved a balance of local power in favor of metropolitan influence—and that kept it cheap. Learning from the history of imperial institution building (while avoiding imperial exploitation and coercion), an effective and affordable strategy for UN peace operations faces a greater challenge. It needs to discover ways to generate *voluntary* cooperation from divided local political actors and mobilize existing local resources for *locally legitimate*, collective purposes.[49] And it must do so *rapidly*. The crucial mark of the success of a peace operation is self-sustaining self-determination.

None of these intrusions into domestic sovereignty would work were it not for the genuinely multilateral character of the United Nations, which in itself serves as guarantee of nonimperial motivation—and nonimperial capacity. The very multilateralism that makes the United Nations such an ineffective war maker is what makes it such an acceptable and reliable peace maker.

Recent peacekeeping experience has suggested a second peacekeeping innovation: an ad hoc, semisovereign mechanism designed to provide effective transitional authority (discussed later) in order to address those new challenges by dynamically managing a peace process and mobilizing local cooperation. Examples of these ad hoc, semisovereign mechanisms include the Supreme National Council (SNC) in Cambodia and the Commission on the Peace (COPAZ) in El Salvador.

It has often been remarked that Chapter VI presents the United Nations with too little authority and Chapter VII offers too much and that Chapter VI is associated with too little use of force and Chapter VII with too much. The value of these ad hoc, semisovereign, artificial bodies is that they provide a potentially powerful, political means of encouraging and influencing the shape of consent. Indeed, these semisovereign, artificial bodies can help contain the erosion of consent and even manufacture it where it is missing. Created by a peace treaty, they permit the temporary consensus of the parties to be formally incorporated in an institution with regular consultation and even, as in the Cambodian Supreme National Council, a semiautonomous sovereign will. These mechanisms have proved crucial in a number of recent UN missions. These transitional authorities can represent the once-warring parties and act in the name of a preponderance of the "nation" without the continuous or complete consent of all the factions. They can both build political support and adjust—in a legitimate way, with the consent of the parties—the mandate in order to respond to unanticipated changes in local circumstances.

In designing these semisovereign, artificial bodies, the United Nations should try (to the extent that its freedom of negotiation allows) to "preview" the peace that the parties and the international community seek. For the Paris peace agreements for Cambodia, seeking a "pluralist democracy" should have meant supplementing the Supreme National Council with other bodies, such as one for civil society. It might have included Buddhist monks, nongovernmental organizations, and other representatives of society outside the state. These supplementary bodies need not perform executive or legislative functions. The important point is that civil society participates in the decision-making process, at a minimum through formally recognized consultative channels.

Peacebuilding

Multidimensional, second-generation peace-keeping pierces the shell of national autonomy by bringing international involvement to areas long thought to be the exclusive domain of domestic jurisdiction. If a peacekeeping operation is to leave behind a legitimate and independently viable political sovereign, it must help transform the political landscape by building a new basis for domestic peace.

Traditional strategies of conflict resolution, when successful, were designed to resolve a dispute between conflicting parties. Successful resolution could be measured by (1) the stated reconciliation of the parties, (2) the duration of the reconciliation, and (3) changes in the way parties behaved toward each other.[50] But successful contemporary peacebuilding not only changes behavior but, more important, also transforms identities and institutional context. More than reforming play in an old game, it changes the game.

This is the grand strategy General Lieutenant John Sanderson invoked when he spoke of forging an alliance with the Cambodian people, bypassing the factions. Reginald Austin, electoral chief of UNTAC, probed the same issue when he asked what are the "true objectives [of UNTAC]: Is it a political operation seeking a solution to the immediate problem of an armed conflict by all means possible? Or does it have a wider objective: to implant democracy, change values and establish a new pattern of governance based on multi-partism and free and fair elections?"[51]

UNTAC helped create new actors on the Cambodian political scene: the electors, a fledgling civil society, a free press, a continuing international and transnational presence. The Cambodian voters gave Prince Ranariddh institutional power and the Khmer Rouge was transformed from an internationally recognized claimant on Cambodian sovereignty to a domestic guerrilla insurgency. The peacebuilding process, particularly the election, became the politically tolerable substitute for the inability of the factions to reconcile their conflicts.

The UN role, mandated by these complex agreements rather than Chapter VII, includes monitoring, substituting for, renovating, and in some cases helping to build the basic structures of the state. The United Nations is called in to demobilize and sometimes to restructure and reform once-warring armies; to monitor or to organize national elections; to promote human rights; to supervise public security and help create a new civilian police force; to control civil administration in order to establish a transitional politically neutral environment; to begin the economic rehabilitation of devastated countries; and, as in the case of Cambodia, to address directly the values of the citizens, with a view to promoting democratic education.

The parties to these agreements, in effect, consent to limitation of their sovereignty for the life of the UN-sponsored peace process. They do so because they need the help of the international community to achieve peace. But acceptance of UN involvement in implementing these agreements is less straightforward than, for example, consenting to observance of a cease-fire. Even when genuine consent is achieved, it is impossible to provide for every contingency in complex peace accords. Problems of interpretation arise, unforeseen gaps in the accords materialize, and circumstances change. The original consent, as the Salvadoran peace process suggests, can become open ended and, in part, a gesture of faith that later problems can be worked out on a consensual basis. In the process the international community, represented by the United Nations, exercises a monitoring pressure to encourage progress on the reform of the judiciary, the expansion of the electoral rolls, and the operation of a free press.

But authentic and firm consent in the aftermath of severe civil strife, such as that which Cambodia endured, is rare. The first clear implication is the consequent importance of risk-spreading multidimensionality. The United

Nations should design in as many routes to peace—institutional reform, elections, international monitoring, economic rehabilitation —as the parties will tolerate.

Second, the international negotiators of a peace treaty and the UN designers of a mandate should attempt, therefore, to design in bargaining advantages for the UN authority. Even seemingly extraneous bargaining chips will become useful as the spirit of cooperation erodes under the pressure of misunderstandings and separating interests. In Mozambique Special Representative Aldo Ajello skillfully deployed a trust fund to assist Renamo's demobilization. In Cambodia the United Nations counted upon the financial needs of the Cambodian factions to ensure their cooperation and designed an extensive rehabilitation component to guarantee steady rewards for cooperative behavior.[52] But the Khmer Rouge's access to illicit trade (with the apparent connivance of elements of the Thai military along the western border) eliminated this bargaining chip. And FUNCINPEC, the royalist faction, was much too suspicious of the dominant so-called State of Cambodia faction (SOC) to allow the latter control of rehabilitation funds in the 80 percent of Cambodia that was under SOC administrative authority.

Third, the architects of the UN operation therefore should also design into the mandate as much independent implementation as the parties will agree to in the peace treaty. In Cambodia the electoral component and refugee repatriation seem to have succeeded simply because they did not depend on the steady and continuous positive support of the four factions. Each had an independent sphere of authority and organizational capacity that allowed it to proceed against everything short of the active military opposition of the factions. Civil administrative control and the cantonment of the factions failed because both relied on the continuous direct and positive cooperation of each of the factions. Each faction, at one time or another, had reason to expect that

the balance of advantages was tilting against itself and so refused to cooperate. A significant source of the success of the election was Radio UNTAC's ability to speak directly to the potential Cambodian voters, bypassing the propaganda of the four factions and invoking a new Cambodian actor, the voting citizen. But voters are only powerful for the five minutes it takes them to vote, if there is not an institutional mechanism to transfer democratic authority to bureaucratic practice. Now, lacking such a mechanism in Cambodia, the voters are vulnerable to the armies, police, and corruption that dominate after the votes are tallied.

In these circumstances the United Nations should try to create new institutions to ensure that votes in UN-sponsored elections "count" more. The United Nations needs to leave behind a larger institutional legacy, drawing, for example, upon the existing personnel of domestic factions, adding to them a portion of authentic independents, and training a new army, a new civil service, a new police force, and a new judiciary. These are the institutions that can be decisive in ensuring that the voice of the people, as represented by their elected representatives, shapes the future.

Peace Enforcing

The United Nations must avoid the trade-offs between too much force and too little.[53] The dangers of Chapter VII enforcement operations, whether in Somalia or Bosnia, lead many observers to think that it is extremely unlikely that troop-contributing countries will actually sign up for such operations. The risks are far more costly than the member-states are willing to bear for humanitarian purposes. But when we look at Chapter VI operations, we see that consent by parties easily dissolves under the difficult processes of peace. UN operations in the midst of civil strife have often been rescued by the *discrete, impartial, but non-neutral use of force*. Rather than attempting to broadly enforce an external solution on a civil war (making war, as in Somalia), "narrow" or "focused enforcement" implements (by force, when needed) a key aspect of a comprehensively agreed-upon peace. Early examples of successfully applied focused force were the operations in Congo, when Katanga's secession was forcibly halted, and the operation in Namibia, when SWAPO's violation of the peace agreement was countered with the aid of South African forces.[54] But both nearly derailed the peace process by eroding local, regional, or global support.

Semisovereign, artificial bodies offer the possibility of midcourse adjustments and "nationally" legitimated enforcement (should it be needed).[55] In Cambodia, for example, UNTAC —operating in full accord with the Paris agreements—appealed to *all* the factions to protect the election. The appeal was impartial and based upon the peace treaty to which all the parties had consented. (In UN circles this is now called "strategic" consent as opposed to "tactical" consent.) The result was distinctly not neutral among the parties as the armies (most effectively, the SOC's army) that were cooperating with the peace plan pushed the Khmer Rouge back from the population centers. This subcontracted use of force permitted a safer vote with a larger—hence more legitimate—turnout in the last week of May 1993.[56]

In 1996 in Eastern Slavonia, relying firmly on the consent of both President Milosevic and President Franjo Tudjman, UNTAES successfully exercised its "executive authority" and employed overwhelming coercive force against the paramilitary gangs controlling the Djeletovici oil fields. In May 2000 in Sierra Leone, force was once again employed to rescue a floundering peace operation as the British Parachute Regiment rushed to Freetown to prevent the cutoff of the UN force and liberate the city from the Revolutionary United Front (RUF), which had terrorized the country. The British force stayed to train one thousand members of the Sierra Leonean army, prop up both the

UN peace operation and the government of President Ahmed Tejan Kabbah, and in July free the remaining 220 UN peacekeepers being held by RUF forces.[57] Discrete, impartial uses of force in the context of a comprehensive peace operation can be effective, and force is often essential to rescue a challenged peace.

In summary, whether in peace making, peacekeeping, peacebuilding, or discrete enforcement, the United Nations' multilateralism —so disadvantageous in making war—contributes significantly to its success in fostering self-sustaining peace. Multilateral impartiality, the principles of equality of states, and universal human rights embedded not just in the UN Charter but deeply in the United Nations' ethos and composition make the quasi-colonial presence that a multidimensional peace operation entails not only tolerable but effective. The United Nations' mere presence guarantees that partial national interests are not in control and thereby makes intrusive peace operations acceptable to the factions of civil war–torn countries. (The United Nations' very inefficiencies make fears of empire mongering seem farfetched.) At their best, UN peace operations mobilize a diverse and complementary set of national talents and serve by their very multinational character to announce that cross-ethnic and cross-ideological cooperation can work.

Transitional Authority

Effective transitional authority that governs how peacekeeping, peacebuilding, and peace enforcement are exercised must be designed to fit the case if it is going to succeed in establishing a self-sustaining peace. The necessary extent of authority is a function, first, of the local root causes of conflict; second, of the local (primarily economic) capacities for change; and, third, of the specific degree of international commitment available to assist change. Effective transitional authority must take into account levels of hostility and factional capacities. Whether

Table 1. Five Ecologies of Transitional Politics

	Hostile Factions		Reconciled Factions	
	Few	*Many*	*Few*	*Many*
Coherent Factions	**Third Ecology** Angola Bosnia I Cambodia Cyprus Georgia Western Sahara (Morocco)		**First Ecology** El Salvador Namibia Tajikistan	
Incoherent Factions	**Fourth Ecology** Brcko (Bosnia) East Slavonia (Croatia) Rwanda	**Fifth Ecology** Bosnia II Congo DRC Liberia Sierra Leone Somalia	**Second Ecology** East Timor Guatemala Haiti Mozambique	

Note: The five ecologies of transitional politics cover cases of predominantly civil war, not interstate wars or invasions by foreign forces (as in, for example, Lebanon).

it in fact does so depends on strategic design and international commitment. Designs for transitional authority incorporate a mix of legal and bureaucratic capacities that integrate in a variety of ways domestic and international commitments.

Authority operates not upon stable states, but instead on unstable factions. These factions (to simplify) come in three dimensions. Examining a conceptual map of the post–Cold War world, we can categorize factions as either *few or many* and *coherent or incoherent* (that is, they do or do not follow the orders of their leaders).[58] They reflect varying degrees of *reconciliation or hostility*. Having reached a "hurting stalemate," they accept the process of peace; or (having been dragged to the conference table) they do not. They also are in conflict in societies that either have very little economic and social capacity (LDCs—less developed in terms of gross

domestic product [GDP], education, and so on) or have more (MDCs—more developed in those capacities). When one examines the mix of these factors in table 1, one can think about differing "ecologies" of transitional authority during peacebuilding that represent differing combinations of those three dimensions and differing levels of international response to them.[59]

There is a *"first ecology"* of peacebuilding in which the factions are *few, semireconciled, and coherent and the capacities are substantial or minimal*. And in the usual more or less ways, El Salvador (more capacity) and, more debatably, Namibia and Tajikistan (less capacity) fall into that pattern. The authority often relies on specific commitments made in the peace treaty by established governments, supplemented by new transitional institutions and an international peace operation. In El Salvador, for example, the government undertook a variety of commitments to engage in judicial, police, military, electoral, and other reforms. The peace agreements also created new transitional institutions, including COPAZ, which was designed to promote dialogue among business, labor, and other elements of civil society. ONUSAL was charged with monitoring and assisting the peace process.

Transitional authority, light as it is, still has a vital role to play in peacebuilding in those circumstances. First, it can create and needs to create transparency. The factions may be reconciled but they do not fully trust each other. The international peacebuilding role consists of monitoring and investigating in order to increase trust so that the parties can believe that the piece of paper they signed has operational significance. In El Salvador ONUSAL helped to increase trust and transparency through the Ad Hoc Commission, which supervised demobilization, and through the Truth Commission, which investigated human rights violations and recommended reforms. Second, in these circumstances the international peacebuilders can also offer capacity building. They can bring in the technical assistance that the parties either lack or do not trust one another to provide, such as electoral assistance or police training. And third, and perhaps most important, the peacebuilders provide assurance of continuing coordination. No matter how well designed the peace treaty happens to have been, and despite whatever reconciliation of the parties may have occurred, the parties know that circumstances will arise that were not anticipated in the treaty. Those circumstances will need to be dealt with if the peacebuilding process is to be kept on track.[60]

In the "*second ecology*" of peacebuilding, the factions are *few* and *reconciled*, but they are *incoherent*. In Guatemala exhaustion and international pressure brought the government and the indigenous communities to the peace table, but soon thereafter the indigenous communities lapsed into their many local components,

the thousands of communities from which war had mobilized them. In Haiti and East Timor war and intervention radically reduced the influence of the opposition, as General Raoul Cedras's forces fled Haiti and the Indonesian militias left East Timor. This left one massive "faction," destitute and lacking in coherent organization. Here factions may be incapable of fulfilling their commitments, even if willing. In Mozambique ONUMOZ appears to have stepped in to play an active, quasi-sovereign, implementing role through a variety of commissions for disarmament, elections, and humanitarian activities.[61] ONUMOZ actually helped to organize a political party as well as to employ demobilized soldiers in building roads, a true capacity, infrastructure-building effort. Proactive peace management oriented toward capacity building was important in both respects, employing the ex-soldiers and building a transportation grid.

In the "*third ecology*" of peacebuilding the factions are *few, hostile, and coherent*. Both Cambodia and Angola fit this space, where the factions were and still are hostile in countries that are poor. In Bosnia, which has greater social and economic capacity, the factions remain very hostile (Muslim-Croat relations resemble Cambodia's SOC-FUNCINPEC relations; Bosnian Serb/Croat Federation–Serb relations resemble SOC-FUNCINPEC relations with the Khmer Rouge). In this third ecology the peacebuilding role includes all the functions that were exercised in that happier first ecology of UN peacebuilding—as in El Salvador, where transparency, coordinating assurance, and capacity building are the keys. But over and above that, because the factions are less than reconciled (the mildest way to describe the Georgian, Cypriot, Western Saharan, and Cambodian experiences), the peace process needs to embody more substantial transitional authority if it is going to have a chance of success.

No faction trusts the established government; alternatively put, the established government is nothing more than another faction, as was the State of Cambodia. Peacebuilding design may thus call for transitional sovereignty institutions, as in the Supreme National Council of Cambodia, to which the sovereignty of Cambodia was temporarily entrusted. The SNC represented each of the factions, with Prince Sihanouk in a trustee, titular head of state role.

International commitment is likely, nonetheless, to be needed to glue the transitional institutions together and provide economic assistance. UNTAC and its special representative, Yasushi Akashi, were given the authority to decide—when the factions were deadlocked and Prince Sihanouk did not act. UNTAC also received the authority to "control" the administrative activities of the factions (most relevantly SOC, which alone had substantial administrative capacity) in five areas of sovereign activity (defense, finance, foreign affairs, information, and public security).

Carrots and sticks may be needed to supplement legal capacities. At the Paris Peace Conference economic rehabilitation assistance was designed for, and only for, those factions that would cooperate within the peace process. Given that their former patrons had cut the factions off from financing, it was thought that this would be a very powerful constraint on defection and an incentive to cooperate in the peace process. Unfortunately, one and then another of the factions discovered alternate sources of financing through illegal sales of gems and logs and other means that removed this particularly important carrot and stick from the peace process.

In addition, in this less happy third ecology the international community may have a very important role in direct implementation. The residual hostility of the factions means that they will not trust one another to implement any crucial element of the peace process. In Cambodia it was absolutely vital that the United Nations itself have the authority to organize from the ground up the electoral process.[62] An election run by one of the factions and only

monitored by the United Nations (as in El Salvador) would have been prone to severe exploitation or manipulation. Instead it was the United Nations, the international community, that organized and ran that election, giving more parties authentic access and guaranteeing a much fairer count of the vote. Despite this substantial authority, there is a growing impression that not enough peacebuilding occurred.[63] Significantly, UNAVEM (United Nations Angola Verification Mission) lacked this kind of authority in Angola and failed.

In the early stages of the Dayton peace process (Bosnia I), the transitional authority available to move the parties to the commitments made at Dayton was far from adequate. Levels of hostility remained high after the signing of the accords. In this strategic situation both formal and effective authority, including the will to use them, were needed. In the military sphere both formal authority and an effective presence on the ground were much in evidence, and the successful separation of forces resulted. However, the narrow interpretation of what constituted security and the lack of coordination between the civilian and military pillars of the Dayton process had debilitating effects on "civilian" implementation. Refugee return to areas in which they would be a minority was stymied, and the forces which had led the campaigns of exclusion and violence stayed in power. Civilian authority, moreover, was both unclear and divided. While the Office of the High Representative (OHR) coordinated many organizations, its authority vis-à-vis the parties and those other implementing organizations was underspecified. The OHR, the Organization for Security and Cooperation in Europe (OSCE), and others were empowered to make determinations of compliance and lack of compliance with the Dayton accords but lacked quasi-sovereign authority to make determinations of policy when the parties disagreed.[64] The mandate in the first phase was interpreted more in lines suited to the degree of genuine reconciliation evidenced in the

Salvadoran or Namibian peace operations, rather than to the hostility that characterized the Bosnian factions. Only with the Bonn Summit of the Peace Implementation Council of December 1997 (Bosnia II) did the OHR begin to acquire the internationally recognized authority to make decisions against the will of the parties. As the factions themselves began to splinter, raising the need for authoritative coordination, the OHR began to make efforts to manage the most blatant spoilers. It instituted neutral license plates, closed hostile media transmitters, targeted the more violent cantonal police forces, and more actively supported minority refugee returns.

In the *"fourth ecology"* of peacebuilding, the factions are *few, incoherent, and hostile*, making the prospects of sustainable peace extraordinarily poor. Only exceptional multilateral and international commitment might succeed in overcoming incentives for resumed armed conflict. On the one hand, in Rwanda such commitment was missing altogether. In Eastern Slavonia, on the other hand, the United Nations acquired "executive authority" through the Erdut Agreement, which gave the transitional administrator, Jacques Klein, the authority to implement the agreement without the consent of the Croatian government or the Krajina Serb entities. Interesting disputes arose over whether that authority was constrained or not, and, if so, by what. On the one hand, Zagreb argued that that Croatian law constrained and UNTAES was "executing" it. On the other hand, certain UNTAES lawyers argued that executive authority was constrained only by international human rights and humanitarian law.[65] Equally noteworthy in the UNTAES operation, however, is the substantial military force at its disposal both locally (in UNTAES) and on call (from NATO's IFOR/SFOR). Ongoing operational consent, too, may be playing a more significant role than legal mandates might suggest; UNTAES officials stress the occasional cooperation they have received from Presidents Tudjman (Croatia)

and Milosevic (Serbia) as well as from various local actors, both official and unofficial.

At the extreme, as a potentially superior solution to hostile factions with either coherent or incoherent leadership, the international community has established "supervisory authority" —fully sovereign rule. In the municipality of Brcko in northern Bosnia, U.S. ambassador William Farrand ruled according to the Arbitral Order authorized by the Dayton accords, exercising with the assistance of SFOR troops fully sovereign authority. So far, Brcko is the only Bosnian municipality with significant minority returns (where the returnees are a minority) and the beginnings of a functioning multiethnic police, judiciary, and town council.[66] Following the final arbitral award, in 1999 Brcko was established as an autonomous district, separate from both the Republika Srpska and the federation, in effect a third entity. To its international administrators, Brcko is an experiment in whether concentrated international authority and substantial international capacity can begin to build self-sustaining, multiethnic peace.

In the *"fifth ecology"* of peacebuilding, in which there are *many incoherent and hostile* factions in a desperately poor economy, as in Bosnia II, Congo, the DRC, Liberia, Sierra Leone, and Somalia, the prospects appear to be even grimmer for effective peacebuilding. What may have been needed in Somalia was a partition that separated it from Somaliland and, for the remainder of the country, a substantial civilian and developmental effort with a long-term horizon and trusteeship-like quasi-sovereign authority. Instead, the international community offered a military mission with a constant eye open for a fast exit.[67]

There appears to be a relation between the depth of hostility and the number and character of the factions, on the one hand, and the extent of effective authority needed to build peace, on the other. There is a functional progression from ONUSAL's monitoring/assisting, to UNTAC's "administrative control," to

Table 2. Four Types of Transitional Authority

	First Ecology	Second Ecology	Third Ecology	Fourth Ecology	Fifth Ecology
Supervisory Authority		*UNTAET*[a]		*UNMIK* Brcko Arbitral Order	
Executive Authority				**UNTAES**	*Bosnia II* *UNOMIL*[b]
Administrative Authority		**ONUMOZ**	**UNTAC** *Bosnia I* MINURSO		*UNOSOM II*
Monitor	**ONUSAL** **UNTAG** **UNMOT**	*UNMIH?* MINUGUA	*UNAVEM* UNOMIG UNFICYP	*UNAMIR*	*UNOSOM I* *MONUC* ***UNPROFOR*** *UNOMSIL*

Note: Successful operations are in bold type, unsuccessful operations in bold italic, ongoing operations in regular type, and recent operations in regular italic.

a. A curious and exceptional case of *excessive* international authority. The Timorese factions are more than ready to cooperate according to a number of accounts, but the United Nations is insisting on full sovereign control. See Jarat Chopra, "The UN's Kingdom of East Timor," *Survival* 42, no. 3 (autumn 2000): 27–39.

b. UNOMIL, the UN monitoring operation in Liberia, was paired with and monitored an ECOMOG operation with authority to maintain order, which it achieved in a sporadic fashion.

UNTAES's "executive authority," to a Brcko-style sovereign "supervision." Authority greater than monitoring/facilitating would have been redundant in El Salvador; authority less than supervisory and sovereign in Brcko would have been insufficient.

When we place transitional authority conceived of as legal authority and effective international capacity (troops and budget) on a vertical axis and the five ecologies on a horizontal axis, a progressive relation holds, as shown in table 2. Successful operations (those that lead to an indigenously sustainable peace) demonstrate a one-to-one relation: the more challenging the factional conflict, the more transitional authority seems to be required.

Optimistically, we can note that the international community seems to be learning from past mistakes: in the trying circumstances of Kosovo and East Timor, extensive authority has been provided. In the equally, if not more, trying Congo, modest promises of monitoring as a step toward a negotiated peace are being offered. No one promises nationbuilding or peace enforcement or humanitarian protection, as was done in Somalia and Bosnia.

This is a wise development. There were few takers for the colonialist role in the late twentieth century. Since all transitional authorities must end, authority and the capacity to make it effective are essential in the transition toward effective national self-determination. While muddling and innovation toward enhanced authority on the Bosnian model is better than stagnation, ideally such authority is written into the peace agreement or imposed by Security Council fiat at the outset of a mission.

THE COSTS OF MAKING PEACE

In El Salvador, the official UN costs were $107.7 million (for three and a half years, 1991–94, including $35 million in 1993 for personnel).[68] Estimates suggest that in Cambodia at least $1 billion in additional costs would have been incurred beyond the official budget of $1.5 billion if the plans for economic rehabilitation had been implemented. The April 1993 NATO estimates of the cost of implementing an agreed-upon peace in Bosnia indicated a requirement for fifty thousand soldiers and $10 billion per year, without including the civilian peacebuilding costs.[69] Actual costs of IFOR ran at about $3.5 billion in the first year.

Good peacebuilding tends to be expensive. Considering the dangers of bluffing with inadequate military operations and the costs of effective peacebuilding in the more expensive operations (and the United Nations' continuously shaky finances), it is reassuring to note a favorable emerging trend and another key strategic consideration. The fortunate trend is that the surge of civil wars that accompanied the waning days of the Cold War and its immediate aftermath appears to be ebbing.[70] If so, there will be less demand for the United Nations' costly peace services. The other consideration is that successful operations need not be large and expensive. Good leadership of course economizes on resources. In addition, political and economic circumstances differ. Factions that have arrived at a negotiated, comprehensive, acceptable peace; countries less than devastated; nations retaining a sense of identity and even traditionally legitimate rulers—all require a smaller and less expensive international presence. ONUSAL was thus cheaper than UNTAC, which in turn will have been much cheaper than a sustainable peace in Bosnia (once achieved).[71]

The inevitably difficult choices concerning UN financing need to be made with a better comparative perspective. For every $1,000 spent by member countries on their own military forces, they spend, on average, $1.40 on the UN peacekeeping budget.[72] In 1994 the United States budgeted $267 billion on the Defense Department, about $28 billion on the intelligence community, and $1 billion for UN peacekeeping (30 percent of the $3.2 billion total). Nor is the United States discriminated against in the assessment of UN costs. The 25 percent U.S. assessment to the UN regular budget (and the peacekeeping rate proposed by the Clinton administration) is .0076 of a percent of U.S. national income. The Netherlands, Austria, and Sweden pay 135 percent of the U.S. rate relative to their national income. Ministates, like São Tomé, pay 330 percent of the U.S. rate relative to their income.[73]

In the end, however, the United States and other large contributors will have to ask whether UN peace operations are worth the cost. Today, for example, although no one calls Cambodia and El Salvador models of a growth-oriented, stable democracy, both governments were chosen in UN-supervised elections that were the freest and fairest in their histories. El Salvador's police were reformed; Cambodia enjoys an effective coalition government that successfully resisted the remaining and dwindling Khmer Rouge guerrillas. When we consider that the U.S. government once thought peace, pro-American states, and democratic development in Southeast Asia were worth more than fifty thousand U.S. lives and about $179 billion (in 1990 dollars) and that as late as the 1980s the U.S. government thought that promoting a friendly regime, peace, and democracy was worth $6.01 billion (1981–90, in 1994 dollars) in El Salvador, both the United Nations' Cambodian and Salvadoran operations look remarkably cheap and successful, even when measured solely in terms of U.S. national interests.[74]

ALTERNATIVES?

When the United Nations cannot negotiate a peace, should the international community abandon the cause? What responses should have been made to acts of overt aggression, such as Iraq's invasion of Kuwait, or to the looming humanitarian disasters in Bosnia and Somalia in 1992 or Rwanda in the spring of 1994?

Delegation to national action has become, as it was in Korea in 1950, the United Nations' answer to extreme emergencies, including international aggression and humanitarian catastrophe. Delegation offers a traditional national solution to the United Nations' typical command-and-control problems. Now delegation to states under Articles 51–53 of the UN Charter is becoming so widespread that it is being designated "fourth-generation" peacekeeping. Stimulated by the temporary success of UNITAF, the U.S.-led precursor to UNOSOM II in Somalia, and by the delegations of enforcement to Russia in Georgia, to France in Rwanda, to the United States in Haiti, and to Australia in East Timor, the United Nations is surmounting contributors' fatigue by assigning mandates to the states willing to accept and perhaps enforce them. This, indeed, may be the best compromise available in difficult circumstances.[75] In itself, however, it does little to address the longer-run problems of leaving behind a stable form of locally legitimate government. Here, as in Haiti, there remains an important "handoff" role for the United Nations. Imposing a scheme of public order should be avoided in favor of mobilizing the peace-making, peacekeeping, and peace-building strategies of enhanced consent that the United Nations exercises well. The UNITAF to UNOSOM II handoff failed in part because peace making stopped short of negotiating a comprehensive, implementable agreement that included both the warlords and civil society. Instead, the United Nations attempted to impose law and order from New York and Washington, with all the consequences. In these cases the United Nations should try to recruit the beginnings of a Friends coalition of interested states to assist and help monitor the intervenor. These Friends will also be needed to help

negotiate, fund, and manage a peace on a multilateral basis.

Delegation raises difficult issues of UN responsibility. Can the Security Council be confident that the mandate it assigns will be implemented in ways that fulfill multilateral principles and serve the interests of the United Nations as a whole? Security Council "licenses" to intervene with preordained but renewable expiration clauses should address some of these concerns. But in our dangerous times will states volunteer in reliably large enough numbers for international public service?

Another alternative centers on new attention to the possibilities of regional peacekeeping —a multilateral, burden-sharing strategy recommended in the secretary-general's 1995 *Supplement to An Agenda for Peace*. Regional peacekeeping appears designed to elicit a more locally sensitive approach to political disputes. Under the aegis of the OSCE and with UN endorsement, Italy played a constructive role in providing security for the transition in Albania. But the lack of institutional, military, and financial capacity of the regional organizations (with the exception perhaps of NATO) remains a considerable hurdle. The United States developed an African Crisis Response Initiative and now is becoming involved in training African peacekeepers in Nigeria.

In yet another alternative, Sir Brian Urquhart has issued an eloquent manifesto in favor of a UN rapid reaction force of five thousand to ten thousand. Small and centrally controlled, this force would be suited for overcoming delays occasioned by the recruiting of peacekeeping forces, enabling the United Nations to engage in rapid interventions that can sometimes prevent an escalating crisis. Had they been available, these forces might have been decisive in Somalia in early 1992 or Rwanda in April 1994.[76] Very few countries, however, have expressed a willingness to establish such a force. Current discussions center on a less global but still valuable ready reaction force consisting of designated national units, trained in peacekeeping and available at short notice, and a mobile headquarters unit.

When no state, group of states, or organization volunteers to intervene, then sometimes the best that can be done is to try to mitigate the consequences of natural disaster or war. Humanitarian assistance from "above"—state efforts to establish "humanitarian corridors," as has been done in Sudan, or protected convoys and even, at the minimum, airdrops, as was essayed in Bosnia—can make a valuable difference. Assistance from "below" by nongovernmental organizations, taking all the considerable risks of independent action, can also provide relief, as the voluntary agencies did in Somalia until they were overwhelmed in late 1992.[77] In these circumstances, the United Nations should continue to attempt to recruit coalitions of states—Friends—who will dedicate their energies to negotiating and managing a peace.

Neither UN peace making nor these alternative strategies will eliminate the formidable challenges of making, keeping, and building peace in the midst of protracted civil wars. Some crises will not find their solution. But today, as the United Nations is under attack in the United States and elsewhere, we should not neglect its authentic peace-making potential. Employing strategies of enhanced consent, the United Nations can play a constructive role in the forging of peace and reconstruction in those areas of the world in need of assistance. Avoiding the dangerous and often counterproductive effects of armed imposition, whether unilateral or multilateral, the United Nations can be the legitimating broker in the making, keeping, and building of a stable peace that takes the first steps toward the opening of political space for human rights and participatory communal self-expression. The very multilateralism that makes the United Nations so ineffective in making war is what makes it so effective in making a peace.

NOTES

This paper draws on research supported by the Christian Johnson Endeavor Foundation, a Hewlett Foundation fellowship at the Center for Advanced Study in the Behavioral Sciences; and on my "Discovering the Limits and Potential of Peacekeeping," in *Peacemaking and Peacekeeping for the New Century*, ed. Olara Otunnu and Michael Doyle (Lanham, Md.: Rowman and Littlefield, 1998).

1. I realize that the United Nations regarded these activities as "peacekeeping" or "peace enforcement," not war making. The parties, however, can have reason to see them differently. Imagine, for example, how the U.S. federal government would have viewed a decision of the European Concert in 1864 to establish Washington, Baltimore, Atlanta, Mobile, and New Orleans as "safe havens" and to ban all interference with U.S. commerce in U.S. territorial waters—a "no-sail zone"—by either the federal government or the Confederacy. None of this questions whether the UNPROFOR measures were justified.

2. The U.S. Congress included provisions in the National Security Revitalization Act (H.R. 7) for charging the United Nations for a wide range of indirect as well as direct costs of U.S. participation in peacekeeping. If these provisions had been adopted in this form, the act (in the eyes of many expert witnesses) would have bankrupted UN peacekeeping as the United States and other states proceeded to charge the United Nations for what have been extensive voluntary commitments in support of UN peacekeeping efforts. See the testimony of Secretary of State Warren Christopher (January 26, 1995) and C. William Maynes (January 19, 1995) before the House International Relations Committee.

3. Boutros Boutros-Ghali, *An Agenda for Peace* (New York: United Nations, 1992), 11, 13–34.

4. Boutros Boutros-Ghali, *Supplement to An Agenda for Peace: Position Paper of the Secretary-General on the Occasion of the Fiftieth Anniversary of the United Nations*, A/50/60; S/1995/1, January 3, 1995, 4.

5. *Vienna Declaration and Program of Action*, United Nations, A/CONF. 157/23, June 1993.

6. For a discussion of the traditional Cold War interpretations of "threats to the peace" and so on, see Leland M. Goodrich, E. Hambro, and Anne Simons,

Charter of the United Nations (New York: Columbia University Press, 1969), 293–300.

7. Mikhail Gorbachev, "Global Human Values" (speech before the UN General Assembly, A/43/PV72, December 7, 1988).

8. It is worth recalling that the time line of evolution has by no means been chronologically straightforward. The most extensive third-generation operation undertaken by the United Nations was ONUC in then-Congo between 1960 and 1964, which preceded the spate of second-generation operations, which began with UNTAG in Namibia in 1989.

The "6 and ½" refers to the fact that peacekeeping per se is nowhere described in the UN Charter and thus falls between Chapter VI, peacemaking (good offices and so on), and Chapter VII, peace enforcement.

9. "Traditional peacekeeping" is a shorthand term that describes many but by no means all Cold War peacekeeping missions (the most notable exception being the Congo operation). For cogent analyses of different types of peacekeeping, see Marrack Goulding, "The Evolution of United Nations Peacekeeping," *International Affairs* 69, no. 3 (July 1993); F. T. Liu, *United Nations Peacekeeping and the Non-Use of Force*, IPA Occasional Paper (Boulder, Colo.: Lynne Rienner, 1992); and Thomas Weiss, ed., *Collective Security in a Changing World* (Boulder, Colo.: Lynne Rienner, 1993).

10. In terms of game theory, they solved both variable sum, "coordination" problems, in which both parties have the same best outcome and will reach it if they can trust each other, and "prisoner's dilemma" problems, in which the parties have an incentive to cheat. The peacekeepers provide the missing transparency in the first and alter the payoffs in the second, making the prisoner's dilemma a coordination game. First-generation operations focus on the first but can include both sorts of games. Second- and third-generation operations focus on the more difficult challenges when achieving cooperation meets much more resistance.

11. Boutros-Ghali, *An Agenda for Peace*, 32.

12. "Success" is of course an ambiguous and contested term. It has been variously defined as implementing the UN Security Council mandate or the peace treaty, ending the war, reestablishing effective sovereignty, and/or promoting democratization, economic development, and other human rights. In this essay I focus on ending the war, reestablishing effective sovereignty, and certain core issues in the mandate as described in each case.

13. For insightful discussions of enforcement and consent problems, see Mats Berdal, *Whither UN Peacekeeping?* Adelphi Paper no. 281 (London: International Institute for Strategic Studies, 1993); Stephen Stedman, "Spoiler Problems in Peace Processes," *International Security* 22, no. 2 (fall 1997): 5–53; and William Durch, "Keeping the Peace: Politics and Lessons of the 1990s," in *UN Peacekeeping, American Policy, and the Uncivil Wars of the 1990s* (New York: St. Martin's Press, 1996), 1–34.

14. Other recent categories include "preventive deployments" deployed with the intention of deterring a possible attack, as in the Former Yugoslav Republic of Macedonia, where the credibility of the deterring force must ensure that the potential aggressor knows that there will be no easy victory. In the event of an armed challenge, the result will be an international war that involves costs so grave as to outweigh the temptations of conquest. Enforcement action against aggression (Korea or the Persian Gulf), conversely, is a matter of victory—"the decisive, comprehensive and synchronized application of preponderant military force to shock, disrupt, demoralize and defeat opponents"—the traditional zero-sum terrain of military strategy. See John Mackinlay and Jarat Chopra, *A Draft Concept of Second-Generation Multinational Operations* (Providence, R.I.: Brown University, Watson Institute, 1993); and John Ruggie, *The United Nations: Stuck in a Fog between Peacekeeping and Peace Enforcement*, McNair Paper no. 25 (Washington, D.C.: National Defense University, Institute for National Strategic Studies, 1993).

15. For further discussion, see Ruggie, *The United Nations*.

16. See Jonathan Stevenson, "Hope Restored in Somalia," *Foreign Policy* (1993): 138–154; Jeffrey Clark, "Debacle in Somalia: The Failure of Collective Response," in *Enforcing Restraint*, ed. Lori Damrosch (New York: Council on Foreign Relations, 1993); and Jane Perlez, "Somalia Self-Destructs and the World Looks On," *New York Times*, December 29, 1991, 1.

17. For this argument, see Mohammed Sahnoun, *Somalia: The Missed Opportunities* (Washington, D.C.: United States Institute of Peace Press, 1994).

18. For President Bush's rationale, see Michael Wines, "Bush Outlines Somalia Mission to Save Thousands," *New York Times*, December 5, 1992, 1.

19. Boutros Boutros-Ghali, *Further Report of the Secretary-General Submitted in Pursuance of Para. 19 Resolution 814 (1993) and Para. 5 (Resolution 865) of 1993,* S/26738, November 12, 1993. For an excellent account of UNOSOM I, see John Hirsch and Robert Oakley, *Somalia and Operation Restore Hope* (Washington, D.C.: United States Institute of Peace Press, 1995); and for UNOSOM II, see Walter Clarke and Jeffrey Herbst, eds., *Learning from Somalia* (Boulder, Colo.: Westview Press, 1997); and Jarat Chopra, *Peace-Maintenance* (New York and London: Routledge, 1999), chap. 6.

20. The figures are controversial. See David Rieff, *Slaughterhouse: Bosnia and the Failure of the West* (New York: Simon and Schuster, 1995); and George Kenney, "Bloody Bosnia," *Washington Monthly* (March 1995): 49–52. One widely publicized estimate is "at least 200,000" deaths or disappearances in Bosnia, more than 2 million displaced persons of Bosnia's prewar population of 4.3 million, 1.1 million of whom now live abroad; see "Bosnia Enters Fourth Year of War," *New York Times,* April 6, 1995, A8.

21. Rosalynn Higgins, "The New United Nations and the Former Yugoslavia," *International Affairs* 69, no. 3 (1993): 468–470; James B. Steinberg, "International Involvement in the Yugoslav Conflict," in *Enforcing Restraint,* ed. Damrosch; Sabrina Ramet, "War in the Balkans," *Foreign Affairs* 71, no. 4 (fall 1992): 79–98; and Misha Glenny, "Yugoslavia: The Great Fall," *New York Review of Books,* March 23, 1995.

22. Michael Gordon, "Pentagon Is Wary of Role in Bosnia," *New York Times,* March 13, 1994. The United States did assist the covert acquisition of light weapons for the Bosnian forces.

23. Andrew Bair, "Yugoslav Lessons for Future Peacekeepers," *European Security* 3, no. 2 (summer 1994): 340–349.

24. For eloquent testimony to all these factors, see the United Nations' *Srebenica Report* (1999); David Rohde's *Endgame* (New York: Farrar, Straus, and Giroux, 1997); and Jan Willem Honig and Norbert Both, *Srebrenica* (Harmondsworth, U.K.: Penguin, 1996).

25. Thorough histories of the political origins of the conflicts can be found in Susan Woodward, *Balkan Tragedy* (Washington, D.C.: Brookings Institution, 1995); and Steven Burg and Paul Shoup, *The War in Bosnia-Herzegovina* (Armonk, N.Y.: M. E. Sharpe, 1999).

26. Eric Schmitt, "Somalia's First Lesson for Military Is Caution," *New York Times,* March 5, 1995.

27. Karl von Clausewitz, *On War,* ed. and trans. Peter Paret (Princeton, N.J.: Princeton University Press, 1976), esp. book 8: "War Plans." For a discussion of strategic categories applied to the Cambodian operation, see Lieutenant General John Sanderson, "Dabbling in War," in *Peacemaking and Peacekeeping for the New Century,* ed. Otunnu and Doyle, 145–168.

28. William Doll and Steven Metz, *The Army and Multinational Peace Operations: Problems and Solutions* (Carlisle Barracks, Pa.: U.S. Army War College, 1993), 14. The problem of field command and control was less severe in first-generation peacekeeping because it did not usually involve the use of force.

29. See Mark Bowden, *Blackhawk Down* (New York: Atlantic Monthly Press, 1999), 90–96.

30. The safe havens were said to require thirty-four thousand troops; the Security Council authorized seventy-six hundred.

31. See the account of the UN decision process concerning Rwanda in Michael Barnett, "The UN Security Council, Indifference, and Genocide in Rwanda," *Cultural Anthropology* 12, no. 4 (1997): 551–578. An added problem is that the use of force in civil wars frequently causes casualties among civilians, opening the United Nations and its members to accusations of neocolonialism and brutality; see Adam Roberts, "The Crisis in Peacekeeping," in *Managing Global Chaos: Sources of and Response to International Conflict,* ed. Chester Crocker and Fen Hampton with Pamela Aall (Washington, D.C.: United States Institute of Peace Press, 1996), 297–319.

32. Richard Betts, "The Delusion of Impartial Intervention," in *Managing Global Chaos,* ed. Crocker and Hampson with Aall, 333–341; a revised version of that chapter appears in this volume (chapter 18).

33. As Abdi Hassan Awale, an Aideed adviser in Mogadishu, complained, "[T]he UN wants to rule this country. They do not want a Somali government to be established. The UN wants to stay and colonize us." *New York Times,* March 2, 1994.

34. For a classic discussion of these problems, see John Stuart Mill, "A Few Words on Nonintervention" (1859), in *Essays on Politics and Culture,* ed. Gertrude Himmelfarb (Gloucester, Mass.: P. Smith, 1973). Also see Edward Mortimer, "Under What Circumstances Should the UN Intervene Militarily in a

Crisis?" in *Peacemaking and Peacekeeping for the New Century*, ed. Otunnu and Doyle, 111–144.

35. The Kurds, for example, won widespread sympathy for their resistance to Saddam Hussein and benefited from a UN-endorsed U.S.-French-British intervention in the aftermath of the war against Iraq. Now the Kurdish factions are so divided that they appear incapable of establishing law and order in their territory. Instead, three factions have divided the region. None appear capable of sustaining themselves against whatever attempts to reincorporate Kurdistan that Saddam Hussein may make. The international community has thus placed itself in the awkward position of either adopting Kurdistan as a long-term ward or returning it to the not-so-tender mercies of Saddam Hussein. See Chris Hedges, "Quarrels of Kurdish Leaders Sour Dreams of a Homeland," *New York Times*, June 18, 1994, A1.

36. For valuable analytic surveys of multilateralism and how it can work, see John Ruggie, "Multilateralism: The Anatomy of an Institution"; and Miles Kahler, "Multilateralism with Small and Large Numbers," *International Organization* 46, no. 3 (summer 1992): 561–598 and 681–708.

37. Before the United Nations became involved, during the Cold War when action by the Security Council was stymied by the lack of consensus among its five permanent members, the international community allowed Cambodia to suffer an auto-genocide and El Salvador a brutal civil war. Indeed, the great powers were involved in supporting factions who inflicted some of the worst aspects of the violence the two countries suffered. We should keep this is mind when we consider the United Nations' difficulties in Somalia and Bosnia.

38. On the need to "enhance" the parties' consent so as to increase the likelihood of peacekeeping and peacebuilding success, see Michael Doyle, *UN Peacekeeping in Cambodia: UNTAC's Civil Mandate* (Boulder, Colo.: Lynne Rienner, 1995); and Steven R. Ratner, *The New UN Peacekeeping: Building Peace in Lands of Conflict after the Cold War* (New York: St. Martin's Press, 1995).

39. The Governors Island Agreement, which produced the first (ineffective) settlement of the Haitian conflict, resulted from economic sanctions on arms and oil imposed by the United Nations and the Organization of American States on Haiti as a whole. Sanctions targeted on the perpetrators (the military

elite and their supporters) might have been much more effective (and were later imposed, in the summer of 1994). Restrictions on the overseas private bank accounts and air travel of the ruling elite would have been more just and perhaps more effective than general economic sanctions whose impact was most severe on the most vulnerable and from which the elite may actually have benefited. David Malone's *UN Decision-Making in Haiti* (Oxford: Oxford University Press, 1998) covers these events in depth.

40. For a wide-ranging collection of recent experience in UN and other peacemaking, see Chester Crocker, Fen Hampson, and Pamela Aall, eds., *Herding Cats: Multiparty Mediation in a Complex World* (Washington, D.C.: United States Institute of Peace Press, 1999).

41. Yasushi Akashi, "UNTAC in Cambodia: Lessons for UN Peace-Keeping" (Charles Rostow Annual Lecture, SAIS, Washington, D.C., October 1993); Richard Solomon, "Bringing Peace to Cambodia," in *Herding Cats*, ed. Crocker, Hampson, and Aall, 275–323; and Doyle, *UN Peacekeeping in Cambodia*.

42. Ian Johnstone and Mark LeVine, "Lessons from El Salvador," *Christian Science Monitor*, August 10, 1993. The examples in these pages from UNTAC and ONUSAL are drawn in part from Michael Doyle, Ian Johnstone, and Robert Orr, eds., *Keeping the Peace* (Cambridge: Cambridge University Press, 1997).

43. The group of Friends for Haiti consisted of France, the United States, Canada, and Venezuela.

44. For a good discussion of the United Nations', and especially the secretary-general's, potential strength as a diplomatic legitimater, see Giandomenico Picco, "The U.N. and the Use of Force," *Foreign Affairs* 73, no. 5 (September-October 1994): 14–18. The "Friends" mechanism seems to answer many of the objections to UN mediation expressed by Saadia Touval, "Why the UN Fails," *Foreign Affairs* 73, no. 5 (September-October 1994): 44–57.

45. See Adam Roberts, "The United Nations and International Security," *Survival* 35, no. 2 (summer 1993); William Durch, ed., *The Evolution of UN Peacekeeping* (New York: St. Martin's Press, 1993); Berdal, *Whither UN Peacekeeping?*; Thomas Weiss, "New Challenges for UN Military Operations," *Washington Quarterly* 16, no. 1 (winter 1993); and Fen Osler Hampson, *Nurturing Peace: Why Peace Settlements*

Succeed or Fail (Washington, D.C.: United States Institute of Peace Press, 1996).

46. I first heard a variation on this point from Edward Luck.

47. See Raymond Vernon, "Long-Run Trends in Concession Contracts," *Proceedings of the Sixty-First Annual Meeting of the American Society of International Law* (Washington, D.C.: American Society of International Law, 1967).

48. Yasushi Akashi, interview in "Peace in the Killing Fields," part 3 of *The Thin Blue Line*, BBC Radio 4, released May 9, 1993.

49. It is interesting in this light to note that some key, early UN experts in peacekeeping were eminent decolonization experts, deeply familiar with the politics of colonial rule, as was Ralph Bunche from the UN Trusteeship Division. See Brian Urquhart, *Ralph Bunche: An American Life* (New York: W. W. Norton, 1993), chap. 5. For a discussion of imperial strategy, see Michael Doyle, *Empires* (Ithaca, N.Y.: Cornell University Press, 1986), chap. 12. But there are key differences. Empires were governed primarily in the interests of the imperial center; UN peace operations explicitly promote the interests of the host country. And what made imperial strategy work was the possibility of coercive violence, the over-the-horizon gunboats that could be and often were offshore. That, for good and bad, is what the United Nations usually lacks, unless it calls in the enforcement capacity of the major powers. Rehabilitation assistance is sometimes an effective carrot, but not the equivalent of the Royal Navy.

50. For a good account of traditional views of reconciliation, see A. B. Fetherston, "Putting the Peace Back into Peacekeeping," *International Peacekeeping* 1, no. 2 (spring 1994). For an approach stressing in various ways the strife involved in strategic political management, see I. William Zartman, "The Unfinished Agenda," in *Stopping the Killing: How Civil Wars End*, ed. Roy Licklider (New York: New York University Press, 1993), 20–34; Chaim Kaufmann, "Possible and Impossible Solutions to Ethnic Civil Wars," *International Security* (spring 1996): 136–175; David Lake and Donald Rothchild, "Containing Fear: The Origins and Management of Ethnic Conflict," *International Security* 21, no. 2 (fall 1996): 41–75; Stephen Stedman, "Spoiler Problems in Peace Processes," *International Security* 22, no. 2 (fall 1997); and Hampson, *Nurturing Peace.*

51. Reginald Austin, unpublished paper, 1993.

52. This link was drawn explicitly by Deputy Secretary Lawrence Eagleburger at the Conference on the Reconstruction of Cambodia, June 22, 1992, Tokyo, where he proposed that assistance to Cambodia be "through the SNC—to areas controlled by those Cambodian parties cooperating with UNTAC in implementing the peace accords—and only to those parties which are so cooperating." (Press Release USUN-44-92, June 23, 1992.) Disbursing the aid through the SNC, however, gave the Khmer Rouge a voice, as a member of the SNC, in the potential disbursement of the aid.

53. For an extensive discussion of the law and tradition of UN doctrine on the use of force, see Katherine E. Cox, "Beyond Self-Defense: United Nations Peacekeeping Operations and the Use of Force," *Denver Journal of International Law and Policy* 27 (spring 1999): 239–273.

54. John Carlin, "Namibia's Independence is UN's Triumph," *The Independent*, March 20, 1990, 11; and William Durch, "The UN Operation in the Congo," in *The Evolution of UN Peacekeeping*, chap. 19, 315–352.

55. The People's Republic of China did not want to see the Khmer Rouge destroyed; the USSR did not want to destroy the SOC; and France and the United States did not want to destroy FUNCINPEC. Each of the great powers is a permanent member of the Security Council and has veto on UN activity. Similar diversity applies with regard to the aims of troop-contributing countries. The gamble is as noted: an impartial intervention will elicit enough support from international actors and from the parties that multilateral assistance will be sufficient to establish a peace, especially when supplemented by impartial use of force as described.

56. Lieutenant General John Sanderson (UNTAC force commander), conversation with author at the Vienna Seminar, March 5, 1995. On May 28, 1993, I observed this in process around the small town of Stoung, which was surrounded by the Khmer Rouge. The Indonesian battalion established an inner perimeter around the town. The Cambodian People's Armed Forces (SOC army) created an outer perimeter and trucked in voters from outlying villages.

57. James Clark and Jon Swain, "SAS Rescue Mission Leads Jungle Hostages to Safety," *Financial Times*, July 16, 2000; and James Clark, "Freetown Parades Its British Army," *Sunday Times*, July 23, 2000.

58. Nick Sambanis and I find the relationship between factions and the difficulty of peacebuilding to be nonmonotonic, in fact U-shaped, in a 128-case statistical analysis of civil wars we conducted. "Few" make coordination problems less difficult; "many" (up to five) make them more difficult. "Very many" make coordination easier, as perhaps crosscutting coalitions emerge and factional salience declines. See Michael Doyle and Nicholas Sambanis, "International Peacebuilding: A Theoretical and Quantitative Analysis," *American Political Science Review* 94, no. 4 (December 2000): 785.

59. I use ecology as a variety of the "worlds" analogy employed by Robert Jervis in "Cooperation under the Security Dilemma," *World Politics* 30 (January 1978).

60. When it was discovered that one of the factions of the FMLN had a weapons cache, ONUSAL impartially investigated and then dismantled the cache. When it was discovered in November 1993 that the death squads seemed to be reemerging, many asked: Was the government behind them? The United Nations was able to investigate, enjoying the trust of the FMLN that it would do as thorough a job as could be done. See Ian Johnstone, *Rights and Reconciliation in El Salvador* (Boulder, Colo.: Lynne Rienner, 1995).

61. Richard Synge, *Mozambique: UN Peacekeeping in Action, 1992–94* (Washington, D.C.: United States Institute of Peace Press, 1997).

62. Doyle, *The UN in Cambodia*.

63. For a recent assessment, see International Crisis Group, *Cambodia: The Elusive Peace Dividend*, Asia Report no. 8 (Phnom Penh and Brussels: ICG, August 11, 2000).

64. Nonetheless, as in Cambodia, there were narrow areas of policy in which the international community possessed effective transitional authority. The International Monetary Fund, for example, had tie-breaking authority on the governing board of the central bank and the Council of Europe appointed a majority of the members of the Human Rights Chamber.

65. Interviews by author, Vukovar, Croatia, July 1997, with Transitional Administrator Jacques Klein, Jaque Grinberg, and others.

66. Interviews by author, Brcko, June 1999 and June 2000, with U.S. ambassador Bill Farrand, Mayor Kisic, and others.

67. For a discussion of transitional authority, see Gerald Helman and Steven Ratner, "Saving Failed States," *Foreign Policy* (winter 1992-93); and Ken Menkhaus, "International Peacebuilding," and Thomas Weiss, "Rekindling Hope," in *Learning from Somalia*, ed. Walter Clarke and Jeffrey Herbst (Boulder, Colo.: Westview Press, 1997). For later developments in Somalia, see Ameen Jan, *Peacebuilding in Somalia*, IPA Policy Briefing Series (New York: IPA, July 1996).

68. In 1994 dollars, as of December 31, 1994 (UN/PS/DPI/15/Rev.6, March 1995), and *Jane's Defence Weekly*, February 5, 1994.

69. The figures for Cambodia include the costs of refugee repatriation and the $800 million pledged by the International Commission on the Reconstruction of Cambodia. Bosnian costs are found in Bair, "Yugoslav Lessons for Future Peacekeepers," 349. The Clinton administration pledged a U.S. contingent of twenty-five thousand soldiers, drawn primarily from the 1st Armored Division and the 3rd Infantry Division.

70. Ted Gurr, "Ethnic Warfare on the Wane," *Foreign Affairs* 29, no. 3 (May-June 2000): 52–64.

71. For a statistical model of the factors determining the probabilities of success of peace operations, see Doyle and Sambanis, "International Peacebuilding." The model is tested against all civil wars since 1944.

72. Shijuro Ogata and Paul Volcker, *Financing an Effective United Nations* (New York: Ford Foundation, 1993). Also see U.S. ambassador Madeleine Albright's testimony to the Senate Committee on Armed Services, May 12, 1994.

73. Commission on Global Governance, *Our Global Neighbourhood* (Oxford: Oxford University Press, 1995), 247. Some countries, such as some of the rapidly developing countries, are paying less than their full share because the UN budget is too slow to adjust to rapid changes in GNP. The United States will be able to shrink its share of the peacekeeping budget from 30 percent to 25 percent with little cost to the United Nations if Japan and Germany join the Security Council as permanent members, paying at the higher rate permanent members have traditionally accepted for their greater privileges and responsibilities in the direction of UN peace operations.

74. Of course, the circumstances, including Cold War competition, were vastly different. For the figures, see James L. Clayton, "The Military Budget and

National Economic Priorities," in *The World Almanac, 1994* (Chicago: J. B. Ferguson, 1994); Central Intelligence Agency, *World Factbook, 1993* (Washington, D.C.: GPO, 1993); United States Agency for International Development, *U.S. Overseas Loans, Grants and Assistance from International Organizations*, Statistical Annex 1, Annual Development Coordination Committee Report to Congress (Washington, D.C.: Statistics and Reports Division, Office of Financial Management, various years); and Michael Switow, "Costs of U.S. Interventions" (research memorandum, Woodrow Wilson School, Princeton, N.J., 1995).

75. For a case for an option similar to this, called "benign spheres of influence," see Charles William Maynes, "A Workable Clinton Doctrine," *Foreign Policy* 93 (winter 1993-94).

76. Brian Urquhart, "For a UN Volunteer Military Force," *New York Review of Books*, June 10, 1993. See also "Four Views," *New York Review of Books*, June 24, 1993.

77. For a valuable discussion, see Stephen Jackson, "Survival of the Cutest," *Irish Reporter*, no. 12 (4th quarter 1993): 5–7.

33

The Role of Regional Organizations in Preventing and Resolving Conflict

Connie Peck

THIS CHAPTER WILL CONSIDER the growing role of regional organizations in the maintenance of regional peace and security. Since the topic is enormous, what follows will not attempt to be comprehensive but will instead simply highlight some of the more interesting and promising mechanisms that regional organizations are developing to prevent, resolve, and manage regional conflict. The intention is to provide a glimpse of the kinds of approaches that regional organizations can most effectively carry out and to show how these methods fit into the complex, multilayered global governance architecture that is emerging. This chapter will also briefly discuss the strengths and weaknesses of regional organizations relative to the United Nations, how they might work together more effectively, and the developing role of subregional organizations.

Regional organizations are, of course, diverse entities, established in response to different historical, political, economic, and cultural contexts and created for different objectives and

purposes. As such, each has developed unique approaches that make it difficult to discuss them as if they were a coherent group. Nonetheless, some commonalities exist.

THE ROLE OUTLINED FOR REGIONAL ORGANIZATIONS BY THE UNITED NATIONS CHARTER

The Charter of the United Nations does not define regional organizations (which it calls regional arrangements), although in practice the United Nations has tended to consider them to be collective or cooperative security arrangements rather than defense alliances. Their importance for the maintenance of international peace and security and their relationship to the United Nations is discussed in Chapter VIII of the UN Charter, which states that nothing in the charter precludes regional arrangements or agencies from dealing with matters that are appropriate for regional action, provided that they are "consistent with the Purpose and Principles of the United Nations." More pro-actively, it instructs that member-states enter-ing into such arrangements shall make every effort to achieve the pacific settlement of local disputes through such regional arrangements before referring them to the Security Council and, further, that the Security Council shall encourage the development of the pacific set-tlement of local disputes through regional arrangements, either on the initiative of the states concerned or by reference from the Secu-rity Council.[1]

Going even further in terms of collective security, Article 53 states that the Security Council shall, where appropriate, utilize such regional arrangements for enforcement action under its authority, but that no enforcement action can be taken by regional arrangements without the authorization of the Security Council.[2] Finally, Article 54 states that "The Security Council shall at all times be kept fully informed of activities undertaken or in contem-plation under regional arrangements or by re-gional agencies for the maintenance of inter-national peace and security."[3]

Thereby, the UN Charter recognizes the vital role that regional organizations can potentially play in the peaceful settlement of disputes, but it firmly places them under the authority of the Security Council with regard to any kind of en-forcement action and even forbids such action without the council's agreement. Interestingly, the charter seems to endorse implicitly a kind of subsidiarity model, where regional organiza-tions are actually encouraged to be the first port of call in trying to resolve regional disputes.

In *An Agenda for Peace,* UN secretary-general Boutros Boutros-Ghali also highlighted the importance of regional arrangements and or-ganizations, suggesting that they can render "great service if their activities are undertaken in a manner consistent with the Purpose and Prin-ciples of the Charter."[4] He noted that the Cold War impaired the proper use of Chapter VIII and that regional organizations sometimes worked against resolving disputes in the manner set out by the charter. Boutros-Ghali's predic-tion that regional arrangements would even-tually have a much greater role to play in the area of peace and security is, indeed, being ful-filled, as various regional organizations have increasingly begun to develop their own ap-proaches and mechanisms for conflict preven-tion, management, and resolution.

THE GROWTH OF REGIONAL AND SUBREGIONAL ORGANIZATIONS

Not all states, of course, are members of a re-gional organization, and some states belong to more than one. Moreover, the term "regional" is somewhat of a misnomer for some of these or-ganizations, whose membership goes beyond a single region.

Regional organizations are more prevalent in some parts of the world than in others. Europe has the most—with the European Union (EU), the Council of Europe (COE), and the Organi-zation for Security and Cooperation in Europe (OSCE)—although the latter not only is Eu-ropean but covers the area from "Vancouver to Vladivostok"—including the United States, Canada, and Central Asia. The North Atlantic Treaty Organization (NATO) is typically con-sidered a defense alliance, rather than a regional organization, and will not be covered in this chapter (although in the case of the Imple-mentation Force [IFOR] in the Republic of Bosnia and Herzegovina, it has acted much like a regional organization in providing a peace mission with enforcement capacity, under the umbrella of Security Council approval). The Commonwealth and La Francophonie are headquartered in Europe and are sometimes considered to be regional organizations, in spite of their being composed of geographically diverse countries that were former colonies of the United Kingdom and France. The Com-monwealth of Independent States (CIS) is composed of the former states of the Soviet

Union. The primary African regional organization is the Organization of African Unity (OAU), and all African countries are members. The League of Arab States (LAS) covers the Arab states of the Middle East and some northern African countries, and the Organization of the Islamic Conference (OIC) draws its members from different regions of the world where Islam is dominant. The Organization of American States (OAS) now has the membership of all states in the Americas (Canada being the last to join).

Asia is the only continent that does not have its own regionwide organization. This means that a number of major states that are involved in serious disputes (for example, China, Japan, the two Koreas, India, Pakistan, and Sri Lanka) have no regional organization to which they can turn for assistance. The Southeast Asian countries, however, have formed the Association of Southeast Asian Nations (ASEAN), which originally had an economic focus but now also deals with peace and security matters. It, in turn, has created a regional "dialogue forum" called the ASEAN Regional Forum (ARF). The purpose of the ARF is to provide a regular means for ASEAN members to interact with their counterparts in other parts of Asia—as well as a few key countries outside Asia. Whether the ARF will eventually evolve into a regional organization for all of Asia remains to be seen. The South Pacific Forum covers the island states of the Pacific as well as Australia and New Zealand.

Two relatively new developments are also of interest. First, subregional arrangements of organizations, such as the Economic Community of West African States (ECOWAS), the Southern African Development Community (SADC), and the Intergovernmental Authority on Development (IGAD), are now beginning to emerge, especially in Africa. Organizations that were originally formed for economic and development reasons have, over the past few years, been developing a peace and security role, because of the inevitable realization that these two issues are closely linked. In Latin America, subregional arrangements founded for economic cooperation are also taking an increasing interest in issues related to peace and security (for example, the Southern Cone Common Market [MERCOSUR] and the Caribbean Community [CARICOM]). In Europe, there is the Council of Baltic Sea States, the Nordic Council, the Central European Initiative, and the Black Sea Cooperative Council.

The second new development is the growing cooperation between regional organizations. In Europe, for example, numerous meetings are taking place to ensure that European regional organizations interact in a way that is "interlocking rather than interblocking." On a broader front, cooperation is just beginning to develop across regions (for example, the European Union has entered into discussions with the OAU and ASEAN). The relationship between regional organizations and the United Nations will be discussed at the end of the chapter.

THE EVOLVING NATURE OF THE CHALLENGE

In order to evaluate whether regional organizations are appropriately addressing the many problems on their agendas, we need to consider briefly the changing nature of the challenges that these organizations are facing in today's world. During the Cold War, the major threats to states were perceived to be "external," and even when internal problems arose, they were frequently blamed on external agents. Security was defined as "state security." In this context, intrastate problems tended to be seen as having less to do with real grievances or a state's own policies and shortcomings than with "communist," "capitalist," or "extremist" influence and support. (In fact, this view was not entirely without foundation, since the superpower rivalry did indeed permeate conflict nearly everywhere.)

In the aftermath of the Cold War, however, conflicts have been largely *within* rather than *between* states. The latest data by Peter Wallensteen and Margaretha Sollenberg, who analyze conflicts since the end of the Cold War, show that 94 percent of the 108 conflicts around the world were intrastate in nature.[5] Consequently, regional organizations and the United Nations have to take a much closer look at the new situation and redefine the underlying causes of conflict. Moreover, these organizations have to search for new ways to meet the objectives that they had set for themselves when they were founded.

This task entailed a number of difficulties, since regional organizations (following the lead of the United Nations) had placed clauses in their charters specifically prohibiting "interference" in the internal affairs of their member-states—clauses that were adopted because the organizations had been established to prevent conflicts *between* states. Now, however, these clauses provide a stumbling block to efforts by regional organizations (and the United Nations) to respond to the new challenges. As will be shown later, some regional organizations have made significant progress in adapting and updating their mandates, while others have not.

Developing a new methodology for preventing conflict within states has required a better understanding of the root causes of this type of conflict. Fortunately, this process has been helped by a shift in scholarly research away from Cold War issues to a more in-depth study of ethnic conflicts. Much of this research has suggested that the kind and the quality of governance are closely related to conflict prevention within states. The data indicate that conflicts are less likely to occur when identity groups have access to opportunities for political and economic participation and cultural and religious expression, and are more likely to occur when these basic human needs are suppressed, especially when groups perceive that they are the object of systematic discrimination and injustice relative to other groups in the same society.[6] Moreover, studies have suggested that when governments recognize, listen to, and accommodate dissatisfied groups, grievances tend to be lessened or resolved and that problems arise largely when governments ignore or repress these concerns.[7]

In response to this analysis, the concept of "human security" has been advanced as the best foundation upon which "state security" can be built. The evidence supports the view that the most secure states are those that are able to provide the greatest human security to their populations.[8] Weak states are those that either do not or cannot provide human security. Consequently, assisting states in their capacity to enhance human security offers a promising approach to conflict prevention within states.

As will be argued, this has led to a new methodology based on cooperative, rather than coercive, means of influence. In considering what makes this "cooperative security" approach effective, four factors seem to emerge. The first involves regional efforts to lay down and establish regional standards, norms, and rules based on internationally recognized principles. The second relates to finding incentive structures that encourage compliance with the group's rules and that can influence those who are beginning to stray. The third involves an assistance approach that helps states live up to their commitments. The fourth is the adoption of a problem-solving approach (as opposed to a hard-bargaining power-based model) that will more effectively resolve differences within and between states, before they turn to conflict.[9] These cooperative security methods can be very powerful incentives for gradual and constructive change within regions. As well, they can provide guidance in helping to direct rapid change at key transitional moments. These general methodologies will be illustrated below by discussing some of the more promising specific methodologies.

A FORUM FOR DIALOGUE AND COLLECTIVE DECISION MAKING REGARDING PEACE AND SECURITY ISSUES

One of the most obvious but useful functions of regional organizations, as they relate to issues of peace and security, is the provision of a regular forum, in which the leadership of member-states can come together to share their different perspectives, discuss their common problems, offer ideas and proposals about how these can be addressed, and—where sufficient consensus exists—respond with appropriate action. In the process, working relationships are formed; habits of communication and dialogue are developed; and narrow perspectives are widened, allowing those involved to see how the problem looks from other points of view. A better understanding is gained of the interests of all parties, and new and innovative options for solutions are explored.

Most regional fora meet at several levels to discuss peace and security issues—at the level of a general assembly of heads of state and government (usually once a year), at the level of ministers of foreign affairs (usually once or twice a year), and at the level of the permanent representative or ambassador (in some cases several times a week; in others, on a weekly or monthly basis). Regular fora provide an opportunity for government officials at various levels to consider how to address both the general issues affecting the peace and security of the region and the specific disputes, crises, or conflicts that arise. In handling the general issues, such fora often agree on certain principles or standards that they may decide to enshrine through declarations, conventions, or treaties (for example, the OAS American Convention on Human Rights, the ASEAN Treaty of Amity and Cooperation in Southeast Asia, and the OSCE Charter of Paris for a New Europe). These create agreed-upon regional norms or rules that are intended to guide the future action

of the group and its members. In other cases, they may establish certain institutional mechanisms for the purpose of addressing regional issues and/or ensuring that the guidelines are adhered to (for example, the Inter-American Commission on Human Rights, the Inter-American Court of Human Rights, and the OSCE Office for Democratic Institutions and Human Rights).

Such fora typically develop a set of procedures for dealing with specific situations or crises, which tend to become a part of institutional practice (resolutions of decision-making bodies; use of special rapporteurs, special representatives, envoys; and so on). Many of these are copied from the practices of the United Nations, but others develop uniquely along regional lines. All of these represent the specific methodology of regional organizations in dealing with peace and security issues.

THE DEVELOPMENT OF AGREED-UPON STANDARDS AND NORMS AND THE CREATION OF INSTITUTIONAL MECHANISMS TO PROMOTE THEM

The development of widely agreed-upon standards and norms for achieving peace and security within states (usually called human rights) began with the United Nations, which has produced more than seventy human rights instruments over the past fifty-five years—creating a broad international consensus on a framework for good governance, whose goal is human security and the satisfaction of basic human needs. These landmark declarations and conventions—the Universal Declaration of Human Rights, the International Covenant on Civil and Political Rights, and the International Covenant on Economic, Social, and Cultural Rights—were followed by many others that have extended and developed their prescription for good governance. A number of regional organizations have followed the United Nations' example and developed their own conventions and standards—deepening the normative and legal framework and extending it to various regional contexts. These human rights documents provide crucial guidelines for conflict prevention within states, spelling out in great detail *how* governments can provide "human security" to their people and reminding governments that it is their *duty* to do so. They thus provide a set of guidelines for governments and for governance.

Probably the best regional example of this is the European Convention on Human Rights (which was concluded in 1950 and entered into force in 1953), which, according to Kruger and Strasser, has "matured into the most effective human rights treaty in existence due to the binding obligations for states in the area of human rights."[10] In Europe, a number of other major conventions have followed, achieving important milestones in the development of standards for human rights and democracy in the region. Two new conventions, which will also greatly strengthen the Council of Europe's standards with regard to minority protection, are the European Charter for Regional or Minority Languages and the Framework Convention for the Protection of National Minorities, which represent the most comprehensive international documents of their kind. Moreover, the Framework Convention is the first legally binding multilateral instrument devoted to the protection of national minorities in general.

The European Convention is enforced by the European Court of Human Rights and the COE Committee of Ministers. The European Court handles cases between states and between an individual and a state. What is unique about the European Convention is that in 1989 compulsory jurisdiction was made a precondition to new membership in the Council of Europe (since all existing members had by then already accepted the convention's jurisdiction). This precondition gave the convention a

significant advantage over similar agreements in other regions, since obligations are universally binding with a kind of enforcement power. Suspension from membership in the Council of Europe may be considered if a state is found to be noncompliant. This represents an important precedent in terms of states as a group agreeing to accept compulsory jurisdiction and could serve as an important model for other regions.

After the Council of Europe, the Organization of American States has the most well-developed and active human rights standards and machinery (some of which are, in fact, modeled on instruments of the COE). The American Convention on Human Rights (which entered into force in 1978) serves as the cornerstone. It is backed up by the Inter-American Commission on Human Rights, which is an organ of the OAS, and the Inter-American Court of Human Rights, which is an autonomous judicial institution created by the American Convention but linked to the Inter-American Commission.

The Inter-American Commission, which has been functioning since 1960, receives approximately fifteen hundred complaints per year from victims, other individuals, and nongovernmental organizations (NGOs). The right of nonvictims to introduce petitions and of individuals to submit petitions against their own governments is an important feature of the commission's procedures. States can also present complaints but seldom do. The commission evaluates a petition upon receipt and, if it is admissible and if local remedies have been exhausted, conducts fact finding, receives evidence and testimony, and seeks a friendly settlement. If the commission cannot obtain a settlement, it examines the evidence and prepares a report, offering its conclusions, as well as proposals and recommendations. The state is then asked to remedy the situation within a given time frame. When the time has expired, the commission decides whether the state has taken suitable measures and whether to publish a report, which it can forward to the OAS

General Assembly for further discussion. In cases in which a state is a party to the American Convention and has accepted the jurisdiction of the Inter-American Court of Human Rights, the commission can also refer the case to the court.

One of the most effective means of responding to serious individual or NGO cases against state bodies is for the Inter-American Commission to issue a precautionary measure—an urgent request to a government (sometimes issued within twenty-four hours of receiving a complaint) to take all necessary measures to ensure the protection of a given individual or group. Precautionary measures can be used with any member-state of the OAS. Although normally confidential, the commission has the option of publicizing its request if a government fails to respond. Precautionary measures are used about two hundred times a year, with generally good results.

The commission can also request that the Inter-American Court of Human Rights issue provisional measures, which have the strength of the court behind them. However, even with a fast-track procedure, these measures tend to take longer. They also require a strong case with sufficient evidence and are limited to states that have agreed to the jurisdiction of the court.

The Inter-American Commission also carries out fact-finding visits to study the situation in a given country. This can provide an opportunity for the commission to play an informal role in mediation, as it did in Guatemala, where it brought about a formal agreement between the government and fifty thousand indigenous people who had been in hiding for a decade.

Finally, analyses and findings with regard to cases are published in the annual report, as well as in "special country" or "special situation" reports, which go to the General Assembly for discussion and/or resolutions—giving the commission both a legal and a political function. General Assembly censure is usually unwelcome and may prompt desired changes in practice within member-states by exposing situations, thereby marshaling moral outrage. This was the effect of the commission's reports on the Somoza regime in Nicaragua and on Haiti, which added to the momentum for action.

Cases can also be submitted to the Inter-American Court of Human Rights, but only by state parties to the American Convention and by the Inter-American Commission. The court normally meets twice a year, although it can also meet in emergency session. A case must first go to the commission, which decides which cases should go to the court. Normally, the commission sends only strong cases, to ensure that they are successful in creating a deterrent. Cases are decided by a simple majority of the seven judges, who give a rationale for the judgment. If the court finds a violation of a right or freedom protected by the convention, it can rule that the injured party be ensured the enjoyment of the right or freedom, that the measure or situation that caused the breach of such right or freedom be remedied, and that fair compensation be paid to the injured party. The court also reports to the General Assembly and can make pertinent recommendations to the assembly if the state does not comply. To date, the court has not earned the same reputation as the commission.

Although the Inter-American system is still evolving, its work has made a significant impact in terms of making governments accountable for human rights violations in a hemisphere where in the past they have been rampant. More and more evidence suggests that human rights violations are one of the major early-warning indicators of intrastate conflict. Thus, the development of strong normative standards for human rights and a means of protecting them is, in effect, a conflict prevention measure sending, as we have seen earlier, clear signals to governments that their actions are not condoned and asking for remedy—and using regional socialization factors (including censure from peer states) as a means of effecting change.

The African Charter on Human and Peoples' Rights was adopted in 1981 in an effort to create a human rights instrument based on African legal philosophy and responsive to African needs. The charter entered into force in 1986 and established the African Commission on Human Rights. This commission, however, was given much weaker powers than its European and OAS counterparts. For example, while the commission can receive complaints from either states or individuals and provides powers of investigation, it does not have the discretion to make its reports public without permission from the Assembly of Heads of States and Governments. The commission must also refer cases to the assembly, which then may request the commission to undertake investigations and make recommendations. The commission is also hampered by a severe shortage of funds, making it unable to fulfill even its limited mandate.

The League of Arab States has an instrument but no mechanism. In Asia, there is no regional human rights standard or regime, apart from that of the United Nations.

THE PROMOTION OF DEMOCRACY

In recent years, a number of regional organizations have become very active in the promotion of democracy. One of the most common means has been through the provision of electoral assistance, which a number of regional organizations now provide, including the OAU, the OAS, the COE, the OSCE, the Commonwealth, and La Francophonie.

One of the most thorough methodologies for providing electoral assistance has been developed by the OSCE Office for Democratic Institutions and Human Rights (ODIHR), which places teams of experts in the field to observe the entire electoral process for a period of six to eight weeks before, during, and after elections. Observers, who are seconded from participating states, are deployed throughout

the country to assess the legal and regulatory framework, the electoral administration, the media environment, and the general situation surrounding the election campaign. They are supplemented by short-term election monitors, who arrive at the end of the campaign to monitor the voting and counting process. The OSCE issues a preliminary statement, sometimes in conjunction with other organizations, shortly after election day, and ODIHR publishes a report within thirty days. In 1998 ODIHR monitored elections in twelve OSCE countries, using more than fifteen hundred observers. Additional electoral assistance is provided either on request or as a follow-up to recommendations included in a final report. Beyond simply monitoring elections, ODIHR helps review and draft electoral law, rules, and regulations; train domestic observers, law enforcement agents, and electoral administrators on new election legislation; and organize voter education.

Some regional organizations have even moved a step further in the active promotion of democracy by offering technical assistance in building democratic institutions. The OAS Unit for the Promotion of Democracy, ODIHR, and the Council of Europe's Programmes for Assistance to Central and Eastern Europe prepare and support key institutional actors in the reforms needed to create good governance. The most active is the Council of Europe, which has a unique status among regional organizations in requiring states to achieve certain standards of democracy and human rights before they can become members. To qualify for membership, a state must show that it has institutions and a legal system in line with the basic principles of democracy, the rule of law, and respect for human rights; a parliament chosen by free and fair elections based on universal suffrage; guaranteed freedom of expression, including a free press; a system for the protection of national minorities; and a record of observance of principles of international law.

Following the dramatic changes that ended the division of Europe, the Council of Europe created several programs to provide extensive technical assistance to twenty-one central and eastern European states to help them develop into full-fledged democracies. These programs aimed to promote the gradual and harmonious integration of these countries into the processes and structures of European cooperation, and sixteen have now, through the assistance provided, become full members of the council. The programs also seek to reinforce, consolidate, and accelerate the democratic reform process in these countries. The central themes include human rights protection (seeking to harmonize national legislation with the European Convention on Human Rights and the case law of the European Court of Human Rights); legal cooperation (aimed at developing institutions and practices based on the rule of law that include legislative and judicial reform); the media (seeking to protect the independence and pluralism of the media); civil society; local government; and education, culture, and youth. These programs cover a wide range of subjects and approaches, including, for example, study visits by government officials to their counterpart organizations in the more established democracies; conferences on government and minorities; study packages promoting tolerance and intercultural learning; the development of manuals for newly elected officials; seminars on the role of the media during electoral campaigns; seminars on human rights for journalists; and so on. The council also has established a joint program with the European Commission that has extended assistance programs to the Russian Federation and Ukraine.

DEFENSE OF DEMOCRACY

In a region where military coups have been a common occurrence, the Organization of American States has made great progress in recent years in instituting changes, unprecedented in any other regional organization—changes that not only allow but actually mandate the organization to become involved in the internal affairs of a member-state when there is a threat to a democratically elected government. This development began in 1985 when the OAS Charter was amended to state: "Representative democracy is an indispensable condition for the stability, peace and development of the region." In 1991 the Santiago Commitment to Democracy and Renewal of the Inter-American System and Resolution 1080 were adopted to give priority to democratic principles and help stabilize democratic governments. Resolution 1080, for example, instructs the secretary-general to call for an immediate meeting of the Permanent Council "in the event of any occurrences giving rise to the sudden or irregular interruption of the democratic political institutional process or the legitimate exercise of power by the democratically elected government in any of its Member States." The Permanent Council then has the power to examine the situation and convene an ad hoc meeting of ministers of foreign affairs or a special session of the General Assembly, which must take place within a ten-day period. The ad hoc meeting of foreign ministers or the special session of the General Assembly is instructed "to look at the events collectively and adopt any decisions deemed appropriate, in accordance with the Charter or international law." Since its adoption, Resolution 1080 has been used four times—in Haiti, Peru, Guatemala, and Paraguay. The Protocol of Washington, approved by the OAS General Assembly in 1992 and ratified in 1997, goes even further, allowing the organization to suspend (by a two-thirds vote) the participation of any regime that comes to power by deposing a democratic government.

The Organization of African Unity has also made pronouncements against unconstitutional changes to government in its Harare Declaration of 1997 and in a resolution of its recent summit in Algiers. Further, a subcommittee of the Central Organ has been mandated to re-view the modalities of response that the OAU should consider in relation to unconstitutional changes of government.

ASSISTANCE IN CONFLICT PREVENTION

Several regional organizations have proclaimed an interest in developing conflict prevention mechanisms, but progress has been slow in most. The OAU, for example, is so overwhelmed with attempts to manage and resolve the many full-blown conflicts in the region that it has not been able to devote much time to prevention per se. In other cases, as with the ASEAN Regional Forum, no real consensus has emerged over how, or even whether, preventive diplomacy should be carried out at the regional level. By contrast, the OSCE has moved decisively in this area. Indeed, the world's most innovative, active, and cost-effective conflict prevention mechanism is the OSCE High Commissioner on National Minorities. The post of the high commissioner was established in 1992, and the first high commissioner, Max van der Stoel, took up the position early in 1993. The task of the high commissioner is to "identify —and seek early resolution of—ethnic tensions that might endanger peace, stability or friendly relations between the participating States of the OSCE." His unique mandate describes him as "an instrument of conflict prevention at the earliest possible stage" and allows him to go wherever he wishes (even without the specific consent of the state concerned) and to gather information from any source (although he is not permitted to speak with any group or person who condones terrorism).

What is particularly interesting is the methodology of this work, which is based on a problem-solving approach, rather than on a traditional hard-bargaining, power-based approach. Typically, the high commissioner begins his work with on-site visits (he travels about one hundred fifty days a year), meeting with representatives from all sides, including senior government officials (such as the president, prime minister, and relevant ministers); the opposition parties; representatives of minority groups; civil society groups; and sometimes even parties in neighboring states.

Through information gathering, he attempts to gain an understanding of the core interests and positions of all parties. He describes what he does as follows: "I always try to look at the specific issues at stake to try to understand why a situation has developed to the point that it has and to therefore see what issues need to be reconciled, both in terms of the substance and the political processes involved."[11] At the same time, he seeks to develop a relationship with the major parties, so that he can engage them in a cooperative problem-solving process. Once he feels that he has a full grasp of the situation, he normally writes a letter to the government involved, making recommendations for possible solutions to the problem.

The letters of the high commissioner make fascinating reading, as they are a model of problem-solving negotiation. They begin by acknowledging and legitimizing the different perspectives and concerns of various sides, providing relevant data, and reminding the parties of their legal obligations and political commitments as well as the international norms and responsibilities that apply. The letters also suggest the consequences of following or not following certain courses of action (as a means of helping governments understand where such problems can lead). Finally, the high commissioner provides new ideas and perspectives, along with a nonobligatory set of recommendations, usually in the form of specific proposals for changes in government policy, practice, or legislation regarding minorities. Copies of his letters are also circulated to participating states via the Permanent Council and eventually made public, so that nonstate actors are aware of his work. The high commissioner then follows up with frequent contact with the parties to discuss his recommendations, to lobby for their implementation, and to work with those involved to overcome obstacles and provide even more specific and detailed assistance where necessary. Van der Stoel describes his approach this way:

> In these and other situations that I have dealt with, one of my philosophies has been that the best way of preventing inter-ethnic tensions is to properly integrate minorities into the wider society. To use the fire fighting analogy again, one can never completely make a structure fire proof, but one can implement effective standards, install internal alarms and avoid combustible situations in order to reduce the chances of igniting a spark. In other words, if minorities feel that they have a stake in society, if they have input into discussion and decision-making bodies, if they have avenues of appeal, and if they feel that their identities are being protected and promoted, the chances of inter-ethnic tensions arising will be significantly decreased. Ideally members of minorities should feel that they belong not only to their particular ethnic or linguistic community, but also that they share and value an important sense of belonging to the wider society. Following this logic, I encourage states to take care of their own problems and to develop institutions, legislation and mechanisms to pre-empt the types of crises which would necessitate my involvement.[12]

The high commissioner is, of course, backed up by support from the rest of the OSCE and even from other regional organizations in Europe. As he notes:

> You may ask, what impact can one man possibly have in such situations? I may have small teeth and few carrots, but I am mandated by 55 States acting as part of a wider framework of European security organizations. I regularly report to the OSCE Permanent Council in Vienna where the representatives of all OSCE participating States meet on a weekly basis. My recommendations usually have the support of the OSCE participating States. In fact, they often follow-up my recommendations in bilateral contacts, through making demarches, strong public statements on my behalf or through other channels. I do not work in isolation. Protection of the rights of persons belonging to national minorities is seen as a reflection of a country's willingness and ability to live up to its international commitments. The way that a country acts toward its own people is a good indicator of how it will act with its neighbors and in the international community. This point is kept in mind by the European Commission when considering accession, and by the Council of Europe which is constantly insisting upon respect for human rights among members and prospective member countries. This is co-operative security in action—co-operative in the sense of my office working with other international organizations and in the sense of working with OSCE participating States to assist them in solving their problems.[13]

Since taking office, the high commissioner has worked with many OSCE participating states, including Albania, Croatia, Estonia, Greece, Hungary, Kazakhstan, Kyrgyzstan, Latvia, Moldova, Romania, Slovakia, the Former Yugoslav Republic of Macedonia, and Ukraine. His work has been widely regarded as highly successful, and among the accomplishments he lists are "preventing an escalation of tensions regarding the Greek minority in Albania in 1994; the improvement of inter-ethnic relations in Latvia and Estonia, especially by widening the opportunities for nationalization of the Russian-speaking populations; acting as a catalyst in the Hungarian-Romanian Treaty of 1996; initiating a solution to the problem of the status of Crimea within Ukraine; guarding against the rolling back of the rights of Hungarians in Slovakia during the Meciar era; and helping to find a compromise solution to the delicate issue of minority education in Romania."[14]

At a recent meeting held in Lund, Sweden, initiated by the Ministry for Foreign Affairs of Sweden, senior representatives of regional organizations and governments from different regions discussed whether the methodology of the high commissioner's work could be usefully replicated (with the appropriate adaptations) in other regions. It was generally agreed that it could be adapted, especially in Africa. John Packer, director of the Office of the High Commissioner on National Minorities, has also written about how such a mechanism might be relevant to the OAU.[15] Most participants at the meeting acknowledged that the OSCE as an organization had the advantage of having advanced further than other organizations in reaching a higher level of consensus on such issues, which made it easier for its participating states to agree to such an intrusive, albeit helpful, mechanism.

FIELD MISSION ASSISTANCE IN PREVENTIVE DIPLOMACY AND PEACEBUILDING

The OSCE employs another operational mechanism that is somewhat unique among regional organizations—long-term missions for both preventive diplomacy and peacebuilding. These are established with a mandate from the Permanent Council, and they report regularly, through the chairman-in-office [sic], on the situation on the ground, as well as on their own activities. This allows the Permanent Council and other OSCE bodies to improve the quality and timeliness of their decision making in regard to matters involving the host country. Currently there are nine active long-term missions, to Bosnia and Herzegovina, Croatia, Estonia, Georgia, Latvia, Kosovo, Moldova, the Former Yugoslav Republic of Macedonia (the mission name refers to Skopje), and Tajikistan. More recently, the OSCE has established other field activities, such as the Liaison Office in Central Asia; the Assistance Group to Chechnya (now relocated to Moscow); a Presence in Albania [sic]; an Advisory and Monitoring Group in Belarus; Centers in Almaty, Ashgabad, and Bishkek; Offices in Yerevan and Baku; and a Project Coordinator in Ukraine.

Most of these operations are relatively small (three to twenty-five persons). Some involve only civilians, while others are composed of both civilians and military personnel. Their minimum mandate is six months, but some have been in existence for up to eight years.

Normally, a mission establishes a small office in the country's capital city, which serves as a base from which staff travel widely to gather information, monitor developments, and help to reduce tension. Mission staff also provide information to the parties. Through their ability to move easily between the parties, they can provide a communications link, reducing suspicion and fear and helping all sides understand one another better. Long-term missions can offer objective factual data, as well as information to minorities about rights and procedures. They also provide advice to governments in formulating legislation or regulations in areas such as constitutional law, citizenship law, minorities' rights, and the establishment of councils for interethnic dialogue, usually in cooperation with the High Commissioner on National Minorities. In some countries, they have established an open-door policy for members of minority communities who wish to complain about government discrimination. By listening to individual cases and bringing these to the attention of the authorities, they have helped to alleviate tension and been able to assess where governments need to change their practice.

Long-term missions, however, are subject to the political consent of the state. The Long-term Mission to Kosovo, Sandjak, and Vojvodina, which agreed to a "continuous presence" in the Memorandum of Understanding signed between the then Conference on Security and Cooperation in Europe and the Federal Republic of Yugoslavia on October 28, 1992, was not extended beyond June 28, 1993, and had to be withdrawn following the Belgrade government's refusal to extend the memorandum in response to Yugoslavia losing its status as a full participating state of the CSCE.

Even in less difficult circumstances, missions must walk a fine line. If a mission becomes viewed as simply an advocate for the minority population, it may be terminated by the government; but if it does not raise sensitive issues, it will not be able to facilitate dialogue and reduce tensions. However, the recent trend to establish offices and centers tends to be more acceptable to governments, as even the terminology appears less intrusive. The general consensus remains that long-term missions have been successful, with preventive diplomacy missions being better able to effect change than those that were dispatched after conflict had already broken out.

In response to the breakup of the former Yugoslavia, three larger field missions have been initiated by the OSCE—those to Bosnia and Herzegovina (established in 1995), to Croatia (established in 1996), and to Kosovo (established in 1999), with up to seven hundred international staff on the books for the Mission in Kosovo alone. These large missions have significantly taxed the small OSCE Secretariat in Vienna, caused numerous operational problems on the ground, and necessarily shifted the focus of the organization away from prevention and toward postconflict peacebuilding. Moreover, the larger missions have faced the complexity of coordinating with the other regional and international actors on the ground.

The OSCE Mission in Kosovo, for example, forms a distinct component within the overall framework of the United Nations Interim Administration Mission in Kosovo, taking the lead role in matters relating to institution and democracy building and human rights. It is charged with the training of a new Kosovo police service, with the establishment and operation of a Kosovo Police School, and with the training of judicial personnel and civil administrators, in cooperation with the Council of Europe. It also has responsibility for democratization and governance, including the development of civil society, NGOs, political parties, and the local media. It is mandated to oversee the organization and supervision of elections and the monitoring, protection, and promotion of human rights, including the establishment of an ombudsman institution, which will be carried out in cooperation with the United Nations High Commissioner for Refugees. Finally, it is generally mandated with such tasks that may be requested by the UN secretary-general and his special representative and that are consistent with the relevant UN resolution and approved by the Permanent Council.

Through this intensive experience, the OSCE is gaining considerable experience and is learning from its mistakes. To refine practice through the sharing of information and discussion of problems, it organizes the annual Heads of Missions Meeting, which is a noteworthy innovation among international organizations.

ASSISTANCE IN PEACEMAKING

Most regional organizations try to assist in bringing about the resolution of the region's conflicts. ASEAN, for example, worked long and hard, with other actors, including the United Nations Security Council, to resolve the problem in Cambodia. The OAS was involved in various ways, in collaboration with other actors, including the United Nations, in resolving conflicts in Central America and in Haiti. The European Union worked in partnership with the United Nations over several years in an attempt to resolve the conflicts in Croatia and in Bosnia and Herzegovina.

Regional organizations use many ad hoc mechanisms for their peacemaking efforts. One of the most common is the use of special or personal representatives or envoys of either the secretary-general of the organization or, in some cases, the political leadership of the organization (for example, in the OSCE, the chairman-in-office appoints personal representatives). These representatives typically attempt to bring the conflicting parties to the negotiating table and to assist them, through good offices and third-party facilitation, in finding a political solution. In some cases, these efforts extend over long periods of time with varying degrees of success. Special and personal representatives and envoys are sometimes backed up by the organization's political forum, which may pass resolutions calling for the parties to cease hostilities and to engage in political dialogue and settlement. As well, various kinds of bilateral pressure may be brought to bear, often orchestrated by the senior leadership of the organization or by the special representative.

When actual talks do get under way, there is a variety of means of organizing them. Sometimes peacemaking efforts are carried out informally. Other times, a more formal procedure is used, which typically requires initial negotiations about the procedure itself, before substantive talks can begin. (In some instances, negotiations have become so bogged down at the procedural stage that they never reach substantive negotiations.) Formal procedures take a variety of forms but usually involve official delegations from the conflicting parties, who are convened by a third party, often with observers from interested governments or organizations. Sometimes smaller working groups are convened to deal with specific issues and bring their proposals back to the full plenary sessions for further consideration and harmonization. Usually, a whole series of outside influences also affect the process, some due to events on the ground, others relating to the efforts by secondary actors to influence the process.

How such negotiations move forward or become bogged down is a fascinating subject that requires much more study. A better understanding of how this kind of negotiation can be better controlled would greatly assist the effectiveness of those who have to act as third parties on behalf of the regional or international community. One of the problems with this kind of formal process is that it often relies on a traditional power-based, hard-bargaining model of negotiation. Parties begin with opening statements—which usually include extreme demands and which sometimes raise, rather than lower, tensions. The effort then becomes one of the parties trying to reach a compromise between opposing sets of demands, often

through a mutual process of coercion and countercoercion—sometimes in front of an audience (the observers). Third parties are often reduced to using "leverage" (rewards and punishment called "carrots" and "sticks") in an attempt to influence the process and the outcome. In too many cases, the root causes of the conflict, which would need to be explored and addressed to find a lasting settlement, and the sharing of perspectives and interests, which allows the gradual emergence of understanding, do not come out of such a process. Given this approach and the fact that most regional organizations have not devoted sufficient attention to conflict prevention and typically only become involved in peacemaking when a conflict has become prolonged and intractable, it is not surprising that there are not a great many successes to discuss.

One of the regions where peacemaking is most urgent is Africa. According to a recent survey by Wallensteen and Sollenberg, the continent had 41 percent of the world's wars in the nine years from 1989 to 1998.[16] To meet this challenge, the OAU Heads of States and Governments committed themselves in their 1990 Declaration on the Political and Socio-Economic Situation in Africa and the Fundamental Changes Taking Place in the World to work together toward a speedy and peaceful settlement of all conflicts on the continent. According to the consensus that emerged, Africans should, as much as possible, rely on their own resources and traditions in resolving regional conflict. At the 1993 summit in Cairo, it was decided that a Mechanism for Conflict Prevention, Management, and Resolution should be established within the OAU in order to assist in implementing this goal.

The mechanism was set up with a Central Organ to provide overall direction and coordination. The Central Organ consists of the state members of the Bureau of the Assembly of Heads of States and Governments, who are elected annually from each of the five subregions, with two representatives from each subregion, as well as the outgoing chairperson and, if known, the incoming chairperson. The secretary-general also attends meetings of the Central Organ. The organ meets at OAU headquarters once a year at the level of heads of state and government, twice a year at the ministerial level, and as often as necessary at the ambassadorial level (since the ambassadors can be convened at any time at the request of the secretary-general or any member-state of the OAU). Recently, more decision-making power has been given to the permanent representatives (as has also been done in the OSCE Permanent Council) in order to increase the timeliness and effectiveness of the Central Organ's action.

Basically, the Central Organ acts as a kind of Security Council to the OAU. Importantly, the mechanism also empowers the secretary-general, under the authority of the Central Organ and in consultation with the parties, to take all appropriate initiatives to prevent, manage, and resolve conflict. The establishing declaration calls upon the organization to build the capacity of the general secretariat to a level commensurate with the magnitude of this task. It also notes that the secretary-general may wish to resort to eminent African personalities or others, in sending special envoys or special representatives and in dispatching fact-finding missions to conflict areas. The importance of close cooperation between the mechanism and African subregional organizations, the United Nations, and other international organizations, as well as NGOs, is also stressed.

A Conflict Management Center was also established to provide information and strategic analysis of policy options to the secretary-general and, through him, to the Central Organ. The Conflict Management Center is funded by the regular budget, as well as by the OAU's Peace Fund, which receives 6 percent of OAU members' contributions to the organization. The small staff of the center now provides logistical support to OAU peace missions. The center has also been attempting to develop an early warning capacity.

The Central Organ, with support from the secretary-general and the Conflict Management Center, has been involved in many conflicts, among them Angola, Burundi, the Comoros, Guinea-Bissau, Liberia, the Central African Republic, the Democratic Republic of the Congo, Sierra Leone, Somalia, and Ethiopia and Eritrea. The OAU's recent success in brokering peace (in conjunction with the United Nations and bilateral actors) in Ethiopia and Eritrea indicates the potential role that regional organizations can play in peacemaking. Anecdotal evidence further indicates that the OAU's involvement in peacemaking has kept a number of other situations from deteriorating and may, in some instances, still lead to breakthroughs that could result in more sustainable political settlements. Given the seriousness of the conflicts on the African continent, the OAU should be assisted in its daunting task to supplement its limited technical and financial resources and, in particular, in putting an emphasis on establishing a more preventive mechanism for early action (such as the OSCE high commissioner—but adapted to Africa).

Following the lead of the OAU, both ECOWAS and SADC have been developing their own mechanisms (called respectively ECOWATCH and the SADC Organ for Politics, Defense, and Security). Even before this, ECOWAS was active, in conjunction with other partners, in attempting to broker peace settlements in Liberia and Sierra Leone. Although there have been significant problems in the implementation of the peace process in Sierra Leone, the coordination between ECOWAS and the United Nations represents a new model for partnership between a subregional organization and the United Nations.

ASSISTANCE IN PEACEKEEPING

The mechanism of peacekeeping is still at an embryonic stage in all regional organizations where, until recently, the United Nations had full hegemony. This was eroded in the 1990s, when the number of peacekeeping missions created by the Security Council far outstripped the organization's resource capacity and when peacekeepers were sent into situations where there was no peace to keep. The backlash has led to more caution in the creation of UN peacekeeping missions. To fill this gap, a few regional organizations have begun to consider the development of a limited peacekeeping role.

The three large OSCE missions have already been described in brief. They are civilian missions, devoted primarily to postconflict peacebuilding, and, in each case, they have worked with missions from the United Nations or NATO. The OAU has also experimented with observer missions in a few instances. The Cairo Declaration on the establishment within the OAU of a Mechanism for Conflict Prevention, Management, and Resolution states that "civilian and military missions of observation and monitoring of limited scope and duration may be mounted and developed by the OAU." In 1993, a Neutral Military Observer Group was sent to Rwanda to monitor and supervise compliance with the cease-fire before being replaced (after three months) by the United Nations. The OAU Observer Mission in Burundi was created in 1996 as a kind of preventive deployment mission, whose purpose was "to restore confidence and promote dialogue with a view to re-establishing constitutional order in Burundi." It was withdrawn in the aftermath of the coup d'état. In 1997 a small OAU Observer Mission to the Comoros was deployed to monitor and observe the prevailing situation there and to report to the secretary-general. More recently, a commitment has been made to deploy observers in the Democratic Republic of the Congo.

The OAU has been involved in considerable debate about whether, or to what extent, it should develop a peacekeeping capacity. One of the major constraints, of course, is resources, as peacekeeping missions are very expensive. For the moment, it seems, the OAU has decided

that it will not venture too far into peacekeeping; however, there is little doubt that the debate will continue and things may change over time.

PEACE ENFORCEMENT

Apart from NATO, which has now undertaken peace enforcement in both Bosnia and Herzegovina and Kosovo (the latter without the consent of the Security Council, causing much concern among UN member-states in terms of international jurisdictional issues), there has been virtually no regional organization involvement in peace enforcement. The only other exception is ECOMOG (the ECOWAS Peace Monitoring Group), which was deployed in Liberia and Sierra Leone. ECOMOG was also deployed without the authority of the Security Council, but it should be noted that the council did not condemn the use of force in the missions in Liberia and Sierra Leone (presumably because the United Nations did not wish to become involved). In fact, in 1998 the council actually commended ECOWAS and ECOMOG for their role in restoring peace and security to Sierra Leone, when the ECOWAS mission overturned the junta and restored the democratically elected government in 1998. Moreover, when ECOMOG threatened to pull out of Sierra Leone before UN peacekeepers could be deployed, negotiations were undertaken to keep the force on the ground until a smoother handover could be effectuated. Nonetheless, there were also problems with ECOMOG. Many considered it to be a Nigerian force (since most of the finances and a majority of its troops were Nigerian), which led to its motives being questioned. ECOMOG also frequently ended up in the middle of the fighting, and ECOMOG troops are widely reported to have committed human rights abuses. This demonstrates some of the difficulties with regional or subregional organizations becoming involved in peacekeeping. Others, however, have argued that, with the permanent members of the Security Council reluctant to risk the lives of their soldiers in African conflicts and the council's general aversion to becoming bogged down in complex African situations, the example of ECOMOG represents one option that should be further explored. If regional or subregional options of this type are to be employed in the future, however, there is a need to consider how troops can be more appropriately trained for such involvement.

If this trend does continue, the United Nations may also wish to continue the practice (started toward the end of the Liberian conflict) of sending its own military observers to monitor the mission, in an attempt to ensure that international standards are being adhered to.

THE ADVANTAGES AND DISADVANTAGES OF REGIONAL ORGANIZATIONS VIS-À-VIS THE UNITED NATIONS

As regional organizations have evolved there has been an ongoing debate about their relative merit vis-à-vis the United Nations. An either/or approach, however, is not very helpful. What is really needed is careful consideration of the comparative advantages of each and a better understanding of how they can work together to achieve a more strategic partnership. A brief review of the advantages and disadvantages should help to illustrate this point.

As the only global intergovernmental organization whose primary function is the peaceful settlement of disputes, the United Nations has a number of distinct advantages over regional organizations. One of these is that all 188 member-states have, by virtue of becoming members of the organization, agreed to resolve their disputes peacefully and to address the root causes of conflict by respecting human rights and working for social and economic justice. Moreover, the nearly universal membership of the organization and the fact that every region of the world is represented

in the collective decision making that is required before action can be taken gives the United Nations a greater degree of legitimacy and moral authority than that enjoyed by either regional organizations or states acting unilaterally. Further, because some regions do not yet have regional organizations and because a number of UN member-states do not belong to any regional arrangement, the coverage of the United Nations is greater than that of regional organizations, singly or collectively.

Through its General Assembly, the United Nations is able to provide a democratic forum where all member-states, regardless of size, have a voice. At the same time, the Security Council, which has the major responsibility for peace and security, tends to be dominated by the "permanent five" (the United States, the United Kingdom, France, the Russian Federation, and China), which still retain veto power, while nonpermanent members are elected on a rotating basis from each region. The veto can slow down the decision-making process or even result in organizational paralysis when there is no consensus (as occurred during the Cold War). On the other hand, decisions, when they are taken by the council, are backed by the considerable weight of the big powers.

A second advantage is that the United Nations provides the most comprehensive dispute settlement system available, with a full range of organs—the secretary-general, the International Court of Justice, and the Security Council—and a wide range of methods—from preventive diplomacy and peacebuilding to peace enforcement. Its systems essentially embody three different approaches to dispute settlement—an interest-based approach, a rights-based approach, and a power-based approach, with each corresponding roughly to the organs of the United Nations—good offices of the secretary-general and his envoys representing the organization's interest-based approach; the judicial functions of the World Court and the United Nations' human rights machinery representing its rights-based approach; and the Security Council and its repertoire of responses under Chapter VII representing its power-based approach. Moreover, the United Nations has immense power (in theory at least), as Security Council resolutions have the effect of international law and the council has the legal capacity to enforce its resolutions through power-based methods, if necessary.

The United Nations' power-based instruments, however, are sometimes a double-edged sword. They can, in certain cases, encourage members to abide by their obligation to resolve their disputes peacefully; but in others, they may actually discourage states from availing themselves of other parts of the system. For example, members may not use the secretary-general's good offices because they fear that the Security Council may become involved. However, it is not only the Security Council's power-based instruments that are of concern, but also the council's great power privileges (for example, permanent membership and the veto) and the council's perceived lack of adequate representation. Some member-states feel that the Security Council acts inconsistently and in the self-interest of its permanent members.

In spite of these problems, the United Nations has more institutional experience than any other organization in attempting to prevent and resolve conflict. Its human and financial resources, although small in relation to its enormous mandate, are considerably greater than those of regional organizations.

Regional organizations have the advantage of being more likely to be familiar with local actors, as well as with the situation on the ground and how it is developing. Proximity itself can make a situation more salient. Neighbors are likely to take a greater interest in conflict prevention in an adjacent state, especially if they fear that fighting could spread or result in uncontrolled flows of arms or refugees through their territories. Neighbors sometimes also have a vested interest in a conflict, such as when members of an aggrieved group in a neighboring state

are ethnic "kin." Many of the conflicts in Africa, in particular, suffer from this problem, because the Congress of Berlin divided up the continent in illogical ways, cutting across the territories of ethnic groups and tribes in an arbitrary manner in the demarcation of state boundaries.

In terms of long-term conflict prevention and resolution, regional organizations can, in some cases, bring even more influence to bear on their neighbors than the United Nations can because of the importance of regional relationships. At the same time, regional politics sometimes play a less helpful role. Regional cleavages can cause some governments to favor one side while other governments favor the other side, which can widen a dispute (as has been occurring recently in the conflict in the Democratic Republic of the Congo). Regional hegemons can also use their weight to unduly influence decision making within the organization. Past examples include Nigeria in ECOWAS, the Russian Federation in the CIS, and the United States in the OAS. Similarity of norms and values among states in a region and a low level of conflict within the regional organization itself may, however, promote consensus and overcome such problems, as has largely been the case in the OSCE.

Of course, it must be remembered that the basic medium of discourse and action within both regional organizations and the United Nations is that of governments. The advantage is that governments can put pressure on one another to conform to regional and international norms, but they do not always do so. Because governments have bilateral and multilateral relationships outside the multilateral organization, they also bring political baggage to their interactions within these organizations, which can lead to political trade-offs (counter to the principles of the organization) and to inconsistent decision making, motivated by personal, national, or coalitional interests rather than "the greater good." There is also a danger that personal relationships among leaders within a region will mean that regional norms and values are not being upheld or enforced and governments might agree to condone or overlook certain abuses by a member-state in the interests of regional harmony. This is why organizations firmly founded on common values that have been codified into well-developed standards, norms, or rules of behavior that their members have agreed to observe are more likely to be successful than those less rigorously based.

Finally, most regional organizations have even more meager human and financial resources than the United Nations, which necessarily limits their reach and effectiveness.

THE ADVANTAGES AND DISADVANTAGES OF MULTILATERAL ACTORS VIS-À-VIS BILATERAL ACTORS

There remains, in some circles, a corresponding debate to that discussed previously on the advantages and disadvantages of multilateral versus bilateral actors and action. But in this realm, as well, the question is not so much either/or, but rather how the two can be coordinated so that they can work more effectively in tandem. Those who argue in favor of bilateral action note that one of its advantages is that single actors (responding to one another) do not become bogged down in collective decision making and so decisions can be made and acted upon more quickly (although, of course, decision making within government departments or ministries can also be complicated). Since action taken bilaterally does not require as much consultation, it is also argued that single actors are freer to pursue their own interests more directly. Moreover, bilateral actors often have more resources at their disposal than multilateral organizations, including both economic resources and standing military forces, as well as other means of influence, such as trade. On the negative side, however, when coercive methods are employed, bilateral actors tend to be accorded less legitimacy, are open

to the claim that they are acting in their own narrow self-interest, and may risk loss of credibility and prestige, leading to long-term damage to their wider self-interest.

The growth of multilateral organizations has not eclipsed bilateral relationships and influence that continue to be an important part of the international architecture for maintaining peace and security. But there has been a shift in recent years toward a more collective security paradigm, as witnessed by the above-mentioned growth of regional organizations and mechanisms, the development of a variety of approaches to UN peacekeeping missions, and the creation of "coalitions of the willing" to carry out peace enforcement under a UN mandate.

Since the United Nations and regional organizations are, in effect, no more than a composite of bilateral actors, what is perhaps most important in this debate is that political commitments to certain international principles, norms, and laws that are undertaken in these larger bodies need to be strictly adhered to in the action of bilateral actors in their relations with their citizens and with one another.

If a democratic process is one of the principles being advocated by the most powerful bilateral actors, it would seem important that democratization also be modeled and practiced at the international level. Hence, although bilateral actors and action will continue to be an important source of influence, both within and outside multilateral institutions, the most important consideration is not which type of actors should be favored, but rather how broad-based, inclusive, multilateral decision making could be enhanced to make the system work most effectively to achieve common goals.

The international response to the violence after the election in East Timor provides an interesting example of multilateral and bilateral pressures being used together to good effect—in this case, to persuade the Indonesian government to allow the deployment of a multinational force to control the violence. Multilateral pressure included a Security Council mission to Jakarta and Dili; an open meeting of the Security Council, where virtually all member-states called upon the Indonesian government to agree; and attempts by the secretary-general and his personal representative to persuade senior members of the Indonesian government of the seriousness of the situation and the need for remedial action. As well, the World Bank and the International Monetary Fund exerted what influence they could. World leaders at the Asia Pacific Economic Cooperation (APEC) meeting in New Zealand spoke out forcefully. At the same time, bilateral influence was exercised by a wide number of bilateral contacts, through diplomatic missions, through leader-to-leader contacts, through military-to-military contacts, and through linkages to future aid and trade. Together, these efforts persuaded leaders in the Indonesian government that it was in their best interest to go along with the strong international consensus that was being expressed.

At a more general level, the need to support multilateral efforts suggests that individual actors need to seriously consider how to build more effective multilateral organizations at the regional and global levels, how to properly support these organizations in terms of resources, and how to streamline decision-making processes, so that they can become increasingly effective.

COOPERATION BETWEEN REGIONAL ORGANIZATIONS AND THE UNITED NATIONS IN PEACE AND SECURITY

Given the respective advantages and disadvantages described, the potential exists for the formation of a more strategic partnership between regional organizations and the United Nations that would allow these organizations to better complement one another. Indeed, cooperation between the United Nations and regional organizations is already on the rise.

A number of cooperative agreements have been signed between the United Nations and regional organizations, and three meetings have taken place over the past several years between the secretaries-general of the United Nations and regional organizations (and another is currently being planned), from which recommendations for greater cooperation have emerged. As well, an additional meeting involved middle-level staff from these organizations. Finally, UN staff members regularly attend certain high-level meetings of regional organizations and vice versa.

The United Nations and some regional organizations have also agreed upon a division of responsibility, with one organization taking the lead in some instances and another organization in others. The United Nations and the OSCE, for example, decided to divide responsibility in relation to Georgia, with the United Nations working on the conflict in Abkhazia and the OSCE working on the conflict in Ossetia. In a few situations, the United Nations and regional organizations have organized joint peace missions or jointly appointed special representatives. In Haiti, for example, the United Nations and the OAS launched a joint peace mission. In the Ethiopian-Eritrean conflict, as in others in Africa, the United Nations and the OAU worked closely together with a jointly appointed special representative. A senior UN political officer has now been posted to the OAU headquarters to ensure greater communication and cooperation.

In spite of these promising developments, many problems still exist between the United Nations and regional organizations and, all too often, these organizations still do not coordinate properly, occasionally even appearing to actively obstruct one another. A problem of *diffusion of responsibility* also sometimes occurs, when the UN Security Council believes a situation should be handled by the regional organization and the regional organization abdicates responsibility to the United Nations. Other times, two or more actors become involved in an uncoordinated manner and work at cross-purposes. Equally problematic are bureaucratic jealousies and interinstitutional rivalries, which can plague efforts at coordination, exacerbate problems, and waste time.

Potentially, however, regional organizations and the United Nations could work together much more effectively. One way to expand on the emerging efforts would be for regional organizations and the United Nations to join in a closer partnership to provide assistance in conflict prevention. In my book *Sustainable Peace: The Role of the United Nations and Regional Organizations in Preventing Conflict,* I have discussed in detail how UN Regional Centers for Sustainable Peace could be established to provide a conflict prevention mechanism that would build this kind of strategic partnership and offer assistance in both dispute resolution and good governance.[17] Such centers would require small teams of expert staff to provide full-time quiet assistance in conflict prevention and good governance to those governments wishing to avail themselves of it, following the example set by the OSCE High Commissioner on National Minorities and ODIHR. Expert knowledge and skill would be *fundamental* to the work of these programs. Senior staff, with specialist knowledge and experience in dispute settlement and governance, would be required, along with regional or country experts, who are well versed in the cultural, historical, and political perspectives of actors in the region.

Regional centers would also work in close cooperation with the relevant regional or subregional organizations. This partnership would allow organizations to pool their expertise, use their comparative advantages, and be better informed about individual situations, as well as about the overall causes of conflict within a region. A joint approach would also provide an opportunity to share responsibility and truly coordinate activities.

Further, UN centers could liaise closely with relevant NGOs, as well as with research institutions and think tanks in the region, to extend their knowledge base and "reach" into all levels of civil society. This would ensure that learning proceeds in both directions—that is, bottom-up and top-down—so that the constructive ideas of those at all levels are heard and incorporated into solutions that are acceptable and well tailored to local concerns, culture, and circumstances. Equally important would be the *horizontal transfer of knowledge and experience within each region.* Those within the region who have found solutions to their local problems or have developed relatively successful models for good governance could be tapped to assist others in this endeavor.

Strategic cooperation between the United Nations, regional and subregional organizations, and NGOs could also be expected to have a synergetic effect. Increasing resources for conflict prevention and shifting the focus to a more preventive, assistance-oriented approach could go a long way to helping regional organizations and the United Nations work together more effectively to ameliorate the many existing and potential conflicts besetting all regions of the world.

Salim Ahmed Salim, secretary-general of the Organization for African Unity, expresses these needs as follows:

> Regional organizations are, in my view, the pillars upon which the United Nations must anchor its global peace agenda. The UN needs the cooperation and, indeed, the partnership of regional organizations if it is to be fully effective in brokering peace and ending conflicts. . . . In this process, it may be necessary to look into the possibility of creating a mechanism within the UN to liaise with regional organizations, exchange information on conflicts and coordinate responses to them.[18]

SUMMARY

As can be seen, some of the most effective roles that can be played by regional organizations are those that involve tackling the root causes of regional conflict. This leads to the conclusion that regional organizations should seriously consider placing more of their efforts upstream on conflict prevention, rather than downstream on conflict management. Addressing root causes—before they create violent and intractable conflicts, which are extremely difficult to resolve, and before large-scale human suffering and misery ensue—would be a wise investment of the scarce resources of regional organizations.

In reviewing the evolving role of regional organizations, it appears that there are four factors that can lead to more powerful and sustainable outcomes in creating and promoting peace and security in the regional context: (1) the development of strong regional standards, norms, and rules of behavior that member-states agree upon as guidelines for their interactions with their citizens and with other states; (2) the creation of regional mechanisms and procedures that can monitor, promote, encourage, support, assist, and (where necessary) enforce the group's agreed-upon rules; (3) the fostering of group socialization, in which incentive structures are devoted to making it attractive for states to comply with these agreed-upon norms; and (4) a more widespread use of problem-solving methods of negotiation and mediation, so that when disputes within or between states do arise, they can be resolved before they escalate beyond control.

This is a difficult challenge (for both regional organizations and the United Nations), primarily because there is constant pressure to give all of an organization's attention to full-blown crises, thereby ignoring tomorrow's conflicts. But as long as the root causes remain unaddressed, the whole process recycles endlessly.

Current crises cannot, of course, be ignored, but it is crucial that regional organizations (and the United Nations) develop mechanisms whose *sole* mandate is prevention. The OSCE provides a good case example. In the early 1990s, much of the organization's work was centered on conflict prevention, but the demands of the conflicts in the Former Republic of Yugoslavia overwhelmed the OSCE and made it difficult to maintain this focus. Fortunately, the organization had put in place mechanisms, such as the OSCE High Commissioner on National Minorities, ODIHR, and Long-term Preventive Diplomacy Missions (dedicated to addressing the root causes of conflicts within the region), which have allowed this vital work to continue, even when the attention of the political bodies was drawn elsewhere. It is hoped that other regional organizations will consider creating similarly sustainable mechanisms for prevention.

The development of this type of approach will not, of course, replace the need to monitor and enforce human rights or the collective security actions that may be needed to influence governments or political entrepreneurs that do not live up to international law and do not respond to a positive socialization process. Hence, to create a more effective dispute settlement system, the development of a full range of cooperative security approaches, backed up by a full complement of collective security instruments, is needed. In its current repertoire, the UN system already has a range of power-based methods available for use—even if the political will has not always been there to employ them. What has been largely missing from the international architecture for dispute settlement is the availability of a full complement of *cooperative* security approaches. This is something that both the United Nations and regional organizations could usefully develop further, along the lines noted previously.

As Max van der Stoel, the OSCE High Commissioner on National Minorities (who has been such a successful model of what can be done within a regional organization), has said, "What we need is a new paradigm to respond to new challenges." That paradigm has begun to emerge—now it needs to be studied, nurtured, and developed.

NOTES

The author wishes to thank John Packer, director of the OSCE Office of the High Commissioner on National Minorities, for his helpful comments on the text and the Carnegie Commission on Preventing Deadly Conflict, and, in particular, David Hamburg, cochair of the commission, who supported this work. It should also be noted that the opinions expressed in this paper are those of the author and do not necessarily reflect those of the United Nations Institute for Training and Research or any other part of the UN system.

1. United Nations Charter, Chapter VIII, Article 52.

2. United Nations Charter, Chapter VIII, Article 53.

3. United Nations Charter, Chapter VIII, Article 54.

4. Boutros Boutros-Ghali, *An Agenda for Peace* (New York: United Nations, 1992), 36.

5. Peter Wallensteen and Margaretha Sollenberg, "Armed Conflict, 1989–98," *Journal of Peace Research* 36 (1999): 593–606.

6. See, for example, Ted Robert Gurr, *Minorities at Risk: A Global View of Ethnopolitical Conflicts* (Washington, D.C.: United States Institute of Peace Press, 1993); M. E. Brown, ed., *Ethnic Conflict and International Security* (Princeton, N.J.: Princeton University Press, 1996); Donald L. Horowitz, *Ethnic Groups in Conflict* (Berkeley: University of California Press, 1985); Joseph Montville, ed., *Conflict and Peacemaking in Multiethnic Societies* (Lexington, Mass.: Lexington Books, 1990); D. A. Lake and D. Rothchild, "Containing Fear: The Origins and Management of Ethnic Conflict," *International Security* 21 (1996): 41–75; John Burton, *Conflict: Human Needs Theory* (New York: St. Martin's Press, 1990).

7. See Gurr, *Minorities at Risk*. Also Ted Robert Gurr, "Peoples against States: Ethnopolitical Conflict and the Changing World System," *International Studies Quarterly* 38 (1994): 347–377.

8. Ibid.

9. Connie Peck, *Sustainable Peace: The Role of the United Nations and Regional Organizations in Preventing Conflict* (Lanham, Md.: Rowman and Littlefield, 1998).

10. H. E. Kruger and W. Strasser, "Combating Racial Discrimination with the European Convention on the Protection of Human Rights and Fundamental Freedoms," in *The Use of International Conventions to Protect the Rights of Migrants and Ethnic Minorities* (Strasbourg: Council of Europe, 1994).

11. Wolfgang Zellner and Falk Lange, eds., *Peace and Stability through Human and Minority Rights: Speeches of the OSCE High Commissioner on National Minorities* (Baden-Baden: Nomos Verlagsgesellschaft, 1999).

12. Ibid.

13. Ibid.

14. Max van der Stoel, "Early Warning and Early Action: Preventing Inter-Ethnic Conflict" (speech by Max van der Stoel, OSCE High Commissioner on National Minorities, Royal Institute of International Affairs, London, July 9, 1999).

15. John Packer, "Conflict Prevention by the OAU: The Relevance of the OSCE High Commissioner on National Minorities," in *African Yearbook of International Law*, vol. 4 (The Hague: Kluwer Law International, 1996), 279–291.

16. Wallensteen and Sollenberg, "Armed Conflict, 1989–98."

17. Peck, *Sustainable Peace*.

18. Salim Ahmed Salim, "The OAU Role in Conflict Management," in *Peacemaking and Peacekeeping for the New Century*, ed. Olara A. Otunnu and Michael W. Doyle (Lanham, Md.: Rowman and Littlefield, 1996).

34

NATO's Contributions to Conflict Management

David S. Yost

THIS CHAPTER CONSIDERS the contributions of the North Atlantic Treaty Organization (NATO) to the management of international crises and conflicts. The roles the Alliance has assumed in this regard were not explicitly anticipated at its founding. During the Cold War, from the founding of the Alliance in 1949 to the breakup of the Soviet empire in 1989–91, NATO was essentially an instrument of collective defense. That is, NATO was an alliance organized to defend its members from external aggression or coercion and, on that basis, to conduct diplomacy with its Soviet-led adversaries to the East and seek a peaceful resolution to East-West differences. While the Alliance has not by any means abandoned its collective defense function, it has since 1990–91 increasingly taken on roles and responsibilities that were no more than implicit in its earlier history. Some of the new roles involve what is sometimes called "collective security," in that the Alliance is prepared to act in support of general international security interests on behalf of larger, more inclusive organizations or in defense of principles such as humanitarian necessity.

This chapter begins with a brief discussion of NATO's origins, structure, and assets, which give it a unique standing among international security institutions. It then examines key distinctions between collective defense and collective security—and, indeed, three meanings of collective security—and discusses their significance for the Alliance. These concepts help to explain NATO's transformation since 1990–91. They also set the scene for considering the implications of the Alliance's interventions in the Balkans, particularly those in the Kosovo crisis. The combat in Operation Allied Force in 1999 made possible the subsequent peacekeeping by the NATO-led Kosovo Force.

NATO's Origins, Structure, and Assets

The North Atlantic Treaty was not initiated by the United States, but by Western European

585

nations, particularly Britain and France. In the aftermath of World War II, London and Paris judged that no satisfactory equilibrium and assurance of security could be constructed without U.S. participation in an organization that would guarantee U.S. involvement in combating aggression. After making a bilateral mutual defense pact in 1947, Britain and France in March 1948 organized the Brussels Pact, which included Belgium, Luxembourg, and the Netherlands as well. This was seen as inadequate, however, in light of threatening Soviet behavior, including the Soviet-orchestrated communist coup d'état in Czechoslovakia in February 1948. The Brussels Pact nations, therefore, initiated talks with the United States about possible defense cooperation. Preliminary meetings involving the Brussels Pact nations, Canada, and the United States took place in July 1948, shortly after Stalin initiated a blockade of the British, French, and U.S. sectors of Berlin. Formal negotiations about the North Atlantic Treaty began in December 1948, and the treaty was signed by twelve founding nations on April 4, 1949, while the Soviet blockade of Berlin was still in force.[1]

At this point, however, the North Atlantic Treaty was seen as little more than a mutual defense commitment that would deter Soviet aggression and reassure Western Europe during its economic recovery. It was assumed that the Western Europeans would rebuild their defense capabilities and that, after some years, they would bear the major military burdens in balancing Soviet power in Europe. The treaty established the Alliance's supreme decision-making body, the North Atlantic Council (the NAC, consisting of representatives of the member nations), and specified that the NAC would establish a defense committee; but the Alliance had almost no institutional structure at the outset.

It took the North Korean invasion of South Korea in June 1950 to "put the 'O' in NATO" —that is, to convince the Allies to organize an integrated military command structure in peacetime and to establish the expectation of a large, long-term U.S. military presence in Europe. Many experts and officials in North America and Western Europe feared that the North Korean invasion was a Soviet stratagem. Pyongyang's attack was interpreted as evidence that the communists (then seen as a unified monolithic bloc, including the Soviet Union, China, North Korea, and other states) were prepared to resort to armed aggression; and some hypothesized that the attack against South Korea was perhaps but a prelude to or distracting feint before a communist attack against Western Europe. The United States and its new allies responded. In December 1950 General Dwight Eisenhower was appointed the first Supreme Allied Commander, Europe (SACEUR). In April 1951 Allied Command Europe became operational, with the Supreme Headquarters Allied Powers Europe (SHAPE) then located at Roquencourt, near Paris.

Since 1951 the Allies have built up a comprehensive and reasonably effective institutional structure. This includes a political headquarters in Brussels for the ambassador-level Permanent Representatives to the NAC, with supporting national delegations; high-level policy bodies in which most Allies participate, such as the Defense Planning Committee and the Nuclear Planning Group; an International Staff reporting to the Secretary General; a Military Committee composed of the Chiefs of Defense Staff of the member nations, with permanent National Military Representatives at the political headquarters in Brussels, supported by an International Military Staff; and an integrated command structure, with two Strategic Commands at present—Allied Command Europe, under SACEUR, with SHAPE now located in Mons, Belgium; and Allied Command Atlantic, under the Supreme Allied Commander, Atlantic (SACLANT), in Norfolk, Virginia. Several subordinate commands are maintained under SACEUR and SACLANT, and the Alliance maintains many specialized agencies, committees, research centers, and schools.[2]

The Allies have adapted their military capabilities and institutional structures to meet evolving challenges over the decades, and they have achieved a level of collective military planning and cooperation unprecedented in a peacetime alliance of sovereign and democratic states. Exchanges of all types of information have promoted an educated awareness of the perceptions and problems of fellow Allies. Smaller and less prosperous Allies have benefited from—and contributed to—the formation of a common political-military culture in the Alliance and have gained access to advanced military technology. Through NATO institutions, European nations (notably Britain, France, and Germany) have substantially influenced the Alliance's political and strategic planning.

Indeed, NATO has to a significant degree institutionalized transparency and dialogue in defense planning. Every year the Allies participating in the collective defense planning process under the Defense Planning Committee (at present, all the Allies except France) submit detailed responses to questionnaires about their forces and plans, engaging in systematic and extensive information exchanges that would have been unthinkable in earlier periods of European history. The Allies work together to define planning targets, looking six or more years forward, for their armed forces on the basis of the Alliance's Strategic Concept and ministerial guidance; and the Allies monitor one another's performance.

Collective decision making regarding the acquisition of certain types of capabilities and in exercises and operations has contributed to the growth of trust among the Allies. Decades of consultations and working together have "socialized" Allies into a shared outlook on security affairs and have given them confidence that they understand one another. This "mutual surveillance" in cooperative institutions can be seen as a form of intra-Alliance reassurance that, in the words of Stephen Flanagan, is "designed to avoid renationalization of defense policies and to take concerns about each other out of the security risk calculus of member states."[3]

NATO's cohesiveness and coherence should not be overstated, however. NATO is composed of distinct powers, each still interested in its own security priorities and influenced by its own internal political debates and dynamics. Although NATO has achieved an unusually high level of institutionalization, it remains an intergovernmental organization. NATO acts only when its member governments can agree to do so. The organization has no supranational authority; its international staff assists in the coordination of Alliance activities but has no directive or coercive powers. Most Alliance decisions are made through consensus on the basis of lowest-common-denominator judgments acceptable to all the member governments.

Although France has popularized a distinction between the North Atlantic Treaty (of which France has always remained a loyal signatory) and NATO's integrated military structure (from which France withdrew in 1966), the degree of "integration" achieved in NATO should not be exaggerated. Maintaining an integrated military structure does not mean that SACEUR, for example, commands Allied forces in Europe in peacetime. Most of the forces of NATO member-states are under complete national command in peacetime. Historically, aside from the headquarters staffs in the integrated military structure, only a few types of forces have been under SACEUR's command in peacetime, such as certain standing naval forces and airborne early warning, communications, and air defense units. Aside from the relatively few units already placed under his command in peacetime, no Ally's forces pass under SACEUR's operational command automatically; an explicit transfer of authority from national to NATO command is required. All NATO governments retain national command authority and may withhold agreement to requests by SACEUR or SACLANT, and these commanders are always subordinate to the

Alliance's political authorities—that is, the North Atlantic Council.

Despite continuing shortcomings in standardization and interoperability, Allied military forces have conducted and refined demanding multinational and multiservice exercises and activities over the decades. NATO forces have thus worked together enough to constitute an instrument capable of effective combined action at the disposition of the Alliance political authorities. These forces have logistics, communications, command-and-control systems, and other military assets on a scale and at a level of readiness unrivaled by any other multinational organization.

The military capabilities include those commonly funded and maintained by the Alliance as a whole as well as those of individual Allies, regularly made available for NATO purposes. The Allies have undertaken collective funding of certain capabilities and assets necessary for the common defense, such as Airborne Warning and Control System (AWACS) aircraft, fuel pipelines and storage, air defense radars and navigation aids, communications and information systems, storage and support facilities for reinforcement, headquarters facilities, airfields, and naval bases. Since the end of the Cold War in 1989–91, such investments have shifted away from the Alliance's historical Central Region (Germany and the Benelux countries) toward Greece, Italy, and Turkey. Since 1996, such investments have also supported infrastructure facilities in support of NATO-led peacekeeping operations in the Balkans, including roads, bridges, airports, and railroads. The Allies have also commonly funded specialized agencies, such as the Central Europe Operating Agency, which maintains and operates the Central Europe Pipeline System; the NATO Maintenance and Supply Organization, which provides assistance with spare parts, maintenance, and repairs; and the NATO Communications and Information Systems Operating and Support Agency (NACOSA), which maintains

and operates communications and information networks.

NATO's military capabilities make possible a division of labor with other international organizations acting in support of collective security. In November 2000 Lord Robertson, the NATO Secretary General, described the division of responsibilities in Bosnia and Kosovo as follows: "NATO is providing a secure environment. The UN is providing overall political direction, and helping to rebuild local institutions. The OSCE [Organization for Security and Cooperation in Europe] is helping to build democracy by running elections, and promoting basic standards of human rights."[4]

Robertson has quoted the August 2000 *Report of the Panel on United Nations Peace Operations* to UN secretary-general Kofi Annan: "No amount of good intentions can substitute for the fundamental ability to project credible force if complex peacekeeping, in particular, is to succeed."[5] As Robertson has pointed out, NATO is now leading two UN-authorized peacekeeping operations (the Stabilization Force in Bosnia and the Kosovo Force in Kosovo), and the Alliance's credibility in doing so "rests, above all, on its military effectiveness. . . . It means air forces and navies with precision guided munitions. It means command and control systems that allow for efficient and effective operations. It means forces that can move fast, hit hard and then stay in the field as long as necessary. And it means that these capabilities are shared across the Alliance, not just in one or two of the most advanced members."[6] Indeed, in an effort to promote military capability improvements and enhanced interoperability in Partnership for Peace forces, the Alliance has opened a number of committees in its Defense Support division to Partner nations. As a result, Sweden (not a NATO Ally, but a NATO Partner) has become the first Partner nation to chair a Defense Support division subgroup, one dealing with virtual prototyping in naval armaments.[7]

Procedures for effective cooperation and consensus building have helped to make the Alliance a useful and adaptable asset, constructed over decades at great cost. As Robert McCalla has noted, "Developing new institutions or consultative frameworks entails start-up costs; NATO's appeal is that these costs already have been paid. . . . The wider the range of functions that an alliance fulfills beyond its core defense function, the less responsive it will be to changes in the threats it faces and the more likely it is to be transformed in purpose as its external environment changes."[8] In other words, because NATO continues to serve multiple security functions for its members, the disappearance of the specific threat that triggered the Alliance's formation—the Soviet Union—did not lead to its atrophy.

NATO's continuing security functions are both external and internal. The Alliance's main external functions during the Cold War, preparedness for collective defense and dialogue with non-NATO countries, have been supplemented since the early 1990s with crisis management and peacekeeping operations in the Balkans as well as extensive programs of security cooperation (above all, Partnership for Peace and the Euro-Atlantic Partnership Council) involving most non-NATO countries in Europe in exercises and other activities.

While NATO's internal functions in support of international security and the interests of the Allies may be categorized and defined in various ways, at least eight have been identified: maintaining U.S. engagement in European security, resolving intra–Western European security dilemmas, reassuring Germany's neighbors and allies, limiting the scope of nuclear proliferation in NATO Europe, promoting a certain "denationalization" of defense planning, providing a forum for the coordination of Western security policies, supplying economic benefits to the Allies, and encouraging and legitimizing democratic forms of government.[9] In other words, the Alliance's internal functions

constitute contributions to international conflict management, above and beyond the defense and deterrence preparedness, conflict prevention, trans-European security cooperation, crisis management, and peacekeeping undertaken by NATO. The Allies envisaged some of these internal functions at the outset in the North Atlantic Treaty (for instance, Article 2's reference to "economic collaboration" and Article 4's allusion to security consultations), but they discovered most of them over time. The Allies have recognized the importance of the planning and coordination functions, among others, by refining and strengthening the Alliance's institutions.

DISTINGUISHING BETWEEN COLLECTIVE DEFENSE AND COLLECTIVE SECURITY

In the interests of clear thinking, fundamental distinctions must be made. Two official statements in 1990–91 illustrate how readily the concepts of collective defense and collective security can be confused. In November 1990 the NATO Allies and the members of the Soviet-led Warsaw Pact agreed in a Joint Declaration in Paris that they were "no longer adversaries" and that they recognized that "security is indivisible and that the security of each of their countries is inextricably linked to the security of all States participating in the Conference on Security and Co-operation in Europe [CSCE]."[10] A year later, in its Strategic Concept, approved in November 1991, NATO declared, "The security of all Allies is indivisible: an attack on one is an attack on all."[11]

Despite the apparent similarity in these statements, the key distinction resides in the difference between declaring that "the security of all Allies is indivisible" and, more broadly, asserting that "security is indivisible" with regard to nations outside the Alliance but in the CSCE, a vast body including all the states in the Euro-Atlantic region. The first phrase helps to define an alliance based on a mutual defense pledge—that is, collective defense; the latter expresses an aspiration toward collective security. The collective security tradition is rooted in an effort to think of interests beyond those of the nation and its allies and to consider those of international society as a whole—on a regional, if not a global, basis. The hallmarks of the collective security tradition include a desire to avoid grouping powers into opposing camps and a refusal to draw dividing lines that would leave anyone out.

Collective Defense

During the Cold War, the Alliance's main mission was preparedness for deterrence and defense in the event of aggression against any of the Allies. The Allies were determined, in other words, to honor the mutual defense commitment in Article 5 of the North Atlantic Treaty, and collective defense remains the bedrock purpose of the Alliance. Since the early 1990s, however, a new phrase has been invented— "non–Article 5" missions—because the Alliance is prepared, on a selective basis, to intervene in external conflicts and to support peacekeeping and other operations, as in the Bosnia and Kosovo conflicts. While the Allies are committed to uphold their mutual defense pledges in the event of aggression against an Ally, they are not necessarily obliged to take action concerning international crises, such as an act of aggression affecting a non-ally.

Collective Security

In contrast to collective defense, NATO operations in support of collective security entail actions on behalf of non-allies. The fundamental idea behind all three meanings of collective security is that of universally shared responsibility for international security. The three meanings of collective security differ, however, as to the nature of the obligation to act, the legitimizing framework of action, and the configuration of international power relationships known as the balance of power.

The first meaning is the model of an ideal international order championed most famously, though with some differences, by Immanuel Kant and Woodrow Wilson—a pact against war by the community of states, an arrangement for effective action against any aggressor from within that community. In a Kantian or Wilsonian collective security system, all states would have a moral, political, and legal obligation to act against any aggressor and restore the peace, because of a shared conviction that "peace is indivisible" and that every state's security interests are affected by any aggression anywhere. Such an obligation to act was made a formal treaty commitment in the Covenant of the League of Nations. Despite persistent allegiance to Kantian and Wilsonian ideals in many quarters, no historical attempt to establish an effective collective security system on this model—such as the League of Nations— has ever worked as its organizers intended. NATO has made clear in its practice that it has no intention of pursuing a Kantian or Wilsonian design.

The second meaning of collective security refers to an intervention, usually undertaken by a coalition of states, against international aggression or internal conflict or disorder with the explicit or implicit approval of a major-power consensus. This intervention can take many forms, including mediation and conciliation, economic sanctions, preventive force deployments, coercive military operations, peace enforcement, and peacekeeping and crisis management. Whatever their sense of moral and political obligation, states today do not have a legal commitment equivalent to the League Covenant obliging them to assist victims of aggression and injustice. In practice, only "coalitions of the willing" act, rather than all states—a reality deviating from the Kantian or

Wilsonian ideal. Moreover, when NATO has undertaken such actions and interventions, it has usually sought political legitimization by referring to a consensus of the major powers —in practice, UN Security Council authorization. This is how NATO justified Operation Deliberate Force in 1995, the use of force that made possible the Dayton accords regarding Bosnia. UN Security Council resolutions have also authorized NATO-led peacekeeping forces: the Implementation Force (IFOR) and the Stabilization Force (SFOR) in Bosnia, and the Kosovo Force (KFOR) in Kosovo.

The third meaning of collective security concerns an intervention by a single state or a coalition of states against international aggression or internal conflict or disorder without the approval of a major-power consensus. In other words, the intervention could involve the use of force for a purpose other than national or collective defense without an explicit UN Security Council authorization. This is what NATO did in Operation Allied Force, the conduct of air operations against the Federal Republic of Yugoslavia from March to June 1999.

All the Allies have agreed since October 1998, when they approved activation orders for air operations, that the Alliance had a sufficient legal basis to use force against Belgrade, but the Allies did not and do not agree on the specific content of that legal basis. Some of the Allies have referred to UN Security Council resolutions that Slobodan Milosevic's regime violated, such as Resolutions 1199 and 1203 (and to the UN secretary-general's report on these violations), even though these resolutions did not explicitly authorize the use of force against Belgrade. Some of the Allies— notably the United Kingdom—have referred to a doctrine of overriding humanitarian necessity. Some of the Allies have even argued that there were elements of collective defense in the situation that justified the use of force, on the grounds that a spillover of fighting could have endangered their national security.

France was one of the Allies that strongly resisted the use of force without an explicit UN Security Council authorization. In the end, however, the French decided that the use of force was unavoidable, and France conducted more air combat sorties than any other Ally, except for the United States. In March 1999 Lionel Jospin, the French prime minister, said that "[m]ilitary intervention was imperative, because the irrationality of the Yugoslav regime left no other choice, [and] because we could not resign ourselves to impotence. . . . once the [UN Security] Council was not in a position to act . . . , [and] once there was an emergency, it was up to us to assume all our responsibilities, notably within the Atlantic Alliance."[12]

The UN Security Council "was not in a position to act"—in Jospin's phrase—because Russia and China had indicated that they would not approve a resolution explicitly authorizing the use of force. The French emphasized the UN Security Council resolutions that Milosevic's regime had violated and the fact that Resolution 1199 had been approved under Chapter VII of the UN Charter, which deals with "Action with Respect to Threats to the Peace, Breaches of the Peace, and Acts of Aggression."

The Kosovo crisis revealed, in other words, a contradiction between two principles of collective security—collectivism and the obligation to take action against injustice. As Inis Claude has pointed out, "Respect for the principle of collectivism would impel a state to remain passive in the face of what it regarded as aggression, if no collective determination of the fact of aggression and authorization of counteraction were forthcoming. Adherence to the collective security maxim that anybody's aggression threatens everybody's stake in world order would impel a state to take action on the basis of its own judgment that aggression had occurred, even without benefit of collective legitimization."[13]

The principle confirming a state's right to take action against aggression and in support of collective security, even in the absence of an explicit authorization from the major powers in a quasi-universal international organization, would seem to apply to the Alliance as well. In some circumstances the only available means of honoring fundamental principles of collective security may be outside the framework of a formal organization nominally committed to that purpose. In Claude's words, "Wilsonian collectivism has been given expression in the function of collective legitimization assigned to the United Nations but . . . too literal and strict adherence to the idea that national policy should be constrained by the requirement of collective approbation may defeat the application of Wilson's most fundamental principle, that aggression must be opposed if world order is to be maintained."[14]

The decision by the NATO Allies to use force for a purpose other than collective defense without an explicit UN Security Council authorization was exceptional. An intervention in support of collective security without a major-power endorsement implies that the intervening states are willing to assume additional political and strategic risks, on grounds of necessity and conviction as to the rightness of their objective. The additional risks could include domestic political controversy and negative reactions from major powers opposed to the intervention. The decision by the Allies to use force without explicit UN Security Council approval was consistent with their insistence since 1949 that the Alliance is not a regional arrangement or agency in the sense of Chapter VIII of the UN Charter; defining the Alliance in these terms might be seen as subordinating it to the UN Security Council.

In short, the ultimate purpose of Kantian and Wilsonian designs for collective security is to abolish war and competitive power relationships—to move beyond the balance of power. In contrast, collective security interventions benefiting from a major-power consensus or undertaken outside such a consensus acknowledge the continuing reality of power relationships in international politics.

NATO's Transformation since 1990–91

During the Cold War the main function of NATO's forces was collective defense. The language of the Alliance's November 1991 Strategic Concept suggests that NATO did not then envisage participating in any crisis management or peacekeeping operations as they came to be understood in subsequent years; the mission remained collective defense against aggression affecting Alliance territory, not intervention beyond that territory. "The Alliance is purely defensive in purpose: none of its weapons will ever be used except in self-defense. . . . The role of the Alliance's military forces is to assure the territorial integrity and political independence of its member states, and thus contribute to peace and stability in Europe."[15]

NATO governments were nonetheless reminded of the Alliance's utility as a forum for policy coordination in matters beyond collective defense by the 1990–91 Persian Gulf War. NATO's formal role in that conflict was limited to collective defense: preparedness to defend NATO territory in the southern region (Turkey in particular) and to defend Allied ships and aircraft in the Mediterranean Sea. Because Iraq did not attack Turkey, the Allies did not have to honor Article 5 of the North Atlantic Treaty in combat operations. Alliance procedures and logistical and communications assets were tested, however, in a number of unprecedented ways. NATO officials concluded that the Alliance "responded effectively to a non-Soviet threat against one of its members emanating from outside of Europe, and it prepared to deal with the possible spillover effects of violence occurring in an adjacent region."[16] Moreover, twelve of the then-sixteen NATO Allies provided forces to the coalition against Iraqi aggression and thereby participated in the liberation of Kuwait. In doing so, they closely coordinated their strategies and policies and drew heavily on forces and military infrastructure assets developed within the Alliance.

In June 1992 NATO foreign ministers formally declared the Alliance's willingness, on a case-by-case basis, to support peacekeeping activities under the auspices of what was then called the CSCE.[17] Later that year, the Alliance agreed to make troops and equipment available to CSCE and UN efforts to bring peace to the former Yugoslavia, initially in activities such as enforcing the arms embargo and monitoring the no-fly zone. Since mid-1995 the Alliance's "peace operations" in the former Yugoslavia have overshadowed those of other international organizations, notably since Operation Deliberate Force in August–September 1995, the Dayton peace talks, and the establishment in late 1995 of the multinational IFOR in Bosnia. In late 1996 the Allies agreed that NATO would lead the post-IFOR Stabilization Force (SFOR) in Bosnia. Operation Allied Force, NATO's forcible intervention in the Kosovo conflict in March–June 1999, led to the establishment of the NATO-led KFOR for peacekeeping in Kosovo.

Since the end of the Cold War, the Alliance has also been engaged in "outreach" to non-NATO countries in Europe, particularly former adversaries—nations that were formerly Eastern European members of the Warsaw Pact or republics of the Soviet Union. The new institutions involved in outreach activities include the North Atlantic Cooperation Council (NACC), established in 1991 and replaced in 1997 by the Euro-Atlantic Partnership Council (EAPC); the Partnership for Peace (PfP), founded in 1994; and the NATO-Russia Permanent Joint Council and the NATO-Ukraine Commission, both established in 1997. The fundamental purpose of all these institutions is the promotion of positive and peaceful relations among the participating nations. In both NACC/EAPC and PfP the major activities have included peacekeeping studies and exercises. Russia, Ukraine, and several other PfP nations (including candidates for NATO membership) have participated in IFOR, SFOR, and KFOR.

Since the NATO summit in January 1994, moreover, the Alliance has been engaged in a complex multidimensional process of redefining its command structure and establishing new institutional mechanisms such as Combined Joint Task Forces (CJTFs), owing in part to the practical challenges of conducting peace operations. Another major incentive for establishing CJTFs has been to respond to the aspirations of European allies to build a European Security and Defense Identity (ESDI, the term favored by NATO) or a Common European Security and Defense Policy (CESDP, the term preferred by the European Union). CJTFs and the new Alliance command structure will have multiple functions in addition to collective defense preparedness. When serving as instruments for peace operations and humanitarian relief, NAC-approved CJTFs are expected to be available for use by NATO, the European Union, or "coalitions of the willing" composed of self-selected Allies and non-NATO countries such as Russia. The non-NATO countries making use of CJTFs could include EAPC and PfP members, as well as countries outside these institutions, as with IFOR and SFOR in Bosnia and KFOR in Kosovo.

The term "collective security" is, of course, not favored by NATO officials. Instead, the tendency in official documents is to speak of "crisis response" or "crisis management" or "peace support" operations. According to the 1991 Strategic Concept, one of the Alliance's aims is "to pursue the development of cooperative structures of security for a Europe whole and free."[18] In April 1999, the Allies employed three terms—"security," "partnership," and "crisis management"—to define NATO's new roles:

Security
To provide one of the indispensable foundations for a stable Euro-Atlantic security environment, based on the growth of democratic institutions and commitment to the peaceful resolution of disputes, in which no country would be able to intimidate or coerce any other through the threat or use of force.

Partnership

To promote wide-ranging partnership, cooperation, and dialogue with other countries in the
Euro-Atlantic area, with the aim of increasing
transparency, mutual confidence and the capacity for joint action with the Alliance.

Crisis Management

To stand ready, case-by-case and by consensus,
in conformity with Article 7 of the Washington Treaty, to contribute to effective conflict
prevention and to engage actively in crisis management, including crisis response operations.[19]

An advantage of the term "collective security" is that it has a long history—going back to
the 1930s—of standing in contrast with "collective defense." Concepts of collective security
clarify how thoroughly the Alliance has been
transformed since the end of the Cold War. The
Alliance originated as, and remains, a group of
nations dedicated to collective defense—that
is, ensuring protection for the Allies against
aggression or coercion by an external adversary.
The core function of collective defense (sometimes called territorial defense) continues to be
paramount for the existing Allies and for prospective Allies. Since the early 1990s, however,
collective security—that is, support for international security beyond the immediate defense of the Allies themselves—has become
increasingly prominent in the Alliance's words
and actions.

The words include NATO's offers, beginning in 1992, to support the United Nations
and the CSCE (later the OSCE) in peacekeeping operations; its commitments since 1994 to
security consultations with the twenty-six non-
NATO nations in the Alliance's Partnership
for Peace; and its declarations that "security is
indivisible" throughout what has since the end
of the Cold War often been called the Euro-
Atlantic area, defined as the territory of all the
OSCE states—that is, Canada and the United
States, Europe, Turkey, and the former Soviet
Union, including Siberian Russia and the former Soviet republics in the Caucasus and Central Asia.

The actions include the many Partnership
for Peace exercises and other activities oriented
toward enhancing interoperability between
Alliance and Partner forces, in support of confidence building and transparency as well as
humanitarian, crisis management, and peacekeeping operations. NATO's most momentous
actions, however, have been its first military
operations involving actual combat, including
Operation Deliberate Force in 1995 and Operation Allied Force in 1999—the interventions
in the former Yugoslavia that made possible
NATO-led peacekeeping operations (IFOR
and SFOR in Bosnia and KFOR in Kosovo).

These words and actions confirm that,
even as NATO remains an instrument of collective defense, it has been transformed into a
vehicle, on a selective basis, for interventions
in support of collective security in the Euro-
Atlantic region. The Allies have thus gone beyond their own self-defense, the commitment
to defend each other in Article 5 of the North
Atlantic Treaty. Now the Allies are prepared
to undertake interventions—on a selective basis,
it should be repeated—in support of general
interests, such as containing the conflict in Kosovo, on the grounds of humanitarian necessity and the potential threat to international
peace and security.

IMPLICATIONS OF KOSOVO

The failure of diplomatic efforts to resolve the
Kosovo crisis in the winter of 1998–99 led to
the largest combat operations in the history of
the Alliance and an acceptance by the Alliance
of huge responsibilities for security in the Balkans. Moreover, NATO's involvement has confirmed the importance of the Alliance's new
roles in collective security. Indeed, the Kosovo
intervention represents an acceptance, at least
on an exceptional basis, of a controversial approach to collective security—using force without an explicit UN Security Council authorization or "mandate" to do so.

The key passage in the 1999 Strategic Concept dealing with the "mandate" question reads as follows: "NATO recalls its offer, made in Brussels in 1994, to support on a case-by-case basis in accordance with its own procedures, peacekeeping and other operations under the authority of the UN Security Council or the responsibility of the OSCE, including by making available Alliance resources and expertise. In this context NATO recalls its subsequent decisions with respect to crisis response operations in the Balkans."[20] This wording is noteworthy because it refers to and repeats the formulas employed in the 1994 Brussels summit declaration. This satisfied France and other Allies that favored a reaffirmation of the UN Security Council's primacy—when it is capable of functioning effectively. The reference to the Alliance's "subsequent decisions with respect to crisis response operations in the Balkans" may be construed as an allusion to the policies adopted regarding the Kosovo crisis—that is, to threaten the use of force and to conduct a military intervention in the absence of a UN Security Council resolution explicitly authorizing these actions.

The Kosovo intervention has significant implications for NATO's two most important new roles: pursuing partnership and cooperation with former adversaries and other non-NATO countries in the Euro-Atlantic area and conducting crisis management and peacekeeping operations.

It has been clear since March 1999 that NATO's intervention in Kosovo has complicated the Alliance's pursuit of effective cooperation with Russia. The Russians immediately suspended their participation in Partnership for Peace (which was already at a low level), removed their personnel from positions at SHAPE and at NATO headquarters in Brussels, withdrew their officers from military schools in NATO countries, and so forth. The Russians agreed to resume meetings of the NATO-Russia Permanent Joint Council in July 1999, but they limited the agenda to SFOR and KFOR matters until March 2000.

Furthermore, NATO's intervention in Kosovo stimulated the already powerful anti-Western currents in Russian politics. The picture of NATO conducting attacks against an Orthodox Slavic nation regarding a supposedly internal matter gave ammunition to nationalist and communist political forces in Russia; some Russians even feared that NATO might soon intervene in former Soviet states, including Russia. According to Alexei Arbatov, deputy chairman of the Russian Duma's defense committee, "NATO's attack on Yugoslavia in March 1999 marked a watershed in Russia's assessment of its own military requirements and defense priorities. For the first time since the mid-1980s, within operational departments of the General Staff and Armed Forces, the Security Council, and Foreign Ministry crisis management groups, and in closed sessions of the *Duma*, serious discussions took place concerning [potential] military conflict with NATO."[21]

The picture of NATO that has sometimes been painted in Russia is fundamentally distorted. Some Russian accounts have portrayed NATO as assertive and precipitate in intervening in the Balkans. In fact, however, the Bosnia conflict dragged on for over three years before Operation Deliberate Force took place, making IFOR and SFOR possible. Similarly, Milosevic's abuses of power in Kosovo go back at least to 1989, when he eliminated Kosovo's autonomy within the Yugoslav federation and introduced direct rule from Belgrade. It was only Milosevic who was finally able to convince the Allies to take action about the situation in Kosovo, and it took him years to do so. The picture of an assertive NATO has nonetheless also aroused anti-Western political forces in other countries, from Belarus and Ukraine to even Bulgaria and Romania, and the long-term impact on PfP programs of cooperation remains to be seen.

The operational demands of the Kosovo intervention have increased NATO's security obligations—on a de facto and practical basis, and on a declaratory, political basis—far beyond the promise of security consultations made to the countries in Partnership for Peace. In March 1999 the NATO Secretary General sent letters to Albania, Bulgaria, the Former Yugoslav Republic of Macedonia, Romania, and Slovenia assuring them that the Alliance would regard any Serbian attack against them as "unacceptable."[22] At the April 1999 Washington summit, the Alliance's heads of state and government met with their counterparts from these five countries and with the foreign ministers of Bosnia and Croatia to assure all of these "front line" countries near the Federal Republic of Yugoslavia that "the security of the neighboring states was of direct and material concern to Alliance member states and that NATO would respond to any challenges by Belgrade to the neighboring states resulting from the presence of NATO forces and their activities on their territory during this crisis."[23]

In short, the Kosovo intervention has simultaneously complicated and impeded cooperation with some non-NATO countries while drawing NATO into much deeper security obligations toward others than were originally contemplated. The situation is especially complex, because some countries—for instance, Bulgaria—are affected by both trends, with some polarization in domestic politics around the questions of increased cooperation with NATO and eventual membership in NATO.

The Kosovo intervention may also affect the Alliance's future crisis management and peace operations. Even though Operation Allied Force achieved much of what was intended, and through air power alone, without any NATO ground force combat operations and without any loss of life in combat among the NATO forces, the operations lasted much longer and incurred political and financial costs much greater than the Allies evidently anticipated at the outset.

Furthermore, the Kosovo combat operations were marked by unanticipated events. Air strikes did not succeed in stopping the expulsion of ethnic Albanian Kosovars, the "ethnic cleansing" that Milosevic pursued, and the Serb forces intensified their deportations of these Kosovars into Albania and Macedonia during the NATO air strikes. NATO therefore undertook huge humanitarian relief operations, in cooperation with other international organizations, in Albania and Macedonia. It was only after the fighting stopped that the NATO-led KFOR, in cooperation with other organizations, was able to assist ethnic Albanian Kosovars in their return to Kosovo.

KFOR's achievements include making possible the return of over 1.3 million refugees to their homes; clearing almost two thousand kilometers of roads of mines and unexploded ordnance; repairing power stations, bridges, roads, and railroads; and providing medical treatment to over forty-three thousand Kosovars. According to a paper by Lord Robertson, NATO's Secretary General, in March 2000 "over 50 per cent of KFOR's manpower is currently dedicated to protecting the minority (mainly Serb) populations of Kosovo. This involves guarding homes and villages, transporting people to schools and shops, patrolling, monitoring checkpoints, protecting patrimonial sites and otherwise assisting local people."[24]

Robertson indicated that the Alliance faces five main challenges in Kosovo: "deterring renewed hostility and threats against Kosovo by Yugoslav and Serb forces; establishing a secure environment and ensuring public safety and order; demilitarizing the Kosovo Liberation Army; supporting the international humanitarian effort; and coordinating with and supporting the international civil presence, the United Nations Mission in Kosovo (UNMIK)."[25] Bernard Kouchner, the head of UNMIK, reported in July 2000 that the local ethnic populations "still hate one another deeply. . . . To make peace takes generations, a deep movement and a change of the spirit."[26]

The unexpected costs and difficulties during the Kosovo crisis and subsequently may lead the Allies to tone down their ambitious rhetoric, drawn from the collective security tradition, including the notion that "security is indivisible." Indeed, frustrations in Kosovo and the Balkans as a whole may even lead the Allies to return to a greater emphasis on the Alliance's traditional mission—collective defense, the Article 5 bedrock on which NATO was founded. By the same token, the distinction between a collective security operation undertaken with the endorsement of a major-power consensus (that is, an explicit UN Security Council mandate) and one lacking such an endorsement may become even more significant to the Alliance. Despite NATO's actions in the Kosovo crisis, some Allies may insist on such an endorsement with respect to future non–Article 5 crisis response actions involving the use of force, out of genuine convictions about international law and/or because of practical considerations in domestic and international politics.

One of the rationales for the engagement in Kosovo is NATO's "strategic interest" in preserving its credibility and its vision of the future European political order. If the Allies decide that this is a much costlier enterprise than they bargained for, that the costs are higher than they are willing to pay to intervene in future crises, they may shift their focus back to the "vital interest" of collective defense and become even more selective about undertaking major interventions in support of collective security. According to Lord Robertson, "Kosovo should not be seen as a model for the future. Ideally, the future should be characterized by more prevention and less intervention. That is why we must strengthen preventive mechanisms, from the OSCE to NATO's Partnership initiatives."[27]

The obligations the Alliance has assumed in Bosnia and Kosovo mean that NATO will probably be involved in peacekeeping, crisis management, and associated activities in the Balkans for many years ahead. The costs of these new Balkan obligations—politically, and in terms of human and financial resources—suggest that the Alliance may become more selective in undertaking interventions beyond NATO territory. The provisional settlements enforced by SFOR and KFOR under NATO leadership may last only as long as the Allies agree that containing these conflicts through a quasi-imposed solution is worth the price.

The NATO Allies would obviously prefer not to be committed indefinitely to imposing provisional order on the local antagonists in Bosnia and Kosovo. As Lord Robertson has observed, NATO's vision for southeastern Europe and the Balkans in particular calls for "a region that shares what NATO countries take for granted: peace and trust between neighboring states; the highest standards of human rights, freedom and democracy; economic cooperation; and deepening integration."[28] The emergence of a democratic government in Zagreb led to Croatia's admission to NATO's Partnership for Peace in May 2000. Slobodan Milosevic's fall from power in Belgrade in October 2000 and his replacement by Vojislav Kostunica, a moderate evidently oriented to more cooperative relations with ethnic minorities and neighboring states, may prove to be even more significant developments in the realization of NATO's vision for the region. Lord Robertson expressed cautious optimism in November 2000: "These are auspicious beginnings. But the real movement will come only when new Serbian and Yugoslav Governments finally begin to address the core issues—facing up to the true history of the recent past, opening up Serbian society and media, positively cooperating with the international community, implementing Dayton [accords on Bosnia] and UNSCR [UN Security Council Resolution] 1244 [on Kosovo]. Only then will we see just how far and how fast Southeast Europe can be transformed."[29]

NATO's intervention in the Kosovo conflict has also stimulated new efforts to improve European political-military cohesion and capabilities. Efforts such as ESDI and CESDP have been pursued under various labels for the past half-century. Basic obstacles have historically proved difficult to surmount: a lack of political cohesion and unity in Europe, an absence of a shared vision of strategic requirements, and (on the part of several NATO European governments) an unwillingness to spend more than minimal levels on military capabilities. The post-Kosovo European Union decisions to seek improved military capabilities—including the December 1999 Helsinki "headline goal" of building up by 2003 an intervention force of fifty thousand to sixty thousand troops, deployable within sixty days and sustainable for at least a year—may be attributed in part to European frustrations during the Kosovo conflict (and during the diplomatic maneuvers that preceded it) with U.S. political dominance, which stemmed directly from U.S. preponderance in military capabilities.

The "headline goal" suggests, however, that the European Union's current aspirations extend to being able to undertake operations like the SFOR and KFOR peacekeeping missions, not combat actions like Operation Allied Force. The capabilities required for such combat actions—including precision-guided munitions, air-to-air refueling tankers, heavy air transport, and electronic warfare systems—are expensive. To the extent that improvements in these capabilities are pursued, they will be sought above all by France, Britain, and a few other European countries. The European Union as a whole is likely, however, to remain heavily dependent on U.S. forces for command and control, communications, aerial refueling, electronic attack, precision strike, intelligence, and other functions.

The European Union countries evidently chose to define their "headline goal" on a lowest-common-denominator basis that they could all endorse politically and contribute to militarily —hence the focus on ground forces for peacekeeping. Moreover, the European Union's "headline goal" was apparently designed to be readily feasible, with minor budgetary consequences. The European Union's limited ambitions are consistent with the continuing

tendency of most NATO European Allies, including major countries such as France and Germany, to cut their defense spending. The key exceptions to this tendency remain Greece, Turkey, and the United Kingdom.

France and the United Kingdom are the European Union nations most committed to gaining more political-military options under national and/or European Union control and greater influence in defining NATO strategy that would flow from increased capabilities. The British have played a leading role in this regard since late 1998, when Prime Minister Tony Blair announced, in a major change in British policy, an unprecedented readiness to bring security and defense matters into the European Union. The British nonetheless remain more inclined than the French to think in terms of developing the European Union's military potential within a broad NATO framework and in close cooperation with the United States. The French are more apt to think of a European Union capability distinct from that of the Alliance and U.S. forces. As in the past, the concept of the European Union as an autonomous great power—what the French call *"l'Europe-puissance"*—commands more interest and respect in France than in any other European Union country. Long-standing patterns of capability dependence in transatlantic relations appear likely, however, to be prolonged and may even be deepened by factors affecting the willingness and ability of governments to spend on military forces, such as the low level of threat perceptions in NATO Europe and the imperatives of other social priorities in the European Union.[30]

From NATO's perspective, the most important principles in European defense cooperation should be, in Lord Robertson's words, "inclusiveness of all NATO allies," because several are not European Union members; "indivisibility of the transatlantic link," because of the imperative of continued U.S. engagement in European security; and "improvement of capabilities," particularly in Europe, because of the U.S.-European asymmetries.[31] Even with improved European capabilities, Robertson has noted, "NATO has assets the EU will need to borrow for larger operations—assets like deployable headquarters, strategic lift, or satellite intelligence."[32] In October 2000 U.S. secretary of defense William Cohen proposed that the twenty-three nations in NATO and/or the European Union establish a consolidated NATO–European Union defense planning mechanism, a "European Security and Defense Planning System," with the European officer serving as Deputy SACEUR functioning as a "strategic coordinator" between NATO and the European Union.[33] Whether this arrangement and/or other institutional mechanisms for NATO–European Union cooperation will be established remains to be seen.

CONCLUSION

Collective defense and actions in support of collective security (with or without benefit of a major-power consensus) can be pursued simultaneously. Collective defense investments ensure that military capabilities are available for selected operations in support of collective security if the Allies choose to undertake them. Such operations, however, remain constrained by the broader configuration of power relationships and by the limited obligations that governments are normally prepared to assume regarding the safety of others. More ambitious aspirations, for a collective security system in the Kantian or Wilsonian sense, would compete with a collective defense orientation, because these aspirations call for replacing balance-of-power arrangements and alliances, which are by definition exclusive, with an inclusive community in which peace and security would be truly "indivisible."

The Alliance's new functions in support of collective security could raise challenges for its long-term cohesion. Participation in non–Article 5 contingencies is, in principle, optional (in contrast with the obligatory nature of Article 5 commitments). This "coalitions-of-the-willing" method of dealing with nonunanimity could undermine Alliance cohesion, because the differences among the Allies could extend to conflicting preferences about the outcomes of conflicts outside NATO territory. While all the Allies have participated in IFOR, SFOR, and KFOR, and all the Allies offered political support and made contributions in some form to the intervention in the Kosovo crisis, such high levels of practical solidarity cannot be taken for granted in future crisis management operations. The Allies themselves have insisted on the voluntary nature of choices to participate in non–Article 5 operations. This implies that a pattern of "free rider" behavior could emerge, with some Allies preferring to "hold the coats," as it were, of the Allies prepared to take greater risks by actually conducting interventions in support of collective security. Those taking the risks might resent such passivity, and this could constitute a centrifugal force.

The Kosovo crisis, it should be recalled, led to public disagreements among the Allies about what course of action to pursue and what outcomes to strive for. Fourteen of NATO's nineteen nations participated in the air operations in the Kosovo intervention. Four nations—the Czech Republic, Iceland, Luxembourg, and Poland—did not participate for lack of relevant capabilities, while Greece chose not to participate in the air operations for political reasons, including the high level of sympathy for Serbia in Greek public opinion.

The Allies could therefore find it harder in future crises to manage NATO's political cohesion problems, owing to differences in interests and priorities, if the Alliance expanded to include some or all of the current nine applicants (Albania, Bulgaria, Estonia, Latvia, Lithuania, Macedonia, Romania, Slovakia, and Slovenia) and/or other countries that may eventually apply for membership, such as Austria, Finland, and Sweden. The tension between inclusiveness and effectiveness, a challenge to some degree for all international organizations, could become even more acute with regard to optional actions in support of collective security, in contrast with cases clearly demanding collective defense—that is, acts of aggression directly threatening the security of one or more members of NATO.[34]

Given the absence of a sense of common interest and community in the Euro-Atlantic region (and pending the development of such a sense), the United States and its NATO Allies will have little choice but to pursue a two-track policy with perseverance and full awareness of the potential pitfalls—pursuing collective security aspirations to the extent that this is feasible and prudent, but maintaining a collective defense posture as a hedge in case those aspirations cannot be fulfilled.

Collective defense remains the only solid foundation for Alliance cohesion and strength, and the most reliable basis for undertaking selected operations in support of collective security. The challenge is to find a via media that maintains collective defense capabilities in good order, given the risk of future threats to Alliance security, while seeking to deepen cooperation and transparency in security matters and to contain the risks inherent in emerging or ongoing rivalries. It is imperative to pursue opportunities for constructive cooperation with Russia while hedging against the continuing risk of grave setbacks in that country's political development.

While the ideas legitimizing crisis management and peace operations will almost certainly reflect the collective security tradition, the Allies will have to recognize the risks and limits inherent in certain ideas. For example, trying to act on the principle that "security is indivisible" with regard to every case of aggression or internal conflict in the Euro-Atlantic region probably would exceed the resources and political will of the Allies, particularly with regard to conflicts in the former Soviet Union. Moreover, as the Allies recognized in the Kosovo crisis, depending on the UN Security Council as the only entity capable of legitimizing an intervention in support of collective security could hamper the Alliance's ability to act in cases in which the gravity of the injustice and the magnitude of the threat to Allied interests demand immediate action.

In short, the Kosovo conflict has demonstrated how long and difficult the road ahead will be for the Alliance, if it is to fulfill its vision. The Allies cannot have credibility regarding the grand project of building cooperative security structures throughout the Euro-Atlantic region unless they demonstrate determination and staying power in Bosnia and Kosovo. NATO must nonetheless meet this challenge. NATO remains the most effective institution for combining the political-military assets of the major Western powers, and its effectiveness must be preserved—for collective defense, above all, but also to enable it to conduct selected operations in support of collective security.

NOTES

The views expressed in this chapter are the author's alone and do not represent those of the Department of the Navy or any U.S. government agency.

1. The original twelve signatories of the 1949 North Atlantic Treaty were Belgium, Canada, Denmark, France, Iceland, Italy, Luxembourg, the Netherlands, Norway, Portugal, the United Kingdom, and the United States. The following countries have subsequently joined the Alliance: Greece and Turkey (1952), the Federal Republic of Germany (1955), Spain (1982), and Hungary, Poland, and the Czech Republic (1999).

2. For details, see the current issue of the *NATO Handbook* (Brussels: NATO Office of Information and Press, 1999) or consult the NATO Web site at http://www.nato.int.

3. Stephen J. Flanagan, "NATO and Central and Eastern Europe: From Liaison to Security Partnership," *Washington Quarterly* (spring 1992): 149.

4. Lord Robertson, "Security in the Wider Europe" (speech at the Centre for European Policy Studies, Brussels, November 10, 2000).

5. *Report of the Panel on United Nations Peace Operations*, A/55/305-S/2000/809 (New York: United Nations General Assembly and Security Council, August 21, 2000), p. viii of executive summary. This report is available on the Internet at http://www.un.org/peace/reports/peace_operations/.

6. Lord Robertson, "NATO's New Agenda: More Progress Than Meets the Eye" (speech at the SACLANT Symposium, Reykjavik, Iceland, September 6, 2000). This is the speech in which Robertson quoted the *Report of the Panel on United Nations Peace Operations.*

7. Luke Hill, "NATO Seeks to Enhance Partner Participation," *Jane's Defence Weekly*, November 8, 2000.

8. Robert B. McCalla, "NATO's Persistence after the Cold War," *International Organization* 50 (summer 1996): 464, 470.

9. For an extensive discussion of NATO's eight internal functions, see David S. Yost, *NATO Transformed: The Alliance's New Roles in International Security* (Washington, D.C.: United States Institute of Peace Press, 1998), 50–72.

10. Joint Declaration of Twenty-Two States, Paris, November 19, 1990, par. 3, in Adam Daniel Rotfeld and Walter Stützle, eds., *Germany and Europe in Transition* (New York: Oxford University Press, 1991), 217–218.

11. North Atlantic Council, Strategic Concept, November 7, 1991, par. 37.

12. Lionel Jospin, statement to the National Assembly on March 26, 1999, *Journal Officiel de la République Française, Débats Parlementaires, Assemblée Nationale*, 2969–2972.

13. Inis L. Claude Jr., "The Collectivist Theme in International Relations," *International Journal* 24 (autumn 1969): 655.

14. Ibid., 656.

15. North Atlantic Council, Strategic Concept, November 7, 1991, par. 36.

16. Admiral Jonathan T. Howe, U.S. Navy, "NATO and the Gulf Crisis," *Survival* 33 (May-June 1991): 255. Admiral Howe was then Commander in Chief of Allied Forces in NATO's southern region.

17. The CSCE was renamed the OSCE (Organization for Security and Cooperation in Europe) in December 1994. There have been no examples to date of NATO peacekeeping operations under OSCE aus-pices. In July 1992 the CSCE heads of state or government declared that "the CSCE is a regional arrangement in the sense of Chapter VIII of the Charter of the United Nations" and that "The rights and responsibilities of the Security Council remain unaffected in their entirety." According to Article 53 of the UN Charter (part of Chapter VIII), "no enforcement action shall be taken under regional arrangements or by regional agencies without the authorization of the Security Council." However, partly because terms such as "enforcement action," "peacekeeping," and "peacemaking" have not yet received authoritative and generally accepted definitions and are subject to diverse interpretations, the possibility of the OSCE someday mandating NATO to perform an operation in support of collective security (e.g., monitoring a cease-fire or border settlement) without UN Security Council authorization cannot be excluded.

18. North Atlantic Council, Strategic Concept, November 7, 1991, par. 19.

19. North Atlantic Council, Washington Summit Communiqué, April 24, 1999, par. 6.

20. North Atlantic Council, Strategic Concept, April 24, 1999, par. 31.

21. Alexei G. Arbatov, *The Transformation of Russian Military Doctrine: Lessons Learned from Kosovo and Chechnya*, Marshall Center Paper no. 2 (Garmisch-Partenkirchen, Germany: George C. Marshall Center, July 2000), 8–9.

22. Craig R. Whitney, "NATO Assures Five Neighbors That Fear Serbian Attack," *New York Times*, March 25, 1999.

23. Chairman's Summary, Meeting of the North Atlantic Council at the Level of Heads of State and Government with Countries in the Region of the Federal Republic of Yugoslavia, Washington, D.C., April 25, 1999.

24. Lord Robertson of Port Ellen, *Kosovo One Year On: Achievement and Challenge*, March 21, 2000, 17. This report is available at http://www.nato.int/kosovo/repo2000/report-en.pdf.

25. Ibid., 18.

26. Bernard Kouchner quoted in Steven Erlanger, "Aide Takes Stock of U.N. in Kosovo," *New York Times*, July 17, 2000.

27. Lord Robertson, "Peacekeeping and Conflict Prevention: What Risks and Threats in Geopolitics in the Future?" (speech at the Transatlantic Century conference, Aspen Institute and Philip Morris Institute, Rome, January 13, 2000).

28. Lord Robertson (speech at the Joint Wilton Park/Atlantic Council Conference, Brdo Castle, Slovenia, May 11, 2000).

29. Lord Robertson (speech to the NATO Parliamentary Assembly, Berlin, Germany, November 21, 2000).

30. For background on ESDI/CESDP issues, see David S. Yost, "The NATO Capabilities Gap and the European Union," *Survival* 42 (winter 2000-2001).

31. Lord Robertson (remarks at the conference Défense Européenne: Le concept de convergence, Brussels, March 29, 2000).

32. Lord Robertson (speech to the NATO Parliamentary Assembly, Berlin, Germany, November 21, 2000).

33. William Cohen quoted in Jim Garamone, "U.S. Proposes 'More Positive' Vision of NATO-EU Partnership," American Forces Press Service, October 10, 2000.

34. The antinomy between inclusiveness and effectiveness is discussed in Yost, *NATO Transformed*, 173–176.

35

International Law and Response to Conflict

William A. Schabas

IN THE FINAL INTERNATIONAL armed conflict of the twentieth century, as bombs fell upon Belgrade and other Yugoslav towns and cities, both sides in the war found themselves being taken to court. Serbian leader Slobodan Milosevic was the first off the mark, suing ten NATO countries for aggression and genocide before the International Court of Justice. An application for a provisional order against his enemies was dismissed by the court. But tension and uncertainty instilled by his arguments, which cut deeply among some NATO members that were profoundly troubled with the legality of their efforts, may well have altered dynamics within the alliance. A few weeks later, Prosecutor Louise Arbour of the International Criminal Tribunal for the Former Yugoslavia announced that Milosevic himself had been charged with crimes against humanity, that an international warrant had been issued against him, and that any foreign assets of his would be seized. She added that this changed the diplomatic landscape for resolving the conflict because it would be inappropriate to negotiate with an indicted war criminal.

For the first time in history, then, a parallel international conflict was being waged in the courtrooms of The Hague while a shooting war raged a thousand miles away. Did international litigation simply continue armed conflict but by other means, to paraphrase von Clausewitz, or was an innovative and promising response to conflict resolution emerging, albeit in a still primitive and imperfect form? In any event, to the extent that legal rules and their implementation by the courts were being injected into a complex international crisis, there was an additional element of unpredictability. While this may represent some degree of triumph of principle over pragmatism, it is certainly questionable whether the insistence that conflicts be waged and resolved in accordance with international law makes their resolution easier and more likely. Indeed, the contrary may well be the case, as some have argued. Debates about "fundamental rights," particularly with respect to sovereignty and minority rights issues, often muddle the search for common ground.[1] Sometimes, states may agree upon terms of a settlement that actually conflict with rules of international law of a peremptory character. They may, for example, agree to grant amnesty to perpetrators of war crimes. Those who seek peace at all costs will accept such concessions, while those who stick to other principles of international law, including a growing insistence in human rights law on resisting impunity, will argue that such settlements are improper and, ultimately, invalid.

PROHIBITION OF WAR, HUMAN RIGHTS, AND STATE SOVEREIGNTY

Sixty years ago, international law textbooks were divided into two principal rubrics: the law of war and the law of peace.[2] There was no general prohibition on the use of force, and indeed international law conceived of war as the ultimate and legitimate exercise of the attributes of state sovereignty. To protect themselves against aggression, states wove a complex web of treaties, pacts, and ententes, many of them secret, some accompanied by full-blown military alliances and duties to intervene if allies were attacked by a third party. Woodrow Wilson expressed the growing disaffection with the system in his Fourteen Points address to Congress on January 8, 1918. But when the victorious allies, gathered in Paris, proposed criminal prosecution of Kaiser Wilhelm II, his alleged crime was not making war as such but rather breaching international agreement. Article 227 of the Treaty of Versailles dictated that he be tried for "a supreme offence against international morality and the sanctity of treaties."[3]

Law was transformed in the interwar years. By the Kellogg-Briand Pact, or Pact of Paris, of August 27, 1928, sixty-three states condemned "recourse to war for the solution of international controversies" and renounced it as an instrument of national policy. Its breach was at the core of convictions at Nuremberg of Nazi leaders for "crimes against peace." The Nuremberg judgment stated: "To initiate a war of aggression, therefore, is not only an international crime; it is the supreme international crime differing only from other war crimes in that it contains within itself the accumulated evil of the whole." Thus, pacific settlement of disputes became the rule. The law of war was studied no more. Yet the dogs of war continued to bark and bite.

Three principles of international law seem to define the contemporary legal framework of conflict prevention: the prohibition of the use of force, the sanctity of national sovereignty, and the protection and promotion of human rights. All three take their bearings from the Charter of the United Nations. But there is much tension and contradiction among them, especially as these three concepts continue to evolve. We may well ask whether their relationship helps to mold the conduct of conflict as well as its resolution, or whether this is simply reactive, an attempt to alter legal norms to fit political realities.

The fundamental norm prohibiting the use of force in international relations is now Article 2(4) of the Charter of the United Nations, reformulating and reaffirming Articles 1 and 2 of the Kellogg-Briand Pact of 1928. It is no longer necessary for states to negotiate separate pacts of nonaggression; probably the last such treaty in history will be that agreed to by Molotov and Ribbentrop in the days immediately before the outbreak of World War II. The Charter of the United Nations recognizes two exceptions: self-defense and collective action under the aegis of the Security Council pursuant to Chapter VII. In theory, the Security Council's intervention is confined to matters of international peace and security, a mandate that appears to eliminate its involvement in internal conflict as a general rule. In any event, the fragile balance of the five permanent members resulted in a power that was rarely used, at least until the end of the Cold War provided a temporary lull in great-power tension. The fall of the Berlin Wall and the breakup of the Soviet Union opened a window of opportunity for an expansive view of the council's mandate. By the early 1990s intervention under Chapter VII was being conducted in the name of the protection of human rights in countries where the threat to *international* peace and security was more virtual than real.

Parallel to this new legal regime prohibiting the use of force was the growth of international human rights law. Human rights language can be found throughout the charter, although the 1945 San Francisco Conference stopped short of including a substantive declaration. That task was undertaken a few years later in the adoption of the Universal Declaration of Human Rights, a document whose guiding light was the American stateswoman Eleanor Roosevelt. The declaration's preamble described it as a "common standard of achievement."[4] It was barely thinkable that the United Nations might one day express opinions and actually condemn human rights violations occurring within the borders of sovereign states. Indeed, in the early years of the United Nations, when individuals from various parts of the world complained to the secretary-general that their rights were being violated, he simply forwarded the complaint to the accused government with an accompanying note explaining that such matters were none of his business. But over time this conservatism and reticence dissolved. Relatively secondary UN organs, principally the Commission on Human Rights, took the lead during this initial phase. In time, human rights percolated up to the General Assembly and, ultimately, the Security Council.

But there was a counterweight to these developments, its spirit crystallized in Article 2(7) of the charter, which cautioned that nothing would "authorize the United Nations to intervene in matters which are essentially within the domestic jurisdiction of any state." The message of respect for state sovereignty is also transmitted in Article 1's reference to the self-determination of peoples. If all of this seemed clear enough in 1945 when the charter was adopted, its significance has weakened over the decades. It is obviously far too soon to speak of the end of sovereignty. Nevertheless, the wall that international law erected around states, in effect ensuring that what goes on within their own borders is immune to international scrutiny and involvement, has been breached.

HUMANITARIAN INTERVENTION

The concept of humanitarian intervention has relatively ancient origins. In the nineteenth century some world powers affirmed a right and in some cases a duty to intervene in the interests of conflict prevention, the promotion of democratic ideals, and securing the rights of minorities. The most frequently cited case is that of France in Lebanon during the 1860s, but the paradigm is large enough to include the Monroe Doctrine. The intervention was unilateral and it was politically colorable, owing to the presence of a rather clear correspondence between the right to intervene and a concept of spheres of influence of major powers.

By the 1950s and 1960s "intervention" had become a dirty word and "sovereignty" a sacred and intangible value, but by the end of the century the pendulum was to swing back in the other direction. Fundamentally, it was the growth of the human rights discourse that authorized the international community to claim the right to involve itself in areas that had been beyond its reach in the past. Although the United Nations provided perhaps the most important forum for these developments, the role of regional organizations must not be overlooked. For example, by the early 1960s the Inter-American Commission on Human Rights was studying the question of human rights within Cuba, needless to say without the express or implied consent of the Cuban government. Basket Three of the Conference on Security and Cooperation in Europe opened the door to Western involvement in human rights–type issues within the Soviet bloc. It did much to prepare and promote the fall of the socialist regimes at the end of the 1980s.[5] Yet as in the Charter of the United Nations, the modest human rights language of the 1975 Helsinki Final Act was couched in the classic references to self-determination and the sanctity of international borders.

Throughout this gestation period, much of the debate centered on the racist regime in South Africa and, to a somewhat lesser extent, in Southern Rhodesia (now Zimbabwe). The new states of the so-called Third World were the most nervous and uncomfortable about any suggestion of a right to intervene. Yet they pushed forward the agenda in the case of apartheid, treating it as a special and exceptional case. Apartheid was, of course, an egregious violation of fundamental rights. UN resolutions and treaties would call such racist domination of the majority a crime against humanity. In any event, intervention in the case of apartheid was confined to relatively modest proportions, principally in the areas of trade and cultural and athletic exchanges. Nevertheless, the fact that apartheid was a subject of international concern set a precedent whose implications might be enormous. Once the principle was recognized, there were other serious violations of human rights that could warrant comparable international efforts.

UN peacekeeping is another dimension in the evolving doctrine of humanitarian intervention. The charter had contemplated the raising of UN forces within the context of Chapter VII and it even provided for the creation of a Military Staff Committee. But the major peacekeeping operations—Suez, Cyprus, Kashmir—relied on Chapter VI and would never have taken place without the consent of the parties. Peacekeeping troops facilitated

conflict resolution, but they did so essentially in situations where willing parties needed a neutral international umpire to help them move the process along. Where this will was lacking, Chapter VII could be the only vehicle. But as long as the Security Council was dominated by power struggles between two great superpowers, intensely suspicious of each other, it could rarely agree upon implementing Chapter VII.

The defining moment in these developments was the Gulf War. When Iraq invaded Kuwait in mid-1991, asserting territorial grievances dating to the time of colonization, the Security Council responded with an ultimatum to withdraw and, when that failed, robust military intervention. Yet Operation Desert Storm was grounded in uncontroversial premises: the right of Kuwait to self-defense and the unchallengeable role of the Security Council in the case of aggression. The precedent here was UN involvement in the Korean War, in the earliest days of the organization. Thus, from a legal standpoint, the ability of the Security Council to authorize intervention had existed since 1945. But from a practical standpoint, the Soviet veto and superpower rivalry had made this impossible in the past. Indeed, during the Korean War a deadlocked Security Council was bypassed in favor of the General Assembly. Forty years later, however, the major powers had lost any enthusiasm for such a role being exercised by a General Assembly whose overwhelming majority now lay in the southern half of the planet.

When Iraq withdrew from Kuwait, the raison d'être of the intervention evaporated. The Security Council then turned to a radically new dimension within its Chapter VII powers, authorizing ongoing intervention including the creation of "no-fly zones" in the name of protection of ethnic and religious minorities within Iraq itself. Resolution 688, adopted in April 1991, provided the legal framework for military attack as well as economic embargo of Iraq that would continue to the end of the decade. The precedent it established rapidly led to a range of initiatives, previously thought unthinkable, in various parts of the world: Somalia, Rwanda, Haiti, Bosnia, Kosovo, East Timor.

What was so radically different about these interventions was the difficult and tenuous link with the Security Council's remit. By what stretch of the imagination did the persecution of minorities within Iraq fall within the ambit of aggression or constitute a breach of the peace? Essentially, the council took the view that internal developments could threaten international peace. The link, though welcomed by human rights advocates, was often unconvincing. A frequent argument was that the refugee flows that usually accompany internal strife have devastating consequences on neighboring states, thereby threatening the peace. But as the 1990s progressed, these rationalizations became less and less important. Massive human rights violations, in and of themselves, were deemed sufficient to trigger the provisions of Chapter VII.

The collapse of the Soviet Union had provided the window of opportunity for Security Council–mandated intervention. Though the agenda during this period was generally set by the three Western permanent members, this was not always the case. In April and May 1994 it was the elected members, particularly New Zealand and the Czech Republic, who urged intervention in the Rwandan genocide while the permanent members dawdled.[6] But it still remained unthinkable that international intervention in an internal conflict could be justified without the imprimatur of the Security Council.

The argument that international law provided a basis for humanitarian intervention irrespective of the provisions of the charter, or even in conflict with them, had been supported by some scholars in the United States since the 1970s, although the weight of international opinion considered such initiatives to be illegal.[7] Opinions rapidly evolved in late 1998 as the United States started mooting the possibility of military intervention in the Federal Republic of Yugoslavia so as to protect the persecuted Kosovar Albanian minority from "ethnic cleansing." A Soviet veto of any Security Council mandate for the use of force seemed inevitable, and in the end the matter was never even tested with a vote. NATO proceeded to attack Yugoslavia on its own and without council authorization.

The legality of the bombing of Yugoslav military targets by NATO aircraft and missiles remains uncertain at best. The broad participation of a major regional organization combined with the lack of condemnation by major international forums, such as the General Assembly of the United Nations, has led some to suggest the permissibility of such practice. They have cited Chapter VIII of the charter, which allows regional arrangements for enforcement action, although the relevant provisions explicitly require Security Council approval. On the other hand, the silence of the charter and the lack of any other "black letter" law on the subject leaves the parameters of such humanitarian intervention vague. Subsequent statements by some of the NATO participants even suggest a profound reluctance to establish a precedent that could be invoked to justify similar initiatives in the future.

Some treaties have been invoked as a basis for humanitarian intervention in the absence of any Security Council authorization. The reasoning is that by accepting certain conventional norms, states have voluntarily recognized the prospect of intervention and furthermore have committed themselves to participate as required by circumstances. The 1948 Convention for the Prevention and Punishment of the Crime of Genocide creates an obligation to both "punish" and "prevent" what has been called the "crime of crimes."[8] But while the convention spells out in some detail its punitive dimension, its preventive side remains enigmatic. In 1994, as genocide raged in Rwanda, uncertainty about the scope of the obligation to prevent genocide influenced some states to eschew use of the "g-word." There was a fear that a direct reference to genocide in a Security Council resolution might generate a legal obligation to intervene, one that some members of the council were not prepared to assume.[9]

A similar argument can be made based on common Article 1 to the four Geneva Conventions of 1949, in its requirement that states both "respect and ensure respect" for the other provisions in those humanitarian law treaties. It seems somewhat contradictory that treaties whose purpose is to humanize the worst abuses of armed conflict and protect noncombatants would also encourage the use of force. However, there are historic roots for such a concept in the notion of belligerent reprisals, by which violations of the laws of war may be tolerated to the extent they are imposed in order to compel the other side's respect for such laws.

LITIGATION BEFORE INTERNATIONAL COURTS

The relationship between international responses to conflict and judicial mechanisms dates back more than a century, to the Hague Conference of 1899. That meeting took a number of initiatives in the direction of regulating armed conflict as well as preventing it. The conference devised the Permanent Court of Arbitration in order to provide states with a judicial institution where disputes could be settled. Before then, arbitration had been undertaken on an ad hoc basis, with a monarch or other head of state often designated as a neutral arbiter.

But the Permanent Court of Arbitration was really only the forerunner of moves to establish an international court, a body created in the aftermath of World War I. Named the Permanent Court of International Justice, it operated until the end of World War II, when it was reconstituted into the International Court of Justice. The International Court of Justice

has its seat in The Hague. The statute of the court is an annex to the Charter of the United Nations. However, while all states have some involvement in the court because it is a UN organ, only contentious cases that involve states that have accepted its jurisdiction can come before the court, and these are still a minority.

During the interwar years, the Permanent Court of International Justice developed a body of jurisprudence in the realm of minority rights, applying and interpreting the web of treaties and declarations governing post-Versailles Eastern Europe. The court's rulings did much to define the rights of minorities. Although the practical significance of the minority rights treaties should not be exaggerated, there is evidence that some of Hitler's anti-Semitic policies were checked temporarily because of special guarantees contained in the applicable instruments.[10]

After World War II, the work of the International Court of Justice began modestly. The Soviet Union and its allies stayed well clear of its jurisdiction during the Cold War. African and other Third World countries became quickly disenchanted after observing the court's reticence to get involved in a series of Namibia cases. But in the mid-1980s, the court's stock rose considerably in these quarters after it condemned the United States for supporting attempts of the Contras to destabilize the Sandinista regime in Nicaragua. The United States, which had successfully challenged Iran in the court over the Tehran embassy occupation a few years earlier, actually refused to participate in the Nicaragua proceedings, arguing that the court was not entitled to exercise jurisdiction. But at the same time, many states recognized the court's jurisdiction or withdrew reservations to its jurisdiction that had been attached to relevant international treaties. Suddenly a court whose docket had never contained more than a couple of cases, and whose judges worked at the most leisurely of paces, found itself overwhelmed with applications, some of them dealing with ongoing conflicts and requiring it to navigate through intensely political waters.[11]

In late March 1993, as war raged in the disintegrating Yugoslavia, the newly created state of Bosnia filed an application directed against Belgrade based on a number of specific treaties, including the old minority treaty adopted in the aftermath of World War I and the 1948 Genocide Convention.[12] The application charged the Milosevic regime with fomenting genocide through its policy of ethnic cleansing, which it said was carried out on Bosnian territory by armed groups taking direction from Belgrade. Bosnia coupled its application with a request for provisional measures. It asked the court to issue an immediate order to Yugoslavia to cease a detailed list of hostile and aggressive acts.

Representations were made by both sides within a matter of days. The court granted Bosnia's request for such an interim order. By its very nature, a provisional order avoids detailed study of the merits of a case. Nevertheless, the court will not issue one unless there is a serious basis for a claim. But Bosnia's victory in court had little or no practical significance on the ground. It was, nevertheless, a useful propaganda tool. Note was taken of the court order in a variety of international documents, including a Security Council resolution. Bosnia returned some months later for a second order, whose real consequences were similarly symbolic. It also threatened to sue the United Kingdom for its failure to prevent genocide, but cooler heads in the Bosnian foreign ministry eventually prevailed.

Since then, Bosnia's case against Yugoslavia has returned periodically to the court's docket as various preliminary matters were addressed pending a full hearing on the Bosnian claim. There were rumors that the case would be dropped as part of the Dayton accords. Although this did not happen, the political compromise made at Dayton has made further progress in the case problematic. In effect, the Republika Srpska, an "entity" of Bosnia and Herzegovina, has not shown any enthusiasm for the case, for obvious reasons. But its unlikely cooperation seems necessary if the matter is to go to trial.

There were other interesting attempts to influence the war in the former Yugoslavia through judicial means. In September 1991, faced with the imminent breakup of Yugoslavia as well as of the Soviet Union, the European Commission issued a declaration setting out its conditions for recognition of any new states that might be created. The European standards included evidence of a democratic manifestation of a desire for any new state and commitments to protect human rights, particularly those of ethnic minorities. In order to assess compliance with these terms, the European Commission established a form of tribunal, chaired by French constitutional judge Robert Badinter.

The Badinter Commission promptly ruled that the European Commission's terms for recognition were fulfilled in Slovenia and Macedonia. In the case of Croatia, it was not satisfied with the human rights and national minority issues. With respect to Bosnia, the Badinter Commission considered that an adequate referendum had not taken place. The results were chaotic and, arguably, provocative. Despite the clean bill of health, Macedonia was not recognized for years, the result of political concerns with Greek objections. Although Badinter had frowned on Croatian recognition, Germany broke ranks and recognized the new state just before the end of 1991. And Bosnia, in order to comply with the ruling, plunged into a referendum campaign that helped provoke the outbreak of armed conflict.

The Badinter Commission applied international law, drawing on precedents of the International Court of Justice and similar bodies and interpreting documents derived from the United Nations and the Conference on Security and Cooperation in Europe. One of the more intriguing and controversial conclusions of the commission was that the possibility of creation of new states was not unlimited. Making an analogy with the decolonization in South America and Africa, Badinter said new states could only be created along preexisting administrative boundaries *(uti possidetis juris)*, effectively ruling out attempts by Bosnian Serbs to join a "Greater Serbia." The same principle would return years later to rule out initiatives for an independent Kosovo or a "Greater Albania."[13]

The European Commission's attempt to govern the process of recognition of new states with rigorous legal norms and judicial institutions appealed to the jurist but shocked many politicians and diplomats. Clearly, it limited the options of negotiators at a time when the utmost flexibility was required. Here, then, judicial intervention is vulnerable to the charge that it may have aggravated conflict and inhibited efforts at peaceful settlement. Yet in the result, political leaders seem to have followed the judicial precedents of the Badinter Commission only when these corresponded to their own intuitions and strategies, suggesting that international law is disposable, a comfortable support when it confirms political judgments but little more than a minor annoyance when it does not.

International human rights courts also have their role to play in dealing with interstate conflict. The European Convention on Human Rights and the American Convention on Human Rights, as well as the International Covenant on Civil and Political Rights, all permit interstate complaints. States have proven themselves reluctant to use such mechanisms and, in practice, there have been only a handful, all of them in the European system. One of the first cases before the European Commission on Human Rights, back in the 1950s, was filed by Greece against the United Kingdom and concerned alleged abuses during the independence struggle in Cyprus. Cyprus has filed a series of applications against Turkey before the commission, all dealing with the 1974 invasion and its aftermath. In the mid-1970s

Ireland successfully sued the United Kingdom about conditions in detention camps in Northern Ireland.

But the most interesting petitions have come, surprisingly, from individuals. In 1996 the European Court of Human Rights ruled in favor of an application from a Greek Cypriot who claimed her right to enjoyment of property had been violated by the Turkish invasion. Two years later the court awarded her damages of approximately $1 million.[14] If other Cypriots file similar claims, judgment debts could extend into the billions of dollars. So far, Turkey has refused to honor the judgment and has even threatened to withdraw from the Council of Europe. But a hostile posture on human rights may irreparably compromise its application to join the European Union. Thus, although this was not its overt purpose, an individual litigant's claim may help advance the peaceful settlement of one of Europe's longest-standing disputes.

PEACEFUL SETTLEMENT OF INTERNATIONAL DISPUTES

Taken in a historical perspective, the examples of violent conflicts being addressed in judicial bodies tend to be the exception, although certainly a growing one. Most dispute settlement by judicial means has actually been unspectacular, helping states to resolve issues relating to boundaries, both territorial and maritime, as well as to the use of rivers, the extent of fishing zones, and similar matters. Potentially, of course, these can quickly spiral into shooting wars. That matters never get to such a stage because they are tackled by arbitration or judicial settlement is not well known.

A look at the docket of the International Court of Justice gives some idea of the importance of this work. In 2000 the court was considering disputes dealing with borders or river rights involving Qatar and Bahrain, Hungary and Slovakia, Cameroon and Nigeria,

Indonesia and Malaysia, and Nicaragua and Honduras. Many more such matters had been considered over the years, some of them leading to binding judgments, others—just as they do before domestic courts in litigation between individuals—being settled out of court, the result of constant reassessment by the parties of the dynamics of the case. Even when the court declines jurisdiction, it often exhorts the parties to seek alternative methods of peaceful settlement, as required by Article 33 of the Charter of the United Nations. Sometimes a judgment of the court will lead to special means of settlement being developed. In 1981, after succeeding in its claim against Iran, the United States renounced its right to compensation under the court's judgment in exchange for the establishment of the Iran-United States Claims Tribunal.[15]

CRIMINAL PROSECUTION OF LEADERS OF A BELLIGERENT PARTY

A very different tack on judicial involvement in the wars of the former Yugoslavia emerged in late 1992 and early 1993 following investigations into atrocities by a United Nations fact-finding commission. The call for an international war crimes tribunal was picked up quickly. The Security Council, whose Resolution 827 of May 1993 actually established the International Criminal Tribunal for the Former Yugoslavia (ICTY),[16] was able to build on work then ongoing within the United Nations International Law Commission aimed at creating a permanent international criminal court. The international criminal court project had been around since 1948 but became obscured during the Cold War and had been revived only in 1989.

Unlike the International Court of Justice, whose litigants were sovereign states, the ICTY was to judge individuals for war crimes, crimes against humanity, and genocide. The prece-

dent, of course, was the Nuremberg trial of 1945–46. But there were some important distinctions: the conflict was ongoing and the tribunal itself had been established not by victors but by an ostensibly impartial international community. And while Nuremberg's philosophical underpinning had been retribution imposed upon the leaders of a defeated regime, the ICTY was focused on deterring future atrocities. Also unlike Nuremberg, the ICTY was plagued with the problem of bringing the main suspects into custody.

The initial indictments were filed against relatively minor players in the conflict. Indeed, there was much speculation that prosecutions of the leaders in the conflict were being stymied by political pressure. How could a peace process be launched and negotiations proceed if the spokespeople for the parties were on the tribunal's most wanted list? In political circles, concern was expressed publicly that prosecution would abort a negotiated settlement. Then in mid-1995, in the days following the summary executions at Srebrenica of thousands of civilian noncombatants, Prosecutor Richard Goldstone announced that charges had been laid against Bosnian Serb leaders Radovan Karadzic and Ratko Mladic. The immediate result was not, as some had feared, to sabotage the peace process. In fact, within weeks encouraging negotiations were under way at Dayton, but those indicted refused to come.[17] Goldstone's indictment had marginalized Karadzic politically, and he would never really recover. Stigmatization of the Karadzic-Mladic leadership, later confirmed in a preliminary hearing on the overall sufficiency of the charges, had been accomplished.

Justice Goldstone's 1995 indictment of Karadzic was only the dress rehearsal. In May 1999, as NATO bombs rained down on Serbia, Prosecutor Louise Arbour indicted Slobodan Milosevic for crimes against humanity. Weeks earlier she had stood on the border of Kosovo and warned him of the consequences, and critics will surely point to this as a failure of the tribunal's deterrent function. The timing of the indictments left Justice Arbour open to charges of political interference, but she was in fact criticized on all sides. Possibly the most troublesome element in the exercise of prosecutorial discretion was the suggestion that her decision to charge Milosevic had been dependent on obtaining high-level communications intercepts from NATO intelligence services. To the extent NATO controlled the evidence, it also helped to set the agenda for the tribunal's prosecutor.

Short of obtaining the diaries of Milosevic's confidants, we will never be able to establish with any precision the role that the ICTY indictment played in bringing an end to the Kosovo conflict. There were some very immediate and practical consequences of the tribunal's initiative, including an order freezing assets of Milosevic that might be located outside Yugoslavia. In announcing the indictment, Justice Arbour also claimed that Milosevic, as an indicted war criminal, could no longer participate legitimately in negotiations. This was a questionable assertion, because until a final judgment is issued he remains entitled to the presumption of innocence. But on a political level, this was also a dangerous and troubling claim. Ruling out a negotiated peace because a leader has been indicted is rather like the judicial equivalent of saying "take no prisoners." It seems destined to prolong a conflict, not shorten it.

Meanwhile, Milosevic was up to some judicial mischief of his own. In late April 1999 he filed an application with the International Court of Justice, borrowing a page from his Bosnian adversaries, whose lawsuit against Yugoslavia launched in 1993 is still pending. Yugoslavia charged ten NATO countries with a breach of the peace, contrary to the Charter of the United Nations, and genocide, in violation of the 1948 Genocide Convention. An order for provisional measures was sought aimed at an injunction to the NATO states to stop bombing. While hostilities continued, lawyers for both sides debated the matter in The Hague. At the very least, Milosevic had an arguable case in his claim that the charter had been violated, because the use of force by NATO had been conducted without authorization from the Security Council. But Yugoslavia had accepted the jurisdiction of the court only a few days before filing suit, a cynical move that discredited its suit. This was only one of several obstacles to the admissibility of the application. Ultimately, the court refused to grant its request for an interim order against the NATO states, although the case itself is proceeding and may still be heard on the merits. Milosevic's lawsuit was not likely to unbalance the more steadfast members of the NATO alliance, but it seems probable that this very visible and credible challenge to the legality of the campaign may well have contributed to wavering among NATO's less determined members.

The idea of a permanent international criminal court has been studied seriously within international organizations since before World War II. The United Nations War Crimes Commission, established by the Allies in 1943 in order to prepare prosecutions of Nazi war criminals, drafted a statute for a permanent international court. But while the prosecutorial efforts that followed the war were bold and innovative in many respects, the international community balked at creating a permanent institution. Further study of the matter was requested of the General Assembly's International Law Commission. With Cold War tensions, the matter fell off its agenda and was reactivated only in 1989. Intense work and negotiations culminated in a diplomatic conference in June and July 1998 and adoption of the Rome Statute of the International Criminal Court. The court will actually be created when sixty states have ratified the Rome Statute, which is expected to take four or five years.[18]

THE INTERNATIONAL CRIMINAL COURT

The International Criminal Court is probably the most significant new international organization to be created since the United Nations. It sits squarely within the three themes that have been addressed throughout this chapter: the decline in state sovereignty, the growth in humanitarian intervention, and the enhanced protection of human rights. Yet because the court is created by treaty, it is consensual in nature. Participation by states in the court system is not a denial of sovereignty but rather its assertion.

The court will have jurisdiction over the "most serious crimes of international concern." Four categories of crime are listed, of which the first three, genocide, crimes against humanity, and war crimes, echo the terms of the ad hoc tribunals for the former Yugoslavia and Rwanda. The final category of crime is aggression, but here the work of the drafters is unfinished. The diplomatic conference that drafted the Rome statute was unable to agree on the subject and left the reference to aggression in the statute as a kind of placeholder, all the while providing that there could be no prosecutions for aggression until the states parties to the statute agreed upon a definition and other issues.

The "aggression" issue highlights the problems that arise when an international criminal court attempts to contribute to furthering international responses to conflict. It is argued that Article 39 of the Charter of the United Nations reserves to the Security Council the authority to determine whether an act of aggression has been committed. To allow another international body to address the same question might lead to inconsistency and conflict. But the alternative, by which prosecution for aggression would be dependent upon a Security Council ruling that the crime had actually taken place, is extremely problematic because it denies a defendant the forum to contest the basic material elements of the crime.

The consequences for international conflict of an International Criminal Court with jurisdiction over the crime of aggression are potentially enormous. The other key international crimes may or may not be committed in the context of international armed conflict. They were alleged during the Kosovo war of 1999, with both sides being accused of crimes against humanity or genocide, as has already been discussed. However, charges of aggression during international armed conflict would seem almost unavoidable. In some future reprise of the Kosovo conflict, a frustrated Milosevic or even an independent prosecutor on his or her own initiative may threaten criminal prosecution of NATO leaders.

Alongside the question of jurisdiction over aggression is the broader issue of the relationship between the International Criminal Court and the Security Council. The initial draft of the court's statute, prepared by the International Law Commission in 1994, stated: "No prosecution may be commenced under this Statute arising from a situation which is being dealt with by the Security Council as a threat to or breach of the peace or an act of aggression under Chapter VII of the Charter, unless the Security Council otherwise decides." In effect, then, matters being considered by the council were simply off-limits as far as the court was concerned, unless the council ruled otherwise. But the provision provoked great controversy as the drafting proceeded. Resentment about the composition of the council, and particularly the veto power of its five permanent members, helped drive efforts to whittle down any role it may have in controlling the prosecutorial agenda. The final result still allows the council to block prosecutions, but this must be done by a positive resolution valid for only one year, a far more demanding standard than the initial draft's requirement that the matter be a "situation being dealt with."

It seems easy to imagine circumstances in which the International Criminal Court and the Security Council may be at cross-purposes. The council may consider that threatened prosecution for aggression or any of the other three crimes risks complicating delicate political negotiations, possibly involving a formal or informal grant of amnesty or some other inherently political decision. As for the court, it may refuse to bow to decisions of the council on the grounds that it would be exceeding its jurisdiction, which is confined to matters of international peace and security.

In the vote at the conclusion of the Rome Conference in July 1998, the court's statute was adopted by 120 to 7. The handful of opponents included the United States, China, and Israel. The United States has been a keen supporter of international criminal justice, dating from the Nuremberg and Tokyo trials in the 1940s to the more recent ad hoc tribunals for the former Yugoslavia and Rwanda. However, it is uncomfortable with a number of aspects of the Rome Statute, including the power granted to the court's prosecutor to initiate prosecution unilaterally and the limitations on the Security Council's right to suspend or defer cases. The most important difficulty for the United States is the enlargement of the court's jurisdiction to cover persons committing crimes within the territory of a state that has ratified the statute. The United States considers that jurisdiction should extend only to nationals of a state that has ratified the statute. The principal concern, it seems, is with the threat of prosecution of U.S. military personnel when engaged in activities beyond U.S. borders. In reply, defenders of the court argue that the statute would not allow it to assume jurisdiction to the extent that the United States shows its willingness to prosecute its own soldiers for war crimes. During the Vietnam War U.S. servicemen, such as those involved in the My Lai atrocity, were prosecuted for war crimes, to much international publicity. There is no reason to believe that military prosecutors would behave differently in future conflicts, should the situation arise.[19]

TRANSITIONAL JUSTICE: PROSECUTE OR FORGIVE?

Historically, conflict resolution has often involved some form of forgiving and forgetting. In this spirit, the Geneva Convention on prisoners of war dictated prompt repatriation at the end of the conflict. In 1977, when the Geneva Conventions were expanded with a protocol addressing noninternational armed conflict, it too called for "the broadest possible amnesty to persons who have participated in the armed conflict." The conventional wisdom reflected in these provisions was that peace could be purchased in exchange for a promise that the past would be forgotten. But self-proclaimed amnesties by repressive rulers in South America during the 1980s gave the concept of amnesty a sour taint. By the 1990s, in an ironic shift, even nongovernmental organizations such as Amnesty International were condemning amnesties as being incompatible with human rights. Accordingly, the Rome Statute of the International Criminal Court leaves little room for amnesty or any alternative approaches to accountability.

This complicates conflict resolution by insisting upon an almost inexorable judicial dimension. The logic of releasing prisoners of war at the end of the conflict was that this promise of fair and humane treatment would encourage them to surrender and therefore shorten the period of hostilities. This same wisdom has been applied with favorable effect in Haiti, where a pledge of asylum elsewhere prompted putschist Raoul Cedras to relinquish power, and in South Africa, where the farsighted Truth and Reconciliation Commission of Nelson Mandela and Desmond Tutu avoided a predictably bloody day of reckoning between the proponents of apartheid and its adversaries, but one whose outcome would be uncertain. These options now seem to be largely foreclosed by the new and rather intransigent insistence upon accountability before criminal courts, be they national or international.

The wisdom of a rigorously judicial approach remains unproven.[20] The drafters of the Rome Statute searched vainly for a formulation that would enable them to distinguish between the amnesties granted by Mandela, which most found acceptable, and those by Augusto Pinochet, which most found repulsive. Ultimately, the matter now seems to rest with the discretion of the prosecutor, a profoundly unsatisfactory situation reflecting the continuing inadequacy of our understanding of this problem. The prosecutor may refuse to proceed with a case, even when submitted by a state party or by the Security Council, when "[t]aking into account the gravity of the crime and the interests of victims, there are nonetheless substantial reasons to believe that an investigation would not serve the interests of justice." The statute also allows the court itself to decline jurisdiction in matters that are "not of sufficient gravity to justify further action." International judges may well be inclined to include here cases in which alternative methods of accountability, such as truth commissions, had functioned in a genuine and sincere fashion. But then again, they may not.

CONCLUSION

International and noninternational conflict is being increasingly judiciarized. This is due in part to a proliferation of norms that simply did not exist a century ago, in particular those belonging to the law of human rights. It was not until after World War I that international law abandoned the idea that states could go to war legally, as long as they did not violate applicable bilateral or multilateral nonaggression pacts, as well as the idea that states could basically do as they pleased as long as they did it within their own borders and to their own nationals. Now, a much broader range of state behavior is actually contemplated by international law. Moreover, various new forums have been created in which this law can be litigated, the principal bodies being the International Court of Justice, the international criminal tribunals, and international human rights courts.

Examples of successful dispute settlement through essentially legal mechanisms abound, but these generally concern boundary disputes and the like. In the early 1980s Canada and the United States went before the International Court of Justice to have a line drawn in the Gulf of Maine along a previously disputed border. The suggestion that they would otherwise have gone to war is preposterous. But some cases get closer to the boundary between peaceful, judicial settlement of disputes and resort to force. In the past, Chad and Libya have crossed swords on a frontier issue. Later, they agreed to submit the matter to the International Court of Justice in The Hague. When the court ruled in Chad's favor, border guards on both sides are said to have had a farewell party before the Libyans politely retreated to the new line. These are clear success stories, but some of the examples discussed in this article—Yugoslavia, Cyprus, South Africa — leave many questions unanswered.

Proving law's effectiveness, in any context, is a formidable challenge. Criminal codes prohibit serious crimes against the person and against property, and yet murder, rape, and theft are frequent occurrences. Does this demonstrate law's failure to influence the behavior of individuals? It is widely believed that punishment deters crime, but we can never prove this because it is impossible to document and quantify the uncommitted crimes. Transposed to an international law context, how can we know whether conflict is prevented, calmed, or perhaps, in some cases, incited by law's participation?

Table 1. Judicial Instruments for Conflict Prevention

Settlement of Disputes between States

International Court of Justice. Established in 1945 as part of the creation of the United Nations. All UN member-states are parties to the statute of the court. However, states must accept the jurisdiction of the court either by making a general declaration or on a case-by-case basis. The court may also issue advisory opinions, a somewhat more indirect technique for resolving legal issues that may lead to potential conflict.

Specialized arbitral tribunals. These are established pursuant to ad hoc arrangements between states that agree that their decisions will be binding. They have included the United Nations Tribunal in Libya, United Nations Tribunal in Eritrea, Supreme Restitution Court of the German Federal Republic, Iran–United States Claims Tribunal, and International Center for Settlement of Investment Disputes.

Arbitration. Individual arbitrators or panels are set up by ad hoc agreement between states to deal with a specific dispute or class of disputes.

Human Rights Courts

European Court of Human Rights. Established in the 1950s pursuant to the European Convention on Human Rights. Although most of its case load involves individual petitions, it is empowered to consider complaints by one state that another has violated the convention. It has jurisdiction over the forty-two member-states of the Council of Europe.

Inter-American Court of Human Rights. Established in the 1970s pursuant to the American Convention on Human Rights. Similar in form to the European Court; while it is empowered to consider interstate complaints, none have ever been filed. It hears cases dealing with member-states of the Organization of American States that have accepted its jurisdiction.

International Criminal Prosecution

International Criminal Court. Yet to be established, its creation is provided for by the Rome Statute of the International Criminal Court, adopted in July 1998. The court will have jurisdiction over genocide, crimes against humanity, war crimes, and aggression committed on the territory of a state that has ratified the statute, or by a national of such a state.

International Criminal Tribunal for the Former Yugoslavia. Established by the Security Council in 1993. The tribunal has jurisdiction over genocide, crimes against humanity, and war crimes committed on the territory of the former Yugoslavia since 1991. The Security Council has yet to determine when its mandate concludes.

International Criminal Tribunal for Rwanda. Established by the Security Council in 1994. The tribunal has jurisdiction over genocide, crimes against humanity, and war crimes committed on the territory of Rwanda or in neighboring states during 1994.

This resort to law and to courts seems to add a degree of rigidity to conflict resolution that may appear counterproductive in some cases. For example, it may in effect veto amnesties and similar compromises that are the price for peace and transition or forbid parlay and negotiation with those condemned or even charged as war criminals. Although it will be wise to be watchful for such deformations, current practice does not suggest that the injection of law and litigation into crises unduly complicates the work of mediators.

On balance, international law's contribution would appear to be generally helpful. How else can we explain the almost universal enthusiasm for the creation of new judicial mechanisms like the International Criminal Court? The gamble, of course, is that increased reliance on and adherence to a law that prohibits aggressive war and the persecution of vulnerable minorities or individuals will ultimately enhance chances for peace and reduce conflict.

NOTES

1. See, for example, Melanie C. Greenberg and John H. Barton, "Lessons of the Case Studies," in *Words over War: Mediation and Arbitration to Prevent Deadly Conflict*, ed. Melanie C. Greenberg and John H. Barton (New York: Carnegie Commission on Preventing Deadly Conflict, 2000), 343–369, esp. 357–360.

2. See, for example, H. Lauterpacht, ed., *Oppenheim's International Law* (London and New York: Longmans, Green, 1944).

3. The kaiser had sought refuge in the Netherlands, a neutral country at the time, and was never extradited to stand trial. He died there shortly after the outbreak of World War II. See M. Cherif Bassiouni, "From Versailles to Rwanda in Seventy-Five Years: The Need to Establish a Permanent International Criminal Court," *Harvard Human Rights Journal* 10 (1997): 11–62. These provisions of the Treaty of Versailles were regularly cited as precedent during the debate surrounding claims of immunity for former Chilean president Augusto Pinochet during 1998 and 1999.

4. On the development of the international law of human rights, see Louis Henkin, *The Age of Rights* (New York: Columbia University Press, 1990).

5. Gérard Cohen-Jonathan and Jean-Paul Jacqué, "Obligations Assumed by the Helsinki Signatories," in *Human Rights, International Law, and the Helsinki Accord*, ed. Thomas Buergenthal (Montclair, N.J.: Allenheld, Osman, 1975), 43–70.

6. See Linda Melvern, "Genocide behind the Thin Blue Line," *Security Dialogue* 28 (1997): 333, 341. Also see Boutros Boutros-Ghali, *Unvanquished: A U.S.-U.N. Saga* (New York: Random House, 1999), 129–140.

7. For the position favorable to a right of humanitarian intervention, see W. Michael Reisman and M. S. McDougal, "Humanitarian Intervention to Protect the Ibos," in *Humanitarian Intervention and the United Nations*, ed. R. B. Lillich (Charlottesville: University of Virginia Press, 1973), 178–183; Bartram S. Brown, "Humanitarian Intervention at a Crossroads," *William and Mary Law Review* 41 (2000): 1683. For a recent review concluding that the Charter of the United Nations leaves no room for humanitarian intervention, see Djamchid Momtaz, "NATO's 'Humanitarian Intervention' in Kosovo and the Prohibition of the Use of Force," *International Review of the Red Cross* 89 (2000): 837. Also see Albrecht Randelzhofer, "Article 2(4)," in *The Charter of the United Nations*, ed. Bruno Simma (Oxford: Oxford University Press, 1995), 106–128, at 123–124.

8. *Prosecutor v. Kambanda* (Case no. ICTR-97-23-S), Judgment and Sentence, September 4, 1998, par. 16.

9. William A. Schabas, *Genocide in International Law* (Cambridge: Cambridge University Press, 2000).

10. In Upper Silesia, for example, the Nazis delayed introduction of racist laws because this would have violated the applicable minorities treaty norms. Jews in the region, protected by a bilateral treaty between Poland and Germany, were sheltered from the Nuremberg laws and continued to enjoy equal rights, at least until the convention's expiry in 1937. See Jacob Robinson, *And the Crooked Shall Be Made Straight* (New York: Macmillan, 1965), 72–73.

11. The current president of the International Court of Justice, Gilbert Guillaume, has penned a lively account of the relationship between litigation before the court and ongoing international crises: *Les grandes crises internationales et le droit* (Paris: Editions du Seuil, 1994).

12. Much has already been written on the early stages of the case: Peter H. F. Bekker and Paul C. Szasz, "Casenote: Application of the Convention on the Prevention and Punishment of the Crime of Genocide," *American Journal of International Law* 91 (1997): 121; Ben Gaffikin, "The International Court of Justice and the Crisis in the Balkans: Application of the Convention on the Prevention and Punishment of the Crime of Genocide (*Bosnia and Herzegovina v. Yugoslavia*)," *Sydney Law Review* 17 (1995): 458; Thomas D. Grant, "Territorial Status, Recognition, and Statehood: Some Aspects of the *Genocide*

Case (*Bosnia and Herzegovina v. Yugoslavia*)," *Stanford Journal of International Law* 33 (1997): 305; Christine Gray, "Application of the Convention on the Prevention and Punishment of the Crime of Genocide (*Bosnia and Herzegovina v. Yugoslavia [Serbia and Montenegro]*)," *International and Comparative Law Quarterly* 43 (1994): 704; William L. Hurlock, "The International Court of Justice: Effectively Providing a Long Overdue Remedy for Engaging State-Sponsored Genocide (*Bosnia-Herzegovina v. Yugoslavia*)," *American University Journal of International Law and Policy* 12 (1997): 299.

13. Marc Weller, "The International Response to the Dissolution of the Socialist Federal Republic of Yugoslavia," *American Journal of International Law* 82 (1992): 569; and Alain Pellet, "L'activité de la Commission d'arbitrage de la Conférence européenne pour la paix en Yougoslavie," *Annuaire français de droit international* 38 (1992): 220.

14. *Loizidou v. Turkey (Article 50)*, Judgment, July 28, 1998.

15. *Claims Settlement Agreement*, January, 19, 1981, *International Legal Materials* 20 (1981): 230.

16. On the ICTY, see M. Cherif Bassiouni and Peter Manikas, *The Law of the International Criminal Tribunal for the Former Yugoslavia* (Irvington-on-Hudson, N.Y.: Transnational Publishers, 1996);

Virginia Morris and Michael P. Scharf, *An Insider's Guide to the International Criminal Tribunal for the Former Yugoslavia: A Documentary History and Analysis* (Irvington-on-Hudson, N.Y.: Transnational Publishers, 1995).

17. See John R. W. D. Jones, "The Implications of the Peace Agreement for the International Criminal Tribunal for the Former Yugoslavia," *European Journal of International Law* 7 (1996): 226.

18. Roy S. Lee, *The International Criminal Court: The Making of the Rome Statute* (The Hague, London, and Boston: Kluwer Law International, 1999); Otto Triffterer, ed., *Commentary on the Rome Statute of the International Criminal Court, Observers' Notes, Article by Article* (Baden-Baden: Nomos, 1999); Flavia Lattanzi and William A. Schabas, eds., *Essays on the Rome Statute of the ICC* (Rome: Editrice il Sirente, 2000).

19. David J. Scheffer, "The United States and the International Criminal Court," *American Journal of International Law* 93 (1999): 12.

20. For the authoritative work on forms of accountability, including a range of nonjudicial mechanisms, see Neil J. Kritz, ed., *Transitional Justice: How Emerging Democracies Reckon with Former Regimes* (Washington, D.C.: United States Institute of Peace Press, 1995).

36

Arms Control Treaties and Confidence-Building Measures as Management Tools

Michael Krepon and Lawrence Scheinman

INTRODUCTION

Arms control treaties and confidence-building measures (CBMs) played an important role during the Cold War in modulating super-power competition over dangerous weapons, establishing norms for responsible states, facilitating the isolation of states seeking weapons of mass destruction, reassuring domestic audiences and allies by means of cooperative threat reduction, and reducing the risks associated with the possession of particularly dangerous weapons.

While arms control, nonproliferation, disarmament, and CBMs are analytically separable undertakings, they are closely related in practical terms. CBM accords such as the "Hotline" both preceded and facilitated treaties. CBMs were also embedded in treaties, reinforcing monitoring arrangements by providing greater transparency and helping participating states to verify whether obligations were being met.

Progress with CBMs usually led to progress in treaty negotiations and vice versa. At times during the Cold War, the United States and the Soviet Union also focused on stand-alone CBM agreements, such as the creation of nuclear risk reduction centers, when negotiations were stalled and when fears of nuclear danger were on the rise.

Arms control agreements impose limits on weaponry and military activities, while disarmament treaties provide for the elimination or prohibition of certain categories of weapons. The strategic arms limitation and strategic arms reduction treaties (SALT and START) are examples of the former, while the Biological Weapons Convention (BWC) and the Chemical Weapons Convention (CWC) are examples of the latter. The 1968 Nuclear Nonproliferation Treaty (NPT) is a unique accord in which states not having a category of weapons pledge forbearance, while states possessing nuclear weapons continue to retain them, committing to work in good faith toward their ultimate elimination, thus removing the treaty-based discrimination.

Arms control and disarmament regimes have been important adjuncts to conflict management and resolution, but they have not substituted for political commitment to improve bilateral relationships and tackle sources of hostility and conflict. For example, by joining the NPT, Argentine and Brazilian leaders underscored prior political commitments to close off nuclear options. Successful arms control and disarmament regimes can strengthen regional security by providing greater predictability, transparency, reciprocal monitoring arrangements, and reassurance. While all of these tools are useful, conflict resolution rests primarily on political undertakings that are reflected in treaties, rather than on the treaties themselves. CBMs can be useful precursors and adjuncts to treaties, facilitating favorable political developments, but they, too, require prior political commitment to change the dynamics of troubling bilateral or regional interactions. Consensual arms control and disarmament regimes are therefore predicated on an already existing political will to transform and consolidate relationships, to establish rules and standards to regulate activity in certain defined spheres, and to provide mechanisms and processes for dealing with conflict.

During the Cold War, the negotiation and the implementation of treaties dealing with weapons of mass destruction were of paramount importance. Only at the latter stages of the superpower competition did the United States, the Soviet Union, and their allies agree upon arms control constraints on conventional weaponry most suitable for seizing and holding territory. The resulting Conventional Forces in Europe (CFE) Treaty required substantive revision soon after its completion, with the breakup of the Soviet Union and the demise of the Warsaw Pact. The CFE Treaty was built upon prior agreements codifying confidence-building measures in Europe, focusing primarily on transparency and risk reduction measures. With the end of the Cold War, the scope of attempted constraints on weaponry expanded to include land mines and small arms transfers. These efforts have been plagued by the lukewarm support of the United States and other key countries, as well as by the difficulties of seeking to control weapons with low cost and multiple sources of supply.

These circumstances are likely to continue to plague efforts to control land mines and small arms, making progress on both fronts primarily contingent on the resolution of regional conflicts rather than on the negotiation and imposition of control regimes. The control regime for heavy conventional arms in Europe has so far weathered the demise of the Soviet Union and the Warsaw Pact, as well as the CFE Treaty's blatant violation by the Russian Federation in prosecuting the war in Chechnya. Even harsh critics of arms control in the United States have not taken aim at the CFE Treaty, which is strongly supported in Eastern and Western Europe. In contrast, bilateral treaties governing nuclear forces and missile defenses have been the subject of intense partisan and executive-legislative-branch wrangling in the United States. A continued breakdown in consensus bodes ill for treaty-mandated control arrangements, which could then increase the utilization of CBMs between Washington and Moscow. CBMs are also likely to be employed increasingly in regions beset with tension where control regimes are nonexistent and where national leaders seek security through alternative means.

ARMS CONTROL AND CBMS AS FOREIGN POLICY TOOLS

The canonical purposes of arms control during the Cold War were to avoid a war that neither side wanted, minimize the costs and risks of an arms competition, and curtail the scope and violence of war in the event of its occurrence.[1] Taken together, arms control treaties and

CBMs contributed to some of these objectives while failing in others.

To be sure, the United States and the Soviet Union managed to avoid detonating nuclear weapons in anger during four harrowing decades. This happy result could be ascribed to a combination of factors, including deterrence strategy, sane political leadership, effective command-and-control arrangements, reliable and trustworthy lines of communication, the reassurance of arms control accords, and perhaps divine intervention or plain dumb luck. Separating these factors and rank ordering them has been a fruitless exercise. It seems self-evident, however, that treaties and CBMs offering intrusive monitoring arrangements, agreed-upon and verifiable reductions in nuclear forces, prior notifications of missile flight tests, and agreed-upon procedures to avoid dangerous military practices contributed to the avoidance of a nuclear war and the reduction of the risks of a nuclear arms competition. Also central to the achievement of these objectives were tacit and formal agreements not to change the status quo in sensitive areas by means of force and a common understanding not to engage in nuclear brinksmanship, especially in each other's backyard. These key elements of avoiding direct conflict and the use of nuclear weapons took decades to put into place, with impetus provided by close calls along the way.

Alongside these successes, arms control treaties and CBMs did not minimize the costs of the competition. While the military utility of nuclear weapons remained unproven during the Cold War, Washington and Moscow presumed the political utility of nuclear weapons to be high. Both capitals jockeyed for advantage —or at least to avoid being placed at a disadvantage—resulting in a costly, closed-loop competition over offensive nuclear forces. Moreover, the buildup of nuclear weapon capabilities did not permit cost savings on conventional forces. Both the United States and the Soviet Union temporarily flirted with this notion, only to reject it as unfeasible and unwise.

The astounding growth of U.S. and Soviet nuclear stockpiles and deployed forces, as well as the mutual embrace of extensive nuclear targeting doctrines, meant that any breakdown in deterrence could result in open-ended and long-lasting destruction—unless concerted efforts by political leaders could be applied to severely limit the number of detonations. Huge nuclear arsenals were also of little help in preventing proxy wars that moved the Cold War competition to faraway places in Africa, Indochina, and Afghanistan. Thus, while treaties and CBMs helped the superpowers to avoid a central strategic conflict, they had little effect in dampening the search for relative geopolitical advantage—an impulse that generated much loss of blood and treasure.

Treaties and CBMs have been useful tools for political leaders in the Middle East, Latin America, and the U.S.-Soviet relationship who have wished to improve bilateral ties, modulate competition, and assist in the conflict management and resolution process. For example, when Chilean officials decided to invest government pension funds in the Argentine power grid, Chile's air force needed to rethink contingency planning. In contrast, CBMs have been hollow instruments in South Asia, with the exception of a World Bank–brokered accord to share Himalayan waters after partition. India and Pakistan have negotiated many CBMs to govern military-to-military interactions, but none have been faithfully implemented. Most were negotiated in the aftermath of crises at the encouragement of outside powers. In other words, successful treaties and CBMs require the prior intent of political leaders to engage in mutual restraint and avoid deadly conflict and dangerous military practices. Political leaders can also utilize treaties and CBMs to signal an intent to chart a new course and to catalyze even more far-reaching changes in policy, as was the case in the Intermediate-Range Nuclear Forces (INF) Treaty signed by Ronald Reagan and Mikhail Gorbachev.

Arms control agreements became a central feature of foreign relations during the Cold War, when the threat of nuclear war between two nuclear superpowers locked in strategic confrontation and intense political hostility was the greatest risk and the prevailing concern. U.S. and Soviet leaders came to rely on an arms control process to reduce the risk of nuclear weapons use, to control escalation, and to reassure domestic publics and allies. Both U.S. and Soviet leaders understood that even if a deliberate attack might be implausible, nuclear war could result from other causes, such as crisis instability arising from perceptions of vulnerability to preemptive attack and escalation from conventional conflicts, or as a consequence of unauthorized or accidental use of nuclear weapons. To diminish these risks, a construct of stable nuclear deterrence was built around mutual acceptance of each other's ability to retaliate from an attack with devastating force.

Arms control treaties were intended as a complement to, rather than a substitute for, military capabilities. Arms control was also viewed as a means of reducing or limiting the threat from adversaries and of reducing dangers that would result if one were to rely exclusively on military preparedness to prevent nuclear war. As succinctly stated by William Perry, former secretary of defense, arms control became a form of "defense by other means."[2]

PUBLIC DEBATES OVER ARMS CONTROL DURING THE COLD WAR

The analytical and philosophical underpinnings of arms control were matters of contention throughout the Cold War. Debates over the value of these control mechanisms were rooted, in part, in fundamentally different assumptions about human nature and the international system. Critics questioned the wisdom of negotiating with potential adversaries arms control agreements that might limit preparedness and therefore be incompatible with national security. They also believed that the perceived value of arms control accords was ephemeral at best and that accords were breached when states concluded that the benefit of cheating exceeded the cost of maintaining strict compliance. Debates over the value of these control mechanisms also extended to their utility for alliance management and reassurance. Critics argued that treaties offered a false sense of security and that strong leadership and articulation of the threat could better serve alliance management. They questioned the extent to which agreements were truly verifiable, denigrating the value of the transparency that flowed from many treaty provisions, particularly the insight and understanding gained about the military programs and deployments from mandatory on-site inspections. In this view, arms control agreements were false alternatives, rather than complements to national defense.

These arguments against an arms control process were unnerving to domestic and allied audiences, particularly at dangerous passages during the Cold War. The potential loss of control over nuclear arsenals during crises was a recurring nightmare. Not surprisingly, the most tense periods of the Cold War were followed by the most substantive accords. Supporters argued that arms control was not an end in itself, nor a moral good to be pursued for its own sake, but rather an integral part of an overall national strategy to enhance international stability and national security. For foreign and domestic audiences, arms control was a highly valued process as well as a preferred outcome. Even when negotiations appeared stuck, dialogue helped to pave the way for rapid agreement when the political climate changed. Arms control discussions kept communication channels open, offering the prospect of cooperation as an alternative to confrontation.

When the arms control process began, important constituencies in the United States and the Soviet Union were strongly opposed.

Dialogue helped to sensitize officials in both countries to each other's security concerns. In the Soviet Union dialogue allowed civilian officials into a domain previously reserved for military leaders. In the United States, military leaders became well versed in arms control issues—a helpful process that cannot be quantified and was often underestimated. While arms control agreements by and large have been the product of favorable political circumstances rather than the reason for political accommodation, arms control accords certainly reinforced positive developments and braked negative trends in bilateral relations.

BILATERAL ARMS CONTROL TREATIES

Bilateral arms control agreements between the United States and the Soviet Union were in many ways "unnatural acts."[3] The notion of limiting the most powerful weapons in one's arsenal—in terms of both military effectiveness and political salience—certainly ran counter to intuition and history. Yet the destructive power of these weapons generated domestic and international demand for controls, against both nuclear proliferation and unrestrained superpower competition that could prompt a nuclear confrontation. Even more counterintuitive was the conclusion reached in the late 1960s by U.S. officials, affirmed by their Soviet counterparts in the early 1970s, that nuclear safety and reassurance required severe limits on defenses and lax constraints on offenses.

The first strategic arms limitation accord and the accompanying Antiballistic Missile (ABM) Treaty enshrined the Cold War construct that stability and safety resided in assured retaliatory capabilities. These accords were negotiated and extravagantly praised by the Nixon administration, a team led by a president with strongly anticommunist credentials. SALT I and the ABM Treaty received overwhelming support in the U.S. Congress. Public

opinion in the United States, the Soviet Union, and allied countries reacted with relief that the nuclear arms race was presumably contained and that the two nuclear superpowers were in general concert on these matters. A few voices in the wilderness argued that the SALT I accords did the right thing—limitations of offenses—badly, and the wrong thing—constraints on defenses—all too well.[4] But most strategic analysts went along with the twin foundations of strategic arms limitation.

Disaffection grew quickly, however, fueled by the pace of Soviet strategic modernization programs permitted under SALT I, the Kremlin's unabated jockeying for advantage in distant Cold War localities, and the suspect credentials of a Democratic administration that appeared to be not vigilant enough in combating communism. The overly optimistic reviews and interpretations of SALT I by the Nixon administration, combined with the Kremlin's strategic overreaching, prompted a predictable backlash. The second strategic arms limitation treaty negotiated by a sclerotic Politburo and the Carter administration failed to be ratified. The Kremlin's invasion of Afghanistan struck the final blow to SALT. By the early 1980s, the reassurance blanket that strategic arms control was supposed to offer lay in tatters.

With SALT mortally wounded, what would follow? In the first few years of the Reagan administration, the answer seemed to be a joint U.S.-Soviet nuclear arms buildup and a powerful new U.S. embrace of strategic defenses. The main theater of jousting was, as usual, Europe, where either the Soviet gambit of deploying medium-range, nuclear-tipped missiles would be called and raised by NATO or a new accord would offer a far different solution. The Cold War nuclear stakes were extremely high, since the cohesion of the NATO alliance hung in the balance. Popular movements to freeze nuclear developments and to combat President Reagan's Strategic Defense Initiative grew in the United States and in Western Europe to levels reminiscent of "ban-the-bomb" demonstrations in the 1950s and early 1960s against atmospheric nuclear testing.

The extraordinary juxtaposition of Ronald Reagan and Mikhail Gorbachev—two anti-nuclear risk takers and outside-the-box thinkers —resolved these crises in reassuring ways. Both leaders believed that control arrangements for nuclear dangers were insufficient and that more proactive and ambitious efforts were needed. Under their aegis, the enterprise of arms control was replaced with strategic arms reductions: SALT was superseded by START. Entire categories of nuclear weapon deployments were removed from the European theater, much to the relief of allied publics and the consternation of nuclear strategists.

With improved relations between the two nuclear superpowers and dramatic reductions in deployed nuclear forces, the perceived need for missile defenses was greatly diminished. While President Reagan's commitment to a defensive shield never wavered, technical constraints and cost factors eventually brought these plans to earth. The impenetrable shield in space that Reagan sought evolved into a modest, ground-based defense against very limited attacks under Presidents Bush and Clinton.

Two strategic arms reduction treaties were negotiated in the last decade of the Cold War. This ambitious agenda—reducing deployments by almost 70 percent from Cold War peaks— required heroic efforts at implementation, since entry into force of these accords would need to take place amid wholesale changes wrought by the demise of the Soviet Union and the Warsaw Pact. Implementation of the first START accord was much delayed, since the Kremlin conditioned this on the acceptance of permanent nonnuclear status by successor states of the Soviet Union.

Just as SALT was replaced by START, now START would become supplemented, if not eclipsed, by a host of cooperative threat reduction initiatives. Government officials, military leaders, and nuclear laboratory experts from the United States and Russia worked together

in extraordinary ways to guard against "loose nukes," to control fissile material, and to provide constructive tasks for skilled workers at impoverished nuclear, chemical, and biological institutes. With Russia in steep decline, an enterprise long fixated on the numbers of deployed nuclear weapons took on a far more complex shape. Cooperative threat reduction initiatives—safeguarding weapons and dangerous material within a weakened Russia— made strategic arms reductions seem simple in comparison. To complicate matters further, the end of the Cold War—unlike the end of World War II—did not prompt a Marshall Plan–like effort to deal with the dangers generated from a vanquished foe.

With the expansion of beneficial cooperative threat reduction initiatives in the 1990s, new linkages between treaties and confidence-building measures became apparent. Cold War treaties, in effect, became the core constructs around which inventive threat reduction programs were implemented. The existence of outdated treaties was reassuring to Russia, even though the equality upon which they were predicated was now a fiction. If the treaties were to be cast aside, cooperative threat reduction initiatives would be placed at risk, with far-reaching potential consequences for proliferation.

The START process, like SALT, initially gathered strong domestic and international support. Treaty-mandated reductions properly symbolized effective management of bloated Cold War nuclear arsenals. The intrusive monitoring provisions embedded in treaties were also reassuring, with respect to both verifying compliance and ensuring close cooperation on nuclear matters. Agreed-upon strategic arms reductions also fulfilled the central provision of the Nuclear Nonproliferation Treaty, which linked continued restraint in acquiring these weapons with the contraction of existing arsenals. In 1995 the NPT was extended indefinitely, an action predicated in part on the promise of the successful conclusion of a comprehensive nuclear test ban. By mid-decade, control and management regimes for nuclear weapons appeared to be strong.

These appearances were deceiving. The Comprehensive Test Ban Treaty (CTBT), banning all nuclear weapon tests, was negotiated in 1996, but with a provision making its entry into force problematic. Likewise, the formal entry into force of the second strategic arms reduction treaty (START II) remains linked with the future of the ABM Treaty. For the latter half of the 1990s, executive leadership in the United States and Russia was distracted and weak, unable to develop or "sell" compromise solutions to resolve nullifying reservations to treaty ratification. At the same time, NATO expansion and severe U.S.-Russian differences over the U.S. use of force against Iraq and the former Yugoslavia compounded distrust and difficulties in arms control.

Domestic divisions on nuclear issues in the United States reached a low point with the summary rejection by Senate Republicans of the CTBT in 1999. Not since the Treaty of Versailles had the Senate rejected an agreement so widely valued by the international community. Most countries were genuinely surprised by the Senate's decision, since it was widely presumed that the United States had more to gain under the CTBT than the other nuclear weapon states, whose "stockpile stewardship" programs were technically inferior and less well funded. U.S. allies—nuclear as well as nonnuclear—who strongly supported the CTBT's entry into force were left to puzzle over the future of nuclear control regimes and the implications of the breakdown of bipartisanship on nuclear treaties.

The CTBT vote reflected a deep domestic divide over the future role of nuclear weapons in U.S. defense posture, extremely poor executive-congressional relations, and growing insular and unilateralist tendencies among some members of Congress. The Clinton administration's inclination toward missile defense deployments (even though prompted by and focused on

"rogue state" threats)—and even stronger tendencies in this regard by Republican leaders—compounded not only allied, Russian, and Chinese concerns but also prospective problems for existing arms control and nonproliferation regimes. At the beginning of a new millennium, prospects for successful management strategies to contain or reduce nuclear and proliferation dangers were clouded, at best.

MULTILATERAL ARMS CONTROL

Multilateral nonproliferation and arms control regimes exist for nuclear, chemical, and biological weapons, as well as for missiles capable of delivering such ordnance a distance of 300 or more kilometers. Over the past decade these regimes have enjoyed important successes, but they also face challenges that, if unresolved, will severely erode their effectiveness and long-term viability.

The Nuclear Nonproliferation Treaty is the most widely adhered-to multilateral arms control treaty: all but four states (India, Pakistan, Israel, and Cuba) are parties. The NPT contained a proviso that, twenty-five years after it entered into force, the parties would convene to decide whether to continue it in force indefinitely or for a fixed period or periods of time. In 1995 the NPT was extended indefinitely. The treaty's extension was part of a package of decisions including a set of principles and objectives for nuclear nonproliferation and disarmament, provisions for a strengthened treaty review process, and a resolution focused on the Middle East.

Since 1990, the NPT has been strengthened in a number of ways: South Africa dismantled nuclear weapons that it had produced, abandoning its nuclear weapon program and joining the NPT; France and China, which for many years had remained outside the treaty, became parties; Argentina and Brazil, which had incipient nuclear weapon programs under way, terminated them and joined the treaty;

and Belarus, Kazakhstan, and Ukraine relinquished control of nuclear weapons left on their territory in the wake of the dissolution of the Soviet Union, transferring them to the Russian Federation and adhering to the NPT. Thus, over the past decade, a proliferator rolled back its program, incipient proliferators abandoned their activities, states instantly endowed with nuclear weapons relinquished them, and the two remaining acknowledged nuclear weapon states joined the treaty.

Following Iraq's defeat in the 1991 Gulf War, the United Nations Security Council mandated the destruction or removal of all of Iraq's weapons of mass destruction capabilities. Moreover, by asserting in 1992 that "the proliferation of all weapons of mass destruction constitutes a threat to international peace and security," the president of the Security Council formally linked compliance with nonproliferation treaties. Based on the discovery of an extensive clandestine nuclear weapon program in Iraq, the Board of Governors of the International Atomic Energy Agency (IAEA) agreed to a series of measures to strengthen nuclear safeguards through increased access to information and increased physical access to facilities and sites.

Nuclear weapon–free zones are an important part of the nonproliferation regime. Four zones now exist covering more than one hundred states in Latin America, the South Pacific, Africa, and Southeast Asia. All but the African zone have entered into force. Nuclear weapon–free zone treaties preclude nuclear weapon states placing nuclear weapons on the territory of states within the zone. Each treaty contains protocols binding states outside the region to respect zonal denuclearization and committing nuclear weapon states not to use or threaten to use nuclear force against any party to the treaty—"negative security assurances." With the exception of the signatories to the Southeast Asian treaty, all of the nuclear weapon states have signed the relevant protocols of regional nuclear weapon–free zones.

The Chemical Weapons Convention, which entered into force in 1997, established a legally binding standard outlawing acquisition, possession, or use of chemical weapons. The CWC incorporated a comprehensive and intrusive verification system, including challenge on-site inspections. As of May 2001, 174 states had signed the CWC and 143 had ratified it. Implementation is entrusted to the Organization for the Prohibition of Chemical Weapons, which has a staff of five hundred, including two hundred inspectors. Inspections of declared former chemical weapon production facilities, chemical munitions plants, and other industrial sites have been taking place on a steady basis since 1997.[5]

The Biological Weapons Convention, like the CWC, is both a nonproliferation and a disarmament treaty, requiring parties not to develop, stockpile, or acquire biological agents other than for peaceful purposes, nor weapons or their means of delivery. Approximately 140 states have ratified the convention; 18 have signed but not ratified. At the time of the BWC's negotiation, there was little concern about the potential military utility of proliferation of biological weapons. As a result, the BWC—unlike the Chemical Weapons Convention—does not have formal verification arrangements, relying instead on consultation and cooperation to resolve problems that arise. Complaints of noncompliance also can be lodged with the UN Security Council. Beginning in the mid-1980s, growing concern with the prospect of biological warfare prompted international efforts to increase transparency and enhance confidence in treaty compliance. Revelations about the extensive biological weapon program in Iraq and growing concern about military or terrorist use of biological agents have prompted efforts to negotiate a formal verification protocol for the BWC. To date, no agreement has been reached.

The CWC, the BWC, and the NPT have the potential to become effective cornerstones of interlocking arms control, disarmament, and nonproliferation regimes. Each treaty regime, however, suffers from weaknesses that can severely erode effectiveness. These regimes will become either stronger or less reliable, depending on how each regime handles issues of universality of membership, implementation, verification, and cases of noncompliance.

Universality

None of the three core multilateral treaties enjoys universal adherence. The NPT lacks only four states, but one of the nonparticipating states, India, which is the largest democracy in the world, has crusaded against the NPT as a discriminatory treaty that fails to move the world toward nuclear disarmament. India conducted a series of nuclear tests in 1998 and declared itself a nuclear state, placing the NPT under significant duress and raising a virtually insuperable barrier to the treaty's universalization. Pakistan followed India's example. Few parties to the NPT would be willing to amend the treaty to formalize nuclear weapon status for India and Pakistan, and both states are highly unlikely to relinquish their nuclear weapons and join the treaty as nonnuclear weapon states. Israel maintains an ambiguous nuclear weapon status and will not join the NPT in the absence of an enduring regional peace. Cuba is the only other nonparty, but it is bound by the Latin American Nuclear Weapon Free Zone, which contains comparable nonproliferation undertakings.

The CWC is considerably further away from universal membership than the NPT. Key states in the Middle East, including Syria, Egypt, Libya, and Iraq, are withholding participation in the absence of Israeli membership in NPT. Israel signed but has not ratified the CWC. In the case of the BWC, Israel is the only significant nonsignatory, although several states parties, including North Korea, Iraq, Iran, and Libya, are suspected of maintaining covert biological weapon programs. The extent of treaty nonuniversality is important, not only for its impact on the strength of the underlying norm, but also for future prospects for collective responses to treaty violations.

Implementation

A second critical factor in the future health of multilateral regimes relates to how states parties implement treaty provisions. The CWC contains highly intrusive monitoring provisions, but these already have been weakened by the treaty's implementing body—at the insistence of a diverse group of states, including Israel, Japan, Germany, China, Russia, Iran, and the United States. The motivations of these states vary greatly. Some may wish to protect covert weapons programs; others appear intent on protecting commercial trade secrets. Conditions weakening the CWC were attached to the U.S. resolution of ratification at the behest of conservative senators concerned about the risk of commercial espionage during international inspections. In addition, a number of crucial states have been slow to implement treaty obligations such as the submission of declarations regarding chemical industry facilities.

Implementation concerns for the NPT are also noteworthy. States parties are supposed to conclude safeguards agreements (which provide assurances that states are not using nuclear power programs for military purposes) within eighteen months of joining the NPT. More than fifty states have yet to do so. The most important case of delay was that of North Korea, where seven years elapsed between joining the NPT and concluding a safeguards agreement. The subsequent confrontation over the accuracy and completeness of North Korea's declared nuclear materials inventory led to a crisis over how to manage and respond to situations of noncompliance.

Another critical implementation issue relates to the NPT's provisions for peaceful nuclear cooperation, including the right of all parties to develop nuclear energy for peaceful purposes as well as the right to participate in the fullest possible exchange of equipment, materials, and information. At the same time, the treaty obliges nuclear weapon states not to assist nonnuclear weapon states in any way to manufacture or otherwise acquire nuclear weapons. The tensions arising from these cross-cutting obligations are most evident in the case of Iran, an oil-rich country with an extensive interest in the infrastructure and skills associated with nuclear technology. U.S. officials contend that Iran has been engaged in a clandestine nuclear weapon program and Washington has sought to persuade others not to engage in nuclear cooperation with Tehran. The Iranian government claims it is being denied treaty-based rights to peaceful nuclear cooperation while being in full compliance with NPT obligations. The Iranian case highlights the limitations of the export control regimes developed in support of nonproliferation.

The most serious implementation question for many nonnuclear weapon states concerns the NPT requirement that nuclear weapon states pursue nuclear disarmament in good faith. Many nonnuclear weapon states have long contended that the NPT must not establish a permanent two-class system of states, those with and those without nuclear weapons. In the post–Cold War period, demands for more progress toward nuclear disarmament have been increasing and have gained broader-based support, including support from some U.S. allies. The indefinite extension of the NPT was predicated on renewed efforts toward disarmament and on a pledge by the nuclear weapon states to conclude negotiations for the Comprehensive Test Ban Treaty.

The implementation of multilateral agreements can be affected by the state of play of key bilateral treaties. For instance, nuclear weapon states agree that the NPT requires good-faith efforts toward nuclear disarmament and contend that much progress was made in this regard, especially during the final phase of the Cold War. Subsequently, however, U.S.-Russian treaties have been weakened, the CTBT has been rejected by the U.S. Senate, and negotiations have yet to begin on a verifiable fissile material cutoff treaty (FMCT). The FMCT, another essential building block for nuclear control, requires states to terminate any further production of such material for weapons purposes and to ensure that any future production for peaceful purposes will be under international safeguards.

Uncertainties over the START process, renewed movement in the United States for missile defenses, a badly wounded CTBT, and continued delay on the cutoff treaty could have grave consequences for the NPT's long-term viability. The loosening of U.S. and Russian controls on nuclear forces is likely to spill over to nonproliferation treaties. Strained U.S.-Russian and U.S.-Chinese relations also spell trouble for UN Security Council efforts to control proliferation. With the weakening of treaties and the worsening of proliferation concerns, other states are more likely to hedge their bets against a more uncertain future with program initiatives for weapons of mass destruction.

Verification

Verification arrangements for the NPT have been strengthened in the wake of the belated discovery of Iraq's weapons of mass destruction (WMD) programs.[6] The CWC contains expansive monitoring provisions, but, as noted, implementation decisions have had a weakening effect. It is very difficult to negotiate effective monitoring arrangements for the Biological Weapons Convention, since many biotechnology and pharmaceutical companies routinely grow large quantities of dangerous pathogens to produce vaccines and treatments for disease. Many of these firms currently oppose intrusive inspections to protect trade secrets. Since 1994, a group of states has been trying unsuccessfully to negotiate a protocol containing legally binding measures to strengthen confidence in compliance with the BWC and to deter violations. There is general awareness that arms control measures alone are unlikely to resolve the problem of the proliferation of biological weapons. While it is important to strengthen the norm of nonproliferation and nonuse, this is a realm in which passive and active defense measures are increasingly relevant.[7]

Noncompliance

Perhaps the most telling indicator of the future effectiveness of multilateral treaties is how states deal with cases of probable or confirmed noncompliance. Nonproliferation and arms control treaties and regimes are judged in the final analysis by the degree to which they meet the security expectations of their parties. In an imperfect world, rule bending and outright forms of noncompliance will occur. How such incidents are dealt with will determine whether treaties succeed or fail as control mechanisms. Administrative or technical noncompliance—such as the U.S. failure to submit declarations required by the CWC on a timely basis, or the failure of a number of states that have no nuclear activity to complete safeguards agreements—weakens but does not disable treaty regimes.

The most serious tests of treaties are cases of substantial noncompliance, such as North Korea's refusal in 1993 to allow IAEA inspectors access to suspect sites not declared by Korean authorities; Iraq's extensive cheating on its NPT, CWC, and BWC obligations by pursuing clandestine weapons development programs; and substantial Soviet noncompliance with the BWC over an extended period of time. Noncompliance of this magnitude nullifies the security objectives sought by other members, undermines confidence in the credibility of the regime, and raises the prospect of countermeasures, including efforts to acquire the very weapons the regime sought to foreclose.

The international community's collective response to Iraq's aggression against Kuwait, followed by Security Council resolutions to eliminate Iraq's weapons of mass destruction and medium-range missile delivery programs, were firm and wide ranging. If properly implemented and accepted by Iraqi authorities, this response would have built confidence in the reliability of arms control and nonproliferation treaties and regimes. The Security Council's actions immediately after the Gulf War reflected the cohesion of its five permanent members (P-5), upon which the effectiveness of collective security measures ultimately rests. The subsequent assertion by the president of the Security Council that proliferation of any kind constituted a threat to international peace and security gave added assurance of Security Council determination to confront and take appropriate measures in the case of violations of undertakings.[8]

With the passage of time, controls on Iraq's WMD programs have eroded badly. Saddam Hussein has persistently refused to fully comply with Security Council resolutions, and the unified front of the permanent members of the UN Security Council has splintered. The United Nations has rejected Iraqi disclosures as incomplete and inadequate. Nine years after the Security Council passed Resolution 687 in 1991, which mandated destroying, removing, or rendering harmless these weapons of mass destruction, sanctions had not brought about Iraqi acquiescence. It was still impossible to certify that all materials and facilities had been declared and destroyed. The inspection regime (UNSCOM) imposed on Iraq by the United Nations ceased its operations in 1998 due to lack of Iraqi cooperation, and its successor (UNMOVIC) is still unable to operate in Iraq, not least because of continued squabbling among the P-5 over how sanctions are to be managed. Just as the International Control Commissions failed to stop German rearmament after World War I, so, too, international efforts to control Iraqi WMD programs are in danger of losing ground.

The international community also reacted more tentatively to the IAEA's notification to the Security Council in 1993 of North Korea's refusal to comply with a demand to permit a special inspection of undeclared sites. China would not agree to the application of collective sanctions on North Korea, and the Security Council limited itself to supporting U.S. bilateral negotiations to bring North Korea into full compliance with its commitments under the NPT. The United States subsequently negotiated an Agreed Framework substituting light-water reactors for Korea's more proliferation-oriented gas graphite reactors, which would be shut down, monitored, and ultimately dismantled.

These developments underscore the increasingly fragile nature of nonproliferation regimes at a time when bilateral accords are under great stress. If states cannot enforce the cooperative security regimes they have constructed to reduce and eliminate threatening weapons, then recourse to more traditional approaches—self-reliance, acquisition of weapons to counter severe threats, and reliance on alliance structures—will once again curtail the scope of international control regimes.

Thus, despite great advances in monitoring technologies and greater acceptance of intrusive verification provisions, multilateral control mechanisms are at increased risk owing to problems of universality, implementation, verification, and compliance. The multiple weaknesses of treaty regimes, and deep domestic divisions in the United States over what strengthening measures to adopt, make remedial steps difficult.

CONFIDENCE-BUILDING MEASURES

The regional adaptation and extension of confidence-building measures that were heavily developed for Central Europe is one of the most useful and poorly appreciated outgrowths of the Cold War.[9] Forged through the crucible of Berlin crises and the German divide, CBMs focused initially on arrangements to provide "credible evidence of the absence of feared threats."[10] Crises provided the impetus

for CBMs as well as treaties. For example, the Cuban missile crisis helped generate both the first nuclear control accord, the Limited Test Ban Treaty, as well as the first significant CBM, the Hotline between U.S. and Soviet leaders.

Other military-to-military arrangements followed, including CBMs to avoid dangerous military practices and incidents at sea. Prior notifications of military exercises were agreed upon and later developed to include provisions for observers. The Hotline was modernized, and, at the last stage of the Cold War, an extraordinarily intrusive cooperative aerial monitoring regime was negotiated.

CBMs between NATO and the Warsaw Pact were by no means limited to military measures. On the contrary, progress in reducing tensions and furthering détente was consciously pursued in crosscutting ways, as evidenced by the work of the Conference on Security and Cooperation in Europe (CSCE), now the Organization for Security and Cooperation in Europe (OSCE). CBM accords beginning at Helsinki in 1975 were expressly designed to cover an expansive waterfront. One "basket" of measures covered military/security issues; a second "basket" dealt with cooperation in economics, science, technology, and the environment; and a third "basket" stipulated a code of conduct for humanitarian issues.[11]

The import of these CBMs was not to constrain military capabilities, although the beginnings of a constraint regime were evident in required prenotifications of major European military exercises. Instead, most of the military-related CBMs were crafted to provide greater transparency and predictability, as well as to create more effective channels of communication for crisis prevention and de-escalation. Codes of conduct for armed forces were written to reduce many instances of dangerous brinksmanship. The exchange of observers at military exercises, prior notification of missile flight tests, and other potentially troubling military activities helped states "read" each other's intentions better, distinguishing between routine military practices and worri-some ones.

Implementation of CBMs in the military/security sphere during the Cold War was gen-erally good, with one notable lapse along the Russian-Polish border in 1980–81, when the Kremlin utilized large-scale military exercises to intimidate the Solidarity movement. While CBM accords did not prevent every dangerous military activity in the later decades of the Cold War, military establishments became active sup-porters of these procedures, which survived serious downturns in U.S.-Soviet relations.

In contrast, the humanitarian measures were poorly implemented, becoming yardsticks for measuring how far Warsaw Pact governments had fallen short of their commitments. The interchanges in economics and other disciplines were widely criticized in some Western circles, but in retrospect, these appear to have had a profound impact on the opening of commu-nist societies. Far from being a "sellout" of Western values and security, the Helsinki pro-cess helped pave the way for the peaceful trans-formation of Europe, formally institutional-ized as the OSCE in 1994.

CBMs naturally complemented arms con-trol during the Cold War. Engagement no less than containment won this contest, and CBMs moved engagement beyond the narrow confines of negotiators and government officials. Arms control enshrined deterrence through assured retaliatory capabilities; CBM accords comple-mented deterrence by providing much-needed reassurance to domestic audiences and allies. Successes in arms control facilitated more am-bitious CBM accords; rough stretches in treaty negotiations made CBMs all the more desir-able to reassure domestic and allied audiences.

With the end of the Cold War, interest in CBMs grew in many other regions, prompted in part by their evident utility in bridging the European divide. Greater interest in CBMs was also due to the fluidity of post–Cold War circumstances, marked by the juxtaposition of centrifugal forces alongside integrative trends

in economics and communications. CBMs like those implemented in Europe, suitably adapted to meet regional conditions, seemed to offer tools for national leaders interested in consolidating gains while providing buffers against losses in changing post–Cold War circumstances.

The utilization of CBMs varied greatly from one region to the next.[12] In the southern cone of Latin America, Argentina, Brazil, and Chile made great strides in securing gains and set-ting aside lingering security concerns by focus-ing on measures to integrate their economies. At the same time, Argentine and Brazilian leaders alleviated concerns over secret nuclear programs by making them transparent. Suc-cessful economic interactions facilitated joint military exercises.

In the Middle East, CBMs were almost entirely restricted to military arrangements, facilitating troop disengagement agreements, and peacemaking. Troop disengagement ac-cords between Israel and Egypt were facili-tated by CBMs, including aerial observation carried out by the United States to confirm declarations relating to the status of forces on both sides. While disengagement accords even-tually led to a treaty of peace, military CBMs did not extend to economic and cultural con-tacts beyond a very modest scale. The result-ing "cold peace" between Israel and Egypt has been criticized in both countries, but it is far superior to "hot wars."

In South Asia, the embrace of CBMs has been mostly declaratory and not substantive. Direct economic linkages remain limited, al-though indirect trade through Gulf states is far more substantial. CBMs in the military sphere have been dubbed "competition-building measures," with both India and Pakistan doing little to increase trust. For example, both coun-tries have agreed to exchange lists of nuclear facilities, but neither believes these annual lists are complete. Very few or none of the key ele-ments for nuclear risk reduction in the U.S.-Soviet experience, such as trustworthy lines of communication, are now in place between India and Pakistan. The growing dangers posed by nuclear and missile programs in close proximity have not yet prompted a serious reconsideration of the utility of CBMs that are properly implemented. In parts of Africa, Central Asia, and Southeast Asia, the utilization of CBMs has been limited and episodic.

THE WAY AHEAD

The last decade of the twentieth century, which started with major treaty success stories and ended with treaties unraveling on many fronts, offers very divergent paths for the future. One path is largely defined by the continued unraveling of existing treaty regimes; the other path involves adaptation and strengthening of these control arrangements. In the first instance, the salience of weapons of mass destruction and their delivery vehicles would grow, both because control regimes would be widely perceived to be weaker reeds and because new states would hedge their bets against a more uncertain future with WMD programs. Under this scenario, alliance and regional security arrangements would become increasingly frayed, giving further impetus to weapons of mass destruction and missile programs.

Major stress fractures in control regimes in the Middle East and South Asia are of growing concern, while the situation in Northeast Asia appeared to be moving in more promising directions at the end of the Clinton administration. External CBM initiatives are unlikely to compensate for structural weaknesses within these regions—unless national leaders in tense regions are willing to make concerted efforts to change regional dynamics and unless these efforts have the strong support of the United States, Russia, and China. In the absence of treaty control regimes that include all key regional actors, creative compensatory steps may be required. For example, North Korea's troubling missile programs and uncertain status

with regard to the NPT have been tackled by bilateral initiatives taken by Washington, Seoul, and Moscow. In addition, multilateral economic incentives are being employed to reduce nuclear dangers on the Korean peninsula by means of the Korean Economic Development Organization, a consortium created to finance construction of two nuclear power reactors.

The situation in the Middle East is fluid, with a dramatic downturn in the peace process between Israel and the Palestinian Authority and Syria coinciding with continuing WMD programs in Iran, Iraq, Israel, and other states in the region. CBMs can help states in the region secure progress on the negotiating front but are no substitute for new territorial accords. In South Asia, overt nuclear and missile programs have heightened insecurity. The level of violence between India and Pakistan over disputed Kashmir has noticeably increased since the May 1998 nuclear tests. Indian and Pakistani adherence to the CTBT and constructive involvement in the negotiation of a fissile material cutoff treaty would serve to reinforce global regimes, but progress on both fronts remains problematic. Regional agreements including China offer creative ways to reduce dangers emanating from South Asian nuclear and missile programs, but Beijing appears uninterested in triangular talks or bilateral discussions that engage India as an equal. After Pakistan and India's brief but intense war in 1999 over the heights dividing Kashmir, many impediments stand in the way of negotiating new CBM accords in South Asia.

The domestic U.S. debate over the continued value of treaties rooted in the Cold War has disturbed foreign audiences. For most of the international community, treaties constitute essential norms and management tools. One paramount goal of these arrangements is to retard further proliferation that creates destabilizing chain reactions. With the further demise of treaties, U.S.-Russian and U.S.-Chinese cooperation is likely to decrease, including cooperation on the toughest proliferation cases.

As a result, the isolation of those few states that remain outside established norms would become harder, as would efforts to build coalitions against states that cheat from within.

It is far from clear what control arrangements critics would construct in lieu of the accords they oppose. Nor is it likely that critics would garner more than grudging international acknowledgment for their preferred remedies, such as the deployment of unconstrained national and theater missile defenses. The deployment of these defenses outside treaty frameworks is likely to increase the distance between the United States and its allies in Europe and Asia. Critics of outdated bilateral treaties have not explained how abrogation would permit the containment of damage to multilateral accords such as the NPT, the CWC, or the BWC. Nor is it clear how reassurance can be maintained—through CBMs or unilateral steps—when treaties are discarded.

At issue are (1) the confidence level states have in existing treaty regimes; (2) whether these regimes will be strengthened or weakened in the future; and (3) how the international community deals with states that refuse to join or that seek to undermine regimes from within. Unratified treaties such as the CTBT pose another set of questions. Will they unravel or will signatories continue to respect their terms? Will countries work together to set up an international monitoring system? Or will weapons development and testing resume, and if so, will there be a chain reaction of testing, resulting in greater salience of and reliance on nuclear weapons in international relations?

Yet another set of questions relates to the uncertain state of bilateral strategic arms reductions and the ABM Treaty. Can new political leaders in the United States and Russia reach an accommodation that would permit treaty-mandated reductions to proceed along with agreed modifications of the ABM Treaty? Or will decisions regarding strategic offensive and defensive forces henceforth proceed mostly outside treaty frameworks? What will be the net effects of these decisions on alliance relations, regional security, and the salience of nuclear weapons on the international system?

One key indicator of the future path for arms control treaties is the status of the NPT. The realist view holds that states belong to the NPT for reasons of self-interest, regardless of whether nuclear weapons states adhere to bilateral accords reducing their arsenals. Treaty supporters argue that the renewed viability of the NPT requires continued, cooperative contraction of existing nuclear arsenals. These contending arguments will be put to the test if U.S.-Russian relations trend downward as bilateral treaties unravel. The NPT is also likely to be severely impacted if nuclear testing resumes in the wake of the CTBT's defeat by Senate Republicans.

The demise of the NPT could take various forms: future review conferences of the NPT could break down in controversy; efforts could be made to assert new conditions for continued adherence to the NPT by selected nonnuclear weapon states; states parties could refrain from endorsing strengthening measures for treaty compliance; more states could hedge their bets by readying nuclear options while remaining in the treaty regime; or states could formally withdraw from the NPT. The implications of the NPT's weakening or demise for national security, regional stability, and international control would be severe.

A second key indicator of the health of arms control regimes in the next decade is whether new administrations in the United States and Russia can adapt and affirm compacts governing strategic offensive and defensive forces. The initial arms control compacts codifying huge nuclear arsenals and placing heavy constraints on missile defenses have been periodically updated, but future adaptation is questionable as bipartisan support for the ABM Treaty erodes in the United States. Some hope for a "grand bargain" between the United States and Russia codifying still deeper reductions in nuclear forces and further relaxation of the ABM

Treaty to permit limited national and upgraded theater missile defenses; others strenuously oppose treating Russia as an equal or constraining defenses in any way.

The transition toward deeper cuts in nuclear forces would be welcomed by U.S. allies and by the international community; the transition toward deployed missile defenses would be greeted with considerable unease, since stability during the Cold War—a period of strenuous controls over missile proliferation—has been widely equated with the absence of missile defenses. In contrast, missile proliferation has been a troubling characteristic of the post–Cold War period, contributing to a renewed interest in missile defense deployments.

What would be the overall impact of missile defenses on regional stability and alliance relations? And what are the likely consequences for regional stability and alliance relations if missile defenses are not deployed because of their presumed adverse impacts? While all of the permutations associated with the phased introduction of missile defenses cannot be confidently predicted, several conclusions seem evident. First, contemporary circumstances suggest that a blanket rejection of missile defenses is no longer supportable on substantive grounds or politically sustainable in the United States. Second, the unsettling consequences of introducing missile defenses could be greatly alleviated by the reaffirmation of treaty regimes, rather than by their continued unraveling or rejection. Third, missile defenses could generate significant perturbations in Russia and China, with consequential impacts on regional stability and alliance relations. A transition strategy that emphasizes cooperative threat reduction while introducing missile defenses holds the best prospect for managing downside risks.

A third key health indicator of treaty control regimes over the next decade will be how states deal with the problem of verification and compliance. Current trend lines suggest

growing cause for concern. Their reversal would require, inter alia, improved relations between the United States and Russia as well as China; reconsideration of national policies in the industrial world placing the protection of trade secrets in opposition to intrusive monitoring; and improved regional security prospects for tension-prone regions.

Whether arms control regimes continue to unravel or are reaffirmed, a broader role for confidence-building measures seems likely. CBMs lend themselves to fluid post–Cold War circumstances. They can be applied to complement and strengthen control regimes, or to partially compensate for their breakdown. The post–Cold War period paradoxically has been marked by greater transparency and repeated surprises. National leaders who wish to avail themselves of more information to avoid surprises and to bolster national security in fluid circumstances will increasingly employ CBMs as well as other means to do so.

This discussion makes clear that arms control regimes and CBMs are best understood as adjuncts to broader policies of defense, security, and conflict management. They complement but do not substitute for political and diplomatic initiatives to address underlying differences between rival states. The rise of nonstate political and economic actors as direct participants in internal conflicts only compounds the challenges facing those who would limit the spread of weapons and associated technologies into unstable zones. At the same time, the determined pursuit of control regimes and CBMs can continue in important ways to shape a political climate in which challenges are more likely to be met.

NOTES

1. Thomas C. Schelling and Morton H. Halperin, *Strategy and Arms Control* (New York: Twentieth Century Fund, 1961), 1.

2. Ashton B. Carter and William J. Perry, *Preventive Defense: A New Security Strategy for America* (Washington, D.C.: Brookings Institution, 1999), 75.

3. This term was often used by Paul Warnke, lead U.S. negotiator for the second strategic arms limitation treaty.

4. Donald G. Brennan, *Arms Treaties with Moscow: Unequal Terms Unevenly Applied?* (New York: National Strategy Information Center, 1975), 12.

5. See Johnathan B. Tucker, "Challenges to the Chemical Weapons Convention," in *Nonproliferation Regimes at Risk,* Occasional Paper, no. 1, ed. M. Barletta and A. Sands (Monterey, Calif.: CNS Monterey Institute of International Studies, 1999); and Amy Smithson, *The CBW Chronicle,* http://www.stimson.org/cwc/cbwchron.html, 1999.

6. Progress in bringing the Additional Protocol to Safeguards Agreements that provides for increased information and increased access to national facilities and activities into force has been slow, and few of the most important states have concluded agreements thus far. Differences also exist over whether the Additional Protocol is additive to or more of a partial substitute for existing safeguards system.

7. See Brad Roberts, "Biological Weapons: New Challenges, New Strategies?" in *Nonproliferation Regimes at Risk.*

8. United Nations Security Council, S/PV.3046, January 31, 1992.

9. For basic readings of the European experience, see Jonathan Alford, *Confidence-Building Measures in Europe: The Military Aspects*, Adelphi Paper no. 149 (London: International Institute for Strategic Studies, 1979); Johan Jørgen Holst, "Confidence-Building Measures: A Conceptual Framework," *Survival* 25, no. 1 (January-February 1983): 2–15; and Stephen Larrabee and Dietrich Stobbe, eds., *Confidence-Building Measures in Europe* (New York: Institute for East-West Studies, 1983).

10. Johan Jørgen Holst and Karen Melander, "European Security and Confidence-Building Measures," *Survival* 19, no. 4 (July-August 1977): 147.

11. See, for example, John J. Maresca, *To Helsinki: The Conference on Security and Cooperation in Europe, 1973–1975* (Durham, N.C.: Duke University Press, 1985); and John Borawski, *From the Atlantic to the Urals: Negotiating Arms Control at the Stockholm Conference* (New York: Pergamon-Brassey's, 1988).

12. For a global survey of CBMs, see Michael Krepon, Michael Newbill, Khurshid Khoja, and Jenny S. Drezin, eds., *Global Confidence Building: New Tools for Troubled Regions* (New York: St. Martin's Press, 2000).

37

Humanitarian NGOs in Conflict Intervention

Mary B. Anderson

- As the civil war in Tajikistan came to an end, the international community provided rebuilding assistance, "targeting" this aid to those whose homes suffered the "greatest destruction." This was seen as a critical first step toward restarting the shattered economy and preparing the way for reconciliation between the two groups that had fought. However, because most of the destroyed homes naturally belonged to people on the losing side of the war, the group that won was angered that the international aid community appeared to be one-sided and favoring their "enemies."

- In Liberia, an international nongovernmental organization (NGO) hired local staff to work in its postwar agricultural program. Months later, the NGO learned that all of its sizable staff were from only one of the many ethnic groups it hoped to reach. This had occurred because the group had dominated the local agricultural college for many years. The NGO was intent on hiring people with appropriate qualifications but was not aware that through hiring out of the agricultural college it was engaged in one-sided hiring. Moreover, the NGO's programs reached villages and groups within villages that also were predominantly from the same group as the staff, which conflicted with the NGO's goal to reach out to all ethnic groups.

Aid agencies that work in conflict areas in the early twenty-first century encounter many complexities. As the vignettes above show, international assistance, provided out of humanitarian concern for the people who live where wars rage, often becomes intertwined with the forces that drive the conflicts that prompted the aid in the first place. In the past ten years, an alarming number of conflicts have prompted an increase in the numbers and types of agencies responding to them. During this time, many humanitarian assistance NGOs have been learning to recognize, and respond creatively to, the complexities of conflict.

In the following pages, we explore the experience of international NGO interventions in conflict settings. We begin by describing briefly who the international NGOs are, suggesting a categorization of these according to their stated purposes. We then briefly review NGO relations to conflicts in the past and in recent settings, again suggesting a categorization of NGO approaches to working in conflicts. Finally, we identify some of the changes that have occurred in conflicts in recent years, making the work of humanitarian assistance both more complex and more promising. We also provide examples of how some agencies have learned to design their aid programs to "do no harm" and encourage and support local disengagement from conflict.

WHAT ARE THE NGOS THAT INTERVENE IN CONFLICT SETTINGS?

Nongovernmental organizations are privately organized and privately financed agencies, formed to perform some philanthropic or other worthwhile task in relation to a need that the organizers feel is not adequately addressed by public, governmental, or UN efforts.[1] Churches, civic groups, labor unions, private foundations, and millions of individuals have established organizations that usually operate as tax-free entities to provide support to some group or some cause. While many of these operate within their own societies, many NGOs have defined their mission as working with people in other countries as an alternative or adjunct to official foreign aid.

NGOs based in Europe and North America that provide assistance in the international sphere operate from what can be categorized as basically four different mandates:

- the provision of humanitarian relief to people in emergencies,

- the promotion of long-term social and economic development in countries where poverty persists,
- the promulgation and monitoring of basic human rights, and
- the pursuit of peace, including promotion of the philosophy and techniques of negotiation, mediation, conflict resolution, and nonviolence.

Some agencies define themselves in terms of only one of these four mandates; others operate from several and design their programs to make explicit connections among them.

Increasingly, the international NGO community recognizes the interrelationships of these four mandates. Agencies that are primarily committed to providing emergency relief assistance, whether in wars or so-called natural disasters,[2] now recognize that the ways in which they provide such aid have profound effects on the recipients' potential to achieve future sustainable development.[3] Similarly, evidence is growing that development assistance programs that are planned without recognizing their impact on the environment or on aspects of social systems often contribute to the probability of disasters[4] or wars,[5] or both. Experiences in the former Yugoslavia, Rwanda, and elsewhere seem to indicate that wide publicity about human rights abuses may actually cause some accused groups to harden their positions as "misunderstood" and "maligned" by the international community, thus reinforcing their pursuit of war (and further abuse of human rights). Finally, peace-mandated NGOs that promote negotiated solutions to conflicts in developing countries have a direct impact on the way in which resources are divided and allocated and, thus, on whether and how development may—or may not—occur.

Action in any sphere of international assistance has repercussions in the recipient society going beyond those that were foreseen and intended by the NGO. This is especially true when the NGO comes from another country or culture distant from the recipient community.[6] These sometimes counterintuitive and negative intermandate impacts of international NGO programs are heightened in conflict settings. Thus we need to understand the relationships between NGO humanitarian interventions in conflict settings and the conflicts themselves.

NGO EXPERIENCES IN CONFLICT INTERVENTIONS

Lives have been saved, postconflict development or redevelopment supported, human rights protected, and conflict resolution skills attained through the interventions of NGOs in conflict settings over the years. Many recipients of NGO aid can attest to the fact that this assistance kept their families alive under desperate circumstances, helped them escape from imprisonment or exile, provided the extra support needed to initiate a self-sustaining enterprise, or supported their pursuit of the values of intergroup harmony. Foreign assistance provided through nongovernmental channels has had a profound impact on the lives of many individuals, has helped spawn the creation of many NGOs in the recipient countries, and has prompted the articulation of operational principles adopted by most donor government and UN agencies. NGOs are valued for their clarity of purpose and the humanitarian basis of their operations; for their encouragement of grassroots participation in economic, social, and political life; for their innovation and creativity in solving problems; and for their ability to cross national boundaries with a message of interdependence and humanitarian concern wherever people are in need.

However, the NGO record is not without problems, and, as noted, circumstances of violent conflict add complexities to the operating environment of international NGOs that often distort the impacts of NGOs' interventions. In the next section, we briefly examine the

historical experience of NGOs in conflict settings and, in more specific terms, the experience of NGOs in the wars of the past decade.

NGOS AND CONFLICTS: A BRIEF HISTORY

Some NGOs had their origins in wars, while others found themselves involved in conflict settings even though they had not been formed to address these circumstances. Examples of the former include the Red Cross, Catholic Relief Services, and CARE, each of which was formed during or immediately after a war, explicitly to provide emergency relief to war victims.[7] Others, such as the American Friends Service Committee, which was started by Quakers in 1917, were formed to provide an alternative to military service for young men whose consciences would not permit them to carry weapons or to sit on the sidelines watching the suffering occur. Later, two other "peace churches," the Mennonites (through the Mennonite Central Committee) and the Church of the Brethren (through the Brethren Service Committee), also undertook war-related responses in the same spirit. Even when these three NGOs later began to provide development assistance in Africa, Asia, and Latin America, they made the link between their development efforts and war "prevention," noting that their development motivation was to address some of the economic and social ills that could become seeds of war.

Other NGOs, such as Oxfam, Acción, and Technoserve (to name only a few of the more than one hundred such agencies in the United States alone), which were formed in the 1960s and 1970s to provide emergency disaster relief and/or development assistance in the countries of Africa, Asia, and Latin America, subsequently found themselves operating in simmering (and sometimes boiling) conflict settings.[8] For example, many of the agencies that responded to the Guatemalan earthquake of

1976 stayed in that country to work with peasant groups after the emergency. Similarly, the Ethiopian famines of the early and mid-1980s prompted emergency responses from NGOs, which continued to provide development assistance to rural communities once the famines had ended. In both countries, NGOs that intended to work only on relief or development found themselves operating in an environment where local conflicts affected their staff and their programming. These NGOs soon realized that, in addition to recognizing the impact of these conflicts on their programs, they had to acknowledge the impact of their programs on the conflicts.

Some international NGOs were founded explicitly to support liberation and/or justice movements in other parts of the world, while others provided humanitarian or development assistance to these movements in direct support of the cause they represent.[9] NGO assistance programs in South Africa, Central America, Eritrea, and Biafra (to name a few of the places where these programs have occurred) have not only provided direct assistance to their "clients," but also assumed an advocacy role on behalf of their cause in the political arenas of North America and Europe. That some of these movements were engaged in violent conflict has been accepted by these NGOs as necessary and justified because of the rightness of their cause.

Thus, a great many of the NGOs operating in recent and current conflict settings have had experience in war-related contexts either because they were formed specifically to provide aid to war victims or because they found themselves operating in such contexts as they pursued other mandates. This experience shapes the work of NGOs in two important ways.

First, founded as many of them were under conditions of life-threatening urgency, NGOs have defined themselves as service agencies. They have adopted a purity of motivation that originally seemed uncomplicated and direct. The suffering of children, who could not in any way be held accountable for the wars that engulfed them, demanded a humanitarian response from those who could provide it. Although subsequent entry by NGOs into longer-term development work raised other issues, some of the same sense of the purity and urgency of their mission continues to shape the work of many NGOs.

Second, except for those that were formed explicitly in solidarity with warring liberation movements, NGOs that entered conflict-ridden settings to provide aid to "innocents" defined themselves as apolitical. Sometimes claims of nonpartisanship and neutrality were necessary to gain access to needy people in a war setting. Sometimes NGOs adopted an apolitical stance out of a sense of disdain for politics and the problems it causes. Following the apparent clarity of academe, which divides knowledge into distinct disciplines, NGOs often acted on the assumption that the realm of politics could be separated from the social, cultural, and economic realms where they work.

These two aspects of NGOs' history shape and influence their ongoing work even though they find themselves increasingly involved in the highly politicized contexts of civil warfare. Most NGOs that operate in these contexts continue to do so out of a basic commitment to humanitarian service. At the same time, they increasingly acknowledge the political ramifications of their work. In the years since the end of the Cold War, they have been the first to recognize, and deal with, the evidence that their activities in conflict settings—even when effective in humanitarian, development, or human rights terms—very often exacerbate the local tensions and suspicions that underlie the violence. We turn now to this evidence.

HOW HUMANITARIAN AID CAN WORSEN CONFLICT

Although many factors lead to and underlie wars, once the fighting starts, conflict is about power, as each side tries to dominate the other through violence. Material resources represent, buttress, and are essential to power. Thus, when NGOs introduce resources—such as food, cash, and equipment—into settings where people are already in conflict, these resources very often become additional foci for struggle and contention. Externally offered resources play into power struggles in several ways.[10]

First, warring factions may demand payment from NGOs (in the form of "tariffs" or "taxes") for the right to deliver their assistance. These direct payments are then used to support armies and subsidize the conflict. Under the chaos of war, NGO resources are often stolen, and these goods may show up in the warehouses of fighting parties, who either organized the theft or bought what was offered by the thieves. In-kind support delivered to civilians, such as food, may be passed on to sons, husbands, brothers, and fathers who are directly engaged in fighting. In the civilian-based wars, attempts by NGOs to ensure that only innocent civilians receive aid are confounded as the lines between civilians and armies are blurred. NGO resources, whether used by civilians or by fighters, relieve the burden of governing bodies and army commanders to support the populations or soldiers under their aegis. This then frees internal resources for the war effort.

Second, NGO interventions can reinforce and worsen intergroup tensions by affecting the distribution of resources. NGOs employ some people (and not others), purchase goods from some (and not others), and target their aid toward some people (and not others); these decisions can fuel separate group identities, inequalities, and jealousies. For example, international assistance in Tajikistan logically focused on rebuilding destroyed homes in a postwar setting, which increased the suspicions of the war's "victors," as they saw most of the aid being directed toward the people they had defeated. Development assistance that is targeted toward specific groups explicitly alters an existing power relationship. While this may appear to be justified as a means for overcoming discrimination and disadvantage, it may also prompt or reinforce intergroup tensions.

Third, NGOs' presence affects wages, prices, and profits. Insofar as the effect is to increase the incentives for pursuing warfare, these influences are also negative. Finally, through their interactions with local authorities, aid agencies legitimate some actors and some activities and delegitimate others. This effect can also feed into intergroup conflict.

Furthermore, the "message" of some international NGOs as they work in conflict settings, expressed in both the publicity they offer and the modes of their programs, can also reinforce tensions that underlie conflict. NGOs' use of horror pictures of war atrocities in fund-raising materials may serve to dehumanize the perpetrators of these atrocities in the minds of the wider public and reinforce their alienation from any peace process. It may do a further disservice to peace efforts by oversimplifying conflict as if there are clear victims and clear demons. While at the extremes this may be true, most wars are more complicated, and guilt is more generalized, than such simple messages imply.

Although the evidence is strong that NGO programming interacts with and often exacerbates local intergroup tensions, this does not mean that NGOs create violence or cause wars. Wars happen for many reasons that are far outside the reach of NGO activities. The atrocities that NGOs cite in their publicity do, in fact, happen and are widely reported to the public by the press, whether NGOs cite them or not. Even though it is not within the power of international assistance agencies to end war, the fact that their aid often feeds into and exacerbates conflict demands their serious attention and specific programming adjustments.

NGO APPROACHES IN CONFLICT SETTINGS

NGOs adopt different approaches for dealing with the negative ramifications that their good works sometimes have in conflict settings. We outline three types of approaches that encompass the ways NGOs carry out their interventions in these circumstances.

The "Mandate Blinders" Approach

When blinders are attached to a horse's bridle, the horse's peripheral vision is restricted so that it can see nothing but the road straight ahead. Some agencies work strictly from their specific, original mandates; like the horse with blinders, these agencies focus entirely on their intended purpose. They are committed to its rightness, and they eschew responsibility for its secondary or tertiary impacts. They think that achieving their primary purpose justifies or outweighs any potential negative side effects that may result from their efforts and that, if such side effects do occur, they should be dealt with by someone else. Very often, these agencies operate in emergency settings and cite the urgency of need to justify their approach. They believe that "it is always right to save the life of a child" or "it is always right to deliver food to people who are starving." Moral imperatives and time pressures drive their efforts.

There is a tendency for such agencies to locate all decision making about and control of aid deliveries entirely in their own hands. The result is that those whom the NGOs mean to help are entirely dependent on the techniques and resources of outsider aid providers, and this inevitably has deleterious long-term effects. While the mandate blinders approach may appear to have advantages in terms of speed and efficiency, it can disempower local people to such an extent that the long-term efficacy of the effort is compromised. Local people are led to depend entirely on outsiders, both for survival assistance and (perhaps worse) for any efforts to achieve peace.

The "Aid on Our Terms Only" Approach

Some agencies (also motivated by their belief in the rightness of their purpose) pursue a specific mandate fully but also monitor and assume responsibility for side effects of their efforts. Because such groups are particularly aware of the ways in which war can distort and disrupt intended efforts, they maintain as their ultimate option the decision to withdraw assistance if they perceive that the negative side effects of their work are becoming too significant to justify its continuation. Agencies that pursue this approach sometimes suspend operations in a given area, notifying local people of their hope to return "when . . ." and spelling out the conditions under which they would resume work. Such agencies use both the aid they give and their potential for withdrawing it to affect processes in ways they deem consistent with their mandate.

Sometimes such a threat to withdraw itself can have negative consequences, however. Rather than being perceived by the people in a conflict area as expressing a moral desire not to worsen a situation, a threat can be seen as another, war-related misuse of power. That is, international NGOs with the power of resources and the freedom of movement not enjoyed by local people can decide when and whether to stay or leave without accountability to those whom they are there to serve. In some cases, also, the act of leaving a crisis can worsen the crisis. For example, after the takeover of Goma in eastern Congo by rebel forces in the summer of 1998, some of the NGOs began to withdraw their international staff. Both local NGOs and their expatriate colleagues, however, knew that a collective pullout of the international NGOs could promote an atmosphere of uncertainty that, in turn, could reinforce tensions and violence.[11]

The "Hippocratic Oath" Approach

Some agencies follow an approach that can be likened to the Hippocratic oath that medical doctors take as they assume their professional practice. Through this oath, doctors pledge to do whatever is within their ability to serve the health of their patients. They recognize that their knowledge—and the knowledge of medical science in general—is imperfect; they assume responsibility for keeping up with current knowledge and using their own experience as the basis for improving their, and their colleagues', practice of medicine.

In this oath, doctors also pledge that they will "first, do no harm."[12] The phrase, widely quoted by other disciplines, connotes recognition that misapplied medical interventions can do harm as well as good. As we have seen, the same holds for NGO interventions in relief, development, human rights, and peace promotion in conflict areas. While no NGO can predict with certainty all the ramifications of its activities in complex settings, recognizing that good intentions can have bad outcomes is a critical step in planning programs, establishing systems for monitoring impacts, and redesigning and altering programs according to experience. Commitment to the Hippocratic oath approach to conflict intervention means that an NGO takes responsibility for its larger and longer-term impacts and that it continually seeks to learn from both the mistakes and the successes of its own programs and those of other agencies. Such an approach is also deeply attentive to the voices and intentions of the people on whose behalf the NGOs work.

These three approaches constitute the basis for ongoing dialogue and debate both within and among NGOs. In every NGO that intervenes internationally, some staff members advocate one of these approaches while others advocate another. Field operations of the same NGO vary, depending on the favored approach of the particular staff at the site. However, because many now accept the evidence that NGO interventions can have a significant negative impact, the NGO community as a whole is moving toward adopting the Hippocratic oath approach.

Before turning to a discussion of how NGOs may avoid "doing harm" in conflict settings, we first briefly describe important characteristics of recent conflicts that affect the programming options available to the operational NGOs.

CHARACTERISTICS OF CONFLICTS: NEW COMPLEXITIES AND NEW OPPORTUNITIES

Wars in the final decade of the twentieth century exhibited certain characteristics that pose new complexities and new opportunities for NGOs working in these settings. As many have noted, few wars in the post–Cold War era were between nations.[13] Instead, many wars were fought within national borders, between groups that had previously lived and worked side by side; in many places, warring groups had been friends and even family members. Shifting arrangements in governance occasioned by the end of the Cold War and the demise of the Soviet Union frequently engendered or exposed political ambitions on the part of aspiring leaders. However, as individuals entered the political arena to compete for power, they very often defined their constituencies according to some subgroup identity and conveyed a message to their supporters that unless one's own group dominated, it would be dominated by others. A number of these putative leaders relied on threats about the risk of oppression by others to prompt their followers into violent conflict with their former neighbors.

Many of these wars have been fought not on distant or defined battlefields, but in the living and work spaces of daily life, and the lines between military and civilian arenas have been increasingly blurred. Civilians have been increasingly targeted and endangered; they are also engaged in the processes of war.

Whereas news reports and the propaganda of warring factions cite entrenched and desperate attitudes reflecting the will "to fight to the death," private conversations and low-key consultations have shown that some of the populace in these wars hold unexpected attitudes.[14]

Many people express deep disaffection with "their" wars and, even more profoundly, with war in general as a means of solving intergroup problems. They note that "this war is not solving our problems." In fact, they observe that the cycles of action, reaction, revenge, and reprisal have themselves become the cause of future conflicts. According to the analysis of such individuals within warring societies, the problems that prompted the first outbreak of violence are often superseded by even worse and more intransigent hatred based on and fueled by the experiences of war.

Citizens in recent war zones often discuss the ways in which their so-called leaders fail to serve the people's interests. Rather than being excited to patriotic fervor by an ideal, expressed and embodied by a popular and heroic leader, many people say they are weary of the endlessness of battle for what they perceive as little purpose. Sometimes such comments are made openly and vigorously; more often they are expressed only in private, and protected, spaces because local pressure for pro-war solidarity makes expressing disaffection extremely dangerous.[15]

Such expressions of disaffection with war characterize many recent wars, as compared with wars of the past. Throughout much of history, although people have always decried war as a "last resort," by the time a nation had actually entered a war, most people could be persuaded that it was worthy of their loyalty and sacrifice. Many people joined wars to fight oppression, overthrow a colonial or despotic rule, or redistribute a basic economic resource such as land; they did so with a commitment to the justice of the cause and pursued war as an effective (if undesirable) mechanism for achieving a just (and desirable) goal. But today, as more and more people in war-torn countries cite the greed of their leaders as the only fuel for continuing battle, they fight (when they must) more for self- and group preservation than for an ideal world that will be realized through fighting.[16]

Given the civilization of warfare (by its location and pervasiveness) and the often wide disaffection (even on the part of those who fight) with warfare as a means for achieving desired societal or political goals, the work of NGOs intervening in conflict settings has become more complex and more promising.

Intervention has become more complex in three basic ways. First, the international conventions that formerly governed the rules of war between states do not apply when wars are fought within countries, largely because fighting factions and their commanders often have little knowledge of or respect for such conventions. Furthermore, international law was not originally written for these circumstances. Second, as groups within nations have fought for power, both the legitimacy and the sovereignty of governmental authority have been challenged. Under these circumstances, the international community has been faced with a need for new rules to guide decisions regarding intervention. Third, when wars are driven by political opportunism rather than clear causes of justice, NGOs (and others) do not know with whom to align themselves. Who is right and who is wrong? How can an NGO decide it is justifiable to negotiate with a given regime and lend its aid to support it? When is it important to withhold support so that local people have the power to choose their leaders without international influence? These issues make intervention by international NGOs (and governments and the United Nations) more complex.

At the same time, the current wars present new opportunities for NGO interventions. We have described the ways in which NGO interventions can exacerbate conflicts through the introduction and potential misuse of resources and through the moral messages associated with NGO interventions. But these mechanisms can also be used to ensure that the impacts of NGO work are positive in relation to conflict—that is, that they enable local people to disengage from fighting or that they link people rather than divide them.

WHAT NGOS CAN DO TO AVOID WORSENING CONFLICT AND HOW NGOS CAN SUPPORT PEACE

When a significant number of people in a war setting do not believe that the war in which they are engaged serves any positive purpose, NGOs that provide assistance in these areas have an opportunity to support local disengagement from conflict.[17] Aid programs can provide safe "space" for people to articulate opposition to the war or to live in "nonwar" ways. In many war environments, locally hired staff people tell of the freedom they gain through employment with international NGOs. For example, an agency in Bosnia and Herzegovina required that all its staff serve people on all sides of the war without regard to ethnicity. When family and friends of these individuals accosted them, demanding to know how they could work with "the enemy," these staff people reported that they could simply explain that, if they refused to do so, they would lose their jobs. This explanation satisfied all complaints because everyone understood the desperate need for employment during the war. These staff people also noted, however, that they very much wanted to maintain a life that connected with people from all ethnicities within their society, and, thus, the "requirement" of their employer became a legitimate "excuse" for why they did what they very much wanted to do anyway.

Though the resources NGOs provide can feed into intergroup conflict, they can also be used to connect people across warring lines. For example, in postconflict Tajikistan, most NGOs assumed that the two groups that had fought—the Garmi and the Kulyabi—could no longer work together. Thus, they worked with each of the mono-ethnic villages to develop economic self-reliance. However, one NGO realized that these people had been economically interdependent for years. Though tensions remained high in some areas, the NGO developed a program that reemphasized mutual interdependence. It helped Garmi women in one village develop a wool-production enterprise; in a nearby village of Kulyabi people, it promoted a carpet-weaving enterprise. The former village was organized to supply the latter with the wool it needed. If either gained, all gained. For anyone to gain, everyone had to gain.

In another tense war zone, one small region was physically cut off from the others on its "side" of the war. Aid agency staff were intent on reaching the civilians in this area because, without aid, they would have no food or health support. However, to reach them, aid trucks had to pass through territory controlled by their enemies, who attacked the trucks along the road. Finally, aid agency staff visited the village leaders in the areas where the attacks occurred. They explained the need of the civilians they were trying to reach. The staff also inquired about surpluses in the attacking territory; were there any food supplies there that the NGO could purchase to supply the civilians who were cut off? These leaders understood the need; they agreed to sell goods to the NGO and ensure safe transport. Because these negotiations were carried out by civilian leaders, the result was that direct benefits were channeled to civilians suffering from the war on two sides of the conflict. Some were able to find a market for the food they could produce; others received food without which they could not have survived. Before this solution, the delivery of aid incited intergroup jealousy and constant violence; with this approach the common interests of the two sides were reinforced.

Understanding that people in war remain linked by some shared values, international humanitarian agencies have been able to negotiate days of tranquillity and zones of peace for carrying out broad campaigns to immunize children against childhood disease or to open and maintain corridors for the delivery of aid goods. Understanding that people separated by civil war often actively seek reconnection with former friends and colleagues, aid agencies have been able to build opportunities for this into their aid programs by offering health services, training programs, or other nonthreatening activities in places to which all sides have access. Building on common cultures and histories, aid agencies have been able to incorporate linking cultural events into their humanitarian programs.

By being conscious of the impacts of their activities on the wages, prices, and profits in the local economy, NGOs can find ways to reward actors and activities that are committed to normal, peacetime survival and exchange and to avoid reinforcing economic incentives for continued pursuit of war. By considering the distributional impacts of their aid, NGOs can ensure that they do not feed into existing intergroup tensions, but rather that they distribute goods in ways that reinforce the common interests and mutual interdependence of divided groups. NGOs can create nonwar space for people to act as they had before the war, as citizens of one land and colleagues in common enterprises. People within war-torn societies report that they need the international agencies as much for these influences to counter the dividedness of warfare as for the humanitarian assistance they provide. Both are seen as important aspects of survival, in the immediate crisis of violence and in the longer-term context of postwar stability and, when possible, reconciliation.

Ending a war requires work at many levels. International forums bring together commanders of warring factions to sign treaties and divide territories. One powerful motivation for these leaders to go to the conference table is the realization that the people on whom they depend for power do not support further war. Increasingly, agencies that implement programs affecting the daily lives of a people have an opportunity (and an obligation) to support these people as they disengage from conflict. To focus on feeding people or on promoting development activities that have long-term prospects is not enough in conflict-ridden societies, because the good that is accomplished

can be overbalanced by the inadvertent exacerbation of the forces of conflict. NGOs that undertake interventions to relieve suffering and promote sustainable development and human rights must also accept responsibility for their impact on intergroup tensions and divisions. The most exciting challenges facing international NGOs today are to recognize where things go wrong in order that they "do no harm" and to explore, develop, and implement programs that support the shared interests and interconnectedness of people divided by war.

NOTES

1. All NGOs receive private contributions or were founded with private funds. Many also rely (sometimes heavily) on funding from their national governments, although a few completely eschew any government funding.

2. The term "natural disaster" is usually used to refer to events that arise from nature such as earthquakes, floods, winds, and fire. However, since disasters occur in relation to human societies and are measured in terms of injury, death, and property loss, we (and many others) feel that there is no such thing as a truly "natural" disaster. Such events only become disasters in relation to human systems and human choices. For example, organization of economies may result in impoverishment of some people, which in turn means that they live in high-risk zones such as coastal plains or cannot afford adequate housing that might better withstand earthquakes or high winds. Thus, we put quotation marks around the word "natural."

3. For the full argument about these connections, see Mary B. Anderson and Peter J. Woodrow, *Rising from the Ashes: Development Strategies in Times of Disaster* (Boulder, Colo., and Paris: Westview and UNESCO Presses, 1989).

4. For fuller discussion of this point, see articles in Alcira Kreimer and Mohan Munasinghe, eds., *Managing Natural Disasters and the Environment* (Washington, D.C.: World Bank, 1991).

5. Mary B. Anderson, *International Assistance and Conflict: An Exploration of Negative Impacts,* Issues Series no. 1, Local Capacities for Peace Project

(Cambridge, Mass.: Collaborative for Development Action, 1994).

6. It is important to remember that all NGOs that come from other countries are not intrinsically "foreign" to the circumstances in which they provide assistance. In some instances, solidarity of purpose and philosophy can mean that an international NGO is more of an "insider" than a local NGO that is based in a distant part of the country and operates out of a stance that is less sensitive to the circumstances of the people whom it purports to help. This occurs sometimes when urban-based, upper-class local NGOs attempt to work in remote and rural areas of their countries. Furthermore, some international NGOs (such as the International Federation of Red Cross and Red Crescent Societies and denominational church groups) always work through local counterpart groups. Thus, there is a blurred line between "insider" and "outsider" NGOs operating in any given context.

7. The Red Cross was formed to provide emergency care to the sick, wounded, and other victims of either "man-made" (that is, war) or natural disasters. Catholic Relief Services was founded in 1943 as the War Relief Services to coordinate relief efforts of a variety of Catholic agencies to victims of World War II.

CARE was started at the close of World War II and represented a cooperative effort of twenty-two U.S. religious, relief, labor, civic, and service groups focused on providing food packages to needy families in postwar Europe. It is from this program that the term "CARE packages" originated. For more on the histories of NGOs in relation to war and development, see Landrum R. Bolling, *Private Foreign Aid: U.S. Philanthropy for Relief and Development*, A Council on Foundations Report (Boulder, Colo.: Westview Press, 1982).

8. See Thomas H. Fox, "NGOs from the United States," *in Development Alternatives: The Challenge for NGOs,* ed. Anne Gordon Drabek, *World Development* 15, supplement (Oxford: Pergamon Press, 1987).

9. The number of NGOs founded explicitly in solidarity with justice movements is small relative to those founded for more general humanitarian reasons. Often these NGOs cease to exist when (if) the cause that they supported achieves its intended aim.

10. The negative impacts of aid resources on conflict discussed in the following pages were articulated through the collaborative Local Capacities for Peace Project. They are more fully reported and described in Mary B. Anderson, *Do No Harm: How Aid Supports Peace or War* (Boulder, Colo.: Lynne Rienner, 1999).

11. Fortunately, the argument was sufficiently well made that many expatriate staff remained in the area.

12. The idea for using this part of the Hippocratic oath as a pledge for international NGOs working in conflict settings was suggested to me by a participant, himself an M.D., at a conference in Toronto in May 1994, organized and sponsored by the Health Reach program at McMaster University. I regret that I do not know the name of the individual, so I cannot cite him adequately; but the idea he gave those of us who were at that conference has proved extremely useful in my examination of NGO approaches to work in conflict settings.

13. For one discussion of these changes, see the preface in Thomas G. Weiss and Larry Minear, eds., *Humanitarianism across Borders: Sustaining Civilians in Times of War* (Boulder, Colo.: Lynne Rienner, 1993).

14. The following paragraphs reflect conversations that I have personally had with people in many parts of the former Yugoslavia, Tajikistan, Afghanistan, Sri Lanka, Pakistan, Lebanon, and elsewhere in the Middle East. As I have discussed these findings with others, many who have experience in other war zones have confirmed that they also hear local people expressing disaffection with both their wars and the so-called leaders who pursue them.

15. Although this idea arises in many settings, two individuals who articulated these dangers most clearly in personal conversations with me were a former mujahideen from Afghanistan and a citizen of a small town in Croatia, both of whom took the risk of initiating important local peace efforts that subsequently engaged a number of their fellow citizens.

16. Obviously, the discussion here is generalized to cover many different circumstances. Still, I believe it accurately reflects realities in many sites, including Somalia, Afghanistan (in the civil war that followed the Soviet withdrawal), Tajikistan, Rwanda, the former Yugoslavia, Angola, Sierre Leone, Liberia, Chechnya, and so on. It does not apply as well to East Timor, Kosovo, or Chiapas. Even in those areas where there is broad disaffection with warfare, people acknowledge that there are real intergroup divisions and inequalities that are easily manipulated by the leadership and cited as root causes of the conflicts. And even in the areas where people are ideologically committed

to the purpose of their warfare, they acknowledge that some leaders manipulate genuine causes for their own personal gain, wealth, and power, often exacerbating intergroup hatreds and prolonging violence.

17. The examples in this section of how NGOs can avoid worsening war and support peace come from the agencies collaborating in the Local Capacities for Peace Project. Fuller details of these findings are included in the project's book *Do No Harm: How Aid Supports Peace or War*.

38

New Institutions for New Times

The Case of the International Crisis Group

Alain Destexhe

Editors' note: *The International Crisis Group (ICG), an international nongovernmental organization, was created in the wake of the savage internal conflicts of the early 1990s. Working in the interstices between the official and nonofficial worlds, and between policy analysis and operational activities, ICG is attempting to improve the way the international community reacts to conflict. The following description, written by its former president, captures ICG's approach and is included here as but one example of a new institutional response to unraveling the complex conflicts and unsettled settlements of our time.*

IN 1995 A GROUP OF PROMINENT international figures gathered in London to discuss plans for the creation of the International Crisis Group. The idea that brought them together was simple but powerful. The Cold War had ended, leaving behind it a backwash of messy internal and regional conflicts and crises—festering sores on the international scene that, to treat effectively, would require a good deal of imagination, patience, and persistence on the part of world policymakers.

Many countries found themselves in a precarious position, and the seeds of potential conflicts were widely spread. The Balkans had dissolved into a long, bloody, and costly war. Somalia had collapsed, dragging down with it the reputation of the international community. And Rwanda had exploded into a terrifying genocide and threatened to destabilize the entire Central African region.

In addition, humanitarian assistance had all too often been used as an alibi for political inaction. Providing relief assistance to the victims is often necessary but never sufficient. In Bosnia, before Dayton, the international community comforted itself by feeding a population that was actually crying out for protection. The human massacre that followed in Srebrenica was evidence of this misguided approach. Similarly, the world fell silent as between eight hundred thousand and a million people were slaughtered in Rwanda in the 1994 genocide and only afterward responded by ordering a multimillion-dollar humanitarian aid operation to help the refugees. That operation, many now believe, actually aggravated the political situation by giving rise to a newly destabilized and highly militarized zone on the border between Rwanda and eastern Zaire. In Central Africa we are continuing to pay the price for mistakes made in Rwanda in 1994.

If the world wanted to avoid slipping into a new era of chaos and violence, policymakers needed first to better understand the problems confronting countries at risk of crisis and then to develop new thinking on ways to overcome those problems and contribute to the creation of stronger, safer, and more stable civil societies. In this respect, ICG was designed to help plug a widening international information gap. The organization seeks to provide governments and others with an independent source of information, analysis, and ideas and, in that way, contribute to the development of more coherent and effective policy responses to international problems.

But ICG's founders recognized that we need more than just greater understanding, new ideas, and policy pamphlets to solve world problems. We also need action—informed, appropriate, and timely action. And so the concept of ICG was born: an independent nonprofit, professional organization, with an influential voice, able to develop serious, credible proposals on how the international community can respond more effectively to signs of impending crises and, at the same time, mobilize support for such proposals among key decision makers.

ICG is committed to strengthening the capacity of the international community to anticipate, understand, and act to prevent and contain conflict. Whenever national or regional stability is threatened by the escalation of a crisis, world decision makers are faced with the difficult challenge of developing an effective response that minimizes the risk of bloodshed and helps restore long-term peace and stability.

The International Crisis Group was founded on the belief that we can stop emerging crises from turning into runaway disasters only if the world acts promptly and effectively.

ICG has a distinct status in the world of conflict management for a number of reasons. First, it is financially independent from any particular donor and receives a wide range of funding from different governments, foundations, and individuals. No single donor provides more than 10 percent of ICG funding. Second, ICG has built a reputation for reliable and independent analysis not influenced by any government, international institution, or local warring party. ICG tries to find the best political solution, both realistic and practical, based mainly but not exclusively on respect for a few key principles like peace, human dignity, and stability. Unlike, for example, Amnesty International or Human Rights Watch, ICG is not driven exclusively by a human rights agenda. Respect for human rights is included in a broader concept involving different aspects —economical, political, military—of the conflict. Another aspect of ICG's work is that it tries to lobby and influence all the players involved at different levels and using all possible tools. For example, ICG puts forward recommendations for the Bosnian situation to members of the international community active in Sarajevo, the local players, and the local Bosnian press as well as to governments in key Western capitals and to the international press through articles to inform public opinion.

ICG's approach can be broken down into three activities: analysis, advocacy, and assistance.

ANALYSIS

ICG's greatest strength lies in its ability to provide policymakers with well-timed, high-quality, balanced analyses of complex crises. Analytical reports, which contain an assessment of key trends and events as well as practical policy recommendations for international decision makers, are prepared by field-based professionals with an intimate knowledge of the countries concerned. During 2000, ICG staff members were stationed in Bosnia, Macedonia, Kosovo, Montenegro, Burundi, the Democratic Republic of the Congo, Algeria, and Indonesia.

ICG's in-country staff builds up a sustained understanding of local conditions by consulting widely at all levels and across all sectors of society. Among those typically approached by ICG are representatives of the political leadership (both government and opposition), public servants, the military, teachers, health workers, economists, journalists, women, young people, various ethnic communities, businesspeople, religious groups, and other groups within civil society. Additional input is sought from the diplomatic representatives of external governments and intergovernmental organizations, UN agencies, and human rights and humanitarian relief organizations active on the ground. As well as mapping the security, social, and economic landscape of a given country, ICG staff undertakes firsthand investigations of potentially incendiary incidents—for example, house burnings and crowd stoning in Bosnia or student demonstrations in Macedonia —seeking to highlight the objective facts and explain the implications of events.

From time to time ICG may commission expert opinion pieces by legal or technical professionals on specific subjects that warrant more detailed specialist attention. Examples include papers on the rights of the substate entities within Bosnia and Herzegovina to succeed to the state assets of the former Yugoslavia and the development of alternative electoral systems that encourage candidates to appeal across ethnic divides.

The end product of this process is a stream of reports, papers, and public statements that seek to identify, dissect, and assess potential problems and, importantly, suggest practical solutions. ICG's reports are targeted at the international community in general—but always with an eye to those key governments and international organizations that have the capacity to make a positive impact on the course of events in a given country.

Examples of ICG Analysis

During the first six months of 1999, the main focus of ICG in the Balkans was the conflict in Kosovo and the confrontation between Belgrade and the West. Since the withdrawal of Yugoslav forces from Kosovo, ICG has turned its attention to the task of peace implementation in Kosovo and the prospects for further conflict and hopes of political change in other parts of the federation. ICG research themes during this period included, among others, former president Slobodan Milosevic's handling of the Kosovo crisis and his strategy of diplomacy; the financial and political mechanism by which he clung to power; the NATO air campaign; prospects for political change in Serbia; assessments of Kosovo's political scenery; the potential for conflict in Montenegro; and reports on policing, security, and the UN Mission in Kosovo (UNMIK). In Macedonia and Albania ICG provided sustained analysis of key trends and events with a special emphasis on the impact of the Kosovo crisis and its aftermath in both countries.

ICG has provided a running analysis of the peace process in Bosnia since 1996, when the organization's first analyst arrived in Sarajevo. The project is intended to support the Dayton Peace Accords by providing the institutions engaged in building peace with an independent assessment of the challenges and a source of practical problem-solving policy ideas. ICG has released a number of reports on refugee return, the justice system, electoral reform, Bosnian Serb and Bosnian Croat politics, the Bosnian bureaucracy, and the future of Brcko.

In April 1999 ICG published a hard-hitting assessment of the barriers to private investment in Bosnia. The report, entitled *Why Will*

No-One Invest in Bosnia and Herzegovina? emphasized the risk to the peace process if steps were not taken to stimulate greater private investment ahead of a likely winding back in the levels of international aid. The report, which was based on extensive interviews with Bosnian and foreign businesspeople, past and potential investors, and government officials, proposed reforms designed to open up the Bosnian economy to private investment and reduce dependency on foreign aid. Its release attracted widespread attention among both the Bosnian press and representatives of the international community in Sarajevo and helped trigger a national and international debate on the issue.

In November 1999, to coincide with the fourth anniversary of the signing of the Dayton Peace Accords, ICG released a comprehensive assessment of the state of the peace process. The report, entitled *Is Dayton Failing?* examined the peace agreement annex by annex—highlighting areas of success and failure, identifying obstacles to continued progress, and setting out the tough choices confronting policymakers. In response to high demand, the report was reissued in book format and distributed to more than twenty-five hundred top international officials.

ADVOCACY

While field research and analysis remain at the heart of ICG's efforts, the organization can make an impact on international policymaking only if it is successful in attracting significant high-level political backing for its policy prescriptions. ICG's advocacy begins at the local level, where ICG staff work closely with key agencies and organizations engaged on the ground to develop and mobilize support for its policy recommendations. In Bosnia, for example, ICG focuses a great deal of its effort on the main international organizations involved in the implementation of the Dayton Peace Accords—including the Office of the

High Representative (OHR), the Organization for Security and Cooperation in Europe (OSCE), the North Atlantic Treaty Organization (NATO), and the European Union.

Copies of ICG reports and policy recommendations are distributed directly to eight hundred high-level decision makers around the world by fax, mail, or e-mail. The organization's global distribution system targets officials in national governments and international organizations, such as NATO, the World Bank, the United Nations, and the European Commission, as well as journalists, diplomats, parliamentarians, and other key opinion makers.

ICG representatives have presented the organization's findings at special briefing sessions organized for NATO and European Commission officials in Brussels and to foreign ministry advisers in Ottawa, Vienna, The Hague, London, Brussels, Stockholm, Copenhagen, Oslo, Helsinki, and Paris. In Washington, ICG staff regularly provide briefings for members of Congress and congressional aides and officials at the World Bank, the Department of State, the Department of Defense, and the White House. In addition, public policy seminars have been held on Kosovo, Bosnia, Algeria, Cambodia, and Central Africa in Paris, Brussels, and Washington. In an effort to reach beyond the specific policy communities, all ICG reports and press releases are posted immediately on the organization's Internet site, Crisisweb (www.crisisweb.org).

Members of the ICG board of directors are invited to throw their weight behind ICG's findings by making private representations to key government officials and urging action along the lines spelled out in ICG's reports. The board includes prominent figures from the fields of politics (former presidents, prime ministers, foreign ministers, members of parliament), diplomacy, business, and the media. From 1995 to the beginning of 2000 the board was chaired by George Mitchell, former U.S. Senate majority leader and peace negotiator in Northern Ireland. Former Finnish president

Martti Ahtisaari took over as chairman in February 2000. ICG board members also seek to raise public awareness of certain problems by publishing articles in the international press, appearing on television programs, and granting interviews to journalists. ICG board members have undertaken trips on behalf of ICG to Bosnia, Macedonia, Yugoslavia, Burundi, and Cambodia, on each occasion meeting with key political leaders as well as international diplomatic representatives to promote ICG's policy prescriptions.

ICG activities are underpinned by an effort to direct media attention to often-neglected issues ICG believes need highlighting. ICG's field offices provide a useful source of information and comment for in-country journalists, while media briefings and press releases set out the organization's position on key issues to editors in world capitals. Reports and policy recommendations generated sustained media attention during the past two years. ICG field correspondents were often quoted in newspaper articles filed by correspondents on location, while ICG representatives in Brussels and Washington took part regularly in television and radio news programs.

Examples of ICG Advocacy

An embargo was imposed on Burundi after Major Pierre Buyoya took power in a coup in July 1996. In 1998 President Buyoya announced the establishment of a transitional government based on a power-sharing agreement between the two main opposing parties and a program of governmental reforms. The same year peace talks between various sides in the Burundian conflict began in the northern Tanzanian town of Arusha.

In April 1998 ICG released *Burundi under Siege—Lift the Sanctions, Relaunch the Peace Process,* an assessment of the performance of the Buyoya government and the political, economic, and humanitarian impact of the embargo on Burundi. The report argued that,

while the military had escaped the misery that sanctions were inflicting on the broader population, the sense of isolation created by the sanctions had helped radicalize certain elements within the army and the ruling Tutsi elite. The report called for sanctions on Burundi to be lifted. At the time ICG was the only organization to argue in favor of such a move. Between May and December 1998, ICG campaigned vigorously for a lifting of the sanctions, holding meetings in the region, Europe, and the United States and publishing opinion pieces in major newspapers around the world. In January 1999 regional leaders agreed to lift sanctions.

In November 1998 the Algerian government forced the country's three leading independent newspapers to close following editorial criticisms of government policy. ICG campaigned to end the ban and flew the editors of the three newspapers to press conferences and meetings in Paris and Brussels to protest the Algerian government's action. In December 1998 the ban on all three newspapers was lifted.

ICG has been particularly successful in Bosnia, where it has enjoyed the respect of both the Bosnian players and the international community. In the spring of 1998, ICG published a report calling for fundamental reform of the electoral system in Bosnia and then spearheaded a national debate on electoral reform. The report examined a number of electoral systems suitable for use in ethnically divided societies such as Bosnia and put forward an alternative system aimed at encouraging the development of greater cross-ethnic political cooperation and collaboration. A few months later the Office of the High Representative established the Election Law Working Group —a mixed group of Bosnian and international officials—to prepare proposals for electoral reform.

The arbitration panel on the disputed town of Brcko, Bosnia's northern flash point, implemented key ICG proposals on its future. In February 1998 ICG published a report on Brcko calling on the arbitration panel to adopt a package of measures designed to build inter-ethnic trust and pave the way for a final settlement. In March the arbitration panel adopted many of ICG's proposals, including an expansion and extension of the mandate of the international supervisor in Brcko and the creation of a special economic zone.

ASSISTANCE

ICG's primary role is to persuade and encourage relevant sectors of the international community—in particular, a number of major governments and regional and international organizations—to respond promptly and effectively in the face of impending instability or conflict.

While such a role can often be useful in helping to forestall or stave off disasters, it is clear that, in the longer term, much more needs to be done to help minimize the risk that future crises will emerge. Real crisis prevention —lasting prevention—requires strong, stable, civil structures to be constructed at a local level. A vibrant and durable civil society, rule of law, robust democracy, and, by extension, strong government accountability are all indispensable hallmarks of stable and peaceful countries. While outside diplomatic pressure and measures such as tying international development aid to the achievement of certain political objectives by recipient governments can be helpful, it is ultimately only through local action and the persistence of local people, organized within democratic political movements and civil organizations, that such objectives can be achieved.

By virtue of being on the ground in a number of countries at risk of crisis, ICG is well placed to help support the work carried out by local civil society groups. First, ICG can provide a certain amount of technical, legal, and, at times, modest financial support for such groups. Second, in cases in which substantial financial and other forms of support are needed, ICG

can assist with fund-raising, putting local groups in touch with international donors and undertaking advocacy on their behalf. Third, ICG can help bring civil society spokespeople to Western capitals to present their case in person before influential officials and to participate in important meetings and conferences.

Examples of ICG Assistance

In 1996 and 1997 ICG supported the Campaign for Good Governance in Sierra Leone, a local group of civic leaders working to raise the level of awareness of good governance and the need for greater government accountability. During the fifteen months between the election of President Ahmed Kabbah and the May 1997 coup, the Campaign for Good Governance ran a program of workshops for members of Parliament, the Cabinet, the judiciary, and the media. A nationwide civic education campaign, combining local workshops with radio broadcasts, was in progress at the time of the coup.

In Algeria, given difficulties of access and poor security conditions, ICG was not able to establish a full-time on-the-ground presence inside the country until the end of 1998 and was therefore obliged initially to conduct field research based on regular, albeit short-term, missions. The lack of a field analyst has inevitably restricted ICG's capacity to gather material and compile detailed reports, and the organization has therefore concentrated on identifying and channeling support to moderate voices and key groups within Algerian society, particularly the independent press and a women's association.

In Kosovo ICG undertook a project in support of the work of the International Criminal Tribunal for the former Yugoslavia, which involved collecting testimonials from nearly five thousand witnesses of atrocities. Up to a hundred legal experts and translators worked on this high-profile project in the second half of 1999. The findings were published in a book entitled *Reality Demands: Documenting Violations of International Humanitarian Law in Kosovo in 1999*. Lastly, ICG arranged and attended a number of high-level meetings between a delegation of civil society leaders from Kosovo and senior officials in Washington and Brussels.

INTERNAL DECISION MAKING

The board of directors decides which countries and conflicts the organization should focus on. Local analysts, a regional expert, the president, and a few board members interested in a particular region jointly set up key objectives. On a day-to-day basis, local staff often take the initiative to propose a statement or an issue to advocate, under the final responsibility of the president. Option papers are often circulated for comments among the Executive Committee of the organization, which meets more often than the board. At the end of the day, the president is responsible for which policies to advocate and is accountable to the board for these decisions.

ANALYSIS VERSUS ADVOCACY

A risk for ICG is that in the effort to cover many countries and issues at once, ICG may come to be seen as just another commentator on the course of current crises and conflicts. As the output of reports and briefing papers has risen from twenty in 1997 to fifty-five last year, it has become increasingly difficult to control and maintain a consistent quality of analysis and policy prescription. But as ICG was designed to be a source of advice on how to prevent crises from escalating into deadly conflicts and humanitarian disasters or how to contain them, rather than be just another think tank, it faces particular challenges.

Having produced clear policy prescriptions, ICG still needs to improve its capacity to attract attention to what it has to say and to actively mobilize political support for its proposals. The increase in the output of ICG reports and briefings has far outstripped the organization's capacity to follow up key policy issues and recommendations with targeted and sustained advocacy initiatives. One particular difficulty for ICG is to become a global player and to influence decision makers in Washington, New York, and the main European capitals. Until recently ICG had an effective advocacy capacity in Washington, but its activities have been limited in Europe, where political decision makers are dispersed over a wide area and where ICG's Brussels-based staff has been overstretched managing projects and raising funds. Some explanations could be given for this situation.

Given the primacy of the U.S. role in many of the crises with which ICG is dealing, the U.S. government has always been a high-priority target for all advocacy. In some ways, Washington is a "village," with a thriving policy community. Nothing comparable exists in Europe, except possibly in Brussels; there, however, the policy community is far more focused on international European Union economic and commercial issues. There is also little tradition of lobbying in Europe in comparison with the United States. This is particularly true in relation to foreign policy and security issues. During the Kosovo crisis, for example, in Brussels, London, and Paris, there was no "Kosovo coalition of NGOs" advocating in the same direction.

However, despite this situation, ICG is filling a niche in Europe as a source of independent analysis for small to medium-sized European governments. While the U.S. or French government might not always need the kind of analysis produced by ICG, many small and medium-sized governments are analysis hungry. Lacking the vast diplomatic resources of large countries, they may be receptive to fresh analysis rather than advocacy initiatives, which tend to put governments on the defensive. For instance, in developing options for

Burundi, where there are no more than five or six Western embassies, foreign ministers in Scandinavian countries may prefer to consult ICG rather than to rely exclusively on information coming from the United States, France, or Belgium, the former colonial power.

IMPARTIALITY VERSUS NEUTRALITY

ICG tries to be impartial in its analysis, which does not mean it will remain neutral when faced with conflicts and humanitarian disasters. It does not hesitate to take sides in a conflict and to speak out against the official policy line of the international community if deemed appropriate. For example, against the predominant view in Washington, Paris, and London during the long period when Milosevic was considered a key element for any long-lasting solution for peace, ICG advocated that he was certainly neither the solution nor part of the solution of the crisis but rather the main problem in the Balkans and the main obstacle to any long-term settlement. During the war in Kosovo, ICG supported in vain the deployment of ground troops against the view of Washington and most European capitals. In the case of Burundi, ICG had to face the opposition of almost all leaders in the region when the organization called for the lifting of the sanctions.

In a way, ICG was created in reaction to the neutral humanitarianism concept that prevailed in Rwanda in 1994 and in Bosnia between 1992 and 1995. In both Rwanda and Bosnia before 1995, neutral humanitarianism—elevated to the status of official policy—encouraged and fostered aggression while bringing public opinion to accept both the fait accompli of the stronger party and an "ethnic" reading of the conflict. It became little more than a conscience-saving gimmick, preventing an articulated political analysis of the situation, sustaining the impression that these supposedly tribal struggles defy comprehension.

For the international community to claim neutrality is often a shaky defense of inaction. A claim of neutrality may make sense in the context of fratricidal civil wars or in countries such as Somalia or Liberia that are falling apart at the center and are sometimes referred to as "failed states." But it makes no sense at all in the case of genocide or crimes against humanity, in which neutrality is reduced to the weakest possible definition of indifference and succeeds only in removing every distinction between the victims and the victimizers. Indeed, neutrality can become a refuge large enough to accept inhuman policies.

IS ICG SUCCESSFUL?

Since its launch in 1995, ICG has, by any measure, come a long way. Neither a think tank nor a human rights organization nor a relief NGO, ICG is a unique organization. It has established a reputation for rigorous research and analysis, particularly in the Balkans, and a broad and growing following among government officials. Measuring the progress of an organization such as ICG—whose ultimate aim is to contribute to the prevention of deadly conflict—is inevitably an inexact science. The most concrete measures relate to the level of activity and output: the increase in the number of countries where ICG is present, the number of publications produced, the number of visits to ICG's Web site, the number of governments providing financial support for ICG's work, and so on.

But any real measure of ICG's progress must also take into account factors that are more difficult to gauge, including the quality and accuracy of the organization's analysis, the relevance and utility of its policy prescriptions, and, critically, the ultimate impact of ICG's work on the policymaking process. We can point to many occasions when ICG made a contribution to the resolution of a specific problem. One is ICG's role in highlighting the negative political and humanitarian impact of sanctions on Burundi and its (successful) campaign to have the sanctions lifted. Another is the adoption by the arbitration panel set up to resolve the dispute over Brcko in Bosnia of most of ICG's proposals for the future of the municipality. In addition, there have been many instances when ICG's analysis and ideas have stimulated debate on important issues and helped move opinion in favor of a particular course of action—from election law and economic reform in Bosnia to international aid strategy in Central Africa.

But measuring progress of this sort is not easy. In the past, ICG has tended to base judgments of this sort on internal evaluation as well as feedback—solicited and unsolicited—from donors, report recipients, journalists, and others. In the future, ICG plans to develop a more systematic process of external evaluation, designed to provide a clearer picture of both the relative quality, accuracy, relevance, and utility of ICG's research and advocacy work and the extent to which these efforts actually influence decision makers and those around them.

Note

Since this text was completed, ICG has been through a substantial period of further change and development. For a full account of the organization as it now operates, see its Web site, www.crisisweb.org.

39

Is There a Role for Business in Conflict Management?

Virginia Haufler

THE DEBATE ABOUT HOW TO CONTROL so-called blood diamonds—diamonds from mines in Africa that are sold by rebels to fund relentless civil war there—has reignited interest in the role of business in conflict. Foreign investors have been linked to the emergence or exacerbation of conflict around the world for centuries. This link became especially prominent in the eighteenth and nineteenth centuries, when colonialism and imperialism brought European investors into "new" corners of the world, where they disrupted existing patterns of political relationships—more often than not with force. During the two world wars of the twentieth century, many companies came to be viewed as "merchants of death," profiting off the arms trade and deeply implicated in the Holocaust.[1] In the past fifty years, investors in extractive industries such as oil have been accused of destabilizing local governments and supporting ongoing or incipient civil conflict.[2] Diamonds are the latest in a string of industries accused of complicity in the ongoing destruction of lives and lands.

In a new twist, a few human rights and humanitarian groups have raised the possibility of working closely with companies on strategies to prevent or mitigate conflict.[3] For instance, the conflict prevention nonprofit International Alert, along with two partners, is working with oil companies in the Caspian Sea region to try to prevent the escalation of violence there in the future.[4] They propose a role for business in protecting human rights, promoting tolerance and democracy, reconstructing economies after war, and participating directly in conflict management. A handful of international businesses have expressed interest in working in partnership with civil society organizations and governments to make a positive contribution to peace and stability. If this becomes a serious trend, it raises new and interesting questions for scholars, policymakers, and business leaders. Why would major corporations seek a role in conflict management? Why would governments and advocacy groups seek to partner with corporations in this way? Would it make a difference in the level of conflict and the character of conflict management programs if business takes on this role? How would this change our framework for understanding the issues surrounding peacekeeping and peacemaking, the role of the state in contemporary world affairs, and global governance more generally?

CONTEXT AND BACKGROUND

The private sector today is *the* major force pushing forward globalization. Multinational corporations are active in every part of the world, either directly through the establishment of subsidiaries or indirectly through links with literally thousands of suppliers. It is almost trite to compare the size of transnational corporations with the size of states, and yet that comparison demonstrates the scale of transnational operations today. The Fortune 500 lists the largest corporation today as General Motors, with revenues of approximately $176,558 million in 2000 (Fortune 2000). This is greater than the national income of a small industrialized state, such as Denmark. It is greater than the combined income of almost all the countries of sub-Saharan Africa, excluding South Africa and Nigeria (World Bank 1997). General Motors alone has a network of over 30,000 suppliers; it manufactures in over 50 countries and has a presence in about 200; and it has over 260 major subsidiaries, joint venture partners, and affiliates (General Motors Corporation 2000). There are over 53,000 transnational corporations in the world with about 450,000 affiliates. The value of international production in 1998 by multinational corporations was $3.5 trillion, and foreign affiliates posted global sales worth $9.5 trillion (World Investment Report 1998).

Despite their global operations, business interests to date have not been involved in conflict management exercises. There is little empirical evidence so far on which to base sound analysis of their potential role. Most of the literature on the role of business in conflict literature

ally assumes that they only create, worsen, or prolong outbreaks of violence within and between countries. Foreign investors have been accused—rightly so in many cases—of supporting repressive regimes in order to protect their investments (Lopez and Stohl 1989; Frynas 1998; Global Witness 1999; Manby 1999; Pegg 1999). The influence of economic agendas and actors on conflict is certainly nothing new, and yet there has been relatively little research into this topic until recently (Keen 1998; Berdal and Malone 2000a).[5] Few lessons can be drawn from history to help us understand the possible consequences of *positive and direct* corporate contributions to conflict resolution.

Most of the following discussion will be about transnational corporations, which operate on a global basis and create supply and distribution channels that penetrate into many corners of the world. The intensification of transnational commerce in recent decades and the links between local resources and international markets allow some groups to develop ties to foreign firms, which can influence the outbreak and prolongation of conflict (Duffield 2000; Reno 2000). Foreign firms in turn bring with them the "spotlight" of outside media and activists, who bring worldwide attention to a conflict—and to the role the company plays in it (Spar 1998). The political and social activities of global business are changing in response to an evolution in the influence of civil society groups on corporate operations and the shifting expectations society holds about the responsibilities of powerful economic actors (Haufler 2001).

This chapter will focus on "legitimate" businesses—ones that are not criminal enterprises and that generally operate within the bounds of law.[6] The distinction between legitimate and illegitimate companies can be hard to determine, however. In fact, this is often the main point of contention between corporations and their critics. For instance, the Canadian oil company Talisman Energy, Ltd., bought a small percentage of an existing multinational oil project in Sudan, despite the civil war there. The government of Sudan is accused of forcibly relocating civilians in order to clear the way for oil development. Talisman Energy, Ltd., is accused of supporting and profiting from these relocations and of allowing government military forces to use company facilities, as detailed in a Canadian government report (the "Harker Report") (Harker 2000). The result is that Talisman is accused by human rights activists of being an illegitimate and perhaps even criminal enterprise.

There are many situations in which the positive contribution that a business can make is to stop what it is doing—stop buying diamonds from regions of conflict, stop investing in countries engulfed in strife, stop paying off corrupt public officials, stop doing business—period. These amount to private economic sanctions, and few executives willingly follow this path.[7] When foreign investors decide to remain in an unstable area, they may be the only ones who have the financial and managerial resources to address some of the problems that lead to unrest, rebellion, and war. The record of recent official multilateral humanitarian interventions has not been very good, owing in part to the dwindling financial resources of the United Nations. The security and economic development agendas have become more closely linked in the past decade, providing for an opening for increased private sector involvement.

WHY WOULD THEY DO IT?

Before we can even begin to explore what the private sector *could* do for conflict management, we first have to ask why they *would* do it. Why would business executives respond positively to invitations and demands that they participate in preventing or managing conflict situations? For that matter, why would public interest groups, governments, and intergovernmental organizations promote the direct participation of companies in conflict management programs? Is it a product of altruistic and philanthropic impulses on the part of both parties or a simple lack of funding on the part of public and nonprofit agencies, or are there more complex mechanisms at play? The following discussion focuses on the private sector and the three general factors that might persuade managers to consider direct participation in conflict prevention or management programs: (1) the level of political and economic risk, (2) how much they need access to resources and markets located in unstable areas, and (3) how important reputation is as a corporate asset (Carnegie Commission on Preventing Deadly Conflict 1997; Butler 2000).

In some ways it seems obvious that most corporate executives *should* be interested in preventing conflict, because it disrupts the normal conduct of business.[8] Commenting on civil wars in the 1990s, Berdal and Malone say that the "staggering number of deaths and the widespread destruction associated with these wars have naturally reinforced a tendency to view them as an unmitigated calamity for all concerned" (Berdal and Malone 2000a, 3). The potential losses from violence from interstate war, civil war, riot, rebellion, and terrorism are only the most dramatic set of political risks corporate executives face, because such violence can lead to destruction of property, the shutting down of business operations, and direct harm to corporate personnel. In Nigeria, for instance, rebels have sabotaged oil pipelines and held workers hostage. In Colombia a pipeline managed by Western oil companies is blown up on a regular basis. But a less drastic but still significant political risk is that there may be a change of government (peacefully or not), which then changes the rules of the game. In general, once violence breaks out the majority of foreign investors will leave the country.

Some political risks are manageable, however, and foreign investors will neither leave the area nor necessarily be interested in conflict management programs. A recent survey of managers pointed to conditions under which businesses will tolerate conflict. If the conflict is geographically isolated and contained or if it is not too severe, the business may be able to maintain operations despite nearby violence. If the government's policies toward the private sector are very favorable overall, the benefits of those policies can outweigh the costs of disruption from conflict. If the industry is unlikely to be targeted by rebels or criminals or can be structured financially in a way that reduces bottom-line risk, then the calculations may favor investment even in conflict-ridden territories (Berman 2000). A major multinational may take a global perspective and diversify its operations or insure its activities to reduce the financial risk to the company (Haufler 1997). In all these cases, the return on investment may outweigh the costs of operating in areas of violent conflict.

There are conditions under which companies do stay in conflict-ridden areas, but where the political risks are not necessarily tolerable and where companies may be persuaded to engage in conflict management activities. Some industries may be tied to a specific location, and the costs of withdrawing would be too high.[9] For instance, extractive industries such as mining cannot pick and choose among locations but must go where nature put the resources. Even nonextractive industries today can have assets tied up in a way that makes a particular location hard to leave; for instance, a high-technology company may be tied to a particular location by the availability of trained personnel or links to other local firms. Most companies today have extensive, long-standing relationships with contractors and subcontractors, and they often depend upon particular links—both physical and human—in those supply chains. Many investments have an unusually long time horizon, extending ten or more years into the future, which makes conflict management appear to be a more reasonable strategy than if the companies intended to stay for only a short period.[10] For all these firms, access to resources,

markets, and people is a critical need that may outweigh any concern about local violence. Companies that are tied to particular places are politically invested in those countries and therefore have a stake in political outcomes, including peace (Butler 2000).

Economic risks also obviously influence corporate strategy. These include calculations of financial risk and return and an assessment of how much competition a company faces. For large companies, particularly those that are leaders in their markets or whose markets are oligopolistic, the calculation of the costs and benefits of both conflict and conflict management activities would be very different from that of smaller companies. The former may be more willing to try new strategies and new projects because they have more resources and less competition. When international economic competition is fierce, companies may be more willing to tolerate higher risks in return for access to resources and markets but less willing to spend money on conflict management.

Both economic and political risks are influenced by the value a company places on its reputation. A good reputation can help a firm market its products, attract good employees, and establish business relations with other firms. If done well, the brand name of the company becomes synonymous with quality and is a major competitive asset. Such a reputation can be very fragile, however. For instance, the De-Beers diamond company knows that a diamond is valuable only to the degree that people believe it is. If diamonds are used to fund bloody conflict, as they have been in Sierra Leone, then they become closely associated with death and people will stop buying them. DeBeers quickly acted to maintain its reputation by promising not to buy diamonds from regions of conflict and promising to certify the source of the diamonds it did buy.

One of the most significant risks today for corporations, especially those with an international brand name, is being targeted by transnational activists (Keck and Sikkink 1998).

Activists use the media (including the Internet), litigation, boycotts, shareholder activism, and social investment to impose costs on businesses that have committed violations. In recent years, some activist groups have brought suit in U.S. courts against companies operating in Burma, arguing that their continuing presence constitutes complicity in the human rights abuses of the current military regime (Butler 2000). Shareholder activism and social investment funds are putting more pressure on company boards of directors (Opinion Leader Research 2000). Transnational activism is facilitated by many aspects of globalization—the global reach of the corporations themselves, global media that bring home to citizens and consumers conditions abroad, and communications technology that makes it easier than ever to establish and maintain international networks (Bray 1997). Many activist campaigns have the goal of forcing foreign investors to withdraw from countries of repression and conflict. Only in recent years have a few nonprofit organizations sought out corporate partners for conflict management activities in areas of emerging or existing violent conflict.

WHAT COULD THEY DO?

What exactly can a business organization do to contribute to conflict management? How can corporate executives participate in a way that is legitimate? Does the entry of the private sector directly into conflict management have the potential to create new sources of division among local interests, or can it help to reconcile them? What is the appropriate relationship between the private sector and public authorities at all levels—local, national, regional, and international—when intervening in conflicts? There are a variety of means by which conflict management in general is undertaken, and some are more or less appropriate for the private sector to use. The following discussion is divided into three sections: the stages and character of the conflict, the types of private sector intervention that are possible; and the character and core competencies of the industry. In each case a firm can choose from a range of positive and negative actions to take.

First, however, we have to acknowledge that business investment can play a role in reducing conflict simply by increasing the level of economic development in a country. Indirectly, without direct intention, the private sector often contributes to peace by reducing the economic sources of conflict. There is a link between general levels of investment, increases in economic development, and long-term improvement in human rights and political stability (Meyer 1996). As noted previously, investment in extractive industries tends to be associated with conflict largely because of the huge revenues involved. But foreign investment in general is also associated with employment, income, and economic growth that could promote stability.

As mentioned, when violence breaks out businesses have three general options: withdraw entirely, stay but try to ignore the conflict, and—as this chapter argues—remain invested in a country but work to prevent the escalation of violence. Most companies leave a society riven by conflict. In fact, many advocacy groups argue that they *should* leave, especially if the existing regime is corrupt or repressive. By leaving or threatening to leave, business sends a signal to the combatants that they should end the conflict if they want economic growth and development. But by leaving, business contributes to a continued downward slide in the economy or economic collapse that worsens the conflict. Companies that stay invested but do nothing to promote peace may actually contribute to worsening conflict, as many critics complain, since they send a message that the violence is tolerable. This chapter focuses primarily on the third option, that companies remain invested but operate their business in ways that reduce conflict or participate directly in conflict prevention/conflict management programs.

Stages and Character of Conflict

To start to understand the potential role of business in conflict management, we need to separate and categorize the different stages of conflict, which determine what kinds of interventions are possible or appropriate.[11] Generally, most analysts point to three broad stages: preconflict, when prevention strategies are most useful; outbreaks of significant violence, when intervention is considered; and postconflict reconstruction, when rebuilding is necessary.[12] Within each stage, there may be points in time when intervention and mediation will be most effective and when the situation is "ripe" for conflicts to be resolved (Regan 2000). The distinctions between these categories are fairly clear in theory, although not always in practice (Berdal and Malone 2000b).

The character of the conflict also shapes possible corporate responses. The underlying causes of a conflict may lie in an inequitable distribution of resources, rival identities and ideologies, or competition for government power —and in many cases they are intertwined (Nelson 2000, 37). Conflicts rooted in ethnic and nationalist hostility would be difficult for the private sector to address effectively, although in both South Africa and Northern Ireland investors have tried to use policies of inclusive employment to promote tolerance and reduce conflict. Ideological conflict, especially when it involves hostility to capitalism and market forces, cannot really be resolved by business. In conflicts over who rules in a given territory, the private sector often cannot take sides in a conflict without becoming part of the conflict itself. Generally, we would expect to see more opportunity for the private sector to contribute directly to conflict management when economic factors are a major source of grievance.

The role of business before the outbreak of violence, in the conflict prevention stage, is potentially the most controversial and yet potentially positive. At the preconflict stage, outside parties can pursue long-term strategies that

attempt to forestall or prevent the conditions that breed discontent or more short-term strategies of preventive diplomacy. Investment by business can directly and indirectly contribute to expanding opportunities and income in ways that help forestall the outbreak of violence. The private sector can adopt policies that promote a more equal distribution of wealth and resources, including land. Investment can, however, exacerbate existing socioeconomic divisions if it leads to uneven levels of economic activity throughout a country or if the central government appropriates revenues from the investment and uses them for narrow, even corrupt, purposes. Distributive policies are primarily a government responsibility, but the private sector can try to ensure that economic benefits reach a wider portion of the population. For instance, Exxon Mobil, the World Bank, and nongovernmental organizations (NGOs) recently committed to an oil project in Chad that includes a system for distributing oil revenues that bypasses the authoritarian central government.

When violent conflict breaks out, transnational activists often demand that a company make a judgment about the legitimacy of the existing regime and those rebelling or protesting against it. Some cases where the government is particularly nasty, such as in Burma, are relatively easy to assess. Other situations can be more difficult, where all sides in a conflict appear equally culpable. When companies, particularly foreign ones, take sides they then become a part of the conflict and may be shut down by public officials or by the rebels. Instead of taking sides, the private sector can attempt to be neutral in supporting democracy, free speech, and the protection of human rights, although exactly how to do this successfully is an open question.

Most people see a justifiable role for business in the final stage of postconflict reconstruction.[13] In fact, many commercial enterprises already are participating in postconflict reconstruction efforts. After a war or outbreak of violence, a nation needs to rebuild the infrastructure, provide employment to citizens, resettle refugees and retrain combatants, repair the infrastructure, remove land mines, ensure food security and agricultural rehabilitation, rebuild medical services, and meet an array of economic and social needs (Forman, Patrick, et al. 2000, 64–65, appendix 4). In almost all of these areas the business community can contribute materials, money, and expertise. One of the keys to successful reconstruction is persuading businesses to invest, to reopen shuttered operations, to jump-start the economy again. This need not be a deliberate and direct attempt to promote the ending of conflict and building of peace, but it may contribute indirectly to those outcomes. In a bid to be a more direct contributor, business interests might agree to operate even where conditions are still unstable. In the Middle East, a number of efforts to build a durable peace depend upon the participation of investors to create a functioning economy, especially in areas under Palestinian control.

Types of Intervention

Conflict prevention and management efforts fall into a number of general categories, from talking to sending in the troops.[14] A business might think of intervention in four different ways. First, a firm can correctly manage the side effects of its own business decisions. For instance, DeBeers can ensure that its diamond suppliers do not come from conflict-ridden areas. Second, a firm can do business with those attempting to manage conflict by selling or donating services, products, or investments. The United Nations now has an independent agency to develop partnerships with the private sector in support of its peacekeeping and other operations. Third, companies can participate as partners in collective efforts to resolve conflict, either in league with other businesses or more especially with governments and civil society organizations. The British government supports a project led by NGOs and a business organization that will provide policy tools for

companies wishing to employ conflict prevention strategies, particularly oil companies in the Caspian Sea region (Short 1999). Fourth, firms can engage in social investment and philanthropic ventures, addressing pressing social needs by donating cash, expertise, and other resources.

Within each of these four categories, there are a number of more specific actions that the private sector can take. These include informational activities, diplomatic intervention, positive inducements, negative sanctions, and direct intervention in a conflict.

INFORMATIONAL ACTIVITIES. The private sector can provide, collect, or facilitate access to information and communication between disputants or to the wider public. As a first step, companies can conduct socioeconomic impact assessments of their own operations. They are increasingly doing this for environmental issues but could extend the activity to include social indicators.[15] This process would involve company managers and employees in dialogue with each other, with the local community, and with international opinion leaders (Nelson 2000). The goal would be to develop a better understanding of whether the operations of the firm make a conflict worse and what to do about it if so. Companies could also participate in or facilitate the launching of multistakeholder dialogues, following the model of a South African business group that played a constructive role in the postapartheid political process. They can look to their own operations and employee policies to ensure they are not contributing to increased tensions. In countries where identity politics are being used to divide the population, companies can adopt tolerant hiring practices. They can try not to favor one group in their buying, selling, and subcontracting operations. In this way they may facilitate dialogue and engagement where neither currently exists.

Investors could try to promote peace by making public appeals to the warring sides to end the bloodshed or to the wider international community to intervene diplomatically. In general, when the private sector speaks out on a divisive political issue it should do so collectively and in partnership with other civil society groups. Business could provide the communications infrastructure that would facilitate information sharing within society, providing a means for citizens, activists, and the media to make public appeals and organize to press politically for peace. The business community could advocate on behalf of free and open media.

In promoting wider dissemination of information, businesses can sponsor fact-finding missions and observe the conduct of each side in a conflict. They could underwrite confidence-building measures that institutionalize mechanisms to enhance transparency and communications in general. If part of postconflict reconstruction includes an agreement to give up arms, then the private sector may be able to contribute technical assistance.[16] All of this has to be done carefully since the private sector would be viewed with suspicion for taking sides or for unduly profiting, for instance, if it participates in election monitoring. When conflict is at relatively low intensity, the business community can make positive contributions by supporting efforts to promote good governance, including protection of human rights, tolerance, and anticorruption policies. It can publicly support the initiatives of other groups that are fighting for democracy and accountability. When the situation deteriorates more significantly, the public role of the private sector becomes a source of conflict itself. In the case of Ken Saro-Wiwa and other Ogoni activists who were tried and hanged by an autocratic regime in Nigeria, many critics argued that Shell representatives should have made public appeals to free the rebels. The Harker Report on the activities of Talisman Energy in Sudan explicitly recommends that it speak out in favor of a cease-fire and conduct its own monitoring and reporting on forced removals, displacements of people, and human rights violations (Harker 2000, 18).

DIPLOMATIC INTERVENTION. The private sector can intervene diplomatically to bring the parties together, promote widespread dialogue, and mediate between different interests. Third parties can intervene directly in a conflict as part of "multitrack diplomacy." Corporate executives could seek to promote peace through open dialogue and pressing for democracy in discussions with political leaders, either public or private. These efforts can be strengthened by incentives and disincentives offered by the company, such as a promise to invest or sell in an area depending on whether the government makes sincere efforts to promote peace. In the past, when governments were weak or illegitimate, foreign investors often "propped up" these governments, creating a deep wellspring of resentment within society (Nelson 2000, 41). But there have been cases in which the business community has been instrumental in bringing conflicting sides to the negotiating table.

POSITIVE INDUCEMENTS. The private sector can help settle conflicts peacefully using positive inducements such as aid, economic development programs, and support for institutional capacity building. Investment itself, and the economic activity and employment it brings, can be an indirect means for promoting peace. It can be an inducement for governments to pursue peace. Unfortunately, it can also lead governments to invite foreign investors to exploit local natural resources at the expense of local inhabitants, as is the case in Sudan. Foreign aid and development programs can reinforce the dominance of particular elites or ethnic groups, change the local balance of power, and draw foreign actors into taking sides in ongoing disputes. When the multinational mining firm Freeport McMoRan decided to put more funds into community development near its operations in Indonesia, it inadvertently strengthened the local leader, who was viewed as a threat by a central government facing movements for autonomy in many regions of the country. At the same time, aid and foreign investment, when appropriately used and evenly distributed, can increase living standards and economic growth in general.

There are other ways that the private sector can contribute more directly to conflict management efforts. Aid—particularly nonmilitary aid—is probably the most acceptable form of direct intervention by the private sector. Humanitarian giving and community development are already a part of private sector philanthropic activities. Technical assistance would be a natural contribution of the private sector. There are dangers involved in distributing such aid, for example, if the government uses the new resources for its own aims, thus prolonging conflict (Keen 1998, 58–59). Nevertheless, positive inducements have been successful, as business can essentially buy peace by providing direct payments to rebels and/or government elites to bring them to the bargaining table. For instance, the international conglomerate Lonrho pledged support to the rebel group Renamo after the cease-fire in Mozambique, which encouraged the rebels to support the transition to peace (Keen 1998, 57).

NEGATIVE SANCTIONS. The private sector can apply negative sanctions, such as closing down operations, refusing to buy or sell, or divesting from a country, as leverage to halt the escalation of violence. This is probably the private sector's least-favored option, as demonstrated by the way the private sector strenuously resisted pressure to divest from South Africa a decade ago.[17] Official sanctions have more often failed than succeeded in their aims. Despite this, as already described, DeBeers did indeed impose private economic sanctions on the diamond-producing regions in Africa where rebels use diamond profits to continue fighting.

DIRECT INTERVENTION. The private sector can contribute to officially sanctioned intervention in violent conflicts, such as in peacekeeping or large-scale humanitarian missions. This usually involves putting military forces on the ground to guard against the eruption of conflict or to deliver a wide variety of services to a war-torn society, including everything from refugee assistance to drug eradication (Diehl, Druckman, et al. 1998). In extreme cases it involves coercive intervention by military force, as in the NATO operations in the Balkans. Private military services companies are actively involved in many aspects of current peacekeeping and police operations (Avant forthcoming). Corporations often are subcontractors for logistical and other support to military, police, and humanitarian missions. This kind of involvement is more in the nature of a commercial venture than an attempt by business to promote conflict management. In most cases only official, legitimate public authorities are in a position to keep opponents apart with force, defend victims from aggression, put down riots, or provide safe havens. Any forceful intervention by the private sector will create a furor over the legitimate use of force. Although there is some role for the private sector in direct interventions into conflict, it has to be a limited one and managed carefully in partnership with others, perhaps authorized by the United Nations.

The Character and Core Competencies of the Industry

The private sector is not one monolithic, homogeneous entity but varies in size, scale, organization, interests, and other characteristics. Three factors will be highlighted here: the particular industry sector, the organization and management of the firm, and whether the corporation is local or foreign. Different industry sectors have different strengths, given what are called their "core competencies." In searching for a role for business in conflict management, it is natural to start there. What does the business sell, and how can it be used for conflict management purposes?

The character of the business determines not just what it can do, but how it affects the local political environment. The most prominent sector in this regard is the extractive sector—oil, gas, mining, even water. These require very large investments and often generate equally large revenues, to be shared with the local government. These revenues almost inevitably become a source of friction within and between countries. A recent World Bank study found a high correlation between the outbreak of conflict and a country's reliance on commodity exports (Collier 2000).

Extractive industries interested in managing their investments in a way that lessens the probability of conflict have to decide whether to attach requirements to their contracts with governments or government-owned firms. The Harker Report on Talisman Energy in Sudan advocated that oil companies assume some responsibility for ensuring that their contracts with the government allow for an equitable distribution of revenues for humanitarian and development purposes (Harker 2000). However, as many corporate executives like to point out, they often do not have as much power in these bargaining situations as others believe. Especially when competition for contracts is high, it will be difficult for any foreign investor to make demands on the government. Only when a government is in a relatively weak position can such demands be made, as happened in Chad when transnational activists pressured Exxon Mobil and the World Bank to put significant restrictions on the government's use of oil revenues.

The prominence and the power of many extractive industries in small developing countries make it difficult for the industries to become active in the political arena, even in pursuit of peace. When the local situation near an oil, gas, or mining operation deteriorates, the international community tends to demand that they halt operations and withdraw from the country. In other situations, however, political instability may be moderate and the industry

can take a different role. In Ecuador, for instance, foreign oil companies exploring or drilling in lands owned by indigenous peoples have provided resources that have helped the groups organize politically and participate more fully in electoral politics (Burke 1999). In such cases the extractive industries invest resources in community development and dialogue in an area that is politically unstable. The extractive industries are not always associated with negative outcomes, fortunately. Botswana, for example, has prospered from a constructive partnership between the government and the leading natural resource companies.

Resource-intensive industries inevitably have an impact on the natural environment around their operations. Mining, petroleum drilling, timber clear-cutting, and similar activities destroy or degrade natural resources, which can worsen local conflicts (Homer-Dixon 1999). In Nigeria Ken Saro-Wiwa and others fought to protect the Ogoni people's right to a clean environment by taking action against oil spills and gas flaring. When oil or timber companies build roads into undeveloped land, they attract developers and others into rural areas and generate opposition, as has happened in the Amazon basin in Brazil. Some oil companies now attempt to explore remote areas with as little impact on the local community as possible, by bringing in all their equipment by air and making sure that everything down to the trash is removed afterward.

Corporate practices that protect the environment, minimize pollution, and preserve natural resources also contribute to conflict management. Such practices apply to large infrastructure projects, especially those that displace people from access to land, water, and resources. In response to international outcries against large dam projects in India and China, companies such as the engineering firm ABB have been forced to participate in what may be viewed as a conflict management exercise—the World Commission on Dams. This commission, made up of representatives from all sides in the debate over dam building, has the goal of resolving conflicts over these megaprojects.

The financial sector is becoming a more active participant in many social issues today. Activists use social investing as a tool to put pressure on companies and countries. For instance, the Chinese government could not raise money in the United States for its dam building because that project generated so much controversy and opposition. Talisman Energy saw its stock price drop after the critical Harker Report. Banks are increasingly under pressure to make sure their facilities are not used to support war, corruption, or criminal activity. The famously secretive Swiss banks now are adopting increasingly open policies in this regard. Social investment funds now control literally billions in investor dollars, and they screen out of portfolios those corporations they judge to be involved in illegitimate activities (human rights abuses, environmental degradation, arms dealing, and so on).

Consumer industries, such as textile, footwear, and carpet manufacturing—and diamond retailing—are the sectors that most need to maintain a positive reputation worldwide. Their brand names cannot be associated with violence and death. At the same time, the firms in these sectors do not need to invest in conflict-ridden regions of the world, and most tend to leave when violence breaks out. Nevertheless, many of the factories that supply brand-name corporations are adopting codes of conduct that state a commitment to human rights, dialogue with local communities, and other values. These light industries, requiring relatively little investment, often are the very ones most needed in the immediate postconflict reconstruction phase, when restarting the economy and generating employment are pressing needs.

Surprisingly little attention has been paid to the travel and tourism sector. This is a truly global industry with an obvious interest in peace. One of the most hurtful aspects of the antiapartheid movement, according to some, was the ban on sports and tourism in South

Africa. Some corporate leaders in the tourism industry have become interested in and active in promoting peace. For example, American Express and others support the International Institute of Peace Through Tourism and at a recent conference supported a commitment to building a culture of peace (Nelson 2000, 69). Although their view is controversial, some see tourism as a way to promote tolerance and respect for different cultures.

Information and media industries can establish better communications and information infrastructure within and between countries involved in conflict. The media can be a tool to promote democracy and human rights, though they can also be a tool for intolerance and conflict. Information and media industries can facilitate the work of civil society groups and international organizations involved in conflict management activities. Cisco Systems is building and running Internet Academies in Rwanda, to train people to use information technologies and to create a regional information center. The project planners provide aid and technology and hope that by helping to create a functioning economy they will also make it more difficult for conflict to recur.

The organization of an industry also can affect its willingness to intervene in conflicts and its capacity to do so. Many multinational corporations struggle to put effective systems in place to convey and implement policies from the top, including those designed to minimize conflict. In order to be more effective in peace promotion, a company has to ensure it has people with the right skills. Engineers make poor diplomats in most cases, as Shell found in Nigeria. In many cases a company has less control over its environment than most people realize. Foreign factories may not be owned or controlled by a major corporation but may be tied to it in a much weaker relationship: partly owned, joint venture, service or management contracts, licenses, leases, concessions, and build-operate-transfer or build-operate-own schemes. Thus, the nominal "owners" may not be in control at all (Nelson 2000). Typically, a company with direct ownership in an operation in an area of conflict will be more willing to participate in conflict management. Small-scale operations also may be more willing and able to work with those promoting a peaceful resolution to conflict, because they cannot afford losses associated with conflict or may have a personal commitment to the local community.

One final important point to make is the difference in context for local versus foreign companies. Local company leaders are more intimately linked to the political system and may be active "players" in the political conflict. This can give them great influence in promoting reform, as in the case of the National Business Initiative in South Africa, or great but negative influence in a corrupt and illegitimate system. Foreign direct investors, even when they do not directly worsen conflict, may find themselves the targets of criticism and active opposition simply because they are foreign. Foreign investors tend to bring a media spotlight with them and are more likely to attract attention for whatever they do, good or bad (Spar 1998). Foreigners may be more likely to respond to transnational activist pressure than local businesses and therefore may be more receptive to conflict management programs, but they may also be bigger targets for criticism. In fact, the private sector may be between a rock and a hard place, criticized both for the actions it does not take in the face of violent conflict and repression and for the actions it does take when it attempts to develop a new role in conflict management.

PUBLIC AND PRIVATE ACTORS IN SITUATIONS OF VIOLENT CONFLICT

The previous sections discussed various reasons why businesses might be motivated to participate in conflict management activities and the types of conflict management activities businesses might do. But do we want the private sector to become a direct participant in managing or preventing violent conflicts? After all, these involve complex political issues in which the legitimacy of the actors is a central factor in the conflict, and the private sector typically is not given this kind of legitimacy. Violent conflicts touch on issues of sovereignty and public authority, which could be undermined by ill-considered outside intervention of any sort, let alone that undertaken by business. Nevertheless, it is appropriate at this point to consider the role of business in conflict management. The corporate community has benefited tremendously from the liberalization of markets around the world. In return for the rewards of globalization, many people argue that the private sector must take up its responsibilities. Kofi Annan, secretary-general of the United Nations, challenged business on this point in launching the new Global Compact between the United Nations and the private sector.

When considering the business role in conflict management, we must remember first that the firm is an organization and that the people within that organization may, with the best will in the world, find it just as difficult to cope with the political, economic, and social challenges they face as any of the other participants in conflict management. Two decades ago, one study had this to say: "Our concern is with conflict of a different sort, a veritable managerial nightmare where the rules of the game are often incoherent, ambiguous, redundant and ever-changing. Where an attempt to resolve conflict in the here and now often leads to even greater conflict in another place or another time. Where managers are often trapped in conflicts not of their own making. And where 'good' and 'bad' solutions are often indistinguishable at the time managerial decisions have to be made" (Gladwin and Walter 1980, 1). Attempts by private sector actors to resolve divisions within and between societies have been beset with unintended side effects, insufficient expertise, and accusations of unaccountability and illegitimacy.

Conflict management and prevention have been criticized, with some observers pointing out that outside interventions produce temporary holding patterns while combatants regroup, instead of leading to lasting peace. Private sector actors may be accused of co-opting local interests in order to "stabilize" the environment for investment, generating significant repression. Any actor considering intervening in situations of conflict has to consider the conditions under which it makes sense and who should lead (Jonge Oudraat 2000, 3). Given this, is there any possibility the private sector could become the leading edge in international interventions? Conceivably we could encounter a situation in which foreign governments are ambivalent, the United Nations is unresponsive, but the business community decides it is in its strategic interest to intervene. This is an unlikely scenario, however. More likely is that when businesses are motivated, they will put pressure on governments and the United Nations to intervene.

The private sector cannot act alone but must act in partnership with others. This has two dimensions: first, individual firms should act in concert with other firms and, second, they should work with more legitimate actors such as the United Nations. If they do not work together, they could work at cross-purposes and weaken their effectiveness. When business interests unite, however, it raises all sorts of questions about anticompetitive behavior, conspiratorial wielding of unelected power, and illegitimate profit making. This is why it is important for businesses to work in partnership with other organizations that have a better claim to represent the broader public interest.[18] These partnerships will depend upon greater accountability by the corporation in assessing its impact on conditions in a country and in reporting publicly on those effects (Nelson 2000).

Appropriate partners can be difficult to identify, especially in complex political situations with foreign cultures, where there may be many different and opposing groups even on the side of peace. Intermediaries such as NGOs, academics, clergy, politicians, and others may create another layer of obscurity in an already difficult-to-diagnose situation. Each of these potential partners may view the corporation as a cash cow and tool for promoting individual and not public interests. The money spent by a company might be viewed as appeasement or bribery. NGOs worry that their membership may view this as a partnership with the devil. Intergovernmental organizations, such as the United Nations Development Programme and the Office of the Secretary-General, have been accused of selling out by critics of their partnerships with the private sector. Corporate executives have in some cases discovered that they are working with the "wrong" community groups or that favoring one leads to criticism from another. Despite all these problems, the private sector can consult with a wide range of experts who can guide them in choosing partners carefully. United Nations agencies will probably be the most effective partners in conflict management.

The home countries of foreign investors clearly can play a role in facilitating conflict management and prevention by the private sector. They can bring pressure to bear on companies accused of supporting conflict and repression, such as the pressure put on Talisman by the Canadian government. The United States and Great Britain recently unveiled a set of voluntary principles for companies hiring private or public security forces in developing countries, with support from seven major oil and mining companies. The goal is to try to ensure that these forces are not used in ways that worsen a conflict (Alden and Buchan 2000). Business could become partners in implementing foreign aid, development, and humanitarian assistance programs, which they do to some degree already. Increasingly, governments view the private sector as a tool—willing or unwilling—to promote foreign policy preferences abroad through everything from sanctions to corporate codes of conduct.

The international community can provide an environment that makes it easier for companies to minimize their effect on unstable societies, promote peaceful resolution of conflict, and become more socially responsible. This could include, for instance, the new OECD Guidelines for Multinational Enterprises, which set out a framework of expectations for corporate behavior on a global basis. Both international and domestic law and regulation can reward companies and support them, and stronger monitoring and verification systems could indicate when to sanction them. If the international community believes it is important to involve the private sector in conflict management, then it will need to promote educational initiatives to convince top management of the benefits of responsible behavior.

Are there any wider implications that we can draw from this speculation about the potential for a corporate role in conflict prevention and management? Certainly, the idea that the private sector could contribute to the resolution of conflict turns our notions of world politics upside down. States are supposed to be sovereign and in charge. They are the central actor in world politics, especially on issues of war and peace. Private interests are traditionally viewed as selfish and uninterested in the impact their operations may have on social and political divisions. Many people equate globalization with the growing power of multinational corporations. They also equate it with the increasing division of the world into haves and have-nots, exacerbating local and international points of contention. Globalizers believe that economic interests have become so strong that markets replace politics at home and abroad. But the bottom line is that, as the Carnegie Commission report says, "It cannot be emphasized enough that governments bear the greatest responsibility to prevent deadly conflict" (Carnegie Commission on Preventing Deadly Conflict 1997). The resolution of conflict lies in the hands of public authorities. Private economic interests cannot perform the functions of governments and should not be asked to do so.

Conflict resolution practitioners are "like physicians in that they work to prevent or control noxious situations. But few of them believe that violent international conflict follows the classical model of infectious disease, in which each condition has a single cause and a small number of effective treatments can be identified and evaluated by scientific analysis and applied independently of the situation" (Stern and Druckman 2000, 33). Perhaps direct action by the private sector to prevent or resolve violent conflict can be looked upon as a risky but potentially fruitful alternative therapy. Its application must be monitored closely, and it should be administered not alone but in conjunction with more traditional methods. Multiple therapies of this sort may cure the disease or at least ameliorate some of the pain. That is the hope of those pressing business to get involved in conflict management.

NOTES

1. This has come back to haunt many companies today. Swiss banks and insurers, German car manufacturers, and others face class action lawsuits and diplomatic negotiations to settle war-related claims from their victims.

2. Research indicates that mineral wealth is positively and significantly correlated with the outbreak of armed conflict (de Soysa 2000).

3. The best, and to date the only, comprehensive work on the role of business in conflict management is *The Business of Peace* by Jane Nelson, published by the Prince of Wales Business Leaders Forum, the Council on Economic Priorities, and International Alert (Nelson 2000).

4. International Alert is a London-based nonprofit that has worked in Sri Lanka and other conflict-torn societies to promote peace and reconciliation. The current project is in partnership with the Prince of Wales Business Leaders Forum, an organization established at the initiative of the Prince of Wales to

promote corporate social responsibility. Its members include top British multinational corporations. The other partner is the Council on Economic Priorities, a New York–based nonprofit that pioneered the concept of social investing and recently sponsored the development of a social accounting standard for businesses. Their joint project is still in its early stages, so there is little information yet on its progress.

5. Commenting on "several dogs that either did not bark or merely whimpered" at a recent conference on economic agendas in civil wars, Berdal and Malone note that "although the role of the private sector in shaping and furthering economic agendas in civil wars was widely accepted as key, only local trading networks were addressed in any depth. . . . Nevertheless, in seeking to come to grips with means for international actors to influence belligerents, the corporate factor looms large in the equation" (Berdal and Malone 2000b, 11).

6. This chapter also will not discuss the arms industry, since it is hard to make the case that the manufacturers and retailers of weapons could have an interest in conflict prevention. But private military services firms (sometimes called "modern mercenaries") do indeed have an interest in conflict management. These companies are hired by governments, international organizations, and multinational corporations to provide logistical support, security, and conflict management services to multinational corporations operating in violence-prone areas. See Avant forthcoming.

7. The business community generally opposes official economic sanctions and has lobbied vigorously against them, especially in the United States. The failure of UN sanctions in areas such as Angola because of smuggling shows that perhaps the best path to eradication of illegally traded goods may be through the private sector (Jonge Oudraat 2000; United Nations 2000).

8. We tend to assume that conflict prevention is valuable to the international community. For a cost-benefit analysis of the value to outsiders of preventing deadly conflict, see Brown and Rosecrance 1999. Jordana Friedman, director of the International Security Program of the Council on Economic Priorities, points out that we need to develop good quantitative evidence that conflict management actually benefits the private sector if we want to convince them to get involved in preventing it (Friedman 2000).

9. "Asset-specificity" is the term that economists use to refer to investments that are tied to locations, persons, or valuable relationships.

10. Even a company with long-term investments, however, may not feel any pressure to deal with local instabilities. The executives of Shell in Nigeria, for instance, could make the argument that they will outlive any particular political regime, good or bad, and any particular level of conflict; they have been there for half a century and plan to be there half a century more.

11. All such categorizations are somewhat arbitrary. No stage is neatly delineated from the next, nor is there some logical progression from one stage to another with no stasis or slipping backward (Allan Gerson, cited in Nelson 2000).

12. We could divide this into further categories. For instance, Nelson uses three roughly similar categories but then subdivides them: the preconflict stage entails prevention strategies such as peacebuilding, good governance, and democracy promotion; the conflict zone stage involves crisis management and diplomacy, preventive deployment of troops, and disarmament of combatants; the postconflict stage involves reconstruction and reconciliation, with activities such as investment, governance, repairs, de-mining, and refugee assistance (Nelson 2000, 58).

13. Only recently have major donors such as the World Bank begun to consider how to incorporate the private sector into postwar reconstruction efforts.

14. The Carnegie Commission Report on Preventing Deadly Conflict divides action into two broad categories: operational prevention, which focuses on crisis activities, and structural prevention, which addresses the fundamental causes of conflict (Carnegie Commission on Preventing Deadly Conflict 1997). Keen (1998, 55) lays out four main types of outside intervention that can reduce violence: emergency aid, use or threat of force, democracy promotion, and reconstruction and development aid; see also Berdal and Malone 2000b. Dixon (1996) discusses seven categories of intervention by third parties in conflicts, while Brown and Rosecrance (1999) propose ten. Regan (2000) presents three forms of conflict management: bilateral, multilateral, and third-party mediation.

15. Current attempts to develop measurable, auditable social indicators include SA8000 and the multistakeholder Global Reporting Initiative. These are intended to measure corporate performance in meeting environmental, labor, and human rights goals and could be adapted for use in conflict prevention programs.

16. Certain types of monitoring and verification programs absolutely require private sector participation. The Chemical Weapons Convention, for instance, entails significant and burdensome reporting by chemical manufacturers.

17. Over thirty major multinational companies withdrew from Burma shortly after the launch of the Free Burma Campaign, owing to the repression there (Nelson 2000). This withdrawal would not have happened ten years ago, demonstrating a change in the way corporate managers define the acceptable conditions for business.

18. According to the report of the Prince of Wales Business Leaders Forum/CEP/International Alert, the principles of corporate engagement in conflict prevention activities include the commitment of corporate leaders embodied in management systems; preparing the appropriate skills, incentives, experts, and evaluation for these activities; dialogue and consultation; working collectively with other companies, civil society, and governments; evaluation and accountability through measurement, verification, reporting, and benchmarking; and working with governments and others to create an enabling environment (Nelson 2000, 4).

REFERENCES

Alden, Edward, and David Buchan. 2000. "Oil Groups Back Initiative to Guard Human Rights." *Financial Times*, December 21.

Avant, Debbi. Forthcoming. *The Market for Force*.

Berdal, Mats, and David M. Malone. 2000a. Introduction to *Greed and Grievance: Economic Agendas in Civil Wars*, ed. Mats Berdal and David M. Malone, 1–18. Boulder, Colo.: Lynne Rienner.

———, eds. 2000b. *Greed and Grievance: Economic Agendas in Civil Wars*. Boulder, Colo.: Lynne Rienner.

Berman, Jonathan. 2000. "Corporations and Conflict: How Managers Think about War." *Harvard International Review* (fall 2000).

Bray, John. 1997. "A Web of Influence." *World Today* (August/September).

Brown, Michael, and Richard Rosecrance, eds. 1999. *The Costs of Conflict: Prevention and Cure in the Global Arena*. Carnegie Commission on Preventing Deadly Conflict. Lanham, Md.: Rowman and Littlefield.

Burke, Pamela. 1999. "Oil Companies and Indigenous Peoples in Ecuador." In *Private Authority and International Affairs*, ed. A. Claire Cutler, Virginia Haufler, and Tony Porter. Albany: State University of New York.

Butler, Nick. 2000. "Companies in International Relations." *Survival* 42, no. 1: 149–164.

Carnegie Commission on Preventing Deadly Conflict. 1997. *Preventing Deadly Conflict: Final Report*. New York: Carnegie Corporation of New York.

Collier, Paul. 2000. *Economic Causes of Civil Conflict and Their Implications for Policy*. Washington, D.C.: World Bank.

Diehl, Paul F., Daniel Druckman, et al. 1998. "International Peacekeeping and Conflict Resolution." *Journal of Conflict Resolution* 42, no. 1: 33–55.

Dixon, William J. 1996. "Third-Party Techniques for Preventing Conflict Escalation and Promoting Peaceful Settlement." *International Organization* 50, no. 4: 653–681.

Duffield, Mark. 2000. "Globalization, Transborder Trade, and War Economies." In *Greed and Grievance: Economic Agendas in Civil War*, ed. Berdal and Malone, 69–90.

Forman, Shepard, Stewart Patrick, et al. 2000. *Recovering from Conflict: Strategy for an International Response*, 1–67. New York: Center on International Cooperation, New York University.

Fortune. 2000. *Fortune 500*. Accessed by the author through the Internet on June 15, 2000, at http://www.fortune.com.

Freeman, Jordan. 2000. Speech to the Business and International Security Conference, sponsored by the International Peace Forum, New York, April 29, 2000.

Frynas, George. 1998. "Political Instability and Business: Focus on Shell and Nigeria." *Third World Quarterly* 19, no. 3: 457–487.

General Motors Corporation. 2000. Web site. Accessed by the author on June 15, 2000, at http://www.gm.com.

Gladwin, Thomas N., and Ingo Walter. 1980. *Multinationals under Fire: Lessons in the Management of Conflict.* New York: John Wiley.

Global Witness. 1999. *A Crude Awakening: The Role of Oil and Banking Industries in Angolan Civil War and the Plunder of State Assets.* London: Global Witness.

Harker, John. 2000. *Human Security in Sudan: The Report of a Canadian Assessment Mission.* Ottawa: Department of Foreign Affairs and International Trade.

Haufler, Virginia. 1997. *Dangerous Commerce: Insurance and the Management of International Risk.* Ithaca, N.Y.: Cornell University Press.

———. 2001. *Industry Self-Regulation and Global Governance.* Washington, D.C.: Carnegie Endowment for International Peace Press.

Homer-Dixon, Thomas. 1999. *Environment, Scarcity, and Violence.* Princeton, N.J.: Princeton University Press.

Jonge Oudraat, Chantal de. 2000. "Making Economic Sanctions Work." *Survival* 42, no. 3: 105–127.

Keck, Margaret E., and Kathryn Sikkink. 1998. *Activists beyond Borders: Advocacy Networks in International Politics.* Ithaca, N.Y.: Cornell University Press.

Keen, David. 1998. *The Economic Functions of Violence in Civil Wars.* Oxford: Oxford University Press for the International Institute for Strategic Studies.

Lopez, George, and Michael Stohl, eds. 1989. *Dependence, Development, and State Repression.* New York: Greenwood Press.

Manby, Bronwen. 1999. *The Price of Oil: Corporate Responsibility and Human Rights Violations in Nigeria's Oil Producing Communities.* New York: Human Rights Watch.

Meyer, William H. 1996. "Human Rights and MNCs: Theory versus Quantitative Analysis." *Human Rights Quarterly* 18: 368–397.

Nelson, Jane. 2000. *The Business of Peace: The Private Sector as a Partner in Conflict Prevention and Resolution.* London: Prince of Wales Business Leaders Forum.

Opinion Leader Research. 2000. *Does the City Have a Social Conscience?* 1–12. London: Control Risks Group.

Pegg, Scott. 1999. "The Cost of Doing Business: Transnational Corporations and Violence in Nigeria." *Security Dialogue* 30, no. 4: 473–484.

Regan, Patrick M. 2000. *Thoughts on How to Organize a Data Set on Diplomatic Methods of Conflict Management.* Workshop on Negotiation, Center for International Development and Conflict Management. College Park: University of Maryland.

Reno, William. 2000. "Shadow States and the Political Economy of Civil Wars." In *Greed and Grievance: Economic Agendas in Civil Wars*, ed. Berdal and Malone, 43–68.

Short, Clare. 1999. *Conflict Prevention, Conflict Resolution, and Post-Conflict Peace-Building: From Rhetoric to Reality: Speech by the Secretary of State for International Development, United Kingdom.* London: International Alert.

Soysa, Indra de. 2000. "The Resource Curse: Are Civil Wars Driven by Rapacity or Paucity?" In *Greed and Grievance: Economic Agendas in Civil Wars*, ed. Berdal and Malone, 113–136.

Spar, Debora L. 1998. "The Spotlight and the Bottom Line: How Multinationals Export Human Rights." *Foreign Affairs* 77, no. 2: 7–12.

Stern, Paul C., and Daniel Druckman. 2000. "Evaluating Interventions in History: The Case of International Conflict Resolution." *International Studies Review* 2, no. 1: 33–63.

United Nations. 2000. *Report of the Panel of Experts on Violations of Security Council Sanctions against UNITA.* New York: United Nations.

United Nations Conference on Trade and Investment. 1998. *World Investment Report: Trends and Determinants.* New York and Geneva: United Nations.

World Bank. 1997. *World Development Report 1997.* Washington, D.C.: World Bank.

40

Information
and Conflict

Warren P. Strobel

CROSSHAIRS ON A TELEVISION SCREEN track a NATO missile to its destination in Serbia, the weapon dissolving in a silent plume of white smoke. A small radio transmitter, broadcasting from the back of a truck in the Rwandan jungle, exhorts Hutus to begin the mass murder of ethnic Tutsi. In the streets of Belgrade, tens of thousands of Serbs with mock "targets" on their torsos gather for journalists' cameras, aiming at Western public opinion during the Kosovo bombing campaign. On a beach outside Mogadishu, Somalia, U.S. special forces are swarmed by reporters clutching video cameras and klieg lights. The reporters have been tipped off about where to wait by U.S. and United Nations officials using the international media for their own purposes.[1]

Information, wielded both by the international media and increasingly by others—civilians, private aid groups, militaries, political leaders in dictatorships and democracies—plays a large and growing role in conflict and conflict prevention. The influence of information can begin before the first shots are fired and last long into the postconflict, reconstruction, and reconciliation phases. This influence, especially of television images, can *seem* sudden, powerful, and unexpected: a (repeatedly rebroadcast) image of a starving child or dead American soldier can grip the public imagination, threatening in a moment to sweep away diplomats' painstakingly constructed policies. So striking and (apparently) unpredictable is the role of information and public opinion that some observers argue that the news media have become independent actors in foreign and national security affairs, on a par with more traditional sources of policy such as nation-states and international law. "For the past two centuries, it was law that provided the source of authority for democracy," observed former UN secretary-general Boutros Boutros-Ghali. "Today, law seems to be replaced by opinion as the source of authority, and the media serve as the arbiter of public opinion."[2]

However, upon closer scrutiny, we see that the role of the news media and information generally in conflict and conflict prevention

677

reveals itself to be more complex—more interactive, to use a popular phrase. In one moment, Cable News Network (CNN) threatens to seize the initiative from official policymakers with emotive images it broadcasts. The next day (or hour), CNN acts as a vital tool for those same policymakers to communicate to domestic publics or foreign audiences. Horrific reports of "ethnic cleansing" in Bosnia had minimal impact on the Bush and Clinton administrations' firm resolve not to intervene with troops in the Balkans until the United States concluded in early 1994 that the risks of inaction outweighed the risks of action.[3] Overnight, the media's insistent coverage of humanitarian horror metamorphosed (if you were sitting in the White House) from bane to boon. In Kosovo, the flood of ethnic Albanian refugees created by Serbian leader Slobodan Milosevic after the start of Operation Allied Force provoked harsh criticism of NATO's actions—and simultaneously provided justification for them. In short, the impact of information is rarely if ever predetermined. It depends on the agility of policymakers and their adversaries; the conviction (and political will) with which a policy position is held and communicated; and, it must be said, the course of events themselves.

The most distinctive trait of information today is its *pervasiveness*.[4] The impact and effects of information can be mitigated, even harnessed to prevent or prevail in conflict. But these potential impacts and their purveyors in the media are ignored at extreme peril: "The media is not an optional add-on; it is key."[5] Complaining about the media's scope and reach is as effective as ruing the weather. Those who participate in conflict management must, in Pentagon lingo, learn to "operate wet."

Two developments over the past decade have fed the increasing centrality of information to conflict. The first is obvious: the emergence of communication technologies such as live, global television networks and the Internet, which offer rapid, worldwide, and increasingly personalized information flows. Indeed, defining just what the media are is increasingly difficult. Typically, past studies of media influence on national security focused on discrete institutions such as prestige papers like the *New York Times* and the *Washington Post;* the "Big Three" broadcast television networks; and CNN. These, particularly television, still hold considerable sway. But the past decade has seen dramatic changes in the media industry and news consumption. A June 2000 survey by the Pew Research Center for the People and the Press found that more and more Americans were turning to the Internet for news and information, primarily at the expense of broadcast television. And fewer Americans were following the news at all.[6] Even more important, new communication tools give anyone from guerrilla leaders to student demonstrators the potential to affect foreign policy, depriving the elite (including the media elite) and officialdom of their monopoly.

For these and other reasons, this chapter looks at media and information in the broadest sense. I use the term "information" to describe the content of a communication, regardless of the medium or audience involved. I use "media" to refer to the tools of communication, although there are obviously wide gaps in levels of commercialization, reliability, and other factors between, say, an Internet radio broadcast and the ABC evening news. Because of television's presumed role in prompting interventions in conflict, and because of the longer time frame involved, the first half of this chapter deals primarily with the "traditional" commercialized international news-gathering industry, which I refer to as the "news media." The second half, which concentrates on the modern humanitarian war in Kosovo, brings the new media onto the stage.

The second development of the past decade is arguably even more instrumental than technology: the changed nature of conflict itself. The current era appears to be one of limited conflicts fought largely on humanitarian grounds. In military operations such as those in Kosovo, Bosnia, East Timor, Haiti, and Somalia, appeals to national interest that function in wartime hold little sway with either Western publics or news media. Consequently, the news media's "room to maneuver" and report what and how they like expands. Each participant's domestic public opinion becomes a primary battleground, with information, through the media, an important weapon. Citizens themselves can now participate in information warfare, as happened in Belgrade's streets and cybercafés. Because public opinion is so vital, TV towers and other media outlets may be considered military targets. Ethnic populations, whose mistreatment may have prompted the conflict, may be further misused for propaganda gains. And because the conflict is moral in nature, the news media may hold Western militaries to the highest standards in terms of minimizing civilian casualties.[7] These are the conflicts not only of the recent past, but, it would appear, of the foreseeable future.

The first half of this chapter will look at how the news media and other sources of information influence decisions by the United States and allied nations on when and how to intervene in foreign conflicts. The second half will look at their role once an intervention is under way, when information is arguably an even more important factor in the dynamics of conflict.[8]

BEFORE THE BEGINNING

The ubiquity of information can be seen in its use to fan the flames of conflict, particularly ethnic conflict, long before most outsiders are more than dimly aware of a crisis that soon may present them with a decision to make about intervening. Such information often comes from indigenous media tools that are as unsophisticated as they are effective: small radio transmitters and propagandistic state-controlled television stations that help turn a precrisis zone into a bloody one.

"Hate radio" is one example. Its most notorious use occurred in Rwanda in 1994. Radio Mille Collines (A Thousand Hills), controlled by the then-Hutu government, helped ignite the Rwandan genocide of an estimated eight hundred thousand ethnic Tutsi and moderate Hutu by exploiting fears and ethnic hatreds. The Tutsi "cruelly kill mankind . . . they kill by dissecting Hutus . . . by extracting various organs from the bodies of Hutus . . . the [Tutsi] eat men," declared one representative broadcast.[9] The radio station also incited attacks against Belgian civilians and the small UN Assistance Mission in Rwanda (UNAMIR). As the genocide began, Belgian troops were withdrawn and the UN Security Council scaled back UNAMIR. Even after Tutsi rebels toppled the government, the radio station continued broadcasting from a mobile transmitter, probably located on the back of a truck.[10] And it continued to have an impact, urging Hutus to flee to neighboring Zaire (now the Democratic Republic of the Congo), a journey that killed many and finally brought large-scale outside intervention in the form of humanitarian aid.

In the Balkans, manipulation of the media in the service of ethnic aims was a hallmark of Slobodan Milosevic's rule in Serbia.[11] This (mis)use of information helped start the conflicts in Croatia, Bosnia, and Kosovo as ethnic groups were vilified, ancient grievances recalled, and moderate voices marginalized. Again, the outside world eventually intervened in the region, with air strikes and international peacekeeping forces.

It has been estimated that several hundred thousand people could have been saved in Rwanda if Radio Mille Collines had been jammed and if the United Nations and United States had mounted more than the minimal counterbroadcasting effort they did.[12] But proposals for early "information intervention" that would jam or counter hateful radio and TV broadcasts before crises erupt remain controversial, raising questions about sovereignty, fairness, and control.[13]

Whether they choose to act preemptively or not, outside intervenors, once they enter a conflict zone, will have to deal with indigenous information campaigns. Information, as much as weapons or diplomacy, can affect the success of an intervention, public support for it at home, and efforts to promote lasting peace and reconciliation between former antagonists.

INFORMATION AND INTERVENTION DECISIONS

A frequent refrain from U.S. military officers in recent years is that CNN and its news media colleagues determine where the United States deploys its soldiers overseas, heartrending images of violence and humanitarian suffering replacing the strategic guiding light provided by the Soviet Union during the Cold War. Such powerful images, they worry, may have little to do with U.S. national security interests in a particular region—and may not reflect the will of the U.S. body politic to stay engaged in the face of casualties or other setbacks. Even worse, this "push" to intervene may be driven by news coverage that is focused on ratings and commercial success.[14]

On one level, such concerns seem legitimate. The international community's intervention in Somalia, the Balkans, East Timor, and elsewhere was preceded by journalists' images and words that seemed to cry out for a response, thereby setting the West's foreign policy agenda. Yet a more detailed look at the news media's impact on intervention decisions suggests that their role is neither as powerful nor as direct as it seems at first glance. That the media generate pressures for intervention is inarguable. Sometimes these pressures help propel policymakers toward *humanitarian* interventions that *seem* to them to present low risk. Examples include providing for the Iraqi Kurds at the end of the Persian Gulf War (1991) and securing relief efforts in Somalia (1992). But even in these cases, other strategic or foreign

policy considerations played a pivotal role in the ultimate U.S. decision to intervene.

If a proposed intervention entails major risk or conflicts with policymakers' strongly held positions, the news media's impact can be minimal and bear little relation to the minutes of broadcast time or pages of newsprint devoted to the region in question. Policymakers find ways, rhetorical and otherwise, to deflect media-generated pressures.[15] This happened with respect to Bosnia from 1992 until 1994, and the Rwandan genocide in 1994. Also, "viewer fatigue" at images of carnage or starvation can dull public pressure on policymakers to "do something." Nor do the news media operate as the independent source of policy inputs that they sometimes appear. Relief groups, members of Congress (or other parliamentary bodies), and even middle-level government officials court the media, particularly television, to draw international attention to a crisis, hoping to pressure senior executive-branch decision makers into action. These third-party attempts to shape policy are seen most clearly in the case of Somalia. Finally, the cases of Haiti and, to some extent, Kosovo serve as reminders that, even absent the Soviet threat, the U.S. president's foreign policy prerogatives easily trump the media's. In both cases, the commander in chief, wielding the argument of "national security interests," ordered U.S. troops overseas without strong media or public backing.

■ ■ ■

The U.S.-led intervention in Somalia in December 1992 to provide security for relief efforts seems like a good place to begin, since it is widely believed that "CNN got us in" (and later, by portraying U.S. casualties, "got us out," too). The Somalia experience gave life to a presumed "CNN effect," in which government officials lose control over policy to the news media.[16] Yet to say that horrific television images of starving innocents in Somalia determined U.S. foreign policy is to caricature the policymaking process. First, television coverage of Somalia tended to *follow* the Bush administration's actions, rather than precede them. Coverage of the famine in the Horn of Africa by the network evening news and CNN was minimal before President George Bush's initial August 12, 1992, decision to mount an airlift of emergency relief supplies to drought-stricken areas. That action drew dozens more journalists to the region—and raised inevitable questions about whether the airlift would be sufficient to meet the need.[17] Among those raising such questions were other policy actors, including U.S. Agency for International Development (AID) officials, members of Congress, and nongovernmental organizations (NGOs) concerned with Africa. They used the media to draw the attention of the world, and particularly Bush and his top aides, to Somalia in hopes of prompting the large-scale intervention that the president in fact ordered in late November. Herman Cohen, then assistant secretary of state for African affairs, observed the weekly strategy sessions between top AID officials and NGOs. "They are all in there, planning strategy . . . how do you inform the world?" Cohen recalled.[18] This is a key point for policymakers to keep in mind: Thanks to a pervasive media, a much wider array of official and nonofficial actors has the *potential* to use information to affect foreign policy. Their efforts are more likely to succeed if official policy suffers from uncertain stewardship.

Most important, the images from Somalia landed in a specific policy environment that gave them weight; they were a necessary, but not sufficient, condition for action. In the summer and fall of 1992, the Bush administration also was facing intense pressure to intervene in the former Yugoslavia, where the president and his top advisers unanimously believed the risks outweighed U.S. national interests. Somalia, by contrast, appeared amenable to a relatively low-risk humanitarian "fix." Acting to stop starvation in Africa would restore faith in Washington's post–Gulf War foreign policy and ease the

pressure to send troops to Bosnia.[19] Indeed, the Pentagon dropped its opposition to a Somalia mission almost at the last minute. The sudden support of General Colin Powell, chairman of the Joint Chiefs of Staff, may have been predicated on the condition that the United States would not also intervene in Bosnia.[20]

The case of Somalia shows how, under very limited conditions and prompted largely by official and nonofficial policy actors, television images and other media-reported information can help persuade policymakers to intervene for humanitarian purposes. Yet the news media alone seem to have little, if any, power to push governments to intervene with military force to stop a conflict. Much more is needed. "Pictures are very useful in getting people to focus on it as a basis for humanitarian support," said former assistant secretary of state Robert Gallucci, who argued in November 1992 for U.S. intervention in *both* Bosnia and Somalia. For anything more than that, he said, "it's gotta answer the question, Why us?"[21]

News media reporting of atrocities in the former Yugoslavia from 1992 to 1994 caused political and diplomatic difficulties for Presidents Bush and Clinton but did not overcome a larger opposing force—their belief that the risks of intervention in Bosnia outweighed the stakes. "It wouldn't have mattered if television was going 24 hours around the clock with Serb atrocities. Bush wasn't going to get in," said Warren Zimmermann, the last U.S. ambassador to Yugoslavia.[22] Even the existence of Serb-run detention camps, revealed in August 1992 first by *Newsday* and then on videotape by Britain's Independent Television Network (ITN), did not change this basic policy. Bush demanded that the Serbs open the camps to international access. The UN Security Council passed Resolution 770, reinforcing that demand and authorizing the use of force, if necessary, to deliver humanitarian supplies. But the basic thrust of Bush's policy remained unchanged, as he made clear in remarks on August 7: "I do not want to see the United States bogged down in any way into some guerrilla warfare. We lived through that once." Leaders in Washington, and in European capitals, responded to news media reports of what were then the worst atrocities in Europe since World War II, but it was a *minimalist response.*

It is often said that the desire of the Western powers not to intervene in Bosnia was overcome by a single media event. The "marketplace massacre" of February 5, 1994, when a mortar shell landed in Sarajevo's central marketplace, killing sixty-eight people and wounding nearly two hundred others, was televised around the world. It prompted public and official demands for action. There had been many such deaths in Bosnia in the preceding two years, but these were captured on camera. Once again, however, a closer look reveals that the images played a role because of the nature of the policy process they impacted upon. That process was suddenly fluid, after months of stasis. By February 1994, the Clinton administration had reluctantly concluded that the West's inability to stop the war in Bosnia was endangering NATO—the cornerstone of U.S. policy in Europe—and U.S. leadership. France was putting intense pressure on the United States for action. On February 4, the day *before* the shelling, Secretary of State Warren Christopher proposed to his peers at the White House and Pentagon that the United States lead a new diplomatic effort to end the fighting, backed by the threat of military force.[23] Before the shelling, "We had already made the psychological determination [about] the direction we wanted to go," recalled a senior State Department official. This official was in meetings about crafting a new Bosnia policy when the mortar attack occurred—and he worried then that the new policy would be seen, incorrectly, as an instant response to the massacre.[24] NATO issued an ultimatum to the Bosnian Serbs to remove their heavy weapons from around the capital, and the five-nation "Contact Group" was formed, giving new momentum to a diplomatic solution to the conflict. Sarajevo

then enjoyed a bit of normalcy after nearly two years of siege. The Sarajevo shelling is a good example of how the media can help officials make the case for intervention—when they are so inclined. "It was a short window. We took advantage of it. We moved the policy forward. And it was successful," said White House spokesperson Dee Dee Myers.[25]

The Rwandan genocide illustrates even more starkly the limits of the news media's power on intervention. Under CNN effect theory, the pressures to act in Rwanda were greater than those in Somalia. There was more coverage of Rwanda on the network evening news in April and May 1994, after a mysterious plane crash had killed the Hutu presidents of Rwanda and Burundi and provided a pretext for the slaughter, than there was of Somalia before President Bush's decision to dispatch U.S. troops there.[26] Yet with the trauma of U.S. casualties in Somalia only months old, and with no clear idea of how to stop the killing in Rwanda, the gruesome television pictures had little impact. Recalling one videotaped report of corpses floating down an African river, a senior administration official said, "None of those provoked or provided the kind of catalyst for a U.S. military intervention."[27] It was only in late July, when the fighting largely was over and hundreds of thousands of mostly Hutu Rwandan refugees were on the move, that the Clinton administration decided it could offer humanitarian assistance at acceptable risk. Significantly, according to a senior NGO representative, it was also at this point, when the images depicted innocents in need rather than brutal civil conflict, that the U.S. public became aroused and began donating funds to relief groups.[28] President Eduard Shevardnadze of Georgia may have put it best: "The dictatorship of the TV picture, horrifying millions of people with images of mass violence, urges us to adopt humanitarian decisions and to avoid political ones."

■ ■ ■

The news media can have another effect on intervention decisions: officials' concern (well grounded or not) over the media's role in publicizing casualties or other setbacks once a mission is under way can, absent compelling interests, argue against getting involved in the first place. In the words of Secretary of State Lawrence Eagleburger, "Those who got you in won't defend you. They will turn on you. . . . What you're worried about is that you'll orient the United States to a policy and you'll have to reverse it" because the media go from cheerleader to critic.[29] Concerns over postintervention media reports, and their presumed impact on U.S. public opinion, may also contribute to delimiting an intervention. This is particularly true if public support for a mission is frail to begin with. In Haiti, for example, President Clinton limited the scope and duration of U.S. involvement and put a major emphasis on keeping casualties to a minimum.[30] After control of the mission was handed over to the United Nations in March 1995, remaining U.S. troops were prohibited from making direct contact with Haitians or from touring Port-au-Prince.[31] Similarly, when he spoke from the Oval Office at the outset of the Kosovo bombing campaign four years later, Clinton circumscribed the mission in a way that his critics felt told Milosevic too much. "I do not intend to put our troops in Kosovo to fight a war," the president reassured the U.S. public.[32] Clinton's statement underscores the challenges, to be discussed later, of communicating in conflict when many audiences are listening.

In Kosovo, Haiti, and elsewhere, it was not media technologies or behaviors that set the mission parameters so much as the very nature of the missions, in which direct national interests that might merit a large loss of blood or treasure were absent.

News media reports usually are presumed to be a factor that tips policymakers' scales toward intervention, inasmuch as television and other media focus on unaddressed human suffering and violence, their reports an unspoken call to

"Do something!"[33] This is often but not always the case. As he prepared to dispatch troops to Haiti in September 1994, President Clinton was faced with media that reflected the many dissenting voices in Congress and among the foreign policy elite. Before former president Jimmy Carter's visit to Port-au-Prince to secure an agreement that allowed U.S. troops an unopposed entry into Haiti, 88 percent of network evening news sources voiced criticism of Clinton's policy.[34] The *New York Times* and the *Washington Post* editorialized against the administration's course of action and criticized its decision not to seek congressional authorization for the Haiti intervention.[35] Even an address from the Oval Office failed to convince the public that U.S. interests were at stake in Haiti, as the president argued.[36] Yet Clinton, who had put his credibility on the line by threatening the Haitian junta, went ahead with the mission. The president and other senior policymakers retain formidable powers to set the intervention agenda in the post–Cold War era, even in the face of media skepticism—as long as they are prepared to live with the postintervention consequences.

The Haiti, Kosovo, and Bosnia cases point to another feature of intervention policymaking in an era of pervasive media. Each of these interventions was preceded by warnings from Washington: in the case of Haiti, for the junta to leave power; in the Balkans, for "ethnic cleansing" to cease. Once made, these sorts of demands help propel their authors toward further action. The media play a role because, with their pervasiveness and speed, they can document in fine detail whether the demands are met or ignored. (Increasingly, those doing the documenting include human rights or other kinds of activists using the Internet and other non–mass media tools.) If the latter is the case, news reports of continuing violence, atrocities, or intransigence pose an uncomfortable question to policymakers: What will you do now? This was the situation when a second mortar shell fell in the same Sarajevo marketplace on

August 28, 1995. This time, the horrifying images played less of a role than they had in February 1994. But several weeks before, following the fall of the UN-declared Srebrenica and Zepa "safe areas" to the Serbs, NATO defense ministers had gathered in London and pledged to protect the remaining safe areas, including Sarajevo, from attack. After the second marketplace attack, the only question, as expressed by White House press secretary Michael McCurry, was "Were we going to make good on those commitments?"[37]

■ ■ ■

A decision about whether to send troops abroad is among the most fundamental a leader can make. Many factors go into the decision-making process, including the national or other interests at stake; the risks of action (or nonaction); the views of allies; domestic public opinion; and the media, which, as we have seen, sometimes can amplify or muffle the other factors. In the early 1990s the international news media both contributed to, and reflected, a newly optimistic mood about the possibilities of humanitarian intervention in the aftermath of the Cold War and the U.S. triumph in Operation Desert Storm. After setbacks in Somalia and the Balkans, a more sober, cautious mood about peacekeeping operations set in, documented in a formal U.S. policy on the subject.[38]

While they reflect the prevailing mood as much as setting it, the media retain a heavy *agenda-setting* function when it comes to potential interventions. In the words of former secretary of state James A. Baker III, the modern news media—particularly television—have a "spatial" function.[39] For both policymakers and the public, they bring onto the agenda far-off conflicts, conflicts that, in the past, officials may have wished (and been able) to ignore. The agenda-setting role was made dramatically clear in September 1999, when pro-Jakarta militias went on a murderous rampage

in East Timor following that territory's vote for independence from Indonesia. The United States had just led an intervention against similar atrocities in Kosovo. Because Washington was not similarly inclined to act in East Timor, journalists questioned whether there wasn't a double standard. The Clinton administration's underlying resistance to involvement was made clear by National Security Adviser Samuel Berger, who famously responded: "My daughter has a very messy apartment up in college, maybe I shouldn't intervene to have that cleaned up."[40] Thanks in part to U.S. policy, the international community responded belatedly to the violence. But while Washington saw no national interest in deploying ground troops in East Timor,[41] the news media had helped put the remote territory on the agenda, where it could not be completely ignored. A week after Berger's remark, Clinton ordered U.S. logistical support for, and a token contribution to, a multinational intervention force.

Being on the media's agenda does not guarantee that policymakers will address a conflict, but being absent from the agenda makes it more likely they will not—particularly when there is no *perceived* national interest that would cause officials to cue the media's attention. Western leaders are hardly looking for more places to intervene. The West African nation of Sierra Leone witnessed a brutal civil war in the 1990s, with gruesome atrocities. U.S. television coverage of the civil war has been spotty: twenty-three mentions in 1997, one in 1998, and twenty in 1999, with 66 percent of the coverage on CNN rather than on the higher-audience ABC, CBS, and NBC evening news.[42] Much the same could be said for Angola, Afghanistan, and many other places ravaged by tragic conflicts.

Finally, media coverage does not seem sufficient to overcome U.S. reluctance to intervene militarily in conflicts, such as in Chechnya and Kashmir, where large, nuclear-armed states are directly involved.

INFORMATION IN CONFLICT

Both before and during an intervention, media can be either a tool in officials' hands or an independent source of policy input. We saw, for example, how U.S. government officials at times used the media to guide intervention policy toward Bosnia and Somalia, while at other times the media led the policy "dance." Information plays the same dual role once an intervention in conflict has occurred, whether it is a peacekeeping mission or the outright use of force. Leaders play "offense" by using real-time television, the Internet, and other media tools to communicate to adversaries and allies; they must also play "defense" against news media reports from the conflict zone and others' attempts to manipulate them.

The principal difference is the intensity of the information environment. When American armed forces deploy in conflict zones, the number of international and local journalists paying attention rises sharply. The number of policy "players" increases, too. Likely to be present are other nations' military forces, many NGOs, and UN agencies, as well as the adversary and its allies. The number of audiences—local, regional, international, and domestic—increases. And so too do the domestic political stakes for U.S. officials. Officials may be able to resist the impact of media and information and decide not to intervene at all (or to intervene in minimalist ways); once the bombs, or peacekeepers, or conflict managers are sent on their way, they have no such luxury.[43]

■ ■ ■

The 1999 war over Kosovo provides the best example to date of information's ubiquitous role in modern conflicts, particularly those fought over humanitarian principles.[44] As NATO bombed the former Yugoslavia for seventy-eight days in Operation Allied Force, information suffused every aspect of the conflict. It was used by all parties and touched all of them. The conflict highlighted important principles of information, including (1) the information challenge and the use of propaganda; (2) the importance of indigenous media; (3) "netwar," a relatively new phenomenon; (4) the challenges of communicating by, and within, a multinational alliance; and (5) the relationship among information, media, and casualties. Kosovo was a potent reminder why nations should not undertake conflict and conflict management without a full understanding of, and a plan for, information in every phase of the effort. Kosovo thus provides an excellent prism to examine these effects, which have shown themselves in other conflicts over the past decade and are almost certain to do so again in the future.

But first, it is important to briefly recall what the news media and other information sources *did not* do in Kosovo. The information environment was an exceedingly challenging one in which Milosevic used civilian casualties and fleeing ethnic Albanian refugees for propaganda value to undercut NATO, while the Western media questioned the alliance's strategy and likelihood of success. Despite this, Clinton, British prime minister Tony Blair, and other alliance leaders prosecuted the conflict as they deemed best—by sustained bombardment, without a ground invasion. Serbia's military withdrawal from Kosovo was achieved by very old-fashioned means: military force coupled, in the final days of Operation Allied Force, with diplomacy. Information, media, and public opinion then were part of the conflict on a daily—if not hourly—basis, helping to define the larger "battlefield" but not, themselves, determining the outcome.

Kosovo also illustrates again how the role of information is tied not just to the technologies in use, but, intimately, to the nature of the conflict. In traditional wars, fought for direct national interests, the public is more directly engaged in the outcome. Controls are imposed, often with public support, on journalists' freedom to report from the conflict area. At home, the news media tend to follow the public mood and, at least initially, to support the war effort. NGOs and other "third parties" play a diminished role until the postconflict phase. These conditions describe World War II and Desert Storm, but few recent conflicts. Peace operations such as those in Somalia, Bosnia, Haiti, and Rwanda could hardly be more different for journalists and officials. The entire nation does not feel itself "at war." There are few, if any, media controls. Indeed, in Somalia, Bosnia, and Haiti, journalists were in the conflict zone before peacekeepers arrived and often had more mobility and information than did soldiers, a reversal of the normal wartime pattern.

This greater media independence, coupled with modern media technologies, can be a significant challenge for conflict managers, especially the military. Commanders worry about media reports that will endanger their soldiers or threaten objectives. In Somalia, the news media were far more mobile than the UN military mission. Military spokespeople frequently learned of significant events from reporters, reducing to zero the time they had to craft a response that fit with the mission's overall message. Somali warlord Mohammed Farah Aideed proved adept at using local and international news media to frustrate UN objectives. From the commanders' perspective, most of the mission took place in a fish bowl of international media attention. Moreover, in peace operations, political objectives often take on added significance over purely military ones. Because political considerations may restrict or even rule out the use of force, information becomes a primary (sometimes *the* primary) means of warfare and conflict management.[45]

Along the spectrum of intervention, Operation Allied Force lies more toward the peacemaking model: a conflict fought for humanitarian reasons (ending Serbia's repression of the ethnic Albanian majority in Kosovo), by a multinational alliance with, in the United States at least, moderate public support at best.

However, there was one decisive difference from the pattern in peace operations: during the bombing campaign, the international press corps could not move freely in Kosovo. That created a vacuum of information that Milosevic exploited, severely complicating NATO's public diplomacy.

The Information Challenge

Real-time global television gives leaders (and other policy actors) a powerful new medium to communicate directly with one another and with one another's publics during international crises. This became clear during the 1990–91 Persian Gulf crisis, when President Bush and his aides used CNN to signal their resolve to Iraqi president Saddam Hussein that his troops leave Kuwait. They had been told that Saddam constantly watched CNN and were concerned about the conclusions he might draw about U.S. fortitude from viewing antiwar protests in the United States.[46]

The medium is also available to adversaries, of course. Whether dictators, with their repressive information policies and frequently incomplete understanding of the outside world, can use it to the same effect is questionable. Saddam's attempts to show that he was not mistreating Western hostages in Iraq backfired badly when TV cameras recorded his overstaged attempts to ingratiate himself with a young British "guest," Stuart Lockwood.[47] Still, global television opens up opportunities for a wider range of policy actors to use information. Former president Carter used CNN to further his extra-official diplomacy in Somalia and North Korea. In Haiti in October 1993, as President Clinton faced a domestic uproar over the deaths of U.S. soldiers in Somalia, thugs loyal to the Haitian junta stage-managed a protest for television cameras on the docks of Port-au-Prince. Threatening "another Somalia," they convinced Clinton to turn around the USS *Harlan County,* which waited offshore with unarmed U.S. and Canadian engineers and police trainers.[48] (Here again, information had an impact because policy was off balance.)

In Kosovo, Milosevic, facing superior NATO military force, clearly saw Western public opinion as a more favorable battleground and propaganda as a key weapon. When Operation Allied Force began, he accelerated the eviction of Kosovar Albanians and blamed the resulting televised humanitarian disaster on the air strikes. Although NATO came in for criticism initially, the images of columns of refugees and teeming camps ultimately boomeranged in favor of the alliance.[49] Incidents in which civilians were killed and maimed by the NATO air strikes appeared to have more impact on alliance decision makers. Milosevic was able to manipulate these mistakes to maximum advantage (he probably planted some of the "evidence") because he had clamped down on independent Serbian media and permitted the international media only supervised visits to Kosovo.[50] NATO could not similarly control the news media. But the alliance's botched explanation of one of the worst such incidents, the attack on a convoy near Djakovica on April 14, 1999, made matters infinitely worse. The resulting uproar (spread worldwide through the media) marred NATO's ability to achieve or enunciate its goals for some time—a clear illustration of how inadequate information policies have real consequences during conflicts. Afterward, NATO belatedly buttressed its public affairs staff with contributions from the United States and other member countries.[51]

Milosevic used a wide variety of information and propaganda techniques, with the apparent aim of dividing NATO's nineteen nations, some of whom were clearly less enthusiastic about the use of force than others. Some of Milosevic's techniques were clever, such as the regime-sponsored rallies and rock concerts where Belgrade residents wore "targets" mocking the NATO bombers. Billboards went up in the capital, showing Paris in flames and declaring, "Just Imagine! Stop the Bombs." NATO's response was less imaginative. The Voice of America and Radio Free Europe increased their programming in the region. U.S. planes dropped fliers warning Serbian military commanders that they could be prosecuted for war crimes and describing the atrocities under way in Kosovo. Secretary of State Madeleine Albright videotaped an address to the Serbian people in the Serbo-Croatian language.

While each side clearly saw the other's public opinion as an important center of gravity, the effect of their efforts to influence it was uncertain. The Serbian people for the most part rejected NATO's account of the conflict and what precipitated it—an illustration, perhaps, of the limits of trying to influence a populace with information while simultaneously using military force against their country.[52] Milosevic's propaganda efforts clearly complicated NATO's efforts to explain its motives and objectives. Picked up and further disseminated by media of all kinds, these tactics led to sharp questioning of NATO actions. But in the United States, at least, they did not significantly damage public support. The U.S. public, which had never been particularly enthusiastic about the Kosovo venture, did not change its view substantially as the weeks went by. Support sagged slowly over time as doubts grew over whether Clinton and NATO could achieve their objectives with air power alone.

Indigenous Media

The role of indigenous media (as opposed to propaganda or communications aimed primarily at an international audience) was touched upon at the beginning of the chapter. Although they often receive less attention, indigenous media also play important roles during an intervention.

In humanitarian and peace operations, the consent and understanding of the local populace may be vital to a mission's success; persuasion often has to be achieved with information rather than from the barrel of a gun. One or more of the previously warring parties may resist the presence of international troops and attempt to portray them as biased or as an occupation force. The international intervention in Somalia illustrates this in both positive and negative ways. At the outset, senior U.S. AID official Andrew Natsios discovered the reach of the BBC's Somali-language radio broadcasts and used them to inform powerful village elders whose consent the mission needed. The U.S.-led United Task Force (UNITAF) established its own newspaper and television station to explain UNITAF's mission and objectives to Somalis, warn against interference, and counteract the growing propaganda of warlord Mohammed Farah Aideed. Unfortunately, the United Nations did not continue these efforts once it assumed command of the Somalia mission.[53] Aideed used his Radio Mogadishu as a weapon, vilifying the UN operation, UNOSOM II. It was the June 5, 1993, inspection of a weapons depot, where the radio also was located, which resulted in the deaths of twenty-three Pakistani peacekeepers and sparked the ill-conceived hunt for Aideed, radically changing the nature of the entire mission. Much later, during the U.S.-assisted UN withdrawal from Somalia in March 1995, the commander, Lieutenant General Anthony Zinni, made communications through the local media a top priority. The message: His troops meant no harm but would respond with deadly force if attacked.[54]

Kosovo provides a good illustration of indigenous media's role in a slightly different context. Milosevic used state-run media to rally the populace, suppress dissent, disseminate the regime's explanation of the conflict, and display a united front to NATO. He coupled this effort with tightened control over the few remaining independent media outlets, such as Radio B92. In the prevailing political atmosphere, these outlets had already found it difficult to provide news critical of the regime. NATO's largely unsuccessful efforts to break through this tight media control already have been noted. In time, NATO spokespeople argued that Serbian state media were part of Milosevic's "war machine" and, after lengthy debate within the alliance, missiles struck the headquarters of Serbian state television a month into the bombing campaign.[55]

Somalia, Kosovo, and other cases suggest that the international community has not yet settled on policies to deal with and, if necessary, counter indigenous media. Efforts by the United Nations to counter "hate radio" or proactively broadcast during peace operations have been hampered by member-states' unwillingness to fund such activities and by concerns that "peace radio" will itself become a well-meaning form of propaganda.[56] The Kosovo bombing campaign showed how the Western democracies are loath to attack civilian media outlets even if they appear to be contributing to the war effort.

Netwar

A frequent theme of this chapter has been how the evolution of communications has allowed a wider range of nonofficial actors to play a role in conflict and conflict management. Nowhere is this more striking than in the development of the Internet, even if it is too soon to gauge its ultimate impact. The term "netwar" refers to information-related conflict between societies, a largely psychological exercise of trying to affect what a target population knows or thinks about itself and the world. By contrast, "cyberwar" refers to conducting military operations according to information-related principles.[57] While it can be argued that both occurred during the Kosovo conflict, this discussion will focus on nonmilitary aspects of conflict using computers, that is, netwar, and particularly those events that have a broader impact in terms of propaganda, information, and publicity.

The use of the Internet for netwar appears to be widespread and growing, although the actual effect of these attacks remains open to debate. Species of netwar have taken place across the Taiwan Strait, between Armenia and

Azerbaijan, against Japan's infrastructure, and between dissident groups and regimes attempting to suppress them.[58] In many cases, the attackers appear to be noncombatants in the traditional sense, with at most a loose affiliation (and perhaps not even geographic proximity) to the nation or people whose cause they seek to advance.

During the NATO bombing campaign, Serbian students led by a "Captain Dragan" used the Internet to disseminate pro-Belgrade messages, network with other anti-NATO groups, and encourage expatriate Serbs to become politically active.[59] Hackers loyal to Belgrade flooded NATO's unclassified computer network with e-mails for several days, forcing it temporarily offline, and struck at Web sites belonging to the White House, the U.S. Navy, and others. After the U.S. bombing of the Chinese embassy in Belgrade, hackers apparently in Asia infiltrated numerous U.S. government and business computer systems.

The combined effect of these activities was a modest propaganda success for the perpetrators. The intrusions embarrassed NATO, while the Internet itself helped those opposed to Operation Allied Force find one another and propagate their message. "Hacking" was hardly decisive, but it does not seem outlandish to suggest that in future conflicts, "civilians" using the Internet could launch more damaging attacks on a nation's domestic infrastructure that would sow confusion or undercut public support for continuing the military effort.

Communicating in a Multinational Alliance

The hackers' messages likely were received differently in the nineteen countries of the NATO alliance, where official and public opinion differed over the use of force against the former Yugoslavia. The multilateral nature of the campaign also posed a challenge for NATO's efforts to communicate among its members and to the world at large.

Multilateral military and peace operations increasingly are the rule rather than the exception. This makes it more difficult for policy actors to speak with one voice or act together to oppose adversary propaganda. During UNOSOM II in Somalia, for instance, Italy, the former colonial power, frequently differed with other UN members over the best tactic for dealing with Aideed. This resulted in different messages being sent to the Somali leader and his Somali National Alliance (SNA). Nor did the United States and the United Nations always see eye to eye. In pre- and postconflict zones, military and civilian NGOs increasingly operate at close quarters, with different priorities, institutional cultures, and methods of communicating to the media and affected populations. As already noted, nations acting together in a multilateral alliance may have sharply differing views of how, if at all, to counter enemy propaganda and hate broadcasting.

The Kosovo campaign reflected these problems in spades. What "played" in London or Washington did not necessarily play in Athens, Berlin, or Prague, where there was much less enthusiasm for Operation Allied Force. This put extra stress on NATO's media organization and operation. As NATO spokesperson Jamie Shea has noted regarding coalition politics, "If you are running a coalition military campaign, if one country has a problem it soon becomes your problem."[60] Clinton's statement that he would not send troops into combat in Kosovo clearly was aimed at soothing domestic U.S. public concern over further involvement in the Balkans. However, many critics thought it revealed too much to a different audience— Milosevic and his military forces in Kosovo. Later, when Clinton and Blair reassessed the alliance's refusal to engage in a ground campaign, they were met with staunch opposition from allies, including German chancellor Gerhard Schroeder, who was in danger of losing his governing coalition over the issue. "There will be no NATO land war," Schroeder said at one point.[61] In multilateral operations, these sorts of differences are inevitable; minimizing them and sending a coherent, unified message to multiple audiences is a time-consuming but vital task. Coordinating information between an alliance's military command on the one hand and political authorities and spokespeople on the other is yet another challenge.[62]

As is usually the case with information and media, challenges can be turned into advantages. In Kosovo, being a multinational alliance meant that NATO could deploy numerous, diverse, and well-recognized faces to fill up the "media space" and fight the battle on the airwaves.[63]

Information and Casualties

This brief survey does not afford sufficient space to fully examine the extensive literature on how casualties affect public support for military operations, and the role of information and media in that process. Nonetheless, no discussion of information and conflict is complete without addressing this crucial issue. Three assumptions appear to be widespread: that the American public, more than European ones, has little stomach for casualties among its soldiers; that television reporting of casualties, especially in real time, exacerbates this condition; and that, as a result, U.S. military forces must now fight quick, low-risk, "sanitized" conflicts using high-tech weaponry that minimizes the threat to U.S. soldiers.[64] Those who make this argument frequently cite as evidence the deaths of eighteen U.S. soldiers in Somalia in October 1993—videotape and still photography captured the body of one soldier being dragged down a dusty street in Mogadishu—and the Clinton administration's subsequent retreat from the mission.[65] Cases where the news media have been barred or controlled also lend credence to the argument that the scope and style of reporting about casualties impacts public opinion. For example, the Russian government severely limited news media reporting of Russian combat forces in Chechnya beginning

in the late 1990s, especially reporting of military and civilian casualties, in what was seen as a successful effort to prevent a recurrence of Russian public opinion's souring on Chechnya in a previous phase of the conflict in the mid-1990s. U.S. adversaries clearly put stock in the U.S. public's lack of steadfastness: Saddam Hussein in Iraq, Milosevic in Serbia, and many others apparently believed that if they could inflict sufficient casualties, public opinion would turn against U.S. leadership, and they would prevail.

Surprisingly, given the argument's prevalence, there is little support for the view that media reporting of casualties alone is responsible for declining levels of public support. Comparisons of public attitudes toward the Korean War, when television was in its infancy, and the Vietnam War, the so-called living room war, found nearly identical patterns of decreasing public support over time, despite the different types and levels of coverage.[66] In Vietnam, the U.S. public endured years of warfare and thousands of casualties before withdrawing its support. Televised casualties were not as ubiquitous as sometimes remembered, appearing in only 2 percent of televised accounts of the war.[67] Clearly the public was focused on the real costs of war (U.S. casualties and resources), not just media accounts.

The Somalia example also falls apart under closer examination. The *fact* of the casualties was responsible for declining levels of public support rather than media reporting, which, while dramatic, focused primarily on the renewed debate over the Somalia mission that the images engendered.[68] The eighteen soldiers' deaths had such a powerful impact because they occurred in a communications vacuum. The loss came during a mission that the American people had never been told was anything other than humanitarian. Modern news media reporting accelerates the potential impact of casualties on public support for military operations; yet leaders still can shape the context in which they occur. In Somalia before the U.S. combat deaths, the executive branch had never fully explained the expanded UN mission. After the deaths (as with Vietnam after the Tet offensive), the executive branch was itself in such shock that it never fully attempted to frame the casualties in any other way.[69] Yet in both Vietnam and Somalia, even as public approval declined, there was residual support for an *escalation* of American involvement (assuming that would lead to a rapid and successful conclusion of objectives). That that course was not chosen was due to other factors weighing on political leaders in Washington. Indeed, recent surveys have found that the general public is far more tolerant of casualties to achieve specific national security objectives than are either political or military leaders.[70]

The United States did not suffer any combat deaths during Operation Allied Force.[71] Had they occurred, it is almost certain that rapid—and perhaps dramatic—media reporting would have presented the Clinton administration with a difficult political problem. Yet it also appears that the U.S. public had, early on, made a rational judgment about the (low) relative importance it attached to Kosovo and the costs it was willing to accept to achieve U.S. goals there, independent of media reporting. That preexisting judgment would have determined the impact of casualties, along with U.S. officials' conduct and explanation of the military operation and its setbacks.

The most notable characteristic of information in conflict today is its pervasiveness. Information, whether purveyed by the international news media or others, potentially can alter the course of events before, during, and after an intervention by outsiders. It can be put to good or ill use by many actors, from a NATO spokesperson to a Serbian youth at his computer keyboard, from a hate-spewing radio in the Rwandan jungle to U.S. government officials trying to change the policy preferences of their own superiors. The potential impact can come at many levels, from the tactical-military level to the political-geostrategic one.

This reality means that the old model, in which military and civilian officials curb and control information during times of conflict, is largely outmoded. To engage in conflict prevention, conflict management, conflict resolution, and reconciliation today, policy actors must integrate media and information into their strategies in a dynamic and proactive manner —while constantly monitoring other parties who seek to do the same. The *good* news for conflict managers in this more complex and challenging environment is that media and information are rarely, if ever, determinative. Their impact depends on who is using them and how. Sophisticated communications strategies that buttress well-built policies can increase the chances of success.

CONCLUSION

The change in the nature of military operations brought about by the end of the Cold War, along with a revolution in communications technology, has transformed information and the news media into an even more vital component of conflict and conflict management. In the past, the use of information was primarily linear and bipolar; today, information is used in a dynamic, multilateral environment, with many more potential actors than merely two opposing nation-states.

NOTES

1. On this last point, see Warren P. Strobel, *Late-Breaking Foreign Policy: The News Media's Influence on Peace Operations* (Washington, D.C.: United States Institute of Peace Press, 1997), 92–93.

2. Boutros Boutros-Ghali, speaking at the Freedom Forum Media Studies Center, New York, March 19, 1995.

3. Strobel, *Late-Breaking Foreign Policy*, 146–159.

4. James F. Hoge, Jr., "Media Pervasiveness," *Foreign Affairs* 73, no. 4 (July-August 1994): 141.

5. Jamie Shea, NATO spokesperson, address to the Summer Forum on Kosovo, Reform Club, London, July 15, 1999.

6. Available at www.people-press.org. Accessed July 2000.

7. Shea, address to the Summer Forum on Kosovo.

8. Strobel, *Late-Breaking Foreign Policy.*

9. Neil Munro, "Inducting Information," *National Journal*, March 27, 1999. See also François Misser and Yves Jaumain, "Death by Radio," *Index on Censorship* 4/5 (1994): 73–74; John-Thor Dahlburg, "Why the World Let Rwanda Bleed," *Los Angeles Times*, September 10, 1994, A2.

10. Ibid.

11. Dusko Doder and Louise Branson, *Milsoevic: Portrait of a Tyrant* (New York: Free Press, 1999), especially 32–62.

12. Munro, "Inducting Information"; Strobel, *Late-Breaking Foreign Policy,* 118.

13. Jamie F. Metzl, "Information Intervention," *Foreign Affairs* 76, no. 6 (November-December 1997): 15–20; Jim Mann, "UN Hate-Radio Jamming Would Send Wrong Signal," *Los Angeles Times*, December 3 1997, A5.

14. Numerous interviews by author.

15. See Nik Gowing, *Real-Time Television Coverage of Armed Conflicts and Diplomatic Crises: Does It Pressure or Distort Foreign Policy Decisions?* Working Paper 94-1 (Cambridge, Mass.: Joan Shorenstein Barone Center on the Press, Politics, and Public Policy, Harvard University, June 1994).

16. Steven Livingston and Todd Eachus, "Humanitarian Crises and U.S. Foreign Policy: Somalia and the CNN Effect Reconsidered," *Political Communication* 12, no. 4 (October-December 1995): 415–416.

17. Ibid.; Strobel, *Late-Breaking Foreign Policy*, 131–137.

18. Herman Cohen, interview by author, June 1, 1995. See also Livingston and Eachus, "Humanitarian Crises."

19. Numerous senior Bush administration officials, interviews by author.

20. "Operation Restore Hope," *U.S. News and World Report*, December 14, 1992, 26.

21. Robert Gallucci, interview by author, May 31, 1995.

22. Warren Zimmermann, interview by author, June 8, 1995.

23. Elizabeth Drew, *On the Edge: The Clinton Presidency* (New York: Simon and Schuster, 1994). See also Elaine Sciolino and Douglas Jehl, "As U.S. Sought a Bosnia Policy, the French Offered a Good Idea," *New York Times*, February 14, 1994, A1.

24. Background interview by author, February 3, 1995.

25. Dee Dee Myers, interview by author, February 27, 1995.

26. Data from Network Evening News Abstracts, Television News Archives, Vanderbilt University, Nashville, Tenn.

27. Background interview by author, November 17, 1994.

28. Senior NGO representative at conference on "Media, Military and the Humanitarian Crises: New Relations for New Challenges," George Washington University, Washington, D.C., May 5, 1995.

29. Lawrence Eagleburger, interview by author, February 1, 1995.

30. See, for example, Michael Gordon, "Pentagon's Haiti Policy Focuses on Casualties," *New York Times*, October 6, 1994.

31. United Nations Association of the United States of America, *A Report on the Fourth Annual Peacekeeping Mission* (Washington, D.C.: United Nations Association, August 1995), 22.

32. President Clinton, Speech to the Nation, March 24, 1999.

33. Gowing, *Real-Time Television Coverage of Armed Conflicts and Diplomatic Crises.*

34. "1994: The Year in Review," *Media Monitor* 9, no. 1 (January-February 1995): 3.

35. "Congress Must Vote on Haiti," *New York Times*, September 13, 1994, A22; "Haiti: Consensus and Consent," *Washington Post*, September 14, 1994, A20.

36. *ABC News Nightline* poll, September 15, 1994.

37. Michael McCurry, interview by author, May 15, 1995.

38. U.S. Department of State, *The Clinton Administration's Policy on Reforming Multilateral Peace Operations*, Publication 10161, May 1994.

39. James A. Baker III, telephone interview by author, September 11, 1995.

40. Transcript, press briefing by Samuel Berger and National Economic Adviser Gene Sperling, The White House, September 10, 1999. (Berger later apologized for the remark.)

41. General Hugh Shelton, chairman of the Joint Chiefs of Staff, quoted in Patrick J. Sloyan, "At Least 200 U.S. Troops Deployed," *Newsday*, September 17, 1999, A20.

42. Data from Network Evening News Abstracts, Television News Archives, Vanderbilt University.

43. See generally Strobel, *Late-Breaking Foreign Policy*.

44. For more on the news media's special impact in humanitarian conflict, see Shea, address to the Summer Forum on Kosovo.

45. U.S. Army, *Peace Operations*, Field Manual 100-23, December 30, 1994, v, 1, 17.

46. James A. Baker III and former national security adviser Brent Scowcroft, interviews by author, February 7, 1995.

47. Ted Koppel, "The Global Information Revolution and TV News" (address to the United States Institute of Peace "Managing Chaos" conference, Washington, D.C., December 1, 1994).

48. See, for example, George J. Church, "In and Out with the Tide," *Time*, October 25, 1993, 26–32.

49. Shea, address to the Summer Forum on Kosovo.

50. Ibid.; Felicity Barringer, "Propaganda Wars: Pictures Can Lie, After All," *New York Times*, April 25, 1999, A5.

51. For more, see Edward Stourton, "Spinning for Victory," *Daily Telegraph*, October 16, 1999, 2.

52. See, for example, Michael Dobbs, "The War on the Airwaves; Serbs Ridicule TV Atrocity Reports," *Washington Post*, April 19, 1999, A1.

53. John L. Hirsch and Robert B. Oakley, *Somalia and Operation Restore Hope: Reflections on Peacemaking and Peacekeeping* (Washington, D.C.: United States Institute of Peace Press, 1995), especially 116–118, 153 (footnote).

54. Strobel, *Late-Breaking Foreign Policy*, 230, 118–119.

55. See, for example, "Support Grows for Bombing Serb TV, Radio Facilities," *Wall Street Journal*, April 20, 1999, A19; "NATO Bombs Destroy Serbian State Television," *Atlanta Journal*, April 23, 1999, A1.

56. For a broader study of UN communications during peace operations, see Ingrid A. Lehmann, *Peacekeeping and Public Information: Caught in the Crossfire* (London: Frank Cass, 1999).

57. John Arquilla and David Ronfeldt, "Cyberwar Is Coming!" *Comparative Strategy* 12 (spring 1993).

58. See Warren P. Strobel, "A Glimpse of Cyberwarfare," *U.S. News and World Report*, March 13, 2000, 32–33.

59. Michael Satchell, "Captain Dragan's Serbian cybercorps," *U.S. News and World Report*, May 10, 1999, 42.

60. Shea, address to the Summer Forum on Kosovo.

61. See, for example, Daniel Schorr, "NATO's Cultural Divide: Clinton's Kosovo See-Sawing versus Schroeder's No-Apologies," *Christian Science Monitor*, April 28, 1999, 11.

62. Shea, address to the Summer Forum on Kosovo.

63. Ibid.

64. See, for example, William Drozdiak, "For Europe, Haiti Confirms U.S. Hesitation," *Washington Post*, September 17, 1994, A12.

65. See Peter D. Feaver and Christopher Gelpi, "How Many Deaths Are Acceptable? A Surprising Answer," *Washington Post*, November 7, 1999, B3.

66. John E. Mueller, *War, Presidents and Public Opinion* (Lanham, Md.: University Press of America, 1985), chap. 3.

67. Hoge, "Media Pervasiveness."

68. Eric V. Larson, "U.S. Casualties in Somalia," vol. 2, "The Public Response: A Grief and Rage" (unpublished manuscript, March 1995).

69. Ibid.; Strobel, *Late-Breaking Foreign Policy*, 166–184; Feaver and Gelpi, "How Many Deaths Are Acceptable?"

70. Feaver and Gelpi, "How Many Deaths Are Acceptable?"

71. Two U.S. soldiers were killed in May 1999 when their Apache helicopter crashed.

PART V
PEACEBUILDING: FROM SETTLEMENT TO RECONCILIATION

41

Obstacles to Peace Settlements

Roy Licklider

WE KNOW MORE ABOUT HOW WARS BEGIN than about how they end. Intellectually, the problem of negotiating an end to a civil war is daunting; how do you make peace and agree to live in the same state with people who have killed your friends and family? How do you live with these people for the rest of your life? How do you trust them enough to work with them economically and socially to create a functioning political system?

The problem is made much more difficult by the likely conditions under which this trust must be created. Typically, war or civil violence has not solved the problems that caused it. If two groups of people have been antagonistic toward each other, large-scale killing is unlikely to have improved relations. If maldistribution of economic resources has been a problem, the destruction of the economy will not help. The list can be extended.

Peace, after all, is not the primary goal of the parties. On the contrary, the violence arose precisely because both sides felt there were other issues more important, things that were

worth dying for and killing for. Nor is this inappropriate. An unjust peace, whatever that means, is not necessarily a good bargain. This analysis does not assume that peace should be the primary goal; it only assumes that peace sometimes is and that, at such times, it is useful to have some idea about the conditions under which peace may be obtained.

An "ideal type" of postwar society might look like this: economically the infrastructure has been destroyed; the currency has been undermined; commerce is at a standstill; agriculture has been devastated; unemployment is high, which means there are no jobs for former soldiers; foreign investment has been frightened off; and there is no basis for exports. The country's society has been undercut by the mutual dislike between warring groups, which is not any weaker than before the war; the wide distribution of weapons within the population; the people's habit of nonobedience to government and authority generally; the undermining of traditional sources of authority; the need to demobilize and disarm at least two armies quickly; and the prevalence of young soldiers with no skills other than killing. The old political process has been discredited (you do not want to re-create the political system that resulted in civil war), there is no single legitimate government, there is a low tolerance for legitimate opposition, there is often little democratic tradition, and the police and judicial systems are seen (usually correctly) as part of the problem rather than as part of the solution because they have no legitimacy for much of the population.

Civil war looks more likely to start than to end under these conditions. It is thus not surprising that a number of analysts have found that civil wars are less likely to end in negotiated settlements than are interstate wars (Pillar 1983; Stedman 1991; Licklider 1995; Walter 1997, 335). Nor is it incredible that most settlements of civil wars do not last (Walter 1997, 2001); it is perhaps surprising that any do. But we also know that historically every major state has gone through at least one such transition (the French Revolution, the Chinese Revolution, the English Civil War, the Russian Revolution, the American Civil War, and the American Revolution), so we know that it does happen. We also know that, since 1945, settlements of civil wars that have lasted about five years have seldom later collapsed into future violence. But we do not know much about the dynamics of these processes or the conditions under which they are more or less likely to succeed.

WHY HAVE COMBATANTS INCREASINGLY SOUGHT SETTLEMENT THROUGH POLITICAL RATHER THAN MILITARY MEANS?

Conventionally, civil wars were expected to end by a military victory for one side or the other, on the model of the American Civil War or the French and Russian Revolutions. The theory was straightforward: in interstate wars foreign conquerors might leave at some point, but in civil wars the stakes were permanent control of the government, losing such control would be fatal to the interests of either side, and therefore compromise was impossible (Iklé 1971). Analyses of civil wars during the Cold War period confirmed that negotiated settlements were rare, although not unknown (Pillar 1983; Stedman 1991; Licklider 1995; Walter 1997).

More recently, however, combatants seem more willing to work out negotiated settlements involving compromises, some of which seem to work (El Salvador, South Africa, and Nicaragua) and some of which do not (Angola and Sudan). Both internal and external factors seem to be contributing to this trend.

Internally, military victories seem harder to come by these days. Increasingly the issues in civil wars tend to be about identity rather than ideology, a trend that began several decades ago (Gurr 2000, 53; Licklider 1995, 685–686). Identity conflicts may be harder to resolve; settlements do not seem to hold as well (Licklider 1995). We can imagine why this may be true. In an ideological conflict (e.g., Cambodia), it is possible to imagine converting the enemy to your own position by reeducation. It is striking that in China, for example, the communists asked thousands of Kuomintang officials to remain in office after the revolution once organized resistance had ceased (Teiwes 1987, 74).

In an identity conflict, on the other hand, conversion is practically impossible. The victor has only a few alternatives: removal of the other group by genocide or ethnic cleansing (which explains why these policies have become more common); repression, which presumably makes a future outbreak of violence more likely in the long run; and conciliation, which can never be fully effective because the victor cannot risk losing control of the state, which is the most important stake. A fourth alternative is integration, which would produce new alliances that cross former divisions and make the identity conflict irrelevant. Integration, however, is attractive in concept but extremely difficult to bring about, especially in the short run.

Thus stalemate is increasingly likely to be the result of civil war. But stalemate by itself does not produce negotiated settlements. As I. William Zartman has pointed out (1989, 1993), stalemate is not necessarily a bad outcome for the parties; one may control the state apparatus and be able to gain some resources from its international connections, while the other may control a substantial part of the state's population and territory and run a shadow state, again benefiting those in control. Thus the elites of both sides may find stalemate a comfortable outcome, although it may be less attractive to those in whose name they govern.

At the same time, external resources for long-term civil wars are generally declining. Because the Cold War has ended, the superpowers are much less interested in financing such activities; thus there was an outbreak of peace in the early 1990s (Gurr 2000; Ayres 2000). Regional powers often remain willing and able to intervene (Syria in Lebanon is a conspicuous example), but the increased stress on economic performance rather than on conventional security issues seems to have reduced this tendency somewhat as well. Both sides in such wars thus increasingly feel under pressure to end the violence as the situation moves to what Zartman (1989) has called a "hurting stalemate," in which each side expects things to get worse in the future unless some change occurs. It is interesting that explanations for the continuation of some current conflicts often stress access to portable economic resources that can be looted, such as diamonds and oil in Zaire and Angola; these ideas in turn are part of a recent, serious interest in the economic basis for civil war (World Bank Web site).

WHY IS IT SO DIFFICULT FOR THESE PEACE SETTLEMENTS TO HOLD?

Negotiated settlements seem an attractive way to end large-scale violence. Presumably, each side gets enough concessions to encourage it to participate in a common government that will alleviate societal problems, build ties with former adversaries, and make future conflict less likely. Negotiated settlements also hold the promise of not enforcing a vindictive peace that may lead to resentment and renewed violence. Indeed, negotiated settlements have become the gold standard for ending civil wars after the Cold War, part of the good practice by which Ted Gurr (2000) explains their recent increase.

However, some theorists and practitioners believe negotiated settlements will not generally hold as well as military victories will. A plausible general argument is that different factors cause groups to (1) initiate negotiations, (2) reach agreement, and (3) implement those agreements and that considerable slippage between these different stages is thus predictable (Walter 2001). Negotiated settlements create a series of veto groups in internal politics, making it difficult for the new government to act decisively. Moreover, the groups remain in existence, so political crises may be followed by renewed resort to violence. Military victory, on the other hand, destroys the internal organization of one side, allowing the winners to take strong actions, although obviously not guaranteeing success, and making it very difficult for the losers to successfully resort to violence (Wagner 1993). Some analysis suggests that this theory may be correct; of the approximately eighty civil wars between 1945 and 1993, 15 percent of the military victories were followed by renewed wars, while 50 percent of the negotiated settlements were (Licklider 1995, 685; cf. Carment and Harvey 2000, 123–146).

Why do negotiated settlements often not work well? Such agreements have a number of serious potential problems, and it is important to remember that the collapse of an agreement need not signal bad faith or irreconcilable differences. Negotiated settlements by definition involve compromises; both sides have to abandon some of their goals to reach agreement.

Negotiated settlements are thus always second-best solutions. As a result, no party is totally committed to the terms of the settlement itself. It may be the best outcome they can get, but it is unlikely to inspire passionate loyalty from either side, at least at the beginning. This lack of automatic support puts it constantly at risk, particularly if circumstances change (Werner 1999).

Often the two sides have effectively developed separate states, areas, and peoples under the control of a working government. The settlement will usually require both sides to abandon these separate structures to create a new structure that those who have been deadly enemies share. It is not surprising that the prospect may be greeted with real concern, even if goodwill is present.

Within each side, a settlement will threaten the interests of individuals and organizations who have the ability to undercut it, those Stephen Stedman (1997, 1998) has called spoilers. Peace may make obsolete the expertise of specialists in violence and diminish their political dominance. They and others often are benefiting economically from the war as well; large amounts of money are being used, and there are a variety of ways, more and less legitimate, to profit from it (Collier and Hoeffler 2000). The settlement is often driven by a new coalition of moderates from both camps. But it may be opposed by a similarly crosscutting coalition of extremists in both camps tacitly allied in opposition to the agreement. Outsiders often assume that the moderates have a natural advantage since they are advocating peace, but the spoilers may have access to important resources and be aided by the inherent difficulties of negotiating an end to a civil war.

ROLES FOR OUTSIDERS

Many of the factors that explain the rise in negotiated settlements are the result of external actions or lack of them: the end of the Cold War with the corresponding decline in support for violence, an international intellectual climate less sympathetic to violence, nongovernmental organizations dedicated to ending violence, and so on. In many cases international pressure has pushed the parties to negotiate when they otherwise might not have done so. Once the process has begun, outsiders have transmitted information, acted as mediators, and offered incentives to reach settlements. Several studies have found that these activities are more common in cases in which settlements are reached (Miall 1992, 186; Richardson and Wang 1993). On the other hand, at least one study found that UN intervention seemed to make interstate disputes more intense (Diehl, Reifschneider, and Hensel 1996).

External pressure does not always promote peace, of course. Ostensibly, internal violence is often promoted or made possible by outside assistance of various sorts, such as provided by the United States in Afghanistan and by South Africa in Mozambique. Borrowing from, among other cases, the settlement for Zimbabwe, outsiders attempting to end wars have frequently tried to resolve the problems with external powers first, in order to have a better chance of success when moving on to the internal disputes that are usually at the heart of the matter.

But external pressure seems increasingly to be oriented toward bringing about peace, which in practice means some sort of negotiated settlement, even if some players want the settlement skewed in favor of one side or another. External diplomatic involvement is not necessary to reach a settlement; in Colombia in 1957 and North Yemen in 1970 the local protagonists negotiated and enforced agreements (Walter 1997). However, external involvement is often helpful in facilitating this process, albeit only when the local parties prove ready to take advantage.

Interestingly, we do not have much systematic research on what qualities of a peace settlement make it more likely to endure. In the absence of parsimonious, empirically supported theory, practitioners and analysts have developed a number of plausible suggestions to guide policy choices of outsiders trying to encourage such behavior.

Inclusiveness

A workable settlement usually has to involve all the major parties (Hampson 1996, 217). This is easy to say but hard to accomplish. Civil wars often involve loose alliances of moderates and extremists on both sides. It is tempting to negotiate with the moderates and try to leave the extremists out; the moderates are much more willing to make agreements, are more likely to keep them, may have more supporters, and are often much more attractive individuals.

But this is often a mistake. Negotiated settlements to civil wars are delicate affairs; persuading enemies to disarm and leave themselves vulnerable is not a simple task, and even after the agreement is reached, implementation remains extremely fragile (Walter 2001). The process can often be derailed by relatively small acts of violence or even symbolic gestures, particularly early in the process, before personal trust has developed among the former antagonists. Civil war settlement is not a democratic process; even a small but dedicated group can commit a series of violent acts that can bring about the collapse of the peace process, as when Ulster Catholic and Protestant militants have undercut popular Ulster peace agreements. It is important, then, to make every effort to include all the major groups involved in the conflict, particularly at first. At the same time, such inclusion need not imply granting the extremists a permanent veto. Over time an effective coalition may develop between the moderates of both sides. If this coalition is strong enough, it may be able to survive the violent defection of extremists. Cambodia is an interesting example; the Khmer Rouge defected

from the settlement and caused considerable trouble, but over time the settlement gained momentum and the Khmer Rouge subsided into irrelevance.

Outsiders have promoted inclusiveness by encouraging the different sides to meet, selecting the meeting places, empowering the weaker groups, and funding the process. In the process they may effectively select the parties who will meet. They should exert every effort to bring all of the important players in the conflict into the process as soon as possible. Experience suggests that they need to resist the temptation to settle for an easy agreement with moderates, even if it means that the killing will go on longer, because such settlements are very likely to fail, reinforcing distrust and making future negotiations more difficult.

Elite Integration

In practice, a coalition of moderates is critical for negotiated settlement. Effectively, this means that the more moderate members of the elites from both sides of the war must be integrated and given a stake in the settlement. Recently two important theories have been developed to explain this process.

Elisabeth Wood's impressive work (2000) focuses particularly on El Salvador and South Africa. Her theory applies to states where elite power depends on control of the labor of the masses in ways that go beyond the conventional employer-employee relationship. The resulting civil war is likely to have a large dose of class conflict, although ethnic issues may also be involved, creating what Ted Gurr (1993, 21) has called an ethnoclass struggle, as in South Africa. If the war continues, this elite control will be weakened, and profits in this sector will decline. Members of the elite will shift their investments to other activities that do not require such control. As these activities become dominant within the elite, its interests change; the elites now have an economic interest in peace, and as a result a new coalition of moderates on both sides becomes possible.

Marie-Joëlle Zahar (1999) proposes an alternate theory in her analysis of militia leaders, who, although usually seen as the most difficult people to work with, have in fact sometimes been amenable to peace settlements in places as highly charged as Lebanon and Bosnia. She argues that militias develop social and political institutions in order to fight their wars successfully, but that these institutions in turn open new opportunities that change the costs and benefits of various strategies. In particular, militias become more vulnerable to military losses and develop economic interests that can be traded off against their original political goals, sometimes making them more amenable to negotiated settlements.

Because of the importance of ethnicity in current violence, it is particularly important that both theories seem to explain settlement in places like South Africa, Bosnia, and Lebanon. If they work in these very unpromising conflicts, they suggest that ethnic conflicts may not be all that different from others in some significant qualities.

The general point of both Wood and Zahar is that interests of the parties may change as the conflict goes on, sometimes making compromise possible. Zartman (1989; cf. Stedman 1996, 351–353) has argued that conflicts may become "ripe for resolution" when a mutual, hurting stalemate occurs, that is, when each side believes that things will get worse if the status quo continues and that another alternative (settlement) is available that will be better than continued war. This concept has been difficult to apply because we have no way to measure the degree of ripeness separate from the success or failure of settlements, but the underlying idea remains important—namely, that there may be times when the interests of elites change, making peace possible.

However, integration does not mean that everyone participates and benefits from a peace settlement; despite the conflict resolution rhetoric, settlements are not a win-win outcome for all the participants. Every peace settlement has losers and winners (Stedman 1993, 159–160); effective settlements include those who have the power to disrupt, often leaving out others who may seem more deserving but are less threatening. Zimbabwe is a good example. The Lancaster House settlement resulted in an election that established a black government led by Robert Mugabe. Mugabe then decided to allow the white settlers to remain and to keep their land and money in return for their allegiance to him and their withdrawal from politics; indeed, he even kept the white heads of the army and intelligence until they became involved in an antigovernment plot. This meant that he could not keep his promises of land reform to his own soldiers; they gained political rights (no small thing, of course), but their economic situation did not change much. The settlement was not necessarily a bad thing; it allowed Zimbabwe to retain the export sector of its economy during the transition and eased the concerns of European powers and the United States. But it is a useful reminder that, despite the conflict resolution rhetoric, negotiated settlements are not simply win-win solutions but political "deals" (Waterman 1993) in which some people win a great deal more than others.

Civil wars go on for a long time because at least some people and institutions find it useful that the wars do so. In order to change this incentive system, outsiders need to find ways to make peace pay more than war for the competing elites. Apparently it does not have to pay equally for everyone; Hugh Miall (1992, 186) found that, as long as one side did not clearly lose outright, agreement was possible with different levels of benefits.

Once the fighting itself has stopped, elites need to be encouraged to work together. This can be done in a variety of ways; aid is often tied to agreements among them or targeted to institutions in which they work together, for example. The key is to develop and strengthen a coalition of moderates from both sides (although they need not have been moderates during the war) because it is practically inevitable that some people will find themselves less well off in peace and form an alternate, if often implicit, coalition of extremists resisting the settlement. Outsiders may be too quick to assume that the moderate coalition, which often has control of the governmental institutions and receives external support, will automatically win such a conflict. This is a bad assumption to make if it encourages outsiders to reduce support for postsettlement governments that face enormous challenges.

Resolve the Security Dilemma

Several studies show that since 1940 civil wars have been much less likely than interstate wars to end in negotiated settlements. Figures vary somewhat with the time and definitions: 15 percent to 68 percent (Miall 1992, 124); 32 percent to 68 percent (Pillar 1983, 25); 15 percent to 68 percent (Stedman [1991, 8] refines Pillar's civil war data and does not dispute the interstate war figure); and 20 percent to 55 percent (Walter 1997, 335). Some analysts have attributed this to the different stakes involved in civil wars (Iklé 1971; Licklider 1995, 682). Barbara Walter (1997, 336–341; 2001) argues persuasively, however, that the difference is that a negotiated end to an interstate war may leave each side with enough military power to defend itself, while a comparable settlement in a civil war requires that both sides disarm themselves, leaving each vulnerable to destruction.

Analysts have borrowed the term "security dilemma" from international politics to describe the situation (Posen 1993; Fearon 1998; Walter and Snyder 1999). Disarmament is necessary for internal security, but for each side it is enormously risky; what if the other side takes advantage of its weakness to destroy it? But if one side does not disarm, the other assumes that it is planning an attack and rearms. More seriously, each side has a strong incentive to rearm even when it has ambiguous information that the other side is doing the same, and of course each side knows this about the other. Thus even people who want to disarm may find it too risky and wind up undercutting the settlement they support. Naturally, those who oppose the settlement on both sides will use these issues as arguments against it.

The importance of the security dilemma can be exaggerated. Many civil war settlements collapse, not because of real fear of attack, but because one or more of the antagonists were unhappy with the outcomes and felt that violence was a preferred alternative. Security dilemma theorists sometimes make it sound as though every civil war could be settled if we could just resolve this particular issue, which is obviously untrue. But the security dilemma remains a major problem, both in the short term during the transition from war to building shared political institutions, and later, as the new government tries to cope with its very substantial problems.

Much attention has focused on the transition period. It usually is very unstable politically. The alliances of the preceding war are coming apart as the rules and rewards change. People with guns are uneasy about their future, which is always a recipe for trouble. The country is often close to anarchy. Some new political structure is being created, but no one is certain what it is or what its effects will be. The existing political institutions cannot be trusted.

It seems reasonable that third parties could play an essential role in bridging the transition, reassuring each side that the other is complying long enough for mutual trust to build and infant institutions to develop, perhaps formally guaranteeing the process. Outsiders may also offer alliances in case the settlement fails, thus reducing the security dilemma (Stedman 1996, 356; Walter 1997, 1999, 2001). In fact, the effects of such guarantees are unclear. Walter (1997, 349–351; cf. Hartzell, Hoddie, and Rothchild 2001) identified sixteen successful civil war settlements between 1940 and 1990;

fourteen of them included third-party guarantees, and every case in which such a guarantee was given was a success. Aside from the raw figures, when nine cases of failed settlements are analyzed, negotiations often foundered on the issue of security during the transition. When peacekeeping troops were in place but withdrawn after settlement—Laos in 1973 and Vietnam in 1975—fighting resumed. Similarly, when peacekeepers failed to arrive—Uganda in 1985, Chad in 1979—the settlements collapsed. In a later version of the analysis, Walter (2001, chapters 4 and 5) identified fifty-nine civil wars ending between 1940 and 1995, twelve by successful settlement; she found that third-party security guarantees were one of the strongest predictors of successful implementation of civil war negotiated settlements. At the same time, Caroline Hartzell (1999) looked at settlements from 1945 to 1997 and Suzanne Werner (1999) examined settlements from 1815 to 1992; both found that third-party guarantees did not matter much.

Outside intervention comes in different forms. Classical conflict resolution theory calls for neutral peacekeepers, but in several of these cases the outsiders were not neutral (the United States in the Dominican Republic and Britain in Zimbabwe are examples). This is probably a good thing; even though outside states with an interest in a civil war are likely to be biased, states without such an interest may not be willing to make the commitment that is useful in ending the violence.

Walter (1997) also argues that foreign troops can help resolve the security dilemma by enforcing the terms of the agreement and providing reliable information to the parties about compliance of the other parties. We now have examples in the former Yugoslavia in which foreign soldiers actually enforced such agreements among locals—a radical change from conventional peacekeeping that is sometimes called peacemaking. Western governments seem to have decided that they can carry out such activities only as long as casualties are low; the

ominous example of Somalia hangs over them, despite research that suggests that the U.S. public in fact did not demand withdrawal after the debacle (Kull and Ramsay 2000). As a result they are inclined to use air power and artillery instead of ground forces when resistance is likely. If one side decides to reopen the civil war, strategies such as these that often produce civilian casualties do not seem the best way to end the violence, as suggested by the vigorous debate over the ethics of the Kosovo intervention.

Establish a Working Government

Postviolence states have major social problems; "[p]ractically all war-torn societies require comprehensive reforms in their political, economic, social, and security sectors" (Kumar 1997, 3). In particular these problems require a strong state, at a minimum able to provide security for its citizens, make decisions in a politically acceptable way, and create organizations that will implement these decisions and extract resources from the population to pay for the whole process. Each set of problems is formidable, and outsiders have attempted to assist with all of them at various times.

SECURITY. Perhaps the most fundamental task of the state is providing security for its population. This is often very difficult for the postconflict state. Civil war armies are often not well disciplined under the best of circumstances, one explanation for the seemingly pointless brutality that often accompanies such conflicts. When the fighting ends, they often disintegrate, releasing thousands of armed young men with no civilian skills at all. At the same time, the public security forces of the old regime were deeply implicated in its bad actions and cannot continue their repressive behavior because of the political settlement. All this happens precisely when people who have often been terribly injured by the war desperately need reassurance in order to resume their normal lives.

In communities tormented by repeated violence . . . safety is the most compelling motive for action. Unstable conditions tend to be exacerbated by the return of community members who fled during earlier bouts of fighting; land disputes, threats, retribution, and intimidation are common. Individuals may be frightened by other individuals or gangs, identity groups as a whole may be afraid of large-scale retribution of attacks based on association, and the community at large may be threatened by other regions, the military, or government persecution. Healing under these conditions can be extremely difficult. Therefore, freedom of movement within the community, absence of personal or group threats or attacks, property security, and access to community resources are necessary first steps on the path to recovery. The principle of safety must apply to all members of the community, regardless of status. (Maynard 1999, 132)

The problem of establishing security for citizens confronts every society after civil war. At one level it seems to be fairly simple: a police force has to be created. But in fact this is extraordinarily difficult. If it seems inappropriate to use personnel from the earlier security forces, where are trained and competent personnel, fluent in the local language and versed in the local customs and geography, to be found in short order? Anarchy in the streets will not wait for the establishment of a new police academy, determination of a curriculum, recruitment of new officers, completion of course work, and initiation into the complexities of police work. Given the time constraints, veterans from the earlier security forces have to be used. Outsiders can encourage purging those guilty of the worst excesses and providing some sort of training to the rest, even if it is only on the job.

In fact, however, a police force is only part of the solution. A police force needs a set of laws to enforce, and the previous set dates from the old regime and is now widely seen as illegitimate. It also needs a judicial system with judges and lawyers, who are likely to be in short supply after a civil war in which they were likely targets. After trials, a prison system is needed, and again this will likely have to be built from the ground up. In other words, it needs a government. But who should control such a government? That is precisely what the civil war was all about. (For a useful collection on this whole process, see Dziedzic, Goldberg, and Oakley 1998.)

At another level, the security system attempts to limit individual violence within the society. The usual upsurge in such violence is the result of fighters who find that crime is the easiest way to prosper economically. Clearly it is more efficient to demobilize and integrate these individuals into the national economy than to try to deal with them as an internal security problem. Obviously this will reduce the security dilemma as well.

Demobilization usually involves assembling the fighters to disarm them and give them some preparation for reentering civilian life, perhaps including some skills and basic education, and providing them with some basic resources for some time. It is a complex and expensive process, and delays often seem inevitable. However, such delays raise the threat that the civil war armies may reform, undermining confidence in the settlement, and they should be avoided if possible (Ball 1996).

Outsiders have often played a central part in such activities, by providing intellectual leadership, resources, and personnel to supervise the process. Demobilization succeeded in Namibia, where 7,500 people from the United Nations were present; it failed in Angola, where there were only 425. On the other hand, numbers are sometimes not enough; the Khmer Rouge refused to be disarmed despite the presence of over 15,000 military personnel associated with the United Nations. This raised the delicate question of whether the United Nations should have been prepared to use force to enforce demobilization; the combat records of the Khmer Rouge and the United Nations suggest this may have been a bad idea (Hampson 1999, 224–227). Nonetheless, the general point remains that demobilization and disarmament are critical and that third parties often play a central role in making it happen.

An interesting alternative is community-based security, in which arms are retained under the authority of local councils. This approach seems to have worked in Somaliland and produced significant disarmament without foreign assistance (Hippel 2000b, 195).

Outsiders have often been reluctant to become involved in these activities. Outsiders do not like to spend money on police and prisons; it is much more satisfying to feed starving children than to establish a justice system that may reduce corruption so they can get food on their own. In addition, some organizations, including the U.S. military, are forbidden to aid police (Kumar 1997, 13). This reluctance may explain why the same sorts of problems seem to confront us repeatedly and why international learning on this subject seems to have been rather slow.

Any outside troops on the scene will be pressed into service as police, but they will not like it. Soldiers and police are not trained to do the same things, even if they both are armed. Moreover, the soldiers as outsiders have no legitimacy. So the military will pressure the civilians to get some sort of police force, almost any kind, on the streets so they can get back to their job. In Panama, for example, the Americans created a special group of reservists who had been police in the United States, some of whom also spoke Spanish, to go on patrol with the new Panamanian police officers. However, this did not last long because the U.S. military is forbidden to train foreign police (Donnelly 1991, 384). In Somalia a police force was created in Mogadishu from former police after the initial intervention by the U.S.–directed UNITAF, but when the United Nations took over, its personnel felt that there should be a government before there was a police force and allowed the rather vestigial force to decay (Hirsch and Oakley 1995, 60–61, 87–95, 103–106). In Haiti an interim police force was formed from diaspora Haitians and members of the armed forces who had been nonpolitical and given a few days of training. Simultaneously a separate, permanent police force was recruited and given more extensive training by both the United States and the United Nations; over time it replaced the interim force (Hippel 2000b, 108–112).

Similar problems arose in Panama, El Salvador, and Haiti, despite different roles for the United States and the United Nations. The new security forces had insufficient physical equipment and fiscal support, first from the external sponsors and later from the local government. They found it extremely difficult to recruit high-level officials who had not been involved in the previous government's security systems and suffered public scandals as a result. They were handicapped by the lack of an effective judicial system, including courts, lawyers, prisons, and so on. They clearly had a much better human rights record than their predecessors (which would not have been difficult), and the local populations generally viewed them fairly favorably initially, but local support declined as crime rose after the settlement and the police seemed unwilling or unable to cope with it (Licklider 1999, 95–99; Stanley and Call 1997; University of Illinois 1990; Hippel 2000b, 109–112).

Some organizations have stepped forward to fill the gap with training, notably the International Criminal Investigative Training Assistance Program, sponsored by the U.S. Department of Justice, and the United Nations CIVPOL; the Stanley Foundation (2000) recently suggested developing an International Legal Assistance Consortium. Nonetheless, the lack of capability within the international community is a major problem, as shown most clearly in Bosnia (Hippel 2000b, 160–161).

POWER SHARING. The most important issue in any civil war settlement is the distribution of political power in the successor state(s). That is, ultimately, what the war has been about. People are willing to fight and die over it because they know it will determine their future and that of their children.

Western governments, particularly the United States, seem to believe that democracy is the form of government most likely to allow people to live together peacefully, and indeed it seems reasonable that people are more likely to be content if they have some say in their government. Several authors have tried to develop empirical theories about how democracy may emerge from civil war. Wood (2000) concludes that changing elite interests in oligarchies make continuation of civil war too expensive and democracy an attractive alternative. Leonard Wantchekon and Zvika Neeman (2000) suggest that elites in conflict prefer basic decisions to be made by the population at large rather than by their opponents, since the interests of the population are more divided and therefore more likely to be neutral.

However, simple majoritarian democracy is unlikely to be acceptable to groups who see themselves as permanent minorities. This means that the conventional parliamentary system, which most European states exported to their colonies, will not work well. The U.S. system of divided powers specified by a written constitution, perhaps reinforced by a federal system, may seem more attractive, but it is not clear how the legal checks on executive authority can be enforced. The more common strategy is a parliamentary system with some sort of proportional representation (Hartzell 1999, 8–10); this guarantees access to the government but risks producing weak governments.

There are two different types of power sharing: assuring all groups a voice in political decisions at the center of the state and dispersing central power to regional or local centers. They may be used together, of course. Timothy Sisk (1996, 49) has argued that dispersal of power is an appropriate response to situations in which groups are regionally concentrated (often these are ethnic groups), while central distribution is more helpful in other cases. Regional autonomy settlements have often been effective in

resolving ethnic and communal conflicts, although they are not a panacea (Gurr 1993, 298–305; Lapidoth 1996).

Power sharing is not necessarily democratic; in fact, it is often designed precisely to prevent simple majorities from ruling. More significantly, it can take place among elites with very little role for other segments of the society (Rothchild and Foley 1988; Rothchild 1997). We do not have good evidence about whether democratic postsettlement governments make renewed civil war less likely, in part because in the post–World War II era there have not been many such governments or renewed civil wars. However, some tentative work suggests that there may not be much of a connection. Democracy was not significantly associated with decreased likelihood of renewed civil war in an analysis of eighty-three cases from 1945 to 1993. Further analysis specified a number of causal processes, including intermediate variables, by which democracy would be expected to have this impact; some of the specified intermediate variables were not uniquely linked to democracy, and others seemed to have little impact on renewed civil war (Licklider 2000). Democracy may be a superior form of government for a variety of reasons, but it is not clear that it prevents renewed civil wars.

Third-party forces may be useful during the transition, but they cannot remain forever. We are usually talking about a period of a few years (although the Syrians who guaranteed the 1989 agreement in Lebanon show no signs of leaving). Aside from stopping the killing, the most important function of the transition is to establish a set of political institutions through which societal conflicts may be pursued without large-scale violence. Boutros Boutros-Ghali (1992, 11–12) has called this postconflict peacebuilding.

Hartzell (1999) has shown that successful settlements are overwhelmingly characterized by agreements that specify in some detail (a) rules about the use of coercive force, particularly during the transitional period, when the security dilemma is the most acute, (b) rules concerning the distribution of political power after the transition, and (c) rules concerning the distribution of economic resources after the transition. This research suggests that (1) power sharing is likely to be essential in a settlement and (2) the time to get the agreement is when the initial settlement is being negotiated, not in a later conference when the urgency to end the violence has passed and compromise has become more difficult (cf. Stedman 1996, 353; Hampson 1996, 206).

Can outsiders significantly increase the chances of stable democratic postsettlement governments? The evidence is thin at this point because there are very few cases; the whole idea of using democracy after civil wars is fairly new. One interesting analysis argues that democracy, like settlement, is a second choice for elites at war, who not surprisingly prefer victory and domination. Democracy, then, is much more likely when a single elite does not feel able to control the situation, as in a negotiated settlement. Democracy is not an automatic result of settlement, but it is more likely here than after a military victory. Outsiders in such a situation may find that incentives to retain democracy are more useful than sanctions against nondemocratic behavior (Krain 2000). At the same time, two large-N (many cases) statistical analyses find that whether a war ended in military victory or not is unrelated to subsequent democratization (Wantchekon and Nickerson 1999, 14; Doyle and Sambanis 2000a, 23), while it does seem to be linked to prewar democratization (Sambanis 2000, 463).

Although often overlooked, the German and Japanese occupations after World War II demonstrated that outsiders could in fact create working democracies that would receive local support for over fifty years. Germany and Japan, of course, were different from our current concerns; they were literate and industrialized and were totally controlled by foreign governments that believed they had a vital national interest in instituting democracy (Hippel 2000b, 12–13,

185–186). At the same time, the outsiders had just killed several million of their citizens, had no clear idea about how to create democracy, and expended relatively limited resources over only a few years (Licklider 1999, 85–90). Certainly the failure of contemporaneous Soviet efforts in Eastern Europe is striking. The failure of the United States in Vietnam suggests the difficulties in establishing democracy even when substantial resources are deployed. Karin von Hippel (2000b, 18–22) attributes the U.S. failure to a lack of coordination and more concern with fighting communism than building democracy.

Building democracy has been a new activity for the United Nations since 1989. Some of its missions have achieved impressive results in unpromising situations, such as El Salvador, Mozambique, and Namibia. Others, such as Somalia, Angola, and Rwanda, have been resounding failures. In these missions, the United Nations works under several handicaps: member concern about the precedent of undermining sovereignty; a neutrality tradition that contradicts peacebuilding, which is inherently political; and the potential conflict between the goals of establishing security and creating a democratic political system (Bertram 1995, 390–400). The record of individual states is similarly mixed. The United States has found itself engaged in similar state-building exercises in Panama, Somalia, Haiti, Bosnia, and Kosovo. In general, the military aspects of these interventions have gone well, but it is not at all clear that the U.S. government knows how to create a working state in a country where none exists, much less how to make it self-sufficient and democratic (Licklider 1999; Hippel 2000a, 2000b).

Part of the problem is simple ignorance.

The international community has accumulated a vast body of technical knowledge in designing and implementing economic and, to some extent, social assistance programs during the past three decades. Although the knowledge is not highly satisfactory, it is nonetheless adequate for all practical purposes. However, no such claims can be made for assistance in the political arena.... Consequently, those charged with designing and implementing political rehabilitation interventions lack appropriate conceptual frameworks, intervention models, concepts, policy instruments, and methodologies for assistance programs to rebuild civil society, establish and nurture democratic institutions, promote a culture favorable to the protection of human rights, reconstruct law enforcement systems, or facilitate ethnic reconciliation in a highly unstable political and social environment. (Kumar 1997, 33–34)

We know that some efforts to build democracy have backfired (Adamson 2000). Moreover, almost all work in this area has been guided by the assumption that democracy is necessary to prevent renewed civil war (much as it was earlier seen as a barrier to communism). As suggested earlier, we do not have much empirical support for this proposition, but its widespread acceptance has meant that a working government is defined as democratic.

This in turn has sometimes allowed outsiders to justify focusing almost exclusively on free elections as the most appropriate strategy to create and legitimize a new, democratic political system. A careful analysis of postconflict elections, however, including those which failed, led Krishna Kumar and Marina Ottaway (1998, 234–235) to suggest that several preconditions are necessary: a working state, a societal consensus on boundaries and how the government should function, a democratic commitment among all parties strong enough so that they are prepared to accept losing, and progress toward demobilization. They suggest that in the absence of these preconditions it may be better to delay elections for some time, using a coalition government or one largely controlled by outsiders, in order to establish the conditions that make elections appropriate (Kumar and Ottaway 1998, 236–237).

Intellectually, it is plausible that democracy may be more trouble than it is worth and that elite power sharing may be a better political strategy in some cases. However, it would be very difficult for Western governments and organizations to support a government that is avowedly not democratic. Under the circumstances, we seem to have no alternative other than to support democracy, although of course the locals may choose to do something else altogether. Given this, a major contribution by outsiders is the development and reinforcement of the norms that are central to democracy, such as tolerance, rule of law, and respect for human rights (Hampson 1996, 229–231).

Can we say anything more that is useful about what works and what does not? A recent analysis of 1815 to 1990 (an unusually long period) finds that multilateral interventions are much more likely to result in a more democratic regime than previously (Wantchekon and Nickerson 1999, 12–13). A sophisticated analysis of 124 post–World War II civil wars concludes that UN mediation by itself is not sufficient to establish basic democratization but that UN operations that involve a variety of activities (traditional peacekeeping, economic development, and building political institutions) have a major positive impact (Doyle and Sambanis 2000b, 789–791). A separate analysis of unilateral interventions concludes that mixed strategies work better than purely military strategies in establishing peace (Regan 2000, 82–99), results that seem similar to those for multilateral interventions, although Regan looks for peace rather than democratization.

CREATING A RESPONSIVE, EFFECTIVE, AND REASONABLY HONEST STATE APPARATUS. Outsiders often focus on the political leadership of the postsettlement government, and this is clearly important. It is difficult to imagine South Africa's peaceful transition without Nelson Mandela, for example. But in order for settlements to hold, governments must be able to deliver services and collect revenues to pay for them in a manner that the population finds acceptable. This is done by state employees, civil servants, bureaucrats, and so on, not elected politicians. For example, the government of Panama after the U.S. invasion essentially consisted of three men: a president and two vice presidents. They had been fairly elected, although the election had been nullified by Manuel Noriega. When the United States invaded, most members of the government, who had naturally been linked to Noriega, decamped, often taking whatever resources were available with them. The three men were powerless; the U.S. military had to step in until locals could be brought in to take over, which took months.

Internal security is so immediate and important that it has been discussed in an earlier section, but many of the same problems appear in other areas of government. Skilled personnel are in short supply. Loyalty to political leaders or groups often is more important than competence in getting jobs. Supporters expect to be rewarded, and this is especially complex when there are several sides to be satisfied at the same time. The prior government has often not offered a useful model of governance, even for those with good intentions.

Taxation policy is particularly critical. In many cases an unjust taxation system was one of the spurs to civil war in the first place; this tradition, combined with a general culture of resistance, makes it very difficult to establish a taxation system based on income and sales taxes across the population, which most economists now see as the best way to encourage economic growth. It is often temptingly easier instead to rely on taxation of export industries and resource producers, since this can be done fairly easily. As Charles Tilly (1992, chapter 4) pointed out, however, this is a dangerous strategy because it allows the state to avoid reaching an agreement with the productive sectors of society, which is the basis for long-term governance. The more recent notion of the "resource curse" suggests that states with resources that can easily be seized (drugs, oil, some kinds of diamonds) will find it very difficult to end civil violence because the rebels can use these resources

to finance their wars; Angola and Congo are examples (Collier and Hoeffler 2000).

The good news is that the new government does not have to produce Weber's ideal-type bureaucrats in large numbers. Standards of governance have usually been abysmal, so fairly low levels of competence can actually look pretty good, and a certain amount of corruption may be acceptable, depending on the society. The important thing is that the new government is perceived to be acting fairly and reasonably competently.

Outsiders can be very helpful by training personnel and sending experienced people to help get the various organizations of modern government established. However, none of this will work unless the locals fairly quickly acquire both access to local resources and a sense of ownership.

Create a Working Economy

A recent sophisticated econometric study links two economic factors to civil war renewal: a high percentage of GDP acquired from natural resources and the lack of economic opportunities, particularly for young men (Collier and Hoeffler 2000; Collier 2000; see also Berdal and Malone 2000). This analysis presents the policymaker with a dilemma, since one way to increase opportunities is to focus on resource extraction. These findings suggest the importance of creating a working economy, both to reduce dependence on easily looted resources and to increase economic opportunities. This opinion is widely supported by anecdotal evidence in various cases. But this is easier to say than to do when the country has been devastated by civil war; the infrastructure is often in ruins; equipment and factories have been destroyed; workers and managers have been dispersed; the banking and financial systems have been destroyed; and the government is weak and without planning expertise or resources.

Economically, outsiders can bring important resources to the table and add incentives to make peace more attractive for everyone (Cortright 1997). Kumar (1997) notes that we have had a lot of experience with economic development assistance, so we do not have a good excuse if it does not work. Moreover, it is commonplace that economic development is critical to the stability of postsettlement governments. Thus most settlements now include economic assistance from states and intergovernmental and nongovernmental organizations.

However, there is no consensus on how such economic assistance should be given. In particular there is disagreement about whether the new governments should be encouraged to establish fiscal responsibility by limiting expenditures quickly or be allowed to respond to the massive social needs for several years, even at the risk of discouraging foreign investment that may be essential for their long-term futures. The International Monetary Fund has become the lightning rod for this issue, and we have not made much progress in resolving it.

The problem would be simplified, although not eliminated, by the provision of economic resources from outsiders, and such commitments are often part of the settlement. Unfortunately, donors often do not deliver on their promises, in part because a successful negotiation ends the violence, which in turn makes the issue seem less pressing to outsiders, whose attention may then shift to another instance of violence. Even when promises are kept, the inability of the international community to coordinate its activities means that the real impact of such aid may be less than expected (Forman and Patrick 2000).

All of this assumes that foreign assistance leads to economic development, which in turn makes renewed civil war less likely. Aside from a good deal of anecdotal argument, a recent study shows that higher levels of net current economic transfers (which include aid of all sorts) and local economic capabilities are indeed associated with a substantially higher probability of achieving a basic level of democracy; they even seem to compensate somewhat for

higher levels of hostility that reduce this probability (Doyle and Sambanis 2000a, 18, 29). At the same time, some analysts argue that economic aid may actually increase conflict on the ground (Anderson 1999).

Transitional Justice/Retribution

Civil war fighters often do terrible things to their enemies and to more or less innocent bystanders: needless killing, torture, rape, robbery, expulsion, and so on. After the war, the people who did these things are still in the country, in many cases living close to their victims. They present two separate questions: What, if anything, should be done about them, and what in fact can be done about them?

WHAT SHOULD BE DONE? One school of thought holds that individuals who have done such things, or have ordered them done, should be punished in courts of law, either in the country where the atrocities occurred or elsewhere, or at least publicly confess and repent. The legal argument rests on the assumption that international norms and conventions increasingly adopt this position; the agreement on the International Criminal Court is perhaps the most striking recent example. There are two political arguments: (a) punishment of such crimes deters future crimes and (b) borrowing from psychology, neither victims nor perpetrators will be able to live with the other until the crimes are acknowledged and some punishment, compensation, or sign of remorse is given. This position dominates the current literature on peacebuilding and has resulted in the creation of a variety of institutions to discover the truth and, in some cases, to administer justice, from international war crimes courts to truth commissions with varying charters (Kritz 1995). An interesting variation of this is communalization, in which victims and perpetrators share memories of what happened in small communities such as villages (Maynard 1999, 134–136).

The opposing argument is that the only way that people live together, whether in families or states, is to forget the things that divide them, that truth is elusive and in the mind of the beholder, and that justice cannot and will not be administered fairly. Tony Judt's comments about World War II apply in recent civil wars as well:

> [H]ow do you punish tens of thousands, perhaps millions of people for activities that were approved, legalized, and even encouraged by those in power . . . ? But how do you justify leaving unpunished actions that were manifestly criminal even before they fell under the aegis of "victors' justice"? How do you choose whom to punish and for what actions? Who does the choosing? At what precise moment is a purge sufficient to meet elementary demands for justice and revenge, and not yet so divisive as to damage still further a rent social fabric? (Judt 2000, 300–301)

In a civil war, everyone has been guilty of collaborating with one side or the other (usually both) at different times; who is to draw the line? Those condemned as criminals by some will be seen as martyrs by others, and the net result may well deepen and harden existing divisions, undermining the settlement, weakening the already fragile postsettlement state, and making future violence more likely rather than less likely. This position is often held by people on the ground in postsettlement situations, although it is not politically popular.

We simply do not know whether transitional justice makes future violence more or less likely. Reconciliation, after all, is likely to take generations. It is, however, interesting to compare two cases from earlier in this century: Germany and the Jews and Turkey and the Armenians. Germany has become the poster child of transitional justice, after the Nuremberg trials embarking on an extensive program of apologies and compensations to both individual Jews and the state of Israel (Gardner Feldman 1984; Wolffsohn 1993; Lavy 1996; Olick and Levy 1997). Turkey has never even acknowledged any responsibility for the deaths of the

Armenians, much less done anything to show remorse (Dadrian 1997; Chorbajian and Shirinian 1999; Hovannisian 1999; Tölöyan 1987). Clearly relations between Germany and Jews are better than relations between Turkey and Armenians, suggesting that something like transitional justice may facilitate reconciliation. However, neither government had to live with large numbers of the victims in its own state afterward, so their experiences are not really comparable to modern cases like Cambodia or Rwanda.

PRACTICAL LIMITS. In practice each situation has different limitations on what can actually be done. There is a fundamental contradiction between negotiating a settlement with someone and subjecting that person to trial for war crimes. If the settlement was negotiated, presumably the leaders of both sides have built in amnesty for themselves and their followers; otherwise they would not have agreed in the first place. More generally, there is always the risk that rigorous transitional justice programs will trigger new violence. The American Civil War, for example, is usually seen as a military victory, but it is hard to imagine that Southerners would have laid down their arms and gone home if the government had announced that every soldier in the rebel army would be tried for treason and executed, as it clearly could have done legally. Often the leaders who signed the peace agreement are among the most complicit, but arresting them may cause a renewed outbreak of civil war; peace and justice may thus be directly opposed.

There are also enormous practical problems. Major human rights violations may involve thousands of people; someone estimated that every Hutu family in Rwanda had at least one member directly involved in the massacres. Postsettlement states do not have the resources to give fair trials to so many people, so decisions about who will be punished are necessarily arbitrary and unfair. The international tribunals have found it difficult to function effectively, both because of the intrinsic difficulty of the task and because of lack of resources. Truth commissions find their reports disregarded or attacked. In the storm of problems confronted by a new government, how important is transitional justice?

Recently there has been a tendency to accept mutual amnesty in order to reach a settlement and then change the terms later, when one side is weaker politically and presumably less able to resist; the Pinochet case has elements of this. Aside from the details of the particular case, this policy has broader and riskier implications for conflict management. Disowning such amnesty guarantees may make political leaders more reluctant to accept future negotiated settlements to civil wars.

Third parties have been extremely important in encouraging transitional justice institutions of various sorts. In many places the whole idea of transitional justice, as opposed to the traditional strategies of direct reprisals or amnesty, has been imported; even when the impulse has been local, information about alternatives and fiscal and political support have come from the outside. When outsiders have this much impact, they take on a correspondingly high level of responsibility for the outcomes. It is particularly troubling that much of this work is being done with no clear evidence of its impact on the prospects for reconciliation within the target society.

Renegotiation of the Settlement

Carrying out the terms of the peace settlement is often seen as one measure of its success. Indeed, its success often depends on the assumption by all concerned that this will happen; this is particularly true for the political and security provisions, as we have seen, and without such assurance the violence may well resume.

However, the settlement itself often is not the best framework for the postwar government. The American Civil War formally ended in 1865 with the Confederacy surrendering

and Reconstruction governments established in Southern states. But in fact resistance was so intense (possibly constituting an extension of the war by our current coding schemes) that a second settlement was reached in 1877, under which white Southerners agreed to abandon slavery and not to secede but were allowed to eliminate all political rights for black Southerners. A civil war ended in Colombia with a model power-sharing agreement that actually worked for decades, but the rise of a new civil war was due in part to the settlement that kept new groups out of power (Hartlyn 1993, 49–58). The Cambodia war ended with a power-sharing settlement that was replaced by a dictatorship but did not develop into a new war. The French, Chinese, and Russian Revolutions all ended in governments that were replaced by more extreme elements within a few years.

Theoretically, this is not hard to understand. Settlements focus on current issues, primarily those of the civil war. But once those issues have been handled, at least for a short time, the political coalitions on both sides break up, and new issues become more important; indeed in several recent cases the first violence after the settlement was between former allies, not former adversaries (Atlas and Licklider 1999). The U.S. constitutional convention almost foundered on the issue of large versus small states, but once the issue was settled by having two houses of Congress, no issue has ever separated the large from the small states. A successful settlement is precisely one that makes its own issues less relevant and thus makes itself obsolete.

Thus there is a paradox: a civil war settlement must seem permanent but in fact should probably be temporary. But the short-term need is stability, expectations that the terms of the settlement will endure. On balance, it is probably not a good idea to try to formally build the possibility of change into the system; the renegotiation process may well trigger new violence (Werner 1999). However, we need to remember that change is inevitable in politics and that civil war settlements must not be immune from such processes. In the short run, ambiguous provisions in the settlement will have to be negotiated. As time goes on, changes will have to be made to make the settlement work, and eventually the intractable issues that were omitted from the settlement will have to be tackled. Presumably the process culminates in a permanent political process within the country itself, but third parties can be critical in encouraging the negotiating process and supporting those who are willing to be involved in it (Hampson 1996, 218–223).

COORDINATION WITHIN THE INTERNATIONAL COMMUNITY

Much of our discussion has assumed that the international community is effectively a single actor, with common goals and strategies, and that the key question is to decide how it should act. Of course this is not true. There is some general agreement on goals (peace is better than war, democracy is better than authoritarianism, economic development is important for peace, and so forth) among most of those involved in interventions in civil war. But once we move beyond this very general consensus, major divisions are quickly revealed.

Karin von Hippel (2000b, 205) identifies five international communities that need to be coordinated: donor governments, militaries, multilateral organizations, the private sector, and nongovernmental organizations. Governments bring the most resources to bear (when they choose to do so) but are not usually well organized to deliver the goods and services that will be helpful in making a civil war settlement work. Militaries are often very good at violence and organization but, especially in the United States, have problems working with civilian organizations on development and political projects. Multilateral organizations (United Nations agencies and regional

organizations) have great potential, but they are necessarily responsive to the often conflicting imperatives of the governments that control them. The private sector has generally been neglected, but it clearly can bring major resources and often has considerable influence with both governments and rebel groups; on the other hand it often has no obvious reason to become involved.

The recent explosion in activities of humanitarian nongovernmental organizations has changed the face of international response to civil wars. Such organizations tend to be highly specialized in function and/or targets (medical care, food, negotiation, civil society, children, refugees, former combatants, AIDS, democracy, legal systems) and independently financed and controlled. They can respond quickly and bring appropriate and vital resources to the task at hand, including experienced personnel, and they are often accepted when governmental organizations are not. On the other hand, their limited missions may encourage rigid standard operating procedures, regardless of the local situation, sometimes disregarding the wishes of the local population. They are also very concerned both to remain independent and to appear to be independent from others. Many of them are particularly concerned not to be associated with military forces and missions, which causes difficulty in those peacemaking activities that require security and humanitarian missions to be carried out in concert.

These divisions are convenient for analysis, but it is important to realize that there is no reason to expect that any two organizations in the same category will agree on policy decisions. Each organization has its own mission and set of goals, organizational culture, sources of support, and dominant constituency. The incentives for cooperation are generally low; indeed, in many cases organizations fear they will suffer if they are associated with others. Advanced planning is an important part of the cultures of the military and, to a lesser extent, the private sector; nongovernmental organizations have great difficulty in getting the necessary resources to indulge in it. Moreover, all of these organizations share a division between those in the field and those at headquarters (Maynard 1999, xii–xiii).

At the same time, there is a general realization that coordination is a problem, and some progress is being made in this area. Reforms in the United Nations seem to have improved things considerably. Groups of representatives from different organizations—such as the Burundi Forum, the Afghanistan Programming Board, the Monitoring and Steering Group in Liberia, and the Somalia Aid Co-ordination Body (Hippel 2000b, 205)—have coalesced around particular countries or problems. Military, governmental, and nongovernmental organizations now participate in common training exercises and planning.

Coordination between the military and political organizations is both particularly critical and particularly difficult; it thus serves as a useful proxy for the more general problem. Clearly all concerned have learned a good deal about how to work together (Hippel 2000b; Weiss 1999; Williams 1998). Given the world we live in, we are likely to see soon whether they have learned enough.

REFERENCES

Adamson, Fiona B. 2000. "International Norms Meet Local Structures: The Dilemmas of Democracy Promotion in Post-Soviet Central Asia." Paper presented at the American Political Science Association, August 30–September 3, Washington, D.C.

Anderson, Mary. 1999. *Do No Harm: How Aid Can Support Peace or War*. Boulder, Colo.: Lynne Rienner.

Atlas, Pierre, and Roy Licklider. 1999. "Conflict among Former Allies after Civil War Settlement in Sudan, Zimbabwe, Chad, and Lebanon." *Journal of Peace Research* 36, no. 1 (January): 35–54.

Ayres, R. William. 2000. "A World Flying Apart? Violent Nationalist Conflicts and the End of the Cold War." *Journal of Peace Research* 37, no. 1 (January): 105–117.

Ball, Nicole. 1996. "Demobilizing and Reintegrating Soldiers: Lessons from Africa." In *Rebuilding Societies after Civil War: Critical Roles for International Assistance*, ed. Krishna Kumar, 85–105. Boulder, Colo.: Lynne Rienner.

Berdal, Mats, and David M. Malone. 2000. *Greed and Grievances: Economic Agendas in Civil Wars*. Boulder, Colo.: Lynne Rienner.

Bertram, Eva. 1995. "Reinventing Governments: The Promise and Perils of United Nations Peacekeeping." *Journal of Conflict Resolution* 39, no. 3 (September): 387-418.

Boutros-Ghali, Boutros. 1992. *An Agenda for Peace*. New York: United Nations.

Carment, David, and Frank Harvey. 2000. *Using Force to Prevent Ethnic Violence: An Evaluation of Theory and Evidence*. Westport, Conn.: Praeger Press.

Chorbajian, Levon, and George Shirinian. 1999. *Studies in Comparative Genocide*. New York: St. Martin's Press.

Collier, Paul. 2000. "Policy for Post-Conflict Societies: Reducing the Risks of Renewed Conflict." Paper presented at the Economics of Political Violence Conference, March 18–19, Princeton University, Princeton, N.J.

Collier, Paul, and Anke Hoeffler. 2000. *Greed and Grievance in Civil War*. Washington, D.C.: World Bank.

Cortright, David. 1997. *The Price of Peace: Incentives and International Conflict Prevention*. Lanham, Md.: Rowman and Littlefield.

Dadrian, Vahakn N. 1997. *The History of the Armenian Genocide: Ethnic Conflict from the Balkans to Anatolia to the Caucasus*. Providence, R.I.: Berghahn Books.

Diehl, Paul F., Jennifer Reifschneider, and Paul R. Hensel. 1996. "United Nations Intervention and Recurring Conflict." *International Organization* 50 (fall): 683–700.

Donnelly, Thomas, Margaret Roth, and Caleb Baker. 1991. *Operation Just Cause: The Storming of Panama*. New York: Lexington Books.

Doyle, Michael W., and Nicholas Sambanis. 2000a. "International Peacekeeping: A Theoretical and Quantitative Analysis." Paper presented at the

Economics of Political Violence Conference, March 18–19, Princeton University, Princeton, N.J.

Doyle, Michael W., and Nicholas Sambanis. 2000b. "International Peacekeeping: A Theoretical and Quantitative Analysis." *American Political Science Review* 94, no. 4 (December): 779–801.

Dziedzic, Michael J., Eliot M. Goldberg, and Robert B. Oakley. 1998. *Policing the New World Order: Peace Operations and Public Security*. Washington, D.C.: National Defense University Press.

Fearon, James D. 1998. "Commitment Problems and the Spread of Ethnic Conflict." In *The International Spread of Ethnic Conflict: Fear, Diffusion, and Escalation*, ed. David A. Lake and Donald Rothchild, 107–126. Princeton, N.J.: Princeton University Press.

Forman, Shepard, and Patrick Stewart. 2000. *Good Intentions: Pledges of Aid for Postconflict Recovery*. Boulder, Colo.: Lynne Rienner.

Gardner Feldman, Lily. 1984. *The Special Relationship between West Germany and Israel*. Boston: George Allen and Unwin.

Gurr, Ted Robert. 1993. *Minorities at Risk: A Global View of Ethnopolitical Conflicts*. Washington, D.C.: United States Institute of Peace Press.

———. 2000. "Ethnic Warfare on the Wane." *Foreign Affairs* 79 (May-June): 52–64.

Hampson, Fen Osler. 1996. *Nurturing Peace: Why Peace Settlements Succeed or Fail*. Washington, D.C.: United States Institute of Peace Press.

Hartlyn, Jonathan. 1993. "Civil Violence and Conflict Resolution: The Case of Colombia." In *Stopping the Killing: How Civil Wars End*, ed. Roy Licklider, 37–61. New York: New York University Press.

Hartzell, Caroline. 1999. "Explaining the Stability of Negotiated Settlements to Intrastate Wars." *Journal of Conflict Resolution* 43 (February): 3–22.

Hartzell, Caroline, Matthew Hoddie, and Donald Rothchild. 2001. "Stabilizing the Peace after Civil War: An Investigation of Some Key Variables." *International Organization* 50, no. 1 (winter): 183–208.

Hippel, Karin von. 2000a. "Democracy by Force: A Renewed Commitment to Nation Building." *Washington Quarterly* 23, no. 1: 95–112.

———. 2000b. *Democracy by Force: U.S. Military Intervention in the Post–Cold War World*. New York: Cambridge University Press.

Hirsch, John L., and Robert B. Oakley. 1995. *Somalia and Operation Restore Hope: Reflections on Peacemaking and Peacekeeping*. Washington, D.C.: United States Institute of Peace Press.

Hovannisian, Richard G. 1999. *Remembrance and Denial: The Case of the Armenian Genocide*. Detroit: Wayne State University Press.

Iklé, Fred C. 1971. *Every War Must End*. New York: Columbia University Press.

Judt, Tony. 2000. "The Past Is Another Country." In *The Politics of Retribution in Europe: World War II and Its Aftermath*, ed. István Deák, Jan T. Gross, and Tony Judt, 293–323. Princeton, N.J.: Princeton University Press.

Krain, Matthew. 2000. *Repression and Accommodation in Post-Revolutionary States*. New York: St. Martin's Press.

Kritz, Neil. 1995. *Transitional Justice: How Emerging Democracies Reckon with Former Regimes*. 3 vols. Washington, D.C.: United States Institute of Peace Press.

Kull, Steven, and Clay Ramsay. 2000. "Challenging U.S. Policymakers' Image of an Isolationist Public." *International Studies Perspectives* 1, no. 1 (April): 105–117.

Kumar, Krishna. 1997. "The Nature and Focus of International Assistance for Rebuilding War Torn Societies." In *Rebuilding Societies after Civil War: Critical Roles for International Assistance*, ed. Krishna Kumar, 1-38. Boulder, Colo.: Lynne Rienner.

Kumar, Krishna, and Marina Ottaway. 1998. "General Conclusions and Priorities for Policy Research." In *Postconflict Elections, Democratization and International Assistance*, ed. Krishna Kumar, 229–237. Boulder, Colo.: Lynne Rienner.

Lapidoth, Ruth. 1996. *Autonomy: Flexible Solutions to Ethnic Conflicts*. Washington, D.C.: United States Institute of Peace Press.

Lavy, George. 1996. *Germany and Israel: Moral Debt and National Interest*. London: Frank Cass.

Licklider, Roy. 1995. "The Consequences of Negotiated Settlements in Civil Wars, 1945–1993." *American Political Science Review* 89: 681–690.

———. 1999. "State-Building after Invasion: Germany, Japan, Panama, and Somalia." *Small Wars and Insurgencies* 10, no. 3 (winter): 82–116.

———. 2000. "False Hopes? Democracy and the Resumption of Civil War." Working paper. Political Science Department, Rutgers University.

Maynard, Kimberly. 1999. *Healing Communities in Conflict: International Assistance in Complex Emergencies*. New York: Columbia University Press.

Miall, Hugh. 1992. *The Peacemakers: Peaceful Settlement of Disputes since 1945*. New York: St. Martin's Press.

Olick, Jeffrey K., and Daniel Levy. 1997. "Collective Memory and Cultural Constraint: Holocaust Myth and Rationality in German Politics." *American Sociological Review* 62 (December): 921–936.

Pillar, Paul R. 1983. *Negotiating Peace: War Termination as a Bargaining Process*. Princeton, N.J.: Princeton University Press.

Posen, Barry. 1993. "The Security Dilemma and Ethnic Conflict." In *Ethnic Conflict and International Security*, ed. Michael E. Brown. Princeton, N.J.: Princeton University Press.

Regan, Patrick M. 2000. *Civil Wars and Foreign Powers: Outside Intervention in Intrastate Conflict*. Ann Arbor: University of Michigan Press.

Richardson, John M., Jr., and Jianxin Wang. 1993. "Peace Accords: Seeking Conflict Resolution in Deeply Divided Societies." In *Peace Accords and Ethnic Conflict*, ed. K. M. de Silva and S. W. R. de A. Samarsinghe, 173–198. London: Pinter Publishers.

Rothchild, Donald. 1997. *Managing Ethnic Conflict in Africa: Pressures and Incentives for Cooperation*. Washington, D.C.: Brookings Institution.

Rothchild, Donald, and Michael W. Foley. 1988. "African States and the Politics of Inclusive Coalitions." In *The Precarious Balance: State and Society in Africa*, ed. Donald Rothchild and Naomi Chazan, 233–263. Boulder, Colo.: Westview Press.

Sambanis, Nicholas. 2000. "Partition as a Solution to Ethnic War: An Empirical Critique of the Theoretical Literature." *World Politics* 52 (July): 437–483.

Sisk, Timothy D. 1996. *Power Sharing and International Mediation in Ethnic Conflicts*. Washington, D.C.: United States Institute of Peace Press.

Stanley Foundation. 2000. *Creating the International Legal Assistance Consortium*. Muscatine, Iowa. April.

Stanley, William, and Charles T. Call. 1997. "Building a New Civilian Police Force in El Salvador." In *Rebuilding Societies after Civil War: Critical Roles for International Assistance*, ed. Krishna Kumar, 107–134. Boulder, Colo.: Lynne Rienner.

Stedman, Stephen John. 1991. *Peacemaking in Civil War: International Mediation in Zimbabwe, 1974–1980*. Boulder, Colo.: Lynne Rienner.

———. 1993. "The End of the Zimbabwean Civil War." In *Stopping the Killing: How Civil Wars End*, ed. Roy Licklider, 125–163. New York: New York University Press.

———. 1996. "Negotiation and Mediation in Internal Conflicts." In *The International Dimensions of Internal Conflict*, ed. Michael E. Brown, 341–376. Cambridge, Mass.: MIT Press.

———. 1997. "Spoiler Problems in Peace Processes." *International Security* 22 (fall): 5–53.

———. 1998. "Conflict Prevention as Strategic Interaction: The Spoiler Problem and the Case of Rwanda." In *Preventing Violent Conflicts: Past Record and Future Challenges*, Report no. 48, ed. Peter Wallensteen. Uppsala, Sweden: Department of Peace and Conflict Research, Uppsala University.

Teiwes, Frederick C. 1987. "Establishment and Consolidation of the New Regime." In *The Cambridge History of China*. Vol. 14, *The People's Republic, Part I: The Emergence of Revolutionary China, 1949–1965*, ed. John K. Fairbank and Denis Twitchett, 51–143. Cambridge: Cambridge University Press.

Tilly, Charles. 1992. *Coercion Capital and European States: A.D. 990–1992*. Cambridge, Mass.: Blackwell Publishers.

Tölöyan, Khachig. 1987. "Cultural Narrative and the Motivation of the Terrorist." *Journal of Strategic Studies* 10, no. 4 (December): 217–233.

University of Illinois. Office of International Criminal Justice. 1990. *Panama City Citizen Survey: Panama's Public Force*. Chicago: University of Illinois. August.

Wagner, Robert Harrison. 1993. "The Causes of Peace." In *Stopping the Killing: How Civil Wars End*, ed. Roy Licklider, 235–268. New York: New York University Press.

Walter, Barbara F. 1997. "The Critical Barrier to Civil War Settlement." *International Organization* 51: 335–364.

———. 1999. "Designing Transitions from Civil War." *International Security* 24 (summer): 127–155.

———. 2001. *Negotiating Settlements to Civil Wars*. Princeton, N.J.: Princeton University Press.

Walter, Barbara F., and Jack Snyder. 1999. *Civil Wars, Insecurity, and Intervention*. New York: Columbia University Press.

Wantchekon, Leonard, and Zvika Neeman. 2000. "A Theory of Post-Civil War Democratization." Working paper. Political Science Department, Yale University. April 25.

Wantchekon, Leonard, and David Nickerson. 1999. "Multilateral Intervention Facilitates Post-Civil War Democratization." Working paper. Political Science Department, Yale University. November 5.

Waterman, Harvey. 1993. "Political Order and the 'Settlement' of Civil Wars." In *Stopping the Killing: How Civil Wars End*, ed. Roy Licklider, 292–302. New York: New York University Press.

Weiss, Thomas G. 1999. *Military-Civilian Interactions: Intervening in Humanitarian Crises*. Lanham, Md.: Rowman and Littlefield.

Werner, Suzanne. 1999. "The Precarious Nature of Peace: Resolving the Issues, Enforcing the Settlement, and Renegotiating the Terms." *American Journal of Political Science* 43, no. 3 (July): 912–934.

Williams, Michael C. 1998. *Civil-Military Relations and Peacekeeping*. Adelphi Paper no. 321. Oxford: Oxford University Press.

Wolffsohn, Michael. 1993. *Eternal Guilt? Forty Years of German-Jewish-Israeli Relations*. New York: Columbia University Press.

Wood, Elisabeth Jean. 2000. *Forging Democracy from Below: Insurgent Transitions in South Africa and El Salvador*. New York: Cambridge University Press.

World Bank Web site at http://www.worldbank.org/research/conflict.

Zahar, Marie-Joëlle. 1999. "Mercenaries, Brigands . . . and Politicians: Militia Decision-Making and Civil Conflict Resolution." Ph.D. diss., Department of Political Science, McGill University.

Zartman, I. William. 1989. *Ripe for Resolution: Conflict and Intervention in Africa*. New York: Oxford University Press.

———. 1993. "The Unfinished Agenda: Negotiating Internal Conflicts." In *Stopping the Killing: How Civil Wars End*, ed. Roy Licklider, 20–61. New York: New York University Press.

42

The Challenge of Rebuilding War-Torn Societies

Nicole Ball

IN THE LAST HALF OF THE TWENTIETH CEN-TURY, an average of nearly 1 million people perished each year as a result of armed conflict. The costs of these wars in terms of missed developmental opportunities are substantial. Although socioeconomic development may not come to a halt during conflict, what is possible to accomplish under conditions of war tends to be both very limited and under constant threat of reversal. What is more, the growing trend of the warring parties to use natural resources to sustain war is further reducing some countries' long-term development potential.

Armed conflict both retards the development process and erodes a country's development foundation—as people abandon their homes, their education, and their livelihoods, flee their countries, or are killed; as infrastructure is damaged or destroyed; as resources are diverted from routine maintenance of existing social and economic infrastructure; and as a country's resource base is depleted. War-related damages are difficult to quantify, but estimates typically run into the billions of dollars. Fundamental requirements for sustainable, poverty-reducing development—such as a state capable of furnishing public goods, of impartially protecting property rights and personal safety, and of providing a predictable, equitable legal framework for investment—are often beyond the capacity of postconflict governments.[1]

Beyond the physical destruction, armed conflict that arises out of internal power imbalances gravely complicates efforts to create an environment conducive to sustainable development. Most wars fought since 1945 have had local roots: political and economic inequality, ethnic and religious rivalry, and struggles to control the levers of power.[2]

Since the early 1990s, as more and more concerted efforts have been made to halt prolonged civil wars, a growing number of countries have been facing the challenge of making a transition from war-weakened economies to rejuvenated economies capable of satisfying the basic needs of all citizens, and from highly

719

polarized political and social relations to political systems that offer all social groups meaningful participation in the decisions shaping their future. Simultaneously, the international development community has been facing a burgeoning number of requests from formerly warring parties for assistance in laying the foundation for renewed development in their countries and overcoming the political, economic, social, and psychological ravages of war.[3]

This chapter examines a number of key issues that must be addressed both by governments of war-torn countries and by the members of the international development community as they confront the task of postconflict rebuilding. The chapter briefly describes the characteristics of postconflict countries and maps out the phases of peace processes. The second section summarizes the priority peacebuilding tasks and underscores the importance of governance for postconflict rehabilitation and development, particularly good governance in the security sector. The chapter concludes by outlining how the donors can assist this process and by briefly assessing the activities of the donors in these key areas.

THE POSTCONFLICT ENVIRONMENT AND THE PHASES OF THE PEACE PROCESS

The Postconflict Environment

Civil wars occur in countries at different levels of political and economic development, with diverse political and social systems and varying physical and human resource endowment, cultures, and historical experiences. The paths these countries follow along the road from war to peace will diverge in many important respects, and the assistance provided by the donor community should reflect individual circumstances. At the same time, the experience of prolonged internal strife produces important similarities in the nature and function of civil institutions and political life, the economy, and the security sector in postconflict environments. These are summarized in table 1. Every country that experiences violent intergroup conflict will not necessarily exhibit all of these characteristics. Most, however, will manifest a significant number of them.

Several additional characteristics of postconflict environments define the context in which war-to-peace transformations occur, and they can have an important influence on donor–host country interactions: the effects of war-induced isolation, the influence of peace treaties on the scope and pace of change, and the magnitude and urgency of the problems confronting postconflict countries.

Civil wars engender isolation at a variety of levels within society. The first is the isolation of the combatant, who is ill equipped for civilian life and has unrealistic expectations about life after discharge. A second level of isolation is manifest in the separation between the areas in which fighting occurred and the rest of the country. The people who make decisions affecting the former conflict zones or who are expected to implement peace-related programs in those areas often reside outside the conflict zones during the war and may be quite unfamiliar with conditions there. Finally, many countries are relatively isolated during civil war and, to varying degrees, face a not insignificant learning curve for dealing with donors and other international institutions. The impact of each level of isolation can be intensified by the monopoly that the parties to the conflict have over information, a monopoly that enables them to create and maintain significant distortions of the truth during the conflict and even into the postsettlement period.[4]

In countries where conflicts have ended through negotiated peace agreements, the scope and pace of peacebuilding is heavily determined by the provisions of the peace accords and the timetables established for implementing them. Peace agreements frequently decree that major

Table 1. Characteristics of War-Torn Societies

Institutional Characteristics	Economic and Social Characteristics	Security Characteristics
• Weak political and administrative institutions • Nonparticipatory political system • Vigorous competition for power at expense of attention to governing • Limited legitimacy of political leaders • Lack of consensus on direction country should follow	• Extensive damage to or decay of economic and social infrastructure • High levels of indebtedness • Unsustainably high defense budgets • Significant contraction of legal economy and expansion of illegal economy • Reversion to subsistence activities • Destruction or exile of human resources • Conflicts over ownership of and access to land • Gender imbalance • Environmental degradation • Weakened social fabric • Poor social indicators	• Bloated security forces • Armed opposition, paramilitary forces • Overabundance of small arms • Need to reassess security environment and restructure security forces accordingly • Lack of transparency in security affairs and accountability to civil authorities and to population • Political role of security forces • History of human rights abuses perpetrated by security forces

institutional changes that normally require a significant amount of time to implement—such as developing an electoral system, restructuring the security forces, or reforming the judicial branch of government—be completed in a year or two, before the peacekeeping mandate of the international community expires.

Finally, postconflict countries face a particularly large and complex set of issues that must be addressed rapidly. Resolving the myriad of economic, social, institutional, and political problems confronting war-torn countries takes on a heightened urgency because many of these problems were related to the conflict. Since the capacity to respond to these critical needs may be limited, it is difficult to address them as rapidly as the political situation requires. Failing to respond in a timely fashion may create the conditions for a return to organized violence.

Stages and Phases of the Peace Process

Just as the experiences of countries emerging from violent conflict share certain characteristics, peace processes based on negotiated settlements with no outright victor exhibit significant similarities. In these countries, two stages of peace processes can be identified, with each stage having two component phases (see table 2).[5] The length of each stage and phase varies according to the situation in each country. Movement from one phase to the next is not automatic, as the numerous false starts toward peace in countries such as Angola, Liberia, Rwanda, and Sierra Leone so clearly underscore.

The first stage—cessation of conflict—aims at reaching agreement on key issues so that fighting can be halted and political, social, and

Table 2. The Peace Process in Countries with Negotiated Peace Settlements

STAGES	Cessation of Conflict		Peacebuilding	
PHASES	*Negotiations*	*Cessation of Hostilities*	*Transition*	*Consolidation*
MAIN OBJECTIVES	Agreeing on key issues to enable fighting to stop	Signing peace accords Establishing cease-fire Separating forces	Establishing a government with adequate legitimacy to enable it to rule effectively Implementing reforms to build political institutions and establish security Inaugurating economic and social revitalization Promoting societal reconciliation	Continuing and deepening reform process Continuing economic and social recovery efforts Continuing promotion of societal reconciliation

economic reconstruction can begin. This stage has two component phases: negotiation and the formal cessation of hostilities.

The peacebuilding stage also consists of two phases: transition and consolidation. Priorities during these two phases center on strengthening political institutions, consolidating internal and external security, and revitalizing the economy and society. The major objectives during the transition phase are to establish a government with a sufficient degree of legitimacy to operate effectively and to implement key reforms mandated by the peace accords.

The first major objective during the consolidation phase is to continue the reform process. Many peace accords—such as those in Angola, Bosnia, Cambodia, El Salvador, and Mozambique—establish transition periods that last between one and two years and conclude with general elections. It has become increas-

ingly evident, however, that this time frame is too short to record significant progress on even the reforms prescribed by the peace accords, let alone those that are necessary to consolidate the peace but are not mandated by the accords.

Furthermore, the balance of forces within society can influence outcomes in ways that may be contrary to the terms or intent of peace agreements. For example, in mid-1993 a former El Salvador army officer was appointed to head the National Civilian Police, which was expressly forbidden by the peace treaty. This decision was eventually reversed, in part due to opposition from the United Nations and some of the bilateral donors, including the United States.

Not infrequently, early elections influence the balance of societal forces in ways that are inimical to the consolidation of peace. In Bosnia, the elections held under the Dayton accords

Table 3. Priority Peacebuilding Tasks

- Provide sufficient level of security to civilians to enable economic activity to recover, to encourage refugees and the internally displaced to reestablish themselves, and to persuade the business community to invest
- Strengthen the government's capacity to carry out key tasks
- Assist the return of refugees and internally displaced persons
- Support the rejuvenation of household economies, especially by strengthening the smallholder agricultural sector
- Assist community recovery, in part through projects that rehabilitate the social and economic infrastructure
- Rehabilitate infrastructure crucial to economic revival, such as major roads, bridges, marketplaces, and power-generation facilities
- Remove land mines from major transport arteries, fields in heavily populated areas, and other critical sites
- Stabilize the national currency and rehabilitate financial institutions
- Promote national reconciliation
- Give priority to social groups and geographic areas most affected by the conflict

consolidated and formalized nationalist divisions within society and served to complicate an already complex and highly contentious peace process.[6] For these reasons, implementing peace accords is often not completed when the transition phase formally ends and the peacekeeping mission is withdrawn.

In addition, while one might expect peace agreements to address the root causes of conflicts, the compromises necessary to produce a document acceptable to all parties generally leave many of the key issues wholly or partly unresolved. During negotiation of the Lusaka Protocol, for example, most of the highly contentious military issues were left for talks to be held immediately after the protocol was signed. The status of Jonas Savimbi, head of the armed opposition whose refusal to accept the outcome of the September 1992 elections mandated by the 1991 Bicesse peace accords had plunged Angola back into two years of brutal war, was glossed over, and the control of the nation's natural resources was not part of the discussions at all. All of these issues subsequently became stumbling blocks to the implementation of the peace process. The choice that the mediator faced, however, was either a flawed agreement or continuation of the violence that

in two years had been responsible for taking a hundred thousand or more lives.[7]

As the Angolan experience indicates, the provisions of a peace accord may constitute necessary steps toward consolidating peace, but they frequently neither deal adequately with the problems that led to the war nor create an environment conducive to resolving future conflicts peacefully. In consequence, the reform process must also be deepened during the consolidation phase to enable fundamental political, economic, and social grievances to be addressed, whether they are enshrined in the peace agreement or not.

Peacebuilding Tasks

In the early 1990s, when the international community first became involved in a significant way in helping countries recover from civil war, the primary emphasis in postconflict rebuilding was on economic and social reconstruction. Apart from the intrinsic desirability of equitably distributed, poverty-reducing development, strengthening economies in transition countries is desirable for at least three other reasons.

To begin with, people require tangible proof that investing in peace or in democratic transitions will change their material situation for the better. Tangible material benefits can help people get through the inevitable rough patches in political transitions. A focus on the economy is also critical because when people are economically disadvantaged, it is easier to mobilize them for partisan political purposes and thus undermine the entire transition process.

Strengthening the *legal* economy of transition countries is important in achieving a degree of peace that will encourage sustainable, poverty-reducing development. War economies —illicit activities that provide the means of continuing armed conflict—have been a major impediment to conflict transformation in places such as Angola, Bosnia, the Democratic Republic of the Congo (DRC), Serbia, Kosovo, and Sierra Leone.

At the same time, it is important not to overestimate the contribution that economic development can make to the creation of societies where disputes are resolved by nonviolent means. There are several particularly important reasons for exercising caution when assigning economic development a role in strengthening national stability in transition countries.

The first is the extreme weakness of many war-torn economies outlined in table 1. In these cases, one can scarcely talk about economic development unless a country has undergone a period of economic rehabilitation and reconstruction.[8] Second, many economies in war-torn countries require "construction," rather than "reconstruction." That is because the economic institutions and structures of the ancien régime served a social and political order that constrained sustainable, poverty-reducing development. The benefits that accrued to elites from the economic and political prerogatives of power associated with that order encouraged either the elites to resort to violence to protect their privileges or others to do so to gain access to those privileges. In these situations,

simply to reconstruct the old institutions and structures would be counterproductive.

Third, a transition from war to peace is virtually impossible as long as the parties to the conflict have access to natural resources that can command a high price on the international market. Angola, DRC, and Sierra Leone are prime examples of conflicts that will continue until access to diamonds, oil, and similar commodities is denied, either militarily or through the refusal of international corporations to deal, directly and indirectly, with the warring parties.

Some progress was made in 2000 toward stigmatizing so-called blood diamonds emanating from conflict zones. Under pressure from nongovernmental organizations (NGOs) such as Global Witness and fearing an international boycott, DeBeers, the South African diamond corporation that controls 60 percent of the global market for uncut diamonds, took some steps in mid-2000 to limit its purchases from conflict zones. It instructed its major rough-diamond buyers to cease purchases from African conflict zones and urged the World Federation of Diamond Bourses and the International Diamond Manufacturers' Association to expel individuals trading in "conflict diamonds." On July 19, 2000, the World Diamond Congress approved tracking measures and sanctions against dealers trading in diamonds from conflict zones. It was hoped that the new regulations would be in force by December. NGOs that had campaigned for such controls announced themselves largely pleased with the proposed regime.[9] Efforts such as these are critical to the rehabilitation, reconstruction, and eventual development of conflict areas, but the role that development assistance can play to support efforts of this nature is relatively limited.

A final reason for caution when assigning economic development a central role in rebuilding transition societies is the relationship among sustainable, poverty-reducing economic development, political development, and security. There can be no sustainable, poverty-reducing development without political development that has as one of its objectives a reasonably equitable distribution of economic and political power and the reasonably equitable sharing of the fruits of development. There can be no such political development without security of individuals, social groups, and society as a whole —in contrast to security for a specific government or security of particular ruling groups, which is prevalent in many war-torn societies. In short, sustainable, poverty-reducing development requires due attention to governance—both economic and political governance.[10]

The centrality of good governance to the achievement of economic development has become increasingly clear to the development community over the past decade. Development agencies, including the World Bank and the International Monetary Fund (IMF), have consequently been seeking to define for themselves what the promotion of good governance entails. For the Bretton Woods institutions, the challenge has been to move beyond narrow economic governance. In this, the World Bank has been more successful than the IMF, although both organizations still have a way to go in putting political governance on a par with economic governance.

In a country attempting to overcome the effects of civil war, promoting good economic and political governance is simultaneously critically important and even more difficult to achieve than in countries that have not experienced civil war. Its importance lies in the close link between the causes of the war and inadequate governance. Its difficulty lies in the enormous pressures that exist to achieve short-term goals in the early stages of the peace process. Thus, a major challenge confronting both the societies emerging from violent conflict and the international development community is to identify ways to incorporate the longer-term objective of strengthening economic and political governance into short-term rehabilitation and reconstruction efforts.

A key component of governance is the establishment of an institutional framework that supports equitable economic and political development. In this regard, the termination of civil war offers a unique opportunity to address fundamental imbalances between the security forces and the rest of society that contribute to conflict and insecurity and make sustainable, poverty-reducing development more difficult to achieve. The priority tasks in the security sector for countries making the transition from civil war to peace are summarized in table 4. In particular, postconflict countries need to internalize a series of rules that support an equitable division of society's political and economic resources and reduce the likelihood of impunity on the part of the security forces. The most important of these are accountability, transparency, comprehensiveness, a commitment to equity, and acceptance of the rule of law.

A number of the priority tasks outlined in table 4 are routinely enshrined in peace agreements. The tasks include the disbanding and disarming of informal security forces and the demobilization of some number of the formal forces, as well as some degree of police reform and judicial system development. Many of the longer-term tasks associated with strengthening good governance in the security sector are most often not mandated by the peace accords and are also not included in efforts to consolidate the peace at the end of the formal peace process.

The security sector includes the military, police, paramilitary, gendarmerie, organizations that support the police in delivering accessible justice (judiciary and penal system), intelligence, customs enforcement, and the civil management and oversight authorities. In many respects, developing a policy for the security sector closely resembles the process by which any sectoral policy is determined. The first step is to identify the needs and key objectives of the security sector as a whole, that is, to conduct an assessment of the country's security environment. The second step is to determine the overall resource framework for the central government. Once that is determined, it will be possible to allocate resources according to

Table 4. Postconflict Priorities in the Security Sector

- Assess the security environment, redefine the doctrine and missions of the security forces, and task the security forces based on this assessment and on the principle of civil management and oversight of the security forces
- Restructure the security forces based on the postconflict doctrines, missions, and budget realities
- Increase transparency and accountability on security-related issues within the security forces, the executive branch, and the legislature, as well as to the public
- Enhance the capacity of the civil authorities to manage and oversee the activities of the security forces
- Pursue parallel development of the criminal justice system
- Train civilian security analysts, in both the public sector and civil society
- Pursue professional development of the security forces that imbues their members with an understanding of democratic accountability and strengthens their internal management capacity to implement and sustain reforms
- Terminate extralegal forms of recruitment to the security sector
- Disband and disarm opposition forces and informal paramilitary forces; demobilize government troops

priorities both within the security sector and between the security sector and other portions of the public sector. Finally, it is critically important that mechanisms be in place to ensure the efficient and effective use of resources allocated to the security sector.[11]

The security forces also need to operate according to democratic principles, which means, among other things, accepting the supremacy of the civil authorities and respecting the rule of law. Although donors have traditionally shied away from engagement with the security sector, they can provide much of the necessary technical assistance to meet these policy, planning, and operational requirements within the terms of current organizational mandates.[12]

DONOR ROLES AND RESPONSIBILITIES IN SUPPORTING THE REBUILDING OF WAR-TORN SOCIETIES

The international community has come to recognize that warring parties require assistance not only in negotiating peace agreements but also in consolidating the peace. As the catalog of characteristics of war-torn societies in table 1 suggests, peacebuilding requires action on a wide variety of fronts. The parties' capacity to meet these demands is, however, severely constrained by institutional weaknesses, limited human and financial resources, profound mistrust and animosity generated by civil war, and economic fragility; thus parties have increasingly turned to the international community for technical assistance, financial advice, and political support, particularly during the transition phase. For these same reasons, repairing the ravages of war is an arduous, complex, and lengthy process.

It is crucial that assistance provided be appropriate for the task at hand. The international community has made progress over the past decade in understanding the needs of postconflict environments and in its ability to deliver what is needed. Nonetheless, considerable work remains to be done. This section surveys progress in four key components of peacebuilding: creating sustained partnerships among international actors; enhancing the effectiveness of peacebuilding assistance; effecting donor coordination; and restarting government.

Creating Sustained Partnerships among External Actors

One lesson that is progressively being incorporated into the policies and programs of international actors relates to the importance of sustained assistance from the entire international community throughout the peace process. At the beginning of the 1990s, there was a tendency to assume that diplomatic and military efforts should be concentrated in the negotiation, cessation of hostilities, and transition phases, while financial and technical assistance should be concentrated in the transition phase.[13] As experience accumulated, development actors came to realize that they needed to devote a relatively modest amount of resources to planning for postwar activities and building collaborative relationships with the parties to the conflict during the negotiation phase. Among the earliest instances of donor engagement in the negotiation phase were the Dayton negotiations regarding Bosnia and the UN-brokered discussions in Guatemala.

The speed with which events occur once peace agreements are signed argues very strongly in favor of donor involvement at the earliest possible moment in a peace process. Furthermore, early engagement by the development community can help the parties to the conflict address relevant economic issues realistically and develop mechanisms for tackling crucial economic issues that are likely to become politicized or ignored once the peace agreement is signed. All of this places a premium on donors who can keep their knowledge base as up-to-date as possible during the conflict and the peace negotiation phase. The World Bank, for example, has developed a watching brief methodology to enable it to keep abreast of developments in countries where the bank has had to suspend operations because of civil war.[14] Previously, when the bank ceased operations, it also ceased collecting information, primarily because staff salaries were largely tied to lending programs. Few managers were willing to dip into their budgets for nonlending activities in order to finance work in a country that may not have an active lending portfolio for many years.

As far as the peacekeeping operation is concerned, it has been evident from the outcome of a number of first-generation peace processes such as those in Cambodia, El Salvador, and Mozambique that a two-year, or shorter, mandate often requires peace missions to be shut down before the accords have been fully implemented. There is still variation, however, in the extent to which this knowledge is being incorporated into peacekeeping mandates. While a lengthy international peacekeeping presence has been accepted for Bosnia and Kosovo, the UN mission in Sierra Leone is working on rolling, six-month mandates. The missions in East Timor and the DRC were authorized for approximately fifteen months each in the first instance.[15]

Restrictions on the length of mandates often arise because of resource constraints. Peace operations are costly, and the United Nations has been in financial crisis for some years. Efforts have been made to use resources more efficiently and accountably within the United Nations as a whole, but such reforms will not by themselves resolve the problem of nonpayment of dues. In addition to financial constraints, there are political ones. Many UN members are leery of what may appear to be a significant open-ended commitment to very troubled countries or regions.

Moreover, very short mandates, even if the intention of the Security Council is to renew them, create significant problems in recruiting and retraining high-quality staff, as well as give the impression to parties seeking to avoid complying with peace agreements that they can "wait out" the international community.[16]

In some cases, notably Bosnia, East Timor, Kosovo, and Sierra Leone, maintaining a proactive and flexible military and police presence is critical to the creation of a durable peace. Bosnia has shown, for example, that sustaining the peace process can require peacekeeping troops to engage in what might be termed non-military activities, for example, arresting indicted war criminals and combating organized crime syndicates that had their roots in the war economy. Similarly, in countries where "negotiated" settlements have essentially been imposed on warring parties—Angola, Bosnia, Kosovo, and Sierra Leone—events have demonstrated that peacekeepers must be prepared to actively keep the peace in order to promote the rule of law in postconflict societies.

More robust and flexible peacekeeping operations may require a greater role for gendarmerie-type forces, to supplement civilian police and military units. As the situation in Sierra Leone demonstrated in 2000, they also require a willingness on the part of military units to engage in peace enforcement. These issues are under discussion within the peacekeeping community, but by no means have they been fully resolved. Some UN member governments are unwilling to allow their units to engage in peace enforcement activities, and some national units have shown themselves to be more effective fighting forces than others. This underscores the importance of being able to choose among troop-contributing countries.

Enhancing the Effectiveness of Peacebuilding Assistance

Donors have sought to improve the effectiveness of the assistance they provide to war-torn countries. They have had mixed results in these efforts.

One of the earliest lessons identified was the need for flexible, quick-disbursing funds that donors could utilize during the transition period. Development assistance funds are slow disbursing, and faster-disbursing humanitarian or emergency relief aid tends to have restrictions on the types of activities donors can support, which render them unavailable for development-type transition activities. Fast-disbursing windows now exist in most donor agencies, and

most donor agencies have also created peace-building or transition units. Some of these units operate only in postconflict environments; others have a preventive mandate as well.

The creation of special funding windows and units for peacebuilding activities is one indication of the seriousness with which the donors are now approaching postconflict assistance. At the same time, it is important that the activities funded meet the needs of war-torn countries. Donors have made significant efforts to learn from the past and incorporate those lessons into ongoing programs. The World Bank, for example, has evaluated its experience with postconflict reconstruction and carried out a major lessons-learned study on demobilization and reintegration of former combatants. Other donors have conducted numerous country- and issue-specific lessons-learned studies and program evaluations.[17] Operational staff involved with peacebuilding activities in twenty-two multilateral and bilateral donor agencies have been meeting twice a year since late 1997. They have created the Conflict Prevention and Post-Conflict Reconstruction Network, which has recently begun compiling the *Compendium of Operational Frameworks for Peacebuilding and Donor Coordination.*[18]

Important as lessons-learned and assessment work is, it is equally important that the lessons and good practices gleaned from these exercises be put into context. There is a tendency within the development community as a whole, not merely that portion dealing with postconflict situations, to seek "solutions" to problems that can be applied more or less universally. Although there are many similarities among postconflict countries, wholesale application of approaches that have proved successful in one postconflict environment may well be ineffective or even counterproductive in another postconflict environment.

In 1997, the U.S. Agency for International Development (USAID) commissioned a lessons-learned study of the South African peace committees that were established in 1992 to help reduce the violence that erupted in South Africa during its transition from apartheid to democratic rule. USAID was interested in the peace committees because of the perception that they were a successful mechanism for managing conflict that could be replicated on other conflict-prone and conflict-affected countries. In fact, the lessons-learned study demonstrated that the peace committees recorded varying degrees of success depending on a variety of conditions. The study concluded that while peace committees can be a valuable conflict management tool, they are not appropriate in every setting and that the environment into which they are to be introduced must be evaluated to determine whether a sufficient number of key enabling factors are present. In addition, the study cautioned against confusing concept with structure. While the *concept* of peace committees—fora in which differences among groups can be aired and solutions to problems sought—is transferrable, the *form* peace committees assume is rooted in social, political, and economic conditions in individual countries and is not necessarily transferrable.[19]

In addition to contextualizing lessons-learned and good-practices work, dissemination of good practices is critically dependent on the quality and motivation of staff. Donors have increasingly sought to strengthen staff assigned to postconflict countries. In some cases, staff with previous experience in one postconflict transition country have been assigned to other war-torn countries, especially within the same region. Staff from El Salvador have transferred to Guatemala; staff from Mozambique have transferred to Angola; staff from Bosnia have transferred to Kosovo. The United Nations Development Programme (UNDP) has recognized the importance of recruiting resident coordinators from outside its own ranks. Once again, however, it is important that staff be aware of the differences that exist between countries and not attempt to re-create exactly the programs that worked well in other countries.

One way to overcome the staff problems of inadequate experience in war-torn countries and the tendency to apply cookie-cutter-type approaches is to ensure that the local stakeholders are included from the beginning.[20] That said, the weakness of human capacity and the extreme politicization and polarization that characterize war-torn societies are important limitations on efforts to include local stakeholders in program design and implementation. An equally serious limitation, however, is the unwillingness of many donor representatives to promote genuine participation by local stakeholders. This is a problem that afflicts nongovernmental actors as well as official actors and appears to derive from a fear of loss of control. Despite considerable rhetoric about "empowerment" and "ownership," most donor agencies and their representatives still want to be able to define what is done, how it is done, and who does it.

Effecting Donor Coordination

The need to act rapidly to take advantage of the relatively short-lived opportunities that the end of war creates for fundamental restructuring and the desirability of presenting a united front on the part of the donor community to prevent backsliding place a premium on aid coordination in postconflict situations. Coordinating aid is notoriously difficult, even in countries that are not moving from war to peace. In postconflict environments, both the need and the constraints are magnified. Also, political considerations that can hinder coordination efforts are more important in the aftermath of protracted civil wars.

The expansion of donor involvement in postwar environments has underscored the serious conflicts of interest that exist within development agencies, among development agencies, and between these agencies and other members of the international community. While efforts have been made to overcome these problems, coordination within the international community remains problematic. Despite the creation of peacebuilding units in many bilateral and multilateral development agencies, a significant number of staff continue to view peacebuilding as a diversion from "true" development objectives, rather than as a crucial foundation for sustainable development. Military establishments continue to be loath to see their resources applied to economic revitalization objectives and to use their military assets for "nonmilitary" activities such as apprehending war criminals. Individual agencies continue to jealously guard their "turf."

A variety of initiatives began in the late 1990s to enhance coordination within the United Nations and among the United Nations and other major development and humanitarian actors.[21] These have had only limited success to date, although given the size and nature of the multiple bureaucracies involved, it would be surprising if rapid progress had been made. A report issued in early 2000 that sets forward a "strategy for international response" to countries recovering from conflict concluded, "In sum, there is a pattern of poor coordination and integration that characterizes global, regional, and national efforts to advance recovery from conflict."[22]

As with so many other aspects of postconflict assistance, the success of coordination efforts depends to a large degree on the qualities of agency field staff. Where staff have a collaborative working style; a high degree of flexibility, patience, and creativity; experience in war-torn environments; political astuteness; and appropriate language skills, the likelihood that they will be able to collaborate effectively with international colleagues as well as with local stakeholders is greatly enhanced. Different peace missions have had different relations with the donor community. The United Nations Operation in Mozambique (ONUMOZ) was one of the first peacekeeping missions that attempted to maintain direct control over the coordination of humanitarian assistance by asking the UN Department of Humanitarian

Affairs (now the Office for the Coordination of Humanitarian Affairs) to establish a special unit within the mission. In doing so, it earned the resentment of the UNDP, which thought that the new UN Office of Humanitarian Assistance Coordination (UNOHAC) had usurped the mandate of its resident representative (who was also humanitarian coordinator). Much of the bilateral donor community viewed UNOHAC as an unnecessary additional layer of bureaucracy. The noncollaborative working style of the first UNOHAC director both contrasted significantly with the style of the UNDP resident representative and added to the donors' unhappiness with UNOHAC.[23]

In Angola, by contrast, two UN special representatives of the secretary-general, Dame Margaret Anstee and the late Maître Alouine Blondin Beye, gave the Humanitarian Assistance Coordination Unit (UCAH) a considerable degree of autonomy. Despite pressure from headquarters in New York, Beye decided that UCAH would not co-locate with the peacekeeping mission. In his view, raising voluntary funding for humanitarian activities would be considerably more difficult if UCAH were located in UNAVEM III headquarters because of the perception among donors and NGOs that UNAVEM was a "military" operation and thus off-limits to humanitarian actors. This was a strategy that paid off in terms of funding and generally good relations between UCAH and the donors, as well as between UCAH and the NGO community.

For the most part, UCAH directors were well versed in the skills necessary for fostering collaborative relationships with local stakeholders and other members of the international community, although this did not always overcome turf battles within the UN family or with other donor agencies. Relations between some UNAVEM III staff and UCAH were problematic because the former could not understand why UCAH was accorded a high degree of autonomy. The UNDP resented the fact that bilateral donors were more generous in the support they offered to UCAH programs than to UNDP programs. While this may have reflected donor assessments of the relative capacity of the two organizations, the situation in Angola was in fact one that required greater attention to humanitarian programs than to development programs.[24]

Coordination is also often enhanced by the willingness of agencies to decentralize responsibility and authority to their field staff. While this approach is only as effective as an agency's field staff, constant second-guessing from headquarters and injunctions on collaboration with other agencies have hampered the development of close working relationships in the field on many occasions. A number of donor agencies have devolved more authority to field staff or are in the process of doing so, and over time this could strengthen field-level coordination.

Restarting Government

One priority area that has generally not received the attention it deserves is strengthening governmental capacity. When wars end, governments are typically seriously overextended, lack capable staff, and are unable to fulfill key functions and deliver critical services. The armed opposition—which retains control of its weapons through a portion of the transition phase —remains highly wary of the government. Opposition leaders frequently believe that the government will fail to deliver benefits in an equitable fashion and may seek to limit the government's role in peacebuilding, particularly in areas formerly controlled by the armed opposition. At the same time, there is significant pressure to implement peacebuilding programs rapidly to keep the peace process on track.

These conditions present donors with a dilemma. In order to implement peacebuilding activities, resources can be channeled either through the government or through nongovernmental bodies and international organizations. The sitting government is simultaneously the government and one of the factions contesting

for political power in the period before any elections mandated under the peace accords. It aspires to fulfill all the functions of government but lacks adequate capacity and may have ceded certain responsibilities to a peacekeeping mission under the terms of a peace agreement. Consequently, donors may view bypassing the government as the desirable course to follow in the name of efficiency and impartiality.

This short-term strategy may, however, create significant problems in the medium to long term. If the donors postpone substantially strengthening institutions and building human-resource capacity until a new government is elected, or if they turn preferentially to non-governmental bodies to design and execute peacebuilding programs, there is a strong probability that the postelection government will be no more prepared to carry out key tasks than was the preelection government. Indeed, since the transition phase lasts between eighteen and twenty-four months, governments may well reach the consolidation phase with their capacity for independent action severely weakened. Cambodia offers an excellent example of the hazards of this approach.

> As urged by the U.S. and France, both UNTAC [the United Nations Transitional Authority in Cambodia] and the bilateral donor agencies adhered to a restrictive definition of political "neutrality" prior to the elections, when it came to dealing with the existing bureaucracy, apart from activities to facilitate the election. Accepting the argument that this bureaucracy was beholden to the SOC faction [State of Cambodia, that is, the ruling Cambodian People's Party], and potentially a SOC instrument for influencing the vote, the donors beginning to be active inside Cambodia severely constrained UNTAC's rehabilitation component and refused to provide financial support that would have enabled the SOC to restore its collapsed capacity to pay civil servant salaries. . . .
>
> One cannot know what effects on the election outcome might have resulted if the "neutrality" policy had allowed for budget support during the UNTAC period. . . . It is clear, however, that the more than two years between (a) the collapse of Soviet aid and the budget

support that had entailed and (b) the start of IFI aid for the RCG [Royal Cambodian Government] budget had significant negative consequence for the post-May 1993 reconstruction and reconciliation processes that were designed to dovetail with legitimation.[25]

Yet, as El Salvador demonstrates, making the government the main vehicle of peacebuilding assistance can be equally problematic. The United States, which had been a major player in the Salvadoran civil war on the side of the sitting government, channeled its economic assistance through the government's National Secretariat for Reconstruction (SRN). The SRN had its roots in the National Commission for the Restoration of Areas, the agency that implemented the U.S.-backed counterinsurgency program during the war. This history made it highly suspect in the eyes of the former armed opposition and many people living in the ex-conflictive zones. The government was able to gain electoral advantage by controlling the distribution of funds through the SRN. Thus, the agency that was meant to provide peace agreement–mandated assistance to the areas most affected by the war in fact was used by the government to perpetuate its rule, fostering a political environment inimical to reconciliation.

The increased emphasis among those involved with development on the importance of governance has made the donors more aware of the general need to strengthen government institutions, but there are still numerous problems inherent in donor approaches. What is necessary—although extremely difficult to achieve in practice—is a nuanced approach that progressively strengthens the central government's capacity to carry out key activities while minimizing its ability to use resources for partisan political purposes. For the most part, however, donors appear to have taken the easier route of avoiding a concerted effort to enhance state capacity.[26]

A notable exception involves the institutions responsible for administering justice—the police and to a lesser extent the judiciary and the penal system. Police reform programs are now part of many peacebuilding efforts. While such reforms take a very long time to implement and frequently have to overcome numerous obstacles, the donor community has understood the critical importance of providing security for individuals in postconflict environments.[27] It has been far less aware of the importance of developing the capacity of the civil authorities to monitor and manage the defense and intelligence services.[28] As of mid-2000, there was only one donor, the U.K. Department for International Development (DFID), that has a policy of support for reforming the defense sector, although other donors were considering their policies in this area and the OECD Development Assistance Committee was contemplating issuing some general guidance to its members on supporting reforms in the entire security sector.[29]

CONCLUSION

The international community has gained valuable experience since the beginning of the 1990s in addressing the needs of postconflict countries and has begun to implement important changes in the content of its assistance and its operating procedures in order to maximize the value of the assistance is provides to wartorn countries.

At the same time, many problems that plagued the earliest peacekeeping missions and peacebuilding efforts remain in evidence nearly a decade later. In March 2000 a joint report on the Balkans from the European Union's foreign policy representative, Javier Solana, and the European Commission noted that "the effectiveness of the EU's policies is affected by the plethora of actors involved. Division of labor is too ad hoc and there is a high degree of duplication. . . . The effectiveness of our policies suffers from the multiplicity of institutions and frameworks in the region, from complex and lengthy procedures for policy formulation."[30] In Kosovo, the three largest donors—United Nations High Commissioner for Refugees (UNHCR), the U.S. Office for Foreign Disaster Assistance, and DFID—gradually evolved methods of coordinating the activities of the foreign donors. But as one of the participants in this process observed, "It isn't clear whether this system will outlive the departure of the individuals who set it up and made it work."

Thus we are confronted by a paradox. High-caliber, experienced individuals are critical to the success of peacebuilding; the right people can often overcome significant institutional and organizational deficits. At the same time, too much continues to depend on individuals. The failure to incorporate good practice into ongoing activities is undermining the international community's efforts to support the transition from war to peace in many parts of the world. The slow and difficult process of institutionalizing an approach to postconflict recovery that puts the local stakeholders—including those who have been the victims of war as well as those who have been the perpetrators of war—at the center of external support for rebuilding must not only continue; it must be accelerated.

Notes

1. Of course, many postconflict governments were unable to fulfill these functions satisfactorily prior to war, but it is nonetheless clear that their capacity is further eroded by lengthy wars.

2. The findings of a major research project conducted under the auspices of the World Institute for Development Economics Research, United Nations University, at the end of the 1990s substantiates this observation. See E. Wayne Nafziger, Frances Stewart, and Raimo Väyrenen, eds., *The Origins of Humanitarian Emergencies: War and Displacement in Developing Countries*, vol. 1 of *War, Hunger and Displacement: The Origins of Humanitarian Emergencies* (Oxford: Oxford University Press, 2000).

3. The international development community consists of bilateral and multilateral development assistance agencies (such as the U.S. Agency for International Development and the United Nations Development Programme), international financial institutions (such as the World Bank), and development-oriented nongovernmental organizations. The word "donors" is used interchangeably with the terms "international development community," "development assistance agencies," and "development cooperation agencies."

4. Some combatants are well connected to the outside world, through the Internet, through commercial connections, through their diaspora. This does not mean, however, that a transition to a postwar civilian way of life will be easy for them.

5. These phases do not apply to countries where civil wars end with the victory of one party. However, the problems confronted by governments and societies in these situations are very similar to those faced by countries where civil wars end with negotiated settlements.

6. The entire Bosnia peace process has been characterized by resistance from all parties to implementing key provisions of the Dayton accords that govern the peace process in Bosnia and Herzegovina, but the elections clearly hardened divisions between the different communities. Dayton was signed in December 1995 and elections were held in September 1996. To a large degree, the timetable was set by the Clinton administration's perceived need to have U.S. troops withdrawn from Bosnia prior to the U.S. presidential election in November 1996, and not by a considered assessment of the costs and benefits of an early election.

7. For a period of time, the loss of civilian life was extremely high. In mid-1993, the UN humanitarian coordinator reported to the UN special representative of the secretary-general, "It is hard to estimate the mortality rate in Angola, as there is no physical presence of UN or NGO staff in most of the more critical areas. However, following extensive consultations with NGOs and Agencies, I have arrived at what I consider to be a *conservative figure* which could be *as much as 1,000 civilians are dying a day*. This is made up by mostly children and old people who are perishing due to the consequences of the effects of war, malnutrition and related disease." Cited in Nicole Ball and Kathleen F. Campbell, *Complex Crisis and Complex Peace: Humanitarian Coordination in Angola*

(New York: UN Office for the Coordination of Humanitarian Affairs, March 1998), 31.

It may be argued, of course, that the parties to the conflict, particularly UNITA, had no intention of implementing the Lusaka Protocol and that the purpose of the "peace implementation period" during 1996–98 was, in fact, to enable UNITA to regroup and rearm.

For one view of the trade-offs facing the mediators, see Paul Hare, *Angola's Last Best Chance for Peace: An Insider's Account of the Peace Process* (Washington, D.C.: United States Institute of Peace Press, 1998).

8. For example, see Nicole Ball with Tammy Halevy, *Making Peace Work: The Role of the International Development Community*, ODC Policy Essay no. 18 (Washington, D.C.: Overseas Development Council, distributed by Johns Hopkins University Press, 1996); and Council on Foreign Relations, *Promoting Sustainable Economies in the Balkans*, Report of an Independent Task Force sponsored by the Council on Foreign Relations (New York: Council on Foreign Relations, 2000).

9. See Timothy Kalyegira, "DeBeers Urges Penalty on 'Rebel' Dealers," United Press International, June 14, 2000, www.lexis-nexis.com; "Gem Manufacturers Seek Global Registry to Halt Illegal Exports: Diamonds Being Used to Fund Africa's Rebel Wars," *San Francisco Examiner*, July 17, 2000 (second edition), www.lexis-nexis.com; Paul Ames, "Diamond Industry Clamps Down," AP Online, July 20, 2000, www.lexis-nexis.com; Global Witness, *A Rough Trade: The Role of Companies and Governments in the Angolan Conflict* (London: Global Witness, December 1998, www.oneworld.org/globalwitness/reports/Angola/cover.html); and Global Witness, *Conflict Diamonds: Possibilities for the Identification, Certification, and Control of Diamonds*, A Briefing Document (London: Global Witness, June 2000, www.oneworld.org/globalwitness/reports/conflict/cover.htm).

10. See, for example, Nicole Ball, *Spreading Good Practices in Security Sector Reform: Policy Options for the British Government* (London: Saferworld, December 1998), 4–5; and Malcolm Chalmers, *Security Sector Reform in Developing Countries: An EU Perspective* (London and Brussels: Saferworld and Stiftung Wissenschaft und Politik/Conflict Prevention Network, January 2000), 6–7.

11. For a brief description of the defense management process, see *Annex 3: Security Sector Reform and the Management of Defence Expenditure: A Conceptual Framework*, Discussion Paper no. 1, in *Security Sector Reform and the Management of Military Expenditure: High Risks for Donors, High Returns for Development. Report on an International Symposium Sponsored by the UK Department for International Development* [hereafter *High Risks for Donors*] (London: Department for International Development, June 2000), 41–55. *Annex 3* is also available at www.dfid.gov.uk by searching on "ssrmilex."

12. See, for example, *Annex 4: Supporting Security Sector Reform: Review of the Role of External Actors*, Discussion Paper no. 2, in *High Risks for Donors*, 57–72; Nicole Ball, "Transforming Security Sectors: The View from Washington," *Journal of Conflict, Security, and Development* 1, no. 1 (2001); Ball, *Spreading Good Practices;* and Chalmers, *Security Sector Reform. Annex 4* is also available at www.dfid.gov.uk by searching on "ssrmilex."

13. Development assistance agencies and the international financial institutions are by no means the only source of financial and technical assistance. Other actors such as ministries of finance, foreign ministries, ministries of justice, national police forces, private enterprise, and civil society also have a role to play.

14. World Bank, *Post-Conflict Reconstruction: The Role of the World Bank* (Washington, D.C.: World Bank, 1998), 42–43. The executive summary of this report is located on the bank's Web site: wbln0018.worldbank.org/essd/kb.nsf/PostConflictHome?OpenView, under "Policies."

15. According to paragraph 19 of UN Security Council Resolution 1244 (1999), June 10, 1999, the Security Council "[d]ecides that the international civil and security presences are established for an initial period of 12 months, to continue thereafter unless the Security Council decides otherwise." The mandates and relevant Security Council resolutions concerning UN missions in East Timor, DRC, and Sierra Leone can be found at www.un.org/peace/pmissions1.htm.

16. On staffing, see Ball and Campbell, *Complex Crisis and Complex Peace*, 56–57. The IFOR mission in Bosnia and Herzegovina provides an excellent example of the latter point.

17. Alcira Kreimer et al., *The World Bank's Experience with Post-Conflict Reconstruction* (Washington, D.C.: World Bank, 1998). Field studies were conducted of Bosnia and Herzegovina, El Salvador, and Uganda. Desk studies were conducted of Cambodia, Eritrea, Haiti, Lebanon, Rwanda, and Sri Lanka.

Selected USAID evaluations and lessons-learned studies are available at www.dec.org/usaid_eval.

18. The Global Peacebuilding Network, managed by the World Bank Post-Conflict Unit, provides access to the Conflict Prevention and Post-Conflict Reconstruction Network (CPR). The CPR's focus is to improve operational capacity of the main multilateral and bilateral actors in helping to prevent conflict and engage in reconstruction, rehabilitation, reconciliation, reintegration, and peacebuilding in countries that have experienced internal conflicts. The Global Peacebuilding Network's Web site is located at wbln0018.worldbank.org/ESSD/pc1.nsf/Home?OpenView. It provides access to the CPR compendium through the link to the Canadian International Development Agency.

19. Nicole Ball, *Managing Conflict: Lessons from the South African Peace Committees*, USAID Evaluation Special Study Report no. 78 (Washington, D.C.: USAID/Center for Development Information and Evaluation, November 1998). This report is also available at www.dec.org/usaid_eval under the heading "USAID Evaluation Special Study Reports."

20. For example, research sponsored by the United States Institute of Peace on peacebuilding in Bosnia demonstrates the importance of local stakeholder involvement. "Virtually every initiative represented in this report, be it policy research, training, or a grassroots initiative, notes the importance of early and substantial involvement by Bosnians in the conception, design, and implementation of reconciliation and reconstruction activities, from the provision of aid to the development of conflict resolution training curricula." Steven M. Riskin, ed., *Three Dimensions of Peacebuilding in Bosnia: Findings from USIP-Sponsored Research and Field Projects*, Peaceworks no. 32 (Washington, D.C.: United States Institute of Peace, December 1999), 2.

21. One effort to bring together the major relief and development donors is the so-called Brookings Process, named after the Brookings Institution, which hosted a senior-level meeting of donor representatives in 1999 to inaugurate a discussion on institutional and funding gaps that were hindering effective donor contributions to the transition from armed conflict to sustainable peace and development. Information on this process can be found at wbln0018.worldbank.org/ESSD/pc1.nsf/Control?OpenView&DN=10&SC=Brookings+Process&.

22. Shepard Forman, Stewart Patrick, and Dirk Solomons, *Recovering from Conflict: Strategy for an International Response* (New York: Center on International Cooperation, New York University, 2000), 34. This publication briefly summarizes a number of multilateral coordination efforts. For insights into aid coordination efforts in war-affected countries, see also the country case studies on Cambodia, El Salvador, Mozambique, the Palestinian Territories, and Bosnia and Herzegovina in Shepard Forman and Stewart Patrick, ed., *Good Intentions: Pledges of Aid for Postconflict Recovery* (Boulder, Colo.: Lynne Rienner, 2000).

23. Nicole Ball and Sam Barnes, "Mozambique," 159–203, in *Good Intentions;* and Sam Barnes, *Humanitarian Aid Coordination during War and Peace in Mozambique: 1985–1995*, Studies on Emergencies and Disaster Relief, Report no. 7 (Uppsala, Sweden: Nordiska Afrikainstitutet in cooperation with the Swedish International Development Agency, 1998).

24. Ball and Campbell, *Complex Crisis and Complex Peace,* 15–19.

25. Frederick Z. Brown and Robert J. Muscat, "The Transition from War to Peace: The Case of Cambodia" (Washington, D.C.: Overseas Development Council Program on Enhancing Security and Development, March 14, 1995), 66–67, cited in Ball and Halevy, *Making Peace Work*, 88.

26. This approach as applied to the Palestinian Authority has been described as follows: "Some Palestinian line ministries, municipalities, and agencies continued to approach donors on an individual basis, rather than operating through MOPIC [Ministry of Planning and International Cooperation] or any other centralized mechanism. Some donors complained about this. Most, however, continued to pursue the path of least resistance, arranging whatever projects seemed easiest with whatever level or branch of Palestinian authority or society seemed most amenable. . . . Some donors responded by citing the need to disburse funds expeditiously. The effect, however, was that donors committed their assistance in those sectors where Palestinian counterpart institutions were strong (for example, education and health), rather than those where institutional capacity or competence was weak (for example, agriculture or tourism). This pattern, of course, exacerbated uneven institutional development and hindered effective economic planning." Rex Brynen, Hisham Awartani, and Clare Woodcraft, "The Palestinian Territories," in *Good Intentions*, 231.

27. Examples of the growing literature on police reform and associated judicial system reform include Robert B. Oakley, Michael J. Dziedzic, and Eliot M. Goldberg, eds., *Policing the New World Disorder: Peace Operations and Public Security* (Washington, D.C.: National Defense University Press, 1998); Chuck Call, "Police Reform, Human Rights, and Democratization in Post-Conflict Settings: Lessons from El Salvador," in *After the War Is Over What Comes Next? Promoting Democracy, Human Rights, and Reintegration in Post-Conflict Societies* (Washington, D.C.: USAID/Center for Development Information and Evaluation, 1997); and Hugh Byrne, William Stanley, and Rachel Garst, *Rescuing Police Reform: A Challenge for the New Guatemalan Government* (Washington, D.C.: Washington Office on Latin America, January 2000).

28. See, for example, *Supporting Security Sector Reform.*

29. Department for International Development, "Poverty and the Security Sector," Policy Statement (London: Department for International Development, 1999); and "Security Sector Reform and the Elimination of Poverty," speech by Clare Short, secretary of state for international development, Centre for Defence Studies, King's College, University of London, March 9, 1999. Both of these items are available on the DFID Web site: www.dfid.gov. Some of the work commissioned by the DAC is available at www.oecd.org/dac.

30. World Bank, "Bureaucracy Hampering Balkans Aid, EU Will Be Told," *Development News,* March 23, 2000.

43

International Implementation of Peace Agreements in Civil Wars

Findings from a Study of Sixteen Cases

Stephen John Stedman

WHEN ANTAGONISTS IN CIVIL WAR sign a peace agreement, what can international actors do to prevent a recurrence of that war? This is a life-or-death question for millions of people. The two worst outbreaks of massive violence in the 1990s—Angola in 1993 and Rwanda in 1994—followed the failure of peace agreements to end those wars. In both cases the death and destruction were staggering: an estimated 350,000 dead in Angola and 800,000 dead in Rwanda. War went on for eight years in Liberia and took 150,000 lives because multiple peace agreements failed to end the civil war there. In 2001 two more countries find themselves back in war after the failure of peace accords—Angola and Sierra Leone.

In all of these cases international actors mediated the agreements and were given prominent roles in implementation. Why did they fail? What could they have done differently? Was implementation in these cases doomed by unworkable peace agreements? Was failure a question of unfulfilled mandates or mandates

inappropriate to the task at hand? Or was failure caused by the lack of an appropriate strategy and/or the unwillingness to anticipate violent challenges and craft an effective response? How did these cases differ from successes such as Namibia, El Salvador, and Mozambique? Were these successes the result of less challenging environments or did international actors do things differently?

Between late 1997 and early 2000, Stanford University's Center for International Security and Cooperation (CISAC) and the International Peace Academy (IPA) conducted research to better understand the determinants of successful peace implementation. The CISAC-IPA project on peace implementation focused on three primary issues:

- the evaluation of international actors and their strategies of peace implementation;
- the evaluation of various subgoals of peace implementation (e.g., demobilization, disarmament, refugee repatriation, human rights,

reconciliation, etc.) and their relationship to overall implementation success; and

- the search for low-cost, possible high-payoff opportunities for linking short-term implementation success to longer-term peacebuilding.

The project found that cases of peace implementation differ dramatically in terms of the difficulty of the implementation environment and in the willingness of international actors to provide resources and risk troops, and that these differences are predictable before a peace operation begins. These two findings mark a dramatic advance in our understanding of peace implementation in three fundamental ways. First, the CISAC-IPA results put to rest glib generalizations about peace operations based on one or few cases. To put it bluntly, the results suggest that there is no reason to assume that what actions and strategies work in a more benign conflict environment such as Guatemala or Namibia will work in a much more demanding implementation environment such as Bosnia or Sierra Leone. Second, the results imply that implementation strategies must be designed based on the level of difficulty of the case. In certain limited situations strategies that derive from traditional peacekeeping (with its underlying emphasis on confidence building) can be effective. In more challenging situations, however, when predation coexists with fear, confidence building will prove inadequate, and implementers will need to compel and deter to ensure compliance with a peace agreement. Third, the results raise the fundamental issue of incentive incompatibility. Tough cases require more resources, greater international involvement, and more coercive strategies, but in many of those cases such resources, involvement, and strategies will not be forthcoming because no major or regional power believes the case affects its security interest. Such incentive incompatibility usually is subsumed under arguments that lack of political will is the problem—that if only more

will were found, then tougher cases would receive the needed care. But the emphasis on political will misleads: it takes a relatively fixed variable—perception of vital national interest of regional and major powers—and treats it as if it were easily manipulated. The CISAC-IPA study argues that this is a vexing analytical error that overstates the commitment of international actors to making peace in civil wars in countries of peripheral security importance.

The project also scrutinized claims that are made about the importance of various implementation subgoals and their role in overall success and failure. Such claims grew in prominence in the 1990s as various international nongovernmental organizations lobbied publics and governments and insisted that their single issue of concern—whether it be disarmament, elections, human rights, or refugee repatriation—was crucial to implementation success. Two major findings emerge from an examination of subgoals and overall implementation success. First, in terms of what can be achieved in any subgoal, desires must be commensurate with resources and permitted strategies. On any dimension we can speculate about the perfect conditions under which elections should be held, or the need for peace with full accountability and prosecution for past atrocities and war crimes, or the need for all refugees to repatriate to their original homes. In the absence of commitment of resources and troops, however, ambitious standards for subgoals are symbolic statements of virtue, not practical means of terminating wars. Second, in terms of investment in subgoals, priority should be given to demobilization of soldiers and demilitarization of politics, that is, the transformation of warring armies into political parties. Without achieving these two subgoals, civil wars cannot be brought to an end, and important normative goals such as the creation and consolidation of democracy and the protection of human rights have little chance of success.

The project also identified two low-cost opportunities that should be pursued during implementation: civilian security through police and judicial reform, and local capacity building for human rights and reconciliation. Although the study cannot point to a single case of failed implementation that resulted from failure to pursue these opportunities, we found that the potential long-term benefits of security reform and local capacity building for peacebuilding warrant the relatively inexpensive investments that such measures require.

IMPLEMENTATION: THE LINK BETWEEN MEDIATION AND PEACEBUILDING

For the most part, analysis of conflict resolution and civil war has paid scant attention to the short-term implementation of peace agreements and has instead focused on the mediation of agreements and/or long-term peacebuilding. Because negotiated termination of civil wars was a relatively rare phenomenon in the Cold War era, studies in the 1980s focused primarily on the conditions and tools for getting parties in civil wars to sign agreements.[1] Rather legalistically, scholars assumed that a contract between state and insurgent leaders would remain binding in the postagreement phase. There was also a tendency to conceive of conflict resolution in a linear fashion, in which successful negotiation signaled an irreversible reduction in conflict. Successful cases in the 1980s—Zimbabwe, Namibia, and Nicaragua —reinforced these assumptions. Before long, however, several civil wars—Angola, Rwanda, and Liberia—defied the linear view of conflict resolution and brought attention to the difficulties of getting parties to live up to their commitments to peace.[2] Far from being a time of conflict reduction, the period immediately after the signing of a peace agreement seemed fraught with risks, uncertainty, and vulnerability for the warring parties and civilians caught in between.

We have rather thin knowledge on this dangerous period because for the most part

scholars asked the wrong question of the cases: When antagonists in a civil war sign a peace agreement, what can international actors do to ensure that the society will not experience war in the future? This is the wrong question because it misses a prior question that is much more causally direct: When antagonists in civil war sign a peace agreement, what can international actors do to prevent a recurrence of *that* war? The difference between preventing the return of a specific war with roughly the same cast of characters and preventing forever the outbreak of war is crucial. The former, albeit extremely difficult, lies in the realm of possibility, while the latter is unachievable in the short term. And it is usually in the short term that combatants return to war and millions die.

Peace implementation is the process of carrying out a specific peace agreement. It focuses on the narrow, short-term (three months in the case of Zimbabwe, five years plus in the case of Bosnia) efforts to get warring parties to comply with their commitments to end a war. Success is measured in relationship to concluding the war on a self-enforcing basis: When the outsiders leave, do the local parties refrain from returning to war? Evaluation criteria are much narrower than the basket of goods associated with peacebuilding (amelioration of root causes of conflict, justice, positive peace, harmony, reconciliation of enemies), but they are broader than the accomplishment of specific mandated tasks.[3]

They are narrower than indicators of positive peace because good things like reconciliation, justice, democracy, and the rule of law cannot be attained in the short run. Moreover, measuring the effect of short-term action by effects ten to fifteen years in the future is problematic because the passage of time is the enemy of inference. As two of our authors argue, "The further away one gets in time from the conclusion of a peace mission, the more likely it is that any number of other extraneous factors (e.g., business cycles, famines, unusually good or bad weather, the policies of a neighboring state, the behavior of the first elected leaders) are actually responsible for what has taken place rather than the technology of the peace mission itself. As the potential impact of such exogenous factors increases, the quality of our inferences about the contribution of the peace operation itself tends to diminish until the point where it breaks down completely."[4]

Some performance indicators, especially those suggested from scholars of peacebuilding, run the further danger of setting such high standards of success that we are left with a world of undifferentiated failure. For example, Roland Paris argues that one should judge the success of peace operations in the 1990s by the standard of "creating conditions that will allow peace to endure long after the peacekeepers have left" and asserts that by this standard only one operation—Namibia—can be judged a success.[5] Correspondingly, the list of failures then includes not only unmitigated disasters such as Rwanda and Angola but also operations in which war has ended such as Mozambique, El Salvador, Bosnia, and Nicaragua. By failing to discriminate between catastrophic failures such as Rwanda and Angola and flawed successes such as El Salvador, Cambodia, and Mozambique, Paris holds evaluation hostage to an unreasonable standard of success and ensures that it will yield very little information that can be used to improve future missions. It is not that attaining good things like economic growth, equitable development, and good governance should not be striven for; it is that they form a useless standard for evaluating implementation actions that take place in a short period of time.

To address the gaps in our understanding of peace implementation, the CISAC-IPA study did not assume that all civil wars were equally difficult to end through negotiation. Our instinct was that some implementation environments were more difficult than others and that successful implementation of peace would be in part a function of easier environments. Second,

we assumed that the greater the amount of international commitment, the more likely implementation would succeed. But we also assumed that not all civil wars receive equal attention or resources. Here we took a step back from the recognition that there was something about international involvement in implementation that favored success to ask which cases get more international involvement in implementation.[6] Again our instinct was that international attention and resources were a function of some other important variable and that knowledge of that variable would allow us to specify when international commitment would be forthcoming. Third, we assumed that there were interaction effects between environment and willingness: that more difficult cases would need greater international commitment and that in the more difficult cases international actors would have to do things differently than in easier cases. In essence, we felt that strategies of international actors mattered—an insight that was lost in vague generalizations about international attention or guarantees. Fourth, given that international actors are called upon to do so much in implementation, we wanted to know which subgoals contained in implementation mandates were more important for success.

DETERMINANTS OF SUCCESSFUL IMPLEMENTATION

Without any knowledge of civil war, peacekeeping, or war termination, the literature on policy implementation provides crucial insight into when a peace agreement might succeed or fail. An implementation perspective posits that some environments are more conducive to implementation than others. Such a perspective also looks to the coalitions that support implementation and their willingness to spend resources. A first cut, therefore, was for our project to ascertain what makes some peace implementation environments more difficult and challenging than others. A second cut was to determine which cases get the most resources.

Based on arguments from the scholarly literature on peacemaking in civil war, we created a difficulty score for peace implementation based on the following eight variables:[7]

- *The number of warring parties.* The difficulty of implementation increases when there are more than two warring parties.[8] Strategies become less predictable, balances of power become more tenuous, and alliances become more fluid. In Cambodia, for example, any action that the United Nations might have taken against the Khmer Rouge had to be weighed against the effects such action would have had on FUNCINPEC, which relied on the Khmer Rouge for balance against the State of Cambodia.[9] In cases in which proliferation of parties occurred, as in Somalia and Liberia, implementers constantly found it difficult to craft solutions that would address all of the concerns of the warring factions. But if any factions found themselves out in the cold, the peace agreement would face their violent opposition.

- *The presence of a peace agreement signed by all major warring parties before intervention.* The United Nations has usually required a detailed peace agreement among the warring parties as a sign of their consent to a peace mission before it would intervene. In the 1980s and 1990s, however, the United Nations had the opportunity to intervene in any number of ongoing wars, and in several instances it or a regional organization or state did intervene in the hope of using force to compel a peace agreement: the United Nations in Somalia, ECOWAS in Liberia and Sierra Leone, India in Sri Lanka, NATO in Bosnia, and Syria in Lebanon. Intervention in the absence of a peace agreement likely will trigger violent opposition by parties who value the preintervention status quo. The absence of a peace agreement implies a lack of problem solving, trust,

and confidence building among the warring factions. Both factors imply a more difficult implementation environment.

- *The likelihood of spoilers.* The presence of spoilers in peace agreements poses daunting challenges to implementation.[10] The critique of the spoiler concept, however, is that spoilers are only recognized after the fact. This criticism can be addressed by attempting to gauge whether implementers judged that they were likely to face violent challenges during implementation. A more sophisticated criticism of the spoiler concept is that potential spoilers are always present and whether or not an actor actually assumes this role depends on the existence of a special opportunity structure.[11] There is, as we shall see, some evidence that this is at least partially the case.

- *Collapsed state.* The lack of state institutions and capacity places great demands on peace implementers. In addition to bringing fighting to a close, the implementers must create and build up levels of state capacity in order for the peace to have a chance to sustain itself.

- *Numbers of soldiers.* At some level numbers matter. High levels of soldiers pose greater demands for verification and monitoring, and hence more likelihood of successful cheating. Moreover, greater numbers of soldiers require more personnel for monitoring and more resources for demobilization. We scored cases with more than fifty thousand soldiers as more difficult to implement.

- *Disposable natural resources.* If warring parties have access to disposable resources such as gems, minerals, or timber, implementation becomes more difficult. Such resources not only provide armies with a means for continuing to fight, but also become the reward against which they weigh the benefits of peace.[12] It is argued plausibly that a key difference between Mozambique and Angola is that in the latter country UNITA's access to diamonds emboldened its spoiler behavior, whereas Renamo's lack of such resources in the former would have effectively limited its chances if it had returned to war.[13]

- *Hostile neighboring states or networks.* Civil wars rarely take place in otherwise stable regions. As Peter Wallensteen and Margareta Sollenberg observe, many civil wars today intersect with regional conflicts and interstate competition.[14] From this it would follow that the attitude of the surrounding states toward a peace agreement in a neighbor's civil war would play a key role in supporting or undermining the prospects of peace. Spoilers to a peace agreement, for example, are likely to be much stronger and vocal if they are confident that they can count on neighboring states for sanctuary, guns, fuel, and capital.[15] Likewise, in regions where weak states have little control over borders, well-organized private or semiofficial networks can take advantage of such state decrepitude and support spoilers in the war-torn country.

- *Wars of secession.* There is at least a plausible argument that negotiated settlements are more difficult to attain and implement in civil wars fought over ethnic or national secession.[16] Such conflicts often dissolve into all-or-nothing stakes, which might make the job of implementers more difficult than in cases in which warring parties share a common identity and at least agree on a unitary future for their country.

The more these variables are present, the greater the difficulty to bring the conflict to an end. The conflict environment, however, is only one aspect of determining implementation success or failure. International willingness is also crucial; low degrees of interest and commitment lead to intervention with an extremely limited strategy set in the sense that the implementer is restricted in the resources it will be permitted to employ and the range of subgoals it will be allowed to pursue. Constraints on the strategy set need not be a problem when the case is easy. But difficult cases and constrained

strategies can be a recipe for disaster: for example, when the United Nations Security Council provides enough willingness to agree to implement an agreement, but not enough resources to succeed.

We scored our cases on three indicators of interest and commitment, what we refer to as a willingness score:

- *Major-power interest.* A key sign of commitment to a mission is whether large, powerful states support intervention and publicly define the conflict as important to their own security interests. The more remote that a mission is from a powerful state's security interests, the more likely it is being undertaken for symbolic reasons that are unlikely to inspire the outlay of more than a very modest amount of resources.

- *Resource commitment.* Crucial for successful implementation is the willingness of states to provide financial resources for a mission. But such resources vary by case, and the amount states are likely to contribute is often known before a mission even begins. In Cambodia, for example, the Security Council provided extreme leeway to planners to judge what resources were needed for a successful mission. In Rwanda, however, the Security Council rejected the figures provided by its own field mission and instead severely limited resources available.

- *Willingness to risk lives.* We score this separately from resource commitment because policymakers treat this differently than a judgment about financial and personnel resources.

Table 1 lists the cases in our study, the principal implementer, the conflict difficulty score, and the international willingness score. The higher the difficulty score, the more difficult the implementation environment; the higher the willingness score, the greater the willingness of international actors to commit to the effort.

If we look at just the bivariate regressions of implementation outcome on each of the eleven

Table 1. Peace Implementation Cases

Case	Time Period	Principal Implementer	Conflict Difficulty Score	International Willingness Score	Outcome
Zimbabwe	1980	United Kingdom	3	1.0	Success
Sri Lanka	1987–89	India	6	1.7	Failure
Namibia	1989–90	UN	0	1.7	Success
Nicaragua	1989–90	UN	1	1.5	Success
Lebanon	1990–	Syria	5	2.7	Partial Success
Liberia	1990–98	ECOWAS	6	2.1	Partial Success
Angola I	1991–93	UN	4	0.4	Failure
Cambodia	1991–94	UN	5	2.2	Partial Success
Mozambique	1992–95	UN	2	1.2	Success
El Salvador	1992–94	UN	1	1.5	Success
Somalia	1993	UN	5	1.4	Failure
Rwanda	1993–94	UN	3	0.4	Failure
Angola II	1994–99	UN	4	0.9	Failure
Guatemala	1994-97	UN	0	1.5	Success
Bosnia	1995–	NATO	6	2.2	Partial Success
Sierra Leone	1996–98	ECOWAS	6	0.7	Failure

Note: Conflict difficulty score ranges from 0 (low) to 8 (high). International willingness score ranges from 0 (low) to 3 (high).

variables, we find that only four variables are significant at the .01 level. These are the existence of a spoiler, the presence of disposable natural resources, the presence of a neighboring state that is hostile to the peace agreement, and the presence of great-power interest. Consistent with expectations, the presence of the first three variables reduces the chances of successful implementation, and the last improves it. The summary variables, conflict difficulty and international willingness, together explain about 65 percent of the variance in mission outcome. All of the other variables have an impact that is in the predicted direction but not significant with the small number of cases.

Figure 1 highlights the intersection of case difficulty, major- or regional-power interest, and success or failure. In the upper left-hand corner of the graph are the cases of Guatemala, El Salvador, Namibia, and Nicaragua—all of which scored as the least difficult implementation environments and high in great- or regional-

power interest. All of them, not surprisingly, were successes. The cases of Mozambique and Zimbabwe also fell among the less difficult cases, and although their interest scores were not as high as for the first four cases, their peace agreements were successfully implemented. On the right side of the graph are the more difficult cases. Where great- or regional-power interest was low, as in Angola, Somalia, and Rwanda, or medium, as in Sri Lanka, implementation failed. In the most difficult cases, great- or regional-power interest was enough to compensate for the difficulty and to produce partial success in Cambodia, Lebanon, Bosnia, and Liberia, but not enough in Sierra Leone.

STRATEGIES, COORDINATION, AND INCENTIVE COMPATIBILITY ISSUES

Our project found that as the difficulty of the conflict increases, there is a need for greater

Figure 1. Interest and Difficulty: Case Outcomes

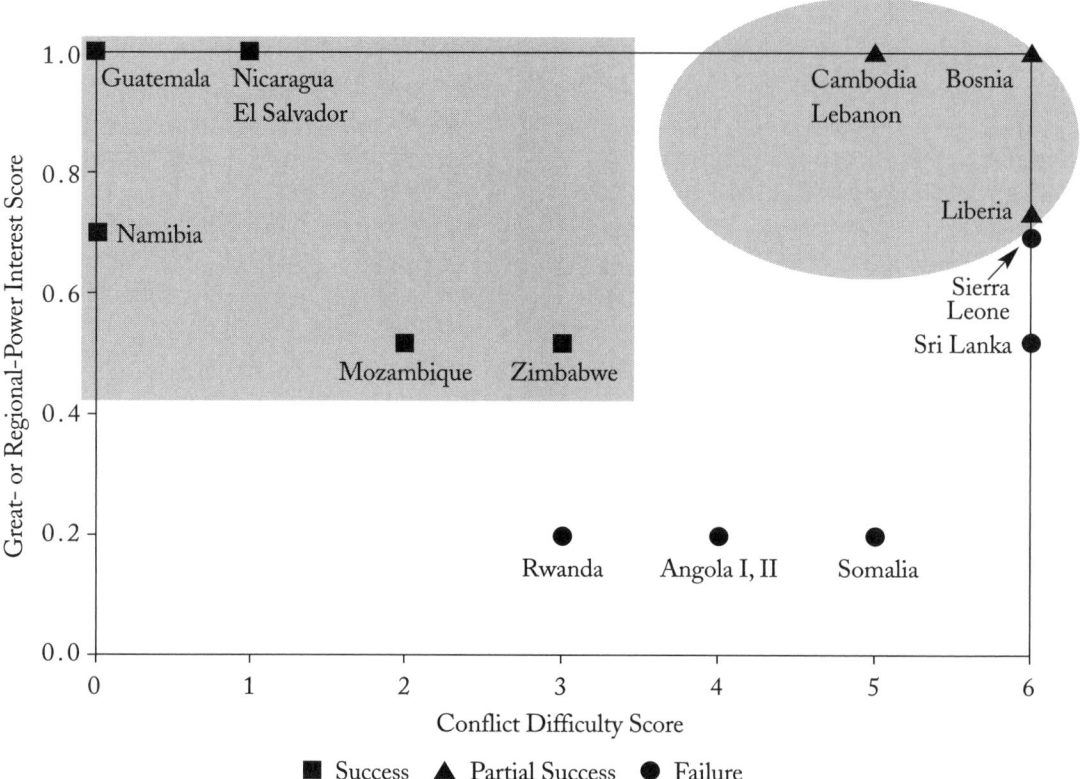

scope and assertiveness from the transitional authority that is supplied by international actors.[17] Similarly, the greater the difficulty of the conflict, the greater the need for coercive strategies of implementation.[18] Yet the availability of strategies to international implementers is a function of major- or regional-power interest. When great or regional powers do not see a particular case as affecting their security interests, they do not provide the resources and commitment necessary for more intrusive, coercive strategies.

Incentive incompatibility affects not only choice of grand strategy but even the availability of mechanisms that are needed to provide strategic coherence and coordination. As Bruce Jones argues, the more difficult the conflict, the greater the need for strategic coordination.[19]

When international actors suffer from a lack of unity or do not fully support an operation, would-be spoilers can take advantage of international splits to attack the peace process and threaten would-be peacemakers. Similarly, the more coercive the strategy, the greater the civil-military tensions in implementation.[20] When international troops are at risk, troop-donating states tend to insist on greater day-to-day interference in the political conduct of the mission. Such interference can defeat the ability of an implementation force to diagnose and respond effectively to spoilers.

Strategies such as "Friends of the Secretary-General" are fundamentally a function of Major-or regional-power interest. The willingness of states to join such a Friends group is indicative of a prior judgment that the specific case is in the state's interest.[21] The result is that such mechanisms for coordination will be unavailable in some cases: there were no Friends of Somalia, as there were no major or regional powers that had security interests in a peaceful Somalia.

Incentive incompatibility and the gap between what is needed in some missions and what the major or regional powers are willing to provide has led to organizational pathologies within the United Nations that, unless addressed, may lead to the end of UN involvement in making peace.[22] The UN Secretariat seems to have learned that there are some cases in which the Security Council will authorize a mission only if it perceives that the case will be safe and easy. Where threats or dangers appear, the reaction of the Security Council is to cut and run. Faced with such knowledge as early as Rwanda, UN bureaucrats became reluctant to share worrisome conflict assessments and tended only to "ask for what the traffic will bear." This led to UN intervention in cases where, if anything went wrong, the United Nations would fail. The need to present optimistic scenarios to the Security Council precluded contingency planning, since the basic premise of such planning signals that less than optimistic scenarios are possible. In some cases the need for the United Nations to present a successful face to its political masters led missions such as Angola in 1997 and Sierra Leone in 1999 to ignore blatant noncompliance by the warring parties. At its worst, as in East Timor in 1999, the Secretariat engaged in reckless gambling by selling the Security Council on a mission by downplaying its difficulty, in the hopes that if it went bad, the Security Council and the member-states would be embarrassed into response.

EVALUATION OF SUBGOALS

The CISAC-IPA project sought to shed light on the importance of various subgoals in peace implementation. The reasons for doing so were twofold. First, when mandates contain multiple tasks and operations face constraints on resources, implementers will likely look at the broad set of tasks that they are asked to accomplish and attempt to decide which ones are primary and which ones are secondary to ending the war. It is possible that in a complex environment the attempt to accomplish all tasks will lead to no overall policy direction or strategy. In such circumstances advice about which subgoals to prioritize is of utmost importance. This assumes even greater importance because of the second reason for evaluation. During the 1990s a cottage industry developed around peace implementation as nongovernmental organizations argued for the overriding importance of particular subgoals, such as human rights, disarmament, economic reconstruction, or civilian security, as the key to peace. Rarely were these claims subjected to empirical evaluation, and when they were, they were often flawed by basic errors. The resulting danger exists when the priorities of implementers are set by appeals to faith and sentiment rather than what will likely work in a given context. This danger was described by one implementer, who stated that for his operation there was never a problem of too few resources; rather, the problem was that the resources were often earmarked for activities that were nonessential to ending the war and that would be unsustainable in the absence of ending the war.

Before we proceed to a discussion of individual subgoals, several points require emphasis. What we have said about incentive incompatibility and overall success pertains also to subgoals. Ambitions concerning justice, accountability, perfect conditions for holding elections, and repatriation of refugees to their previous homes have to be commensurate with overall resources and permitted strategies. A demand for some combatants to be tried as war criminals, for example, makes sense and indeed is only feasible if implementers are willing to employ a robust coercive strategy. But as we pointed out earlier, unless a case is perceived by a regional or major power as in its security interest, there will be little coercive capability or will to prevail if a coercive strategy is challenged.

A second point concerns the difficulty of evaluating the contributions of various subgoals to overall success. Different subgoals interact in the sense that success in one area can affect success in another area, but the importance of this interaction will be missed when analyzing subgoals in isolation.[23] This can lead to any number of mistaken inferences. For example, Human Rights Watch not too surprisingly asserts that the failure to protect and further human rights in Angola best explains the United Nations' failure to implement peace there.[24] But as Tonya Putnam demonstrates, the protection and furtherance of human rights during peace implementation rests completely on the ability of the implementers to persuade the warring parties to demobilize their soldiers and turn their armies into political parties.[25] In the absence of progress in demobilization and demilitarization of politics, implementers have little chance to achieve higher standards of human rights.

Finally, context also matters greatly in the evaluation of subgoals. Again to use the human rights example, the ability of peacekeepers to successfully pursue human rights during implementation differs dramatically according to the conflict environment. Pursuing human rights in Somalia, for example, where there was no existing rule of law, no civil society, no functioning state, and spoilers who sought to destroy the peace agreement, was much more difficult than pursuing human rights in El Salvador, where the two warring parties agreed to make reform of judiciary and police institutions a key aspect of the peace agreement.

Demobilization and Reintegration of Combatants

The study found that demobilization of soldiers and their reintegration into civilian life are the most important subgoals of peace implementation.[26] The ending of a civil war hinges on the willingness of competing armies to refute self-help solutions to their insecurity, demobilize their soldiers, and in some circumstances create a new, integrated, army. These are processes, however, that are filled with dangers and risks for antagonists. Third-party implementers can eliminate such risks by acting as guarantors and deterring any party from taking advantage of their adversary's vulnerability or protecting any party that is taken advantage of during demobilization. Our study, however, found that such guarantees are seldom forthcoming from implementers. With the exceptions of NATO in Bosnia, Syria in Lebanon, and ECOWAS (on occasion) in Liberia and Sierra Leone, implementers in our study did not commit to such guarantees. This is understandable and goes to the heart of incentive compatibility and willingness of outsiders to implement an agreement: the costs and risks of becoming a direct combatant in a civil war are often too high for implementers. Most of our implementers limited their role to monitoring, verifying, and facilitating demobilization.

Such monitoring as has been practiced in most of the missions that we studied has been flawed by the lack of an intelligence capacity to assess motives behind violations of agreements and unwillingness of implementers to set strict standards of compliance. Assessment of motives is important because cheating is pervasive in demobilization of soldiers. Our study, however, found different motives for cheating, motives that had important implications for prospects of successful war termination. Starting with the most benign motives for cheating, warring parties may withhold troops from demobilization as a self-help protection should their adversary attack them. A less benign motive is seen in parties that withhold troops to gain a potential advantage in elections, by using their soldiers for intimidation purposes. Finally, the most malignant motive for cheating is the attempt to sucker opponents and to take advantage of their vulnerability to win an outright victory.

Since motives are important for outcomes, there should be a premium placed on robust monitoring and verification of demobilization. The greatest danger stems from implementers who pull their punches in terms of acknowledging, reporting, or responding to violations of demobilization agreements. In Angola implementers did not call the parties on violations for fear that such renunciations would hinder their ability to act as impartial brokers. Later the implementers falsely verified UNITA's demobilization in order to claim the mission as a success. In Rwanda the Department of Peacekeeping Operations prohibited its peacekeepers from aggressively investigating reports of hidden arms caches for fear that such investigation might provoke violence by extremists.

Disarmament

Unlike demobilization of soldiers, large-scale disarmament does not appear to be crucial to implementation success.[27] Disarmament, when it occurred, followed demobilization; in the absence of demobilization, disarmament did not occur. Furthermore, there were cases, such as Mozambique, in which demobilization was largely successful but disarmament was a failure; hundreds of thousands of weapons were said to have been cached by the warring sides and these weapons were not eliminated by the United Nations Operation in Mozambique (ONUMOZ).

Successful disarmament is greatly affected by the implementation environment. Where there is a lack of a functioning state to provide individual security, or where the police are believed to be "owned" by particular ethnic groups and unwilling to provide impartial justice, disarmament will be extremely difficult. In such circumstances groups turn to gun ownership as a means of security self-help.

Elections

The study found that implementers often hold elections for multiple, sometimes contradictory goals: war termination, democratization, and internal organizational purposes.[28] Our study advocates the importance of war termination when such goals are in conflict. The problem for an implementer is to accurately gauge what is possible from holding elections and to carefully consider what alternatives may be available. Critics of settlement elections often compare the effects of such elections against impossibly high standards or against alternatives that were not politically feasible. In terms of the process of carrying out elections, our study emphasizes the need for investment in demilitarizing politics. Resources spent on transforming armies into viable political parties can play a crucial role in persuading rebels to compete for power within the political arena and therefore strengthen the prospects of war termination. Even in elections whose short-term results are unlikely to further democratization, process can matter. The construction of electoral authorities and institutions with legitimacy and effectiveness can serve as a bridge to long-term democratization.

Elections may decide who will rule in a country emerging from civil war and how power will be concentrated, absolute fundamental conditions for war termination. But what might be necessary to bring a war to a close may or may not forward the goal of democratization, depending primarily on who wins the election and how it is carried out and perceived by the new electorate. Liberia is a case in point; most international observers believe that the election of Charles Taylor in 1998 was necessary to bring the country's civil war to a close. But few analysts saw those elections, given Taylor's authoritarian and corrupt behavior before and during the war, as holding out much hope for democracy in Liberia. Indeed, Liberians themselves saw the election as a referendum on the terms of bringing the war to an end: a vote for Taylor was a vote for ending the war.

Conversely, elections may produce results that are favorable for democracy—the opportunity for citizens to express preferences over who should rule—but prove antithetical to war termination. If a losing party, such as Jonas Savimbi and UNITA, is committed to returning to war in the absence of winning an election, no matter how legitimate the election is seen by a citizenry, the war will not end.

Human Rights

Our study found that international human rights organizations have asked for too much and for too little with regard to human rights and peace implementation.[29] They have asked for too much by insisting on a doctrinaire approach to human rights protection in environments that are ill suited for such an approach. They have asked for too little by dogmatically refusing to help new governments work toward greater human rights standards and to see that all subgoals of peace implementation should have a human rights component.

Although the promotion of human rights and the establishment of institutions capable of advocating and protecting human rights are desirable for societies emerging from civil war, the demands and the challenges of implementing peace in war-torn countries require more nuanced strategies than those typically chosen by international human rights organizations (IHROs). The CISAC-IPA study argues that "exclusive reliance on the enforcement approach to human rights protection is entirely unsuited to the early stages of peace implementation."[30] Typically, IHROs have failed to appreciate the specific challenges posed by war-torn societies and have used strategies designed for contexts in which there are functioning governments and rule of law. This has led IHROs to commit three common errors: (1) to place undue

importance on achieving formal expression of human rights provisions in the body of peace settlements; (2) to demand individual responsibility for human rights violations in societies that lack even rudimentary investigative, adjudicative, and compensatory institutions; and (3) to isolate human rights concerns from direct involvement with postsettlement governments and other key tasks of peace implementation.

Evidence from cases of peace implementation suggests that "the formal enumeration of human rights provisions in peace settlements correlates only weakly, if at all, with the quantity and quality of human rights protection during and after peace implementation." Moreover, the ability of mediators to insist on the inclusion of human rights language in peace agreements is extremely constrained.

The findings in our study do not imply that human rights are irrelevant to the achievement of peace. Rather, they point to the need for a changed approach by those who care about the promotion and protection of human rights. Two aspects of change stand out. First, human rights objectives must be linked to other instrumental tasks of implementation. Second, human rights groups must work to build the capacity of locally based human rights advocates, who will have to do the heavy lifting over the long haul.

Refugee Repatriation

The study challenged two strongly held beliefs concerning the relationship between refugee repatriation and reintegration and successful implementation of peace—one that holds that there can be no peace without repatriation and one that dismisses refugee concerns as peripheral to war termination.[31] Instead, the study found a complicated relationship between refugee repatriation and successful peace implementation, one that depends greatly on the context of the conflict and the rhetoric of the implementers. In some cases, for example, El

Salvador, the fact that many refugees were re-settled in other countries and not repatriated contributed to successful implementation of the peace accords. Refugees who were resettled became a crucial source of needed capital at home through remittances of income. And because so many refugees were resettled, those who did repatriate faced less competition for scarce jobs and land.

The study found that the type of civil war affected the relationship between refugee repatriation and implementation success. In wars that are about exclusion of peoples, for example, Bosnia, the insistence on repatriation to areas where ethnic cleansers were successful can lead to resumption of violence. This of course creates a daunting ethical dilemma: where implementation success is measured simply by the absence of war, the surest way to avoid new hostilities is to avoid repatriation. In practice, in Bosnia, at least, the reluctance of policymakers to repatriate refugees to original homes and their unease with the ethical implications of that choice has led to a worse outcome: a proclaimed right to return without enforcement, which, in the words of Howard Adelman, "is no real right to return and leads . . . to no repatriation and no resettlement."[32]

BRIDGES TO PEACEBUILDING

Although our study focused on the short-term efforts of international implementers and judged their performance accordingly, we do care about long-term peacebuilding and therefore sought recommendations on action that could bridge between short-term implementation and the long-term consolidation of peace. Our study identified two important contributions that implementers can make in the short term that, at relatively low cost, could prove to have large payoffs for longer-term peacebuilding: reform of civilian police and judiciaries and strengthening local civil society organizations.

Civilian Security

For good reasons, international implementers of peace agreements focus on ensuring the security of ex-combatants. But our study found that ensuring the security of the general population is often lacking in peace implementation.[33] This is problematic, however, given that many civil war settlements that are based on liberal norms and institutions depend on citizens' accepting individual assurances rather than group-based protections. In the absence of a police force that can effectively provide those assurances, new postwar arrangements seem unjust and in violation of group rights. In an insecure environment, political entrepreneurs can engage in protection racketeering that undermines the credibility and authority of the new state.

As Charles Call and William Stanley point out, "virtually all post-1989 cases of negotiated civil war termination experienced perceptions of heightened public insecurity, often as a result of documented increases in violent crime."[34] As they point out, civil war settlements offer unique opportunities for redesigning and reforming civilian security institutions. The inclusion of civilian security reform in peace agreements provides implementers with clear guidelines for assistance programs. Our cases suggest important lessons for such programs: the need to design and implement judicial, penal, and police reforms in tandem and the importance of creating specialized police units, especially criminal investigative units and oversight offices (e.g., internal affairs, inspectors-general, and civilian commissions).

Local Capacity Building: Civil Society Organizations

At relatively low cost, implementers can support local civil society organizations that can play key roles in sustaining peace after the implementers leave.[35] Civil society organizations can help to sustain peace agreements by working at the grassroots level to legitimize peace and make it more than an elite concern. Local organizations can address key issues such as reconciliation, justice, and human rights that go to the heart of what many consider to be the root causes of civil wars. Moreover, local organizations tend to have a longer time horizon and are more adept at sustaining long-term processes that are integral to peacebuilding.

POLICY RECOMMENDATIONS

Several policy recommendations follow from our study. These recommendations cluster into three dimensions: (1) when international actors should become involved in attempting to implement peace; (2) the capabilities that are needed for international actors to succeed in peace implementation; and (3) priorities to be undertaken during peace implementation.

When to Become Involved

- When selecting which peace agreements the United Nations should implement, great- or regional-power interest should be treated as a hard constraint.
- Without great- or regional-power interest, the United Nations should not implement hard cases.
- Before attempting to implement a peace agreement in a country where there are easily marketed, valuable commodities (spoils), the implementer should have the strategy, resources, and commitment to regulate such commodities.

Needed Capabilities

- Given the importance of judgment about the difficulty of the conflict, there is a need at the United Nations for better strategic assessment concerning possible peace implementation missions.

- Given the importance of the role that spoilers play in implementation failure, there is a need for intelligence gathering and assessment concerning the motives, intentions, and capabilities of parties that sign peace agreements and parties that are omitted from peace agreements.
- Given that such intelligence is fallible and that there will be missions in which unanticipated violent challenges may erupt during implementation, there is a need for the United Nations to improve its contingency planning for peace operations.

Priorities

- Emphasis must be given to demilitarizing politics: demobilization of armies, returning soldiers to civilian life, and transforming armies into political parties.

NOTES

1. See, for example, I. William Zartman, *Ripe for Resolution* (New York: Oxford University Press, 1985); Richard Haass, *Conflicts Unending* (New Haven: Yale University Press, 1990); and Stephen John Stedman, *Peacemaking in Civil War* (Boulder, Colo.: Lynne Rienner, 1991).

2. Stephen John Stedman, "UN Intervention in Civil Wars: Imperatives of Choice and Strategy," in *Beyond Traditional Peacekeeping*, ed. Donald C. F. Daniel and Bradd C. Hayes (New York: St. Martin's Press, 1994), 40–64; Fen Osler Hampson, *Nurturing Peace: Why Peace Settlements Succeed or Fail* (Washington, D.C.: United States Institute of Peace Press, 1996); Stephen John Stedman, "Mediation and Negotiation in Internal Conflicts," in *International Dimensions of Internal Conflicts*, ed. Michael Brown (Cambridge, Mass.: MIT Press, 1996), 341–376; and Barbara Walter, "The Critical Barrier to Civil War Settlement," *International Organization* 51, no. 3 (summer 1997): 335–364.

3. For a critical but sympathetic review of the peacebuilding literature, see Elizabeth Cousens, introduction to *Peacebuilding as Politics: Cultivating Peace in Fragile Societies*, ed. Elizabeth Cousens and

Chetan Kumar, with Karin Wermester (Boulder, Colo.: Lynne Rienner, 2000), 1–20.

4. George Downs and Stephen John Stedman, "Evaluating the International Implementation of Peace Agreements in Civil Wars," in *Implementation of Peace Agreements*, vol. 2 of *Ending Civil Wars*, ed. Stephen John Stedman, Donald Rothchild, and Elizabeth Cousens (forthcoming).

5. Roland Paris, "Peacebuilding and the Limits of Liberal Internationalism," *International Security* 22, no. 2 (fall 1997): 54–89.

6. Fen Hampson and Barbara Walter argue that international attention (Hampson) or international guarantees (Walter) are crucial for negotiated termination of civil wars. See Hampson, *Nurturing Peace*, and Walter, "Crucial Barrier to Civil War Settlement."

7. This section draws from Downs and Stedman, "Evaluating the International Implementation of Peace Agreements in Civil Wars."

8. Gerardo L. Munck and Chetan Kumar, "Civil Conflicts and the Conditions for Successful International Intervention: A Comparative Study of Cambodia and El Salvador," *Review of International Studies* 21, no. 2 (1995): 159–181; and Michael Doyle and Nicholas Sambanis, "International Peacebuilding: A Theoretical and Quantitative Analysis," *American Political Science Review* 94, no. 4 (December 2000).

9. Sorpong Peou, "Implementing Cambodia's Peace Agreement: Challenges, Strategy, and Outcome" in *From Mediation to Implementation*, vol. 1 of *Ending Civil Wars*, ed. Stephen John Stedman, Donald Rothchild, and Elizabeth Cousens (forthcoming); and Stephen John Stedman, "Spoiler Problems in Peace Processes," *International Security* 22, no. 2 (fall 1997): 32–36.

10. Stedman, "Spoiler Problems in Peace Processes."

11. Paul Collier and Anke Hoeffler have made a similar argument in connection with the factors that inspire rebellion in the first place. See *Greed and Grievance in Civil War,* Policy Research Working Paper no. 2355 (Washington, D.C.: World Bank Development Group, May 2000).

12. There is a burgeoning literature on the political economy of civil wars and its effect on prospects for war termination. See, for example, Mats Berdal and David Malone, eds., *Greed and Grievance: Economic Agendas in Civil Wars* (Boulder, Colo.: Lynne Rienner, 2000).

13. Stedman, "Spoiler Problems in Peace Processes," 47–48.

14. Peter Wallensteen and Margareta Sollenberg, "Armed Conflicts, Conflict Termination, and Peace Agreements, 1989–96," *Journal of Peace Research* 34, no. 3 (fall 1997): 339–358.

15. Stedman, "Spoiler Problems in Peace Processes," 51.

16. Chaim Kaufman, "Possible and Impossible Solutions to Civil Wars," *International Security* 20, no. 4 (spring 1996): 136–175.

17. Michael Doyle, "Transitional Authority," in *Implementation of Peace Agreements*, vol. 2 of *Ending Civil Wars*.

18. Stephen John Stedman, "From Mediation to Implementation: The Strategy Gap," in *From Mediation to Implementation*, vol. 1 of *Ending Civil Wars*.

19. Bruce Jones, "The Challenge of Strategic Coordination: Containing Opposition and Sustaining Implementation," in *Implementation of Peace Agreements*, vol. 2 of *Ending Civil Wars*.

20. Karen Guttieri, "Civil-Military Relations," in ibid.

21. Jones, "Challenge of Strategic Coordination."

22. Downs and Stedman, "Evaluating the International Implementation of Peace Agreements in Civil Wars."

23. Ibid.

24. Human Rights Watch, *Angola Unravels: The Rise and Fall of the Lusaka Peace Process* (New York: Human Rights Watch, 1999).

25. Tonya Putnam, "Human Rights and Sustainable Peace," in *Implementation of Peace Agreements*, vol. 2 of *Ending Civil Wars*.

26. Joanna Spear, "Demobilization and Disarmament: Key Implementation Issues," in ibid.

27. Ibid.

28. Terrence Lyons, "Implementing Peace and Building Democracy: The Role of Elections," in ibid.

29. Putnam, "Human Rights and Sustainable Peace."

30. Ibid.

31. Howard Adelman, "Peace Agreements: Refugee Repatriation and Reintegration," in *Implementation of Peace Agreements*, vol. 2 of *Ending Civil Wars*.

32. Ibid.

33. Charles Call and William Stanley, "A Sacrifice for Peace? Security for the General Public during Implementation of Peace Agreements," in *Implementation of Peace Agreements*, vol. 2 of *Ending Civil Wars*.

34. Ibid.

35. John Prendergast and Emily Plumb, "Civil Society Organizations and Peace Agreement Implementation," in *Implementation of Peace Agreements*, vol. 2 of *Ending Civil Wars*.

44

Conflict Resolution versus Democratic Governance

Divergent Paths to Peace?

Pauline H. Baker

CONTRARY TO THE PUBLIC IMPRESSION that "small wars" do not significantly threaten U.S. interests, internal conflicts based on ethnic, religious, or linguistic identities constitute one of the biggest dangers to world peace since the end of the Cold War.[1] While the perils of nuclear proliferation are real and there is a compelling need for the United States to retain the military capabilities to reform the military to address the new international threats, actual military engagements of U.S. forces since the collapse of the Soviet Union have primarily occurred in response to internal conflicts.

None of the thirty-one instances of active hostilities around the world in 1994, for example, were "classical" interstate wars.[2] Yet in the five years following Operation Desert Storm, the U.S. military was involved in twenty-seven overseas operations, ranging in scope from a noncombat evacuation in Sierra Leone in May 1992 to Operation Restore Democracy in Haiti in September 1994.[3]

Internal conflicts have spawned unprecedented responses from the international community as a whole. In its first military operation since it was founded, NATO bombed Serbian forces to stop Yugoslavia's "ethnic cleansing" of the majority Albanian population in Kosovo. The International Criminal Tribunal on Yugoslavia indicted Yugoslavian president Slobodan Milosevic for war crimes, the first time a sitting head of state was indicted for actions taken against his own citizens, effectively preventing the Serbian leader from traveling outside his own country and contributing to his ultimate downfall. In Asia, an Australian-led peacekeeping mission intervened in East Timor after Indonesia was pressured into agreeing to let an outside force come in to bring order to the territory, which had erupted into violence after the Timorese voted overwhelmingly in favor of self-determination. In Africa, violence has been equal to or greater than that in Yugoslavia and Indonesia. Smaller UN operations were deployed in Sierra Leone, where rebel forces of the Revolutionary United Front killed and mutilated civilians in a senseless war, and in the Great Lakes region of Africa, the site of what some have described as the continent's "first world war," involving at least six countries and several rival militia groups.

There were also fresh attempts to hold accountable those who had committed human rights abuses in past conflicts. The United Nations urged Cambodia to try Khmer Rouge leaders who were blamed for the deaths of more than one million people from 1975 to 1979. When Cambodian prime minister Hun Sen offered his own version of a tribunal, the United Nations rejected it on the grounds that it did not meet international standards. Later, a novel agreement was reached between the United Nations and the government of Cambodia that would establish a court in Cambodia with co-prosecutors (one foreign and one Cambodian) and co-judges (three Cambodian and two foreign) on a judicial panel to resolve disputes between the prosecutors by a "supermajority" of four votes, giving independent judges the power to block efforts by the Cambodian government to squash indictments. In perhaps the most stunning action, Spain indicted former Chilean military ruler General Augusto Pinochet for crimes he committed in the early 1970s. This led to his arrest in London and a long legal battle over extradition. Never before had a country indicted a former head of state while he was abroad for human rights violations that he had committed in his own country. The case was considered by human rights groups to be a historic breakthrough. Indeed, it sparked a similar move in Africa, where several deposed leaders have escaped justice by going into exile with stolen state funds. Senegal indicted Hissene Habré, a dictator who had ruled Chad for most of the 1980s, for torture and "barbarity" after several Chadian citizens testified before a Senegalese judge that they had been tortured under Habré's rule. The case was dismissed. Even the United Nations came under scrutiny for its failure to prevent human rights abuses. It admitted that it had failed to stop the 1994 genocide in Rwanda and to protect thousands of civilians in 1995 from being massacred in Srebrenica, Bosnia.

Kosovo and East Timor raise still more complicated questions of international responsibility in preventing revenge killings in ongoing or recent conflicts. Consistent application of human rights standards means that a rapid turn of events on the ground could make international engagement tricky, with local allies, such as the Kosovar Albanians, unwilling to respect international standards of human rights. Local allies may prefer to exact vengeance, repeat the cycle of violence, and thus undermine political domestic support for peacekeeping if it appears to be facilitating reciprocal, albeit less extensive, abuses. In Indonesia, the international community faced yet another complex dilemma: dealing with militias that were exacting vengeance in the refugee camps in West Timor, where peacekeepers had no jurisdiction. Imposing accountability in countries in which there is a fragile peace must take into account the context, sequence, and timing of events on the ground, as initial assumptions may be wrong about who has dirty hands. History abounds with examples of the oppressed becoming the oppressors.

As these examples demonstrate, the long-term political consequences of internal conflicts have been greatly underestimated. Ethnic conflicts and internal wars have endangered emerging democracies from Mexico to Russia, led to the worst atrocities since World War II, shaken public confidence in multilateral organizations, and strained bilateral relations with some of our closest allies, and they are eroding long-standing international norms such as respect for sovereignty and noninterference in the internal affairs of other states.

Nonetheless, there have also been some positive responses to these conflicts. Effective short-term relief strategies to reduce human suffering have been developed; progress has been made in mediating long-simmering conflicts, such as in the Middle East and Ireland; the U.S. military is developing new peacekeeping capabilities; and many Western countries have peacekeeping training programs for areas, such as Africa, that are in severe conflict. The Pinochet and Habré cases, the interventions in Kosovo and East Timor, and the candor with which the United Nations acknowledged its own failures represent new standards of international conduct in man-made humanitarian crises. When civilians are being killed, the world is beginning to recognize, something must be done to stop the carnage.

But the international community is no closer to reaching a political consensus about who should lead in shouldering the burden, or how peacekeeping should be conducted, than it was when the U.S. Marines landed on the beaches of Somalia in December 1992, the first post–Cold War peace enforcement intervention. As Assistant Secretary of State Richard Holbrooke observed with respect to Bosnia, peace is being invented as we go along, often with uncertain domestic and international support. UN secretary-general Kofi Annan argues forcefully that national borders are not inviolable and that the world has the right to intervene in the internal affairs of nation-states when leaders abuse their own people, preferably under UN authority. However, Senator Jesse Helms (R-N.C.), chairman of the U.S. Senate Foreign Relations Committee, told the United Nations on January 21, 2000, that the United States was moving away from what he described as utopian international arrangements like the international criminal court and supranational institutions like the United Nations. He asserted the right of the United States to intervene unilaterally, citing President Ronald Reagan's interventions to oppose communist oppression, with or without the approval of the United Nations to legitimize its actions. While U.S. involvement in peacekeeping is often encouraged, the unilateralist sentiment expressed by Helms and many others in the United States rankles most other nations.

In fact, within the United States there is also considerable confusion. Most polls show that the general U.S. public tends to support humanitarian military intervention to stop atrocities. But a majority of U.S. foreign policy elites vowed never to get involved in such crises again after the Somalia experience. When—inevitably—other crises followed, the United States reacted with varying responses. The first challenge was Rwanda, which erupted in an orgy of ethnic bloodletting shortly after the misadventure in Somalia. The Canadian commander of the UN peacekeeping force in Rwanda argued that he could stem the violence. But the United Nations, backed by the United States, ordered UN troops to withdraw after some Belgian peacekeepers were killed. What followed was the worst genocidal violence since the Nazi era, with between five hundred thousand and 1 million people slaughtered in four months of unrelenting butchery. To his credit, Kofi Annan placed the blame on himself, the Security Council, and the UN staff for the lack of rapid and effective responses.

In other crises, the reluctance of the United States to get involved similarly led to deteriorating circumstances. It was only after refugees fled to U.S. shores in droves and domestic pressure for action mounted that Washington responded to the crisis in Haiti. Likewise, U.S. leadership in Bosnia occurred only after Serbian forces overran UN safe havens and held UN peacekeepers hostage and the conflict threatened to split NATO. Dire circumstances, not preventive diplomacy, are driving the United States in those instances. By the time circumstances demand a response, however, massive military intervention is often unavoidable, very costly, and the most dangerous.

The failure of the international community to address the problems posed by small wars at an earlier stage has made matters worse. Ethnic crises do not rapidly burn themselves out, at least not without enormous human and material damage. The Great Lakes region shows how a conflict can spiral out of control. Nor does a reluctance to intervene necessarily relieve the international community of the burden of involvement. Often, as the carnage mounts, human rights groups and relief agencies call for action, and the media drive home the brutalities, the imperative for intervention becomes even more compelling. Better predictive capabilities and a wider range of preventive measures must be developed so that full-scale catastrophic explosions can be avoided and nonmilitary options explored.

In confronting the problem, however, the international community faces a dilemma. It is not so much a question of whether to engage in nation building, but rather how to get involved —specifically, how to reconcile the two imperatives of peace: conflict resolution, on the one hand, and democracy and human rights, on the other.

Should peace be sought at any price to end the bloodshed, even if power-sharing arrangements fail to uphold basic human rights and democratic principles? Or should the objective be a democratic peace that respects human rights, a goal that may prolong the fighting and risk more atrocities in the time that it takes to reach a negotiated solution?

The need to create power-sharing arrangements with rival factions and to include all major groups in a peace process often clashes with the need to bring human rights abusers to justice, establish political legitimacy, establish the rule of law, and build new state structures that can earn the confidence and trust of the people. This dilemma is at the heart of the current debate about how best to pursue peace in the twenty-first century.

A NEW TERRAIN OF CONFLICT

It is not surprising that difficulties arise in crafting policies toward peacemaking. Indeed, this has become a central issue in the U.S. debate between isolationists and internationalists.

However, adding to the complexity of the problem is a nascent rift within the internationalist community itself. In one camp are those who stress conflict resolution to end destructive wars as soon as possible; in the other are those who believe that democracy and human rights must be the overriding objective of peace efforts.

Theoretically, isolationists should largely be out of this debate, because they oppose international involvement on all but the most narrow criteria. But they nevertheless cast their shadow because they set limits, particularly in the U.S. Congress, on the resources available for meaningful action. Hence, peacemakers may tilt toward the most expedient resolution of conflict not because they necessarily believe in that approach, but because they need to dampen domestic opposition, silence critics, and minimize American culpability if anything goes wrong. The architects of peace have to assuage combatants at home as much as they have to assuage combatants abroad.

Aside from these political considerations, the two types of peacemakers diverge in substantive ways as well. What are these groups and what, precisely, are their differences?

For the purposes of this discussion, they will be described as "conflict managers" and "democratizers." The term "conflict managers" is used to denote those who are involved in a range of activities, from preventive diplomacy and mediation to dispute resolution of various sorts (including efforts that go under various other names such as conflict or dispute regulation and conflict mitigation). The "democratizers" include those who advocate human rights, democratic institutions, the rule of law, and the prosecution of those who commit war crimes and atrocities.

In practice, these groups often overlap and share many perspectives, especially on the larger questions of U.S. engagement and leadership. For this reason, it may not always be easy to separate them. But in concrete cases, from Rwanda to the former Yugoslavia, conflict managers and democratizers have emphasized different values, goals, and strategies. At times, their differences may appear to be partisan in nature or to echo the Cold War rivalry between realists and idealists. But however much such factors may be present, this is largely a nonpartisan dialogue between people who share a common concern with ending conflict but favor different strategies for achieving it.

That there is an emerging problem is evident not only in the controversies that have surrounded the various wars that have preoccupied peacemakers since the late 1980s, but also in the political evolution of one of the world's leading mediators, former president Jimmy Carter.

Carter's thematic emphasis on human rights was the cornerstone of his presidency. As a result of his advocacy, Congress began to attach human rights conditions to various foreign policies, an Office of Humanitarian Affairs and a Bureau of Human Rights were created in the State Department, and nongovernmental organizations—among them Freedom House, Human Rights Watch, and Amnesty International—issued public reports on the human rights records of other countries. More than any other president, Carter placed human rights on the agenda of U.S. foreign policy.

After he left office, Carter became a skilled conflict resolution mediator, building on his Camp David experience. He defused a looming crisis between the United States and North Korea, mounted an eleventh-hour successful diplomatic mediation in Haiti, and initiated a confidence-building effort in Central Africa to hasten the return of 2 million refugees displaced by the genocide in Rwanda. Yet in doing so, Carter began to be criticized for unnecessarily offering deals, making concessions, or offering legitimacy to oppressive leaders. Despite the pivotal role he played in facilitating a peaceful transition in Haiti, for example, Carter was castigated by the Haitian people for granting too many concessions to the deposed military dictator, Raoul Cedras, who

was allowed to go into exile with his family and live comfortably off his property without being held accountable for his crimes. Moreover, although Carter, along with Senator Sam Nunn and General Colin Powell, restored an elected president to power, Haiti was far from stable. In total, the Clinton administration sent twenty thousand troops and invested over $2 billion in the restoration of Haitian democracy, but a standoff between the opposing political parties, escalating political violence, an increase in the drug trade, and lingering poverty made the future of constitutional rule uncertain. One may ask whether the net effect of Carter's intervention was to tilt Haiti toward democracy and peace at the cost of justice or to simply buy time, postponing the moment of reckoning when both democracy and justice will have to be adopted to promote a truly enduring peace.

That Jimmy Carter could be attacked on human rights grounds is a mark of how far the wheel of history has turned in the new international environment. Unlike during the Cold War, peace is no longer acceptable on any terms; it is intimately linked with the notion of justice. During the Cold War, human rights were often trumped by geostrategic considerations, a formula hard to justify today outside of some areas, such as China and Russia. Conflict resolution is not measured now simply by the absence of bloodshed; it is assessed by the moral quality of the outcome. And while pragmatism and flexibility continue to be admired, they are seen not as virtues in their own right, but as skills whose value is determined by the ends to which they are applied.

The need to ensure public accountability and entrench basic human and political rights is not only a luxury of the rich and stable; it is a demand being made by victims of oppression in societies around the world. Indeed, hard choices between the imperatives of peace and the demands for justice are being made in countries as far apart as Ethiopia, Honduras, the Philippines, and Sierra Leone. These demands are reflected in amnesties, judicial commissions, and Nuremberg-like tribunals in Latin America, Eastern Europe, Asia, and Africa.

For the United States, the tensions emanating from these opposing objectives have perhaps been drawn most dramatically in the former Yugoslavia, which history may see as a critical test of U.S. diplomacy in the post–Cold War era. "Some people are concerned that pursuing peace in Bosnia and prosecuting war criminals are incompatible goals," stated President Clinton. "But I believe they are wrong. There must be peace for justice to prevail, but there must be justice when peace prevails."[4]

Several observers believe that these goals are, in fact, not compatible in the former Yugoslavia, at least not in the long term. Some Serbian leaders—including Milosevic—have been indicted by the International Criminal Tribunal in The Hague, but they represent only a fraction of the parties who may ever be brought to justice for atrocities. Moreover, the Dayton accords recognized borders defined by ethnic cleansing and later converted those who were seen as warmongers into latter-day peacemakers. This created problems when the crisis arose in Kosovo. In the aftermath of that war, the conventional wisdom was that it would be easier to administer and bring about reconciliation between the warring parties. Yet here, too, ethnic separation was the reality as peacekeepers were unable to contain the reciprocal cycle of vengeance between Serbs and Albanians, who continued to launch attacks on each other.

U.S. leaders have swung back and forth on the question of how to deal with the guilty. In 1992, former secretary of state Lawrence S. Eagleburger stated that Milosevic should be tried for crimes against humanity, and the former U.S. ambassador to Belgrade, Warren Zimmermann, called the Serbian leader "the slickest con man in the Balkans."[5] By 1995, however, U.S. policymakers argued that pragmatism requires putting aside those sentiments. "If you want to end the conflict, you

have to deal with Milosevic," observed one diplomat.[6] Thus, in merely three years, the politician most closely associated with starting the war and initiating ethnic cleansing had turned condemnation into praise for cooperating in the Dayton accords. Richard Holbrooke, who engineered the Bosnian agreement, singled out Milosevic, who negotiated on behalf of Bosnian Serb leaders who had been indicted by the UN tribunal. By clearing the way for talks to proceed, Milosevic became a pivotal figure on whom the success of U.S. diplomacy and the peace settlement then depended.[7]

"Should we not be pursuing some measure of principled or agreed consistency?" mused Stephen Rosenfeld in his assessment of this diplomatic ploy, which obviously raised eyebrows. Not necessarily, he concluded. "If this is what 'peace' takes, then pragmatism needs no defending," even if it "may be the enemy of the multiethnic ideal that appeals deeply to many Americans" and violates our sense of justice.[8] General Charles G. Boyd, the former deputy commander in chief, U.S. European Command, who served in Bosnia, argued that there is no room for justice in the Balkans because there are no clean hands. Balkan diplomacy, as he put it, meant "making peace with the guilty."[9] "A heartbreaking outcome," concurred columnist Jim Hoagland, "but the lesser of competing evils."[10]

Then came Kosovo. Opinions shifted again, this time coming full circle, back to Eagleburger's original view. There was no U.S. criticism of the indictment of Milosevic, even from those who had argued that there was no room for justice in the Balkans. Milosevic had finally pushed the limits of international tolerance, even for the so-called pragmatists. The collapse in May 2000 of the Sierra Leone peace agreement, which gave Foday Sankoh, a notorious warlord, a central role in the government and control over the country's diamond resources, stiffened the view that warmongers should be brought to justice. This time, oddly,

Table 1. Peacemaker Profiles

Conflict Managers	Democratizers
Inclusive approach	Exclusive approach
Goal is reconciliation	Goal is justice
Pragmatic focus	Principled focus
Emphasis on the process	Emphasis on the outcome
Particular norms and cultures of the societies in conflict	Universal norms endorsed by the international community
Assume moral equivalence	Insist on moral accountability
Conflict resolution is negotiable	Justice is not negotiable
Outside actors should be politically neutral	Outside actors cannot be morally neutral

it came to the point of putting other peace-keeping missions at risk. Sankoh's forces had refused to disarm and took five hundred UN peacekeepers hostage, resurrecting the violence in that country. In response, Senator Judd Gregg (R-N.H.), chairman of the Senate Appropriations Committee, announced that he would hold up disbursements of peacekeeping funds approved by Congress in 1999 that were designated for use in half a dozen hotspots around the world, to protest what he felt was the Clinton administration's capitulation to rebel forces who had not been brought to justice.

PEACE OR JUSTICE?

In some respects, the debate over Milosevic and Sankoh is reminiscent of the traditional debate during the Cold War between realists and idealists, in which the former argued for pragmatism over too rigid adherence to morality. But that would be rendering the contemporary debate too simplistically. Although there are parallels, the tension between peace and justice is not simply a replay of the usual tensions in foreign policy, such as the trade-offs that often must be made between human rights and resource dependence (for example, in Saudi Arabia) or human rights and trade (for

example, in China).[11] In these cases, the dilemma boils down to defining which conflicting interest should take precedence. The debate over peace strategies, by contrast, arises in areas in which the United States often has few strategic or economic interests, except peace itself. It is precisely on this issue—how best to pursue peace—that the differences arise.

The major traits of the two types of peacemakers are presented in table 1. This list is not intended to be exhaustive and, in specific instances, there may be agreement between the two types. In fact, during negotiations, diplomats may employ elements of both.[12] Moreover, it is important to note that it is not always easy to separate the "good guys" from the "bad guys" since all major parties in a conflict may be guilty of human rights violations, as in Afghanistan, and the policy alternatives between justice and achieving peace may in some cases overlap. Nonetheless, the distinctive approaches of the two types of peacemakers lead to sharply different approaches.

- Conflict managers tend to be inclusive, to neutralize those who might obstruct negotiations. Democratizers tend to be exclusive, to punish or purge human rights offenders. Simply put, conflict managers want to keep an eye on the "bad guys" while making them part of power-sharing arrangements;

democratizers want to sideline the "bad guys," holding them accountable for their crimes and excluding them from power.

- Conflict managers stress reconciliation as the primary goal of peace; democratizers stress justice as the primary objective of peace.
- Conflict managers focus on pragmatic, confidence-building steps to build trust among the leaders personally; democratizers focus on principles that institutionalize the rule of law to build trust in the system.
- Conflict managers are preoccupied with the process, emphasizing negotiating skills to facilitate dialogue and end the violence; democratizers are preoccupied with the outcome, emphasizing constitutionalism and the legal protection of political and civil rights.
- Conflict managers call attention to the importance of the particular cultural values of the societies in conflict; democratizers call attention to the importance of the universal values and standards of the international community.
- Conflict managers assume the moral equivalence of the belligerents and do not attribute blame; democratizers identify human rights offenders and hold them morally accountable.
- Conflict managers argue that conflict resolution is negotiable; democratizers argue that justice is nonnegotiable.
- Conflict managers insist on the political neutrality of outside actors as a necessary condition of effective mediation; democratizers insist that outside mediators cannot be morally neutral and must take sides, supporting those who stand for democracy and human rights.

In summary, conflict managers tend to concentrate on short-term solutions that address the precipitous events that sparked the conflict; above all, they seek a swift and expedient end to the violence. Democratizers tend to concentrate on longer-term solutions that address

the root causes of the conflict; they search for enduring democratic stability. The former see peace as a precondition for democracy; the latter see democracy as a precondition for peace.

In reality, these approaches rarely appear in a "pure" form but usually tilt in favor of one direction or the other. Illustrations of conflict resolution that tilted toward the conflict managers' model are Cambodia, Mozambique, Angola, and Sierra Leone. Elections were held as part of the peace agreement, but there has been, to date, no accountability for war crimes committed by the Khmer Rouge (although a Cambodian tribunal may change that), the Mozambique Resistance Movement (Renamo), the National Union for the Total Independence of Angola (UNITA), or the Revolutionary United Front (RUF) in Sierra Leone (although a new tribunal, the world's fourth such body, has now been set up), even though all these rebel groups were accused of atrocities. Basically, settlements in these countries represented power-sharing arrangements with weak democratic foundations. While they may have ended brutal wars, or tried to do so, they are unfinished agreements that are inherently fragile. The duration of the settlements rests primarily on the continued goodwill of the parties, not on the legal authority of the agreements they signed or the representative institutions they created.

Examples of conflicts settled along the lines of the democratizers' model are South Africa, Namibia, and El Salvador, where real political change included measures to ensure moral accountability and justice in the long term. Indeed, in these conflicts, recognition that the crises were basically human rights struggles, rather than mere power grabs by disgruntled interests, enabled real power sharing to go forward.

In some cases, the outcome tilts too far in one direction, leaving many issues unresolved. In Chile, for example, which returned to democracy in 1990, the military was included as a powerful partner in the government despite accusations of widespread human rights abuses by the security forces. As a result, Chile experienced two near-rebellions by Pinochet, who was allowed to serve as commander of the army until 1998. Moreover, only one military commander has been jailed for actions taken during seventeen years of military rule: Manuel Contreras, the former head of the secret police who ordered the 1976 assassination of ex–foreign minister Orlando Letelier in Washington. Fundamental issues of civilian-military relations and moral accountability for past crimes are not fully resolved, despite the Pinochet indictment. The "protected democracy" (as the junta defined it) or "imperfect democracy" (as President Eduardo Frei described it) failed to address human rights abuses committed during military rule by all military officers. This omission casts a long shadow on Chile's ability to complete its transition to a full democracy, though there are promising signs that in the wake of the Pinochet case the country is finally willing to confront its past.

In the immediate post–Cold War era, there appears to be an inclination toward solutions that favor the conflict managers' model. In Liberia, for example, Charles Taylor, who started the civil war, was part of the 1995 settlement, a feature that was widely regarded as enhancing the chances for peace. Previous cease-fires and negotiations collapsed, it was believed, largely because he had been left out. (Unfortunately, the 1995 agreement also collapsed.) In Ethiopia, where a battlefield solution created another power-sharing experiment based on ethnic lines, a Tigre-dominated government staged Nuremberg-type trials for members of the previous regime. But Ethiopia may not be stable either, because it has not succeeded in building confidence among all the major communal groups, particularly the Oromos, the country's largest ethnic group. Similar concerns surrounded the peace settlement in Sierra Leone, where the RUF claimed a significant portion of influential positions in the new government, a flaw that many felt

was a key weakness in the power-sharing agreement. International envoys continued to talk about reaching some kind of agreement with Sankoh, even after his capture following the collapse of the peace pact. Sankoh was replaced by another RUF leader, but a stable outcome is still uncertain.

Each conflict must be looked at on its own terms, and the solutions adopted must meet its particular needs. However, settlements built on solid democratic foundations have a far better chance of achieving sustainable security. While South Africa and Cambodia are considered "successes," for example, having made the historic transition from civil strife to peace through elections, their long-term prospects for a sustainable democratic peace are different.

South Africa adopted a power-sharing arrangement in conjunction with a new constitution negotiated by the internal parties themselves. Political violence diminished substantially following the first election held on the basis of universal suffrage, although fighting continued in KwaZulu-Natal, much of it tied to local issues. Nevertheless, the country moved forward, particularly on the question of balancing justice with reconciliation. On the justice side of the ledger, for example, former defense minister General Magnus Malan and ten other retired senior officials were arrested in connection with 1987 murders, and a Truth and Reconciliation Commission was launched with the power to offer amnesty (including to Malan and the others arrested) in exchange for disclosure of crimes. On the reconciliation side of the ledger, local elections that included proportional representation for minorities were successfully held only eighteen months after the general election, and racial reconciliation was a hallmark of the first government of national unity headed by Nelson Mandela. Clearly, democracy is taking root and is likely to endure in the post-Mandela era under the new president, Thabo Mbeki, in large part because South Africa is actively dealing with both justice and reconciliation.

Cambodia's settlement, by contrast, may be troubled for some time. Its power-sharing arrangement was largely forged by external parties, and it has failed to address the issue of accountability for two decades. As one observer noted after the agreement was reached, "the current leadership of the Khmer Rouge is identical, to a man, to that which produced the killing fields."[13] Though the threat from the Khmer Rouge diminished after the settlement, its violence continued for some time, it maintained a large stockpile of weapons and tens of millions of dollars safely deposited in banks in Thailand, and (as of this writing) none of its leaders have been prosecuted.[14] Hun Sen, a former Khmer Rouge officer himself, has not aggressively pursued accountability. The agreement reached with the United Nations to put surviving leaders who were responsible for more than a million deaths on trial in a hybrid judicial mechanism with no precedent leaves many questions unanswered, including whether Hun Sen will uphold the spirit of this arrangement and be committed to seeing justice done.

CONCLUSION

The tensions between justice and reconciliation are confronted not only by local players, but also by external parties who want to contain the costs of war. Diplomats, soldiers, relief workers, international organizations, nongovernmental organizations, and concerned private citizens each in their own way face common problems in today's internal wars: How do we deal with the guilty and achieve justice while advancing peace? Should diplomats rehabilitate warmongers? Should military assistance and training be given to professionalize militias that perpetrated human rights violations? Should relief workers feed refugees who committed atrocities? Should international organizations assume the moral equivalence of belligerents known to be responsible for war crimes? Should individuals involved in "track-two diplomacy"

(unofficial mediation or good offices provided by nongovernmental groups or individuals) legitimize leaders associated with violence in the name of healing? These are not easy questions, and they will not be answered soon.

As if these tensions were not enough, new dilemmas are confronting the international community. Majority populations in both East Timor and Kosovo wanted independence and had historical justifications for their positions. They were both victims of oppression. While the historical situations were different, the international community supported independence in East Timor, recognizing that anything short of self-determination could further destabilize Indonesia, while it supported an ambiguous autonomy for Kosovo, fearing that independence might spark a wider struggle for a Greater Albania and further fragment the Balkans. The outcome in East Timor is consistent with the position of the democratizers, while the Kosovo outcome is consistent with the position of the conflict managers. On what grounds, then, can oppressed groups expect their calls for self-determination to be recognized in the future? Which outcome is likely to be more stable in the long term? Which is likely to lead to sustainable security without military intervention? There are no universal criteria for recognizing or denying claims of self-determination and each case seems to cloud the picture even further.

Another new dilemma concerns the wrenching question of how to choose among competing crises. Why Kosovo but not Sierra Leone? On what grounds is the international community going to triage dying states? Democratizers have called attention to the inequity of international intervention in divergent regions; conflict managers point out that there are limits to what the international community can do. Strategic considerations come into play in the case of the United States, but this is a global issue, not a national one. There needs to be more thinking about the appropriate authorities and institutions that can respond to humanitarian emergencies. Otherwise, we will see more small wars engulfing entire regions, and we will continue to respond on a case-by-case basis, risking lives and treasure in ever-increasing levels.

One development working against advance planning is a new backlash or disillusionment that has arisen, first, from the number of peace-keeping burdens, many of which do not yield clear long-term successes, and, second, from what some have alleged as exaggerated claims of atrocities. In East Timor and Kosovo, fewer mass graves and bodies have been found than were expected. Whether this shows that intervention curtailed the violence before the death toll mounted or was caused by inflated stories of atrocities is uncertain. But the controversy highlights the political difficulties of dealing with questions of internal war and peace.

In spite of these difficulties, it is important to underscore that justice and democracy need not be antithetical. If both camps work together, they should be able both to resolve their differences and to address the new dilemmas that confront the international community.

For example, we need not impose, nor reasonably expect to have, instant democracy in postconflict situations. Democracy is reached in stages and will probably be more deeply rooted if introduced gradually, as long as the transition is credible, has the support of the majority of the people, and maintains the same political goal. By the same token, the sequence and timing of power-sharing arrangements and judicial inquiries can also be incremental, allowing cooling-off periods among combatants and the building of a culture that is based on fundamental human rights and the rule of law. Precisely how and when the twin goals of conflict resolution and democracy are reconciled, and which will take precedence under what circumstances, are issues that should be resolved on a case-by-case basis. However, experience thus far should serve as a cautionary tale. The pursuit of peace in the post–Cold War period will be an infinitely more complex and morally ambiguous process than anyone ever imagined it would be.

NOTES

1. The term "small wars" denotes internal disputes (within states) that do not affect geostrategic interests of the major powers or risk interstate warfare. However, the death rate in such conflicts often exceeds that of conventional wars. The term is therefore a misnomer, since the costs in human life are enormous. For more on this subject, see William J. Olson, special ed., "Small Wars," *Annals of the American Academy of Political and Social Science* (September 1995).

2. *SIPRI Yearbook 1995* (Oxford: Oxford University Press, 1995), 1.

3. *Strategic Assessment 1995: U.S. Security Challenges in Transition* (Washington, D.C.: Institute for National Strategic Studies, National Defense University, 1995), 14–15. The inventory of overseas military operations covered the period from March 1991 to October 1994.

4. President Bill Clinton in a speech at the University of Connecticut. "Clinton Pushes for U.N. War Crimes Tribunal," *Washington Post*, October 16, 1995, A4.

5. "Milosevic Transformed into Peace Talks Partner," *Washington Post*, September 24, 1995, A31.

6. Ibid.

7. See "Peace in the Balkans Now Relies on Man Who Fanned Its Wars," *New York Times*, October 31, 1995, A1.

8. Stephen S. Rosenfeld, "Ethnic Diplomacy," *Washington Post*, September 29, 1995, A27.

9. See Charles G. Boyd, "Making Peace with the Guilty," *Foreign Affairs* 74, no. 5 (September-October 1995): 22–38.

10. Jim Hoagland, "Bosnia: The Ego Factor," *Washington Post*, October 15, 1995, C7.

11. See the discussion on the tension between trade and human rights in "U.S. Shifts Goals in Markets of Asia," *Washington Post*, August 9, 1995, A14.

12. An example of using parallel tracks occurred in the Bosnian negotiations in Dayton, Ohio, when U.S. diplomats proposed to the three Bosnian presidents that suspected war criminals should be constitutionally barred from running for office in any part of the future Bosnian state. This demonstrated a U.S. commitment to prosecuting the Bosnian Serb leaders who had already been indicted. However, the proposal seemed to conflict with complaints made by the chief prosecutor of the tribunal, Judge Richard Goldstone, that the United States had not been forthcoming in handing over open-source intelligence information that could be used to build criminal cases against those suspected of atrocities. Moreover, while the proposed prohibition would prevent Bosnian Serb leaders Radovan Karadzic and General Ratko Mladic from running for office, it could also eventually apply to the Balkan leaders at the table if it were determined that any of them had command responsibility for massacres and killings. Then they, too, could be indicted as war criminals, as members of the Bush administration had originally recommended. But if the United States protected some Balkan leaders while indicting others, it would represent unequal justice, a clear decision of the mediators to take sides in the dispute and a factor that could inflame passions in Bosnia itself. See "War Crimes Prosecutor Says U.S. Information Insufficient," *Washington Post,* November 7, 1995, A19; and "U.S. Says It Is Withholding Data from War Crimes Panel," *New York Times,* November 8, 1995, A10.

13. Marvin C. Ott, as quoted in Janet E. Heininger, *Peacekeeping in Transition* (New York: Twentieth Century Fund, 1994), 2. For a further discussion of this issue, see United States Institute of Peace, "Accounting for War Crimes in Cambodia," *PeaceWatch,* October 1995, 1–3.

14. Ibid., 3.

45

Wilson's Ghost

The Faulty Assumptions of Postconflict Peacebuilding

Roland Paris

WHEN STUDENTS OF INTERNATIONAL RELA-
TIONS talk about Wilsonianism, they are usually
referring to the foreign policy of President
Woodrow Wilson and his thoughts about international affairs. One of Wilson's strongest
beliefs was that democracies were more peaceful than nondemocracies—more peaceful both
in their domestic affairs *and* in their relations
with other states. Democracy, he wrote, promotes the "ascendancy of reason over passion"
and promises "the supreme and peaceful rule
of counsel," or rational debate, which is the
recipe for "peace and progress" in political life.[1]
Drawing upon these ideas, Wilson insisted
that the only way to establish a durable peace
in Europe after World War I was to emanci-
pate the various nationalities that lived under
authoritarian rule and to make the conduct
of international relations more open to public
scrutiny and accountability. World peace, he
argued, "must be planted on the tested foundations of political liberty."[2]

There is an interesting parallel between
the period immediately after World War I and
the post–Cold War years. In both eras, the international community faced a security threat
to which it responded with a Wilsonian remedy. The leaders who gathered at the Palace
of Versailles in 1919 faced the challenge of preventing a recurrence of general war in Europe.
At Wilson's urging, they agreed to a number
of measures, including the creation of the
League of Nations and the liberation of national groups ruled by the Austro-Hungarian
and Ottoman Empires. Unless these nationalities, or "peoples," were permitted to exercise
their right of self-government, the U.S. president argued, unrequited grievances would
continue to foment new conflicts. Wilson insisted that any attempt to secure peace that
did not "recognize and accept the principle
that governments derive all their just powers
from the consent of the governed" was bound
to fail.[3]

At the end of the Cold War, the international community faced a different security challenge: the "apparently remorseless rise of ethnic and communal conflict" in many parts of the world.[4] In response to this challenge, Wilson's ideas about war and peace once again led the way. There was no grand Versailles-like conference to define the principles for conflict management in the post–Cold War era, but in practice many international organizations and actors began pursuing a broadly common strategy for dealing with states suffering from civil violence. The strategy centered around the assumption that "liberalizing" these states would promote domestic peace. In the political realm, liberalization meant democratization, or the transformation of war-shattered states into liberal democratic polities with periodic and genuine elections, constitutional limitations on the exercise of governmental power, and respect for basic civil liberties, including freedom of speech, assembly, and conscience. Democratization was expected to promote peace in these states, as the old saying goes, by replacing the breaking of heads with the counting of heads. In the economic realm, liberalization meant marketization, or the transformation of war-shattered states into market-oriented economies. Marketization was expected to create conditions that were most conducive to long-term economic growth, which would, in turn, also help to reduce tensions in these states.

This liberalization strategy was most noticeable in the "postconflict peacebuilding" operations that the international community conducted after the Cold War in several countries that were just emerging from civil conflicts. Peacebuilding operations seek, in the words of former UN secretary-general Boutros Boutros-Ghali, "to identify and support structures which will tend to strengthen and solidify peace in order to avoid a relapse into conflict."[5] Between 1989 and the turn of the century, twelve such operations were deployed to war-shattered states: Namibia, Angola,

Mozambique, Rwanda, Cambodia, Bosnia, Croatia, Nicaragua, El Salvador, Guatemala, Kosovo, and East Timor.[6] All these operations promoted free and fair elections, the construction of democratic political institutions, respect for civil liberties, and market-oriented economic reforms, on the assumption that these reforms would help consolidate peace in countries that were just emerging from civil wars.

The Wilsonian assumption, however, turned out to be flawed: international efforts to transform war-shattered states into liberal market democracies gave rise to unanticipated and destabilizing side effects in several of the states that hosted peacebuilding missions. In the most extreme cases, Angola and Rwanda, the liberalization process contributed to a resurgence of fighting, while in many other cases the deleterious effects of liberalization were less severe but still visible. The Wilsonian approach to peacebuilding, in other words, wrongly assumes that rapid liberalization in the immediate aftermath of civil conflicts will have a pacifying effect on the states undergoing these reforms.

If Wilsonianism is a faulty foundation for peacebuilding, as I argue in this chapter, then the states and international agencies that sponsor these operations have two options: either abandon the practice of postconflict peacebuilding or fix it. In my view, some form of peacebuilding remains necessary because civil wars, now the most prevalent form of armed conflict in the world, routinely inflict terrible suffering on civilian populations and often spill over into neighboring states. Although international intervention in most *ongoing* civil conflicts may not be practicable, as Richard Betts argues in another chapter of this volume, outside actors can and should assist war-shattered states in the implementation of peace agreements once local parties have agreed to stop fighting. Devising effective methods of preventing such conflicts from reigniting would be a modest and feasible first step toward addressing the larger problem of pervasive civil violence in the post–Cold War era. I therefore advocate fixing the peacebuilding mechanism, not abandoning it.

But what principles, other than those of Wilsonianism, should guide the design and conduct of peacebuilding operations? Instead of assuming that liberalization will moderate societal conflicts in war-shattered states, peacebuilders must recognize that efforts to transform these states into liberal market democracies can serve to exacerbate societal conflicts. Rapid liberalization is the wrong way to promote peace in the immediate aftermath of a civil war; instead, peacebuilders should delay liberalization until they have constructed political and economic institutions that are capable of managing the societal tensions that naturally arise from the process of democratization and marketization. During this period of institution construction, the international community should *curb* political and economic freedoms in war-shattered states, because failing to do so in the absence of effective domestic institutions risks renewed conflict. What is needed in the immediate postconflict period is not elections and democratic ferment but political stability and the establishment of an effective international administration over the territory. Successful peacebuilding, then, requires that the international community not shy away from acting "illiberally" by constraining civil liberties and political activity in the short run, in order to build the institutional foundations for more peaceful and democratic societies in the long run.

The first part of the chapter evaluates the Wilsonian approach to peacebuilding and describes, with reference to several recent peacebuilding operations, how unforeseen problems arising from the process of political and economic liberalization have impeded the consolidation of peace in several war-shattered states. The second part of the chapter sets out an alternative strategy, called "institutionalization before liberalization."

THE HAZARDS OF HASTY LIBERALIZATION

The long-term consequences of peacebuilding remain to be seen; it is still too early to conclude definitively that any operation launched since 1989 has been "successful" in establishing a stable and lasting peace. Some peacebuilding host states that are at peace today may slip back into war, while those that remain riven by internal violence may ultimately have a brighter future. But we can reach some conclusions, including the following: contrary to the expectations of the peacebuilders themselves, international efforts to transform war-shattered states into liberal market democracies have often exacerbated rather than moderated societal conflicts in many of the countries that hosted peacebuilding missions.

The mission in *Angola,* for example, illustrates the dangers of conducting elections in the immediate aftermath of a civil conflict. Angolans have been fighting one another (with periodic breaks) since the country gained independence from Portugal in 1975. Hopes for peace were raised in 1991 when international negotiators secured a cease-fire between the two warring parties—the Popular Movement for the Liberation of Angola (MPLA) and the National Union for the Total Independence of Angola (UNITA)—and concluded an agreement to hold multiparty elections in late September 1992. The elections took place on schedule under international supervision and were judged to be "generally free and fair." The results gave MPLA presidential candidate José Eduardo dos Santos 49.6 percent of the votes and UNITA's Jonas Savimbi 40.1 percent, thereby requiring a second round of elections.[7] Savimbi, apparently fearing defeat in the runoff election, rejected the first-round results and resumed a full-scale civil war in January 1993 that was "as bloody as anything seen since independence."[8] After several months of fighting, a new cease-fire was negotiated among the parties, but by the end of the decade Angola was at war again. The 1992 Angolan elections, in short, did not serve as a basis for reconciliation, but rather helped to rekindle war.[9] Several observers have suggested that the elections would have been less destabilizing if the parties had been fully disarmed before the elections were held, or if provision had been made for power-sharing arrangements after the elections so that the losing party would not be completely shut out of the new government.[10] Whether or not these measures could have averted violence, the fact remains that political liberalization had a negative effect on Angola's peace process—a result that was not anticipated by the peacebuilding agencies. Elections forced the latent conflict between Savimbi and dos Santos back out into the open, encouraging a climate of competition between the two parties that escalated into renewed fighting.

In *Rwanda,* plans for political liberalization and democratic elections also contributed to the collapse of a fragile peace. In August 1993 Rwanda's Hutu-led government signed a peace agreement with the Rwandan Patriotic Front, the Tutsi opposition group that had been fighting an insurgency war against the government since 1990. The agreement, dubbed the "Arusha Declaration," formally ended hostilities and initiated a peacebuilding process that involved power-sharing arrangements, integration of the two armies, the return of refugees, and a transition to democracy culminating in multiparty elections scheduled for 1995, all of which were to be supervised by the United Nations. Efforts to implement the agreement collapsed in April 1994, however, when Hutu extremists in the Rwandan government orchestrated a mass slaughter of Tutsi civilians that lasted three months and killed an estimated eight hundred thousand people. The genocide represented a conscious attempt by Hutu officials to thwart the planned elections and other elements of the Arusha Declaration that would have required them to share power with their adversaries.[11] Although responsibility for the killings rests with the perpetrators, plans for political liberalization in Rwanda not only failed to facilitate the reconciliation of the parties, but apparently helped to induce the genocide by threatening Hutu elements with the prospect of losing power.

Some commentators have argued that *greater* political liberalization could have averted the tragedy in Rwanda. A freer press, for example, might have countered and neutralized the inflammatory propaganda broadcast by Hutu leaders, which openly incited violence against Tutsi civilians in the period leading up to the genocide.[12] Jack Snyder and Karen Ballentine persuasively argue, however, that the partial liberalization of Rwanda's popular media, which followed the signing of the Arusha Declaration, actually helped to reignite the conflict: Although the Hutu regime monopolized the radio, the growth of a vibrant but irresponsible antigovernment press appeared to reinforce the Hutu extremists' determination not to share power with the opposition or permit the elections to proceed.[13] In other words, greater press freedom may have served to intensify, not moderate, civil violence in Rwanda.

In *Bosnia,* political liberalization also seems to have worked against the goal of building a lasting peace. The Dayton accords, signed in November 1995, provided for multiparty elections to newly created pan-Bosnian political institutions. The agreement also empowered the Organization for Security and Cooperation in Europe (OSCE) to certify whether "social conditions" for "effective" elections existed and then to administer the elections themselves.[14] Under considerable pressure from the United States, the OSCE certified on June 25, 1996, that these conditions existed, despite the warnings of many observers that elections held so soon after the cessation of hostilities would merely consolidate the power of extremist nationalists and reinforce Bosnia's de facto division into separate ethnic conclaves.[15] In fact, this is precisely what happened. The period leading up to the elections triggered renewed low-level conflict between the parties, and when elections were finally held in September 1996, nationalist political parties dominated the federal and regional legislative races.[16] As one observer in Sarajevo commented, even though elections were intended to create mechanisms that would facilitate cooperation among Bosnia's ethnic groups, they served instead to reaffirm "the ethnic fault lines that tore the country apart."[17] The well-respected International Crisis Group, chaired by former U.S. Senate majority leader George Mitchell, similarly concluded in October 1999 that one of the "greatest flaws" of the Dayton accords was the insistence on early elections, which resulted in most exclusionist nationalist leaders "cementing their power via the ballot box."[18] Because the elections consolidated and legitimized the power of exclusionist parties who were least willing to cooperate with their former adversaries, the task of building an effective central government in Bosnia became considerably more difficult. Although plans for an effective central government were an integral part of the Dayton plan—they were supposed to provide the "common roof" of political, judicial, and economic institutions that would permit the country's three communities to coexist peacefully in a single state—today these pan-Bosnian agencies exist "largely on paper."[19] Whether these new institutions will survive—or, perhaps more to the point, whether they will encourage the reconciliation of the Bosnian parties instead of stimulating further hostility—remains to be seen. It seems clear, however, that early elections in Bosnia served to drive the parties further apart, not to draw them closer together as was intended.

The effects of internationally sponsored democratization efforts in *Cambodia* are more difficult to discern. Peacebuilders arrived in the country in 1992 to implement a peace settlement that prescribed political liberalization as a remedy for the country's long-standing internal conflict, and although the weeks leading up to the UN-run elections in 1993 witnessed a sharp rise in political violence and killings that the United Nations peacebuilding mission was ill prepared to handle, election day was relatively calm.[20] One of the former belligerents in Cambodia, the notorious Khmer Rouge, refused to participate in the vote and resumed a low-intensity guerrilla campaign from its jungle redoubts along the Thai border. Two other parties—the Cambodian People's Party (CPP) and the National Front for an Independent, Neutral, Prosperous, and Cooperative Cambodia (FUNCINPEC)—formed a coalition government, but anticipation of the next set of elections in 1998 soon contributed to a deterioration in relations between the two parties. CPP leader Hun Sen was determined to weaken FUNCINPEC before the 1998 elections and launched a military campaign against top FUNCINPEC officials in July 1997. As one Western journalist who was in Cambodia during this period commented, "The only reason that there was a coup [in 1997] was that Hun Sen saw himself as being politically outflanked and realized that he would have lost the election [if he had not taken action]."[21]

Hun Sen's strategy was successful: the CPP won the election by a margin of more than 10 percent over FUNCINPEC, and Cambodia has since enjoyed greater peace than at any time in its modern history. But what role can we attribute to the electoral process in yielding this outcome? On the one hand, two national elections allowed Hun Sen to consolidate and legitimize his power, both within Cambodia and on the international stage, which has given him a freer hand to establish domestic peace by using the resources of the state to dominate and debilitate his political adversaries. On the other hand, elections simultaneously stimulated further competition and conflict among the Cambodian parties that, in the absence of such a crafty operator as Hun Sen, could have easily rekindled (and many times threatened to rekindle) the civil war. At the very least, then, the democratization process did not have the pacifying influence that the Cambodian peace agreement had anticipated. Rather, the elections exacerbated tensions among the formerly warring parties, though these tensions did not result in a return to continuous armed conflict.

In *El Salvador,* by contrast, it was the process of economic rather than of political liberalization that generated unexpected and destabilizing side effects. Twelve years of civil war between the national government and the Farabundo Marti Liberation Front ended with the signing of a UN-mediated peace accord in 1992. Since then, the formerly warring parties have remained at peace with each other, but El Salvador has experienced a sharp increase in criminal violence that many analysts link to the effects of economic liberalization programs that the government of El Salvador implemented at the behest of international donor agencies, including the World Bank and the International Monetary Fund (IMF). These agencies routinely impose conditions on the delivery of financial assistance to economically distressed countries. They almost always require that recipient states adopt market-oriented economic policies, such as eliminating government subsidies and price controls, privatizing state-owned enterprises, lowering barriers to the free flow of goods and services, and reducing government spending and public-sector employment—reforms that are intended to remove obstacles to the efficient operation of markets and thus to create conditions for sustainable economic growth within the recipient states. Although international donors have imposed conditions on aid disbursements for decades, only in the 1980s did the IMF pioneer "structural adjustment" lending, which requires recipient countries to undertake comprehensive programs of market-oriented reforms in exchange for international financial assistance. In addition, many of the world's largest national development agencies—including those of the United States, Canada, Japan, and the states of Western Europe—began to attach similar conditions to their bilateral aid programs during the 1980s and 1990s.[22]

While economic liberalization and structural adjustment programs aim at fostering economic growth in the long run, they can also cause social and economic dislocations in the short run, as changes in government policy affect different segments of a reforming country's population. For example, because economic liberalization and structural adjustment policies often call for reductions in redistributive payments to the poor, these reforms tend to exacerbate economic inequalities within societies, which can contribute to social tensions.[23] Some countries successfully weather this stormy transitional period; others do not.[24] But war-shattered states like El Salvador tend to be in a particularly precarious position, because the demands of maintaining domestic peace require them to moderate, not exacerbate, internal social divisions.

Here is what happened in El Salvador: Internationally mandated cutbacks in social spending and government employment had disproportionately detrimental effects on the less affluent members of society, particularly the rural poor and the urban working class. In the first six years of structural adjustment, El Salvador's "human development index"—a measure of general social welfare—fell by more than 10 percent, while the percentage of the urban population living in "extreme poverty" increased, and the income gap between the richest 20 percent and the poorest 20 percent of the population widened.[25] In the same period, the incidence of criminal violence soared. The annual number of violent deaths reported in the late 1990s far exceeded the estimated yearly figure during the civil war years, including both civilian and military deaths.[26] By some measures, El Salvador has the highest per capita homicide rate in the world, and a large proportion of Salvadorans themselves blame difficult economic conditions, including high unemployment, for this crime wave.[27] Many foreign analysts of

Salvadoran politics have reached the same conclusion.[28] If they are right, economic liberalization has not had a pacifying effect on El Salvador. The war is over, but the society has experienced greater violence than during the war years.

Nicaragua and *Guatemala* have experienced similar social unrest. Both countries hosted international peacebuilding missions after negotiating an end to their respective civil wars, pursued fiscal austerity programs at the behest of the international financial institutions, and experienced violent crime waves that were attributed to austerity-induced economic hardship. In Nicaragua, reductions in social expenditures that accompanied the introduction of structural adjustment in 1990 led to a 50 percent drop in real wages and a 31 percent decline in per capita food consumption between 1990 and 1992.[29] Hardship continued through the rest of the decade. Between 1992 and 1997, for example, per capita income in Nicaragua fell from $920 to $340.[30] Meanwhile, the income and the private consumption of a narrow segment of the urban population—specifically, those involved in the newly deregulated and thriving financial and export sectors—increased during this period of general impoverishment, thus widening the income gap, already one of the widest in the world, between the richest and poorest Nicaraguans.[31] This deterioration in living standards appears to have fueled an increase in criminal and gang-related violence. According to Nicaraguan government statistics, armed bands roaming the countryside were responsible for an estimated one thousand deaths and six hundred kidnappings between 1990 and 1996.[32] Even the army chief, charged with controlling the violence, linked the problem to the pervasiveness of poverty and unemployment.[33] Another factor contributing to the violence was the presence of large numbers of ex-combatants, who had few legitimate economic opportunities but ready access to automatic weapons. Former fighters from both sides in the civil war had been promised access

to land, credit, and other resources, but few received these benefits, in part because of continuing conflicts over land titles and because the Nicaraguan government was under pressure from international financial agencies to reduce spending.[34]

Commentators commonly point to the Central American states as peacebuilding "success stories." If the standard for success is whether armed conflict among the former belligerents has resumed, the operations in El Salvador, Nicaragua, and Guatemala were clearly successful, because the formerly warring parties are no longer fighting. If, however, the main goal of peacebuilding is to establish a *durable* peace by addressing the underlying sources of conflict in a country, these operations lose some of their sheen, because economic liberalization and structural adjustment policies have exacerbated the very conditions that have historically precipitated social unrest and revolutionary violence in Central America: namely, economic hardship and distributional inequalities. As the *New York Times* editorialized in March 1999, "The conflicts are over, but Central America's warring nations have essentially returned to the conditions of misery and inequality that caused the wars to begin with."[35] Even the World Bank, one of the sponsors of fiscal austerity, acknowledges that El Salvador's civil war was "largely related to extreme inequalities" within the society.[36] To the extent that the economic policies of peacebuilding have contributed to this state of affairs, these policies have not worked to promote a stable and lasting peace in Central America. On the contrary, they have perpetuated (and perhaps even worsened) socioeconomic conditions that are at the root of the region's long history of instability and violence. Indeed, if large-scale fighting does recur in El Salvador, Nicaragua, or Guatemala, the economic liberalization policies that are a central component of the prevailing peacebuilding paradigm will likely share part of the blame.

When observers point to peacebuilding successes, they also often cite *Namibia* and

Mozambique, both of which share borders with South Africa. Namibia was administered by South Africa until the UN-sponsored peacebuilding operation oversaw its transition to independence in 1989. Before that date, the South African–run government of Namibia had been at war with the South West African People's Organization (SWAPO), which demanded that South African forces and administrators leave the territory. Elections were held in 1989, in 1994, and again in 1999. SWAPO won each election and maintains a tight hold on power—so tight a hold that some observers are concerned that Namibia is in danger of becoming a one-party state.[37] Nevertheless, the country remains largely at peace (although Angola's war occasionally spills over the border into Namibia) and the Namibian economy is performing very well by African standards, having grown by 2 percent in 1998.

Mozambique is doing even better than Namibia economically. In December 1999 the governor of the Bank of Mozambique reported that the country's economy had grown by approximately 10 percent in 1999.[38] This followed several years of higher than 7 percent per annum growth.[39] Indeed, the International Monetary Fund, which oversaw the country's liberalization policies in the 1990s, presents Mozambique as a model for other developing states to emulate. Mozambique has also enjoyed the longest period of peace and stability in its twenty-five-year history as an independent state. The two formerly warring parties —the Mozambique Liberation Front (Frelimo) and the Mozambican National Resistance (Renamo)—succeeded in shifting their rivalry from the battlefield to the political arena in time for the UN-sponsored election in 1994. Frelimo, which had governed Mozambique throughout the civil war, won the 1994 election and a subsequent one in 1999. With some reluctance, Renamo gave up its armed struggle, accepted the results of the elections, and assumed the role of democratic opposition party.

How can we account for the apparent success of peacebuilding in Mozambique and Namibia when similar peacebuilding policies have produced less favorable results in so many other host states? There are two possible explanations, both related to the fact that Mozambique and Namibia are neighbors of South Africa. First, the civil wars in Mozambique and Namibia were not primarily indigenous or "home-grown" conflicts—they were not instigated or sustained chiefly by local parties. When outside support for these conflicts ceased, there was little domestic "demand" for continued fighting. As a result, the political environment for postconflict peacebuilding was less precarious in Mozambique and Namibia than in many other peacebuilding host states.

South Africa, the key foreign actor in Namibia's and Mozambique's wars, worked tirelessly during the apartheid era to install friendly regimes and eliminate its enemies in neighboring states. Namibia's conflict, for instance, was principally between SWAPO and the South African armed forces. When the South African army left Namibia at the country's independence, one of the warring parties effectively disappeared from the scene, and the principal impetus behind the conflict— South African control of the territory—ceased to exist. Perhaps for this reason, Namibia has been less vulnerable to the roiling effects of political and economic liberalization than have many other war-shattered states. In Mozambique, the warring groups comprised Mozambicans, not foreigners, but the conflict still lacked deep indigenous roots. Renamo, the rebel group, began its existence in 1975 as an instrument of Ian Smith's white-minority government of Rhodesia. Smith's goal was to overthrow Mozambique's black-led government, which criticized white minority rule in both Rhodesia and South Africa. To this end, Smith organized a group of Mozambican dissidents and expatriates, provided them with safe haven and arms on Rhodesian territory, and organized their guerrilla raids into Mozambican territory with the support of the Rhodesian army. As one scholar writes, Renamo was "simply a mercenary group of a white colonial army" and not a genuine "political movement" when it was founded.[40] After the fall of Ian Smith's government in 1979, Renamo was adopted by South Africa, and most of the group's membership and equipment were transferred to South African territory. The rebel organization still lacked a political program and received little encouragement from within Mozambique —when Renamo did eventually acquire territorial bases inside Mozambique, it maintained them primarily by terrorizing the local population. While the group did gain some measure of popular support in the latter stages of the war, which translated into electoral support in the postconflict period, the guerrilla campaign that Renamo conducted against the government—in other words, the war itself— was inspired and supported primarily by foreign, not domestic, actors.[41] Thus, when the rebel group lost its foreign backing in the early 1990s, there was virtually no popular support within Mozambique for a continuation of the armed struggle, which in turn reduced the danger of renewed fighting in the postconflict period.[42]

The second possible explanation for the relative stability of Namibia and Mozambique is, paradoxically, the economic benefits they experienced in the postconflict period from being adjacent to South Africa, a wealthy industrialized state. In particular, these economic benefits may have insulated Namibia and Mozambique from some of the more destabilizing effects of rapid economic liberalization that were prescribed by peacebuilding agencies. As noted earlier, economic liberalization policies are intended to create conditions for economic growth in the long run, but they often cause social and economic dislocations in the short run, which can work against the goal of consolidating peace in war-shattered states. Mozambique and Namibia were fortunate, as compared with many other war-shattered states,

because proximity to South Africa literally paid off in terms of access to foreign investment, which financed massive industrial and infrastructure projects, and contributed to economic expansion in both countries during the most precarious, early, period of economic reform.[43] Indeed, many observers attribute the relatively high rates of economic growth in Mozambique and Namibia to their success in obtaining foreign investment, the bulk of which has come from South Africa.[44] Nor is this investment a form of charity: South African investment has concentrated on projects that are designed to process South African raw materials into more valuable export commodities or to transport South African export goods through Namibian and Mozambican ports.

Whether the relative stability of Mozambique and Namibia is primarily due to the economic benefits of proximity to a wealthy industrialized state or to the fact that their now-terminated wars were not "home grown," the larger point to emphasize, for the purposes of this chapter, is that Mozambique and Namibia are *unlike* most of the states that have hosted peacebuilding missions, where the destabilizing effects of rapid political and economic liberalization appear to have exacerbated, not moderated, rivalries and tensions among formerly warring parties. Indeed, any lingering doubts about the dangers of rapid liberalization in war-shattered states should have been put to rest by the violence surrounding *East Timor's* independence referendum in August 1999. Many international observers predicted that there would be bloodshed leading up to the election and that anti-independence gangs supported by the Indonesian army would not allow East Timor to secede from Indonesia without a fight.[45] Despite these warnings, the United Nations proceeded with the referendum and deployed only a small number of foreign observers and security forces (three hundred soldiers and four hundred police) to oversee the elections, leaving the primary responsibility for protecting civilians to the

Indonesian army. As expected, violence escalated in the days leading up to the vote. When it became clear that the results of the referendum strongly favored secession, anti-independence groups that were backed by the army began a campaign of violence against their political opponents in which scores of civilians were killed and as many as five hundred thousand displaced from their homes. Many commentators criticized the international community's lack of foresight, including the editorial writers for France's *Le Monde* newspaper: "By taking on the organization of the referendum, the UN implicitly guaranteed not only the security of the voting operation, but also that of the voters in the aftermath of the poll. It has betrayed their trust; it has abandoned them without defense."[46] The United Nations did not authorize the deployment of a multinational force to restore peace and security in East Timor until two weeks after the vote, and foreign troops started arriving in large numbers only at the end of September. Why the United Nations failed to foresee this outcome, even after the organization's experience with abortive elections in other deeply divided societies such as Angola, remains unclear. According to Secretary-General Kofi Annan, "Nobody in his wildest dreams thought that what we are witnessing could have happened."[47] As I have argued in this chapter, however, the peacebuilding record alone should have provided Annan with good reasons to anticipate the problems that occurred in East Timor.

There is some evidence that the United Nations may be in the process of backing away from its previously unqualified support for the rapid democratization of war-shattered states. On October 19, 1999, two months after the debacle in East Timor, Annan hinted that the United Nations might not push for quick elections in Kosovo, where the international community had deployed yet another peacebuilding operation in June 1999. While not mentioning East Timor explicitly, Annan did express his wish that the United Nations not

repeat the "mistakes" made in Bosnia, where the results of the 1996 elections "legitimized those who caused the war."[48] These comments, and other recent developments, described in greater detail below, suggest that the United Nations may be discovering the limits of the Wilsonian approach to peacebuilding. Although the goals of the Kosovo mission include democratization and marketization—specifically, the establishment of "democratic self-governing institutions" and "the creation of a viable market economy"[49]—there appears to be a growing recognition that hasty liberalization can endanger the domestic peace of war-shattered states.

A PRESCRIPTION FOR BETTER PEACEBUILDING: TEMPORARY DIRECTORSHIP

In the long run, there are many good reasons to encourage war-shattered states to adopt the principles of liberal market democracy: values such as the rule of law, governmental accountability, freedom of speech, and other principles that are central to liberal democracy. The eventual democratization of war-shattered states extends the benefits of democracy to people who currently do not live in societies that honor these principles. Support for liberal democracy usually implies support for a market-oriented economic system as well. Although one may be able to imagine a state possessing a liberal democratic polity and a nonmarket economy, such a system has never existed and probably never could exist, owing to the difficulty of guaranteeing individual liberty in the political realm and simultaneously restricting it in the economic realm. As Sanford Lakoff writes, "economic freedom is as much a part of democracy as any other freedom."[50] Promoting capitalism in war-shattered states *in the long run* also appears to increase the prospects for economic growth in these societies: the second half of the twentieth century demonstrated that centrally planned and state-dominated development strategies (including not only Soviet-style communism but also import substitution strategies pursued in many parts of Latin America and Africa) produce lower levels of economic growth than market-oriented development strategies. Although debates continue over the appropriate balance between the market and the state in economic development, there is now widespread agreement that nonmarket-oriented economic policies, which do not allow the market to set prices and allocate scarce resources, are too inefficient to generate sustained economic growth. As T. N. Srinivasan put it, "ignoring or restricting the role of competitive markets is a sure prescription for failure to develop."[51]

All of these reasons for seeking to transform war-shattered states into liberal market democracies are sensible and valid; yet we have also noted that the process of political and economic liberalization can do more harm than good in states that have just emerged from civil wars. The dilemma, then, is to figure out how to set war-shattered states on the path toward liberal market democracy in the long term while avoiding the destabilizing effects of political and economic liberalization in the short term.

Resolving this dilemma will require peacebuilders to abandon the Wilsonian belief that liberalization necessarily fosters peace—an assumption that is not only empirically incorrect, as I have argued, but also theoretically defective. It overlooks the fact that both democracy and capitalism are built on a paradox: the notion that *encouraging* societal competition can, under the right conditions, limit the intensity of intercommunal tensions and conflicts. If this seems a strange observation, consider the following: Democracy requires a politically active and involved citizenry, or what some commentators call a vibrant "civil society," to counterbalance and scrutinize the power of the state and to provide channels for political expression.[52] An energetic civil society is characterized by a profusion of citizen organizations and associations, such as unions, churches, political parties and movements, cooperatives, neighborhoods, and schools of thought. The existence of these organizations presupposes sustained mobilization on the part of a large number of citizens and serves to stimulate political debate by catalyzing competing societal interests—a debate that, in turn, feeds into the policymaking process and, in principle, permits democratic governments to devise policies and practices that reflect shifting public attitudes. Thus, as Robert Dahl notes, "in democratic countries political conflict is not merely normal, it is generally thought to be rather healthy."[53] A similar paradox exists in the logic of capitalism, which encourages individuals and firms to pursue their own economic interests and compete for profits, on the grounds that doing so will allocate scarce resources most efficiently and thus benefit the entire society.

However, in order for the conflict-inducing effects of democracy and capitalism to produce peace and prosperity rather than war and impoverishment, one underlying condition must be present: there must be a rough balance between the intensity of existing conflicts in the society and the ability of that society's political and economic institutions to manage these conflicts. The logical flaw in the Wilsonian approach to peacebuilding lies in its failure to recognize that this condition of balance rarely exists in states that are just emerging from civil wars. War-shattered states typically suffer from deep and abiding societal conflicts (defined by the groups that were recently killing each other) and often possess few functioning political or economic institutions. Given these conditions, why should we expect the process of political and economic liberalization, which encourages societal competition, to have a stabilizing effect on war-shattered states? If anything, we should expect the opposite.

Elections, as we have seen, may reinforce rather than moderate conflicts by inducing populations to polarize along existing lines of social cleavage and by providing opportunities for opportunistic politicians to play upon intergroup hostilities in order to build a following. This problem is not limited to Angola, Rwanda, and Bosnia; other examples abound. In Sudan during the 1980s, elections provided an opportunity for fundamentalist groups such as the Islamic National Front to use the rhetoric of Islamic revival in order to gain political power, thereby reinforcing the ethnic, regional, and religious tensions that continue to fuel the country's civil war. In Ethiopia, an attempt by the Tigrean People's Liberation Front to exclude other ethnic parties from participating in the June 1992 elections elicited renewed violence from the excluded parties. In Sri Lanka, voters helped precipitate civil war in the 1950s by turning out in large numbers for radical Sinhala-based parties and Tamil-supported movements. In Papua New Guinea, democratic elections have invariably exacerbated communal tensions and fueled political violence in the country by reinforcing the tribalization of electorates. Elections have also served as an "indispensable prelude to civil war" in Nigeria, Uganda, Chad, and Pakistan.[54] What this suggests is that the adversarial politics of democratic elections can precipitate large-scale fighting in divided societies rather than providing a mechanism for the peaceful resolution of intercommunal differences.

Fortunately, the shortcomings of Wilsonianism also point toward possible solutions to the dilemma of placing war-shattered states on a long-term path to liberal democracy and market-oriented economics while avoiding the destabilizing effects of democratization and economic liberalization in the short term. If the principal impediment to successful liberalization in recently warring societies is the imbalance between the intensity of societal conflicts and the regulatory capacity of domestic institutions, then peacebuilders need to devise a strategy that helps to suppress societal conflict for as long as it takes to construct the foundations of effective political and economic institutions. Only then should peacebuilders gradually encourage free political and economic competition in the society. The goal of peacebuilding, therefore, should be to establish a stable and lasting peace by using "illiberal" methods in the short run—a kind of temporary tutelary directorship—in order to create the conditions for liberal market democracy in the long run.

In the rest of the chapter, I lay out the principal elements of this alternative approach to peacebuilding, which I label "institutionalization before liberalization." First I shall describe a political and economic strategy; then I will recommend organizational guidelines for future peacebuilding operations.

Political Strategy

The central goal of the political strategy should be to build effective governmental institutions while promoting the growth of moderate, cross-factional political parties and curbing the power of extremist parties. This is what peacebuilders have attempted to do in Bosnia: as the Bosnia mission has progressed, international civilian authorities have grown bolder in asserting their rights under the Dayton accords to remove from office local officials who obstruct the peace process. In November 1999, for example, the international community's "high representative" in charge of monitoring the implementation of the Dayton accords, Wolfgang Petritsch, dismissed nine Serbs, seven Muslims, and six Croats from office, including cantonal ministers, a governor, members of parliaments, heads of municipalities, mayors, and housing officials, on the grounds that they had "violated the law and obstructed peace implementation."[55] International officials have also issued administrative fiats on issues such as housing, tariff laws, border police, and the design for a common flag, thus establishing some of the institutional foundations of the Bosnian state.

This movement toward more assertive foreign rule is a positive development in Bosnia, where obstructionist local politicians have blocked the implementation of many aspects of Dayton. But it may turn out to be too little, too late. The international community has been reluctant to compel local parties to live by the rules of Dayton, and the result has been that important goals such as the repatriation of refugees and the creation of effective and functioning national institutions—goals that are essential to the restoration of a pluralist and peaceful Bosnian state—remain largely unmet, while picayune matters like license plates receive a great deal of attention. Part of the problem is that international officials do not directly control Bosnia's political institutions; rather, they monitor the performance of locally run institutions. As Ivo Daalder and Michael Froman point out, one result of this arrangement is that "international civilian authorities in Bosnia possess little more than the power of persuasion."[56] UN officials faced a similar problem in Cambodia in the early 1990s. On paper, they had the power to exercise "direct supervision and control" over the actions of the Cambodian government, but in practice the governmental bureaucracy was too partial to the regime in power to be "controlled" by international officials, and the United Nations never attempted to exercise its full powers in this area. In order to create political institutions that are effective (in the sense that they can make authoritative decisions) and are sufficiently neutral and professional to channel societal conflicts though a peaceful policymaking process, the international community needs to *rebuild* the governmental institutions of war-shattered states from scratch and, at least initially, exert direct control over these new institutions by staffing them primarily with foreign officials.

At the same time, peacebuilders should be promoting the growth of moderate, cross-factional political parties and constraining the activities of groups that are not committed to building cooperation across factional lines. To some extent this is already being done in Bosnia and Kosovo. In Bosnia, not only have recalcitrant officials been dismissed, but perceived moderates such as Serbian politician Milorad Dodik have received financial and rhetorical backing from the international community. In Kosovo, the OSCE established a political party "service center" in Pristina to promote the development of "mature, democratic political parties" by providing office space, basic infrastructure, and communication facilities. These measures, which are very assertive by the standards of other peacebuilding missions, still do not go far enough. Rather than merely offering assistance to moderate parties and occasionally dismissing local officials who blatantly oppose the goals of the peacebuilding mission, international administrators should require political parties to secure a license, without which they may not sponsor large public gatherings or be eligible for governmental positions. In order to obtain a license, parties should be obliged to have members from all of the formerly warring groups and to espouse cross-factional compromise and coexistence as a principal goal. After constructing and staffing new political institutions, international administrators could gradually open the doors of governmental power to representatives of political parties that have met these criteria in order to begin the process of transferring governmental authority back to local control and to build up a coterie of local officials with experience and training in public administration.

Similarly, before liberalizing popular media in war-shattered states, peacebuilders should establish mechanisms to limit the promulgation of inflammatory propaganda, including ethnic "hate media." In Rwanda, for example, radio broadcasts by Hutu extremists on Radio Rwanda and Radio-télévision libre des mille collines (RTML) are considered by many observers to have played a key role in inciting ethnic hatred and initiating the genocide. As Snyder and Ballentine argue, international agencies can support "media that strive to attract a politically and ethnically diverse audience, invite the expression of various viewpoints, and hold news stories to rigorous standards of objectivity."[57] The goal of such policies would be to reduce the danger of malevolent and erroneous journalism sparking renewed conflict in the fragile period following the cessation of hostilities. As in the case of political parties, television and radio stations should be licensed (indeed, this is currently the practice in Kosovo). In cases where incendiary broadcasts or publications appear to be inciting large-scale violence, international authorities should have both the means and the mandate to block the distribution or transmission of these messages, as they have in some cases in Bosnia.

Elections can be delayed until moderate, cross-factional political parties and media outlets are well established and moderate candidates are likely to gain widespread electoral support, as reflected in opinion polls conducted by international agencies. Even after moderate parties and candidates have become viable contenders, peacebuilders would be well advised to design electoral rules that reward moderation, not extremism; in particular, parties or candidates that advocate violence during an election campaign must be immediately disqualified. Successful candidates should also be required to secure a minimum level of support from each of the formerly warring groups before being declared victors in an election. Presidential votes in Nigeria, for example, have in the past required presidential aspirants to win not only an absolute majority of ballots cast nationally, but at least 25 percent of votes cast in no fewer than two-thirds of the nineteen states—a requirement that encouraged serious candidates to "reach out and conciliate and propitiate the interests of groups other than the ones [that they were] accustomed to appealing to."[58] If this kind of arrangement had existed in Bosnia from 1996 onward, national elections might have produced legislators who advocated tolerance and compromise rather

than intolerance and intransigence and facilitated the rise of cross-factional political movements instead of reinforcing the power of the nationalist parties that fought the war.

Even after a new government is formed through democratic elections, international peacebuilders can retain partial control over certain government functions that are critical to the peace process, including arrangements for future elections, the selection of judges, the training and retraining of local police forces, communications and transportation policy, and school curricula. Indeed, international administration of the planning and conduct of future elections may help to reassure local parties of the fairness of the electoral arrangements and avoid situations in which the parties struggle among themselves for control of these arrangements. Having peacebuilders select judges would ensure that appointees are politically moderate and impartial and willing to uphold the rule of law without bending to political interference. Moreover, international administration of communications and transportation policy can help to promote cross-factional interchange in both the economic and cultural spheres; and some control over school curricula can be a useful method of encouraging intercommunal tolerance in future generations.

Economic Strategy

As noted earlier, economic liberalization programs promoted by the World Bank and the IMF under the rubric of structural adjustment have exacerbated instabilities in some war-shattered states by increasing poverty and widening distributional inequalities. The relationship between structural adjustment and poverty has been a controversial topic in the development field for more than a decade; much of the controversy centers around the question of whether structural adjustment programs increase or decrease poverty levels in the long run. Some scholars argue that structural adjustment creates conditions for economic growth over the long term and the eventual reduction of poverty, while others deny that it benefits the poor in the long run. There is widespread agreement, however, that *in the short term* such policies tend to increase poverty and income inequalities in societies undergoing these reforms. This is what makes these reforms problematic for countries just emerging from civil conflicts: countries are most vulnerable to the destabilizing effects of rapid economic liberalization in the immediate postconflict period, yet this is exactly the period in which economic liberalization policies are most likely to produce destabilizing effects.

International lenders and financial institutions could do a better job of tailoring their economic reform programs to the particular needs and fragilities of war-shattered states. Devoting greater resources to reducing distributional inequalities, for example, would likely reduce the conflict-inducing effects of market-oriented adjustment. Furthermore, greater attention to poverty and inequality may also enhance the prospects for economic growth. Several recent econometric studies have concluded that societies with more equitable distributions of income tend to experience higher levels of economic growth over the long term.[59] However, even if the opposite were true—if efforts to narrow the gap between rich and poor ultimately reduced the rate of economic growth—the trade-off would be sensible if it reduced the risk of renewed civil war.

In a commendable effort to soften the effects of economic reform for the most vulnerable populations, the World Bank and the IMF have supported social "safety net" funds in a number of states undergoing structural adjustment—funds that have, among other things, subsidized housing, education, and health care projects for the poor. As the Danish government concluded in 1995, however, these funds are "of little financial significance compared to the overall magnitude of adjustment lending." They are underresourced, in part, because the international financial institutions fear that larger social funds would diminish the effectiveness of adjustment by diverting resources away from more fundamental structural reforms. So, while the World Bank and the IMF have become more sensitive to the social effects of adjustment, they have not substantially altered their established adjustment model, which emphasizes the importance of *rapid* economic reform, or what is sometimes called "shock therapy." As long as international lenders emphasize rapid liberalization and macroeconomic balance as the primary goals of economic adjustment, the problems associated with short-term increases in poverty and income inequality will continue. These problems may be tolerable, and surmountable, for many developing countries, but they pose a particular danger to war-shattered states, which are often in no condition to withstand economic "shock therapy."

War-shattered states merit a special adjustment model—a *peace-oriented* adjustment model—that should be based on the following principles. First, economic liberalization should be implemented more gradually than in other developing states in order to reduce the destabilizing effects of these reforms by spreading them out over time. Second, peacebuilders should reduce the prevailing emphasis on market rationality and macroeconomic balance and increase the emphasis on poverty reduction and distributional equity, particularly in countries where civil conflict is associated with socioeconomic disparities in the population. For instance, food subsidies, which can help maintain the general health of a population and eliminate the most extreme forms of poverty, should be considered in the immediate postconflict period, even at the cost of delaying adjustment in the agricultural sector. Third, in order to stimulate renewed economic activity and employment, internationally sponsored reconstruction projects should take precedence over demands for fiscal austerity and disinflation in the short term. To date, international financial institutions have insisted on delaying reconstruction programs or extended them over longer periods to reduce their inflationary effects. But war-shattered states should be permitted to generate higher levels of inflation in exchange for economic growth in the short run instead of requiring vulnerable groups in these states to suffer through an artificially induced economic recession. Finally, the construction of domestic financial institutions and regulatory and judicial structures, including bankruptcy laws and functioning courts, is a precondition for the successful operation of a market economy. Delaying economic liberalization in war-shattered states can buy time during which peacebuilders can create these institutional structures.

Organizational Issues

In order to implement the political and economic strategy that I have outlined, the organization of peacebuilding operations needs to be changed in at least two ways. First, missions must remain in place for a longer period than has been typical; most operations have lasted from one to three years, with the exception of the Bosnia mission, which at this writing has existed for just over four years. The termination of peacebuilding operations should be linked to the accomplishment of specific policy objectives, not to dates; if conditions are not suitable for holding elections, they should be delayed. The duration of each mission will vary according to local conditions. These longer missions—ten years is probably a minimum in most circumstances—will admittedly be more costly, but scrimping on peacebuilding is false economy if fighting resumes because operations have failed to create conditions for durable peace.

A second requirement is greater central coordination of peacebuilding operations. Given the number and diversity of international agencies that participate in these operations, coordination has—not surprisingly, perhaps —been a problem. Peacebuilding agencies have often worked at cross-purposes. In El

Salvador and Mozambique, for example, while the United Nations was urging local governments to increase spending on peacebuilding-related programs, the IMF was demanding fiscal restraint. It is also true that few independent or quasi-independent organizations are eager to relinquish their independence; nongovernmental organizations, in particular, are often reluctant to be associated with governmental and intergovernmental agencies in field operations. Nevertheless, some mechanism to improve coordination will be required before the "institutionalization before liberalization" strategy that I have proposed can be implemented.

An effective way to accomplish this goal may be to establish an explicit division of labor among peacebuilding agencies and identify lines of authority in advance of a mission's deployment. This is what the international community is currently attempting in Kosovo, where the UN secretary-general's special representative has the formal authority "to coordinate the activities of all United Nations agencies and other international organizations" that are participating in the mission.[60] In practice, however, there is so much overlap and conflict in the activities of the various peacebuilding agencies in Kosovo that the mission is being "undermined by the international civilian agencies that are supposed to serve it."[61] One difficulty is the sheer number of actors involved in the operation—an "impenetrable tangle of international organizations" in the words of one observer.[62] This problem is compounded by normal interagency rivalries and by the fact that many of these organizations possess significant resources—both financial and human —that they can deploy at their own discretion. Even clear directives from the national governments that fund these agencies have failed to overcome these organizational hurdles.

Bolder measures are necessary. Perhaps the best way to surmount the coordination problem would be to centralize not only the management but also the execution of peacebuilding in the hands of a new international agency that specializes in conducting postconflict peacebuilding missions and administering war-shattered states. This new agency could take over many of the tasks now performed by the myriad organizations engaged in peacebuilding, reducing the prospect of interagency turf battles. Further, in order to tap into the expertise of the many organizations that already operate in many fields of peacebuilding, such as the resettlement of refugees, these existing organizations should be required by leading states to second personnel to the new international peacebuilding agency. Just as the colonial powers of yesteryear created specific agencies dedicated to administering foreign territories, the international community today should establish a single authority to conduct the more benign and altruistic form of international trusteeship that current conditions demand. This appears to be the most promising solution to the problem of coordinating the activities of peacebuilding agencies in the field.

CONCLUSION

The Wilsonian approach to peacebuilding places too much faith in the pacifying effects of liberalization. Democratization and marketization engender societal competition and conflict, which can pose a danger to the domestic peace of states that are emerging from civil wars. To minimize these dangers, peacebuilders should pursue a strategy of "institutionalization before liberalization." By constructing a firm institutional foundation for democratic politics and market-oriented economics in war-shattered states, peacebuilders can lay the groundwork for a smoother and less hazardous transition to democracy and capitalism and ultimately for a more stable peace.

Pursuing this strategy will require international peacebuilding agencies and their principal backers—the industrialized democracies—to behave in ways that may be viewed as illiberal or even imperialistic, but this, it seems to me, is the short-term price of an effective peacebuilding policy. Unless peacebuilders are willing to govern with a firmer hand in the immediate postconflict period—restricting political and economic freedoms and political activity while building effective domestic institutions—we can expect the problems of recent peacebuilding operations to recur in future missions.

NOTES

1. Woodrow Wilson, "The Modern Democratic State," in *The Papers of Woodrow Wilson*, vol. 5, ed. Arthur S. Link (Princeton, N.J.: Princeton University Press, 1968), 90.

2. Woodrow Wilson, quoted in Thomas J. Knock, *To End All Wars: Woodrow Wilson and the Quest for a New World Order* (Princeton, N.J.: Princeton University Press, 1992), 121.

3. Woodrow Wilson, Second Inaugural Address, March 15, 1917, quoted in Michla Pomerance, "The United States and Self-Determination: Perspectives on the Wilsonian Conception," *American Journal of International Law* 70, no. 1 (January 1976): 2.

4. Adam Roberts, "Ethnic Conflict: Threat and Challenge to the UN," in *Ethnic Conflict and International Security*, ed. Anthony McDermott (Oslo: Norwegian Institute of International Affairs, 1994), 6.

5. Boutros Boutros-Ghali, *An Agenda for Peace* (New York: United Nations, 1992), 32, par. 55.

6. I exclude Somalia from this list because the fighting there did not stop and a *postconflict* operation never started; I also exclude Haiti because the operation there did not follow a conflict.

7. Alex Vines, *Angola and Mozambique: The Aftermath of Conflict*, Conflict Studies Series, no. 200 (London: Research Institute for the Study of Conflict and Terrorism, May-June 1995), 3.

8. Anthony W. Pereira, "The Neglected Tragedy: The Return to War in Angola, 1992–93," *Journal of Modern African Studies* 32, no. 1 (March 1994): 17.

9. See Marina Ottaway, "Democratization in Collapsed States," in *Collapsed States: The Disintegration and Restoration of Legitimate Authority*, ed. I. William Zartman (Boulder, Colo.: Lynne Rienner, 1995), 236.

10. See, for example, Jim Wurst, "Mozambique: Peace and More," *World Policy Journal* 11, no. 3 (fall 1994): 79–80; Bertram, "Reinventing Governments," 398–399; Vines, *Angola and Mozambique*, 8; and Pereira, "Neglected Tragedy," 15–16.

11. Bruce D. Jones, "Humanitarian Intervention in Rwanda, 1990–94," *Journal of International Studies* 24, no. 2 (summer 1995): 243; and Matthew J. Vaccaro, "The Politics of Genocide: Peacekeeping and Disaster Relief in Rwanda," in *UN Peacekeeping, American Politics, and the Uncivil Wars of the 1990s*, ed. William J. Durch (New York: St. Martin's Press, 1996), 372.

12. This argument is made in Human Rights Watch, *Slaughter among Neighbors: The Political Origins of Communal Violence* (New Haven, Conn.: Yale University Press, 1995).

13. Jack Snyder and Karen Ballentine, "Nationalism and the Marketplace of Ideas," *International Security* 21, no. 2 (fall 1996): 30–34.

14. Annex 3, Article 1 (2) of the Dayton accords, reprinted in *International Legal Materials* 35, no. 1 (January 1996): 115.

15. See, for example, Anthony Borden's prediction in Anthony Borden, Slavenka Drakulic, and George Kenny, "Bosnia's Democratic Charade," *Nation*, September 23, 1996, 14; and Human Rights Watch/Helsinki, "Bosnia-Hercegovina: A Failure in the Making: Human Rights and the Dayton Agreement," *Human Rights Watch/Helsinki Report* 8, no. 8 (June 1996): 2.

16. Chris Hedges, "Bosnia's Nationalist Parties Dominate Election Results," *New York Times*, September 22, 1996, 12.

17. Colin Soloway, "Bosnia's Freely Elected Fanatics: And the Winner Is . . . Ethnic Hatred," *U.S. News and World Report*, September 30, 1996, 48.

18. International Crisis Group, *Is Dayton Failing? Bosnia Four Years after the Peace Agreement* (Sarajevo: International Crisis Group, October 1999), 2, 11.

19. Ibid., 3.

20. James A. Schear, "Riding the Tiger: The United Nations and Cambodia's Struggle for Peace," in *UN Peacekeeping, American Politics, and the Uncivil Wars of the 1990s*, 174; and Mark Plunkett, "The Establishment of the Rule of Law in Post-Conflict Peacekeeping," in *International Peacekeeping: Building on*

the Cambodian Experience, ed. Hugh Smith (Canberra: Australian Defence Studies Centre, 1994), 71.

21. Nate Thayer, correspondent for the *Far Eastern Economic Review*, in a personal communication with the author, May 15, 1998.

22. On the evolution of development lending policies, see John Rapley, *Understanding Development: Theory and Practice in the Third World* (Boulder, Colo.: Lynne Rienner, 1996).

23. For example, Samuel A. Morley, *Poverty and Inequality in Latin America: The Impact of Adjustment and Recovery in the 1980s* (Baltimore: Johns Hopkins University Press, 1995).

24. See John Walton and David Seddon, *Free Markets and Food Riots: The Politics of Global Adjustment* (Oxford: Blackwell, 1994).

25. James K. Boyce and Manuel Pastor, Jr., "Macroeconomic Policy and Peace Building in El Salvador," in *Rebuilding Societies after Civil War: Critical Roles for International Assistance*, ed. Krishna Kumar (Boulder, Colo.: Lynne Rienner, 1997), 304; Jack Spence et al., *Chapultepec: Five Years Later: El Salvador's Political Reality and Uncertain Future* (Cambridge, Mass.: Hemisphere Initiatives, 1997), 34; Development Group for Policy Alternatives (DGPA), *Structural Adjustment and the Spreading Crisis in Latin America* (Washington, D.C.: DGPA, 1995); and Elisabeth Wood and Alexander Segovia, "Macroeconomic Policy and the Salvadoran Peace Accords," *World Development* 23, no. 12 (December 1995): 2085.

26. Ken Guggenheim, "Rising Violence Disturbs Post–Civil War Peace," Associated Press, June 14, 1998; and Economist Intelligence Unit, *Country Profile: El Salvador, 1997–98* (London: Economist Intelligence Unit, 1997), 71.

27. Tommie Sue Montgomery, "Constructing Democracy in El Salvador," *Current History* 96, no. 607 (February 1997): 61.

28. For example, Jenny Pearce, "From Civil War to 'Civil Society': Has the End of the Cold War Brought Peace to Central America?" *International Affairs* 74, no. 3 (July 1998): 587–615; and Kimbra L. Fishel, "From Peace Making to Peace Building in Central America: The Illusion versus the Reality of Peace," *Small Wars and Insurgencies* 9, no. 1 (spring 1998): 32–49.

29. William I. Robinson, *Promoting Polyarchy: Globalization, U.S. Intervention, and Hegemony* (New York: Cambridge University Press, 1996), 251–252.

30. Mark Everingham, "Neoliberalism in a New Democracy: Elite Politics and State Reform in Nicaragua," *Journal of Developing Areas* 32, no. 2 (winter 1998): 251.

31. W. Thiesenhusen and S. Hendrix, "Poverty and Progress: The Cases of El Salvador and Nicaragua," *Harvard International Review* 17, no. 2 (spring 1995): 59; Mario Arana, "General Economic Policy," in *Nicaragua without Illusions: Regime Transition and Structural Adjustment in the 1990s,* ed. Thomas W. Walker (Wilmington, Del.: Scholarly Resources, 1997), 84; and Rose J. Spalding, "Nicaragua: Poverty, Politics, and Polarization," in *Constructing Democratic Governance: Mexico, Central America, and the Caribbean in the 1990s,* ed. Jorge I. Dominguez and Abraham F. Lowenthal (Baltimore: Johns Hopkins University Press, 1996), 21.

32. Reuters, "Nicaraguan Army Chief Gives Gangs Ultimatum," January 28, 1997.

33. Joaquin Cuadra (the army chief), quoted in ibid.

34. James Dunkerly, *The Pacification of Central America: Political Change in the Isthmus, 1987–1993* (New York: Verso, 1994), 58.

35. "Peace and Poverty in Central America," *New York Times,* March 11, 1999, A30.

36. World Bank, *Poverty Reduction and the World Bank: Progress in Fiscal 1994* (Washington, D.C.: World Bank, 1995), 62.

37. Victor Mallet, "Nujoma's Third Term Makes Namibia's Democracy Look Third Rate," *Financial Times* (London), December 1, 1998, 6.

38. "Mozambique Economy Growing at 10 Percent," *Panafrican News Agency,* December 30, 1999.

39. Kurt Schiller, "A Tale of Two Countries," *Boston Globe,* December 6, 1999, A2.

40. Malyn Newitt, *A History of Mozambique* (Indianapolis: Indiana University Press, 1995), 564.

41. Scholars have disagreed about the sources and depth of support for Renamo within Mozambique; for an overview of this debate, see Tom Young, "From the MNR to RENAMO: Making Sense of an African Counter-Revolutionary Insurgency," in *The Dynamics of Change in Southern Africa,* ed. Paul B. Rich (New York: St. Martin's Press, 1994), chap. 7. My own view is that (1) Mozambique's civil war was primarily, though not entirely, a foreign imposition on the country; (2) Renamo did gain a measure of popular support within Mozambique, but it did so primarily by threatening its own "supporters"; (3) available evidence suggests that there was little popular support for Renamo's guerrilla war—rather, the vast majority of ordinary Mozambicans wanted to have nothing to do with the conflict; and (4) Renamo would not have posed a serious military, or even political, threat to the government without Rhodesian and South African prodding and material assistance. For further discussion, see James Ciment, *Angola and Mozambique: Postcolonial Wars in Southern Africa* (New York: Facts on File, 1997); and William Finnegan, *A Complicated War: The Harrowing of Mozambique* (Berkeley: University of California Press, 1992).

42. By contrast, although the insurgencies in El Salvador, Nicaragua, and Guatemala also received large amounts of foreign assistance, these guerrilla movements represented important constituencies of disaffected people within each of the Central American societies, who were themselves reacting to socioeconomic conditions inside these countries. Because these conditions and the disaffected constituencies have continued to exist in Central America, even after the formal termination of armed conflict, we should not be surprised that Namibia and Mozambique have experienced relatively fewer problems of domestic unrest in the postconflict period relative to Central America.

43. In Mozambique, foreign investment has been concentrated in the so-called Maputo Development Corridor—a strip of Mozambican territory that links Johannesburg and its nearest ocean port, which happens to be Maputo, the capital of Mozambique—and has included not only road and railway improvement, but the construction of hydroelectric generation plants, an aluminum smelter plant valued at $1.3 billion, and a planned iron and steel production project that will use South African and Mozambican inputs and will cost an estimated $2.4 billion to build. Namibia has also benefited from South African investment in infrastructure projects, including port and roadway improvements that were intended to facilitate exports to Europe and the Americas.

44. For example, Tony Hawkins, "Private Investment Key to Impressive Growth," *Financial Times,* October 18, 1999, 2.

45. Paul Knox, "UN Shortcomings Thrown into Spotlight: Earlier Action Could Have Averted Bloodbath, UNAMET Official Says," *Globe and Mail*

(Toronto), September 14, 1999; "Timor-Oriental: l'ONU Savait," *Le Monde,* September 14, 1999.

46. "L'ONU Defiée," *Le Monde,* September 9, 1999.

47. Quoted in Sander Thoenes and Minh Vo, "Peacekeepers Were Finally Invited to East Timor Sunday; But Has the UN Been Naïve?" *Christian Science Monitor,* September 13, 1999, 1.

48. Quoted in Jane Perlez, "Annan Says Quick Elections in Kosovo May Not Help Tensions," *New York Times,* October 20, 1999.

49. UN Security Council Resolution 1244 (June 10, 1999), article 11(a); and *Report of the Secretary-General on the United Nations Interim Administration in Kosovo,* UN Security Council document S/1999/779 (July 12, 1999), para. 105.

50. Sanford Lakoff, *Democracy: History, Theory, Practice* (Boulder, Colo.: Westview Press, 1996), 6.

51. T. N. Srinivasan, "Democracy, Markets and Development" (paper presented at Yale University, April 4, 1997).

52. On the importance of an active "civil society" for democratic governance, see Seymour Martin Lipset, "The Social Requisites of Democracy Revisited," *American Sociological Review* 59, no. 1 (February 1994): 12; and Robert D. Putnam, *Making Democracy Work: Civic Traditions in Modern Italy* (Princeton, N.J.: Princeton University Press, 1993).

53. Robert A. Dahl, *Democracy, Liberty, and Equality* (Oslo: Norwegian University Press, 1986), 14.

54. Donald L. Horowitz, *A Democratic South Africa? Constitutional Engineering in a Divided Society* (Berkeley: University of California Press, 1991), 97. For further reading on the relationship between elec-

tions and violence in deeply divided societies, see Georg Sorenson, "Development as a Hobbesian Dilemma," *Third World Quarterly* 17, no. 5 (December 1996): 903–916; and Marina Ottaway, *Democracy and Ethnic Nationalism: African and Eastern European Experiences* (Washington, D.C.: Overseas Development Council, 1994).

55. "The High Representative's Television Address on Dismissals of Officials," November 29, 1999, reproduced on the Internet Website of the Office of the High Representative in Bosnia and Herzegovina, http://www.ohr.int/speeches/s991129a.htm, accessed on February 19, 2000.

56. Ivo H. Daalder and Michael B. G. Froman, "Dayton's Incomplete Peace," *Foreign Affairs* 78, no. 6 (November-December 1999): 111.

57. Snyder and Ballentine, "Nationalism and the Marketplace of Ideas," 39–40.

58. Donald L. Horowitz, "Ethnic Conflict Management for Policymakers," in *Conflict and Peacemaking in Multiethnic Societies,* ed. Joseph V. Montville (Toronto: Lexington Books), 127.

59. For a review of this literature, see Nancy Birdsall and Frederick Jaspersen, eds., *Pathways to Growth: Comparing East Asia and Latin America* (Washington, D.C.: Inter-American Development Bank, 1997).

60. UN Security Council document S/1999/672 (June 12, 1999), pars. 2–3.

61. Steven Erlanger, "In Victory's Wake, a Battle of Bureaucrats," *New York Times,* November 28, 1999, sec. 4, 5.

62. Matthias Rueb, "Reconstructing Kosovo: On the Right Track—But Where Does It Lead?" *NATO Review* 47, no. 3 (autumn 1999): 20–23.

46

Democratization and Peacebuilding

Perils and Promises

Timothy D. Sisk

WHEN THE GUNS FALL SILENT after today's civil wars, groups in conflict often resolve their differences at the negotiating table in a usually turbulent and tortured "peace process." When these talks succeed, the peace settlements reached routinely feature measures to introduce a process of democratization as a long-term system of managing deep social conflicts. Democratization is a process of gradually introducing more participatory politics, including elections and the creation of a civil society supportive of tolerant, pluralistic politics through adherence to constitutional rules of the game.[1] International mediators in today's civil wars often argue (and often insist), and the parties embroiled in war often agree, that democratic solutions are a feasible way to re-create a legitimate system of postwar governance.

Whether in failed states, such as East Timor, or in protracted wars such as Bosnia's, elections are seen as an immediate way to legitimate a negotiated settlement and establish some semblance of postwar governance. Elec-tions after a civil war are especially risky because the competition for power through the ballot box sharpens social differences—usually along the lines over which the war was fought. At the same time, they seem desirable, even necessary, at some point in the postwar reconciliation process. When no side is able to prevail on the battlefield and exhaustion leads the parties to make peace, negotiating with foes and moving toward a new system of non-violent conflict management is the only realistic way out. Democratic institutions establish new rules of the game that may allow for a period of power sharing that involves the principal protagonists in the war in a collective government.

In recent years, internationally assisted efforts to democratize after bitter internal conflicts have featured prominently in Angola, Bosnia, Croatia, East Timor, El Salvador, Ethiopia, Guatemala, Nicaragua, Northern Ireland, Sierra Leone, South Africa, and Zimbabwe, to name a few. Hopes are pinned on the ballot box replacing the battlefield as the principal way in which social conflicts are waged.

The international community's efforts to promote peace through democracy in traumatized societies have been fraught with peril. Once so many lives have been lost, how can trust in peaceful politics be built? In this chapter we examine

- *lessons learned* in recent instances of postwar democratization in societies that have experienced deep-rooted social violence, especially along ethnic, racial, or religious lines;
- *options* on the table for helping ameliorate social differences, and some recent political solutions that have been proposed;
- the *perils* of democratization, and why efforts to introduce formal power sharing as a solution to stubbornly intractable conflicts have been inherently unstable in recent years; and
- the *promises* of democratization, or ways in which certain types of democratic institutions may help alleviate, not exacerbate, divisions in a war-torn society.

In sum, there is simply no more just or legitimate way to peacefully manage differences among contending social groups than democracy, however difficult it may seem to move from violent to electoral competition. Democracy is a system of government that allows for conflict to continue, albeit in institutions such as the parliament and courts rather than on the battlefield. The alternatives to democracy in postwar situations—partition or political divorce, dominance of one group over others, long-term international trusteeship, personal or military rule—may work to contain differences in the short run, as they have in times past.[2] But over time these alternatives do not offer a legitimate and sustainable method for fostering multiethnic consensus and promoting reconciliation so desperately needed after a bitter, fratricidal war.

The critical debate, therefore, is how to craft postwar democratic institutions to foster reconciliation. For the international community, the question is how to prod the protagonists in civil wars to design a democratic system that may help manage and ameliorate the underlying causes of conflict over the long term. Such a settlement should also avoid winner-take-all outcomes in elections. Building appropriate, trust-building political systems in divided societies is key to healing social wounds and to preventing new wars from emerging, in today's diverse world. As the *Economist* recently reported:

> Few countries are ethnically homogenous, and all too many are riven by ethnic or religious animosity. If mankind could devise a system that would accept this animosity and somehow turn it to good effect—as well-regulated capitalism accepts human greed and turns it to the business of creating wealth—the world would be a better place. That, however, is an invention still to come.[3]

LESSONS LEARNED

As Roy Licklider writes in this volume, in the past decade many more conflicts than before have ended at the negotiating table; as a result, there have been several lessons learned about the relationships between peace processes and postwar democratization. Many recent civil wars have come to an end through negotiation. Among the most successfully perceived negotiated settlements in civil wars are the democratization pacts that ended fighting in Namibia, Cambodia, El Salvador, Nicaragua, Mozambique, South Africa, and, haltingly, Northern Ireland. These agreements have featured diverse patterns of settlement including independence and the creation of new states (or partition), autonomy or the territorial devolution of power, "intermediate sovereignty" or transitional arrangements, formal power sharing along essentially ethnic lines, and democracy by majority rule. The track record on making peace through building democracy in recent years is decidedly mixed and thus difficult to assess.

- *Some wars seem intractable.* Several civil wars today grind on despite unfailing attempts by the international community to foster a settlement that features a tolerant multi-ethnic democracy. These situations such as in Chechnya, Sri Lanka, or Sudan do not seem "ripe" for peace or for fully inclusive democracy.

- *Apparent successes can be illusory.* Even when a peace accord is clinched, horrific tragedy can still occur. The August 1993 Arusha Accords for Rwanda were meant to end a bloody civil war and lead to a power-sharing government with some democratic features; instead, the agreements collapsed in the hundred-day genocide that left eight hundred thousand dead and many more deeply scarred survivors because militants of the Hutu majority refused to consider sharing power with the militarily powerful Tutsi minority.

- *Tragedy can happen.* UN–supervised elections to end the civil war in Angola in 1992 failed palpably when ill-considered elections went ahead without full demobilization of the rebel forces. The likely loser in the presidential poll, Jonas Savimbi, refused to accept defeat and the war resumed; since then, an estimated one hundred fifty thousand Angolans have died in the renewed fighting.

- *Cold peace is a common outcome.* Other peace accords have produced an unsatisfactory, frustrating, and often violent, or "cold," peace. A foundation for peace in postwar Bosnia was laid in the 1995 Dayton accords—two national-level elections, in 1996 and 1998, have been held—yet reconciliation is halting and ethnic nationalist forces that eschew reconciliation still dominate the postwar landscape.

- *Nevertheless, success can be won.* Some peace agreements have produced profound inspiration and a heartwarming national elation; peace agreements have ended wars and laid the basis for democracy and postwar reconciliation. The pacts that ended apartheid in South Africa in 1994, averting a cataclysmic race war there, are seen as a model of step-by-step measures to promote a just peace in a society deeply divided during the course of a profoundly unjust history.

Most practitioners and scholars agree that civil wars today need a peace *process,* or step-by-step reciprocal moves to build confidence, resolve gnarly issues such as disarmament, and carefully define the future through the design of new political institutions. In other terms, a peace process is an intricate dance of steps—choreographed by third-party mediators—among parties in conflict that help to gradually exchange war for peace. These processes define the nature and type of the postwar democracy, and they lay out a specific path to getting there. In this chapter we are especially concerned with the outcome dimensions of these processes—the political terms of settlement. One of the most important functions of this process is to define the terms of the postwar society and, in particular, how the warring factions can feasibly live together.

A final lesson learned is that there are many more options on the table for structuring a postwar political system for divided societies than is appreciated by most observers of these conflicts. Some options may move us closer to a promising scenario in which a carefully crafted set of democratic institutions can engender moderation and promote reconciliation rather than exacerbate social tensions.

OPTIONS

The political solutions that peace agreements embody, in effect, describe the most feasible form for a postwar peace. The solutions reached at the bargaining table are simply "feasible" because they usually represent the middle ground among the opposing positions of the parties to the war. In the negotiations over

Bosnia's Dayton accords, Serbian parties wanted partition, Croatian leaders wanted accession to Croatia, and the Bosniacs (Bosnian Muslims) generally wanted a rather centralized government leaning more toward majority rule (in which they would be the numerical majority). In brokering a peace among these factions, the international community insisted on maintaining the territorial integrity of the independent Bosnian state with highly devolved federal units. Thus, none of the factions got their preferred solution; the Dayton outcome can be described as "shared sovereignty."

Similarly, in Northern Ireland the April 1998 Good Friday Agreement reflects a solution of "integrative sovereignty," a formula that obscures the hotly contested question of ultimate ownership of the six contested counties. In that settlement, institutions were created that allow the United Kingdom, Ireland, and a power-sharing Northern Ireland Assembly to jointly administer the territory, all within the context of broader European integration. In Cyprus advocates of peace have argued for a "bizonal, bifederal" reunited country, which is seen as the median point between Turkish claims for an independent republic and Greek Cypriot claims for an indivisible territory. The best possible solution for Cyprus is something that approaches a principle of "divided sovereignty." These examples illustrate that a principal challenge is to devise innovative, creative, conflict-specific solutions to widely varied claims in deeply divided societies, which means examining a broad range of options from which to potentially choose in any given setting.

Partition

Partition refers to the creation of an entirely new state that enjoys full sovereignty and international recognition. Some of the civil wars of the 1990s did end in effective partition, including the breakup of the former Yugoslavia, the independence of Eritrea and East Timor, and the likely trajectory of the Israeli-Palestinian

dispute. Many others—such as Azerbaijan (Nagorno-Karabakh) and southern Sudan—have ended in a de facto partition, one that exists in reality but is not internationally recognized. The legal partitions remain anomalies in the general trend of international policies. In each of these cases, resolutions of the United Nations Security Council pertaining to them assert the primacy of international principles of territorial integrity and state sovereignty to argue that current borders should not be changed. Some question the wisdom of policies that seek to keep states together after the deep injuries of civil war. Chaim Kaufman writes:

> Stable resolutions of ethnic civil wars are possible, but only when the opposing groups are demographically separated into defensible enclaves. Separation reduces both incentives and opportunity for further combat, and largely eliminates both reasons and chances for ethnic cleansing of civilians. . . . This means to save lives threatened by genocide, the international community must abandon attempts to save war-torn multiethnic states.[4]

Others strongly disagree. Partition, in the opposing view, undercuts the essential reality of the modern world: most societies are multiethnic and highly diverse. The principle of tolerant, multiethnic diversity should not be sacrificed in the pursuit of peace to end an ethnically charged civil war in which the aim of ethnic "purity" is the goal of any disputant. The granting of partition is tantamount to rewarding disputants with territorial ambitions—who may well have committed war crimes. These arguments are the principal reasons why the United States insisted upon the maintenance of Bosnia's territorial integrity when it mediated the Dayton talks in November 1995.

Moreover, recent cases of partition underscore that in the newly created state, multiethnicity and tolerance are still critical to social peace. Partition does not resolve ethnic conflict; it usually just rearranges the patterns of majorities and minorities, often creating new sources of social divisions. East Timor must still resolve its problems of ethnic coexistence, even after it has become politically independent of Indonesia on its UN-guided route to full recognition and state sovereignty.

The lesson learned on partition is clear: while undesirable—unyielding claims for independence and self-determination for ethnic groups often generate violence—it should be left on the list of options in particularly intractable disputes. Sometimes partition, as in the situation in East Timor under UN administration, is a feasible way to de-escalate the violence, even if the challenges of building a new, tolerant, multiethnic society thereafter are incredibly challenging.

Autonomy

Autonomy is not a term on which there is a consensus definition.[5] Nonetheless, scholar Yash Ghai's best effort at one is useful: "Autonomy is a device to allow an ethnic group or other groups claiming a distinct identity to exercise direct control over important affairs of concern to them while allowing the larger entity to exercise those powers which are the common interests of both sections."[6] The forms of autonomy include symmetrical federalism, in which all units enjoy similar powers, and asymmetrical federalism, which might provide enhanced powers to a particular region.

As noted, autonomy seems a reasonable solution between groups in ethnic conflicts in which territorial and ethnic boundaries largely overlap. As a United States Institute of Peace Special Report noted:

> The U.S. preference for "enhanced status" for Kosovo and meaningful self-administration, combined with Milosevic's reluctance to oversee independence, makes autonomy for Kosovo an option. Autonomy, however, is rejected by all Albanians. . . . Belgrade is thought to be willing to accept a large measure of autonomy. The key issue will be police and security, functions that Belgrade will not want to yield and that the Albanians will insist upon.[7]

President Vojislav Kostunica and the new leadership in Belgrade have shown a greater willingness to negotiate with the Kosovar Albanians, limiting the likelihood that independence will be forthcoming. The Kosovo problem underscores autonomy's desirability as a compromise between self-determination and territorial integrity; however, as a compromise, autonomy is inherently limited because it requires both sides in territorial disputes to jeopardize their primary aims in waging the war.

Power Sharing

Power sharing is often conceived as a system to ensure group security in a multiethnic society. Essentially, this system of governance seeks to include all segments of a diverse society in a decision-making process that aims for the broadest possible consensus. Critical to the success of power sharing is proportional representation of all groups in the policymaking and administrative institutions and especially in the police and military. The principles of power sharing are representation and a say in decision making for all groups in society, with an emphasis on discussion, respect, and equal representation.

With formal power sharing guaranteed, some of the heat can be taken off of elections.[8] When the campaigns begin under proportional representation, the fight is over a party or minority group's share in collective decision making rather than a struggle for exclusive power. Power-sharing agreements, worked out before the polls, are widely viewed as a viable alternative to winner-take-all democracy in which the winner at the ballot box alone controls the reins of authority. In South Africa in April 1994, for example, the first all-race elections were held with the certain knowledge by opposition parties that they would have a seat in government and in cabinet and that they would win a proportional number of seats in parliament for their strength in the population. Although it was certain that the African

Table 1. Political Outcomes in Peace Agreements: A Typology

Type	Features	Examples	Perils and Promises
Partition	• Political divorce • Creation of a new state • International recognition	• East Timor • Eritrea • Yugoslavia	• May create new majorities and minorities in the new state, with potential for violence • Separates antagonistic populations
Autonomy (Territorial)	• Asymmetric federalism (special status for certain territories) • Negotiations occur over the extent to which each political unit exercises competency, or control, over what kinds of issues • Complicated on tax, revenue, and often policing/security issues • Can also be devised as nonterritorial, or "corporate," federalism for widely dispersed, yet still distinct, groups	• Israel-Palestine • Proposed by some as a compromise outcome in Kosovo, Kashmir, Sudan, Turkey, Russia (Chechnya), Azerbaijan (Nagorno-Karabakh), and Sri Lanka	• A dangerous interregnum (intermediate sovereignty) on the slow path to partition, which might evoke violence (Israel-Palestine) • Provides reasonable compromise solutions when claims for group self-determination clash with state demands for territorial integrity
Group-Based/ Mandatory Power-Sharing Democracy	• Grand coalition • Parliamentary rule • Cultural autonomy/ minority veto • Proportionality in elected representation and civil service, military • Ethnic or linguistic federalism for areas that are ethnically homogeneous	• Bosnia • Sierra Leone • Lebanon	• Perpetuates ethnic divisions and may invite alleged war criminals into government (Sierra Leone); leads to gridlock • Provides vulnerable groups constitutional guarantees of their security

Table 1. *(cont.)*

Type	Features	Examples	Perils and Promises
Integrative Power-Sharing Democracy	• Incentives to form multi-ethnic coalitions • Presidential rule • Vote pooling • Federalism that primarily features multiethnic districts • The use of voting systems that encourage the pooling of votes across group lines (through the use of electoral systems that give voters multiple choices of candidates) • Individual-based rights, rather than group-based rights, that aim to protect minority culture, religion, language, and education	• Fiji • Nigeria • South Africa • Northern Ireland	• Incentives to moderate are weak; democracy is vulnerable to ethnic extremism (Fiji) • Politicians may moderate in pursuit of electoral success (South Africa, Northern Ireland, Nigeria)
Majority-Rule Democracy	• Parties enter postwar elections without an agreement to share power • Winner-take-all in a government-versus-opposition scenario • Often, single-member district electoral system, yielding disproportionate electoral results	• Mozambique • El Salvador • Nicaragua	• Losers at the ballot box might turn to violence if they are excluded from power • Clear majorities emerge with mandates to undertake difficult social reform

National Congress would win, power sharing was a necessary step on the route to broader democratization.[9]

There are two principal variants of power sharing: consociational and integrative. The *consociational power-sharing approach* relies on accommodation by ethnic group leaders at the political center and guarantees of group autonomy and minority rights. The key institutions are federalism and the devolution of power to ethnic groups in territory that they control, minority vetoes on issues of particular importance to them, grand coalition cabinets in a parliamentary framework, and proportionality in all spheres of public life (for example, budgeting and civil service appointments). Like Bosnia, Lebanon (after the 1990 Ta'if Agreement) has a political system in which representation and autonomy for the country's main religious groups are guaranteed in the constitution. Systems of communal representation have been attempted in many settings over the years, as described by scholar Arend Lijphart, an advocate of consociationalism, in his seminal book *Democracy in Plural Societies*.[10] Lijphart argues that time and again, protagonists in deeply divided societies have arrived at power sharing as the best way to promote inclusion of all groups in society and an accommodative, consensus-seeking form of democracy.

Power sharing is a flexible and widely varied form of government. In Lebanon power sharing recognizes groups on a "confessional" or religious basis and assures them representation at the highest levels. In South Africa cultural practices and language are protected for individuals, but minority representation occurs less formally and often outside the political arena. Thus consociationalism is just one type of design option for democratization in civil wars.

The *integrative power-sharing approach* rejects providing guarantees of group security and instead proposes that peace settlements feature *incentives* for multiethnic cooperation.[11] It eschews ethnic groups as the basis for building a common society. In South Africa's 1993 interim constitution, for example, ethnic group representation was explicitly rejected in favor of institutions and policies that deliberately promote social integration across group lines. Election laws (in combination with the delimitation of provincial boundaries) have had the effect of encouraging political parties to put up candidate slates—if they want to maximize the votes they get—that reflect South Africa's highly diverse society. And the federal provinces were created so as not to overlap with ethnic group boundaries (South Africa's groups are more widely dispersed in any event). Similarly, the process in Northern Ireland that led to the 1998 Good Friday Agreement also included provisions to encourage moderation on divisive themes. In fact, early research shows that in the 1998 elections in Northern Ireland voters were willing to support candidates and parties other than those clearly associated with their own sectarian identity.

The integrative approach seeks to build multiethnic political coalitions (usually political parties), to create incentives for political leaders to be moderate on divisive ethnic themes, and to enhance minority influence in majority decision making. The elements of an integrative approach include electoral systems that encourage preelection pacts across ethnic lines, nonethnic federalism that diffuses points of power, and public policies that promote political allegiances that transcend groups.[12] On the one hand, integrative power sharing is superior in theory, in that it seeks to foster ethnic accommodation by promoting crosscutting interests. However, incentives to promote conciliation will run aground when faced with deep-seated enmities that underlie ethnic disputes and that are hardened during the course of a brutal civil war.

It is reasonable to be skeptical that any institutional "fix" can help moderate the deeply bitter politics of many societies at war today. Both consociational and integrative forms of power sharing have their potential disadvantages. It is fair to criticize a consociational approach that structures the political system around ethnic identities, as in Bosnia. Mechanisms such as communal representation reify and help harden ethnic differences and the mutual veto can lead to gridlock in decision making. Then again, integrative approaches do not always work, as has been the case following the deplorable abrogation of the carefully crafted constitutional agreement in Fiji; ethnic chauvinist rebels vitiated a broadly negotiated and thoughtfully implemented agreement to share power between Fiji's two principal communities, the Fijians and the Indo-Fijians.[13]

Is sharing power, with its inherent problems of long discussions to reach agreement, or in futile attempts to find common ground, too unwieldy for effective governance? After some civil wars, protagonists have plunged into democracy without the constitutional assurances provided by power sharing. Some peace settlements in recent years have featured *majority-rule democracy,* despite a wide body of scholarship that suggests that postwar societies cannot contain the fissiparous tendencies that electoral competition generates. The real possibility of losing power through an election that was not lost on the battlefield arguably limits the desirability of majority-rule democracy, or winner-take-all politics, as a political solution.

Yet, curiously, postwar settlements in Mozambique, El Salvador, and Nicaragua have proven durable so far even though they feature democracy by majority rule as a principal component of the political solution. Is majority rule not as bad for nascent postwar democracies as had been generally believed? A potential answer to the riddle seems to lie with the nature of these particular disputes. Majority-rule democracy may be better suited for managing postwar settlements following peasant rebellions or class-based struggles than it is for settlements following wars fought among well-defined ethnic groups. When coupled with other measures such as land reform and basic protection of individual human rights, liberal or majority-rule democracy may be a more desirable solution than one that is primarily designed to reconcile deep-rooted ethnic conflict. Parties are more comfortable with government-versus-opposition roles than they are with trying to hammer out a consensus policy.

Which options are best? There is no way to prejudge the "best" outcome to any given conflict. Those seeking to promote peace in contemporary civil wars need to carefully develop a strategic idea that reinforces the domestic dynamics most conducive to peace. *What type of outcome—from partition to majority rule—is feasible and most desirable for establishing the basis of a self-reinforcing postwar peace?* This strategic concept that informs a peace process must clarify the way out of a war's quagmire and the overall direction of the difficult journey of postwar peacebuilding ahead. Whether this means that after a civil war the country will stay together, or whether partition is desirable and feasible, has less to do with the wishes of external mediators than in the perceptions and positions of the parties at the table. Whether they can live together is really a consequence of the war itself: the depth of enmity that developed, the intensity and nature of the fighting, the extent of civilian atrocities, the division of spoils and territory, and the realities of personality and politics.

PERILS

Even with a reasonable settlement on power, and a plan for managed democratization, implementation of peace agreements that feature democracy faces some inherent perils.

LACK OF TRUST. Surely the lack of trust among parties who were only recently at war is the principal peril for embracing democracy as a postwar system of conflict management. The meaning and logic of war often overtake the desirability and logic of peace. Why lose at the ballot box what was not lost on the battlefield?

That is, wars today are often seen as "intractable" because of the dynamics that fuel the war itself and the inherent uncertainty of a newfound peace.[14]

THE AGONY OF DEFEAT. The potential agony of defeat—either in war or at the ballot box—is a peril that limits the willingness of disputants in a civil war to consider peace and embrace democracy. Consider the position of the Bosniacs in Bosnia during the war there between 1992 and 1995. To agree to an uncertain peace such as that offered during the course of talks through the International Conference on the Former Yugoslavia would have risked survival of the community. After so many war crimes had been committed against the Bosniacs, how could they trust their foes in a peace process or envision a future in which they could peacefully live together?

THE PERSISTENCE OF DEEP DIVISIONS. If the conflict is over exclusively defined ethnic identity as the basis of the state, this position is not easily reconciled with inclusive views of the state. Sudan is an example of such irreconcilable views. While it may be possible to conjure up any number of scenarios for a more peaceful, democratic Sudan, unless and until the parties can agree on the core identity of the Sudanese state—Islamic, in many Northern views, or multiethnic, as many moderates seek, or binational, as some Southerners seek—peace and democracy will be elusive.[15] In many other places the claims of the parties also seem rather irreconcilable. When absolute claims for self-determination and independence clash with inflexible positions on territorial integrity, as in Russia/Chechnya, there is little room for compromise on basic principles.

THE INSIDE GAME OF POLITICS. It is critically important to look inside conflicting groups in civil wars today. The inside game within groups is just as important as the competition between groups. What are the *factions and*

frictions within a party at the table? What happens inside organizations such as governments and rebel groups explains why moderates who seek peace may rise to the level of leadership and "deliver" their constituencies in the rough-and-tumble of postwar politics. In Northern Ireland the most important point in the teetering balance between war and peace, and an exclusive versus inclusive democracy, lies not with the relationship between the political leaders, but between the "hard" armed men of the IRA and the Unionist militias. The relative balance of power between moderates and hard-liners—those who will fight to the bitter end—is the most important factor in explaining when the peace process moves or teeters on a return to the violent struggle. Is there a moderate core of political leaders, able to carry their military backers and with sufficient clout to make the concessions necessary for peace and the courage necessary to rely on the democratic impulses of the people?

THE LACK OF CREDIBLE COMMITMENT. Even when the protagonists in the war are ready to explore peace, the absence of skilled and/or resourceful mediation by third parties is sometimes the last obstacle to a peace process. In every major peace agreement reached since the end of the Cold War, and especially those that have been successful, there has been extensive and active external mediation. Yet many mediators are limited because they cannot guarantee the terms of settlement. Although there are many variables involved in successful mediation in civil wars, providing the parties with credible commitment—resources and personnel for a long-term commitment to assist a country on the path to accepting the inherent uncertainties of democracy and security—is at the top of the list. Long-term commitment is the key to nurturing peace and sustaining the underlying trust necessary for democracy to prevail.[16]

If a third party can provide guarantees that former enemies will abide by the terms of a peace agreement—for example, in ensuring a free and fair postwar election—the warriors can be less fearful of the uncertain peace. A lack of true commitment and an inability to solve the credible commitment puzzle mean that in many conflicts—such as Burundi in the past few years—negotiations drag on but so does the war. Today, former South African president Nelson Mandela is seeking to mediate an end to the war, a slow but promising process that may ultimately yield a new peace agreement there.[17]

The perils of introducing democracy after civil war are many and serious. Trust is weak, the issues are emotionally strong, the parties are faction ridden and incoherent, and much is required of outside parties to guarantee a settlement. Should relative successes like El Salvador and South Africa inspire our thinking about democratization after civil war, or should the perils revealed by Cambodia (which suffered setbacks to democracy after a period of failed power sharing) and Bosnia inform our views? The answer, of course, is both.

PROMISES

If the perils to democratization after conflict could not be overcome, there would not have been the rather extensive number of relatively successful negotiated settlements in recent years.[18] Most peace processes really make progress when the parties are utterly exhausted with the war. For all sides simultaneously, there must exist an expectation that future escalation of the conflict will not decisively defeat the opponent nor will further commitment of resources fundamentally affect the eventual outcome should a negotiated settlement be reached. The alternatives to cooperating—especially returning to the armed struggle—are really much worse than working through deeply difficult and painful issues in a wrenching search for consensus. What lessons offer promise of improving the ability to create

democratic institutions to manage deep-seated, postwar social differences?

Defining the goal of democracy clearly and early on, creating a plan, and defining the path. To start democratization, agreement must be reached early in negotiations that the process is moving toward an inclusive, and maybe power-sharing, democracy and that compromise early will set the stage for greater cooperation down the road. Yet usually security concerns preoccupy negotiators in peace talks; without security guarantees, there is no basis for political cooperation. One side will demand an agreement on a conflict's outcome before a cease-fire, whereas other parties demand a cessation of violence before talking about outcomes. If parties can surmount this difficult dilemma that links the outcome of talks with the process of de-escalation, cooperation and the move to less violent forms of political competition have begun. For example, in Northern Ireland the ultimate outcome of the shaky peace process—a power-sharing assembly in Northern Ireland, along with North-South (Northern Ireland and Ireland) and East-West (Ireland and Britain) institutions—has remained the same since the early stages of prenegotiation (the Hume-Adams and Sinn Fein–Britain talks) in 1993. This early point of agreement has kept the process going despite many hurdles since that time.

Assertive peacemaking. There has been a tendency in several recent cases for international mediators, especially the United States, to engage in coercive peacemaking. This refers to the threat of coercive action, for example, sanctions or force, if the protagonists in the civil war fail to make peace. Western powers seeking to broker peace in Kosovo in 1999 at the Rambouillet negotiations put together an integrated package of sanctions and incentives to coax the reticent Albanians and the dug-in Serbs to sign a peace agreement. For the Albanians, failure to sign meant ostracism and a withdrawal of support for their cause; for Yugoslavia's government, it meant a NATO bombing campaign. As the Rambouillet experience shows, coercive peacemaking entails certain risks. If the talks fail, the mediator must then become one of the parties to the armed conflict itself.

Managing factionalism. Players emerging from a civil war need many different opportunities, or "tracks" (arenas of interaction), to discover confidence and build cooperation. Multiple tracks at which top- and mid-level leaders negotiate are essential to success. Peace processes set up bargaining institutions that allow problems such as stakes, issues, sovereignty, identity, and economics to be negotiated in a participatory way. A proliferation of opportunities for facilitated interaction was an essential component of South Africa's transition from war to peace. At the same time, opportunities for interaction do not guarantee that talks will progress. In Cyprus peace is not yet at hand despite many opportunities in the past decade to establish multiple arenas for bargaining.

Using local-level processes to resolve conflict. The need for multiple tracks also suggests that elite-level negotiations need to be accompanied by a local-level process for conflict mitigation. A multitiered approach is called for in which top-level bargaining bolsters the work of community-level mediators and local-level confidence reinforces the pressures for peace at the top. This also raises the notion of complementarity in peace processes, in which efforts at different levels of society reinforce each other.[19]

Consulting the people. Another lesson is that sometimes it is desirable to negotiate in secret, announcing a "done deal" to a surprised world. While of course transparency is desirable when leaders are negotiating peace, sometimes parties participating in talks must quickly cooperate in keeping the very existence of negotiation secret. Once the nature and the extent of risky concessions have been determined and the trade-offs identified, the precise terms are announced to the world. Both the 1993 Oslo Middle East agreement and the 1995 Dayton accords that ended the war in Bosnia were negotiated mostly in secret. Especially in the Middle East talks, it was believed that if details of the talks were leaked while they were being negotiated, the opponents of the peace process would be better able to act to scuttle negotiations.

On the other hand, for long-term peace, open participatory peacemaking may arguably build stronger support for the settlement. In South Africa many initial agreements in 1991 and 1992 were made in secret among top political leaders such as Nelson Mandela and F. W. de Klerk, but the final constitution was adopted in 1996, only after unprecedented public participation in the drafting process. The conclusion is that secret agreements make sense early, but, in the long run, if the search for peace does not broaden, the agreement may not be sustainable over time. A useful lens for analyzing tasks of postwar peacemaking is "conflict transformation," in which coherent efforts are put into place to build democracy and conflict resolution from the bottom up, over time.[20]

Fostering inclusion. The experiences of Northern Ireland, South Africa, and Bosnia help clarify some of the essential questions to be asked in structurig peace processes.

- Does the structure of talks (bilateral or multilateral) lend itself to the eventual inclusion of some rejectionist parties, either in formal or informal (that is, NGO-sponsored) negotiations?
- Do negotiations proceed in secret or in public, or both? Do the parties reach agreement at the highest levels first, or do negotiators bicker until impasse and then request intervention by higher authorities?
- To what extent and in what manner should military commanders be included in talks, along with would-be guarantors of the agreement such as UN peacekeepers?
- How visual or public is the role of the mediator, and to what extent and in what manner

do mediators intervene to help move the parties beyond impasses?

Although there are no universally applicable lessons learned with regard to inclusion and exclusion, it is clear that sometimes the table needs to be enlarged to incorporate more negotiators, while at other times chairs need to be taken away.

Keeping momentum. An important lesson on process options is that the momentum of peace must be maintained. When peace processes lag, when progress is not readily visible, when talks collapse or drag on incessantly, frustration builds. Supporters of the peace begin to lose faith in the process, moderate political leaders become vulnerable to charges that the risks they have taken have not borne fruit, and fatigue sets in. At the same time, opponents of peace see the vulnerability and interpret lack of progress as a sign that the peace process is weak and faltering. This problem has beset the Middle East: the lack of progress in talks angered Palestinians and has been one of the factors behind the October 2000 "intifadah" in the Middle East.

Innovative solutions. The core issue of sovereignty is the key to agreements in most of today's civil wars. Although the interests and power of the disputants generally frame the terms of a settlement in an internal conflict, international mediators clearly influence the political solutions that form the core of peace agreements. By insisting on the territorial integrity of a state, such as in Bosnia or Chechnya, powers in the international community tilt toward power sharing, as in the Good Friday Agreement, over partition. International intervention limits the options on the table for power sharing in most instances.[21] This being the case, international intervention should be more proactive in helping parties to consider the full range of options at their disposal if the parties in conflict really want to devise a system that might help them exit the devastating traps of ethnic hatred.

CONCLUSION

The depressing fact that so many peace processes in the 1990s went awry reveals that it is much easier to argue that the perils to postwar democratization outweigh the opportunities. Many democratization processes—like a troubled birthing—have "failed to progress." Efforts to consolidate democracy in Bosnia, Cambodia, Guatemala, and Zimbabwe are shaky or deeply troubled. However, all is not lost. Many deep-rooted wars were brought to an end, as in El Salvador, Mozambique, and South Africa, as were many other less intense disputes. What innovations in peacemaking through democratization can provide hope that new opportunities exist to prevent new civil wars and bring those currently raging to an end?

First, there is a new space for creativity in addressing some of the underlying causes of internal conflicts and the dynamics that fuel them. If the war is waged over state sovereignty and territory, then rapid changes in the international system may render these putative values more elusive in any event. Economic globalization, expanding trade and investment, migration, and regional economic and political integration have made the notion of sovereign states increasingly less important in practical terms. As global governance emerges, control over national life is less possible for all national states; the best approach to democratization may well be to start at the local level.[22] With the emergence of new global norms on democracy and fair treatment of minorities, state sovereignty, independence, autonomy, and borders may mean very different things in the years ahead than they did during the era of the so-called Westphalian (or state-centered) international system. If sovereignty is less meaningful in today's globalized world, is it still worth fighting for?

Second, the continued erosion of national-level sovereignty in today's interdependent world means that opportunities for creatively resolving self-determination disputes will grow commensurately. For example, in terms of the 1998 Good Friday Agreement in Northern Ireland, it is altogether impossible—especially within the European Union context—to determine precisely who is "sovereign" in the disputed territories. Similar arrangements may offer pathways for fruitful talks on other complicated disputes, such as Chechnya, Cyprus, or Kashmir. Although these proposals may seem impossible now, no war lasts forever.

Third, opportunities also exist to introduce a more expansive notion of peacemaking and to develop new capacities for managing complex exits to civil wars. Recent innovative proposals include the creation of regional conflict amelioration centers, where comparative learning, trained mediators, and institutionalized forums for bargaining can directly address regional problems and offer immediate solutions.[23] The regionalization of international responses to civil wars may also provide opportunities for quickly and effectively providing the external military forces—through regional peacekeeping operations—necessary to provide credible commitments to negotiated settlements. Innovations have been made in administering elections, providing and fielding international monitors, resolution of election disputes, electoral system design, methods for parallel balloting, and organizing democratic political parties.[24]

Fourth, until the international community's ability to serve as a guarantor of peace agreements is bolstered, promoting postwar democratization will be inherently limited. Recent experience reveals an international community confused about the necessity of quickly reinforcing peace through external military intervention. In Kosovo a strong, resolute, well-armed NATO is deployed to enforce de facto autonomy, a force that was deployed without the government of Yugoslavia's consent. A similarly strong military force was deployed in East Timor (although in that case the government of Indonesia had reluctantly agreed to

its deployment). With UNTAET (United Nations Transitional Authority in East Timor) deployed, the process of peacemaking is moved forward with the clear understanding that external powers will in fact provide the types of commitments required to help the warring protagonists overcome their deep-seated insecurities. At least democratization has a chance in East Timor. Yet in many countries the international community is reluctant to intervene (as in the Democratic Republic of the Congo) or already has been stung by warbent factions (as in Sierra Leone).

Promoting democracy in postwar societies entails significant risks, particularly in advocating elections in situations that are likely to reinforce, rather than mitigate, conflict. Yet the necessity of elections even in the most unfavorable circumstances seems, in the long term, imperative. Elections, for all their real and perceived flaws, provide some basic source of legitimacy to postwar rules, backing that they need to implement rehabilitation and reconciliation policies.

Finally and fortunately, international norms on the promotion of democracy in divided societies evolved rapidly in the 1990s, and their further development is critical to maintaining peace in today's multiethnic societies. In 1992 the United Nations General Assembly adopted a resolution on the fair treatment of minorities and indigenous groups. The Organization for Security and Cooperation in Europe established a High Commissioner on National Minorities, who seeks to prevent the eruption of ethnic violence in Europe through quiet diplomacy, particularly in the newly democratic states of the former Eastern bloc. Electoral assistance is now readily available from the United Nations, the Commonwealth, regional organizations, and a plethora of nongovernmental groups. Conditionalities are also employed by Western governments, international financial institutions, and regional organizations when they tie political aid to progress toward democratic rights and freedoms.

Most policymakers recognize that democracy cannot save many of today's deeply divided countries, at least in the short run. The pressure of gaining or losing power is too intense; the incentives to use violence instead are too many. And few deeply conflicted multiethnic societies will become consolidated democracies in the near term. In most instances, efforts to promote democracy after war are thwarted by lingering enmities and structural barriers to peace, such as entrenched economic inequality among ethnic groups.

The imperatives of today's violent conflicts demand that the efforts to promote democracy in deeply divided societies proceed. International mediation and monitoring should continue to be developed; new norms on democracy, such as an international right to local freedom of choice, should be put into place. Sustained peace in deeply divided societies requires a formula for the recognition and tolerance of ethnic differences, strong legal protections for individual and group rights, and political institutions that encourage bargaining, compromise, and inclusive coalitions. The "invention" that—through the design of political institutions—would magically turn animosity into cooperation has, unfortunately, remained elusive. But progress has been made in considering ways in which peace settlements can be self-reinforcing over time. When a political system can encourage politicians to be moderate in their drive to office, eschewing the turn to ethnic politics for their personal or party political gain, multiethnic democracy at least has a better chance.

NOTES

The author acknowledges the support of the John D. and Catherine T. MacArthur Foundation, the Norwegian Nobel Institute, and the Carnegie Corporation of New York for their support of the research on which this chapter is based. The views expressed in this chapter reflect those of the author alone.

1. See Georg Sorensen, *Democracy and Democratization* (Boulder, Colo.: Lynne Rienner, 1998).

2. For example, in the Ottoman Empire, the "millet system" offered considerable autonomy to minority groups, reducing ethnic conflict, albeit certainly not in a democratic framework. See Jason Goodwin, *Lords of the Horizons: A History of the Ottoman Empire* (New York: Henry Holt, 1998).

3. "Forlorn Fiji," *Economist*, July 22, 2000, 21.

4. Chaim Kaufman, "Possible and Impossible Solutions to Ethnic Civil Wars," *International Security* 20, no. 4 (1996): 137.

5. See Ruth Lapidoth, *Autonomy: Flexible Solutions to Ethnic Conflicts* (Washington, D.C.: United States Institute of Peace Press, 1997); and Hurst Hannum, *Autonomy, Sovereignty, and Self-Determination: The Accommodation of Conflicting Rights* (Philadelphia: University of Pennsylvania Press, 1990).

6. Yash Ghai, *Autonomy* (Washington, D.C.: National Research Council, Committee on International Conflict Resolution, 2001).

7. United States Institute of Peace, *Kosovo Dialogue: Too Little, Too Late*, Special Report (Washington, D.C.: United States Institute of Peace, June 1998).

8. For further information on the relationship between elections and conflict management, see Timothy Sisk and Andrew Reynolds, *Elections and Conflict Management in Africa* (Washington, D.C.: United States Institute of Peace Press, 1998); and Ben Reilly and Andrew Reynolds, *Electoral Systems and Conflict Resolution in Divided Societies* (Washington, D.C.: National Academy Press, 1999).

9. See Timothy Sisk, *Democratization in South Africa: The Elusive Social Contract* (Princeton, N.J.: Princeton University Press, 1995).

10. Arend Lijphart, *Democracy in Plural Societies* (New Haven, Conn.: Yale University Press, 1977).

11. See Donald Horowitz, *Ethnic Groups in Conflict* (Berkeley and Los Angeles: University of California Press, 1985).

12. See Andrew Reynolds and Ben Reilly, eds., *The International IDEA Handbook of Electoral Systems* (Stockholm: International Institute for Democracy and Election Assistance [IDEA], 1998).

13. The Fiji Constitutional Review Commission was arguably one of the best and most thorough efforts of informed specialists to help design a constitution and political system that would ameliorate

ethnic conflict through democracy. In theory, the resulting constitution was an ideal system of managing Fiji's struggle between indigenous Fijians and Indo-Fijians. Before rebels overthrew the government in June 2000, the constitution never had the chance to prove whether it could engender and manage multiethnic harmony as designed. See *Our Common Future*, 2 vols. (Suva, Fiji: Fiji Constitution Commission, 1999).

14. On the definition and management of intractable conflicts (those seen as resistant to resolution), see the University of Colorado's Conflict Resolution Consortium Web site at http://www.colorado.edu./conflict/.

15. See Francis Deng, *War of Visions: Conflicts of Identities in the Sudan* (Washington, D.C.: Brookings Institution, 1995).

16. Fen Osler Hampson, *Nurturing Peace: Why Peace Agreements Succeed or Fail* (Washington, D.C.: United States Institute of Peace Press, 1996).

17. On Burundi, see Stephen R. Weissman, *Preventing Genocide in Burundi: Lessons from International Diplomacy*, Peaceworks no. 22 (Washington, D.C.: United States Institute of Peace Press, July 1998). Ethical dilemmas for mediators seeking to choreograph a peace process also abound. Should peace be made with war criminals? The July 1999 peace agreement in Sierra Leone, brokered by Togo, drew widespread criticism for its provisions to give amnesty to the rebel forces, whose trail of widespread, grotesque human rights abuses is well documented.

18. Successful in that they have stopped the fighting. Defining success in negotiated settlements is a conceptually difficult enterprise. For a consideration of this debate, see Hampson, *Nuturing Peace*, 8–11.

19. See David Bloomfield, *Peacemaking Strategies in Northern Ireland: Building Complementarity in Conflict Management Theory* (New York: St. Martin's Press, 1997).

20. See John Paul Lederach, *Building Peace: Sustainable Reconciliation in Divided Societies* (Washington, D.C.: United States Institute of Peace Press, 1997).

21. For an overview of power-sharing options, see Timothy Sisk, *Power Sharing and International Mediation in Ethnic Conflicts* (Washington, D.C.: United States Institute of Peace Press, 1995); and Peter Harris and Ben Reilly, eds., *Democracy and Deep-Rooted Conflict: Options for Negotiators* (Stockholm: International IDEA, 1998).

22. See Timothy Sisk, *Local Democracy: Representation, Participation, and Conflict Management* (Stockholm: International IDEA, 2001).

23. For an elaboration of these proposals, see Connie Peck, *Sustainable Peace: The Role of the United Nations and Regional Organizations in Preventing Conflict* (Lanham, Md.: Rowman and Littlefield, 1998).

24. See the Web site of International IDEA at http://www.idea.int.

47

The Rule of Law
in the Postconflict Phase

Building a Stable Peace

Neil J. Kritz

THE CHANGED NATURE OF WAR at the end of the twentieth century requires a fresh perspective on the methods of managing conflict, on the one hand, and of making and maintaining peace, on the other. Today, the overwhelming majority of wars around the world are intranational rather than international. Wars fought between the military forces of two sovereign countries are increasingly the exception to the norm. In their stead, ethnic and religious conflicts, disputes over self-determination or secession, and violent power struggles between opposing domestic political factions account for 93 percent of the major armed conflicts recorded in recent years worldwide.[1] This statistic has profound ramifications for the processes of conflict prevention, conflict resolution, and postconflict peacebuilding. Tools and techniques that may be appropriate for resolving "classical" wars between state actors are often inadequate for achieving a meaningful accommodation and reconciliation between domestic adversaries, who together must build a durable national union. One element that assumes far greater importance in this changed context of war is the development of the rule of law.

It is essential at the outset to distinguish between the rule of law and simply rule *by* law. Broad concepts like democracy and the rule of law can easily be distorted. Even totalitarian regimes frequently use law as a tool in their arsenal of mechanisms for social control. The Nazis clothed many of their atrocities with a veneer of legality. The Soviet constitution of 1936 reads like a litany of legal entitlements, yet it served Stalin well with its wide loopholes for contortion.[2] During its final weeks in power, the Ceausescu regime in Romania invoked the law even while killing its citizens. These are all examples of rule *by* law, in which courts, statutes, and regulations are manipulated in the service of tyranny. In contrast, the rule of law does not simply provide yet one more vehicle by which government can wield and abuse its awesome power; on the contrary, it establishes principles that constrain the power of government, oblige it to conduct itself according to a series of prescribed and publicly known rules, and, in the postconflict setting, enable wary former adversaries all to play a vital role in keeping the new order honest and trustworthy.

Adherence to the rule of law entails far more than the mechanical application of static legal technicalities; it involves an evolutionary search for those institutions and processes that will best facilitate authentic stability through justice. Beyond its focus on limited government, the rule of law protects the rights of all members of society. It establishes rules and procedures that constrain the power of all parties, hold all parties accountable for their actions, and prohibit the accumulation of autocratic or oligarchic power. It also provides a variety of means for the nonviolent resolution of disputes, whether between private individuals, between groups, or between these actors and the government. In this way it is integrally related to the attempt to secure a stable peace. At a historic meeting in Copenhagen in 1990, the thirty-five nations then composing the Conference on Security and Cooperation in Europe (CSCE) affirmed this linkage, declaring that "societies based on . . . the rule of law are prerequisites for . . . the lasting order of peace, security, justice, and cooperation."[3]

The shift from international to intranational conflict engages the rule of law in two significant ways. First, international law is tracking and adapting to these new circumstances through evolutionary changes in the rules of warfare. There is now a growing consensus that many of the normative standards that had previously governed only wars between states, proscribing a variety of wartime abuses as violations of international law, are increasingly applicable to intrastate conflicts as well.[4] A half-century ago, when the world held individuals to account for war crimes and crimes against humanity at Nuremberg, those crimes were generally understood in international law as engendering liability only when perpetrated in the context of battles between states. By

November 1994, when the United Nations Security Council established an international criminal tribunal to prosecute the recent genocide in Rwanda, that understanding had changed. As approved by the Security Council, the charter of the Rwanda tribunal severed any nexus requirement between the international prosecution and punishment of crimes against humanity, on the one hand, and the international or noninternational character of the conflict in which they were committed, on the other hand, applying these international prohibitions to purely domestic conflict.[5] The treaty adopted in 1998 to establish a permanent International Criminal Court similarly incorporates this approach, defining genocide, crimes against humanity, and a range of war crimes as international offenses over which the court will have jurisdiction even when they are committed in conflicts of a noninternational character.[6]

At the same time (and in contrast to many formal militaries), irregular forces and insurgent groups engaged in civil wars, to whom these international rules of conduct now apply, do not generally receive any training in the laws of war. A challenge in the coming years is the need to more effectively disseminate and enforce these rules vis-à-vis such nonstate actors.

The second sense in which law is pertinent to the changed nature of war—and the principal focus of the present essay—is the central role played by the rule of law in establishing stability and a durable peace following an intranational conflict. It is completely plausible—and often the case—that a classical war between two independent states can be resolved and a durable peace developed without any modification to the internal rules, structures, or institutions of either party to the conflict. The 1980–88 war between Iran and Iraq, the border conflict between Peru and Ecuador, and the Ethiopia-Eritrea war all demonstrate this proposition.[7] In none of these six combatant countries did conclusion of the conflict entail any significant degree of internal reorganization. On the other hand, resolving violent conflicts between groups within a state and preventing their recurrence require the nurturing of societal structures and institutions to assure each combatant group that their interests will be protected through nonviolent means. This is rarely, if ever, possible without attention to the establishment of the rule of law. As stated by then UN secretary-general Boutros Boutros-Ghali in his description of peacebuilding, "Peacemaking and peacekeeping operations, to be truly successful, must come to include comprehensive efforts to identify and support structures which will tend to consolidate peace and advance a sense of confidence and well-being among people. . . . There is an obvious connection between . . . the rule of law and . . . the achievement of true peace and security in any new and stable political order."[8]

EMERGING INTERNATIONAL STANDARDS AND INTERNATIONAL ASSISTANCE

In recent years, international standards have evolved to define the meaning of the rule of law with ever-greater detail, providing an increasingly nuanced road map for those engaged in peacebuilding efforts. This articulation of explicit standards results primarily from the convergence of trends in two areas—democracy and human rights—each of which is closely related to, but distinct from, the rule of law.

During the past few decades, one school of thought focused on democratic systems as the best guarantor not only of freedom, but also of peace. (This school was largely, but not exclusively, the domain of Western political conservatives who advocated democracy in a Cold War context.) Extensive research demonstrated what was to some an obvious postulate: Democracies are less likely to go to war with one another than are totalitarian or authoritarian regimes.[9] But promoting democracy as a paradigm for the organization of society invites further inquiry. How does one create and ensure

a democratic polity? Answering this question requires a shift from democracy as a macro concept to an examination of those specific institutional structures and mechanisms that are essential to democracy and that distinguish it from a nondemocratic system. The result is a recognition and articulation of the basic elements of the rule of law, which is the ultimate guarantor of democracy.

The human rights stimulus followed an opposite path of analysis, moving from the specific to the general. Prompted in part by the atrocities of World War II, international law, as defined by the United Nations and various regional organizations, provided guarantees for an ever-widening catalogue of human rights. Over time, however, the international human rights movement (dominated to some degree by more liberal perspectives) increasingly recognized a basic fact: While an international campaign could often free a political prisoner from detention, he or she could quickly be replaced by many new victims unless the system and structures that permitted their abuse was changed. Stated differently, fundamental guarantees of individual human rights, already provided in international law, could most effectively be secured by more detailed guidelines on the institutions and procedures through which these rights should be enforced. The result once again was a recognition of the need to elaborate on the meaning of the rule of law.

As a consequence, a growing corpus of UN conventions, resolutions, declarations, and reports today elaborate standards on the rule of law. Various regional organizations have similarly contributed to the articulation of these guidelines. The Organization for Security and Cooperation in Europe (OSCE, formerly CSCE) has produced a detailed definition of the institutional and procedural elements of the rule of law—the most comprehensive catalogue of this sort ever adopted by an international organization—which serves as a standard for its fifty-five member-states.[10] The Council of Europe long ago made adherence to the rule of law an explicit requisite of membership in the organization and has similarly developed a sophisticated series of standards. Both the Organization of American States and the Council of Europe have developed and enforced their rule of law standards in part through the jurisprudence of a regional commission and court on human rights. (In the case of the Council of Europe, these two bodies have recently been merged into one.) As articulated through these various sources, the obligations imposed by the rule of law include the following:

- a representative government in which the executive is accountable to the elected legislature or to the electorate,
- the duty of the government to act in compliance with the constitution and the law,
- a clear separation between the state and political parties,
- accountability of the military and the police to civilian authorities,
- consideration and adoption of legislation by public procedure,
- publication of administrative regulations as the condition for their validity,
- effective means of redress against administrative decisions and provision of information to the person affected on the remedies available,
- an independent judiciary,
- protection of the independence of legal practitioners,
- detailed guarantees in the area of criminal procedure,
- compensation of victims of official abuse,
- free and fair elections at regular intervals, and
- comprehensive rights of political participation.

In elaborating the principle of the rule of law, some of these documents reiterate and expand on traditional human rights commitments, including freedoms of association, religion, expression, and movement, and protection against torture.

Beyond the articulation of standards on the rule of law, there has been a vast expansion in recent years of assistance programs to facilitate their implementation, particularly in countries emerging from conflict. Assessments, technical assistance, training, expert consultations on drafting of legislative and regulatory reforms, observer and advisory missions, and donation of resources and materials for the enhancement of the rule of law are now increasingly standard features of the postconflict scene. Those providing such assistance routinely include various agencies of the United Nations (in particular, the United Nations Development Programme and the Office of the High Commissioner for Human Rights), regional organizations, the World Bank, several bilateral governmental donors, and an assortment of foreign nongovernmental organizations.[11] Lawyers in military peacekeeping units have at times played an active role. There are so many providers of rule of law assistance that it has become necessary in a number of postconflict locations to convene rule of law donor coordination meetings on a regular basis to share information, avoid duplication, and attempt to provide sequenced assistance in keeping with the often-limited absorption capacity of postconflict local legal institutions. (Arguably, even with this heightened level of activity, the aggregate level of resources available for postconflict legal rebuilding has generally been much less than the amount needed, and donors often still pursue differing agendas.)

It must be kept in mind that the standards outlined above provide an important road map for development of the rule of law in a postconflict society but are seldom maintained to perfection in circumstances that are so far from perfect. In a country emerging from a protracted and bloody civil war, the justice system is generally in severe disrepair. Even if the courts had once been credible, the institutions and personnel of the system have typically been destroyed or corrupted. Notwithstanding significant foreign assistance, rebuilding an effective justice system (or, in the case of some countries, constructing one for the first time) will not occur overnight. The need to recruit and train investigators, prosecutors, judges, and court personnel; adopt needed legislative and regulatory reforms; develop a robust independent legal profession; put in place the material resources and equipment necessary to the operation of the system; and create a culture of respect for the law can take years. The international capacity to provide rapid-response legal assistance in such countries is developing but still has far to go. Postconflict evolution of the rule of law, like many other postconflict processes, may be somewhat messy and slow; in such circumstances, however, insistence on the perfect before the system moves forward can be the enemy of the good.

Even when the international community intervenes so thoroughly as to take over the task of local judicial administration, it is incapable of satisfying its own rules. A telling case in point is that of postwar Kosovo, where the UN mission is vested with all executive and legislative powers, and foreign experts imported by the United Nations have the mandate to administer the system of justice. Even in this case, an October 2000 report by the OSCE Kosovo office complained of common practices in the UN-run courts, and provisions of UN-imposed regulations, that fell short of international standards.[12]

SOME MAJOR STRUCTURAL AND PROCEDURAL ELEMENTS

The rule of law incorporates many of the elements necessary to ease tension and lessen the likelihood of further conflict. While a comprehensive review of all aspects of the rule of law is far beyond the scope of this essay, an examination of some of the major elements is warranted to understand their vital role in postconflict peacebuilding and conflict prevention.

An Independent Judiciary

A primary requisite for the functioning of the rule of law, of course, is an independent judiciary. At the most fundamental level, the principal purpose of the courts in virtually any system is to serve as a forum for the peaceful resolution of disputes. Conflict and disagreement are inevitable in any human system; it would be foolhardy to construct an idyllic model that did not assume disagreements between individuals and between groups. To forge a durable peace, it is necessary to channel those conflicts into a routinized and accepted mode of amelioration before they become violent and less tractable.

In any country emerging from armed conflict, numerous claims and grievances will remain. These may include demands for punishing the perpetrators of war crimes and other atrocities. Wars frequently displace large numbers of people, and the subsequent return of refugees or prisoners will often result in competing claims to property. In the postconflict context, courts are also often called upon to resolve disputes regarding the use of minority languages or the eligibility of various factions to participate in elections. Each of these is a highly volatile issue; an independent judiciary provides a peaceful and trustworthy means of addressing them. The judiciary also addresses, of course, the normal, everyday disputes between people, hopefully contributing to an overall culture that resolves its conflicts through such nonviolent means.

It is important to note that not every dispute is amenable to judicial resolution. Some points of conflict are purely political, not addressed by any law that the courts might apply. To make the courts the arbiter of such disputes —particularly if the judiciary is still a fragile institution—risks politicizing the very institution that must be blind to politics, undermining the credibility and independence of the judicial system. Several analysts have suggested that this sort of politicization characterized the

Russian constitutional court in the early 1990s, rendering it a more high-profile but less effective institution for facilitating Russia's difficult democratic transition.

Law Enforcement and Criminal Justice

The rule of law requires a system of criminal justice that deters and punishes banditry and acts of violence, allowing the citizenry to live with a sense of security. At the same time, the criminal justice system must be immune from abuse for political purposes and must adhere to a lengthy list of internationally recognized rights of criminal procedure.[13] In other words, if societal tensions and the likelihood of further conflict are to be minimized, people must become confident that they will not be abused either by private sector criminals or by the authorities.

An additional problem confronting many countries emerging from war or from a repressive regime to a democracy is the hiatus in enforcement capabilities. A transitional period unfolds during which the old police and security forces (as well as the system of authority in general) are eliminated or weakened, but the new order has yet to take hold. Retaining the old police and judiciary, many of whom were part of the problem rather than of the solution, undercuts the credibility of the new order and could threaten the ability of the new government to manage the transition. It takes a couple of years or more to train new personnel, establish new lines of command, and build a new and credible criminal justice system. In Russia, Georgia, South Africa, and El Salvador, to cite a few examples, this time lag has resulted in a security vacuum readily capitalized upon by criminal elements. In each of these four countries, the transition has produced a soaring crime rate; the same trend occurs in numerous states in the postconflict phase. While people's daily fear of being caught in the cross fire of war or of being viciously repressed by the authorities because of their political views has dramatically receded, it has been partially replaced by

a new fear of the thieves, gangs, and mafias that operate with relative impunity in the interim period. In some cases these new criminals are demobilized combatants and officers of the conflict just ended, still possessing their weapons but no new livelihood. In El Salvador, for example, an official inquiry determined that the death squads that killed thousands of leftists and moderates during the war transformed themselves into new criminal bands, unchecked and undaunted by an ineffective criminal justice system. Uncontrolled, this dramatic rise in crime poses a very real threat to the stability of the new peace.

Because of this vacuum of effective law enforcement, postconflict settings provide fertile ground for the growth of transnational criminal operations, which then become difficult to uproot and can undermine the stability not only of the country in question but of other nations as well. The postconflict absence of an effectively functioning government in Kosovo provides a poignant recent example. In January 2001, the British government sent a special criminal intelligence squad to Kosovo to focus on the entrenchment of criminal gangs involved in smuggling illegal immigrants, prostitutes, and drugs to Western Europe.[14] The postconflict government's incapacity to deal effectively with this problem may be viewed as complacency toward transnational crime and may put at risk some of the international assistance and investment it badly needs.

To address these problems, postconflict reconstruction has to move quickly to establish courts that are above corruption and intimidation by criminal elements; police forces need to be supported, and individual officers must be held accountable for violations of the rule of law; and training and cleansing of the law enforcement and criminal justice systems need to begin promptly following the conflict. The Dayton accords, for example, attempt to integrate this lesson, addressing each of these points explicitly in the terms for the postconflict phase.[15]

In addition, international police operations have expanded significantly in the past few years, becoming commonplace in postconflict scenarios to help fill the void in law enforcement. By 2000, approximately nine thousand UN civilian police were authorized for deployment in various postwar locations. The organization and fielding of such police operations are gradually becoming more professionalized, but numerous challenges remain with respect to the recruitment, training, coordination, and clarification of the law to be applied by these forces in the future.

Transparency and Predictability

It is accepted and proven that transparency and predictability of action by adversaries reduce the likelihood of international conflict. Confidence-building measures have been instituted to reduce tensions in a variety of regions, under which certain actions that might agitate an opposing party (troop movements or missile testing, for instance) can only be taken according to prescribed procedures that facilitate communication and reduce suspicion.

Traditionally, diplomats and those involved in conflict resolution and conflict prevention have applied this principle primarily to conflicts between states. As conflicts have become increasingly intranational, however, the principle is equally valid. Confidence and trust will be increased—and the potential for suspicion, surprise, and tension reduced—when parties are required to conduct their activities in the open. The rule of law requires that governments adhere to principles of transparency and predictability, and it establishes several mechanisms to ensure that this is so. These include requirements that laws be adopted through an open and public process by a representative body, all regulations be published, no rules be applied retroactively, government agencies conduct their affairs according to prescribed rules, and the whole system be subject to judicial scrutiny to ensure compliance with these rules.

As articulated by the conservative Austrian-born economist Friedrich von Hayek:

> Nothing distinguishes more clearly conditions in a free country from those in a country under arbitrary government than observance in the former of the great principles known as the Rule of Law. Stripped of all its technicalities, this means that government in all its actions is bound by rules fixed and announced beforehand—rules which make it possible to foresee with fair certainty how the authority will use its coercive powers in given circumstances and to plan one's individual affairs on the basis of this knowledge.[16]

Controlling the Bureaucracy

Even when the relationship between securing the rule of law and avoiding further conflict is recognized, attention and foreign assistance tend to focus fairly exclusively on the courts and the legislature. These may be the primary institutions, but as technology advances and as society becomes more complex, parliaments are able to address a decreasing proportion of the issues with which governments must deal. Legislative bodies can generally paint only with broad brushstrokes, leaving more and more of the details, as well as the implementation, to be provided by the administrative bureaucracy of the modern state.

In many countries the average citizen will most frequently experience the presence or absence of the rule of law (and will accordingly feel less or more alienated from the system) not through any interaction with the legislative or judicial process, not through any involvement in broad constitutional questions, but through encounters with the administrative state. Resolving a problem with their social security benefits, obtaining a license to fish and support their family, getting a permit to build a house or a church or register a political party, obtaining state certification and funding for an ethnic language school—these are the sorts of events that bring most people into contact with the state, and they are not generally in the purview of the legislative branch. Unless the rule of law is extended to administrative decision making, these interactions are unlikely to be subject to public scrutiny and thus are open to corruption, manipulation, and discrimination. For most nationals and foreign advisers engaged in reconstructing war-torn societies, administrative procedure is hardly as glamorous as constitution writing or elections, but they are ill advised to neglect it, for it is in this realm that, unnoticed, the seeds of grievance and confrontation may quietly, even unwittingly, be sown.

In Peru in 1984, some correlation was believed to exist between the level of public confidence in the government, on the one hand, and the effectiveness of the violent opposition, on the other hand. Peru had a functioning democratic legislature, with laws adopted and published following public debate; to the casual observer, the system adhered to the rule of law. Despite this appearance, economist Hernando de Soto found that 99 percent of the rules governing daily life in the country never went through the legislative process. They were, instead, the result of regulations issued by executive branch agencies, a process that was not subject to public participation, procedural controls, or any oversight.[17] This kind of situation is not unique to Peru. Insofar as the power of these administrative bureaucracies continues unchecked in the postconflict period, it makes it more likely that individuals and groups will feel disenfranchised from the system, individual and national economic growth will be hampered, and administrative regulations or decisions may discriminate on the basis of political affiliation, ethnicity, religion, race, or geography.

In implementing these principles of the rule of law, those involved in postconflict peace building will often need to focus on two challenges of particular urgency for the process of reconciliation. These are discussed in the next two sections.

RECKONING WITH WAR CRIMES AND OTHER PAST ABUSES

A basic question confronting many societies in the postconflict phase is how to deal with the legacy of massive abuses that may have been inflicted by those on each side of the conflict. The worst of these offenses are those classified by international law as war crimes, crimes against humanity, and genocide. Nations also need to come to terms with the question of accountability for those abuses that, while not constituting such international crimes, still give rise to deeply felt resentment and antagonism in the postconflict phase. Some of these abuses may have been perpetrated in the heat of the conflict; others may have taken place earlier, fanning the resentments that led to the conflict. A variety of approaches need to be considered in contemplating the issue.

Criminal Accountability

Some argue not only that the trial and punishment of these offenses are essential to achieve some degree of justice, but also that a public airing and condemnation of the crimes are the best way to draw a line between times past and present, lest the public perceive the new order as simply more of the same. Others claim that these are simply show trials unbefitting a search for peace and democracy, that a public review of wartime atrocities will inflame passions rather than calm them, and that the best way to rebuild and reconcile the nation is to leave the past behind by forgiving and forgetting the sins of all parties to the conflict.

In many countries, prosecutions for abuses committed during the conflict can serve several functions. They provide victims with a sense of justice and catharsis—a sense that their grievances have been addressed and can more easily be put to rest rather than smoldering in anticipation of the next round of conflict. In addition, they can establish a new dynamic in society, an understanding that aggressors and those who attempt to abuse the rights of others will be held accountable.

Because these trials tend to receive much attention from both the local population and foreign observers, they often provide an important focus for rebuilding the judiciary and the criminal justice system in accordance with rule of law principles. Perhaps most important for purposes of long-term reconciliation, this approach underscores that specific individuals— not entire ethnic or religious or political groups —committed atrocities for which they need to be held accountable. In so doing, it rejects the dangerous culture of collective guilt and retribution that too often produces further cycles of resentment and violence.

When prosecutions are undertaken, how widely should the net be cast in imposing sanctions on those who committed war crimes or similar abuses? How high up the chain of command should superiors be responsible for wrongs committed by their underlings? Conversely, how far down the chain should soldiers or bureaucrats be held liable for following the orders of their superiors in facilitating these abuses?

International legal standards are evolving that help address these questions; there is a growing consensus that, at least for the most heinous violations of human rights and international humanitarian law, a sweeping amnesty is impermissible.[18] On the other hand, offenses like genocide or crimes against humanity generally require the participation of a vast number of people, and international law does not demand the prosecution of every individual implicated in the atrocities. Putting all of the hundreds and sometimes thousands of such individuals on trial, whether before a local or international court, would be financially, politically, and logistically untenable. A symbolic or representative number of prosecutions of those most culpable may satisfy international

obligations, especially if an overly extensive trial program would threaten the stability of the country. Argentina, Ethiopia, and some of the countries of Central and Eastern Europe, for example, have adopted this approach in dealing with the legacy of massive human rights abuses by their ousted regimes.

In several cases the challenge has been made slightly more manageable by distinguishing distinct categories of culpability and designing different approaches for each. Roughly, these classifications break down into (1) the leaders, those who gave the orders to commit war crimes, and those who actually carried out the worst offenses (inevitably the smallest category numerically); (2) those who perpetrated serious abuses but not rising to the first category; and (3) those whose offenses were minimal. The severity of treatment then follows accordingly. The Dayton accords concluding the war in the former Yugoslavia more or less adopted this approach. In the first category, the warring parties committed themselves to cooperating with the international criminal tribunal established to prosecute those on each side of the conflict who perpetrated the most heinous offenses (that is, genocide, war crimes, and crimes against humanity). The accords also prohibit any individuals indicted by the tribunal from holding public office. In the second tier of culpability, the agreement characterizes as a confidence-building measure the obligation to immediately undertake "the prosecution, dismissal, or transfer, as appropriate, of persons in military, paramilitary, and police forces, and other public servants responsible for serious violations of the basic rights of persons belonging to ethnic or minority groups."[19] Finally, all returning refugees and displaced persons charged with any crime related to the conflict "other than a serious violation of international humanitarian law" are guaranteed amnesty for their offenses.[20] While the implementation of these provisions has been lacking, the basic framework is sound.

The Rwandan case demonstrates the need for pragmatism to temper an absolutist approach to prosecution. For decades, elites maneuvering for power manipulated ethnic rivalries between Hutu majorities and Tutsi minorities for political ends, without any fear of being called to account for their actions. This culminated in 1994 in one of the most horrific genocidal massacres in recent memory, as five hundred thousand to a million Tutsis and moderate Hutus were brutally slaughtered in just fourteen weeks.

To break this cycle of violence, the new Rwandan government correctly insisted that it was necessary to replace the endemic culture of impunity with a sense of accountability. To achieve this, many senior members of the new government insisted throughout their first year in office that every person who participated in the atrocities should be prosecuted and punished. The result was the multiyear pre-trial detention of some 125,000 alleged *génocidaires* in prisons built to house a small fraction of that number—far fewer than the total number of potential defendants but vastly more than can be handled by any criminal justice system in a reasonable amount of time. To compound the problem, Rwanda's criminal justice system was decimated during the genocide, with most lawyers and judges either killed, in exile, or in prison. In the past three years, the Rwandan courts processed more than three thousand genocide cases—a Herculean feat matched by virtually no society in history, let alone one still reeling from destruction—in proceedings that have been evaluated as generally fair by independent observers, including those representing the defense. By late 2001, the Rwandan government plans to move the overwhelming majority of the caseload to a new village-level system called *gacaca*, loosely based on an indigenous model of traditional justice. Local residents in each of thousands of villages will select their own *gacaca* panel; genocide defendants will appear before these bodies in hearings that will include the active participation of the

members of their local community. The program will not satisfy all the criteria set by the international standards described earlier in this essay. There will likely be some shortcomings, in particular in terms of compliance with contemporary international standards for criminal procedure and criminal defense rights. Some victims fear that in communities where the genocide was so sweeping that no victim-witnesses remain, *gacaca* will be a whitewash process conducted by neighbors of the defendant who supported the genocide; some defendants fear drumhead justice before *gacaca* tribunals in communities dominated by victims; local and international human rights groups point to several concerns, including the exclusion of any defense counsel from *gacaca* proceedings. Nonetheless, most Rwandans in the justice system feel that they have no alternative: the caseload cannot be handled by the courts in any timely manner; politically it is not an option to throw open the prisons and release over one hundred thousand alleged *génocidaires;* and it is not acceptable to continue to keep people locked up for years without trial. Although the *gacaca* program will be controversial, Rwandan advocates argue that it will engage local villages in the process of justice, return and reintegrate perpetrators into their home communities, and empty the prisons of untried cases within a relatively short time.

With rare exceptions, it is arguable that capital punishment should not be available in these transitional trials. Given the high emotion and political pressures inherent in these trials, the death penalty may further aggravate tensions the society faces in the immediate post-conflict phase.

The issue of accountability versus impunity is not only relevant to the resolution of conflict within a war-torn country; it also may have grave consequences for future, seemingly unrelated conflicts in other parts of the world. In explaining his confidence that he could proceed with his diabolical campaign of genocide without fear of retribution by the international community, Adolf Hitler infamously scoffed, "Who remembers the Armenians?"—referring to the victims of a genocide twenty-five years earlier for which no one had been brought to account. Recent evidence suggests that the Bosnian Serb leadership, in pursuing a campaign of ethnic cleansing and genocide in the 1990s, was emboldened by the fact that the Khmer Rouge leadership has never been prosecuted or punished for the atrocities it committed in Cambodia in the 1970s.[21]

Cleansing the Structures of Government

Holding individuals accountable may entail more than criminal trials. In many countries, limitations may be placed on participation in the public sector by those associated with past abuses. A durable peace requires the establishment of public confidence in the institutions of the new order. That confidence can be seriously undercut if these institutions are staffed by the same personnel who gave rise to prior or current resentments. Those who kept the engine of an abusive but now-ousted government running may be perceived as of uncertain loyalty, and supporters of discriminatory positions or abusive tactics of former antigovernment groups may not be seen as credible candidates for unbiased public administration. Some conflicts may lack this element of clear perpetrator and victim groups, but most post–Cold War civil conflicts have included patterns of atrocities or gross violations of human rights by one or both sides. Even where they are not liable in a criminal sense, those who facilitated past abuses should not be permitted to infect or represent the new governmental structures. At the same time, it may be argued that in the immediate postconflict phase, when seasoned talent from the level of junior bureaucrat to senior minister may be scarce, some of these people, particularly from the former government, are vital to national reconstruction, that their knowledge and experience are indispensable to making the new order function.

There are several examples of such attempts at screening. In El Salvador, the peace agreement provided for a special Ad Hoc Commission, which identified one hundred senior military officers for retirement due to their implication in past human rights abuses. In Bosnia, the International Police Task Force is assigned the responsibility of excluding from the newly reconstituted local police any candidate who has previously engaged in abuse of ethnic minorities. Even if such individuals are not prosecuted for their crimes, permitting them to occupy positions in which their presence would be cause for a sense of greater insecurity among their former victims would be unjust and detract from peacebuilding efforts.

Administrative purges do not, however, provide the same level of due process protection as does a criminal proceeding. Because they involve a large number of people, purges tend to be conducted in summary fashion and can easily be misused to mete out a form of victor's justice in the allocation of government jobs. In stressing the importance of individual responsibility and accountability, the rule of law rejects any notion of collective guilt. When large numbers of people are removed from their places of employment solely because they had worked there during the conflict or because of their membership in a particular political party, without any demonstration of individual wrongdoing, they may legitimately cry foul and question the democratic underpinnings of the new government. Rather than contributing to reconciliation and rebuilding, such purges may create a substantial ostracized opposition that threatens the stability of the new system. In some cases, the dislocational effects of such a measure have been tempered by limiting any ban on public service by implicated individuals to a cooling-off period of a few years, permitting their entry (or reentry) only after the initial postconflict phase and after stable and trustworthy public institutions are in place. This problem requires a careful balancing of interests.

Establishing a Historical Record

In the transitional period after an intranational conflict, history is always controversial. Each side will still have its defenders who will deny that the abuses of which it is accused ever took place, will claim that they were actually perpetrated by others, or will suggest that they were justified by exigent circumstances. Left uncontested, these competing claims may undermine the new order and the effort at peacebuilding; they may also add insult to the injury already inflicted on the victims, deeply sowing seeds of resentment that can result in a new round of violence. The Bosnian war displayed unresolved issues of history and resentment dating back some seven centuries.

As a consequence, in addition to the focus on individual perpetrators, establishing an official overall accounting of the past is often an important element to a successful transition, providing a sense of national justice, reckoning, and catharsis. Fairly conducted criminal trials are one way to establish the facts and figures of past abuses; the formation of a "truth commission" is another. While the two processes can complement each other, a truth commission may be all the more useful for healing and reconciliation if the country is not equipped to conduct fair and credible trials. Long-term reconciliation requires a careful examination of the mix that will best fit the society in question.

In El Salvador, the twelve-year civil war between the government and the Farabundo Martí National Liberation Front (FMLN) left some seventy-five thousand people dead. "As the peace negotiations advanced, the charges and countercharges relating to [atrocities committed by each side] threatened to become serious obstacles to any peaceful resolution of the conflict. It was soon recognized, therefore, that the hate and mistrust built up over the years required . . . some mechanism permitting an honest accounting of these terrible deeds."[22] At the war's conclusion in 1992, the judiciary was intact, but it was highly politicized and compromised and incapable of credibly addressing the difficult issue of accountability for war crimes or egregious violations of human rights in an objective manner. The three-member United Nations Commission on the Truth, established by the peace agreements between the warring parties, was seen as an alternative vehicle through which to attain some sense of justice and accountability.[23]

Although not a court, the commission—like similar entities that have been created in several countries facing a legacy of abuses on a mass scale—investigated and reported on abuses that had been committed by both sides during the war, giving both victims and perpetrators an opportunity to make their testimony part of the official record. Because of the absence of a credible criminal justice system, the commission also felt obliged to render certain judgments in its 1993 report that would otherwise have been left to the Salvadoran judiciary. A prime example was the commission's decision to publicly name those individuals it determined were guilty of particularly egregious abuses, even though the commission process had not afforded these individuals all the due process protections to which they would be entitled in a judicial proceeding. Had a credible national justice system been functioning, the commission might have kept all such names confidential in its report and instead turned them over to the authorities for prosecution.[24] In its report, the commission analyzed the ways in which the militarization of Salvadoran society had eviscerated all three branches of government; it also made recommendations to enhance the prospects for each of these institutions and the military to function in accord with the precepts of the rule of law.

Truth commissions have provided a forum and a voice for the hundreds or thousands of victims who will never be called to testify at trial. They have been used in several countries to look not simply at individual cases but also at the systemic problems that made abuses possible, at the role of various sectors—the security forces, religious leadership, the media, the educational system, the judiciary, and so on—in engendering, through acts of omission and commission, the environment for these offenses to occur. Based on their analyses, the commissions have been tasked with developing detailed recommendations for appropriate governmental and societal reforms. Truth commissions established or contemplated in postconflict settings have recently been charged, to a greater degree than those created in the transition from a repressive regime, with developing ways to contribute to the process of reconciliation. In Guatemala, where a civil war raged for thirty-five years and cost over one hundred thousand lives, the peace agreement provided for appointment of a truth commission and stressed the importance of establishing the "whole truth" about past abuses by all parties, presenting this as part of a process that "will help lay the basis for a peaceful coexistence" and that "will eliminate all forms of retaliation or revenge as a prerequisite for a firm and lasting peace."[25] In Sierra Leone it is hoped that the truth commission will be able to deal with the vexing problem of child combatants who perpetrated atrocities. In Bosnia, the truth commission will also expose the positive stories of individuals on all sides of the conflict who took risks to protect fellow citizens of other ethnic groups from abuse.

Compensation, Restitution, and Rehabilitation

Finally, from the perspective of the rule of law, a reckoning of past abuses must focus not only on the perpetrators but also on the victims. Notwithstanding the competing demands for limited resources, which is always an aspect of the war-torn economy, issues of compensation and rehabilitation of victims should be incorporated into most plans for postconflict reconstruction. Compensation serves at least three functions in the process of national reconciliation. First, it helps the victims to

manage the material aspect of their loss. Second, it constitutes an official acknowledgment of their pain by the nation. Both of these facilitate the societal reintegration of people who may have long suffered in silence. Third, it may deter the state from future abuses, by imposing a financial cost to such misdeeds. There is a growing consensus in international law that the state is obligated to provide compensation to victims of egregious human rights abuses perpetrated by the government; if the regime that committed the acts in question does not provide compensation, the obligation carries over to the successor government.

In a few countries new legal entities have been established to deal with this complex aspect of justice in the postconflict phase. In the aftermath of the war in the former Yugoslavia, the peace accords provided for the establishment of a commission to restore land to those displaced by the war, resolve countless disputes over property, and provide compensation to dislocated victims of the conflict. In Rwanda there are thousands of competing claims to property made by several groups: returning Tutsi exiles who departed the country over a thirty-five-year period, those displaced during the genocide, and Hutu refugees who left in 1994; before long, these will be joined by returning detainees. In both Rwanda and the former Yugoslavia, the rule of law requires equitable restitution or compensation, which are also essential for the construction of a durable peace. Depending on the situation, compensation may range from return of lost property or educational benefits to pensions for survivors of those killed or funds for minority group cultural activities.[26]

The Need for an Integrated Approach

Massive and systemic atrocities often either are an outgrowth of complex problems in a society or contribute to the creation of the same. They are generally not amenable to simplistic solutions. It has become increasingly clear that effective postconflict peacebuilding generally requires not just one of the mechanisms outlined above but a nuanced and integrated approach that combines and sequences various approaches to address the particular case. For more than two years in postwar Bosnia, many people argued that a truth and reconciliation commission should be created to complement the work of the International Criminal Tribunal in the The Hague, to provide a forum for thousands of victims, to develop recommendations for systemic reforms, and to undertake other tasks. The effort was stymied by those who insisted that no such body should be established until the tribunal had concluded its work. The result would have been an implicit statement that, if a postconflict society is determined to be incapable of conducting its own credible war crimes trials, and if that function is assumed by the international community, that society should then be blocked for several years from pursuing any other program to deal with its own troubled past. Similarly, in Sierra Leone, the 1999 Lomé peace agreement provided for the establishment of a truth and reconciliation commission. Subsequently, the UN Security Council mandated the establishment of a special war crimes court in Sierra Leone—at which point many international actors suggested that the commission effort could be abandoned. In both cases, extensive discussions among local and international actors have, by the end of 2000, produced consensus on the need for both trials and truth commissions, proceeding concurrently to fulfill different functions in a complementary manner, to move these troubled countries forward. In addressing accountability for mass violence in East Timor, UN and local authorities have similarly adopted an integrated, multitrack approach.

THE CONSTITUTION-MAKING PROCESS

In many countries in transition from civil war to a new government, one of the first important tasks is drafting a new constitution. The constitution is, of course, the foundational legal document from which the entire national system of rules will derive; it is the cornerstone for the rule of law. In addition, insofar as the constitution enshrines the vision of a new society, articulates the fundamental principles by which the political system will be reorganized, and redistributes power within the country, both its substantive provisions and the process by which it is created can play an important role in the consolidation of peace.

When a constitution is drafted and imposed by a small group of elites from the victorious party, a foundation may result that is not only less democratic but also less stable. Alternatively, given the nature of this document, constitution making can involve a process of national dialogue, allowing competing perspectives and claims within the postwar society to be aired and incorporated, thus facilitating reconciliation among these groups. It can also be a process of national education with respect to concepts of government, the problems and concerns of different groups within the country, the development of civil society and citizen responsibility, and international norms of human rights, nondiscrimination, and tolerance that have been incorporated into recent constitutions. In short, the process of constitution making can contribute to peace and stability.

In Eritrea, following a thirty-year war for independence, the constitution-making process was intentionally structured to facilitate the consolidation of peace—a two-year effort that was proclaimed "a historic process of a coming together of Eritreans for a creative national discourse."[27] The Constitutional Commission included a variety of religious, ethnic, and regional constituencies. Offices were established in five regions of the country, with an additional office responsible for involving the estimated 750,000 Eritreans living abroad in the process. The Constitutional Commission adopted a strategy "which involves the widest possible public consultation, a strategy which eschews the top-down approach."[28] Discussions were initiated through an extensive series of civic education seminars, debates, and town and village meetings reaching over a hundred thousand people. Pamphlets, newspapers, television, and radio were used to facilitate public education and dialogue. Articulation of basic principles and of a draft constitution was the subject of further public debate and input.

In Cambodia, although not accompanied by the same wide-scale public consultation, the drafting and adoption of a new constitution after the Paris Peace Accords also included a degree of national dialogue, with rival factions all shaping the distribution of power and rights within Cambodian society. Constitution making in South Africa provides a further example of the usefulness of this approach. During one session in the spring of 1995, for instance, the Constitutional Assembly spent hours deliberating over provisions in the new draft constitution concerning the security forces in the new South Africa, hardly a minor or noncontroversial topic for opponents emerging from years of conflict. A variety of sensitive issues—such as emergency powers and their limits, the authorization of soldiers to disobey orders that violate international law, and civilian control of the security forces—were all respectfully discussed and debated by former enemies now in Parliament, ranging from Pan-African Congress members on the left of the political spectrum to those of the Freedom Front on the right. Several participants subsequently acknowledged that as little as a year earlier, such a discussion would have been inconceivable.[29] In the context of the transition, however, the lengthy Constitutional Assembly process provided an important avenue for previously violent adversaries to negotiate and collaborate in constructing each piece of their new order.

Developing a constitution through this process of national dialogue also has certain limitations. It is far less efficient than the alternative model, in which the terms of this crucial social compact are determined by a small group behind relatively closed doors and handed down to the people like contemporary tablets from Mount Sinai. A drawn-out process of constitution making could be destabilizing, for example, if it means a lengthy transition governed by no basic rules or a transition still governed by an old constitutional system that had exacerbated the conflict. In such situations interim arrangements may first be needed for the consolidation of peace. Such was the case in South Africa, where a negotiated interim constitution established the basis for transition, and a lengthier process then followed to debate the tough issues and develop the final document. In addition, it is essential to recognize that not all of society's problems can be resolved through the constitution. As was suggested earlier with respect to the courts, viewing constitution making as a means of redressing all group grievances may force onto the plate issues that are not appropriate to this process. This can result either in rejection of the process by disgruntled factions or inclusion of promises in the new document that cannot be fulfilled, either of which would damage the credibility of the process and of the new constitution.

Enabling a broad spectrum of society to participate in shaping the compact means that the process will take significantly longer to complete, entail higher administrative costs and greater debate, and possibly result in some compromises that might otherwise be avoided. At the same time, it may also produce a constitutional system that is more widely understood and accepted, more stable, and more supportive of peace. Decisions regarding the process will necessarily be affected by the nature of the particular conflict and the circumstances of its resolution.[30]

HOW LARGE A FOREIGN ROLE?

As noted, while the challenge of demonstrating a new beginning founded on justice and the rule of law will likely present itself very early in the postconflict phase, constructing new institutions and training new lawyers, judges, police, and other personnel can take years. This is a recurring quandary.

In some instances, the solution has been to pursue justice and reconciliation through the medium of an international entity. In El Salvador, for example, the country's relatively small population was felt to be too polarized to achieve any consensus on the abuses committed during the conflict. As a consequence, the UN truth commission was composed entirely of non-Salvadorans in order to achieve a degree of neutrality, objectivity, and acceptability that could not be garnered by any domestic body at that early stage in the transition from war.

The United Nations Security Council created two international criminal tribunals to respond to civil war and genocide in Rwanda and the former Yugoslavia—the first such bodies established since the Nuremberg tribunal a half-century earlier. Several factors militated in favor of internationalizing the response in these cases:

- the crimes were so horrific and so great a challenge to basic precepts of international law;
- the need for justice as an essential ingredient in achieving reconciliation and breaking the cycle of violence was so apparent; and
- the domestic justice systems (particularly in Rwanda) were so thoroughly decimated.

In addition, an international tribunal was better positioned than a domestic court to (1) convey a clear message that the international community will not tolerate such atrocities, hopefully deterring future carnage of this sort, not only in Rwanda and Bosnia but worldwide; (2) be staffed by experts able to apply and interpret evolving international law standards; (3) be more likely to have the necessary human and material resources at its disposal; (4) function—and be perceived as functioning—on the basis of independence and impartiality rather than retribution; (5) advance the development and enforcement of interna-

tional criminal norms; and (6) obtain jurisdiction over many of the worst perpetrators who were no longer in the country. The two tribunals have produced several important advances in the understanding and treatment of war crimes, crimes against humanity, and genocide.

In rare circumstances such as these, creating an international entity to provide a sense of justice is vital. In the vast majority of instances, however, this should only be the second choice. Even in cases such as Rwanda and Bosnia, where the establishment of international criminal tribunals was appropriate, durable peace requires that robust domestic institutions be established, developing within the states in question the capacity to undertake efforts at justice and reconciliation. Although it is hardly a zero-sum equation, the relative allocation of resources makes a statement regarding international priorities in the area of postwar justice and the rule of law: while total contributions to the two international tribunals is approaching the $1 billion mark, allocations to develop the legal institutions within the countries in question have totaled only a small fraction of that amount.

Whether accountability and justice are achieved through a court or through a truth commission, they are generally best achieved through a domestic process managed by the country in question. If it can be conducted in accord with the protections afforded by the rule of law, prosecution before domestic courts can enhance the legitimacy of the new postconflict government and of the judiciary, be more sensitive than outsiders to nuances of the local community, emphasize that the nation will henceforth hold all individuals accountable for their crimes, and stress a viable alternative to vigilante justice. In addition, the state and the body politic will generally be most likely to integrate these lessons of justice, accountability, and reconciliation following a cathartic *domestic* process that includes representatives of all parties. This internalization is extremely important to building peace. Conversely, if the state is relieved of the need to face these issues, leaving them to be handled and concluded by outsiders (and therefore easily disowned by local leaders if that becomes politically expedient), then the experience may contribute less to a durable peace and the entrenchment of the rule of law.

A UN Commission of Experts that preceded creation of the Rwanda tribunal acknowledged this point, noting that domestic courts could be more sensitive to individual cases and that resulting decisions "could be of greater and more immediate symbolic force, because verdicts would be rendered by courts familiar to the local community."[31]

Two developments suggest a gradual acknowledgment of the priority to be given to domestic ownership of the process. First, since 1995, there has been no purely international body established along the lines of the El Salvador commission or the Yugoslavia and Rwanda tribunals. Instead, where an international role is deemed necessary, the trend has been toward creation of hybrid international-domestic bodies, with local members generally forming the majority. Examples include the truth commission recently concluded in Guatemala, the one under consideration in Bosnia, and proposed special courts in Cambodia and Sierra Leone. Second, unlike the international tribunals for the former Yugoslavia and Rwanda, which were given primacy of jurisdiction that trumps the ability of any domestic court to pursue a prosecution, the 1998 Rome treaty to establish a permanent International Criminal Court (ICC) correctly shifted that primacy. The ICC is complementary to national justice systems and can only assert its jurisdiction over a case of genocide, war crimes, or crimes against humanity when the national system is incapable of doing so or unwilling to do so.[32]

A related trend vis-à-vis the foreign role is represented by proceedings such as those brought against former Chilean dictator Augusto Pinochet. As a result of the growing acceptance of the principle of universal jurisdiction over certain international crimes, some countries have begun to assert the jurisdiction of their national courts to prosecute genocide, war crimes, crimes against humanity, and torture even when committed in an internal armed conflict in a second country, with the perpetrators and victims both citizens of the second country. In the past decade, criminal cases have been opened in at least eleven countries against foreign nationals for crimes against humanity and related abuses allegedly committed in their home countries. In several of these cases, victims have circumvented the unwillingness or incapacity of their own authorities to pursue the prosecution. In the Pinochet case, in which a Spanish judge sought the former president's extradition from London, victims and judges were able to force the matter forward over the wishes of all three of the governments involved (Chile, Spain, and Great Britain). A key result of the embarrassing specter of a Spanish judge finally doing what Chilean society had been unable to do for itself for two decades was the unleashing of a torrent of activity and emotion in Chile. The consequent efforts to prosecute Pinochet at home, open criminal investigations against many others, and force the military to meet at long last with human rights lawyers and begin to determine and reveal the fate of the disappeared displayed the extent to which the trigger of the external proceedings helped stimulate the completion of Chile's democratic transition. Developments in the next few years in such exercise of universal jurisdiction will no doubt be a somewhat messy process.

CONCLUSION

New challenges to peace require new tools. As war in all parts of the globe changes its complexion, becoming preponderantly intranational, establishing the rule of law plays an increasingly critical role, particularly in the immediate postconflict construction of peace.

There are those who, even today, imply that emphasis on the establishment of the rule of law is irrelevant, or at best tangential, to the real work of conflict resolution and postconflict peacebuilding—a belief that the imposition of legal regulations and institutions will by itself erase deep-seated resentments, hatreds, and power struggles. Nothing could be less accurate. The rule of law has at its core a hard-nosed and not particularly optimistic assessment of human nature and the prospects for conflict. It assumes that pacific pledges and conciliatory rhetoric are obviously important to peacebuilding but can be too tenuous. In the worst case, the rule of law imposes a network of institutions, mechanisms, and procedures that check sources of tension at an early phase, constrain the ability of any party to engage in violent or abusive action, and force an open process and a relatively level playing field. In the best case, when diligently nurtured, this system of accountability, conflict resolution, limits on power, and the airing and processing of opposing views—all undertaken through nonviolent channels—becomes habit forming, reducing the likelihood of another civil war.

NOTES

1. Taylor B. Seybolt, "Major Armed Conflicts," in *SIPRI Yearbook 2000: Armaments, Disarmament and International Security* (New York: Oxford University Press, 2000), 15. The SIPRI study defines a major armed conflict as "the use of armed force between the military forces of two or more governments, or of one government and at least one organized armed group, resulting in the battle-related deaths of at least 1000 people in any single year and in which the incompatibility concerns control of government and/or territory" (ibid.). This figure is based on 1999 data. A review of comparable surveys for 1992–99 finds that wars of the classical interstate variety only made up, on average, slightly more than 3 percent of the major armed conflicts in any one year.

2. "The proclamation of this constitution . . . not only did not stop lawless and arbitrary rule, but also

served to camouflage it, allowing the torture and killing of innocent people while praising Stalin's law for all the people." Aleksandr Iakovlev, "Constitutional Socialist Democracy: Dream or Reality," *Columbia Journal of Transnational Law* 28 (1990): 117.

3. "Concluding Document of the CSCE Copenhagen Conference on the Human Dimension," June 29, 1990. The CSCE member-states explained that "the rule of law does not mean merely a formal legality which assumes regularity and consistency in the achievement and enforcement of democratic order, but justice based on the recognition and full acceptance of the supreme value of the human personality and guaranteed by institutions providing a framework for its fullest expression." *International Legal Materials* 29 (1990): 1305, 1306.

4. See, for example, Theodor Meron, "International Criminalization of Internal Atrocities," *American Journal of International Law* 89 (1995): 554.

5. "Statute of the International Tribunal for the Prosecution of Persons Responsible for Genocide and Other Serious Violations of International Humanitarian Law Committed in the Territory of Rwanda and Rwandan Citizens Responsible for Genocide and Other Such Violations Committed in the Territory of Neighboring States, between 1 January 1994 and 31 December 1994," UN Doc. S/RES/955, annex, 1994. Even though the war in the former Yugoslavia was treated as international in nature, the international criminal tribunal created to address the abuses of that conflict stated its conviction that its jurisdiction also extended to crimes perpetrated in both internal and international conflicts. Annual Report, UN Doc. A/49/342-S/1994/ 1007, par. 19, 1994.

6. Rome Statute of the International Criminal Court, UN Doc. A/CONF.183/9, arts. 6–8.

7. Although Peru and Ecuador have experienced important regime changes, with accompanying political shifts that affect the dynamics of the conflict, these are distinct from the sort of internal structural reforms discussed here.

8. Boutros Boutros-Ghali, *An Agenda for Peace* (New York: United Nations, 1992), 32–34.

9. See, for example, Melvin Small and J. David Singer, "The War-Proneness of Democratic Regimes," *Jerusalem Journal of International Relations* 1, no. 4 (summer 1976): 50–69; Rudolph J. Rummel, *War, Power, Peace*, vol. 4 of *Understanding Conflict and War*

(Newbury Park, Calif.: Sage, 1979); Rudolph J. Rummel, "Libertarianism and International Violence," *Journal of Conflict Resolution* 27, no. 1 (March 1983): 27–71; Bruce Russett, *Grasping the Democratic Peace: Principles for a Post–Cold War World* (Princeton, N.J.: Princeton University Press, 1993); Zeev Maoz and Nasrin Abdolali, "Regime Types and International Conflict, 1815–1976," *Journal of Conflict Resolution* 3 (1989): 3–35; and William J. Dixon, "Democracy and the Peaceful Settlement of International Conflict," *American Political Science Review* 88, no. 1 (March 1994): 14–32. Much of the research on the "democratic peace" finds its roots in the theory propounded nearly two hundred years ago by Immanuel Kant. But see, for example, Edward D. Mansfield and Jack Snyder, "Democratization and War," *Foreign Affairs* 74, no. 3 (May-June 1995): 79–97. They suggest that although fully democratized nations are less likely to go to war with one another, the process of transition to democracy exacerbates instability and thereby enhances the possibility of entry into conflict in the short term.

10. *Concluding Document of the CSCE Copenhagen Conference on the Human Dimension.* In 1994, to reflect a series of structural changes as the Helsinki process moved from a series of periodic meetings to a permanent organization with several institutional components and full-time staff, the name of the Conference on Security and Cooperation in Europe was formally changed to the Organization for Security and Cooperation in Europe.

11. As one observer of rule of law assistance has noted,

> Assistance in this field has mushroomed in recent years, becoming a major category of international aid. . . . Russia's legal and judicial reforms, for example, have been supported by a variety of U.S. assistance projects, extensive German aid, a $58 million World Bank loan, and numerous smaller World Bank and European Bank for Reconstruction and Development initiatives, as well as many efforts sponsored by Great Britain, the Netherlands, Denmark, and the European Union. . . .
> Almost every major bilateral donor, a wide range of multilateral organizations—especially development banks—and countless foundations, universities, and human rights groups are getting into the act. In most countries, U.S. rule-of-law assistance is a small part of the aid pool, although Americans frequently assume it

is of paramount importance. They mistakenly believe that rule-of-law promotion is their special province, although they are not alone in that. German and French jurists also tend to view their country as the keeper of the flame of civil code reform. British lawyers and judges point to the distinguished history of the British approach. Transitional countries are bombarded with fervent but contradictory advice on judicial and legal reform.

Thomas Carothers, "The Rule of Law Revival," *Foreign Affairs* 77, no. 2 (March-April 1998): 103–104.

12. *Kosovo: A Review of the Criminal Justice System* (Organization for Security and Cooperation in Europe, October 18, 2000).

13. For a comprehensive review of this category of rights, see Stanislav Chernichenko and William Treat, *The Administration of Justice and the Human Rights of Detainees: The Right to a Fair Trial—Current Recognition and Measures Necessary for Its Strengthening,* UN Doc. E/CN.4/Sub.2/1994/24, June 3, 1994; and William M. Cohen, "Principles for Establishment of a Rule of Law Criminal Justice System," *Georgia Journal of International and Comparative Law* 23 (summer 1993): 269–287.

14. Radio Free Europe/Radio Liberty, *Balkan Report*, vol. 5, no. 3 (January 12, 2001).

15. "General Framework Agreement for Peace in Bosnia and Herzegovina," annex 7, art. I, par. 3, and annex 11, November 21, 1995 (hereafter Dayton Agreement).

16. Friedrich A. von Hayek, *The Road to Serfdom* (Chicago: University of Chicago Press, 1944), 72.

17. Hernando de Soto, *The Other Path: The Invisible Revolution in the Third World* (New York: Harper and Row, 1989), 253.

18. See, for example, Diane F. Orentlicher, "Settling Accounts: The Duty to Prosecute Human Rights Violations of a Prior Regime," *Yale Law Journal* 100 (June 1991): 2537–2615.

19. Dayton Agreement, annex 7, art. I, par. 3(e).

20. Ibid., annex 7, art. VI.

21. The Vietnamese-installed People's Revolutionary Council of Kampuchea did create a "revolutionary tribunal" that tried the two top leaders of the Khmer Rouge for genocide in absentia in 1979, but most observers characterized this as a show trial lacking in credibility. The issue of legal accountability for atrocities perpetrated by the Khmer Rouge regime of Pol Pot continues to be a volatile point in Cambodia twenty years after the acts in question. In interviews during the conflict in the former Yugoslavia, Bosnian Serb leaders quickly dismissed any possibility of their being brought to account for war crimes or genocide by pointing to the absence of any trials or punishment in these earlier cases.

22. Thomas Buergenthal, "The United Nations Truth Commission for El Salvador," *Vanderbilt Journal of Transnational Law* 27, no. 3 (October 1994): 503.

23. As Thomas Buergenthal, one of the three members of the commission, has noted, the "establishment of the Truth Commission marks the first time that the parties to an internal armed conflict, in negotiating a peace agreement, conferred on a commission composed of foreign nationals designated by the United Nations the power to investigate human rights violations committed during the conflict and to make binding recommendations. . . . National reconciliation is often difficult to achieve in countries trying to overcome the consequences of a bloody, internal armed conflict or an especially repressive regime without an appropriate accounting for or acknowledgment of past human rights violations. To the extent that the Truth Commission as an institution met the demands of the Salvadoran peace process, it has become a model the international community is likely to draw upon in the years to come" (ibid., 501–502). In his article, Professor Buergenthal provides an insightful firsthand description and analysis of the Truth Commission and its relationship to the peace process.

24. *Report of the Commission on the Truth for El Salvador: From Madness to Hope*, UN Doc. S/25500, annex, 1993, 25; and Buergenthal, "UN Truth Commission for El Salvador," 522.

25. "Agreement between the Government of Guatemala and the Guatemalan National Revolutionary Unity on the Establishment of the Commission for Historical Clarification," June 23, 1994.

26. For a comprehensive overview of this issue, see Theo van Boven, *Study Concerning the Right to Restitution, Compensation, and Rehabilitation for Victims of Gross Violations of Human Rights and Funda-*

mental Freedoms: Final Report, UN Doc. E/CN.4/Sub.2/1993, July 8, 1993.

27. Government of Eritrea, Proclamation no. 55/1994, March 15, 1994.

28. Bereket Habte Selassie, "Constitution Making as a Historic Moment" (keynote speech to the International Symposium on the Making of the Eritrean Constitution, Asmara, Eritrea, January 7, 1995).

29. Interviews by author.

30. During 2001–2002, a United States Institute of Peace interdisciplinary working group on constitution making and national reconciliation is examining numerous case studies to derive guidelines for the process of postconflict constitutional development.

31. "Preliminary Report of the Independent Commission of Experts Established in Accordance with Security Council Resolution 935," 1994, 31.

32. Rome Statute of the International Criminal Court, UN Doc. A/CONF.183/9, preamble and art. 17. A UN-sponsored study on postconflict reconstruction proceeds from the same premise: "Wartorn societies inevitably depend to a large degree on external assistance for reconstruction. . . . The question of the relative role, responsibility and authority of external donors and actors, as opposed to local ones, in bringing about and maintaining peace and in rebuilding the country is one of the most important and most delicate questions. . . . External assistance, rather than being subsidiary to local efforts, tends to become a substitute, and worse, destroys local coping and resistance mechanisms and controls emerging local institutions and solutions. A large-scale foreign presence . . . is obviously not sustainable in the long term, neither politically for the local actors nor financially for the external ones. A policy of 'betting on the local' may in the short term be more laborious, less spectacular, and take more time, but in the long term may be the only realistic option." "Rebuilding Wartorn Societies: Problems of International Assistance in Conflict and Postconflict Situations" (United Nations Research Institute for Social Development and the Programme for Strategic and International Security Studies of the Geneva Graduate Institute of International Studies, Geneva, August 1994), 17.

48

Religion as an Agent of Conflict Transformation and Peacebuilding

R. Scott Appleby

THE IRONY IS PAINFUL. During the 1970s and 1980s, a small but increasingly vocal group of scholars and public intellectuals in the United States and Europe—the epicenter, as it were, of the secularized West—argued for the integration of the professional study of religion into the academic mainstream; for more sophisticated media coverage of religion, especially by journalists on the political beat; and for greater attention to religion by diplomats and policymakers. Prominent religionists such as Harvey Cox, Martin Marty, Robert Coles, and Hans Küng pointed out the flaws in the secularization theory years before José Casanova provided a definitive version of the revised theory in his landmark book, *Public Religion in the Modern World*.[1] The original secularization theorists were correct, Casanova acknowledged, in predicting an ever-deepening differentiation between religious and state institutions and organizations in the modern world. But they were demonstrably wrong in also predicting the wholesale privatization of religion, followed by its gradual and inevitable decline.

Today, at the dawn of a new century, religion has indeed achieved greater prominence in public discourse and political debate. The attention has focused almost exclusively, however, on the deleterious impact of faith on political order, human rights, and ethnic conflict —on "terror in the mind of God," as Mark Juergensmeyer's year 2000 survey of religious violence put it.[2] Intense interest in "fundamentalism" followed the 1978–79 Islamic revolution in Iran, the rise of the New Christian Right in the United States, the dual emergence of mirror-image radical Jewish and Islamic cells in Israel and Palestine, the momentum established by Hindu nationalists and Sikh extremists in India, and numerous other manifestations of religious resurgence in the final quarter of the twentieth century.

The irony lies in the fact that religion is a source not only of intolerance, human rights violations, and extremist violence, but also of nonviolent conflict transformation, the defense of human rights, integrity in government, and reconciliation and stability in divided societies.

If religions have legitimated acts of political violence, they have also attempted to limit the frequency, scope, and targets of those acts. Although religious movements have embraced violence as an instrument of self-defense and enforcement of religious norms, they have also acknowledged its potential for uncontrollable destructiveness.

In recent years, moreover, religious leaders and faith-based nongovernmental organizations, sometimes acting in collaboration with governmental and policymaking agencies, have initiated a new round of efforts to develop the constructive roles that religions and religious actors are capable of playing across the range of activities that make up peacebuilding. "Peacebuilding," as I use the term in this essay, encompasses a broad range of activities, including conflict prevention and management; the transformation of conflict through mediation, the implementation of negotiated settlements, and the longer-term rebuilding of civil society and democratic institutions; and, not least, "second order" efforts, such as the building of human rights regimes and the promulgation of secular and religious laws and ethical traditions conducive to peaceful relations. Religious actors have played and are increasingly playing important and sometimes essential roles at each stage of peacebuilding. Indeed, the longer-term salience of religion in the transnational era of globalization may lie in its promise as an agent of peacebuilding.[3]

RELIGIOUS EXTREMISM

The precise role of religion in promoting violent conflict is a matter of intense debate. In addition to influencing broader cultural notions, including attitudes toward ethnic, religious, or social "outsiders," religions produce social movements with explicit political agendas. Scholarly and media discourse about the Middle East, ethnic and religious animosity in the Balkans, communal violence in India, and other conflicts generated or exacerbated by religion relies on broad categories such as "fundamentalism," "religious nationalism," and "liberation theology." Such categories are inadequate to portray reality in its complexity and may be seriously misleading if used carelessly. Some commentators, for example, automatically equate "fundamentalism" with extremism and use the term as a broad brush with which to tar every religiously orthodox, literate, and committed believer. In that wrongheaded view, every believer is a militant, every militant a fundamentalist, every fundamentalist an extremist. Thus the enormous distance between ordinary, pious Muslims and bomb-throwing "Islamic terrorists" is all but erased, not to mention the finer distinction between nonviolent militants and violence-legitimating extremists.

Mainstream Muslims, Christians, and Jews object to "fundamentalism" for a different reason: It implies that their extremist coreligionists, who are a minority in every religious tradition, are actually upholding or defending the basic "fundamentals" of the faith; the majority of believers do not see it that way. Finally, historians rightly object when the extravagant use of the term encourages nonspecialists to ignore the details of individual movements and their contexts and thus to downplay the vast differences among these movements, which are far greater than their similarities. When describing particular movements, then, the term "fundamentalism" is best applied only to those Protestant Christians of North America who coined the term in the early twentieth century and their contemporary ideological heirs; Muslim "fundamentalists" are best described as "Islamists," Jewish "fundamentalists" by specific Jewish designations, and so on.

Carefully defined, however, such comparative constructs as "fundamentalism" do help us differentiate broader patterns of religious militance in the real world. They establish reliable criteria by which to interrogate the generalizable findings of case studies and generate a cross-cultural vocabulary by which to make specific comparisons of movements and groups.

In addition to nuancing these categories, one must apply them judiciously. In most religions, for example, there is a tension between the use of violence and its sublimation or outright rejection. Finding the proper language to convey this ambivalence is complicated by the indiscriminate use of "extremist," "radical," "fundamentalist," and "terrorist" to describe fundamentally different phenomena. None of these terms, moreover, accurately describes militant believers who reject violence as a means for settling disputes, but who risk their livelihoods or their very lives in pursuit of justice, reconciliation, and peace.

In what follows I use the word "extremist" to describe religious actors who employ violence as a privileged means of purifying the community and waging war against threatening outsiders. The extremist sees the conversion, suppression, or elimination of the enemy as a sacred right or obligation. If this goal is achievable through political means, religious extremists may practice what David Little calls "civic intolerance," whereby they rely on the "legitimate violence" of the state to meet their objectives.[4] When the established legal and political system does not support their goals, however, religious extremists may resort to extralegal violence.

Fundamentalism

The specific goals and patterns of religious extremism vary. Those religious extremists who are properly called "fundamentalists" react primarily against the marginalization of religion. By creating viable alternatives to secular structures and processes, they seek to restore religion to its rightful place at the center of society, culture, politics, and law.

The penetration of the religious community by secular or religious outsiders has stimulated the rise of fundamentalist movements. Western businesspeople, heedless of Islamic codes and culture, brought their casinos and luxury hotels, wine and women to Cairo. The theory of evolution, despite its seeming subversion of the Christian doctrines of creation and divine providence, infiltrated the curriculum of U.S. public schools. The shah of Iran inaugurated and accelerated a cultural revolution apparently designed to glorify a Persian and pagan past at the expense of Shiism. The secular Zionist government of Israel abandoned and then bulldozed the Jewish settlements of Yamit on the Sinai peninsula in order to preserve the peace agreement with Egypt. In an increasingly secularized Israel, support for Jewish religious education and strict Sabbath observance erodes.

Among the religious a corresponding sense of being in exile in one's own land has given rise to groups that seek to bolster and reshape the religious community and its social environment in order to retain members and reverse decline. Islamists from West Africa to South Asia, segments of the Christian Right, and the religious Zionists and ultra-Orthodox haredim of Israel have emerged from Orthodox and conservative religious environments in order to preserve them from erosion. Prepared to give their lives to the struggle for divine sovereignty, they blame the religious establishment for failing to stem an increasingly aggressive, secular, religiously plural, materialist, amoral, feminist tide.

Fundamentalist groups such as the Taliban of Afghanistan, the Armed Islamic Group (GIA) of Algeria, and the terrorist cadres of Osama bin Laden, the Saudi exile, wage overt or covert war in order to annihilate religious and political enemies and impose religious law. Other fundamentalists, such as segments of the New Christian Right in the United States, or the Jama'at-i-Islami of Pakistan, employ constitutional and legal methods to obtain their goals.

Still other fundamentalist movements combine violence and civic intolerance, as did Hizbullah, the infamous "Party of God" formed in 1982, in its attempt to purge southern Lebanon of Israel and other purported enemies of the Shiite community.[5] Hizbullah's campaign of political violence in the eighties was enacted by suicide bombers—"self-martyrs" who destroyed the command facilities of Israeli forces in the occupied South and devastated the barracks of American and French peacekeeping troops. But Hizbullah also accumulated political capital through its social service work among the suffering poor of southern Lebanon. In response to the 1990 Ta'if accords, which ended Lebanon's sixteen-year civil war, Hizbullah decided to enter mainstream politics. Accordingly, the movement underscored its Lebanese character by shedding many of its Iranian trappings (including its overt reliance on Iranian religious scholars and military advisers) and by strengthening its Lebanese contacts and alliances with politicians and other public figures outside the Lebanese Shiite community. In 1992 and 1996 the movement won parliamentary seats; by the mid-nineties, it had evolved into a bona fide political party.[6]

Ethnoreligious Nationalism

While fundamentalism accounts for much of the religious violence in the world today, ultranationalism is also a significant source of extremism. Religious nationalists identify their religious tradition so closely with the fate of a people or a nation that they perceive a threat to either as an assault on the sacred. Like fundamentalists, they may demonize missionaries of other faiths, foreign businesspeople, troops stationed on the country's sacred soil, educational and social service volunteers, relief workers, and international peacekeepers. In

this indirect sense, ethnoreligious nationalists are concerned, like fundamentalists, with the marginalization of religion. But religious nationalists believe that the most direct route to strengthening the host religion is not the purification of the religion, per se, but the establishment of a political collective within which the religion is privileged and its enemies disadvantaged. In such cases, when religion is subordinated to and placed at the service of ethnic or nationalist ideologies, the collaborators, motivations, objectives, timing, and patterns of violence are different.

Ethnoreligious nationalists are therefore more likely to be members of a larger coalition whose objectives are not primarily religious. Although they draw upon Catholic symbols, myths, and rituals, the IRA and other Irish nationalist paramilitaries are not fighting to preserve or extend the influence of Roman Catholicism in Northern Ireland; the same can be said, mutatis mutandis, for the Ulster Volunteer Force in its relationship to Ulster Protestantism. Nor were Slobodan Milosevic and his ultranationalist political allies in the former Yugoslavia motivated by religious concerns when they tapped fanatical religious tendencies within the Serbian Orthodox community on the eve of the Bosnian war.[7]

Communalism in South Asia also features religion turned to ultranationalist causes. The competition for resources and benefits among the region's numerous ethnic groups, writes Stanley Tambiah, "requires the formation of coalitions of ethnic concerns and interests acting as a monolithic principle, vertically integrating a people differentiated by class."[8] Coalition builders in India and Sri Lanka have employed religion to bind together racial, linguistic, class, and territorial markers of identity. For over a century Hindu nationalists in India, for example, have cultivated boundary-setting and discriminatory practices that once seemed incompatible with Hinduism. Driven by an ethnonationalist ideology that employs the rhetoric and imagery of blood, soil, and birth, the Hindutva movement in India seeks to establish a representative structure resembling the secular nation-state but pursuing a policy of civic intolerance toward "non-Hindus."[9] The inflammatory and diffuse appeals to "Hindu national pride" in the face of perceived Muslim encroachments have also stimulated numerous episodes of mob violence.[10]

To complicate matters, elements of both fundamentalism and ethnonationalism may coexist within an extremist movement or organization. In 1993, for example, the Union of Rabbis for the People and Land of Israel, an organization of religious Zionist rabbis founded to coalesce opposition to the Oslo Accord, issued a rabbinic *psak,* a binding judgment based on halakha, which declared the accords null and void. In so doing the rabbis created new divisions within the Jewish community as well as within Israeli society in general. Their subsequent agitations, including the ruling that the proposed withdrawal from the occupied territories created "*pikuach nefesh,*" a situation threatening Jewish existence, unleashed the forces of Jewish extremism. The tragic process led to the assassination of Prime Minister Yitzhak Rabin by Yigal Amir, a Bar Ilan student, army veteran, and former "yeshiva boy."

In demonizing the prime minister and the Israeli government, the rabbis acted in the manner of fundamentalists seeking to preserve religious orthodoxy and "purity" against compromises offered by misguided secular politicians. Their legitimation of violence against fellow Israelis was predicated upon a fundamentalist interpretation of what they called "our sacred obligation to strengthen and deepen our people's connection to the Torah and to Jewish tradition as passed down through the generations." Yet the rabbis also claimed to represent "true Zionism" and thus to be the arbiters of the legal and moral warrants for government policy. In this respect they behaved like religious nationalists by "wrapping their political

stand in the mantle of religion and a rabbinic *da'at Torah* (Torah wisdom)."[11]

RELIGIOUS PEACEBUILDING

Contesting the Religious Tradition

It would be gratifying to report that religious peacebuilders have been effective in neutralizing the religious extremists within their own community. The impact of nonviolent religious actors on their violent or civically intolerant coreligionists is, however, difficult to demonstrate. A more defensible claim is that courageous religious leaders who advocate nonviolent social change, while they often seem to be in the minority, perform an invaluable function when they contest and refuse to cede the religious and moral high ground. In fact, coalitions of moderate Sunni religious leaders have repeatedly and openly condemned extremists operating under the banner of Islam. "Socially engaged" Buddhists such as Sulak Sivaraksa (Thailand) and Aung San Suu Kyi (Burma) have denounced the military extremism of their respective governments, as well as the complicity of their fellow Buddhists in supporting, or failing to resist, political leaders who ignored the basic needs of their people, courted graft, and allowed corporations to despoil the natural environment. Judaism, Christianity, and Hinduism have also produced influential figures of moral authority who describe the nonviolent struggle for justice and reconciliation as a religious obligation.[12]

Such *nonviolent religious militants*—believers and practitioners who strive to sublimate violence and resist efforts to legitimate it on religious or nationalist grounds—may also "go to extremes" of self-sacrifice in devotion to the sacred. Like the fundamentalists, they, too, claim to be "radical," or rooted in and renewing the fundamental truths of their religious traditions. For the mass of believers, especially the young men who are candidates for the extremist cadres, this competition between extremists and moderates for the mantle of religious orthodoxy or "authenticity" is all-important. Control of the institutions of education and religious formation—which currently include religiously based health care clinics and social service networks, as well as seminaries, madrasas, and yeshivot—is the key to the outcome, which will in turn determine whether "religious peacebuilding" can develop into a substantial and enduring force.

This hermeneutical war currently being waged within religious communities—the battle over the proper interpretation of the scriptures, traditions, and norms that shape the believer's self-understanding and behavior—is the context for understanding the contemporary efforts of Christian theologians who are refining the just-war tradition in light of the horrendous realities of chemical, nuclear, and biological warfare; Muslim jurists who are seeking principles of nonviolent conflict resolution within the Qur'an, the Hadith, and Islamic law; Jewish, Buddhist, Hindu, and Confucian scholars who are "translating" into second-order, broadly accessible language the insights and values of their respective traditions, especially as they address the question of human rights; and courageous religious officials who join cross-cultural and interreligious dialogues, often in the face of internal opposition from their coreligionists.

Religion and Conflict Transformation

Internal measures to strengthen religious resources for peacebuilding are noteworthy because they both reflect and seek to shape the practice of religious actors directly engaged in conflict transformation. One of the contributors to this volume, John Paul Lederach, exemplifies this point. Drawing upon his Mennonite Christian theological heritage as well as his considerable experience in the field as a

mediator and conciliator, Lederach has developed a model of peacebuilding that reflects and responds to the realities of contemporary conflicts. Not least among these realities is the salience of religion.

Contemporary conflicts tend to be internal, precipitated by the failure of states to address fundamental needs and ensure an equitable distribution of resources and benefits to a variety of competing ethnic or religious groups. Opposition movements take refuge in neighboring countries and engage in international weapons trading and supply. Displaced refugee populations cross immediate and distant borders: the enemy is only a village or, in some cases, a block away. Collective identity issues loom large. Thus, "social-psychological perceptions, emotions, and subjective experiences" play a central role, even though they may be totally independent of the substantive or originating issues in the dispute. A sociological dynamic of "reciprocal causation" develops, whereby the response mechanism within the cycle of violence and counterviolence perpetuates the conflict.[13] In such disputes, therefore, issues of substance, such as territory or governance, are intimately rooted in cultural and psychological elements driving and sustaining the conflict. Fighting is intended to achieve collective rights in opposition to other groups of often differing ethnicity, religion, or race.

In this context, Lederach argues, peacebuilding "must take into account the long-term horizon of protracted intermediate conflicts and wars, and develop a comprehensive, multifaceted strategy for ending the violence and for achieving and sustaining reconciliation."[14] Thus, it involves a wide range of activities and functions that both precede and follow formal peace accords.

For Lederach, the key to this process is middle-level community leadership, operating according to the "nested paradigm" of conflict transformation—a method by which local actors, people already embedded or "nested" in the conflicted community, collaborate to resolve the conflict peacefully. The mid-level leaders who enable this process to succeed are highly respected as individuals and/or as formal office-holders in sectors such as religion, education, business, agriculture, or health. They tend to control primary academic, religious, and humanitarian networks and therefore are likely to know and be known by the top-level leadership. Yet these mid-level leaders also know the experience of people living at the grassroots level.[15]

Leaders at the grassroots level must deal with the crisis on a day-to-day basis, witnessing firsthand the deep-rooted hatred and animosity sustaining the conflict. Because identity forms around ethnicity, religion, or region rather than class, divisions cut down through the levels of the social pyramid rather than pitting one level against the other. Leaders within each level have connections to their "own people" up and down the pyramid and, at the same time, have counterparts within their own level who are perceived as enemies.

Accordingly, mid-level and grassroots-level leaders must be engaged in the peacebuilding process from the outset. They must foster sufficient trust and flexibility among the antagonists to permit new options to emerge and compromises to take place. In this sense they are the critical link in a comprehensive network that involves multiple levels of leadership and sectors of the population in differing but simultaneous peacebuilding activities.

The potential role of religious actors in Lederach's model of peacebuilding seems obvious. Rooted in local communities with representatives operating in regional, national, and often international organizational structures, religions inhabit a unique social location, display a powerful and pervasive institutional presence, and exercise significant cultural power. Their daily contact with the masses, long record of charitable service, and reputation for integrity in most settings have earned religious leaders and institutions a privileged status and an unparalleled legitimacy, especially in societies where

they enjoy a measure of independence from the state. And because so many violent conflicts occur among people living in proximity to one another, local religious actors enjoy a decided advantage in conflict management over most governments and their remote bureaucracies.[16]

Thus mid-level and grassroots-level religious actors drawn from the communities in conflict—local pastors, ministers, rabbis, religious scholars, lay leaders, and monks—are well positioned to serve as agents of conflict transformation. Already in some cases they have contributed not only to resolving the immediate crisis, but also to reforming the long-term social structures that fostered and perpetrated the religious hatred, racism, or other forms of discrimination at the root of the conflict. Religiously motivated practitioners have helped to defuse the immediate face-to-face tensions, worked to repair the broken relationships, and moved the process toward confrontation of the inequities in the political and economic system.

THREE CASES OF RELIGIOUS PEACEBUILDING

It is not yet possible, however, to draw unqualified conclusions about religious agency in conflict transformation. In a 1997 article on the subject, Cynthia Sampson was able to provide numerous examples of religious involvement in virtually every phase of peacebuilding; subsequent authors extended the sketch—but it remains a sketch.[17] For the purposes of systematic analysis the types of religious involvement remain inadequately detailed and documented. We also need to learn more about the various kinds of relationships the religious actors have with their secular and religious partners in peacebuilding, as well as the various sides of the conflict.

If we focus on three significant modes of religious peacebuilding in the nineties, however, it is possible to derive some general lessons about its advantages as well as weaknesses, and the circumstances under which it has been most effective.

Mediation

Some religious communities have become adept at bridging the highly particular world and discourse of religion, their own as well as others, and the larger secular world defined by a variety of competing interests. The Community of Sant'Egidio, a movement of mostly lay Roman Catholics that now numbers approximately thirty thousand members worldwide, originated in 1968 as a voluntary charitable organization committed to ecumenical and interreligious dialogue and social concern for the poor. Their international headquarters, provided by the Vatican, is a sixteenth-century Carmelite convent (from which the community takes its name), located in the ancient Roman district of Trastevere, a neighborhood traditionally known as a meeting place of nationalities and cultures. The Italian government subsequently renovated the convent, transforming it into a complex of meeting rooms, offices, and reception areas.

Feeling a special vocation to immigrants from the developing world, Sant'Egidio's founders befriended the poor, Gypsies, addicts, orphans, AIDS victims, and the handicapped. They fostered outreach to the Third World by developing contacts in Argentina, Guatemala, Mexico, Albania, Algeria, Mozambique, Ethiopia, Burundi, Rwanda, Somalia, and Vietnam. Eventually, approximately half of Sant'Egidio's members lived in Italy, with half diffused in small communities in Northern Europe (Belgium, the Netherlands, Germany), Africa (Ivory Coast, Cameroon, Mozambique), and the Americas. In these settings Sant'Egidio's charitable works, activism on behalf of the marginalized, and initiatives in conflict resolution are rooted in its corporate spiritual identity as a community of prayer and fellowship. Members strive to integrate their local and international presences; each local community seeks a way to serve the poor, even while expanding its contacts with other religious and political communities and with states. Sant'Egidio's network of *scuole popolari* teaches volunteers that local problems are connected to regional stability, which is enhanced by equitable social policies. The Community therefore lobbies governments and policymakers.[18]

The Community's vitality derives from its emphasis on "friendship"—characteristically, Sant'Egidio prefers to use secular-friendly or bridge terms to articulate convictions and principles with deep religious roots—and its attitude of openness, hospitality, and respect for all people. This ethos of friendship finds expression in practically every aspect of the members' individual lives and corporate life, including the Community's penchant for networking and establishing relationships with political and religious actors at every level. Thus Sant'Egidio has enjoyed close relations not only with the dispossessed, but with numerous government officials in Europe and Africa, with the Holy See and with Pope John Paul II.

The members of Sant'Egidio believe that interreligious dialogue is both a good in itself and a powerful resource for peacebuilding. The Community excels in building up "networks for peace"—personal and organizational contacts across religious boundaries. Having established a strong reputation in the Islamic world through its programs on behalf of Muslim immigrants newly arrived in Rome and other European urban centers from the Middle East and North Africa, Sant'Egidio has been particularly successful in arranging Muslim-Christian interaction and collaboration. Moreover, the Community's record of social service, ecumenical and political networks, and interfaith collaboration enabled it to become one of the most successful conflict mediators of the 1990s.

This evolution began in 1982, when the Lebanese Druze leader Walid Jumblatt and the patriarch of the Lebanese Melichites, Maximos V, met at Sant'Egidio headquarters and signed an agreement to end the war between Christians and Druze in the Shuf mountains south of Beirut. It reached a new level in the early nineties when Sant'Egidio mediated the negotiations that ended the civil war in Mozambique, where the Community had enjoyed a presence since 1976, when a young Mozambican priest studying in Rome, Don Jaime Gonçalves, joined the community.

The story of the Mozambican conflict and Sant'Egidio's role in mediating the peace accords has been told elsewhere.[19] Three aspects of the community's involvement, however, hold implications for our understanding of religious peacebuilding. First and foremost, Sant'Egidio's religious ethos earned it the trust not only of the combatants (Frelimo, the marxist independence movement that came to power in 1975, and Renamo, the Mozambique National Resistance movement), but also of the religious communities of Mozambique and other participants in the peace process. Sant'Egidio's religious ethos was expressed in the Community's unimpeachable record for integrity and good offices, in its nonpartisan social action for the common good, and in its repeated striving to understand each point of view in a conflict.[20]

Second, Sant'Egidio acted in concert with a variety of governmental, intergovernmental, nongovernmental, cultural, and religious agencies and individuals both inside and outside Mozambique. The Community saw its own mediating and facilitating role in the peace process as limited and quite specific, but it also played an important bridging or coordinating role at crucial moments in the process. Sant'-Egidio representatives became personally familiar with leaders of both warring parties and established ties to missionaries serving in the war zones controlled by Renamo. In 1981 Gonçalves, now the archbishop of Beira, met with Enrico Berlinguer, the secretary general of Italy's Communist Party, who opened a channel of dialogue between Frelimo and Sant'Egidio. In 1982 representatives of the community

negotiated the release of missionaries Renamo had taken captive; the occasion provided Sant'Egidio the opportunity to build a relationship of trust and credibility with the insurgents that would prove invaluable in the subsequent peace talks. In 1985 Sant'Egidio arranged a critical meeting between Samora Machel, Mozambique's president, and the pope.[21]

The Community persisted in its efforts over the long term of the conflict. The growing perception of Sant'Egidio as an impartial agent of constructive dialogue was reinforced by the way the community used its influence with governments and churches. It established networks in Italy to obtain funds and supplies for Mozambique and to spread information in Europe on Mozambique's crisis; a parallel network soon appeared inside Mozambique itself, where Sant'Egidio members made overtures to the Islamic and Christian communities, extending the Community's social services and educational network across denominational and traditional lines. In 1984 Community leaders went to Maputo, Mozambique's capital, to discuss humanitarian needs with government ministers. The meeting led to the establishment of a program, supported by the Italian government at Sant'Egidio's request, to deliver massive shipments of food and medicine to the war-torn nation.[22]

Third, the cumulative impact of Sant'Egidio's neutrality, its connections, and its disinterested participation in the peace process enabled the Community to serve effectively as host, facilitator, and mediator of the negotiations that led to the General Peace Agreement of 1992. The first direct contact between Renamo leadership and the Frelimo government took place at Sant'Egidio headquarters in Rome on July 8, 1990. In concert with the Italian government, U.S. advisers, the United Nations, the Mozambican Council of Churches, and several other governmental and nongovernmental organizations, the representatives of Sant'Egidio were able to create and maintain a momentum for peace among the two parties over the course of the ten rounds of talks.

There was, in short, both humility and pragmatism on display in Sant'Egidio's willingness to play a circumscribed but essential role in conflict transformation in Mozambique. The Community's success also resulted from repeated demonstrations of its commitment to a long-term relationship to Mozambique and to the peace process in its fullest sense.

These virtues served Sant'Egidio well in other settings where it displayed effectiveness as a mediator of conflict.[23] The Algerian civil war has raged since the government canceled the results of the 1991 elections, which brought the major Islamist party, the Islamic Salvation Front (FIS), to the brink of controlling the state. In response to the government crackdown, the opposition went underground and splintered into various Muslim, ethnic, and secular factions. Chaos and seemingly random violence followed. Sant'Egidio was able to bring together representatives of these various factions for the purpose of formulating a common framework for negotiations with the government. These meetings, held in November 1994 at Sant'Egidio headquarters in Rome, created an atmosphere of trust that allowed the Islamists as well as the secular parties to offer major concessions.[24] The result was the "Rome Platform," an agreement signed in January 1995 by all the participants at the Sant'Egidio meetings. Regrettably, however, the Algerian government refused to participate in the desired peace talks.[25]

Conflict Management

In the spring of 1993 Samdech Preah Maha Ghosananda, the sixty-eight-year-old Buddhist primate of Cambodia, led hundreds of Buddhist monks, nuns, and laity on a dramatic monthlong march from Siam Reap in the northwest section of Cambodia throughout the central regions to the capital, Phnom Penh. Held on the eve of the United Nations–sponsored elections of a new National Assembly and government, the Peace March, known as Dhammayietra ("Pilgrimage of Truth") II, traversed dangerous territory marked by land mines and firefights. The marchers hoped to build popular confidence in the elections and overcome the fear that had been aroused by Khmer Rouge threats of violence and disruption. By the time Maha Ghosananda and his supporters reached Phnom Penh, hundreds of thousands of Cambodians had encouraged the marchers along their path, and more than ten thousand people had joined their ranks.[26]

Ninety percent of the Cambodian electorate voted in the ensuing free and fair elections, the first in the country's history. While the United Nations Transitional Authority in Cambodia (UNTAC) had created the conditions necessary for the holding of the elections, many Cambodians and NGO workers also attributed the extraordinary level of popular participation to the success of the Dhammayietra.[27]

A year later, on April 24, 1994, Maha Ghosananda led Dhammayietra III. The political circumstances, and thus the immediate purpose of the march, had changed. Held in support of national reconciliation, the 1994 march came less than a month after Khmer Rouge troops had recaptured their strategic stronghold and nominal "capital" of Pailin, a lucrative gem-mining area, and only days after peace talks between the Khmer Rouge and the coalition government (formed after the 1993 elections) had been postponed indefinitely. Eight hundred people began the march, including four hundred monks, two hundred nuns, and a dozen NGO workers. On April 30, in the Bavel district about twenty-four miles northwest of the provincial capital of Battambang, the marchers were caught in a firefight between soldiers of the Royal Cambodian Army and the Khmer Rouge guerrillas occupying territory near the Thai border. Two peace marchers, a Buddhist monk and a nun, were fatally wounded in the cross fire.[28]

Despite the casualties sustained during the 1994 march, and a loss of nerve by some of Ghosananda's fellow pilgrims, the monk continued to lead the annual pilgrimages. The theme of Dhammayietra IV, in May 1995, was the need to end global land mine production. Ghosananda, now lauded internationally as the "Gandhi of Cambodia," hoped that his greater visibility would help secure international help in removing the estimated ten million mines in Cambodian soil that continued to kill or maim hundreds of farmers each year.[29]

One important sign of hope in Cambodia at the time was the presence of more than two hundred nongovernmental organizations, many of which had arrived during the 1980s to provide emergency relief after the Khmer Rouge had been routed by a Vietnamese-backed army. Several of the most effective NGOs working in Cambodia were religiously sponsored and religiously motivated. These included Catholic Relief Services, Lutheran World Service, and the American Friends Service Committee. Like UNICEF (the largest relief organization in Cambodia, with over two hundred staff in the mid-nineties), some of the NGOs were large multiservice operations, while others focused on specific areas such as women's issues, de-mining operations, AIDS education and treatment, the provision of prosthetic devices for those who had lost limbs, agricultural development, and environmental protection. Without the substantial and sustained contributions that such NGOs made during the 1980s, "it is hard to see how this country, devastated by its own leaders in the immediate past, and almost completely ostracized by western governments, could have survived at all."[30]

Survival was a significant accomplishment for a country whose older generations had been virtually wiped out, leaving a society populated primarily by children and young adults; where property ownership remained in a state of confusion, and the capital city was largely in ruins despite the presence of isolated foreign embassies and businesses, royal residences, and tourist attractions; where starvation, disease, a growing traffic in narcotics, government corruption, and foreign corporate exploitation of Cambodia's rich natural resources were the most obvious legacies of the years of lawlessness. The brief presence of the UN peacekeeping teams was followed by the unraveling of the election results in a makeshift coalition government that exacerbated rather than solved Cambodia's systemic problems (and arguably created new ones such as the international drug trade and money laundering).[31]

In this context the Western-based NGOs expanded their operations in the 1990s; among their many services, they worked with Cambodians to build the foundations of a legal system, including local and national courts. Indigenous NGOs sprouted as well, relying on collaboration with the more experienced organizations. Buddhist-affiliated groups were prominent in this effort. Ghosananda's Dhammayietra Center in Phnom Penh and the Coalition for Peace and Reconciliation (CPR), run by a Catholic priest, Bob Maat, and a Jewish activist, Liz Bernstein, built upon the fame of the annual peace walks by enrolling Cambodians in conflict prevention training programs. In Battambang in 1996, for example, the CPR established the Dhammayietra Peacemakers Program for Cambodian students from the ages of fifteen to thirty. Staffed by volunteer teachers who formed the embryonic cell of a Dhammayietra Volunteer Corps, the program offered short courses on the lives of peacemakers in world history. CPR recruited these students and other Cambodians to attend workshops in active nonviolence, Buddhist peacemaking skills, and conflict resolution; more than seven hundred people attended such workshops in 1996. Foreign NGOs contributed trainers for the workshops and provided financial support.[32]

Such incipient networks took the first steps in addressing the structural impediments to stability, including the lack of monastic leaders trained in conflict resolution techniques, the weakness of monastic disciplines, and the absence of educational resources (both Buddhist and secular) following the Khmer Rouge destruction of Buddhist institutes, libraries, and manuscripts.

Religious exemplars do not make competent policymakers. Nor are they accomplished organizational leaders. Seldom, however, do religious leaders act alone in translating their vision of justice into concrete procedures, policies, or laws. The descent from prophecy to the politics of social reform means that even a guru or archbishop must negotiate practicalities with his followers and other members of the religious community and the nation. This was certainly true for Maha Ghosananda. His supporters in the NGO community criticized him less for his approach to fundamental issues of justice and reconciliation than for his lack of organizational skills and his failure to use modern management techniques—or, to be fair, to develop a permanent staff possessing such abilities. (The monk was, after all, a charismatic leader, not a modern bureaucrat.) The general sense of such concerns was that Ghosananda's movement, rooted in his militant religiosity and powerful moral example, was not being translated as effectively as it could have been into enduring institutions and widespread social practices.

Ghosananda did not participate in the day-to-day training of recruits in the methods of nonviolent conflict resolution, and the Buddhist trainers themselves remained too few in number. Philanthropic offers of computers were refused for lack of staff capable of using them. The Dhammayietra events suffered at times from poor planning and inadequate flow of information. Strikingly, there was little advance discussion of procedures to follow in case of violence, and inadequate provision of safe houses in which marchers could take refuge.[33]

As peacebuilders, in short, the Buddhists were not sufficiently organized or well equipped. This led them to rely heavily on foreign NGO workers and inhibited the growth of the indigenous expertise necessary to make peacebuilding a long-term social effort. The large number of NGOs in Cambodia was a mixed blessing, therefore, for they kept Cambodians in a state of dependence and even complacency. In addition, some NGOs replicated the condescending attitudes and relational patterns of colonists. United Church of Christ minister Peter Pond, who was involved for decades in human rights and pro-democracy training in Southeast Asia, contends that NGO workers should have been devoting a greater portion of their funds and energies to publicizing and building up the indigenous peacemaking efforts under way. The five hundred Buddhist supporters of the Dhammayietra Center, he argues, could have been five thousand. Greater visibility would have allowed the peace movement to attract external financial and organizational support to train Cambodians in conflict resolution techniques. The cost of such programs, Pond believes, would be miniscule in comparison to the benefit to be realized from the presence of thousands of indigenous trained peacemakers. "With no more than one million U.S. dollars per year for the training of indigenous, middle-level leaders, from mayors to school teachers," he argues, "stability can be achieved within a decade and the foundations of lasting peace built over a fifty-year period."[34]

Transitional Justice

On the occasions when religious leaders have been directly involved in recommending or interpreting laws or policies of the state, as in Anglican archbishop Desmond Tutu's leadership of South Africa's Truth and Reconciliation Commission (TRC), they have nonetheless been one voice among many.

Tutu and his associates were charged with the delicate task of discovering "truth" and promoting "reconciliation." Genuine reconciliation is something more than forgiveness, as the biblical theologian Walter Wink observes, for forgiveness can be unilateral, while reconciliation is always mutual.[35] If this is true, then reconciliation can be sustained only in a society that is addressing the social inequalities that inspired the insurrection or civil war. While reconciliation is primarily an attitude or spiritual quality that cannot be coerced or manufactured, it can be stimulated by the provision of economic and political incentives for collaboration and power sharing. In this view reconciliation is not a utopian goal that gets in the way of the more pragmatic, hardheaded negotiations that assume enlightened self-interest on the part of the conflicted parties. Political scientists are beginning to recognize that reconciliation serves "enlightened self-interest" and that altruism offers distinct social and economic advantages in an interdependent world.[36]

Critics of the TRC charged that it was not a suitable vehicle for ensuring that white South Africans would come to recognize the evils of apartheid and their own complicity in them. Even with an offer of amnesty in exchange for "truth-telling," the TRC had difficulty getting people to come forward. Most perpetrators of apartheid-era abuses refused to acknowledge their guilt and ask for or accept forgiveness from those families and individuals willing to offer it. Under such circumstances many victims of the white Afrikaner regime's policies declared themselves unwilling or unable to offer forgiveness. As a result, the "truth" uncovered by the process was partial and ambiguous.

The legislation that established the commission required all individuals involved in "gross human rights abuses" to apply for amnesty in order to avoid prosecution; it did not distinguish sufficiently between the violence used to maintain the system that legitimated such abuses and the violence employed to oppose it. In what many saw as a moral failure, the TRC exacerbated this problem by seeming to regard the excesses of the African National Congress (ANC), a liberation movement fighting for freedom, in the same light

as the systematic atrocities committed by the white supremacist government. Critics traced this supposed flaw to the Christian doctrine of original sin that informed the thinking of many commissioners, leading them to believe that no South African involved in the conflict was entirely free of guilt. In this view, rather than expose the sordid mechanisms of the structural violence, the TRC took refuge from the difficult work of discerning culpability in a blanket notion of universal guilt and therefore offered cheap forgiveness.

The test for granting amnesty—the political motivation of the deed—further threatened to abolish the distinction between state functionaries and dissidents. It begged important questions: What are the limits of ideologically motivated action? What may *not* be done in the name of politics? Most damning in the eyes of the critics was the possibility that the perpetrators might benefit more than the victims from the work of the TRC. Some individuals made decisions to work for the security apparatus, to inform upon friends, to engage in violent behavior, while others did not. Was the TRC contributing to the creation of a society in which those distinctions count? By failing to punish perpetrators of serious human rights violations, the critics charged, the Mandela government, by means of the TRC, was forgoing not only the opportunity to restore order to the lives of the victims, but also the obligation to assert the inviolability of human rights and the rule of law.[37]

Defenders of the TRC claimed that the crucial issue facing South Africa was a decision about whether to use the past as a club to punish others or as a tool to build a better future, and that public acts of forgiveness were the most powerful way to liberate the victims of apartheid from their tortured past. As the work of the commission unfolded, these supporters argued, its salutary effects became more visible, extending even to those conservative whites who eventually came forward to admit culpability.[38]

A strong case can be made for the long-term political efficacy of both the juridical and symbolic acts of the TRC when one considers the specific religious and cultural setting in which they resonated. In South Africa, a predominantly Christian country, citizens accord theological discourse on political matters a significant measure of respect, and Christian theological and ethical principles informed the work of the TRC. Tutu chaired the commission, Alex Boraine, former president of the Methodist Church of South Africa, was deputy chair, and several commissioners came from the churches. The hearings "resembled a church service more than a judiciary proceeding, with Bishop Tutu dressed in his purple clerical robes and clearly operating as a religious figure."[39]

This description is not the insult it may seem to be. Traditional African thought, which places great emphasis on rehabilitating rather than punishing evildoers, reinforces Christian sensibilities on the issue of forgiveness. The concept of *ubuntu* holds that humanity, the common possession of the entire people, is diminished when even one individual is lost to inhumanity. African jurisprudence is restorative rather than retributive, in that ubuntu teaches that the dignity of one is linked to the dignity of all.[40]

To address the abuse of human rights experienced by millions of ordinary South Africans as a result of political and legal measures taken by the regime—the violence of pass laws, the forced removals of South Africans, the exploitation of the poor—the TRC set up special hearings, outside the purview of the regular work of its three committees, on the role of the media, the medical profession, the judiciary, the business community, and the churches. In December 1997 the TRC encouraged members of the general public to sign a register of reconciliation to express their regret at failing to prevent human rights violations and to pledge their commitment to a future South Africa in which human rights abuses will not take place.

In terms of accountability, the massive final report of the TRC, extending over some five volumes and more than thirty-five hundred pages, documents gross human rights violations and victims' testimonies, examines the broader institutional and social environment—the role of the media, the military, the churches, and so on—in which apartheid-era crimes occurred, and offers findings, conclusions, and a series of policy recommendations that take into account and attempt to overcome the limitations and weaknesses of the commission itself. The final report advances a strong concept of reconciliation, in that it emphasizes the need for the perpetrators of the crimes, including those who were granted amnesty by the state for appearing before the TRC, to contribute concretely to restoring the social fabric and repairing relations, whether by financial compensation, community service, or some other form of commitment. "Restorative justice demands that the accountability of perpetrators be extended to making a contribution to the restoration of the well-being of their victims," the report states. "The fact that people are given their freedom without taking responsibility for some form of restitution remains a major problem with the amnesty process. Only if the emerging truth unleashes a social dynamic that includes redressing the suffering of victims will it meet the ideal of restorative justice."[41]

CONCLUSION: CONDITIONS FOR EFFECTIVE RELIGIOUS AGENCY

Our examples of religiously affiliated peacebuilding suggest general lessons that are confirmed by other cases not examined here. First, religious actors stand the best chance of being effective as facilitators of peace processes and as mediators when they are perceived as acting independently from the state, on their own authority, and beholden to no larger governmental, cultural, or religious power. At the same time, religious figures or organizations acting alone, without the benefit of logistical, technical, political, and diplomatic support from governmental or intergovernmental agencies, cannot be expected to succeed in either bringing parties to the negotiating table or providing the incentives for disputants to strike a deal and live by it.

The case of Sant'Egidio illustrates a second and related dimension of successful religious conflict transformation, namely, the ability to "exploit" religious convictions, qualities, and behaviors for the purposes of peacebuilding. The word "exploit" in this context does not imply "manipulate," "misuse," or "distort." To the contrary, religious militants for peace see their work in conciliation and mediation as a natural and even an obligatory expression of their faith. To put the point negatively: It hardly matters whether peacebuilders come from a religious background, if that background and set of perceptions and sensibilities do not consciously and carefully inform their work.

The religious ethos may be expressed in a variety of ways. Religious actors are effective when they or their coreligionists have established a reputation for integrity and have demonstrated a long-term, open-ended institutional and moral commitment to the community experiencing the deadly conflict. Sant'Egidio provides one model of this presence on the ground through its nonpartisan, nonproselytizing, indiscriminate social service and charitable work, coupled with a vigorous practice of dialogue and relationship building with all parties over time.

In Afghanistan a different model of religious cooperation obtained when representatives of the Organization of the Islamic Conference (OIC), the United Nations, and the warring factions in Afghanistan laid the groundwork for a cease-fire and talks between the Taliban and the forces of the Afghan Muslim leader, Ahmed Shah Masud. The Taliban, an extremist movement led by Muslim religious scholars (ulema) from the rural southern region around the city of Kandahar, had occupied two-thirds of the country after driving Masud's army from Kabul in October 1996. During the spring 1998 negotiations the two sides exchanged prisoners and agreed to appoint a commission of forty ulema, twenty to be selected by each side. The Muslim religious scholars would serve as mediators of the conflict, their expertise in the sharia and Islamic norms of warfare providing a common framework for negotiations between the rival Islamist parties.[42] This was a case of coreligionists sharing the same general theological worldview and common sources for dispute resolution in the Qur'an, the Hadith of the Prophet, and the sharia, or Islamic law.

Lederach's nested paradigm of conflict transformation relies, it will be recalled, on local and grassroots leaders, including religious figures, whose knowledge of the local culture and status within the community must be complemented by formal training in the techniques and methods of conflict management and resolution.

Keeping Lederach's overall goal in view, the second lesson learned from the cases of religious peacebuilding is that there is no one privileged or universally reliable formula for translating religious conviction and ethos into functional parts of a peacemaking process. In some settings of interreligious conflict, as in the example of Afghanistan, recondite (to outsiders) legal and theological matters will be relevant, and mediators and conciliators will need to be drawn from the theological/religious communities in dispute. In other cultural environments and social settings, where two or more religious traditions and ethnic groups are at war, the ecumenical, low-ecclesiological approach typical of Sant'Egidio will be more appropriate. (It should be mentioned that Sant'Egidio is so nonthreatening, and wears its religious identity so unassumingly, that it has been effective with secular as well as religious interlocutors.) Simply put, religious mediators and conciliators must be allowed and encouraged to draw fully upon the spiritual and religious resources of their tradition in the task of bringing enemies together to discern ways of resolving the conflict.

A third lesson—the necessity of building alliances between religious communities, organizations, and individuals, on the one hand, and faith-based as well as secular NGOs, on the other—is illustrated by the vignette on the would-be Buddhist peacebuilders of Cambodia. The story of Maha Ghosananda is telling because it combines one of the most frustrating aspects of religious agency—namely, the otherworldliness and impracticality (and, in some cases, deliberate obtuseness) of some charismatic or prophetic religious leaders—with one of the most promising developments of our times, namely the explosion of nongovernmental humanitarian organizations. A significant minority of these NGOs (including, increasingly, faith-based organizations such as Catholic Relief Services, World Vision, and the World Conference on Religion and Peace) are led and staffed by people who possess technical skills and are dedicated to the kind of education, training, and mobilization that many religious communities are sorely lacking—despite their often relatively well developed theologies of social justice.[43]

The belief or ideological system underlying the work of an NGO influences its mission, programs, and choice of tactics. The few organizational studies of religious or faith-based NGOs suggest that their leadership strategies, organizational cultures, management of human resources, and fund-raising techniques are distinctively shaped by the dual goal of providing effective services and advancing a set of social values developed within a religio-moral framework.[44]

In several important respects, faith-based NGOs stand in relation to their host religious traditions as do secular NGOs to the governments that provide the majority of their funding. Faith-based NGOs have the advantage of drawing on the material and symbolic resources of the host religion while retaining some measure of independence from its offi-

cial leadership and bureaucratic or hierarchical constraints. A faith-based NGO's mission and methods often reflect the values of the sponsoring religious tradition or denomination; religious identity can determine whether the NGO works in relief, development, or peacebuilding, for example, or what areas of expertise it develops within any or all of these realms.[45] A widely recognized feature of faith-based NGOs is their extensive networking capacity at all levels of society—another reflection of their privileged access to, and roles within, religious communities.[46] While faith-based NGOs and secular NGOs differ in several important respects, however, there are also significant areas of overlap and complementarity in their respective missions, organizational structures, and methods of operation.[47]

A final lesson is derived from our brief consideration of South Africa's Truth and Reconciliation Commission. In that story we can perceive the simultaneous cultural power and political ambiguity of religious attitudes toward transitional justice and other politically charged elements of postconflict peacebuilding. In this phase of peacebuilding, collaboration with secular and other religious actors is essential but also destined to be unsatisfying in societies where a dizzying variety of secular and faith-based worldviews coexist—which is to say, most of the societies in the modern world. In religious societies—again, the majority of societies in the world—religious communities will seek and deserve a prominent voice in any deliberations about how to come to terms with the past, how to seek justice, and whether forgiveness and reconciliation between erstwhile enemies are possible or even desirable. But theirs will not be the only or even the predominant voice; the necessary alliances with the state ensure that religious as well as secular actors must abandon expectations of a pure or untroubled reckoning with the past.

Such a reckoning may nonetheless have powerful cultural resonance and lend an aura of legitimacy to the postconflict political culture, if not the state itself. The ultimate viability of truth and reconciliation commissions as tools of transitional justice depends in large part on the culture of the society in question. In this regard religion frequently has a potentially decisive role to play. In light of South Africa's cultural and religious background, it is not surprising that South Africans demonstrated an extraordinary willingness to confront the past in an effort to bring about reconciliation. Africanist Lyn S. Graybill notes that representations of the apartheid era—including instruments of torture—have taken center stage in the new, postapartheid museums of the nation.[48] Equally remarkable is the zeal with which South Africans approached the rewriting of history texts. In apartheid-era textbooks blacks were virtually absent, and apartheid was described as the nation's crowning achievement. Following the 1994 elections, the Mandela government asked for a review of the curriculum to purge all elements of racism and to change the portrayals of the history of the resistance.

The TRC must be evaluated with these cultural conditions in mind, and its flaws weighed in light of the fact that the act authorizing it did not make an expression of remorse or the offering of a public apology a requirement for amnesty. Nor did the commissioners believe that such apologies, if coerced, could be considered sincere. Hindered by its inability to raise the bar for the granting of amnesty, the TRC nonetheless offered victims a forum and created a momentum toward disclosure of at least some portion of the details of human rights abuses under the apartheid regime, thereby inaugurating a public "narrative of oppression and recovery" that continues to unfold and gather moral weight in the aftermath of the commission's formal work. For good or ill, South African Christianity, like religions in other parts of the world, will play a central role in shaping and interpreting the public narrative of the sins of the past as well as the redemptive possibilities of the present.

NOTES

1. José Casanova, *Public Religion in the Modern World* (Chicago: University of Chicago Press, 1994).

2. Mark Juergensmeyer, *Terror in the Mind of God: The Global Rise of Religious Violence* (Berkeley: University of California Press, 2000).

3. For a detailed defense of this claim, see R. Scott Appleby, *The Ambivalence of the Sacred: Religion, Violence, and Reconciliation* (Lanham, Md.: Rowman and Littlefield, 2000). Parts of this chapter are excerpted from that discussion.

4. David Little, "Religious Militancy," in *Managing Global Chaos: Sources of and Responses to International Conflict,* ed. Chester A. Crocker and Fen Hampson with Pamela Aall (Washington, D.C.: United States Institute of Peace Press, 1996), 83.

5. On Hizbullah, see R. K. Ramazani, *Revolutionary Iran: Challenge and Response in the Middle East* (Baltimore: Johns Hopkins University Press, 1986), 175–195; and Martin Kramer, "Hizbullah: The Calculus of Jihad," in *Fundamentalisms and the State: Remaking Polities, Economies, and Militance,* ed. Martin E. Marty and R. Scott Appleby (Chicago: University of Chicago Press, 1993), 539–556.

6. By 1996 its former coalition partners, Amal and the Progressive Socialist Party, were calling Hizbullah "extremist" and accusing it of "damaging the nation's welfare" through its "exclusivist resistance" to Israel in the south. "Hizbullah in Politics," *Economist,* September 7, 1996, 38.

7. See Michael A. Sells, *The Bridge Betrayed: Religions and Genocide in Bosnia* (Berkeley: University of California Press, 1996), 25–45 passim.

8. Stanley J. Tambiah, *Leveling Crowds: Ethnonationalist Conflicts and Collective Violence in South Asia* (Berkeley: University of California Press, 1996), 12.

9. See Robert Eric Frykenberg, "Accounting for Fundamentalisms in South Asia: Ideologies and Institutions in Historical Perspective," in *Accounting for Fundamentalisms,* ed. Martin E. Marty and R. Scott Appleby (Chicago: University of Chicago Press, 1994), 601–602; and Ainslie Embree, "The Function of the Rashtriya Swayamsevak Sangh: To Define the Hindu Nation," in ibid., 641.

10. Daniel Gold, "Rational Action and Uncontrolled Violence: Explaining Hindu Communalism," *Journal of Religion* 21 (1991): 357–370.

11. Samuel Heilman, "Guides of the Faithful: Contemporary Religious Zionist Rabbis," in *Spokesmen for the Despised: Fundamentalist Leaders of the Middle East*, ed. R. Scott Appleby (Chicago: University of Chicago Press, 1987), 347.

12. See Daniel L. Smith-Christopher, *Subverting Hatred: The Challenge of Nonviolence in Religious Traditions* (Cambridge, Mass.: Boston Research Center for the 21st Century, 1998). Also see Catherine Ingram, *In the Footsteps of Gandhi: Conversations with Spiritual Social Activists* (Berkeley, Calif.: Parallax Press, 1990); Albert J. Raboteau, "Martin Luther King, Jr., and the Tradition of Black Religious Protest," in *Religion and the Life of the Nation: American Recoveries*, ed. Rowland A. Sherrill (Urbana: University of Illinois Press, 1990), 46–63; and Daniel L. Buttry, *Christian Peacemaking: From Heritage to Hope* (Valley Forge, Pa.: Judson Press, 1994), 45–59. For a comparative overview of peacemakers in Islam, Judaism, and Christianity, see Marc Gopin, "Religion, Violence, and Conflict Resolution," *Peace and Change* 22, no. 1 (January 1997): 1–31.

13. John Paul Lederach, *Building Peace: Sustainable Reconciliation in Divided Societies* (Washington, D.C.: United States Institute of Peace Press, 1997), 22.

14. Ibid., 25.

15. Ibid., 33.

16. Cynthia Sampson, "Religion and Peacebuilding," in *Peacemaking in International Conflict: Methods and Techniques*, ed. I. William Zartman and J. Lewis Rasmussen (Washington, D.C.: United States Institute of Peace Press, 1997), 275.

17. Ibid. See also Appleby, *Ambivalence of the Sacred*; and Marc Gopin, *Between Eden and Armageddon: The Future of World Religions, Violence, and Peacemaking* (New York: Oxford University Press, 2000).

18. The following account of Sant'Egidio is adapted from Appleby, *Ambivalence of the Sacred*, 155–164.

19. Cameron Hume, *Ending Mozambique's War: The Role of Mediation and Good Offices* (Washington, D.C.: United States Institute of Peace Press, 1994). For additional background, see Ruth Brandon Miller, "Mozambique's War of Terror," *Christianity and Crisis*, September 14, 1987, 286; Carl F. Nielsen, "The Devastation of Mozambique," *One World* (April 1992): 14; Malyn Newitt, *A History of Mozambique* (Bloomington: Indiana University Press, 1995), 517–540;

Hilary Andersson, *Mozambique: A War against the People* (New York: St. Martin's Press, 1992), 1–45; and William Finnegan, *A Complicated War: The Harrowing of Mozambique* (Berkeley: University of California Press, 1992).

20. "We do not approve or condemn, but search out the grain of reason and goodness we believe persists in even the hardest criminal." Andrea Bartoli, interview by author, New York City, January 23, 1997.

21. Hume, *Ending Mozambique's War*, 17–18.

22. In 1985, Hume reports, Sant'Egidio sent Mozambique a "ship of solidarity" with thirty-five hundred tons of humanitarian aid, and in 1988 a second ship arrived with seven thousand tons.

23. The community also brokered limited settlements in Guatemala, Burundi, and Albania. In each of these cases, however, the agreements eventually fell apart with changes in the political climate or the political leadership. See Paul Lewis, "Not Just Governments Make War and Peace," *New York Times*, November 28, 1998, A21.

24. Marco Impagliazzo and Mario Giro, "Algeria Held Hostage: The Army, Fundamentalism, and the History of a Troublesome Peace" (unpublished manuscript).

25. Subsequently, however, the government rejected the Sant'Egidio platform for peace talks. Milton Viorst, "Algeria's Long Night," *Foreign Affairs* 76, no. 6 (November-December 1997): 96.

26. The account of Ghosananda and the Dhammayietra is adapted from Appleby, *Ambivalence of the Sacred*, 123–131.

27. Coalition for Peace and Reconciliation, "Letter from Cambodia," January 1997.

28. *Providence Journal-Bulletin*, May 3, 1994, 7C.

29. "Former R. I. Buddhist Leads Cambodia Walk," *Providence Journal-Bulletin*, May 6, 1995, 7C.

30. Frank Reynolds and Winifred Sullivan, "Report from Cambodia," *Criterion* 33, no. 3 (August 1994): 16–23.

31. *Christian Science Monitor*, May 20, 1994, 5; "Medellin on the Mekong," *Far Eastern Economic Review*, November 23, 1995, 12.

32. Coalition for Peace and Reconciliation, *CPR Update: A Newsletter of the Dhammayietra Center*, January 1997, 6.

33. Peter Pond, interview by author, March 26, 1998.

34. Ibid.

35. Walter Wink, *When the Powers Fall: Reconciliation in the Healing of Nations* (Minneapolis, Minn.: Fortress, 1998), 14.

36. See Kristen Renwick Monroe, *The Heart of Altruism: Perceptions of a Common Humanity* (Princeton, N.J.: Princeton University Press, 1996).

37. Lyn S. Graybill, "South Africa's Truth and Reconciliation Commission: Ethical and Theological Perspectives," *Ethics and International Affairs* 12 (1998): 45. Also, cf. "South Africa: Indemnity Act" and "South Africa: 1993 Constitution" in *Transitional Justice: How Emerging Democracies Reckon with Former Regimes,* vol. 3, *Laws, Rulings, and Reports,* ed. Neil J. Kritz (Washington, D.C.: United States Institute of Peace Press, 1995), 593–597.

38. Andre du Toit, "No Rest without the Wicked," *Indicator* 14 (summer 1997): 9.

39. Graybill, "South Africa's Truth and Reconciliation Commission," 44–47. Not only academics but some victims as well have complained about "the imposition of a Christian morality of forgiveness," Graybill notes. "While some critics find the Christian framework and verbiage unacceptable, for many South Africans—77 percent of whom identify themselves as Christians—the Biblical language resonates."

40. Similarly, Wink recounts the story of his experience leading a workshop on nonviolence with a group of South African church leaders, half of them black, in 1988. "Every black person there had been tortured," he recalls, "and all had forgiven their torturers." Their Christian faith, reinforced by their cultural heritage, literally required them to forgive. Wink, *When the Powers Fall,* 15.

41. *The Report of the Truth and Reconciliation Commission,* vol. 1 (South Africa, 1998), para. 100.

42. On May 3 the peace talks broke down after the Taliban refused to lift a blockade of Hazarajat, the central region where tens of thousands of Afghans were threatened by food shortages, until the commission of religious scholars was in place. Fighting between the two sides resumed on May 20. See "Fighting Resumes in Afghanistan," *New York Times,* May 21, 1998, A11; "Afghan Peace Talks Break Off, Bringing Fear of New Fighting," *New York Times,* May 4, 1998; "Afghans Hold Peace Talks; Signs of Hope and Pessimism," *New York Times,* April 27, 1998, A6.

43. There is now a substantial body of literature on NGOs and how they operate within a world of traditionally state-centric international relations. The peacebuilding potential of NGOs has been widely recognized despite disagreement over the particulars of their roles. Indeed, the United Nations, expanding its operations in the post–Cold War era to include refugee aid, humanitarian relief, preventive diplomacy, peacekeeping, and postconflict peacebuilding, entered into partnerships with NGOs in each of these areas. See, inter alia, Anne Marie Clark, "Non-Governmental Organizations and Their Influence on International Society," *Journal of International Affairs* 48, no. 2 (1995): 507–525; Peter Willetts, ed., *The Conscience of the World: The Influence of Non-Governmental Organizations in the U.N. System* (Washington, D.C.: Brookings Institution, 1995); Jackie Smith, Charles Chatfield, and Ronald Pagnucco, eds., *Transnational Social Movements and Global Politics: Solidarity beyond the State* (Syracuse, N.Y.: Syracuse University Press, 1997); Jackie Smith, Ronald Pagnucco, and George Lopez, "Globalizing Human Rights: The Work of Transnational Human Rights NGOs in the 1990s," *Human Rights Quarterly* 20 (1998): 379–412; and Farouk Mawlawi, "New Conflict, New Challenges: The Evolving Role for Non-Governmental Actors," *Journal of International Affairs* 46, no. 2 (1993): 391–413. On the United Nations, see Elise Boulding and Jan Oberg, "United Nations Peacekeeping and NGO Peacebuilding: Towards Partnership," in *The Future of the United Nations System: Potential for the Twenty-First Century,* ed. Chadwick F. Alger (New York: United Nations University Press, 1998), 127–154.

44. One study of the work of SERPAJ, an NGO promoting nonviolent direct action in Latin America, presents evidence that faith-based groups are more likely to participate in such initiatives than other groups. Ronald Pagnucco and John D. McCarthy, "Advocating Nonviolent Direct Action in Latin America: The Antecedents and Emergence of SERPAJ," in *Religion and Politics in Comparative Perspective,* ed. Bronislaw Misztal and Anson Shupe (Westport, Conn.: Praeger, 1992), 127–128. Also see Loramy Conradi, "Faith-Based and Secular NGOs: A Comparative Study of Peacebuilding" (Ph.D. diss., University of Notre Dame, 2001); and Thomas H. Jeavons, *When the Bottom Line Is Faithfulness: Management of Christian Service Organizations* (Bloomington: Indiana University Press, 1994).

45. Fred Kniss and David Todd Campbell, "The Effect of Religious Orientation on International Relief and Development Organizations," *Journal for the Scientific Study of Religion* 36, no. 1 (1997): 93–103.

46. Douglas Johnston and Cynthia Sampson, eds., *Religion: The Missing Dimension of Statecraft* (New York: Oxford University Press, 1994); William Demars, "Helping People in a People's War: Humanitarian Organizations and the Ethiopian Conflict, 1980–1988" (Ph.D. diss., University of Notre Dame, 1993); Elizabeth Ferris, *Beyond Borders: Refugees, Migrants, and Human Rights in the Post–Cold War Era* (Geneva: WCC Publications, 1993).

47. Loramy Conradi, after surveying the literature comparing religious and secular NGOs and interviewing representatives from both types of organizations, concluded that while some generalizable differences between them can be traced to a religious orientation or lack thereof, others turn on differing economic, psychological, and sociological factors. See Loramy Conradi, "A Comparative Study of Faith-Based and Secular NGOs Working in Conflict Resolution" (unpublished paper, University of Notre Dame, 1998).

48. Graybill, "South Africa's Truth and Reconciliation Commission."

49

Civil Society
and Reconciliation

John Paul Lederach

INTRODUCTION

At the writing of this chapter we are just a short way into the new century and millennium. Over the past months our minds have turned numerous times toward reflection on the meaning of the past century, the events that riveted our attention, and the direction of global relationships. For those of us who have had the opportunity and privilege to work at the forging of peace processes, we witnessed in the past few years extraordinary events.

Over the course of decades we watched the ebb and flow of destructive cycles of violence in the Irish context. At some points over the past thirty years it seemed that political negotiations might render a peaceful solution, but nearly as soon as the hopes were raised, a new cycle of violence would break out. Then came the declaration of cease-fires in the 1990s, nudged through a maze of people and decision makers by a series of mostly unnamed internal actors, but soon supported by a much broader coalition of peace supporters. Against all odds, and most surprisingly, in spite of numerous explosive moments of violence that in early years rekindled the destructive patterns and destroyed the fledgling peace initiatives, the process has made its way forward. The flame of peace refused to die.

Throughout nearly the whole of the century we were witnesses to the injustices, open warfare, and structural violence that were built on an exclusionist political model of apartheid in South Africa. Pressures rose for change within and from the international community. We held our breath as Nelson Mandela walked from prison to the presidency. We watched as a nation moved through monumental change affecting every one of its citizens, teetering between the choices of escalated and uncontrolled violence and moving toward rebuilding their political, economic, and social structures on the basis of respect and dialogue. Against all odds, in what had to be the situation with the greatest potential for centuries of pent-up anger and injustice to be unleashed in untold proportions, the process made its way forward. The flame of peace refused to die.

What kept the flame alive in these situations, when in earlier instances under similar situations it was quickly snuffed under the pressures of destructive conflict? The conflict was no less great. I would speculate that in these cases, as in numerous other peace processes our global community has forged and followed in the past decade, for the first time people began to understand peacebuilding as an organic ecosystem rather than as a narrow and hierarchically defined political event or agreement. A systemic view provides lenses that help us look across the whole of the interrelated parts in any system, as opposed to lenses that posit causal analysis only on the aspects that are most visible, or, in the case of social systems, those vested with higher formal or political authority. Such an ecosystemic view will suggest that war is not just politics by other means and that peace is process by multiple means. It will bring us full face toward the title of this chapter: civil society and reconciliation.

Before proceeding further I should be clear that I consider myself better described as being driven by the impulses of a conflict transformation practitioner than an academic researcher. This has the advantage that my eyes and heart are cast toward the practical question, So what exactly does this suggest we do? It has the disadvantage that scientific exactitude, particularly in reference to the definition of terms, may not reach the rigorous standards upheld in some academic quarters. Thus I understand the much used and increasingly abused terms "civil society" and "reconciliation" in rather simple, straightforward ways.

I understand civil society to refer to a web of human relationships made up of individual people, their networks, organizations, and institutions around which social and community life is built. It is dynamic, adaptive, at times nebulous, at times well structured, though much of it is informal. The only thing civil society is not is the formal structures of official political governance, particularly at national levels.

I understand reconciliation to be dynamic, adaptive processes aimed at building and healing the torn fabric of interpersonal and community lives and relationships. The "re" in reconciliation is not aimed at putting Humpty Dumpty back together again. Humpty was an egg. Reconciliation is first and last about people and their relationships. Hence reconciliation is never about returning to a former state, though there is often great longing to do so. It is about building relationships, and relationships are about real people in real situations who must find a way forward together. To be more precise, reconciliation is made up of processes that build relationships in a context of interdependence.

When we take a relationship-centric approach it is possible to envision why reconciliation is so difficult following intense periods of violence and civil war. Peace agreements and conflict resolution generally orient themselves toward dealing with content-specific issues requiring short-term immediate action from the people enmeshed in the disputes. Reconciliation, by contrast, orients its energy toward understanding the deeper psychological and subjective aspects of people's experiences, not just in connection to their recent past but often based on generations of pain, loss, and suffering. Reconciliation requires that people not only decide what to do about particular issues, but also address and reconsider their understanding of self, community, and enemy. Building a relationship with a mortal enemy is always accompanied with a change in how you perceive yourself and your community, and how you perceive the other and their community. In short, reconciliation based on the building of relationships requires that people begin a process of reconstructing their identities. The monumental task is that this reconstruction must be done in a period of rapid, volatile, and unpredictable change and more often than not in physical proximity to the enemy.

To understand civil society and reconciliation under the broad rubric of "consolidating peace," we need to explore two things. First, we must look briefly at a comprehensive framework that helps us understand peace as a process, a dynamic social ecosystem. Second, we must give consideration to the kind of social energies and directions that reconciliation processes engender within deeply divided societies. These two broad explorations form the main body of this chapter. Throughout I shall address myself to a broad audience of people concerned with peacebuilding: those engaged in the conflicts, those functioning as third parties, and those who study these phenomena.

A COMPREHENSIVE FRAMEWORK FOR PEACEBUILDING

In a recent book I suggested that peacebuilding may be best understood using the metaphor of building a house (Lederach 1997). A house requires a vision, often contemplated early on in the architectural design, which provides an image and a direction. The design, however, usually evolves through changes that emerge as specific needs and structural issues (like the lay of the land) are addressed. There are stages and sets of interrelated though very different skills that must be coordinated. A strong foundation is needed and strategically placed pillars reinforced with crosscutting beams and boards that hold and strengthen the structure. If we draw a parallel to peacebuilding, this approach suggests a number of lenses that enhance our capacity to visualize the process in broader and more strategic ways. Several key understandings are particularly important for our purposes in this chapter.

1. *Peacebuilding must be undertaken simultaneously at numerous levels of the society.*
   If we are to move beyond settlement and toward reconciliation, or toward what I refer to as sustainable peace processes, we must

not limit our lenses to only the highest level of political actors and the peace negotiations they forge. I have graphically depicted this as a pyramid that describes three interrelated but different processes (see figure 1). The first process is top-down negotiations conducted by a few representative and usually highly visible leaders. The second is bottom-up approaches that involve the forging of understanding and peace at local levels according to the unique characteristics of those local settings. The third is middle-out approaches that can support both of the other two in unique ways and that often provide linkages vertically in the society and horizontally across the lines of conflict.

The key from this perspective is to understand sustainability as a dynamic process built on active interdependence and interaction of leadership across the levels of the affected society. Simultaneity suggests a web of relationships such that this process not be envisioned as sequential and linear. In other words, peacebuilding has multiple activities, at multiple levels, carried on by different sets of people at the same time. This is differentiated from a view that says peace is controlled at one place, by one set of people, who put in motion a series of sequential steps. Experience in peacebuilding initiatives that have shown themselves resilient against the many storms and pressures of the long term and destructive cycles of violence prevalent in protracted conflict suggests that no one level of leadership within a society is capable of delivering and sustaining a peace process on its own. Thus, while different levels have distinct needs, requirements, and time frames, each is related to the others. They are systemically linked and must be understood as such. This is particularly true of the civil society and processes of reconciliation, in which local participation of those affected by the conflict, constructive responsibility by recognized leaders, and contextualized approaches

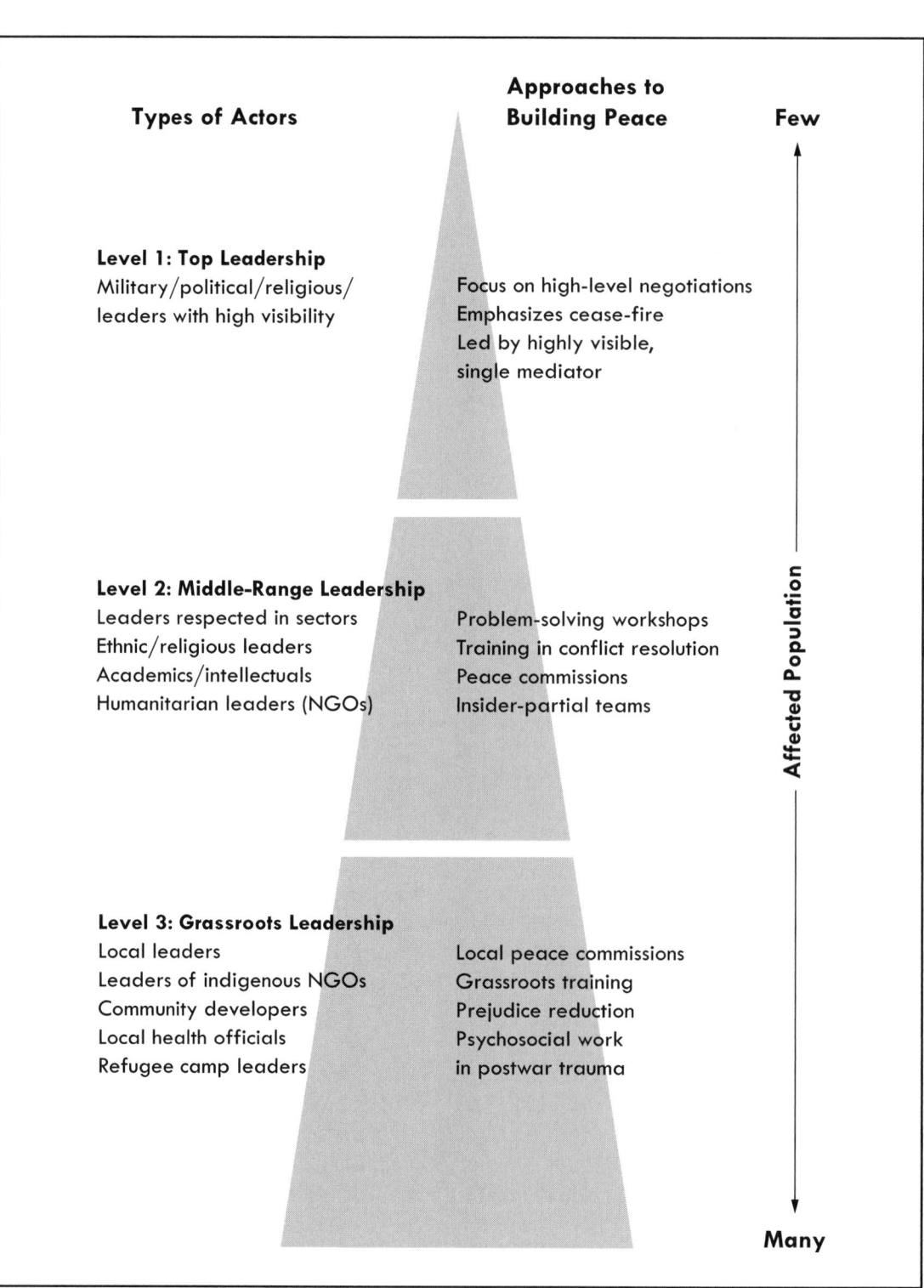

Figure 1. Actors and Approaches to Peacebuilding
Source: John Paul Lederach, *Building Peace: Sustainable Reconciliation in Divided Societies* (Washington, D.C.: United States Institute of Peace Press, 1997), 39.

are the elements, sine qua non, of responsive and sustainable design.

Let us take a concrete example. Throughout the peace process over the past years in the Irish context the interdependence of levels can be clearly seen. A stalemate or a collapse in the peace talks at the highest level of leadership, or a particular set of inflammatory statements by one or another of the visible leaders, often affected how people responded to local issues: they became more contentious. But it was equally true that at any given moment decisions and struggles over a local parading issue that turned violent immediately affected the higher-level negotiations and process. The levels of action and activity were different but linked and mutually dependent. Each level needed an infrastructure to support its respective processes. The local community needed support for dealing with a particular set of concerns that faced it, while the negotiations needed a support system for working through the variety of concerns facing the broader agenda. In the end, the capacity of the peacebuilding system to sustain a constructive and resilient process had to do with creating an infrastructure of support responsive to various levels, working simultaneously at multiple processes, and finding creative, adaptive mechanisms that permitted each to move forward. In the end, the key was that stalemates or even breakdowns at one level could not derail the whole process. Rather, while each level was linked and mutually affected the other, each continued to work at the adaptations necessary to keep moving forward in a constructive manner.

What I have just outlined is descriptive of an ecosystem. From this view we do not envision that conflicts end, as if they go away. Rather, we understand the key to be the set of ongoing relationships and the discovery and practice of new ways of relating that do not center or rely on violence. Conflict, however, is still a part of the ecosystem. Over time, from a multiplicity of places, people, and processes, as was the case in Northern Ireland, new capacities and mechanisms for dealing with those differences and conflicts emerge and take precedence over the old. What has diminished and eventually ended is violence as the primary mechanism for expressing and handling the conflict.

2. *Short-term needs and long-term vision must be linked.*

One of the unique challenges of peacebuilding is how we conceptualize time and timing. In settings that have experienced long-term destructive conflict, people often mark their history by the ebb and flow of crises. Each new day brings the possibility of some new twist in the cycles of violence that will rivet attention on an urgent, often life-or-death crisis. Protracted conflict settings are crisis-driven systems, and correspondingly, peacebuilding too often takes on this same characteristic. Crisis driven means that the process defines itself by hopping from one urgent task to the next, frequently at the expense of having a strategic focus and design for the longer-term change needed. Peacebuilding easily becomes a "firefighting" process, rushing from one explosion to the next in an effort to prevent any single fire from escalating back into full-blown violence. The impact of being crisis driven is that our lenses become narrow, myopic, and very short term. We too often assume that if we can just get out of this mess, we can turn our attention to the more important things. We discover too late that most settings of protracted, violent conflict are wrapped up in a permanently emerging crisis.

I have suggested that a critical shift in our thinking, one that is readily apparent in peace processes that have sustained themselves over time, is the capacity to develop a strategic design framework. Such a framework provides a space for envisioning a desired future and pushes us to reflect critically about the nature of change processes required to move from immediate crisis to longer-term hope. It is only within a framework that thinks ahead that we are able to shift from being crisis driven to being crisis responsive. Crisis responsive means that we are able to recognize within any given moment and urgent task the opportunity for maximizing our potential that both responds to the immediate need and at the same time increases the overall movement toward the desired change. Being crisis responsive changes how we ask questions. We move from the simpler question—How do we solve this crisis?—to the more complex dilemma formulation—How do we respond to the immediate crisis and at the same time build capacities and relationships that will be needed for longer-term change we hope to create?

Experience suggests that in the places that have created a capacity to sustain an adaptive peace process over time, for example, South Africa, Nicaragua, or Northern Ireland, their time frame of reference shifted conceptually to match the practicalities of their respective realities. They were required to shift from a short-term, task-oriented view toward a longer-term, change-oriented view. This is what I refer to as "decade" thinking. In conflicts that have been expressed through violent cycles of interaction that date across decades or even generations we must think in longer blocks, in decades, in reference to the peacebuilding processes required to move toward the desired change in relationships. This does not mean we think in idealistic but irrelevant terms about peace, thereby making dreams an untouchable utopia. Rather, we build from dreams the strategic frameworks that clarify and concretize the social, political, economic, community, and interpersonal changes those dreams would entail. This, in turn, sharpens our capacity to recognize at any given moment the potential inherent in the crisis that permits us to

simultaneously respond to the crisis and build our overall capacity for desired change.

The key in peacebuilding lies not in whether we are proficient at putting out fires, nor in whether we are adept at articulating our hopes. The key lies in whether we are capable of strategically linking the potential in the crisis with the changes needed to move us toward the dream.

3. *Critical issues must find response while broader structural change is envisioned and set in motion.* The landscape of conflict terrain is never flat and smooth. Rather, it is spiked with a series of contentious issues that function nearly like lightning rods rising above the peaks of inhabitants. These issues are often the recipients of spectacular energy mobilizing people's attention. In protracted conflict, issues can range from "parades" in a particular neighborhood in Ireland, to the redrawing of a national "map" in Ethiopia, to the struggle in a local community in Guatemala over a particular "parcel of land." Or, as I write this paper in the year 2000, to the rights of citizenship and family responsibility for a small Cuban boy found in the waters off Miami.

In the professional fields that address the handling of conflict, finding responses to these issues is often referred to as "conflict resolution." The guiding metaphor is finding a way to forge a creative solution to the particular problem posed at any given time. For the most part, the energy of the response system is given over to working out an agreement that ends the contentiousness, and in particular the violence. Here the focus is on how to find a solution that ends something not desired.

Reconciliation and the strengthening of civil society must think beyond this more limited metaphor. I believe reconciliation requires us to think about how to end things not desired, how to find creative solutions to specific problems, and how to use both to build something desired. This broader thinking I would refer to as peacebuilding and conflict transformation. Peacebuilding suggests forging structures and processes that redefine violent relationships into constructive and cooperative patterns. Conflict transformation suggests that such a redefinition will require change processes at multiple levels.

Reconciliation as a process of change and redefinition of relationships therefore pushes beyond the resolution of a particular issue and toward a framework that embeds that issue in the context of the broader system and the root causes that underlie the symptomatic expression of the conflict. In concrete terms, reconciliation processes always envision the issue as a potential opportunity to explore, understand, and change the deeper patterns and causes that have given rise to violent expressions of conflict in the relationship. This requires that we link the content of a particular issue with the systemic patterns and structures that have historically guided and defined the relationships. Changes in historic patterns push us into the realm of seeking change in the root causes while addressing the content of specific issues.

Similar to the holistic approach in reference to the time frame, linking symptomatic issues with systemic patterns requires us to think in reference to the interdependence within a system of relationships rather than focus exclusive energy on the most visible aspect. The key is not whether we are adept at solving a particular issue, nor whether we have envisioned a broad macrochange of the policies. The key lies in our capacity to link the seeking of the potential inherent in the discrete issues as a portal creating pathways forward on the journey toward changing destructive systemic patterns and structures.

In both points 2 and 3, we may usefully return to the metaphor of building a house as an analogy of forging reconciliation processes. When a house is built, longer-term

vision and short immediate intensive work represent distinct aspects of the process but are never disconnected. Builders, particularly contractors, operate with a complexity approach rather than strictly a linear understanding. Thus while in the morning concrete is poured for the foundation of a house and people labor fast and furious, that activity fits within a bigger picture and simultaneously is juggled with others. Just before the cement truck arrives the contractor may be ordering the trusses, finalizing a subcontract with the plumber, asking for bids from several cabinetmakers. The actual work of building and installing the kitchen cabinets is done well after the pouring of the cement, but putting in motion what is needed to design, build, and prepare the cabinets happens simultaneously with it. This is precisely how reconciliation processes can be envisioned: the capacity to see the whole, understand different sets of needs and activities, move with intensity to respond to key immediate needs while simultaneously preparing the way for other sets of activities to have their place and time. This approach requires an understanding of complexity and simultaneity of action.

THE SOCIAL ENERGIES OF RECONCILIATION

I lived and worked in Central America for several years in the mid-1980s. During that time an opportunity emerged to work with a national conciliation process between the East Coast resistance leaders and the Sandinista government in Nicaragua that became the primary focus of my work for the rest of the decade. The team was made up of Moravian and Baptist church leaders. It was an intense time of learning in a very violent situation, which eventually led to the design and support of negotiations, a cease-fire, and an end to the war raging in that part of Nicaragua.

It was through this experience that I found myself moving beyond the narrower lenses of conflict resolution and toward deeper understandings of the practices of reconciliation. I saw reconciliation through the way these indigenous East Coast and Nicaraguan conciliators thought and developed their work. They did not see their principal goal to be resolving a particular issue, nor did they see themselves as even operating with a certain approach to negotiation. They envisioned themselves as people located in a set of relationships, most of which were lifelong relationships between friends who were enemies. As I have written in other texts, in the best of indigenous and Latin traditions, they were more like older siblings handling a family conflict than professional mediators brokering a negotiation. For them, reconciliation was finding a way to restore and heal the broken web of relationships.

One of the requests made to our group was to accompany the negotiators on several tours throughout the East Coast of Nicaragua where the higher-level officials on both sides made presentations about the peace process to the local communities. On these travels we invariably arrived by river unannounced in the remote villages and within hours found ourselves in an open community forum. Almost all of the meetings started with one of the conciliator-pastors reading Psalm 85. In this poetic verse the psalmist beseeches the Lord, requesting restoration and mercy in a context of a people who are seeking return to their homeland after exile, violence, and suffering. In verse 10, the psalmist weaves together four voices that, in the Spanish translation based on the old English of the King James Version, reads:

> Truth and Mercy have met together,
> Justice and Peace have kissed.

Hearing these words repeated nearly every day in a new village, in the context of a war-torn society, moving with fits and starts toward the construction of peace, provided intriguing insight. I noticed the psalmist treats the concepts as if they were people, as if they were alive. In the context of the violence, suffering, and efforts of peace, I could hear these different voices. I began to think about these voices of Truth, Mercy, Justice, and Peace as social energies that are alive and present in any conflict. Over the years I have developed exercises that help elucidate and call forward in more explicit ways the concerns and impulses of the four.

My conviction is this. The single greatest challenge of all conflicts, particularly those with a long history of violence and suffering, is to create the social space where it is possible to hold together and interdependent, not separate and isolated, the impulses of these four social energies. Where they meet, are connected, and relate, we create the pathway leading toward reconciliation. Where they are ignored, isolated from one another, or chosen one over the other, we often are unable to create sustainable peace processes.

The key question then becomes how we understand the impulses and energy represented by each of the voices, and how we move to thinking in a more comprehensive way about their relationship. What I have discovered is that they are best linked when each is given a voice, as if they were people, and invited to speak and advocate for what they need, but in the active presence of the others (Lederach 1999). Thus a reconciliation process must be dynamic, adaptable, and practical, weaving back and forth between the different but interdependent energies pushing for Truth, Mercy, Justice, and Peace. For the purposes of this chapter I propose to briefly outline some of what I feel each voice requires and the energy it brings to reconciliation as a process that goes beyond the formal peace accord and toward the rebuilding of relationships.

Truth

Within the bigger picture of the conflict setting, Sister Truth casts her eyes toward the past. In essence she wants the community to know what occurred, to bring to public light the actions and responsibilities of those involved. In social-political terms Truth is organized around commissions of inquiry, sometimes in the form of tribunals. Too often this is seen for its formalistic role: establishing facts and attaching those to individual persons. In reality, Sister Truth as a social energy is about the retelling of a story in the public square, in its fullest version, so that all eyes and ears can hear and know. To go further, the impulse of Truth related to reconciliation has some very specific needs.

We must start with the deepest impulse of Sister Truth, for she is not driven so much by the requirements of legal or human rights standards as by the fundamental need to know and make known. Particularly from the eyes and hearts of those who have suffered, who have lost family and loved ones in the course of a violent conflict, Truth represents the avenue of alleviating the haunting and seemingly endless guesswork, the ambiguity of speculation. People just want to know what happened, and usually also ask, Why?

Here the social organization of Truth is oriented toward creating a transparency of history, with a straightforward exploration of the intentions and meaning that created the events and actions. While this exploration may lead to impulses related to justice, or forgiveness, or prevention of this kind of action in the future, the primary impulse of Truth is to make transparent, open, and clear what was opaque, shrouded in secrecy, and hidden.

There is a world of difference—in reference to social meaning, not etymology—between *knowing* and *acknowledging*. While the initial impulse of Sister Truth is to make known, perhaps the greater energy she brings is the need to have that which is known be declared, recognized, and acknowledged. At a phenomenological level we move here from the realm of the subjective—"I know these things took place" —to the terrain of the intersubjective: "We acknowledge that this happened in this way." Further, the acknowledgment desired is only complete if the recognition of the action indicates directly that not only is this known, not only is it openly stated, but that it was wrong and unacceptable by decent human standards. Truth as acknowledgment is whole if it states the action committed openly, creates a clarity of public recognition, and establishes that it had detrimental and destructive impact on real people that is not acceptable.

Truth as acknowledgment is therefore not a passive, static, or individual experience. Nor can it ever be bureaucratized, though all too often passive and static bureaucracy defines the ways we have chosen to organize Sister Truth in our public processes. Acknowledgment moves Truth into the arena of social processes where a person (or group) recognizes and takes account for his or her actions that have affected others, in the presence of the other. It reintroduces the other in the form of a live, feeling person; it reintroduces the victim as a human being into the process. To acknowledge what was done, or what I did, means that I recognize the other not as an object but as a person who was hurt. In religious terms such a process of acknowledgment is akin to confession; in legal terms it is direct admission of action.

The keys to acknowledgment would seem to be multifaceted. From the standpoint of reconciliation and relationship, far more than knowing the objective facts of what occurred, acknowledgment is measured by the authenticity, honesty, and genuineness of the persons revealing the nature of their actions and the capacity of recognizing the impact of that action on another. In the absence of even minimal acknowledgment, or the perception that it is not authentic, or that it does not recognize the damage and the effect, then engaging the voice of Truth in an open forum attested to by others becomes critical. In simple terms, for the person or community affected by the destructive action, acknowledgment needs to be public. "These things happened to you. It was not right. It will not be forgotten." Truth as acknowledgment thus covers both the content of a given history and the rendering of that story into a public arena where it can be seen, attested to, and recognized. Thus the push of victim-centered groups is toward having leadership and visible figures publicly name the wrong, the wrongdoing, and the wrongdoer. It is then more than knowing. Truth has been afforded a place; it is legitimate; it has received a recognized status.

However, as is the case in so many long-term conflicts, where all sides have experienced violence and incomprehensible and unjustifiable loss, it becomes extremely difficult to create the space for mutual acknowledgment of the loss. Each side moves to justify and protect its loss, expecting the acknowledgment to be forthcoming from the other. Paradoxically, what each needs from the other to liberate the cycle of recrimination and violence is the hardest to give. This is coupled with the inherent difficulty that Truth is more than facts; it involves recognition and an interactive quality, and it means that the forms for socially organizing the voice, impulses, and needs of Truth rarely match the needs and expectations of those who have been victimized and suffered. At a practical level we therefore often find ourselves engaged in public processes aimed at giving flesh to the impulse of Sister Truth that at best are incomplete and symbolic, leaving many with the perception that Truth is mute and the community deaf. The social energy she represents, however, pushes us to look back in transparent and honest ways toward the experience and impact of the past. It asks us to acknowledge through open and public fora what was done, by whom and to whom, and the consequences of those actions in the context of the conflict. And it requires us to create mechanisms that legitimate and recognize the pain suffered through the wrongdoing. To the extent the impulse of Sister Truth is not given voice and flesh, the peace process will be experienced as superficial, manipulated, and covering up the depth of the injustice suffered.

Mercy

Over the past few years I have worked closely with colleagues who founded and now provide leadership with the West Africa Network for Peacebuilding (WANEP). Many of them, like Sam Doe, Marion Subeh, or Emmanuel Bombande, come from practical experiences of working at peacebuilding in Liberia and Sierra Leone, some of the harshest challenges facing reconciliation across our globe. In particular, they have worked for years with child soldiers, young children kidnapped at the ages of nine to eleven, drugged, forced into committing severe atrocities against their own families and villages, and now severely traumatized in the aftermath of the wars. The question that crops up time and again in these situations, hidden from the cameras and publicity of CNN, is simple. How do we reintegrate the child soldier into the community against which he or she has committed the atrocity? How do we not lose a generation of children to the trauma of this violence?

The question is the voice of Brother Mercy. His energy is forward looking, aimed toward the future and based fundamentally on two impulses. The first is to discover how to socially organize the space that makes possible a new start. The second is to discover how to do this in the context of interdependent, often face-to-face, relationships in which the victim of the violence must find a way to coinhabit a local geography with the perpetrator of the violence. And both of these tasks must be accomplished in a context in which the perpetrator himself or herself has been severely traumatized at a young age.

Brother Mercy often feels misunderstood. Maligned as soft and running from the past (Sister Truth), he is easily accused of covering up or refusing to engage in the hard changes needed. In reality, the impulse of Mercy is driven by a paradox: To the degree people feel safe, they can engage in the vulnerability of transparency; to the degree there is understanding and hope for change in the future, they can journey through the past. Ironically, Brother Mercy holds up hope and a new start as means to engage responsibility and accountability.

Within much of Western jurisprudence we have systematized punishment as the measuring stick of accountability. This system is oriented toward the question of what someone should pay in order to account for his or her wrongdoing. We have not equally systematized the pathway for individuals, much less for whole groups, to reintegrate into the community. There is no vision at the end of the path of punishment for how reintegration and healing will take place, neither in the preparation of the individual nor in the preparation of the affected community.

Brother Mercy, however, addresses himself precisely to these concerns. The impulses are aimed at thinking ahead, creating the space for rebuilding individuals and the communities affected, providing a pathway forward that leads toward a great wholeness. This begins with small starts, taking risks to venture back into relationship or initiate relationship for the first time, as is the case in many settings of generational conflict.

In reference to practice, the efforts to organize mercy across the whole of an affected setting involve programmatic initiatives. Amnesty, in one form or another, for past actions provides the reintegration of individuals or armed groups into civilian life and the release of those who participated in and were captured during periods of violence with a way back into the society. Once politicized and made into a program, however, the deeper quality of Brother Mercy is replaced by the pragmatic push for the society to hide or quickly rid itself of the very face of its past history.

The formidable task that Brother Mercy places before us as a social energy is to discover the deeper meaning of personal and social change. At a first level is the logistical challenge of how former enemies encounter and coin-

habit a common social and physical geography. More important, at a second level it holds before us the process of how individuals and whole societies move toward changing patterns of behavior and relationships. And this must be done in a context in which memories of personal trauma are still very much etched in the minds and hearts of those involved. With the horizon of reconciliation within sight Brother Mercy asks us to take steps each day, even when the possibility of reaching the horizon seems remote. The long process of change initiates with the small steps of taking the risk to create opportunity, knowing full well there is no guarantee of success.

Justice

Over the course of the hearings of the South African Truth and Reconciliation Commission, I found it a powerful experience to listen to the voices of the families who were living through the recounting of the atrocities committed against members of their family and community. Invariably, you would hear in one interview a mother who would plead, "What I need most is simply to know what happened to my son. Where can I find his remains?" This is clearly the voice of Sister Truth. The commission established the guideline that if people involved in the inhumane crimes came forward and gave a full public testimony about their actions, they would then be afforded amnesty in the new South Africa. Here we can see the way Brother Mercy was organized programmatically. Soon, however, we would hear in the next interview "the violence perpetrated against our families goes beyond comprehension. Those who committed these crimes must be held accountable, and we must be compensated for our losses." And herein we begin to feel the deep pulse and energy of Brother Justice.

As it relates to conflict transformation and reconciliation the impulse of Justice is carried through three different energies. As can be heard in the voice above, the first energy is often that of accountability. Perhaps more than any other concern, during and in the aftermath of violence, Brother Justice cries for something to be done to both account for and prevent the inhumane treatment and suffering that destroys families and communities. An accounting requires that those who were involved in the violence be held responsible for the actions. There are multiple forms that accountability can take, though the most common in our structure of jurisprudence has been that of punishment.

This leads to the second major impulse, recompense for the damage done. In conflict, and particularly violent conflict, the voice of Justice pursues the idea that the perpetrator not only should be held accountable but should also "pay" to restore in some form what has been lost to those who lost it. When we consider more closely the ideas of accountability and recompense we find an intriguing set of underlying concerns that often get lost in the typical forms or solutions these take under our modern systems of law. This is precisely where a paradigm shift from retributive toward restorative justice has emerged (Zehr 1990).

Typically, retributive justice assumes that the violent wrongdoing, while taking place against a person or group, is best handled as if it were a crime or violence against the laws of a state or against humanity. The burden is then on the shoulders of the state to prove the case. Subsequently, accountability and recompense are achieved when the state punishes the perpetrators, who pay their dues to the state or the society. This quickly translates into a process whereby the conflict is removed from the actual relationships where the damage and harm were done and the victims are placed at a distance from access to and participation in the very thing that has most affected their lives. Often we find that the victims then feel powerless and marginalized, not only from the formal process but more important from the process of their own healing.

The restorative approach, on the other hand, suggests that the key in the pursuit of justice is to retain a victim-centered orientation. Restorative justice proposes to address victims' needs and offers ways for the perpetrators to take a greater level of responsibility for their actions. Perpetrators do not face a nameless bureaucracy that represents the state, often affording perpetrators the luxury of feeling justified as victims vis-à-vis the "system," but they must face the reality of the consequences of their actions in the lives of real people. Accountability and recompense are thus embedded in the realities of individual and community relationships. In practical terms, we again find that the voice of Brother Justice from this perspective works from the meaning structure of those victimized and the context within which the relationships must move forward.

The third major impulse of Brother Justice relates to equality and fairness. In settings of protracted violent conflict, we find that the "roots" are dug deep in the soils of relationships defined historically by inequality, lack of access to basic resources, and exclusion from decision-making processes. The conflict initiates and experiences its ebbs and flows as people seek to gain a voice, respect, and participation. In peace and reconciliation processes a significant "justice" gap is felt if the outcome of the efforts reduces open violence (stops the shooting) but does not adequately increase access to resources, participation, and protection of rights.

Taken at its deepest core, the practice of Justice in settings of prolonged conflict addresses the need to organize and channel three different social spaces and processes. First, how do we create processes that increase accountability and responsibility for the consequences of past actions that have harmed others in ways that are responsive to victims' needs? Second, how do we create alternative spaces that provide mechanisms by which participants in violence can be reintegrated into the community? And third, how do we reduce reliance on violence as a means of protecting or pursuing goals and at the same time increase fairness, equality, and the meeting of basic human needs?

Peace

When I was traveling extensively in Somalia in the early 1990s a newspaper article came out in our hometown describing my work as a mediator's effort to bring peace in a war-torn country. At the time, my son Joshua was four and in a preschool program. His teacher, having read the article that morning, asked him what his dad was doing in Somalia. Josh responded with the direct insight of children, saying, "My daddy is going to tell those folks to put away their guns and eat their food." Such is the wisdom of innocence with which the voice of Peace often speaks. The time has come to stop fighting, gather around the table, and put our lives back together.

As I have heard her, in the context of deep-rooted conflicts, the impulse of Sister Peace speaks with two broad metaphors. First, she moves to stop the violent patterns through which the conflict has been conducted. This is typically referred to as the "peace process." The peace process is much like a choir of voices, trumpeting out the concern and plight of those who suffer and begging for the fighting to stop. This is often connected to the narrower activity of peace talks, negotiations, moving from guns to words, from separation and distance toward encounter and dialogue.

The second major energy is to create a space where it is possible for people to be together, to begin the long process of weaving back together the fabric of a human community. Sometimes this is articulated as harmony heard in the plea, "Can't we just all get along?" Sometimes this is put forward as the metaphor of the table where we actually come together to eat, as the voice of mother making sure that everyone is taken care of, present, and cared for. Peacebuilding, as I described earlier in this chapter, connects these ideas by suggesting that peace is both ending something that is destructive, painful, and inhumane and building something that is dynamic, feeding people and their relationships.

Central to this impulse is the focus on people and relationships. Sister Peace organizes around people, and while she may propose events and the signing of agreements, her thrust is to keep alive a longer-term process that spins out over generations. We find, therefore, that if Peace is a person, she may well be a grandmother who looks back across numerous generations and forward to those that come. In a seminar exercise I conduct, where we stage a discussion between these four people—Truth, Mercy, Justice, and Peace—Grandma Peace, more often than not, extends her arms around the other three and says, "We need all of you to be a family."

If we move these concerns toward practice we find that Sister Peace must think first and foremost about how to create the space to develop and sustain relationships between enemies and in the face of all the pressures that wish to tear them apart. While at times this can be done publicly, Sister Peace must nurture people through real-life encounters that provide them safety and opportunity to experience themselves and each other in a new light. She does not judge herself on the basis of success and failure of any given event or effort, but rather by the measure of the slow and sure building of interdependence and cooperation that must break through the repetitive cycles of negative and violent interaction.

THE SOCIAL ORGANIZATION OF RECONCILIATION

The intriguing challenge of reconciliation lies not so much with hearing or recognizing any one of the four voices. The key is how to create the social space and processes where they meet and are held together. If we have Truth at the expense of Mercy or Peace, we fall quickly into negativism, stuck in past repetitive cycles of criticism and failure with no hope for a way forward. If we have Mercy at the expense of Truth, we fall prey to manipulation, impunity, and complete lack of accountability. Justice without Mercy is a sharp sword controlled only by the victor, but Peace without Justice is a facade and a betrayal, for it requires no change. Peace then easily becomes a dream deferred, as Langston Hughes once put it, that dries like a raisin in the sun, or a sore that can only seep and run.

Likewise, in the midst of conflict we cannot channel these social energies as if they are contradictory forces voiced by different persons within the conflict. In too many conflicts I find that those who cry out for Truth and Justice are pitted against those who plead for Mercy and Peace. Reconciliation suggests that the place where these four are held together is a dynamic process and space, where they are recognized as different and interdependent social energies. We have tended to understand these phenomena as principles or values, as if they were static and abstract, whereas we need to recognize them as continual sources of power, forces of change. From this view, the practice of reconciliation requires us to move in *polychronic* rather than *monochronic* terms. This means we have to broaden our approaches to think beyond narrow, short-term, time-bounded programs, one isolated from the other. Within settings of deep-rooted conflict, reconciliation pushes us to build and support a *multiplicity* of needed activities, *simultaneity* of action, and *interdependence* of the energies though each is qualitatively different from the other. Reconciliation and the building of civil society requires systemic rather than linear perspectives on people, relationships, processes, and context.

An intriguing question that has not been addressed directly in this chapter emerges from the assumption of the role played by civil society in reconciliation. Are the kinds of sugges-

tions and observations I made about reconciliation equally valid in situations where there is little civil society, such as North Korea, or where it is under great oppression and stress, such as Colombia? My arguments would remain much the same. Ultimately peace is sustained on the shoulders of relationships of people and communities that go beyond a narrow definition of politics and political actors. In conflicts like Colombia and North and South Korea the intractable nature of the situation and the difficulties faced by a weak civil society do not invalidate the approaches of reconciliation as an ecosystem. In fact the inverse may be true. We have to think strategically about planting and cultivating this missing nucleus precisely because, sooner or later, it will be the one ingredient capable of sustaining the kind of changes needed over the long haul.

As discussed earlier, reconciliation and the building of civil society are not peripheral activities to sustaining a peace process. They are the fundamental ingredients that make up the ecosystem in which peace must live. Key to this perspective is the understanding that peace is not a static outcome but rather a set of dynamic processes embedded in the real-life context of people's lives and relationships, perceptions, hopes, and fears. While negotiations may broker unique opportunities that take the form of peace accords and agreements, ultimately these opportunities are given flesh and life to the degree they create social energies and spaces that sustain change processes in people's relationships and communities.

REFERENCES

Lederach, John Paul. 1997. *Building Peace: Sustainable Reconciliation in Divided Societies.* Washington, D.C.: United States Institute of Peace Press.

———. 1999. *The Journey toward Reconciliation.* Scottdale, Pa.: Herald Press.

Zehr, Howard. 1990. *Changing Lenses: New Perspectives on Crime and Punishment.* Scottdale, Pa.: Herald Press.

Credits

The following publishers have generously given permission to reprint or adapt previously published work. The numbers refer to chapters in this book.

2. Reprinted from Michael Howard, *The Causes of War and Other Essays* (Cambridge, Mass.: Harvard University Press, 1983), 7–22. Copyright © 1983 by Michael Howard. Reprinted by permission.

6. Reprinted from *Survival* 40, no. 4 (winter 1998-99): 5–19. Copyright © 1999 by Oxford University Press. Used by permission.

8. Adapted from "Democratization and War," *Foreign Affairs* 74, no. 3 (May-June 1995): 79–97. Copyright © 1995 by the Council on Foreign Relations, Inc. Used by permission.

9. Adapted from the author's chapter in *Between Development and Destruction: An Enquiry into the Causes of Conflict in Post-Colonial States,* ed. Rupesinghe, Sciarone, and van de Good (London: Macmillan, 1996).

18. Adapted from *Foreign Affairs* 73, no. 6 (November-December 1994): 21–33. Copyright © 1994 by the Council on Foreign Relations, Inc. Used by permission.

19. Parts of this chapter first appeared in *Intervention: The Use of American Military Force in the Post–Cold War* (Washington, D.C.: Carnegie Endowment for International Peace, 1994). They appear here with the permission of the Carnegie Endowment for International Peace.

26. Adapted from "Mediation: The Role of Third-Party Diplomacy and Informal Peacemaking," in *Resolving Third World Conflict,* ed. Sheryl J. Brown and Kimber M. Schraub (Washington, D.C.: United States Institute of Peace Press, 1992), 239–261. It draws on the authors' previous work, especially the chapter in *Mediation Research,* ed. Kenneth Kressel, Dean G. Pruitt, and Associates (San Francisco: Jossey-Bass, 1989).

Index

United States Institute of Peace

The United States Institute of Peace is an independent, nonpartisan federal institution created by Congress to promote research, education, and training on the peaceful management and resolution of international conflicts. Established in 1984, the Institute meets its congressional mandate through an array of programs, including research grants, fellowships, professional training, education programs from high school through graduate school, conferences and workshops, library services, and publications. The Institute's Board of Directors is appointed by the President of the United States and confirmed by the Senate.

Chairman of the Board: Chester A. Crocker
Vice Chairman: Seymour Martin Lipset
President: Richard H. Solomon
Executive Vice President: Harriet Hentges

Board of Directors

Chester A. Crocker (Chairman), James R. Schlesinger Professor of Strategic Studies, School of Foreign Service, Georgetown University

Seymour Martin Lipset (Vice Chairman), Hazel Professor of Public Policy, George Mason University

Betty F. Bumpers, President, Peace Links, Washington, D.C.

Holly J. Burkhalter, Advocacy Director, Physicians for Human Rights, Washington, D.C.

Marc E. Leland, Esq., President, Marc E. Leland & Associates, Arlington, Va.

Mora L. McLean, Esq., President, Africa-America Institute, New York, N.Y.

María Otero, President, ACCION International, Somerville, Mass.

Barbara W. Snelling, State Senator and former Lieutenant Governor, Shelburne, Vt.

Shibley Telhami, Anwar Sadat Chair for Peace and Development, University of Maryland

Harriet Zimmerman, Vice President, American Israel Public Affairs Committee, Washington, D.C.

Members ex officio
Paul G. Gaffney II, Vice Admiral, U.S. Navy; President, National Defense University
Colin L. Powell, Secretary of State
Donald H. Rumsfeld, Secretary of Defense
Richard H. Solomon, President, United States Institute of Peace (nonvoting)

Turbulent Peace

This book is set in Adobe Caslon. Kim Hasten Design Studio, Inc., designed the book's cover, and Mike Chase designed the interior. Pages were made up by Helene Y. Redmond. David Sweet copyedited the text, which was proofread by Karen Stough. The index was prepared by Sonsie Conroy. The book's editor was Nigel Quinney.